EUROPE in 1715 after the Treaties of Utrecht & Rastadt

0 100 200 300 400
SCALE OF MILES

Hapsburg Dominions
Piedmont (House of Savoy)
Prussia
Hanover (House of Brunswick)
Bavaria and the Palatinate
Venice
Boundary of the Empire

Stockholm

RUSSIA

St. Petersburg

BALTIC SEA

POLAND

Königsberg

Thorn

Warsaw

Lublin

eslau

RUSSIA

MOLDAVIA

Budapest

HUNGARY

Temesvar

WALLACHIA

NIA

SERVIA

TURKISH

BLACK SEA

Constantinople

EMPIRE

EA

al)

Athens

MOREA

Smyrna

RHODES

BY WILL DURANT

The Story of Philosophy
Transition
The Pleasures of Philosophy
Adventures in Genius

THE STORY OF CIVILIZATION
BY WILL AND ARIEL DURANT

I. *Our Oriental Heritage*
II. *The Life of Greece*
III. *Caesar and Christ*
IV. *The Age of Faith*
V. *The Renaissance*
VI. *The Reformation*
VII. *The Age of Reason Begins*
VIII. *The Age of Louis XIV*
IX. *The Age of Voltaire*
X. *Rousseau and Revolution*

THE STORY OF CIVILIZATION: PART X

ROUSSEAU
AND
REVOLUTION

*A History of Civilization in France, England, and
Germany from 1756, and in the Remainder of
Europe from 1715, to 1789*

by

Will and Ariel Durant

SIMON AND SCHUSTER

NEW YORK · 1967

LIBRARY OF CONGRESS CATALOG CARD NUMBER: 67-14239
DESIGNED BY EVE METZ
MANUFACTURED IN THE UNITED STATES OF AMERICA
PRINTED BY MAHONY & ROESE, NEW YORK, N. Y.
BOUND BY H. WOLFF BOOK BINDERY, NEW YORK, N. Y.

Dear Reader:

This is the concluding volume of that *Story of Civilization* to which we devoted ourselves in 1929, and which has been the daily chore and solace of our lives ever since.

Our aim has been to write *integral history:* to discover and record the economic, political, spiritual, moral, and cultural activities of each civilization, in each age, as interrelated elements in one whole called life, and to humanize the narrative with studies of the protagonists in each act of the continuing drama. While recognizing the importance of government and statesmanship, we have given the political history of each period and state as the oft-told background, rather than the substance or essence of the tale; our chief interest was in the history of the mind. Hence in matters economic and political we have relied considerably upon secondary sources, while in religion, philosophy, science, literature, music, and art we have tried to go to the sources: to see each faith at work in its own habitat, to study the epochal philosophies in their major productions, to visit the art in its native site or later home, to enjoy the masterpieces of the world's literature, often in their own language, and to hear the great musical compositions again and again, if only by plucking them out of the miraculous air. For these purposes we have traveled around the world twice, and through Europe unnumbered times from 1912 to 1966. The humane reader will understand that it would have been impossible, in our one lifetime, to go to the original sources in economics and politics as well, through the sixty centuries and twenty civilizations of history. We have had to accept limits, and acknowledge our limitations.

We regret that we allowed our fascination with each canto of man's epic to hold us too willingly, with the result that we find ourselves exhausted on reaching the French Revolution. We know that this event did not end history, but it ends us. Unquestionably our integral and inclusive method has led us to give to most of these volumes a burdensome length. If we had written shredded history—the account of one nation or period or subject— we might have spared the reader's time and arms; but to visualize all phases in one narrative for several nations in a given period required space for the details needed to bring the events and the personalities to life. Each reader will feel that the book is too long, and that the treatment of his own nation or specialty is too brief.

French and English readers may wish to confine their first perusal of this volume to Chapters I–VIII, XIII–XV, and XX–XXXVIII, leaving the rest for another day, and readers in other tongues may choose their chapters likewise. We trust, however, that some heroes will go the course with us, seeking to vision Europe as a whole in those thirty-three eventful years from the Seven Years' War to the French Revolution.

We shall not sin at such length again; but if we manage to elude the Reaper for another year or two we hope to offer a summarizing essay on "The Lessons of History."

WILL AND ARIEL DURANT

Los Angeles
May 1, 1967

We are grateful to Yale University and the McGraw-Hill Book Company for permission to quote from *Boswell on the Grand Tour: Germany and Switzerland*, and from *Boswell in Holland*. It would be difficult to write about Boswell without nibbling at the feast offered by the Yale Editions of the Private Papers of James Boswell, so carefully edited and so handsomely published.

We are indebted also to the author and to W. W. Norton & Company for permission to quote a letter from Marc Pincherle's excellent *Vivaldi*.

Our warm appreciation to Sarah and Harry Kaufman for their long and patient help in classifying the material, and to our daughter Ethel for not only typing the manuscript immaculately, but for improving the text in many ways. Our thanks to Mrs. Vera Schneider for her scholarly editing of the manuscript.

NOTES ON THE USE OF THIS BOOK

1. Dates of birth and death are in the Index.
2. Italics in excerpts are never ours unless so stated.
3. We suggest the following rough equivalents, in terms of United States dollars of 1965, for the currencies mentioned in this book:

carolin, $22.50	guilder, $5.25	pistole, $12.50
cigliato, $6.25	guinea, $26.25	pound, $25.00
crown, $6.25	gulden, $5.25	reale, $.25
doppio, $25.00	kreutzer, $2.50	ruble, $10.00
ducat, $6.25	lira, $1.25	rupee, $4.00
écu, $3.75	livre, $1.25	shilling, $1.25
florin, $6.25	louis d'or, $25.00	sol, $1.25
franc, $1.25	mark, $1.25	sou, $.05
groschen, $1.25	penny, $.10	thaler, $5.00

4. The location of works of art, when not indicated in the text, will be found in the Notes. In allocating such works the name of the city will imply its leading gallery, as follows:

Amsterdam—Rijksmuseum	The Hague—Mauritshuis
Berlin—Staatsmuseum	Kansas City—Nelson Gallery
Bologna—Accademia di Belle Arti	Leningrad—Hermitage
Budapest—Museum of Fine Arts	London—National Gallery
Chicago—Art Institute	Madrid—Prado
Cincinnati—Art Institute	Milan—Brera
Cleveland—Museum of Art	Naples—Museo Nazionale
Detroit—Institute of Art	New York—Metropolitan Museum of Art
Dresden—Gemälde-Galerie	
Dulwich—College Gallery	San Marino, California—Huntington Art Gallery
Edinburgh—National Gallery	
Frankfurt—Städelsches Kunstinstitut	Vienna—Kunsthistorisches Museum
Geneva—Musée d'Art et d'Histoire	Washington—National Gallery

Table of Contents

BOOK I: PRELUDE

Chapter I. Rousseau Wanderer: 1712–56 3

I. The *Confessions* 3
II. Homeless 5
III. Maman 9
IV. Lyons, Venice, Paris 14
V. Is Civilization a Disease? . . . 19
VI. Paris and Geneva . . 24
VII. The Crimes of Civilization . 28
VIII. The Conservative 32
IX. Escape from Paris 33

Chapter II. The Seven Years' War: 1756–63 38

I. How to Start a War 38
II. The Outlaw 44
III. From Prague to Rossbach . . 46
IV. The Fox at Bay 51
V. The Making of the British
Empire 57
VI. Exhaustion 59
VII. Peace 62

BOOK II: FRANCE BEFORE THE DELUGE: 1757–74

Chapter III. The Life of the State 67

I. The Mistress Departs 67
II. The Recovery of France . . 69
III. The Physiocrats 71
IV. The Rise of Turgot 77
V. The Communists 80
VI. The King 84
VII. Du Barry 86
VIII. Choiseul 88
IX. The Revolt of the
Parlements 89
X. The King Departs 95

Chapter IV. The Art of Life 97

I. Morality and Grace 97
II. Music 100
III. The Theater 101
IV. Marmontel 104
V. The Life of Art 106
1. Sculpture 106
2. Architecture 109
3. Greuze 111
4. Fragonard 115
VI. The Great Salons 118
1. Mme. Geoffrin 118
2. Mme. du Deffand 121
3. Mlle. de Lespinasse 125

xi

Chapter V. VOLTAIRE PATRIARCH: 1758–78 132

I. The Good Lord 132
II. The Scepter of the Pen 136   IV. The Reformer 145
III. Voltaire *Politicus* 140   V. Voltaire Himself 147

Chapter VI. ROUSSEAU ROMANTIC: 1756–62 152

I. In the Hermitage 152   IV. The Break with the
II. In Love 155   *Philosophes* 161
III. Much Ado 159   V. The New Héloïse ...165

Chapter VII. ROUSSEAU PHILOSOPHER 171

I. *The Social Contract* 171
II. *Émile* 178   2. Religion 182
    1. Education 178   3. Love and Marriage 185

Chapter VIII. ROUSSEAU OUTCAST: 1762–67 189

I. Flight 189
II. Rousseau and the Arch-   V. Boswell Meets Rousseau ...201
      bishop 192   VI. A Constitution for Corsica 204
III. Rousseau and the Calvinists 197   VII. Fugitive 205
IV. Rousseau and Voltaire 199   VIII. Rousseau in England 209

BOOK III: THE CATHOLIC SOUTH: 1715–89

Chapter IX. *Italia Felix:* 1715–59 217

I. The Landscape 217
II. Music 220   4. Tiepolo 237
III. Religion 224   5. Goldoni and Gozzi 239
IV. From Turin to Florence ...226   VI. Rome 244
V. Queen of the Adriatic 228   VII. Naples 249
    1. Venetian Life 229   1. The King and the People 249
    2. Vivaldi 232   2. Giambattista Vico 251
    3. Remembrances 235   3. Neapolitan Music 254

Chapter X. PORTUGAL AND POMBAL: 1706–82 259

I. John V 259   III. Pombal the Reformer 268
II. Pombal and the Jesuits 261   IV. The Triumph of the Past ..270

Chapter XI. Spain and the Enlightenment: 1700–88 273

I. Milieu 273
II. Philip V 276
III. Ferdinand VI 279
IV. The Enlightenment Enters
    Spain 280
V. Charles III 281
   1. The New Government 281
   2. The Spanish Reforma-
     tion 283
   3. The New Economy 286

VI. The Spanish Character . . .290
VII. The Spanish Mind 293
VIII. Spanish Art 297
IX. Francisco de Goya y
    Lucientes 300
   1. Growth 300
   2. Romance 302
   3. Zenith 304
   4. Revolution 306
   5. Decrescendo 308

Chapter XII. *Vale, Italia:* 1760–89 310

I. Farewell Tour 310
II. Popes, Kings, and Jesuits . .316
III. The Law and Beccaria 319
IV. Adventurers 321
   1. Cagliostro 321

   2. Casanova 322
V. Winckelmann 325
VI. The Artists 331
VII. *I Musici* 332
VIII. Alfieri 335

Chapter XIII. The Enlightenment in Austria: 1756–90 341

I. The New Empire 341
II. Maria Theresa 342
III. Joseph Growing 346
IV. Mother and Son 348

V. The Enlightened Despot . . .354
VI. The Emperor and the
    Empire 360
VII. *Atra Mors* 364

Chapter XIV. Music Reformed 367

I. Christoph Willibald Gluck 367

II. Joseph Haydn 373

Chapter XV. Mozart 382

I. The Wonderful Boy 382
II. Adolescence 385
III. Music and Marriage 389
IV. In Paris 392
V. Salzburg and Vienna 393

VI. The Composer 395
VII. Spirit and Flesh 400
VIII. Apogee 402
IX. Nadir 405
X. Requiem 407

Book IV: ISLAM AND THE SLAVIC EAST: 1715–96

Chapter XVI. Islam: 1715–96 411

I. The Turks 411
II. African Islam 415

III. Persia 417

Chapter XVII. RUSSIAN INTERLUDE: 1725–62 422

    I. Work and Rule 422   IV. Elizabeth Petrovna 431
    II. Religion and Culture 424   V. Peter and Catherine 432
    III. Russian Politics 428   VI. Peter III 437

Chapter XVIII. CATHERINE THE GREAT: 1762–96 441

    I. The Autocrat 441   VI. The Warrior 456
    II. The Lover 444   VII. The Woman 461
    III. The Philosopher 446   VIII. Literature 463
    IV. The Statesman 450   IX. Art 466
    V. The Economist 454   X. Journey's End 469

Chapter XIX. THE RAPE OF POLAND: 1715–95 472

    I. Polish Panorama 472   IV. The First Partition 481
    II. The Saxon Kings 475   V. The Polish Enlightenment 484
    III. Poniatowski 477   VI. Dismemberment 487

BOOK V: THE PROTESTANT NORTH: 1756–89

Chapter XX. FREDERICK'S GERMANY: 1756–86 495

    I. Frederick Victorious 495   VI. The Romantic Reaction . . .517
    II. Rebuilding Prussia 499   VII. Sturm und Drang 520
    III. The Principalities 502   VIII. The Artists 523
    IV. The German Enlightenment 505   IX. After Bach 525
    V. Gotthold Lessing 508   X. Der Alte Fritz 528

Chapter XXI. KANT: 1724–1804 531

    I. Prolegomena 531
    II. *Critique of Pure Reason* . . .535   V. Religion and Reason 544
    III. *Critique of Practical Reason* 540   VI. The Reformer 547
    IV. *Critique of Judgment* 543   VII. Posthumous 549

Chapter XXII. ROADS TO WEIMAR: 1733–87 552

    I. The Athens of Germany . .552   2. *Götz* and *Werther* 560
    II. Wieland 553   3. The Young Atheist 564
    III. Goethe Prometheus 555   IV. Herder 567
      1. Growth 555   V. Schiller's *Wanderjahre* 569

Chapter XXIII. WEIMAR IN FLOWER: 1775–1805 576

 I. Wieland Sequel 576
 II. Herder and History 577   V. Goethe Waiting 589
 III. Goethe Councilor 580   VI. Schiller Waiting 591
 IV. Goethe in Italy 586   VII. Schiller and Goethe 596

Chapter XXIV. GOETHE NESTOR: 1805–32 606

 I. Goethe and Napoleon 606
 II. *Faust:* Part I 607   V. The Philosopher 618
 III. Nestor in Love 611   VI. *Faust:* Part II 623
 IV. The Scientist 615   VII. Fulfillment 625

Chapter XXV. THE JEWS: 1715–89 629

 I. The Struggle for Existence 629   III. Moses Mendelssohn 637
 II. The Mystic Solace 635   IV. Toward Freedom 641

Chapter XXVI. FROM GENEVA TO STOCKHOLM 643

 I. The Swiss: 1754–98 643
 II. The Dutch: 1715–95 645   2. Gustavus III 655
 III. The Danes: 1715–97 649   3. The Swedish Enlighten-
 IV. The Swedes: 1718–97 653   ment 658
    1. Politics 653   4. Assassination 662

BOOK VI: JOHNSON'S ENGLAND: 1756–89

Chapter XXVII. THE INDUSTRIAL REVOLUTION 669

 I. Causes 669   III. Conditions 676
 II. Components 671   IV. Consequences 680

Chapter XXVIII. THE POLITICAL DRAMA: 1756–92 683

 I. The Political Structure 683
 II. The Protagonists 687   VI. England and India 715
 III. The King versus Parliament 697   VII. England and the French
 IV. Parliament versus the People 701   Revolution 721
 V. England versus America . . .708   VIII. The Heroes Retire 726

Chapter XXIX. THE ENGLISH PEOPLE: 1756–89 728

I. English Ways 728
II. English Morals 730
III. Faith and Doubt 734
IV. Blackstone, Bentham, and
    the Law 736
V. The Theater 739
  1. The Performance 739
  2. Garrick 741
VI. London 743

Chapter XXX. THE AGE OF REYNOLDS: 1756–90 746

I. The Musicians 746
II. The Architects 747
III. Wedgwood 748
IV. Joshua Reynolds 750
V. Thomas Gainsborough 755

Chapter XXXI. ENGLAND'S NEIGHBORS: 1756–89 759

I. Grattan's Ireland 759
II. The Scottish Background   762
III. The Scottish Enlightenment 764
IV. Adam Smith 768
V. Robert Burns 772
VI. James Boswell 778
  1. The Cub 778
  2. Boswell Abroad 781
  3. Boswell at Home 783

Chapter XXXII. THE LITERARY SCENE: 1756–89 786

I. The Press 786
II. Laurence Sterne 787
III. Fanny Burney 790
IV. Horace Walpole 791
V. Edward Gibbon 795
  1. Preparation 795
  2. The Book 800
  3. The Man 804
  4. The Historian 806
VI. Chatterton and Cowper . . .808
VII. Oliver Goldsmith 813

Chapter XXXIII. SAMUEL JOHNSON: 1709–84 818

I. Deformative Years 818
II. The Dictionary 820
III. The Charmed Circle 825
IV. Ursus Major 828
V. The Conservative Mind 831
VI. Autumn 835
VII. Release 837
VIII. Boswell *Moriturus* 840

BOOK VII: THE COLLAPSE OF FEUDAL FRANCE: 1774–89

Chapter XXXIV. THE FINAL GLORY: 1774–83 845

I. The Heirs to the Throne . .845
II. The Government 848
III. The Virgin Queen 850
IV. *Le Roi Bonhomme* 855
V. The Ministry of Turgot . . .858
VI. Necker's First Ministry 865
VII. France and America 867

Chapter XXXV. DEATH AND THE PHILOSOPHERS: 1774–1807 873

I. Voltaire Finale 873
  1. Twilight in Ferney 873
  2. Apotheosis 875
  3. The Influence of
      Voltaire 880
II. Rousseau Epilogue 881
  1. The Haunted Spirit 881
  2. The Influence of
      Rousseau 887
III. *Marche Funèbre* 892
IV. The Last *Philosophe* 894
V. The Philosophers and the
    Revolution 897

Chapter XXXVI. ON THE EVE: 1774–89 900

I. Religion and the Revolution 900
II. Life on the Edge 902
III. The *Salonnières* 906
IV. Music 909
V. Art under Louis XVI 910
VI. Literature 914
VII. Beaumarchais 920

Chapter XXXVII. THE ANATOMY OF REVOLUTION: 1774–89 927

I. The Nobles and the
    Revolution 927
II. The Peasants and the
    Revolution 930
III. Industry and the Revolution 931
IV. The Bourgeoisie and the
    Revolution 934
V. The Gathering of the
    Forces 937

Chapter XXXVIII. THE POLITICAL DEBACLE: 1783–89 941

I. The Diamond Necklace ...941
II. Calonne 943
III. Loménie de Brienne 945
IV. Necker Again 948
V. Enter Mirabeau 951
VI. The Last Rehearsal 954
VII. The States-General 956
VIII. To the Bastille 961

ENVOI 964

BIBLIOGRAPHICAL GUIDE 967

NOTES 983

INDEX 1023

List of Illustrations

The page number in the captions refers to a discussion in the text of the subject or the artist, and sometimes both.

Part I.   This section follows page 108

Fig.   1—Maurice-Quentin de La Tour: *Jean-Jacques Rousseau*
Fig.   2—Carmontelle: *Melchior von Grimm*
Fig.   3—Carmontelle: *Mme. d'Épinay*
Fig.   4—Louis Tocqué: *Count Wenzel Anton von Kaunitz*
Fig.   5—Engraving after a painting by F. Bock: *Frederick the Great in Old Age*
Fig.   6—Augustin Pajou: *Mme. du Barry*
Fig.   7—J.-F. Oeben and J.-H. Riesener: *Bureau du Roi*
Fig.   8—Louis-Michel Vanloo: *Louis XV in Later Life*
Fig.   9—*Sèvres soft-paste porcelain*
Fig. 10—Jacques-Ange Gabriel: *The Petit Trianon*
Fig. 11—Jean-Jacques Caffieri: *Jean de Rotrou*
Fig. 12—Jacques-Germain Soufflot: *The Panthéon, Paris*
Fig. 13—After a painting by Jean-Marc Nattier: *Mme. Geoffrin*
Fig. 14—Jean-Honoré Fragonard: *Self-Portrait*
Fig. 15—Carmontelle: *Mme. du Deffand Visited by Mme. de Choiseul*
Fig. 16—Jean-Baptiste Greuze: *Sophie Arnould*
Fig. 17—Greuze: *The Broken Pitcher (La Cruche Cassée)*
Fig. 18—Fragonard: *The Swing*
Fig. 19—Antonio Canaletto: *View of St. Mark's, Venice*
Fig. 20—Giambattista Tiepolo: *The Banquet of Cleopatra*
Fig. 21—Tiepolo: *Apollo Bringing the Bride to Barbarossa*
Fig. 22—Rosalba Carriera: *Self-Portrait*
Fig. 23—Giovanni Battista Piazzetta: *Rebecca at the Well*
Fig. 24—A. Longhi: *Carlo Goldoni*
Fig. 25—*The Royal Palace, Madrid*
Fig. 26—*Façade of the Church of Santiago de Compostela, Spain*
Fig. 27—Francisco José de Goya y Lucientes: *Charles IV and His Family*
Fig. 28—Goya: *Charles III*
Fig. 29—Goya: *The Duchess of Alba*
Fig. 30—Goya: *Self-Portrait*
Fig. 31—Goya: *The Tribunal of the Inquisition*
Fig. 32—Goya: *La Maja Desnuda*
Fig. 33—Goya: *La Maja Vestida*
Fig. 34—Goya: *Saturn Devouring His Offspring*
Fig. 35—Francesco Guardi: *Concert in the Sala dei Filarmonici*
Fig. 36—Anton Raphael Mengs: *Parnassus*
Fig. 37—Jean-Antoine Houdon: *Gluck*
Fig. 38—Xavier-Pascal Fabre: *Vittorio Alfieri*
Fig. 39—Franz von Zauner: *Emperor Joseph II*

FIG. 40—FABRE: *The Countess of Albany*

FIG. 41—JOHN HOPPNER: *Joseph Haydn*

FIG. 42—*Esterházy Castle at Eisenstadt*

FIG. 43—JOHANN NEPOMUK DELLA CROCE: *The Mozart Family*

FIG. 44—ÉTIENNE-MAURICE FALCONET: *Statue of Peter the Great*

FIG. 45—ARTIST UNKNOWN: *Czar Peter III*

FIG. 46—ENGRAVING BY G. SKORODUMOV AFTER A PAINTING BY F. S. ROKOTOV: *Catherine the Great*

FIG. 47—F. S. ROKOTOV: *Grigori Orlov*

FIG. 48—IVAN STAROV: *Potemkin's Taurida Palace*

Part II.   This section follows page 236

FIG. 49—JOHANN GOTTFRIED SCHADOW: *The Quadriga on the Brandenburg Gate*

FIG. 50—KARL GOTTHARD LANGHANS: *The Brandenburg Gate*

FIG. 51—ANGELICA KAUFFMANN: *The Vestal Virgin*

FIG. 52—ANGELICA KAUFFMANN: *Stanislas Poniatowski*

FIG. 53—DANIEL CHODOWIECKI: *A Gathering in the Zoological Garden*

FIG. 54—JOHANN HEINRICH TISCHBEIN: *Lessing in Youth*

FIG. 55—ANTON RAPHAEL MENGS: *Self-Portrait*

FIG. 56—ENGRAVING BY KARL BARTH AFTER A DRAWING BY STOBBE: *Immanuel Kant*

FIG. 57—JOHANN FRIEDRICH AUGUST TISCHBEIN: *Schiller*

FIG. 58—ANTON GRAFF: *The Actress Korona Schröter*

FIG. 59—JOHANN HEINRICH WILHELM TISCHBEIN: *Goethe in the Roman Campagna*

FIG. 60—ASMUS JAKOB CARSTENS: *The Birth of Light*

FIG. 61—ALEXANDER ROSLIN: *Gustavus III*

FIG. 62—*The Bridgewater Canal at Barton Bridge*

FIG. 63—THOMAS GAINSBOROUGH: *George III*

FIG. 64—SIR JOSHUA REYNOLDS: *Edmund Burke*

FIG. 65—ENGRAVING BY JOHN JONES AFTER A PAINTING BY SIR JOSHUA REYNOLDS: *Charles James Fox*

FIG. 66—JOHN HOPPNER: *William Pitt the Younger*

FIG. 67—GEORGE ROMNEY: *Actress Mary Robinson*

FIG. 68—ROBERT PINE: *David Garrick*

FIG. 69—ENGRAVING BY JOHN HALL AFTER A PAINTING BY REYNOLDS: *Richard Brinsley Sheridan*

FIG. 70—FROM A PRINT AFTER A DRAWING BY CANALETTO: *An Inside View of the Rotunda in Ranelagh Gardens*

FIG. 71—SIR JOSHUA REYNOLDS: *Portrait of the Artist as a Deaf Man*

FIG. 72—CHIPPENDALE AND HAIGH IN THE STYLE OF ROBERT ADAM: *Side Table of Gilt and Silvered Wood*

FIG. 73—THOMAS GAINSBOROUGH: *Mrs. Sarah Siddons*

FIG. 74—ROSALBA CARRIERA: *Horace Walpole*

FIG. 75—PAUL SANDBY: *Strawberry Hill*

FIG. 76—THOMAS GAINSBOROUGH: *The Honorable Mrs. Graham*

FIG. 77—ARCHIBALD SKIRVING: *Robert Burns*

FIG. 78—HENRY RAEBURN: *Lord Newton*

FIG. 79—THOMAS GAINSBOROUGH: *The Market Cart*

FIG. 80—SIR JOSHUA REYNOLDS: *Georgiana, Duchess of Devonshire*

FIG. 81—GEORGE DANCE: *James Boswell*

FIG. 82—SIR JOSHUA REYNOLDS: *Laurence Sterne*

FIG. 83—GEORGE ROMNEY: *William Cowper*

FIG. 84—STUDIO OF REYNOLDS: *Oliver Goldsmith*

FIG. 85—MME. VIGÉE-LEBRUN: *Marie Antoinette*

FIG. 86—SIR JOSHUA REYNOLDS: *Dr. Samuel Johnson*

FIG. 87—JEAN-ANTOINE HOUDON: *The Artist's Wife*

FIG. 88—JEAN-BAPTISTE PIGALLE: *Denis Diderot*

FIG. 89—HOUDON: *Voltaire*

FIG. 90—HOUDON: *Mme. de Sérilly*

FIG. 91—HOUDON: *Mirabeau*

FIG. 92—CLODION (CLAUDE MICHEL): *The Intoxication of Wine (Nymph and Satyr)*

FIG. 93—JACQUES-LOUIS DAVID: *The Oath of the Horatii*

FIG. 94—HOUDON: *Diana*

FIG. 95—NATTIER: *Beaumarchais*

FIG. 96—HOUDON: *George Washington*

FIG. 97—MME. VIGÉE-LEBRUN: *Portrait of the Artist and Her Daughter*

FIG. 98—ENGRAVING BY J. E. NOCHEZ AFTER A PAINTING BY ALLAN RAMSAY: *Jean-Jacques Rousseau*

BOOK I

PRELUDE

CHAPTER I

Rousseau Wanderer

1712–56

I. THE *CONFESSIONS*

HOW did it come about that a man born poor, losing his mother at birth and soon deserted by his father, afflicted with a painful and humiliating disease, left to wander for twelve years among alien cities and conflicting faiths, repudiated by society and civilization, repudiating Voltaire, Diderot, the *Encyclopédie*, and the Age of Reason, driven from place to place as a dangerous rebel, suspected of crime and insanity, and seeing, in his last months, the apotheosis of his greatest enemy—how did it come about that this man, after his death, triumphed over Voltaire, revived religion, transformed education, elevated the morals of France, inspired the Romantic movement and the French Revolution, influenced the philosophy of Kant and Schopenhauer, the plays of Schiller, the novels of Goethe, the poems of Wordsworth, Byron, and Shelley, the socialism of Marx, the ethics of Tolstoi, and, altogether, had more effect upon posterity than any other writer or thinker of that eighteenth century in which writers were more influential than they had ever been before? Here, if anywhere, the problem faces us: what is the role of genius in history, of man versus the mass and the state?

Europe was ready for a gospel that would exalt feeling above thought. It was tired of the restraints of customs, conventions, manners, and laws. It had heard enough of reason, argument, and philosophy; all this riot of unmoored minds seemed to have left the world devoid of meaning, the soul empty of imagination and hope; secretly men and women were longing to believe again. Paris was weary of Paris, of the turmoil and hurry, the confinement and mad competition of city life; now it idealized the slower pace of the countryside, where a simple routine might bring health to the body and peace to the mind, where one might see modest women again, where all the village would meet in weekly armistice at the parish church. And this proud "progress," this vaunted "emancipation of the mind"—had they put anything in place of what they had destroyed? Had they given man a more intelligible or inspiring picture of the world and human destiny? Had they improved the lot of the poor, or brought consolation to bereavement or pain? Rousseau asked these questions, gave form and feeling to these doubts; and after his voice was stilled all Europe listened to him. While Voltaire was being idolized on the stage and at the Academy (1778), and while Rousseau, berated and despised, hid in the obscurity of a Paris room, the age of Rousseau began.

In the decline of his life he composed the most famous of autobiographies, the *Confessions*. Sensitive to every criticism, suspecting Grimm, Diderot, and others of a conspiracy to blacken him in Paris salons and in the *Mémoires* of Mme. d'Épinay, he began in 1762, on the urging of a publisher, to write his own account of his history and character. All autobiography, of course, is vanity, but Rousseau, condemned by the Church, outlawed by three states, and deserted by his closest friends, had the right to defend himself, even at great length. When he read some passages of this defense to gatherings in Paris, his foes secured a government ban on further public readings of his manuscript. Discouraged, he left it at his death with a passionate plea to posterity:

> Here is the sole human portrait—painted exactly after nature in all truth—that now exists or that will probably ever exist. Whoever you are, whom my fate and confidence have made the arbiter of this record, I beg you, by my misfortunes and by your fellow feeling, and in the name of all mankind, not to destroy a work useful and unique, which can serve as a first piece of comparison for the study of man, . . . and not to take from the honor of my memory the only sure monument of my character that has not been disfigured by my enemies.[1]

His extreme sensitivity, subjectivity, and sentiment made the virtues and the faults of his book. "A feeling heart," he said, ". . . was the foundation of all my misfortunes";[2] but it gave a warm intimacy to his style, a tenderness to his recollections, often a generosity to his judgments, that melt our antipathy as we read. Here everything abstract becomes personal and alive; every line is a feeling; this book is the fountainhead of the Mississippi of introspective self-revelations that watered the literature of the nineteenth century. Not that the *Confessions* had no forebears; but even St. Augustine could not match the fullness of this self-denudation, or its claim to truth. It begins with a burst of challenging eloquence:

> I am forming an enterprise which has had no example, and whose execution will have no imitator. I wish to show my fellow men a man in all the truth of nature; and this man shall be myself.
> Myself alone. I know my heart, and I am acquainted with men. I am not made like any one of those who exist. If I am not better, at least I am different. If nature has done well or ill in breaking the mold in which I was cast, this is something of which no one can judge except after having read me.
> Let the trumpet of the Last Judgment sound when it will, I shall come, this book in hand, to present myself before the Sovereign Judge. I shall say loudly: "This is how I have acted, how I have thought, what I have been. I have told the good and the bad with the same candor. I have concealed nothing of evil, added nothing of good. . . . I have shown myself as I was: despicable and vile when I was so, good, generous, sublime, when I was these; and I have unveiled my inmost soul . . ."[3]

This claim to complete sincerity is repeated again and again. But Rousseau admits that his remembrance of things fifty years past is often fragmentary and unreliable. In general Part I has an air of candor that is disarming; Part II is disfigured by wearisome complaints of persecution and conspiracy. Whatever else the book is, it is one of the most revealing psychological studies known to us, the story of a sensitive and poetic spirit in painful conflict with a hard and prosaic century. In any case, "the *Confessions*, if it were not an autobiography, would be one of the great novels of the world."[4]*

II. HOMELESS: 1712–31

"I was born at Geneva in 1712, son of Isaac Rousseau and Suzanne Bernard, citizens." This last word meant much, for only sixteen hundred of Geneva's twenty thousand souls had the name and rights of citizen, and this was to enter into Jean-Jacques' history. His family was of French origin, but had been settled in Geneva since 1529. His grandfather was a Calvinist minister; the grandson remained basically a Calvinist through all the wanderings of his faith. The father was a master watchmaker, imaginative and unstable, whose marriage (1704) brought him a dowry of sixteen thousand florins. After the birth of a son François he left his wife (1705) and traveled to Constantinople, where he remained for six years. Then he came back, for reasons unknown, and "I was the sad fruit of this return."[8] The mother died of puerperal fever within a week of Jean-Jacques' birth. "I came into the world with so few signs of life that little hope was entertained of preserving me"; an aunt nursed and saved him, for which, he said, "I freely forgive you." This aunt sang well, and may have given him his lasting taste for music. He was precocious and soon learned to read, and, since Isaac loved romances, father and son read together the romances left in the mother's little library; Jean-Jacques was brought up on a mixture of French love stories, Plutarch's *Lives,* and Calvinist morality, and the mixture unsteadied him. He described himself accurately enough as "at once haughty and

---

* The debate as to the truthfulness of the *Confessions* is still warm on two continents. It turns chiefly on Rousseau's charge that Grimm and Diderot had conspired to give a false account of his relations with Mme. d'Épinay, Mme. d'Houdetot, and themselves. The balance of critical judgment before 1900 was against Rousseau. About 1850 Sainte-Beuve, with unwonted acerbity, decided that "Rousseau, whenever his self-esteem and his diseased vanity are at stake, has not the slightest hesitation about lying, and I have arrived at the conclusion that with respect to Grimm he was a liar."[5] And the most learned of French literary historians, Gustave Lanson, agreed (1894): "We surprise Rousseau on every page in flagrant falsehoods—falsehood, not mere error; yet the book as a whole burns with sincerity—a sincerity not of facts but of feeling."[6] These judgments preceded the publication of Mrs. Frederika Macdonald's *Jean-Jacques Rousseau: A New Study in Criticism* (London, 1906), which "makes out a good case for regarding Mme. d'Épinay's *Mémoires* as colored, if not actually dictated, by the malevolent attitude of Grimm and Diderot; and her study of the documents undoubtedly qualifies a good many of the assumptions that had been previously made."[7] Cf. Masson, *La Religion de Rousseau* (I, 184): "We shall see with what caution we must use this recital [the *Mémoires*], which was so strongly retouched [*remanié*] by Diderot." Similar judgments favorable to Rousseau were reached by Matthew Josephson (*Jean-Jacques Rousseau*, 434-35, 531), Émile Faguet (*Vie de Rousseau*, 189), Jules Lemaître (*Jean-Jacques Rousseau*, 9-10), and C. E. Vaughn (*Political Writings of Rousseau*, II, 295, 547-48, 552 f.).

tender, a character effeminate and yet invincible, which, fluctuating between weakness and courage, luxury and virtue, has ever set me in contradiction to myself."[9]

In 1722 the father quarreled with a Captain Gautier, gave him a bloody nose, was summoned by the local magistrate, fled from the city to escape imprisonment, and took up residence at Nyon, thirteen miles from Geneva. A few years later he married again. François and Jean-Jacques were taken over by their uncle Gabriel Bernard. François was apprenticed to a watchmaker, ran away, and disappeared from history. Jean-Jacques and his cousin Abraham Bernard were sent to a boarding school operated by Pastor Lambercier at the neighboring village of Bossey. "Here we were to learn Latin, with all the insignificant trash that has obtained the name of education."[10] The Calvinist catechism was a substantial part of the curriculum.

He liked his teachers, especially the pastor's sister, Mlle. Lambercier. She was thirty, Jean-Jacques was eleven, so he fell in love with her, after his own queer fashion. When she whipped him for some misbehavior he took delight in suffering at her hands; "a degree of sensuality mingled with the smart and shame, which left more desire, than fear, of a repetition."[11] When he offended further, the pleasure he took in the chastisement became so obvious that she resolved never to whip him again. A masochistic element remained in his erotic make-up till the end.

> Thus I passed the age of puberty, with a constitution extremely ardent, without knowing or even wishing for any other gratification of the passions than what Miss Lambercier had innocently given me an idea of; and when I became a man that childish taste, instead of vanishing, only associated with the other. This folly, joined to a natural timidity, has always prevented me from being very enterprising with women, so that I have passed my days languishing in silence for those I most admired, without daring to disclose my wishes. . . .
>
> I have now made the first and most difficult step in the obscure and painful maze of my Confessions. We never feel so great a degree of repugnance in divulging what is really criminal, as what is merely ridiculous.[12]

It is possible that in later life Rousseau found an element of pleasure in feeling himself buffeted by the world, by his enemies, and by his friends.

Next to Mlle. Lambercier's chastisements he enjoyed the magnificent scenery that surrounded him. "The country was so charming . . . that I conceived a passion for rural life which time has not been able to extinguish."[13] Those two years at Bossey were probably the happiest that he ever experienced, despite his discovery of injustice in the world. Punished for an offense that he had not committed, he reacted with lasting resentment, and thereafter he "learned to dissemble, to rebel, to lie; all the vices common to our years began to corrupt our happy innocence."[14]

He never advanced further in formal or classical education; perhaps his lack of balance, judgment, and self-control and his subordination of reason to feeling were in part due to the early end of his schooling. In 1724, aged twelve, he and his cousin were recalled to the Bernard household. He visited his father at Nyon, and there fell in love with a Mlle. Vulson, who rejected him, and then with Mlle. Goton, who, "while she took the greatest liberties with me, would never permit any to be taken with her in return."[15] After a year of vacillations he was apprenticed to an engraver in Geneva. He liked drawing, and learned to engrave watchcases, but his master beat him severely for some minor offenses, and "drove me to vices I naturally despised, such as falsehood, idleness, and theft." The once happy boy turned into a morose and unsociable introvert.

He consoled himself with intense reading of books borrowed from a nearby library, and with Sunday excursions into the countryside. On two occasions he dallied so long in the fields that he found the city gates closed when he tried to return; he spent the night in the open, reported for work half dazed, and received a special thrashing. On a third such occasion the memory of these beatings made him resolve not to return at all. Not yet sixteen (March 15, 1728), without money, and with nothing but the clothes on his back, he marched on to Confignon in Catholic Savoy, some six miles away.

There he knocked at the door of the village priest, Père Benoît de Pontverre. Perhaps he had been told that the old curé was so anxious to convert stray Genevans that he fed them well on the theory that a full stomach makes for an orthodox mind. He gave Jean-Jacques a good dinner, and bade him "go to Annecy, where you will find a good and charitable lady whom the bounty of the king enables to turn souls from those errors she has happily renounced."[16] This, Rousseau adds, was "Mme. de Warens, a new convert, to whom the priests contrived to send those wretches who were disposed to sell their faith; and with these she was in a manner constrained to share a pension of two thousand francs bestowed upon her by the King of Sardinia." The homeless youth thought a part of that pension might be worth a Mass. Three days later, at Annecy, he presented himself to Mme. Françoise-Louise de La Tour, Baronne de Warens.

She was twenty-nine, pretty, gracious, gentle, generous, charmingly dressed; "there could not be a more lovely face, a finer neck, or handsome arms more exquisitely formed";[17] altogether she was the best argument for Catholicism that Rousseau had ever seen. Born in Vevey of good family, she had been married, quite young, to M. (later Baron) de Warens of Lausanne. After some years of painful incompatibility she left him, crossed the lake into Savoy, and won the protection of King Victor Amadeus, then at Evian. Domiciled at Annecy, she accepted conversion to Catholicism, with the conviction that if her religious ritual were correct God would pardon her an occasional amour; besides, she could not believe that the gentle Jesus would send men—surely not a beautiful woman—to everlasting hell.[18]

Jean-Jacques would gladly have stayed with her, but she was occupied; she gave him money, and bade him go to Turin and receive instruction in the Hospice of the Holy Spirit. He was received there on April 12, 1728, and on April 21 he was baptized into the Roman Catholic faith. Writing thirty-four years later—eight years after his return to Protestantism—he described with horror his experience in the hospice, including an attempt upon his virtue by a Moorish fellow catechumen; he imagined that he had approached conversion with revulsion, shame, and long delays. But apparently he adjusted himself to the conditions that he found in the hospice, for he remained there, uncompelled, over two months after being received into the Church of Rome.[19]

He left the hospice in July, armed with twenty-six francs. After a few days of sightseeing he found work in a store to which he had been drawn by the good looks of the lady behind the counter. He fell in love with her at once; soon he knelt before her and offered her a lifetime of devotion. Mme. Basile smiled, but let him go no further than her hand; besides, her husband was expected at any minute. "My want of success with women," says Rousseau, "has ever proceeded from my having loved them too well";[20] but it was his nature to find greater ecstasy in contemplation than in fulfillment. He relieved his tumescence by "that dangerous supplement which deceives nature, and saves young men of my temperament from many disorders, but at the expense of their health, their vigor, and sometimes their life."[21] This practice, made hectic by terrifying prohibitions, may have played a secret role in promoting his irritability, his romantic fancies, his discomfort in society, his love of solitude. Here the *Confessions* are frank beyond precedent:

> My thoughts were incessantly occupied with girls and women, but in a manner peculiar to myself. These ideas kept my senses in a perpetual and disagreeable activity. . . . My agitation rose to the point where, unable to satisfy my desires, I inflamed them with the most extravagant maneuvers. I went about seeking dark alleys, hidden retreats, where I might expose myself at a distance to persons of the [other] sex in the state wherein I would have wished to be near them. That which they saw was not the obscene object—I did not dream of that; it was the ridiculous object [the buttocks]. The foolish pleasure which I had in displaying it before their eyes cannot be described. From this there was but a step to the desired treatment [whipping]; and I do not doubt that some resolute woman, in passing, would have given me the amusement, if I had had the audacity to continue. . . .
>
> One day I went to place myself at the back of a court in which was a well where the young women of the house often came to fetch water. . . . I offered to the girls . . . a spectacle more laughable than seductive. The wisest among them pretended to see nothing; others began to laugh; others felt insulted, and raised an alarm.

Alas, no girl offered to beat him; instead a guardsman came, with heavy sword and frightful mustache, followed by four or five old women armed with brooms. Rousseau saved himself by explaining that he was "a young stranger of high lineage, whose mind was deranged," but whose means might enable him later to reward their forgiveness. The "terrible man was touched," and let him go, much to the discontent of the old women.[22]

Meanwhile he had found employment as a liveried footman in the service of Mme. de Vercellis, a Turinese lady of some culture. There he committed a crime which weighed on his conscience through the rest of his life. He stole one of Madame's colorful ribbons; when charged with the theft he pretended that another servant had given it to him. Marion, who was quite innocent of the theft, reproached him prophetically: "Ah, Rousseau, I thought you were of a good disposition. You render me very unhappy, but

I would not be in your situation."[23] Both were dismissed. The *Confessions* adds:

> I do not know what became of the victim of my calumny, but there is little probability of her having been able to place herself agreeably after this, as she labored under an imputation cruel to her character in every respect. . . . The painful remembrance of this transaction . . . has remained heavy on my conscience to this day; and I can truly say that the desire to relieve myself in some measure from it has contributed greatly to the resolve to write my Confessions.[24]

Those six months as a footman left a mark on his character; with all his consciousness of genius he never achieved self-respect. A young priest whom he met while serving Mme. de Vercellis encouraged him to believe that his faults could be overcome if he would sincerely seek to approach the ethics of Christ. Any religion, said "M. Gaime," is good if it spreads Christian conduct; hence he suggested that Jean-Jacques would be happier if he returned to his native habitat and faith. These views of "one of the best men I ever knew" lingered in Rousseau's memory, and inspired famous pages in *Émile*. A year later, in the Seminary of St.-Lazare, he met another priest, Abbé Gâtier, a "very tender heart," who missed advancement because he had conferred pregnancy upon a maiden in his parish. "This," remarks Rousseau, "was a dreadful scandal in a diocese severely good, where the priests (being under good regulation) ought never to have children—except by married women."[25] From "these two worthy priests I formed the character of the Savoyard Vicar."

Early in the summer of 1729 Rousseau, now seventeen, felt again the call of the open road; moreover, he hoped that with Mme. de Warens he might find some employment less galling to his pride. Along with a jolly Genevan lad named Bâcle, he marched from Turin to and through the Mont Cenis pass of the Alps to Chambéry and Annecy. His romantic pen colored the emotions with which he approached Mme. de Warens' dwelling. "My legs trembled under me, my eyes were clouded with a mist, I neither saw, heard, nor recollected anyone, and was obliged frequently to stop that I might draw breath and recall my bewildered senses."[26] Doubtless he was uncertain of his reception. How could he explain to her all his vicissitudes since leaving her? "Her first glance banished all my fears. My heart leaped at the sound of her voice. I threw myself at her feet, and in transports of the most lively joy I pressed my lips upon her hand."[27] She did not resent adoration. She found a room for him in her house; and when some eyebrows rose she said, "They may talk as they please, but since Providence has sent him back, I am determined not to abandon him."

III. MAMAN: 1729–40

He was intensely attracted to her, like any youth in proximity with a *femme de trente ans*. He furtively kissed the bed on which she had slept, the chair she had sat on, "nay, the floor itself when I considered she had walked there"[28] (here we suspect that romance got the better of history); and he was furiously jealous of all who competed with him for her time. She let him purr, and called him *petit chat* (little cat) and *enfant;* gradually he resigned himself to calling her *Maman*. She employed him to write letters, keep her accounts, gather herbs, and help in her alchemical experiments. She gave him books to read—*The Spectator*, Pufendorf, Saint-Évremond, Voltaire's *Henriade*. She herself liked to browse in Bayle's *Dictionnaire historique et critique*. She did not let her theology discommode her; and if she enjoyed the company of Father Gros, superior of the local seminary, it might be because he helped to lace her stays. "While he was thus employed she would run about the room, this way or that as occasion happened to call her. Drawn by the laces, M. le Supérieur followed grumbling, repeating at every moment, 'Pray, Madame, do stand still'; the whole forming a scene truly diverting."[29]

It was perhaps this jolly priest who suggested that though Jean-Jacques gave every sign of stupidity he might digest enough education to make him a village curé. Mme. de Warens, glad to find a career for him, agreed. So in the fall of 1729 Rousseau entered the Seminary of St.-Lazare, and prepared for priesthood. By this time he had become accustomed to Catholicism, even fond of it;[30] he loved its solemn ritual, its processions, music, and incense, its bells that seemed to proclaim, every day, that God was in his heaven, and that all was—or would be—right with the world; besides, no religion could be bad that charmed and forgave Mme. de Warens. But he had received so little formal education that he was first subjected to a concentrated course in the Latin language. He could not suffer its declensions, conjugations, and exceptions patiently; after five months of effort, his teachers sent him back to Mme. de Warens with the report that he was "a tolerably good lad," but not fit for holy orders.

She tried again. Having observed his flair for music, she introduced him to Nicoloz Le Maître, organist at the Annecy cathedral. Jean-Jacques went to live with him through the winter of 1729–30, consoled by being only twenty paces from Maman. He sang in the choir and played the flute; he loved the Catholic hymns; he was well fed, and happy. All went well except that M. Le Maître drank too much. One day the little choirmaster quarreled with his employers, gathered his music in a box, and left Annecy. Mme. de Warens bade Rousseau accompany him as far as Lyons. There Le Maître, overcome with delirium tremens, fell senseless in the street. Frightened, Jean-Jacques called the passers-by to his aid. He gave them the address which the music master was seeking, and then fled back to Annecy and Maman. "The tenderness and truth of my attachment to her had uprooted from my heart every imaginable project, and all the follies of ambition. I conceived no happiness but in living near her, nor could I take a step without feeling that the distance between us was increased."[31] We must remember that he was still only eighteen years old.

When he reached Annecy he found that Madame had left for Paris, and no one knew when she would return. He was desolate. Day after day he walked aimlessly into the countryside, comforting himself with the colors of spring and the pretty chatter of doubtless amorous birds. Above all he loved to rise early and watch the sun lifting itself triumphantly above the horizon. On one of these rambles he saw two damsels on horseback, urging their reluctant mounts to ford a stream. In a burst of heroism he caught one horse by the bridle and led it across, while the other followed. He was about to go on his way, but the girls insisted upon his accompanying them to a cottage where he might dry his shoes and stockings. At their invitation he leaped up behind Mlle. G. "When it became necessary to clasp her in order to hold myself on, my heart beat so violently that she perceived it",[32] at that moment he began to outgrow his infatuation for Mme. de Warens. The three youngsters spent the day picnicking together; Rousseau progressed to kissing one girl's hand; then they left him. He returned to Annecy exalted, and hardly minded that Maman was not there. He tried to find those mademoiselles again, but failed.

Soon he was on the road once more, this time accompanying Mme. de Warens' maid to Fribourg. Passing through Geneva "I found myself so affected that I could scarcely proceed, . . . the image of [republican] liberty so elevated my soul."[33] From Fribourg he walked to Lausanne. Of all writers known to history he was the most devoted walker. From Geneva to Turin to Annecy to Lausanne to Neuchâtel to Bern to Chambéry to Lyons he knew the road and drank in gratefully the sights, odors, and sounds.

> I love to walk at my ease, and stop at leisure; a strolling life is necessary for me. Traveling on foot, in a fine country, with fine weather, and having an agreeable object to terminate my journey, is the manner of living most suited to my taste.[34]

Uncomfortable in the society of educated men, shy and wordless before beautiful women, he was happy when alone with woods and fields, water and sky. He made Nature his confidante, and in silent speech told her his loves and dreams. He imagined that the moods of Nature entered at times into a mystic accord with his own. Though he was not the first to make men feel the loveliness of Nature, he was her most fervent and effective apostle; half the nature poetry since Rousseau is part of his lineage. Haller had felt and described the majesty of the Alps, but Rousseau made the slopes of Switzerland along the northern shore of the Lake of Geneva his special realm, and he sent down through the centuries the fragrance of their terraced vines. When he came to choose a site for the home of his Julie and Wolmar he placed them here, at Clarens between Vevey and Montreux, in a terrestrial paradise mingling mountains, verdure, water, sun, and snow.

Unsuccessful in Lausanne, Rousseau moved to Neuchâtel: "Here, . . . by teaching music, I insensibly gained some knowledge of it."[35] At nearby Boudry he met a Greek prelate who was soliciting funds for restoring the Holy Sepulcher in Jerusalem; Rousseau joined him as interpreter, but at Soleure he left him and walked out of Switzerland into France. On this walk he entered a cottage and asked might he buy some dinner; the peasant offered him barley bread and milk, saying this was all he had; but when he saw that Jean-Jacques was not a tax collector he opened a trapdoor, descended, and came up with wheat bread, ham, eggs, and wine. Rousseau offered to pay; the peasant refused, and explained that he had to hide his better food lest he suffer additional taxation. "What he said to me . . . made an impression on my mind that can never be effaced, sowing seeds of that inextinguishable hatred which has since grown up in my heart against the vexations these unhappy people bear, and against their oppressors."[36]

At Lyons he spent homeless days, sleeping on park benches or the ground. For a time he was engaged to copy music. Then, hearing that Mme. de Warens was living at Chambéry (fifty-four miles to the east), he set out to rejoin her. She found work for him as secretary to the local intendant (1732–34). Meanwhile he lived under her roof, his happiness only moderately lessened by the discovery that her business manager, Claude Anet, was also her lover. That his own passion had subsided appears from a unique passage in the *Confessions:*

> I could not learn, without pain, that she lived in greater intimacy with another than with myself. . . . Nevertheless, instead of feeling any aversion to the person who had this advantage over me, I found the attachment I felt for her actually extended to him. I desired her happiness above all things, and since he was concerned in her plan of felicity, I was content he should be happy likewise. Meantime he entered perfectly into the views of his mistress; he conceived a sincere friendship for me; and thus . . . we lived in a union which rendered us mutually happy, and which death alone could dissolve. One proof of the excellence of this amiable woman's character is that all who loved her loved each other, even jealousy and rivalry submitting to the more powerful sentiment with which she inspired them; and I never saw any of those who surrounded her entertain the least ill will among themselves. Let the reader pause a moment in this encomium, and if he can recollect any other woman who deserves it, let him attach himself to her if he would obtain happiness.[37]

The next step in this polygonal romance was just as contrary to all the rules of adultery. When she perceived that a neighbor, Mme. de Menthon, aspired to be the first to teach Jean-Jacques the art of love, Mme. de Warens, refusing to surrender this distinction, or desiring to keep the youth from less tender arms, offered herself to him as mistress, without prejudice to her similar services for Anet. Jean-Jacques took eight days to think it over; long acquaintance with her had made him filial rather than sensual in his thoughts of her; "I loved her too much to desire her."[38] He was already suffering from the ailments that were to pursue him to the end—inflammation of the bladder and stricture of the urethra. Finally, with all due modesty, he agreed to her proposal.

> The day, more dreaded than hoped for, at length arrived. . . . My heart confirmed my engagements without desiring the prize. I obtained it nevertheless. I saw myself for the first time in the arms of a woman, and a woman whom I adored. Was I happy? No. I tasted pleasure, but I know not what invincible sadness poisoned the charm. I felt as if I had committed incest. Two or three times, while pressing her with transport in my arms, I deluged her bosom with

my tears. As for her, she was neither sad nor gay; she was caressingly tranquil. Since she was hardly at all sensual, and had not at all sought pleasure, she had in this no ecstasy, and she never felt remorse.[39]

Recalling this epochal event, Rousseau ascribed Madame's maneuvers to the poison of philosophy.

> I repeat, all her failings were the result of her error, never of her passions. She was well born, her heart was pure, her manners noble, her desires regular and virtuous, her taste delicate; she seemed formed for that elegant purity of manners which she ever loved but never practiced, because, instead of listening to the dictates of her heart, she followed those of her reason, which led her astray. . . . Unhappily, she piqued herself on philosophy, and the morality which she drew from it spoiled that which her heart proposed.[40]

Anet died in 1734. Rousseau left his post with the intendant and took over the management of Madame's business affairs. He found them perilously confused, near bankruptcy. He brought in some income by teaching music; in 1737 he received three thousand francs falling due from his mother's legacy; he spent part of this on books, and gave the rest to Mme. de Warens. He fell ill, and Maman nursed him tenderly. As her dwelling had no garden, she rented (1736) a suburban cottage, Les Charmettes. There "my life passed in the most absolute serenity." Though he "never loved to pray in a chamber," the outdoors stirred him to thank God for the beauty of nature, and for Mme. de Warens, and to ask the divine blessing on their union. He was at this time firmly attached to the Catholic theology, with a somber Jansenist tinge. "The dread of hell frequently tormented me."[41]

Bothered by "the vapors"—a then fashionable form of hypochondria—and thinking that he had a polypus near his heart, he traveled by stagecoach to Montpellier. En route he eased his melancholy by allegedly consummating a liaison with Mme. de Larnage (1738), mother of a fifteen-year-old girl. Returning to Chambéry, he found that Mme. de Warens was trying a similar cure, having taken as her new lover a young wigmaker named Jean Wintzenried. Rousseau protested; she called him childish, and assured him that there was room in her love for two Jeans. He refused to "thus degrade her," and proposed to resume his *status quo ante* as son. She professed consent, but her resentment at being so readily surrendered cooled her affection for him. He retired to Les Charmettes and took to philosophy.

Now for the first time (c. 1738) he became conscious of the Enlightenment breezes that were blowing from Paris and Cirey. He read some works of Newton, Leibniz, and Pope, and browsed in the maze of Bayle's *Dictionnaire*. He took up Latin again, made more progress by himself than formerly with teachers, and managed to read bits of Virgil, Horace, and Tacitus, and a Latin translation of Plato's *Dialogues*. Montaigne, La Bruyère, Pascal, Fénelon, Prévost, and Voltaire came to him as a dizzy revelation. "Nothing that Voltaire wrote escaped us"; indeed, it was Voltaire's books that "inspired me with a desire to write elegantly, and caused me to endeavor to imitate the colorings of that author, with whom I was so enchanted."[42] Insensibly the old theology that had been the frame of his thoughts lost its form and rigor; and he found himself entertaining without horror a hundred heresies that would have seemed scandalous to his youth. An almost passionate pantheism replaced the God of the Bible. There was a God, yes, and life would be meaningless and unbearable without him; but he was not the external, vengeful deity conceived by cruel and fearful men, he was the soul of Nature, and Nature was fundamentally beautiful, and human nature was basically good. On this and Pascal Rousseau would build his philosophy.

In 1740 Mme. de Warens found a post for him as tutor to the children of M. Bonnot de Mably, grand provost of Lyons. He parted from her with no reproach on either side; she prepared his wardrobe for the trip, and wove some garments for it with her own once entrancing hands.

IV. LYONS, VENICE, PARIS: 1740–49

The Mably family was a new intellectual stimulus for Rousseau. The provost was the eldest of three distinguished brothers; one was the almost communist Gabriel Bonnot de Mably; another was the almost materialist Abbé Étienne Bonnot de Condillac; and Rousseau met all three. Of course he fell in love with Mme. de Mably, but she was gracious enough to take no notice of it, and Jean-Jacques had to mind his business of educating her two sons. He drew up for M. de Mably a statement of his pedagogical ideas; in part these accorded with the libertarian principles that were to receive their classical romantic exposition in *Émile* twenty-two years later; in part they contradicted his later rejection of "civilization," for they recognized the value of the arts and sciences in the development of mankind. Meeting frequently men like Professor Bordes of the Lyons Academy (who was a friend of Voltaire), he imbibed more of the Enlightenment, and learned to laugh at popular ignorance and superstition. But he remained ever adolescent. Peeping into the public baths one day, he saw a young woman quite unencumbered; his heart stopped beating. Back in the stealth of his room he addressed to her a bold but anonymous note:

> I hardly dare confess to you, Mademoiselle, the circumstances to which I owe the happiness of having seen you, and the torment of loving you. . . . It is less that figure, light and svelte, which loses nothing by nudity; it is less that elegant form, those graceful contours; . . . it is not so much the freshness of lilies spread with such profusion over your person—but that soft blush . . . which I saw covering your brow when I offered myself to your sight after having unmasked you too mischievously by singing a couplet.[43]

He was now old enough to fall in love with *young* women. Almost any presentable girl set him longing and dreaming, but especially Suzanne Serre. "Once—alas, only once in my life!—my mouth touched hers. O memory! shall I lose you in the grave?" He began to think of marriage, but he confessed, "I have nothing but my heart to offer."[44] As this was not legal tender Suzanne accepted another hand, and Rousseau retired to his dreams.

He had not been made to be either a successful lover or a good teacher.

> I had almost as much knowledge as was necessary for a tutor, . . . and the
> natural gentleness of my disposition seemed calculated for the employment, if
> hastiness had not mingled with it. When things went favorably, and I saw the
> pains, which I did not spare, succeed, I was an angel; but when they went
> contrary I was a devil. If my pupils did not understand me I was hasty; when
> they showed any symptoms of an untoward disposition I was so provoked that
> I could have killed them. . . . I determined to quit my pupils, being convinced
> that I should never succeed in educating them properly. M. de Mably saw this
> as clearly as myself, though I am inclined to think he would never have dis-
> missed me had I not spared him the trouble.[45]

So, sadly resigning or gently dismissed, he took the diligence back to
Chambéry, seeking again the solace of Maman's arms. She received him
kindly, and gave him a place at her table with her paramour; but he was not
happy in the situation. He buried himself in books and music, and contrived
a system of musical notation that used figures instead of notes. When he
resolved to go to Paris and submit his invention to the Academy of Sciences
everybody applauded his resolution. In July, 1742, he returned to Lyons to
seek letters of introduction to notables in the capital. The Mablys gave him
letters to Fontenelle and the Comte de Caylus, and Bordes introduced him to
the Duc de Richelieu. From Lyons he took the public coach to Paris, dreaming of greatness.

France was at this time engaged in the War of the Austrian Succession
(1740–48); but as the conflict was fought on foreign soil, Paris went on with
its life of gilded gaiety, intellectual agitation, theaters mouthing Racine,
salons sparkling with heresy and wit, bishops reading Voltaire, beggars competing with prostitutes, hawkers crying their wares, artisans sweating for
bread. Into this maelstrom came Jean-Jacques Rousseau, aged thirty, in
August, 1742, with fifteen livres in his purse. He took a room in the Hotel
St.-Quentin, Rue des Cordeliers, near the Sorbonne—"a vile street, a miserable hotel, a wretched apartment."[46] On August 22 he presented to the
Academy his *Projet concernant de nouveaux signes pour la notation musicale*. The savants rejected his project with handsome compliments. Rameau
explained: "Your signs are very good, . . . but they are objectionable on
account of their requiring an operation of the mind, which cannot always
accompany the rapidity of execution. The position of our notes is described
to the eye without the concurrence of this operation." Rousseau confessed
the objection to be insurmountable.[47]

Meanwhile his letters of introduction had given him access to Fontenelle,
who, now eighty-five, was too cautious of his energy to take him seriously;
and to Marivaux, who, though busy with success as both novelist and dramatist, read Rousseau's manuscript comedy *Narcisse*, and suggested improvements. The newcomer met Diderot, who, one year younger than Jean-
Jacques, had as yet published nothing of importance.

> He was fond of music, and knew it theoretically; . . . and he communi-
> cated to me some of his literary projects. This soon formed between us a more
> intimate connection, which lasted fifteen years, and which probably would still
> exist were not I, unfortunately, . . . of the same profession as himself.[48]

With Diderot he went to the theater, or played chess; in that game Rousseau met Philidor and other experts, and "had no doubt but in the end I should become superior to them all."[49] He found entrance to the home and salon of Mme. Dupin, daughter of the banker Samuel Bernard, and struck up a friendship with her stepson, Claude Dupin de Francueil. Meanwhile he could see the bottom of his purse.

He began to look about him for some occupation that would supplement his friends in feeding him. Through the influence of Mme. de Besenval he was offered the post of secretary to the French embassy in Venice. After a long journey made hazardous by the war, he reached Venice in the spring of 1743, and reported to the ambassador, the Comte de Montaigu. This count, Rousseau assures us, was almost illiterate; the secretary had to decipher as well as to compose documents; he presented the messages of the French government to the Venetian Senate in his own person—not having forgotten the Italian he had learned in Turin. He was proud of his new status, and complained that a merchant vessel which he visited gave him no cannonade in salute, though "people of less consequence received it."[50] Master and man quarreled as to who should pocket the fees paid for the secretary's issuance of passports to France. With his share Rousseau prospered, ate unusually well, attended theater and opera, and fell in love with Italian music and girls.

One day, "not to appear too great a blockhead among my associates," he visited a prostitute, La Padoana. He asked her to sing; she did; he gave her a ducat, and turned to leave; she refused to take the coin without having earned it. He satisfied her, and returned to his lodgings "so fully persuaded that I should feel the consequences of this step that the first thing I did was to send for the King's surgeon to ask him for medicine"; but the doctor "persuaded me that I was formed in such a manner as not to be readily infected."[51] Some time later his friends gave him a party, at which the pretty harlot Zulietta was to be the prize. She invited him to her room, and disrobed. "Suddenly, instead of being devoured by flame, I felt a deadly chill run through my veins, and sick at heart, I sat down and wept like a child." He later explained his incapacity on the ground that one of the woman's breasts was deformed. Zulietta turned upon him in scorn and bade him "leave women alone, and study mathematics."[52]

M. de Montaigu, his own salary being in arrears, withheld Rousseau's. They quarreled again; the secretary was dismissed (August 4, 1744). Rousseau complained to his friends in Paris; an inquiry was sent to the ambassador; he replied: "I must inform you how greatly we have been deceived by the Sire Rousseau. His temper and his insolence, caused by the high opinion he has of himself, and by his madness, are the things that hold him in the state in which we found him. I drove him out like a bad valet."[53] Jean-Jacques returned to Paris (October 11), and presented his side of the matter to officials in the government; they offered him no redress. He appealed to Mme. de Besenval, she refused to receive him. He sent her a passionate letter in which we can feel the heat of the distant Revolution:

I was wrong, Madame; I thought you just, and you are only *noble* [titled]. I should have remembered that. I should have perceived that it was improper for me, a foreigner and plebeian, to complain against a gentleman. If my destiny should ever again put me in the grip of an ambassador of the same stuff, I shall suffer without complaint. If he is wanting in dignity, without elevation of soul, it is because nobility dispenses with all that; if he is associated with all that is vile in one of the most immoral of cities, it is because his ancestors have created enough honor for him; if he consorts with knaves, if he is one himself, if he deprives a servitor of wages, ah, then, Madame, I shall think only how fortunate it is *not* to be the son of one's own deeds! Those ancestors —who were they? Persons of no repute, without fortune, my equals; they had talent of some kind, they made a name for themselves; but nature, which sows the seed of good and evil, has given them a pitiful posterity.[54]

And in the *Confessions* Rousseau added:

The justice and futility of my complaints left in my mind seeds of indignation against our foolish social institutions, by which the welfare of the public and real justice are always sacrificed to I know not what appearance of order, which does nothing more than add the sanction of public authority to the oppression of the weak and the iniquity of the powerful.[55]

Montaigu, returning to Paris, sent Rousseau "some money to settle my account. . . . I received what was offered me, paid all my debts, and remained as before, with not a franc in my pocket." Re-established at the Hotel St.-Quentin, he supported himself by copying music. When the current Duc d'Orléans, hearing of his poverty, gave him music to copy and fifty louis, Rousseau kept five and returned the rest as overpayment.[56]

He earned too little to support a wife, but he thought that with stoic economy he could afford a mistress. Among those who ate at his table in the Hotel St.-Quentin were the landlady, some impecunious abbés, and a young woman who served the hotel as laundress or seamstress. Thérèse Levasseur was as timid as Jean-Jacques, and as conscious—though not so proud—of poverty. When the abbés teased her he defended her; she came to look upon him as her protector; soon they were in each other's arms (1746). "I began by declaring to her that I would never either abandon or marry her."[57] She confessed that she was not a virgin, but assured him that she had sinned only once, and long ago. He forgave her magnanimously, assuring her that a virgin twenty years old was a rarity in Paris in any case.

She was a simple creature, devoid of all charm, free of all coquetry. She could not talk philosophy or politics like a *salonnière*, but she could cook, keep house, and put up patiently with his strange moods and ways. Usually he spoke of her as his "housekeeper," and she spoke of him as "my man." He rarely took her with him on visits to his friends, for she remained permanently adolescent mentally, as he remained permanently adolescent morally.

I at first tried to improve her mind, but in this my pains were useless. Her mind is as nature formed it; it was not susceptible of cultivation. I do not blush in acknowledging she never knew how to read well, although she writes tolerably. . . . She could never enumerate the twelve months of the year in order, or distinguish one numeral from another, notwithstanding all the trouble I took endeavoring to teach her. She neither knows how to count money, nor to reckon the price of anything. The word which, when she speaks, comes to her mind is frequently the opposite of that which she means to use. I formerly made a dictionary of her phrases to amuse M. de Luxembourg, and her *qui pro quos* often became celebrated among those with whom I was most intimate.[58]

When she became pregnant he "was thrown into the greatest embarrassment"; what could he do with children? Some friends assured him it was quite customary to send unwanted offspring to a foundling asylum. When the infant came this was done, over Thérèse's protests but with the co-operation of her mother (1747). In the next eight years four other children came, and were disposed of in the same way. Some skeptics have suggested that Rousseau never had any children, and that he invented this story to hide his impotence, but his many apologies for this shirking of responsibility make this theory improbable. He privately confessed his behavior in this matter to Diderot, Grimm, and Mme. d'Épinay;[59] he implicitly acknowledged it in *Émile*; he raged against Voltaire for making it public; in the *Confessions* he admitted it explicitly, and expressed remorse. He was not made for family life, being a skinless mass of nerves, and a wanderer in body and soul. He missed the sobering care of children, and never quite became a man.

He had the good fortune, about this time, to find lucrative employment. He served as secretary to Mme. Dupin, then to her nephew; and when Dupin de Francueil became receiver-general Rousseau was promoted to cashier at a thousand francs a year. He adopted the gold braid, white stockings, wig, and sword by which men of letters, to get entrance to aristocratic homes, imitated aristocratic dress;[60] we can imagine the discomfort of his divided personality. He was received in several salons, and made new friends: Raynal, Marmontel, Duclos, Mme. d'Épinay, and, most intimately and fatally, Friedrich Melchior Grimm. He attended the exciting dinners at the home of Baron d'Holbach, where Diderot slew gods with what his enemies called the jawbone of an ass. In that den of infidels most of Jean-Jacques' Catholicism melted away.

Meanwhile he wrote music. In 1743 he had begun a combination of opera and ballet which he called *Les Muses galantes*, celebrating the loves of Anacreon, Ovid, and Tasso; this was produced in 1745, with some éclat, at the home of the tax collector La Popelinière. Rameau shrugged it off as a *pasticcio* of plagiarisms from Italian composers, but the Duc de Richelieu liked it, and commissioned Rousseau to revise an opera-ballet, *Les Festes de Ramire*, tentatively prepared by Rameau and Voltaire. On December 11, 1745, Rousseau wrote his first letter to the literary monarch of France:

> For fifteen years I have been working to render myself worthy of your regard, and of the kindness with which you favor young Muses in whom you discover talent. But, through having written the music for an opera, I find myself metamorphosed into a musician. Whatever success my feeble efforts may have, they will be glorious enough for me if they win me the honor of being known to you, and of having shown the admiration and profound respect with which I have the honor of being, sir, your humble and most obedient servitor.[61]

Voltaire replied: "Sir, you unite in yourself two talents which have always been found separate till now. Here are two good reasons why I should esteem and like you."

With such love letters began their famous enmity.

V. IS CIVILIZATION A DISEASE?

In 1749 Diderot was imprisoned at Vincennes for some offensive passages in his *Letters on the Blind*. Rousseau wrote to Mme. de Pompadour pleading for his friend's release, or permission to share his imprisonment. Several times during that summer he made the round trip of ten miles between Paris and Vincennes to visit Diderot. On one such journey he took an issue of the *Mercure de France* to read as he walked. So he came upon the announcement of a prize offered by the Academy of Dijon for the best essay on the question: "Has the restoration of the sciences and the arts contributed to corrupt or to purify morals?" He was tempted to compete, for he was now thirty-seven years old, and it was time he should make a name for himself. But did he know enough of science or art or history to discuss such topics without revealing the defects of his education? In a letter to Malesherbes, January 12, 1762, he described with characteristic emotion the revelation that came to him on this walk:

> All at once I felt myself dazzled by a thousand sparkling lights. Crowds of vivid ideas thronged into my mind with a force and confusion that threw me into unspeakable agitation; I felt my head whirling in a giddiness like that of intoxication. A violent palpitation oppressed me. Unable to walk for difficulty in breathing, I sank down under one of the trees by the road, and passed half an hour there in such a condition of excitement that when I rose I saw that the front of my waistcoat was all wet with tears. . . . Ah, if ever I could have written a quarter of what I saw and felt under that tree, with what clarity I should have brought out all the contradictions of our social system! With what simplicity I should have demonstrated that man is by nature good, and that only our institutions have made him bad![62]

That last sentence was to be the theme song of his life, and those tears that streaked his vest were among the headwaters of the Romantic movement in France and Germany. Now he could pour out his heart against all the artificiality of Paris, the corruption of its morals, the insincerity of its fine manners, the licentiousness of its literature, the sensuality of its art, the snobbishness of class divisions, the callous extravagance of the rich financed by exactions from the poor, the desiccation of the soul by the replacement of religion with science, of feeling with logic. By declaring war on this degeneration he could vindicate his own simplicity of culture, his village manners, his discomfort in society, his disgust with malicious gossip and irreverent wit, his defiant retention of religious faith amid the atheism of his friends. In his heart he was again a Calvinist, remembering with a kind of homesickness the morality expounded to him in his youth. By answering Dijon he would exalt his native Geneva above Paris, and would explain to himself and others why he had been so happy in Les Charmettes, and was so miserable in the salons.

Arrived at Vincennes, he revealed to Diderot his intention to compete. Diderot applauded him, and bade him attack the civilization of their time with all possible force. Hardly any other competitor would dare take that line, and Rousseau's position would stand out as individual.* Jean-Jacques returned to his lodgings eager to destroy the arts and sciences that Diderot was preparing to exalt in the *Encyclopédie, ou Dictionnaire raisonné des sciences, des arts, et des métiers* (1751 f.).

> I composed the *Discourse* in a very singular manner. . . . I dedicated to it the hours of the night in which sleep deserted me; I meditated in bed with my eyes closed, and in my mind I turned over and over again my periods with incredible labor and care. . . . As soon as the *Discourse* was finished I showed it to Diderot. He was satisfied with the production, and pointed out some corrections he thought should be made. . . . I sent off the piece without mentioning it to anybody [else], except, I think, to Grimm.[65]

The Dijon Academy crowned his essay with the first prize (August 23, 1750)—a gold medal and three hundred francs. Diderot, with characteristic enthusiasm, arranged for the publication of this *Discours sur les arts et les sciences*, and soon he reported to the author: "Your *Discours* is taking beyond all imagination; never was there an instance of a like success."[66] It was as if Paris realized that here, at the very mid-point of the Enlightenment, a man had risen to challenge the Age of Reason, and to challenge it with a voice that would be heard.

The essay seemed at first to applaud the victories of reason:

> It is a noble and beautiful spectacle to see man raising himself, so to speak, from nothing by his own exertions; dissipating by the light of reason all the thick clouds by which he was by nature enveloped; mounting above himself, soaring in thought even to the celestial regions, encompassing with giant strides, like the sun, the vast extent of the universe; and what is still grander and more wonderful, going back into himself, there to study man and get to know his own nature, his duties, and his end. All these miracles we have seen renewed within the last few generations.[67]

Voltaire must have shed an approving smile over this initial ecstasy; here was a new recruit to the *philosophes*, to the good companions who would slay superstition and *l'infame;* and was not this young Lochinvar already contributing to the *Encyclopédie?* But a page later the argument took a distressing turn. All this progress of knowledge, said Rousseau, had made governments more powerful, crushing individual liberty; it had replaced the simple virtues and forthright speech of a ruder age with the hypocrisies of *savoir-faire.*

---

* A minor controversy obscures the narrative at this point. Diderot, in 1782, reported Rousseau's visit in a manner reconcilable with Rousseau's account: "When . . . Rousseau came to consult me about the view he should adopt, 'The part you will take,' I said, 'is that which others would reject.' 'You are right,' said he."[63] Marmontel, about 1793, quoted Diderot as having dissuaded Rousseau from taking the affirmative stand. " 'I shall follow your advice,' said Rousseau."[64]

Sincere friendship, real esteem, and perfect confidence are banished from among men. Jealousy, suspicion, fear, coldness, reserve, hate, and fraud lie constantly concealed under that uniform and deceitful veil of politeness, that boasted candor and urbanity, for which we are indebted to the light and leading of this age. . . . Let the arts and sciences claim the share they have had in this salutary work![68]

This corruption of morals and character by the progress of knowledge and art is almost a law of history. "Egypt became the mother of philosophy and the fine arts; soon she was conquered."[69] Greece, once peopled by heroes, twice vanquished Asia; "letters" were then in their infancy, and the virtues of Sparta had not been replaced, as the Greek ideal, by the refinement of Athens, the sophistry of the Sophists, the voluptuous forms of Praxiteles; when that "civilization" had reached its height it was overthrown at a blow by Philip of Macedon, and then supinely accepted the yoke of Rome. Rome conquered the whole Mediterranean world when she was a nation of peasants and soldiers inured to a stoic discipline; but when she relaxed into epicurean indulgence, and praised the obscenities of Ovid, Catullus, and Martial, she became a theater of vice, "a scorn among the nations, an object of derision even to barbarians."[70] And when Rome revived in the Renaissance, arts and letters again sapped the strength of governed and governors, and left Italy too feeble to meet attack. Charles VIII of France mastered Tuscany and Naples almost without drawing a sword, "and all his court attributed this unexpected success to the fact that the princes and nobles of Italy applied themselves with greater earnestness to the cultivation of their understandings rather than to active and martial pursuits."[71]

Literature itself is an element of decay.

It is related that the Caliph Omar, being asked what should be done with the library of Alexandria, answered . . . , "If the books in the library contain anything contrary to the Koran, they are evil and ought to be burned; if they contain only what the Koran teaches, they are superfluous." This reasoning has been cited by our men of letters as the height of absurdity; but if Gregory the Great had been in the place of Omar, and the Gospel in the place of the Koran, the library would still have been burned, and it would have been perhaps the finest action of his life.[72]

Or consider the disintegrating effect of philosophy. Some of these "lovers of wisdom" tell us that there is no such thing as matter; another assures us that nothing but matter exists, and no other God but the universe itself; a third group announces that virtue and vice are mere names, and nothing counts but strength and skill. These philosophers "sap the foundations of our faith, and destroy virtue. They smile contemptuously at such old words as *patriotism* and *religion*, and consecrate their talents . . . to the destruction and defamation of all that men hold most sacred."[73] In antiquity such nonsense did not long survive its author, but now, thanks to print, "the pernicious reflections of Hobbes and Spinoza will last forever." Consequently, the invention of printing was one of the greatest disasters in the history of mankind, and "it is easy to see that sovereigns will hereafter take as much pains to banish this dreadful art from their dominions as they ever took to encourage it."[74]

Note the vigor and excellence of those peoples who never knew philosophy or science, literature or art: the Persians of Cyrus' time, the Germans as described by Tacitus, or, "in our own time, that rustic nation [Switzerland] whose renowned courage not even adversity could conquer, and whose fidelity no example could corrupt." To these the proud Genevan adds "those happy nations, which did not know even the names of many vices that we find it hard to suppress—the savages of America, whose simple and natural mode of government Montaigne preferred, without hesitation, not only to the laws of Plato, but to the most perfect visions of government that philosophy can suggest."[75]

What, then, should be our conclusion? It is that

> luxury, profligacy, and slavery have been in all ages the scourge of the efforts of our pride to emerge from that happy state of ignorance in which the wisdom of Providence has placed us. . . . Let men learn for once that nature would have preserved them from science as a mother snatches a dangerous weapon from the hands of her child.[76]

The answer to the question of the learned Academy is that learning without virtue is a snare; that the only real progress is moral progress; that the advancement of learning has corrupted, rather than purified, the morals of mankind; and that civilization is not an ascent of man to a nobler state, but the fall of man from a rural simplicity that was a paradise of innocence and bliss.

Toward the end of the *Discourse* Rousseau checked himself, and looked with some trepidation at the shambles of science, art, literature, and philosophy that he had left in his wake. He recalled that his friend Diderot was preparing an encyclopedia dedicated to the progress of science. Suddenly he discovered that some philosophers—e.g., Bacon and Descartes—were "sublime teachers," and he proposed that living specimens of the breed should be welcomed as counselors by the rulers of states. Had not Cicero been made consul of Rome, and the greatest of modern philosophers been made chancellor of England?[77] Perhaps Diderot had slipped these lines in, but Jean-Jacques had the last word:

> As for us, ordinary men, upon whom Heaven has not been pleased to bestow such great talents, . . . let us remain in our obscurity. . . . Let us leave to others the task of instructing mankind in their duty, and confine ourselves to the discharge of our own. . . . Virtue! sublime science of simple minds, . . . are not your principles graven upon every heart? Need we do more, to learn your laws, than . . . listen to the voice of conscience? . . . This is the true philosophy, with which we must learn to be content.[78]

Paris did not know whether to take this *Discourse* seriously or to interpret it as a mischievous essay in hyperbole and paradox, tongue in cheek. It was said by some (Rousseau tells us[79]) that he did not believe a word of it. Diderot, who believed in science but fretted under the restraints of convention and morality, apparently approved of Rousseau's exaggerations as a needed chastisement of Parisian society; and members of the court applauded the essay as a long-deserved rebuke to insolent and subversive philosophers.[80] There must have been many sensitive spirits who were, like this eloquent author, ill at ease in the babble and sparkle of Paris. Rousseau had expressed a problem that appears in every advanced society. Are the fruits of technology worth the haste, strains, sights, noises, and smells of an industrialized life? Does enlightenment undermine morality? Is it wise to follow science to mutual destruction, and philosophy to disillusionment with every fortifying hope?

A dozen critics rose to the defense of civilization: Bordes of the Lyons Academy, Lacat of the Rouen Academy, Formey of the Berlin Academy, and not least the genial Stanislas Leszczyński, once king of Poland, now duke of Lorraine. Scholars pointed out that the diatribe merely enlarged the doubts that Montaigne had voiced in his essay "On Cannibals." Others heard the voice of Pascal retreating from science to religion, and of course a thousand "doctors and saints" had long since condemned civilization as a disease or a sin. Theologians could claim that the "innocence" and happiness of the "state of nature" from which, in Rousseau's theory, man had lapsed was only the Eden story retold; "civilization" took the place of "original sin" as causing the fall of man; in both cases the desire for knowledge had ended bliss. Sophisticates like Voltaire wondered that a man thirty-seven years old should have written such a juvenile jeremiad against the achievements of science, the boon of good manners, and the inspirations of art. Artists like Boucher might well have squirmed under Rousseau's lash, but artists like Chardin and La Tour could have charged him with indiscriminate generalization. Soldiers smiled at the tender musician's exaltation of martial qualities and perpetual readiness for war.

Rousseau's friend Grimm protested against any return to "nature." "What devilish nonsense!" he exclaimed, and asked a thorny question: "What is 'nature'?"[81] Bayle had remarked: "There is scarcely a word that is used more vaguely than . . . *nature*. . . . The conclusion is not certain that because 'this comes from nature, therefore this is good and right.' We see in the human species many very bad things, although it cannot be doubted that they are the work of nature."[82] Rousseau's conception of primitive nature was of course a romantic idealization; nature (life without social regulation and protection) is "red in tooth and claw," and its ultimate law is, Kill or be killed. The "nature" that Jean-Jacques loved, as in Vevey or Clarens, was a nature civilized—tamed and refined by man. In truth, he did not want to go back to primitive conditions, with all their filth, insecurity, and physical violence; he wished to return to the patriarchal family cultivating the soil and living on its fruits. He longed to be freed from the rules and restraints of polished society—and from the classic style of moderation and reason. He hated Paris and yearned for Les Charmettes. Toward the end of his life, in *Les Rêveries d'un promeneur solitaire*, he idealized his maladaptation:

> I was born the most confiding of men, and for forty years together never was this confidence deceived for a single time. Falling suddenly among another

order of persons and things, I slipped into a thousand snares. . . . Once convinced that there was nothing but deceit and falsity in the grimacing demonstrations which had been lavished upon me, I passed rapidly to the other extreme. . . . I became disgusted with men. . . . I have never been truly accustomed to civil society, where all is worry, obligation, duty, and where my natural independence renders me always incapable of the subjections necessary to whoever wishes to live among men.[83]

And in the *Confessions* he bravely admitted that this first *Discourse,* "though full of force and fire, was absolutely wanting in logic and order; of all the works I ever wrote it is the weakest in reasoning, and the most devoid of number [prose rhythm?] and harmony."[84]

Nevertheless he replied vigorously to his critics, and reaffirmed his paradoxes. He made an exception as a courtesy to Stanislas: on second thought he decided not to burn the libraries or close the universities and academies; "all we should gain by this would be to plunge Europe once more into barbarism";[85] and "when men are corrupt it is better for them to be learned than ignorant."[86] But he recanted no item in his indictment of Parisian society. To mark his withdrawal from it he discarded sword and gold braid and white stockings, and dressed in the simple garb and smaller wig of the middle class. "Thus," said Marmontel, "from that moment he chose the role he was to play, and the mask he was to wear."[87] If it was a mask it was so well and persistently worn that it became part of the man, and changed the face of history.

VI. PARIS AND GENEVA: 1750–54

In December, 1750, Rousseau suffered so severely from his bladder ailment that he was confined to his bed for six weeks. This misfortune increased his tendency to melancholy and privacy. His rich acquaintances sent him their own physicians, but the medical science of the time had not equipped them to help him. "The more I submitted to their direction, the yellower, thinner, and feebler I became. My imagination . . . presented to me, on this side of the tomb, nothing but continued sufferings from the gravel, stone, and retention of urine. Everything which gave relief to others—ptisans, baths, and bleeding—increased my tortures."[88]

Early in 1751 Thérèse presented him with a third child, which followed its predecessors to the foundling asylum. He later explained that he was too poor to bring up children, that they would have been ruined by being reared by the Levasseurs, and that they would have played havoc with his work as a writer and a musician. His sickness had compelled him to resign his position and income as cashier for Dupin de Francueil; henceforth he supported himself chiefly by copying music at ten sous the page. Through the negligence of Diderot, or the parsimony of the publishers, Rousseau received nothing from the sale of his *Discourse.* His music proved more profitable than his philosophy.

On October 18, 1752, through Duclos' influence, Rousseau's operetta, *Le Devin du village,* was presented before King and court at Fontainebleau, and with such success that it was repeated there a week later. A performance for the public in Paris (March 1, 1753) won a wider acclaim, and the retiring author found himself again a celebrity. The little *intermède,* for which Rousseau had written both words and music, was almost an *obbligato* to the *Discourse:* the shepherdess Colette, saddened by the flirtations of Colin with urban demoiselles, is instructed by the village soothsayer to win him back by flirtations of her own; Colin, jealous, returns, and together they sing ballads praising rural as against city life. Rousseau attended the première, and was almost reconciled to society:

> There is no clapping before the King; therefore everything was heard, which was advantageous to the author and the piece. I heard about me the whispering of women, who appeared as beautiful as angels. They said to one another, in a low voice: "This is charming; this is ravishing; there is not a sound that does not go to the heart." The pleasure of giving this emotion to so many amiable persons moved me to tears; and these I could not restrain in the first duet, when I observed that I was not the only person who wept.[89]

That evening the Duc d'Aumont sent him word to come to the palace the next morning at eleven to be presented to the King; and the messenger added that the King was expected to give the composer a pension. But Rousseau's bladder vetoed the plan.

> Will it be believed that the night of so brilliant a day was for me a night of anguish and perplexity? My first thought was that after being presented I should frequently want to retire; this had made me suffer very considerably at the theater, and might torment me the next day, when I should be in the gallery or in the King's apartment, amongst all the great, waiting for the departure of his Majesty. My infirmity was the principal cause which prevented me from mixing in polite companies and enjoying the conversation of the fair. . . . None but persons who are acquainted with this situation can judge of the horror which being exposed to the risk of it inspires.[90]

So he sent word that he could not come. Two days later Diderot reproved him for missing such a chance to provide more fitly for himself and Thérèse. "He spoke of the pension with more warmth than, on such a subject, I should have expected from a philosopher. . . . Although I was obliged to him for his good wishes, I could not relish his maxims, which produced a heated dispute, the first I ever had with him."[91] He was not without some profit from his *Devin.* Mme. de Pompadour liked it so well that she herself played the part of Colette in its second presentation at the court; she sent him fifty louis d'or, and Louis sent him a hundred.[92] The King himself, "with the worst voice in his kingdom," went around singing Colette's sad aria "J'ai perdu mon serviteur"—a premonition of Gluck.

Meanwhile Rousseau prepared articles on music for the *Encyclopédie.* "These I executed in great haste, and consequently very ill, in the three months that Diderot had allowed me." Rameau criticized these contributions severely in a pamphlet, *Erreurs sur la musique dans l'Encyclopédie* (1755). Rousseau amended the articles, and made them the basis of a *Dictionnaire de la musique* (1767). His contemporaries, excepting Rameau, rated him "a musician of the very first order";[93] we should now consider him as a good composer in a minor genre; but he was without question the most interesting writer on music in that generation.

When a troupe of Italian opera singers invaded Paris in 1752, a controversy flared up on the relative merits of French versus Italian music. Rousseau leaped into the fray with a *Lettre sur la musique française* (1753), "in which," said Grimm, "he proves that it is impossible to compose music to French words; that the French language is altogether unfit for music; that the French have never had music, and never will."[94] Rousseau was all for melody. "We sang some old song," he wrote in his *Rêveries*, "which was far better than modern discord";[95] what age has not heard that plaint? In the article "Opéra" in his *Dictionnaire de la musique* he gave a cue to Wagner: he defined opera as "a dramatic and lyrical spectacle which seeks to reunite all the charms of the *beaux arts* in the representation of a passionate action. . . . The constituents of an opera are the poem, the music, and the decoration: the poetry speaks to the spirit, the music to the ear, the painting to the eye. . . . Greek dramas could be called operas."[96]

About this time (1752) Maurice-Quentin de La Tour portrayed Rousseau in pastel.[97] He caught Jean-Jacques smiling, handsome, and well-groomed; Diderot condemned the portrait as unfair to the truth.[98] Marmontel described Rousseau as seen in these years at d'Holbach's dinners: "He had just gained the prize . . . at Dijon. . . . A timid politeness, sometimes . . . so obsequious as to border on humility. Through his fearful reserve distrust was visible; his lowering eyes watched everything with a look full of gloomy suspicion. He seldom entered into conversation, and rarely opened himself to us."[99]

Having so forcefully denounced science and philosophy, Rousseau was ill at ease among the *philosophes* who dominated the salons. His *Discourse* had committed him to the defense of religion. Mme. d'Épinay tells how, at a dinner given by Mme. Quinault, the hostess, finding the talk too irreverent, begged her guests to "respect at least natural religion." "No more than any other," retorted the Marquis de Saint-Lambert, lately Voltaire's rival for Mme. du Châtelet, and soon to be Rousseau's for Mme. d'Houdetot. Mme. d'Épinay continues:

> At this answer Rousseau became angry, and muttered something which made the company laugh at him. "If," he said, "it is cowardice to allow anyone to speak ill of an absent friend, it is a crime to allow anyone to speak ill of his God, who is present; and I believe in God, Messieurs." . . . Turning to Saint-Lambert I said, "You, Monsieur, who are a poet, will agree with me that the existence of an eternal being, all powerful and supremely intelligent, is the germ of the most beautiful enthusiasm." "I confess," he replied, "that it is beautiful to see this God inclining his face to the earth, . . . but it is the germ of the follies—" "Monsieur," interrupted Rousseau, "if you say one word more I shall leave the room." In fact he had left his seat, and was seriously meditating flight, when the Prince de —— was announced,[100]

and everybody forgot the subject of the debate. If we may believe Mme. d'Épinay's *Memoirs*, Rousseau told her that these atheists well deserved eternal hell.[101]

In the preface to his comedy *Narcisse*—which was played by the Comédie Française on December 18, 1752—Rousseau renewed his war on civilization. "The taste for letters always announces in a people the commencement of a corruption which it very soon accelerates. This taste arises in a nation only from two evil sources . . . : idleness, and the desire for distinction."[102] Nevertheless he continued till 1754 to attend d'Holbach's "synagogue" of freethinkers. There one day Marmontel, Grimm, Saint-Lambert, and others heard the Abbé Petit read a tragedy that he had composed. They found it lamentable, but praised it handsomely; the abbé had too much wine in him to perceive their irony, and swelled with content. Rousseau, resenting the insincerity of his friends, fell upon the abbé with a merciless tirade: "Your piece is worthless; . . . all these gentlemen are mocking you; go away from here, and return to be vicar in your village."[103] D'Holbach reproved Rousseau for his rudeness; Rousseau left in anger, and for a year he stayed away.

His companions had destroyed his Catholicism, but not his faith in the fundamentals of Christianity. His boyhood Protestantism came to the surface again as his Catholicism subsided. He idealized the Geneva of his youth, and thought that he would be more comfortable there than in a Paris that irked his soul. If he returned to Geneva he would regain the proud title of citizen, with the exclusive privileges that this implied. In June, 1754, he took the coach to Chambéry, found Mme. de Warens poor and unhappy, opened his purse to her, and went on to Geneva. There he was welcomed as a repentant prodigal son; he seems to have signed a statement reaffirming the Calvinist creed;[104] the Genevan clergy rejoiced in the reclamation of an Encyclopedist to their evangelical faith. He was reinstated as a citizen, and thereafter proudly signed himself "Jean-Jacques Rousseau, *Citoyen*."

> I was so impressed with the kindness shown me . . . by the [civic] council and the [ecclesiastical] consistory, and by the great civility and obliging behavior of the magistrates, ministers, and citizens, that . . . I did not think of going back to Paris except to break up housekeeping, find a situation for Monsieur and Madame Levasseur, or provide for their subsistence, and then return with Thérèse to Geneva, there to settle for the rest of my days.[105]

He could now appreciate more thoroughly than in his boyhood the beauty of the lake and its shores. "I preserved a lively remembrance of . . . the farther end of the lake, and of this, some years afterward, I gave a description in *La Nouvelle Héloïse*." The Swiss peasants entered into the bucolic idyl he was to write in that novel: they owned their farms, were free from poll tax and *corvée*, busied themselves with domestic crafts in winter, and stood contentedly apart from the noise and strife of the world. He had in mind the small city-states of Switzerland when he described his political ideal in *Le Contrat social*.

In October, 1754, he left for Paris, promising to be back soon. Voltaire arrived in Geneva two months after Rousseau's departure, and settled down at Les Délices. In Paris Jean-Jacques resumed his friendship with Diderot and Grimm, but not as trustfully as before. When he learned that Mme. d'Holbach had died, he wrote the Baron a tender letter of condolence; the two men were reconciled, and Rousseau again sat at table with the infidels. For three years more he was, to all appearances, one of the *philosophes;* his new Calvinist creed sat lightly on his thoughts. He was absorbed now in seeing through the press his second *Discourse,* which was to be more world-shaking than the first.

VII. THE CRIMES OF CIVILIZATION

In November, 1753, the Dijon Academy announced another competition. The new question was: "What is the origin of inequality among men, and is it authorized by natural law?" "Struck with this great question," says Rousseau, "I was surprised that the Academy had dared to propose it; but since it had shown the courage, . . . I immediately undertook the discussion."[106] He entitled his contribution *Discours sur l'origine et les fondements de l'inégalité parmi les hommes.* At Chambéry on June 12, 1754, he dedicated this second *Discourse* "to the Republic of Geneva," and added an address to the "most honorable, magnificent, and Sovereign Lords," voicing some notable opinions on politics:

> In my researches after the best rules common sense can lay down for the constitution of a government, I have been so struck at finding them all in actuality in your own, that even had I not been born within your walls I should have thought it indispensable for me to offer this picture of human society to that people which of all others seems to be possessed of its greatest advantages, and to have best guarded against its abuses.[107]

He complimented Geneva in terms quite applicable to Switzerland today:

> A country diverted, by a fortunate lack of power, from the brutal love of conquest, and secured, by a still more fortunate situation, from the fear of becoming itself the conquest of other states: a free city situated between several nations, none of which should have any interest in attacking it, while each had an interest in preventing it from being attacked by the others.[108]

And the future idol of the French Revolution approved the limitations placed upon democracy in Geneva, where only eight per cent of the population could vote:

> In order to prevent self-interest and ill-conceived projects, and all such dangerous innovations as finally ruined the Athenians, each man should not be at liberty to propose new laws at pleasure; this right should belong exclusively to the magistrates. . . . It is above all the great antiquity of the laws which makes them sacred and venerable; men soon learn to despise laws which they see daily altered; and states, by accustoming themselves to neglect their ancient customs under the pretext of improvement, often introduce greater evils than those they endeavor to remove.[109]

Was this only a plea for readmission to Genevan citizenship?

This aim having been achieved, Rousseau submitted his essay to the Dijon Academy. He was not awarded the prize, but when, in June, 1755, he published the *Discours,* he had the satisfaction of becoming again the exciting topic of Paris salons. He had left no paradox unturned to stir debate. He did not deny "natural" or biological inequality; he recognized that some individuals are by birth healthier or stronger than others in body or character or mind. But he argued that all other inequalities—economic, political, social, moral—are unnatural, and arose when men left the "state of nature," established private property, and set up states to protect property and privilege. "Man is naturally good";[110] he becomes bad chiefly through social institutions that restrain or corrupt his tendencies to natural behavior. Rousseau pictured an ideal primitive condition in which most men were strong of limb, fleet of foot, clear of eye,* and lived a life of action in which thought was always a tool and incident of action, and not an enfeebling substitute for it. He contrasted this natural health with the proliferating diseases engendered in civilization by wealth and sedentary occupations.

> The greater part of our ills are of our own making, and we might have avoided them, nearly all, by adhering to that simple, uniform, and solitary manner of life which nature prescribed. If she destined man to be healthy, I venture to declare that a state of reflection is a state contrary to nature, and that a thinking man is a depraved animal [*l'homme qui médite est un animal dépravé*]. When we think of the good constitution of the savages—at least of those whom we have not ruined with our spirituous liquors—and reflect that they are troubled with hardly any disorders save wounds and old age, we are tempted to believe that in following the history of civil society we shall be telling that of human sickness.[112]

Rousseau admitted that his ideal "state of nature . . . perhaps never existed, and probably never will";[113] he offered it not as a fact of history but as a standard of comparison. This is what he meant by the startling proposal: "Let us begin, then, by laying facts aside, as they do not affect the question. The investigations we may enter into . . . must not be treated as historical truths, but only as conditional and hypothetical reasonings."[114] However, we may form some idea of man's life before the rise of social organization, by observing the condition and conduct of modern states, for "states today remain in a state of nature"[115]—each individually sovereign, and knowing in actuality no law but those of cunning and force; we may suppose that presocial man lived in a like condition of individual sovereignty, insecurity, collective chaos, and intermittent violence. Rousseau's ideal was not such an imaginary presocial existence [for society may be as old as man], but a later stage of development in which men lived in patriarchal families and tribal groups, and had not yet instituted private property. "The most ancient of all societies, and the only one that is natural, is the family."[116] That was the time of maximal happiness for mankind; it had defects, pains, and punishments, but it had no laws beyond parental authority and family discipline; "it was altogether the best state that man could experience, so that he can have departed from it only through some fatal accident."[117] That accident was the establishment of individual property, from which came economic, political, and social inequality, and most of the evils of modern life.

---

* "What I am not, that for me is God and virtue."—Nietzsche.[111]

The first man who, having enclosed a piece of ground, bethought himself of saying, *This is mine*, and found people simple enough to believe him, was the real founder of civil society. From how many crimes, wars, and murders, from how many horrors and misfortunes, might not anyone have saved mankind, by pulling up the stakes, or filling up the ditch, and crying to his fellows: "Beware of listening to this impostor; you are undone if you once forget that the fruits of the earth belong to us all, and the earth itself to nobody."[118]

From that permitted usurpation came the curses of civilization: class divisions, slavery, serfdom, envy, robbery, war, legal injustice, political corruption, commercial chicanery, inventions, science, literature, art, "progress" —in one word, degeneration. To protect private property, force was organized, and became the state; to facilitate government, law was developed to habituate the weak to submit to the strong with a minimum of force and expense.[119] Hence it came about that "the privileged few gorge themselves with superfluities, while the starving multitude lack the bare necessaries of life."[120] Added to these basic inequities is a mass of derivative iniquities: "shameful methods sometimes practiced to prevent the birth of human beings," abortion, infanticide, castration, perversions, "the exposure or murder of multitudes of infants who fall victims to the poverty of their parents."[121] All these calamities are demoralizing; they are unknown to animals; they make "civilization" a cancer on the body of mankind. In comparison with this polymorphous corruption and perversity, the life of the savage is healthy, sane, and humane.

Should we therefore go back to savagery? "Must societies be totally abolished? Must *mine* and *thine* be annulled, and must we return to the forests to live among bears?" That is no longer possible for us; the poison of civilization is in our blood, and we shall not eradicate it by flight to the woods. To end private property, government, and law would be to plunge the people into a chaos worse than civilization. "Once man has left it he can never return to the time of innocence and equality."[122] Revolution may be justified, for force may justly overthrow what force has set up and maintained;[123] but revolution is not now advisable. The best we can do is to study the Gospels again, and try to cleanse our evil impulses by practicing the ethics of Christianity.[124] We can make a natural sympathy for our fellow men the basis of morality and social order. We can resolve to live a less complicated life, content with necessaries, scorning luxuries, shunning the race and fever of "progress." We can slough off, one by one, the artificialities, hypocrisies, and corruptions of civilization, and remold ourselves to honesty, naturalness, and sincerity. We can leave the noise and riot of our cities, their hatreds, licentiousness, and crimes, and go to live in rural simplicity and domestic duties and content. We can abandon the pretensions and blind alleys of philosophy, and return to a religious faith that will uphold us in the face of suffering and death.

Today, having heard all this a hundred times, we sense a certain artificiality in this righteous indignation. We are not sure that the evils Rousseau described arise from corrupt institutions rather than from the nature of man;

after all, it is human nature that made the institutions. When Jean-Jacques wrote his second *Discourse* the idealization of the "friendly and flowing savage" had reached its peak. In 1640 Walter Hamond had published a pamphlet "proving that the inhabitants of Madagascar are the happiest people in the world."[125] Jesuit accounts of Huron and Iroquois Indians seemed to bear out Defoe's picture of Robinson Crusoe's amiable man Friday. Voltaire generally laughed at the legend of the noble savage, but he used it gaily in *L'Ingénu*. Diderot played with it in the *Supplément au Voyage de Bougainville*. But Helvétius ridiculed Rousseau's idealization of the savage,[126] and Duclos, though a faithful friend of Jean-Jacques, argued that "it is among savages that crime is most frequent; the childhood of a nation is not its age of innocence."[127] All in all, the intellectual climate favored Rousseau's thesis.

The victims of Rousseau's invective calmed their consciences by representing the *Discourse*, like its predecessor, as a pose. Mme. du Deffand openly called him a charlatan.[128] Skeptics laughed at his professions of Christian orthodoxy, at his literal interpretation of Genesis.[129] The *philosophes* began to distrust him as upsetting their schemes to win the government to their ideas of social reform; they were not in favor of appealing to the resentments of the poor; they recognized the reality of exploitation, but they saw no constructive principle in the replacement of magistrates with mobs. The government itself made no protest against Rousseau's denunciations; probably the court took the essay as an exercise in declamation. Rousseau was proud of his eloquence; he sent a copy of the *Discourse* to Voltaire, and anxiously awaited a word of praise. Voltaire's reply is one of the gems of French literature, wisdom, and manners:

> I have received, Monsieur, your new book against the human race. I thank you for it. You will please men, to whom you tell truths that concern them, but you will not correct them. You paint in very true colors the horrors of human society; . . . no one has ever employed so much intellect to persuade men to be beasts. In reading your work one is seized with a desire to walk on four paws [*marcher à quatre pattes*]. However, as it is more than sixty years since I lost that habit, I feel, unfortunately, that it is impossible for me to resume it. . . .
>
> I agree with you that literature and the sciences have sometimes been the cause of much evil. . . . [But] admit that neither Cicero, nor Varro, nor Lucretius, nor Virgil, nor Horace had the least share in the proscriptions of Marius, Sulla, Antony, Lepidus, Octavius. . . . Confess that Petrarch and Boccaccio did not cause the intestine troubles of Italy, that the badinage of Marot did not cause the Massacre of St. Bartholomew, and that Corneille's *Le Cid* did not produce the wars of the Fronde. The great crimes were committed by celebrated but ignorant men. That which has made, and will always make, this world a vale of tears is the insatiable cupidity and indomitable pride of men. . . . Literature nourishes the soul, corrects it, consoles it; it makes your glory at the same time that you write against it. . . .
>
> M. Chapuis informs me that your health is quite bad. You must come and restore it in your native air, to enjoy freedom, to drink with me the milk of our cows, and browse on our herbs. I am, very philosophically and with the tenderest esteem, Monsieur, your very humble and very obedient servant.[130]

Rousseau replied with equal courtesy, and promised to visit Les Délices when he returned to Switzerland.[131] But he was deeply disappointed by the reception of his *Discourse* in the Geneva to which he had dedicated it with such ingratiating praise. Apparently the tight little oligarchy that ruled the republic felt some of the barbs of that essay, and did not relish Rousseau's wholesale condemnation of property, government, and law. "I did not perceive that a single Genevan was pleased with the hearty zeal found in the work."[132] He decided that the time was not ripe for his return to Geneva.

VIII. THE CONSERVATIVE

The same year 1755 that witnessed the publication of the second *Discourse* saw the appearance, in Volume V of the *Encyclopédie*, of a long article by Rousseau—"Discours sur l'économie politique." It requires note because it diverged from the earlier discourses in some vital particulars. Here society, government, and law are honored as natural results of man's nature and needs, and private property is described as a social boon and a basic right. "It is certain that the right of property is the most sacred of all the rights of citizenship, and even more important in some respects than liberty itself. . . . Property is the true foundation of civil society, and the real guarantee of the undertakings of citizens";[133] i.e., men will not work beyond the provision of their simplest needs unless they may keep the surplus product as their own, to consume or transmit as they may desire. Now Rousseau approves the bequest of property from parents to children, and cheerfully accepts the class divisions that result. "Nothing is more fatal to morality and the republic than the continual shifting of rank and fortune among the citizens; such changes are both the proof and the source of a thousand disorders, and overturn and confound everything."[134]

But he continues to inveigh against social injustice and the class favoritism of the law. Just as the state should protect private property and its lawful inheritance, so "the members of a society ought to contribute from their property to the support of the state." A rigorous tax ought to be laid upon all persons in graduated proportion to their property and "the superfluity of their possessions."[135] There should be no tax on necessaries, but a heavy tax on luxuries. The state should finance a national system of education. "If the children are brought up in common [in national schools] in the bosom of equality, if they are imbued with the laws of the state and the precepts of the general will, . . . we cannot doubt that they will cherish one another mutually as brothers, . . . to become in time defenders and fathers of the country of which they will have been the children."[136] Patriotism is better than cosmopolitanism or a watery pretense of universal sympathy.[137]

As the two earlier discourses were overwhelmingly individualistic, so the article on political economy is predominantly social-istic. Now for the first time Rousseau announces his peculiar doctrine that there is in every society a "general will" over and above the algebraic sum of the wishes and dislikes of its constituent individuals. The community, in Rousseau's developing philosophy, is a social organism with its own soul:

> The body politic is also a moral being, possessed of a will; and this general will, which tends always to the preservation and welfare of the whole and of every part, is the source of the laws, and constitutes for all the members of the state, in their relations to one another, the rule of what is just or unjust.[138]

Around this conception Rousseau builds the ethics and the politics that will henceforth dominate his views of public affairs. The rebel who thought of virtue as the expression of the free and natural man now defines it as "nothing more than the conformity of particular wills with the general will";[139] and he who so recently saw law as one of the sins of civilization, as a convenient tool for keeping exploited masses in docile order, now declares that "it is to law alone that men owe justice and liberty; it is that salutary organ of the will of all which establishes, in civil right, the natural equality between men; it is the celestial voice which dictates to each citizen the precepts of public reason."[140]

Perhaps the harassed editors of the *Encyclopédie* had cautioned Rousseau to moderate, in this article, his attack upon civilization. Seven years later, in *The Social Contract*, we shall find him defending the community against the individual, and building his political philosophy upon the notion of a sacred and supreme general will. Meanwhile, however, he continued to be an individualist and a rebel, hating Paris, asserting himself against his friends, and making fresh enemies every day.

IX. ESCAPE FROM PARIS: 1756

His closest friends now were Grimm, Diderot, and Mme. d'Épinay. Grimm was born at Ratisbon in 1723, and was therefore eleven years younger than Rousseau. He was educated at Leipzig in the closing decade of Bach's life, and received from Johann August Ernesti a solid grounding in the languages and literature of ancient Greece and Rome. Coming to Paris in 1749, he learned French with German thoroughness, and was soon writing articles for *Le Mercure*. In 1750 he became private secretary to Count von Friesen. His love of music attached him to Rousseau, while a deeper hunger brought him to the feet of Mlle. Fel, a singer at the opera. When she preferred M. Cahusac, Grimm, says Rousseau,

> took this so much to heart that the appearances of his affliction became tragical. . . . He passed days and nights in a continued lethargy. He lay with his eyes open, . . . without speaking, eating, or stirring. . . . The Abbé Raynal and I watched over him; the Abbé, more robust than I, and in better health than I was, by night, and I by day, without ever both being absent at one time.[141]

Von Friesen summoned a doctor, who refused to prescribe anything except time. "At length, one morning, Grimm rose, dressed himself, and returned to his regular way of life, without either then or later mentioning . . . this irregular lethargy."[142]

Rousseau introduced Grimm to Diderot, and the three dreamed of going to Italy together. Grimm absorbed avidly the stream of ideas spouting from the cornucopia of Diderot's mind; he learned the language of the irreverent *philosophes*, wrote an agnostic *Catéchisme pour les enfants*, and advised von Friesen to take three mistresses at one time "in memory of the Holy Trinity."[143] Rousseau was irked by the growing intimacy between Grimm, whom Sainte-Beuve was to call "the most French of Germans," and Diderot, "the most German of Frenchmen."[144] "Grimm," Jean-Jacques complained, "you neglect me, and I forgive you for it." Grimm took him at his word. "He said I was right, . . . and shook off all restraint; so that I saw no more of him except in company with our common friends."[145]

In 1747 the Abbé Raynal had begun to send to French and foreign subscribers a fortnightly newsletter, *Nouvelles littéraires*, reporting events in the French world of letters, science, philosophy, and art. In 1753 he turned the enterprise over to Grimm, who, with help from Diderot and others, carried it on till 1790. Under Grimm the letters had many distinguished subscribers, including Queen Louisa Ulrika of Sweden, former King Stanislas Leszczyński of Poland, Catherine II of Russia, the Princess of Saxe-Gotha, the Prince and Princess of Hesse-Darmstadt, the Duchess of Saxe-Coburg, the Grand Duke of Tuscany, Duke Karl August of Saxe-Weimar. Frederick the Great held back for a time, having several correspondents in France; finally he consented to receive the letters, but he never paid. Grimm's first number (May, 1753) announced his plan:

> In the sheets which are requested of us we shall not spend time over the brochures with which Paris is daily inundated; . . . rather we shall seek to give an exact account, a logical analysis (*critique raisonnée*) of the books which deserve to hold the attention of the public. The drama, which constitutes so brilliant a part of French literature, will be a considerable part of our report. In general we shall let nothing escape us which is worthy of the curiosity of other peoples.[146]

This famous *Correspondance littéraire* is now a chief and precious record for the intellectual history of France in the second half of the eighteenth century. Grimm could be forthright in his critiques, since these were not known to the French public or to the author discussed. He was usually fair, except, later, to Rousseau. He made many judicious judgments, but misjudged *Candide* as "unable to bear serious criticism"; this, however, was without prejudice, for he described Voltaire as "the most fascinating, the most agreeable, and the most famous man in Europe."[147] Voltaire returned the compliment in his impish way: "What is this Bohemian thinking about, to have more wit than we?"[148] It was Grimm's *Correspondance*, more than any other writings except Voltaire's, that spread through Europe the ideas of the French Enlightenment. Yet he had his doubts of the *philosophes* and their faith in progress. "The world," he said, "is made up of nothing but abuses which none but a madman would try to reform."[149] And in 1757 he wrote:

> It seems to me that the eighteenth century has surpassed all others in the eulogiums that it has heaped upon itself. . . . A little more, and the best minds

will persuade themselves that the mild and peaceful empire of philosophy is about to succeed the long tempests of unreason, and to establish forever the repose, the tranquillity, and the happiness of mankind. . . . But unluckily the true philosopher has less consoling but more accurate notions. . . . I am a long way from believing that we are approaching the age of reason, and I lack but little of believing that Europe is threatened by some fatal revolution.[150]

We catch here a hint of the pride and vanity that sometimes irritated Grimm's friends. More Gallic than the Gauls, he spent hours on grooming himself, powdering his face and hair, and so sprinkling himself with perfume that he was nicknamed "the musk bear."[151] His *Correspondance* shows him scattering compliments with expectant hand. Frederick the Great made it a condition of subscribing to the letters that Grimm should "spare me his compliments."[152] Such flattery, of course, was part of epistolary style in the Old Regime.

Grimm, usually cold and calculating, caught the attention of Paris by almost dying for Mlle. Fel, and fighting a duel for Mme. d'Épinay. Louise-Florence Tardieu d'Esclavelles was the daughter of a Valenciennes baron who died in the King's service in 1737. Eight years later Louise, aged twenty, married Denis-Joseph Lalive d'Épinay, son of a rich tax collector. They came to live in the handsome Château de la Chevrette, nine miles from Paris, near the Forest of Montmorency. Her happiness bubbled. "Will my heart ever be able to endure such happiness?" she wondered. She wrote to a cousin: "He was playing the harpsichord, I was sitting on the arm of his chair, my left hand resting on his shoulder, and my other hand turning over the leaves; he never missed kissing it each time it passed in front of his lips."[153]

She was not beautiful, but she was charmingly petite, *très bien faite* (she tells us);[154] and her big black eyes would later ravish Voltaire. But "always to feel the same thing" is soon "the same as to feel nothing";[155] after a year M. d'Épinay no longer noticed those eyes. He had been promiscuous before marriage, he became so again. He drank heavily, gambled heavily, and spent a fortune on the sisters Verrières, whom he installed in a cottage near La Chevrette. Meanwhile his wife bore him two children. In 1748 he returned from a trip in the provinces, slept with his wife, and infected her with syphilis. Broken in health and spirits, she secured a legal separation from her husband. He agreed to a generous settlement; she inherited the fortune of her uncle; she kept La Chevrette; she tried to forget her unhappiness by caring for her children and helping her friends. When one of these, Mme. de Julli, fell mortally ill of smallpox, Louise went to nurse her, and stayed with her to the end, running the risk of an infection that might have killed her or disfigured her for life.

All her friends agreed that she should take a lover. One came (1746), that same Dupin de Francueil who gave employment to Rousseau. He began with music, and ended with syphilis; he was soon cured, while she continued to suffer.[156] He joined her husband in sharing the Desmoiselles de Verrières. Duclos told her bluntly, "Francueil and your husband have the two sisters between them."[157] She fell into a delirium that lasted thirty hours. Duclos sought to take Dupin's place, but she sent him away. To these misfortunes another was added. Mme. de Julli, dying, had given Louise a batch of papers revealing her amours, with an earnest request to burn them. Louise did. Then M. de Julli accused her of having knowingly burned the certificates of her own indebtedness to him. She denied the charge, but appearances were against her, for it was known that despite separation she was giving her husband financial help.

It was at this juncture that Grimm entered the drama. He had been introduced to Louise by Rousseau in 1751; the three had several times played or sung music together. One evening at a party given by Count von Friesen, a guest expressed conviction of Mme. d'Épinay's guilt. Grimm defended her; argument rose to the point of honor; accuser and defender fought a duel; Grimm was slightly wounded. Soon afterward the lost documents were found; Madame was exonerated; she thanked Grimm as her *preux chevalier*, and their mutual esteem ripened into one of the most enduring loves of that fitful age. When Baron d'Holbach sickened with grief over the death of his wife, and Grimm went off to take care of him in the countryside, Louise asked him: "But who will be my knight, monsieur, if I am attacked in your absence?" Grimm answered: "The same as before—your past life."[158] The reply was not beyond cavil, but it was beyond praise.

Rousseau had met Mme. d'Épinay in 1748 at Mme. Dupin's. She invited him to La Chevrette. Her *Memoirs* describe him fairly:

> He pays compliments, yet he is not polite, or at least he is without the air of politeness. He seems to be ignorant of the usages of society, but it is easily seen that he is infinitely intelligent. He has a brown complexion, white eyes that overflow with fire and give animation to his expression. . . . They say he is in bad health, and endures agony which he carefully conceals. . . . It is this, I fancy, which gives him from time to time an air of sullenness.[159]

His picture of her is not very gallant:

> Her conversation, though agreeable enough in mixed company, was uninteresting in private. . . . I was happy to show her little attentions, and gave her little fraternal kisses, which seemed not to be more sensual than herself. . . . She was very thin, very pale, and had a bosom like the back of her hand. This defect alone would have been sufficient to moderate my most ardent desires.[160]

For seven years he was welcomed in Mme. d'Épinay's home. When she saw how uncomfortable he was in Paris, she thought of ways to help him, but she knew that he would refuse money. One day, as they were walking through her park behind La Chevrette, she showed him a cottage, called L'Hermitage, which had belonged to her husband. It was unused and in disrepair, but its situation, on the very edge of the Forest of Montmorency, excited Rousseau to exclaim: "Ah, madame, what a delightful habitation! This asylum was expressly prepared for me."[161] Madame made no reply, but when, in September, 1755, they walked again to the cottage, Rousseau was surprised to find it repaired, the six rooms furnished, and the grounds cleared and neat. He quotes her as saying: "My dear, here behold your refuge; it is you who have chosen it; friendship offers it to you. I hope this will remove your cruel idea of separating from me." She knew that he had thought of residing in Switzerland; perhaps she did not know that his enthusiasm for Geneva had cooled. He "bathed with tears the beneficent hand" of his friend, but hesitated to accept her offer. She won Thérèse and Mme. Levasseur to her plan, and "at length she triumphed over all my resolutions."

On Easter Sunday, 1756, adding grace to her gift, she came to Paris in her coach, and took her "bear," as she called him, along with his mistress and his mother-in-law, to the Hermitage. Thérèse did not relish separation from Paris, but Rousseau, sniffing the air, was happier than at any time since his idyl with Mme. de Warens. "On April 9, 1756, I began to live."[162] Grimm darkened the occasion with a warning to Mme. d'Épinay:

> You do Rousseau a very ill service by giving him the Hermitage, but you do yourself a very much worse one. Solitude will complete the work of blackening his imagination; all his friends will be, in his eyes, unjust and ungrateful, and you first of all, if you refuse a single time to place yourself at his orders.[163]

Then Grimm, now secretary to Maréchal d'Estrées, went off to play his part in the war that was to remake the map of the world.

CHAPTER II

The Seven Years' War

1756–63

I. HOW TO START A WAR

BY 1756 Europe had known eight years of peace. But the War of the Austrian Succession had settled nothing. It had left Austria insecure in Bohemia and Italy, Prussia insecure in Silesia, Britain insecure in Hanover, France insecure in India, America, and on the Rhine. The Treaty of Aix-la-Chapelle (1748) had achieved no territorial settlement comparable in stability with that reached by the Treaty of Westphalia a century before. The old balance of power had been disturbed by the growth of the Prussian army and the British navy; that army might sally forth on new absorptions; that navy needed only time to capture the colonies of France, Holland, and Spain. The rising spirit of nationalism was fed in England by the profits and prospects of commerce, in Prussia by successful war, in France by a cultural superiority uncomfortably conscious of martial decline. The conflict between Catholicism and Protestantism had ended in a stalemate; both sides waited for some turn of chance to renew the Thirty Years' War for possession of the European soul.

Austria took the initiative in preparing a new throw of the human dice. Maria Theresa, the thirty-nine-years-old but still fair head of the Austrian empire, had all the pride of her Hapsburg ancestry, all the anger of a woman scorned; how could she live with Silesia amputated from her inherited realm—whose territorial integrity all the major states of Europe had guaranteed? Even the Frederick who had humiliated her would later praise her "courage and ability," and the way in which "when it seemed that events were conspiring to ruin her, this . . . younger ruler caught the spirit of government, and became the soul of her council."[1] Defeated, yielding Silesia as the price of peace, she made the peace only a truce, and devoted herself to the reform of administration, the restoration of her shattered armies, and the acquisition of strong allies. Frequently she visited the camps where her troops were being trained; for this purpose she traveled to Prague in Bohemia, to Olmütz in Moravia; she inspired the soldiers with rewards and distinctions, and even more by her regal and yet womanly presence. Her generals did not have to swear fidelity to her, for this was in their blood and chivalry; so the Prince of Liechtenstein spent 200,000 écus ($1,500,000?) of his fortune in recruiting and equipping for her a complete artillery corps. She founded near Vienna a War College for the younger nobility, and brought to its staff the best teachers of geometry, geography, fortification, and history. "Under her," said Frederick, "the military of Austria acquired a degree of perfection never known to her predecessors, and a woman carried out designs worthy of a great man."[2]

Diplomacy was the other side of the design. She sent agents everywhere to win friends for Austria and stir up hostility to Frederick. She noted the rising strength of Russia, which had been organized by Peter the Great and was now commanded by the Czarina Elizaveta Petrovna; she saw to it that Frederick's sarcastic remarks about the amours of the Russian Empress should reach her ears. Maria Theresa would gladly have renewed her alliance with England, but that entente had been soured by England's separate peace with Prussia (1745), which had compelled Austria to surrender Silesia. Now England's foreign policy was turning to protect her trade in the Baltic against the power of Russia, and her hold on Hanover against any threat from Prussia or France. She depended upon Russia for the timber of her navy, and she depended upon her navy for victory in war. So on September 30, 1755, England signed a treaty that bound Russia, in return for English subsidies, to maintain 55,000 troops in Livonia; these, the English hoped, would deter Frederick from any expansionist adventures to the west.

But how should England deal with France? For hundreds of years France had been her enemy. Time and again France had fomented or financed Scottish hostilities to England; repeatedly she had prepared or threatened to invade the British Isles. Now she was the only state that challenged Britain on the seas and in the colonial world. To defeat France decisively would be to win her colonies in America and India; it would be to destroy her navy or render it impotent; the British Empire would then be not only secure but supreme. So William Pitt the Elder argued to Parliament day after day, in the most forceful oratory that that body had ever heard. But could France be defeated? Yes, said Pitt, by allying Prussia to England. Would it not be dangerous to let Prussia grow stronger? No, Pitt answered; Prussia had a great army, which on this plan would help England to protect Hanover, but she had no navy, and therefore could not rival Britain on the sea. It seemed wiser to let Protestant Prussia replace Catholic France or Catholic Austria as the dominant power on the Continent, if that would let "Britannia rule the waves" and capture colonies. Any victories of Frederick in Europe would strengthen England overseas; hence Pitt's boast that he would win America and India on the battlefields of the Continent. England would supply money, Frederick would fight the land battles, England would win half the world. Parliament consented; Britain proposed to Prussia a pact for mutual defense.

Frederick had to accept this plan, for the development of events had clouded his victories. He knew that France was flirting with Austria; if France and Austria—worse yet, if Russia too—should unite against him he could hardly resist them all; in such a predicament only England could help him. If he signed the pact that England offered he could call upon her to keep Russia from attacking him; and if Russia abstained Austria might be dissuaded from war. On January 16, 1756, Frederick signed the Treaty of

Westminster, which pledged both England and Prussia to oppose the entry of foreign troops into Germany. That single clause, they hoped, would protect Prussia from Russia and Hanover from France.

France, Austria, and Russia all felt that this treaty was a betrayal by their allies. There had been no formal termination of the alliances that had bound England with Austria, and France with Prussia, in the War of the Austrian Succession. Maria Theresa, as she informed the British ambassador, was shocked to learn that her English friends had signed a pact with "the mortal and constant enemy of my person and my family."[3] Louis XV complained that Frederick had deceived him; Frederick replied that the treaty was purely defensive, and should give no offense to any power not meditating offense. Mme. de Pompadour, who chose and dominated French ministries, remembered that Frederick had charged her with depositing great sums in British banks, and had called her "*la demoiselle Poisson*" (Miss Fish) and "Cotillon IV" (Petticoat IV—fourth mistress of Louis XV). Louis remembered that Frederick had ridiculed the barnyard morals of the French King. The desertion struck France just when her armies and treasury were exhausted, and when her navy was only beginning to recover from the neglect it had suffered under the pacific ministry of Cardinal Fleury. In 1756 France had forty-five ships of the line, England had 130;[4] naval supplies were clogged with corruption and theft, naval discipline had been ruined by the invidious promotion of titled incompetents and the frequency of defeats. To whom now could France turn for an ally? To Russia?—but England had forestalled her. To Austria?—but in the last war France had violated her pledge to guarantee Maria Theresa's inheritance, had joined Prussia in attacking her, and had continued to attack her even when Frederick had made peace. Austria under the Hapsburgs, France under the Bourbons, had been foes for centuries; how could they and their peoples, long trained to mutual hatred, suddenly become friends?

Yet that was precisely the "reversal of alliances" that the Austrian government now proposed to France. So far as we can now trace its history, the plan took form in the mind of Count Wenzel Anton von Kaunitz, the ablest, most penetrating, most persevering diplomat produced on the European Continent in the eighteenth century. The Seven Years' War was to be a contest in arms between Frederick the Great and Marshal Daun, and a contest in brains between Kaunitz and Pitt. "Prince Kaunitz," said Frederick, "has the wisest head in Europe."[5]

Being a second son, Kaunitz was told to become a priest; instead, privately, he became a disciple of Voltaire.[6] As his father served as ambassador to the Vatican and as governor of Moravia, the son inherited diplomacy. At thirty-one he was Austrian envoy at Turin. His first dispatch to his government was so logically reasoned on such careful observation of political realities that Count von Uhlfeld, presenting it to Maria Theresa, said, "Behold your first minister."[7] At thirty-seven he was Austrian plenipotentiary at the Congress of Aix-la-Chapelle. There he defended the interests of Maria Theresa with such pertinacity and skill that even in her defeat the Empress was grateful for his services and devotion. And when, as early as 1749, he broached to her his plan for an alliance with France, she met with an open mind the idea of embracing the traditional enemy of her house. Her heart was set on defeating Frederick and regaining Silesia. But this, Kaunitz explained, could not be done by alliance with England, whose power was on the seas; it required alliance with France and Russia, whose power was on the land. Between these and Austria Frederick could be crushed. The Empress bade Kaunitz labor to this end.

In 1751 he was sent as ambassador to Paris. He astonished the nobility by the splendor of his official entry to the city; he pleased the populace by giving alms; he amused the salons with his luxurious raiment, his assortment of cosmetics, and his laboriously powdered curls;[8] "a most high-sniffing, fantastic, slightly insolent fellow," thought Carlyle;[9] but he impressed the King, his mistress, and their ministers by his knowledge of affairs and his appraisal of policies. Gradually he prepared their minds for an entente with Austria. He pictured the possibility of bringing Russia, Poland, and Saxony into taking part in disciplining Frederick. He asked what France had gained by her alliance with Prussia—only the aggrandizement of a land power that challenged the Continental hegemony of France; and had not Frederick repeatedly broken his pledge when it suited his interest?

Kaunitz was making good headway when Maria Theresa called him back to Vienna to be her chancellor, with full power over both domestic and foreign affairs (1753). His plan was long opposed by the aging nobles at the Viennese court; patiently he expounded and defended it; the Empress supported him; and on August 21, 1755, the proposal for an alliance with France received the formal approval of the Imperial ministry. Count Georg von Starhemberg, who had succeeded Kaunitz as Austrian ambassador at Paris, was instructed to promote the grand design at every opportunity with Louis XV and Mme. de Pompadour. Kaunitz sent a flattering letter to the *maîtresse-en-titre* (August 30, 1755), and attached to it a note which she was requested to hand secretly to the King. She did so. The note was from Maria Theresa, and read:

> As an empress and a queen, I promise that nothing will ever be disclosed of all that is going to be offered in my name by Count Starhemberg to the most Christian King, and that the deepest secrecy in this respect will always be maintained, whether negotiations succeed or fail. It will be understood, of course, that the King will give a similar declaration and promise.
>
> Vienna, June 21, 1755[10]

Louis appointed the Abbé de Bernis and the Marquise de Pompadour to confer privately with Starhemberg at her pavilion "Babiole." There the ambassador proposed, in the name of the Empress, that France should renounce her alliance with Prussia, and should pledge at least financial aid to Austria in case of war. He argued that Frederick was a useless and unreliable ally, and he hinted that Frederick was even now engaged in clandestine dealings with the British ministry. Austria, for her part, would refrain from any hostile action against France if France should make war upon England; in case of such a war Austria would allow France to occupy Ostend and Nieuport, and she might ultimately allow the Austrian Netherlands to fall to France.

Louis noted that the pact would involve him in an Austrian war against Prussia, but would not pledge Austrian aid to France against England. He had good reason to fear Frederick's army more than the Austrian—so often defeated and so badly led in the recent war. He instructed Bernis to reply that France would make no change in her alliance with Prussia until proofs were offered of Frederick's dealings with England. Kaunitz could as yet offer no such proofs, and was temporarily checked in his course. But when Louis received Frederick's acknowledgment of the Anglo-Prussian Treaty of Westminster, he saw that his alliance with Prussia was factually dead. Perhaps, amid his sins, it occurred to him that he might appease the Almighty by uniting the Catholic powers—France, Austria, Poland, and Spain—in a plan to control the destinies of Europe.[11] On May 1, 1756, the Treaty of Versailles completed the reversal of alliances. The preamble professed that the sole aim of the convention was to maintain the peace of Europe and the balance of power. If either of the contracting parties should be threatened in its European possessions by any power but England, the other would come to its aid by diplomatic intercession and, if necessary, by subsidies or troops. Austria would not promise aid to France against England, and France would not aid Austria against Prussia unless Prussia should be clearly the aggressor. As Louis saw no likelihood of Prussia endangering her gains by again attacking Austria, he and his mistress could deceive themselves into believing that the new alliance made for peace on the Continent.

Kaunitz had as yet fallen short of his aim to secure French aid against Prussia. But he was patient; perhaps he could prod Frederick into attacking Austria. Meanwhile he had little difficulty in persuading the Czarina into the new alliance. Elizaveta was eager to remove the Prussian obstacle to Russia's expansion westward. She offered to attack Prussia before the end of 1756 if Austria would promise to do likewise; and she promised, in that event, to make no peace with Prussia until Silesia was completely restored to Austria. She learned with delight that France had signed the Treaty of Versailles. Kaunitz had to check her enthusiasm; he knew that her armies would not be ready for a major campaign till 1757. Not until December 31, 1756, did he sign the agreement by which Russia formally joined the Franco-Austrian entente.

Meanwhile England, confident that her alliance with Frederick would immobilize Austria, had already begun naval operations against France, without any declaration of war. From June, 1755, English men-of-war seized French shipping wherever possible. France retaliated by preparing an invasion of England, and by sending a squadron of fifteen vessels, under the Duc de Richelieu, to attack Minorca. This island had been captured by the British in the War of the Spanish Succession (1709). To reinforce the small garrison there Britain dispatched ten ships under Admiral John Byng; three additional vessels joined these at Gibraltar. On May 20, 1756, the hostile fleets engaged near Minorca. The French were repulsed, but the English squadron suffered such damage that Byng led it back to Gibraltar, making no attempt to land reinforcements at Minorca. The helpless garrison surrendered; France had now a strategic post in the Mediterranean; Richelieu was hailed as a hero in Paris and Versailles, and Byng was executed on his own quarterdeck in Portsmouth Harbor (March 14, 1757) on the charge of failure to do his utmost for victory; Voltaire and Richelieu interceded for him in vain. This, said Voltaire, was England's way of "encouraging the others" who held British commands. On May 17, 1756, England declared war on France, but the official inception of the Seven Years' War was left to Frederick.

He knew that his conquest of Silesia had left him subject to *revanche* whenever Maria Theresa should find new resources and allies. His own resources were perilously limited. His kingdom was an assortment of *disjecta membra:* East Prussia was severed from Prussia proper by Poland, and the Prussian provinces in Westphalia and East Frisia were separated from Brandenburg by independent German states. Including these scattered fragments and Silesia, all Prussia had in 1756 some four million population, England eight million, France twenty. A large part of Prussia's population was in Silesia, which was still half Catholic and pro-Austrian. Only seven miles from Berlin lay the border of hostile Saxony, whose Elector, the Catholic King Augustus III of Poland, looked upon Frederick as an insolent and rapacious infidel. How could one survive in that caldron of enmity?

Only by wits, economy, a good army, and good generals. His own wits were as keen as any; he was the best-educated ruler of his age; he came off with honors in correspondence, conversation, and controversy with Voltaire. But his tongue was too sharp to be loosed; he might have had calmer seas had he not spoken of Elizaveta Petrovna, Maria Theresa, and Mme. de Pompadour as the "three first whores of Europe",[12] it is comforting to see that even the Great can be foolish now and then. As to the economy of Prussia, Frederick subjected it to state control and what seemed to him the unavoidable needs of possible war. He did not dare, in the circumstances, to change the feudal structure of Prussian life, lest it disturb the feudal organization of his army. That army was his salvation and his religion. Ninety per cent of his revenues went to its maintenance.[13] He called it the Atlas whose strong shoulders carried the state.[14] He built it up from the 100,000 men bequeathed him by his father to 150,000 in 1756. He disciplined it with severe punishments to immediate and precise obedience, to march steadily toward the opposing line without firing a shot till ordered, to change direction, and maneuver en masse, under fire. It had, at the beginning of the war, the best generals in Europe after Frederick himself—Schwerin, Seydlitz, and James Keith.

Almost as important as his generals were the spies that he had scattered among his enemies. They left him no doubt that Maria Theresa was forming a cordon of hostile powers around him. In 1753–55 his agents in Dresden and Warsaw secured copies of secret correspondence, between the Saxon and Austrian ministries, which convinced him that these courts were conspiring to attack and—if fortune favored—dismember Prussia, and that France was conniving at the scheme.[15] On June 23, 1756, he ordered the Prussian general in Königsberg to be prepared for an attack from Russia. He notified the British government that "the court of Vienna has three designs to which its present steps are tending: to establish its despotism in the Empire, to ruin the Protestant cause, and to reconquer Silesia."[16] He learned that Saxony was planning to enlarge its army from seventeen thousand to forty thousand during the winter;[17] he guessed that the allies were waiting for the spring of 1757 to advance upon him from three directions; and he resolved to strike before their mobilization was complete.

He felt that his only chance of escaping from his peril was to disable at least one of his foes before they could unite in action. Schwerin agreed with him, but one of his ministers, Count von Podewils, begged him not to give his enemies excuse for branding him as the aggressor; Frederick called him *"Monsieur de la timide politique."*[18] Long ago, in a secret "Political Testament" (1752), he had advised his successor to conquer Saxony and thereby give Prussia the geographical unity, the economic resources, and the political power indispensable to survival.[19] He had put the idea aside as beyond himself to realize; now it seemed to him a military necessity. He must protect his western frontier by disarming Saxony. Even in his almost idealistic *Anti-Machiavel* (1740) he had sanctioned an offensive war to forestall a threatened attack.[20] Mitchell, the Prussian minister in England, informed him that while the British government strongly desired the maintenance of peace on the Continent, it recognized the emergency that Frederick faced, and would not hold him "in the least to blame if he tried to forestall his enemies instead of waiting until they carried out their hostile intentions."[21]

In July, 1756, he sent an envoy to Maria Theresa soliciting assurance that Austria intended no attack upon Prussia either in the current year or in the next. A member of the Austrian cabinet thought such assurance should be given; Kaunitz refused to send it; all that Maria Theresa would say was that "in the present crisis I deem it necessary to take measures for the security of myself and my allies, which tend to the prejudice of no one."[22] Frederick sent a second message to the Empress, asking for a clearer reply to his request for assurance; she answered that she "had concluded no offensive alliance; and although the critical situation of Europe compelled her to arm, she had no intention to violate the Treaty of Dresden [which pledged her to peace with Frederick], but she would not bind herself by any promise from acting as circumstances required."[23] Frederick had anticipated such a reply; before it reached him he led his army into Saxony (August 29, 1756). So began the Seven Years' War.

II. THE OUTLAW: 1756–57

He made a halfhearted attempt to enlist the Saxon Elector as an ally, offering him Maria Theresa's Bohemia as a bribe. Augustus scorned this vicarious philanthropy; he ordered his generals to stop Frederick's advance, and fled to Warsaw. The Saxon force was too small to resist the finest army in Europe; it withdrew to the citadel at Pirna; Frederick entered Dresden unopposed (September 9, 1756). At once he bade his agents open the Saxon archives and bring him the originals of those documents that had revealed Saxony's participation in the plan to chasten, perhaps to dismember, Prussia. The aging Electress-Queen with her own person barred access to the archives, and demanded that Frederick should respect her royal inviolability; he ordered her to be removed; she fled; the documents were secured.

Maria Theresa sent an army from Bohemia to dislodge the invader; Frederick met it and defeated it at Lobositz, on the road from Dresden to Prague (October 1). He returned to besiege Pirna; it surrendered (October 15); he impressed the fourteen thousand captive Saxon soldiers into his own divisions, arguing that this was cheaper than feeding them as prisoners; the German appetite was notorious. He declared Saxony a conquered country, and applied its revenues to his own needs. During the winter he published the Saxon documents to the world. Maria Theresa called them forgeries, and appealed to France, Russia, and all God-fearing Christians to aid her against the man who, by flagrant aggression, had again plunged Europe into war.

Europe generally agreed in condemning Frederick. The German principalities, fearing a fate like Saxony's if Frederick should triumph, declared war upon Prussia (January 17, 1757), and raised a Reichsarmee, or Imperial Army, for action against the Prussian King. Kaunitz lost no time in reminding Louis XV that France had promised help in case Austria should be threatened. The Dauphine, daughter of the Saxon Elector, pleaded with her father-in-law to rescue her father. Mme. de Pompadour, who had hoped to enjoy her reign in peace, now inclined to war. In appreciation of her aid Maria Theresa sent her a royal portrait decorated with gems valued at 77,-278 livres;[24] Pompadour became martial. Louis, usually slow to decide, decided with impetuous vigor. By a second Treaty of Versailles (May 1, 1757) France bound herself in defensive-offensive alliance with Austria, pledged her an annual subsidy of twelve million florins, agreed to equip two German armies, and proposed to devote a French force of 105,000 men to the "*destruction totale de la Prusse.*" She promised never to make peace with Prussia until Silesia had been restored to Austria. When that restoration had been consummated France was to receive five frontier towns in the Austrian Netherlands, and these southern Netherlands were to be transferred to the Bourbon Infante of Spain in return for Spanish duchies in Italy. Perhaps France was knowingly writing off her colonies to British conquest by devoting nearly all her resources to absorbing "Belgium." Kaunitz could feel that he had won a vital diplomatic victory.

He found it easy now to draw Russia into active aid. The Convention of St. Petersburg (February 2, 1757) committed Russia and Austria each to put eighty thousand troops into the field, and to make war until Silesia had been reunited with Austria, and Prussia had been reduced to a minor power. Turning to Sweden, Kaunitz brought her into the alliance by guaranteeing to her, in the event of victory, all that part of Pomerania which had been conceded to her in the Treaty of Westphalia. Sweden was to contribute 25,000 men, Austria and France were to finance them. Poland, under its refugee King Augustus III, pledged her modest resources to the Franco-Austrian alliance. Now nearly all of Europe except England, Hanover, Denmark, Holland, Switzerland, Turkey, and Hesse-Cassel was united against Frederick.

And England was tempted to leave Frederick to his fate. George II saw with horror that his beloved Hanover, the electorate from which his father had come to rule Britain, lay defenseless in the path of overwhelming armies, with Frederick too distant and harassed to send substantial aid. The temptation was made almost irresistible when Kaunitz offered to leave Hanover inviolate if England would keep out of the Continental war; at that moment Frederick's fate was touch and go. Pitt, who was appointed secretary of state on November 19, 1756, was at first inclined to let Prussia and Hanover shift for themselves, while England would concentrate all her martial resources upon the contest for colonies; little wonder that George II, loving Hanover, hated Pitt. Soon Pitt changed his mind, and declared that a France victorious against Frederick would be master of Europe, and soon of England too; Parliament must vote money for Frederick and troops for Hanover; France must be made to spend herself in Europe, while England would pluck colonies and markets out of the conquered seas.

So in January, 1757, Britain signed a second alliance with Prussia, promising subsidies to Frederick and soldiers to Hanover. But then, suddenly, Pitt was dismissed (April 5), politics befuddled policy, help to Frederick was delayed, and for almost a year he stood alone, with 145,000 men, against armies converging from every quarter upon him: in the west 105,000 troops from France and 20,000 from the German states; in the south 133,000 from Austria; in the east 60,000 from Russia; in the north 16,000 from Sweden. And on that same day which saw Pitt fall, the Emperor Francis I—the usually amiable and docile husband of Maria Theresa—officially branded Frederick as an outlaw, and called upon all good men to hunt him out as an impious enemy of mankind.

III. FROM PRAGUE TO ROSSBACH: 1757

On January 10 Frederick sent to his ministers in Berlin some secret instructions: "If I am killed, affairs must continue without the slightest alteration. . . . If I have the bad luck to be captured, I forbid the smallest consideration for my person, or the slightest attention to anything I may write in captivity."[25]

It was a useless gesture, for without his military genius Prussia was lost. His only hope lay in facing his foes one at a time before they could unite. The French were not yet ready for battle, and perhaps the regiments that England was sending to Hanover could hold them for a while. The Austrians were accumulating in nearby Bohemia and Moravia immense magazines of arms and provisions to equip their armies for an invasion of Silesia. Frederick decided first to capture those precious stores, fight the Austrians, then march back to face the French. He led his own force from Saxony, and ordered the Duke of Brunswick-Bevern from East Germany, and Marshal Schwerin from Silesia, to advance into Bohemia and meet him in the hills overlooking Prague from the west. It was so done; the magazines were captured; and on May 6, near Prague, 64,000 Prussians met 61,000 Austrians under Prince Charles of Lorraine in the first great battle of the war.

The issue was decided not by numbers, nor by strategy, but by courage. Schwerin's regiments, under Austrian fire, marched waist-deep, shoulder-deep, through morasses. For a time they lost heart and turned in flight; then Schwerin, aged seventy-three, rallied them, wrapped the colors about his body, rode straight in the face of the foe, was struck by five balls at once, and fell dead. His men, loving him almost more than they feared death, charged in fury against the enemy, and turned defeat into victory. The slaughter on both sides was enormous, and Frederick's losses included four hundred officers and his best general; in this war generals did not die in bed. The 46,000 surviving Austrians retired into their citadel in Prague, and prepared to resist siege.

But Frederick found siege difficult, for Marshal Leopold von Daun, ablest of the Austrian commanders, was coming up from Moravia with another 64,000 men. Leaving part of his army to blockade the citadel, Frederick marched eastward with 32,000 troops, and met the advancing masses at Kolin (June 16). The odds against him were too great, and the generalship of Daun was in this case superior to his own. Two of Frederick's generals disobeyed his orders, causing confusion; Frederick lost his temper, and shouted to his retreating cavalry, "Would you live forever?"[26] The infantry, overwhelmed by carnage, refused to advance. Frederick, despondent, withdrew from the field, leaving 14,000 Prussians dead, wounded, or prisoners. He led his 18,000 survivors back to Prague, abandoned the siege, and returned with his remnants toward Saxony.

At Leitmeritz he rested his army for three weeks. There, on July 2, he received word that his mother, Sophia Dorothea, had died. The iron man of war broke down, wept, and secluded himself for a day. Perhaps he wondered, now, whether his assault on Silesia, seventeen years before, had been a foolish tempting of Nemesis. He shared his grief with his sister Wilhelmine, margravine of Bayreuth, whom he loved beyond any other soul. On July 7, his pride nearly spent, he sent her a desperate appeal:

> Since you, my dear sister, insist upon undertaking the great work of peace, I beg you to be good enough to send M. de Mirabeau to . . . offer the favorite [Mme. de Pompadour, formerly Cotillon IV] as much as 500,000 crowns for peace. . . . I leave it all to you . . . whom I adore, and who, although far more accomplished than I, is another myself.[27]

Nothing came of this approach. Wilhelmine tried another way: she wrote to Voltaire, then living in Switzerland, and begged him to use his influence. Voltaire transmitted her proposal to Cardinal de Tencin, who had opposed

the Franco-Austrian alliance. Tencin tried and failed.[28] The allies were sniffing the scent of victory. Maria Theresa talked now of completely dismembering Frederick's realm: not only must Silesia and Glatz be restored to
her, but Magdeburg and Halberstadt were to go to Augustus III, Pomerania
was to revert to Sweden, and Cleves and Ravensburg were to reward the
Elector Palatine.

Her hopes seemed reasonable. A French "army of the Dauphine" had
entered Germany; part of it, under Pompadour's favorite general, the Prince
de Soubise, was coming to join with the Imperial army at Erfurt; another
part, under Maréchal d'Estrées, advanced to meet a Hanoverian force under
George II's son, the Duke of Cumberland. Near the village of Hastenbeck
the French so badly defeated this army (July 26) that the Duke signed at
Kloster-Zeven (September 8) a "convention" by which he promised to keep
his Hanoverian troops from any further action against France.

Word of this humiliating capitulation may have reached Frederick at approximately the same time as news that a Swedish army had landed in
Pomerania, and a Russian army of 100,000 men under Marshal Stepan Apraksin had invaded East Prussia and overwhelmed a force of 30,000 Prussians at
Gross-Jägersdorf (July 30). These reverses, added to his own debacle in
Bohemia, almost destroyed Frederick's hope of overcoming enemies so
numerous and so fortified with reserves of materials and men. Having abandoned the morality as well as the theology of Christianity, he fell back upon
the ethics of the Stoics, and meditated suicide. To the end of the war he
carried on his person a phial of poison; he was resolved that his foes should
never take him except as a corpse. On August 24 he sent to Wilhelmine a
semihysterical paean to death:

> And now, ye promoters of sacred lies, go on leading cowards by the nose;
> . . . to me the enchantment of life is ended, the charm disappears. I see that all
> men are but the sport of Destiny, and that if there do exist some Gloomy and
> Inexorable Being, who allows a despised herd of creatures to go on multiply-
> ing here, he values them as nothing; he looks down upon a Phalaris crowned
> and a Socrates in chains, upon our virtues and our misdeeds, upon the horror
> of war and the cruel plagues that ravage the earth, as things indifferent to him.
> Wherefore my sole refuge and only haven, dear sister, is in the arms of death.[29]

She answered (September 15) by vowing to join him in suicide:

> My dearest brother, your letter, and the one you wrote to Voltaire, . . .
> have almost killed me. What fatal resolutions, great God! Ah, my dear brother,
> you say you love me, and yet you drive a dagger into my heart. Your letter . . .
> made me shed rivers of tears. Now I am ashamed of such weakness. . . . Your
> lot shall be mine. I will not survive either your misfortunes or those of the
> House I belong to. You may calculate that such is my firm resolution.
> But after this avowal let me entreat you to look back at what was the pitiable
> state of your enemy when you lay before Prague. It is the sudden whirl of
> Fortune for both parties. . . . Caesar was once the slave of pirates, and became
> lord of the earth. A great genius like yours finds resources even when all seems
> lost. I suffer a thousand times more than I can tell you; nevertheless hope does
> not abandon me. . . . I must finish, but I shall never cease to be, with the most
> profound respect, your Wilhelmine.[30]

She appealed to Voltaire to support her plea, and early in October, in his first letter to Frederick since 1753, he seconded her arguments:

> The Catos and Othos, whose death your Majesty thinks noble, had nothing else they could do but fight or die. . . . You must keep in mind how many courts there are that see in your invasion of Saxony a violation of international law. . . . Our morality and your situation are far from requiring such an act [as suicide]. . . . Your life is needed; you know how dear it is to a numerous family. . . . The affairs of Europe are never long on the same basis, and it is the duty of a man like you to hold himself in readiness for events. . . . If your courage led you to that heroic extremity it would not be approved. Your partisans would condemn it, your enemies would triumph.[31]

To which Frederick replied in prose and verse:

> *Pour moi, menacé du naufrage,*
> *Je dois, en affrontant l'orage,*
> *Penser, vivre, et mourir en roi—*

"as for me, menaced with shipwreck, I must, confronting the storm, think, live, and die like a king."[32]

Between poems (always in French) he searched for the French army; now he longed for a battle that would settle for him the question of life or death. At Leipzig, October 15, he sent for Johann Christoph Gottsched (who wrote verses in German), and tried to convince him that German poetry was impossible. So many explosions—*Knap, Klop, Krotz, Krok;* so many gutturals, so many consonants—even in the professor's name five in a row; how could you make a melody with such a language? Gottsched protested; Frederick had to prepare for another march; but ten days later, back in Leipzig, he received the old poet again, found time to listen to a Gottsched ode in German, and gave him a gold snuffbox as a parting token of good will.

During that literary interlude more bad news came: a force of Croats under Count Hadik was advancing upon Berlin, and rumor said that Swedish and French battalions were converging upon the Prussian capital. Frederick had left a garrison there, but far too small to buffet such an avalanche. If Berlin should fall, his principal source of supplies in arms, powder, and clothing would be in the hands of the enemy. He hurried with his army to rescue the city and his family. On the march he received word that no French or Swedish force was moving toward Berlin; that Hadik, halting in the suburbs, had exacted a ransom of £27,000 from Berlin, and had led his Croats contentedly away (October 16). There was other comforting intelligence: the Russians under Apraksin, racked with disease and famishing for food, had withdrawn from East Prussia into Poland. Less pleasant messages informed Frederick that the main French army under Soubise had entered Saxony, had plundered the western cities, and had united with the Imperial army under the Duke of Saxe-Hildburghausen. The weary King turned back in his tracks, and led his troops to the vicinity of Rossbach, some thirty miles west of Leipzig.

There his tired army, reduced to 21,000 men, came at last face to face with the 41,000 troops of France and the Reich. Even so, Soubise advised against risking battle; better, he said, to continue evading Frederick and wearing him out with fruitless marches until the overwhelming superiority of the allies in manpower and materials should force him to yield. Soubise knew the breakdown of discipline in his ranks, and the lack of enthusiasm, in the mostly Protestant soldiers of the Reichsarmee, for fighting against Frederick.[33] Hildburghausen pleaded for action, and Soubise gave in. The German marshal led his men on a long detour to attack the Prussians on their left flank. Frederick, watching from a housetop in Rossbach, ordered his cavalry under Seydlitz to execute a countermovement against the right flank of the enemy. Screened by hills, and proceeding with disciplined speed, the Prussian cavalry, 3,800 strong, charged down upon the allied troops and overcame them before they could re-form their ranks. The French came up too late, and were shattered by the Prussian artillery; in ninety minutes the crucial battle of Rossbach was over (November 5, 1757). The allies retreated in disorder, leaving 7,700 dead on the field; the Prussians lost only 550 men. Frederick ordered the prisoners to be well treated, and invited the captured officers to share his table. With French grace and wit he excused the limited fare: *"Mais, messieurs, je ne vous attendais pas sitôt, en si grand nombre"* (But, gentlemen, I did not expect you so soon, in so great number).[34]

Military men on all sides marveled at the disproportion of the losses, and at the superior generalship that had made this possible. Even France confessed admiration, and the French people, so lately allied with Prussia, could not yet look upon Frederick as their foe. Did he not speak and write good French? The *philosophes* applauded his victories and claimed him as their champion of free thought against the religious obscurantism that they were fighting at home.[35] Frederick responded to the gallant emotions of the French by saying, "I am not accustomed to regard the French as enemies."[36] But privately he composed—in French—a poem expressing his pleasure at having given the French a kick in the *cul*, which Carlyle delicately translated as "the seat of honor."[37]

England rejoiced with him, and put new faith in her ally. London celebrated his birthday with bonfires in the streets, and devout Methodists acclaimed the infidel hero as the savior of the one true religion. Pitt had been brought back to head the government (July 29, 1757); henceforth he was the unswerving support of the Prussian King. "England has taken long to produce a great man for this contest," said Frederick, "but here is one at last!"[38] Pitt denounced the Convention of Kloster-Zeven as cowardice and treason—though the King's son had signed it; he persuaded Parliament to send a better army to protect Hanover and help Frederick (October); and whereas it had voted only £164,000 for Cumberland's "Army of Observation," now it voted £1,200,000 for an "Army of Operations." Pitt and Frederick united in choosing, as leader of this new force, Frederick's brother-in-law and military pupil, Duke Ferdinand of Brunswick, thirty-six years old, handsome, cultured, brave, who played the violin so well, said

Burney, that "he might have made his fortune by it."[39] Here was an instrument nobly fit to play second fiddle to Frederick's flute!

IV. THE FOX AT BAY: 1757–60

Frederick had not much leisure for rejoicing. A French army under Richelieu still held much of Hanover. On the very day of Rossbach 43,000 Austrians laid seige to Schweidnitz, the principal stronghold and storehouse of the Prussians in Silesia; Frederick had left 41,000 men there, but they had been reduced by desertion and death to 28,000; these were poorly led by the Duke of Brunswick-Bevern, who ignored the King's order to attack the besiegers; on November 11 he surrendered the fortress, yielding to the Austrians 7,000 prisoners, 330,000 thalers, and provisions sufficient to maintain 88,000 men for two months. The victors, amplified to 83,000 troops by union with forces under Prince Charles and Marshal Daun, went on to Breslau; on November 22 they overwhelmed a small force of Prussians; Breslau fell, and most of Silesia was now restored to the triumphant Maria Theresa. Frederick might well feel that his victory at Rossbach had been annulled.

But that victory had renewed his courage, and he no longer spoke of suicide. His army too had recovered from its marches and battles, and seemed usefully resentful of the ravages with which French soldiers had desecrated Protestant churches in Saxony. Frederick appealed to his men to help him recapture Silesia. They marched 170 miles in twelve wintry days through difficult terrain. En route they were joined by the remains of the Prussian forces that had been defeated at Schweidnitz and Breslau. On December 3 Frederick, with 43,000 men, sighted the 72,000 Austrians who were encamped near Leuthen on the road to Breslau. That evening Frederick addressed his captains in a speech prefiguring the martial harangues of Napoleon:

> It is not unknown to you, gentlemen, what disasters have befallen here while we were busy with the French and Imperial armies. Schweidnitz is gone, . . . Breslau is gone and all our war stores there; most of Silesia is gone. . . . My embarrassments would be beyond recovery if it were not for my unbounded confidence in your courage, your constancy, and your love for the Fatherland. . . . There is hardly one among you who has not distinguished himself by some conspicuous deed of valor. . . . I flatter myself, therefore, that in the coming opportunity you will not fail in any sacrifice that your country may demand of you.
>
> This opportunity is close at hand. I should feel that I had accomplished nothing if Austria were left in possession of Silesia. Let me tell you, then, that I propose, in defiance of all the rules in the art of war, to attack the army of Prince Charles, three times as large as ours, wherever I find it. The question is not of his numbers or the strength of his position; all this, by the courage of our troops, and the careful execution of our plans, I hope to overcome. I must take this step, or all will be lost; we must defeat the enemy, or we shall lie buried under his batteries. So I read the case; so I shall act.

Make my determination known to all officers of the army; prepare the men for the work that is to come, and tell them that I feel justified in demanding exact fulfillment of orders. For you, when I reflect that you are Prussians, can I think that you will act unworthily? But if there should be one or another among you who dreads to share all dangers with me [here Frederick looked into each face in turn], he can have his discharge, this evening, and shall suffer not the least reproach from me. . . .

I knew that none of you would desert me. I count, then, absolutely on your faithful help, and on certain victory. Should I not survive to reward you for your devotion, the Fatherland must do it. Return now to camp, and report to your troops what you have heard from me.

The cavalry regiment that does not at once, on receipt of the order, throw itself upon the enemy I will, directly after the battle, unhorse, and make it a garrison regiment. The infantry battalion that even begins to hesitate, no matter what the danger may be, shall lose its colors, its swords, and the gold lace from its uniforms.

And now, gentlemen, good night. Soon we shall have beaten the enemy, or we shall see each other no more.[40]

Heretofore the Austrians, following a Fabian policy, had avoided battle with Frederick, hesitating to pit their troops and generals against Prussian discipline and Frederick's tactical genius; but now, inspired by superior numbers and recent victories, they decided, against the advice of Marshal Daun, to face the King in battle. And so, on December 5, 1757, the human pawns of dynastic rivalry—43,000 against 73,000—advanced upon each other's swords and guns in the greatest battle of the war. "That battle," said Napoleon, "was a masterpiece. Of itself it suffices to entitle Frederick to a place in the first rank among generals."[41] He sought first to gain the hills, from which his artillery could fire over the heads of his infantry into the enemy's ranks. He deployed his troops in an oblique order anciently used by Epaminondas of Thebes: separate columns were to move at approximately forty-five-degree angles to strike the enemy sidewise and so disorder his line of defense. Frederick pretended to be aiming his strongest pressure against the Austrian right; Prince Charles weakened his left wing to reinforce the right; Frederick poured his best troops upon the diminished left, routed it, and then turned to attack the right wing on its flank, while the Prussian cavalry rode down upon that same wing from concealment in the hills. Order triumphed over disorder; the Austrians surrendered or fled; 20,000 of them were taken prisoner—a catch unprecedented in military history;[42] 3,000 more were left dead, and 116 pieces of artillery fell into Prussian hands. The Prussians too lost heavily—1,141 dead, 5,118 wounded, 85 captured. When the carnage was over Frederick thanked his generals: "This day will bring the renown of your name, and of the nation, to the latest posterity."[43]

The victor pursued his victory with passionate resolve to regain Silesia. Within a day after the battle his army besieged the Austrian garrison in Breslau; Sprecher, its commander, posted placards through the town proclaiming instant death for anyone who breathed a word of surrender; twelve days later (December 18) he surrendered. Frederick took there 17,000 prisoners and precious military stores. Soon all Silesia, except heavily garrisoned and fortified Schweidnitz, was back in Prussian hands. Prince Charles, humble before Daun's silent reproaches, retired to his estate in Austria. Bernis and other French leaders advised Louis XV to make peace; Pompadour overruled them, and replaced Bernis with the Duc de Choiseul as minister for foreign affairs (1758); but France, suspecting that she was fighting for Austria while sacrificing her colonies, lost heart for the war. Richelieu showed so little enthusiasm, so little fervor in pursuing his advantage in Hanover, that he was recalled from his command (February, 1758).

He was replaced by the Comte de Clermont, an abbé licensed by the Pope to keep his benefice while playing general.[44] The French evacuated Hanover before the resolute advances of Duke Ferdinand of Brunswick; they yielded Minden to him in March; soon all Westphalia was freed from the French, who there too had made themselves hated by plunder and desecration.[45] Ferdinand marched west and, with half as many men, defeated Clermont's main force at Krefeld on the Rhine (June 23). Clermont yielded his post to the Duc de Contades; the defeated army was joined by Soubise with new French levies and the survivors of Rossbach; before this united force Ferdinand withdrew to Münster and Paderborn.

Encouraged by a season of victories, England signed (April 11) a third treaty with Frederick, promising him a subsidy of £670,000 by October, and pledging herself against a separate peace.[46] Meanwhile Frederick, his own Prussia having been taxed to exhaustion, taxed Saxony and other conquered territory likewise. He issued debased currencies, and (like Voltaire) hired Jewish financiers to make profitable deals for him in foreign exchange.[47] By the spring of 1758 he had rebuilt his army to 145,000 men. In April he attacked and recovered Schweidnitz. Eluding the main Austrian army (reconstituted under Daun), he moved south with 70,000 men to Olmütz in Moravia; if he could capture this Austrian stronghold he hoped to march against Vienna itself.

But about this same time 50,000 Russians under the Count of Fermor swept over East Prussia and attacked Cüstrin, only fifty miles east of Berlin. Frederick abandoned the siege of Olmütz and hurried north with 15,000 men. On the way he learned that Wilhelmine was critically ill; he stopped at Grüssau to send her an anxious note: "O you, dearest of my family, you whom I have most at heart of all beings in this world—for the sake of whatever is most precious to you, preserve yourself, and let me have the consolation of shedding my tears on your breast!"[48]

After days and nights on the march he joined a Prussian force under Count zu Dohna near Cüstrin. On August 25, 1758, with 36,000 men, he faced Fermor's 42,000 Russians at Zorndorf. His favorite tactic of a flank attack was here made impossible by marshy ground; Fermor proved as resourceful in command as Frederick, and the Russians fought with a courage and pertinacity that the Prussians seldom encountered in the Austrians or the French. Seydlitz and his cavalry won whatever honors could come from a day of rival butchery. The Russians retreated in good order, leaving 21,000 dead, wounded, or captured; the Prussians lost 12,500 killed or wounded, and 1,000 prisoners.

But who could continue to fight on so many fronts at once? While Frederick was in the north Daun had led his army to a junction with the Imperial regiments, and was now besieging Dresden, where Frederick had left a garrison under Prince Henry. A force of 16,000 Swedes marched through Pomerania, joined the Russians in ravaging a great part of the Mark of Brandenburg, and might with them endanger Berlin again. A new army of 30,000 Austrians and Hungarians, under General Harsch, entered Silesia and headed for Breslau. Which of the three capitals should be defended first? Reorganizing his dispirited and now rebellious troops, Frederick marched them twenty-two miles a day across Prussia into Saxony, and reached his beleaguered brother just in time to discourage Daun from attack. After giving his men two weeks' rest, he set out to drive Harsch from Silesia. At Hochkirch in Silesia Daun blocked his path. Frederick pitched camp close to the enemy, and waited four days for provisions to arrive from Dresden. Suddenly, at five o'clock on the morning of October 14, 1758, Daun, whom Frederick had relied upon to avoid the initiative, fell upon the Prussian right wing. The movement of the Austrians had been concealed by a thick fog, the Prussians were literally caught napping; they had no time to form the tactical lines that Frederick had designed. Frederick exposed himself recklessly in his efforts to restore order; he succeeded, but too late to retrieve the situation. After five hours of battle, 37,000 pawns against 90,000, he gave the signal for retreat, leaving on the field 9,450 men, to the Austrian loss of 7,590.

Again he contemplated suicide. With so able a general as Daun leading the Austrians, with so able a general as Saltykov forming a new Russian army, and with his own forces declining in number, quality, and discipline, while his foes could make up any loss, it seemed clear that a Prussian victory could come only through a miracle; and Frederick did not believe in miracles. On the day after Hochkirch he showed to his reader, de Katt, an *Apology for Suicide* which he had composed, and said, "I can end the tragedy when I choose."[49] On that day (October 15, 1758) Wilhelmine died, leaving instructions that her brother's letters to her might be laid on her breast in her tomb.[50] Frederick appealed to Voltaire to write something in her memory; Voltaire responded well, but his ode to the *"âme héroïque et pure"*[51] could not match the simple fervor of the King's tribute in his *Histoire de la Guerre de sept ans:*

> The goodness of her heart, her generous and benevolent inclinations, the nobility and elevation of her soul, the sweetness of her character, brought together in her the brilliant gifts of the mind with a foundation of solid virtue. . . . The tenderest and most constant friendship united the King [Frederick wrote in the third person] and this worthy sister. These ties had been formed in their earliest childhood; the same education and the same sentiments had further bound them, and a mutual fidelity in every test had rendered these ties indissoluble.[52]

Spring brought new French armies into the field. On April 13, 1759, at Bergen (near Frankfurt-am-Main), a French force ably led by the Duc de Broglie gave Ferdinand of Brunswick a taste of defeat, but Ferdinand redeemed himself at Minden. There (August 1), with 43,000 Germans, English, and Scots, he routed 60,000 French under Broglie and Contades so decisively, and with relatively so little loss, that he was able to send 12,000 troops to Frederick to make good the weakening of the King's army by a disastrous campaign in the east.

On July 23 Saltykov's 50,000 Russians, Croats, and Cossacks overwhelmed at Züllichau the 26,000 Prussians whom Frederick had left to guard the approaches from Poland to Berlin; nothing there now stood in the way of a Russian avalanche upon the Prussian capital. The King had no choice but to rely upon his brother to hold Dresden against Daun, while he himself marched to face the Russians. Reinforced on the way, he was able to muster 48,000 men, but meanwhile 18,000 Austrians under General Laudon had joined the Russians, raising Saltykov's total to 68,000. On August 12, 1759, these two armies—the largest masses of expendable human flesh since the competitive slaughters of the War of the Spanish Succession—fought at Kunersdorf (sixty miles east of Berlin) the most merciless, and for Frederick the most tragic, battle of the war. After twelve hours of fighting he seemed to have the advantage; then Laudon's 18,000 men, who had been kept in reserve, fell upon the exhausted Prussians and drove them into a rout. Frederick dared every danger to rally his troops; three times he led them personally to the attack; three horses were shot under him; a small gold case in his pocket stopped a bullet that might have ended his career. He was not happy over his escape; "Is there not," he cried, "one devil of a ball that can reach me?"[53] His soldiers begged him to retire to safety, and soon they gave him every example. He appealed to them: "Children, don't abandon me now, your king, your father!" But no urging could get them to advance again. Many of them had fought six hours under a burning sun, and without time or chance for a cup of water. They fled, and at last he joined them, leaving behind him 20,000 captured, wounded, or dead, against an enemy loss of 15,700. Among the mortally wounded was Ewald von Kleist, the finest German poet of that age.

As soon as Frederick could find a place to rest he dispatched a message to Prince Henry: "Of an army of 48,000 men I have at this moment not more than 3,000, and I am no longer master of my forces. . . . It is a great calamity, and I will not survive it." He notified his generals that he was bequeathing his command to Prince Henry. Then he dropped upon some straw and fell asleep.

The next morning he found that 23,000 fugitives from the battle had returned to their regiments, ashamed of their flight, and ready to serve him again if only because they longed to eat. Frederick forgot to kill himself; instead he reorganized these and other poor souls into a new force of 32,000 troops, and took a stand on the road from Kunersdorf to Berlin, expecting to make a last attempt to protect his capital. But Saltykov did not come. His men, too, had to eat; they were in enemy country and found foraging dangerous, and the line of communications with friendly Poland was long and hazardous. Saltykov thought it was time for the Austrians to take their turn against Frederick. He gave the order to retreat.

Daun agreed that the next move should be his. Now, he felt, was the time to take Dresden. Prince Henry had withdrawn a force from that city to go to Frederick's help; he had left only 3,700 men to guard the citadel, but powerful defenses had been raised to stave off attack. The new commander in Dresden, Kurt von Schmettau, was a loyal servant of the King, but when he received word from Frederick himself, after Kunersdorf, that all seemed lost, he gave up hope of successful resistance. An Imperial army, fifteen thousand strong, was approaching Dresden from the west; Daun was actively cannonading the city from the east. On September 4 Schmettau surrendered; on September 5 a message reached him from Frederick that he should hold out, that help was on the way. Daun, with 72,000 men, now made Dresden his winter quarters. Frederick came up to nearby Freiberg and wintered there with half that number.

The winter of 1759–60 was exceptionally severe. For several weeks snow covered the ground to the knee. Only the officers found shelter in homes; Frederick's common soldiers lived in makeshift cabins, hugged their fires, laboriously cut and brought wood to feed them, and themselves had scarcely any other food than bread. They slept close together for mutual warmth. Disease, in both camps, took almost as many lives as battle had done; in sixteen days Daun's army lost in this way four thousand men.[54] On November 19 Frederick wrote to Voltaire: "If this war continues much longer, Europe will return to the shades of ignorance, and our contemporaries will become like savage beasts."[55]

France, though immeasurably richer than Prussia in money and men, was near bankruptcy. Choiseul nevertheless equipped a fleet to invade England, but it was destroyed by the English at Quiberon Bay (November 20, 1759). Taxes were multiplied with all the ingenuity of governments and financiers. On March 4, 1759, the Marquise de Pompadour had secured the appointment of Étienne de Silhouette as controller general of finance. He proposed curtailment of pensions, a tax on the estates of nobles, the conversion of their silver into money, and even a tax on the tax-collecting farmers general. The rich complained that they were being reduced to mere shadows of their former selves; thenceforth *silhouette* became the word for a figure reduced to its simplest form. On October 6 the French treasury suspended payment on its obligations. On November 5 Louis XV melted his silver to give good example; but when Silhouette suggested that the King should get along without the sums usually allotted him for his gambling and games, Louis agreed with such visible pain that Choiseul vetoed the idea. On November 21 Silhouette was dismissed.

Like almost every Frenchman, the King felt that he had had enough of war; he was ready to hear proposals of peace. Voltaire had sounded out Frederick on the matter in June; Frederick replied (July 2): "I love peace quite as much as you could wish, but I want it good, solid, and honorable"; and on September 22 he added, again to Voltaire: "For making peace there are two conditions from which I will never depart: first, to make it conjointly with my faithful allies; . . . second, to make it honorable and glorious."[56] Voltaire transmitted these proud replies (one dated after the debacle at Kunersdorf) to Choiseul, who found in them no handle for negotiation. And faithful ally Pitt, who was busy absorbing French colonies, how could he make peace before he had built the British Empire?

V. THE MAKING OF THE BRITISH EMPIRE

The most important phase of the Seven Years' War was not fought in Europe, for there it effected only minor changes in the map of power. It was fought on the Atlantic, in North America, and in India. In those areas the results of the war were immense and enduring.

The first step in the formation of the British Empire had been taken in the seventeenth century, by the passage of naval supremacy from the Dutch to the English. The second was marked by the Treaty of Utrecht (1713), which granted England the monopoly of supplying African slaves to the Spanish and English colonies in America. The slaves produced rice, tobacco, and sugar; part of the sugar was turned into rum; the trade in rum shared in enriching the merchants of England (old and New); the profits of trade financed the expansion of the British fleet. By 1758 England had 156 ships of the line; France had seventy-seven.[57] Hence the third step in building the Empire was the reduction of French power on the seas. This process was interrupted by Richelieu's success at Minorca, but it was resumed by the destruction of a French fleet off Lagos, Portugal (April 13, 1759), and of another in Quiberon Bay. Consequently the commerce of France with her colonies dropped from thirty million livres in 1755 to four million in 1760.

Supremacy on the Atlantic having been won, the way was open for the British conquest of French America. This included not only the basin of the St. Lawrence River and the region of the Great Lakes, but also the basin of the Mississippi from the Lakes to the Gulf of Mexico; even the Ohio River Valley was in French hands. French forts dominated Chicago, Detroit, and Pittsburgh—whose change of name from Fort Duquesne symbolized the results of the war. The French possessions blocked the westward expansion of the English colonies in America; had England not won the Seven Years' War, North America might have been divided into a New England in the East, a New France in the center, and a New Spain in the West; the divisions and conflicts of Europe would have been reproduced in America. The pacific Benjamin Franklin warned the English colonists that they could never be safe in their possessions, nor free in their growth, unless the French were checked in their American expansion; and George Washington came into history by attempting to take Fort Duquesne.

Canada and Louisiana were the two doors to French America; and the nearer to England and France was Canada. Through the St. Lawrence came supplies and troops for the *habitants*, and that door was guarded by the French fort of Louisbourg on Cape Breton Island at the mouth of the great river. On June 2, 1758, Louisbourg was besieged by an English flotilla of forty-two vessels, bearing 18,000 soldiers, under Admiral Edward Boscawen.

The fort was defended by ten ships and 6,200 men; reinforcements sent from France were intercepted by the British fleet. The garrison fought bravely, but soon its defenses were shattered by British guns. The surrender of the fort (July 26, 1758) began the British conquest of Canada.

The process was only slightly retarded by the strategy and heroism of the Marquis de Montcalm. Sent from France (1756) to command the French regulars in Canada, he advanced from one success to another until frustrated by corruption and discord in the French-Canadian administration, and by the inability of France to send him aid. In 1756 he captured an English fort at Oswego, giving the French control of Lake Ontario; in 1757 he besieged and took Fort William Henry, at the head of Lake George; in 1758, with 3,800 men, he defeated 15,000 British and colonial troops at Ticonderoga. But he met his match when, with 15,000 men, he defended Quebec against the English general James Wolfe, who had only 9,000 soldiers under his command. Wolfe himself led his troops in scaling the heights to the Plains of Abraham. Montcalm was mortally wounded in directing the defense; Wolfe was mortally wounded on the field of victory (September 12–13, 1759). On September 8, 1760, the French governor of Canada, Vaudreuil-Cavagnal, surrendered, and the great province passed under British control.

Turning their ships south, the English attacked the French islands in the Caribbean. Guadeloupe was taken in 1759, Martinique in 1762; all the French possessions in the West Indies—St.-Domingue excepted—fell to Britain. To add to the profits of victory Pitt sent squadrons to Africa to capture the French slave-trading stations on the west coast; it was done; the French trade in slaves collapsed; Nantes, its chief port in France, decayed. The price of slaves in the West Indies rose, and British slave merchants made new fortunes in supplying the demand.[58] We should add that the English were not any more inhumane in this imperial process than the Spanish or the French; they were merely more efficient; and it was in England that the antislavery movement first took effective form.

Meanwhile British enterprise—naval, military, commercial—was busy absorbing India. The English East India Company had set up strongholds at Madras (1639), Bombay (1668), and Calcutta (1686). French merchants established domination at Pondicherry, south of Madras (1683), and at Chandernagore, north of Calcutta (1688). All these centers of power expanded as Mogul rule in India declined; each group used bribery and soldiery to extend its area of influence; already, in the War of the Austrian Succession (1740–48), France and England had fought each other in India. The Peace of Aix-la-Chapelle had merely interrupted the conflict; the Seven Years' War renewed it. In March, 1757, an English fleet under Admiral Charles Watson, aided by troops of the East India Company under a Shropshire lad named Robert Clive, took Chandernagore from the French; on June 23, with only 3,200 men, Clive defeated 50,000 Hindus and French at Plassey (eighty miles north of Calcutta) in a battle that assured British mastery in northeast India. In August, 1758, an English fleet under Admiral George Pococke drove from Indian waters the French squadron that had been protecting French possessions along the coast; thereafter, with the British free, the French unable, to bring in men and supplies, the triumph of England was only a matter of months. In 1759 the French siege of Madras by the Comte de Lally was frustrated by the arrival of British provisions and reinforcements by sea. The French were decisively defeated at Wandiwash on January 22, 1760; Pondicherry surrendered to the British on January 16, 1761. This last French outpost was restored to France in 1763, but everyone understood that French possession continued only by British consent.

India and Canada remained, until our own time, two bastions, east and west, of an empire that was built with money, courage, cruelty, and brains, in full accord with the international morals of the eighteenth century. In tardy retrospect we now perceive that that empire was a natural product of human nature and material conditions, and that the alternative to it was not the independence of helpless peoples, but a similar empire established by France. In the long run, despite its Clives and Hastingses and Kiplings, the rule of half the world by the British navy—the comparatively humane and urbane maintenance of order amid ever-threatening chaos—was a blessing rather than a bane to mankind.

VI. EXHAUSTION: 1760–62

What was the hunted Prussian fox doing in that harsh winter of 1759–60? He was raising and debasing money, conscripting and training men, writing and publishing poetry. In January a pirate Parisian publisher issued *Oeuvres du philosophe de Sans-Souci,* joyfully printing those reckless poems which Voltaire had carried off with him from Potsdam in 1753, and for which Frederick had had him intercepted and detained at Frankfurt-am-Main. Those poems would amuse uncrowned heads, but would make royal wigs tremble with rage, including those of Frederick's ally George II. Frederick protested that the pirated publication was corrupted by malignant interpolations; he bade his friend the Marquis d'Argens (director of fine arts at the Berlin Academy) to issue at once an "authentic edition" carefully purged. It was so done in March, and Frederick could turn back to war. On February 24 he wrote to Voltaire:

> Steel and death have made terrible ravages among us, and the sad thing is that we are not yet at the end of the tragedy. You can easily imagine the result of such cruel shocks upon me. I wrap myself up in stoicism as well as I can. . . . I am old, broken, gray, wrinkled; I am losing my teeth and my gaiety.[59]

Vast masses of soldiery were being marshaled to determine which ruler should tax most men. Saltykov, in April, was returning from Russia with 100,000; Laudon had 50,000 Austrians in Silesia, against Prince Henry's 34,000; Daun at Dresden, with 100,000, hoped to break through Frederick's 40,000, who were now encamped near Meissen; the French, with 125,000, were waiting to advance against Ferdinand's 70,000; altogether 375,000 men were being aimed at Berlin. On March 21, 1760, Austria and Russia renewed their alliance, with a secret clause giving Prussia to Russia as soon as Silesia should be restored to Austria.[60]

Laudon drew first blood of the year 1760, overwhelming 13,000 Prussians at Landeshut (June 23). On July 10 Frederick began to besiege Dresden with heavy artillery, laying most of Germany's then loveliest city in ruins. The bombardment availed him nothing; hearing that Laudon was approaching Breslau, he abandoned the siege, marched his men one hundred miles in five days, encountered Laudon's army at Liegnitz (August 15, 1760), inflicted upon it a loss of 10,000 men, and entered Breslau. But on October 9 an army of Cossacks under Fermor captured Berlin, ransacked its military stores, and exacted a ransom of two million thalers—equal to half the British subsidy that Frederick was receiving annually. He marched to relieve his capital; the Russians fled on hearing of his approach, and Frederick turned back to Saxony. On the way he wrote to Voltaire (October 30): "You are fortunate in following Candide's advice, and limiting yourself to the cultivation of your garden. 'Tis not granted to everyone to do so. The ox must plow the furrow, the nightingale must sing, the dolphin must swim, and I must fight."[61]

At Torgau on the Elbe (November 3) his 44,000 Prussians met 50,000 Austrians. Frederick sent half his army under Johann von Ziethen to detour and attack the enemy in the rear. The maneuver did not succeed, for Ziethen was delayed by an enemy detachment on the way. Frederick led his own divisions personally into the fury of the battle; here too three horses were shot under him; a shell struck him in the chest, but with spent force; he was knocked unconscious to the ground, but soon recovered; "It is nothing," he said, and returned to the fray. He won a Pyrrhic victory; the Austrians gave way, with a loss of 11,260 men, but Frederick left 13,120 Prussians on that field. He retired to Breslau, now his main center of supplies. Daun still held Dresden, waiting patiently for Frederick to die. Winter again gave the survivors rest.

The year 1761 was one of diplomacy rather than war. In England the death of George II (October 25, 1760), who had cared deeply for Hanover, and the accession of George III, who cared for it much less, gave a royal sanction to popular resentment of a war that was weighing heavily upon English pounds. Choiseul put out feelers from France for a separate peace; Pitt refused, and kept full faith with Frederick; but the British contingent in Hanover was reduced, and Ferdinand had to yield Brunswick and Wolfenbüttel to the French. Choiseul turned to Spain, and in a "Pacte de Famille"— a family pact between Bourbon kings—persuaded her to join in the alliance against Prussia. Military developments concurred with these diplomatic reverses to bring Frederick again to the verge of debacle. Laudon with 72,000 men affected a junction with 50,000 Russians; they completely severed Frederick from Prussia, and laid plans to take and keep Berlin. On September 1, 1761, the Austrians again took Schweidnitz and its stores. On October 5 Pitt, overwhelmed by the popular demand for peace, resigned rather than betray

Frederick. His successor, the Earl of Bute, thought Frederick's cause hopeless, and saw, in the negotiation of peace, a means of strengthening George III against Parliament. He pleaded with Frederick to admit defeat at least to the extent of surrendering part of Silesia to Austria. Frederick demurred; Bute refused him any further subsidy. Nearly all Europe, including many Prussians, called upon Frederick to make concessions. His troops had lost any hope of victory; they warned their officers that they would not attack the enemy again, and, if attacked, would surrender.[62] As the year 1761 ended Frederick found himself alone against a dozen foes. He admitted that only a miracle could save him.

A miracle saved him. On January 5, 1762,[63] Czarina Elizaveta, who hated Frederick, died, and was succeeded by Peter III, who admired him as the ideal conqueror and king. When Frederick heard the news he ordered all Russian prisoners to be clad, shod, fed, and freed. On February 23 Peter declared the war with Prussia at an end. On May 5 he signed a treaty of peace drawn up, at his request, by Frederick himself; on May 22 Sweden followed suit; on June 10 Peter re-entered the war, but as an ally of Prussia. He donned a Prussian uniform and volunteered for service "under the King my master." It was one of the most remarkable overturns in history.

It warmed Frederick's heart, and restored morale in his army, but he half agreed with his enemies that Peter was crazy. He was alarmed when he heard that Peter proposed to attack Denmark to recover Holstein; Frederick used every effort to dissuade him, but Peter insisted; finally, Frederick tells us, "I had to keep silent, and abandon this poor prince to the self-confidence that destroyed him."[64]

Bute, now actively hostile to Frederick, asked Peter to let the twenty thousand Russians now in the Austrian army continue there; Peter sent a copy of this message to Frederick, and ordered the Russian troops to join and serve Frederick. Bute offered Austria a separate peace, promising to support the cession of Prussian territory to Austria; Kaunitz refused; Frederick denounced Bute as a scoundrel.[65] He was pleased to learn that France had ended her subsidies to Austria, and that the Turks were attacking the Austrians in Hungary (May, 1762).

On June 28 Peter was deposed by a *coup d'état* that established Catherine II as "Empress of all the Russias"; on July 6 Peter was assassinated. Catherine ordered Czernichev, who commanded the Russians under Frederick, to bring them home at once. Frederick was just preparing an attack upon Daun. He asked Czernichev to conceal for three days the news of the Czarina's instructions. Without using these Russian auxiliaries Frederick defeated Daun at Burkersdorf (July 21). Czernichev now withdrew his troops, and Russia took no further part in the war. Relieved of danger in the north, the King drove the Austrians before him, and recaptured Schweidnitz. On October 29 Prince Henry, with 24,000 men, defeated 39,000 Austrians and Imperials at Freiberg in Saxony; this was the only major action of the war in which the Prussians were victorious when not under Frederick's command. It was also the last important battle of the Seven Years' War.

VII. PEACE

All Western Europe was exhausted. Prussia most of all, where boys of fourteen had been conscripted, and farms had been devastated, and merchants had been ruined by the stifling of trade. Austria had more men than money, and had lost vital Russian aid. Spain had lost Havana and Manila to the English, and nearly all her navy had been destroyed. France was bankrupt, her colonies were gone, her commerce had almost disappeared from the sea. England needed peace to consolidate her gains.

On September 5, 1762, Bute sent the Duke of Bedford to Paris to negotiate a settlement with Choiseul. If France would yield Canada and India England would restore Guadeloupe and Martinique, and France might keep, with British consent, Frederick's western provinces of Wesel and Gelderland.[66] Pitt denounced these proposals with passionate eloquence, but public opinion supported Bute, and on November 5 England and Portugal signed with France and Spain the Peace of Fontainebleau. France gave up Canada, India, and Minorca; England restored to France and Spain her conquests in the Caribbean; France promised to maintain neutrality between Prussia and Austria, and to withdraw her armies from Prussian territory in western Germany. A further Peace of Paris (February 10, 1763) confirmed these arrangements, but left France her fishing rights near Newfoundland, and some trading posts in India. Spain ceded Florida to England, but received Louisiana from France. Technically these agreements violated Britain's pledge against a separate peace; actually they were a boon to Frederick, for they left him with only two adversaries—Austria and the Reich; and he was now confident that he could hold his own against these disheartened enemies.

Maria Theresa resigned herself to peace with her most hated foe. All her major allies had abandoned her, and 100,000 Turks were marching into Hungary. She sent an envoy to Frederick, proposing truce. He accepted, and at Hubertusburg (near Leipzig), February 5–15, 1763, Prussia, Austria, Saxony, and the German princes signed the treaty that ended the Seven Years' War. After all the shedding of blood, ducats, rubles, thalers, kronen, francs, and pounds the *status quo ante bellum* was restored on the Continent: Frederick kept Silesia and Glatz, Wesel and Gelderland; he evacuated Saxony, and promised to support the candidacy of Maria Theresa's son Joseph as King of the Romans and therefore emperor-to-be. At the final signing Frederick's aides congratulated him on "the happiest day of your life"; he replied that the happiest day of his life would be the last one.[67]

What were the results of the war? To Austria, the permanent loss of Silesia, and a war debt of 100,000,000 écus. The prestige of the Austrian rulers as traditional holders of the Imperial title was ended; Frederick dealt with Maria Theresa as ruler of an Austro-Hungarian, rather than a Holy Roman, Empire. The German princes of the Empire were now left to their resources, and would soon submit to the Prussian hegemony in the Reich;

the Hapsburg power declined, the Hohenzollern power rose; the road was open for Bismarck. Patriotism and nationalism began to think in terms of Germany instead of each proudly separate state; German literature was stimulated to Sturm und Drang, and mounted to Goethe and Schiller.

Sweden lost 25,000 men, and gained nothing but debts. Russia lost 120,000 men to battle, hardship, and disease, but would soon reproduce them; she had opened a new era in her modern history by marching into the west; the partition of Poland was now inevitable. For France the result was enormous losses in colonies and commerce, and a near-bankruptcy that moved her another step toward collapse. For England the results were greater than even her leaders realized: control of the seas, control of the colonial world, the establishment of a great empire, the beginning of 182 years of ascendancy in the world. For Prussia the results were territorial devastation, thirteen thousand homes in ruins, a hundred towns and villages burned to the ground, thousands of families uprooted; 180,000 Prussians (by Frederick's estimate[68]) had died in battle, camp, or captivity; even more had died through lack of medicine or food; in some districts only women and old men were left to till the fields. Out of a population of 4,500,000 in 1756, only 4,000,000 remained in 1763.

Frederick was now the hero of all Germany (except Saxony!). He entered Berlin in triumph after an absence of six years. The city, though destitute, with every family in mourning, blazed with illuminations to welcome him, and acclaimed him as its savior. The iron spirit of the old warrior was moved: "Long live my dear people!" he cried. "Long live my children!"[69] He was capable of humility; in his hour of adulation he did not forget the many mistakes he had made as a general—he the greatest of modern generals excepting Napoleon; and he could still see the thousands of Prussian youths whose bloody deaths had paid for Silesia. He himself had paid. He was now prematurely old at fifty-one. His back was bent, his face and figure lean and drawn, his teeth lost, his hair white on one side of his head, his bowels racked with colic, diarrhea, and hemorrhoids.[70] He remarked that now his proper place was in a home for elderly invalids.[71] He lived twenty-three years more, and tried to redeem his sins with peaceful and orderly government.

Politically the main results of the Seven Years' War were the rise of the British Empire, and the emergence of Prussia as a first-class power. Economically, the chief result was an advance toward industrial capitalism: those Gargantuan armies were glorious markets for the mass consumption of mass-produced goods; what client could be more desirable than one that promised to destroy the purchased goods at the earliest opportunity, and order more? Morally, the war made for pessimism, cynicism, and moral disorder. Life was cheap, death was imminent, suffering was the order of the day, pillage was permissible, pleasure was to be seized wherever it could for a moment be found. "But for this campaign," said Grimm in Westphalia, 1757, "I should never have conceived how far the horrors of poverty and the injustice of man can be carried";[72] and they had only begun. The suffering helped, as well as hindered, religion: if a minority was turned to atheism by the stark

reality of evil, the majority was moved to piety by the need to believe in the
ultimate triumph of the good. A reaction to religion would soon come in
France, England, and Germany. Protestantism in Germany was saved from
destruction; probably, if Frederick had lost, Prussia would have experienced,
like Bohemia after 1620, a compulsory restoration of Catholic faith and
power. The triumph of imagination over reality is one of the humors of
history.

BOOK II

FRANCE BEFORE THE DELUGE

1757–74

CHAPTER III

The Life of the State

I. THE MISTRESS DEPARTS

MME. DE POMPADOUR was among the casualties of the war. For
some time the charm of her personality kept the King in thrall while
the nation mourned; but after the attempt of Damiens to assassinate him (January 5, 1757) Louis XV, suddenly conscious of God, sent word to her that
she must leave at once. He made the humane mistake of coming to say good-
bye; he found her quietly and sadly packing. Some surviving tenderness
overcame him; he asked her to remain.[1] Soon all her former privileges and
powers were restored. She negotiated with diplomats and ambassadors; she
raised and lowered ministers and generals. Marc-Pierre de Voyer, Comte
d'Argenson, had opposed her at every step; she had sought to appease him
and had been repulsed; she had him replaced by the Abbé de Bernis as minister for foreign affairs, and then by Choiseul (1758). Reserving her tenderness
for her relatives and the King, she faced all others with a heart of steel within
an ailing frame. She sent some enemies to the Bastille, and let them stay there
for years.[2] Meanwhile she feathered her nests, adorned her palaces, and ordered a stately mausoleum for herself beneath the Place Vendôme.

She bore, among the people, in the Parlement, and at court, the chief blame
for French reverses in the war, but she received no credit for the victories.
She was held accountable for the unpopular alliance with Austria, though
she had been only a minor factor in that mating. She was condemned for the
disaster at Rossbach, where her man Soubise had commanded the French; her
critics did not know—or considered it irrelevant—that Soubise had advised
against giving battle, and had been forced into it by the precipitancy of the
German general. If Soubise had had his way, if his plan of wearing out Frederick with marches and desertions had been followed, if Czarina Elizaveta
had not died so inopportunely and left Russia to a young idolator of Frederick—perhaps the Prussian resistance would have collapsed, France would
have received the Austrian Netherlands, and Pompadour would have been
carried on a sea of blood to national acclaim. She had failed to placate the
great god Chance.

The Parlement hated her for encouraging the King to ignore the Parlement. The clergy hated her as friend of Voltaire and the *Encyclopédistes*;
Christophe de Beaumont, archbishop of Paris, said he would "like to see her
burn."[3] When the Paris populace suffered from the high price of bread they
cried out that "that prostitute who governs the kingdom is bringing it to
ruin." "If we had her here," said a voice in the mob at the Pont de la Tournelle, "there would soon not be enough left of her to make relics."[4] She
dared not show herself in the streets of Paris, and she was surrounded by

67

enemies at Versailles. She wrote to the Marquise de Fontenailles: "I am quite alone in the midst of this crowd of *petits seigneurs*, who loathe me and whom I despise. As for most of the women, their conversation gives me a sick headache. Their vanity, their lofty airs, their meannesses, and their treacheries make them insupportable."[5]

As the war dragged on, and France saw Canada and India snatched from her, and Ferdinand of Brunswick kept French armies at bay, and returning soldiers, wounded or maimed, appeared in the streets of Paris, it became clear to the King that he had made a tragic mistake in listening to Kaunitz and Pompadour. In 1761 he consoled himself with a new mistress, Mlle. de Romans, who bore him the future Abbé de Bourbon. Gossip said that Pompadour revenged herself by accepting Choiseul as her lover,[6] but she was too weak, and Choiseul too clever, for such a liaison; to Choiseul she surrendered her power rather than her love. Now, it may be, she uttered the despondent prophecy, "*Après moi le déluge.*"[7]

She had always been frail. Even in her youth she had spit blood; and though we are not certain that she had tuberculosis, we know that her coughing increased painfully as she turned forty. The singing voice that had once thrilled King and court was now hoarse and strained. Her friends were shocked by her emaciation. In February, 1764, she took to her bed with high fever and bloody inflammation of the lungs. In April her condition became so serious that she summoned a notary to draw up her last testament. She left gifts to her relatives, friends, and servants, and added: "If I have forgotten any of my relatives in this will I beg my brother to provide for them." To Louis XV she deeded her Paris mansion, which, as the Élysée Palace, is now occupied by the President of France. The King spent many hours at her bedside; during her last days he seldom left the room. The Dauphin, who had always been her foe, wrote to the bishop of Verdun: "She is dying with a courage rare for either sex. Her lungs are full of water or pus, her heart is congested or dilated. It is an unbelievably cruel and painful death."[8] Even for this last battle she kept herself richly attired, and her parched cheeks were rouged. She reigned almost to the end. Courtiers thronged around her couch; she distributed favors, and nominated persons to high office; and the King acted on many of her recommendations.

At last she admitted defeat. On April 14 she accepted gratefully the final sacraments that sought to solace death with hope. So long the friend of philosophers, she tried now to recapture the faith of her childhood. Like a child she prayed:

> I commend my soul to God, imploring Him to have pity on it, to forgive my sins, to grant me the grace to repent of them and die worthy of His mercy, hoping to appease His justice through the glory of the precious blood of Jesus Christ my Saviour, and through the intercession of the Virgin Mary and all the saints in Paradise.[9]

To the priest who was departing as she entered her final agony, she whispered, "Wait a moment; we will leave the house together."[10] She died on April 15, 1764, choked by the congestion in her lungs. She was forty-two years old.

It is not true that Louis took her death with indifference; he merely concealed his grief.[11] "The King," said the Dauphin, "is in great affliction, though he controls himself with us and with everybody."[12] When, on April 17, the woman who had been half of his life for twenty years was carried from Versailles Palace in a cold and driving rain, he went out on the balcony to see her depart. "The Marquise will have very bad weather," he said to his valet Champlost. It was not a frivolous remark, for Champlost reported that there were tears in the royal eyes, and that Louis added sadly, "This is the only tribute I can pay her."[13] By her own wishes she was buried by the side of her child Alexandrine, in the now vanished church of the Capucines in the Place Vendôme.

The court rejoiced to be freed from her power; the populace, which had not felt her charm, cursed her costly extravagance, and soon forgot her; the artists and writers whom she had helped lamented the loss of a gracious and understanding friend. Diderot was harsh: "So what remains of this woman who cost us so much in men and money, who left us without honor and without energy, and who overthrew the whole political system of Europe? A handful of dust." But Voltaire, from Ferney, wrote:

> I am very sad at the death of Mme. de Pompadour. I was indebted to her, and I mourn out of gratitude. It seems absurd that while an ancient pen-pusher, hardly able to walk, should still be alive, a beautiful woman, in the midst of a splendid career, should die at the age of forty. Perhaps if she had been able to live quietly, as I do, she would be alive today. . . . She had justice in her mind and heart. . . . It is the end of a dream.[14]

II. THE RECOVERY OF FRANCE

Not until Napoleon did France fully recover from the Seven Years' War. High taxes had discouraged agriculture under Louis XIV; they continued to the same effect under Louis XV; thousands of acres farmed in the seventeenth century were left uncultivated in 1760, and were reverting to wilderness.[15] Livestock was depleted, fertilizer was lacking, the soil was starved. Peasants kept to old clumsy methods of tillage, for taxes rose with every improvement that increased the peasants' wealth. Many peasants had no heat in their houses in winter except from the cattle that lived with them. Abnormal frosts in 1760 and 1767 ruined crops and vineyards in their growth. One bad harvest could condemn a village to near-starvation, and to terror of the famished wolves that lurked about.

Nevertheless economic recovery began as soon as peace was signed. The government was inefficient and corrupt, but many measures were taken to help the peasantry. Royal intendants distributed seed and built roads; agronomic societies published agricultural information, established competitions, awarded prizes; some tax collectors distinguished themselves by their humane moderation.[16] Stimulated by the physiocrats, many seigneurs interested themselves in improving agricultural methods and products. Peasant proprietors grew in number. By 1774 only six per cent of the French population still labored under serfdom.[17] But every increment of production brought a rise in population; the land was rich, yet the average peasant holding was small; poverty remained.

Out of peasant loins came the human surplus that went to man the industries in the growing towns. With a few exceptions industry was still in the domestic and handicraft stage. Large-scale capitalistic organizations dominated metallurgy, mining, soap-making, and textiles. Marseilles in 1760 had thirty-five soap factories, employing a thousand workers.[18] Lyons was already dependent for its prosperity upon the shifting market for the product of its looms. English carding machines were introduced about 1750, and toward 1770 the jenny, working forty-eight spindles at once, began to replace the spinning wheel in France. The French were quicker to invent than to apply, for they lacked the capital that England, enriched by commerce, could use to finance mechanical improvements in industry. The steam engine had been known in France since 1681.[19] Joseph Cugnot used it in 1769 to operate the first known automobile; a year later this was employed to transport heavy loads at four miles an hour; however, the machine got out of hand and demolished a wall, and it had to stop every fifteen minutes to replenish its water.[20]

With such bizarre exceptions, transport was by horse, cart, coach, or boat. Roads and canals were much better than in England, but inns were worse. A regular postal service was established in 1760; it was not quite private, for Louis XV ordered postmasters to open letters and report any suspicious content to the government.[21] Internal trade was hampered by tolls, external trade by war and loss of colonies. The Compagnie des Indes went bankrupt, and was dissolved (1770). Trade with European states, however, increased substantially during the century, from 176,600,000 livres in 1716 to 804,300,000 livres in 1787; but some of the increase merely reflected inflation. Trade with the French West Indies flourished in sugar and slaves.

A gradual inflation, due partly to debasement of the currency, partly to rising world production of gold and silver, had a stimulating effect upon industrial and commercial enterprise; the businessman could usually expect to sell his product at a higher price level than that on which he had bought his labor and materials. So the middle classes swelled their fortunes, while the lower classes had all they could do to keep income in sight of prices. The same inflation that enabled the government to cheat its creditors reduced the value of its revenues, so that taxes rose as livres fell. The King became dependent upon bankers like the brothers Paris, particularly Paris-Duverney, who so delighted Pompadour with his fiscal prestidigitation that he was able, during the war, to make or break ministers and generals.

The basic economic development in eighteenth-century France was the passage of pre-eminent wealth from those who owned land to those who controlled industry, commerce, or finance. Voltaire noted in 1755: "Owing to the increasing profits of trade . . . there is less wealth than formerly among the great, and more among the middle classes. The result has been to lessen the distance between classes."[22] Businessmen like La Popelinière could build palaces that were the envy of nobles, and adorn their tables with the best poets and philosophers in the realm; it was the bourgeoisie that now gave patronage to literature and art. The aristocracy consoled itself by hugging its privileges and displaying its style; it insisted upon noble birth as prerequisite to army commissions or episcopal posts; it flaunted its armorial bearings and proliferated pedigrees; it strove—often in vain—to keep able or distinguished commoners out of high administrative office and the court. The rich bourgeois demanded that career should be open to talent of whatever birth; and when his demand was ignored he flirted with revolution.

All but the peasant phase of the class war took visible form in the tumult and splendor of Paris. Half the wealth of France was siphoned into the capital, and half the poverty of France festered there. Paris, said Rousseau, "is perhaps the city in the world where fortunes are most unequal, and where flaunting wealth and the most appalling penury dwell together."[23] Sixty paupers were part of the official escort for the corpse of the Dauphin's eldest son in 1761.[24] Paris toward 1770 contained 600,000 of France's 22,000,000 souls.[25] It housed the most alert, the best-informed, and the most depraved people in Europe. It had the best-paved streets, the most splendid avenues and promenades, the busiest traffic, the finest shops, the lordliest palaces, the dingiest tenements, and some of the most beautiful churches in the world. Goldoni, coming to Paris from Venice in 1762, marveled:

> What crowds! What an assemblage of people of every description! . . . With what a surprising view my senses and mind were struck on approaching the Tuileries! I saw the extent of that immense garden, which has nothing comparable to it in the universe, and my eyes were unable to measure the length of it. . . . A majestic river, numerous and convenient bridges, vast quays, crowds of carriages, an endless throng of people.[26]

A thousand stores tempted purses and the purseless; a thousand vendors hawked their goods in the streets; a hundred restaurants (the word first appears in 1765) offered to *restore* the hungry; a thousand dealers collected, forged, or sold antiques; a thousand hairdressers trimmed and powdered the hair or wigs of even the artisan class. In the narrow alleys artists and craftsmen produced paintings, furniture, and finery for the well-to-do. Here were a hundred printing shops producing books, sometimes at mortal risk; in 1774 the book trade at Paris was estimated at 45,000,000 livres—four times that of London.[27] "London is good for the English," said Garrick, "but Paris is good for everybody."[28] Said Voltaire in 1768, "We have over thirty thousand people in Paris who take an interest in art."[29] There, beyond challenge, was the cultural capital of the world.

III. THE PHYSIOCRATS

In an apartment at Versailles, under the rooms and the favoring eye of Mme. de Pompadour, that economic theory took form which was to stir and mold the Revolution, and shape the capitalism of the nineteenth century.

The French economy had been struggling to grow despite the swaddling clothes of regulations—by guilds and Colbert—and the Midas myth of a mercantilism that mistook gold for wealth. To increase exports, diminish imports, and take the "favorable balance" in silver and gold as a prop of political and military power, France and England had subjected their national economies to a mesh of rules and restraints helpful to economic order but harming production by hampering innovation, enterprise, and competition. All this— said men like Gournay, Quesnay, Mirabeau *père*, Du Pont de Nemours, and Turgot—was quite contrary to nature; man is by nature acquisitive and competitive; and if his nature is freed from unnecessary trammels he will astonish the world with the quantity, variety, and excellence of his products. So, said these "physiocrats," let nature (in Greek, *physis*) rule (*kratein*); let men invent, manufacture, and trade according to their natural instincts; or, as Gournay is said to have said, *laissez faire*—"let him do" as he himself thinks best. The famous phrase was already old, for about 1664, when Colbert asked businessman Legendre, "What should we [the government] do to help you?" he answered, *"Nous laisser faire*—let us do it, let us alone."[30]

Jean-Claude Vincent de Gournay was the first clear voice of the physiocrats in France. Doubtless he knew of the protests that Boisguillebert and Vauban had made to Louis XIV against the stifling restrictions laid upon agriculture under the feudal regime. He was so impressed by Sir Josiah Child's *Brief Observations Concerning Trade and Interest* (1668) that he translated it into French (1754); and presumably he had read Richard Cantillon's *Essay on the Nature of Commerce* (c. 1734) in its French form (1755). Some would date from this last book the birth of economics as a "science"—a reasoned analysis of the sources, production, and distribution of wealth. "Land," said Cantillon, "is the source or material from which wealth is extracted," but "human labor is the form which produces wealth"; and he defined wealth not in terms of gold or money, but as "the sustenance, conveniences, and comforts of life."[31] This definition was itself a revolution in economic theory.

Gournay was a well-to-do merchant operating at first (1729–44) in Cadíz. After extensive business dealings in England, Germany, and the United Provinces, he settled in Paris, and was appointed *intendant du commerce* (1751). Traveling through France on tours of inspection, he observed at first hand the restraints put by guild and governmental regulations upon economic enterprise and exchange. He left no written formulation of his views, but they were summarized after his death (1759) by his pupil Turgot. He urged that existing economic regulations should be reduced, if not removed; every man knows better than the government what procedure best favors his work; when each is free to follow his interest more goods will be produced, wealth will grow.[32]

> There are laws unique and primeval, founded on nature alone, by which all existing values in commerce balance one another and fix themselves at a determined price, just as bodies left to their own weight arrange themselves according to their specific gravity;[33]

that is, values and prices are determined by the relations of supply and demand, which in turn are determined by the nature of man. Gournay concluded that the state should intervene in the economy only to protect life, liberty, and property, and to stimulate, with distinctions and awards, the quantity and quality of production. M. Trudaine, heading the Bureau of Commerce, accepted these doctrines, and Turgot gave them the force of his eloquence and acknowledged probity.

François Quesnay followed a slightly different physiocratic line. Son of a landed proprietor, he never lost his interest in land, though he was trained to be a physician. He made a fortune by his skill in medicine and surgery, and rose to be physician to Mme. de Pompadour and the King (1749). In his rooms at Versailles he gathered a coterie of heretics—Duclos, Diderot, Buffon, Helvétius, Turgot . . . ; there they discussed everything freely except the King, whom they dreamed of transforming into an "enlightened despot" as the agent of peaceful reform. Immersed in the Age of Reason, Quesnay felt that the time had come to apply reason to economics. Though he was a self-confident dogmatist in his works, he was in person a kindly soul, distinguished by integrity in an immoral milieu.

In 1750 he met Gournay, and soon became more interested in economics than in medicine. Under careful pseudonyms he contributed essays to the *Encyclopédie* of Diderot. His article "Farms" ascribed their desertion to high taxes and conscription. The article "Grains" (1757) noted that small farms were incapable of profitably using the most productive methods, and favored large plantations managed by "entrepreneurs"—an anticipation of the agricultural mammoths of our time. The government should improve roads, rivers, and canals, remove all tolls on transportation, and free the products of agriculture from all restraints of trade.

In 1758 Quesnay published a *Tableau économique* that became the basic manifesto of the physiocrats. Though printed by the government press in the Palace of Versailles under the supervision of the King, it condemned luxury as a wasteful use of wealth that might have been employed to produce greater wealth. In Quesnay's view only the products of the earth constituted wealth. He divided society into three classes: a *classe productive*, of farmers, miners, and fishermen; a *classe disponible*—persons available for military or administrative offices; and a *classe stérile*—artisans who work up the products of the earth into useful objects, and tradesmen who bring the products to the consumer. Since taxes laid upon the second or third class ultimately (in Quesnay's view) fall upon the owners of land, the most scientific and convenient impost would be a single tax (*impôt unique*) upon the annual net profit of each parcel of land. Taxes should be collected directly by the state, never by private financiers (*fermiers généraux*). The government should be an absolute and hereditary monarchy.

Quesnay's proposals now seem to be vitiated by their underestimation of labor, industry, commerce, and art, but to some of his contemporaries they appeared as an illuminating revelation. The most colorful of his followers, Victor Riqueti, Marquis de Mirabeau, thought that the *Tableau économique* rivaled writing and money as among the noblest inventions of history. Born in 1715, dying in 1789, the Marquis precisely spanned the age of Voltaire. He inherited a comfortable estate, lived like a lord, wrote like a democrat, entitled his first book *L'Ami des hommes, ou Traité de la population* (1756), and earned the name he had taken, "Friend of Mankind." After publishing his chef-d'oeuvre he came under the influence of Quesnay; he revised his book accordingly, and enlarged it into a six-volume treatise that went through forty editions and shared in preparing the mind of France for 1789.

The Marquis was not as disturbed by human multiplication as Malthus was to be in 1798. He held that a nation is made great by a large population, and that this is made possible by "men multiplying like rats in a barn if they have the means of subsistence"[34]—as we still see. He concluded that every encouragement should be given to those who grow food. The unequal distribution of wealth, he thought, discourages food production, for the estates of the rich take up land that could be fertile farms. Mirabeau's preface told the King that the peasants were

> the most productive class of all, those who see beneath them nothing but their nurse and yours—Mother Earth; who stoop unceasingly beneath the weight of the most toilsome labors; who bless you every day, and ask nothing from you but peace and protection. It is with their sweat and (you know it not!) their very blood that you gratify that heap of useless people who are ever telling you that the greatness of a prince consists in the value and number . . . of favors that he divides among his courtiers. I have seen a tax-gathering bailiff cut off the hand of a poor woman who clung to her saucepan, the last utensil of the household, which she was defending from distraint. What would you have said, great prince?[35]

In *Théorie de l'impôt* (1760) the revolutionary Marquis attacked the tax-collecting farmers general as parasites preying upon the vitals of the nation. The angry financiers persuaded Louis XV to imprison him in the Château de Vincennes (December 16, 1760); Quesnay induced Mme. de Pompadour to intercede; Louis released the Marquis (December 25), but ordered him to remain on his estate at Le Bignon. Mirabeau made a virtue of necessity by studying agriculture at first hand and in 1763 he issued *Philosophie rurale*, "the most comprehensive treatise on economics prior to Adam Smith."[36] Grimm called it "the Pentateuch of the [physiocratic] sect."[37]

Altogether this unique Marquis wrote forty books, right up to his dying year—all despite the trouble given him by his son, whom in desperation he sent to prison as a measure of safety for both. Like that son he was violent and dissolute, married for money, charged his wife with adultery, let her return to her parents, and took a mistress. He denounced *lettres de cachet* as intolerable tyranny, and later prevailed upon the ministry to issue fifty of them to help him discipline his family.[38]

We find it hard to realize today the commotion raised by the publications of the physiocrats, and the ardor of their campaigns. Quesnay's disciples looked up to him as the Socrates of economics; they submitted their writings to him before going to print, and in many cases he contributed to their books. In 1767 Lemercier de la Rivière, sometime governor of Martinique, issued what Adam Smith considered "the most distinct and best connected account of the doctrine,"[39] *L'Ordre naturel et essentiel des sociétés politiques.* In economic relations (ran the argument) there are laws corresponding to those that Newton found in the universe; economic ills arise from ignorance or violation of those laws.

> Do you wish a society to attain the highest degree of wealth, population, and power? Trust, then, its interests to freedom, and let this be universal. By means of this liberty (which is the essential element of industry) and the desire to enjoy—stimulated by competition and enlightened by experience and example —you are guaranteed that everyone will always act for his own greatest possible advantage, and consequently will contribute with all the power of his particular interest to the general good, both to the ruler and to every member of the society.[40]

Pierre-Samuel du Pont summed up the gospel in *Physiocratie* (1768), which gave the school its historic name. Du Pont spread the theory also in two periodicals whose influence was felt all the way from Sweden to Tuscany. He served as inspector general of manufactures under Turgot, and fell with Turgot's fall (1776). He helped to negotiate with England the treaty that recognized American independence (1783). He was elected to the Assembly of Notables (1787) and the Constituent Assembly (1789). There, to distinguish him from another member called Du Pont, he was called Du Pont de Nemours, from the town that he represented. Having opposed the Jacobins, he was endangered by their rise to power; in 1799 he exiled himself to America. He returned to France in 1802, but in 1815 he made his final home in the United States, where he founded one of America's most famous families.

On the face of it the physiocratic doctrine appeared to favor feudalism, since feudal lords still owned, or drew feudal dues from, at least a third of the land of France. But they—who had paid hardly any taxes before 1756— were appalled at the notion that all taxes should fall upon the landowners; nor could they accept the removal of feudal tolls on the transport of goods through their domains. The middle classes, which were thinking of new dignities, resented the idea that they were a sterile, unproductive, part of the nation. And the *philosophes*, though mostly agreeing with the physiocrats about relying on the King as an agent of reform, could not accompany them in making peace with the Church.[41] David Hume, who visited Quesnay in 1763, thought the physiocrats "the most chimerical and arrogant set of men to be found nowadays since the destruction of the Sorbonne."[42] Voltaire lampooned them (1768) in *L'Homme aux quarante écus* (*The Man with Forty Crowns*).[43] In 1770 Ferdinando Galiani, an Italian habitué of d'Holbach's "synagogue" of atheists, issued *Dialoghi sul commercio dei grani*, which Diderot in that same year translated into French. Voltaire said that Plato and Molière must have joined in writing this excellent contribution to the already "dismal science" of economics. Galiani ridiculed with Parisian wit the physiocratic notion that only the land produces wealth. To free the trade in grains from all regulation would (he argued) ruin the farmers of

France, and could produce a famine at home while clever merchants exported French grain to other states. This is precisely what happened in 1768 and 1775.

A story tells how Louis XV asked Quesnay what he would do if he were king. "Nothing," answered Quesnay. "Who, then, would govern?" "The laws"[44]—by which the physiocrat meant the "laws" inherent in the nature of man and governing supply and demand. The King agreed to try them. On September 17, 1754, his ministry abolished all tolls and restraints on the sale and transport of grains—wheat, rye, and corn—within the kingdom; in 1764 this freedom was extended to the export of grains except when these should reach a stated price. Left to the operation of supply and demand, the price of bread dropped for a time, but a bad harvest in 1765 raised it far beyond normal. The shortage of grains reached the famine stage in 1768–69; peasants grubbed for food in pigsties, and ate weeds and grass. In a parish of 2,200 souls 1,800 begged for bread. The people complained that while they faced starvation, speculators were exporting grain. Critics charged the government with profiting from the operations of these *monopoleurs* in a "Pacte de Famine," and this bitter variation on the Pacte de Famille of 1761 rang through subsequent years to accuse even the kindly Louis XVI of benefiting from the high price of bread. Some officials were apparently guilty, but Louis XV was not. He had commissioned certain dealers to buy grain in good years, store it, and put it on the market in years of scarcity; but when this was sold it was at prices too high for the impoverished to pay. The government took tardy remedial measures; it imported grain and distributed it to the neediest provinces. The public clamored for restoration of state control over the trade in grain; the Parlement joined in the demand; it was at this juncture that Voltaire published his *L'Homme aux quarante écus*. The government yielded; on December 23, 1770, the edicts permitting free trade in grain were revoked.

Despite this setback, physiocratic notions made their way, at home and abroad. An edict of 1758 had established free trade in wool and woolen products. Adam Smith visited Quesnay in 1765, was attracted by his "modesty and simplicity," and was confirmed in his own predilection for economic liberty. He judged "the capital error of this system . . . to lie in its representing the class of artificers, manufacturers, and merchants as altogether barren and unproductive," but he concluded that "this system, with all its imperfections, is perhaps the nearest approximation to the truth that has yet been published on the subject of political economy."[45] The ideas of the physiocrats accorded well with the desire of England—already the greatest exporter among the nations—to reduce export and import dues. The doctrine that wealth would grow faster under freedom from governmental restrictions on production and distribution found sympathetic hearing in Sweden under Gustavus III, in Tuscany under Grand Duke Leopold, in Spain under Charles III. Jefferson's affection for a government that governed least was in part an echo of physiocratic principles. Henry George acknowledged the influence of the physiocrats on his advocacy of a single tax falling upon realty.[46] The philosophy of free enterprise and trade charmed the American business class, and gave an added stimulus to the rapid development of industry and wealth in the United States. In France the physiocrats provided a theoretical basis for freeing the middle classes from feudal and legal impediments to domestic trade and political advancement. Before Quesnay died (December 16, 1774) he had the comfort of seeing one of his friends made controller general of finance; and had he lived fifteen years more he would have seen the triumph of many physiocratic ideas in the Revolution.

IV. THE RISE OF TURGOT: 1727–74

Was Turgot a physiocrat? His rich and diverse background repels every label. He came of an old family—"*une bonne race*," Louis XV called it—which had through generations filled with distinction important posts. His father was a councilor of state and *prévôt des marchands*—the highest administrative office in Paris. His older brother was *maître des requêtes* (secretary for petitions and claims), and a leading member, of the Parlement of Paris. As a younger son, Anne-Robert-Jacques Turgot was intended for the priesthood. In the Collège Louis-le-Grand, in the Seminary of St.-Sulpice, and in the Sorbonne he passed all tests with credit, and at the age of nineteen he became Abbé de Brucourt. He learned to read Latin, Greek, Hebrew, Spanish, Italian, German, and English, and to speak the last three of these languages fluently. In 1749 he was elected a prior of the Sorbonne, and in that capacity he delivered lectures two of which made a stir beyond the ramparts of theology.

In July, 1750, he addressed the Sorbonne in Latin on "The Advantages that the Establishment of Christianity Has Conferred upon the Human Race": it had rescued antiquity from superstition, had preserved many arts and sciences, and had presented to mankind the liberating conception of a law of justice transcending all human prejudices and interests. "Could one hope for this from any other principle than religion? . . . The Christian religion alone has . . . brought to light the rights of humanity."[47] There is an echo of philosophy in this piety; apparently the young prior had read Montesquieu and Voltaire, with some effect upon his theology.

In December, 1750, he addressed the Sorbonne with a *Tableau philosophique des progrès successifs de l'esprit humain*. This historic enunciation of the new religion of progress was a remarkable performance for a youth of twenty-three. Anticipating Comte—perhaps following Vico—he divided the history of the human mind into three stages: theological, metaphysical, and scientific:

> Before man understood the causal connection of physical phenomena, nothing was so natural as to suppose they were produced by intelligent beings, invisible, and resembling themselves. . . . When philosophers recognized the absurdity of these fables about the gods, but had not yet gained an insight into natural history, they thought to explain the causes of phenomena by abstract

expressions such as essences and faculties. . . . It was only at a later period that, by observing the reciprocal mechanical action of bodies, hypotheses were formed which could be developed by mathematics and verified by experience.[48]

Animals, said this brilliant youth, know no progress; they remain the same from generation to generation; but man, by having learned to accumulate and transmit knowledge, is able to improve the tools by which he deals with his environment and enriches his life. As long as this accumulation and transmission of knowledge and technology continues, progress is inevitable, though it may be interrupted by natural calamities and the vicissitudes of states. Progress is not uniform, nor is it universal; some nations advance while others retreat; art may stand still while science moves on; but the sum of the movement is forward. For good measure Turgot predicted the American Revolution: "Colonies are like fruit, which clings to the tree only until it is ripe. By becoming self-sufficient, they do what Carthage did, what America will sometime do."[49]

Inspired by the idea of progress, Turgot, while still in the Sorbonne, planned to write a history of civilization. Only his notes for some sections of the project survive; from these it appears that he had intended to include the history of language, religion, science, economics, sociology, and psychology as well as the rise and fall of states.[50] His father's death having left him an adequate income, he determined, late in 1750, to leave the ecclesiastical career. A fellow abbé protested, and promised him rapid advancement, but Turgot replied, according to Du Pont de Nemours, "I cannot condemn myself to wear a mask throughout my life."[51]

He had taken only minor orders, and was free to enter a political career. In January, 1752, he became substitute attorney general, and in December counselor in the Parlement; in 1753 he bought the office of *maître des requêtes*, in which he won a reputation for industry and justice. In 1755–56 he accompanied Gournay on tours of inspection in the provinces; now he learned economics by direct contact with farmers, merchants, and manufacturers. Through Gournay he met Quesnay, and through him Mirabeau *père*, Du Pont de Nemours, and Adam Smith. He never listed himself as of the physiocratic school, but his money and his pen were main supports of Du Pont's magazine, *Éphémérides*.

Meanwhile (1751) his mind and manners won him welcome in the salons of Mme. Geoffrin, Mme. de Graffigny, Mme. du Deffand, and Mlle. de Lespinasse. There he met d'Alembert, Diderot, Helvétius, d'Holbach, and Grimm. One early result of these contacts was his publication (1753) of two *Lettres sur la tolérance*. To Diderot's *Encyclopédie* he contributed articles on existence, etymology, fairs, and markets, but when the enterprise was condemned by the government he withdrew as a contributor. Traveling in Switzerland and France, he visited Voltaire (1760), beginning a friendship that lasted till Voltaire's death. The sage of Ferney wrote to d'Alembert: "I have scarcely ever seen a man more lovable or better informed."[52] The *philosophes* claimed him as their own, and hoped through him to influence the King.

In 1766 he wrote, for two Chinese students who were about to return to China, a hundred-page outline of economics—*Réflexions sur la formation et la distribution des richesses*. Published in the *Éphémérides* (1769–70), it was acclaimed as one of the most concise and forceful expositions of physiocratic theory. Land, said Turgot, is the only source of wealth; all classes but cultivators of the soil live on the surplus that these produce beyond their own need; this surplus constitutes a "wages fund" from which the artisan class can be paid. Here follows an early formulation of what came to be known as "the iron law of wages":

> The wages of the worker are limited to his subsistence by competition among the workmen. . . . The mere worker, who has only his arms and his industry, has nothing except in so far as he succeeds in selling his toil to others. . . . The employer pays him as little as he can; and as he has a choice among a great number of workers, he prefers the one who works for the least wage. The workers are therefore obliged to lower their price in competition with one another. In every kind of work it cannot fail to happen, and actually it does happen, that the wages of the worker are limited to what is necessary for his subsistence.[53]

Turgot went on to stress the importance of capital. Someone through his savings must supply the tools and materials of production before the worker can be employed, and he must keep the workers alive until the sale of the product replenishes his capital. As an enterprise is never sure of success, profits must be allowed to balance the risk of losing the capital. "It is this continual advance and return of capital which constitutes . . . the circulation of money, that useful and fruitful circulation which gives life to all the labors of the society, . . . and is with great reason compared to the circulation of the blood in the animal body."[54] This circulation must not be interfered with; profits and interest, like wages, must be allowed to reach their natural level according to supply and demand. Capitalists, manufacturers, merchants, and workingmen should be free from taxation; this should fall only upon landowners, who will reimburse themselves by charging more for their products. No duty should be charged on the transport or sale of any article of consumption.

In these *Réflexions* Turgot laid down the theoretical basis of nineteenth-century capitalism—before the effective organization of labor. One of the kindest and most honest men of his time could see for the workers no better future than a subsistence wage. Yet this same man became a devoted public servant. In August, 1761, he was appointed intendant—the king's supervisor —of the *généralité* of Limoges, one of the poorest regions of France. He estimated that forty-eight to fifty per cent of the income of the land went in taxes to the state and tithes to the Church. The local peasants were sullen, the nobles uncouth. "I have the misfortune," he wrote to Voltaire, "of being an intendant. I say the misfortune, for in this age of quarrels and remonstrances there is happiness only in living the philosophic life among one's books and friends." Voltaire answered: "You will win the hearts and the purses of Limousins . . . I believe that an intendant is the only person who can be useful. Can he not have the highways repaired, the fields cultivated, the marshes drained, and can he not encourage manufactures?"

Turgot did all that. He labored zealously in Limoges for thirteen years, winning affection from the people and dislike from the nobility. He repeatedly—vainly—petitioned the Council of State to reduce the tax rate. He improved the allotment of taxes, remedied injustices, organized a civil service, freed the trade in grain, and built 450 miles of roads; they were part of that nationwide road-building program (begun by the French government in 1732) to which we owe the lovely tree-shaded highways of France today. Before Turgot the roads had been built by *corvée*—the forced and unpaid labor of the peasantry; he abolished *corvée* in Limoges, and paid for the labor by a general tax on all the laity. He persuaded the inhabitants to grow potatoes as human food, instead of only for animals. His vigorous measures of relief in the famine periods of 1768–72 won universal admiration.

On July 20, 1774, a new King invited him to join the central government. All France rejoiced, and looked to him as the man who would save the crumbling state.

V. THE COMMUNISTS

While the physiocrats were laying the theoretical basis of capitalism, Morelly, Mably, and Linguet were expounding socialism and communism. As the educated classes surrendered their hopes of heaven they consoled themselves with earthly substitutes: the well-to-do, ignoring religious prohibitions, indulged themselves with wealth and power, women and wine and art; the commoners found solace in visions of a utopia in which the goods of the earth would be equally shared between simple and clever, weak and strong.

There was no socialist movement in the eighteenth century, no such definite group as the Levellers in Cromwell's England, or the communistic Jesuits of Paraguay; there were only individuals here and there adding their voices to a mounting cry that would become, in "Gracchus" Babeuf, a factor in the French Revolution. We recall that the priestly skeptic Jean Meslier, in his *Testament* of 1733, pleaded for a communistic society in which the national product would be equally shared, and men and women would mate and part as they pleased; meanwhile, he suggested, it would help if a few kings should be killed.[55] Seven years before this proclamation came to print, Rousseau, in his second *Discourse* (1755), denounced private property as the source of all the evils of civilization; but even in that outburst he disclaimed any socialistic program, and by 1762 the heroes of his books were well equipped with property.

In the same year with Rousseau's *Discourse on the Origin of Inequality* appeared the *Code de la nature* of an obscure radical of whom, aside from his books, we know hardly anything but his last name, Morelly. We must not confuse him with André Morellet, whom we have seen as a contributor to the *Encyclopédie.* Morelly first roused the wits with a *Traité des qualités d'un grand roi* (1751), which pictured a communistic king. In 1753 he gave his dream poetic form as *Naufrage des îles flottantes, ou La Basiliade;* here the good king, perhaps after reading Rousseau's first *Discourse,* leads his people back to a simple and natural life. The best and fullest exposition of the communistic ideal was Morelly's *Code de la nature* (1755–60). Many ascribed it to Diderot, and the Marquis d'Argenson pronounced it superior to Montesquieu's *L'Esprit des lois* (1748). Morelly thought, like Rousseau, that man is by nature good, that his social instincts incline him to good behavior, and that the laws corrupted him by establishing and protecting private property. He praised Christianity for inclining to communism, and mourned that the Church had sanctioned property. The institution of private property had generated "vanity, fatuity, pride, ambition, villainy, hypocrisy, viciousness . . . ; everything evil resolves itself into this subtle and pernicious element, the desire to possess."[56] Then sophists conclude that the nature of man makes communism impossible, whereas in real sequence it was the violation of communism that perverted the natural virtues of man. If it were not for the greed, egoism, rivalries, and hatreds engendered by private property, men would live together in peaceful and co-operative brotherhood.

The road to reconstruction must begin by clearing all obstacles to the free discussion of morals and politics, "allowing full liberty to wise men to attack the errors and prejudices that maintain the spirit of property." Children should be taken from their parents at six years of age and brought up communally by the state until they are sixteen years old, when they should be returned to their parents; meanwhile the schools will have trained them to think in terms of the common good rather than personal acquisition. Private property should be permitted only in articles pertaining to the individual's intimate needs. "All products will be collected in public storehouses to be distributed to all citizens for the needs of life."[57] Every able-bodied individual must work; from twenty-one to twenty-five he must help on the farms. There is to be no leisure class, but everyone will be free to retire at forty, and the state will see that he is well cared for in old age. The nation will be divided into garden cities with a shopping center and a public square. Each community is to be governed by a council of fathers over fifty years old; and these councils will elect a supreme senate to rule and co-ordinate all.

Perhaps Morelly underestimated the natural individualism of men, the strength of the acquisitive instinct, and the opposition that the hunger for freedom would offer to the tyranny required for the maintenance of an unnatural equality. Nevertheless his influence was considerable. Babeuf declared that he had imbibed his communism from Morelly's *Code de la nature,* and Charles Fourier probably took from the same source his plan (1808) for co-operative "phalansteries," which in turn led to such communist experiments as Brook Farm (1841). In Morelly's *Code* occurs the famous principle that came down to inspire and plague the Russian Revolution: *"chacun selon ses facultés, à chacun selon ses besoins"*—from each according to his ability, to each according to his needs.[58]

The *philosophes* generally rejected Morelly's system as impracticable, and accepted private property as an unavoidable consequence of human nature. But in 1763 Morelly found a vigorous ally in Simon-Henri Linguet, a lawyer who attacked both law and property. Disbarred from practice, Linguet published (1777–92) *Annales politiques*, a journal in which he delivered a running fire upon social abuses. Law, he thought, had become an instrument for legalizing and maintaining possessions originally won by force or fraud.

> Laws are destined above all to safeguard property. Now, as one can take away much more from the man who has than from him who has not, they are obviously a guarantee accorded to the rich against the poor. It is difficult to believe, and yet it is clearly demonstrable, that the laws are in some respects a conspiracy against the majority of the human race.[59]

Consequently there is an inevitable class war between the owners of property or capital and the workers who, in competition with one another, must sell their labor to propertied employers. Linguet scorned the claims of the physiocrats that the liberation of the economy from state controls would automatically bring prosperity; on the contrary, it would accelerate the concentration of wealth; prices would rise, and wages would lag behind. The control of prices by the rich perpetuates the slavery of the wage earner even after slavery has been "abolished" by law; "all that they [the former slaves] have gained is to be constantly tormented by the fear of starvation, a misfortune from which their predecessors in this lowest rank of humanity were at least exempt";[60] slaves were lodged and fed all the year round; but in an uncontrolled economy the employer is free to throw his employees into beggary whenever he can make no profit from them; then he makes begging a crime. There is no remedy against all this, Linguet thought, but a communist revolution. He did not recommend it for his time, since it would lead more likely to anarchy than to justice, but he felt that the conditions for such a revolt were rapidly taking form.

> Never has want been more universal, more murderous for the class which is condemned to it; never, perhaps, amidst apparent prosperity, has Europe been nearer to a complete upheaval. . . . We have reached, by a directly opposite route, precisely the point which Italy had reached when the slave war [led by Spartacus] inundated it with blood and carried fire and slaughter to the very gates of the mistress of the world.[61]

The Revolution came in his time despite his advice, and sent him to the guillotine (1794).

The Abbé Gabriel Bonnot de Mably kept his head by dying four years before the Revolution. He came of a prominent family in Grenoble; one of his brothers was the Jean Bonnot de Mably with whom Rousseau stayed in 1740; another was the Condillac who made a sensation of psychology. Still another famous relative, Cardinal de Tencin, tried to make a priest out of him, but Gabriel stopped short at minor orders, attended the salon of Mme. de Tencin in Paris, and succumbed to philosophy. In 1748 he quarreled with the Cardinal and withdrew into scholarly retirement; thereafter the only events in his life were his books, all of them once renowned.*

His seven years in Paris and Versailles gave him a knowledge of politics, of international relations, and of human nature. The result was a unique mixture of socialistic aspirations with pessimistic doubts. Mably insisted (contrary to Machiavelli) that the same moral standards that are applied to individuals should be applied to the conduct of states, but he recognized that this would require an enforceable system of international law. Like Voltaire and Morelly he was a theist without Christianity, but he believed that morality cannot be maintained without a religion of supernatural punishments and rewards, for most persons "are condemned to the permanent infancy of their reason."[62] He preferred the Stoic ethics to those of Christ, and the Greek republics to modern monarchies. He agreed with Morelly in deriving the vices of man not from nature but from property; this is "the fountainhead of all the ills that afflict society."[63] "The passion for enriching oneself has taken a growing place in the human heart, stifling all justice";[64] and that passion is intensified as inequality of fortunes increases. Envy, covetousness, and class divisions poison the natural amity of mankind. The rich multiply their luxuries, the poor sink into humiliation and degradation. Of what good is political liberty if economic slavery persists? "The freedom which every European thinks he enjoys is only the freedom to leave one master and give himself to another."[65]

How much happier and finer would men be if there were no *mine* and *thine!* Mably thought that the Indians were happier under Jesuit communism in Paraguay than the Frenchmen of his time; that the Swedes and the Swiss of that age, who had given up the quest for glory and money and were content with a moderate prosperity, were happier than the English who were conquering colonies and trade. In Sweden, he contended, character was held in greater honor than fame, and a modest contentment was valued above great wealth.[66] Real freedom is possessed only by those who are not anxious to be rich. In the kind of society advocated by the physiocrats there would be no happiness, for men would always be agitated by the desire to equal, in possessions, those more affluent than themselves.

So Mably concluded that communism is the only social order that will promote virtue and happiness. "Establish community of goods, and nothing is thence easier than to establish equality of conditions, and to affirm on this double foundation the well-being of man."[67] But how can such communism be established with men so corrupted as they now are? Here the skeptic in Mably raises his head, and despondently admits that "no human force today could re-establish equality without causing greater disorders than those one

---

* Chiefly *Droit public de l'Europe* (1748); *Observations sur les Grecs* (1749); *Observations sur les Romains* (1751); *Droits et devoirs des citoyens* (1758); *Entretiens de Phocion sur le rapport de la morale avec la politique* (1763); *Observations sur l'histoire de France* (1765); *Doutes proposés aux philosophes économistes* (1768, against the physiocrats); *De la Législation, ou Principes des lois* (1776); *De la Manière d'écrire l'histoire* (1783, demanding accurate and contemporary documentation); *Principes de la morale* (1784); *Observations sur le gouvernement et les lois des États-Unis de l'Amérique* (1784).

wished to avoid."[68] Democracy is theoretically splendid, but in practice it fails through the ignorance and acquisitiveness of the masses.[69] All that we can do is to hold up communism as an ideal toward which civilization should gradually and cautiously move, slowly changing the habits of modern man from competition to co-operation. Our goal should be not the increase of wealth, nor even the increase of happiness, but rather the growth of virtue, for only virtue brings happiness. The first step toward a better government would be the summoning of a States-General, which should draw up a constitution giving supreme power to a legislative assembly (this was done in 1789–91). The acreage possessed by any one person should be limited; large estates should be broken up to spread peasant proprietorship; there should be strict curbs on the inheritance of wealth; and "useless arts" like painting and sculpture should be banned.

Many of these proposals were adopted in the French Revolution. Mably's collected works were published in 1789, again in 1792, again in 1793; and a book published soon after the Revolution listed Helvétius, Mably, Rousseau, Voltaire, and Franklin, in that order, as the principal inspirers of that event, and the true saints of the new dispensation.[70]

VI. THE KING

Louis XV, so far as he knew them, smiled at these communists as negligible dreamers, and passed amiably from bed to bed. The court continued its reckless gambling and extravagant display; the Prince de Soubise spent 200,000 livres to entertain the King for one day; and every "progress" of his Majesty to one of his country seats cost the taxpayers 100,000 livres. Half a hundred dignitaries had their *hôtels*, or palaces, at Versailles or Paris, and ten thousand servants labored proudly to meet the wants and foibles of nobles, prelates, mistresses, and the royal family. Louis himself had three thousand horses, 217 carriages, 150 pages garbed in velvet and gold, and thirty physicians to bleed and purge and poison him. The royal household in one year 1751 spent 68,-000,000 livres—almost a quarter of the government's revenue.[71] The people complained, but for the most part anonymously; every year a hundred pamphlets, posters, satirical songs displayed the King's unpopularity. "Louis," said one brochure, "if you were once the object of our love, it was because your vices were still unknown to us. In this kingdom, depopulated because of you, and given over as a prey to the mountebanks who rule with you, if there are Frenchmen left, it is to hate you."[72]

What had led to this transformation of Louis le Bien-Aimé into a despised and insulted king? He himself, aside from his extravagance, negligence, and adulteries, was not quite as bad as vengeful history has painted him. He was physically handsome, tall, strong, capable of hunting all afternoon and entertaining women at night. His educators had spoiled him; Villeroi had given him to understand that all France belonged to him by inheritance and divine right. The pride of sovereignty was moderated and confused by the shadow and tradition of Louis XIV; the young King was obsessed and made timid by a sense of his inability to meet that august standard of grandeur and will; he became incapable of resolution, and gladly left decisions to his ministers. His boyhood reading and his tenacious memory gave him some acquaintance with history, and he acquired in time a considerable knowledge of European affairs; through many years he kept his own secret diplomatic correspondence. He was languidly intelligent, and judged well and mercilessly the character of the men and women about him. He could keep pace with the best minds in his court in conversation and wit. But apparently he accepted even the most absurd dogmas of the theology that Fleury had poured into his youth. Religion became an intermittent fever with him as he alternated between piety and adultery. He suffered from fear of death and hell, but gambled on absolution *in articulo mortis*. He halted the persecution of the Jansenists, and in retrospect we perceive that the *philosophes*, on and off, enjoyed considerable leeway in his reign.

He was sometimes cruel, but more often humane. Pompadour and Du Barry learned to love him for himself as well as for the power he gave them. His coldness and taciturnity were part of his shyness and self-distrust; behind that reserve lay elements of tenderness, which he expressed especially in his affection for his daughters; these loved him as a father who gave them everything except good example. Usually his manners were gracious, but at times he was callous, and talked too calmly about the ailments or approaching death of his courtiers. He quite forgot to be a gentleman in his abrupt dismissals of d'Argenson, Maurepas, and Choiseul; but that too may have been the result of diffidence; he found it hard to say no to a man's face. Yet he could face danger bravely, as in the hunt or at Fontenoy.

Dignified in public, he was pleasant and sociable with his intimate friends, preparing coffee for them with his own anointed hands. He observed the complex etiquette that Louis XIV had established for royalty, but he resented the formalism that it laid upon his life. Often he rose before the official *lever*, and made his own fire so as not to awaken the servants; more often he lingered in bed till eleven. At night, after having been put to bed with the official *coucher*, he might slip away to enjoy his mistress or even to visit, incognito, the town of Versailles. He avoided the artificialities of the court by hunting; on those days when he did not run off to the chase the courtiers said, "The King is doing nothing today."[73] He knew more about his hounds than about his ministers. He thought that his ministers could take care of matters better than he could; and when he was warned that France was moving toward bankruptcy and revolution, he comforted himself with the thought that "*les choses, comme elles sont, dureront autant que moi*" (things as they are will last through my time).[74]

Sexually he was a monster of immorality. We can forgive him the mistress that he took when the Queen was oppressed by his virility; we can understand his fascination with Pompadour, and his sensitivity to the beauty and grace and bright vivacity of women; but there is little in royal history so despicable as his serial passage through the girls prepared for his bed in the Parc aux Cerfs. The coming of Du Barry was, by comparison, a return to normalcy.

VII. DU BARRY

She began in the Champagne village of Vaucouleurs about 1743 as Marie-Jeanne Bécu, daughter of Mlle. Anne Bécu, who, it appears, never revealed the father's identity. Such mysteries were quite frequent in the lower classes. In 1748 Anne moved to Paris and became a cook to M. Dumonceux, who arranged to have Jeanne, aged seven, boarded in the Convent of St.-Anne. There the pretty girl remained for nine years and, it seems, not unhappily; she kept pleasant memories of this well-ordered nunnery, received instruction in reading, writing, and embroidery, and retained throughout her life a simple and unquestioning piety, and a reverence for nuns and priests; the shelter that she gave to hunted priests in the Revolution shared in leading her to the guillotine.[75]

When she emerged from the convent she took as her surname that of her mother's new mate, M. Rançon. She was sent to a hairdresser to learn his art, but this included seduction, and Jeanne, irresistibly beautiful, knew not how to resist. Her mother transferred her to Mme. de La Garde as a companion, but Madame's visitors paid too much attention to Jeanne, and she was soon dismissed. The millinery shop in which she became a salesgirl attracted an unusual number of male patrons. She became the kept woman of a succession of rakes. In 1763 she was taken up by Jean du Barry, a gambler who procured women for aristocratic roués. Under the elegant name of Jeanne de Vaubernier she served this pimp for five years as hostess at his parties, and added some refinement to her charms. Du Barry thought that he too, like Mme. Poisson, had discovered a "morsel for the King."

In 1766 good King Stanislas died in Lorraine, which thereby became a province of France. His daughter, Marie Leszczinska, the modest, pious Queen of France, fell into a rapid decline after his death, for their mutual love had upheld her in her long servitude to a faithless husband in an alien environment; and on June 24, 1768, she passed away, mourned even by the King. He gave his daughters hope that he would take no more mistresses. But in July he saw Jeanne, who happened to be straying through the Palace of Versailles as innocently as La Pompadour had driven in the Sénart hunting park twenty-four years before.

He was struck by her voluptuous beauty, her gaiety and playfulness; here was someone who could amuse him again, and warm his cold and melancholy heart. He sent his valet Lebel for her; "Comte" du Barry readily agreed to part with her for a royal consideration. To appease appearances Louis insisted that the girl should have a husband. The "Comte" married her in short time to his brother Guillaume, the real but impoverished Comte du Barry, who was brought from Lévignac in Gascony for the purpose. Jeanne bade him farewell immediately after the ceremony (September 1, 1768), and never saw him again. Guillaume was awarded a pension of five thousand livres. He took a mistress of his own, carried her off to Lévignac, lived with her there for twenty-five years, and married her on learning that his wife had been guillotined.

Jeanne, new-named Comtesse du Barry, joined the King secretly at Compiègne, then publicly at Fontainebleau. The Duc de Richelieu asked Louis what he saw in this new toy. "Only this," his Majesty answered, "that she makes me forget that soon I shall be sixty."[76] The courtiers were horrified. They could readily understand a man's need of a mistress; but to take a woman whom several of them had known as a prostitute, and elevate her to a place above marquises and duchesses! Choiseul had hoped to offer his sister to the King as *maîtresse en titre;* this rejected lady goaded her usually cautious brother into open hostility to the pretty upstart, and La Barry never forgave him.

The new mistress was soon swimming in livres and gems. The King dowered her with a pension of 1,300,000 francs, plus an annuity of 150,000 more, levied on the city of Paris and the state of Burgundy. Jewelers hurried to supply her with rings, necklaces, bracelets, tiaras, and other sparkling adornments, for which they billed the King 2,000,000 francs in four years. Altogether, in those four years, she cost the treasury 6,000,375 livres.[77] The people of Paris heard of her brilliance, and mourned that a new Pompadour had come to swallow their taxes.

On April 22, 1769, entering in a blaze of jewelry and on the arm of Richelieu, she was formally presented at court. The men admired her charms, the women received her as coldly as they dared. She bore these slights quietly, and appeased some courtiers by the modesty of her behavior and the melodious laughter with which she regaled the King. Even to her enemies (except Choiseul) she showed no malice; she gained favor by bending his Majesty to issue pardons more frequently than before. Bit by bit she gathered around her titled men and women who used her intercession with the King. Like Pompadour, she took good care of her relatives; she bought property and title for her mother, and secured pensions for her aunt and her cousins. She paid the debts of Jean du Barry, gave him a fortune, and bought for him a sumptuous villa at L'Isle-Jourdain. She herself won from the King the Château of Louveciennes, which the Prince and Princesse de Lamballe had occupied, on the edge of the royal park at Marly. She engaged the greatest architect of that generation, Jacques-Ange Gabriel, to remodel the château to her convenience, and the meticulous cabinetmaker Pierre Gouthière to decorate it with furniture and objects of art to the value of 756,000 livres.

She lacked the background of education and association that had made Pompadour a willing and discriminating patron of literature, philosophy, and art. But she collected a library of well-bound books, from Homer to pornography, from Pascal's pious *Pensées* to Fragonard's spicy illustrations; and in 1773 she sent her homage and portrait to Voltaire with "a kiss for each cheek." He replied with a poem, as clever as ever:

Quoi! deux baisers sur la fin de ma vie!
Quelle passeport vous daignez m'envoyer!
Deux! c'est trop d'un, adorable Égérie.
Je serai mort de plaisir au premier.*78

She asked Louis XV to let Voltaire return to Paris; he refused; she had to content herself with buying an assortment of watches from Ferney. In 1778, when the old Master came to Paris to die, she was among the many who climbed the stairs in the Rue de Beaune to pay her respects to him. He was charmed, and ended by rising from his bed to escort her to the door. On the way down she met Jacques-Pierre Brissot, the future revolutionist; he was hoping to submit to Voltaire a manuscript on criminal law; he had sought entry the day before and had been refused; he was trying again. She led him back to Voltaire's door, and arranged for his admittance. In his *Mémoires* he recalled her "smile so full of warmth and kindness."[79]

She was unquestionably good-natured and generous. She bore without recrimination the enmity of the royal family, and the refusal of Marie Antoinette to speak to her. Choiseul alone she could not forgive, and that was because he never ceased his efforts to drive her from the court. Soon he or she would have to go.

VIII. CHOISEUL

He came of an old Lorraine family, and was already in early life the Comte de Stainville. He earned distinction for his bravery in the War of the Austrian Succession. In 1750, aged thirty-one, he replenished the fortunes of his family by marrying a wealthy heiress. His brilliant mind and gay wit soon won him prominence at court, but he interrupted his rise by opposing Pompadour. In 1752 he changed sides and gained her gratitude by revealing to her a plot to get her dismissed. She secured his appointment as ambassador to Rome, then to Vienna. In 1758 he was summoned to Paris to replace Bernis as minister for foreign affairs, and was made a duke and peer of France. In 1761 he transferred his ministry to his brother César, but continued to direct foreign policy; he himself took the ministries of war and marine. He became so powerful that at times he overruled and intimidated the King.[80] He rebuilt both the army and the navy; he reduced speculation and corruption in military payments and supplies, restored discipline in the ranks, and replaced superannuated dignity with untitled competence in the officer corps. He developed French colonies in the West Indies, and added Corsica to the French crown. He sympathized with the *philosophes*, defended the publication of the *Encyclopédie*, supported the expulsion of the Jesuits (1764), and winked at the reorganization of the Huguenots in France. He protected Voltaire's security at Ferney, furthered his campaign for the Calas family, and won from Diderot an apostrophe of praise: "Great Choiseul, you watch sleeplessly over the fortunes of the Fatherland."[81]

---

* "What! Two kisses at the close of my life! What a passport you deign to send me! Two! —it is one too many, adorable Egeria; I shall die with pleasure at the first."

All in all, his policies rescued France in modest measure from the disaster brought upon her by the Austrian *mésalliance*. He reduced the subsidies that France habitually paid to Sweden, Switzerland, Denmark, and some German princes. He encouraged the efforts of Charles III to bring Spain into the eighteenth century, and sought to strengthen both France and Spain by the Pacte de Famille (1761) between the Bourbon kings. The plan went awry, but Choiseul negotiated peace with England on much better terms than the military situation appeared to support. He foresaw the revolt of the English colonies in America, and strengthened the French position in St.-Domingue, Martinique, Guadeloupe, and French Guiana, in the hope of establishing a new colonial domain that would compensate France for the loss of Canada. The two Napoleons adopted the same policy in 1803 and 1863.

Against these achievements we must weigh his failure to stop the Russian penetration of Poland, and his insistence upon leading France and Spain into renewed hostilities with England. Louis had had enough of war, and gave an open mind to those who were working for Choiseul's fall. The clever Minister charmed many by his courtesy to courtiers, his prodigal entertainment of friends, and his resourcefulness and industry in the service of France; but he intensified rivalries into enmities by open criticism and careless speech, and his unabated opposition to Du Barry gave his foes an intimate access to the King. The inexhaustible Richelieu supported Du Barry, and his nephew the Duc d'Aiguillon itched to replace Choiseul as head of the government. The royal family, resenting Choiseul's activity against the Jesuits, condescended to use the scorned mistress as a tool in deposing the impious Minister.

Louis repeatedly asked him to avoid war with England and with Du Barry; Choiseul continued secretly to plot war and openly to scorn the mistress. Finally she joined all her forces against him. On December 24, 1770, the irritated King sent a curt message to Choiseul: "My cousin, my dissatisfaction with your services compels me to exile you to Chanteloupe, to which you shall take yourself within the next twenty-four hours." Most of the court, shocked by so abrupt a dismissal of one who had done great things for France, dared the royal ire by expressing their sympathy for the fallen Minister. Many nobles rode off to Chanteloupe to solace Choiseul in his exile. It was a comfortable banishment, for the Duke's estate included one of the finest palaces and most spacious private parks in France; and it was placed in Touraine, not far from Paris. There Choiseul lived in state and elegance, for Du Barry induced the King to send him 300,000 livres at once, and a pledge of 60,000 livres per year.[82] The *philosophes* mourned his fall; "*Tout est perdu!*" cried the diners *chez* d'Holbach, and Diderot described them as melting in tears.

IX. THE REVOLT OF THE *PARLEMENTS*

Choiseul was succeeded by a "Triumvirat" in which d'Aiguillon was foreign minister, René-Nicolas de Maupeou was chancellor, and Abbé Joseph-

Marie Terray was *contrôleur des finances*. Terray gave Du Barry all the funds that she demanded; otherwise, however, he reduced expenditures heroically. He suspended amortization, and lowered the rate of interest on governmental obligations; he devised new taxes, dues, and fees, and doubled the tolls on internal transport; altogether he saved 36,000,000 livres, and added 15,000,000 to income. In effect he delayed financial collapse by partial bankruptcy, but many men suffered through governmental defaults, and added their voices to an unsettling discontent. Soon the deficit grew again, and reached 40,000,000 livres in the last year of the reign (1774). What would today seem to be a modest national debt for a nation with fiscal stability was an added cause for anxiety to those who had lent money to the government, and who now heard with less hostility the mounting cries for change.

The culminating crisis in the final decade of Louis XV was the struggle of his ministers to preserve the absolute power of the king against the active rebellion of the *parlements*. These (as we have seen) were not representative or legislative bodies like the British Parliament; they were judicial chambers serving as appellate courts in thirteen cities of France. In addition, like the English Parliament versus Charles I, they claimed to defend, against royal absolutism, the "fundamental law," or established customs, of their regions; and since the Regent Philippe d'Orléans had confirmed their "right of remonstrance" against royal or ministerial edicts, they advanced to the claim that no such edict could become law unless they accepted and registered it.

If the *parlements* had been elected by the people, or by an educated and propertied minority (as in Britain), they might have served as a transition to democracy, and in some measure they were a wholesome check upon the central government; generally, therefore, the people supported them in their conflicts with the king. Actually, however, the *parlements*, almost entirely composed of rich lawyers, were among the most conservative forces in France. As the "nobility of the robe," these lawyers became as exclusive as the "nobility of the sword"; "*parlement* after *parlement* decreed that new posts carrying nobility were to be restricted to . . . families already noble."[83] The Paris Parlement was the most conservative of all. It competed with the clergy in opposing freedom of thought or publication; it banned, and sometimes burned, the books of the *philosophes*. It had been won to Jansenism, which brought a Calvinist theology into the Catholic Church. Voltaire noted that the Jansenist Parlement of Toulouse tortured and killed Jean Calas, and that the Parlement of Paris approved the execution of La Barre, while the ministry of Choiseul reversed the Calas judgment and protected the Encyclopedists.

Christophe de Beaumont, archbishop of Paris, aggravated the conflict between the Jansenists and the orthodox Catholics by ordering the clergy under his jurisdiction to administer the sacraments only to persons who had confessed to a non-Jansenist priest. The Paris Parlement, with wide public approval, forbade the priests to obey this order; it accused the Archbishop of fomenting a schism, and seized some of his temporal possessions. The King's

Council of State called this procedure illegally confiscatory, and bade the Parlement withdraw from religious disputes. The Parlement refused; on the contrary, it drew up "Grandes Remontrances" (May 4, 1753) which in a degree foreshadowed the Revolution: they professed loyalty to the King, but told him that "if subjects owe obedience to kings, these on their side owe obedience to the laws";[84] the implication was that the Parlement, as guardian and interpreter of the law, would act as a supreme court over the king. On May 9 the Council of State issued *lettres de cachet* banishing most members of the Paris Parlement from the capital. The provincial *parlements* and the people of Paris rose to the support of the exiles. The Marquis d'Argenson noted, in December, that "the Parisians are in a state of subdued excitement."[85] The government, fearing a popular rising, ordered its soldiery to patrol the streets and protect the house of the Archbishop. In March, 1754, d'Argenson wrote: "Everything is preparing for civil war."[86] Cardinal de La Rochefoucauld devised a face-saving compromise; the government recalled the exiles (September 7), but ordered the Parlement and the clergy to refrain from further dispute. The order was not obeyed. The Archbishop of Paris continued his campaign against Jansenism, and so vigorously that Louis banished him to Conflans (December 3). The Parlement declared that the papal bull against Jansenism was not a rule of faith, and bade the clergy ignore it. The government vacillated, but finally, needing a loan from the clergy to prosecute the Seven Years' War, it ordered the Parlement to accept the papal bull (December 13, 1756).

The violent debate turned many heads. On January 5, 1757, Robert-François Damiens attacked the King in a Versailles street, and stabbed him with a large penknife; then he stood by, awaiting arrest. Louis told his negligent bodyguard, "Secure him, but let no one do him any harm."[87] The wound proved minor, and the assailant claimed: "I had no intention to kill the King. I might have done this had I been so inclined. I did it only that God might touch the King's heart, and work on him to restore things to their former footing."[88] In a letter from prison to the King he repeated that "the Archbishop of Paris is the cause of all the disturbance about the sacraments, by having refused them."[89] He had (he said) been aroused by the speeches he had heard in the Parlement; "if I had never entered a court of justice . . . I should never have gotten here."[90] Those speeches had so excited him that he had sent for a physician to come and bleed him; none came; had he been bled (he claimed), he would not have attacked the King.[91] The Grand' Chambre of the Parlement tried, convicted, and sentenced him, and condemned his father, mother, and sister to perpetual banishment. Damiens suffered the tortures prescribed by law for regicides: his flesh was torn by red-hot pincers, he was splashed with boiling lead, he was torn apart by four horses (March 28, 1757). Highborn ladies paid for points of vantage from which to see the operation. The King expressed disgust with the tortures, and sent pensions to the banished family.

The attempt won some sympathy for the King: Jews and Protestants joined in prayers for his speedy recovery; but when it was learned that the wound was, in Voltaire's phrase, only a "pinprick" (*piqûre d'épingle*), the tide of public support turned back to the Parlement. People began to discuss representative government versus absolute monarchy. "They see in the *parlements*," wrote d'Argenson, "a remedy for the vexations they suffer. . . . Revolt is smoldering." In June, 1763, the Paris Parlement again affirmed that "the verification of the laws by Parlement is one of those laws that cannot be violated without violating that law by which the kings themselves exist."[92] The Parlement of Toulouse went further, declaring that the law required "the free consent of the nation";[93] but by "nation" it meant the *parlements*. On July 23, 1763, an important judicial body, the Cour des Aides, under the presidency of the brave and honest Malesherbes, submitted to the King a report on national poverty and the incompetence and corruption in the administration of the national finances; it begged him to "listen to the people themselves through the voice of their deputies in a convocation of the States-General of the realm."[94] Here was the first clear demand for that national assembly which had not been called since 1614.

In the crucial struggle that resulted in the expulsion of the Jesuits from France (1764)[95] the Paris Parlement seized the offensive, and forced the hand of the King. In June and November the Parlement of Rennes, supreme judicial court of Brittany, dispatched strong remonstrances to Louis against the oppressive taxes levied by the Duc d'Aiguillon, then governor of the province. Receiving no satisfaction, it suspended its sittings, and most of its members resigned (May, 1765). Its *procureur général*, Louis-René de La Chalotais, published an attack upon the central government. He, his son, and three counselors were arrested and charged with sedition. The King ordered the Rennes Parlement to try them; it refused, and all the *parlements* of France, backed by public opinion, supported the refusal. On March 3, 1766, Louis appeared before the Parlement of Paris, warned it against conniving at sedition, and proclaimed his resolve to rule as an absolute monarch.

> In my person alone resides the sovereign power. . . . To me alone belongs the legislative power, unconditional and undivided. All public order emanates from me. My people and I are one, and the rights and interests of the nation, which some dare to make a body separate from the monarch, are necessarily united with mine, and rest in my hands alone.[96]

His vows, he added, had been not to the nation, as the Parlement asserted, but only to God. The Parlement of Paris continued to defend that of Rennes, but on March 20 it officially accepted, as "inevitable maxims," the doctrine that "the sovereignty belongs to the king alone; he is accountable only to God; . . . the legislative power resides entirely in the person of the sovereign."[97] Choiseul and others urged the King to make responsive concessions. La Chalotais and his fellow prisoners were released, but were exiled to Saintes, near La Rochelle. D'Aiguillon was recalled from Brittany, and joined Choiseul's foes. The Parlement of Rennes resumed its sittings (July, 1769).

Voltaire entered the conflict by issuing in 1769 his *Histoire du Parlement de Paris, par M. l'abbé Big*. He denied authorship of the book, and wrote a letter criticizing it as "a masterpiece of errors and awkwardness, a crime against the language";[98] even so, it was his. Though written in haste, it showed considerable historical research, but it lacked impartiality; it was a long arraignment of the Parlement as a reactionary institution that had at every turn opposed progressive measures—e.g., the establishment of the French Academy, inoculation for smallpox, and free administration of justice. Voltaire accused the *parlements* of class legislation, superstition, and religious intolerance. They had condemned the earliest printers in France; they had applauded the St. Bartholomew's Day Massacre; they had sentenced the Maréchal d'Ancre to be burned as a witch. They had been instituted, said Voltaire, for purely judicial functions, and had no authority to legislate; if they took this authority they would replace the autocracy of the king with an oligarchy of rich lawyers, entrenched beyond any popular control. Voltaire had written this long brief during the ascendancy of Choiseul, whose liberal tendencies encouraged the belief that progress could most readily be made through a king enlightened by an enlightened minister. Diderot did not agree with Voltaire; he argued that however reactionary the *parlements* had been, their claim of the right to supervise legislation served as a desirable check on royal tyranny.[99]

The return of d'Aiguillon to Paris brought on a new crisis. The Parlement of Rennes accused the Duke of malfeasance; he submitted to a trial of these charges by the Parlement of Paris; when it became clear that he would be pronounced guilty Mme. du Barry appealed to the King to intervene. Chancellor Maupeou supported her, and on June 27, 1770, Louis announced that the hearings were revealing state secrets and must be terminated. He annulled the reciprocal complaints, pronounced both d'Aiguillon and La Chalotais innocent, and ordered all parties to the dispute to refrain from further agitation. Defying these commands as an arbitrary interference with the lawful course of justice, the Parlement declared that the testimony had seriously compromised the honor of d'Aiguillon, and recommended his abstention from all functions as a peer until he had been cleared by due process of law. On September 6 the Parlement published an *arrêté*, or decision, that flung down the gauge to the King:

> The multiplicity of the actions of an absolute power exercised everywhere against the spirit and letter of the constitutive laws of the monarchy is unequivocal proof of a premeditated project to change the form of government, and to substitute, for the always equal force of the laws, the irregular actions of arbitrary power.[100]

Then the Parlement adjourned till December 3.

Maupeou used the interval to prepare an uncompromising defense of royal power. On November 27 he issued, over the King's signature, a decree that, while admitting the right of remonstrance, forbade any rejection of an edict renewed after remonstrances had been heard. The Parlement replied by requesting the King to surrender the evil counselors of the throne to the vengeance of the laws.[101] On December 7 Louis summoned the Parlement to Versailles, and in an official *lit de justice* he bade them accept and register the November 27 decree. On returning to Paris the magistrates decided to abstain from all functions of the Parlement until the November decree should be withdrawn. Louis ordered them to resume their sittings; the order was ignored. Choiseul tried to make peace at home to wage better war abroad; Louis dismissed him; now Maupeou dominated the Council of State while Du Barry fluttered about the King. She showed him Vandyck's portrait of England's Charles I, and warned him of a like fate: "Your Parlement too will cut off your head."[102]

On January 3, 1771, Louis again ordered the acceptance of the November edict. The Parlement replied that the edict violated the basic laws of France. On January 20, between one and four o'clock in the morning, the musketeers of the King delivered to each magistrate a *lettre de cachet* giving him a choice between obedience and exile from Paris. The great majority of them protested love of the King, but remained obdurate. Within the next two days 165 members of the Paris Parlement were banished to divers parts of France. The people cheered them as they left their Palais de Justice.

Maupeou now moved to supplant the *parlements* with a new judicial organization. By a royal decree he set up in Paris a supreme court composed of the Council of State and some complaisant jurists; and at Arras, Blois, Châlons, Clermont-Ferrand, Lyons, and Poitiers he established *conseils supérieurs* as appellate courts for the provinces. Some judiciary abuses were reformed, venality was interrupted, justice was henceforth to be administered without charge. Voltaire hailed the reforms and rashly predicted: "I am absolutely sure that the Chancellor will carry off a complete victory, and that the people will love it."[103] But the people could not contentedly accept the destruction of so ancient an institution as the *parlements;* there is nothing so often condemned, and so deeply loved, as the past. The majority of the public scorned the new courts as added tools of royal autocracy. Diderot, though he had no delusions about the *parlements*, mourned their passing as "the end of constitutional government. . . . In one moment we have jumped from the monarchical state to the most complete despotic state."[104] Eleven peers of the realm, and even some members of the royal family, expressed their disapproval of Maupeou's attempt to replace the *parlements*. There was no visible commotion among the people, but the words *liberté, droits* (laws), and *légalité*, which had lately been much heard in the Parlement, now ran from mouth to mouth. Satires on the lecher King took on new audacity and bitterness. Placards called upon the Duc d'Orléans to lead a revolution.

Almost without willing it the *parlements*, despite their conservatism, were caught up in a ferment of revolutionary ideas. The *Discourses* of Rousseau, the communism of Morelly, the proposals of Mably, the secret meetings of Freemasons, the *Encyclopédie*'s exposure of abuses in the government and the Church, the flock of pamphlets circulating through the capital and the provinces: all these stood in violent opposition to the claim of absolute power and divine right by a do-nothing and sexually promiscuous King. "M. Tout le Monde"—i.e., public opinion—was on the move as a force in history.

Until 1750 the brunt of criticism had fallen upon the Church, but thereafter, goaded by the suppression of the *Encyclopédie*, it fell increasingly upon the state. Wrote Horace Walpole from Paris in October, 1765:

Laughing is out of fashion. . . . Good folks, they have no time to laugh. There is God and the King to be pulled down first; and men and women, great and small, are devoutly engaged in the demolition. . . . Do you know who the *philosophes* are, or what the term means here? In the first place, it comprehends almost everybody; and, in the next, means men who, vowing war against popery, aim, many of them, at a subversion of all religion, and still many more at the destruction of regal power.[105]

This, of course, was an exaggeration; most of the *philosophes* (Diderot particularly excepted) were supporters of monarchy, and fought shy of revolution. They attacked the nobility and all hereditary privilege; they pointed out a hundred abuses and called for reform; but they shuddered at the thought of giving all power to the people.[106] Nevertheless Grimm wrote in his *Correspondance* for January, 1768:

The general weariness with Christianity, which is manifested in all parts, and especially in Catholic states; the disquiet which is vaguely agitating the minds of men, and leading them to attack religious and political abuses—[all this] is a phenomenon characteristic of our century, as the spirit of reform was of the sixteenth, and it foreshadows an imminent and inevitable revolution.[107]

X. THE KING DEPARTS

Louis XV, like Louis XIV, lacked the art of dying in due time. He knew that France was waiting for him to disappear, but he could not bear to think of death. The Austrian ambassador reported in 1773: "From time to time the King remarks concerning his age, health, and the frightful account that he must one day render to the Supreme Being."[108] Louis was transiently touched by the retirement of his daughter Louise-Marie to a Carmelite convent, allegedly to atone for her father's sins; there, we are told, she scrubbed floors and washed laundry. When he came to see her she reproved him for his way of life, begged him to dismiss Du Barry, marry the Princesse de Lamballe, and make his peace with God.

Several of his friends died in the final years of the reign; two of them, their hearts failing, fell dead at his feet.[109] Yet he seemed to take a macabre pleasure in reminding aged courtiers of their approaching demise. "Souvré," he said to one of his generals, "you are growing old; where do you wish to be buried?" "Sire," answered Souvré, "at the feet of your Majesty." We are told that the reply "made the King gloomy and pensive."[110] Mme. du Hausset thought that "a more melancholy man was never born."[111]

The King's death was a long-delayed revenge unwittingly taken by the sex that he had adored and debased. When his lust found even Du Barry inadequate, he took into his bed a girl so young as to be barely nubile; she carried the germs of smallpox, and infected the King. On April 29, 1774, the disease began to mark him. His three daughters insisted on staying with him and nursing him, though they had acquired no immunity. (They all contracted the disease, but recovered.) At night they left, and Du Barry took their place. But on May 5 the King, wishing to receive the sacraments, gently dismissed her: "I realize now that I am seriously ill. The scandal of Metz must not be repeated. I owe myself to God and to my people. So we must part. Go to the Duc d'Aiguillon's château at Rueil, and await further orders. Please believe that I shall always hold you in the most affectionate regard."[112]

On May 7 the King, in a formal ceremony before the court, declared that he repented of having given scandal to his subjects; but he maintained that he "owed no accounting of his conduct to anyone but God."[113] At last he welcomed death. "Never in my life," he told his daughter Adélaïde, "have I felt happier."[114] He passed away on May 10, 1774, aged sixty-four, having reigned fifty-nine years. His corpse, which infected the air, was hurried to the royal vaults at St.-Denis without pomp, and amid the sarcasms of the crowd that lined the route. Once more, as in 1715, France rejoiced at the death of her king.

CHAPTER IV

The Art of Life

I. MORALITY AND GRACE

H E who has not lived in the years around 1780," said Talleyrand, "has not known the pleasure of life."* Provided, of course, one belonged to the upper classes, and had no prejudices in favor of morality.

It is hard to define morality, for each age makes its own definition to suit its temper and sins. Frenchmen had through centuries relieved monogamy with adultery, as America relieves it with divorce; and in the Gallic view judicious adultery does less hurt to the family—or at least to the children— than divorce. In any case adultery flourished in eighteenth-century France, and was generally condoned. When Diderot, in his *Encyclopédie*, wished to distinguish *bind* and *attach*, he gave as example: "One is bound to one's wife, attached to one's mistress."[2] "Fifteen out of twenty of the noble lords about the court," according to a contemporary, "are living with women to whom they are not married."[3] To have won a mistress was as necessary to status as to have money. Love was frankly sensual: Boucher painted it *en rose*, Fragonard gave it lace and grace; Buffon said, brutally, "There is nothing good in love but the flesh."[4]

Here and there the finer love appeared, even in Crébillon *fils*;[5] and among the *philosophes* Helvétius dared to be enamored of his wife, while d'Alembert remained faithful to Julie de Lespinasse through all the variations on her absorbing theme. Jean-Jacques Rousseau undertook in this age a one-man reform of morals; and shall we also credit the novels of Samuel Richardson? Some women put on virtue as a fashion,[6] but some received gratefully the recollected gospel of premarital chastity and postmarital fidelity as saving them from the indignity of serving as steppingstones for philanderers. At least monogamy ceased to be a badge of shame. Roués, married, rediscovered old pleasures in family life; better to plumb the depths of unity than be forever scratching the surface of variety. Many women who had begun as frivolous surfaces settled down when children came; some nursed their children, even before Rousseau's exhortations; and often those children, growing up under maternal love, returned it with filial interest. The Maréchale de Luxembourg, after an adventurous youth, became a model wife, faithful to her husband while gently mothering Rousseau. When the Comte de Maurepas died (1781), after serving both Louis XV and Louis XVI and suffering a long exile between his ministries, his wife recalled that they "had spent

---

* "*Qui n'a pas vécu dans les années voisine de 1780 n'a pas connu le plaisir de vivre.*" So this famous remark appears in P. Dupré's *Encyclopédie des citations* (Paris, 1959), 1, 635, which quotes, as source, Fr. Guizot's *Mémoires pour servir à l'histoire de mon temps* (Paris, 1858–68), I, 6.[1]

fifty years together, and not one day apart."[7] We hear too much—we ourselves have spoken too much—of women who gained entrance into history
by breaking marriage vows; we hear too little of those who could not be
made unfaithful even by infidelity. Mlle. Crozat, betrothed at twelve to the
future Duc de Choiseul, bore with patience his infatuation with his ambitious
sister; she accompanied him in exile, and even the sophisticated Walpole
honored her as a saint. The Duchesse de Richelieu continued to love her husband through all his adulteries, and was grateful that fate allowed her to die
in his arms.[8]

Perversions, pornography, and prostitution continued. French law required the penalty of death for sodomy, and indeed two pederasts were
burned in the Place de Grève in 1750;[9] but usually the law ignored voluntary
and private homosexual acts between adults.[10] Economic morality was then
as now; note the passage in Rousseau's *Émile*[11] (1762) about the adulteration
of food and drinks. Political morality was then as now; there were many
devoted public servants (Malesherbes, Turgot, Necker), but also many who
secured their posts by money or connections, and reimbursed themselves, in
office, beyond the letter of the law. Many idle nobles lived luxuriously on the
blood of their peasants; but public and private charity abounded.

All in all, the French of the eighteenth century were a kindly people, despite a code of sexual ethics that violated Christian norms by its candor. See,
in the career of Rousseau, the number of people who came to his aid and
comfort despite the difficulty of pleasing him; and often these sympathetic
souls belonged to that aristocracy which he had reviled. Chivalry had declined
in the relation of men to women, but it survived in the conduct of French
officers to war captives of their class. The irritable and hostile Smollett, traveling in France in 1764, wrote: "I respect the French officers in particular for
their gallantry and valor, and especially for that generous humanity which
they experience to their enemies, even amidst the horrors of war."[12] Goya
pictured, but probably exaggerated, the cruelty of French soldiers to Spanish
commoners in the Napoleonic Wars. Certainly the French could be callously
cruel, presumably because they had been inured to brutality by war and the
penal code. They were turbulent, given to knife-wielding college brawls, and
to street riots as a substitute for elections. They were impetuous, and plunged
into good or evil with little loss of time in deliberation. They were chauvin-
ists who could not understand why the rest of the world was so barbarous
as to speak any other language but French. Mme. Denis refused to learn the
English word for bread—"Why can't they all say *pain?*"[13] Perhaps more than
any other people they loved glory. Soon they would die by the thousands
crying, "*Vive l'Empereur!*"

Of course the French were supreme in manners. The customs of courtesy
established under Louis XIV were tarnished by hypocrisy, cynicism, and
superficiality, but essentially they survived, and gave to life in the educated
classes a grace which no society can rival today. "The French are so polite,
so obliging," said Casanova, "that one feels drawn to them at once"—but he
adds that he could never trust them.[14]

They excelled in cleanliness; in the Frenchwoman this became one of the cardinal virtues, practiced till death. And it was a part of good manners to be neatly dressed. The men and women of the court sometimes sinned against good taste by extensive finery or extravagant coiffures. Men wore their hair in a queue, which Maréchal de Saxe deprecated as dangerous in war, giving a handle to the enemy; and they powdered their hair as assiduously as did their ladies. The women raised their hair to such elevation that they feared to dance, lest they catch fire from chandeliers. A German visitor calculated that the chin of a French lady lay exactly midway between her feet and the top of her hair.[15] Hairdressers made fortunes by changing hair fashions frequently. Cleanliness did not extend to the female hair, for this took hours to arrange, and all but the fanciest women kept the same hairdos for days without disturbing them with a comb. Some ladies carried *grattoirs* of ivory, silver, or gold, to scratch the head with piquant grace.

Facial make-up was as complex as now. Leopold Mozart wrote to his wife from Paris in 1763: "You ask if Parisian ladies are beautiful. How can one say, when they are painted like Nuremberg dolls, and so disfigured by this repulsive trick that the eyes of an honest German cannot tell a naturally beautiful woman when he sees her?"[16] Women carried their cosmetics with them, and renewed their complexions in public as brazenly as today. Mme. de Monaco rouged herself before riding off to be guillotined. Corpses were made up, powdered, and rouged, as in our time. Feminine dress offered a challenging mixture of invitations and impediments: low necklines, lacy bodices, hypnotizing gems, great spreading skirts, and high-heeled shoes, usually of linen or silk. Buffon, Rousseau, and others protested against corsets, but these remained *de rigueur* till the Revolution discarded them.

The variety and gaiety of social life were among the attractions of Paris. The cafés Procope, La Régence, and Gradot entertained intellectuals and rebels, men about town and women about men, while the luminaries of literature, music, and art shone in the salons. The lords of pedigree or wealth kept Versailles and Paris dancing with dinners, receptions, and balls. In the upper classes the arts included eating and conversation. The French cuisine was the envy of Europe. French wit had now reached a refinement where it had worn all topics thin, and boredom clouded brilliance. The art of conversation declined in the second half of the eighteenth century; declamation overheated it, speakers outran listeners, and wit was cheapened by its own profusion and its careless stings. Voltaire, who himself could sting, reminded Paris that wit without courtesy is crudity;[17] and La Chalotais thought that "the taste for cleverness . . . has banished science and true learning" from the salons.[18]

In the parks—which were neatly groomed and alive with statuary—people strolled at their ease, or followed their children or their dogs, and gay blades pursued damsels skilled in vain retreat. The Gardens of the Tuileries were probably more beautiful then than now. Hear Mme. Vigée-Lebrun:

> The Opéra was close by in those days, bordering on the Palais-Royal. In summer the performance ended at half-past eight o'clock, and all the elegant people came out, even before the end, to walk about the grounds. It was the

fashion for women to carry very large nosegays, which, together with the scented powder in their hair, literally perfumed the air. . . . I have known these gatherings, before the Revolution, to continue till two in the morning. There were musical performances by moonlight in the open. . . . There was always a great crowd.[19]

II. MUSIC

France took music as part of its *gaieté Parisienne*. She did not care to rival Germany in Masses and solemn chorales; she almost ignored Mozart when he came to Paris, but she forgot to be chauvinistic when her ears were charmed by Italian melodies. She made *fêtes galantes* out of her music; she specialized in forms fit for, or recalling, the dance—courantes, sarabandes, gigues, gavottes, minuets. Her music, like her morals, her manners, and her arts, circled around woman, and often took names that recalled her image— *L'Enchanteresse, L'Ingénue, Mimi, Carillon de Cythère*.

In France, as in Italy, *opera buffa* was more popular than *opera seria* before Gluck came (1773). A troupe calling itself Opéra-Comique had installed itself in Paris in 1714; in 1762 it merged with the Comédie-Italienne; in 1780 this enlarged Opéra-Comique moved to a permanent home in the Salle Favart. The man who made its fortune was François-André Philidor, who traveled through Europe as chess champion, and composed twenty-five operas, nearly all of a humorous turn, like *Sancho Pança* and *Tom Jones*, but showing good taste and finished art. His operas are now forgotten, but "Philidor's defense" and "Philidor's legacy" are still remembered as classic moves in chess. Ballet was a favorite interlude in French opera; here French grace found another outlet, and motion became poetry. Jean-Georges Noverre, ballet master at the Paris Opéra, wrote a once famous treatise on choreography—*Lettres sur la danse et les ballets* (1760); this prepared the way for Gluck's reforms by advocating a return to Greek ideals of the dance, with naturalness of movement, simplicity of costume, and emphasis on dramatic significance rather than on abstract configurations or virtuoso feats.

Public concerts were now a part of life in all the major cities of France. In Paris the Concerts Spirituels (established in the Tuileries in 1725) set a high standard of instrumental music. While the Opéra-Comique played Pergolesi's *La serva padrona*, the Concerts performed his *Stabat Mater*, which was so well received that it was repeated annually till 1800.[20] The Concerts brought the compositions of Handel, Haydn, Mozart, Jommelli, Piccini, and the Bachs to French acceptance, and provided a platform for the leading virtuosos of the day.

These visiting performers agreed in one thing—that France lagged behind Germany, Austria, and Italy in music. The *philosophes* joined in this judgment. "It is a pity," wrote Grimm (a German) "that people in this country understand so little of music";[21] he excepted Mlle. Fel, who sang with a lovely throat. Grimm concurred with Rousseau and Diderot in asking for a "return to nature" in opera; these three led the Italian faction in that Guerre des

Bouffons which had begun with the presentation of an *opera buffa* by an Italian company in Paris. We have noted elsewhere this debate between French and Italian musical styles; it was not yet over, for Diderot was still fighting the "War of the Buffoons" in his *Le Neveu de Rameau;* and in his *Troisième Entretien sur Le Fils naturel* (1757) he called for a Messiah to redeem French opera from pompous declamation and fanciful artifice. "Let him come forward, who is to put true tragedy and true comedy upon the lyric [operatic] stage!"—and he gave as example of a fit text the *Iphigenia in Aulis* of Euripides.[22] Did Gluck, then in Vienna, hear that call? Voltaire repeated it prophetically in 1761:

> It is to be hoped that some genius may arise, strong enough to convert the nation from this abuse [of artifice], and to impart to a stage production . . . the dignity and ethic spirit that it now lacks. . . . The tide of bad taste is rising, insensibly submerging the memory of what was once the glory of the nation. Yet again I repeat: the opera must be set on a different footing, that it may no longer deserve the scorn with which it is regarded by all the nations of Europe.[23]

In 1773 Gluck arrived in Paris, and on April 19, 1774, he conducted there the French première of *Iphigénie en Aulide*. But that story must bide its time.

III. THE THEATER

France produced in this period no plays that have defied oblivion—perhaps excepting a few of those that Voltaire sent up from Les Délices or Ferney. But France gave the drama every encouragement of staging and acclaim. In 1773 Victor Louis raised at Bordeaux the finest theater in the realm, with a pompous portico of Corinthian columns, classic balustrade, and sculptural embellishments. The Comédie-Française, acknowledged by Garrick to be the best group of actors in Europe, was housed in the Théâtre-Français built in 1683 in the Rue des Fosses, St.-Germain-des-Prés: three tiers of galleries in a narrow oblong that compelled declamation and set the oratorical style of acting in France. Hundreds of families staged private theatricals, from Voltaire at Ferney to the Queen at Trianon—where Marie Antoinette played Colette in Rousseau's *Le Devin du village*—and the Prince de Ligne thought that "more than ten ladies of quality play and sing better than any in the playhouse."[24] "Little theaters" sprouted everywhere in France. A Bernardine monastery, hidden in the woods of Bresse, built a small theater for its monks, "without" (said one of them) "the knowledge of bigots and small minds."[25]

Despite amateur competition, the stars of the Comédie-Française shone brightly over France. We have seen how the people of Geneva and Ferney came out to see Lekain when he played for Voltaire at Châtelaine. His real name was Henri-Louis Cain, but this was a cursed cognomen which he forgivably changed. Neither was his face his fortune; Mlle. Clairon took some time to warm to him even in a play. Voltaire had discovered his ability in an amateur performance, had coached him, and had found a place for him at the

Théâtre-Français. On September 14, 1750, Lekain made his debut as Titus in Voltaire's *Brutus;* and for a generation thereafter he took the male lead in Voltaire's plays. The irascible patriarch loved him to the end.

But Voltaire's stage favorite (now that Adrienne Lecouvreur had passed away) was Mlle. Clairon. Legally she was Claire-Josèphe Hippolyte Léris de La Tude. Born without benefit of marriage in 1723, and not expected to survive, she lived to be eighty—which is not always a blessing for the heroines of the stage. It was not thought worth while to educate her, but she stole her way into the Théâtre-Français, was entranced by the scenery-plus-orations, and never quite overcame a tendency to make speeches even in the ecstasy of love. She announced that she would be an actress; her mother threatened to break her arms and legs if she persisted in so sinful a resolve;[26] she persisted and joined a traveling troupe. She soon acquired the morals that were customary in her new profession. "Thanks to my talent, my good looks, and the ease with which I could be approached, I saw so many men at my feet that it would have been impossible for me, being endowed with a naturally tender heart, . . . to be inaccessible to love."[27]

Back in Paris, she charmed M. de La Popelinière; he enjoyed her, and then used his influence to get her a place at the Opéra; four months later the Duchesse de Châteauroux, current mistress to the King, secured her admission to the Comédie-Française. The company asked her to choose her first role, expecting her to follow custom and select a minor part; she proposed to play Phèdre; the company protested, but let her have her way; she carried off the adventure triumphantly. Henceforth she starred in tragic roles, in which her only rival was Mlle. Dumesnil. She gained a reputation for acquisitive promiscuity. She entertained a roster of nobles, made them pay well, hoarded her gains, and then yielded much of them to her favorite lover, the Chevalier de Jaucourt, who wrote articles on economics for the *Encyclopédie*. She paid a price, too, for the attentions of Marmontel, whom we shall soon meet as the author of *Moral Tales*. Consider the woman's side of it in her letter to him: "Is it possible that you did not know what troubles you caused me (unintentionally, but I had them all the same), and that those troubles have kept me in bed for six weeks, in critical danger? I cannot believe that you were aware of this, else you would not have gone out in society while everybody knew what condition I was in."[28] Nevertheless she and Marmontel remained fast friends for thirty years.

It was he whose criticisms and suggestions led her to make an important change in acting. Till 1748 she had followed the method usual at the Théâtre-Français—forceful and emotional speech, grand gestures, trembling passion. Marmontel found this unnatural and distasteful. Amid her liaisons Clairon had done much reading, and had become one of the best-educated women of her day; her fame and *esprit* had won her admission to cultivated society; she perceived that the emptiest vessels were the most resonant. In 1752 an attack of syphilis compelled her to withdraw for a time from the stage. Recovering, she accepted an engagement to give thirty-five performances in Bordeaux. On her first night there, she tells us, she played Phèdre in the traditional manner, "with all the noise, fury, and unreason which then were so applauded in Paris." She was applauded. But on the next night she played Agrippine in Racine's *Britannicus* in quiet voice and restrained gestures, leaving emotions pent up until the final scene. She received an ovation. Returning to Paris, she won the old audience to her new style. Diderot warmly approved; he had her in mind when he wrote *The Paradox of the Actor*—that a good actor is inwardly calm and self-possessed even in the most passionate moments of his roles; and he asked, "What acting was ever more perfect than Clairon's?"[29] She liked to shock her admirers by telling them that she mentally reviewed her monthly bills while conveying to an audience a pathos that moved it to tears.[30] Voltaire did not welcome the new method, but he effectively supported her, and she him, in reforming costume and furniture on the stage. Heretofore all actresses had played their roles—of any nation or age—in the dress of eighteenth-century Paris, with hoopskirts and powdered hair; Clairon startled her audience by dressing her body and hair in the style of the time in the play; and when she played Idamé in Voltaire's *Orphan of China* the costume and furniture were Chinese.

In 1763 Clairon went to Geneva to consult Dr. Tronchin. Voltaire asked her to stay with him at Les Délices. "Madame Denis is ill; so am I. Monsieur Tronchin will come to our hospital to see the three of us."[31] She came, and the old sage liked her so much that he lured her to Ferney for a longer visit, and persuaded her to join him in several performances in his theater. An old drawing shows him, in his seventieth year, kneeling before her in a passionate avowal.

She retired from the stage in 1766, having already at forty-three lost her health, and even the precision of her speech. Like Lecouvreur, she fell in love with a dashing young noble; she sold nearly all her possessions to rescue him from his creditors; he repaid her by giving his love, and her livres, to other women. Then, aged forty-nine, she received from the thirty six-years-old Christian Friedrich Karl Alexander, Margrave of Ansbach and Bayreuth, an invitation to live with him at Ansbach as his mentor and mistress. She went (1773), and for thirteen years she kept her hold on him. He had imbibed in France some ideals of the Enlightenment; with her encouragement he effected several reforms in his principality—abolishing torture and establishing religious liberty. Her final accomplishment was to persuade him to sleep every night with his wife. In time Clairon grew bored, and longed for Paris. The Margrave took her there occasionally; on one of those trips he adopted a new mistress, and left Clairon in Paris, handsomely endowed. She was now sixty-three.

She was welcomed in the salons, even by the virtuous Mme. Necker; she gave lessons in elocution to the future Mme. de Staël. She took on new lovers, including later the husband of Mme. de Staël herself, who was glad to get rid of him. He set up the aging actress in comfort, but the Revolution deflated her livres, and she lived in poverty until Napoleon reinflated her pension in 1801. In that year a Citizen Dupoirier offered her a last liaison. She discouraged him in a pitiful note that summarizes the tragedy of many an old actress: "It is likely that your memory still recalls me as brilliant, young, and surrounded with all my prestige. You must revise your ideas. I can scarcely see; I am hard of hearing; I have no more teeth; my face is all wrinkled; my dried-up skin barely covers my weak frame."[32] He came nevertheless, and they comforted each other by recalling their youth. She died in 1803 by falling out of bed.

She had long outlived the classic tragic drama whose greatest eighteenth-century exponent, Voltaire, had acclaimed her as its supreme interpreter. The Paris audience, predominantly middle-class, was surfeited with the rhyming speeches of princes, princesses, priests, and kings; those majestic alexandrines of Corneille and Racine, marching pompously on six feet, seemed now to be a symbol of aristocratic life; but were there none but nobles in history? Yes, of course, a Molière had shown those others; but that was in comedy; were there not tragedies, profound trials and noble feelings, in the homes and hearts of people without pedigree? Diderot thought the time had come for dramas of the bourgeoisie. And whereas the nobility had shunned sentimentality, and required emotion to wear a stately mask, the new drama, said Diderot, should liberate feeling, and should not be ashamed to move audiences to handkerchiefs and tears. So he, and some others after him, wrote *drames larmoyants*—weeping plays. Moreover, several of the new playwrights not only portrayed and exalted middle-class life, they attacked the nobility, the clergy, at last even the government—its corruption, taxes, luxury, and waste; they did not merely denounce despotism and bigotry (Voltaire had done this well), they praised republics and democracy; and those passages were applauded with special warmth.[33] The French stage joined a hundred other forces in preparing revolution.

IV. MARMONTEL

"Authors are everywhere," wrote Horace Walpole from Paris in 1765, and they "are worse than their own writings, which I don't mean as a compliment to either."[34] Certainly the age could not compare, in literature, with the age of Molière and Racine, nor with that of Hugo, Flaubert, and Balzac; in this brief period between 1757 and 1774 we have, as memorable authors, only Rousseau and Marmontel, and the living embers of Voltaire's fire, and the secret, unpublished ebullience of Diderot. Men and women gave themselves so intensely to conversation that their wits were spent before they took to ink. Aristocratic polish was out of print; philosophy, economics, and politics held the stage; content now dominated form. Even poetry tended to propaganda; Saint-Lambert's *Les Saisons* (1769) imitated James Thomson, but denounced fanaticism and luxury unseasonably, and, like Lear, thought of winter in terms of icy blasts whistling about the hovels of the poor.

Jean-François Marmontel owed his rise to his shrewdness, to women, and to Voltaire. Born in 1723, he wrote in his old age amiable *Mémoires d'un père* (1804), which offer us a tender picture of his childhood and youth.

Though he became a skeptic, and almost an idolator of Voltaire, he had nothing but good to say of the pious people who had brought him up, and of the kindly and devoted Jesuits who had educated him. He loved these so much that he took the tonsure, aspired to join their order, and taught in their colleges at Clermont and Toulouse. But like many another fledgling of the Jesuits, he flew off on the winds of enlightenment, and lost at least his intellectual virginity. In 1743 he submitted verses to Voltaire, who so relished them that he sent Marmontel a set of his works corrected in his own hand. The young poet kept these as a sacred heirloom, and gave up all notions of a priestly career. Two years later Voltaire secured a place for him in Paris, and free admission to the Théâtre-Français; indeed, in the hidden goodness of his parental-childless heart, Voltaire sold Marmontel's poems, and sent him the proceeds. In 1747 Marmontel's play *Denys le Tyran* (*Dionysius*)— dedicated to Voltaire—was accepted and produced; it succeeded beyond his hopes; "in one day I became famous and rich."[35] Soon he was a minor lion in the salons; he feasted on dinners and paid with wit, and found a route to Clairon's bed.

His second play, *Aristomène*, brought him more money, friends, and mistresses. At Mme. de Tencin's gatherings he met Fontenelle, Montesquieu, Helvétius, Marivaux; at the table of Baron d'Holbach he heard Diderot, Rousseau, and Grimm. Guided by women, he made his way up in the world. Having praised Louis XV in clever verses, he was admitted to the court. Pompadour was charmed by his handsome face and blooming youth; she persuaded her brother to employ him as secretary, and in 1758 she made him editor of the official journal, *Mercure de France*. He wrote a libretto for Rameau, and articles for the *Encyclopédie*. Mme. Geoffrin liked him so well that she offered him a cozy apartment in her home, where he remained for ten years as a paying guest.

To the *Mercure* he contributed (1753–60) a series of *Contes moraux* (*Moral Tales*), which lifted that periodical into literature. *Ex uno judice omnes*. Soliman II, tiring of Turkish delights, asks for three European beauties. The first one resists for a month, yields for a week, and is then put aside. Another sings beautifully, but her conversation is soporific. Roxalana does not merely resist, she berates the Sultan as a lecher and a criminal. "Do you forget who I am and who you are?" he cries. Roxalana: "You are powerful, I am beautiful; so we are even." She is not surpassingly beautiful, but she has a retroussé nose, and this overwhelms Soliman. He tries every device to break down her resistance, but fails. He threatens to kill her; she proposes to spare him the trouble by killing herself. He insults her; she insults him more cuttingly. But also she tells him that he is handsome, and that he needs only her guidance to be as fine as a Frenchman. He is offended and pleased. Finally he marries her and makes her his queen. During the ceremony he asks himself, "Is it possible that a little turned-up nose should overthrow the laws of an empire?"[36] Marmontel's moral: It is little things that cause great events, and if we knew those secret trivia we should completely revise history.

Nearly everything prospered with Marmontel until he published (1767) a novel, *Bélisaire*. It was excellent, but it advocated religious toleration, and questioned "the right of the sword to exterminate heresy, irreligion, and impiety, and to bring the whole world under the yoke of the true faith."[37] The Sorbonne condemned the book as containing reprehensible doctrine. Marmontel appeared before the Syndic of the Sorbonne and protested, "Come, sir, is it not the spirit of the age, not mine, that you are condemning?"[38] The spirit of the age showed in his boldness, and in the mildness of his punishment. Ten years earlier he would have been sent to the Bastille, and his book would have been suppressed; actually the sale of his novel proceeded famously, still bearing the "permission and privilege of the King"; and the government contented itself with recommending that he should keep silence on the matter.[39] However, Mme. Geoffrin was much disturbed when the Sorbonne's decree banning *Bélisaire* was not only read in the churches but posted on her door. She gently suggested that Marmontel should find other lodgings.

He landed on his feet as usual. In 1771 he was appointed royal historiographer, with a good salary; in 1783 he became "perpetual secretary" of the French Academy; in 1786 he was professor of history at the Lycée. In 1792, aged sixty-nine and sickened by the excesses of the Revolution, he retired to Évreux, then to Abloville; there he composed his *Mémoires*, in which even the Sorbonne was forgiven. He spent his final years in uncomplaining poverty, grateful for having lived a full and zestful life. He died on the last day of 1799.

V. THE LIFE OF ART

1. Sculpture

The King had a fine taste in art; so did the lords and ladies of his court, and the millionaires who were now itching to control the state. It was an event in French history when the Sèvres factories, which Mme. de Pompadour had established, began in 1769 to produce hard-paste porcelain; and though the Germans at Dresden and Meissen had done this sixty years earlier, the Sèvres products soon gained a European market. Great artists like Boucher, Caffieri, Pajou, Pigalle, Falconet, and Clodion were not above making designs for Sèvres porcelain. Meanwhile faïence and soft-paste porcelain of exquisite design continued to come from the potters of Sèvres, St.-Cloud, Chantilly, Vincennes . . .

Potters, metalworkers, cabinetmakers, and tapestry weavers combined their resources to adorn the rooms of royalty, nobility, and financiers. Clocks, like that which Boizot designed and Gouthière cast in bronze,[40] were a characteristic ornament of this age. Pierre Gouthière and Jacques Caffieri excelled in "ormolu"—literally, "ground gold," actually an alloy composed chiefly of copper and zinc, carved and chased and inlaid into furniture. The master cabinetmakers formed a proud and powerful guild, whose members were required to stamp their work with their names as an emblem of responsibility. The best of them in France came from Germany: Jean-François Oeben and his pupil Jean-Henri Riesener; these two joined their skills in making for Louis XV (1769) a magnificent "Bureau du Roi," a rococo orgy of design, carving, inlay, and gilt, for which the King paid 63,000 livres. It was enjoyed by Napoleons I and III, and was surrendered to the Louvre in 1870. It is now valued at £50,000.[41]

In this age, which set such store by tactile values, sculpture was esteemed at almost its classic estimate, for its essence was form, and France was learning that form, not color, is the soul of art. Here again women outshone the gods; not in the natural imperfections of reality, but in the ideal shapes and drapery that sensitive sculptors could assemble and conceive. Sculpture embellished not only palaces and churches but gardens and public parks; so the statues in the Jardins des Tuileries were among the most popular figures in Paris; and Bordeaux, Nancy, Rennes, and Reims emulated Paris in terra cotta, marble, and bronze.

Guillaume Coustou II (only one year younger than the reign) now produced his finest work. In 1764 Frederick the Great commissioned him to make statues of Venus and Mars; in 1769 Coustou sent them to Potsdam for the Palace of Sanssouci. Also in 1769 he began the stately tomb of the Dauphin and the Dauphine (parents of Louis XVI) for the cathedral of Sens; on this he labored till his death (1777). In his last decades he saw the rise of as brilliant a quartet of sculptors as France has ever known: Pigalle, Falconet, Caffieri, and Pajou.

Failing to win the *grand prix* that paid for an art education in Rome, Pigalle went there at his own expense, helped by Coustou. Returning to Paris, he won admission to the Académie des Beaux-Arts with his first chef-d'oeuvre, *Mercure Attachânt Ses Talonnières* (*Mercury Attaching His Heelpieces*). Seeing it, the old sculptor Jean-Baptiste Lemoyne cried out, "*Je voudrais l'avoir fait!*" (I wish I had done that!) Louis XV liked it, too, and sent it to his ally, Frederick II, in 1749. Somehow it found its way back to the Louvre, where we may contemplate the remarkable skill with which the young artist suggested the impatience of the Olympian herald to be up and off. Mme. de Pompadour found Pigalle's work congenial, and gave him many commissions. He made a bust of her, which is now in the Metropolitan Museum of Art in New York; and when her amour with the King subsided into friendship he carved her likeness as *Déesse de l'Amitié* (1753).[42] He made a statue of Louis as plain *Citoyen* for the Place Royale at Reims, and finished Bouchardon's *Louis XV* for what is now the Place de la Concorde. He portrayed Diderot in bronze, as a man torn by conflicting philosophies. But he let himself go histrionic in the tomb that he carved for the remains of the Maréchal de Saxe in the Church of St. Thomas at Strasbourg—the amorous warrior striding to death as to a victory.

The most talked-of statue of this period was that which the intelligentsia of Europe chose Pigalle to make of Voltaire. Mme. Necker suggested it at one of her soirees on April 17, 1770. All of her seventeen guests (who included d'Alembert, Morellet, Raynal, Grimm, and Marmontel) welcomed the proposal, and the public was invited to subscribe to the cost. Some objections were raised, for it was unusual to raise statues to any living persons except royalty, and none had been made of Corneille or Racine before their death. Nevertheless subscriptions poured in, even from half the sovereigns of Europe; Frederick sent in two hundred louis d'or to commemorate his old friend and foe. Rousseau asked permission to contribute; Voltaire objected; d'Alembert persuaded him to consent. Fréron, Palissot, and other *anti-philosophes* offered their tribute, but were refused; the *philosophes* proved slower than their opponents to forgive. As for Voltaire himself, he warned Mme. Necker that he was no fit subject for statuary:

> I am seventy-six years old, and I have scarcely recovered from a severe malady which treated my body and soul very badly for six weeks. M. Pigalle, it is said, is to come and model my countenance. But, madame, it would be necessary that I should *have* a countenance, and the place where it was can hardly be divined. My eyes are sunk three inches; my cheeks are of old parchment, badly stuck upon bones that hold to nothing; the few teeth I had are all gone. What I say to you is not coquetry; it is pure truth. A poor man has never been sculptured in that condition; M. Pigalle would believe that he was being played with; and for my part I should have so much self-love that I should never dare to appear in his presence. I would advise him, if he wished to put an end to this strange affair, to take his model, with slight alterations, from the little figure in Sèvres porcelain.[43]

Pigalle doubled the problem by proposing to make a nude statue of the famous imp, but he was dissuaded. He went to Ferney in June, and for eight days the bashful philosopher sat for him, on and off, but so restlessly—dictating to a secretary, making grimaces, blowing peas at various objects in the room—that the sculptor came close to a nervous breakdown.[44] Returning to Paris with a mold, he labored on the task for two months, and revealed the result on September 4; half the elite came to marvel and smile. It is now in the vestibule of the library of the Institute.

Pigalle's only rival for sculptural primacy in this period was Étienne-Maurice Falconet, and Diderot tells us a pretty story of their enmity. Two years younger, Falconet avoided direct competition at first by making figures in porcelain. Especially delightful was the *Pygmalion* which Duru modeled after Falconet's design, showing the Greek sculptor's astonishment as his marble Galatea bends to speak to him. That figure could symbolize a half-forgotten truth: unless a work of art speaks to us it is not art. When Pigalle was shown this bit of clay transformed into enduring significance, he uttered the traditional compliment of one great artist to another: "I wish I had done that!" But Falconet, seeing Pigalle's *Louis XV Citoyen*, did not entirely return the compliment. "Monsieur Pigalle," he said, "I do not like you, and I believe you return my feeling. I have seen your *Citoyen*. It was possible to create such a work, since you have done it; but I do not believe that art can go one line beyond it. This does not prevent us from remaining as we were."[45]

Falconet was soured by forty years of trials before full recognition came

FIG. 1—MAURICE-QUENTIN DE LA TOUR: *Jean-Jacques Rousseau*, pastel portrait (1752). Musée de Saint-Quentin, France.   PAGE 26

FIG. 2—CARMONTELLE (1717–1806): *Melchior von Grimm*. Musée Condé, Chantilly, France. (Photo Giraudon.) PAGE 33

FIG. 3—CARMONTELLE: *Mme. d'Épinay*. Musée Condé, Chantilly. (Photo Giraudon.) PAGE 35

FIG. 4—LOUIS TOCQUÉ (1696–1772): *Count Wenzel Anton von Kaunitz*. National Library, Vienna. PAGE 40

FIG. 5—ENGRAVING AFTER A PAINTING BY F. BOCK: *Frederick the Great in Old Age*. (Bettmann Archive.)

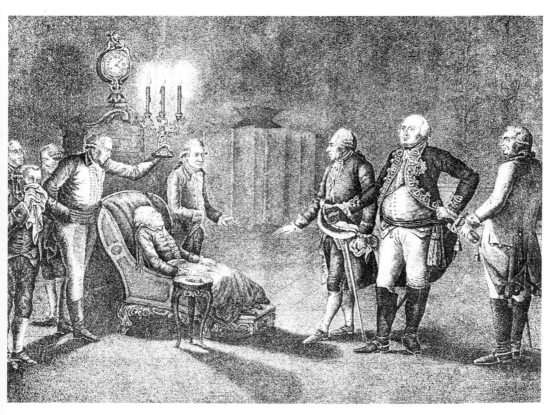

FIG. 6—AUGUSTIN PAJOU: *Mme. du Barry*, marble bust. Louvre, Paris.

PAGES 86, 109

FIG. 7—J.-F. OEBEN AND J.-H. RIESENER: *Bureau du Roi* (1769). Louvre, Paris.

PAGE 107

Fig. 8—Louis-Michel Vanloo: *Louis XV in Later Life*. The Mansell Collection, London. PAGE 84

FIG. 9—*Sèvres soft-paste porcelain*, 1784. The Metropolitan Museum of Art, New York, gift of R. Thornton Wilson, 1950, in memory of Florence Ellsworth Wilson.   PAGE 106

FIG. 10—JACQUES-ANGE GABRIEL: *The Petit Trianon* (1762–68). French Embassy Press and Information Division.

PAGE 111

FIG. 11—JEAN-JACQUES CAFFIERI: *Jean de Rotrou*. Comédie Française, Paris. Reproduced from Max Osborn, *Die Kunst des Rokoko* (Berlin: Propyläen Verlag, 1929).

PAGE 109

FIG. 12—JACQUES-GERMAIN SOUFFLOT: *The Panthéon, Paris* (1757–90). French Embassy Press and Information Division.　　PAGE 110

FIG. 13—AFTER A PAINTING BY JEAN-MARC NATTIER: *Mme. Geoffrin.*

PAGE 118

FIG. 14—JEAN-HONORÉ FRAGONARD: *Self-Portrait*. Louvre, Paris.　PAGE 117

FIG. 15 CARMONTELLE: *Mme. du Deffand Visited by Mme. de Choiseul.* From a drawing by G. P. Harding.
PAGE 125

FIG. 17—GREUZE: *The Broken Pitcher* (*La Cruche Cassée*). Louvre, Paris.　　PAGE 113

Fig. 18—Fragonard: *The Swing*. Reproduced by permission of the Trustees of the
Wallace Collection, London.

FIG. 19—ANTONIO CANALETTO: *View of St. Mark's, Venice*. Collection of Baron von Thyssen, Castagnola-Lugano. (Foto Brunel, Lugano.) PAGE 236

Fig. 20—Giambattista Tiepolo: *The Banquet of Cleopatra*. Palazzo Labia, Venice. (Fotografo Rossi, Venice.)

FIG. 21—TIEPOLO: *Apollo Bringing the Bride to Barbarossa*. The Residenz, Würzburg. (Photo-Verlag Gundermann.)

PAGE 239

FIG. 22—ROSALBA CARRIERA: *Self-Portrait*. Windsor Castle. Copyright reserved. 　　　　PAGE 235

FIG. 23—GIOVANNI BATTISTA PIAZ-ZETTA: *Rebecca at the Well*. Brera, Milan. 　　　　PAGE 236

FIG. 24—A. LONGHI: *Carlo Goldoni*. Museo Correr, Venice.   PAGES 239, 331

FIG. 25—*The Royal Palace, Madrid*. Spanish National Tourist Office.   PAGE 297

FIG. 26—Façade of the Church of Santiago de Compostela, Spain (1738). Spanish National Tourist Office.

Fig. 27—Francisco José de Goya y Lucientes: *Charles IV and His Family*.
Prado, Madrid. page 304

FIG. 28—GOYA: *Charles III*. Prado, Madrid.

FIG. 29—GOYA: *The Duchess of Alba*. Prado, Madrid.

FIG. 30—GOYA: *Self-Portrait*. Prado, Madrid. PAGE 304

FIG. 31—GOYA: *The Tribunal of the Inquisition*. Prado, Madrid. PAGE 306

Fig. 32—Goya: *La Maja Desnuda*. Prado, Madrid.   PAGE 305

Fig. 33—Goya: *La Maja Vestida*. Prado, Madrid.   PAGE 305

FIG. 34—GOYA: *Saturn Devouring His Offspring*. Prado, Madrid. PAGE 308

FIG. 35—FRANCESCO GUARDI: *Concert in the Sala dei Filarmonici*. Alte Pinakothek, Munich.   PAGE 332

FIG. 36—ANTON RAPHAEL MENGS: *Parnassus*. Villa Albani, Rome.   PAGE 249

FIG. 37—JEAN-ANTOINE HOUDON: *Gluck*. Louvre, Paris.   PAGE 367

FIG.   38—XAVIER-PASCAL   FABRE (1766–1837): *Vittorio Alfieri*. Uffizi, Florence.   PAGE 335

FIG. 39—FRANZ VON ZAUNER (1746–1822): *Emperor Joseph II*. Kunsthistorisches Museum, Vienna.   PAGE 346

FIG. 40—FABRE: *The Countess of Albany*. Uffizi, Florence.   PAGE 339

Fig. 41—John Hoppner (1758–1810): *Joseph Haydn*. Windsor Castle. Copyright reserved.   PAGE 373

Fig. 42—*Esterházy Castle at Eisenstadt*. Austrian Information Service.   PAGE 375

FIG. 43—JOHANN NEPOMUK DELLA CROCE: *The Mozart Family*. Original in Mozart's dwelling house in Salzburg, Austria.   PAGE 382

FIG. 44–ÉTIENNE-MAURICE FALCONET: *Statue of Peter the Great*, Leningrad (1782).

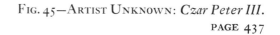

FIG. 45—ARTIST UNKNOWN: *Czar Peter III.*
PAGE 437

FIG. 46—ENGRAVING BY G. SKO-
RODUMOV AFTER A PAINTING BY
F. S. ROKOTOV: *Catherine the
Great.* State Historical Museum,
Moscow. (Sovfoto.)   PAGE 441

FIG. 47—F. S. ROKOTOV: *Grigori Orlov.*
PAGE 437

FIG. 48—IVAN STAROV: *Potemkin's Taurida Palace* (1783), Leningrad. (Sovfoto.)
PAGE 469

to him. He retired into himself, lived in Diogenic simplicity, quarreled readily, belittled his own work, and expressed contempt for fame, living or posthumous. Fame came at last with his *Baigneuse* (1757)—a pretty bather trying the water's temperature with her toes.[46] Now Mme. de Pompadour warmed to him; for her he carved *Amour Menaçant*—Cupid threatening to loose an arrow infected with love. For a time Falconet became the Boucher and Fragonard of sculpture, turning out such charming titillations as *Venus and Cupid, Venus Disrobing before Paris* . . . He excelled in designing candelabra, small fountains, and figurines; he carved in marble the Clock of the Three Graces now in the Louvre; and he pleased Pompadour by representing her as *Music*.[47] In 1766 he accepted Catherine II's invitation to Russia; in St. Petersburg he carved his masterpiece, Peter the Great on a prancing horse. He shared with Diderot and Grimm the favor of the Empress; labored for her through twelve years; quarreled with her and her ministers; left in a huff and returned to Paris. In 1783 he suffered a paralytic stroke; during the eight years that remained to him he kept to his room, confirmed in his gloomy view of life.

Jean-Jacques Caffieri could be more cheerful, having been nursed into success by his father, Jacques, one of the leading bronze workers of the preceding age. He gained early entry into the Academy of Fine Arts with his figure of an old man, clad only in whiskers, and entitled *Le Fleuve* (*The River*). The Comédie-Française engaged him to adorn its halls with busts of the French dramatists; he delighted everyone with his idealized representations of Corneille, Molière, and Voltaire. His masterpiece is a bust of the playwright Jean de Rotrou, which he made from an engraving preserved in the family; it is d'Artagnan in middle age—flowing hair, flashing eyes, pugnacious nose, bristling mustache; this is one of the finest busts in sculpture's history. Jealous of the Comédie, the Company of the Opéra persuaded Caffieri to portray their heroes, too; he made busts of Lully and Rameau, but these have disappeared. A lovely *Portrait of a Young Girl* remains,[48] perhaps a member of the Opéra ballet, a charming reconciliation of modest eyes and proud breasts.

Mme. du Barry's favorite sculptor was Augustin Pajou. After the customary novitiate in Rome, he achieved early prosperity with royal commissions and orders from abroad. He made a dozen portraits of the new mistress; the one in the Louvre has a classic costume wondrously carved. At the King's request he portrayed Buffon for the Jardin du Roi;[49] then he commemorated Descartes, Turenne, Pascal, and Bossuet. His finest work survives in the reliefs with which he adorned the lower tier of boxes at the opera house in Versailles. He lived long enough to work for Louis XVI, to mourn that King's execution, and to watch Napoleon bestride the Continent.

2. Architecture

Was there any memorable building in the France of these eighteen years? Not much. The churches were already too spacious for the remaining faithful, and the palaces were arousing the jealousy of the famine-stricken multi-

tude. The renewal of interest in Roman architecture by the excavations at
Herculaneum (1738) and Pompeii (1748–63) was nourishing a revival of
classical styles—lines of simplicity and dignity, façade of columns and pedi-
ment, and sometimes a spacious dome. Jacques-François Blondel, professor
at the Académie Royale de l'Architecture, was all for such classic forms, and
his successor, Julien-David Le Roy, issued in 1754 a treatise, *Les plus Beaux
Monuments de la Grèce*, which accelerated the intoxication. Anne-Claude
de Tubières, Comte de Caylus, after much traveling in Italy, Greece, and
the Near East, published (1752–67) seven epochal volumes, *Recueil d'antiquités égyptiennes, étrusques, grècques, romaines, et gauloises*, carefully
illustrated from some of his own drawings; the whole world of French art,
even of French manners, was powerfully influenced by this book toward
rejecting the irregularities of baroque and the frivolities of rococo to seek
again the purer lines of classic styles. So in 1763 Grimm told his clientele:

> For some years past we have been making keen inquiry for antique monu-
> ments and forms. The predilection for them has become so universal that now
> everything is to be done *à la grècque*, from architecture to millinery; our ladies
> have their hair dressed *à la grècque*, our fine gentlemen would think themselves
> dishonored if they did not hold in their hands a little box *à la grècque*.[50]

And Diderot, the apostle of bourgeois romanticism, suddenly surrendered to
the new wave (1765) on reading a translation of Winckelmann's *History of
Ancient Art*. "It seems to me," he wrote, "that we must study the antique
in order that we may learn to see nature."[51] That sentence itself was a
revolution.

In 1757 Jacques-Germain Soufflot began to build the Church of Ste.-
Geneviève, which Louis XV, when ill at Metz, had vowed to raise to the
patron saint of Paris as soon as he should recover. The King himself laid the
first stone, and the erection of this edifice "became the great architectural
event of the second half of the eighteenth century" in France.[52] Soufflot designed it in the form of a Roman temple, with a portico of sculptured pedi-
ment and Corinthian columns, and four wings meeting in a Greek cross in a
central choir under a triple dome. Controversy marked almost every stage
of the construction. Harassed and disheartened by attacks upon his design,
Soufflot died in 1780, leaving the structure incomplete. The four piers designed by him to support the dome proved too weak, and Charles-Étienne
Cuvillier replaced them by a much more beautiful circle of columns. This
chef-d'oeuvre of the classical revival was secularized by the Revolution; it
was renamed the Panthéon in memory of Marcus Agrippa's masterpiece at
Rome, as the burial place "of all the gods" of the new order, even of Voltaire, Rousseau, and Marat; it ceased to be a Christian church, and became a
pagan tomb; it symbolized, in its architecture and its fate, the progressive
triumph of paganism over Christianity.

The classic style won another victory in the first Church of the Madeleine
(Magdalen), begun in 1764; colonnades and flat-ceiled aisles took the place
of arches and vaults, and a dome covered the choir. Napoleon swept it away
unfinished, to make way for the still more classical Madeleine that occupies
the site today.

This reversion to grave classic modes, after the rebellious exuberance of baroque under Louis XIV and the playful elegance of rococo under Louis XV, was part of the transition, under Louis XV himself, to *le style Louis Seize*—the style of building, furniture, and ornament that was to take the name of the guillotined King. Art disciplined itself from incalculable curves and superfluous decoration to the sober simplicity of straight lines and structural form. It was as if the decline of Christianity had taken the heart out of the Gothic exaltation, and had left art no recourse but to a Stoic reserve shorn of gods and clinging to the earth.

The greatest of French builders in this generation was Jacques-Ange Gabriel, whose ancestry had put architecture in his blood. Commissioned by Louis XV (1752) to rebuild an old castle at Compiègne, he graced the entrance with a Greek portico of Doric columns, dentil cornice, and unembellished balustrade. He followed similar designs in rebuilding the right wing of the palace at Versailles (1770). To the same palace he added (1753–70) an exquisite opera house. The flushed columns, the delicately carved cornices and handsome balustrade, make this one of the loveliest interiors in France. Tired of court publicity and formality, Louis appealed to Gabriel to build him a *petite maison* hidden in the woods; Gabriel chose a site a mile from the palace, and raised there in French Renaissance style the Petit Trianon (1762–68). Here Pompadour had hoped to enjoy privacy and ease; Du Barry romped there for a while; then Marie Antoinette made it her favorite retreat as the royal shepherdess in those happy, careless days when the sun still shone upon Versailles.

3. Greuze

In the intimacy of aristocratic homes paintings were a favored decoration. Statues were cold and colorless; they pleased the eye and mind rather than heart and soul; paintings could reflect the flux of moods and tastes, and they could transport the spirit to open spaces, shady trees, or distant scenes while the body remained immured. So Claude-Joseph Vernet pictured so many ships riding in French waters that Louis XV, in a famous quip, thought it unnecessary to build more. The French government hired Vernet to visit the ports and make paintings of the vessels anchored there; he did, and made France proud of her fleets. Diderot secured one of Vernet's seascapes and landscapes, and prized it so highly that he prayed to an extemporized God: "I abandon all to thee, take all back; yes, all, except Vernet!"[53] — And there was Hubert Robert, who was called "Robert des Ruines" because he equipped nearly all his landscapes with Roman ruins, like *The Pont du Gard at Nîmes*. Nevertheless, Mme. Vigée-Lebrun assures us, he was "very much in demand" in Paris salons, though he was ruinously fond of eating.[54] — And there was François-Hubert Drouais, who preserved for us, with sensitive portraiture, the loveliness of the Marquise de Sorau and the innocent childhood of the future Charles X and his sister Marie-Adélaïde.[55] But let us look more intimately at Greuze and Fragonard.

Jean-Baptiste Greuze was the Rousseau and Diderot of the brush, who rosied his colors with sentiment, and made himself the Apelles of the bour-geoisie. Sentiment is happier than sophistication, and not as shallow; we must forgive Greuze for seeing and painting the pleasant sides of life, for loving the gay gambol of children, the fragile innocence of pretty girls, and the modest contentment of middle-class homes. Without Greuze and Chardin we might have supposed that all France was decadent and corrupt, that Du Barry was its model, that Venus and Mars were its only gods. But it was the nobles who were decadent, it was Louis XV who was corrupt; and it was the aristocracy and the monarchy that fell in the Revolution. The masses of the people—excepting the rural and city mobs—retained the virtues that save a nation, and Greuze portrayed them. Diderot hailed Chardin and Greuze, not Boucher and Fragonard, as the voice and health of France.

We have the usual stories about the artist's youth: he wanted to draw; his father forbade it as a cover for idleness; the boy crept from his bed at night to draw pictures; the father, coming upon one, relented, and sent him to study with an artist in Lyons. Jean-Baptiste was not long satisfied with what he could learn there; he made his way to Paris. He worked for some time in the poverty that tests young talent. He had good reason later to show the better side of men, for, like most of us, he found much kindness mingled with the busy inattentiveness of the world. About 1754 an art collector, La Live de Jully, bought Greuze's *Père de Famille* (Diderot used the same title for his second play, 1758), and encouraged him to persevere. The art instructor of the royal family, seeing a picture by Greuze, recommended him as a candidate for the Academy. But every candidate was expected to present, within six months, a painting of some scene in history. Such "histories" were not in Greuze's line; he let his candidacy drop, and accepted the offer of Abbé Gougenot to finance his trip to Rome (1755).

He was now thirty, and must long since have felt the magnetism of woman; is not half of art a by-product of that irresistible force? He experi-enced it in Rome to the point of agony. He was engaged to teach drawing to Laetitia, daughter of a duke; she was in the full bloom of youth; what could he do but fall in love? And he was handsome, with curly hair and cheerful, ruddy face; Fragonard, his fellow student, called him an "amorous cherub"; see in the Louvre his self-portrait in old age, and imagine him at thirty; inevitably Laetitia, with blood that could not count ducats, played Héloïse to his Abélard, surgery omitted. He took no advantage of her. She proposed marriage; he longed for her, but realized that the marriage of a poor artist with the heiress of a duke would soon be a tragedy for the girl; and, uncertain of his self-control, he resolved not to see her again. She fell ill; he visited and comforted her, but returned to his resolution. We are assured that for three months he lay in bed with fever and frequent delirium.[56] In 1756 he returned to Paris, quite untouched by classic art or the neoclassical revival.

"A few days after my arrival in Paris," he tells us, "I happened to be pass-ing, I know not by what fatality, down the Rue Saint-Jacques, when I no-ticed Mlle. Babuti at her counter."[57] Gabrielle Babuti worked in a bookshop; Diderot had bought her books and "loved her well" (his words) some years before. Now (1756–57) she was "over thirty years old" (Greuze's account), and feared spinsterhood; she found Jean-Baptiste not affluent but delectable; after he had paid her a few visits she asked him, "Monsieur Greuze, would you marry me if I were willing?" Like any decent Frenchman he replied, "Mademoiselle, would not any man be too happy to spend his life with such a charming woman as you are?" He thought no more of it, but she let the neighborhood understand that he was her betrothed. He had not the heart to contradict her; he married her, and for seven years they were reasonably happy. She had a luscious beauty, and willingly served as his model in many poses that revealed nothing but suggested all. She gave him in those years three children; two survived and inspired his art.

The world knows him for his pictures of children. We must not expect here the supreme excellence of Velázquez' *Don Balthasar Carlos*[58] or Vandyck's *James II as a Boy;*[59] and we are sometimes repelled, in Greuze's girls, by an exaggerated and weepy sentiment, as in the Berlin *Portrait of a Maiden;* but why should we reject the curls and rosy cheeks and wistful-trustful eyes of *Innocence,*[60] or the unrouged simplicity of *A Young Peasant Girl?*[61] There is no pose in the *Boy with a Lesson Book;*[62] it is any lad weary of a task seemingly irrelevant to life. Of 133 extant pictures by Greuze, thirty-six are of girls. Johann Georg Wille, a German engraver living in Paris, bought as many as he could of these childhood idealizations, and "held them more precious than the finest paintings of the period."[63] Greuze repaid the compliment by portraying the unprepossessing Saxon as an exemplar of virility. As these girls grow up in Greuze's art they become more artificial; *La Laitière (The Milkmaid)*[64] is all dressed up as if for a ball, and the lass of *La Cruche Cassée (The Broken Pitcher)*[65] has no excuse (except beauty) for exposing a nipple on her way from the well. But in a portrait of Sophie Arnould[66] the feathered hat, saucy pose, and carmine lips seem all in character.

Greuze was a minor Chardin touched with Boucher; a man honestly admiring virtue and middle-class life, but dressing it up, now and then, with a sensuous lure that Chardin would have shunned. When Greuze forgot the flesh of his women he could achieve an idyl of bourgeois domesticity, as in *The Village Bride (L'Accordée de Village).*[67] Exhibited in the final week of the 1761 Salon, it won the highest honors, and became the talk of Paris. Diderot extolled it for its *émotion douce;* and the Théâtre des Italiens paid it the unprecedented compliment of representing it in a "living picture" on the stage. Connoisseurs found flaws in it—ill-managed light, discordant colors, imperfect drawing and execution; aristocrats laughed at its sentiment; but the Paris public, which had swilled adultery to the dregs, and was in this very year weeping over Rousseau's *Julie,* was in a mood to respect the moral admonitions that were almost audibly coming from the father of the bride to the promised spouse. Every middle-class matron knew the feelings of the mother as she surrendered her daughter to the trials and hazards of marriage; and any peasant would have felt at home in that cottage where a hen and her chicks pecked for corn on the floor, or drank in safety from the bowl at the father's feet. The Marquis de Marigny bought the picture at once, and the King later paid 16,650 livres for it to prevent its being sold abroad. It is now in one of the less-frequented rooms of the Louvre, spoiled by the deterioration of its too superficial colors, and passed by in the reaction of realism and cynicism against optimistic sentiment.

Nearly all the artists of Paris felt that Greuze had lowered art by making it preach through romances instead of revealing truth and character with penetration and impartiality. Diderot defended him as "the first of our artists who gave morals to art, and arranged his pictures to tell a story."[68] He mounted to exclamation points over the tender tragedies that Greuze depicted; "*Délicieux! Délicieux!*" he cried over *The Young Girl Weeping for Her Dead Bird*. He himself was campaigning for middle-class subjects and feelings in drama; he saw in Greuze a precious ally, and praised him even above Chardin. Greuze took him too seriously; he stereotyped himself as the apostle of virtue and sentiment; he sent to Paris journals long expositions of the moral lessons in the pictures that he was producing. Finally he wore out his welcome with the art public, even while sentiment was the rising mood of the age.

During all the twelve years since the acceptance of his candidacy for the Academy, he had neglected to submit to it the historical picture required for full membership. In the judgment of the Academy a genre picture, describing domestic or everyday life, called for a less mature talent than the imaginative reconstruction and competent representation of some historical scene; hence it accepted genre painters only as *agréés* (literally, agreeable), but not yet eligible to academic honors or professorships. In 1767 the Academy announced that Greuze's pictures would no longer be exhibited in the biennial Salon until he had submitted an historical picture.

On July 29, 1769, Greuze sent in a painting of Septimius Severus reproaching his son Caracalla for attempting to assassinate him.[69] The picture was shown to the members of the Academy. After an hour the director informed him that he had been accepted, but added, "Monsieur, you have been received into the Academy, but it is as a painter of genre. The Academy took into consideration the excellence of your previous productions; it has closed its eyes to the present work, which is unworthy both of it and of you."[70] Shocked, Greuze defended his picture, but one of the members demonstrated the faults in the drawing. Greuze appealed to the public in a letter to the *Avant-Courier* (September 25, 1769); his explanation failed to impress connoisseurs, and even Diderot admitted the justice of the criticism.

Diderot suggested that the inadequacy of the painting was due to the disturbance of the artist's mind by the collapse of his marriage. He charged that Gabrielle Babuti had degenerated into an arrogant vixen, exhausting her husband's funds by her extravagance, wearing him down with vexations, and destroying his pride by her repeated infidelities.[71] Greuze himself submitted to the commissioner of police (December 11, 1785) a deposition charging his wife with persistently receiving her lovers into his home and over his protests. In a later letter he accused her of stealing large sums from him, and of attempting to "batter in my head with a chamber pot."[72] He secured a legal separation, took their two daughters with him, and left her half his fortune and an annuity of 1,350 livres.

His character deteriorated under these blows. He became resentful of any criticism, and lost all modesty in the exaltation of his pictures. The public, however, agreed with his self-estimate; it flocked to his studio, and made him rich with purchases of his paintings, and of the prints derived from them. He invested his earnings in government bonds—*assignats*; the Revolution left these bonds worthless, and Greuze found himself a poor man, while the absorption of France in class violence, political ecstasy, and the neoclassical reaction destroyed the market for his pictures of domestic felicity and peace. The new government rescued him moderately (1792) with a pension of 1,537 livres, but he soon outran this, and appealed for an advance. A woman of the streets, named Antigone, came to live with him and care for his failing health. When he died (1805) nearly all the world had forgotten him, and only two artists attended his corpse to the grave.

4. Fragonard

Jean-Honoré Fragonard survived better than Greuze the trials of success, for he surpassed Greuze in both sensuality and technique. His elegant art is the final exaltation of the woman of eighteenth-century France.

Born at Grasse in Provence (1732), he carried the perfumes and flowers of his birthplace into his art, along with the romantic love of the troubadours; to which he added Parisian gaiety and philosophic doubt. Brought to Paris at fifteen, he asked Boucher to take him as a pupil; Boucher told him, as kindly as possible, that he took only advanced students. Fragonard went to work for Chardin. In his off hours he copied masterpieces wherever he could find them. Some of these copies he showed to Boucher, who, much impressed, now accepted him as a pupil, and enlisted his youthful imagination in making designs for tapestry. The lad improved so rapidly that Boucher urged him to compete for the Prix de Rome. Fragonard submitted an historical painting—*Jeroboam Sacrificing to the Idols*.[73] It was a remarkable product for a boy of twenty—magnificent Roman columns, flowing robes, old heads bearded, turbaned, or bald; Fragonard had learned so soon that there is more character in an old face than in one that has not yet been carved by sensation and response. The Academy awarded him the prize; he studied three years in the studio of Carle Vanloo, and then (1765) went off in ecstasy to Rome.

At first he was discouraged by the masterpieces abounding there.

> The energy of Michelangelo terrified me—I experienced an emotion which I could not express; and on seeing the beauties of Raphael I was moved to tears, and the pencil fell from my hands. In the end I remained in a state of indolence which I lacked the strength to overcome. Then I concentrated upon the study of such painters as permitted me to hope that I might some day rival them. It was thus that Baroccio, Pietro da Cortona, Solimena, and Tiepolo attracted and held my attention.[74]

Instead of copying Old Masters he drew plans or sketches of palaces, arches, churches, landscapes, vineyards, anything; for already he had acquired that skill with the pencil which was to make him one of the most facile and finished draftsmen of an age rich in that basic art.* Few drawings catch more of nature's life than the green trees of the Villa d'Este as seen by Fragonard at Tivoli.[75]

On his return to Paris he set himself to satisfy the Academy with a "history" as the indispensable *morceau de réception*. Like Greuze he found historical subjects uncongenial; present Paris with its entrancing women drew him more powerfully than the past; the influence of Boucher was still warm in his mood. After much delay he submitted *Le Grand Prêtre Corésus Se Sacrifie pour Sauver Callirhoé;* let us not stop to inquire who this priest and maiden were; the Academy found them vivid and well drawn, and granted Fragonard associate membership. Diderot raved—"I do not believe that any other artist in Europe could have conceived this painting";[76] Louis XV bought it as a design for tapestry. But Fragonard was finished with historical subjects; indeed, after 1767 he refused to exhibit in the Salon; he worked almost wholly on private commissions, where he could indulge his own taste, freed from academic restraints. Long before the French romantics he rebelled against the "brown sauce" of the Renaissance, and moved out gaily into less charted seas.

Not quite uncharted. Watteau had opened the way with his radiantly robed women starting out with easy conscience for Venus' isle; Boucher had followed with romping senses; Greuze had mated sensuality and innocence. Fragonard combined them all: delicate raiment blowing in the breeze; dainty tarts offering unimpeded sweets; stately ladies hypnotizing men with the rustle of a dress or the fragility of a blouse, or with some rhythmic grace or melting smile; and children plump and rosy and tousle-haired, who had never yet discovered death. In his drawings and miniatures he pictured almost every aspect of child life—babes caressing their mothers, girls fondling their dolls, boys mounting a donkey or playing with a dog . . .

Fragonard's Gallic amorousness responded congenially to the requests of aging courtiers and tired mistresses for pictures celebrating and stirring the flesh. He ranged through the pagan mythology for goddesses whose rosy bodies were immune to time; now it was Venus, not the Virgin, who was raised in triumphant assumption to the skies. He stole half the ritual of religion for the ceremonies of love: *The Kiss*[77] is a prayer, *The Vow of Love* is a sacred pledge, *The Sacrifice of the Rose* is the ultimate offering. Among four pictures painted by Fragonard for Mme. du Barry's château at Louveciennes one had a title that might have covered half the artist's work: *L'Amour Qui Embrasse l'Univers* (*Love That Sets the World on Fire*). He fingered the *Gerusalemme liberata* to find the scene where nymphs flaunted their charms before the chaste Rinaldo. He became the Boucher of the bed,

---

* This was the age of such master engravers and etchers as Charles-Nicolas Cochin, Gabriel de Saint-Aubin, Jean-Jacques Boissieu, and Charles Eisen—who was the outstanding book illustrator of the 18th century.

revealing women in half or all their nudity, as in *La Dormeuse* (*The Sleeping Beauty*), *La Chemise Enlevée* (*The Blouse Removed*), or *La Bacchante Endormie*.[78] Then, realizing that nudity can be disillusioning, he returned from revelation to suggestion, and painted his most famous picture, *Les Hasards de l'Escarpolette* (*The Hazards of the Swing*);[79] the lover gazes in delight at the mysteries of lingerie revealed as his lady swings higher and higher, kicking one slipper with laughing abandon into the air. — Finally, Fragonard could be Greuze, and even Chardin: he pictured modest women, as in *L'Étude*, *La Lecture*,[80] and *Les Baisers Maternels;* and in *Mademoiselle Colombe* he discovered that women have souls.

In 1769, aged thirty-seven, he submitted to marriage. When Mlle. Gérard came up from Grasse to study art in Paris, she had only to name her birthplace to win admission to Fragonard's studio. She was not beautiful, but she was a woman in full bloom; and "Frago" (as he called himself) decided, like Mme. Bovary, that there could not be much more boredom in monogamy than in adultery. He found a new pleasure in working together with her on such pictures as *The Child's First Steps*, and joining his signature with hers. When she bore their first child she asked might she bring her fourteen-year-old sister up from Grasse to help her with the infant and the house; he agreed, and for years this ménage lived in precarious peace.

Now he rivaled Greuze in portraying domestic life, and Boucher in conveying the tranquillity of rural scenes. He painted some religious pictures, and made portraits of his friends. He was more constant as a friend than as a lover, remaining always fond of Greuze and Robert and David despite their success. When the Revolution came he dedicated a patriotic picture, *La Bonne Mère*, to the nation. His savings were mostly annulled by inflation and governmental defaults, but David, favorite artist of the new era, secured his appointment to some minor sinecure. It was about this time that he painted the remarkable self-portrait that hangs in the Louvre: strong and burly head, white hair cropped close, eyes still calm with confidence. The Terror frightened and disgusted him, and he fled to his native Grasse, where he received shelter in the home of his friend Maubert. He decorated the walls with panels collectively known as *Roman d'Amour et de la Jeunesse* (*A Story of Love and Youth*). These he had intended for Mme. du Barry, but she, no longer affluent, had refused them; now they are among the treasures of the Frick Gallery in New York.

One summer day, returning hot and perspiring from a walk in Paris, he stopped at a café and ate an ice. He was seized almost immediately by a cerebral congestion, and died with blessed suddenness (August 22, 1806). Grasse raised a pretty monument to him, with a naked urchin at his feet and, behind him, a young woman swirling her skirts in a joyous dance.

An artist must pay a price for symbolizing an age; his fame fades with its passions, and can return only when the pathos of distance ennobles him, or some turn in the tide brings a past mode into present taste. Fragonard prospered because his art, *desnuda* or *vestida*, pleased his time, soothing and gracing decay; but the stern code of a Revolution fighting for its life against all the rest of Europe needed other gods than Venus to inspire it, and found them in the stoic heroes of republican Rome. The reign of woman ended, the rule of the warrior returned. Greco-Roman models, redeified by Winckelmann, served a new generation of artists, and the neoclassical style swept away baroque and rococo in a tidal wave of ancient forms.

VI. THE GREAT SALONS

1. Mme. Geoffrin

The reign of woman ended, but only after the zenith of the salons. That unique institution reached its climax with Mme. Geoffrin, and subsided in a fever of romance with Mlle. de Lespinasse. It would revive after the Revolution, with Mesdames de Staël and Récamier, but never again with the zest and fullness of the time when political celebrities met on Saturdays at Mme. du Deffand's, artists met on Mondays and philosophers and poets on Wednesdays at Mme. Geoffrin's, philosophers and scientists on Tuesdays at Mme. Helvétius' and on Sundays and Thursdays at Baron d'Holbach's, and literary and political lions on Tuesdays at Mme. Necker's, and any of these might meet any night at Julie de Lespinasse's. Besides these there were many minor salons: *chez* Mesdames de Luxembourg, de La Vallière, de Forcalquier, de Talmont, de Broglie, de Bussy, de Crussol, de Choiseul, de Cambis, de Mirepoix, de Beauvau, d'Anville, d'Aiguillon, d'Houdetot, de Marchais, Dupin, and d'Épinay.

It was not beauty that distinguished these Junos of the salons; nearly all of them were middle-aged or older; it was that complex of intelligence, tact, grace, influence, and unobtrusive money that enabled a hostess to assemble women of charm and men of mind who could make a gathering or causerie sparkle with wit or wisdom without setting it on fire with passion or prejudice. Such a salon was no place for flirtations, or for erotic themes or *double-entendres*.[81] Every man there might have a mistress, every woman a lover, but this was politely veiled in the civilized give and take of courtesies and ideas. Platonic friendships could find acceptance there, as with Du Deffand and Horace Walpole, or with Lespinasse and d'Alembert. As the Revolution neared, the salons tended to lose their dispassionate elevation, and became centers of revolt.

Mme. Geoffrin's salon won the highest repute because she was the most skillful of lion tamers among the *salonnières*, allowed more freedom of discussion, and knew how—without appearing oppressive—to keep liberty from passing the bounds of good manners or good taste. She was one of the few women who rose from the middle class to maintain a distinguished salon. Her father, *valet de chambre* to the Dauphine Marie-Anne, had married the daughter of a banker; their first child, born in 1699, was Marie-Thérèse, who became Mme. Geoffrin. The mother, a woman of culture with some talent for painting, laid great plans for her daughter's development, but died in

1700 giving birth to a son. The two children were sent to live with their grandmother in the Rue St.-Honoré. Half a century later, in reply to Catherine II's request for a brief autobiography, Mme. Geoffrin explained her lack of erudition:

> My grandmother . . . had very little education, but her mind was so observant, so clever, so quick, that . . . it always served her instead of knowledge. She spoke so agreeably of the things she knew nothing of, that no one desired she should know them better. . . . She was so satisfied with her lot that she regarded education as superfluous for a woman. "I have managed so well," she said, "that I have never felt the need of it. If my granddaughter is a fool, knowledge will make her self-confident and unbearable; if she has wit and sense she will do as I did; she will make up the deficiency by her tact and perception." Therefore, in my childhood, she taught me simply how to read, but she made me read a great deal. She taught me to think, and made me reason; she taught me to know men, and made me say what I thought of them, and told me how she herself judged them. . . . She could not endure the elegancies that dancing masters teach; she only desired me to have the grace which nature gives to a well-formed person.[82]

Religion, Grandma felt, was more important than education; so the two orphans were taken to Mass every day.

Grandma attended also to Marie's marriage. A wealthy businessman, François Geoffrin, aged forty-eight, offered to marry the thirteen-year-old girl; Grandma thought it a good match, and Marie was too well brought up to object. She insisted, however, on taking her brother with her to join M. Geoffrin in the comfortable home, also in the Rue St.-Honoré, which she was to keep to the end of her life. In 1715 she gave birth to a daughter, and in 1717 to a son—who died at the age of ten.

In that same fashionable street Mme. de Tencin opened a famous salon. She invited Mme. Geoffrin to attend. M. Geoffrin objected; La Tencin's past had made some noise, and her favorite guests were such dangerous freethinkers as Fontenelle, Montesquieu, Marivaux, Prévost, Helvétius, and Marmontel. Mme. Geoffrin went nevertheless. She was fascinated by these untrammeled minds; how tiresome, by comparison, were the merchants who came to visit her aging husband! He was sixty-five now, and she was Balzac's *femme de trente ans*. She too began to entertain. He objected, she overruled him; finally he consented to preside at her dinners, usually silent and always polite. When he died (1749), aged eighty-four, her diners hardly noticed his absence. One who returned from a journey inquired what had become of the old gentleman who had sat so unobtrusively at the head of the table. Mme. Geoffrin answered softly, "It was my husband. He is dead."[83]

Mme. de Tencin also completed her course in 1749, to the dismay of her accustomed guests. We must record again the remark of the ninety-two-year-old Fontenelle: "Such a good woman! [She had been a veritable synthesis of sins.] What a worry! Where shall I dine on Tuesdays now?" But he brightened up: "Well, on Tuesdays now I must dine at Mme. Geoffrin's."[84] She was glad to have him, for he had been a *philosophe* before Montesquieu and Voltaire, he had memories stretching back to Mazarin, he had seven years left in him, and could bear teasing without taking offense, being hard of hearing. Most of the celebrities who had shone at Tencin's table followed his example, and soon the Geoffrin Wednesday midday dinners brought together, at one time or another, Montesquieu, Diderot, d'Holbach, Grimm, Morellet, Raynal, Saint-Lambert, and the witty little Neapolitan, Abbé Ferdinando Galiani, secretary to the Neapolitan ambassador in Paris.

After her husband's death, and despite her daughter's scandalized opposition, Mme. Geoffrin allowed Diderot, d'Alembert, and Marmontel to set the line and tone of discussion at her Wednesday dinners. She was a patriot and a Christian, but she admired the courage and vivacity of the *philosophes*. When the *Encyclopédie* was organized she contributed over 500,000 livres to its costs. Her home became known as "the salon of the *Encyclopédie*"; and when Palissot satirized the rebels in his comedy *Les Philosophes* (1760), he made fun of her as Cydalize, the fairy godmother of the coterie. Thereafter she asked her lions to roar more courteously, and checked wild eloquence with a deflating compliment—"Ah, there's something good!"[85] At last she withdrew her standing invitation to Diderot, but she sent him a suite of new furniture and an uncomfortably gorgeous dressing gown.

She discovered that artists, philosophers, and men of affairs did not mix well; the philosophers liked to talk, the statesmen expected discretion and good manners; the artists were a tempestuous tribe, and only artists could understand them. So Madame, who collected art and had caught some aesthetic glow from the Comte de Caylus, invited the leading artists and connoisseurs of Paris to special dinners on Monday evenings. Boucher came, La Tour, Vernet, Chardin, Vanloo, Cochin, Drouais, Robert, Oudry, Nattier, Soufflot, Caylus, Bouchardon, Greuze. Marmontel was the only *philosophe* admitted, for he lived in Mme. Geoffrin's house. The amiable hostess not only entertained these guests; she bought their works, posed for their portraits of her, and paid them well. Chardin pictured her best, as a stout and kindly matron in a lace bonnet.[86] After the death of Vanloo she bought two of his pictures for four thousand livres; she sold them to a Russian prince for fifty thousand livres, and sent the profit to the widow.[87]

To round out her hospitality Mme. Geoffrin gave *petits soupers* for her women friends. But no woman was invited to the Monday dinners, and Mlle. de Lespinasse (perhaps as d'Alembert's *alter ego*) was one of the few women who came to the Wednesday soirees. Madame was somewhat possessive, and besides she found that female presences distracted her lions from philosophy and art. Her policy of segregation seemed justified by the high repute her assemblies gained for interesting and significant discussions. Foreigners in Paris angled for invitations; to be able to say, when they returned home, that they had attended Mme. Geoffrin's salon was a distinction second only to being received by the King. Hume, Walpole, and Franklin were among her grateful guests. Ambassadors to Versailles—even the lordly Count von Kaunitz—made it a point to present themselves at the famous house in the Rue St.-Honoré. In 1758 Prince Cantemir, the Russian ambassador, brought with him the Princess of Anhalt-Zerbst, who told of the accomplishments of her daughter; four years later this daughter became Catherine II, and for many years thereafter the Empress of All the Russias carried on a charming correspondence with the bourgeois *salonnière*. A handsome and brilliant Swede who attended some of Madame's dinners went home to be Gustavus III.

A still handsomer youth, Stanislas Poniatowski, was a frequent visitor, almost a devotee of Mme. Geoffrin (who sometimes paid his debts);[88] soon he was calling her *Maman;* and when he became King of Poland (1764) he invited her to visit Warsaw as his guest. Though now sixty-four years old, she accepted. She made a triumphal stay in Vienna on the way: "I am better known here," she wrote, "than a couple of yards from my own house."[89] For a while, in the royal palace at Warsaw (1766), she played at mothering and advising the King. The letters that she sent to Paris were passed from hand to hand there, like the letters of Voltaire from Ferney; "those who had not read Mme. Geoffrin's letters," Grimm wrote, "were not fit to go into good society."[90] When she came back to Paris and resumed her dinners, a hundred celebrities rejoiced; Piron and Delille wrote poems celebrating her return.

The trip had been arduous—riding in a coach through half the length of Europe and back; Mme. Geoffrin was never again as alert and sprightly as before. She who had once expressed her disbelief in life after death,[91] and had reduced religion to charity, now renewed her observance of Catholic worship. Marmontel described her peculiar piety:

> To be in favor with heaven without being out of favor with her society, she used to indulge in a kind of clandestine devotion. She went to Mass as secretly as others go to an intrigue; she had an apartment in a nunnery, . . . and a pew in the church of the Capuchins, with as much mystery as the *galante* women of that day had their *petites maisons* for their amours.[92]

In 1776 the Catholic Church announced a jubilee in which all who visited certain churches at stated times would receive dispensations and indulgences. On March 11 Mme. Geoffrin attended a long service in the Cathedral of Notre Dame. Soon after reaching home she fell in an apoplectic fit. The *philosophes* were angry that her illness should have followed an act of worship; the mordant Abbé Morellet remarked, "She has confirmed, by her own example, the maxim which she frequently repeated: 'One dies only through an act of stupidity.' "[93] The daughter, Marquise de La Ferté-Imbault, took possession of her sick mother, and warned the *philosophes* away. Madame never saw d'Alembert or Morellet again; however, she arranged that the pensions she had given them should be increased after her death. She lingered on for another year, paralyzed and dependent, but distributing charity to the end.

2. Mme. du Deffand

There was only one salon in Europe that could rival Geoffrin's in fame and votaries. We have studied elsewhere the career and character of Marie de Vichy-Chamrond: how as a girl she dismayed nuns and priests with her freethinking; how she wed the Marquis du Deffand, left him, and solaced her solitude with a salon (1739 f.), at first in the Rue de Beaune, then (1747) in the Convent of St. Joseph in the Rue St.-Dominique. Her new site frightened away all but one of the *philosophes* who had previously come to enjoy her wine and wit; d'Alembert remained, being the least pugnacious of the tribe; for the rest, her habitués were men and women of the aristocracy, who tended to snub La Geoffrin as bourgeoisie. When the Marquise became blind at the age of fifty-seven (1754), her friends still came to her dinners; but during the rest of the week she felt loneliness with a rising despondency, until she persuaded her niece to stay with her and serve as assistant hostess at her soirees.

Julie de Lespinasse was the illegitimate daughter of the Comtesse d'Albon and Gaspard de Vichy, brother of Mme. du Deffand. The Comtesse acknowledged her, brought her up with her other children, gave her an exceptionally good education, and sought to have her legitimized; but one of the daughters objected, and it was never done. In 1739 this half sister married Gaspard de Vichy and went to live with him in the Château de Chamrond in Burgundy. In 1748 the Comtesse died, leaving an annuity of three hundred livres for Julie, then sixteen. Mme. de Vichy took Julie to Chamrond, but treated her as an illegitimate orphan who served as governess for the children. When Mme. du Deffand visited Chamrond she was struck by the excellent mind and manners of Mlle. de Lespinasse; she won the girl's confidence, and learned that she was so unhappy in her present position that she had decided to enter a convent. The Marquise proposed that Julie come and live with her in Paris. Objections were raised by the family, in fear that Du Deffand would arrange Julie's legitimation, thus entitling her to a share in the Albon estate. The Marquise promised that she would not so offend her relatives. Meanwhile Julie entered a convent (October, 1752), not as a novice but as a boarder. The Marquise renewed her proposal. After a year of hesitation, Julie agreed. On February 13, 1754, the Marquise sent her a strange letter, which must be remembered in judging the sequel:

> I shall introduce you as a young lady from my province who intended to go into a convent, and will say that I offered you a lodging until you should find one which would suit you. You will be treated with politeness, and even with compliment, and you can count upon me that your self-respect will never be offended.
>
> However, . . . there is another point which I must explain to you. The least artifice, even the most trifling little art, if you were to put it into your conduct, would be intolerable to me. I am naturally distrustful, and all those in whom I detect slyness become suspect to me until I lose all confidence in them. I have two intimate friends—Formont and d'Alembert. I love them passionately, but less for their agreeable charms and their friendship than for their absolute truthfulness. Therefore you must, my queen, resolve to live with me with the utmost truth and sincerity. . . . You may think that I preach, but I assure you that I never do so except in regard to sincerity. On that point I am without mercy.[94]

In April, 1754, Julie came to live with Mme. du Deffand, first above a carriage shed, then in a room over the Marquise's apartment in the Convent of

St. Joseph. Perhaps at Madame's suggestion, the Duc d'Orléans settled upon her a pension of 692 livres.[95] She helped the blind hostess to receive and place her guests at the salon assemblies; she brightened the proceedings with her pleasant manners, her quick intelligence, her fresh and modest youth. She was no beauty, but her bright black eyes and rich brown hair made an arresting combination. Half the men who came there fell half in love with her, even Madame's old faithful chevalier, Charles-Jean-François Hénault, president of the Court des Enquêtes, who was seventy, always ailing, always rubicund with a flow of wine. Julie took their compliments with proper discount, but even so the Marquise, doubly sensitive in her blindness, must have felt that some worship had passed from her throne. Perhaps another element entered: the older woman had begun to love the younger one with an affection that would not share. Both were vessels of passion, despite the fact that the Marquise had one of the most penetrating minds of the time.

It was inevitable that Julie should fall in love. First (?) with a young Irishman of whom we know only the name Taaffe. Once admitted to the salon, he came almost every day, and it was soon obvious to the Marquise that he had come to see not her but Mademoiselle. She was alarmed to see that Julie received his advances favorably. She warned Julie against compromising herself. The proud girl resented the motherly advice. Fearing to lose her, and anxious to protect her against an impetuous attachment that promised no permanence, the Marquise commanded Julie to keep to her room when Taaffe called. Julie obeyed, but was so excited by the quarrel that she took opium to calm her nerves. Many persons in the eighteenth century used opium as a sedative. Mlle. de Lespinasse increased her doses with each new romance.

She learned to forget Taaffe, but her next love entered history, for it fell upon the man whom Mme. du Deffand had taken to herself with a maternal but possessive attachment. Jean Le Rond d'Alembert was in 1754 at the peak of his renown as mathematician, physicist, astronomer, and collaborator in that *Encyclopédie* that was the talk of all intellectual Paris. Voltaire, in a modest moment, called him "the foremost writer of the century."[96] Yet he had none of Voltaire's advantages. He was of illegitimate birth; his mother, Mme. de Tencin, had disowned him, and he had not seen his father since childhood. He lived like a simple bourgeois in the home of the glazier Rousseau. He was handsome, neat, courteous, sometimes gay; he could talk with almost any specialist on any subject, but he could also hide his learning behind a façade of stories, mimicry, and wit. Otherwise he made few compromises with the world. He preferred his independence to the favor of kings and queens; and when Mme. du Deffand campaigned to get him into the French Academy he refused to assure himself of Hénault's vote by praising Hénault's *Abrégé chronologique de l'histoire de France* (1744). There was a strain of satire in him that made his wit bite now and then;[97] he could be impatient, "sometimes violently choleric against opponents."[98] He never found out what to say or do when alone with women; yet his shyness attracted them, as if by challenging the efficacy of their charms.

When Mme. du Deffand first met him (1743) she was struck by the range and clearness of his mind. She was then forty-six, he twenty-six. She adopted him as her "wildcat" (*chat sauvage*);[99] invited him not only to her salon but to private dinners tête-à-tête; she vowed her willingness to "sleep for twenty-two hours of the twenty-four, so long as we pass the remaining two hours together."[100] It was after eleven years of this warm friendship that Julie came into their lives.

There was a natural bond between the natural son and the natural daughter. D'Alembert noted it in retrospect:

> Both of us lacked parents and family, and having suffered abandonment, misfortune, and unhappiness from our birth, nature seemed to have sent us into the world to find each other, to be to each other all that each had missed, to stand together like two willows, bent by the storm but not uprooted, because in their weakness they have intertwined their branches.[101]

He felt this "elective affinity" almost at first sight. "Time and custom stale all things," he wrote to her in 1771, "but they are powerless to touch my affection for you, an affection which you inspired seventeen years ago."[102] Yet he waited nine years before declaring his love, and then he did it by indirection: he wrote to her from Potsdam in 1763 that in refusing Frederick's invitation to become president of the Berlin Academy of Sciences he had had "a thousand reasons, one of which you haven't the wits to guess"[103]— a strange lapse of intelligence in d'Alembert, for was there ever a woman who did not know when a man was in love with her?

Mme. du Deffand felt the growing warmth between her prized guest and her guarded niece; she noticed, too, that Julie was becoming the center of discussion and interest in the salon. For a while she uttered no reproach, but in a letter to Voltaire (1760) she made some bitter remarks on d'Alembert. She allowed a friend to read to her guests, before d'Alembert had arrived, Voltaire's reply, referring to these remarks. D'Alembert came in soon after the reading had begun, and heard the telltale passage; he laughed with the others, but he was hurt. The Marquise tried to make amends, but the wound remained. When he visited Frederick in 1763 his letters were almost daily to Mlle. de Lespinasse, seldom to Madame. After his return to Paris he fell into the habit of visiting Julie in her apartment before they came down to the salon; and sometimes Turgot or Chastellux or Marmontel accompanied him in these intimate visits. The aging hostess felt that she was being betrayed by those whom she had helped and loved. Now she looked upon Julie as her enemy, and she revealed her feelings in a dozen irritating ways— cold tone, petty demands, occasional reminders of Julie's dependence. Julie grew daily more impatient with this "blind and vaporous old woman," and with the obligation to be always on hand or nearby to attend to the Marquise at any hour. Every day increased her unhappiness, for each day had its sting. "All pain strikes deep," she later wrote, "but pleasure is a bird of quick passage."[104] In a final outburst Madame accused her of deceiving her in her own home and at her expense. Julie replied that she could no longer live with one who so considered her; and on a day early in May, 1764, she left to seek other lodgings. The Marquise made the breach irreparable by insisting that d'Alembert should choose between them; d'Alembert left, and never returned.

For a time the old salon seemed mortally wounded by these amputations. Most of the habitués continued to come to the Marquise, but several of them —the Maréchale de Luxembourg, the Duchesse de Châtillon, the Comtesse de Boufflers, Turgot, Chastellux, even Hénault—went to Julie to express their sympathy and continued interest. The salon was reduced to old and faithful friends, and newcomers who sought distinction and good food. Madame described the change in 1768:

> Twelve people were here yesterday, and I admired the different kinds and degrees of futility. We were all perfect fools, each in his kind. . . . We were singularly wearisome. All twelve departed at one o'clock, but none left a regret behind. . . . Pont-de-Veyle is my only friend, and he bores me to death three quarters of the time.[105]

She had never, since her light went out, had any love for life, but now that her dearest friends were gone she sank into a hopeless and cynical despair. Like Job, she cursed the day of her birth. "Of all my sorrows my blindness and age are the least. . . . There is only one misfortune, . . . and that is to be born."[106] She laughed equally at the dreams of romantics and philosophers—not only at Rousseau's Héloïse and Savoyard Vicar, but at Voltaire's long campaign for "truth." "And you, Monsieur de Voltaire, the declared lover of Truth, tell me in good faith, have you found it? You combat and destroy errors, but what do you put in their place?"[107] She was a skeptic, but she preferred genial doubters like Montaigne and Saint-Évremond to aggressive rebels like Voltaire and Diderot.

She thought herself finished with life, but life had not yet quite finished with her. Her salon had a fitful resurrection during the ministry of Choiseul, when the leading men in the government gathered around the old Marquise, and the friendship of the kindly Duchesse de Choiseul brought some brightness to darkened days. And in 1765 Horace Walpole began to come to her gatherings, and gradually she developed for him an affection that became her last desperate hold upon life. We hope to meet her again in that final and amazing avatar.

3. Mlle. de Lespinasse

Julie chose as her new home a three-story house at the meeting of the Rue de Bellechasse with the Rue St.-Dominique—only a hundred yards from the Marquise's conventual home. She was not reduced to poverty; besides several small pensions, she had received pensions of 2,600 livres out of "the King's revenues" (1758 and 1763), apparently at the urging of Choiseul; and now Mme. Geoffrin, at d'Alembert's suggestion, dowered her with separate annuities of two thousand livres and one thousand crowns. The Maréchale de Luxembourg gave her a complete suite of furniture.

Soon after settling in these new quarters Julie came down with a severe case of smallpox. "Mlle. de Lespinasse is dangerously ill," wrote David Hume to Mme. de Boufflers, "and I am glad to see that d'Alembert has come out of his philosophy at such a moment."[108] Indeed, the philosopher walked a long distance every morning to watch at her bed till late at night, and then walked back to his own room at Mme. Rousseau's. Julie recovered, but was left permanently weak and nervous, her complexion coarsened and blotched. We can imagine what this meant to a woman thirty-two years old and still unmarried.

She was cured just in time to care for d'Alembert, who took to his bed in the spring of 1765 with a stomach ailment that brought him near death. Marmontel was shocked to find him living in a "little room ill-lit, ill-aired, with a very narrow bed like a coffin."[109] Another friend, the financier Watelet, offered d'Alembert the use of a commodious home near the Temple. The philosopher now sadly consented to leave the woman who had housed and fed him since his childhood. "Oh, wondrous day!" exclaimed Duclos; "d'Alembert is weaned!" To his new quarters Julie commuted daily, repaying his recent care of her with her own unstinted devotion. When he was well enough to move she begged him to occupy some rooms on the upper floor of her house. He came in the fall of 1765, and paid her a moderate rental. He did not forget Mme. Rousseau; he visited her frequently, shared some of his income with her, and never ceased apologizing for their separation. "Poor foster mother, fonder of me than of your own children!"[110]

For a while Paris assumed that Julie was his mistress. Appearances warranted the assumption. D'Alembert took his meals with her, wrote letters for her, managed her business affairs, invested her savings, collected her income. Publicly they were always together; no host dreamed of inviting one without the other. Nevertheless it gradually dawned even upon the gossipers that Julie was neither mistress nor wife nor lover to d'Alembert, but only a sister and friend. She seems never to have realized that his love for her, though he could not put it into words, was complete. Mesdames Geoffrin and Necker, both of exemplary morals, accepted the relationship as Platonic. The aging salonnière invited both of them to both of her gatherings.

It was a severe test of Mme. Geoffrin's motherly kindness that she made no known protest when Mlle. de Lespinasse developed a salon of her own. Julie and d'Alembert had made so many friends that within a few months her drawing room was filled almost daily, from five to nine o'clock, with chosen visitors, women as well as men, nearly all of fame or rank. D'Alembert led the conversation, Julie added all the charms of womanhood, all the warmth of hospitality. No dinner or supper was offered, but the salon gained the reputation of being the most stimulating in Paris. Here came Turgot and Loménie de Brienne, soon to be high in the government; aristocrats like Chastellux and Condorcet, prelates like de Boismont and Boisgelin, skeptics like Hume and Morellet, authors like Mably, Condillac, Marmontel, and Saint-Lambert. At first they came to see and hear d'Alembert; then to enjoy the sympathetic skill with which Julie drew out each guest to shine in his or her special excellence. No topics were barred here; the most delicate problems of religion, philosophy, or politics were discussed; but Julie—

trained in this art by Mme. Geoffrin—knew how to calm the excited, and return dispute to discussion. The desire not to offend the frail hostess was the unwritten law that generated order in this liberty. At the close of Louis XV's reign the salon of Mlle. de Lespinasse, in Sainte-Beuve's judgment, was "the most in vogue, the most eagerly frequented, at an epoch that counted so many that were brilliant."[111]

No other salon offered such a double lure. Julie, though pockmarked and fatherless, was becoming the second love of a dozen distinguished men. And d'Alembert was at the height of his powers. Grimm reported:

> His conversation offered all that would instruct and divert the mind. He lent himself with as much facility as good will to whatever subject would please most generally, bringing to it an almost inexhaustible fund of ideas, anecdotes, and curious memories. There was no topic, however dry or frivolous in itself, that he had not the secret of making interesting. . . . All his humorous sayings had a delicate and profound originality.[112]

And hear David Hume, writing to Horace Walpole:

> D'Alembert is a very agreeable companion, and of irreproachable morals. By refusing offers from the Czarina and the King of Prussia he has shown himself above personal gain and vain ambition. . . . He has five pensions: one from the King of Prussia, one from the King of France, one as a member of the Academy of Sciences, one as a member of the French Academy, and one from his own family. The whole amount is not above six thousand livres a year; on half of this he lives decently; the other half he gives to poor people with whom he is connected. In a word I scarce know a man who, with some few exceptions, . . . is a better model of a virtuous and philosophical character.[113]

Julie was at opposite poles to d'Alembert in everything but facility and elegance of speech. But whereas the *Encyclopédiste* was one of the last heroes of the Enlightenment, seeking reason and measure in thought and action, Julie, after Rousseau, was the first clear voice of the Romantic movement in France, a creature (Marmontel described her) of "the liveliest fancy, the most ardent spirit, the most inflammable imagination which has existed since Sappho."[114] None of the romantics, in flesh or print—no Héloïse of Rousseau nor Rousseau himself, no Clarissa of Richardson or Manon of Prévost—exceeded her in keenness of sensibility, or in the ardor of her inner life. D'Alembert was objective, or tried to be; Julie was subjective to the pitch of a sometimes selfish self-absorption. Yet she "suffered with those that she saw suffer."[115] She went out of her way to comfort the sick or aggrieved, and she labored feverishly to get Chastellux and Laharpe elected to the Academy. But when she fell in love she forgot everything and everybody else—in the first case Mme. du Deffand, in the second and third d'Alembert himself.

In 1766 a young noble, Marquês José de Mora y Gonzaga, son of the Spanish ambassador, entered the salon. He was twenty-two, Julie was thirty-four. He had been married at twelve to a girl of eleven, who died in 1764. Julie soon felt the charm of his youth, possibly of his fortune. Their mutual attraction ripened rapidly to a pledge of marriage. Hearing of this,

his father ordered him to military duty in Spain. Mora went, but soon resigned his commission. In January, 1771, he began to spit blood; he went to Valencia, hoping for relief; not cured, he rushed up to Paris and Julie. They spent many happy days together, to the amusement of her little court and the secret suffering of d'Alembert. In 1772 the ambassador was recalled to Spain, and insisted on his son coming with him. Neither parent would consent to his marrying Julie. Mora broke away from them and started north to rejoin her, but he died of tuberculosis at Bordeaux, May 27, 1774. On that day he wrote to her: "I was on my way to you, and I must die. What a horrible doom! . . . But you have loved me, and the thought of you still gives me happiness. I die for you." Two rings were removed from his fingers; one contained a strand of Julie's hair; the other was engraved with the words, "All things pass, but love endures." The magnanimous d'Alembert wrote of Mora: "I regret on my own account that sensitive, virtuous, and high-minded man, . . . the most perfect being that I have ever known. . . . I shall ever remember those priceless moments when a soul so pure, so noble, so strong, and so sweet loved to mingle with mine."[116]

Julie's heart was torn by the news of Mora's death, and all the more because she had in the meantime given her love to another man. In September, 1772, she met Comte Jacques-Antoine de Guibert, twenty-nine, who had made a notable record in the Seven Years' War. Moreover, his *Comprehensive Study of Tactics* was acclaimed as a masterpiece by generals and intellectuals; Napoleon was to carry a copy of it, annotated by his own hand, through all his campaigns; and its "Preliminary Discourse," denouncing all monarchies, formulated, twenty years before the Revolution, the basic principles of 1789. We can judge the admiration that poured upon Guibert from a topic selected for discussion in a leading salon: "Is the mother, the sister, or the mistress of M. de Guibert to be most envied?"[117] He had, of course, a mistress—Jeanne de Montsauge, the latest and longest of his amours. Julie, in a bitter moment, judged him harshly:

> The levity, even hardness, with which he treats women comes from the small consideration in which he holds them. . . . He thinks them flirtatious, vain, weak, false, and frivolous. Those whom he judges most favorably he believes romantic; and though obliged to recognize good qualities in some, he does not on that account value them more highly, but holds that they have fewer vices rather than more virtues.[118]

However, he was handsome, his manners were perfect, his speech combined substance with feeling, and erudition with clarity. "His conversation," said Mme. de Staël, was the "most varied, the most animated, and the richest that ever I knew."[119]

Julie considered herself fortunate in the preference that Guibert showed for her gatherings. Fascinated by each other's fame, they developed what on his side became an incidental conquest, and on her side a mortal passion. It was this consuming love that gave her letters to Guibert a place in French literature and among the most revealing documents of the time; there, even more than in Rousseau's *Julie, ou La Nouvelle Héloïse* (1761), the proto-Romantic movement in France finds its living expression.

Her earliest extant letter to Guibert (May 15, 1773) shows her already in his toils. But she was torn with remorse over the violation of her pledge of fidelity to Mora. So she wrote to Guibert, who was leaving for Strasbourg:

> Ah, mon Dieu! by what charm, by what fatality, have you come to distract me? Why did I not die in September? I could have died then without . . . the reproaches that I now make to myself. Alas, I feel it, I could still die for him; there is no interest of mine that I would not sacrifice to him. . . . Oh, he will pardon me! I had suffered so much! My body and soul were so exhausted by the long continuance of sorrow. The news I received of him threw me into a frenzy. It was then that I first saw you; then that you received my soul, then that you brought pleasure into it. I know not which was sweetest—to feel it, or to owe it to you.[120]

Eight days later she took down all her defenses: "If I were young, pretty, and very charming, I should not fail to see much art in your conduct to me; but as I am nothing of all that, I find a kindness and an honor in it which have won you right over my soul forever."[121] At times she wrote with all the abandon of Héloïse to Abélard:

> You alone in the universe can possess and occupy my being. My heart, my soul, can henceforth be filled by you alone. . . . Not once has my door been opened today that my heart did not beat; there were moments when I dreaded to hear your name; then again I was brokenhearted not to hear it. So many contradictions, so many conflicting emotions, are true, and three words explain them: I love you.[122]

The conflict of the two loves increased the nervous agitation that perhaps had come from the starvation of her hopes for womanly fulfillment, and from a growing tendency to consumption. She wrote to Guibert on June 6, 1773:

> Though your soul is agitated, it is not like mine, which passes ceaselessly from convulsion to depression. I take poison [opium] to calm myself. You see that I cannot guide myself; enlighten me, strengthen me. I will believe you; you shall be my support.[123]

Guibert returned to Paris in October, severed his relations with Mme. de Montsauge, and offered his love to Julie. She accepted gratefully, and yielded to him physically—in the antechamber of her box at the opera (February 10, 1774).[124] She claimed later that this, when she was forty-two, was her first lapse from what she called "honor" and "virtue,"[125] but she did not reproach herself:

> Do you remember the condition in which you put me, and in which you believed you left me? Well, I wish to tell you that, returning quickly to myself, I *rose again* [italics hers], and I saw myself not one hair's-breadth lower than before. . . . And what will astonish you, perhaps, is that of all the impulses that have drawn me to you, the last is the only one for which I have no remorse. . . . In that abandonment, that last degree of abnegation of myself and of all personal interests, I proved to you that there is but one misfortune on earth that seems to me unbearable—to offend you and lose you. That fear would make me give my life.[126]

For a time she experienced transports of happiness. "I have thought of you constantly," she wrote to him (for they kept their liaison secret, and dwelt apart). "I am so engrossed in you that I understand the feeling of the devotee for his God."[127] Guibert inevitably tired of a love that poured itself out so profusely, leaving no challenge to his power. Soon he was paying attention to the Comtesse de Boufflers, and resuming his affair with Mme. de Montsauge (May, 1774). Julie reproached him; he replied coldly. Then, on June 2, she learned that Mora had died on his way to her, blessing her name. She sank into a delirium of remorse, and tried to poison herself; Guibert prevented her. Now her letters to him were mostly about Mora, and how superior the young Spanish nobleman had been to every other man she had ever known. Guibert saw her less frequently, Montsauge more. Hoping to remain at least one of his mistresses, Julie planned marriages for him; he rejected her choices, and on June 1, 1775, he married Mlle. de Courcelles, seventeen and rich. Julie wrote him letters of hatred and disdain, ending with protestations of undying love.[128]

Through all the fever of her passion she was able to conceal the nature of it from d'Alembert, who thought the absence, then death, of Mora was its cause. He welcomed Guibert to her salon, developed a sincere friendship for him, and personally mailed the sealed letters which she wrote to her lover. But he noted that she had lost interest in him, that at times she resented his presence. And indeed she wrote to Guibert: "Did it not seem too ungrateful, I would say that M. d'Alembert's departure would give me a sort of pleasure. His presence weighs upon my soul. He makes me ill at ease with myself; I feel too unworthy of his friendship and his goodness."[129] When she was dead he wrote to her "manes":

> For what reason, which I can neither imagine nor suspect, did that feeling, [once] so tender for me, . . . change suddenly to estrangement and aversion? What had I done to displease you? Why did you not complain to me if you had anything to complain of? . . . Or, my dear Julie, . . . had you done me some wrong of which I was ignorant, and which it would have been so sweet to pardon had I known of it? . . . Twenty times have I been on the point of throwing myself into your arms, and asking you to tell me what was my crime; but I feared that those arms would repulse me. . . .
>
> For nine months I sought the moment to tell you what I suffered and felt, but during those months I always found you too feeble to bear the tender reproaches I had to make to you. The only moment when I could have shown to you, uncovered, my dejected and discouraged heart was that dreadful moment, a few hours before your death, when you asked me, in so heartrending a manner, to forgive you. . . . But then you had no longer the strength to either speak to me or hear me; . . . and thus I lost, without recovery, the moment of my life which would have been to me the most precious—that of telling you, once more, how dear you were to me, how much I shared your woes, and how deeply I desired to end my woes with you. I would give all the moments that remain to me to live, for that one instant which I can never have again, that instant when, by showing you all the tenderness of my heart, I might perhaps have recovered yours.[130]

The collapse of Julie's dream helped tuberculosis to kill her. Dr. Bordeu (whom we have met in Diderot's *Dream of d'Alembert*) was called in, and pronounced her condition hopeless. From April, 1776, she never left her bed. Guibert came to see her every morning and evening, and d'Alembert left her bedside only to sleep. The salon had been discontinued, but Condorcet came, and Suard, and the good Mme. Geoffrin, herself dying. On the last days Julie would not let Guibert come, for she did not wish to let him see how convulsions had disfigured her face; but she sent him frequent notes; and now he too protested: "I have always loved you; I have loved you from the first moment that we met; you are dearer to me than anything else in the world."[131] This, and d'Alembert's silent fidelity, and the solicitude of her friends, were her only solace in her suffering. She made her will, of which she appointed d'Alembert executor, and she entrusted to him all her papers and effects.*

Her brother, the Marquis de Vichy, came up from Burgundy, and urged her to make her peace with the Church. To the Comte d'Albon he wrote: "I am happy to say that I persuaded her to take the sacraments, in spite of, in the face of, the entire *Encyclopédie*."[132] She sent a last word to Guibert: "My friend, I love you. . . . Farewell." She thanked d'Alembert for his long devotion, and begged him to forgive her ingratitude. She died that night, in the early hours of May 23, 1776. She was buried that same day, from the Church of St.-Sulpice, and as she had desired in her will—"like the poor."

---

* Her letters to Guibert were preserved by his wife, and were published in 1811.

CHAPTER V

Voltaire Patriarch

1758–78

I. THE GOOD LORD

IN October, 1758, Voltaire bought an ancient estate at Ferney, in the *pays*, or county, of Gex, which bordered on Switzerland. Soon thereafter he added, by a life purchase, the neighboring seigneury of Tournay; now he became legally a lord, and in legal matters he signed himself "Comte de Tournay"; he displayed his coat of arms over his portal and on his silver plate.[1]

He had lived at Les Délices in Geneva since 1755, and had played with pleasure and acclaim the role of a millionaire philosopher who entertained handsomely. But d'Alembert's *Encyclopédie* article on Geneva, revealing the private heresies of its clergymen, subjected Voltaire to charges that he had betrayed them to his friend. He ceased to be *persona grata* on Swiss soil, and looked about him for another residence. Ferney was in France, but only three miles from Geneva; there he could thumb his nose at the Calvinist leaders; and if the Catholic leaders in Paris—250 miles away—should renew their campaign for his arrest, he could in an hour be across the frontier; meanwhile (1758–70) his friend the Duc de Choiseul was heading the French ministry. Perhaps to guard against confiscation through a veering of the political wind, he bought Ferney in the name of his niece Mme. Denis, merely stipulating with her that she should recognize him as master of the estate as long as he lived. Till 1764 Les Délices remained his principal home; he took his time remodeling the house at Ferney, and finally moved into it in that year.

The new mansion was of stone, was largely designed by Voltaire, and contained fourteen bedrooms; the seigneur had prepared for his court. "It is not a palace," he wrote, "but a commodious country house, with lands adjacent that produce much hay, wheat, straw, and oats. I have some oaks as straight as pines, which touch the sky."[2] Tournay added an old château, a farm, a barn, stables, fields, and woods. Altogether his stables sheltered horses, oxen, and fifty cows; his barns were spacious enough to store the produce of his lands and yet leave room for wine presses, poultry yards, and a sheep fold; four hundred beehives kept the plantation humming; and the trees gave wood to warm the Master's bones against the winter winds. He bought and planted young trees, and grew many more from seedlings in his hothouses. He extended the gardens and grounds around his home till they measured three miles in circuit; they included fruit trees, grapevines, and a great variety of flowers. All these structures, plants, and fields, and their thirty caretakers, he supervised in person. Now again, as when he entered Les Délices, he was so content that he forgot to die. He wrote to Mme. du Deffand: "I owe my life and health to the course I have taken. If I dared I would believe myself wise, so happy am I."[3]

Over the thirty or more servants and guests who lived in the château Mme. Denis ruled with an uneven hand. She was good-natured, but she had a temper, and loved money just a little bit more than she loved anything else. She called her uncle stingy; he denied it; in any case he "transferred to her, little by little, the greater part of his fortune."[4] He had loved her as a child, then as a woman; now he was glad to have her as his *maîtresse d'hôtel*. She acted in the plays that he staged, and so well that he compared her to Clairon. This praise went to her head; she took to writing dramas herself, and Voltaire was hard put to dissuade her from exposing them to public view. She was bored by country life, and longed for Paris; it was partly to amuse her that Voltaire invited and tolerated so long a succession of guests. She did not care for his secretary Wagnière, but she was fond of Père Adam, the old Jesuit whom Voltaire welcomed to his household as a genial foe at chess—and whom he surprised one day at the feet of servant Barbara.[5] Once, perhaps by letting Laharpe depart with one of the Master's manuscripts, Denis so angered Voltaire that he sent her off to Paris—with an annuity of twenty thousand francs.[6] After eighteen months he broke down, and begged her to return.

Ferney became a goal of pilgrimage for those who could afford travel and had savored enlightenment. Here came minor rulers like the Duke of Württemberg and the Elector Palatine, lords like the Prince de Ligne and the Ducs de Richelieu and Villars, notables like Charles James Fox, gleaners like Burney and Boswell, rakes like Casanova, and a thousand lesser souls. He lied lamely when the uninvited came: "Tell them I am very sick," "Tell them that I am dead"; but no one believed. "My God!" he wrote to the Marquis de Villette, "deliver me from my friends; I will take care of my enemies myself."[7]

He had hardly settled down at Ferney when Boswell appeared (December 24, 1764), still warm with his visits to Rousseau. Voltaire sent down word that he was still in bed, and could not be disturbed. This was but a slight discouragement to the eager Scot; he stayed on doggedly till Voltaire came forth; they conversed briefly, then Voltaire retired to his study. On the following day, from an inn in Geneva, Boswell wrote to Mme. Denis:

> I must beg your interest, Madam, in obtaining for me a very great favor from M. de Voltaire. I intend to have the honor to return to Ferney Wednesday or Thursday. The gates of this sober city shut at a most . . . absurd hour, so that one is obliged to post away after dinner before the illustrious landlord has had time to shine upon his guests. . . .
> Is it possible, Madam, that I may be allowed to lodge one night under the roof of M. de Voltaire? I am a hardy and vigorous Scot. You may mount me to the highest and coldest garret. I shall not even refuse to sleep upon two chairs in the bedchamber of your maid.[8]

Voltaire bade his niece tell the Scot to come; there would be a bed for him. He came on December 27, spoke with Voltaire while Voltaire was playing chess, was charmed by the Master's English conversation and curses, and then was "very genteelly lodged" in "a handsome room."[9] On the morrow he undertook to convert Voltaire to orthodox Christianity; soon Voltaire, almost fainting, had to beg a respite. A day later Boswell discussed his land-lord's religion with Père Adam, who told him, "I pray for Monsieur de Vol-taire every day. . . . It is a pity that he is not a Christian. He has many Christian virtues. He has the most beautiful soul. He is benevolent; he is charitable; but he is very strongly prejudiced against the Christian religion."[10]

To entertain his guests Voltaire provided food, wisdom, wit, and drama. Near his home he built a small theater; Gibbon, seeing it in 1763, described it as "very neat and well contrived, situated just by his chapel, which is far inferior to it."[11] The philosopher laughed at Rousseau and the Genevan min-isters, who condemned the stage as the Devil's rostrum. He trained not only Mme. Denis but his servants and guests to take parts in his and other plays; he himself pranced across the boards in principal roles; and professional actors were readily persuaded to perform for the most famous writer in the world.

Visitors found his appearance almost as fascinating as his conversation. The Prince de Ligne described him as muffled up in a flower-patterned dressing gown, an immense wig topped with a bonnet of black velvet, jacket of fine cotton reaching to his knees, red breeches, gray stockings, shoes of white cloth.[12] His eyes were "brilliant and filled with fire," according to Wagnière; and the same devoted secretary reported that his master "often washed his eyes with pure, cool water," and "never used spectacles."[13] In the later years of his life, tired of shaving, he pulled out his beard with pincers. "He had a singular love for cleanliness and neatness," Wagnière continues, "and was himself scrupulously clean."[14] He made frequent use of cosmetics, perfumes, and pomades; his keen sense of smell suffered from any offensive odor.[15] He was "unbelievably thin," with just enough flesh to cover his bones. Dr. Burney, after visiting him in 1770, wrote: "It is not easy to con-ceive it possible for life to subsist in a form so nearly composed of skin and bone. . . . He supposed I was anxious to form an idea of . . . one walking after death."[16] He described himself as "ridiculous for not being dead."[17]

He was sick half his life. He had an especially sensitive epidermis; he com-plained frequently of various itches,[18] perhaps from nervousness or excessive cleanliness. He suffered at times from strangury—slow and painful urination; in this regard he and Rousseau, so often at odds, were brothers under the skin. He drank coffee at every turn: fifty times a day, according to Frederick the Great;[19] three times a day, said Wagnière.[20] He laughed at doctors, and noted that Louis XV had outlived forty of his physicians; and "who ever heard of a centenarian doctor?"[21]—but he himself used many medicines. He agreed with Molière's candidate for the M.D. that the best remedy in any serious illness is *clisterium donare*;[22] he purged himself thrice a week with a cassia solution, or with a soapy enema.[23] The best medicine, he thought, was preventive, and the best preventive was to clean the internal organs and the external integument.[24] Despite his years, ailments, and visitors, he worked with the energy that comes to a man who does not carry surplus flesh. Wagnière reckoned that his master slept "not more than five or six hours" a day.[25] He worked far into the night, and sometimes he roused Father Adam from bed to help him hunt a Greek word.[26]

He held action to be a good remedy for philosophy and suicide. Still better, action outdoors. Voltaire literally cultivated his garden; sometimes he plowed or sowed with his own hands.[27] Mme. du Deffand detected in his letters the pleasure with which he saw his cabbages grow. He hoped that posterity would remember him at least for the thousands of trees that he had planted. He reclaimed wastelands and drained swamps. He set up a breeding stable, brought in ten mares, and welcomed the Marquis de Voyer's offer of a stallion. "My seraglio is ready," he wrote, "nothing is wanting but the sultan. . . . So much has been written of late years on population that I wish at least to people the land of Gex with horses, since I am little able to have the honor of increasing my own species."[28] To the physiologist Haller he wrote: "The best thing we can do on this earth is to cultivate it; all other experiments in physics are by comparison children's play. Honor to those who sow the earth; woe to the miserable man—crowned or helmeted or tonsured—who troubles it!"[29]

Not having enough land to give agricultural employment to all the population around him, he organized in Ferney and Tournay shops for watchmaking and the weaving of stockings—for which his mulberry trees grew silk. He gave employment to all who asked for it, until he had eight hundred persons working for him. He built a hundred houses for his workers, lent them money at four per cent, and helped them find markets for their products. Soon crowned heads were buying the watches of Ferney, and titled ladies, seduced by his letters, wore stockings some of which he claimed to have woven with his own hand. Catherine II bought Ferney watches to the value of 39,000 livres, and offered to help him find outlets in Asia. Within three years the watches, clocks, and jewelry made in Ferney went in regular shipments to Holland, Italy, Spain, Portugal, Morocco, Algeria, Turkey, Russia, China, and America. As a result of the new industries Ferney grew from a village of forty peasants to a population of twelve hundred during Voltaire's stay. "Give me a fair chance," he wrote to Richelieu, "and I am the man to build a city."[30] Catholics and Protestants lived in peace on the lands of the infidel.

His relations with his "vassals" were those of a *bon seigneur*. He treated them all with conscience and courtesy. "He talked with his peasants," said the Prince de Ligne, "as if they were ambassadors."[31] He exempted them from the taxes on salt and tobacco (1775).[32] He fought in vain but persistently to have all the peasants of the Pays de Gex freed from serfdom. When the region was threatened with famine he imported wheat from Sicily and sold it far below what it had cost him.[33] While carrying on his war against *l'infâme*—against superstition, obscurantism, and persecution—he spent much of his time in practical administration. He excused himself for not leaving Ferney to visit his friends: "I have eight hundred people to guide and sustain; . . . I cannot absent myself without having everything relapse into chaos."[34] His success as an administrator astonished all who saw the results. "He showed clear judgment and very good sense," said one of his severest critics.[35] Those whom he governed learned to love him; on one occasion they threw laurel leaves into his coach as he passed.[36] The young people were especially fond of him, for he opened his château to them every Sunday for dancing and refreshments;[37] he urged them on, and rejoiced in their joy. "He was very happy," reported Mme. de Gallatin, "and did not perceive that he was eighty-two years old."[38] He perceived it, but was content. "*Je deviens patriarche*," he wrote—"I am becoming a patriarch."[39]

II. THE SCEPTER OF THE PEN

Meanwhile he continued to write, to send forth an incredible quantity, variety, and quality of histories, treatises, dramas, stories, poems, articles, pamphlets, letters, and critical reviews to an international audience that waited eagerly for his every word. In the one year 1768 he wrote *L'Homme aux quarante écus, La Princesse de Babylone* (one of his best tales), *Épître à Boileau, Profession de foi d'un théiste, Le Pyrrhonisme de l'histoire*, two comic-opera librettos, and a play. Almost every day he composed some "fugitive verse"—short, light, graceful epigrams in rhyme; in this department he has no equal in all literature, not even in the composite excellence of the *Greek Anthology*.

His writings on religion and philosophy have occupied us elsewhere. We look only briefly at the plays that he wrote at Ferney—*Tancrède, Nanine, L'Écossaise, Socrate, Saul, Irène;* they are the least alive of his progeny, though they were the talk of Paris in his day. *Tancrède*, presented at the Théâtre-Français September 3, 1759, won universal applause, even from Voltaire's bitter enemy Fréron. Mlle. Clairon as Déborah and Lekain as Tancrède reached in this drama the peak of their art. The stage had been cleared of spectators, and allowed a spacious and striking décor; the medieval and chivalric subject was a welcome deviation from classic themes; indeed, the disciple of Boileau here wrote a romantic play. *Nanine* revealed that Voltaire, like Diderot, had been influenced by Richardson; Rousseau himself praised it. *Socrate* contained a treasurable line: "It is the triumph of reason to live well with those who have none."[40]

Hailed in his time as the equal of Corneille and Racine, Voltaire studied them endlessly, and long hesitated as to which of the two he preferred; finally he voted for Racine. He boldly placed both above Sophocles and Euripides, and he ranked "Molière, in his best pieces, superior to the pure but cold Terence, and to the buffoon Aristophanes."[41] He was aroused when he learned that Marie Corneille, grand-niece of the dramatist, was living in poverty near Évreux; he offered to adopt her and provide for her education; and when he learned that she was pious he assured her that every opportunity would be given to practice her religion. She came to him in December, 1760; he adopted her, taught her to write good French, corrected her pronunciation, and went to Mass with her. To raise a dowry for her he proposed to the French Academy that it should commission him to edit the works of Corneille. It agreed. He began at once to reread the plays of his predecessor, to supply introductions and notes; and, being a good businessman, he advertised the project and solicited subscriptions. Louis XV, Czarina Elizaveta, Frederick of Prussia each subscribed for two hundred copies, Mme. de Pompadour and Choiseul for fifty, and additional subscriptions came from Chesterfield and other foreign notables. The result was that Marie Corneille had many suitors. She married twice, and became in 1768 the mother of Charlotte Corday.

Voltaire was the greatest historian, as well as the greatest poet and dramatist, of his time. In 1757 the Empress Elizaveta asked him to write a biography of her father, Peter the Great. She invited Voltaire to St. Petersburg, and promised him a world of honors. He replied that he was too old to undertake such travel, but that he would write the history if her minister, Count Shuvalov, would send him documents illustrating Peter's career and the changes produced by the Czar's reforms. He had in his youth seen Peter at Paris (1716); he considered him a great man, but still a barbarian; and to avoid going too perilously into his faults he decided to write not a biography but a history of Russia in that memorable reign—a much more difficult task. He undertook considerable researches, labored on the work from 1757 to 1763, and published it in 1759–63 as *Histoire de la Russie sous Pierre le Grand*. It was a creditable performance for its time, and remained the best treatment of the subject before the nineteenth century; but honest Michelet found it "a bore."[42] The Czarina saw parts of it; she sent Voltaire some "big diamonds" on account, but they were stolen en route, and the Czarina died before the book was complete.

On and off, while the Seven Years' War raged around him, he undertook to bring up to date his *Histoire générale*, or *Essai sur les moeurs*, by adding (1755–63) a *Précis du siècle de Louis XV*. It was a delicate operation, for he was still formally under the ban of the French government; we must forgive him if he glided cautiously over the faults of the reigning King; even so it was an excellent narrative, simple and clear; in telling the story of Prince Charles Edward Stuart (Bonnie Prince Charlie) he almost rivaled his own *Charles XII*. True to his conception of history as being best when recording the advances of the human mind, he added a concluding discourse "On the Progress of the Understanding in the Age of Louis XV," and noted what seemed to him to be signs of growth:

> A whole order [the Jesuits] abolished by the secular power, the discipline of other orders reformed by this power, the divisions between the [jurisdiction of] magistrates and bishops, plainly reveal how much prejudice has been dissipated, how far the knowledge of government is extended, and to what degree our minds are enlightened. The seeds of this knowledge were sown in the last

century; in the present they are everywhere springing, even in the remotest provinces. . . . Pure science has illuminated the useful arts, and these have already begun to heal the wounds of the state caused by two fatal wars. . . . The knowledge of nature, and the discrediting of ancient fables once honored as history; sound metaphysics freed from the absurdities of the schools: these are products of this age, and human reason is greatly improved.

Having paid his debt to history, Voltaire returned to philosophy, and to his campaign against the Catholic Church. He issued in rapid succession those little books which we have already examined, as light artillery in the war against *l'infâme: The Ignorant Philosopher, Important Examination of Milord Bolingbroke, L'Ingénu* (or *The Huron*), *Histoire de Jenni*, and *La Raison par alphabet*. Amid all these labors he carried on the most remarkable correspondence ever maintained by one man.

When Casanova visited him in 1760 Voltaire showed him a collection of some fifty thousand letters that he had received to that year; there were to be, thereafter, almost as many more. As the recipient paid the postage, Voltaire sometimes spent a hundred livres for the mail that he received in one day. A thousand admirers, a thousand enemies, a hundred young authors, a hundred amateur philosophers, sent him gifts, bouquets, insults, curses, queries, and manuscripts. It was not unusual for an anxious inquirer to beg him to say, by return post, whether there was a God, or whether man had an immortal soul. Finally he inserted a warning in the *Mercure de France*: "Several persons having complained of not receiving acknowledgment of packages sent to Ferney, Tourney, or Les Délices, notice is given that, on account of the immense number of those packages, it has become necessary to decline receiving all that do not come from persons with whom the proprietor had the honor to be acquainted."[43]

In the definitive edition by Theodore Besterman Voltaire's correspondence fills ninety-eight volumes. Brunetière thought it "the most living portion of his entire work."[44] And in truth there is not a dull page in the whole immensity, for in these letters we can still hear the most brilliant conversationalist of his time talk with all the intimacy of a friend. Never before or since has a writer caught on his running pen—*currente calamo*—so much courtesy, vivacity, charm, and grace. It is a feast not only of wit and eloquence but of warm friendship, humane feeling, and incisive thought. Beside them the letters of Mme. de Sévigné, delightful though they are, seem to flutter casually over the surface of trivial and transitory things. Doubtless there was something of convention in the flourishes of Voltaire's epistolary style, but he seems to mean it when he writes to d'Alembert: "I embrace you with all my strength, and I regret that it must be at so great a distance." (To which d'Alembert replied: "Farewell, my dear and illustrious friend; I embrace you tenderly, and am more than ever *tuus in animo*"—yours in spirit.)[45] And hear Voltaire to Mme. du Deffand: "Adieu, madame. . . . Of all the truths that I seek, that which seems to be surest is that you have a soul which is congenial to me, and to which I shall be tenderly attached during the little time that remains to me."[46]

His letters to his acquaintances in Paris were prized by the recipients, and were passed from hand to hand as nuggets of news and gems of style. For it was in his letters that Voltaire's style reached its fullest brilliance. It was not at its best in his histories, where a smooth and flowing narrative is more desirable than eloquence or wit; it ran to pompous declamation in his plays; but in his letters he could let the diamond point of his pen flash into epigram, or illuminate a topic with incomparable precision and brevity. He added the learning of Bayle to the elegance of Fontenelle, and took a touch of irony from the *Lettres provinciales* of Pascal. He contradicted himself in his seventy years of writing, but he was never obscure; we can hardly believe that he was a philosopher, he is so clear. He goes directly to the point, to the vital spot of an idea. He is sparing of adjectives and similes, lest he complicate the thought, and almost every other sentence is a flash of light. Sometimes there are too many flashes, too many strokes of wit; now and then the reader tires of the sparkle, and loses some darts of Voltaire's agile mind. He realized that this excess of brilliance was a fault, like gems on a robe. "The French language," he modestly confessed, "was carried to the highest point of perfection in the age of Louis XIV."[47]

Half the notables of the time were among his correspondents—not only all the *philosophes*, and all the major authors of France and England, but cardinals, popes, kings, and queens. Christian VII apologized to him for not installing all Voltairean reforms at once in Denmark; Stanislas Poniatowski of Poland mourned that he had been precipitated into royalty just as he was on the way to Ferney; Gustavus III of Sweden thanked Voltaire for occasionally casting a glance at the cold North, and prayed that "God may prolong your days, so precious to humanity."[48] Frederick the Great scolded him for cruelty to Maupertuis, and for insolence to kings;[49] but a month later he wrote: "Health and prosperity to the most malign and most seductive man of genius who has ever been or ever will be in this world";[50] and on May 12, 1760, he added:

> For my part I shall go there [Hades] and tell Virgil that a Frenchman has surpassed him in his own art. I shall say as much to Sophocles and Euripides; I shall speak to Thucydides of your histories, to Quintus Curtius of your *Charles XII;* and perhaps I shall be stoned by these jealous dead because a single man has united all their different merits in himself.[51]

On September 19, 1774, Frederick continued his lauds: "After your death there will be no one to replace you; it will be the end of good letters in France."[52] (A mistake, of course; there is never an end of good literature in France.) And finally, on July 24, 1775, Frederick lowered his scepter before Voltaire's pen: "For my part, I am consoled by having lived in the age of Voltaire; that suffices me."[53]

Catherine the Great wrote to Voltaire as one crowned head to another—indeed, as a pupil to a teacher. She had read him with delight for sixteen years before cleaving her way to the throne of Russia; then, in October, 1763, she began their correspondence by replying in the first person to a letter in verse which he had sent to a member of her diplomatic corps.[54]

Voltaire called her the Semiramis of the North, glided gracefully over her crimes, and became her apologist to France. She begged to be spared his compliments, he extended them. She prized his partisanship, for she knew that it was largely through him—and then through Grimm and Diderot— that she obtained a "good press" in France. French philosophy became a tool of Russian diplomacy. Voltaire recommended Assyrian-style scythe-armed chariots to Catherine for use against the Turks; she had to explain that the unco-operative Turks would not attack in sufficiently close forma-tion to be conveniently mowed down.[55] He forgot his hatred of war in his enthusiasm for the possibility that Catherine's armies would liberate Greece from the Turks; he called upon *"Français, Bretons, Italiens"* to support this new crusade; and he mourned when Semiramis stopped short of his goal. Byron took up his cause.

Many Frenchmen berated Voltaire for his flirtations with royalty; they felt that he lowered himself in fluttering about thrones and mouthing com-pliments. And doubtless this fluttering sometimes went to his head. But he too was playing a diplomatic game. He had never pretended to republican sentiments; he repeatedly argued that more progress could be made through "enlightened" kings than by enthroning the unstable, unlettered, supersti-tious masses. He was warring not against the state but against the Catholic Church, and in that battle the support of rulers was a precious aid. We have seen how precious that support was in his triumphant campaigns for the Calas and the Sirvens. It was of much moment to him that in his fight for religious toleration he had both Frederick and Catherine on his side. Nor did he give up hope of winning Louis XV. He had won Mme. de Pompadour and Choiseul; he wooed Mme. du Barry. He had no scruples in his strategy; and indeed, before the end of the reign, he had the support of half the gov-ernment of France. The battle for religious toleration was won.

III. VOLTAIRE *POLITICUS*

What, in politics and economics, did he hope to accomplish? He set his sights both high and low: his great aim was to free men from theological myths and priestly power—a task difficult enough; for the rest he asked for some reforms, but no utopia. He smiled at "those legislators who govern the universe, . . . and from their garrets give orders to kings."[56] Like nearly all the *philosophes*, he was opposed to revolution; he would have been shocked by it—perhaps guillotined.* Besides, he was scandalously rich, and doubtless his wealth colored his views.

In 1758 he proposed to invest 500,000 francs ($625,000?) in Lorraine.[58]

---

* See Robespierre's description of the Encyclopedists: "As far as politics were concerned, this party drew the line at the Rights of the People. . . . Its leaders sometimes held forth against despotism, and were fed by despots; sometimes they wrote articles on kings, some-times dedications in their honor. They penned speeches for courtiers, and madrigals for courtesans."[57]

On March 17, 1759, he wrote to Frederick: "I derive sixty thousand livres [$75,000?] of my [annual] income from France. . . . I admit that I am very rich." His fortune had been made through "tips" from financier friends like the brothers Paris; through winning lotteries in France and Lorraine; through sharing in his father's estate; through buying government bonds; through taking shares in commercial ventures; and through lending money to individuals. He was content with a six per cent return, which was moderate considering the risks and losses. He lost a thousand écus ($3,750?) in the bankruptcy of the Gilliart firm in Cadíz (1767).[59] In 1768, referring to the eighty thousand francs ($100,000?) that Voltaire had lent to the Duc de Richelieu, Gibbon noted: "The Duke is ruined, the security worth nothing, and the money vanished";[60] at Voltaire's death a fourth of the loan had been repaid. Pensions brought Voltaire four thousand francs per year. Altogether, in 1777, his income came to 206,000 francs ($257,500?).[61] He graced this wealth with commensurate generosity, but he felt called upon to defend it as not necessarily unbecoming a philosopher.

> I saw so many men of letters poor and despised that I made up my mind that I would not increase their number. In France a man must be anvil or hammer; I was born anvil. A slender patrimony becomes smaller every day, because in the long run everything increases in price, and government often taxes both income and money. . . . You must be economical in your youth, and you find yourself in your old age in possession of a capital that surprises you; and that is the time when fortune is most necessary to us.[62]

As far back as 1736, in his poem *Le Mondain*, he had confessed: "I love luxury, and even a soft life, all the pleasures, all the arts." He held that the demand of the rich for luxuries brought their money into circulation among artisans; and he suspected that without wealth there would have been no great art.[63] When Voltaire published Meslier's atheistic-communistic *Testament* he omitted the section against property. He believed that no economic system could succeed without the stimulus of ownership. "The spirit of property doubles a man's strength."[64] He hoped to see every man a property owner; and while Rousseau sanctioned serfdom in Poland, Voltaire wrote: "Poland would be thrice as populous and wealthy if the peasants were not slaves."[65] However, he was not in favor of peasants' becoming rich; who, then, would be strong soldiers for the state?[66]

He did not share Rousseau's enthusiasm for equality; he knew that all men are created unfree and unequal. He rejected Helvétius' notion that if equal education and opportunity were given to all, all would soon be equal in education and ability. "What folly to imagine that every man could be a Newton!"[67] At all times there will be strong and weak, clever and simple, and therefore rich and poor.

> It is impossible in our melancholy world to prevent men who live in a society from being divided into two classes—one of the rich who command, the other of the poor who obey. . . . Every man has a right to entertain a private opinion of his own equality to other men, but it does not follow that a

cardinal's cook should take it upon him to order his master to prepare his dinner. The cook, however, may say: "I am a man as well as my master; I was born like him in tears, and shall die like him in agony. . . . We both perform the same animal functions. If the Turks get possession of Rome and I then become a cardinal and my master a cook, I will take him into my service." This language is perfectly reasonable and just, but, while waiting for the Grand Turk to take Rome, the cook is bound to do his duty, or all human society is subverted.[68]

As the son of a notary, and only lately become a seigneur, he had mingled views about aristocracy, apparently preferring the English type.[69] He accepted monarchy as the natural form of government. "Why is almost the whole earth governed by monarchs? . . . The honest answer is: Because men are rarely worthy of governing themselves."[70] He laughed at the divine right of kings, and traced them and the state to conquest. "A tribe, for its pillaging expeditions, chooses a chief; it accustoms itself to obey him, he accustoms himself to command; I believe this is the origin of monarchy."[71] Is it natural? Look at a farmyard.

> A farmyard exhibits the most perfect representation of a monarchy. There is no king comparable to a cock. If he marches haughtily and fiercely in the midst of his flock it is not out of vanity. If the enemy is advancing he does not content himself with issuing an order to his subjects to go out and get killed for him . . . ; he goes in person, ranges his troops behind him, and fights to the last gasp. If he conquers, it is himself who sings the *Te Deum*. . . . If it be true that bees are governed by a queen to whom all her subjects make love, that is a more perfect government still.[72]

Living in Berlin and then in Geneva, he could study monarchy and "democracy" in their living operation. Like the other *philosophes*, he was prejudiced by the fact that several monarchs—Frederick II, Peter III, Catherine II—and some ministers—Choiseul, Aranda, Tanucci, Pombal—had listened to appeals for reforms, or had given pensions to philosophers. In an age when the Russian peasant was so primitive, when the masses everywhere were largely illiterate and too tired to think, it seemed absurd to propose popular rule. Actually the "democracies" in Switzerland and Holland were oligarchies. It was the populace that loved the old myths and ceremonies of religion, and stood as a massive army in the path of intellectual freedom and development. Only one force was strong enough to resist the Catholic Church in France, as it had successfully resisted the Protestant churches in England, Holland, and Germany; and that was the state. Only through the existing monarchical governments in France, Germany, and Russia could the *philosophes* hope to win their struggle against superstition, bigotry, persecution, and an infantile theology. They could not expect support from the *parlements*, for these rivaled the Church and exceeded the King in obscurantism, censorship, and intolerance. On the other hand, consider what Henry the Navigator had done for Portugal, what Henry IV had done for France, or Peter the Great for Russia, or Frederick the Great for Prussia. "Almost nothing great has ever been done in the world except by the genius and firmness of a single man combating the prejudices of the multitude."[73] So the *philosophes* prayed for enlightened kings. "Virtue on the throne," Voltaire wrote in *Mérope*, "is the fairest work of heaven."[74]*

Voltaire's politics stemmed partly from a suspicion that many people would be incapable of digesting education even if it were offered them. He referred to "the thinking portion of the human race—i.e., the hundred-thousandth part."[76] He feared the mental immaturity and emotional excitability of the people at large. "*Quand le populace se mêle de raisonner, tout est perdu*" (When the populace takes to reasoning, all is lost).[77] And so, until his mellower years, he had little sympathy with democracy. When Casanova asked him, "Would you see the people possessed of sovereignty?" he answered, "God forbid!"[78] And to Frederick: "When I begged you to be the restorer of the fine arts of Greece, my request did not go so far as to beg you to re-establish the Athenian democracy. I do not like government by the rabble."[79] He agreed with Rousseau that "democracy seems to agree only with small countries," but he added further limitations: "only with those happily situated, . . . whose liberty is assured by their situation, and whom it is to the interest of their neighbors to preserve."[80] He admired the Dutch and Swiss republics, but there too he had some doubts.

> If you remember that the Dutch ate on a grill the heart of the two brothers De Witt; if you . . . recall that the republican John Calvin, . . . after having written that we should persecute no man, even such as deny the Trinity, had a Spaniard, who thought otherwise than he about the Trinity, burned alive by green [slow-burning] fagots; then, in truth, you will conclude that there is no more virtue in republics than in monarchies.[81]

After all these antidemocratic pronouncements we find him actively supporting the Genevan middle class against the patricians (1763), and the unfranchised *natifs* of Geneva against both the aristocracy and the bourgeoisie (1766); let us defer this story to its locale.

Indeed, Voltaire seemed to become more radical as he aged. In 1768 he sent forth his *L'Homme aux quarante écus—The Man with Forty Crowns.* It went through ten printings in its first year, but was burned by the Parlement of Paris, which sent the printer to the galleys. This severity was due not to the ridicule which the story lavished upon the physiocrats, but to its vivid picture of peasants reduced to destitution by taxation, and of monks living in idleness and luxury on properties tilled by serfs. In another pamphlet in 1768, called *L'A, B, C* (which Voltaire was at great pains to disavow), he made "Monsieur B" say:

> I could adjust quite easily to a democratic government. . . . All those who have possessions in the same territory have the same right to maintain order in that territory. I like to see free men make the laws under which they live. . . . It pleases me that my mason, my carpenter, my blacksmith, who have helped me to build my lodging, my neighbor the farmer, my friend the manu-

---

* Michelet has a charming passage on this *thèse royale:* "It is the chimera of the *philosophes* and the economists—of such men as Voltaire and Turgot—to accomplish the revolution—to achieve the happiness of mankind—by means of the king. Nothing is more curious than to behold this idol disputed by both parties. The *philosophes* pull him to the right, the priests to the left. Who will carry him off? Women."[75]

facturer, will raise themselves above their trade, and know the public interest better than the most insolent Turkish official. In a democracy no laborer, no artisan, need fear either molestation or contempt. . . . To be free, to have only equals, is the true, the natural life of man; all other ways of life are unworthy artifices, bad comedies in which one man plays the part of master, the other that of slave, one that of parasite, the other that of procurer.[82]

In or soon after 1769 (aged seventy-five), in a new edition of the *Dictionnaire philosophique*, Voltaire gave a bitter description of governmental tyrannies and abuses in France,[83] and praised England by comparison:

The English constitution has in fact arrived at that point of excellence whereby all men are restored to those natural rights of which, in nearly all monarchies, they are deprived. These rights are: entire liberty of person and property; freedom of the press; the right of being tried in all criminal cases by a jury of independent men; the right of being tried only according to the strict letter of the law; and the right of every man to profess, unmolested, what religion he chooses while he renounces offices which only the members of the Established Church may hold. These are . . . invaluable privileges. . . . To be secure, on lying down, that you will rise in possession of the same property with which you retired to rest; that you will not be torn from the arms of your wife and your children in the dead of night, to be thrown into a dungeon or be buried in exile in a desert; that . . . you will have the power to publish all your thoughts; . . . these privileges belong to every one who sets foot on English soil. . . . We cannot but believe that states not established upon such principles will experience revolutions.[84]

Like so many observers, he foresaw revolution in France. On April 2, 1764, he wrote to the Marquis de Chauvelin:

Everywhere I see the seeds of an inevitable revolution, which, however, I shall not have the pleasure to witness. The French come late to everything, but finally they do come. Enlightenment has been so widely spread that it will burst out at the first opportunity; and then there will be quite a pretty explosion. The young are fortunate; they will see great things.

And yet, when he recalled that he was living in France by sufferance of a King whom he had offended by taking up residence in Potsdam; when he saw Pompadour and Choiseul and Malesherbes and Turgot turning the French government toward religious toleration and political reform—and perhaps because he longed for permission to return to Paris—he took, generally, a more patriotic tone, and deprecated violent revolution:

When the poor strongly feel their poverty, wars follow such as those of the popular party against the Senate at Rome, and those of the peasantry in Germany, England, and France. All these wars ended sooner or later in the subjection of the people, because the great have money, and money in a state commands everything.[85]

So, instead of an upheaval from below, where ability to destroy would not be followed by ability to rebuild, and the simple many would soon again be subject to a clever few, Voltaire preferred to work for a nonviolent revolution through enlightenment passing from thinkers to rulers, ministers and magistrates, to merchants and manufacturers, to artisans and peasants. "Reason must first be established in the minds of leaders; then gradually it descends and at length rules the people, who are unaware of its existence, but who, perceiving the moderation of their superiors, learn to imitate them."[86] In the long run, he thought, the only real liberation is education, the only real freedom is intelligence. *"Plus les hommes sont éclairés, plus ils seront libres"* (The more enlightened men are, the more they will be free).[87] The only real revolutions are those that change the mind and heart, and the only real revolutionists are the sage and the saint.

IV. THE REFORMER

Instead of agitating for a radical political revolution, Voltaire labored for moderate, piecemeal reform within the existing structure of French society; and within this self-denying circle he achieved more than any other man of his time.

His most basic appeal was for a thorough revision of French law, which had not been revised since 1670. In 1765 he read, in Italian, the epochal *Trattato dei delitti e delle pene* of the Milanese jurist Beccaria, who in turn had been inspired by the *philosophes*. In 1766 Voltaire issued a *Commentaire sur le livre des délits et des peines*, frankly acknowledging Beccaria's lead; and he continued to attack the injustices and barbarities of French law till 1777, when, aged eighty-two, he published *Prix de la justice et de l'humanité*.

He demanded, to begin with, the subordination of ecclesiastical to civil law; a check on the power of the clergy to require degrading penances or to enforce idleness on so many holydays; he asked for a mitigation of the penalties for sacrilege, and a repeal of the law insulting the body, and confiscating the property, of suicides. He insisted on distinguishing sin from crime, and ending the notion that the punishment of crime should pretend to avenge an insulted God.

> No ecclesiastical law should be of any force until it has received the express sanction of the government. . . . Everything relating to marriages depends solely upon the magistrates, and priests should be confined to the august function of blessing the union. . . . Lending money at interest is purely an object of civil law. . . . All ecclesiastics, in all cases whatsoever, should be under the perfect control of the government, because they are subjects of the state. . . . No priest should possess authority to deprive a citizen of even the smallest of privileges under pretense that that citizen is a sinner. . . . The magistrates, cultivators, and priests should alike contribute to the expenses of the state.[88]

He compared the law of France to the city of Paris—a product of piecemeal building, of chance and circumstance, a chaos of contradictions; a traveler in France, said Voltaire, changed his laws almost as often as he changed his post horses.[89] All the laws of the various provinces should be unified and brought into general harmony. Every law should be clear, precise, and as far as possible immune to legalistic chicanery. All citizens should be equal in the eyes of the law. Capital punishment should be abolished as barbarous and wasteful. It is surely barbarous to punish forgery, theft, smuggling, or arson with death. If theft is punishable with death, the thief will have no reason for avoiding murder; so in Italy many highway robberies are accompanied by assassination. "If you hang on the public gallows [as happened at Lyons in 1772] the servant girl who stole a dozen napkins from her mistress, she will be unable to add a dozen children to the number of your citizens. . . . There is no proportion between a dozen napkins and a human life."[90] To confiscate the property of a man condemned to death is plain robbery of the innocent by the state. If Voltaire sometimes argued from a merely utilitarian standpoint, it was because he knew that such arguments would outweigh, with most lawmakers, any humanitarian appeal.

But on the subject of judicial torture his humanitarian spirit spoke out forcefully. Judges were allowed by French law to apply torture to elicit confessions before a trial, if suspicious clues suggested guilt. Voltaire sought to shame France by referring to Catherine II's edict abolishing torture in supposedly barbarous Russia. "The French, who are considered—I know not why—to be a very humane people, are astonished that the English, who have had the inhumanity to take all Canada from us, have renounced the pleasure of using torture."[91]

Some judges, he charged, were bullies who acted like prosecutors instead of judges, apparently on the assumption that the accused was guilty until proved innocent. He protested against keeping the accused in foul jails, sometimes in chains and for months, before bringing him to trial. He noted that a person accused of a major crime was forbidden to communicate with anyone, even with a lawyer. He related again and again the treatment of the Calas and the Sirvens as illustrating the hasty condemnation of innocent persons. He argued that the evidence of only two persons, even if eyewitnesses, should no longer be held sufficient to convict a man of murder; he adduced cases of false witness, and urged that capital punishment be abolished if only to prevent the execution of one innocent in a thousand instances. Death sentences could in France be passed by a majority of two among the judges; Jean Calas had been sent to death by a vote of eight to five. Voltaire demanded that a death sentence require an overwhelming majority, preferably unanimity. "What an absurd horror, to play with the life and death of a citizen in a game of six to four, or five to three, or four to two, or three to one!"[92]

By and large the reforms suggested by Voltaire were a compromise between his middle-class heritage, his hatred of the Church, his experience and investments as a businessman and a landholder, and his sincere sentiments as a humanitarian. His demands were moderate, but they were in many cases effective. He campaigned for freedom of the press, and it was immensely extended—if only by governmental winking—before he died. He asked for an end to religious persecution, and in 1787 it was practically ended in France. He proposed that Protestants be permitted to build churches and transmit or inherit property, and enjoy the full protection of the laws; this was done before the Revolution. He asked that marriages between persons of different religions be legalized; they were. He denounced the sale of offices, the taxes on necessaries, the restrictions on internal trade, the survival of serfdom and mortmain; he advised the state to recapture from the Church the administration of wills and the education of youth; and in all these matters his voice had influence on events. He led the campaign to exclude spectators from the stage of the Théâtre-Français; it was done in 1759. He recommended that taxes fall upon all classes, and in proportion to their wealth; this had to wait for the Revolution. He wanted a revision of French law; it was done in the Code Napoléon (1807); the most permanent achievement of the warrior-statesman, who determined the legal structure of France till our own time, was made possible by jurists and philosophers.

V. VOLTAIRE HIMSELF

How shall we sum him up, this most amazing man of the eighteenth century? We need no longer speak of his mind—it has revealed itself in a hundred pages of these volumes. No one has ever challenged him in quickness and clarity of thought, in sharpness and abundance of wit. He defined wit with fond care:

> What is called wit is sometimes a startling comparison, sometimes a delicate allusion; or it may be a play upon words—you use a word in one sense, knowing that your interlocutor will [at first] understand it in another. Or it is a sly way of bringing into juxtaposition ideas not usually considered in association. . . . It is the art of finding a link between two dissimilars, or a difference between two similars. It is the art of saying half of what you mean and leaving the rest to the imagination. And I would tell you much more about it if I had more of it myself.[93]

No one had more, and perhaps, as we have said, he had too much. His sense of humor sometimes passed out of control; too often it was coarse, and occasionally it verged on buffoonery.

The quickness of his perceptions, correlations, and comparisons left him no pause for consistency, and the swift succession of his ideas did not always allow him to penetrate a subject to its humanly attainable depths. Perhaps he disposed too readily of the masses as "canaille"; we could not expect him to foresee the time when universal education would be necessary to a technologically progressive economy. He had no patience with the geological theories of Buffon, or the biological speculations of Diderot. He recognized his limits, and had his moments of modesty. "You think that I express myself clearly enough," he told a friend; "I am like the little brooks—they are transparent because they are not deep."[94] He wrote to Daquin in 1766:

> Since I was twelve years old I divined the enormous quantity of things for which I have no talent. I know that my organs are not arranged to go very far in mathematics. I have shown that I have no inclination for music. Rely upon the esteem of an old philosopher who has the folly . . . to think himself a very good farmer, but has not that of thinking that he has all the talents.[95]

It would be unfair to ask of a man who dealt with so many matters that he should have exhausted all available data on every topic before tossing it on the point of his pen. He was not all scholar; he was a warrior, a man of letters who made letters a form of action, a weapon of transformation. Yet we can see from his library of 6,210 volumes, and their marginal comments, that he studied eagerly and painstakingly an astonishing variety of subjects, and that in politics, history, philosophy, theology, and Biblical criticism he was a very learned man. The range of his curiosity and his interests was immense; so were the wealth of his ideas and the retentiveness of his memory. He took no tradition for granted, but examined everything for himself. He had a proper skepticism which did not hesitate to oppose common sense to the absurdities of science as well as the legends of the popular faith. An unprejudiced scholar called him "a thinker who amassed more accurate information about the world in all its aspects than any man since Aristotle."[96] Never elsewhere has one mind transposed into literature and action so extensive a mass of materials from such a diversity of fields.

We have to picture him as the strangest amalgam of emotional instability with mental vision and power. His nerves kept him always on the jump. He could not sit still except when absorbed in literary composition. When the lady with only one buttock asked, "Which is worse—to be ravished a hundred times by Negro pirates, to have one's rump gashed, . . . to be cut to pieces, to row in the galleys, . . . or to sit still and do nothing?," Candide answered thoughtfully, "That is a great question."[97] Voltaire had days of happiness, but he seldom knew peace of mind or body. He had to be busy, active, buying, selling, planting, writing, acting, reciting. He feared boredom worse than death, and in a bored moment he maligned life as "either ennui or whipped cream."[98]

We could draw an ugly picture of him if we described his appearance without noting his eyes, or listed his faults and follies without his virtues and his charm. He was a *bourgeois gentilhomme* who felt that he had as much right to a title as his dilatory debtors. He rivaled the lordliest seigneur in grace of manners and speech, but he was capable of haggling over small sums, and bombarded Président de Brosses with vituperative missiles over fourteen cords of wood—which he insisted on accepting as a gift and not a sale. He loved money as the root of his security. Mme. Denis accused him of parsimony in no measured terms: "The love of money torments you. . . . You are, in heart, the lowest of men. I shall hide as well as I can the vices of your heart";[99] but when she wrote this (1754) she was living extravagantly in Paris on funds that were a serious drain on his purse; and for the rest of her years with him she lived in state at Ferney.

Before and after becoming a millionaire he cultivated the socially or politically powerful with a flattery that sometimes came close to sycophancy. In an *Épître au Cardinal Dubois* he called that vessel of vices a greater man than Cardinal Richelieu.[100] When he was seeking admission to the French Academy and needed ecclesiastical support, he assured the influential Père de La Tour that he wished to live and die in the Holy Catholic Church.[101] His printed lies would make a book; many were not printed, some were unprintable. He held this procedure justifiable in war; he felt that the Seven Years' War was merely the sport of kings compared with his thirty years' war against the Church; and a government that could jail a man for telling the truth could not justly complain if he lied. On September 19, 1764, at the top of his war, he wrote to d'Alembert: "As soon as the slightest danger comes up, kindly notify me, so that I may disown my writings in the public press with my habitual candor and innocence." He denied almost all his works except the *Henriade* and the poem on the battle of Fontenoy. "One must show the truth to posterity with boldness, and to his contemporaries with circumspection. It is very hard to reconcile these two duties."[102]

It goes without saying that he was vain: vanity is the spur of development, and the secret of authorship. Usually Voltaire kept his vanity under control; he frequently revised his writings according to suggestions and criticism offered in good spirit. He was generous in praise of authors who did not compete with him—Marmontel, Laharpe, Beaumarchais. But he could be childishly jealous of competitors, as in his slyly critical *Éloge de Crébillon* [*père*]; Diderot thought he had "a grudge against every pedestal."[103] His jealousy led him to scurrilous abuse of Rousseau: he called him "the clockmaker's boy," "a Judas who betrayed philosophy," "a mad dog who bites everybody," "a madman born of a chance mating of Diogenes' dog with that of Erasistratus."[104] He thought the first half of *Julie, ou La Nouvelle Héloïse* had been composed in a brothel, and the second in a madhouse. He predicted that *Émile* would be forgotten after a month's time.[105] He felt that Rousseau had turned his back upon that French civilization which, with all its sins and crimes, was precious to Voltaire as the very wine of history.

Being nerves and bones with little flesh, Voltaire was even more sensitive than Rousseau. And as we must feel our pains more keenly than our pleasures, so he took commendation in his stride but was "reduced to despair" by an adverse critique.[106] He was seldom wise enough to restrain his pen; he answered every opponent, however small. Hume described him as one "who never forgives [?], and never thinks an enemy beneath his notice."[107] Against persistent foes like Desfontaines and Fréron he fought without restraint or truce; he used every device of satire, ridicule, and vituperation, even crafty distortion of the truth.[108] His rancor shocked old friends and made new enemies. "I know how to hate," he said, "because I know how to love."[109] "By my stars [I am] a bit inclined to malice";[110] so he successfully moved all his cohorts to defeat de Brosses' candidacy for the Academy (1770). He summed up the matter in a mixture of d'Artagnan and Rabelais:

> As for my puny self, I make war up to the last moment—Jansenists, Molinists, Frérons, Pompignans to the right and to the left, and preachers, and Jean-Jacques Rousseau. I receive a hundred thrusts and give back two hundred, and I laugh. . . . God be praised! I look upon the whole world as a farce which sometimes becomes tragic. All is the same at the end of the day, and all is still the same at the end of days.[111]

In his anti-Semitism he turned upon an entire people the resentment generated by his encounters with a few individuals. From the standpoint of those memories Voltaire interpreted the history of the Jews, noting their faults meticulously, and seldom giving them the benefit of a doubt. He could not forgive the Jews for having begotten Christianity. "When I see Christians cursing Jews methinks I see children beating their fathers."[112] He saw in the Old Testament hardly anything but a record of murder, lechery, and wholesale assassination. The Book of Proverbs seemed to him "a collection of trivial, sordid, incoherent maxims, without taste, without selection, and without design"; and the Song of Songs was to him "an inept rhapsody."[113] However, he praised the Jews for their ancient disbelief in immortality, for refraining from proselytism, and for relative tolerance; the Sadducees denied the existence of angels, but suffered no persecution for heresy.

Did his virtues outweigh his vices? Yes, and even if we do not place in the scale his intellectual with his moral qualities. Against his parsimony we must place his generosity, against his love of money his cheerful acceptance of losses and his readiness to share his gains. Hear Collini, who as his secretary for many years must have known his faults:

> Nothing is more baseless than the reproach of avarice made against him. . . . Stinginess never had a place in his home. I have never known a man whom his domestics could more easily rob. He was a miser only of his time. . . . He had, with regard to money, the same principles as for time: it was necessary, he said, to economize in order to be liberal.[114]

His letters reveal some of the many gifts he distributed, usually without revealing his name, and not only to friends and acquaintances, but even to persons whom he had never seen.[115] He allowed the booksellers to keep the profit from his books. We have seen him helping Mlle. Corneille; we shall see him helping Mlle. Varicourt. We have seen him helping Vauvenargues and Marmontel; he did the same to Laharpe, who failed as a dramatist before developing into the most influential critic in France; Voltaire asked that half of his own governmental pension of two thousand francs be given to Laharpe, without letting him know who was the donor.[116] "Everyone knows," wrote Marmontel, "with what kindness he received all young men who showed any talent for poetry."[117]

If Voltaire, conscious of his puny size, had little physical courage (allowing himself to be caned by Captain Beauregard in 1722[118]), he had astonishing moral courage (attacking the most powerful institution in history, the Roman Catholic Church). If he was bitter in controversy, he was quick to forgive opponents who sought reconciliation; "his fury vanished with the first appeal."[119] He lavished affection upon all who asked for it, and was loyal to his friends. When, after twenty-four years of association, he parted from Wagnière, "he cried like a child."[120] As to his sexual morality, it was above the level of his time with Mme. du Châtelet, below that level with his niece. He was tolerant of sexual irregularity, but rose in fine fury against injustice, fanaticism, persecution, hypocrisy, and the cruelties of the penal law. He defined morality as "doing good to mankind"; for the rest he laughed at prohibitions, and enjoyed wine, woman, and song in philosophical moderation. In a little story called "Bababec" he disposed of asceti-cism with characteristic pungency. Omni asks the Brahmin if there is any chance of his eventually reaching the nineteenth heaven.

> "It depends," replied the Brahmin, "on what kind of life you lead."
> "I try to be a good citizen, a good husband, a good father, a good friend. I sometimes lend money without interest to the rich; I give to the poor; I pre-serve peace among my neighbors."
> "But," asked the Brahmin, "do you occasionally stick nails into your behind?"
> "Never, reverend father."
> "I am sorry," the Brahmin replied; "you will certainly never attain to the nineteenth heaven."[121]

Voltaire's crowning and redeeming virtue was his humanity. He stirred the conscience of Europe with his campaigns for the Calas and the Sirvens. He denounced war as "the great illusion": "The victorious nation never profits from the spoils of the conquered; it pays for everything; it suffers as much when its armies are successful as when they are defeated";[122] whoever wins, humanity loses. He pleaded with men of diverse needs and states to remember that they were brothers; and that plea was heard with gratitude in the depths of Africa.[123] Nor was he subject to Rousseau's charge that those who preached love of mankind spread their love so widely that they had little left for their neighbor; all who knew him remembered his kindness and courtesy to the lowliest persons around him. He respected every ego, know-ing its sensitivity from knowing his own.[124] His hospitality survived the excessive calls upon it. "How moved I was," wrote Mme. de Graffigny, "to find you always as perfectly good as you are great, and to see you doing all about you the good that you would have liked to do to all humanity."[125] He could be irascible and break out in a temper, but "you could never imag-ine," wrote another visitor, "how lovable this man is in his heart."[126]

As the fame of his help to persecuted persons spread through Europe, and reports circulated through France of his private charities and beneficence, a new image of Voltaire took form in the public mind. He was no longer Anti-christ, no longer the warrior against a faith beloved by the poor; he was the savior of the Calas, the good seigneur of Ferney, the defender of a hundred victims of intolerant creeds and unjust laws. Genevan clergymen expressed their wonder whether, at the Last Judgment, their faith would balance the works of this impious man.[127] Educated men and women forgave his impiety, his quarrels, his vanity, even his malice; they saw him grow out of hostility into benevolence; and they thought of him now as the venerable patriarch of French letters, the glory of France before the literate world. This was the man whom even the populace would acclaim when he came to Paris to die.

CHAPTER VI

Rousseau Romantic

1756–62

I. IN THE HERMITAGE: 1756–57

ROUSSEAU had moved into Mme. d'Épinay's cottage on April 9, 1756, along with his common-law wife Thérèse Levasseur and her mother. For a while he was happy, loving the song and chatter of the birds, the rustling and fragrance of the trees, the peace of solitary walks in the woods. On his walks he carried pencil and notebook to catch ideas in their flight.

But he was not made for peace. His sensitivity doubled every trouble, and invented more. Thérèse was a faithful housewife, but she could not be a companion for his mind. "The man who thinks," he wrote in *Émile*, "should not ally himself with a wife who cannot share his thoughts."[1] Poor Thérèse had small use for ideas, and little for written words. She gave him her body and soul; she bore with his tantrums, and probably replied in kind; she allowed him to skirt the edge of adultery with Mme. d'Houdetot, and was herself, so far as we know, humbly faithful except for an episode vouched for only by Boswell. But how could this simple woman respond to the range and wild diversity of a mind that was to unsettle half the Continent? Hear Rousseau's own explanation:

> What will the reader think when I tell him . . . that from the first moment in which I saw her, until that wherein I write, I have never felt the least love for her, that I never desired to possess her, . . . and that the physical wants which were satisfied with her person were to me solely those of the sex, and by no means proceeded from the individual? . . . The first of my wants, the greatest, strongest, and most insatiable, was wholly in my heart: the want of an intimate [spiritual] connection, as intimate as it could possibly be. This singular want was such that the closest corporal union was not sufficient; two souls would have been necessary.[2]

Thérèse might have made countercomplaints, for Rousseau had by this time ceased to perform his conjugal duties. In 1754 he had stated to a Geneva physician: "I have been subject for a long time to the cruelest sufferings, owing to the incurable disorder of retention of the urine, caused by a congestion in the urethra, which blocks the canal to such an extent that even the catheters of the famed Dr. Daran cannot be introduced there."[3] He claimed to have ceased all sexual intercourse with Thérèse after 1755.[4] "Until then," he added, "I had been good; from that moment I became virtuous, or at least infatuated with virtue."

The presence of his mother-in-law made the triangle painfully acute. He maintained her and his wife as well as he could with the income from his copying of music and the sale of his writings. However, Mme. Levasseur had other daughters, who required marriage portions, and were always in need. Grimm, Diderot, and d'Holbach made up, for the two women, an annuity of four hundred livres, pledging them to hide this from Rousseau lest his pride be hurt. The mother (according to Rousseau[5]) kept most of the money for herself and her other daughters, and contracted debts in Thérèse's name. Thérèse paid these debts, and long concealed the annuity; finally Rousseau found it out, and flared into anger at his friends for so humiliating him. They fed his wrath by urging him to move from the Hermitage before the winter set in; the cottage (they argued) was not adapted for cold weather; and even if his wife could bear it, would the mother survive? Diderot, in his play Le Fils naturel,[6] had written: "The good man lives in society; only the bad man lives alone." Rousseau took this as applying to himself; now began a long quarrel in which reconciliations were only armistices. Rousseau felt that Grimm and Diderot, envious of the peace he had found in the woods, were trying to lure him back to a corrupt city. In a letter to his benefactress, Mme. d'Épinay (then in Paris), he revealed his character with candor and insight:

> I want my friends to be my friends and not my masters; to advise me but not to try to rule me; to have every claim upon my heart but none upon my liberty. I consider it extraordinary the way people interfere, in friendship's name, in my affairs, without telling me of theirs. . . . Their great eagerness to do me a thousand services wearies me; there is a touch of patronage about it that wearies me; besides, anyone else could do as much. . . .
>
> As a recluse, I am more sensitive than other men. Suppose I fall out with one who lives amid the throng; he thinks of the matter for a moment, then a hundred and one distractions will make him forget it for the rest of the day. But nothing takes my thoughts off it. Sleepless, I think of it all night long; walking by myself, I think of it from sunrise to sunset. My heart has not an instant's respite, and a friend's unkindness will cause me to suffer, in a single day, years of grief. As an invalid I have a right to the indulgence due from his fellow men to the little weaknesses and temper of a sick man. . . . I am poor, and my poverty (or so it seems to me) entitles me to some consideration. . . .
>
> So do not be surprised if I hate Paris yet more and more. Nothing for me, from Paris, except your letters. Never shall I be seen there again. If you care to state your views on this subject, and as vigorously as you like, you have a right to do so. They will be taken in good part, and will be—useless.[7]

She answered him vigorously enough: "Oh, leave these petty complaints to the empty-hearted and empty-headed!"[8] Meanwhile she made frequent inquiries about his health and comfort, shopped for him, and sent him small gifts.

> One day, when it froze to an extreme degree, in opening a packet of several things I had asked her to buy for me, I found a little under-petticoat of English flannel, which she told me she had worn, and desired I should make of it an under-waistcoat. This more than friendly care appeared to me so tender—as if she had stripped herself to clothe me—that in my emotion I repeatedly kissed both the note and the petticoat, while shedding tears. Thérèse thought me mad.[9]

During his first year at the Hermitage he compiled a *Dictionnaire de musique*, and summarized in his own language the twenty-three volumes of the Abbé de Saint-Pierre on war and peace, education, and political reform. In the summer of 1756 he received from the author a copy of Voltaire's poem on the earthquake that had killed fifteen thousand persons, and wounded fifteen thousand more, at Lisbon on All Saints' Day, November 1, 1755. Voltaire, like half the world, wondered why a presumably beneficent Providence had chosen for this indiscriminate slaughter the capital of a country completely Catholic, and an hour—9:40 A.M.—when all pious people were worshiping in church. In a mood of utter pessimism Voltaire painted a picture of life and nature as being heartlessly neutral between evil and good. A passage in the *Confessions* gives us Rousseau's reaction to this powerful poem.

> Struck by seeing this poor man, overwhelmed (if I may so speak) with prosperity and honor, bitterly exclaiming against the miseries of this life, and finding everything to be wrong, I formed the mad project of making him turn his attention to himself, and of proving to him that everything was right. Voltaire, while he appeared to believe in God, never really believed in anything but the Devil, since his pretended deity is a malicious being who, according to him, has no pleasure but in evil. The glaring absurdity of this doctrine is particularly disgusting from a man enjoying the greatest prosperity, who, from the bosom of happiness, endeavors, by the frightful and cruel image of all the calamities from which he is exempt, to reduce his fellow creatures to despair. I, who had a better right than he to calculate and weigh all the evils of human life, impartially examined them, and proved to him that of all possible evils there was not one to be attributed to Providence, and which had [not] its source rather in the abusive use man made of his faculties than in nature.[10]

So, on August 18, 1756, Rousseau sent to Voltaire a twenty-five-page "Lettre sur la Providence." It began with a handsome acknowledgment:

> Your latest poems, monsieur, have come to me in my solitude; and though all my friends know the love I have for your writings, I do not know who could have sent me this book unless it be yourself. I have found in it both pleasure and instruction, and have recognized the hand of the master; . . . I am bound to thank you at once for the volume and for your work.[11]

He urged Voltaire not to blame Providence for the misfortunes of mankind. Most evils are due to our own folly, sin, or crime.

> Note that Nature did not assemble twenty thousand houses of six or seven stories, and that if the inhabitants of that great city had been more evenly dispersed and more lightly lodged, the damage would have been much less, perhaps nothing. All would have fled at the first tremor, and we should have seen them, on the morrow, twenty leagues away, as gay as if nothing had happened.[12]

Voltaire had written that few persons would want to be reborn to the same conditions; Rousseau replied that this is true only of rich people surfeited with pleasures, bored with life, and shorn of faith; or of literary men sedentary, unhealthy, reflective, and discontent; it is not true of simple people like the French middle class or the Swiss villagers. It is only an abuse of life that makes life a problem to us.[13] Moreover, the evil of the part may be the good of the whole; the death of the individual makes possible the rejuvenated life of the species. Providence is universal, not particular: it watches over the whole, but leaves specific events to secondary causes and natural laws.[14] Early death, such as came to Lisbon's children, may be a boon; in any case it is unimportant if there is a God, since He will recompense all for unmerited suffering.[15] And the question of God's existence is beyond solution by reason. We may choose between belief and unbelief; and why reject an inspiring and consolatory faith? As for himself, "I have suffered too much in this life not to hope for another. All the subtleties of metaphysics will not make me doubt for a moment a beneficent Providence and the immortality of the soul. I feel this, I believe it, I wish it; . . . I will defend these beliefs to my last breath."[16]

The letter ended amiably: Rousseau expressed his agreement with Voltaire on religious toleration, and assured him, "I would rather be a Christian after your fashion than in the style of the Sorbonne."[17] He begged Voltaire to compose, with all the force and charm of his verse, a "catechism for the citizen," which would inculcate a code of morals to guide men through the confusion of the age. — Voltaire wrote a polite acknowledgment, and invited Rousseau to be his guest at Les Délices.[18] He made no formal attempt to refute Rousseau's arguments, but replied to them indirectly with *Candide* (1759).

II. IN LOVE

The winter of 1756–57 was heavy with events for Rousseau. At some time during those months he began to write the most famous novel of the eighteenth century: *Julie, ou La Nouvelle Héloïse*. He conceived it first as a study in friendship and love: cousins Julie and Claire both love Saint-Preux, but when he seduces Julie Claire remains the loyal friend of both. Ashamed to write merely a romance, Rousseau proposed to raise the story to philosophy by having Julie become religious, and live in exemplary monogamy with Wolmar, a gentleman agnostic who has succumbed to Voltaire and Diderot. According to Rousseau's *Confessions:*

> The storm brought on by the *Encyclopédie* . . . was at this time at its height. Two parties, exasperated against each other to the last degree of fury, soon resembled enraged wolves . . . rather than Christians and philosophers who had a reciprocal wish to enlighten and convince each other and lead their brethren to the way of truth. . . . Being by nature an enemy to all spirit of party, I had freely spoken severe truths to each, but they had not listened. I thought of another expedient, which in my simplicity appeared to be admirable: this was to abate their mutual hatred by destroying their prejudices, and showing to each party the virtue and merit which in the other deserved public esteem and respect. This project . . . had the success that was to be expected: it drew together and united the rival parties for no other purpose than that of crushing the author. . . . Satisfied with . . . my plan, I returned to the situations in detail, . . . and there resulted Parts I and II of *Héloïse*.[19]

Every evening, by the fireside, he read some pages to Thérèse and Mme. Levasseur. Encouraged by the tears Thérèse shed, he submitted the manuscript to Mme. d'Épinay when she returned to her château, La Chevrette, a mile from the Hermitage. Her memoirs recall: "On our arrival here . . . we found Rousseau awaiting us. He was calm, and in the best temper in the world. He brought me an installment of a romance which he has commenced. . . . He returned to the Hermitage yesterday in order to continue this work, which he says constituted the happiness of his life."[20] Soon afterward she wrote to Grimm:

> After dinner we read Rousseau's manuscript. I do not know whether I am ill-disposed, but I am not satisfied with it. It is wonderfully well written, but it is too elaborate, and seems to be unreal and wanting in warmth. The characters do not say a word of what they ought to say; it is always the author who speaks. I do not know how to get out of it. I should not like to deceive Rousseau, and I cannot make up my mind to grieve him.[21]

Somehow, during that winter, Rousseau poured warmth into *Julie*. Was it because a living romance had come into his life? About January 30, 1757, he was visited by a lady whom he had met in Paris as the sister-in-law of Mme. d'Épinay. Élisabeth-Sophie de Bellegarde had married Comte d'Houdetot, had left him, and had now for several years been the mistress of the Marquis de Saint-Lambert—once the rival of Voltaire for Mme. du Châtelet. Both her husband and her lover were off to the war. In the summer of 1756 the Comtesse had leased the Château of Eaubonne, some two and a half miles from the Hermitage. Saint-Lambert wrote to her that Rousseau was within riding distance of her, and suggested that she might mitigate her solitude by visiting the famous author who had put all civilization on the defensive. She went in a coach; when this stuck in the mire she continued on foot, and arrived with her shoes and her dress soiled with mud. "She made the place resound with laughter, in which I most heartily joined."[22] Thérèse gave her a change of clothing, and the Marquise stayed for "a rustic collation." She was twenty-seven, Rousseau was forty-five. She had no special beauty of face or form, but her kindliness, good temper, and gay spirit brightened his somber life. The next afternoon she sent him a pretty letter, addressing him by the title he had taken after his repatriation in Geneva:

> My dear Citizen, I return the garments which you were kind enough to lend me. In leaving I found a much better road, and I must tell you of my joy over that, because it makes it much more possible to see you again. I am sorry to have seen so little of you. . . . I would be less sorry if I were more free, and always sure of not disturbing you. Farewell, my dear Citizen, and I beg you to thank Mlle. Levasseur for all the kindness she showed me.[23]

A few days later Saint-Lambert returned from the front. In April he was recalled to service, and soon afterward the sprightly Comtesse pranced to the Hermitage on horseback, dressed like a man. Rousseau was shocked by the costume, but was soon conscious that it contained a charming woman. Leaving Thérèse to her housewifely chores, he and his guest walked out into the woods, and Mme. d'Houdetot told him how passionately she loved Saint-

Lambert. In May he returned her visit, going to Eaubonne at a time when, she had told him, she would be "quite alone." "In my frequent excursions to Eaubonne," he says, "I sometimes slept there. . . . I saw her almost every day during three months. . . . I saw my Julie in Mme. d'Houdetot, and I soon saw nothing but Mme. d'Houdetot [in Julie], but with all the perfections with which I had adorned the idol of my heart."[24]

For a time he so abandoned himself to "my delirium" that he ceased to work on his novel; instead he composed love letters, which he took care that she should find in the niches of Eaubonne's trees. He told her that he was in love, not saying with whom; of course she knew. She reproved him, and protested that she belonged body and soul to Saint-Lambert, but she allowed his visits and ardent attentions to continue; after all, a woman exists only when she is loved, and doubly so when loved by two. "She refused me nothing that the most tender friendship could grant; yet she granted me nothing that rendered her unfaithful." He tells of their "long and frequent conversations . . . during the four months we passed together in an intimacy almost without example between two friends of different sexes who contain themselves within the bounds which we never exceeded."[25] In his account of this liaison we find the Romantic movement in full swing: nothing in his novel could rival these ecstasies:

> We were both intoxicated with the passion—she for her lover, I for her; our sighs and delicious tears were mingled together. . . . Amid this delicious intoxication she never forgot herself for a moment, and I solemnly protest that if ever, led away by my senses, I have attempted to render her unfaithful, I was never really desirous of succeeding. . . . The duty of self-denial had elevated my mind. . . . I might have committed the crime; it had been a hundred times committed in my heart; but to dishonor my Sophie! Ah, was ever this possible? No! I have told her a hundred times it was not. . . . I loved her too well to possess her. . . . Such was the sole enjoyment of a man of the most combustible constitution, but who was, at the same time, perhaps one of the most timid mortals Nature ever produced.[26]

Mme. d'Épinay noticed that her "bear" rarely came to see her now, and she soon learned of his trips to her sister-in-law. She was hurt. "It is hard, after all," she wrote to Grimm in June, "that a philosopher should escape from you at the moment when you least expect it."[27] One day at Eaubonne Rousseau found "Sophie" in tears. Saint-Lambert had been informed of her flirtation, and (as she put it to Jean-Jacques) "ill informed of it. He does me justice, but he is vexed. . . . I am much afraid that your follies will cost me the repose of the rest of my days."[28] They agreed that it must have been Mme. d'Épinay who had told the secret to Saint-Lambert, for "we both knew that she corresponded with him." Or she might have revealed it to Grimm, who occasionally saw Saint-Lambert in Westphalia. If we may accept Rousseau's account, Mme. d'Épinay tried to secure from Thérèse the letters he had received from Mme. d'Houdetot. In a wild letter to his hostess he accused her of betraying him:

> Two lovers [Sophie and Saint-Lambert], closely united and worthy of each other's love, are dear to me. . . . I presume that attempts have been made to

disunite them, and that I have been made use of to inspire one of the two with jealousy. The choice was not judicious, but it appeared convenient to the purposes of malice; and of this malice it is you whom I suspect to be guilty. . . . Thus the woman whom I most esteem would . . . have been loaded with the infamy of dividing her heart and her person between two lovers, and I with that of being one of these wretches. If I knew that but for a single moment in your life you ever had thought this, either of her or of myself, I should hate you until my last hour. But it is with having said, and not [merely] with having thought it, that I charge you.

Do you know in what manner I will make amends for my faults during the short space of time I have to remain near you? By doing what nobody but myself would do: by telling you freely what the world thinks of you, and the breaches that you have to repair in your reputation.[29]

Mme. d'Épinay, guilty or not (we do not know), was distressed by the violence of these accusations. She reported them to her distant lover Grimm. He replied that he had warned her against the "devilish scrapes" she would be involved in by letting the moody and incalculable Rousseau into the Hermitage.[30] She invited Jean-Jacques to La Chevrette; she greeted him with an embrace and tears; he responded tear for tear; she gave him no explanation that we know of; he dined with her, slept in her house, and departed the next morning with expressions of friendship.

Diderot complicated the mess. He advised Rousseau to write to Saint-Lambert confessing his tenderness for Sophie, but assuring him of her fidelity. Rousseau (according to Diderot) promised to do so. But Mme. d'Houdetot begged him not to write, and to let her extricate herself in her own way from the difficulties in which his infatuation and her dalliance had placed her. When Saint-Lambert returned from the front Diderot spoke to him of the affair, assuming that Rousseau had confessed it. Rousseau reproached Diderot with betraying him; Diderot reproached Rousseau for deceiving him. Only Saint-Lambert behaved philosophically. He came with Sophie to the Hermitage; he "invited himself to dinner with me, . . . treated me severely but in a friendly manner," and inflicted no worse punishment than to sleep and snore while Jean-Jacques read aloud his long letter to Voltaire. Mme. d'Houdetot, however, discouraged any further meetings with Rousseau. At her request he returned the letters she had written him, but when he asked for those that he had written to her she said she had burned them. "Of this," he tells us, "I dared to doubt, . . . and doubt still. No such letters as mine to her were ever thrown into the fire. Those of Héloïse [to Abélard] have been found ardent; good heavens! what would have been said of these?"[31] Wounded and ashamed, he retired into his imaginary world; he resumed the writing of *La Nouvelle Héloïse*, and poured into it the passions of his letters to Mme. d'Houdetot.

New humiliations awaited him when Grimm returned from the war (September, 1757). "I could scarcely recognize the same Grimm who" formerly had "thought himself honored when I cast my eyes upon him."[32] Rousseau could not understand Grimm's coldness to him; he did not know that Grimm knew of the insulting letter to Mme. d'Épinay. Grimm was almost as self-centered as Jean-Jacques, but was otherwise antipodal to him in mind and character—skeptical, realistic, blunt, and hard.[33] Rousseau with one letter had lost two friends.

III. MUCH ADO

A new crisis developed when, in October, 1757, Mme. d'Épinay decided to visit Geneva. This is Rousseau's story:

> "My friend," she said to me, "I am immediately going to set out for Geneva; my chest is in a bad state, and my health so deranged, that I must go and consult Tronchin." I was the more astonished at this resolution so suddenly taken, and at the beginning of the bad season of the year. . . . I asked her whom she would take with her. She said her son and [his tutor] M. de Linant; and then she carelessly added: "And you, dear, will not you go also?" As I did not think she spoke seriously, knowing that at this season I was scarcely able to go to my chamber [i.e., to travel between La Chevrette and the Hermitage], I joked upon the utility of one sick person to another. She herself had not seemed to make the proposition seriously, and there the matter dropped.[34]

He had excellent reasons for not wishing to accompany Madame; his ailments forbade it, and how could he leave Thérèse? Moreover, gossip whispered that his hostess was pregnant, presumably by Grimm; Rousseau for a time believed the tale, and complimented himself on escaping from a ridiculous situation. The poor woman was telling the truth: she was suffering from tuberculosis; she seems to have sincerely desired Rousseau to accompany her; and why should he not be glad to revisit, at her expense, the city of which he was so proudly *Citoyen?* Aware of her feelings, Diderot wrote to Rousseau urging him to take her request seriously and accede to it, if only as some return for her benefactions. He replied in his characteristic style:

> I perceive that the opinion you give comes not from yourself. Besides my being but little disposed to suffer myself to be led by the nose under your name by any third or fourth person, I observe in this secondary advice a certain underhand dealing which ill agrees with your candor, and from which you will, on your account as well as mine, do well in future to abstain.[35]

On October 22 he took Diderot's letter and his own reply to La Chevrette and read them "in a loud, clear voice" to Grimm and Mme. d'Épinay. On the twenty-fifth she left for Paris; Rousseau went to bid her an awkward goodbye; "fortunately," he tells us, "she set out in the morning, and I still had time to go and dine with her sister-in-law" at Eaubonne.[36] On the twenty-ninth (according to Mme. d'Épinay's *Memoirs*) he wrote to Grimm:

> Tell me, Grimm, why do all my friends declare that I ought to accompany Mme. d'Épinay? Am I wrong, or are they all bewitched? . . . Mme. d'Épinay starts in a nice postchaise, accompanied by her husband, her son's tutor, and five or six servants. . . . Should I be able to endure a postchaise? Can I hope to accomplish so long a journey so speedily without a mishap? Shall I have it stopped every moment that I may get down, or shall I accelerate my torments and my last hours by being obliged to put restraint upon myself? . . . My devoted friends . . . [seem] intent upon worrying me to death.[37]

On October 30 Mme. d'Épinay left Paris for Geneva. On November 5 Grimm (according to the *Memoirs*) replied to Rousseau:

> I have done my utmost to avoid replying definitely to the horrible apology which you have addressed to me. You press me to do so. . . . I never thought that you ought to have accompanied Mme. d'Épinay to Geneva. Even if your first impulse had been to offer her your company, it would have been her duty to refuse your offer, and to remind you of what you owe to your position, your health, and the women whom you have dragged into your retreat; that is my opinion. . . .
> You dare to speak to me of your slavery, to me who, for more than two years, have been the daily witness of all the proofs of the most tender and generous friendship which this woman has given you. If I were able to pardon you, I should think myself unworthy to have a friend. I will never see you again in my life, and I shall think myself happy if I can banish from my mind the memory of your behavior. I ask you to forget me, and not to disturb me any more.[38]

From Geneva Mme. d'Épinay wrote to Grimm: "I have received the thanks of the Republic for the way in which I have treated Rousseau, and a formal deputation of watchmakers on the same subject. The people here hold me in veneration on his account."[39] Tronchin warned her that she would have to remain under his care for a year. She was a frequent visitor at Voltaire's homes in Geneva and Lausanne. After some delay Grimm joined her, and they had eight months of happiness.*

On November 23, 1757, Rousseau (he tells us) wrote to her as follows:

> Were it possible to die of grief I should not now be alive. . . . Friendship, madame, is extinguished between us, but that which no longer exists still has its rights, and I respect them. I have not forgotten your goodness to me, and you may expect from me as much gratitude as it is possible to have toward a person I can no longer love. . . .
> I wished to quit the Hermitage, and I ought to have done it. My friends pretend I must stay there till spring; and since my friends desire it I will remain there till then if you will consent.[40]

Early in December Diderot came to see Rousseau, and found him in wrath and tears at the "tyranny" which his friends exercised over him. Diderot's report of this visit appears in his letter of December 5 to Grimm:

> The man is a madman (*forcené*). I have seen him; I reproached him, with all the force given me by honesty, for the enormity of his conduct. He put into his defense of himself an angry passion which afflicted me. . . . This man comes between me and my work, and troubles my mind; it is as though I had one of the damned near me. . . . Oh, what a spectacle it is—that of a wicked and ferocious man! Let me never see him again; he would make me believe in devils and hell.[41]

Rousseau received an answer from Mme. d'Épinay on December 10. Apparently Grimm had told her of Rousseau's comments on his "slavery" at the Hermitage, for she wrote with unusual bitterness:

---

* They returned to Paris in October, 1759; her home there became one of the minor salons. Her book on education was crowned by the Academy.

After having for several years given you every possible mark of friendship, all I can now do is to pity you. You are very unhappy. . . .

Since you are determined to quit the Hermitage, and are persuaded that you ought to, I am astonished that your friends have prevailed upon you to stay there. For my part I never consult mine on my duty, and I have nothing further to say to you on your own.[42]

On December 15, though winter was closing in, Rousseau left the Hermitage with Thérèse and all their belongings. Her mother he sent to live in Paris with the other daughters, but he promised to contribute to her support. He moved to a cottage in Montmorency, leased to him by an agent of Louis-François de Bourbon, Prince de Conti. There, turning his back upon his former friends, he produced in five years three of the most influential books of the century.

IV. THE BREAK WITH THE *PHILOSOPHES*

His new home was in what he called the *jardin de Mont-Louis;* a "single chamber" fronted with a lawn, and, at the end of the garden, an old tower with an "alcove quite open to the air." When visitors came he had to receive them "in the midst of my dirty plates and broken pots," and he trembled lest "the floor, rotten and falling to ruin," should collapse under his guests. He did not mind his poverty; he earned enough by copying music; he rejoiced in being a competent artisan,[43] no longer a rich woman's retainer. When kindly neighbors sent him gifts he resented them; he felt that to receive more than one gives is a humiliation. The Prince de Conti twice sent him pullets; he told the Comtesse de Boufflers that a third gift would be returned.

We should note, in passing, how many aristocrats helped the rebels of the Enlightenment, not so much through agreement with their views as through generous sympathy with genius in need. There were many elements of nobility in the nobles of the Old Regime. And Rousseau, who denounced the aristocracy, was especially befriended by it. Sometimes the proud artisan forgot himself, and boasted of his titled friends. Speaking of his lawn he wrote:

That terrace was my drawing room, wherein I received M. and Mme. de Luxembourg, the Duc de Villeroi, the Prince de Tingry, the Marquis d'Armentières, the Duchesse de Montmorency, the Duchesse de Boufflers,* the Comtesse de Valentinois, the Comtesse de Boufflers, and other persons of the same rank, who . . . deigned to make the pilgrimage to Mont-Louis.[44]

Not far from Rousseau's cottage was the home of the Maréchal and Maréchale de Luxembourg. Soon after his arrival they invited him to dinner;

---

* In the profusion of Boufflers who entered history in the 18th century we may distinguish (1) the Duchesse de Boufflers, who became the Maréchale de Luxembourg, (2) the Marquise de Boufflers, mistress of Stanislas Leszczyński, and (3) the Comtesse de Boufflers, friend of David Hume and Horace Walpole.

he refused. They repeated the invitation in the summer of 1758; he again refused. Toward Easter of 1759 they came, with half a dozen titled friends, to beard him in his retreat. He was frightened; the Maréchale, as Duchesse de Boufflers, had earned a reputation for charming too many men. But she had outlived her sins, and had matured into a woman of maternal rather than merely sexual charm; soon she thawed his shy reserve, and aroused him into lively conversation. The visitors wondered why a man of such parts should be living in such poverty. The Maréchal invited Rousseau and Thérèse to come and live with him until the cottage could be repaired; Jean-Jacques still resisted; finally he and Thérèse were persuaded to occupy for a time the "Petit Château" on the Luxembourg estate. They moved into it in May, 1759. Sometimes Rousseau visited the Luxembourgs in their luxurious home; there he was easily induced to read to them and their guests some parts of the novel that he was completing. After a few weeks he and Thérèse returned to their own cottage, but he continued to visit the Luxembourgs, and they remained loyal to him through all the perturbations of his moods. Grimm complained that Rousseau "had left his old friends and replaced us with people of the highest rank,"[45] but it was Grimm who had rejected Rousseau. In a letter of January 28, 1762, to Malesherbes Jean-Jacques answered those who accused him of both denouncing and courting the nobility:

> Sir, I have a violent aversion to the social classes that dominate others. . . . I have no trouble admitting this to you, scion of illustrious blood. . . . I hate the great, I hate their position, their harshness, their prejudices, . . . their vices. . . . It was in such a frame of mind I went as one dragged along to the château [of the Luxembourgs] at Montmorency. Then I saw the masters; they loved me, and I, sir, loved them, and will love them as long as I live. . . . I would give them, I will not say my life, for that gift would be a feeble one; . . . but I will give them the only glory that has ever touched my heart—the honor I expect from posterity, and which it will certainly pay me, because this is due me, and posterity is always just.

One former friend he had hoped to keep—Mme. d'Houdetot; but Saint-Lambert reproached her for the gossip in which Paris linked her name with Rousseau's, and she bade Rousseau refrain from addressing letters to her. He remembered that he had confessed his passion for her to Diderot; now he concluded that it was Diderot who had babbled about it in the salons, and "I resolved to break with him forever."[46]

He chose the worst possible moment and means. On July 27, 1758, Helvétius had published, in De l'Esprit, a powerful attack upon the Catholic clergy. The resultant furor led to a rising demand for the suppression of the Encyclopédie (then seven volumes old) and all writings critical of Church or state. Volume VII contained d'Alembert's rash article on Geneva, lauding the Calvinist clergy for their secret Unitarianism, and pleading with the Genevan authorities to allow the establishment of a theater. In October, 1758, Rousseau published his Lettre à M. d'Alembert sur les spectacles. Moderate in tone, it was nevertheless a declaration of war against the Age of Reason, against the irreligion and immorality of mid-eighteenth-century France. In the preface Rousseau went out of his way to repudiate Diderot, without naming him: "I had an Aristarchus, severe and judicious. I have him no more; I want no more of him; but I shall regret him unceasingly, and my heart misses him even more than my writings." And in a footnote he added, believing that Diderot had betrayed him to Saint-Lambert:

> If you have drawn a sword against a friend, don't despair, for there is a way to return it to him. If you have made him unhappy by your words, fear not, for it is possible to be reconciled with him. But for outrage, hurtful reproach, the revelation of a secret, and the wound done to his heart by betrayal, there is no grace in his eyes; he will go away from you and never return.[47]

The letter, 135 pages in translation, was in part a defense of religion as publicly preached in Geneva. As his *Émile* would soon indicate, Rousseau was himself a Unitarian—rejecting the divinity of Christ; but in applying for Genevan citizenship he had professed the full Calvinist creed; in this *Lettre* he defended the orthodox faith, and belief in a divine revelation, as indispensable aids to popular morality. "What can be proved by reason to the majority of men is only the interested calculation of personal benefit"; hence a merely "natural religion" would let morality degenerate into nothing more than avoidance of detection.

But theology was a minor issue in Rousseau's argument; his frontal assault was upon d'Alembert's proposal that a theater should be legalized in Geneva. Here the secret enemy was not d'Alembert but Voltaire: Voltaire whose fame as a resident of Geneva irritably outshone Rousseau's glory as *Citoyen de Genève;* Voltaire who had dared to stage plays in or near Geneva, and who doubtless had prompted d'Alembert to insert a plea for a Genevan theater in an *Encyclopédie* article. What? Introduce into a city famous for its Puritan morals a form of entertainment that had almost everywhere glorified immorality? Tragic dramas nearly always pictured crime; they did not purge the passions, as Aristotle thought; they inflamed the passions, especially of sex and violence. Comedies seldom represented wholesome married love; often they laughed at virtue, as even Molière had done in *Le Misanthrope*. All the world knew that actors led lawless and immoral lives, and that most of the alluring actresses of the French stage were paragons of promiscuity, serving as centers and sources of corruption in a society that idolized them. Perhaps, in large cities like Paris and London, these evils of the stage affect only a small part of the population, but in a small city like Geneva (with only 24,000 population) the poison would spread through all ranks, and the representations would stir up newfangled notions and party strife.[48]

So far Rousseau had echoed the Puritan, or Calvinist, view of the theater; he was saying in France in 1758 what Stephen Gosson had said in England in 1579, William Prynne in 1632, Jeremy Collier in 1698. But Rousseau did not confine himself to denunciation. He was no Puritan; he advocated balls and dances under public sponsorship and supervision. There should be public amusements, but of a social and wholesome kind, like picnics, open-air games, festivals, parades. (Here Rousseau added an animated description of a regatta on Lake Geneva.[49])

The *Letter*, he tells us, "had a great success." Paris was beginning to tire of immorality; there was no further zest in unconventional deviations that had themselves become conventional. The city was surfeited with men who behaved like women, and women who itched to be like men. It had had enough of classic drama and its stilted forms. It saw how poor a showing Mme. de Pompadour's generals and soldiers were making against Frederick's Spartan troops. To hear a philosopher speak well of virtue was a refreshing experience. The moral influence of the *Letter* would grow until, with Rousseau's other writings, it would share in producing an almost revolutionary return to decency under Louis XVI.

The *philosophes* could not foresee this. What they felt in Rousseau's proclamation was an act of betrayal: he had attacked them in the moment of their greatest danger. In January, 1759, the government finally forbade the publication or sale of the *Encyclopédie*. When Rousseau denounced the morals of Paris his former intimates, recalling his pursuit of Mme. d'Houdetot, condemned him a hypocrite. When he denounced the stage they pointed out that he had written *Le Devin du village* and *Narcisse* for the stage, and had frequented the theater. Saint-Lambert rejected with a harsh message (October 10, 1758) the copy which Rousseau had sent him of the *Letter*:

> I cannot accept the present you have offered me. . . . You may, for aught I know to the contrary, have reason to complain of Diderot, but this does not give you a right to insult him publicly. You are not unacquainted with the nature of the persecutions which he suffers. . . . I cannot refrain from telling you, sir, how much this heinous act of yours has shocked me. . . . You and I differ too much in our principles ever to be agreeable to each other. Forget that I exist. . . . I promise to forget your person, and to remember nothing about you but your talents.[50]

Mme. d'Épinay, however, on her return from Geneva, thanked Rousseau for the copy that he had directed to her, and invited him to dinner. He went, and met Saint-Lambert and Mme. d'Houdetot for the last time.

From Geneva came a dozen letters of praise. Encouraged by Rousseau's stand, the Genevan magistrates forbade Voltaire to stage any further theatricals on Genevan soil. Voltaire removed his dramatic properties to Tourney, and transferred his residence to Ferney. He felt the sting of defeat. He branded Rousseau as a deserter and apostate, and mourned that the little flock of *philosophes* had fallen into a self-consuming strife. "The infamous Jean-Jacques," he wrote, "is the Judas of the brotherhood."[51] Rousseau retorted in a letter (January 29, 1760) to the Genevan pastor Paul Moultou:

> You speak to me of that man Voltaire? Why does the name of that buffoon sully your correspondence? That miserable fellow has ruined my country [Geneva]. I would hate him more if I despised him less. I only see in his great gifts something additionally shameful, which dishonors him by the use he makes of them. . . . Oh, citizens of Geneva, he makes you pay well for the refuge you have given him![52]

It grieved Rousseau to learn that Voltaire was producing plays at Tourney, and that many citizens of Geneva were crossing the frontiers into France to witness these performances—some even to take part in them. His resentment found an added *casus belli* when his letter to Voltaire on the

Lisbon earthquake was printed in a Berlin journal (1760), apparently through Voltaire's careless lending of the manuscript to a friend. Now (June 17) Rousseau sent to Voltaire one of the most extraordinary letters in the correspondence of this turbulent age. After reproaching Voltaire for the unauthorized publication, he proceeded:

> I don't like you, monsieur. To me, your disciple and enthusiast, you have done the most painful injuries. You have ruined Geneva as a reward for the asylum that you received there. You have alienated my fellow citizens from me as a reward for the praises I gave you among them. It is you who make it unbearable for me to live in my own country; you who will compel me to die on foreign soil, deprived of all the consolations of the dying, and thrown dishonored upon some refuse heap, while all the honors that a man can expect will attend you in my native land. In short, I hate you, since you have willed it so; but I hate you with the feelings of one still capable of loving you, if you had desired it. Of all the feelings with which my heart was filled for you, there remains only admiration for your fine genius, and love for your writings. If I honor in you only your talents it is not my fault. I shall never be found wanting in the respect which is due them, nor in the behavior which that respect demands.[53]

Voltaire did not answer, but privately he called Rousseau "charlatan," "madman," "little monkey," and "miserable fool."[54] In correspondence with d'Alembert he showed himself quite as sensitive and passionate as Jean-Jacques.

> I have received a long letter from Rousseau. He has gone completely mad. . . . He writes against the stage after having written a bad comedy himself; he writes against France, which nourishes him; he finds four or five rotten staves from the barrel of Diogenes and climbs into them in order to bark at us; he abandons his friends. He writes to me—to me!—the most insulting letter that a fanatic ever scrawled. . . . If he were not an inconsequential poor pygmy of a man, swollen with vanity, there would be no great harm done; but he has added to the insolence of his letter the infamy of intriguing with Socinian pedants here in order to prevent me from having a theater of my own at Tourney, or at least preventing the citizens from playing there with me. If he meant by this base trick to prepare for himself a triumphant return to the low streets whence he sprang, it is the action of a scoundrel, and I shall never pardon him. I would have avenged myself on Plato if he had played a trick of that sort on me; even more on the lackey of Diogenes. The author of the *Nouvelle Aloïsa* is nothing but a vicious knave.[55]

In these two letters of the two most famous writers of the eighteenth century we see, behind the supposedly impersonal currents of the time, the nerves that felt keenly every blow in the conflict, and the common human vanity that throbs in the hearts of philosophers and saints.

V. THE NEW HÉLOÏSE

The book that Voltaire misnamed had been for three years Rousseau's refuge from his enemies, his friends, and the world. Begun in 1756, it was finished in September, 1758, was sent to a publisher in Holland, and appeared in February, 1761, as *Julie, ou La Nouvelle Héloïse, Lettres de deux amants, recueillies et publiées par J.-J. Rousseau.* The letter form for a novel was already old, but was probably determined in this instance by the example of Richardson's *Clarissa.*

The story is improbable but unique. Julie is the daughter, seventeen or so years old, of Baron d'Étange. Her mother invites the young and handsome Saint-Preux to be her tutor. The new Abélard falls in love with the new Héloïse, as any real mother would have foreseen. Soon he is sending his pupil love letters that set the tune for a century of romantic fiction:

> I tremble as often as our hands meet, and I know not how it happens, but they meet constantly. I start as soon as I feel the touch of your finger; I am seized with a fever, or rather delirium, in these sports; my senses gradually forsake me; and when I am thus beside myself what can I say, what can I do, where hide myself, how be answerable for my behavior?[56]

He proposes to go away, but lets the word do for the deed.

> Adieu, then, too charming Julie. . . . Tomorrow I shall be gone forever. But be assured that my violent spotless passion for you will end only with my life; that my heart, full of so divine an object, will never debase itself by admitting a second impression; that it will divide all its future homage between you and virtue; and that no other flame shall ever profane the altar at which Julie was adored.[57]

Julie may smile at this adoration, but she is too womanly to send so delightful an acolyte from the altar. She bids him postpone his flight. In any case the electric contact of male with female has set her in similar agitation; soon she confesses that she too has felt the mysterious sting: "The very first day we met I imbibed the poison which now infects my senses and my reason; I felt it instantly, and thine eyes, thy sentiments, thy discourse, thy guilty pen, daily increase its malignity."[58] Nevertheless he is not to ask for anything more sinful than a kiss. "Thou shalt be virtuous, or despised; I will be respectable, or be myself again; it is the only hope I have left that is preferable to the hope of death." Saint-Preux agrees to unite delirium with virtue, but believes that this will require supernatural aid:

> Celestial powers! . . . Inspire me with a soul that can bear felicity! Divine love! spirit of my existence, oh, support me, for I am ready to sink down under the weight of ecstasy! . . . Oh, how shall I withstand the rapid torrent of bliss which overflows my heart?—and how dispel the apprehensions of a timorously loving girl [*une craintive amante*]?[59]

—and so on for 657 pages. At page 91 she kisses him. Words fail to tell "what became of me a moment after, when I felt—my hands shook—a gentle tremor —thy balmy lips—my Julie's lips—pressed to mine, and myself within her arms! Quicker than lightning a sudden fire darted from my frame."[60] By Letter xxix he has seduced her, or she him. He meanders through reams of rapture, but she thinks all is lost. "One unguarded moment has betrayed me to endless misery. I am fallen into the abyss of infamy, from which there is no return."[61]

Julie's mother, having learned of her deflowering, dies of grief. The Baron vows to kill Saint-Preux, who thereupon begins a circumnavigation of the globe. In remorse and in obedience to her father, Julie marries Wolmar, a

Russian of high birth and considerable years. Clandestinely she continues to correspond with Saint-Preux, and to feel for him a sentiment stronger than her dutiful attachment to her husband. She is surprised to find that Wolmar, though an atheist, is a good man, faithful to her, solicitous for her comfort, just and generous to all. In one of her letters to Saint-Preux she assures him that man and wife can find content in a *mariage de convenance*. But she never again knows full happiness. Her premarital deviation weighs on her memory. Finally she confesses to her husband that moment of sin. He has known of it, and resolved never to mention it; he tells her it was no sin at all; and to confirm her absolution he invites Saint-Preux to come and stay with them as tutor of their children. Saint-Preux comes, and we are assured that the three live together in harmony till death does them part. The incredible husband absents himself for several days. Julie and Saint-Preux go boating on the Lake of Geneva; they cross to Savoy, and he shows her the rocks upon which, in his banishment, he wrote her name; he weeps, she holds his trembling hand, but they return sinless to her home in Clarens, in the Pays de Vaud.[62]

They wonder how Wolmar can be so good without religious belief. Saint-Preux, who, like Julie, is a pious Protestant, explains the anomaly:

> Having resided in Roman Catholic countries, he [Wolmar] has never been led to a better opinion of Christianity by what he found professed there. Their religion, he saw, tended only to the interest of their priests; it consisted entirely of ridiculous grimaces and a jargon of words without meaning. He perceived that men of sense and probity were unanimously of his opinion, and that they did not scruple to say so; nay, that the clergy themselves, under the rose, ridiculed in private what they inculcated and taught in public; hence he has often assured us that, after taking much time and pains in the search, he has never met with above three priests who believed in God.[63]

Rousseau adds, in a footnote: "God forbid that I should approve these hard and rash assertions!" Despite them, Wolmar regularly goes to Protestant services with Julie, out of respect for her and his neighbors. Julie and Saint-Preux see in him "the strangest absurdity"—a man "thinking like an infidel and acting like a Christian."[64]

He did not deserve the final blow. Julie, dying of a fever contracted while saving her son from drowning, entrusts to Wolmar an unsealed letter to Saint-Preux, which declares to Saint-Preux that he has always been her only love. We can understand the permanence of that first impression, but why reward her husband's long fidelity and trust with so cruel a deathbed rejection? It is hardly consistent with the nobility with which the author has invested Julie's character.

Nevertheless she is one of the great portraits in modern fiction. Though it was probably suggested by Richardson's Clarissa, it was inspired by Rousseau's own recollections: the two girls whose horses he had led across the stream at Annecy; the memories he treasured of Mme. de Warens in his first years under her protection; and then Mme. d'Houdetot, who had made him feel the overflow of love by damming his desire. Of course Julie is none of these women, and perhaps no woman that Rousseau had ever met, but only the composite ideal of his dreams. The picture is spoiled by Rousseau's insistence upon making nearly all his characters talk like Rousseau; Julie, as motherhood deepens her, becomes a sage who discourses lengthily on everything from domestic economy to mystic union with God. "We will examine into the validity of this argument," she says; but what lovable woman ever descended to such bathos?

Saint-Preux, of course, is especially Rousseau, sensitive to all the charms of women, longing to kneel at their idealized feet, and to pour out the eloquent phrases of devotion and passion that he has rehearsed in his loneliness. Rousseau describes him as "always perpetrating some madness, and always making a start at being wise."[65] Saint-Preux is an unbelievable prig compared with the frankly villainous Lovelace of Richardson. He too must mouth Rousseau: he describes Paris as a maelstrom of evils—great wealth, great poverty, incompetent government, bad air, bad music, trivial conversation, vain philosophy, and the almost total collapse of religion, morality, and marriage; he repeats the first *Discourse* on the natural goodness of man and the corrupting and degrading influences of civilization; and he compliments Julie and Wolmar on preferring the quiet and wholesome life of the countryside at Clarens.

Wolmar is the most original character in Rousseau's gallery. Who was his model? Perhaps d'Holbach, the "amiable atheist," the philosopher baron, the virtuous materialist, the devoted husband of one wife and then of her sister. And perhaps Saint-Lambert, who had shocked Rousseau by preaching atheism but had forgiven him for making love to his mistress. Rousseau candidly avows his use of living prototypes and personal memories:

> Full of that which had befallen me, and still affected by so many violent emotions, my heart added the sentiment of its sufferings to the ideas with which meditation had inspired me. . . . Without perceiving it I described the situation I was then in, gave portraits of Grimm, Mme. d'Épinay, Mme. d'Houdetot, Saint-Lambert, and myself.[66]

Through these character portraits Rousseau expounded nearly all facets of his philosophy. He gave an ideal picture of a happy marriage, of an agricultural estate managed with efficiency, justice, and humanity, and of children brought up to be exemplary mixtures of freedom and obedience, restraint and intelligence. He anticipated the arguments of his *Émile:* that education should be first of the body to health, then of the character to a Stoic discipline, and only then of the intellect to reason. "The only means of rendering children docile," says Julie, "is not to reason with them, but to convince them that reason is above their age";[67] there should be no appeal to reason, no intellectual education at all, before puberty. And the story went out of its way to discuss religion. Julie's faith becomes the instrument of her redemption; the religious ceremony that sanctified her marriage brought her a sense of purification and dedication. But it is a strongly Protestant faith that pervades the book. Saint-Preux ridicules what seems to him the hypocrisy of the Catholic clergy in Paris, Wolmar denounces sacerdotal celibacy as a cover for adultery, and Rousseau in his own person adds: "To impose celibacy upon a group so numerous as the Roman clergy is not so much to forbid them to have women of their own, as to order them to satisfy themselves with the women of other men."[68] In passing Rousseau declares in favor of religious toleration, extending it even to atheists: "No true believer will be either intolerant or a persecutor. If I were a magistrate, and if the law pronounced the penalty of death against atheists, I would begin by burning, as such, whoever should come to inform against another."[69]

The novel had an epochal influence in arousing Europe to the beauties and sublimities of nature. In Voltaire, Diderot, and d'Alembert the fever of philosophy and urban life had not encouraged sensitivity to the majesty of mountains and the kaleidoscope of the sky. Rousseau had the advantage of being born amid the most impressive scenery in Europe. He had walked from Geneva into Savoy, and across the Alps to Turin, and from Turin into France; he had savored the sights and sounds and fragrances of the countryside; he had felt every sunrise as the triumph of divinity over evil and doubt. He imagined a mystic accord between his moods and the changing temper of the earth and the air; his ecstasy of love embraced every tree and flower, every blade of grass. He climbed the Alps to midway of their height, and found a purity of air that seemed to cleanse and clear his thoughts. He described these experiences with such feeling and vividness that mountain climbing, especially in Switzerland, became one of Europe's major sports.

Never before in modern literature had feeling, passion, and romantic love received so detailed and eloquent an exposition and defense. Reacting against the adoration of reason from Boileau to Voltaire, Rousseau proclaimed the primacy of feeling and its right to be heard in the interpretation of life and the evaluation of creeds. With *La Nouvelle Héloïse* the Romantic movement raised its challenge to the classic age. Of course there had been romantic moments even in the classic heyday: Honoré d'Urfé had played with bucolic love in *L'Astrée* (1610–27); Mlle. de Scudéry had stretched amours to reams in *Artamène, ou Le Grand Cyrus* (1649–53); Mme. de La Fayette had married love and death in *La Princesse de Clèves* (1678); Racine had brought the same theme into *Phèdre* (1677)—the very apex of the classic age. We recall how Rousseau had inherited old romances from his mother, and had read them with his father. As for the Alps, Albrecht von Haller had already sung their majesty (1729), and James Thomson had celebrated the beauty and terror of the seasons (1726–30). Jean-Jacques must have read Prévost's *Manon Lescaut* (1731), and (since he could read English with difficulty) he must have been familiar with Richardson's *Clarissa* (1747–48) in Prévost's translation. From that two-thousand-page (still incomplete) seduction he took the letter form of narrative as congenial to psychological analysis; and he gave Julie a cousin confidante in Claire as Richardson had given Clarissa Miss Howe. Rousseau noted with resentment that Diderot published an ecstatic *Éloge de Richardson* (1761) soon after *Julie*, dimming *Julie*'s glory.

Julie is quite equal to *Clarissa* in originality and faults, far superior to it in style. Both are rich in improbabilities and heavy with sermons. But France, which excels the world in style, had never known the French language to take on such color, ardor, smoothness, and rhythm. Rousseau did not merely preach feeling, he had it; everything he touched was infused with sensitivity and sentiment, and though we may smile at his raptures we find ourselves warmed by his fire. We may resent, and hurry over, the untimely disquisitions, but we read on; and every now and then a scene intensely felt renews the life of the tale. Voltaire thought in ideas and wrote with epigrams; Rousseau saw in pictures and composed with sensations. His phrases and periods were not artless; he confessed that he turned them over in bed while the passion of the artist frightened sleep.[70] "I must read Rousseau," said Kant, "until his beauty of expression no longer distracts me, and only then can I examine him with reason."[71]

Julie succeeded with everyone except the *philosophes*. Grimm called it "a feeble imitation" of *Clarissa*, and predicted that it would soon be forgotten.[72] "No more about Jean-Jacques' romance, if you please," growled Voltaire (January 21, 1761); "I have read it, to my sorrow, and it would be to his if I had time to say what I think of this silly book."[73] A month later he said it in *Lettres sur La Nouvelle Héloïse*, published under a pseudonym. He pointed out grammatical errors, and gave no sign of appreciating Rousseau's descriptions of nature—though he would later imitate Jean-Jacques by climbing a hill to worship the rising sun. Paris recognized Voltaire's hand, and judged the patriarch to be bitten with jealousy.

Barring these pricks, Rousseau was delighted with the reception of his first full-length work. "In all literary history," thought Michelet, "there had never been so great a success."[74] Edition followed edition, but printings fell far behind demand. Lines formed at the stores to buy the book; eager readers paid twelve sous per hour to borrow it; those who had it during the day rented it to others for the night.[75] Rousseau told happily how one lady, all dressed to go to a ball at the Opéra, ordered her carriage, took up *Julie* meanwhile, and became so interested that she read on till four in the morning while maid and horses waited.[76] He ascribed his triumph to the pleasure women took in reading of love; but there were also women who were tired of being mistresses, and longed to be wives and to have fathers for their children. Hundreds of letters reached Rousseau at Montmorency, thanking him for his book; so many women tendered him their love that his imagination concluded: "There was not one woman in high life with whom I might not have succeeded had I undertaken to do it."[77]

It was something new that a man should so completely reveal himself as Rousseau had done through Saint-Preux and Julie; and there is nothing so interesting as a human soul, even partly or unconsciously bared to view. Here, said Mme. de Staël, "all the veils of the heart have been rent."[78] Now began the reign of subjective literature, a long succession, lasting to our own days, of self-revelations, of hearts broken in print, of "beautiful souls" publicly bathing in tragedy. To be emotional, to express emotion and sentiment, became a fashion not only in France but in England and Germany. The classic mode of restraint, order, reason, and form began to fade away; the reign of the *philosophes* neared its end. After 1760 the eighteenth century belonged to Rousseau.[79]

CHAPTER VII

Rousseau Philosopher

I. *THE SOCIAL CONTRACT*

TWO months before the publication of *La Nouvelle Héloïse*, Rousseau wrote to M. Lenieps (December 11, 1760):

> I have quit the profession of author for good. There remains an old sin to be expiated in print, after which the public will never hear from me again. I know of no happier lot than that of being unknown save only to one's friends. . . . Henceforth copying [music] will be my only occupation.[1]

And again on June 25, 1761:

> Until the age of forty I was wise; at forty I took up the pen; and I put it down before I am fifty, cursing, every day of my life, the day when my foolish pride made me take it up, and when I saw my happiness, my repose, my health, all go up in smoke without hope of recapturing them again.[2]

Was this a pose? Not quite. It is true that in 1762 he published both *Du Contrat social* and *Émile;* but these had been completed by 1761; they were the "old sin to be expiated in print." And it is true that he later wrote replies to the Archbishop of Paris, to the Geneva Consistory, and to the requests from Corsica and Poland to propose constitutions for them; but these compositions were *pièces d'occasion*, induced by unforeseen events. The *Confessions*, the *Dialogues*, and the *Rêveries d'un promeneur solitaire* were published after his death. Essentially he kept to his novel vow. It is no wonder that in 1761 he felt exhausted and finished, for in the space of five years he had composed three major works, each of which was an event in the history of ideas.

Far back in 1743, when he was secretary to the French ambassador in Venice, his observation of the Venetian government in contrast with the Genevan and the French had led him to plan a substantial treatise on political institutions. The two *Discourses* were sparks from that fire, but they were hasty attempts to get attention by exaggeration, and neither of them did justice to his developing thought. Meanwhile he studied Plato, Grotius, Locke, and Pufendorf. The *magnum opus* that he dreamed of was never completed. Rousseau did not have the ordered mind, patient will, and quiet temper needed for such an enterprise. It would have required him to reason as well as feel, to conceal passion rather than reveal it; and such self-denial was beyond his reach. His renunciation of authorship was his admission of defeat. But he gave the world in 1762 a brilliant fragment of his plan in the 125 pages published at Amsterdam as *Du Contrat social, ou Principes du droit politique.*

Everyone knows the bold cry that opened the first chapter: *"L'homme est*

né libre, et partout il est dans les fers" (Man is born free, and he is everywhere
in chains). Rousseau began with conscious hyperbole, for he knew that logic
has a powerful *virtus dormitiva;* he judged rightly in striking so shrill a note,
for that line became the watchword of a century. As in the *Discourses,* he
assumed a primitive "state of nature" in which there were no laws; he
charged existing states with having destroyed that freedom; and he proposed,
in their place, "to find a form of association which will defend and protect,
with the whole common force, the person and goods of each associate, and
in which each, while uniting himself to all, may still obey himself alone, and
remain as free as before. . . . This is the fundamental problem of which
The Social Contract provides the solution."[3]

There is a social contract, says Rousseau, not as a pledge of the ruled to
obey the ruler (as in Hobbes's *Leviathan*), but as an agreement of individuals to subordinate their judgment, rights, and powers to the needs and
judgment of their community as a whole. Each person implicitly enters into
such a contract by accepting the protection of the communal laws. The
sovereign power in any state lies not in any ruler—individual or corporate—
but in the *general will* of the community; and that sovereignty, though it
may be delegated in part and for a time, can never be surrendered.

But what is this *volonté générale?* Is it the will of all the citizens, or only
of the majority?—and who are to be considered citizens? It is not the will of
all (*volonté de tous*), for it may contradict many an individual will. Nor is
it always the will of the majority living [or voting] at some particular moment; it is the will of the community as having a life and reality additional
to the lives and wills of the individual members. [Rousseau, like a medieval
"realist," ascribes to the collectivity, or general idea, a reality additional to
that of its particular constituents. The general will, or "public spirit," should
be the voice not only of the citizens now living, but of those dead or yet to
be born; hence its character is given to it not only by present wills but by
the past history and future aims of the community. It is like some old family
that thinks of itself as one through generations, honors its ancestors, and protects its progeny. So a father, out of obligation to grandchildren yet unborn, may overrule the desires of his living children, and a statesman may
feel himself bound to think in terms not of one election but of many generations.]* Nevertheless "the vote of the majority always binds all the rest."[4]
Who may vote? Every citizen.[5] Who is a citizen? Apparently not all male
adults. Rousseau is especially obscure on this point, but he praises d'Alembert for distinguishing "the four orders of men . . . who dwell in our town
[Geneva], of which only two compose the public; no other French writer
. . . has understood the real meaning of the word *citizen*."[6]

Ideally, says Rousseau, law should be the expression of the general will.
Man is by nature predominantly good, but he has instincts that must be controlled to make society possible. There is no idealization of a "state of nature"
in *The Social Contract.* For a moment Rousseau talks like Locke or Montesquieu, even like Voltaire:

---

* The material in brackets is tentative interpretation, and is not explicitly in Rousseau.

The passage from the state of nature to the civil state produces a very remarkable change in man, by substituting law for instinct in his conduct, and
giving his actions the morality they had formerly lacked. . . . Although, in
this [civil] state, he deprives himself of some advantages which he had from
nature, he gains in return others so great, his faculties are so stimulated and
developed, his ideas so extended, and his whole soul so uplifted, that, did not
the abuses of his new condition often degrade him below that which he left,
he would be bound to bless continually the happy moment which took him
from it forever, and instead of a stupid and unimaginative animal, made him
an intelligent being and a man.[7]

So Rousseau (who once talked like a not quite philosophical anarchist) is
now all for the sanctity of law, if the law expresses the general will. If, as
often happens, an individual does not agree with that will as expressed in
law, the state may justly force him to submit.[8] This is not a violation of freedom, it is a preservation of it, even for the refractory individual; for in a
civil state it is only through law that the individual can enjoy freedom from
assault, robbery, persecution, calumny, and a hundred other ills. Hence, in
compelling the individual to obey the law, society in effect "forces him to be
free."[9] This is especially so in republics, for "obedience to a law which we
prescribe to ourselves is liberty."[10]

Government is an executive organ to which the general will provisionally
delegates some of its powers. The state should be thought of not as only
the government, but as the government, the citizens, and the general will or
communal soul. Any state is a republic if it is governed by laws and not by
autocratic decrees; in this sense even a monarchy can be a republic. But if
the monarchy is absolute—if the king makes as well as executes the laws—
then there is no *res publica*, or commonwealth, there is only a tyrant ruling
slaves. Hence Rousseau refused to join those *philosophes* who praised the
"enlightened despotism" of Frederick II or Catherine II as means of advancing civilization and reform. He thought that peoples living in arctic or tropical climates might need absolute rule to preserve life and order;[11] but in
temperate zones a mixture of aristocracy and democracy is desirable. Hereditary aristocracy is "the worst of all governments"; "elective aristocracy" is
the best;[12] i.e., the best government is one in which the laws are made and
administered by a minority of men periodically chosen for their intellectual
and moral superiority.

Democracy, as direct rule by all the people, seemed to Rousseau impossible:

If we take the term in the strict sense, there never has been a real democracy,
and there never will be. It is against the natural order for the many to govern
and the few to be governed. It is unimaginable that the people should remain
continually assembled to devote their time to public affairs, and it is clear that
they cannot set up commissions for that purpose without changing the form of
administration. . . .
Besides, how many conditions difficult to unite are presupposed by such a
government? First, a very small state, where the people can be readily assembled, and where each citizen can with ease know all the rest; secondly, great
simplicity of manners, to prevent business from multiplying and raising thorny

problems; next, a large measure of equality in rank and fortune, without which equality of rights and authority cannot long subsist; and lastly, little or no luxury, for luxury corrupts at once the rich and the poor—the rich by possession and the poor by covetousness. . . . This is why a famous writer [Montesquieu] has made virtue the fundamental principle of republics, for all these conditions could not exist without virtue. . . . If there were a people of gods, their government would be democratic, but so perfect a government is not for men.[13]

These passages invite misinterpretation. Rousseau uses the term *democracy* in a sense rarely ascribed to it in politics or history, as a government in which all laws are made by the whole people meeting in national assemblies. Actually the "elective aristocracy" that he preferred is what we should call representative democracy—government by officials popularly chosen for their supposedly superior fitness. However, Rousseau rejects representative democracy on the ground that the representatives will soon legislate for their own interest rather than for the public good. "The people of England regards itself as free, but it is grossly mistaken; it is free only during the election of members of Parliament; as soon as they are chosen, slavery overtakes the people, and it ceases to count."[14] Representatives should be elected to administrative and judicial offices, but not to legislate; all laws should be made by the people in general assembly, and that assembly should have the power to recall elected officials.[15] Hence the ideal state should be small enough to allow all the citizens to assemble frequently. "The larger the state, the less the liberty."[16]

Was Rousseau a socialist? The second *Discourse* derived almost all the evils of civilization from the establishment of private property; yet even that essay judged the institution to be too deeply rooted in the social structure to permit its removal without a chaotic and desolating revolution. *The Social Contract* allows for private ownership, but subject to communal control; the community should retain all basic rights, it may seize private property for the common good, and it should fix a maximum of property allowable to any one family.[17] It may sanction the bequest of property, but if it sees wealth tending to a disruptive concentration it may use inheritance taxes to redistribute wealth and diminish social and economic inequality. "It is precisely because the force of things tends always to destroy equality that legislation should always tend to maintain it."[18] One purpose of the social contract is that "men who may be unequal in strength or intelligence shall all become equal in social and legal rights."[19] Taxes should fall heavily upon luxuries. "The social state is advantageous to men only when all have something and no one has too much."[20] Rousseau did not commit himself to collectivism, and never thought of a "dictatorship of the proletariat"; he despised the nascent proletariat of the cities, and agreed with Voltaire in calling it "canaille"—rabble, scum.[21] His ideal was a prosperous, independent peasantry and a virtuous middle class composed of families like Wolmar's in *La Nouvelle Héloïse*. Pierre-Joseph Proudhon was to accuse him of enthroning the bourgeoisie.[22]

What place should religion have in the state? Some religion, Rousseau felt, was indispensable to morality; "no state has ever been established without a religious basis."[23]

> Wise men, if they try to speak their language to the common herd instead of its own, cannot possibly make themselves understood. . . . For a young people to be able to prefer sound principles of political theory . . . the effect would have to become the cause: the social spirit which should be created by these institutions would have to preside over their very foundation; and men would have to be before law what they should become by means of law. The legislator, therefore, being unable to appeal to either force or reason, must have recourse to an authority of a different order, capable of constraining without violence. . . . This is what in all ages compelled the fathers of nations to have recourse to divine intervention, and credit the gods with their own wisdom, in order that the peoples, submitting to the laws of the state as to those of nature, . . . might obey freely, and bear with docility the yoke of the public good.[24]

Rousseau would not always hold to this old political view of religion, but in *The Social Contract* he made supernatural belief an instrument of the state, and considered priests to be at best a kind of celestial police. However, he rejected the Roman Catholic clergy as such agents, for their Church claimed to be above the state, and was therefore a disruptive force, dividing the citizen's loyalty.[25] Moreover (he argued), the Christian, if he takes his theology seriously, focuses his attention upon the afterlife, and puts little value upon this one; to that extent he is a poor citizen. Such a Christian makes an indifferent soldier; he may fight for his country, but only under constant compulsion and supervision; he does not believe in waging war for the state, because he has only one fatherland—the Church. Christianity preaches servitude and docile dependence; hence its spirit is so favorable to tyranny that tyrants welcome its co-operation. "True Christians are made to be slaves."[26] Here Rousseau agreed with Diderot, anticipated Gibbon, and was for the moment more violently anti-Catholic than Voltaire.

Nevertheless, he felt, some religion is necessary, some "civil religion" formulated by the state and made compulsory upon all its population. As to creed:

> The dogmas of the civil religion ought to be few, simple, and precisely worded, but without explanation or commentary. The existence of a mighty, intelligent, and beneficent Divinity, possessed of foresight and providence; the life to come, the happiness of the just, the punishment of the wicked, the sanctity of the social contract and the laws; these are its positive dogmas.[27]

So Rousseau, at least for political purposes, professed the basic beliefs of Christianity, while rejecting its ethics as too pacifistic and international—just the reverse of the usual philosophic procedure of retaining the ethics of Christianity while discarding its theology. He allowed other religions in his imaginary state, but only on condition that they did not contradict the official creed. He would tolerate those religions "that tolerate others," but "whoever dares to say, 'Outside the Church there is no salvation,' ought to be driven from the state, unless the state is the Church, and the prince is the pontiff" thereof.[28] No denial of the articles in the religion of the state is to be permitted.

> While the state can compel no one to believe them, it can banish him, not for impiety, but as an antisocial being, incapable of truly loving the laws and justice, and of sacrificing, at need, his life to his duty. If anyone, after publicly recognizing these dogmas, behaves as if he does not believe them, let him be punished by death.[29]

Next to "Man is born free, and is everywhere in chains," this last is the most famous sentence in *The Social Contract*. Taken literally, it would put to death any person acting as if he had no belief in God, heaven, or hell; applied to the Paris of that time, it would have almost depopulated the capital. Rousseau's love of startling and absolute statements probably misled him into saying more than he meant. Perhaps he recalled the Diet of Augsburg (1555), at which the signatory princes agreed that each of them should have the right to banish from his territory any person not accepting the prince's faith—*cuius regio eius religio;* and the laws of Geneva, taken literally (as in the case of Servetus), provided an antecedent for Rousseau's sudden savagery. Ancient Athens had made *asebeia*—failure to recognize the official gods—a capital crime, as in exiling Anaxagoras and poisoning Socrates; the persecution of Christians by Imperial Rome was similarly excused; and on Rousseau's penology the order for his arrest, in this year 1762, could be described as an act of Christian charity.

Was *The Social Contract* a revolutionary book? No and yes. Here and there, amid Rousseau's demand for a government responsible to the general will, some moments of caution calmed him, as when he wrote: "None but the greatest dangers can counterbalance that of changing the public order; and the sacred power of the laws should never be arrested save when the existence of the country is at stake."[30] He blamed private property for nearly all evils, but he called for its maintenance as made necessary by the incorrigible corruption of mankind. He wondered whether the nature of man would, after a revolution, reproduce old institutions and servitudes under new names. "People accustomed to masters will not let mastery cease. . . . Mistaking liberty for unchained license, they are delivered by their revolutions into the hands of seducers who will only aggravate their chains."[31]

Nevertheless his was the most revolutionary voice of the time. Though elsewhere he belittled and distrusted the masses, here his appeal was to the multitude. He knew that inequality is inevitable, but he condemned it with force and eloquence. He announced unequivocally that a government persistently contravening the general will might justly be overthrown. While Voltaire, Diderot, and d'Alembert were curtsying to kings or empresses, Rousseau raised against existing governments a cry of protest that was destined to be heard from one end of Europe to the other. While the *philosophes*, already embedded in the status quo, called only for piecemeal reform of particular ills, Jean-Jacques attacked the whole economic, social, and political order, and with such thoroughness that no remedy seemed possible but revolution. And he announced its coming: "It is impossible that the great kingdoms of Europe should last much longer. Each of them has had its period of splendor, after which it must inevitably decline. The crisis is approaching: we are on the edge of a revolution."[32] And beyond this he predicted far-reaching transformations: "The Empire of Russia will aspire to conquer Europe, and will itself be conquered. The Tatars—its subjects or neighbors—will become its masters and ours, by a revolution which I consider inevitable."[33]

The Social Contract, which in hindsight we perceive to have been the most revolutionary of Rousseau's works, made far less stir than *La Nouvelle Héloïse*. France was ready for emotional release and romantic love, but it was not ready to discuss the overthrow of the monarchy. This book was the most sustained argument that Rousseau had yet produced, and it was not as easy to follow as the sparkling vivacities of Voltaire. Impressed by its later vogue, we are surprised to learn that its popularity and influence began after, not before, the Revolution.[34] Even so we find d'Alembert writing to Voltaire in 1762: "It will not do to speak too loudly against Jean-Jacques or his book, for he is rather a king in the Halles"[35]—i.e., among the burly workers in the central market of Paris, and, by implication, among the populace. This was probably an exaggeration, but we may date from 1762 the turn of philosophy from attack upon Christianity to criticism of the state.

Few books have ever aroused so much criticism. Voltaire marked his copy of *Du Contrat social* with marginal rejoinders; so, on Rousseau's prescription of death for active unbelief: "All coercion on dogma is abominable."[36] Scholars have reminded us how old was the claim that sovereignty lies in the people: Marsilius of Padua, William of Ockham, even Catholic theologians like Bellarmine, Mariana, and Suárez had put forth that claim as a blow behind the knees of kings. It had appeared in the writings of George Buchanan, Grotius, Milton, Algernon Sidney, Locke, Pufendorf . . . *The Social Contract*, like nearly all of Rousseau's political and moral philosophy, is an echo and reflex of Geneva by a citizen distant enough to idealize it without feeling its claws. The book was an amalgam of Geneva and Sparta, of Calvin's *Institutes* and Plato's *Laws*.

A hundred critics have pointed out the inconsistency between the individualism of Rousseau's *Discourses* and the legalism of *The Social Contract*. Long before Rousseau's birth Filmer, in *Patriarcha* (1642), had disposed of the notion that man is born free; he is born subject to paternal authority and to the laws and customs of his group. Rousseau himself, after that initial cry for freedom, moved further and further from liberty toward order—toward submission of the individual to the general will. Basically the contradictions in his works lay between his character and his thought; he was a rebel individualist by temperament, ailment, and lack of formal discipline; he was a communalist (never a communist, not even a collectivist) by his tardy perception that no operative society can be composed of mavericks. We must allow for development: a man's ideas are a function of his experience and his years; it is natural for a thinking person to be an individualist in youth—loving liberty and grasping for ideals—and a moderate in maturity, loving order and reconciled to the possible. Emotionally Rousseau remained always a child, resenting conventions, prohibitions, laws; but when he reasoned he came to realize that within the restrictions necessary for social order many freedoms can remain; and he ended by perceiving that in a community liberty is not the victim but the product of law—that it is enlarged rather than lessened by general obedience to restraints collectively self-imposed. Philosophical anarchists and political totalitarians alike can quote Rousseau to their purpose,[37] and alike unjustly, for he recognized that order is freedom's first law, and the order that he spoke for was to be the expression of the general will.

Rousseau denied any real contradictions in his philosophy. "All my ideas are consistent, but I cannot expound them all at once."[38] He admitted that his book "needs rewriting, but I have neither the strength nor the time to do it";[39] when he had the strength, persecution took away his time, and when persecution ceased, and time was given, strength had been worn away. In those later years he grew doubtful of his own arguments. "Those who pride themselves on thoroughly understanding *The Social Contract* are cleverer than I am."[40] In practice he quite ignored the principles he had there laid down; he never thought of applying them when asked to draw up constitutions for Poland or Corsica. Had he continued in the line of change that he followed after 1762 he would have ended in the arms of the aristocracy and the Church, perhaps under the knife of the guillotine.

II. ÉMILE

1. Education

We can forgive much to an author who could, within fifteen months, send forth *La Nouvelle Héloïse* (February, 1761), *The Social Contract* (April, 1762), and *Émile* (May, 1762). All three were published in Amsterdam, but *Émile* was published also in Paris, with governmental permission secured at great risk by the kindly Malesherbes. Marc-Michel Rey, the Amsterdam publisher, deserves a passing salute. Having made unexpected profits from *Héloïse*, he settled upon Thérèse a life annuity of three hundred livres; and foreseeing a greater sale for *Émile* than for *Du Contrat social* (which he had bought for a thousand livres), he paid Jean-Jacques six thousand livres for the new and longer manuscript.

The book originated partly from discussions with Mme. d'Épinay on the education of her son, and took its first form as a minor essay written "to please a good mother who was able to think"—Mme. de Chenonceaux, daughter of Mme. Dupin. Rousseau thought of it as a sequel to *La Nouvelle Héloïse*: how should Julie's children be brought up? For a moment he doubted whether a man who had sent all his children to a foundling asylum, and who had failed as a tutor in the Mably family, was fit to talk on parentage and education; but as usual he found it pleasant to give his imagination free rein, unhampered by experience. He studied Montaigne's *Essays*, Féne-lon's *Télémaque*, Rollin's *Traité des études*, and Locke's *Some Thoughts on Education*. His own first *Discourse* was a challenge to him, for it had pictured man as good by nature but spoiled by civilization, including education. Could that natural goodness be preserved and developed by right education? Helvétius had just given an affirmative answer in *De l'Esprit* (1758), but he had presented an argument rather than a plan.

Rousseau began by rejecting existing methods as teaching, usually by rote, worn-out and corrupt ideas; as trying to make the child an obedient automaton in a decaying society; as preventing the child from thinking and judging for himself; as deforming him into a mediocrity and brandishing platitudes and classic tags. Such schooling suppressed all natural impulses, and made education a torture which every child longed to avoid. But education should be a happy process of natural unfolding, of learning from nature and experience, of freely developing one's capacities into full and zestful living. It should be the "art of training men":[41] the conscious guidance of the growing body to health, of the character to morality, of the mind to intelligence, of the feelings to self-control, sociability, and happiness.

Rousseau would have wanted a system of public instruction by the state, but as public instruction was then directed by the Church, he prescribed a private instruction by an unmarried tutor who would be paid to devote many years of his life to his pupil. The tutor should withdraw the child as much as possible from its parents and relatives, lest it be infected with the accumulated vices of civilization. Rousseau humanized his treatise by imagining himself entrusted with almost full authority over the rearing of a very malleable youth called Émile. It is quite incredible, but Rousseau managed to make these 450 pages the most interesting book ever written on education. When Kant picked up *Émile* he became so absorbed that he forgot to take his daily walk.[42]

If nature is to be the tutor's guide, he will give the child as much freedom as safety will allow. He will begin by persuading the nurse to free the babe from swaddling clothes, for these impede its growth and the proper development of its limbs. Next, he will have the mother suckle her child instead of turning it over to a wet nurse; for the nurse may injure the child by harshness or neglect, or may earn from it, by conscientious care, the love that should naturally be directed to the mother as the first source and bond of family unity and moral order. Here Rousseau wrote lines that had an admirable effect upon the young mothers of the rising generation:

> Would you restore all men to their primal duties?—begin with the mother; the results will surprise you. Every evil follows in the train of this first sin. . . . The mother whose children are out of sight wins scanty esteem; there is no home life, the ties of nature are not strengthened by those of habit; fathers, mothers, brothers, and sisters cease to exist. They are almost strangers; how should they love one another? Each thinks of himself.
>
> But when mothers deign to nurse their own children, there will be a reform in morals; natural feeling will revive in every heart; there will be no lack of citizens for the state; this first step will by itself restore mutual affection. The

> charms of home are the best antidote of vice. The noisy play of children, which we thought so trying, becomes a delight; mother and father . . . grow dearer to each other; the marriage tie is strengthened. . . . Thus the cure of this one evil would work a widespread reformation; nature would regain her rights. When women become good mothers men will become good husbands and fathers.[43]

These famous paragraphs made breast feeding by mothers part of the change in manners that began in the final decade of Louis XV's reign. Buffon had issued a similar appeal a decade before, but it had not reached the women of France. Now the fairest breasts in Paris made their debut as organs of maternity as well as bewitchments of sex.

Rousseau divided the educational career of his pupil into three periods: twelve years of childhood, eight of youth, and an indeterminate age of preparation for marriage and parentage, for economic and social life. In the first period education is to be almost entirely physical and moral; books and book learning, even religion, must await the development of the mind; till he is twelve Émile will not know a word of history, and will hardly have heard any mention of God.[44] Education of the body must come first. So Émile is brought up in the country, as the only place where life can be healthy and natural.

> Men are not made to be crowded together in anthills, but scattered over the earth to till it. The more they are massed together, the more corrupt they become. Disease and vice are the sure results of overcrowded cities. . . . Man's breath is fatal to his fellows. . . . Man is devoured by our towns. In a few generations the race dies out or becomes degenerate; it needs renewal, and is always renewed from the country. Send your children out to renew themselves; send them to regain in the open field the strength lost in the foul air of our crowded cities.[45]

Encourage the boy to love nature and the outdoors, to develop habits of simplicity, to live on natural foods. Is there any food more delectable than that which has been grown in one's own garden? A vegetarian diet is the most wholesome, and leads to the least ailments.[46]

> The indifference of children toward meat is one proof that the taste for meat is unnatural. Their preference is for vegetable foods, milk, pastry, fruit, etc. Beware of changing this natural taste and making your children flesh-eaters. Do this, if not for their health, then for the sake of their character. How can we explain away the fact that great meat-eaters are usually fiercer and more cruel than other men?[47]

After proper food, good habits. Émile is to be taught to rise early. "We saw the sun rise in midsummer, we shall see it rise at Christmas; . . . we are no lie-abeds, we enjoy the cold."[48] Émile washes often, and as he grows stronger he reduces the warmth of the water, till "at last he bathes winter and summer in cold, even in ice water. To avoid risk, this change is slow, gradual, imperceptible."[49] He rarely uses any headgear, and he goes barefoot all the year round except when leaving his house and garden. "Children should be accustomed to cold rather than heat; great cold never does them any harm if they are exposed to it soon enough."[50] Encourage the child's natural liking for activity. "Don't make him sit still when he wants to run about, nor run when he wants to be quiet. . . . Let him run, jump, and shout to his heart's content."[51] Keep doctors away from him as long as you can.[52] Let him learn by action rather than by books or even by teaching; let him do things himself; just give him materials and tools. The clever teacher will arrange problems and tasks, and will let his pupil learn by hitting a thumb and stubbing a toe; he will guard him from serious injury but not from educative pains.

Nature is the best guide, and should be followed this side of such injury:

> Let us lay it down as an incontrovertible rule that the first impulses of nature are always right. There is no original sin in the human heart. . . . Never punish your pupil, for he does not know what it means to do wrong. Never make him say, "Forgive me." . . . Wholly unmoral in his actions, he can do nothing morally wrong, and he deserves neither punishment nor reproof. . . . First leave the germ of his character free to show itself; do not constrain him in anything; so you will better see him as he really is.[53]

However, he will need moral education; without it he will be dangerous and miserable. But don't preach. If you want your pupil to learn justice and kindness, be yourself just and kind, and he will imitate you. "Example! Example! Without it you will never succeed in teaching children anything."[54] Here too you can find a natural basis. Both goodness and wickedness (from the viewpoint of society) are innate in man; education must encourage the good and discourage the bad. Self-love is universal, but it can be modified until it sends a man into mortal peril to preserve his family, his country, or his honor. There are social instincts that preserve the family and the group as well as egoistic instincts that preserve the individual.[55] Sympathy (*pitié*) may be derived from self-love (as when we love the parents who nourish and protect us); but it can flower into many forms of social behavior and mutual aid. Hence some kind of conscience seems universal and innate.

> Cast your eyes over every nation of the world, peruse every volume of its history; amid all these strange and cruel forms of worship, in this amazing variety of manners and customs, you will everywhere find the same [basic] ideas of good and evil. . . . There is, at the bottom of our hearts, an inborn principle of justice and virtue by which, despite our maxims, we judge our own actions, or those of others, to be good or evil; and it is this principle that we call conscience.[56]

Whereupon Rousseau breaks out into an apostrophe which we shall find almost literally echoed in Kant:

> Conscience! Conscience! Divine instinct, immortal voice from heaven; sure guide of a creature ignorant and finite indeed, yet intelligent and free, infallible, judge of good and evil, making man like to God! In thee consists the excellence of man's nature and the morality of his actions; apart from thee I find nothing in myself to raise me above the beasts—nothing but the sad privilege of wandering from one error to another by the help of an unbridled intellect and reason which knows no principle.[57]

So intellectual education must come only after the formation of moral character. Rousseau laughs at Locke's advice to reason with children:

> Those children who have been constantly reasoned with strike me as excep-
> tionally silly. Of all human faculties reason . . . is the last and choicest growth
> —and you would use this for the child's early training? To make a man reason-
> able is the coping stone of a good education, and yet you profess to train a
> child through his reason. You begin at the wrong end.[58]

No; we must, rather, retard mental education. "Keep the child's mind [in-
tellect] idle as long as you can."[59] If he has opinions before he is twelve you
may be sure they will be absurd. And don't bother him yet with science;
this is an endless chase, in which everything that we discover merely adds to
our ignorance and our foolish pride.[60] Let your pupil learn by experience
the life and workings of nature; let him enjoy the stars without pretending
to trace their history.

At the age of twelve intellectual education may begin, and Émile may read
a few books. He may make a transition from nature to literature by reading
Robinson Crusoe, for that is the story of a man who, on his island, went
through the various stages through which men passed from savagery to
civilization. But by the age of twenty Émile will not have read many books.
He will quite ignore the salons and the *philosophes*. He will not bother with
the arts, for the only true beauty is in nature.[61] He will never be "a musician,
an actor, or an author."[62] Rather, he will have acquired sufficient skill in some
trade to earn his living with his hands if that should ever be necessary. (Many
a tradeless émigré, thirty years later, would regret having laughed, as Voltaire did, at Rousseau's *"gentilhomme menuisier"*—gentleman carpenter.[63]) In
any case Émile (though he is heir to a modest fortune) must serve society
either manually or mentally. "The man who eats in idleness what he has not
earned is a thief."[64]

2. Religion

Finally, when Émile is about eighteen, we may talk to him about God.

> I am aware that many of my readers will be surprised to find me tracing the
> course of my scholar through his early years without speaking to him of reli-
> gion. At fifteen he will not even know that he has a soul; at eighteen he may
> not yet be ready to learn about it. . . . If I had to depict the most heartbreak-
> ing stupidity I would paint a pedant teaching children the catechism; if I
> wanted to drive a child crazy I would set him to explain what he learned in
> his catechism. . . . No doubt there is not a moment to be lost if we must de-
> serve eternal salvation; but if the repetition of certain words suffices to obtain
> it, I do not see why we should not people heaven with starlings and magpies as
> well as with children.[65]

Despite this proclamation, which infuriated the Archbishop of Paris, Rousseau now aimed his sharpest shafts at the *philosophes*. Picture Voltaire or
Diderot reading this:

> I consulted the *philosophes*. . . . I found them all alike proud, assertive, dog-
> matic; professing—even in their so-called skepticism—to know everything; prov-
> ing nothing, scoffing at one another. This last trait . . . struck me as the only
> point in which they were right. Braggarts in attack, they are weaklings in de-

fense. Weigh their arguments, they are all destructive; count their voices, each speaks for himself alone. . . . There is not one of them who, if he chanced to discover the difference between falsehood and truth, would not prefer his own lie to the truth which another had discovered. Where is the *philosophe* who would not deceive the whole world for his own glory?[66]

While he continued to condemn intolerance, Rousseau, reversing Bayle, denounced atheism as more dangerous than fanaticism. He offered to his readers a "profession of faith" by which he hoped to turn the tide from the atheism of d'Holbach, Helvétius, and Diderot back to belief in God, free will, and immortality. He remembered the two abbés—Gaime and Gâtier— whom he had met in his youth; he welded them into an imaginary vicar in Savoy; and he put into the mouth of this village curé the feelings and arguments that justified (in Rousseau's view) a return to religion.

The *vicaire savoyard* is pictured as the priest of a small parish in the Italian Alps. He privately admits to some skepticism: he doubts the divine inspiration of the Prophets, the miracles of the Apostles and the saints, and the authenticity of the Gospels;[67] and, like Hume, he asks, "Who will venture to tell me how many eyewitnesses are required to make a miracle credible?"[68] He rejects petitional prayer; our prayers should be hymns to the glory of God, and expressions of submission to His will.[69] Many items in the Catholic creed seem to him to be superstition or mythology.[70] Nevertheless he feels that he can best serve his people by saying nothing of his doubts, and practicing kindness and charity to all (believers and unbelievers alike), and performing faithfully all the ritual of the Roman Church. Virtue is necessary to happiness; belief in God, free will, heaven, and hell is necessary to virtue; religions, despite their crimes, have made men and women more virtuous, at least less cruel and villainous, than they might otherwise have been. When these religions preach doctrines that seem unreasonable, or weary us with ceremony, we should silence our doubts for the sake of the group.

Even from the standpoint of philosophy religion is essentially right. The Vicar begins like Descartes: "I exist, and I have senses through which I receive impressions; this is the first truth that strikes me, and I am forced to accept it."[71] He makes short work of Berkeley: "The cause of my sensations is outside of me, for they affect me whether I have any reason for them or not; they are produced and destroyed independently of me. . . . Thus other entities exist besides myself." A third step answers Hume and anticipates Kant: "I find that I have the power of comparing my sensations, so I am endowed with an active force" for dealing with experience.[72] This mind cannot be interpreted as a form of matter; there is no sign of a material or mechanical process in the act of thought. How an immaterial mind can act upon a material body is beyond our understanding; but it is a fact immediately perceived, and not to be denied for the sake of some abstract reasoning. Philosophers must learn to recognize that something may be true even if they cannot understand it—and especially when it is of all truths the one most immediately perceived.

The next step (the Vicar admits) is mere reasoning. I do not perceive

God, but I reason that just as in my voluntary actions there is a mind as the perceived cause of motion, so there is probably a cosmic mind behind the motions of the universe. God is unknowable, but I *feel* that He is there and everywhere. I see design in a thousand instances, from the structure of my eyes to the movements of the stars; I should no more think of attributing to chance (however often multiplied [à la Diderot]) the adjustment of means to ends in living organisms and the system of the world, than I would ascribe to chance the delectable assemblage of letters in printing the *Aeneid*.[73]

If there is an intelligent deity behind the marvels of the universe, it is incredible that He will allow justice to be permanently defeated. If only to avoid the desolating belief in the victory of evil, I must believe in a good God assuring the triumph of good. Therefore I must believe in an afterlife, in a heaven of reward for virtue; and though I am revolted by the idea of hell, and would rather believe that the wicked suffer hell in their own hearts, yet I will accept even that awful doctrine if it is necessary for controlling the evil impulses of mankind. In that case I would implore God not to make the pains of hell everlasting.[74] Hence the doctrine of purgatory, as a place of abbreviable punishment for all but the most persistent and unrepentant sinners, is more humane than the division of all the dead between the forever blessed and the eternally damned. Granted that we cannot prove the existence of heaven, how cruel it is to take from the people this hope that solaces them in their grief and sustains them in their defeats![75] Without belief in God and an afterlife morality is imperiled and life is meaningless, for in an atheistic philosophy life is a mechanical accident passing through a thousand sufferings to an agonizing and eternal death.

Consequently we must accept religion as, all in all, a vital boon to mankind. Nor need we make much account of the different sects into which Christianity has been torn; they are all good if they improve conduct and nourish hope. It is ridiculous and indecent to suppose that those who have other creeds, gods, and sacred scriptures than our own will be "damned." "If there were but one religion on earth, and all beyond its pale were condemned to eternal punishment, . . . the God of that religion would be the most unjust and cruel of tyrants."[76] So Émile will not be taught any particular form of Christianity, "but we will give him the means to choose for himself according to the right use of his reason."[77] The best way is to continue in the religion that we inherited from our parents or our community. And to Rousseau himself his imaginary Vicar's counsel is: "Return to your own country, go back to the religion of your fathers, follow it in sincerity of heart, and never forsake it; it is very simple and very holy; in no other religion is the morality purer, or the doctrine more satisfying to reason."[78]

Rousseau, in 1754, had anticipated this counsel—had returned to Geneva and its creed; however, he had not kept his promise to come and dwell there after settling his affairs in France. In the *Letters from the Mountain* which he wrote ten years later he repudiated, as we shall see, most of the faith of his fathers. In his final decade we shall find him advising religion to others, but giving hardly any sign of religious belief or practice in his daily life. Protestants and Catholics, Calvinists and Jesuits, joined in attacking him and his vicarious "Profession of Faith" as essentially un-Christian.[79] The education he proposed for Émile shocked Christian readers as in effect irreligious, for they suspected that an average youth brought up to no religion would not adopt one later except for social convenience. Despite his formal acceptance of Calvinism Rousseau rejected the doctrine of original sin and the redemptive role of the death of Christ. He refused to accept the Old Testament as the word of God, and thought the New Testament "full of incredible things, things repugnant to reason,"[80] but he loved the Gospels as the most moving and inspiring of all books.

> Can a book at once so grand and so simple be the work of men? Is it possible that he whose history is contained therein is no more than a man? . . . What gentleness and purity in his actions, what a touching grace in his teachings! How lofty are his sayings, how profoundly wise are his sermons, how just and discriminating are his replies! What man, what sage can live, suffer, and die without weakness or ostentation? . . . If the life and death of Socrates are those of a philosopher, the life and death of Christ are those of a God.[81]

3. Love and Marriage

When Rousseau ended the fifty pages of the Savoyard Vicar and turned back to Émile, he faced the problems of sex and marriage.

Should he tell his pupil about sex? Not till he asks about it; then tell him the truth.[82] But do everything consistent with truth and health to retard sexual consciousness. In any case don't stimulate it.

> When the critical age approaches, present to young people such spectacles as will restrain rather than excite them sexually. . . . Remove them from great cities, where the flaunted attire and boldness of the women hasten and anticipate the promptings of nature, where everything offers to their view pleasures of which they should know nothing till they are of an age to choose for themselves. . . . If their taste for the arts keeps them in town, guard them . . . from a dangerous idleness. Choose carefully their company, their occupations, and their pleasures; show them nothing but modest and pathetic pictures, . . . and nourish their sensibility without stimulating their senses.[83]

Rousseau worried about the dire results of a practice about which he seems to have had firsthand experience:

> Never leave the young man night or day, and at least share his room. Never let him go to bed till he is sleepy, and let him rise as soon as he awakes. . . . If once he acquires this dangerous habit he is ruined. From that time forward body and soul will be enervated; he will carry to the grave the effects of . . . the most fatal habit which a young man can acquire.

And he lays down the law to his pupil:

> If you cannot master your passions, dear Émile, I pity you, but I shall not hesitate for a moment; I will not permit the purposes of nature to be evaded. If you must be a slave I prefer to surrender you to a tyrant from whom I may deliver you; whatever happens, I can free you more easily from slavery to women than from yourself.[84]

But don't let your associates tease you into a brothel! "Why do these young men want to persuade you? Because they wish to seduce you. . . . Their only motive is a secret spite because they see you are better than they are; they want to drag you down to their level."

It is better to marry. But whom? The tutor describes his ideal of a girl, a woman, and a wife, and strives to imprint that ideal upon Émile's mind as a guide and a goal in searching for a mate. Rousseau feared masculine, domineering, immodest women; he saw the fall of civilization in the rule of increasingly masculine women over increasingly feminine men. "In every land the men are the sort that the women make them; . . . restore women to womanhood, and we shall be men again."[85] "The women of Paris usurp the rights of one sex without wishing to renounce those of the other; consequently they possess none in their fullness."[86] They do these things better in Protestant countries, where modesty is not a jest among sophists but a promise of faithful motherhood.[87] A woman's place is in the home, as among the ancient Greeks; she should accept her husband as a master, but in the home she should be supreme.[88] In that way the health of the race will be preserved.

The education of girls should aim to produce such women. They should be educated at home, by their mothers; they should learn all the arts of the home, from cooking to embroidery. They should get much religion, and as early as possible, for this will help them to modesty, virtue, and obedience. A daughter should accept without question the religion of her mother, but a wife should accept the religion of her husband.[89] In any case let her avoid philosophy and scorn to be a *salonnière*.[90] However, a girl should not be suppressed into a dull timidity; "she should be lively, merry, and eager; she should sing and dance to her heart's content, and enjoy all the innocent pleasures of youth"; let her go to balls and sports, even to theaters—under proper supervision and in good company.[91] Her mind should be kept active and alert if she is ever to be a fit wife for a thinking man. And she "may be allowed a certain amount of coquetry" as part of the complex game by which she tests her suitors and chooses her mate.[92] The proper study of womankind is man.[93]

When this ideal of girlhood and womanhood has been fixed in Émile's hopes he may go out and seek a mate. He, not his parents or his tutor, shall make the choice, but he owes it to them, and to their loving care of him through many years, to consult them respectfully. You wish to go to the big city and look at the girls who are on display there? Very well; we shall go to Paris; you will see for yourself what these exciting demoiselles are. So Émile lives a while in Paris, mingles in "society." But he finds there no girl of the kind his sly tutor has described. "Then farewell, Paris, far-famed Paris, with all your noise and smoke and dirt, where the women have ceased to believe in honor and the men in virtue. We are in search of love, happiness, innocence; the farther we go from Paris, the better."[94]

And so tutor and pupil are back in the country; and lo, in a quiet hamlet far from the madding crowd they come upon Sophie. Here ("Book V")

Rousseau's treatise becomes a love story, idealized but delightful, and told with the skill of an accomplished writer. After those long discourses on education, politics, and religion he returns to romance, and while Thérèse is busy with housework he resumes his dreams of that gentle woman whom he has found only in scattered moments of his wanderings; and he names her from his latest flame.

This new Sophie is the daughter of a once prosperous gentleman who now lives in contented retirement and simplicity. She is healthy, lovely, modest, tender—and useful; she helps her mother with quick and quiet competence in everything; "there is nothing that she cannot do with her needle."[95] Émile finds reason to come again, and she finds reason for his further visits; gradually it dawns upon him that Sophie has all the qualities that his tutor pictured as ideal; what a divine coincidence! After several weeks, he reaches the dizzy height of kissing the hem of her garment. More weeks, and they are betrothed. Rousseau insists that this shall be a formal and solemn ceremony; every measure must be taken—by ritual and elsewise—to exalt, and fix in memory, the sanctity of the marriage bond. Then, when Émile trembles on the edge of bliss, the incredible tutor, throwing liberty and nature to the winds, makes him leave his betrothed for two years of absence and travel to test their affection and fidelity. Émile weeps and obeys. When he returns, still miraculously virginal, he finds Sophie dutifully intact. They marry, and the tutor instructs them on their duties to each other. He bids Sophie be obedient to her husband except in bed and board. "You will long rule him by love if you make your favors scarce and precious; . . . let Émile honor his wife's chastity without complaining of her coldness."[96] The book concludes with a triune victory:

> One morning . . . Émile enters my room and embraces me, saying, "My master, congratulate your son; he hopes soon to have the honor of being a father. What a responsibility will be ours, how much we shall need you! Yet God forbid that I should let you educate the son as well as the father; God forbid that so sweet and holy a task should be fulfilled by any but myself. . . . But continue to be the teacher of the young teachers. Advise and control us; we shall be easily led; as long as I live I shall need you. . . . You have done your duty; teach me to follow your example, while you enjoy the leisure you have earned so well.[97]

After two centuries of laudation, ridicule, and experiment, the world is generally agreed that *Émile* is beautiful, suggestive, and impossible. Education is a dull subject, for we remember it with pain, we do not care to hear about it, and we resent any further imposition of it after we have served our time at school. Yet of this forbidding topic Rousseau made a charming romance. The simple, direct, personal style captivates us despite some flowery exaltations; we are drawn along and surrender ourselves to the omniscient tutor, though we should hesitate to surrender our sons. Having extolled maternal care and family life, Rousseau takes Émile from his parents and brings him up in antiseptic isolation from the society in which he must later live. Never having brought up children, he does not know that the average child is by "nature" a jealous, acquisitive, domineering little thief; if we wait till he learns discipline without commandments, and industry without instruction, he will graduate into an indolent, shiftless, and anarchic misfit, unwashed, unkempt, and unbearable. And where shall we find tutors willing to give twenty years to educating one child? "That kind of care and attention," said Mme. de Staël (1810), ". . . would compel every man to devote his whole life to the education of another being, and only grandfathers would at last be freed to attend to their own careers."[98]

Probably Rousseau recognized these and other difficulties after he recovered from the ecstasy of composition. At Strasbourg in 1765 an enthusiast came to him bursting with compliments: "You see, sir, a man who brings up his sons on the principles which he had the happiness to learn from your *Émile*." "So much the worse, sir, for you and your son!" growled Rousseau.[99] In the fifth of his *Letters from the Mountain* he explained that he had written the book not for ordinary parents but for sages: "I made clear in the preface . . . that my concern was rather to offer the plan of a new system of education for the consideration of sages, and not a method for fathers and mothers."[100] Like his master Plato, he took the child away from the contagion of his parents in the hope that the child, graduating from a saving education, would then be fit to rear his own children. And like Plato, he "laid up in heaven a pattern" of a perfect state or method, so that "he who desires may behold it, and beholding, may govern himself accordingly."[101] He announced his dream, and trusted that somewhere, to some men and women, it would carry inspiration and make for betterment. It did.

CHAPTER VIII

Rousseau Outcast

1762–67

I. FLIGHT

IT is remarkable that a book containing, as did *Émile*, so open an attack upon all but the fundamentals of Christianity should have passed the censor and been printed in France. But the censor was the tolerant and sympathetic Malesherbes. Before allowing publication he urged Rousseau to delete some passages that would almost certainly rouse the Church to active hostility. Rousseau refused. Other heretics had escaped personal prosecution by using pseudonyms, but Rousseau bravely stated his authorship on the title pages of his books.

While the *philosophes* denounced *Émile* as further treason to philosophy, the prelates of France and the magistrates of Paris and Geneva condemned it as apostasy from Christianity. The anti-Jansenist Archbishop of Paris prepared for August, 1762, a powerful *mandemant* against the book. The pro-Jansenist Parlement of Paris was engaged in expelling the Jesuits; it wished, nevertheless, to display its zeal for Catholicism; the appearance of *Émile* offered an opportunity to strike a blow for the Church. The Council of State, at war with the Parlement, and unwilling to lag behind it in zeal for orthodoxy, proposed to arrest Rousseau. Getting wind of this, his aristocratic friends advised him to leave France at once. On June 8 Mme. de Créqui sent him an excited message: "It is only too true that an order has been issued for your arrest. In the name of God, go away! . . . The burning of your book will do no harm, but your person cannot stand imprisonment. Consult your neighbors."[1]

The neighbors were the Maréchal and Maréchale de Luxembourg. They feared involvement if Rousseau were arrested;[2] they and the Prince de Conti urged him to flee, and gave him funds and a carriage for the long ride across France to Switzerland. He yielded reluctantly. He commended Thérèse to the Maréchale's care, and left Montmorency on June 9. On that day a decree was issued for Rousseau's arrest, but it was executed with merciful tardiness, for many in the government were glad to let him escape. On that same day Maître Omer Joly de Fleury, brandishing a copy of *Émile*, told the Parlement of Paris

> That this work appears to have been composed solely with the aim of reducing everything to natural religion, and of developing that criminal system in the author's plan for the education of his pupil; . . .

That he regards all religions as equally good, and as all having their reasons in the climate, the government, and the character of the people; . . .

That in consequence he dares seek to destroy the truth of Sacred Scripture and the prophecies, the certitude of the miracles described in the Holy Books, the infallibility of revelation, and the authority of the Church. . . . He ridicules and blasphemes the Christian religion, which alone has God for its author. . . .

The author of this book, who has had the boldness to sign his name to it, should be arrested as soon as possible. It is important that . . . justice should make an example, with all severity, both of the author and of those who . . . have shared in printing or distributing such a work.

Thereupon the Parlement ordered that

the said book shall be torn and burned in the court of the Palace [of Justice], at the foot of the grand staircase, by the High Executioner; all those who have copies of the book shall deliver them to the Register, to be destroyed; no publisher shall print or sell or distribute this book; all sellers or distributors thereof shall be arrested and punished according to the rigor of the law; . . . and J.-J. Rousseau shall be apprehended and brought to the Conciergerie prison of the Palace.[3]

On June 11 *Émile* was "torn and burned" as ordered, but by June 11 Rousseau had reached Switzerland. "The moment I was in the territory of Bern I bade the postilion stop; I got out of my carriage, prostrated myself, kissed the ground, and exclaimed in a transport of joy: 'Heaven, protector of virtue, be praised; I touch a land of liberty!' "[4]

He was not quite sure. He drove on to Yverdon, near the south end of the Lake of Neuchâtel, in the canton of Bern; there he stayed for a month with his old friend Roguin. Should he seek a home in Geneva? But on June 19 the Council of Twenty-five, ruling Geneva, condemned both *Émile* and *The Social Contract* as

impious, scandalous, bold, full of blasphemies and calumnies against religion. Under the appearance of doubts the author has assembled everything that could tend to sap, shake, and destroy the principal foundations of the revealed Christian religion. . . . These books are so much the more dangerous and reprehensible as they are written in French [not in esoteric Latin], in the most seductive style, and appear over the name of "Citizen of Geneva."[5]

Accordingly the Council ordered both books to be burned, prohibited their sale, and decreed arrest for Rousseau should he ever enter the territory of the republic. The Genevan clergy made no protest against this repudiation of Geneva's most famous living son; doubtless they feared that any sympathy shown by them to the author of "The Savoyard Vicar's Profession of Faith" would confirm d'Alembert's revelation of their secret Unitarian sentiments. Jacob Vernes, Rousseau's friend of many years, turned against him and demanded a retraction. "If [Rousseau recalled] there was any rumor amongst the populace, it was unfavorable to me, and I was publicly treated by all the gossips and pedants like a pupil threatened with a flogging for not having recited his catechism rightly."[6]

Voltaire was touched by the situation of his rival. He had read *Émile;* his comments can still be seen on his copy in the Bibliothèque de Genève. In a letter of June 15 he had written of the book: "It is a hodgepodge of a silly wet nurse in four volumes, with forty pages against Christianity, among the boldest ever known. . . . He says as many hurtful things against the philosophers as against Jesus Christ, but the philosophers will be more indulgent than the priests."[7] In any case he admired the "Profession of Faith": "fifty good pages," he called them, but added: "it is regrettable that they should have been written by . . . such a knave [*coquin*]."[8] To Mme. du Deffand he wrote: "I shall always love the author of the 'Vicaire savoyard' whatever he has done, and whatever he may do."[9] When he heard that Jean-Jacques was homeless he cried out: "Let him come here [to Ferney]! He must come! I shall receive him with open arms. He shall be master here more than I. I shall treat him like my own son."[10] He sent this invitation to seven different addresses; it must have reached one address, for Rousseau later expressed regret that he had made no reply.[11] In 1763 Voltaire renewed the invitation; Rousseau declined it, and accused Voltaire of having incited the Council of Twenty-five to condemn *The Social Contract* and *Émile*. Voltaire denied this, apparently with truth.

Early in July, 1762, the Senate of Bern notified Rousseau that it could not tolerate his presence on Bernese soil; he must leave it within fifteen days or face imprisonment. Meanwhile he received a kindly note from d'Alembert advising him to seek domicile in the principality of Neuchâtel; this was under the jurisdiction of Frederick the Great, and was governed by Earl Marischal George Keith, who, said d'Alembert, "would receive and treat you as the patriarchs of the Old Testament received and treated persecuted virtue."[12] Rousseau hesitated, for he had spoken critically of Frederick as a tyrant in philosophic disguise.[13] Nevertheless, on July 10, 1762, he accepted the invitation of Roguin's niece, Mme. de La Tour, to occupy a house belonging to her in Môtiers-Travers, fifteen miles southwest of the city of Neuchâtel, in what Boswell was to describe as "a beautiful wild valley surrounded by immense mountains."[14] About July 11 Jean-Jacques appealed to the governor, and, with characteristic humility and pride, wrote to

> THE KING OF PRUSSIA:
> I have said a good deal that is bad about you; I shall probably say more such things; however, chased from France, from Geneva, from the canton of Bern, I have come to seek an asylum in your states. . . . Sir, I have not merited grace from you, and I do not ask any; but I have felt that I ought to declare to your Majesty that I am in your power, and that I have willed to be so. Your Majesty may dispose of me as you like.

At an uncertain date Frederick, still in the Seven Years' War, wrote to Keith:

> We must succor this poor unfortunate. His only offense is to have strange opinions which he thinks are good ones. I will send a hundred crowns, from which you will be kind enough to give him as much as he needs. I think he will accept them in kind more readily than in cash. If we were not at war, if we were not ruined, I would build him a hermitage with a garden, where he could live as I believe our first fathers did. . . . I think poor Rousseau has missed his vocation; he was obviously born to be a famous anchorite, a desert father, celebrated for his austerities and flagellations. . . . I conclude that the morals of your savage are as pure as his mind is illogical.[15]

The Marischal, whom Rousseau speaks of as a gaunt, aged, absent-minded saint, sent him provisions, coal, and wood, and proposed to "build me a little house." Jean-Jacques interpreted this offer as coming from Frederick, and refused it, but "from that moment I became so sincerely attached to him that I interested myself as much in his glory as until then I had thought his successes unjust."[16] On November 1, as the war was nearing its end, he wrote to Frederick prescribing the tasks of peace:

> SIRE:
>   You are my protector and my benefactor, and I have a heart made for gratitude; I want to acquit myself with you if I can.
>   You want to give me bread; is there none of your subjects who lacks it?
>   Take away from before my eyes that sword that flashes and wounds me. . . . The career of kings of your mettle is great, and you are still far from your time. But time is pressing; there is not a moment left you to lose. . . . Can you resolve to die without having been the greatest of men?
>   Could I ever be permitted to see Frederick the Just and Feared cover his states at last with a happy people whose father he would be, then Jean-Jacques Rousseau, the enemy of kings, would go to die of joy at the foot of his throne.[17]

Frederick made no known answer, but when Keith went to Berlin the King told him he had received a "scolding" from Rousseau.[18]

Apparently assured of a home, Jean-Jacques sent for Thérèse to join him. He was not certain that she would come, for he "had long perceived her affection to grow colder." He ascribed this to his having ceased to have sexual relations with her, since "a connection with women was prejudicial to my health."[19] Perhaps now she would prefer Paris to Switzerland. But she came. They had a tearful reunion, and looked forward at last to some years of peace.

II. ROUSSEAU AND THE ARCHBISHOP

Their next four years were their unhappiest. The Calvinist clergy of Neuchâtel publicly denounced Rousseau as a heretic, and the magistrates forbade the sale of *Émile*. Perhaps to appease them, or in sincere desire to follow the precepts of his "Vicar," Rousseau asked the pastor at Môtiers might he join the congregation. (Thérèse remained Catholic.) He was accepted, attended worship, and received Communion "with an emotion of heart, and my eyes suffused with tears of tenderness."[20] He gave a handle to ridicule by adopting Armenian costume—fur bonnet, caftan, and girdle; the long robe allowed him to conceal the effects of his urinary obstruction. He attended church in this garb, and wore it in visiting Lord Keith, who made no comment upon it except to wish him *salaam aleikum*. He continued to add to his income by copying music; now he added needlework, and learned to make lace. "Like the women, I carried my cushion with me when I made visits, or sat down to work at my door. . . . This enabled me to pass my time with my female neighbors without weariness."[21]

Probably about this time (late 1762) his publishers prevailed upon him to begin writing his *Confessions*. He had forsworn authorship, but this would not be authorship so much as a defense of his character and conduct against a world of enemies, and especially against charges of the *philosophes* and the gossip of the salons. Furthermore, he had to answer a great variety of correspondence. Women especially offered him the consoling incense of their adoration, and not only because of their sympathy with the hunted author of a famous romance, but because they longed to revert to religion, and saw in the Savoyard Vicar and his creator no real foe of faith but its brave champion against a desolating atheism. For such women, and several men, he became a father confessor, a director of souls and consciences. He advised them to remain in, or return to, the religion of their youth, regardless of all the difficulties that science and philosophy had suggested; those incredibilities were not of the essence, and might be silently put aside; what mattered was trust in God and immortality; with that faith and hope one could rise above all the unintelligible disasters of nature, all the pains and griefs of life. A young Catholic in rebellion against his religion asked for sympathy; Rousseau, forgetting his own rebellions, told him not to make so much ado about incidentals: "if I had been born Catholic I would have remained Catholic, knowing well that your Church puts a very salutary restraint upon the wanderings of human reason, which finds neither bottom nor bank when it would sound the abysses of things."[22] To nearly all these suitors for wisdom he advised a flight from the city to the country, from artifice and complexity to a natural simplicity of life, and a modest contentment with marriage and parenthood.

Women who had been shocked by worldly priests and agnostic abbés fell in love, if only through correspondence, with this unworldly heretic whom all the churches denounced. Mme. de Blot, titled and respected, exclaimed to a company of lords and ladies, "Only the loftiest virtue could keep a woman of true sensibility from devoting her life to Rousseau, if she were certain he would love her passionately."[23] Mme. de La Tour mistook some compliments in his letters for an avowal of love; she responded tenderly, warmly, effusively; she sent him her portrait, protesting that it did not do her justice; she grew despondent when he replied with the calmness of a man who had never seen her.[24] Yet other worshipers wished to kiss the ground he walked on; some raised altars to him in their hearts; some called him the reborn Christ. At times he took them seriously, and thought of himself as the crucified founder of a new faith.[25]

Amid these exaltations, and as if to confirm the analogy, a high priest of the Temple aroused the people to condemn him as a dangerous revolutionary. On August 20, 1762, Christophe de Beaumont, archbishop of Paris, issued a mandate to all priests in his diocese to read to their congregations, and to publish to the world, his twenty-nine-page denunciation of *Émile*. He was a man of rigorous orthodoxy and saintly repute; he had fought against the Jansenists, the *Encyclopédie*, and the *philosophes;* now it seemed to him that Rousseau, after apparently breaking away from the infidels, had joined them in attacking the faith upon which, in the Archbishop's view, rested the whole social order and moral life of France.

He began by quoting St. Paul's Second Epistle to Timothy: "There will come perilous days of men enamored of themselves, bold and proud blasphemers, impious calumniators swollen with arrogance, lovers of pleasure rather than God, men corrupt in spirit and perverse in faith."[26] Surely those times had come!

> Unbelief, emboldened by all the passions, presents itself under every form to adapt itself in some way to all ages, characters, and degrees. Sometimes . . . it borrows a style light, agreeable, and frivolous; hence so many tales, as obscene as they are impious [Voltaire's *romans*], amusing the imagination as a means of seducing the mind and corrupting the heart. Sometimes, affecting profundity and sublimity in its views, it pretends to go back to the first principles of knowledge, and to assume divine authority, in order to throw off a yoke which, they say, dishonors mankind. Sometimes it declaims like a raging woman against religious zeal, and yet with enthusiasm preaches universal toleration. And sometimes, uniting all these diverse manners of speech, it mixes the serious with the playful, pure maxims with obscenities, great truths with great errors, the Faith with blasphemy; in a word, it undertakes to reconcile light with darkness, Jesus Christ with Belial.[27]

This, said the Archbishop, was especially the method of *Émile*, a book full of the language of philosophy without being truly philosophy; replete with bits of knowledge which have not enlightened the author and must only confuse his readers; a man given to paradoxes of opinions and conduct, allying simplicity of manners with pomp of thought, ancient maxims with a madness of innovation, the obscurity of his retreat with the desire to be known by all the world. He denounces the sciences, and cultivates them; he praises the excellence of the Gospel, and destroys its teachings. He has made himself the Preceptor of the Human Race to deceive it, the Monitor of the Public to mislead the world, the Oracle of the Century to destroy it. What an enterprise![28]

The Archbishop was appalled by Rousseau's proposal to make no mention of God or religion to Émile before the age of twelve, or even eighteen. So, then, "all nature would in vain have declared the glory of their Creator," and all moral instruction would forfeit the support of religious faith. But man is not by nature good, as the author supposed; he is born with the taint of original sin; he shares in the general corruption of humanity. The wise educator—best of all, a priest guided by divine grace—will use every just means to nourish the good impulses in men, and to weed out the evil; therefore he will feed the child with "the spiritual milk of religion, that it may grow toward salvation"; only by such education can the child develop into a "sincere worshiper of the true God, and a faithful subject of the sovereign."[29] So much sin and crime survive even this assiduous instruction; imagine what they would be without it. A torrent of wickedness would engulf us.[30]

For these reasons, concluded the Archbishop,

> after having consulted several persons distinguished for their piety and wisdom, and having invoked the holy name of God, we condemn the said book as con-

taining an abominable doctrine subversive of natural law and the foundations of the Christian religion; as establishing principles contrary to the moral teaching of the Gospels; as tending to disturb the peace of states and lead the revolt against the authority of the sovereign; as containing a very great number of propositions false, scandalous, full of hatred against the Church and her ministers. . . . Therefore we expressly forbid each and every person in our diocese to read or keep the said book, under the penalties of the law.[31]

This mandate was printed "with the privilege of the King," and soon reached Môtiers-Travers. Rousseau, always resolving to write no more, decided to reply. Before he put down his pen (November 18, 1762) he had let his answer run to 128 pages. It was printed at Amsterdam in March, 1763, as *Jean-Jacques Rousseau, Citoyen de Genève, à Christophe de Beaumont, Archevêque de Paris*. It was soon condemned by the Parlement of Paris and the Council of Geneva. Attacked by both the leading religions of Europe, Rousseau retaliated by assailing them both; now the shy romantic who had disowned the *philosophes* repeated their arguments with reckless audacity.

He opened with a question that all opponents in the unending debate still ask of each other: "Why must I say anything to you, monseigneur? What common language can we speak, how can we understand each other?"[32] He regretted that he had ever written books; he had not done this till he was thirty-eight, and he had fallen into this error by the accident of noticing that "miserable question" of the Dijon Academy. The critics of his *Discourse* had led him to reply; "dispute led to dispute, . . . and I found myself, so to speak, becoming an author at an age when one usually abandons authorship"; from that time to this, "repose and friends have disappeared."[33] In all his career, he claimed, he had been

> more ardent than enlightened, . . . but sincere in everything; . . . simple and good, but sensitive and weak, often doing evil and always loving the good; . . . adhering rather to my sentiments than to my interests; . . . fearing God without fearing hell; reasoning on religion, but without libertinage; loving neither impiety nor fanaticism, but hating the intolerant more than the free-thinkers; . . . confessing my faults to my friends and my opinions to all the world.[34]

He mourned less the Catholic than the Calvinist condemnation of *Émile*. He who had proudly called himself *Citoyen de Genève* had fled from France hoping to breathe in his native city the air of freedom, and to find there a welcome that would console him for his humiliations. But now "what am I to say? My heart closes up, my hand trembles, the pen falls from it. I must be silent; . . . I must consume in secret the bitterest of my griefs."[35] Behold the man who, "in the century so celebrated for philosophy, reason, and humanity," dared to "defend the cause of God"—behold him "branded, proscribed, hunted from country to country, from refuge to refuge, without regard for his poverty, without pity for his infirmities"; finding asylum at last under "an illustrious and enlightened prince," and secluding himself in a little village hidden among the mountains of Switzerland; thinking at last to find obscurity and peace, but pursued even there by the anathemas of priests. This Archbishop, "a virtuous man, as noble in soul as in birth,"

should have reproved the persecutors; instead, he authorized them shame-
lessly, "he who should have pleaded the cause of the oppressed."[36]

Rousseau perceived that the Archbishop was particularly offended by the
doctrine that men are born good, or at least not evil; Beaumont realized that
if this were true, if man is not tainted at birth by inheriting the guilt of Adam
and Eve, then the doctrine of atonement by Christ would fall; and this doctrine was the very heart of the Christian creed. Rousseau answered that the
doctrine of original sin is nowhere clearly stated in the Bible. He realized that
the Archbishop was shocked by the proposal to defer religious instruction;
he replied that the education of children by nuns and priests had not lessened
sin or crime; those pupils, grown up, had lost their fear of hell, and preferred
a small pleasure at hand to all Paradise in promise; and those priests themselves—were they models of virtue in contemporary France?[37] Nevertheless,
"I am a Christian, sincerely Christian, according to the doctrine of the Gospel; not a Christian as a disciple of the priests, but as a disciple of Jesus
Christ." Then, with an eye on Geneva, Rousseau added: "Happy to have
been born in the holiest and most reasonable religion on the earth, I remain
inviolably attached to the faith of my fathers. Like them, I take Scripture
and reason as the sole rules of my belief."[38] He felt the reproach of those who
told him that "though all men of intelligence think as you do, it is not good
that the commonalty [*le vulgaire*] should think so."

> This is what they cry out to me on every side; this perhaps is what you your-
> self would tell me if we two were alone in your study. Such are men; they
> change their language with their clothes; they speak the truth only in their
> dressing gowns; in their public dress they know only how to lie. And not only
> are they deceivers and impostors in the face of mankind, but they are not
> ashamed to punish, against their own conscience, whoever refuses to be public
> cheats and liars like themselves.[39]

This difference between what we believe and what we preach is at the heart
of the corruption in modern civilization. There are prejudices which we
should respect, but not if they turn education into a massive deception and
undermine the moral basis of society.[40] And if those prejudices become murderous shall we still be silent about their crimes?

> I do not say, nor do I think, that there is no good religion, . . . but I do say
> . . . that there is none, among those which have been dominant, that has not
> inflicted cruel wounds upon humanity. All sects have tormented others, all
> have offered to God the sacrifice of human blood. Whatever may be the source
> of these contradictions, they exist; is it a crime to wish to remove them?[41]

Toward the end of his reply Rousseau defended his *Émile* lovingly, and
wondered why no statue had been raised to its author.

> Assuming that I have made some mistakes, even that I have always been
> wrong, is no indulgence due to a book in which one feels everywhere—even
> in its errors, even in the harm that may be in it—a sincere love of the good and
> a zeal for the truth? . . . A book which breathes only peace, gentleness, pa-
> tience, love of order, and obedience to the laws in everything, even in the mat-
> ter of religion? A book in which the cause of religion is so well established,
> where morals are so respected, . . . where wickedness is painted as folly, and

virtue as so lovable? . . . Yes, I do not fear to say it: if there were in Europe a single government truly enlightened, . . . it would render public honors to the author of *Émile*, it would raise statues to him. I know men too well to expect such recognition; I did not know them well enough to expect that which they have done.[42]

They have raised statues to him.

III. ROUSSEAU AND THE CALVINISTS

The *Letter to Christophe Beaumont* pleased only a few freethinkers in France and a few political rebels in Switzerland. Of twenty-three "refutations" addressed to the author, nearly all were from Protestants. The Calvinist clergy of Geneva saw in the *Letter* an attack upon miracles and Biblical inspiration; to condone such heresies would be to invite again the danger to which they had been exposed by d'Alembert. Angry at the failure of Genevan liberals to speak out in his defense, Rousseau (May 12, 1763) sent to the Grand Council of Geneva a renunciation of his citizenship.

This action won some audible support. On June 18 a delegation submitted to the First Syndic of the republic a "Very Humble and Respectful Representation of Citizens and Burghers of Geneva," which, among other grievances, complained that the judgment against Rousseau had been illegal, and that the confiscation of copies of *Émile* from Genevan bookstores had invaded property rights. The Council of Twenty-five rejected the protest, and in September the public prosecutor, Jean-Robert Tronchin (cousin of Voltaire's doctor) issued *Lettres écrites de la campagne*, defending the disputed actions of the Council. The "Représentants" appealed to Rousseau to answer Tronchin. Never willing to let bad enough alone, Rousseau published (December, 1764) nine *Lettres écrites de la montagne*—a retort from his mountain home to the oligarchy of the Genevan plain. Furious against clergy as well as Council, he attacked Calvinism as well as Catholicism, and burned nearly all his bridges behind him.

Formally he addressed the letters to the leader of the Représentants. He began by dealing with the harm done to himself through the hasty condemnation of his books and his person, without any opportunity for defense. He admitted the imperfections of his books: "I myself have found a great number of errors in them; I doubt not that others may see many more, and that there are still others that neither I nor others have perceived. . . . After having heard both parties the public will judge; . . . the book will triumph or fall, and the case is closed."[43] But was the book "pernicious"? Could anyone read *La Nouvelle Héloïse* and the "Profession de foi du vicaire savoyard" and really believe that their author intended to destroy religion? True, these writings sought to destroy superstition as "the most terrible plague of mankind, the sorrow of sages and the tool of tyranny";[44] but did they not affirm the necessity of religion? The author is accused of not believing in Christ; he believes in Christ, but in a different way from his accusers:

> We recognize the authority of Jesus Christ because our intelligence agrees with his precepts and we find them sublime. . . . We admit revelation as emanating from the Spirit of God, without our knowing how. . . . Recognizing a divine authority in the Gospel, we believe that Jesus Christ was clothed with this authority; we recognize a more than human virtue in his conduct, and a more than human wisdom in his teaching.

The second letter (forgetting *The Social Contract*) denied the right of a civic council to judge in matters of religion. A basic principle of the Protestant Reformation, the right of the individual to interpret Scripture for himself, had been violated in condemning *Émile*.[45] "If you prove to me today that in matters of faith I am obliged to submit to the decisions of someone else, tomorrow I shall become a Catholic."[46] Rousseau admitted that the Reformers in their turn had become persecutors of individual interpretation,[47] but this did not invalidate the principle without which the Protestant revolt against the papal authority would have been unjust. He accused the Calvinist clergy ("except my pastor") of taking over the intolerant spirit of Catholicism; if they had been true to the spirit of the Reformation they would have defended his right to publish his own interpretation of the Bible. He now had a good word to say for d'Alembert's view of the Genevan clergy:

> A philosopher casts a quick glance upon them; he penetrates them, sees that they are Arians, Socinians; he says so, and thinks to do them honor; but he does not see that he is endangering their temporal interests—the only matter that generally determines, here below, the faith of men.[48]

In his third letter he took up the charge that he had rejected miracles. If we define a miracle as a violation of the laws of nature we can never know if anything is a miracle, for we do not know all the laws of nature.[49] Even then every day saw a new "miracle" achieved by science, not in contravention, but through greater knowledge, of nature's laws. "Anciently the Prophets made fire descend from the sky at their word; today children do as much with a little piece of [burning] glass." Joshua made the sun stop; any almanac maker can promise the same result by calculating a solar eclipse.[50] And as Europeans who perform such wonders among barbarians are thought by these to be gods, so the "miracles" of the past—even those of Jesus—may have been natural results misinterpreted by the populace as divine interruptions of natural law.[51] Perhaps Lazarus, whom Christ raised from the dead, had not really been dead. — Besides, how can the "miracles" of a teacher prove the truth of his doctrine when teachers of doctrines generally considered false have performed "miracles" reported as equally real, as when the magicians of Egypt rivaled Aaron in turning wands into serpents?[52] Christ warned against "false Christs" who "shall show great signs as wonders."[53]

Rousseau had begun his letters with a view to helping the middle-class Représentants; he made no plea for the further extension of the franchise in a democratic direction. Indeed, in Letter vi he again committed himself to an elected "aristocracy" as the best form of government, and he assured the rulers of Geneva that the ideal which he had sketched in *The Social Contract* was essentially one with the Genevan constitution.[54] But in Letter vii he told his friends of the protesting bourgeoisie that that constitution acknowledged the sovereignty of the enfranchised citizens only during the elections to the General Council and its annual assembly; for the remainder of the year the citizens were powerless.[55] In all that long interval the small Council of Twenty-five was the "supreme arbiter of the laws, and thereby of the fate of all individuals." In effect the *citoyens et bourgeois*, who appeared sovereign in the Conseil Général, became, after its adjournment, "the slaves of a despotic power, delivered defenseless to the mercy of twenty-five despots."[56] This was almost a call to revolution. However, Rousseau deprecated such a last resort. In his final letter he praised the bourgeoisie as the sanest and most peace-loving class in the state, caught between an opulent and oppressive patriciate and a "brutish and stupid populace";[57] but he advised the Représentants to keep their patience and trust to justice and time to right their wrongs.

The *Lettres de la montagne* offended Rousseau's enemies and displeased his friends. The Genevan clergy were alarmed by his heresies, and still more by his claim that they shared them. Now he turned violently against the Calvinist ministers, called them "canaille, swindlers, stupid courtiers, mad wolves," and expressed preference for the simple Catholic priests of the French villages and towns.[58] The Représentants made no use of the *Letters* in their successful campaign for more political power; they considered Rousseau a dangerous and incalculable ally. He resolved to take no further part in Genevan politics.

IV. ROUSSEAU AND VOLTAIRE

He had wondered, in Letter v, why "M. de Voltaire," whom the Genevan councilors "so often visit," had not "inspired them with that spirit of tolerance which he preaches without cease, and of which he sometimes has need." And he put into Voltaire's mouth an imaginary speech[59] favoring freedom of speech for philosophers on the ground that only a negligible few read them. The imitation of Voltaire's light and graceful manner was excellent. But the sage of Ferney was represented as avowing his authorship of a recently published *Sermon des cinquantes* (*Sermon of the Fifty*), whose paternity Voltaire had repeatedly denied—for it was heavy with heresies. We do not know whether Rousseau's revelation of the secret was deliberate and malicious; Voltaire thought so, and was furious, for it subjected him to the possibility of renewed expulsion from France just as he was settling into Ferney.

"The miscreant!" he exclaimed when he read the telltale letter. "The monster! I must have him cudgeled—yes, I will have him cudgeled in his mountains at the knees of his nurse!"

"Pray calm yourself," said a bystander, "for I know that Rousseau means to pay you a visit, and will very shortly be at Ferney."

"Ah, only let him come!" cried Voltaire, apparently meditating mayhem.

"But how will you receive him?"

"I will give him supper, put him into my own bed, and say, 'There is a good supper; this is the best bed in the house; do me the pleasure to accept one and the other, and to make yourself happy here.' "[60]

But Rousseau did not come. Voltaire revenged himself by issuing (December 31, 1764) an anonymous pamphlet, *Sentiments des citoyens* (*Feelings of the Citizens*), which is one of the blackest marks on his character and career. It must be quoted to be believed.

> We take pity on a fool, but when his dementia becomes fury we tie him up. Tolerance, which is a virtue, then becomes a vice. . . . We pardoned this man's romances, in which decency and modesty are as damaged as good sense. . . . When he mixed religion with his fiction, our magistrates were of necessity obliged to imitate those of Paris . . . and Bern. . . . Today is not patience exhausted when he publishes a new book wherein he outrages with fury the Christian religion, the Reformation that he professes, all the ministers of the Holy Gospel, and all the agencies of the state? . . . He says clearly, in his own name, "There are no miracles in the Gospel which we can take literally without abandoning good sense." . . .
>
> Is he a scholar who debates with scholars? No, . . . he is a man who still carries the tragic marks of his debauches, and who . . . drags along with him from town to town, and from mountain to mountain, the unhappy woman whose mother he made die, and whose children he exposed at the door of a hospital, . . . abjuring all the feelings of nature, as he discards those of honor and religion. . . .
>
> Does he wish to overthrow our constitution by disfiguring it, as he wishes to overthrow the Christianity that he professes? It suffices to warn him that the city which he troubles disavows him. . . . If he thought that we would draw the sword [make a revolution] because of [the condemnation of] *Émile*, he can put this idea into the class of his absurdities and his follies. But he should be told that if we punish lightly an impious romance we punish capitally a vile traitor.[61]

This was a disgraceful performance, hardly to be excused by Voltaire's anger, ailments, and age. (He was now seventy.) No wonder Rousseau never believed (even today we can hardly believe) that Voltaire wrote it; he ascribed it instead to the Genevan minister Vernes, who protested in vain that he was not the author. Rousseau, in one of his finest moments, published a reply to the *Sentiments* (January, 1765):

> I wish to make with simplicity the declaration that seems required of me by this article. No malady small or great, such as the author speaks of, has ever soiled my body. The malady that affects me has not the slightest resemblance to the one indicated; it was born with me, as those who took care of my childhood, and who still live, know. It is known to MM. Malouin, Morand, Thierry, Daran. . . . If they find in this [ailment] the least sign of debauchery, I beg them to confound me and shame me. . . . The wise and world-esteemed woman who takes care of me in my misfortunes . . . is unhappy only because she shares my misery. Her mother is in fact full of life, and in good health, despite her old age [she lived to be ninety-three]. I have never exposed, nor caused to be exposed, any children at the door of a hospital, nor anywhere else. . . . I will add nothing more . . . except to say that, at the hour of death, I would prefer to have done that of which the author accuses me, than to have written a piece like this.[62]

Though Rousseau's delivery of his children to a foundling asylum (not quite precisely their "exposure") had been known to Paris gossip (he had admitted it to the Maréchale de Luxembourg), Voltaire's pamphlet was the first public disclosure. Jean-Jacques suspected Mme. d'Épinay of having revealed it on her visit to Geneva. Now he was convinced that she and Grimm and Diderot were conspiring to blacken his reputation. Grimm at this time repeatedly attacked Rousseau in the *Correspondance littéraire,*[63] and in his letter of January 15, 1765, speaking of the *Letters from the Mountain,* he joined Voltaire in accusing Rousseau of treason: "If there be anywhere on earth such a crime as high treason, it is found surely in attacking the fundamental constitution of a state with the arms that M. Rousseau has employed to overthrow the constitution of his country."

The long quarrel between Voltaire and Rousseau is one of the sorriest blemishes on the face of the Enlightenment. Their birth and status set them far apart. Voltaire, son of a prosperous notary, received a good education, especially in the classics; Rousseau, born to an impoverished and soon to be broken home, received no formal education, inherited no classical tradition. Voltaire accepted the literary norms laid down by Boileau—"Love reason, let all your writings take from reason their splendor and their worth";[64] to Rousseau (as to Faust seducing Marguerite with Rousseau) "feeling is all."[65] Voltaire was as sensitive and excitable as Jean-Jacques, but usually he thought it bad manners to let passion discolor his art; he sensed in Rousseau's appeal to feeling and instinct an individualistic anarchic irrationalism that would begin with revolt and end with religion. He repudiated—Rousseau echoed—Pascal. Voltaire lived like a millionaire, Rousseau copied music to earn his bread. Voltaire was the sum of all the graces in society; Rousseau was ill at ease in social gatherings, and too impatient and irritable to keep a friend. Voltaire was the son of Paris, of its gaiety and luxuries; Rousseau was the child of Geneva, a somber and Puritan bourgeois resentful of class distinctions that cut him, and of luxuries that he could not enjoy. Voltaire defended luxury as putting the money of the rich in circulation by giving work to the poor; Rousseau condemned it as "feeding a hundred poor people in our towns, and causing a hundred thousand to perish in our villages."[66] Voltaire thought that the sins of civilization are outweighed by its comforts and arts; Rousseau was uncomfortable everywhere, and denounced almost everything. Reformers listened to Voltaire; revolutionists heard Rousseau.

When Horace Walpole remarked that "this world is a comedy to those who think, a tragedy to those who feel,"[67] he unwittingly compressed into a line the lives of the two most influential minds of the eighteenth century.

V. BOSWELL MEETS ROUSSEAU

We get an exceptionally pleasant picture of Jean-Jacques in Boswell's report of five visits to him in December, 1764. The inescapable idolator had solemnly sworn (October 21) "neither to talk to an infidel, nor to enjoy a

woman, before seeing Rousseau."[68] On December 3 he set out from Neuchâtel for Môtiers-Travers. At Brot, halfway, he stopped at an inn, and asked
the landlord's daughter what she knew about his prey. Her reply was disconcerting:

> "Monsieur Rousseau often comes and stays here several days with his house-
> keeper, Mademoiselle Levasseur. He is a very amiable man. He has a fine face.
> But he doesn't like to have people come and stare at him as if he were a man
> with two heads. Heavens! The curiosity of people is incredible. Many, many
> people come to see him, and often he will not receive them. He is ill, and doesn't
> wish to be disturbed."[69]

Of course Boswell went ahead. At Môtiers he put up at the village inn and

> prepared a letter to M. Rousseau, in which I informed him that an ancient Scots
> gentleman of twenty-four was come hither with the hopes of seeing him. I
> assured him that I deserved his regard. . . . Towards the end of my letter I
> showed him that I had a heart and soul. . . . The letter is really a masterpiece.
> I shall ever preserve it as proof that my soul can be sublime.[70]

His letter—in French—was a subtle mixture of deliberate naïveté and irresistible adulation:

> Your writings, Sir, have melted my heart, have elevated my soul, have fired
> my imagination. Believe me, you will be glad to have seen me. . . . O dear
> Saint-Preux! Enlightened Mentor! Eloquent and amiable Rousseau! I have a
> presentiment that a truly noble friendship will be born today. . . . I have
> much to tell you. Though I am only a young man, I have experienced a variety
> of existence that will amaze you. . . . But I beg you, be alone. . . . I know
> not if I would not prefer never to see you than to see you for the first time in
> company. I await your reply with impatience.[71]

Rousseau sent word that he might come if he promised to make his visit
short. Boswell went, "dressed in a coat and waistcoat, scarlet with gold lace,
buckskin breeches, and boots. Above all, I wore a greatcoat of green camlet
lined with foxskin fur." The door was opened by Thérèse, "a little, lively,
neat French girl." She led him upstairs to Rousseau—"a genteel black [dark-
complexioned] man in the dress of an Armenian. . . . I asked him how he
was. 'Very ill, but I have given up doctors.'" Rousseau expressed admiration
for Frederick, scorn for the French—"a contemptible nation," but "you will
find great souls in Spain." Boswell: "And in the mountains of Scotland."
Rousseau spoke of theologians as "gentlemen" who "provide a new explanation of something, leaving it as incomprehensible as before." They discussed
Corsica; Rousseau said he had been asked to draw up laws for it; Boswell
began his lasting enthusiasm for Corsican independence. Presently Rousseau
dismissed him, saying that he wished to go for a walk by himself.

On December 4 Boswell returned to the siege. Rousseau talked with him
for a while, then dismissed him: "You are irksome to me. It's my nature, I
cannot help it." Boswell: "Do not stand on ceremony with me." Rousseau:
"Go away." Thérèse saw Boswell to the door. She told him, "I have been
twenty-two years with Monsieur Rousseau; I would not give my place to be
queen of France. I try to profit by the good advice he gives me. If he should
die, I shall have to go into a convent."[72]

Boswell was at the door again on December 5. Rousseau sighed, "My dear sir, I am sorry not to be able to talk with you as I would wish." Boswell "waived such excuses," and stirred conversation by saying "I had turned Roman Catholic and intended to hide myself in a convent." Rousseau: "What folly!" . . . Boswell: "Tell me sincerely, are you a Christian?" Rousseau "struck his breast and replied, 'Yes, I pique myself on being one.' " Boswell (who suffered from melancholy): "Tell me, do you suffer from melancholy?" Rousseau: "I was born placid. I have no natural disposition to melancholy. My misfortunes have infected me with it." Boswell: "What do you think of cloisters, penances, and remedies of that sort?" Rousseau: "Mummeries, all of them." Boswell: "Will you, sir, assume [spiritual] direction of me?" Rousseau: "I cannot." Boswell: "I shall come back." Rousseau: "I don't promise to see you. I am in pain. I need a chamber pot every minute."[73]

That afternoon, in the *maison du village*, Boswell wrote a fourteen-page "Sketch of My Life," and sent it to Rousseau. It confessed one of his adulteries, and asked, "Is it possible for me yet to make myself a man?" He returned to Neuchâtel, but was back at Rousseau's door on December 14. Thérèse told him her master was "very ill." Boswell persisted; Rousseau received him. "I found him sitting in great pain." Rousseau: "I am overcome with ailments, disappointments, and sorrow. I am using a probe [a urethral dilator]. Everyone thinks it my duty to attend to him. . . . Come back in the afternoon." Boswell: "For how long?" Rousseau: "A quarter of an hour, and no longer." Boswell: "Twenty minutes." Rousseau: "Be off with you!" —but he could not help laughing.

Boswell was back at four, dreaming of Louis XV. "Morals appear to me an uncertain thing. For instance, I should like to have thirty women. Could I not satisfy that desire?" "No." "But consider, if I am rich, I can take a number of girls; I get them with child; propagation is thus increased. I give them dowries, and I marry them off to good peasants who are very happy to have them. Thus they become wives at the same age as would have been the case if they had remained virgins, and I, on my side, have had the benefit of enjoying a great variety of women." Then, having made no impression with this royal hypothesis, he asked, "Pray tell me how I can expiate the evil I have done?" Rousseau made a golden answer: "There is no expiation for evil except good."[74] Boswell asked Rousseau to invite him to dinner; Rousseau said, "Tomorrow." Boswell returned to the inn "full of fine spirits."

On December 15 he dined with Jean-Jacques and Thérèse in the kitchen, which he found "neat and cheerful." Rousseau was in good humor, with no sign of the mental disturbances that were later to appear. His dog and cat got along well together and with him. "He put some victuals on a trencher, and made his dog dance around it. He sang . . . a lively air with a sweet voice and great taste." Boswell talked about religion. "The Anglican Church is my choice." Rousseau: "Yes, but it is not the Gospel." "You have no liking for Saint Paul?" "I respect him, but I think he is partly responsible for muddling your head. He would have been an Anglican clergyman."

Mlle. Levasseur: "Shall you, sir, see Monsieur de Voltaire?" Boswell:

"Most certainly." Then to Rousseau: "Monsieur de Voltaire has no liking for you." Rousseau: "One does not like those whom one has greatly injured. His talk is most enjoyable; it is even better than his books." Boswell overstayed his welcome, but when he left, Rousseau "kissed me several times, and held me in his arms with elegant cordiality." When Boswell reached the inn the landlady said, "Sir, I think you have been crying." "This," he adds, "I retain as a true eulogium of my humanity."[75]

VI. A CONSTITUTION FOR CORSICA

Perhaps at Rousseau's prompting, Boswell, after visiting Voltaire at Ferney, went on to Italy, Naples, and Corsica. Corsica, under the leadership of Pasquale di Paoli, had freed itself from Genoese domination (1755). Rousseau, in *The Social Contract*, had hailed the birth of the new state:

> There is still one country in Europe open to the Lawgiver. It is the island of Corsica. The valor and firmness with which this brave people has shown itself able to regain and defend its freedom richly deserve the aid of some wise man who will teach them how to preserve it. I have a premonition that some day this little island will astonish Europe.[76]

Voltaire would have thought Rousseau the last man in Europe to be invited as a lawgiver; but on August 31, 1764, Jean-Jacques received the following letter from Matteo Buttafuoco, Corsican envoy to France:

> You mentioned Corsica, sir, in your *Contrat social*, in a way most flattering to our country. Such praise from a pen so sincere as yours . . . has suggested the strong wish that you could be the wise legislator who would assist the nation to maintain the liberties obtained at the cost of so much blood. I recognize, of course, that the task I dare press you to undertake needs a special knowledge of details. . . . If you deign to accept this charge, I would supply you with all the illumination necessary; and M. Paoli . . . will use his best endeavors to send you from Corsica all the information you may want. This distinguished chief, and indeed all my compatriots who have the advantage to know your works, share my desire, and the sentiments of respect that all Europe has for you, and which are due you on so many grounds.[77]

Rousseau's reply (October 15, 1764) accepted the assignment and asked for material illustrating the character, history, and problems of the Corsican people. He confessed that the task might be "beyond my power, though not beyond my zeal"; but "I promise you," he wrote to Buttafuoco on May 26, 1765, "that for the rest of my life I shall have no other interest but myself and Corsica; all other matters will be completely banished from my thoughts."[78] He began work at once on his *Projet de constitution pour la Corse*.

With the "social contract" in mind, Rousseau proposed that every citizen should sign a solemn and irrevocable pledge of himself—"body, goods, will, and all my powers"—to the Corsican nation.[79] He hailed the *braves Corses* who had won their independence, but he warned them that they had many vices—laziness, banditry, feuds, ferocity—mostly derived from hatred of their foreign masters. The best cure for these vices is a completely agricultural life. The laws should give every inducement to the people to remain on the land rather than gather in cities. Agriculture makes for individual character and national health; trade, commerce, finance open the doors to all sorts of chicanery, and should be discouraged by the state. All travel should be on foot or beast. Early marriage and large families are to be rewarded; men unmarried by the age of forty should lose their citizenship. Private property should be reduced, state property increased. "I should wish to see the state the sole owner, the individual taking a share of the common property only in proportion to his services."[80] If necessary, the population should be conscripted to till the lands of the state. The government should control all education, and all public morality. The form of government should model itself on the Swiss cantons.

In 1768 France bought Corsica from Genoa, sent in an army, deposed Paoli, and subjected the island to French law. Rousseau abandoned his *Projet*, and denounced the French invasion as violating "all justice, all humanity, all political right, all reason."[81]

VII. FUGITIVE

For two years Rousseau lived modestly and quietly at Môtiers, reading, writing, treating his ailment, suffering an attack of sciatica (October, 1764), and receiving courteously the visitors who passed Thérèse's scrutiny. One of these described him gratefully:

> You have no idea how charming his society is, what true politeness there is in his manners, what a depth of serenity and cheerfulness in his talk. Did you not expect quite a different picture, and figure to yourself an eccentric creature, always grave and sometimes even abrupt? Ah, what a mistake! To an expression of great mildness he unites a glance of fire, and eyes the vivacity of which was never seen. When you handle any matter in which he has taken an interest, then his eyes, his lips, his hands—everything about him—speak. You would be quite wrong to picture in him an everlasting grumbler. Not at all; he laughs with those who laugh, he chats and jokes with children, he rallies his housekeeper.[82]

But the local ministers had discovered the heresies in *Émile* and the *Letters from the Mountain*, and it seemed to them a scandal that such a monster should further contaminate Switzerland with his presence. To appease them he offered (March 10, 1765) to bind himself, by a formal document, "never to publish any new work on any topic of religion, never even to deal with it incidentally in any other new work; . . . and, further, I shall continue to testify, through my feelings and my conduct, to the great store I set on the happiness of being united with the church."[83] The Neuchâtel Consistory summoned him to appear and answer charges of heresy; he begged to be excused: "It would be impossible for me, in spite of all my good will, to suffer a long sitting"[84]—which was painfully true. His own pastor turned against him, and denounced him in public sermons as Antichrist.[85] The attacks of the clergy inflamed their parishioners; some villagers took to stoning Rousseau when he went out for a walk. About midnight of September 6–7 he and Thérèse were awakened by stones pelting their walls and breaking the windows; one large rock came through the glass and fell at his feet. A neighbor—a village official—summoned some guards to his rescue; the crowd dispersed; but Rousseau's remaining friends in Môtiers advised him to leave the town.

He had several offers of asylum, "but I was so attached to Switzerland that I could not resolve to quit it as long as it was possible for me to live there."[86] He had visited, a year before, the tiny Île de St.-Pierre, in the middle of the Lake of Bienne; there was but one house on the island—the home of the caretaker; here, thought Rousseau, was an ideal spot for an unpopular lover of solitude. It was in the canton of Bern, which had ejected him two years before, but he received informal assurances that he might move to the island without fear of arrest.[87]

And so, about the middle of September, 1765, after twenty-six months in Môtiers, he and Thérèse left the home that had become dear to them, and went to board with the caretaker's family in a place so isolated that "neither the populace nor the churchmen can trouble it."[88] "I thought I should in that island be more separated from men . . . and sooner forgotten by mankind."[89] To meet his expenses he gave the printer Du Peyrou the right to publish all his works, "and made him the depositary of all my papers, under the express condition of making no use of them until after my death, having it at heart to end my days quietly, without doing anything which would again bring me back to the recollection of the public."[90] He was offered an annuity of twelve hundred livres by Marischal Keith; he agreed to take half. He arranged another annuity for Thérèse. He settled down with her on the island, expecting nothing further of life. He was now fifty-three years old.

Thirteen years later—in the final year of his life—he composed one of his finest books, *Rêveries d'un promeneur solitaire*. It described with subdued eloquence his existence on the Island of St. Peter. "A delicious idleness was the first and principal enjoyment that I wished to taste in all its sweetness."[91] We have seen elsewhere how he admired Linnaeus; now, with one of the Swedish botanist's books in his hand, he began to list and study the plants on his little domain. Or on fair days, like Thoreau on Walden Pond,

> I threw myself alone into a boat which I rowed out to the middle of the lake when the water was calm. There, stretching myself out at full length in the boat, my eyes toward heaven, I let myself go and wander about slowly at the will of the water, sometimes for several hours, plunged into a thousand delightful reveries.[92]

Even on these waters he could not long rest. On October 17, 1765, the Senate of Bern ordered him to leave the island and the canton within fifteen days. He was bewildered and overwhelmed. "The measures I had taken to secure the tacit consent of the government, the tranquillity with which I

had been left to make my establishment, the visits of several people from
Bern," had led him to believe that he was now safe from molestation and
pursuit. He begged the Senate for some explanation and delay, and suggested a desperate alternative to banishment:

> I see but one resource for me, and however frightful it may appear, I will
> adopt it not only without repugnance, but with eagerness, if their Excellencies
> will be good enough to consent. It is that it should please them for me to pass
> the rest of my days in prison in one of their castles, or such other place in their
> estates as they may think fit to select. I will live there at my own expense, and
> I will give security never to put them to any cost. I submit to be without paper
> or pen, or any communication from without. . . . Only let me keep, with a
> few books, the liberty to walk occasionally in a garden, and I am content.

Was his mind beginning to break down? He assures us to the contrary:

> Do not suppose that an expedient so violent in appearance is the fruit of
> despair. My mind is perfectly calm at this moment. I have taken time to de-
> liberate, and it is only after profound consideration that I have brought myself
> to this decision. Mark, I pray you, that if this seems an extraordinary resolu-
> tion, my situation is still more so. The distracted life I have been made to lead
> for several years without intermission would be terrible for a man in full health;
> judge what it must be for a miserable invalid worn down with weariness and
> misfortune, and who has now no wish but to die in peace.[93]

The answer from Bern was an order to leave the island, and all Bernese territory, within twenty-four hours.[94]

Where should he go? He had invitations to Potsdam from Frederick, to
Corsica from Paoli, to Lorraine from Saint-Lambert, to Amsterdam from
Rey the publisher, and to England from David Hume. On October 22
Hume, then secretary to the British embassy in Paris, wrote to Rousseau:

> Your singular and unheard-of misfortunes, independent of your virtue and
> genius, must interest the sentiments of every human creature in your favor; but
> I flatter myself that in England you could find an absolute security against all
> persecution, not only from the tolerating spirit of our laws, but from the re-
> spect which everyone there bears to your character.[95]

On October 29 Rousseau left the Île de St.-Pierre. He arranged for Thérèse to remain for the time being in Switzerland; he himself moved on to
Strasbourg. There he stayed a full month, hesitating. Finally he decided to
accept Hume's invitation to England. The French government gave him a
passport to come to Paris. There Hume met him for the first time, and soon
became fond of him. All Paris talked about the exile's return. "It is impossible," wrote Hume, "to express or imagine the enthusiasm of this nation in
Rousseau's favor. . . . No person ever so much enjoyed their attention.
. . . Voltaire and everybody else are quite eclipsed."[96]

The new friendship was flawed at its birth. It is difficult here to determine
the facts with accuracy, or to report them impartially. On January 1, 1766,
Grimm sent to his clientele the following report:

> Jean-Jacques Rousseau made his entry into Paris on the 17th of December.
> The following day he promenaded in the Luxembourg Gardens in his Armenian

costume; as no one had been warned, no one profited by the spectacle. M. le Prince de Conti has lodged him in the Temple, where the said Armenian holds his court daily. He also promenades daily at an appointed hour on the boulevards near his residence.* . . . Here is a letter that went the rounds of Paris during his stay here, and which has had a great success.[98]

At this point Grimm transcribed a letter purporting to have come to Rousseau from Frederick the Great. It had been composed as a hoax on Rousseau by Horace Walpole. Let Walpole himself tell of it in his letter to H. S. Conway, January 12, 1766:

My present fame is owing to a very trifling composition, but which has made incredible noise. I was one evening at Mme. Geoffrin's joking on Rousseau's affectations and contradictions, and said some things that diverted them. When I came home I put them in a letter, and showed it next day to Helvétius and the Duc de Nivernois; who were so pleased with it that, after telling me some faults in the language, . . . they encouraged me to let it be seen. As you know, I willingly laugh at mountebanks, political or literary, let their talents be ever so great; I was not averse. The copies have spread like wildfire, *et me voici à la mode* [and behold, I am in fashion] . . . Here is the letter [literally translated from Walpole's French]:

"THE KING OF PRUSSIA TO M. ROUSSEAU: *My dear Jean-Jacques:*
You have renounced Geneva, your fatherland; you have had yourself chased from Switzerland, a country so much praised in your writings; France has issued a warrant against you. Come, then, to me; I admire your talents; I am amused by your dreams, which (be it said in passing) occupy you too much and too long. You must at last be wise and happy. You have had yourself talked of enough for peculiarities hardly fitting to a truly great man. Show your enemies that you can sometimes have common sense; this will annoy them without doing you harm. My states offer you a peaceful retreat; I wish you well, and would like to help you if you can find it good. But if you continue to reject my aid, be assured that I shall tell no one. If you persist in racking your brains to find new misfortunes, choose such as you may desire; I am king, and can procure any to suit your wishes; and—what surely will never happen to you among your enemies—I shall cease to persecute you when you cease to find your glory in being persecuted.

Your good friend,
FREDERICK."[99]

Walpole had never met Rousseau. His sophisticated intellect and inherited fortune found no sense in Jean-Jacques' writings. He knew of Rousseau's faults and follies from the dinners at Mme. Geoffrin's, where he met Diderot and Grimm. He probably did not realize that Rousseau, sensitive to the point of neurosis, had been brought near to mental collapse by a succession of controversies and tribulations. If Walpole knew this, his *jeu d'esprit* was disgracefully cruel. We should add, however, that when Hume asked for his advice in finding a retreat for Rousseau in England, Walpole undertook to provide the exile with every assistance.[100]

Did Hume know of this letter? Apparently he had been present at Mme. Geoffrin's when it was first concocted; he has been accused of "taking part"

---

* *Cf.* Rousseau to his friend de Luze: "I wish I could go and see you, but in order not to show off my Armenian cap in the streets, I am obliged to ask you to come to me."[97]

in its composition.[101] He wrote to the Marquise de Brabantane on February 16, 1766: "The only pleasantry I permitted myself in connection with the pretended letter of the King of Prussia was made by me at the dinner table of Lord Ossory."[102] On January 3, 1766, Hume made a farewell visit to the diners at Baron d'Holbach's. He told them of his hopes to free "the little man" from persecution, and to make him happy in England. D'Holbach was skeptical. "I am sorry," he said, "to dispel the hopes and illusions that flatter you, but I tell you it will not be long before you are grievously undeceived. You don't know your man. I tell you plainly, you're warming a viper in your bosom."[103]

The next morning Hume and Rousseau, with Jean-Jacques de Luze and Rousseau's dog Sultan, left Paris in two post chaises for Calais. Rousseau paid his own expenses, having refused offers by Hume, Mme. de Boufflers, and Mme. de Verdelin to supply him with funds. When they reached Dover (January 10), Rousseau embraced Hume, and thanked him for bringing him to a land of freedom.

VIII. ROUSSEAU IN ENGLAND

They arrived at London on January 13, 1766. Passers-by remarked Rousseau's costume—fur cap, purple robe, and girdle; he explained to Hume that he had an infirmity which made breeches inconvenient for him.[104] Hume persuaded his friend Conway to suggest a pension for the distinguished foreigner; George III agreed to one hundred pounds a year, and expressed a desire to get an informal glimpse of him. Garrick reserved for Rousseau and Hume a box at the Drury Lane Theatre opposite the royal box, for a night when the King and Queen were to attend. But when Hume called for Rousseau he had great difficulty in persuading him to leave his dog, whose howls at being locked up tore the exile's heart. At last "I caught Rousseau in my arms, and . . . partly by force, I engaged him to proceed."[105] After the performance Garrick gave a supper for Rousseau, who complimented him on his acting: "Sir, you have made me shed tears at your tragedy, and smile at your comedy, though I scarce understood a word of your language."

Altogether, Hume was thus far pleased with his guest. Soon after reaching London he wrote to Mme. de Brabantane:

> You have asked me my opinion of Jean-Jacques Rousseau. After having watched him in every aspect, . . . I declare that I have never known a man more amiable and virtuous. He is gentle, modest, affectionate, disinterested, of exquisite sensitivity. Seeking faults in him, I find none but extreme impatience, and a disposition to nurse unjust suspicions against his best friends . . . As for me, I would pass my life in his company without a cloud arising between us. There is in his manners a remarkable simplicity. In ordinary affairs he is a veritable child. This makes it easy . . . for those who live with him to govern him.[106]

And again:

He has an excellent warm heart, and in conversation kindles often to a degree of heat which looks like inspiration. I love him much, and hope to have some share in his affections. . . . The philosophers of Paris foretold to me that I could not conduct him to Calais without a quarrel; but I think I could live with him all my life in mutual friendship and esteem. I believe one great source of our concord is that neither he nor I are disputatious, which is not the case with any of them. They are also displeased with him because they think he overabounds in religion; and it is indeed remarkable that the philosopher of this age who has been most persecuted is by far the most devout.[107] . . . He has a hankering after the Bible, and is indeed little better than a Christian.[108]

But there were difficulties. As in Paris, so in London, lords, ladies, authors, commoners flocked to the house of Mrs. Adams, in Buckingham Street, where Rousseau had been lodged by Hume. Soon he wearied of these attentions, and begged Hume to find him a home away from London. An offer came to take care of him in a Welsh monastery; he wished to accept it, but Hume prevailed upon him to board with a grocer at Chiswick on the Thames, six miles from London. Thither Rousseau and Sultan moved on January 28. Now he sent for Thérèse, and troubled his host and Hume by insisting that she should be allowed to sit at table with him. Hume complained in a letter to Mme. de Boufflers:

M. de Luze . . . says that she passes for wicked and quarrelsome and tattling, and is thought to be the chief cause of his quitting Neuchâtel [Môtiers]. He himself owns her to be so dull that she never knows in what year of the Lord she is, nor in what month of the year, nor in what day of the month or week; and that she can never learn the different values of the pieces of money in any country. Yet she governs him as absolutely as a nurse does a child. In her absence his dog has acquired this ascendancy. His affection for that creature is beyond all expression or conception.[109]

Meanwhile Thérèse had come to Paris. Boswell met her there, and offered to escort her to England. On February 12 Hume wrote to Mme. de Boufflers: "A letter has come to me by which I learn that Mademoiselle sets out post in company with a friend of mine, a young gentleman, very good-humored, very agreeable, and very mad. . . . He has such a rage for literature that I dread some event fatal to our friend's honor."[110] Boswell claimed to have justified this premonition. According to pages, now destroyed,[111] in his diary, he shared the same bed with Thérèse at an inn on the second night out from Paris, and several nights thereafter. They reached Dover early on February 11. The diary proceeds: "Wednesday, 12 February: Yesterday morning had gone to bed very early, and had done it once; thirteen in all. Was really affectionate to her. At two [P.M.] set out on the fly." That same evening he took Thérèse to Hume in London, and promised her "not [to] mention *affaire* till after her death, or that of the philosopher." On the thirteenth he "delivered her over" to Rousseau. "*Quanta oscula*. He seemed so oldish and weak you [Boswell] had no longer your enthusiasm for him."[112] Naturally.

At Chiswick, as at Môtiers, Rousseau received more mail than he wished, and complained of the postage he had to pay. One day, when Hume brought him a "cargo" from London, he refused to take it, and bade him return it to the post office. Hume warned him that in that case the postal officials would open the rejected mail and learn his secrets. The patient Scot offered to open such of Rousseau's correspondence as came to London, and to bring him only so much as seemed important. Jean-Jacques agreed, but soon suspected Hume of tampering with his mail.

Invitations to dinner, usually including Mlle. Levasseur, came from notables in London; Rousseau refused them on the score of ill health, but probably because he was loath to reveal Thérèse to elevated company. He repeatedly expressed a wish to retire farther into the country. Hearing of this from Garrick, Richard Davenport offered him a home at Wootton in Derbyshire, 150 miles from London. Rousseau accepted gladly. Davenport sent a coach to transport him and Thérèse; Rousseau complained that he was being treated like a beggar, and he added to Hume: "If this be really a contrivance of Davenport's you are acquainted with it and consenting to it, and you could not possibly have done me a greater displeasure." An hour later (according to Hume),

> he sat suddenly on my knee, threw his hands about my neck, kissed me with the greatest warmth, and, bedewing all my face with tears, exclaimed: "Is it possible you can ever forgive me, dear friend? After all the testimonies of affection I have received from you, I reward you at last with this folly and ill behavior. But I have, notwithstanding, a heart worthy of your friendship; I love you, I esteem you; and not an instance of your kindness is thrown away upon me." . . . I kissed him and embraced him twenty times, with a plentiful effusion of tears.[113]

The next day, March 22, Jean-Jacques and Thérèse set off for Wootton, and Hume never saw them again. Soon afterward Hume wrote to Hugh Blair a perceptive analysis of Rousseau's condition and character:

> He was desperately resolved to rush into this solitude, notwithstanding all my remonstrances; and I foresee that he will be unhappy in that situation, as he has indeed been always in all situations. He will be entirely without occupation, without company, and almost without amusements of any kind. He has read very little in the course of his life, and has now totally renounced all reading; he has seen very little, and has no manner of curiosity to see or remark; . . . he has not, indeed, much knowledge. He has only felt, during the whole course of his life; and in this respect his sensibility rises to a pitch beyond what I have seen any example of, but it still gives him a more acute feeling of pain than of pleasure. He is like a man who were stript not only of his clothes but of his skin, and turned out in that situation to combat with the rude and boisterous elements, such as perpetually disturb this lower world.[114]

Rousseau and Thérèse arrived at Wootton on March 29. At first he was well pleased with his new home. He described it in a letter to a friend in Neuchâtel: "A solitary house, . . . not very large but very suitable, built halfway up the side of a valley"; before it "the loveliest lawn in the universe," and a landscape of "meadows, trees, or scattered farms," and, nearby, pleasant walks along a brook. "In the worst weather in the world I go tranquilly botanizing."[115] The Davenports occupied part of the house on their infrequent stops there, and their servants remained to take care of the philosopher and his "housekeeper." Rousseau insisted on paying Davenport thirty pounds a year for rent and service.

His happiness lasted a week. On April 3 a London journal, the *St. James Chronicle*, published in French and English the supposed letter of Frederick the Great to Rousseau, with no indication of the real author. Jean-Jacques was deeply hurt when he learned of this, and all the more when he found that the editor, William Strahan, had long been a friend of Hume. Moreover, the tone of the British press toward Rousseau had distinctly changed since his departure from Chiswick. Articles critical of the eccentric philosopher multiplied; some contained items which he thought only Hume knew and could have supplied; in any case, he felt, Hume should have written something in defense of his former guest. He heard that the Scot was living in London in the same house with François Tronchin, son of Jean-Jacques' enemy in Geneva; presumably Hume was now plentifully informed of Rousseau's faults.

On April 24 Rousseau wrote to the *St. James Chronicle* as follows:

> You have offended, sir, against the respect which every private person owes to a sovereign, by publicly attributing to the King of Prussia a letter full of extravagance and spite, which consequently you should have known could not have had this author. You have even ventured to transcribe his signature, as though you have seen it written by his hand. I inform you, sir, that this letter was fabricated in Paris; and what grieves and tears my heart especially is that the impostor who wrote it has accomplices in England. You owe it to the King of Prussia, to the truth, and also to me, to print this letter, signed by me, in reparation of an error which no doubt you would reproach yourself for having committed, did you know of what a wicked design you have been made the instrument. I offer you my sincere salutation.
>
> JEAN-JACQUES ROUSSEAU[116]

We can understand now why Rousseau thought there was a "conspiracy" against him. Who but his old foes, Voltaire, Diderot, Grimm, and other lanterns of the Enlightenment, could have engineered the sudden change of tone in the British press from one of welcome and honor to one of ridicule and belittlement? About this time Voltaire published, anonymously, a *Letter to Dr. J.-J. Pansophe*, reproducing the unfavorable references to the English people in Jean-Jacques' writings—that they were not really free, they cared too much for money, they were not "naturally good." The most damaging items in Voltaire's pamphlet were reprinted in a London periodical, *Lloyd's Evening News*.[117]

On May 9 Rousseau wrote to Conway asking that the pension offered him be withheld for the time being. Hume urged him to accept it; Rousseau replied that he could not accept any benefit obtained through Hume's mediation. Hume demanded an explanation. Brooding in his isolation, Rousseau seems now to have passed into a frenzy of suspicion and resentment. On July 10 he sent Hume a letter of eighteen folio pages, too long for total quotation, but so pivotal to a famous quarrel that some central passages must be borne in mind:

I am ill, sir, and little disposed for writing; but as you ask for an explanation, it must be given you. . . .

I live outside the world, and I remain ignorant of much that goes on in it. . . . I only know what I feel. . . .

You ask me, confidently, who is your accuser? Your accuser, sir, is the one man in the whole world whom . . . I would believe: it is yourself. . . . Naming David Hume as a third person, I will make you the judge of what I ought to think of him.

Rousseau acknowledged at length Hume's benefactions, but added:

As for the real good done me, these services are more apparent than weighty. . . . I was not so absolutely unknown that, had I arrived alone, I should have gone without help or counsel. . . . If Mr. Davenport has been good enough to give me this habitation, it was not to oblige Mr. Hume, whom he did not know. . . . All the good that has befallen me here would have befallen me in much the same way without him [Hume]. But the evil that has befallen me would not have happened. For why should I have any enemies in England? And how and why does it happen that these enemies are precisely Mr. Hume's friends? . . .

I heard also that the son of the mountebank Tronchin, my most mortal enemy, was not only the friend but the protégé of Mr. Hume, and that they lodged together. . . .

All these facts together made an impression upon me which rendered me anxious. . . . At the same time the letters I wrote did not reach their destination; those I received had been opened; and all these had passed through Mr. Hume's hands. . . .

But what became of me when I saw in the public press the pretended letter from the King of Prussia? . . . A ray of light revealed to me the secret cause of the astonishingly sudden change toward me in the disposition of the British public; and I saw in Paris the center of the plot which was being executed in London. . . . When this pretended letter was published in London Mr. Hume, who certainly knew that it was fictitious, said not one word, wrote to me nothing. . . .

There remains only one word for me to say to you. If you are guilty, do not write to me; it would be useless; be assured you would not deceive me. But if you are innocent deign to justify yourself. . . . If you are not—farewell forever.[118]

Hume replied briefly (July 22, 1766), not meeting the charges, for he had come to the conclusion that Rousseau was verging upon insanity. "If I may venture to give my advice," he wrote to Davenport, "it is that you would continue the charitable work you have begun, till he be shut up altogether in Bedlam."[119] Hearing that Rousseau had denounced him in letters to Paris (e.g., to the Comtesse de Boufflers, April 9, 1766), he sent to Mme. de Boufflers a copy of Jean-Jacques' long letter. She replied to Hume:

Rousseau's letter is atrocious; it is to the last degree extravagant and inexcusable. . . . But do not believe him capable of any falsehood or artifice; nor imagine that he is either an impostor or a scoundrel. His anger has no just cause, but it is sincere; of that I feel no doubt.

Here is what I imagine to be the cause of it. I have heard it said, and he has perhaps been told, that one of the best phrases in Mr. Walpole's letter was by you, and that you had said in jest, speaking in the name of the King of Prussia, "If you wish for persecutions, I am a king, and can procure them for you of any sort you like," and that Mr. Walpole . . . had said you were its author. If this be true, and Rousseau knows of it, do you wonder that, sensitive, hot-headed, melancholy, and proud, . . . he has become enraged?[120]

On July 26 Walpole wrote to Hume taking full blame—not expressing any repentance—for the false letter, and condemning Rousseau's "ungrateful and wicked heart";[121] but he did not deny that Hume had had a hand in the letter. Hume wrote to d'Holbach, "You are quite right; Rousseau is a monster," and withdrew the kindly words he had formerly used of Rousseau's character.[122] When he learned from Davenport that Jean-Jacques was writing *Confessions* he assumed that Rousseau would air his side of the affair. Adam Smith, Turgot, and Marischal Keith advised Hume to bear the attack in silence, but the *philosophes* of Paris, led by d'Alembert, urged him to publish his own account of a *cause* already *célèbre* in two capitals. So he issued (October, 1766) an *Exposé succinct de la contestation qui s'est élevée entre M. Hume et M. Rousseau*, which had been put into French by d'Alembert and Suard; a month later it appeared in English. Grimm gave its essence wide circulation in his subscription letter of October 15, so that the quarrel resounded in Geneva, Amsterdam, Berlin, and St. Petersburg. A dozen pamphlets redoubled the *bruit*. Walpole printed his version of the dispute; Boswell attacked Walpole; Mme. de La Tour's *Précis sur M. Rousseau* called Hume a traitor; Voltaire sent him additional material on Rousseau's faults and crimes, on his frequentation of "places of ill fame," and on his seditious activities in Switzerland.[123] George III "followed the battle with intense curiosity."[124] Hume sent the pertinent documents to the British Museum.[125]

Amid all this furor Rousseau maintained a somber silence. But he resolved now to return to France at whatever risk and cost. The damp climate of England, the reserve of the English character, depressed him; the solitude he had sought was greater than he could bear. Having made no attempt to learn English, he found it difficult to get along with the servants. He could converse only with Thérèse—who daily pleaded with him to take her to France. To further her plans she assured him that the servants were planning to poison him. On April 30, 1767, he wrote to his absent landlord, Davenport:

> Tomorrow, sir, I leave your house. . . . I am not unaware of the ambushes which are laid for me, nor of my inability to protect myself; but, sir, I have lived; it remains for me only to finish bravely a career passed with honor. . . . Farewell, sir. I shall always regret the dwelling which I leave now; but I shall regret even more having had in you so agreeable a host, and yet not having been able to make of him a friend.[126]

On May 1 he and Thérèse fled in haste and fear. They left their baggage behind, and money to pay for thirteen months' lodging. Unfamiliar with English geography, they took various circuitous conveyances, traveled part of the way on foot, and for ten days were lost to the world. The newspapers advertised their disappearance. On May 11 they turned up at Spalding in Lincolnshire. Thence they found their way to Dover, and there, on May 22, they embarked for Calais, after sixteen months in England. Hume wrote to Turgot and other friends,[127] asking them to help the outcast who, still technically under warrant of arrest, now returned desolate to France.

BOOK III

THE CATHOLIC SOUTH

1715–89

CHAPTER IX

Italia Felix

1715–59

I. THE LANDSCAPE

DIVIDED into a dozen jealous states, Italy could not unite for its own defense; the Italians were so busy relishing life that they allowed immature aliens to kill one another for the bitter fruit of politics and the tainted spoils of war. So the golden peninsula became the battleground of Bourbon Spain and France against Hapsburg Austria. A succession of wars of succession ended in 1748 with Spain again holding the kingdom of Naples and the duchy of Parma; the popes kept control of the Papal States; Savoy, Venice, and San Marino remained free; Genoa and Modena were French protectorates; Austria retained the Milanese and Tuscany. Meanwhile the sun shone, the fields, vineyards, and orchards gave food and drink, the women were beautiful and passionate, and arias filled the air. Foreigners came as tourists and students to enjoy the climate, the scenery, the theaters, the music, the art, and the society of men and women dowered with the culture of centuries. Half conquered, half despoiled, Italy, at least in the north, was the happiest country in Europe.

Its population stood at some fourteen millions in 1700, about eighteen millions in 1800. Less than half the land was arable, but of that half every square foot was tilled with patient labor and skillful care. Sloping terrain was terraced to hold the earth, and vines were hung from tree to tree, garlanding the orchards. In the south the soil was poor; there the sardonically smiling sun dried up the rivers, the earth, and man, and feudalism kept its medieval hold. A bitter proverb said that "Christ had never gotten south of Eboli"—which was just south of Sorrento. In central Italy the soil was fertile, and was tilled by sharecroppers under ecclesiastical lords. In the north— above all in the valley of the Po—the soil was enriched with irrigation canals; these required capital outlays and a peasantry disciplined to dredge the beds and shore the banks; here too the farmers tilled another man's land for a share in the crops. But in those teeming fields even poverty could be borne with dignity.

A thousand villages took form on the plains, in the hills, by the sea: dirty and dusty in the summer, noisy in the morning with talkative labor slowing its pace to the heat, silent at noon, alive in the evening with gossip, music, and amorous pursuits. More than money the Italians loved their midday siesta, when, said Père Labat, "one saw nothing in the streets but dogs, fools, and Frenchmen."[1] A hundred towns rich in churches, palaces, beggars, and art; half a dozen cities as beautiful as Paris; thousands of artisans still at the top of their craft. Capitalistic industry was again developing in textiles, especially in Milan, Turin, Bergamo, and Vicenza; but even in textiles most of the work was done at domestic looms as part of family life. A small middle class (merchants, bankers, manufacturers, lawyers, physicians, functionaries, journalists, writers, artists, priests) was growing up between the aristocracy (landowners and ecclesiastical hierarchy) and the "populace" (shopkeepers, artisans, and peasantry), but it had as yet no political power.

Class distinctions, except in Venice and Genoa, were not painfully pronounced. In most Italian cities the nobles entered actively into commerce, industry, or finance. The fact that any Italian peasant could become a bishop or a pope infused a democratic element into social life; at the court the possessor of an awesome pedigree rubbed elbows with a prelate of humble birth; in the academies and universities intellectual excellence outweighed the claims of caste; in the Carnival melee men and women, at ease behind their masks, forgot their social grades as well as their moral codes. Conversation was as gay as in France, except for a tacit agreement not to disturb a religion that brought international tribute to Italy, even—especially—from her conquerors.

There was nothing puritanic about that religion; it had made its peace with the nature of man and the climate of Italy. It allowed, in the carnivals, a moratorium on modesty, but it labored to preserve the institutions of marriage and the family against the credulity of women and the imagination of men. In the literate classes girls were sent to a convent at an early age—as early as their fifth year—not chiefly for education but for moral surveillance. The eager product was released only when a dowry had been raised for her, and some suitor, approved by her parents or guardians, was prepared to offer her marriage. Occasionally, if we may credit Casanova, a concupiscent nun could elude the mother superior—or the mother superior could elude her nuns—and find a way to meet a concupiscent male between dusk and dawn; but these were rare and perilous escapades. We cannot say as much for the morals of the monks.

Generally the unmarried male, if he could not seduce a wife, patronized prostitutes. The Comte de Caylus estimated eight thousand of them at Naples in 1714 in a population of 150,000. Président de Brosses, in Milan, found that "one cannot take a step in the public squares without encountering pimps [*courtiers de galanterie*] who offer you women of whatever color or nationality you may desire; but you may believe that the effect is not always as magnificent as the promise."[2] In Rome the prostitutes were excluded from the churches and public assemblies, and were forbidden to sell their charms during Advent or Lent, or on Sundays and holydays.

Their greatest cross was the accessibility of married women to illicit devotion. These revenged themselves on their guarded adolescence and unchosen mates by indulging in liaisons, and by adopting a *cavaliere servente*. This custom of *cicisbeatura*, imported from Spain, allowed a married woman, with her husband's consent and in his absence, to be attended by a "serving gentleman" who accompanied her to dinner, to the theater, to society, but rarely to bed. Some husbands chose *cavalieri serventi* for their wives to keep these from unlawful loves.[3] The wide circulation of Casanova's *Memoirs*, and the hasty reports of French travelers accustomed to French laxity, led to an exaggerated foreign conception of Italian immorality. Crimes of violence or passion abounded, but by and large the Italians were devoted children, jealous husbands, hard-working wives, and fond parents, living a united family life, and facing the tribulations of marriage and parentage with dignity, volubility, and resilient good cheer.

The education of women was not encouraged, for many men considered literacy dangerous to chastity. A minority of girls received in convents some instruction in reading, writing, embroidery, the arts of dressing and pleasing. Yet we hear of well-educated women conducting salons in which they conversed at ease with writers, artists, and men of affairs. In Palermo Anna Gentile translated Voltaire into good Italian verse, and published *Lettere filosofiche* in which she boldly defended the nonreligious ethics of Helvétius. At Milan Président de Brosses heard Maria Gaetana Agnesi, aged twenty, lecture in Latin on hydraulics;[4] she learned Greek, Hebrew, French, and English, and wrote treatises on conic sections and analytical geometry.[5] At the University of Bologna Signora Mazzolini taught anatomy, and Signora Tambroni taught Greek.[6] At that same university Laura Bassi received the doctorate in philosophy at the age of twenty-one (1732); she soon acquired such erudition that she was appointed to a professorship; she lectured on Newton's *Opticks*, and wrote treatises on physics; meanwhile she gave her husband twelve children, and educated them herself.[7]

The great majority in both sexes remained illiterate without social contumely. If a village lad showed an alert and eager mind the priest would usually find some way of getting him an education. Various religious "congregations" organized schools in the towns. The Jesuits had a great number of colleges in Italy—six in Venice, seven in the Milanese, six in Genoa, ten in Piedmont, twenty-nine in Sicily, and many in the kingdom of Naples and the Papal States. There were universities at Turin, Genoa, Milan, Pavia, Pisa, Florence, Bologna, Padua, Rome, Naples, and Palermo. All these were under control of Catholic ecclesiastics, but there were many laymen on the faculties. Teachers and students alike were sworn not to teach, read, say, or do anything contrary to the doctrine of the Roman Church. At Padua, says Casanova, "the Venetian government paid well-known professors very highly, and left the students absolute liberty to follow their lessons and lectures or not as they liked."[8]

In addition the Italian mind was stimulated by many academies devoted to literature, science, or art, and usually free from priestly control. Chief of these in fame was the Arcadian Academy, which was now in genteel decay. There were public libraries, like the beautiful Biblioteca Ambrosiana at Milan, or the Biblioteca Magliabechiana (now Nazionale) at Florence; and many private libraries, like that of the Pisani at Venice, were opened to the public on stated days of the week. De Brosses reported that the libraries of

Italy were more frequently and zealously used than those of France. Finally, there were periodicals of every sort—scholarly, literary, or humorous. The *Giornale dei letterati d'Italia*, established in 1710 by Apostolo Zeno and Francesco Scipione di Maffei, was one of the most learned and respected journals in Europe.

All in all, Italy was enjoying a lively intellectual life. Poets abounded, living from dedication to dedication; the air was powdered with lyrics still echoing Petrarch; *improvisatori* competed in spawning verses on the spur of the invitation; but there was no great poetry till Alfieri closed the century. There were theaters at Venice, Vicenza, Genoa, Turin, Milan, Florence, Padua, Naples, Rome; to these elegant structures the elite and the commonalty came to converse and ogle as well as to hear the opera or the play. There were great scholars like Maffei, industrious historians like Muratori; soon there would be great scientists. It was a slightly artificial culture, cautious under censorship, and too courteous to be brave.

Even so, some fitful breezes of heresy came over the Alps or the sea. Foreigners—chiefly Jacobite Englishmen—established in Genoa, Florence, Rome, and Naples, from 1730 onward, Freemason lodges with a tendency to deism. Popes Clement XII and Benedict XIV condemned them, but they attracted numerous adherents, especially from the nobility, occasionally from the clergy. Some books of Montesquieu, Voltaire, Raynal, Mably, Condillac, Helvétius, d'Holbach, and La Mettrie were imported into Italy. Editions of the *Encyclopédie*, in French, were published at Lucca, Leghorn, and Padua. In a modest degree, in a form available to persons who could read French, the Enlightenment reached Italy. But the Italian deliberately, and for the most part contentedly, refrained from philosophy. His bent and skill lay in the creation or appreciation of art and poetry or music; a tangible or visible or audible beauty seemed preferable to an elusive truth that was never guaranteed to please. He let the world argue while he sang.

II. MUSIC

Europe acknowledged the supremacy of Italian music, accepted its instruments and forms, welcomed its virtues, crowned its *castrati*, and surrendered to its melodious opera before, despite of, and after Gluck. Gluck, Hasse, Mozart, and a thousand others went to Italy to study its music, to learn the secrets of *bel canto* from Porpora, or to receive Padre Martini's accolade.

In Venice, said Burney, "if two persons are walking together arm in arm, it seems as though they converse only in song. All the songs there are duets."[9] "In the Piazza di San Marco," reported another Englishman, "a man from the people—a shoemaker, a blacksmith—strikes up an air; other persons of his sort, joining him, sing this air in several parts, with an accuracy and taste which one seldom encounters in the best society of our Northern countries."[10]

Lovers under a window plucked at a guitar or mandolin and a maiden's heart. Street singers carried their strains into coffeehouses and taverns; in the gondolas music caressed the evening air; salons, academies, and theaters gave concerts; churches trembled with organs and choirs; at the opera men melted and women swooned over some diva's or *castrato*'s aria. At a symphony concert given in Rome under the stars (1758) Morellet heard such exclamations as "*O benedetto! O che gusto! Piacer di morir!*—O blessed one! Oh, what delight! One could die of pleasure!"[11] It was not unusual, at the opera, to hear sobbing in the audience.

Musical instruments were loved with more than sexual fidelity. Money was lavished to make them objects of art, precisely fashioned in precious wood, inlaid with ivory, enamel, or jewelry; diamonds might be seen on harps or guitars.[12] Stradivari had left in Cremona pupils like Giuseppe Antonio Guarneri and Domenico Montagnana, who carried on the secret of making violins, violas, and violoncellos with souls. The harpsichord (which the Italians called *clavicembalo*) remained to the end of the eighteenth century the favorite keyboard instrument in Italy, though Bartolommeo Cristofori had invented the *piano-forte* at Florence about 1709. Virtuosi of the harpsichord like Domenico Scarlatti, or of the violin like Tartini and Geminiani, had in this age an international reputation. Francesco Geminiani was the Liszt of the violin, or, as his rival Tartini called him, Il Furibondo—"the madman" of the bow. Coming to England in 1714, he became so popular in the British Isles that he stayed there through most of his final eighteen years.

The rise of such virtuosi encouraged the production of instrumental music; this was the golden age of Italian compositions for the violin. Now—chiefly in Italy—overture, suite, sonata, concerto, and symphony took form. All of them stressed melody and harmony rather than the polyphonic counterpoint which was culminating and dying with Johann Sebastian Bach. As the suite grew out of the dance, so the sonata grew out of the suite. It was something sounded, as the cantata was something sung. In the eighteenth century it became a sequence of three movements—fast (allegro or presto), slow (andante or adagio), and fast (presto or allegro), with sometimes the interpolation of a scherzo ("joke") recalling the merry gigue, or a graceful minuet recalling the dance. By 1750 the sonata, at least in its first movement, had developed "sonata form"—the exposition of contrasting themes, their elaboration through variation, and their recapitulation toward the close. Through the experiments of G. B. Sammartini and Rinaldo di Capua in Italy, and of Johann Stamitz in Germany, the symphony evolved by applying sonata form to what had formerly been an operatic overture or recitative accompaniment. In these ways the composer provided pleasure for the mind as well as for the senses; he gave to instrumental music the added artistic quality of a definite structure limiting and binding the composition into logical order and unity. The disappearance of structure—of the organic relation of parts to a whole, or of beginning to middle and end—is the degeneration of an art.

The concerto (Latin *concertare*, to contend) applied to music that principle of conflict which is the soul of drama: it opposed to the orchestra a solo performer, and engaged them in harmonious debate. In Italy its favorite form was the *concerto grosso*, where the opposition was between a small orchestra of strings and a *concertino* of two or three virtuosi. Now Vivaldi in Italy, Handel in England, and Bach in Germany brought the *concerto grosso* to ever finer form, and instrumental music challenged the pre-eminence of song.

Nevertheless, and above all in Italy, the voice continued to be the favorite and incomparable instrument. There it had the advantage of a euphonious language in which the vowel had conquered the consonant; of a long tradition of church music; and of a highly developed art of vocal training. Here were the alluring prima donnas who yearly mounted the scales in weight and wealth, and the plump *castrati* who went forth to subdue kings and queens. These male sopranos or contraltos combined the lungs and the larynx of a man with the voice of a woman or a boy. Emasculated at the age of seven or eight, and subjected to a long and subtle discipline of breathing and vocalization, they learned to perform the trills and flourishes, the quavers and runs and breathtaking cadenzas, that sent Italian audiences into a delirium of approval, sometimes expressed by the exclamation *"Evviva il coltello!"* (Long live the little knife!)[13] The ecclesiastical opposition (especially at Rome) to the employment of women on the stage, and the inferior training of female singers in the seventeenth century, had created a demand which the little knife supplied by cutting the seminal ducts. So great were the rewards of successful *castrati* that some parents, with the victim's induced consent, submitted a son to the operation at the first sign of a golden voice. Expectations were often disappointed; in every city of Italy, said Burney, numbers of these failures could be found, "without any voice at all."[14] After 1750 the vogue of the *castrati* declined, for the prima donnas had learned to surpass them in purity of tone and rival them in vocal power.

The most famous name in eighteenth-century music was not Bach, nor Handel, nor Mozart, but Farinelli—which was not his name. Carlo Broschi apparently assumed the name of his uncle, who was already well known in musical circles. Born in Naples (1705) of pedigreed parentage, Carlo would not normally have entered the ranks of the unmanned; we are told that an accident that befell him while riding compelled the operation that resulted in the finest voice in history. He studied singing with Porpora, accompanied him to Rome, and appeared there in Porpora's opera *Eumene*. In one aria he competed with a flutist in holding and swelling a note, and so outpuffed him that invitations came to him from a dozen capitals. In 1727, at Bologna, he met his first defeat; he divided a duo with Antonio Bernacchi, acknowledged him as "King of Singers," and begged him to be his teacher. Bernacchi consented, and was soon eclipsed by his pupil. Farinelli now went from triumph to triumph in city after city—Venice, Vienna, Rome, Naples, Ferrara, Lucca, Turin, London, Paris. His vocal technique was a wonder of the age. The art of breathing was one secret of his skill; more than any other singer he knew how to breathe deeply, quickly, imperceptibly, and could hold a note while all musical instruments gave out. In the aria "Son qual nave" he began the first note with almost inaudible delicacy, expanded it gradually to full volume, and then reduced it by degrees to its first faintness. Sometimes an audience, even in staid England, would applaud this *curiosa felicitas* for five minutes.[15] He won his hearers also by his pathos, grace, and tenderness; and these qualities were in his nature as well as in his voice. In 1737 he made what he thought would be a brief visit to Spain; he remained in or near Madrid for a quarter of a century. We shall look for him there.

With *castrati* like Farinelli and Senesino, with divas like Faustina Bordoni and Francesca Cuzzoni, opera became the voice of Italy, and, as such, was heard with delight everywhere in Europe except in France, where it stirred a war. Originally *opera* was the plural of *opus*, and meant works; in Italian the plural became singular, still meaning work; what we now call opera was termed *opera per musica*—a musical work; only in the eighteenth century did the word take on its present meaning. Influenced by traditions of the Greek drama, it had been designed originally as a play accompanied by music; soon, in Italy, the music dominated the play, and arias dominated the music. Operas were planned to give display solos to each prima donna and each *primo uomo* in the cast. Between these exciting peaks the auditors conversed; between the acts they played cards or chess, gambled, ate sweets, fruit, or hot suppers, and visited and flirted from box to box. In such feasts the libretto was regularly drowned in an intermittent cascade of arias, duets, choruses, and ballets. The historian Lodovico Muratori denounced this submergence of poetry (1701);[16] the librettist Apostolo Zeno agreed with him; the composer Benedetto Marcello satirized this tendency in *Teatro alla moda* (1721). Metastasio for a time stemmed the torrent, but rather in Austria than in Italy; Jommelli and Traëtta struggled against it, but were repudiated by their countrymen. The Italians frankly preferred music to poetry, and took the drama as mere scaffolding for song.

Probably no other art form in history ever enjoyed such popularity as opera in Italy. No enthusiasm could compare with an Italian audience welcoming an aria or a cadenza by a singer of renown. To cough during such a ceremony was a social felony. Applause began before the familiar song was finished, and was reinforced by canes beating upon floors or the backs of chairs; some devotees tossed their shoes into the air.[17] Every Italian town of any pride (and which of them was without pride?) had its opera house; there were forty in the Papal States alone. Whereas in Germany opera was usually a court function closed to the public, and in England it limited its audience by high prices of admission, in Italy it was open to all decently dressed persons at a modest charge, sometimes at no charge at all. And as the Italians were devoted to the enjoyment of life, they insisted that their operas, however tragic, should have a happy ending. Moreover, they liked humor as well as sentiment. The custom grew to interpolate comic intermezzi between the acts of an opera; these interludes developed into a genus of their own, until they rivaled *opera seria* in popularity, and sometimes in length. It was an *opera buffa*—Pergolesi's *La serva padrona*—that charmed Paris in 1752, and was acclaimed by Rousseau as attesting the superiority of Italian music over French.

Buffa or *seria*, Italian opera was a force in history. As Rome had once conquered Western Europe with her armies, as the Roman Church had conquered it again with her creed, so Italy conquered it once more, with opera. Her operas displaced native productions in Germany, Denmark, England, Portugal, Spain, even in Russia; her singers were the idols of almost every European capital. Native singers, to win acceptance at home, took Italian names. That enchanting conquest will go on as long as vowels can outsing consonants.

III. RELIGION

After the prima donnas and the great *castrati*, the dominant class in Italy was the clergy. In their distinctive cassocks and under their broad-rimmed hats they walked or rode in proud freedom across the Italian scene, knowing that they dispensed the most precious boon known to humanity—hope. Whereas in France there was in this century approximately one ecclesiastic for each two hundred souls, in Rome there was one for fifteen, in Bologna one for seventeen, in Naples and Turin one for twenty-eight.[18] A contemporary Neapolitan, professedly orthodox, complained:

> So greatly have the clergy increased in number that the princes must either take measures to restrict them, or allow them to engulf the whole of the state. Why is it necessary that the smallest Italian village should be controlled by fifty or sixty priests? . . . The great number of campaniles and convents shuts out the sun. There are cities with as many as twenty-five convents of friars or sisters of St. Dominic, seven colleges of Jesuits, as many of Theatines, about twenty or thirty monasteries of Franciscan friars, and a good fifty others of different religious orders of both the sexes, not to speak of four or five hundred churches and chapels.[19]

Perhaps these figures were exaggerated for argument. We hear of four hundred churches in Naples, 260 in Milan, 110 in Turin; these, however, included small chapels. The monks were relatively poor, but the secular clergy, as a whole, possessed more wealth than the nobility. In the kingdom of Naples the clergy received a third of the revenues. In the duchy of Parma one half, in Tuscany almost three quarters, of the soil belonged to the clergy. In Venice, in the eleven years from 1755 to 1765, new legacies added 3,300,-000 ducats' worth of property to the Church.[20] Some cardinals and bishops were among the richest men in Italy, but cardinals and bishops were primarily administrators and statesmen, only occasionally saints. Several of them, in the second half of the century, renounced their wealth and luxury, and led lives of voluntary poverty.

The Italian people, barring a few publicists or satirists, made no significant protest against the wealth of the clergy. They took pride in the splendor of their churches, monasteries, and prelates. Their contributions seemed a small price to pay for the order that religion brought to the family and the state. Every home had a crucifix, and an image of the Virgin; before these the family—parents, children, and servants—knelt in prayer each evening;

what could replace the moral influence of those unifying prayers? The abstinence from meat on Fridays, and on Wednesdays and Fridays in Lent, was a wholesome discipline of desire—and was a boon to health and fishermen. The priests, who themselves knew the charms of women, were not too hard on sins of the flesh, and winked an eye at the laxities of Carnival. Even the prostitutes, on Saturdays, lit a candle before the Virgin, and deposited money for a Mass. De Brosses, attending a play in Verona, was astonished to see the performance stop when church bells rang the Angelus; all the actors knelt and prayed; an actress who had fallen in a dramatic faint rose to join in the prayer, and then fainted again.[21] Seldom has a religion been so loved as Catholicism in Italy.

There was another side to the picture—censorship and Inquisition. The Church demanded that every Italian, at least once a year, perform his or her "Easter duty"—go to confession on Holy Saturday, and receive Communion on Easter morn. Failure to do this brought—in all but the largest cities—priestly reproof; failure of private reproof and exhortation brought public listing of the recusant's name on the doors of the parish church; continued refusal brought excommunication and, in some towns, imprisonment.[22] The Inquisition, however, had lost much of its power and bite. In the larger centers ecclesiastical surveillance could be evaded, censorship was reduced, and there was a silent spread of doubt and heresy in the intelligentsia, even in the clergy themselves—for some of these, despite papal bulls, were secret Jansenists.

While many priests and monks led easy lives, and were no strangers to sin, there were also many who were faithful to their vows, and kept the faith alive by devotion to their tasks. New religious foundations testified to the survival of the monastic impulse. St. Alfonso de' Liguori, a lawyer of noble lineage, founded in 1732 the "Redemptorists"—i.e., the Congregation of the Most Holy Redeemer; and St. Paul of the Cross (Paolo Danei), who practiced the most severe asceticism, founded in 1737 the "Passionist Order"—i.e., the Clerks of the Holy Cross and Passion of Our Lord.

The Society of Jesus (the Jesuits) had in 1750 some 23,000 members, 3,622 of them in Italy, half of them priests.[23] Their power was quite out of proportion to their number. As confessors to kings, queens, and prominent families they often influenced domestic and international politics, and they were sometimes the most urgent force—next to the populace itself—in the persecution of heresy. Yet they were the most liberal of the Catholic theologians; we have seen elsewhere how patiently they sought a compromise with the French Enlightenment. A similar flexibility marked their foreign missions. In China they converted "several hundred thousands" to Catholicism,[24] but their intelligent concessions to ancestor worship, to Confucianism, and to Taoism shocked the missionaries of other orders; and these persuaded Pope Benedict XIV to check and reprove the Jesuits in the bull *Ex quo singulari* (1743). They remained nevertheless the most able and learned defenders of the Catholic faith against Protestantism and unbelief, and the most loyal supporters of the popes against the kings. In the conflicts of jurisdiction and power between the national states and the supernational Church, the kings saw in the Society of Jesus their subtlest and most persistent enemy. They resolved to destroy it. But the first act of this drama belongs to Portugal.

IV. FROM TURIN TO FLORENCE

Entering Italy from France by Mont-Cenis, we descend the Alps into "foot-of-the-mountain" Piedmont, and pass through vineyards, fields of grain, and orchards of olive or chestnut trees to two-thousand-year-old Turin, ancient citadel of the house of Savoy. This is one of the oldest royal families in existence, founded in 1003 by Umberto Biancamano—Humbert of the White Hand. Its head in this period was among the ablest rulers of the time. Victor Amadeus II inherited the ducal throne of Savoy at the age of nine (1675), took charge at eighteen, fought now for, now against, the French in the wars of Louis XIV, shared with Eugene of Savoy in driving the French from Turin and Italy, and emerged from the Treaty of Utrecht (1713) with Sicily added to his crown. In 1718 he exchanged Sicily for Sardinia; he took the title of King of Sardinia (1720), but kept Turin as his capital. He governed with brusque competence, improved public education, raised the general prosperity, and, after fifty-five years of rule, abdicated in favor of his son Charles Emmanuel I (r. 1730–73).

During these two reigns, covering almost a century, Turin was a leading center of Italian civilization. Montesquieu, seeing it in 1728, called it "the most beautiful city in the world"[25]—though he loved Paris. Chesterfield, in 1749, praised the court of Savoy as the best in Europe for forming "well-bred and agreeable people."[26] Part of Turin's splendor was due to Filippo Iuvara, an architect who still breathed the afflatus of the Renaissance. On the proud hill of Superga, towering 2,300 feet above the city, he built (1717–31) for Victor Amadeus II, to commemorate the liberation of Turin from the French, a handsome basilica in classic style of portico and dome, which for a century served as a tomb for Savoyard royalty. To the old Palazzo Madama he added (1718) a lordly staircase and massive façade; and in 1729 he designed (Benedetto Alfieri completed) the immense Castello Stupinigi, whose main hall displayed all the ornate splendor of baroque. Turin remained the capital of the Savoy dukes until, in their final triumph (1860 f.), they moved to Rome to become kings of united Italy.

Milan, long stifled by Spanish domination, revived under the milder Austrian rule. In 1703 Franz Tieffen, in 1746 and 1755 Felice and Rho Clerici, aided by the government, established textile factories that extended the replacement of handicrafts and guilds with large-scale production under capitalistic financing and management. — In the cultural history of Milan the great name was now Giovanni Battista Sammartini, whom we can still hear occasionally over the affluent air. In his symphonies and sonatas the contrapuntal solemnity of the German masters was replaced by a dynamic interplay of contrasted themes and moods. The young Gluck, coming to Milan (1737) as chamber musician to Prince Francesco Melzi, became the pupil and friend of Sammartini, and adopted his method of constructing an opera. In 1770 the Bohemian composer Josef Mysliveček, listening with the youthful Mozart to some of Sammartini's symphonies in Milan, exclaimed, "I have found the father of Haydn's style!"[27]—and therefore one of the fathers of the modern symphony.

Genoa had a bad eighteenth century. Its commerce had declined through the competition of the oceans with the Mediterranean, but its strategic location on a defensive hill overlooking a well-equipped port attracted the dangerous attention of neighboring powers. Placed between enemies without and an uneducated but passionate populace within, the government fell into the hands of old commercial families ruling through a closed council and an obedient doge. This self-perpetuating oligarchy taxed the people into a sullen and impatient poverty, and was in turn dominated and fleeced by the Banco di San Giorgio. When the allied forces of Savoy and Austria besieged Genoa in 1746 the government did not dare arm the people to resist, for fear they would kill the rulers; it preferred to open the gates to the besiegers, who exacted indemnities and ransoms that broke the bank. The commonalty, preferring indigenous exploiters, rose against the Austrian garrison, bombarded it with tiles and stones torn from roofs and streets, and drove it ignominiously out. The old tyranny was resumed.

The Genoese patriciate built new mansions like the Palazzo Deferrari, and shared with Milan in supporting a painter who has come to a second fame in our time. Almost every extant picture by Alessandro Magnasco strikes us with the dark originality of its style. *Punchinello Playing the Guitar*[28]—an elongated figure in careless patches of black and brown; the graceful *Girl and Musician before the Fire*,[29] *The Barber*,[30] apparently eager to cut his client's throat; the massive *Refectory of the Monks*,[31] attesting the culinary prosperity of the Church: all these are masterpieces, recalling El Greco in their gaunt forms and tricks of light, anticipating Goya in macabre exposure of life's cruelties, and almost modernistic in rough disdain of prim detail.

Florence in this age saw the end of one of history's most famous families. The prolonged reign of Cosimo III (1670–1723) as Grand Duke of Tuscany was a misfortune for a people still proud with memories of Florentine grandeur under the earlier Medici. Obsessed with theology, Cosimo allowed the clergy to govern him and draw from his ailing revenues rich endowments for the Church. Despotic rule, incompetent administration, and exorbitant taxation forfeited the popular support that the dynasty had enjoyed for 250 years.

Cosimo's eldest son, Ferdinand, preferred courtesans to courtiers, ruined his health with excesses, and died childless in 1713. Another son, "Gian" (John) Gastone, took to books, studied history and botany, and lived a quiet life. In 1697 his father forced him to marry Anne of Saxe-Lauenburg, a widow of unfurnished mind. Gian went to live with her in a remote Bohemian village, bore boredom for a year, then consoled himself with adulteries in Prague. When Ferdinand's health failed, Cosimo called Gian back to Florence; when Ferdinand died Gian was named heir to the grand-ducal crown. Gian's wife refused to live in Italy. Cosimo, fearing extinction of the Medici line, persuaded the Florentine Senate to decree that on the death of the childless Gian Gastone, Gian's sister Anna Maria Ludovica should succeed to the throne.

The European powers fluttered eagerly around the dying dynasty. In 1718 Austria, France, England, and Holland refused to recognize Cosimo's arrangement, and declared that on Gian's death Tuscany and Parma should be given to Don Carlos, eldest son of Elizabeth Farnese, Queen of Spain. Cosimo protested, and belatedly reorganized the military defenses of Leghorn and Florence. His death left to his son an impoverished state and a precarious throne.

Gian Gastone was now (1732) fifty-two years old. He labored to remedy abuses in the administration and the economy, dismissed the spies and sycophants who had fattened under his father, reduced taxes, recalled exiles, released political prisoners, assisted the revival of industry and commerce, and restored the social life of Florence to security and gaiety. The enrichment of the Uffizi Gallery by Cosimo II and Gian Gastone, the flourishing of music under the lead of Francesco Veracini's violin, the masked balls, the parades of decorated carriages, the popular battles of confetti and flowers, made Florence rival Venice and Rome in attracting foreign visitors; here, for example, about 1740, Lady Mary Wortley Montagu, Horace Walpole, and Thomas Gray gathered around Lady Henrietta Pomfret in the Palazzo Ridolfo. There is something wistfully attractive in a society in decay.

Exhausted by his efforts, Gian Gastone in 1731 turned the government over to his ministers, and slipped into sensual degradation. Spain sent an army of thirty thousand men to ensure Don Carlos' succession; Charles VI of Austria sent fifty thousand troops to escort his daughter Maria Theresa to the grand-ducal throne. War was averted by an agreement (1736) among Austria, France, England, and Holland that Carlos should have Naples, and that Tuscany should go to Maria Theresa and her husband, Francis of Lorraine. On July 9, 1737, the last of the Medici rulers died, Tuscany became a dependency of Austria, and Florence flowered again.

V. QUEEN OF THE ADRIATIC

Between Milan and Venice some minor cities lolled in the sun. Bergamo had to be content, in this half century, with painters like Ghislandi, composers like Locatelli. Verona presented operas in her Roman theater, and had an outstanding man in Marchese Francesco Scipione di Maffei. His poetic drama *Merope* (1713) was imitated by Voltaire, who honorably dedicated his own *Mérope* to him as "the first who had courage and genius enough to hazard a tragedy without gallantry, a tragedy worthy of Athens in its glory, wherein maternal affection constitutes the whole intrigue, and the most tender interest arises from the purest virtue."[32] Even more distinguished was Maffei's scholarly *Verona illustrata* (1731–32), which set a pace for archaeology. His city was so proud of him that it raised a statue to him in his lifetime. — Vicenza, with its buildings by Palladio, was a goal of pilgrimage for architects reviving the classic style. — Padua had a university then especially noted for its faculties of law and medicine, and it had Giuseppe Tartini, acknowledged by all (except Geminiani) to be at the head of Europe's violinists; who has not heard Tartini's "Devil's Trill"?

All these cities were part of the Venetian Republic. So, in the north, were Treviso, Friuli, Feltre, Bassano, Udine, Belluno, Trento, Bolzano; so in the east was Istria; in the south the state of Venezia extended through Chioggia and Rovigo to the Po; across the Adriatic it held Cattaro, Preveza, and other parts of today's Yugoslavia and Albania; and in the Adriatic it held the islands of Corfu, Cephalonia, and Zante. Within this complex realm dwelt some three million souls, each the center of the world.

1. Venetian Life

Venice herself, as the capital, contained 137,000 inhabitants. She was now in political and economic decline, having lost her Aegean empire to the Turks, and much of her foreign commerce to Atlantic states. The failure of the Crusades; the unwillingness of the European governments, after the victory at Lepanto (1571), to help Venice defend the outposts of Christendom in the East; the eagerness of those governments to accept from Turkey commercial privileges denied to her bravest enemy[33]—these developments had left Venice too weak to maintain her Renaissance splendor. She decided to cultivate her own garden—to give to her Italian and Adriatic possessions a government severe in law, political censorship, and personal supervision, but competent in administration, tolerant in religion and morals, liberal in internal trade.

Like the other republics of eighteenth-century Europe, Venice was ruled by an oligarchy. In the flotsam of diverse stocks—Antonios, Shylocks, Othellos—with a populace poorly educated, slow to think and quick to act, and preferring pleasure to power, democracy would have been chaos enthroned. Eligibility to the Gran Consiglio was generally restricted to some six hundred families listed in the *Libro d'oro;* but to that native aristocracy some judicious additions were made from the ranks of merchants and financiers, even though of alien blood. The Great Council chose the Senate, which chose the powerful Council of Ten. A swarm of spies circulated silently among the citizens, reporting to the *Inquisitori* any suspicious action or speech of any Venetian—of the doge himself. The doges were now usually figureheads, serving to polarize patriotism and adorn diplomacy.

The economy was fighting a losing battle against foreign competition, import dues, and guild restraints. Venetian industry did not expand into free enterprise, free trade, and capitalistic management; it was content with the fame of its crafts. The wool industry, which had fifteen hundred employees in 1700, had only six hundred at the end of the century; the silk industry declined in the same period from twelve thousand to one thousand.[34] The glass workers of Murano resisted any change in the methods that had once brought them European renown; their secrets escaped to Florence, France, Bohemia, England; their rivals responded to advances in chemistry, to experiments in manufacture; the Murano ascendancy passed. The lace industry similarly succumbed to competitors beyond the Alps; by 1750 the Venetians themselves were wearing French lace. Two industries flourished: fisheries, which employed thirty thousand men, and the importation and sale of slaves.

Religion was not allowed to interfere with the profits of trade or the pleasures of life. The state regulated all matters concerning ecclesiastical property and clerical crime. The Jesuits, expelled in 1606, had been recalled in 1657, but under conditions that checked their influence in education and politics. Despite a governmental ban on the importation of works by the French philosophers, the doctrines of Voltaire, Rousseau, Helvétius, and Diderot found their way, if only by visitors, into Venetian salons, and in Venice, as in France, the aristocracy toyed with the ideas that sapped its power.[35] The people accepted religion as an almost unconscious habit of ritual and belief, but they played more often than they prayed. A Venetian proverb described Venetian morals with all the inadequacy of an epigram: "In the morning a little Mass, after dinner a little gamble, in the evening a little woman."[36] Young men went to church not to worship the Virgin but to examine the women, and these, despite ecclesiastical and governmental fulminations, dressed décolleté.[37] The perennial war between religion and sex was giving sex the victory.

The government permitted a regulated prostitution as a measure of public safety. The courtesans of Venice were famous for their beauty, good manners, rich raiment, and sumptuous apartments on the Grand Canal. The supply of *cortigiane* was considerable, but still fell short of the demand. Thrifty Venetians, and aliens like Rousseau, clubbed together, two or three, to maintain one concubine.[38] Despite these facilities, and not content with *cavalieri serventi*, married women indulged in *liaisons dangereuses*. Some of them frequented the casinos, in which every convenience was provided for assignations. Several noble ladies were publicly reproved by the government for loose conduct; some were ordered confined to their homes; some were exiled. The middle classes showed more sobriety; a succession of offspring kept the wife busy, and filled her need for receiving and giving love. Nowhere did mothers lavish more ardent endearments upon their children— *"Il mio leon di San Marco! La mia allegrezza! Il mio fior di primavera!"* (My lion of St. Mark! My joy! My flower of spring!)

Crime was less frequent in Venice than elsewhere in Italy; the arm ready to strike was held back by the abundance and watchfulness of constables and gendarmes. But gambling was accepted as a natural occupation of mankind.

The government organized a lottery in 1715. The first *ridotto*, or gambling casino, was opened in 1638; soon there were many, public or private, and all classes hastened to them. Clever sharpers like Casanova could live on their gambling gains; others could lose the savings of a year in a night. The players, some masked, bent over the table in a silent devotion more intense than love. The government looked on amiably (till 1774), for it taxed the *ridotti*, and received some 300,000 lire from them in annual revenue.[39]

Moneyed idlers came from a dozen states to spend their savings, or their declining years, in the relaxed morals and plein-air gaiety of the piazzas and the canals. The abandonment of empire lowered the fever of politics. No one here talked of revolution, for every class, besides its pleasures, had its stabilizing customs, its absorption in accepted tasks. Servants were pliant and faithful, but they brooked no insult or contumely. The gondoliers were poor, but they were the lords of the lagoons, standing on their gilded barks in the confident pride of their ancient skill, or rounding a turn with lusty esoteric cries, or murmuring a song to the sway of their bodies and the rhythm of their oars.

Many different nationalities mingled in the piazzas, each keeping its distinctive garb, language, and profanity. The upper classes still dressed as in the heyday of the Renaissance, with shirts of finest linen, velvet breeches, silk stockings, buckled shoes; but it was the Venetians who in this century introduced to Western Europe the Turkish custom of long trousers—pantaloons. Wigs had come in from France about 1665. Young fops took such care of their dress, hair, and smell that their sex was imperceptible. Women of fashion raised upon their heads fantastic towers of false or natural hair. Men as well as women felt undressed without jewelry. Fans were works of art, elegantly painted, often encrusted with gems or enclosing a monocle.

Every class had its clubs, every street its *caffè;* "in Italy," said Goldoni, "we take ten cups of coffee every day."[40] All kinds of amusement flourished, from prize fights (*pugni*) to masked balls. One game, *pallone*—tossing an inflated ball about with the palm of the hand—gave us our word *balloon*. Water sports were perennial. Ever since 1315 a regatta had been held on January 25 on the Grand Canal—a race between galleys rowed by fifty oars and decorated like our "floats"; and the festival was climaxed by a water polo game in which hundreds of Venetians divided into shouting and competing groups. On Ascension Day the doge sailed in glory from San Marco to the Lido on the richly decorated ship of state, the *Bucintoro* (*Bucentaur*), amid a thousand other craft, to remarry Venice to the sea.

Saints and historical anniversaries lent their names and memories to frequent holidays, for the Senate found that bread and circuses were an acceptable substitute for elections. On such occasions picturesque processions passed from church to church, from square to square; colorful carpets, garlands and silks were hung from windows or balconies on the route; there was intelligible music, pious or amorous song, and graceful dancing in the streets. Patricians chosen for high office celebrated their victories with parades, arches, trophies, festivities, and philanthropies costing sometimes thirty thousand ducats. Every wedding was a festival, and the funeral of a dignitary was the grandest event in his career.

And there was Carnival—the Christian legacy from the Saturnalia of pagan Rome. Church and state hoped that by allowing a moral holiday they could reduce, for the remainder of the year, the tension between the flesh and the Sixth Commandment. Usually, in Italy, Carnevale extended only through the last week before Lent; in eighteenth-century Venice, from December 26 or January 7 to Martedì Grasso ("Fat Tuesday," Mardi Gras); perhaps from that final day of permissible meat-eating the festival took its name— *carne-vale*, farewell to flesh food. Almost every night in those winter weeks the Venetians—and visitors converging from all Europe—poured into the piazzas, dressed in gay colors, and hiding age, rank, and identity behind a mask. In that disguise many men and women laughed at laws, and harlots thrived. Confetti flew about, and artifical eggs were cast around to spread their scented waters when they broke. Pantalone, Arlechino, Columbine, and other beloved characters from the comic theater pranced and prattled to amuse the crowd; puppets danced, rope walkers stopped a thousand breaths. Strange beasts were brought in for the occasion, like the rhinoceros, which was first seen in Venice in the festivities of 1751. Then, at midnight before Ash Wednesday (Mercoledì della Ceneri), the great bells of San Marco tolled the end of Carnival; the exhausted reveler returned to his legal bed, and prepared to hear his priest tell him on the morrow, *"Memento, homo, quia pulvis es, et in pulverem redieris"* (Remember, man, that thou art dust, and unto dust thou shalt return).

2. Vivaldi

Venice and Naples were the rival foci of music in Italy. In its theaters Venice heard twelve hundred different operas in the eighteenth century. There the most renowned divas of the age, Francesca Cuzzoni and Faustina Bordoni, fought their melodious battles for supremacy; and each from one foot of board moved the world. Cuzzoni sang opposite Farinelli in one theater, Bordoni sang opposite Bernacchi in another, and all Venice was divided between their worshipers. If all four had sung together the Queen of the Adriatic would have melted into her lagoons.

At antipodes to these citadels of opera and joy were the four *ospedali*, or asylums, in which Venice cared for some of her orphan or illegitimate girls. To give function and meaning to the lives of these homeless children they were trained in vocal and instrumental music, to sing in choirs, and to give public concerts from behind their semi-monastic grills. Rousseau said he had never heard anything so touching as these girlish voices singing in disciplined harmony;[41] Goethe thought he had never heard so exquisite a soprano, or music "of such ineffable beauty."[42] Some of the greatest of Italy's composers taught in these institutions, wrote music for them, and conducted their concerts: Monteverdi, Cavalli, Lotti, Galuppi, Porpora, Vivaldi . . .

To supply her theaters with operas, to furnish her *ospedali*, orchestras, and virtuosi with vocal and instrumental music, Venice called upon the cities of Italy, sometimes of Austria and Germany. She herself was the mother or nurse of Antonio Lotti, organist and then *maestro di capella* at St. Mark's, author of indifferent operas but of a Mass that brought tears to Protestant Burney's eyes; of Baldassare Galuppi, famous for his *opera buffe*, and for the splendor and tenderness of his operatic airs; of Alessandro Marcello, whose concertos rank high in the compositions of his time; of his younger brother Benedetto, whose musical setting of fifty psalms "constitute one of the finest productions of musical literature";[43] and of Antonio Vivaldi.

To some of us the first hearing of a Vivaldi concerto was a humiliating revelation. Why had we been ignorant of him so long? Here was a stately flow of harmony, laughing ripples of melody, a unity of structure and a cohesion of parts, which should have won this man an earlier entry into our ken, and a higher place in our musical histories.*

He was born about 1675, son of a violinist in the orchestra of the Doges' Chapel in St. Mark's. His father taught him the violin, and obtained a place for him in the orchestra. At fifteen he took minor orders; at twenty-five he became a priest; he was called Il Prete Rosso because his hair was red. His passion for music may have conflicted with his sacerdotal ministrations. Enemies said that "one day, when Vivaldi was saying Mass, a subject for a fugue came to his mind; he at once left the altar, . . . and repaired to the sacristy to write out the theme; then he came back to finish Mass."[44] A papal nuncio charged him with keeping several women, and finally (it was said) the Inquisition forbade him to say Mass. Antonio in later years gave quite a different account:

> It was twenty-five years ago that I said Mass for . . . the last time, not due to interdiction, . . . but by my own decision, because of an ailment that has burdened me since birth. After being ordained a priest I said Mass for a year or a little more; then I ceased to say it, having on three occasions been compelled by this ailment to leave the altar without completing it.
>
> For this same reason I nearly always live at home, and I only go out in a gondola or coach, because I can no longer walk on account of this chest condition, or rather this tightness in the chest [*strettezza di petto*, probably asthma]. No nobleman invites me to his house, not even our prince, because all are informed of my ailment. My travels have always been very costly because I have always had to make them with four or five women to help me.

These women, he added, were of spotless repute. "Their modesty was admitted everywhere. . . . Every day of the week they made their devotions."[45]

He could not have been much of a rake, for the Seminario Musicale dell' Ospedale della Pietà kept him through thirty-seven years as violinist, teacher, composer, or *maestro di coro*—rector of the choir. For his girl students he composed most of his nonoperatic works. The demands were great; hence he wrote in haste and corrected at what leisure he could find; he told de Brosses

---

* The 1928 edition of *Grove's Dictionary of Music and Musicians* gave him one column; the 1954 edition gave him twelve; judge from this the sudden expansion of Vivaldi's reputation. Is fame a whim of chance?

that he could "compose a concerto faster than a copyist could copy it."[46] His operas were equally hurried; one of them bore on the title page the boast (or excuse) *"Fatto in cinque giorni"*—Done in five days. Like Handel, he saved time by borrowing from himself, adapting past performances to meet present needs.

In the interstices of his work at the Ospedale he composed forty operas. Many contemporaries agreed with Tartini that they were mediocre; Benedetto Marcello made fun of them in his *Teatro alla moda;* but audiences in Venice, Vicenza, Vienna, Mantua, Florence, Milan, and Vienna welcomed him, and Vivaldi often deserted his girls to travel with his women through northern Italy, even to Vienna and Amsterdam, to perform as a violinist, or to conduct one of his operas, or to supervise its staging and décor. His operas are now dead, but so are nearly all those composed before Gluck. Styles, manners, heroes, voices, sexes have changed.

History knows of 554 compositions by Vivaldi; of these 454 are concertos. A clever satirist said that Vivaldi had not written six hundred concertos, but had written the same concerto six hundred times;[47] and sometimes it seems so. There is in these pieces much sawing of strings, much hurdy-gurdy *continuo,* an almost metronomic beating of time; even in the famous series called *The Seasons* (1725) there are some deserts of monotony. But there are also peaks of passionate vitality and wintry blasts, oases of dramatic conflict between soloists and orchestra, and grateful streams of melody. In such pieces[48] Vivaldi brought the *concerto grosso* to an unprecedented excellence, which only Bach and Handel would surpass.

Like most artists, Vivaldi suffered from the sensitivity that fed his genius. The power of his music reflected his fiery temper, the tenderness of his strains reflected his piety. As he aged he became absorbed in religious devotions, so that one fanciful record described him as leaving his rosary only to compose.[49] In 1740 he lost or resigned his post at the Ospedale della Pietà. For reasons now unknown he left Venice and went to Vienna. We know nothing further of him except that there, a year later, he died, and received a pauper's funeral.

His death passed unnoticed in the Italian press, for Venice had ceased to care for his music, and no one ranked him near the top of his art in his land and time. His compositions found a welcome in Germany. Quantz, flutist and composer for Frederick the Great, imported Vivaldi's concertos, and frankly accepted them as models. Bach so admired them as to transpose at least nine for the harpsichord, four for the organ, and one for four harpsichords and a string ensemble.[50] Apparently it was from Vivaldi and Corelli that Bach derived the tripartite structure of his concertos.

Throughout the nineteenth century Vivaldi was almost forgotten except by scholars tracing the development of Bach. Then in 1905 Arnold Schering's *Geschichte des Instrumentalkonzerts* restored him to prominence; and in the 1920s Arturo Toscanini gave his passion and prestige to Vivaldi's cause. Today the Red Priest takes for a time the highest place among the Italian composers of the eighteenth century.

3. Remembrances

From the Indian summer of Venetian art a dozen painters rise up and ask for remembrance. We merely salute Giambattista Pittoni, whom Venice placed only after Tiepolo and Piazzetta; and Jacopo Amigoni, whose voluptuous style passed down to Boucher; and Giovanni Antonio Pellegrini, who carried his colors to England, France, and Germany; it was he who decorated Kimbolton Castle, Castle Howard, and the Banque de France. Marco Ricci makes a more striking figure, since he killed a critic and himself. In 1699, aged twenty-three, he stabbed to death a gondolier who had slighted his paintings. He fled to Dalmatia, fell in love with its landscapes, and caught them so skillfully with his colors that Venice forgave him and hailed him as Tintoretto reborn. His uncle Sebastiano Ricci took him to London, where they collaborated on the tomb of the Duke of Devonshire. Like so many artists of the seventeenth and eighteenth centuries, he loved to paint real or imaginary ruins, not forgetting himself. In 1729, after several attempts, he succeeded in committing suicide. In 1733 one of his paintings was sold for $500; in 1963 it was resold for $90,000,[51] illustrating both the appreciation of art and the depreciation of money.

Rosalba Carriera is more pleasant to contemplate. She began her career by designing patterns for *point de Venise* lace; then (like the young Renoir) she painted snuffboxes; then miniatures; finally she found her forte in pastel. By 1709 she had won such fame that when Frederick IV of Denmark came he chose her to paint for him pastel portraits of the most beautiful or celebrated ladies of Venice. In 1720 Pierre Crozat, millionaire art collector, invited her to Paris. There she was welcomed and feted as no other foreign artist since Bernini. Poets wrote sonnets about her; Regent Philippe d'Orléans visited her; Watteau painted her, and she him; Louis XV sat for her; she was elected to the Académie de Peinture, and offered, as her diploma piece, the *Muse* that hangs in the Louvre. It was as if in her the soul of rococo had been made flesh.

In 1730 she went to Vienna, where she made pastel portraits of Charles VI, his Empress, and the Archduchess Maria Theresa. Back in Venice, she so absorbed herself in her art that she forgot to marry. The Accademia there has a roomful of her portraits, the Gemäldegalerie of Dresden has 157, almost all characterized by pink faces, blue backgrounds, rosy innocence, dimpled delicacy; even when she pictured Horace Walpole[52] she made him look like a girl. She flattered every sitter but herself; the self-portrait in Windsor Castle shows her in her later years, white-haired, a bit somber, as if foreseeing that she would soon be blind. For the last twelve of her eighty-two years she had to live without the light and color that had been to her almost the essence of life. She left her mark on the art of her time: La Tour may have taken fire from her; Greuze remembered her idealization of young women; her rosy tints—*la vie en rose*—passed down to Boucher and Renoir.

Giovanni Battista Piazzetta was a greater artist, superior to sentiment, disdaining decoration, seeking not so much to please the public as to conquer the difficulties, and honor the highest traditions, of his métier. His fellow craftsmen recognized this, and though Tiepolo had led in establishing (1750) the Venetian Accademia di Pittura e Scultura, it was Piazzetta whom they chose as its first president. His *Rebecca at the Well*[53] is worthy of Titian, and makes even less concession to conventional conceptions of beauty; enough of Rebecca is revealed to stir the savage breast, but her Dutch face and snub nose were not fashioned for Italian ecstasies. It is the man who moves us here, a figure worthy of the Renaissance: a powerful face, an insinuating beard, a feathered hat, a gleam of sly inducement in his eyes— and all the picture a masterpiece of color, texture, and design. It was characteristic of Piazzetta that he was the most respected of Venetian painters in his day, and died the poorest.

Antonio Canale, called Canaletto, is more famous, for half the world knows Venice through his *vedute*, or views, and England knew him in the flesh. He followed for a while his father's profession of scene painting for theaters; in Rome he studied architecture; returning to Venice, he applied compass and T square to his drawing, and made architecture a feature of his pictures. From these we know the Queen of the Adriatic as she looked in the first half of the eighteenth century. We note from his *Baccino di San Marco*[54] how crowded with vessels was the main lagoon; we watch *A Regatta on the Grand Canal*,[55] and see that life was as full and eager then as it had ever been; and we are pleased to find the *Ponte di Rialto*,[56] the *Piazza San Marco*,[57] the *Piazzetta*,[58] the *Palazzo dei Dogi*,[59] and *Santa Maria della Salute*[60] almost as we find them today, except for the rebuilt Campanile. Such pictures were precisely what tourists needed in the cloudy north to remember gratefully the sun and magic of Venezia la Serenissima. They bought and paid, and took their mementos home, and soon England demanded Canaletto himself. He came in 1746, and painted extensive views of *Whitehall*[61] and *The Thames from Richmond House;* this last, astonishing in its combination of space, perspective, and detail, is Canaletto's masterpiece. Not till 1755 did he return to Venice. There in 1766, aged sixty-nine, he was still hard at work, and proudly wrote, on *The Interior of St. Mark's,* "Done without spectacles."[62] He handed down his technique of precise measurement to his nephew Bernardo Bellotto Canaletto, and his flair for *vedute* to his "good scholar," Francesco Guardi, whom we shall meet again.

As Canaletto showed the outer view of the splendid city, so Pietro Longhi revealed the life within the walls by applying genre painting to the middle class. The lady at breakfast *en négligé*, the abbé tutoring her son, her little girl fondling a toy dog, the tailor coming to display a frock, the dancing master putting the lady through the steps of a minuet, the children wide-eyed at a menagerie, the young women frolicking at blindman's buff, the tradesmen in their shops, the maskers at Carnival, the theaters, the coffee-houses, the literary coteries, the poets reciting their verses, the quack doctors, the fortunetellers, the vendors of sausages and plums, the promenade in the piazza, the hunting party, the fishing party, the family on its *villeggiatura*

FIG. 49—JOHANN GOTTFRIED SCHADOW: *The Quadriga on the Brandenburg Gate.* German Information Center.

PAGE 523

FIG. 50—KARL GOTTHARD LANGHANS: *The Brandenburg Gate* (1788–91). German Information Center. PAGE 525

Fig. 52—Angelica Kauffmann: *Stanislas Poniatowski*. Uffizi, Florence. PAGE 477

Fig. 53—Daniel Chodowiecki: *A Gathering in the Zoological Garden*. Museum der Bildenden Künste, Leipzig.

PAGE 524

FIG. 56—ENGRAVING BY KARL BARTH AFTER A DRAWING BY STOBBE: *Immanuel Kant*.   PAGE 531

FIG. 57—JOHANN FRIEDRICH AUGUST TISCHBEIN: *Schiller*.

PAGE 569

Fig. 58—Anton Graff: *The Actress Korona Schröter*. Schlossmuseum, Weimar.   PAGE 524

Fig. 59—Johann Heinrich Wilhelm Tischbein: *Goethe in the Roman Campagna*. Städelsches Kunstinstitut, Frankfurt-am-Main.   PAGES 523, 587

Fig. 60—Asmus Jakob Carstens: *The Birth of Light*, drawing. Schlossmuseum, Weimar.

Fig. 61—Alexander Roslin (1718?–53): *Gustavus III*. National Museum, Stockholm.   PAGE 655

Fig. 62—*The Bridgewater Canal at Barton Bridge* (1794). Reproduced from A. S. Turberville, *Johnson's England* (Oxford: Clarendon Press, 1933); Vol. I.   PAGE 672

FIG. 63—THOMAS GAINSBOROUGH: *George III*. Windsor Castle. Copyright reserved.

FIG. 64—SIR JOSHUA REYNOLDS: *Edmund Burke*, 1774. The National Gallery of Ireland, Dublin.   PAGE 689

FIG. 65—ENGRAVING BY JOHN JONES AFTER A PAINTING BY SIR JOSHUA REYNOLDS: *Charles James Fox*. The Metropolitan Museum of Art, New York, Harris Brisbane Dick Fund, 1953.   PAGES 693, 752

FIG. 66—JOHN HOPPNER: *William Pitt the Younger*. The Tate Gallery, London.

PAGE 696

FIG. 67—GEORGE ROMNEY: *Actress Mary Robinson*. Reproduced by permission of the Trustees of the Wallace Collection, London.

PAGE 740

FIG. 68—ROBERT PINE (1742–90): *David Garrick*. National Portrait Gallery, London.   PAGE 741

FIG. 69—ENGRAVING BY JOHN HALL
(1739–97) AFTER A PAINTING BY
REYNOLDS: *Richard Brinsley Sheridan*. National Portrait Gallery, London.   PAGES 694, 752

FIG. 70—FROM A PRINT AFTER A DRAW-
ING BY CANALETTO: *An Inside View
of the Rotunda in Ranelagh Gardens*.
Reproduced from A. S. Turberville,
Johnson's England, Vol. I.   PAGE 744

FIG. 71—SIR JOSHUA REYNOLDS: *Portrait of the Artist as a Deaf Man.* Reproduced by courtesy of the Trustees of the Tate Gallery, London. PAGE 754

FIG. 72—CHIPPENDALE AND HAIGH IN THE STYLE OF ROBERT ADAM: *Side Table of Gilt and Silvered Wood.* Courtesy of Lord Harewood, Leeds. (Photo by Mr. Bertram Unné.) PAGE 748

FIG. 73—THOMAS GAINSBOROUGH: *Mrs. Sarah Siddons*. National Gallery, London.

PAGES 740, 756

FIG. 74—Rosalba Carriera: *Horace Walpole*. Lord Walpole Collection, Wolterton Hall, Norwich.   PAGE 791

FIG. 75—Paul Sandby, *Strawberry Hill c. 1774*, drawing. Reproduced from the original drawing, engraved by E. Rooker.   PAGES 747, 750

FIG. 76—THOMAS GAINSBOROUGH: *The Honorable Mrs. Graham*. National Gallery of Scotland.

PAGE 756

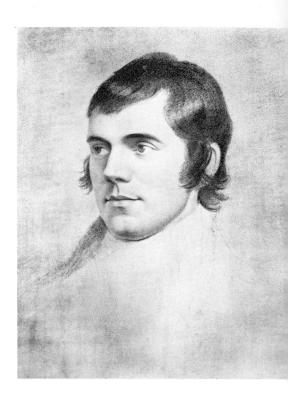

FIG. 77—ARCHIBALD SKIRVING: *Robert Burns*. National Gallery of Scotland.

PAGE 772

FIG. 78—HENRY RAEBURN: *Lord Newton*. National Gallery of Scotland.

PAGE 765

Fig. 79—Thomas Gainsborough: *The Market Cart*. Reproduced by courtesy of the Trustees of the Tate Gallery, London.

FIG. 80—SIR JOSHUA REYNOLDS: *Georgiana, Duchess of Devonshire.* Devonshire Collection, Chatsworth. Reproduced by permission of the Trustees of the Chatsworth Settlement.

PAGE 753

FIG. 81—GEORGE DANCE (1741–1825): *James Boswell.* National Portrait Gallery, London. PAGE 778

Fig. 82—Sir Joshua Reynolds: *Laurence Sterne*. Reproduced with permission. (Photograph courtesy of the University of London, Courtauld Institute of Art, London.)

PAGES 752, 787

FIG. 83—GEORGE ROMNEY: *William Cowper*. National Portrait Gallery, London.   PAGE 810

FIG. 84—STUDIO OF REYNOLDS: *Oliver Goldsmith*. National Portrait Gallery, London.

PAGES 752, 813

Fig. 85—Mme. Vigée-Lebrun: *Marie Antoinette*. Reproduced from Max Osborn, *Die Kunst des Rokoko*.

PAGES 850, 913

Fig. 86—Sir Joshua Reynolds: *Dr. Samuel Johnson*. Reproduced by courtesy of the Trustees of the Tate Gallery, London.

PAGES 752, 818

Fig. 87—Jean-Antoine Houdon: *The Artist's Wife*. Louvre, Paris. Reproduced from Max Osborn, *Die Kunst des Rokoko*.   PAGE 911

Fig. 88—Jean-Baptiste Pigalle: *Denis Diderot*. Louvre, Paris. From Max Osborn, *Die Kunst des Rokoko*.

PAGES 107, 892

VOLTAIRE.

FIG. 89—HOUDON: *Voltaire*. Comédie Française. (Photo Jean Roubier.)

PAGES 873, 912

FIG. 90—HOUDON: *Mme. de Sérilly*. Reproduced by permission of the Trustees of the Wallace Collection, London. PAGE 911

FIG. 91—HOUDON: *Mirabeau*.

PAGES 911, 951

FIG. 92—CLODION (CLAUDE MICHEL): *The Intoxication of Wine* (*Nymph and Satyr*), terra-cotta statue. The Metropolitan Museum of Art, New York, bequest of Benjamin Altman, 1913.

Fig. 93—Jacques-Louis David: *The Oath of the Horatii*. Louvre, Paris.　PAGE 912

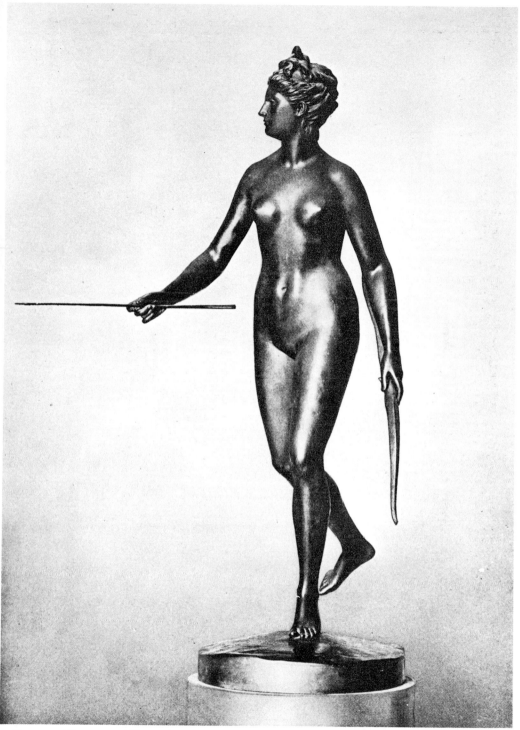

FIG. 94–HOUDON: *Diana*, bronze. Louvre, Paris. Reproduced from Max Osborn, *Die Kunst des Rokoko*.

FIG. 95—NATTIER: *Beaumarchais*. Private Collection. Reproduced from *French Art of the 18th Century*, ed. Stéphane Faniel (New York: Simon and Schuster, 1957). PAGE 920

FIG. 96—HOUDON: *George Washington*. Louvre, Paris. PAGE 912

FIG. 97—MME. VIGÉE-LEBRUN: *Portrait of the Artist and Her Daughter*. Louvre, Paris.

FIG. 98—ENGRAVING BY J. E. NOCHEZ AFTER A PAINTING BY ALLAN RAMSAY: *Jean-Jacques Rousseau*. The Metropolitan Museum of Art, New York, gift of Edith Root Grant, E. W. Root, and Elihu Root, Jr., 1937.

holiday: all the mentionable activities of the bourgeoisie are there, even more fully than in the comedies of Goldoni, Longhi's friend. It is not great art, but it is delightful, and shows a society more orderly and refined than we should have imagined from the aristocrats of the gambling casinos or the cursing stevedores of the wharves.

4. Tiepolo

The Venetian who made Europe believe for a moment that the Renaissance had returned was Giambattista Tiepolo. Any summer's day will see a procession of students and tourists entering the Residenz of the Bishop of Würzburg to see the staircase and ceiling frescoed by Tiepolo in 1750–53; these are the peak of Italian painting in the eighteenth century. Or look at *The Trinity Appearing to St. Clement* in the National Gallery at London; observe its skillful composition, its precise drawing, its subtle handling of light, its depth and glow of color; surely this is Titian? Perhaps, if Tiepolo had not wandered so, he might have joined the giants.

Or, possibly, he was handicapped by good fortune. He was the last child of a prosperous Venetian merchant who, dying, left a substantial patrimony. Handsome, bright, frolicsome, Gian "soon acquired an aristocratic scorn of anything plebeian."[63] In 1719, aged twenty-three, he married Cecilia, sister of Francesco Guardi. She gave him four daughters and five sons, of whom two became painters. They lived in "a fine house" in the parish of Santa Trinità.

His talent had already bloomed. In 1716 he exhibited his *Sacrifice of Isaac*,[64] crude but powerful; he was visibly at this time under Piazzetta's influence. He studied Veronese too, and assumed a *maniera Paolesca* of sumptuous raiment, warm colors, and sensuous lines. In 1726 the Archbishop of Udine invited him to adorn his cathedral and palace. Tiepolo chose themes from the story of Abraham, but the treatment was not quite Biblical: Sarah's face, emerging from a Renaissance ruff, is a corrugation of wrinkles revealing two vestigial teeth; the angel, however, is an Italian athlete with an engaging leg. Tiepolo seems to have felt that in a century that was beginning to laugh at angels and miracles he could let his humor play with reverend traditions, and the amiable archbishop indulged him. But the artist had to be careful, for the Church was still one of the chief sources of pictorial commissions in the Catholic world.

The other source was the layman with a palace to be adorned. In the Palazzo Casali-Dugnani at Milan (1731) Gian told in frescoes the story of Scipio. These were not typical Tiepolo, for he had not yet formed his characteristic style of figures moving easily and loosely in undefined space, but they showed a skill that made a stir in northern Italy. By 1740 he found his forte, and achieved what some[65] have thought his chef-d'oeuvre—the ceiling and banquet hall of the Palazzo Clerici in Milan. Here he chose, as vehicles for his fancy, *The Four Parts of the World*, *The Course of the Sun*, and *Apollo with the Pagan Gods*. He was happy to leave the somber world of

Christian legend and disport himself on Olympian heights where he could use the Greco-Roman divinities as figures in a realm free from the laws of motion, the chains of gravity, and even the academic rules of design. Like most artists, whose moral code melts in the heat of their feelings, he was at heart a pagan; moreover, a fine body might be the product of a resolute and formative soul, and be therefore itself a spiritual fact. For thirty years now Tiepolo would send gods and goddesses—garbed in gauze and nonchalantly nude—frolicking through space, chasing one another among the planets, or making love on a cushion of clouds.

Back in Venice, he returned to Christianity, and his religious pictures absolved his mythologies. For the Scuola di San Rocco he painted a canvas, *Hagar and Ishmael*, notable for the fine figure of a sleeping boy. In the Church of the Gesuati—renamed by the Dominicans Santa Maria del Rosario —he pictured *The Institution of the Rosary*. For the Scuola dei Carmini, or School of the Carmelite Monks, he depicted *The Madonna of Mount Carmel*; this almost rivaled Titian's *Annunciation*. For the Church of St. Alvise he made three pictures; one of these, *Christ Carrying the Cross*, is crowded with powerful figures vividly portrayed. Tiepolo had paid his debt to his native faith.

His fancy moved more freely on palace walls. In the Palazzo Barbaro he showed *The Apotheosis of Francesco Barbaro*—now in the Metropolitan Museum of Art in New York. For the Palace of the Doges he portrayed *Neptune Offering to Venus the Riches of the Sea*. To the Palazzo Papadopoli he contributed two delightful snatches of Venice in Carnival—*The Minuet* and *The Charlatan*. And (topping all his palace pictures in Venice) he embellished the Palazzo Labia with frescoes telling the story of Antony and Cleopatra in magnificent scenes brilliantly realized. A fellow artist, Girolamo Mengozzi-Colonna, painted the architectural backgrounds in a burst of Palladian splendor. On one wall the meeting of the two rulers; on the opposite wall their banquet; on the ceiling a wild array of flying figures representing Pegasus, time, beauty, and the winds—these blown about by jolly puffing imps. In *The Meeting* Cleopatra descends from her barge in dazzling raiment revealing twin mounds calculated to lure a tired triumvir to fragrant rest. In the still more effulgent *Banquet* she drops a pearl without price into her wine; Antony is impressed by this careless wealth; and on a balcony musicians strum their lyres to double the jeopardy and triple the intoxication. This masterpiece, recalling and rivaling Veronese, was one of the pictures that Reynolds copied in 1752.

Such work in the grand style raised Tiepolo to a height visible across the Alps. Count Francesco Algarotti, friend of Frederick and Voltaire, spread his name through Europe. As early as 1736 the Swedish minister in Venice informed his government that Tiepolo was just the man to decorate the royal palace in Stockholm; "he is full of wit and zest, easy to deal with, bubbling over with ideas; he has a gift for brilliant color, and works at a prodigious speed; he paints a picture in less time than it takes another artist to mix his colors."[66] Stockholm was already beautiful, but it seemed so far away.

In 1750 a closer invitation came: Karl Philipp von Greiffenklau, Prince-Bishop of Würzburg, asked him to paint the Imperial Hall of his newly built *Residenz*, or administrative palace. The proffered fee moved the aging master. Arriving in December with his sons Domenico, twenty-four, and Lorenzo, fourteen, he found an unexpected challenge in the splendor of the Kaisersaal, which Balthasar Neumann had designed; how could any picture catch the eye amid that radiance? Tiepolo's success here was the crown of his career. On the walls he depicted the story of the Emperor Frederick Barbarossa (who had kept tryst with Beatrice of Burgundy at Würzburg in 1156), and on the ceiling he showed *Apollo Bringing the Bride;* here he reveled in an ecstasy of white horses, gay gods, and the play of light upon prancing cherubs and filmy clouds. On a slope of the ceiling he represented *The Wedding:* handsome faces, stately figures, flowered drapery, garments recalling Veronese's Venice rather than medieval styles. The Bishop was so pleased that he enlarged the contract to include the ceiling of the grand staircase, and two altarpieces for his cathedral. Over the majestic stairway Tiepolo pictured the continents, and Olympus—the happy hunting ground of his fancy—and a lordly figure of Apollo the Sun God circling the sky.

Rich and weary, Giambattista returned to Venice (1753), leaving Domenico to finish the assignment at Würzburg. Soon he was elected president of the Academy. He was of so amiable a disposition that even his rivals were fond of him, and called him Il Buon Tiepolo. He could not resist all the demands made upon his waning time; we find him painting in Venice, Treviso, Verona, Parma, and doing a large canvas commissioned by "the court of Muscovy." We should hardly have expected another major work from him, but in 1757, aged sixty-one, he undertook to decorate the Villa Valmarana near Vicenza. Mengozzi-Colonna drew the architectural setting, Domenico signed some pictures in the guest house, Giambattista deployed his brush in the villa itself. He chose subjects from the *Iliad*, the *Aeneid*, the *Orlando furioso*, the *Gerusalemme liberata*. He gave his airy illusionism full rein, losing color in light, and space in infinity, letting his gods and goddesses float at their ease in an empyrean raised above all care and time. Goethe, marveling before these frescoes, exclaimed, *"Gar fröhlich und brav"* (Very joyful and bold). It was Tiepolo's last riot in Italy.

In 1761 Charles III of Spain asked him to come and paint in the new royal palace at Madrid. The tired Titan pleaded age, but the King appealed to the Venetian Senate to use its influence. Reluctantly, aged sixty-six, he set out once more with his faithful sons and his model Christina, again leaving his wife behind, for she loved the casinos of Venice. We shall find him on a scaffold in Spain.

5. Goldoni and Gozzi

Four figures, paired, stand out in the Venetian literature of this age: Apostolo Zeno and Pietro Metastasio, both of whom wrote librettos that were poetry; Carlo Goldoni and Carlo Gozzi, who fought over Venetian comedy a comedy that became Goldoni's tragedy. Of the first pair Goldoni wrote:

These two illustrious authors effected the reform of Italian opera. Before them nothing but gods, devils, machines, and wonders were to be found in these harmonious entertainments. Zeno was the first who conceived the possibility of representing tragedy in lyrical verse without degradation, and singing it without producing exhaustion. He executed the project in a manner most satisfactory to the public, reflecting the greatest glory on himself and his nation.[67]

Zeno carried his reforms to Vienna in 1718, retired amiably in favor of Metastasio in 1730, and returned to Venice and twenty years of peace. Metastasio, as Goldoni noted, played Racine to Zeno's Corneille, adding refinement to power, and bringing operatic poetry to an unprecedented height. Voltaire ranked him with the greatest French poets, and Rousseau thought him the only contemporary poet who reached the heart. His real name was Pietro Trapassi—Peter Cross. A dramatic critic, Gian Vincenzo Gravina, heard him singing in the streets, adopted him, rechristened him Metastasio (Greek for Trapassi), financed his education, and, dying, left him a fortune. Pietro ran through the fortune with poetic license, then articled himself to a lawyer who exacted the condition that he should not read or write a line of verse. So he wrote under a pseudonym.

At Naples he was asked by the Austrian envoy to provide lyrics for a cantata. Porpora composed the music; Marianna Bulgarelli, then famous under the name of La Romanina, sang the lead; all went well. The diva invited the poet to her salon; there he met Leo, Vinci, Pergolesi, Farinelli, Hasse, Alessandro and Domenico Scarlatti; Metastasio developed rapidly in that exciting company. La Romanina, thirty-five, fell in love with him, twenty-three. She rescued him from the toil of the law, took him into a *ménage à trois* with her complaisant husband, and inspired him to write his most famous libretto, *Didone abbandonata*, which twelve successive composers set to music between 1724 and 1823. In 1726 he wrote *Siroe* for his inamorata; Vinci, Hasse, and Handel independently made operas of it. Metastasio was now the most sought-after librettist in Europe.

In 1730 he accepted a call to Vienna, leaving La Romanina behind. She tried to follow him; fearing that her presence would compromise him, he secured an order forbidding her to enter Imperial territory. She stabbed her breast in an attempt at suicide; this effort to play Dido failed, but she lived only four years more. When she died she left to her unfaithful Aeneas all her fortune. Stricken with remorse, Metastasio renounced the legacy in favor of her husband. "I have no longer any hope that I shall succeed in consoling myself," he wrote, "and I believe that the rest of my life will be savorless and sorrowful."[67a] He sadly enjoyed triumph after triumph till the War of the Austrian Succession interrupted operatic performances in Vienna. After 1750 he repeated himself aimlessly. He had exhausted life thirty years before his death (1782).

Opera, as Voltaire had predicted, drove the tragic drama from the Italian stage, and left it to comedy. But Italian comedy was dominated by the *com-*

media dell' arte—the play of improvised speech and characterizing masks. Most of the characters had long since become stereotyped: Pantalone, the good-humored, trousered bourgeois; Tartaglia, the stammering Neapolitan knave; Brighella, the simpleton schemer caught in his own intrigues; Truffal- dino, the genial, carnal *bon vivant*; Arlecchino—our Harlequin; Pulcinello— our Punch; diverse towns and times added several more. Most of the dia- logue, and many incidents in the plot, were left to extempore invention. In "those improvised comedies," according to Casanova, "if the actor stops short for a word, the pit and the gallery hiss him mercilessly."[68]

There were usually seven theaters operating in Venice, all named after saints, and housing scandalously behaved audiences. The nobles in the boxes were not particular about what they dropped upon the commoners below. Hostile factions countered applause with whistling, yawns, sneezes, coughs, cockcrows, or the meowing of cats.[69] In Paris the theater audience was mostly composed of the upper classes, professional men, and literati; in Ven- ice it was chiefly middle-class, sprinkled with gaudy courtesans, ribald gon- doliers, priests and monks in disguise, haughty senators in robe and wig. It was hard for a play to please all elements in such an *olla-podrida* of human- ity; so Italian comedy tended to be a mixture of satire, slapstick, buffoonery, and puns. The training of the actors to portray stock characters made them incapable of variety and subtlety. This was the audience, this the stage, that Goldoni strove to raise to legitimate and civilized comedy.

Pleasant is the simple beginning of his *Memoirs*:

> I was born at Venice in 1707. . . . My mother brought me into the world with little pain, and this increased her love for me. My first appearance was not, as is usual, announced by cries; and this gentleness seemed then an indica- tion of the pacific character which from that day forward I have ever pre- served.[70]

It was a boast, but true; Goldoni is one of the most lovable men in literary history; and despite this exordium his virtues included modesty—a quality uncongenial to scribes. We may believe him when he says, "I was the idol of the house." The father went off to Rome to study medicine, and then to Perugia to practice it; the mother was left at Venice to bring up three children.

Carlo was precocious; at four he could read and write; at eight he com- posed a comedy. The father persuaded the mother to let Carlo come and live with him in Perugia. There the boy studied with the Jesuits, did well, and was invited to join the order; he declined. The mother and another son joined the father, but the cold mountain air of Perugia disagreed with her, and the family moved to Rimini, then to Chioggia. Carlo went to a Domini- can college in Rimini, where he received daily doses of St. Thomas Aquinas' *Summa theologiae*. Finding no drama in that masterpiece of rationalization, he read Aristophanes, Menander, Plautus, and Terence; and when a com- pany of actors came to Rimini he joined it long enough to surprise his par- ents in Chioggia. They scolded him, embraced him, and sent him to study law at Pavia. In 1731 he received his degree, and began to practice. He married, and "was now the happiest man in the world,"[71] except that he came down with smallpox on his wedding night.

Gravitating back to Venice, he succeeded in law, and became consul there for Genoa. But the theater continued to fascinate him; he itched to write, and to be produced. His *Belisarius* was staged on November 24, 1734, with inspiring success; it ran every day till December 14, and his old mother's pride in him doubled his joy. Venice, however, had no taste for tragedy; his further offerings in that genre failed, and he sadly took to comedy. Nevertheless he refused to write farces for the *commedia dell' arte;* he wanted to compose comedies of manners and ideas in the tradition of Molière, to put upon the stage no stock characters frozen into masks, but personalities and situations drawn from contemporary life. He chose some actors from a *commedia* troupe in Venice, trained them, and produced in 1740 his *Momolo cortesan* (*Momolo the Courtier*). "The piece was wonderfully successful, and I was satisfied."[72] Not quite, for he had compromised by leaving all the dialogue unwritten except for the leading part, and by providing roles for four of the traditional masked characters.

He advanced his reforms step by step. In *La donna di garbo* (*The Woman of Honor*) he for the first time wrote out action and dialogue completely. Hostile companies rose to compete with his, or to mock his plays; the classes that he had satirized, like the *cicisbei,* plotted against him; he fought them all with success after success. But no other author could be found to furnish his troupe with suitable comedies; his own, too often repeated, forfeited favor; he was compelled, by the competition, to write sixteen plays in one year.

He was at his peak in 1752, hailed by Voltaire as the Molière of Italy. *La locandera* (*The Mistress of the Inn*) had in that year "a success so brilliant that it was . . . preferred to everything else that had yet been done in that kind of comedy." He prided himself on having observed the "Aristotelian unities" of action, place, and time; otherwise he judged his plays realistically: "Good," he said, "but not yet Molière."[73] He had written them too rapidly to make them works of art; they were cleverly constructed, pleasantly gay, and generally true to life, but they lacked Molière's reach of ideas, force of speech, power of presentation; they remained on the surface of character and events. The nature of the audience forbade him to try the heights of sentiment, philosophy, or style; and he was by nature too cheerful to plumb the depths that had tortured Molière.

Once at least he was shocked out of his genial humor and touched to the quick: when Carlo Gozzi challenged him for theatrical supremacy in Venice, and won.

There were two Gozzi involved in the literary turmoil at this time. Gasparo Gozzi wrote plays that were chiefly adaptations from the French; he edited two prominent periodicals, and began the revival of Dante. Not so genial was his brother Carlo: tall, handsome, vain, and ever ready for a fight. He was the wittiest member of the Accademia Granelleschi, which campaigned for the use of pure Tuscan Italian in literature, rather than the Venetian idiom which Goldoni used in most of his plays. As the lover or *cavaliere servente* of Teodora Ricci, he may have felt the sting when Goldoni satirized the *cicisbei*. He too wrote *Memoirs*—the white paper of his wars. He judged Goldoni as one author sees another:

> I recognized in Goldoni an abundance of comic motives, truth, and natural-ness. Yet I detected poverty and meanness of intrigue; . . . virtues and vices ill-adjusted, vice too often triumphant; plebeian phrases of low double mean-ing; . . . scraps and tags of erudition stolen Heaven knows where, and brought to impose upon a crowd of ignoramuses. Finally, as a writer of Italian (except in the Venetian dialect, of which he showed himself a master) he seemed not unworthy to be placed among the dullest, basest, and least correct authors who have used our language. . . . At the same time I must add that he never produced a play without some excellent comic trait. In my eyes he had always the appearance of a man who was born with a natural sense of how sterling comedies should be composed, but who—by defect of education, by want of discernment, by the necessity of satisfying the public and supplying new wares to the poor comedians through whom he gained his livelihood, and by the hurry in which he produced so many pieces every year to keep himself afloat—was never able to fabricate a single play which does not swarm with faults.[74]

In 1757 Gozzi produced a volume of verses expressing kindred criticisms in "the style of good old Tuscan masters." Goldoni replied in *terza rima* (Dante's medium) to the effect that Gozzi was like a dog baying at the moon —"*come il cane che abbaja la luna.*" Gozzi retorted by defending the *commedia dell' arte* from Goldoni's strictures; he charged that Goldoni's plays were "a hundred times more lascivious, indecent, and harmful to morals" than the comedy of masks; and he compiled a vocabulary of "obscure ex-pressions, dirty *double-entendres*, . . . and other nastinesses" from Gol-doni's works. The controversy, Molmenti tells us, "threw the city into a kind of frenzy; the case was discussed in playhouses, homes, shops, coffee-houses, and streets."[75]

Abate Chiari, another dramatist stung by Gozzi's Tuscan asp, challenged him to write a better play than those he had condemned. Gozzi answered that he could do this easily, on even the most trivial themes, and by using only the traditional comedy of masks. In January, 1761, a company at the Teatro San Samuele produced his *Fiaba dell' amore delle tre melarancie* (*Fable of the Love of the Three Oranges*)—merely a scenario that showed Pantalone, Tartaglia, and other "masks" seeking three oranges believed to have magic powers; the dialogue was left to be improvised. The success of this "fable" was decisive: the Venetian public, living on laughter, relished the imagination of the tale and the implied satire of Chiari's and Goldoni's plots. Gozzi followed with nine other *fiabe* in five years; but in these he supplied a poetic dialogue, thereby in part admitting Goldoni's criticism of the *commedia dell' arte*. In any case, Gozzi's victory seemed complete. The attendance at the San Samuele remained high, that at Goldoni's Teatro Sant' Angelo fell toward bankruptcy. Chiari moved to Brescia, and Goldoni ac-cepted an invitation to Paris.*

---

* Two of Gozzi's "fables" were made into operas: *Re Turandote* by Weber, Busoni, and Puccini, *The Love of the Three Oranges* by Prokofiev.

As his farewell to Venice Goldoni produced (1762) *Una delle ultime sere di Carnevale* (*One of the Last Evenings of Carnival*). It told of a textile designer, Sior Anzoleto, who with a heavy heart was leaving in Venice the weavers whose looms he had so long provided with patterns. The audience soon saw in this an allegory for the dramatist regretfully leaving the actors whose stage he had so long supplied with plays. When Anzoleto appeared in the final scene, the theater (Goldoni tells us) "rang with thunderous applause, amid which could be heard, . . . 'A happy journey!' 'Come back to us!' 'Don't fail to come back to us!' "[76] He left Venice on April 15, 1762, and never saw it again.

In Paris he was engaged for two years in writing comedies for the Théâtre des Italiens. In 1763 he was sued for seduction,[77] but a year later he was engaged to teach Italian to the daughters of Louis XV. For the wedding of Marie Antoinette and the future Louis XVI he composed in French one of his best plays, *Le Bourru bienfaisant* (*The Benevolent Boor*). He was rewarded with a pension of twelve hundred francs, which was annulled by the Revolution when he was eighty-one years old. He solaced his poverty by dictating to his wife his *Memoirs* (1792)—inaccurate, imaginative, illuminating, entertaining; Gibbon thought them "more truly dramatic than his Italian comedies."[78] He died on February 6, 1793. On February 7 the National Convention, on a motion by the poet Marie-Joseph de Chénier, restored his pension. Finding him in no condition to receive it, the Convention gave it, reduced, to his widow.

Gozzi's victory in Venice was brief. Long before his death (1806) his *Fiabe* had passed from the stage, and Goldoni's comedies had been revived in the theaters of Italy. They are still played there, almost as frequently as Molière's in France. His statue stands on the Campo San Bartolommeo in Venice, and on the Largo Goldoni in Florence. For, as his *Memoirs* said, "humanity is everywhere the same, jealousy displays itself everywhere, and everywhere a man of a cool and tranquil disposition in the end acquires the love of the public, and wears out his enemies."[79]

VI. ROME

South of the Po, along the Adriatic and spanning the Apennines, were the states of the Church—Ferrara, Bologna, Forlì, Ravenna, Perugia, Benevento, Rome—forming the central and largest part of the Magic Boot.

When Ferrara was incorporated into the Papal States (1598) its Estense dukes made Modena their home, and gathered there their archives, books, and art. In 1700 Lodovico Muratori, priest, scholar, and doctor of laws, became curator of these treasures. From them in fifteen years of labor and twenty-eight volumes, he compiled *Rerum italicarum scriptores* (*Writers of Italian Affairs*, 1723–38); later he added ten volumes of Italian antiquities and inscriptions. He was rather an antiquarian than an historian, and his twelve-volume *Annali d'Italia* was soon superseded; but his researches in documents and inscriptions made him the father and source of modern historical writing in Italy.

Aside from Rome the most flourishing of these states was Bologna. Its renowned school of painting continued under Giuseppe Crespi ("Lo Spagnuolo"). Its university was still one of the best in Europe. The Palazzo Bevilacqua (1749) was among the most elegant structures of the century. A remarkable family, centering in Bologna, brought theatrical architecture and scene painting to their highest excellence in modern times. Ferdinando Galli da Bibiena built the Teatro Reale at Mantua (1731), wrote famous texts on his art, and begot three sons who carried on his skill in deceptive and sumptuous ornament. His brother Francesco designed theaters in Vienna, Nancy, and Rome, and Verona's Teatro Filarmonico—often rated the finest in Italy. Ferdinando's son Alessandro became chief architect for the Elector of the Palatinate. Another son, Giuseppe, designed the interior of the opera house at Bayreuth (1748)—"the most beautiful of its kind in existence."[80] A third son, Antonio, drew the plans for the Teatro Communale at Bologna.

That theater, and the massive old Church of San Petronio, heard the best instrumental music in Italy, for Bologna was the chief Italian center of musical education and theory. There Padre Giovanni Battista Martini held his modest but austere court as the most respected music teacher in Europe. He had a music library of seventeen thousand volumes; he composed classic texts on counterpoint and musical history; he corresponded with a hundred celebrities in a dozen lands. The accolade of the Accademia Filarmonica, of which he was for many years the head, was coveted by all musicians. Here the boy Mozart would come in 1770 to face the prescribed tests; here Rossini and Donizetti were to teach. The annual festival of new compositions, performed by the hundred-piece orchestra of the Accademia, was, for Italy, the supreme event of the musical year.

Gibbon estimated the population of Rome in 1740 at some 156,000 souls. Recalling the brilliance of the Imperial past, and forgetting its paupers and slaves, he found the charm of the Catholic capital uncongenial to his taste:

> Within the spacious enclosures of the [Aurelian] walls the largest portion of the seven hills is overspread with vineyards and ruins. The beauty and splendor of the modern city may be ascribed to the abuses of the government, and to the influence of superstition. Each reign (the exceptions are rare) has been marked by the rapid elevation of a new family, enriched by the childless pontiff at the expense of the Church and country. The palaces of these fortunate nephews are the most costly monuments of elegance and servitude: the perfect arts of architecture, painting, and sculpture have been prostituted in their service; and their galleries and gardens are decorated with the most precious works of antiquity which taste or vanity has prompted them to collect.[81]

The popes of this period were distinguished by their high morality; their morals rose as their power fell. They were all Italians, for none of the Catholic monarchs would allow any of the others to capture the papacy. Clement XI (r. 1700–21) justified his name by reforming the prisons of Rome. Innocent XIII (1721–24), in the judgment of the Protestant Ranke,

possessed admirable qualifications for the spiritual as well as the temporal government, but his health was extremely delicate. . . . The Roman families connected with him, and which had hoped to be promoted by him, found themselves completely deceived; even his nephew could not obtain without difficulty
the enjoyment of those twelve thousand ducats annually, which had now become the usual income of a nephew.[82]

Benedict XIII (1724–30) was "a man of great personal piety,"[83] but (says a
Catholic historian) he "allowed far too much power to unworthy favorites."[84] Clement XII (1730–40) flooded Rome with his Florentine friends,
and, when old and blind, allowed himself to be ruled by his nephews, whose
intolerance further embittered the conflict between Jesuits and Jansenists in
France.

Macaulay thought Benedict XIV (1740–58) "the best and wisest of the
250 successors of St. Peter."[85] A sweeping judgment, but Protestants, Catholics, and unbelievers join in acclaiming Benedict as a man of wide learning,
lovable character, and moral integrity. As archbishop of Bologna he had
seen no contradiction between attendance at the opera three times a week
and strict attention to his episcopal tasks;[86] and as a pope he reconciled the
purity of his personal life with gaiety of humor, freedom of speech, and an
almost pagan appreciation of literature and art. He added a nude *Venus* to
his collection, and told Cardinal de Tencin how the Prince and Princess of
Württemberg scratched their names on a gracefully rounded portion of
the anatomy not often mentioned in papal correspondence.[87] His wit was
almost as keen as Voltaire's, but it did not prevent him from being a careful
administrator and a far-seeing diplomat.

He found papal finances in chaos: half the revenue was lost in transit, and
a third of Rome's population consisted of ecclesiastics far more numerous
than the business of the Church required, and more expensive than the
Church could properly afford. Benedict reduced his own staff, dismissed
most of the papal troops, ended papal nepotism, lowered taxes, introduced
agricultural improvements, and encouraged industrial enterprise. Soon his
probity, economies, and efficiency brought a surplus to the papal treasury.
His foreign policy made genial concessions to turbulent kings: he signed
with Sardinia, Portugal, Naples, and Spain concordats allowing their Catholic
rulers to nominate to episcopal sees. He strove to quiet the doctrinal furor
in France by a lax enforcement of the anti-Jansenist bull *Unigenitus;* "since
infidelity progresses daily," he wrote, "we must rather ask whether men
believe in God than whether they accept the bull."[88]

He made brave efforts to find a *modus vivendi* with the Enlightenment.
We have noted his cordial acceptance of the dedication of Voltaire's *Mahomet,* though this play was under ecclesiastical fire in Paris (1746). He appointed a commission to revise the Breviary and to eliminate some of the
more incredible legends; however, the recommendations of this commission
were not carried out. He secured by his personal activity the election of
d'Alembert to the Bologna Institute.[89] He discouraged the hasty prohibition
of books. When some aides advised him to denounce La Mettrie's *L'Homme*

machine he replied, "Should you not refrain from reporting to me the audacities of fools?" And he added, "Know that the pope has a free hand only to give blessings."[90] The revised Index Expurgatorius which he issued in 1758 abandoned all attempts to keep track of non-Catholic literature; with a few exceptions it confined itself to prohibiting some books by Catholic authors. No condemnation should be made until the author, if available, had been given a chance to defend himself; no book on a learned subject should be condemned except after consultation with experts; men of science or scholarship should be readily given permission to read prohibited books.[91] These rules were followed in subsequent editions of the Index, and were confirmed by Leo XIII in 1900.

The popes found it almost as difficult to govern Rome as to rule the Catholic world. The populace of the city was probably the roughest and most violent in Italy, perhaps in Europe. Any cause could lead to a duel in the nobility, or to a bloody conflict between the sectionally patriotic gangs that divided the Holy City. At the theater the judgment of the audience could be merciless, especially when wrong; we shall see an instance with Pergolesi. The Church strove to appease the people with festivals, processions, indulgences, and Carnival. During the eight days preceding Lent they were allowed to don gay and fanciful disguises, and frolic on the Corso; nobles sought popular favor by parades of horses or chariots bearing skilled riders or beautiful women, all richly adorned; prostitutes offered their wares at temporarily raised rates; and masked flirtations relieved for some hours the strain of monogamy. Carnival over, Rome resumed its uneven tenor of piety and crime.

Art did not prosper amid the diminishing returns of a declining faith. Architecture made some minor contributions: Alessandro Galilei gave the old Church of San Giovanni in Laterano a proud façade, Ferdinando Fuga put a new face upon Santa Maria Maggiore, and Francesco de Sanctis raised the stately, spacious Scala di Spagna from the Piazza di Spagna to the shrine of Santissima Trinità dei Monti. Sculpture added a famous monument, the Fontana di Trevi—where the pleased tourist throws a coin over his shoulder into the water to ensure a further visit to Rome. This "Fountain of the Three Outlets" had a long history. Bernini may have left a sketch for it; Clement XII opened a competition for it; Edme Bouchardon of Paris and Lambert-Sigisbert Adam of Nancy submitted plans; Giovanni Maini was chosen to design it; Pietro Bracci carved the central group of Neptune and his team (1732); Filippo della Valle molded the figures of Fertility and Healing; Niccolò Salvi provided the architectural background; Giuseppe Pannini completed the work in 1762; this collaboration of many minds and hands through thirty years may suggest some faltering of will or failure of funds, but it bars any thought that art in Rome was dead. Bracci added to his honors the tomb (now in St. Peter's) of Maria Clementina Sobieska, the unhappy wife of the Stuart Pretender James III; and della Valle left in the Church of St. Ignatius a delicately carved relief of the Annunciation, worthy of the High Renaissance.

Painting produced no marvels at Rome in this age, but Giovanni Battista Piranesi made engraving a major art. Born to a stonemason near Venice, he read Palladio and dreamed of palaces and shrines. Venice had more artists than money, Rome had more money than artists; so Giovanni moved to Rome, and set up as architect. But buildings were not in demand. He designed them anyway; or, rather, he drew imaginary structures that he knew no one would build, including fantastic jails that looked as if the Spanish Steps had fallen upon the Baths of Diocletian. He published these drawings in 1750 as *Opere varie di architettura* and *Carceri (Prisons)*, and people bought them as they bought puzzles or mysteries. In loftier mood Piranesi turned his skill to engraving his sketches of ancient monuments. He fell in love with them, as Poussin and Robert did; he mourned to see these classic ruins disintegrating further, day by day, through spoliation or neglect; for twenty-five years, almost daily, he went out to draw them, sometimes missing meals; even when he was dying of cancer he continued to draw, engrave, and etch. His *Roman Antiquities* and *Views of Rome* went out as prints over Europe, and shared in the architectural revival of classic styles.

That revival was powerfully stimulated by excavations at Herculaneum and Pompeii—towns that had been overwhelmed by the eruption of Vesuvius in A.D. 79. In 1719 some peasants reported that they had found statues embedded in the earth at Herculaneum. Nineteen years passed before funds could be secured for systematic exploration of the site. In 1748 similar excavations began to reveal the wonders of pagan Pompeii, and in 1752 the massive and majestic Greek temples of Paestum were cleared from the jungle. Archaeologists came from a dozen countries to study and describe the findings; their drawings stirred the interest of artists as well as historians; soon Rome and Naples were invaded by enthusiasts for classic art, especially from Germany. Mengs came in 1740, Winckelmann in 1755. Lessing longed to go to Rome, "to remain there at least for a year, and, if possible, forever."[92] And Goethe—but let that story wait.

Anton Raphael Mengs is hard to place, for he was born in Bohemia (1728), worked chiefly in Italy and Spain, and chose Rome for his home. His father, a painter of miniatures at Dresden, named him after Correggio and Raphael, and pledged him to art. The boy showed talent, and the father took him, aged twelve, to Rome. There, we are told, he shut him up in the Vatican day after day, with bread and wine for lunch, and told him, for the rest, to feed on the relics of Raphael, Michelangelo, and the classic world. After a brief stay in Dresden Anton returned to Rome, and won attention by a painting of the Holy Family. For this he took as his model Margarita Guazzi, "a poor, virtuous, and beautiful maiden."[93] He married her in 1749, and in the same embrace he accepted the Roman Catholic faith. Again in Dresden, he was appointed court painter to Augustus III at a thousand thalers a year. He agreed to paint two pictures for a Dresden church, but he persuaded the Elector-King to let him do these in Rome, and in 1752, aged twenty-four, he settled there. At twenty-six he was made director of the Vatican School of Painting. In 1755 he met Winckelmann, and agreed with him that baroque was a mistake, and that art must chasten itself with neoclassic forms. Probably about this time he executed in pastel the self-portrait now in the Dresden Gemäldegalerie—the face and hair of a girl, but eyes flashing with the pride of a man sure that he could shake the world.

When Frederick the Great chased Augustus from Saxony (1756), Mengs's royal salary stopped, and he had to live on the modest fees offered him in Italy. He tried Naples, but the local artists, following an old Neapolitan custom, threatened his life as an alien invader, and Mengs hurried back to Rome. He adorned the Villa Albani with once famous frescoes; still visible there is his *Parnassus* (1761), technically excellent, coldly classical, emotionally dead. Nevertheless the Spanish minister at Rome felt that this was the man to decorate the royal palace in Madrid. Charles III sent for Mengs, promised him two thousand doubloons per year, plus a house and a coach, and free passage on a Spanish man-of-war soon to sail from Naples. In September, 1761, Mengs arrived in Madrid.

VII. NAPLES

1. The King and the People

The kingdom of Naples, comprising all Italy south of the Papal States, was buffeted about in the struggle for power among Austria, Spain, England, and France. But that is the dreary logic-chopping of history, the bloody seesaw of victory and defeat; let us merely note that Austria took Naples in 1707; that Don Carlos, Bourbon duke of Parma and son of Philip V of Spain, drove out the Austrians in 1734, and, as Charles IV, king of Naples and Sicily, ruled till 1759. His capital, with 300,000 population, was the largest city in Italy.

Charles matured slowly into the royal art. At first he took kingship as a license for luxury: he neglected government, spent half his days in hunting, and ate himself into obesity. Then, toward 1755, inspired by his Minister of Justice and Foreign Affairs, Marchese Bernardo di Tanucci, he undertook to mitigate the harsh feudalism that underlay the toil and ecstasy of Neapolitan life.

Three interlocking groups had long ruled the kingdom. Nobles owned almost two thirds of the land, held four fifths of its five million souls in bondage, dominated the parliament, controlled taxation, and frustrated all reform. The clergy owned a third of the land, and held the people in spiritual subjection with a theology of terror, a literature of legends, a ritual of stupefaction, and such miracles as the semiannual manipulated liquefaction of the congealed blood of St. Januarius, Naples' patron saint. Administration was in the hands of lawyers beholden to nobles or prelates, and therefore pledged to the medieval status quo. A small middle class, mostly of merchants, was politically impotent. Peasants and proletaires lived in a poverty that drove some into brigandage and many into beggary; there were thirty thousand beggars in Naples alone.[94] De Brosses called the masses of the capital "the most abominable riffraff, the most disgusting vermin"[95]—a judgment that condemned the result without stigmatizing the cause. We must admit, however, that those ragged, superstitious, and priest-ridden Neapolitans seemed to have more of the salt and joy of life in them than any other populace in Europe.

Charles checked the power of the nobles by attracting them to the court to be under the royal eye, and by creating new nobles pledged to his support. He discouraged the flow of youth into monasteries, reduced the ecclesiastical multitude from 100,000 to 81,000, laid a tax of two per cent upon church property, and limited the legal immunities of the clergy. Tannuci restricted the jurisdiction of the nobles, fought judicial corruption, reformed legal procedure, and moderated the severity of the penal code. Freedom of worship was allowed to the Jews, but the monks assured Charles that his lack of a male heir was God's punishment for this sinful toleration, and the indulgence was withdrawn.[96]

The King's passion for building gave Naples two famous structures. The vast Teatro San Carlo was raised in 1737; it is still one of the largest and most beautiful opera houses in existence. In 1752 Luigi Vanvitelli began at Caserta, twenty-one miles northeast of the capital, the enormous royal palace that was designed to rival Versailles, and to serve the similar functions of housing the royal family, the attendant nobility, and the main administrative staff. Slaves black or white toiled on the task for twenty-two years. Curved buildings flanked a spacious approach to the central edifice, which spread its front for 830 feet. Within were a chapel, a theater, countless rooms, and a broad double stairway of which every step was a single marble slab. Behind the palace, for half a mile, lay formal gardens, a population of statues, and majestic fountains supplied by an aqueduct twenty-seven miles long.

Other than this Caserta (for the palace, like the Escorial and Versailles, took the name of its town) there was no outstanding art in the Naples of this age, nor anything memorable in drama or poetry. One man wrote a bold *Istoria civile del regno di Napoli* (1723), a running attack upon the greed of the clergy, the abuses of the ecclesiastical courts, the temporal power of the Church, and the claim of the papacy to hold Naples as a papal fief; its author, Pietro Giannone, was excommunicated by the Archbishop of Naples, fled to Vienna, was thrown into prison by the King of Sardinia, and died in Turin (1748) after twelve years of confinement.[97] — Antonio Genovesi, a priest, lost his faith while reading Locke, and in *Elementa metaphysicae* (1743) tried to introduce the Lockian psychology into Italy. In 1754 a Florentine businessman established in the University of Naples the first European chair of political economy on two conditions: that it should never be held by an ecclesiastic, and that its first occupant should be Antonio Genovesi. Genovesi repaid him (1756) with the first systematic economic treatise in Italian, *Lezioni di commercio*, which voiced the cry of merchants and manufacturers for liberation from feudal, ecclesiastical, and other restraints on free enterprise. In that same year Quesnay raised the same demand for the French middle class in his articles for Diderot's *Encyclopédie*.

Perhaps some liaison had been established between Genovesi and Quesnay by Ferdinando Galiani, of Naples and Paris. Galiani published in 1750 a *Trattato della moneta*, in which, with the innocence of a twenty-two-year-old economist, he determined the price of a product by the cost of its production. More brilliant was his *Dialoghi sul commercio dei grani*, which we have noted as a criticism of Quesnay. When he had to come home after his exciting years in Paris, he mourned that Naples had no salons, no Mme. Geoffrin to feed him and stir his wit. It had, however, a philosopher who left a mark on history.

2. Giambattista Vico

At the age of seven, says his autobiography, he fell from a ladder, struck the ground head first, and remained unconscious for five hours. He suffered a cranial fracture over which a massive tumor formed. This was reduced by successive lancings; however, the boy lost so much blood in the process that the surgeons expected his early death. "By God's grace" he survived, "but as a result of this mischance I grew up with a melancholy and irritable temperament."[98] He also developed tuberculosis. If genius depends upon some physical handicap Vico was richly endowed.

At seventeen (1685) he earned his bread by tutoring at Vatolla (near Salerno) the nephews of the bishop of Ischia. There he remained nine years, meanwhile feverishly studying jurisprudence, philology, history, and philosophy. He read with special fascination Plato, Epicurus, Lucretius, Machiavelli, Francis Bacon, Descartes, and Grotius, with some injury to his catechism. In 1697 he obtained a professorship in rhetoric at the University of Naples; it paid him only a hundred ducats yearly, to which he added by tutoring; on this he raised a large family. One daughter died in youth; one son showed such vicious tendencies that he had to be sent to a house of correction. The wife was illiterate and incompetent; Vico had to be father, mother, and teacher.[99] Amid these distractions he wrote his philosophy of history.

Principi di una scienza nuova d'intorno alla commune natura delle nazioni (1725) offered the "principles of a new science concerning the common nature of the nations," and proposed to find in the jungle of history regularities of sequence that might illuminate past, present, and future. Vico thought that he could discern three main periods in the history of every people:

> (1) The age of the gods, in which the Gentiles believed that they lived under divine governments, and that everything was commanded them by [gods through] auspices and oracles. . . . (2) The age of heroes, when these reigned in aristocratic commonwealths, on account of a certain superiority of nature which they held themselves to have over the plebs. (3) The age of men, in which all recognized themselves as equal in human nature, and therefore established the first popular commonwealths, and then monarchies.[100]

Vico applied the first period only to "Gentiles" and "profane" (non-Biblical) history; he could not, without offending sacred tradition, speak of the Old Testament Jews as merely *believing* that they "lived under divine governments." Since the Inquisition (severer in Naples than in northern Italy) had prosecuted Neapolitan scholars for talking of men before Adam, Vico laboriously reconciled his formula with Genesis by supposing that all the descendants of Adam, except the Jews, had relapsed, after the Flood, into an almost bestial condition, living in caves, and copulating indiscriminately in a communism of women. It was from this secondary "state of nature" that civilization had developed through the family, agriculture, property, morality, and religion. At times Vico spoke of religion as a primitive animistic way of explaining objects and events; at times he exalted it as a peak of evolution.

To the three stages of social development correspond three "natures," or ways of interpreting the world: the theological, the legendary, the rational.

> The first nature, by an illusion of imagination (which is strongest in those who are weakest in reasoning power), was a poetic or creative nature, which we may be allowed to call divine, since it conceived physical things as animated by gods. . . . Through the same error of their imagination men had a terrible fear of the gods whom they themselves had created. . . . The second nature was the heroic: the heroes believed themselves to be of divine origin. . . . The third was the human nature [way], intelligent and therefore modest, benign, and rational, recognizing conscience, reason, and duty as laws.[101]

Vico strove to fit the history of language, literature, law, and government into this triadic scheme. In the first stage men communicated through signs and gestures; in the second, through "emblems, similitudes, images"; in the third, through "words agreed upon by the people, . . . whereby they might fix the meaning of the laws." Law itself passed through a corresponding development: at first it was divine, god-given, as in the Mosaic code; then heroic, as in Lycurgus; then human—"dictated by fully developed human reason."[102] Government, too, has gone through three stages: the theocratic, in which the rulers claimed to be the voice of God; the aristocratic, in which "all civil rights" were confined to the ruling order of "heroes"; and the human, wherein "all are accounted equal before the laws. . . . This is the case in the free popular cities, and . . . also in those monarchies that make all their subjects equal under their laws."[103] Vico evidently recalled Plato's summary of political evolution from monarchy through aristocracy to democracy to dictatorship (*tyrannis*), but he varied the formula to read: theocracy, aristocracy, democracy, monarchy. He agreed with Plato that democracy tends toward chaos, and he looked upon one-man rule as a necessary remedy for democratic disorder; "monarchies are the final governments . . . in which nations come to rest."[104]

Social disorder may come through moral deterioration, luxury, effeminacy, loss of martial qualities, corruption in office, a disruptive concentration of wealth, or an aggressive envy among the poor. Usually such disorder leads to dictatorship, as when the rule of Augustus cured the democratic chaos of the Roman Republic.[105] If even dictatorship fails to stem decay, some more vigorous nation enters as conqueror.

> Since people so far corrupted have already become slaves of their unrestrained passions, . . . Providence decrees that they become slaves by the

natural law of nations; . . . they become subject to better nations which, having conquered them, keep them as subject provinces. Herein two great lights of natural order shine forth: first, that he who cannot govern himself must let himself be governed by another who can; second, that the world is always governed by those who are naturally fittest.[106]

In such cases the conquered people falls back into the stage of development reached by its conquerors. So the population of the Roman Empire, after the barbarian invasions, relapsed into barbarism, and had to begin with theocracy [rule by priests and theology]; such were the Dark Ages. With the Crusades came another heroic age; the feudal chieftains correspond to the heroes of Homer, and Dante is Homer again.

We hear in Vico echoes of the theory that history is a circular repetition, and of Machiavelli's law of *corsi e ricorsi*, development and return. The idea of progress suffers in this analysis; progress is merely one half of a cyclical movement in which the other half is decay; history, like life, is evolution and dissolution in an ineluctible sequence and fatality.

On his way Vico offered some striking suggestions. He reduced many heroes of classic legend to eponyms—afternames—post-factum personifications of long impersonal or multipersonal processes; so Orpheus was the imaginary consolidation of many primitive musicians; Lycurgus was the embodiment of the series of laws and customs that congealed Sparta; Romulus was a thousand men who had made Rome a state.[107] Likewise Vico reduced Homer to a myth by arguing—half a century before Friedrich Wolf's *Prolegomena to Homer* (1795)—that the Homeric epics are the accumulated and gradually amalgamated product of groups and generations of rhapsodes who sang, in the cities of Greece, the sagas of Troy and Odysseus.[108] And almost a century before Barthold Niebuhr's *History of Rome* (1811–32) Vico rejected as legendary the first chapters of Livy. "All the histories of the Gentile nations have had fabulous beginnings."[109] (Again Vico carefully avoids impugning the historicity of Genesis.)

This epochal book reveals a powerful but harassed mind struggling to formulate basic ideas without getting himself into an Inquisition jail. Vico went out of his way, time after time, to profess his loyalty to the Church, and he felt that he merited ecclesiastical commendation for explaining the principles of jurisprudence in a manner compatible with Catholic theology.[110] We hear a sincerer tone in his view of religion as the indispensable support of social order and personal morality: "Religions alone have the power to cause the people to do virtuous works . . ."[111] And yet, despite his frequent use of "Providence," he seems to eliminate God from history, and to reduce events to the unimpeded play of natural causes and effects. A Dominican scholar attacked Vico's philosophy as not Christian but Lucretian.

Perhaps the emerging secularism of Vico's analysis had something to do with its failure to win a hearing in Italy, and doubtless the disorderly discursiveness of his work and the confusion of his thought doomed his "new science" to a still but painful birth. No one agreed with his belief that he had written a profound or illuminating book. He appealed in vain to Jean Le Clerc to at least mention it in the periodical *Nouvelles de la république des lettres.* Ten years after the *Scienza nuova* appeared, Charles IV came to Vico's aid by appointing him historiographer royal with a yearly stipend of a hundred ducats. In 1741 Giambattista had the satisfaction of seeing his son Gennaro succeed to his professorship in the University of Naples. In his final years (1743–44) his mind gave way, and he lapsed into a mysticism bordering on insanity.

A copy of his book was in Montesquieu's library.[112] In private notes the French philosopher acknowledged his debt to Vico's theory of cyclical development and decay; and that debt, unnamed, appears in Montesquieu's *Greatness and Decadence of the Romans* (1734). For the rest Vico remained almost unknown in France until Jules Michelet published (1827) an abridged translation of the *Scienza nuova.* Michelet described Italy as "the second mother and nurse who in my youth suckled me on Virgil, and in my maturity nourished me with Vico."[113] In 1826 Auguste Comte began the lectures that became his *Cours de philosophie positive* (1830–42), wherein the influence of Vico is felt at every stage. It was left for a Neapolitan, Benedetto Croce, to give Vico his full due,[114] and to suggest again that history must take its place beside science as the ground and vestibule of philosophy.

3. Neapolitan Music

Naples reversed Pythagoras, and judged music to be the highest philosophy. Said Lalande, the French astronomer, after a tour of Italy in 1765–66:

> Music is the special triumph of the Neapolitans. It seems as if in that country the membranes of the eardrum are more taut, more harmonious, more sonorous than elsewhere in Europe. The whole nation sings. Gestures, tone, voice, rhythm of syllables, the very conversation—all breathe music. . . . So Naples is the principal source of Italian music, of great composers and excellent operas; it is there that Corelli, Vinci, Rinaldo, Jommelli, Durante, Leo, Pergolesi, . . . and so many other famous composers have brought forth their masterpieces.[115]

Naples, however, was supreme only in opera and vocal melody; in instrumental music Venice led the way; and music fanciers complained that the Neapolitans loved the tricks of the voice more than the subtleties of harmony and counterpoint. Here reigned Niccolò Porpora, "perhaps the greatest singing teacher who ever lived."[116] Every Italian warbler aspired to be his pupil, and, once accepted, bore humbly with his imperious eccentricities; so, said a story, he kept Gaetano Caffarelli for five years at one page of exercises, and then dismissed him with the assurance that he was now the greatest singer in Europe.[117] Second only to Porpora as a teacher was Francesco Durante, who taught Vinci, Jommelli, Pergolesi, Paisiello, and Piccini.

Leonardo Vinci seemed handicapped by his name, but he won early acclaim by his setting of Metastasio's *Didone abbandonata;* Algarotti felt that "Virgil himself would have been pleased to hear a composition so animated and so harrowing in which the heart and soul were at once assailed by all the powers of music."[118] Still more famous was Leonardo Leo, in *opera seria* and *buffa,* oratorio, Masses, and motets; Naples oscillated for some time between laughing at his comic opera *La finta Fracastana* and weeping over the "Miserere" that he composed for the Lenten services of 1744.

When, about 1735, Leo heard a cantata by Niccolò Jommelli, he exclaimed, "A short time, and this young man will be the wonder and admiration of Europe."[119] Jommelli almost verified the prophecy. At twenty-three he won the plaudits of Naples with his first opera; at twenty-six he earned a similar triumph in Rome. Passing to Bologna, he presented himself as a pupil to Padre Martini; but when that reverend teacher heard him extemporize a fugue in all its classic development he cried out, "Who are you, then? Are you making fun of me? It is I who should learn from you."[120] At Venice his operas aroused such enthusiasm that the Council of Ten appointed him music director of the Scuola degli Incurabili; there he wrote some of the best religious music of that generation. Moving on to Vienna (1748) he composed in close friendship with Metastasio. After further victories in Venice and Rome he settled down in Stuttgart and Ludwigsburg (1753–68) as *Kapellmeister* to the Duke of Württemberg. Here he modified his operatic style in a German direction, giving more complexity to his harmony, more substance and weight to the instrumental music; he discarded the *da capo* repetition of arias, and provided orchestral accompaniment for recitatives. Probably under the influence of Jean-Georges Noverre, the French ballet master at Stuttgart, he gave ballet a prominent part in his operas. In some measure these developments in Jommelli's music prepared the way for the reforms of Gluck.

When the aging composer returned to Naples (1768) the audience resented his Teutonic tendencies, and decisively rejected his operas. Mozart, hearing one of them there in 1770, remarked: "It is beautiful, but the style is too elevated, as well as too antique, for the theater."[121] Jommelli fared better with his church music; his "Miserere" and his *Mass for the Dead* were sung throughout the Catholic world. William Beckford, after hearing the *Mass* in Lisbon in 1787, wrote: "Such august, such affecting music I never heard, and perhaps may never hear again."[122] Having saved his earnings with Teutonic care, Jommelli retired to his native Aversa, and spent his final years in opulent corpulence. In 1774 all the prominent musicians of Naples attended his funeral.

Naples laughed even more than it sang. It was with a comic opera that Pergolesi conquered Paris after that proud city, alone among the European capitals, had refused to submit to Italy's *opera seria.* Giovanni Battista Pergolesi did not fight that battle in person, for he died in 1736 at the age of twenty-six. Born near Ancona, he came to Naples at sixteen. By the age of twenty-two he had written several operas, thirty sonatas, and two Masses much admired. In 1733 he presented an opera, *Il prigioniero,* and as an interlude to this he offered *La serva padrona*—"the maid" become "mistress" of the house. The libretto is a jolly story of how Serpina, the servant, maneuvers her master into marrying her; the music is an hour of gaiety and agile arias. We have seen how this artful frolic captured the mood and heart of

Paris in the Guerre des Bouffons of 1752, when it ran for a hundred performances at the Opéra, and then, in 1753, for ninety-six more at the Théâtre-Français. Meanwhile Pergolesi conducted his opera *L'Olimpiade* in Rome (1735). It was hailed with a storm of hoots, and with an orange accurately aimed at the composer's head.[123] A year later he went to Pozzuoli to be treated for tuberculosis, which had been made worse by his profligate life. His early death atoned for his sins, and he was buried in the local cathedral by the Capuchin friars among whom he had spent his last days. Rome, repentant, revived *L'Olimpiade*, and applauded it rapturously. Italy honors him not so much for his joyous intermezzi as for the tender sentiment of his "Stabat Mater," which he did not live to complete. Pergolesi himself was made the subject of two operas.

Domenico Scarlatti, like Pergolesi, has been slightly inflated by the winds of taste, but who can resist the sparkle of his prestidigitation? Born in the *annus mirabilis* of Handel and Bach (1685), he was the sixth child of Alessandro Scarlatti, then the Verdi of Italian opera. He breathed music from his birth. His brother Pietro, his cousin Giuseppe, his uncles Francesco and Tommaso, were musicians; Giuseppe's operas were produced in Naples, Rome, Turin, Venice, Vienna. Fearing lest Domenico's genius be stifled by this plethora of talent, the father sent him, aged twenty, to Venice. "This son of mine," he said, "is an eagle whose wings are grown. He must not remain in the nest, and I must not hinder his flight."[124]

In Venice the youth continued his studies, and met Handel. Perhaps together they passed to Rome, where, at the urging of Cardinal Ottoboni, they engaged in an amiable competition on the harpsichord and then on the organ. Domenico was already the best harpsichordist in Italy, but Handel, we are told, equaled him; while on the organ Scarlatti frankly owned *il caro Sassone*'s superiority. The two men became fast friends; this is extremely difficult for leading practitioners of the same art, but, a contemporary tells us, "Domenico had the sweetest temper and the genteelest behavior,"[125] and Handel's heart was as big as his frame. The shy modesty of the Italian deterred him from giving public displays of his harpsichord mastery; we know it only from reports of private musicales. One auditor in Rome (1714) "thought ten thousand devils had been at the instrument"; never before had he heard "such passages of execution and effect."[126] Scarlatti was the first to develop the keyboard potentialities of the left hand, including its crossing over the right. "Nature," he said, "gave me ten fingers, and as my instrument has employment for all, I see no reason why I should not use them."[127]

In 1709 he accepted appointment as *maestro di capella* to the former Queen of Poland, Maria Kazimiera. On the death of her husband, Jan Sobieski, she had been banished as a troublesome intriguer; coming to Rome in 1699, she resolved to set up a salon as brilliant with genius as that of Queen Christina of Sweden, who had died ten years before. In a palace on the Piazza della Trinità dei Monti she gathered many of Christina's former circle, including several members of the Arcadian Academy. There (1709–14) Scarlatti produced several of his operas. Encouraged by their success, he presented *Amleto* (*Hamlet*) in the Teatro Capranico. It was not well received, and Domenico never again offered an opera to an Italian public. His father had set a standard too high for him to reach.

For four years (1715–19) he directed the Cappella Giulia at the Vatican, and officiated at the organ in St. Peter's; now he composed a "Stabat Mater" which has been pronounced "a genuine masterpiece."[128] In 1719 he conducted his opera *Narciso* in London. Two years later we find him in Lisbon as chapelmaster to John V, and as teacher to the King's daughter Maria Barbara, who became a skilled harpsichordist under his tutelage; most of his extant sonatas were composed for her use. Returning to Naples (1725), he married, age forty-two, Maria Gentile, age sixteen; and in 1729 he took her to Madrid. In that year Maria Barbara married Ferdinand, Crown Prince of Spain. When she moved with him to Seville Scarlatti accompanied her, and he remained in her service till her death.

Scarlatti's wife died in 1739, leaving him five children. He married again, and soon the five were nine. When Maria Barbara became queen of Spain (1746) she brought the Scarlatti family with her to Madrid. Farinelli was the favorite musician of the royal pair, but the singer and the virtuoso became good friends. Scarlatti's position was that of a privileged servitor, providing music for the Spanish court. He obtained leave to go to Dublin in 1740 and to London in 1741; but mostly he lived in quiet content in or near Madrid, almost secluded from the world, and probably with no suspicion that he would become a favorite with pianists in the twentieth century.

Of the 555 "sonatas" that now precariously support his fame on their tonal filigree, Scarlatti in his lifetime published only thirty. Their modest title, *Esercizii per gravicembalo,* indicated their limited aim—to explore the possibilities of expression through harpsichord technique. They are sonatas only in the older sense of the term, as instrumental pieces to be "sounded," not sung. Some have contrasted themes, and some are paired in major and minor keys, but they are all in single movements, with no attempt at thematic elaboration and recapitulation. They represent the emancipation of harpsichord music from the influence of the organ, and the reception, by keyboard compositions, of influences from opera. The vivacity, delicacy, trills, and tricks of sopranos and *castrati* are here surpassed by agile fingers obeying a playful and prodigal imagination. Scarlatti literally "played" the harpsichord. "Do not expect," he said, "any profound learning, but rather an ingenious jesting with art."[129] Something of the Spanish dance—its prancing feet and swirling skirts and tinkling castanets—is in these ripples and cascades, and everywhere in the sonatas is the abandon of a performer to pleasure in mastery over his instrument.[130]

That joy in the instrument must have been one source of solace to Scarlatti in those serving years in Spain. It was rivaled by his delight in gambling, which consumed much of his pension; the Queen had repeatedly to pay his debts. After 1751 his health failed, and his piety increased. In 1754 he returned to Naples, and there, three years later, he died. The good Farinelli provided for his friend's impoverished family.

We have left to a later chapter the strange career of Farinelli in Spain. He and Domenico Scarlatti, Giambattista and Domenico Tiepolo, were among the gifted Italians who, with the almost Italianate Mengs, brought Italian music and art into the Spanish quickening. In 1759 the King of Naples followed or preceded them. In that year Ferdinand VI died without issue, and his brother Charles IV of Naples inherited the Spanish throne as Charles III. Naples was sorry to see him go. His departure, in a fleet of sixteen ships, was a sad holiday for the Neapolitans; they gathered in great throngs along the shore to see him sail away, and many, we are told, wept in bidding farewell to "a sovereign who had proved himself the father of his people."[131] He was to crown his career by rejuvenating Spain.

CHAPTER X

Portugal and Pombal

1706–82

I. JOHN V: 1706–50

WHY had Portugal declined since the great days of Magellan, Vasco da Gama, and Camões? Once her flesh and spirit had sufficed to explore half the globe, leaving bold colonies in Madeira, the Azores, South America, Africa, Madagascar, India, Malacca, Sumatra; now, in the eighteenth century, she was a tiny promontory of Europe, tied in trade and war to England, and nourished by Brazilian gold and diamonds reaching her by permission of the British fleet. Had her loins been exhausted by furnishing brave men to hold so many outposts precariously poised on the edges of the world? Had that influx of gold washed the iron out of her veins, and relaxed her ruling classes from adventure into ease?

Yes, and it had enervated Portuguese industry as well. What was the use of trying to compete in handicrafts or manufactures with artisans or entrepreneurs of England, Holland, or France, when imported gold could be paid out for imported clothing, food, and luxuries? The rich, handling the gold, grew richer and more gorgeously accoutered and adorned; the poor, kept at a distance from that gold, remained poor, and had only hunger as a prod to toil. Negro slave labor was introduced on many farms, and beggars made the cities noisy with their cries. William Beckford, hearing them in 1787, reported: "No beggars equal those of Portugal for strength of lungs, luxuriance of sores, profusion of vermin, variety and arrangement of tatters, and dauntless perseverance. . . . Innumerable, blind, dumb, and scabby."[1]

Lisbon was not then the lovely city that it is today. The churches and the monasteries were magnificent, the palaces of the nobility were immense, but fully a tenth of the population was homeless, and the tortuous alleys reeked with rubbish and filth.[2] Yet here, as elsewhere in southern lands, the poor had the consolations of sunny days, starry evenings, music, religion, and pious women with tantalizing eyes. Undeterred by fleas on their flesh and mosquitoes in the air, the people poured into the streets after the heat had subsided, and there they danced, sang, strummed guitars, and fought over a damsel's smile.

Treaties (1654, 1661, 1703) had bound Portugal to England in a strange symbiosis that allied them in economy and foreign policy while keeping them enthusiastically diverse in manners and hostile in creed. England promised to protect Portugal's independence, and to admit Portuguese wine (port from Oporto) at a greatly reduced tariff. Portugal pledged herself to admit

English textiles duty free, and to side with England in any war. The Portuguese thought of the English as damned heretics with a good navy; the English looked upon the Portuguese as benighted bigots with strategic ports.
British capital dominated Portuguese industry and trade. Pombal complained,
with some exaggeration:

> In 1754 Portugal scarcely produced anything toward her own support. Two
> thirds of her physical necessities were supplied by England. England had be-
> come mistress of our entire commerce, and all our foreign trade was managed
> by English agents. . . . The entire cargo of vessels sent from Lisbon to Brazil,
> and consequently the riches that were returned in exchange, belonged to them.
> Nothing was Portuguese except in name.[3]

Nevertheless enough of colonial gold, silver, and gems reached the Portuguese government to finance its expenses and make the king independent of
the Cortes and its taxing power. So John V, in his reign of forty-four years,
lived in sultanic ease, gracing polygamy with culture and piety. He gave or
lent enormous sums to the papacy, and received in return the title of His
Most Faithful Majesty, and even the right to say Mass—though not to change
bread and wine into the body and blood of Christ. "His pleasures," said Frederick the Great, "were in priestly functions; his buildings were convents, his
armies were monks, his mistresses were nuns."[4]

The Church prospered under a King who owed her so many absolutions.
She owned half the land,[5] and her devotees filled nine hundred religious
houses. Of the nation's two million population some 200,000 were ecclesiastics of some degree, or attached to a religious establishment. The Jesuits were
especially prominent, at home and in the colonies; they had shared in winning Brazil for Portugal, and were pleasing even Voltaire by their administration of Paraguay; several of them were welcomed at court, and some of
them acquired ascendancy over the King. In the great procession of Corpus
Christi the King bore one of the poles of the canopy under which the
Patriarch of Lisbon carried the Blessed Sacrament. When Englishmen marveled to see the route of the procession lined with troops and worshipers, all
bareheaded and kneeling, it was explained to them that such ceremonies, and
the display of precious vessels and miraculous relics in the churches, were a
main factor in keeping social order among the poor.

Meanwhile the Inquisition watched over the purity of the nation's faith
and blood. John V checked the power of the institution by securing from
Pope Benedict XIII a bull allowing its prisoners to be defended by counsel,
and requiring that all its sentences be subject to review by the king.[6] Even
so the authority of the tribunal sufficed to burn sixty-six persons in Lisbon
in eleven years (1732–42). Among them was the leading Portuguese dramatist of the age, Antônio José da Silva, who was charged with secret Judaism.
On the day of his execution (October 19, 1739) one of his plays was performed in a Lisbon theater.[7]

John V loved music, literature, and art. He brought French actors and
Italian musicians to his capital. He founded the Royal Academy of History.
He financed the great aqueduct that supplies Lisbon with water. He built,

at a cost of fifty million francs, the Convent of Mafra (1717–32), vaster than the Escorial, and still among the most imposing structures in the Iberian Peninsula. To adorn the interior he summoned back from Spain the greatest Portuguese painter of the century.

The eighty-four years of Francisco Vieira mingled love and art in a romance that stirred all Portugal. Born at Lisbon in 1699, he fell in love with Ignez Elena de Lima when both were children. Enamored also of painting, he went to Rome at the age of nine, studied there for seven years, and, aged fifteen, won the first prize in a competition offered by the Academy of St. Luke. Returning in 1715, he was chosen by John V to paint a *Mystery of the Eucharist*. This, we are told, he finished in six days; then he set out to find Ignez. Her titled father turned him away, and immured the girl in a convent. Francisco appealed to the King, who refused to intervene. He went to Rome and secured a bull annulling Ignez' conventual vows and authorizing the marriage. The bull was ignored by Portuguese authorities. Francisco, back in Lisbon, disguised himself as a bricklayer, entered the convent, carried off his beloved, and married her. Her brother shot him; he recovered and forgave his assailant. John V made him court painter and gave him commissions to decorate not only the Mafra Convent but the royal palaces. After Ignez died (1775), Francisco spent his remaining years in religious retreat and works of charity. How many such romances of soul and blood are lost behind the façades of history!

II. POMBAL AND THE JESUITS

John V died in 1750 after eight years of paralysis and imbecility, and his son Joseph I (José Manoel) began an eventful reign. He appointed to his cabinet, as minister for war and foreign affairs, Sebastião José de Carvalho e Mello, whom history knows as the Marquês de Pombal, the greatest and most terrible minister who ever governed Portugal.

He was already fifty-one years old when Joseph reached the throne. Educated by the Jesuits at the University of Coimbra, he won his first fame as an athletic and pugnacious leader of the "Mohocks" gang that infested the streets of Lisbon. In 1733 he persuaded the highborn Dona Teresa de Noronha to elope with him. Her family denounced him, then recognized his talent and promoted his political career. His wife brought him a small fortune; he inherited another from an uncle. He made his way by influence, persistence, and obvious ability. In 1739 he was appointed minister plenipotentiary to London. His wife retired to a convent, and died there in 1745. In his six years in England Pombal studied the English economy and government, noted the obedience of the Anglican Church to the state, and perhaps shed some of his Catholic faith. He returned to Lisbon (1744), was sent as envoy to Vienna (1745), and there married a niece of Marshal Daun, who was to earn immortality by defeating Frederick once. Pombal's new bride remained devoted to him through all his triumphs and defeats.

John V had distrusted him as having "a hairy heart,"[8] as "coming from a cruel and vindictive family,"[9] and as capable of defying a king. Nevertheless Pombal was called home in 1749, and was raised to ministerial office with Jesuit support. Joseph I confirmed the appointment. Intelligence combined with industry soon gave Pombal dominance in the new cabinet. "Carvalho," reported a French chargé d'affaires, "may be looked upon as the chief minister. He is indefatigable, active, and expeditious. He has won the confidence of the King his master, and in all political matters none has it more than he."[10]

His superiority became evident in the great earthquake of November 1, 1755. At 9:40 A.M. on All Saints' Day, when most of the population were worshiping in the churches, four convulsions of the earth laid half of Lisbon in ruins, killing over fifteen thousand people, destroying most of the churches, sparing most of the brothels,[11] and Pombal's home. Many inhabitants ran in terror to the shores of the Tagus, but a tidal wave fifteen feet high drowned thousands more, and wrecked the vessels that lay in the river. The fires that broke out in every quarter of the city claimed additional lives. In the resultant chaos the scum of the populace began to rob and kill with impunity. The King, who himself had narrowly escaped death, asked his ministers what should be done. Pombal is reported to have answered, "Bury the dead and relieve the living." Joseph gave him full authority, and Pombal used it with characteristic energy and dispatch. He stationed troops to maintain order, set up tents and camps for the homeless, and decreed immediate hanging for anyone found robbing the dead. He fixed the prices of provisions at those that had prevailed before the earthquake, and compelled all incoming ships to unload their cargoes of food and sell them at those prices. Helped by an undiminished influx of Brazilian gold, he supervised the rapid rebuilding of Lisbon with wide boulevards and well-paved and well-lit streets. The central part of the city as it is today was the work of the architects and engineers who worked under Pombal.[12]

His success in this demoralizing catastrophe confirmed his power in the ministry. Now he undertook two far-reaching tasks: to free the government from domination by the Church, and to free the economy from domination by Britain. These enterprises required a man of steel, of patriotism, ruthlessness, and pride.

If his anticlericalism struck especially at the Jesuits, it was primarily because he suspected them of fomenting the resistance to Portuguese appropriation of that Paraguayan territory where the Jesuits had since 1605 been organizing over 100,000 Indians into thirty-one *reductiones*, or settlements, on a semicommunistic basis in formal submission to Spain.[13] Spanish and Portuguese explorers had heard of (quite legendary) gold in Paraguayan soil, and merchants complained that the Jesuit fathers were monopolizing the export trade of Paraguay and were adding the profits to the funds of their order. In 1750 Pombal negotiated a treaty by which Portugal surrendered to Spain the rich colony of San Sacramento (at the mouth of the Rio de la Plata) in exchange for seven of the Jesuit "reductions" adjacent to the Brazilian frontier. The treaty stipulated that the thirty thousand Indians in these communities should emigrate to other regions, and relinquish the land to the incoming Portuguese. Ferdinand VI of Spain ordered the Paraguayan Jesuits to leave the settlements, and to instruct their subjects to depart in peace. The Jesuits claimed to have obeyed these orders, but the Indians resisted with a passionate and violent tenacity, which it took a Portuguese army three years to overcome. Pombal accused the Society of Jesus of secretly encouraging this resistance. He resolved to end all Jesuit participation in Portuguese industry, commerce, and government. Perceiving his intention, the Jesuits of Portugal joined in efforts to overthrow him.

Their leader in this movement was Gabriel Malagrida. Born in Menaggio (on Lake Como) in 1689, he distinguished himself at school by biting his hands till the blood flowed; so, he said, he prepared himself to bear the pains of martyrdom. He joined the Society of Jesus, and sailed as a missionary to Brazil. From 1724 to 1735 he preached the Gospel to Indians in the jungle. Several times he escaped death—from cannibals, crocodiles, shipwreck, disease. His beard turned white in early middle age. He was credited with miraculous powers, and expectant crowds followed him whenever he appeared in the cities of Brazil. He built churches and convents, and founded seminaries. In 1747 he came to Lisbon to solicit funds from King John. He received them, sailed back to Brazil, and established more religious houses, often sharing in the manual labor of construction. In 1753 he was in Lisbon again, for he had promised to prepare the Queen Mother for death. He attributed the earthquake of 1755 to the sins of the people, called for a reform of morals, and, with others of his order, predicted further earthquakes if morals did not improve. His house of religious retreat became a focus of plots against Pombal.

Some noble families were involved in these plots. They protested that the son of an insignificant country squire had made himself master of Portugal, holding their lives and fortunes in his hands. One of these aristocratic factions was led by Dom José de Mascarenhas, Duke of Aveiro; another was headed by the Duke's brother-in-law, Dom Francisco de Assiz, Marquis of Tavora. Tavora's wife, the Marchioness Dona Leonor, a leader of Portuguese society, was a fervent disciple and frequent visitor of Father Malagrida. Her oldest son, Dom Luis Bernardo, the "younger Marquis" of Tavora, was married to his own aunt. When Luis went off to India as a soldier, this lovely and beautiful "younger Marchioness" became the mistress of Joseph I; this too the Aveiros and the Tavoras never forgave. They heartily agreed with the Jesuits that should Pombal be removed the situation would be eased.

Pombal struck back by persuading Joseph that the Society of Jesus was secretly encouraging further revolt in Paraguay, and was conspiring not only against the ministry but against the King as well. On September 19, 1757, a decree banished from the court the Jesuit confessors of the royal family. Pombal instructed his cousin, Francisco de Almada e Mendonça, Portuguese envoy to the Vatican, to leave no ducat unturned in promoting and financing the anti-Jesuit party in Rome. In October Almada presented to Benedict

XIV a list of charges against the Jesuits: that they had "sacrificed all Christian, religious, natural, and political obligations in a blind wish . . . to make themselves masters of the government"; and that the Society was actuated by "an insatiable desire to acquire and accumulate foreign riches, and even to usurp the dominion of sovereigns."[14] On April 1, 1758, the Pope ordered Cardinal de Saldanha, patriarch of Lisbon, to investigate these charges. On May 15 Saldanha published a decree declaring that the Portuguese Jesuits carried on commerce "contrary to all laws divine and human," and he bade them desist. On June 7, probably at Pombal's urging, he ordered them to abstain from hearing confessions or preaching. In July the superior of the Lisbon Jesuits was banished sixty leagues from the court. Meanwhile (May 3, 1758) Benedict XIV died; his successor, Clement XIII, appointed another commission of inquiry; and this body reported that the Jesuits were innocent of the charges brought against them by Pombal.[15]

There was some doubt whether Joseph I would support his minister in attacking the Jesuits; but a dramatic turn of events drove the King completely to Pombal's side. On the night of September 3, 1758, Joseph was returning to his palace near Belém from a secret rendezvous, probably with the young Marchioness of Tavora.[16] Shortly before midnight three masked men emerged from the arch of an aqueduct and fired into the coach, without effect. The coachman put his horse to the gallop, but a moment later two shots came from another ambush; one shot wounded the coachman, the other wounded the King in his right shoulder and arm. According to a later court of inquiry a third ambush, by members of the Tavora family, awaited the coach farther on the highway to Belém. But Joseph ordered the coachman to leave the main road and drive to the house of the royal surgeon, who dressed the wounds. The resultant events, which made a noise throughout Europe, might have been very different if the third ambush had succeeded in the attempted assassination.

Pombal acted with subtle deliberation. Rumors of the attack were officially denied; the King's temporary confinement was ascribed to a fall. For three months the secret agents of the minister gathered evidence. A man was found who testified that Antônio Ferreira had borrowed a musket from him on August 3 and had returned it on September 8. Another man was reported as saying that Ferreira had borrowed a pistol from him on September 3 and had returned it a few days later. Ferreira, said both these witnesses, was in the service of the Duke of Aveiro. Salvador Durão, a servant in Belém, testified that on the night of the attack, while he was keeping an assignation outside the Aveiro home, he had overheard some members of the Aveiro family returning from a nocturnal enterprise.

Pombal prepared his case with caution and audacity. He set aside the procedure required by law, which would have tried the suspected nobles by a court of their peers; such a court would never condemn them. Instead, as the first public revelation of the crime, the King issued on December 9 two decrees: one nominated Dr. Pedro Gonçalves Pereira as judge to preside over a Special Tribunal of High Treason; the other ordered him to discover, arrest, and execute those responsible for the attempt to kill the King. Gon-çalves Pereira was empowered to disregard all customary forms of legal proc-ess, and the tribunal was told to execute its decrees on the day of their announcement. To these decrees Pombal added a manifesto, posted through-out the city, relating the events of September 3, and offering rewards to any person who would give evidence leading to the arrest of the assassins.[17]

On December 13 government officers arrested the Duke of Aveiro, his sixteen-year-old son the Marquis of Gouveia, his servitor Antônio Ferreira, the old and the younger Marquis of Tavora, the old Marchioness of Tavora, all servants of these two families, and five other nobles. All Jesuit colleges were on that day surrounded by soldiers; Malagrida and twelve other leading Jesuits were jailed. To accelerate matters, a royal decree of December 20 permitted (against Portuguese custom) the use of torture to elicit confes-sions. Under torture or threat of it fifty prisoners were examined. Several confessions implicated the Duke of Aveiro; he himself, under torture, ad-mitted his guilt; Antônio Ferreira acknowledged that he had fired at the coach, but swore that he had not known that the prospective victim was the King. Under torture several servants of the Tavoras compromised that entire family; the younger Marquis confessed complicity; the older Marquis, tor-tured to the point of death, denied his guilt. Pombal himself assisted at the examination of witnesses and prisoners. He had had the mails examined; he claimed to have found in them twenty-four letters by the Duke of Aveiro, by several Tavoras, by Malagrida and other Jesuits, notifying their friends or relatives in Brazil of the abortive attempt, and promising renewed efforts to overturn the government. On January 4, 1759, the King nominated Dr. Eusebio Tavares de Sequeira to defend the accused. Sequeira argued that the confessions, elicited under torture, were worthless as evidence, and that all the accused nobles could prove alibis for the night of the crime. The defense was judged unconvincing; the intercepted letters were held to be genuine and to corroborate the confessions; and on January 12 the court declared all indicted persons guilty.

Nine of them were executed on January 13 in the public square of Belém. The first to die was the old Marchioness of Tavora. On the scaffold the executioner bent to tie her feet; she repelled him, saying, "Do not touch me except to kill me!"[18] After being compelled to see the instruments—wheel, hammer, and faggots—by which her husband and her sons were to die, she was beheaded. Her two sons were broken on the wheel and strangled; their corpses lay on the scaffold when the Duke of Aveiro and the old Marquis of Tavora mounted it. They suffered the same shattering blows, and the Duke was allowed to linger in agony until the last of the executions—the burning alive of Antônio Ferreira—was complete. All the corpses were burned, and the ashes were thrown into the Tagus. Portugal still debates whether the nobles, though admittedly hostile to Pombal, had meant to kill the King.

Were the Jesuits involved in the attempt? There was no doubt that Mala-grida, in his passionate fulminations, had predicted the fall of Pombal and the early death of the King;[19] and no doubt that he and other Jesuits had held conferences with the minister's titled foes. He had implied his awareness of a plot by writing to a lady of the court a letter begging her to put Joseph on his guard against an imminent danger. Asked, in jail, how he had learned of such a peril, he replied, In the confessional.[20] Aside from this (according to an anti-Jesuit historian) "there is no positive evidence to connect the Jesuits with the outrage."[21] Pombal accused them, by their preaching and teaching, of having excited their allies to the point of murder. He persuaded the King that the situation offered the monarchy an opportunity to strengthen itself as against the Church. On January 19 Joseph issued edicts attaching all Jesuit property in the kingdom, and confining all Jesuits to their houses or colleges pending settlement, by the Pope, of the charges against them. Meanwhile Pombal used the government press to print—and his agents to distribute widely, at home and abroad—pamphlets stating the case against the nobles and the Jesuits; this was apparently the first time that a government had made use of the printing press to explain its actions to other nations. These publications may have had some influence in leading to the expulsion of the Jesuits from France and Spain.

In the summer of 1759 Pombal sought from Clement XIII permission to submit the arrested Jesuits to trial before the Tribunal of High Treason; moreover, he proposed that henceforth all ecclesiastics accused of crimes against the state should be tried in secular, not ecclesiastical, courts. A personal letter from Joseph to the Pope announced the King's resolve to expel the Jesuits from Portugal, and expressed the hope that the Pope would approve the measure as warranted by their actions and as necessary for the protection of the monarchy. Clement was shocked by these messages, but he feared that if he directly opposed them Pombal would induce the King to sever all relations between the Portuguese Church and the papacy. He recalled the action of Henry VIII in England, and knew that France too was developing hostility against the Society of Jesus. On August 11 he sent his permission to try the Jesuits before the secular tribunal, but explicitly confined his consent to the present case. To the King he made a personal appeal for mercy to the accused priests; he reminded Joseph of the past achievements of the order, and trusted that all Portuguese Jesuits would not be punished for the mistakes of a few.

The papal appeal failed. On September 3, 1759—the anniversary of the attempted assassination—the King issued an edict giving a long list of alleged offenses by the Jesuits, and decreeing that

> these religious, being corrupt and deplorably fallen away from their holy institute [rule], and rendered manifestly incapable, by such abominable and inveterate vices, of returning to its observance, must be properly and effectually banished, . . . proscribed, and expelled from all his Majesty's dominions, as notorious rebels, traitors, adversaries, and aggressors of his royal person and realm; . . . and it is ordered, under the irremissible pain of death, that no person, of whatever state or condition, is to admit them into any of his possessions, or hold any communication with them by word or writing.[22]

Those Jesuits who had not yet made their solemn profession, and who should petition to be released from their preliminary vows, were exempted from the

decree. All Jesuit property was confiscated by the state; the exiles were forbidden to take anything with them but their personal clothing.[23] From all
sections of Portugal they were led in coaches or on foot to ships that took
them to Italy. Similar deportations were carried out from Brazil and other
Portuguese possessions. The first shipload of expatriates reached Civitavecchia on October 24, and even Pombal's representative there was moved to
pity by their condition. Some were weak with age, some were near starvation, some had died on the way. Lorenzo Ricci, general of the Society, arranged for the reception of the survivors into Jesuit houses in Italy, and the
Dominican friars shared in extending hospitality. On June 17, 1760, the
Portuguese government suspended diplomatic relations with the Vatican.

The victory of Pombal seemed complete, but he knew that it was unpopular with the nation. Feeling insecure, he expanded his power to full dictatorship, and began a reign of absolutism and terror that continued till 1777.
His spies reported to him every detected expression of opposition to his
policies or his methods; soon the jails of Lisbon were crowded with political
prisoners. Many nobles and priests were arrested on charges of new plots
against the King, or of implication in the old plot. The Junqueira fort, midway between Lisbon and Belém, became the special jail of aristocrats, many
of whom were kept there till their death. Other prisons held—some for
nineteen years—Jesuits brought from the colonies and charged with resisting
the government.

Malagrida languished in prison for thirty-two months before being brought
to trial. The old man solaced his confinement by writing *The Heroic Life
of St. Anne, the Mother of Mary, Dictated to the Reverend Father Malagrida by St. Anne Herself.* Pombal had the manuscript seized, and found in
it several absurdities that could be labeled heresies; St. Anne, said Malagrida,
had been conceived, like Mary, without the stain of original sin, and she had
spoken and wept in her mother's womb.[24] Having made his own brother,
Paul de Carvalho, head of the Inquisition in Portugal, Pombal had Malagrida
summoned before its tribunal, and drew up with his own hand an indictment
charging the Jesuit with cupidity, hypocrisy, imposture, and sacrilege, and
with having menaced the King with repeated predictions of death. Made
half insane by his sufferings, Malagrida, now seventy-two years old, told the
Inquisitors that he had spoken with St. Ignatius Loyola and St. Theresa.[25] One
judge, moved to pity, wished to stop the trial; Pombal had him removed.
On January 12, 1761, the Holy Office pronounced Malagrida guilty of
heresy, blasphemy, and impiety, and of having deceived the people by pretended divine revelations. He was allowed to live eight months more. On
September 20 he was led to a scaffold in the Praça Rossio, was strangled, and
was burned at the stake. Louis XV, hearing of the execution, remarked, "It
is as if I burned the old lunatic in the Petites [Maisons] asylum, who says
that he is God the Father."[26] Voltaire, recording the event, pronounced it
"folly and absurdity joined to the most horrible wickedness."[27]

The French *philosophes*, who in 1758 had looked upon Pombal as an "enlightened despot," were not pleased with his development. They welcomed
the overthrow of the Jesuits, but they deprecated the arbitrary methods of

the dictator, the violent tone of his pamphlets, and the barbarity of his punishments. They were shocked by the treatment of the Jesuits during their deportation, by the wholesale execution of ancient families, and by the inhumane treatment of Malagrida. We have, however, no record of their protesting the eight-year imprisonment of the bishop of Coimbra for condemning Pombal's Censorship Board, which had allowed the circulation of such radical works as Voltaire's *Philosophical Dictionary* and Rousseau's *Social Contract.*

Pombal himself preached no heresies, and went to Mass regularly. He aimed not at the destruction of the Church but at its subjection to the King; and when, in 1770, Clement XIV agreed to let the government nominate to bishoprics, he made his peace with the Vatican. Joseph I, as he neared death, rejoiced in the thought that, after all, he might die with full benefit of clergy. The Pope sent a cardinal's hat to Pombal's brother Paul, and to Pombal himself a ring bearing the papal portrait, and a miniature framed in diamonds, and the entire cadavers of four saints.

III. POMBAL THE REFORMER

Meanwhile the dictator had left his mark upon the economy, administration, and cultural life of Portugal. With the help of English and German officers he reorganized the army, which turned back a Spanish invasion in the Seven Years' War. Like Richelieu in seventeenth-century France, he reduced the disruptive power of the aristocracy, and centralized the government in a monarchy that could give the nation political unity, educational development, and some protection from ecclesiastical domination. After the execution of the Tavoras the nobles ceased to plot against the king; after the expulsion of the Jesuits the clergy submitted to the state. During the alienation from the Vatican Pombal appointed the bishops, and his bishops ordained priests without reference to Rome. A royal decree curtailed the acquisition of land by the Church, and restrained Portuguese subjects from burdening their estates with bequests for Masses.[28] Many convents were closed, and the rest were forbidden to receive novices under twenty-five years of age. The Inquisition was brought under government control: its tribunal was made a public court, subject to the same rules as the courts of the state; it was shorn of censorship powers; its distinction between Old Christians and New Christians (Christianized Jews or Moors, and their descendants) was abolished, for Pombal took it for granted that most Spaniards and Portuguese had now some Semitic strain in their blood.[29] A decree of May 25, 1773, made all Portuguese subjects eligible to civil, military, and ecclesiastical office.[30] There was no burning of persons by the Portuguese Inquisition after that of Malagrida in 1761.[31]

In that year Pombal abolished three quarters of the petty offices that had hampered the administration of justice; the law courts were made more accessible, litigation was made less expensive. In 1761 he reorganized the Treasury, required it to balance its books every week, ordered yearly audits of municipal revenues and expenditures, and made some progress in the most difficult reforms of all—the reduction of personnel and extravagance at the royal court. The eighty cooks that had fed John V and his entourage were weeded out; Joseph I had to content himself with twenty. An edict of May 25, 1773, in effect abolished slavery in Portugal, but allowed it to continue in the colonies.

The reformer's hand moved everywhere. He gave governmental support to agriculture and fisheries, and introduced the silkworm into the northern provinces. He established potteries, glassworks, cotton mills, woolen factories, and paper plants, to end the dependence of Portugal upon the importation of such products from abroad. He abolished internal tolls in the movement of goods, and established free trade between Portugal and her American colonies. He founded a College of Commerce to train men for business management. He organized and subsidized companies to take over Portuguese trade from foreign merchants and carriers; here he or the Portuguese—failed, for in 1780 the commerce of Portugal was still mostly in foreign, chiefly in British, hands.

The expulsion of the Jesuits necessitated a thorough reconstruction of education. New elementary and secondary schools, to the number of 837, were scattered over the land. The Jesuit college at Lisbon was transformed into a College of Nobles under secular administration. The curriculum at Coimbra was enlarged with additional courses in science. Pombal persuaded the King to build an opera house and to invite Italian singers to lead the casts. In 1757 he founded the Arcádia de Lisboa for the stimulation of literature.

For an exciting half century (1755–1805) Portuguese literature enjoyed a relative freedom of ideas and forms. Liberating itself from Italian models, it acknowledged the spell of France, and felt some zephyrs of the Enlightenment. Antônio Diniz da Cruz e Silva won national fame by a satire, *O Hissope* (1772), describing in eight cantos the quarrel of a bishop with his dean. João Anastasio da Cunha translated Pope and Voltaire, for which he was condemned by the Inquisition (1778) soon after Pombal's fall. Francisco Manoel do Nascimento, son of a longshoreman, took passionately to books, and became the center of a group that rebelled against the Arcadian Academy as a drag on the development of national poetry. In 1778 (again taking advantage of Pombal's fall) the Inquisition ordered his arrest as being addicted "to modern philosophers who follow natural reason." He escaped to France, where he spent nearly all his remaining forty-one years; there he wrote most of his poems, ardent for freedom and democracy, including an ode "To the Liberty and Independence of the United States." His followers ranked him as second only to Camões in Portuguese poetry. — The most elegant and melodious verse of the age was in a volume of love poems, *A Marilia*, bequeathed by Tomaz Antônio Gonzaga, who suffered imprisonment (1785–88) for political conspiracy, and died in exile. — José Agostinho de Macedo, an Augustinian friar unfrocked because of his dissipated life, boldly took for the subject of his epic, *O Oriente*, the same subject as Camões

—the voyage of Vasco da Gama to India; he judged his poem superior to the *Lusiads* and the *Iliad*, but we are assured that it is a dreary performance. More interesting was a satire in six cantos, *Os Burros*, in which Macedo pilloried by name men and women of all ranks, living or dead. — His favorite enemy was Manuel Maria Barbosa de Bocage, who was imprisoned by the Inquisition (1797) on a charge of spreading Voltairean ideas in his verse and plays. The execution of Marie Antoinette turned him back to conservatism in religion and politics; he recaptured his youthful piety, and saw in the mosquito a proof of the existence of God.[32]

The great event in the art history of Pombal's regime was the statue raised to Joseph I, which still stands in Lisbon's Black Horse Square. Designed by Joaquim Machado de Castro, cast in bronze by Bartolommeo da Costa, it represented the King riding a steed victoriously over serpents symbolizing the evil forces overcome during his reign. Pombal made the inauguration of the monument (June 6, 1775) a celebration of his triumphant ministry. Troops of soldiery lined the square; the diplomatic corps, the judiciary, the Senate, and other dignitaries were assembled in full costume; then came the court, then the King and the Queen; finally Pombal came forward and unveiled the figures and the massive pedestal, on which a medallion pictured the minister wearing the Cross of Christ. Everyone but the King understood that the real subject of the celebration was Pombal.

A few days after the unveiling he sent to Joseph I a rosy-colored description of the progress made by Portugal since 1750: the spread of education and literacy, the growth of manufactures and trade, the development of literature and art, the general rise in the standard of living. Truth must make many deductions from his account: industry and trade were growing, but very slowly, and were in financial difficulties; the arts were stagnant, and half of Lisbon still lay (1774) in the ruins caused by the earthquake of 1755. The natural piety of the people was restoring ecclesiastical power. Pombal's lordly manners and dictatorial methods were making new enemies every day. He had enriched himself and his relatives; he had built for himself an extravagantly costly palace. There was hardly a noble family in the kingdom that did not have a beloved member wasting away in jail. Everywhere in Portugal there were secret hopes and prayers for Pombal's fall.

IV. THE TRIUMPH OF THE PAST

The King was sixty years old in 1775. Illnesses and mistresses had aged him beyond his years, and he spent hours in meditation on sin and death. He wondered had he been right in following the policies of his minister. Had he been just to the Jesuits? Those nobles and priests in prison—he would gladly have pardoned them, now that he sought pardon for himself, but how could he mention such an idea to the unrelenting Pombal, and what could he do without Pombal? On November 12, 1776, he suffered an apoplectic stroke, and the court almost visibly rejoiced in expectation of a new reign and a new ministry. The heir to the throne was his daughter Maria Francisca, who had married his brother Pedro. She was a good woman, a good wife and mother, a kind and charitable soul, but she was also a fervent Catholic, who had so resented Pombal's anticlericalism that she had left the court to live quietly with Pedro at Queluz, a few miles from the capital. The foreign diplomats notified their governments to expect an early reversal of Portuguese policies.

On November 18 the King received the sacraments; on November 29 Maria became regent. One of her first acts was to end the bishop of Coimbra's long imprisonment; the seventy-four-year-old prelate was restored to his see amid almost universal rejoicing. Pombal saw his authority waning, and noted with somber premonitions that courtiers lately subservient to him now looked upon him as politically moribund. In a final act of despotism he took a wild revenge upon the village of Trefaria, whose fisherfolk had opposed the forcible impressment of their sons into the army; he ordered a platoon of soldiers to burn the village down; they did it by flinging lighted torches through the windows of the wooden cottages in the dark of night (January 23, 1777).

On February 24 Joseph I died; the regent became Queen Maria I (r. 1777–1816), and her husband became King Pedro III (r. 1777-86). Pedro was a man of weak mind; Maria absorbed herself in piety and charity. Religion, which was half the life of the Portuguese people, rapidly recovered its power. The Inquisition resumed its activity in censorship and the suppression of heresy. Queen Maria sent forty thousand pounds to the papacy to partially reimburse it for expenses incurred in caring for the banished Jesuits. On the day after Joseph's burial Queen Maria ordered the release of eight hundred prisoners, most of them incarcerated by Pombal for political opposition. Many of them had been in the dungeons for twenty years; when they emerged their eyes could not bear the sun; nearly all were in rags; many looked twice their age. Hundreds of prisoners had died in jail. Of the 124 Jesuits who had been imprisoned eighteen years before, only forty-five still lived.[33] Five nobles condemned for alleged complicity in the plot to kill Joseph refused to leave prison until their innocence had been officially declared.

The sight of the released victims of Pombal's hostility, and the news of the burning of Trefaria, brought his unpopularity to the point where he no longer ventured to show himself in public. On March 1 he sent to Queen Maria a letter resigning all his offices and asking permission to retire to his estate in the town of Pombal. The nobles who surrounded the Queen demanded his imprisonment and punishment; but when she discovered that all the measures which they resented had been signed by the late King, she decided that she could not punish Pombal without laying a public stain upon her father's memory. She accepted the minister's resignation, and allowed him to retire to Pombal, but she ordered him to remain there. On March 5 he left Lisbon in a hired chaise, hoping to escape notice; some people recognized him and stoned his carriage, but he escaped. At the town of Oeiras his wife joined him. He was seventy-seven years old.

Now that he was only a private citizen he was assailed from every side by suits for debts he had neglected to pay, for injuries he had inflicted, for properties he had taken without adequate compensation. Bailiffs besieged his doors at Pombal with a succession of writs. "There is not a hornet or a gnat in Portugal," he wrote, "that does not fly to this remote spot and buzz in my ears."[34] The Queen helped him by granting continuance for life of the salary he had received as minister, and added to it a modest pension. Nevertheless countless enemies urged the Queen to summon him to trial on charges of malfeasance and treason. She compromised by allowing judges to visit him and subject him to examination on the charges. They questioned him for hours at a time through three and a half months, until the old dictator, exhausted, begged for mercy. The Queen delayed action on the report of the examination, hoping that Pombal's death might relieve her embarrassment; meanwhile she sought to appease his foes by ordering retrial of those who had been convicted of complicity in the attempt upon her father. The new court confirmed the guilt of the Duke of Aveiro and three of his servants, but exonerated all the rest of the accused. The Tavoras were declared innocent, and all their honors and property were remitted to their survivors (April 3, 1781). On August 16 the Queen issued a decree condemning Pombal as an "infamous criminal," but adding that since he had begged for pardon he was to be left at peace in his exile and in the possession of his property.

Pombal was entering upon his final illness. His body was almost covered with pus-oozing sores, apparently from leprosy.[35] Pain kept him from sleeping more than two hours in a day; dysentery weakened him; and his doctors, as if to add to his torments, persuaded him to drink a broth made from the flesh of snakes. He prayed for death, received the sacraments, and ended his sufferings on May 8, 1782. Forty-five years later a party of Jesuits, passing through the town, stopped at his grave and recited a requiem, in triumph and pity, for the repose of his soul.

CHAPTER XI

Spain and the Enlightenment

1700–88

I. MILIEU

AT his death in 1700 Charles II, last of the Spanish Hapsburgs, bequeathed Spain and all its global empire to the age-long enemy of the Hapsburgs —Bourbon France. The grandson of Louis XIV, as Philip V of Spain, fought bravely during the War of the Spanish Succession (1702–13) to maintain that empire unimpaired; nearly all Europe rose in arms to prevent so dangerous an aggrandizement of Bourbon power; in the end Spain had to yield Gibraltar and Minorca to England, Sicily to Savoy, and Naples, Sardinia, and "Belgium" to Austria.

Moreover, the loss of sea power left Spain only a precarious hold on the colonies that nourished her commerce and her wealth. Wheat in Spanish America gave from five to twenty times the yield per acre that came from the soil of Spain. From those sunny lands came mercury, copper, zinc, arsenic, dyes, meat, hides, rubber, cochineal, sugar, cocoa, coffee, tobacco, tea, quinine and a dozen other medicaments. In 1788 Spain exported to her American colonies goods valued at 158,000,000 reales; she imported from them goods valued at 804,000,000 reales; this "unfavorable balance of trade" was wiped out by a stream of American silver and gold. The Philippines sent cargoes of pepper, cotton, indigo, and sugar cane. At the end of the eighteenth century Alexander von Humboldt estimated the population of the Philippines at 1,900,000, of Spanish America at 16,902,000; Spain herself, in 1797, had 10,541,000.[1] It is one credit to Bourbon rule that this last figure almost doubled the population of 5,700,000 in 1700.

Geography favored Spain only for maritime commerce. In the north the land was fertile, fed with rains and the melting snows of the Pyrenees; irrigation canals (mostly bequeathed to their conquerors by the Moors) had reclaimed Valencia, Murcia, and Andalusia from aridity; the rest of Spain was discouragingly mountainous or dry. The gifts of nature were not developed by economic enterprise; the most venturesome Spaniards went to the colonies; Spain preferred to buy industrial products from abroad with her colonial gold and the yield of her own mines of silver, copper, iron, or lead; her industries, still in the guild or domestic stage, lagged far behind those of the industrious North; and many of her rich mines were operated by foreign management for the profit of German or English investors. The production of wool was monopolized by the Mesta, an association of flock owners privileged by the government, entrenched in tradition, and dominated by a small minority of nobles and monasteries. Competition was stifled, improvements lagged. A meager proletariat festered in the towns, serving as domestics to the great or as journeymen in the guilds. Some Negro or Moorish slaves adorned affluent homes. A small middle class lived in dependence upon the government, the nobility, or the Church.

Of the agricultural land 51.5 per cent was owned in vast tracts by noble families, 16.5 per cent by the Church, 32 per cent by communes (towns) or peasants. The growth of peasant proprietorship was retarded by an old law of entail, which required that an estate should be bequeathed intact to the eldest son, and that no part of it should be mortgaged or sold. Through most of the century, except in the Basque provinces, three quarters of the soil was tilled by tenants paying tribute in rent, fees, service, or kind to aristocratic or ecclesiastical landlords whom they rarely saw. As rents were raised according to the productivity of the farm, the tenants had no incentive to inventiveness or industry.[2] The owners defended the practice by alleging that the progressive depreciation of the currency forced them to raise rents to keep pace with rising prices and costs. Meanwhile a sales tax on such necessaries as meat, wine, olive oil, candles, and soap fell heavily upon the poor (who spent most of their income on necessaries), more lightly upon the rich. The result of these procedures, of hereditary privilege, and of the natural inequality of human ability, was a concentration of· wealth at the top, and at the bottom a somber poverty that continued from generation to generation, alleviated and abetted by supernatural consolations.

The nobility was jealously divided into grades of dignity. At the top (in 1787) were 119 grandees—*grandes de España*. We may guess at their wealth from the probably exaggerated report of the contemporary British traveler Joseph Townsend that "three great lords—the dukes of Osuna, Alba, and Medinaceli—cover [own] almost the whole province of Andalusia."[3] Medinaceli received one million reales yearly from his fisheries alone; Osuna had an annual income of 8,400,000 reales; the Count of Aranda had nearly 1,600,000 reales a year.[4] Below the grandees were 535 *titulos*—men who had been given hereditary titles by the king on condition of remitting half their income to the Crown. Below these were the *caballeros*—chevaliers or knights named by the king to lucrative membership in one of the four military orders of Spain: Santiago, Alcántara, Calatrava, and Montesa. The lowliest of the nobles were the 400,000 hidalgos, who owned modest tracts of land, were exempt from military service and from imprisonment for debt, and had the right to display a coat of arms and be addressed as *Don*. Some of them were poor, some joined the beggars in the streets. Most of the nobles lived in the cities, and named the municipal officials.

As the divine guardian of the status quo the Spanish Church claimed a comfortable share of the gross national product. A Spanish authority reckoned its annual income, after taxes, at 1,101,753,000 reales, and that of the state at 1,371,000,000.[5] A third of its revenues came from land; large sums from tithes and first fruits; petty cash from christenings, marriages, funerals, Masses for the dead, and monastic costumes sold to pious people who thought that if they died in such robes they might slip unquestioned into Paradise. Monastic mendicants brought in an additional 53,000,000 reales. The average priest, of course, was poor, partly because of his number; Spain had 91,258 men in orders, of whom 16,481 were priests and 2,943 were Jesuits.[6] In 1797 sixty thousand monks and thirty thousand nuns lived in three thousand monasteries or convents. The Archbishop of Seville and his staff of 235 aides enjoyed an annual revenue of six million reales; the Archbishop of Toledo, with six hundred aides, received nine million. Here, as in Italy and Austria, ecclesiastical wealth aroused no protest from the people; the cathedral was their creation, and they loved to see it gorgeously adorned.

Their piety set a standard for Christendom. Nowhere else in the eighteenth century was the Catholic theology so thoroughly believed, or the Catholic ritual so fervently observed. Religious practices rivaled the pursuit of bread, and probably exceeded the pursuit of sex, as part of the substance of life. The people, including the prostitutes, crossed themselves a dozen times a day. The worship of the Virgin far surpassed the adoration of Christ; images of her were everywhere; women lovingly sewed robes for her statues, and crowned her head with fresh flowers; in Spain above all rose the popular demand that her "immaculate conception"—her freedom from the stain of original sin—be made a part of the defined and required faith. The men almost equaled the women in piety. Many men, as well as women, heard Mass daily. In some religious processions (until it was forbidden in 1777) men of the lower classes flogged themselves with knotted cords ending in balls of wax containing broken glass; they professed to be doing this to prove their devotion to God or Mary or a woman; some thought such bloodletting was good for the health[7] and kept Eros down.

Religious processions were frequent, dramatic, and colorful; one humorist complained that he could not take a step in Madrid without coming upon such a solemnity; and not to kneel when it passed was to risk arrest or injury. When the people of Saragossa rose in revolt in 1766, sacking and looting, and a religious procession appeared with a bishop holding the Sacrament before him, the rioters bared their heads and knelt in the streets; when the retinue had filed by they resumed the sack of the town.[8] In the great Corpus Christi procession all the departments of the government took part, sometimes led by the king. Throughout Holy Week the cities of Spain were draped in black, theaters and cafés were closed, churches were crowded, and supplementary altars were set up in public squares to accommodate the overflow of piety. In Spain Christ was king, Mary was queen, and the sense of divine presence was, in every waking hour, part of the essence of life.

Two religious orders especially prospered in Spain. The Jesuits, through their learning and address, dominated education and became confessors to royalty. The Dominicans controlled the Inquisition, and though this institution had long since passed its heyday it was still strong enough to terrify the people and challenge the state. When some remnants of Judaism appeared under Bourbon laxity the Inquisition snuffed them out with autos-da-fé. In seven years (1720–27) the Inquisitors condemned 868 persons, of whom 820 were accused of secret Judaism; seventy-five were burned, others were sent to the galleys, or merely scourged.[9] In 1722 Philip V testified his adoption of Spanish ways by presiding over a sumptuous auto-da-fé in which nine heretics were burned in celebration of the coming of a French princess to Madrid.[10] His successor, Ferdinand VI, showed a milder spirit; during his reign (1746–59) "only" ten persons—all "relapsed" Jews—were burned alive.[11]

The Inquisition exercised a strangling censorship over all publication. A Dominican monk reckoned that there was less printing in Spain in the eighteenth century than in the sixteenth.[12] Most books were religious, and the people liked them so. The lower classes were illiterate, and felt no need for reading or writing. Schools were in the hands of the clergy, but thousands of parishes had no schools at all. The once great Spanish universities had fallen far behind those of Italy, France, England, or Germany in everything but orthodox theology. Medical schools were poor, ill-staffed, ill-equipped; therapy relied upon bloodletting, purging, relics, and prayer; Spanish physicians were a peril to human life. Science was medieval, history was legend, superstition flourished, portents and miracles abounded. The belief in witchcraft survived to the end of the century, and appeared among the horrors that Goya drew.

Such was the Spain that the Bourbons came from France to rule.

II. PHILIP V: 1700–46

Felipe Quinto was a good man within his lights, which had been limited by his education. As a younger son to the Dauphin he had been trained to modesty, piety, and obedience, and he never overcame these virtues sufficiently to meet half a century of challenges in government and war. His piety led him to accept in Spain a religious obscurantism that was dying in France; his docility made him malleable by his ministers and his wives.

María Luisa Gabriela, daughter of Victor Amadeus II of Savoy, was only thirteen when she married Philip (1701), but she was already adept in feminine wiles; her beauty and vivacity, her tantrums and tears reduced the King to an exhausted subjection, while she and her chief lady in waiting manipulated the politics of their adopted land. Marie Anne de La Trémoille, Princesse des Ursins, French widow of a Spanish grandee, had helped the girl Queen to marriage and power. Ambitious but tactful, she became for a decade a power behind the throne. She could not rely upon beauty, for she was fifty-nine in 1701, but she provided the knowledge and subtlety lacking in the Queen, and after 1705 she determined policy. In 1714 María Luisa, aged twenty-six, died, and Philip, who had learned to love her devotedly, sank into a morbid melancholy. Mme. des Ursins thought to salvage her power by arranging his marriage with Isabella (Elizabeth) Farnese, daughter of Duke Odoardo II of Parma and Piacenza. She went to meet the new Queen at the Spanish border, but Isabella curtly ordered her to leave Spain. She withdrew to Rome and died eight years later in wealth and oblivion.

Isabella did not admit that the Renaissance was over; she had all the force of will, keenness of intellect, fire of temper, and scorn of scruples that had marked the women, as well as the men, who had dominated sixteenth-century Italy. She found in Philip a man who could not make up his mind, and who could not sleep alone; their bed became her throne, from which she ruled a nation, directed armies, and won Italian principalities. She had known almost nothing of Spain, nor did she ever take to the Spanish character, but she studied that character, she made herself familiar with the needs of the country, and the King was surprised to find her as informed and resourceful as his ministers.

In his first years of rule Philip had used Jean Orry and other French aides to reorganize the government on lines set by Louis XIV: centralized and audited administration and finance, with a trained bureaucracy and provincial intendants, all under the legislative, judicial, and executive authority of the royal council, here called the Consejo de Castilla. Corruption diminished, extravagance was checked—except in the building operations of the King. To these French ministers there succeeded in 1714 an able and ambitious Italian, the Abate Giulio Alberoni, whose energy made the Spanish shudder. Son of a Piacenza gardener, he had reached Spain as secretary to the Duc de Vendôme. He had been the first to suggest Isabella Farnese as Philip's second wife; grateful, she eased his way to power. Together they kept the King away from affairs, and from any counsel but their own. Together they planned to build up Spain's armed forces, and use them to drive the Austrians out of Italy, restore Spanish ascendancy in Naples and Milan, and set up ducal thrones to be graced, someday, by the farseeing Isabella's sons.

Alberoni asked five years for preparation. He replaced titled sluggards with middle-class ability in the leading posts; he taxed the clergy and imprisoned rebellious priests;[13] he scrapped worn-out vessels and built better ones; he set up forts and arsenals along coasts and frontiers; he subsidized industry, opened up roads, accelerated communication, abolished sales taxes and traffic tolls. The British ambassador in Madrid warned his government that with a few more years of such advances Spain would be a danger to other European powers.[14] To soothe such fears Alberoni pretended that he was raising forces to help Venice and the papacy against the Turks. Indeed, he sent six galleys to Clement XI, who rewarded him with a red hat (1717). "The Spanish monarchy," wrote Voltaire, "has resumed new life under Cardinal Alberoni."[15]

Everything was granted him but time. He hoped to win French and English consent to Spanish aims in Italy, and offered substantial concessions in return, but the careless King spoiled these maneuvers by revealing his desire to replace Philippe d'Orléans as ruler of France. Philippe turned against Felipe, and joined England and the United Provinces in a pact to maintain the territorial arrangements fixed by the Treaty of Utrecht. Austria violated that treaty by compelling Savoy to give her Sicily in exchange for Sardinia. Alberoni protested that this placed athwart the Mediterranean a power whose head still claimed the crown of Spain. Cursing the undue acceleration of events, he resigned himself to premature war. His newborn fleet captured

Palermo (1718), and his troops soon brought all Sicily under Spanish control. Austria thereupon joined England, France, and Holland in a Quadruple Alliance against Spain. On August 11, 1718, a British squadron under Admiral Byng destroyed the Spanish fleet off the coast of Sicily; Spain's best troops were bottled up in that island while French armies invaded Spain. Philip and Isabella sued for peace; it was granted on condition of Alberoni's banishment. He fled to Genoa (1719), made his way in disguise through Austrian-held Lombardy to Rome, took part in the conclave that elected Innocent XIII, and died in 1752, aged eighty-eight. On February 17, 1720, a Spanish envoy signed in London a treaty by which Philip resigned all claim to the throne of France, Spain surrendered Sicily to Austria, England promised to restore Gibraltar to Spain, and the Allies pledged to Isabella's offspring the right of succession to Parma and Tuscany.

In the kaleidoscope of international politics allies soon become enemies, and foes may formally become friends. To cement peace with France, Philip had betrothed his two-year-old daughter, María Ana Victoria, to Louis XV in 1721, and had sent her—all wondering—to France (1722). But in 1725 France sent her back so that Louis might marry a woman who could at once undertake the task of giving him an heir. Insulted, Spain allied herself with Austria; the Emperor Charles VI promised to help recapture Gibraltar; when a Spanish army tried to take that bastion Austrian help did not come; the attempt failed, and Spain not only made peace with England, but restored to her the Asiento monopoly of selling slaves to Spanish colonies; in return Britain pledged to put Isabella's son Don Carlos on the ducal throne of Parma. In 1731 Carlos and six thousand Spanish troops were escorted to Italy by an English fleet. Austria, to secure British and Spanish support for the accession of Maria Theresa to the Imperial throne, yielded Parma and Piacenza to Carlos. In 1734 Carlos promoted himself to Naples. Isabella's triumph was complete.

Philip, however, sank into a melancholy mood that, after 1736, lapsed now and then into insanity. He shrank into a corner of his room, thinking that all who entered planned to kill him. He was loath to eat for fear of being poisoned. For a long time he refused to leave his bed or be shaved. Isabella tried a hundred ways to heal or soothe him; all failed but one. In 1737 she coaxed Farinelli to come to Spain. One night, in an apartment adjoining the King's, she arranged a concert in which the great *castrato* sang two arias by Hasse. Philip rose from his bed to look through a doorway and see what agency could make such captivating sounds. Isabella brought Farinelli to him; the monarch praised and caressed him, and bade him name his reward; nothing would be refused. Previously instructed by the Queen, the singer asked only that Philip should let himself be shaved and dressed, and should appear at the royal council. The King consented; his fears subsided; he seemed miraculously healed. But when the next evening came he called for Farinelli, and begged him to sing those same two songs again; only so could he be calmed to sleep. So it continued, night after night, for ten years. Farinelli was paid 200,000 reales a year, but was not allowed to sing except at the court. He accepted the condition gracefully, and though his power over the King was greater than that of any minister, he never abused it, always used it for good; he remained untouched by venality, and won the admiration of all.[16]

In 1746 Philip ordered 100,000 Masses to be said for his salvation; if so many should not be needed to get him into heaven the surplus should be applied to poor souls for whom no such provision had been made.[17] In that year he died.

III. FERDINAND VI: 1746–59

His second son by his first wife succeeded him, and gave Spain thirteen years of healing rule. Isabella survived till 1766; she was treated with kindness and courtesy by her stepson, but she lost her power to influence events. Ferdinand's wife, Maria Barbara, Scarlatti's pupil, was now the woman behind the throne; though she loved food and money beyond reason, she was a gentler spirit than Isabella, and gave most of her energies to encouraging music and art. Farinelli continued to sing for the new rulers, and Scarlatti's harpsichord could not rival him. King and Queen worked to end the War of the Austrian Succession; they accepted the Treaty of Aix-la-Chapelle (1748), though it gave Tuscany to Austria; and a year later they terminated the 136-year-old Asiento by paying £100,000 to the South Sea Company for the loss of its privileges in the slave trade.

Ferdinand was a man of good will, kindly and honest, but he had inherited a delicate constitution and was subject to fits of passion, of which he was painfully ashamed.[18] Conscious of his limitations, he left administration to two able ministers—Don José de Carvajal and Zenón de Somodevilla, Marqués de la Ensenada. Ensenada improved agricultural methods, subsidized mining and industry, built roads and canals, abolished internal tolls, rebuilt the navy, replaced the hated sales tax by a tax on income and property, reorganized the finances, and broke down the intellectual isolation of Spain by sending students abroad. Partly through Ensenada's diplomacy a concordat was signed with the papacy (1753), reserving to the King the right to tax ecclesiastical property and to appoint bishops to Spanish sees. The power of the Church was reduced, the Inquisition was subdued, public autos-da-fé were abolished.

The two ministers diverged in foreign policy. Carvajal felt the charm of the devoted British ambassador, Sir Benjamin Keene, and took a peaceful pro-British line; Ensenada favored France, and moved toward war with England. Ferdinand, appreciating his energy and ability, was long patient with him, but finally dismissed him. While nearly all Europe fell into seven years of war, Ferdinand gave his people a longer period of tranquillity and prosperity than Spain had enjoyed since Philip II.

In 1758 Maria Barbara died. The King, who had loved her as if politics had had nothing to do with their marriage, fell into a state of melancholy and unshaved dishevelment strangely recalling that of his father; in his final year he too was insane. Toward the end he refused to go to bed, fearing that he would never get up again. He died in his chair, August 10, 1759. Everyone mourned the royal lovers, for their rule had been a rare blessing to Spain.

IV. THE ENLIGHTENMENT ENTERS SPAIN

The story of the Enlightenment in Spain is a case of a resistible force encountering an immovable body. The Spanish character, and its blood-written pledge to its medieval faith, turned back sooner or later all winds of heresy or doubt, all alien forms of dress or manners or economy. Only one economic force favored foreign thought—Spanish merchants who daily dealt with strangers, and who knew to what power and wealth their like had risen in England and France. They were willing to import ideas if these could weaken the hold that nobles and clergy had inherited on the land, life, and mind of Spain. They knew that religion had lost its power in England; some had heard of Newton and Locke; even Gibbon was to find a few readers in Spain.[19]

Of course the strongest Enlightenment breezes came from France. The French aristocrats who followed Philip V to Madrid were already touched by the irreligion that hid its head under Louis XIV but ran rampant during the Regency. In 1714 some scholars founded the Real Academia Española in emulation of the French Academy; soon it began work on a dictionary; in 1737 the *Diario de los literatos de España* undertook to rival the *Journal des savants*. The Duke of Alba, who directed the Real Academia for twenty years (1756–76), was a warm admirer of Jean-Jacques Rousseau.[20] In 1773 he subscribed eight louis d'or for Pigalle's statue of Voltaire; "Condemned to cultivate my reason in secret," he wrote to d'Alembert, "I take this opportunity to give public testimony to my gratitude and admiration for the great man who first showed me the way."[21]

Gratuitous advertisement was given to Rousseau's *Émile* by its ceremonious burning in a Madrid church (1765).[22] Young Spaniards acquainted with Paris, like the Marqués de Mora who loved Julie de Lespinasse, came back to Spain with some rubbing of the skepticism that they had encountered in the salons. Copies of works by Voltaire, Diderot, or Raynal were smuggled into Spain, and aroused some innovating minds. A Spanish journalist wrote in 1763: "Through the effect of many pernicious books that have become the fashion, such as those of Voltaire, Rousseau, and Helvétius, much cooling of faith has been felt in this country."[23] Pablo Olavide openly expressed Voltairean ideas in his Madrid salon (c. 1766).[24] On the shelves of the Sociedades Económicas de los Amigos del País in Madrid were works by Voltaire, Rousseau, Bayle, d'Alembert, Montesquieu, Hobbes, Locke, and Hume.[25] Abbé Clément, touring Spain in 1768, reported a wide spread of religious indifference, even unbelief, covered with external observance of Catholic ritual.[26] In 1778 the Inquisition was informed that the highest officials of the court read the French *philosophes*.[27]

It was of considerable importance to Spanish history that Pedro Abarca,

Conde de Aranda, traveling in France, became a friend of Voltaire. We may judge of his connections by his later activity as Spanish ambassador to Versailles; he mixed freely with the Encyclopedists in Paris, formed an admiring intimacy with d'Alembert, and crossed France to visit Voltaire at Ferney. In Spain he professed fidelity to the Church, but it was he who persuaded Charles III to expel the Jesuits. Under his guidance Charles joined the ranks of those "enlightened despots" to whom the *philosophes* were looking as their likeliest aides in the spread of education, liberty, and reason.

V. CHARLES III: 1759–88

1. The New Government

When he arrived from Naples he was forty-three years old. He was welcomed by all but the Jesuits,[28] who resented the sale of their Paraguayan settlements by Spain to Portugal (1750). Otherwise he won all hearts by remitting arrears of taxes, and restoring some of the privileges that the provinces had lost under the centralizing policy of Philip V. His first year as king of Spain was saddened by the death of his wife, Maria Amalia. He never married again. It is to the credit of the Spanish Bourbons of the eighteenth century that they gave the monarchs of Europe an example of marital devotion and stability.

A British diplomat drew a British picture of Charles, who had had some encounters with the English in Naples:

> The King has a very odd appearance in person and dress. He is of diminutive stature, with a complexion the color of mahogany. He has not been measured for a coat these thirty years, so that it sits on him like a sack. His waistcoat and breeches are generally leather, with a pair of cloth spatterdashes on his legs. . . . He goes out a-sporting every day of the year, rain or blow.[29]

But the Earl of Bristol added, in 1761:

> The Catholic King has good talents, a happy memory, and uncommon command of himself on all occasions. His having been often deceived renders him suspicious. He ever prefers carrying a point by gentle means, and has the patience to repeat exhortations rather than exert his authority. . . . Yet, with the greatest air of gentleness, he keeps his ministers and attendants in the utmost awe.[30]

His personal piety gave no warning that he would attack the Jesuits or undertake religious reforms. He heard Mass daily. His "honest and obstinate adherence to all his treaties, principles, and engagements" astonished an English enemy.[31] He devoted a large part of each weekday to governmental affairs. He rose at six, visited his children, breakfasted, worked from eight to eleven, sat in council, received dignitaries, dined in public, gave several hours to hunting, supped at nine-thirty, fed his dogs, said his prayers, and went to bed. His hunting was probably a health measure, aimed to dispel the melancholy that ran in the family.

He began with some serious mistakes. Unfamiliar with Spain, which he had not seen since his sixteenth year, he took as his first aides two Italians who had served him well in Naples: the Marchese de' Grimaldi in foreign policy, the Marchese de' Squillaci in domestic affairs.

The Earl of Bristol described Squillaci as "not bright. He is fond of business, and never complains of having too much, notwithstanding the variety of departments that center in him. . . . I believe he is incapable of taking any bribes, but I would not be equally responsible for his wife."[32] Squillaci did not like the crime, odor, and gloom of Madrid; he organized a zealous police and a street-cleaning squad, and lighted the capital with five thousand lamps. He legalized monopolies for supplying the city with oil, bread, and other necessities; a drought raised prices, and the populace called for Squillaci's head. He offended the clergy by regulations that checked their privileges and power. He lost a thousand supporters by banning concealed weapons. Finally he stirred up a revolution by attempting to change the dress of the people. He persuaded the King that the long cape, which hid the figure, and the broad hat with turned-down rim, which hid much of the face, made it easier to conceal weapons, and harder for the police to recognize criminals. A succession of royal decrees forbade the cape and the hat, and officers were equipped with shears to cut the offending garments down to legal size.[33] This was more government than the proud Madrilenos could stand. On Palm Sunday, March 23, 1766, they rose in revolt, captured ammunition stores, emptied the prisons, overwhelmed soldiers and police, attacked Squillaci's home, stoned Grimaldi, killed the Walloon guards of the royal palace, and paraded with the heads of these hated foreigners held aloft on pikes and crowned with broad-rimmed hats. For two days the mob slaughtered and pillaged. Charles yielded, repealed the decrees, and sent Squillaci, safely escorted, back to Italy. Meanwhile he had discovered the talents of the Conde de Aranda, and appointed him president of the Council of Castile. Aranda made the long cape and wide sombrero the official costume of the hangman; the new connotation made the old garb unfashionable; most Madrilenos adopted French dress.

Aranda came of an old and wealthy family in Aragon. We have seen him imbibing Enlightenment in France; he went also to Prussia, where he studied military organization. He returned to Spain eager to bring his country abreast of those northern states. His Encyclopedist friends rejoiced too publicly over his accession to power; he mourned that they had thereby made his course more difficult,[34] and he wished they had studied diplomacy. He defined political diplomacy as the art of

> recognizing the strength, resources, interests, rights, fears, and hopes of the different powers, so that, as the occasion warrants it, we may appease these powers, divide them, defeat them, or ally ourselves with them, depending on how they serve our advantage and increase our security.[35]

The King was in a mood for ecclesiastical reforms because he suspected the clergy of secretly encouraging the revolt against Squillaci.[36] He had permitted the government press to print in 1765 an anonymous *Tratado de la regalia de l'amortización,* which questioned the right of the Church to amass real property, and argued that in all temporal matters the Church should be subject to the state. The author was Conde Pedro Rodríguez de Campomanes, a member of the Consejo de Castilla. In 1761 Charles had issued an order requiring royal consent for the publication of papal bulls or briefs in Spain; later he rescinded this order; in 1768 he renewed it. Now he supported Aranda and Campomanes in a succession of religious reforms that for one exciting generation remade the intellectual face of Spain.

2. The Spanish Reformation

The Spanish reformers—perhaps excepting Aranda—had no intent to destroy Catholicism in Spain. The long wars to drive out the Moors (like the long struggle for the liberation of Ireland) had made Catholicism a part of patriotism, and had intensified it into a faith too sanctified by the sacrifices of the nation to admit of successful challenge or basic change. The hope of the reformers was to bring the Church under control of the state, and to free the mind of Spain from terror of the Inquisition. They began by attacking the Jesuits.

The Society of Jesus had been born in Spain in the mind and experiences of Ignatius Loyola, and some of its greatest leaders had come from Spain. Here, as in Portugal, France, Italy, and Austria, it controlled secondary education, gave confessors to kings and queens, and shared in forming royal policies. Its expanding power aroused the jealousy, sometimes the enmity, of the secular Catholic clergy. Some of these believed in the superior authority of ecumenical councils over the popes; the Jesuits defended the supreme authority of the popes over councils and kings. Spanish businessmen complained that Jesuits engaging in colonial commerce were underselling regular merchants because of ecclesiastical exemption from taxation; and this, it was pointed out, lessened royal revenues. Charles believed that the Jesuits were still encouraging the resistance of the Paraguayan Indians to the orders of the Spanish government.[37] And he was alarmed when Aranda, Campomanes, and others showed him letters which, they alleged, had been found in the correspondence of the Jesuits; one of these letters, supposedly from Father Ricci, general of the order, declared that Charles was a bastard and should be superseded by his brother Luis.[38] The authenticity of these letters has been rejected by Catholics and unbelievers alike;[39] but Charles thought them genuine, and concluded that the Jesuits were plotting to depose him, perhaps to have him killed.[40] He noted that an attempt had been made, allegedly with Jesuit complicity, to assassinate Joseph I of Portugal (1758). He determined to follow Joseph's example, and expel the order from his realm.

Campomanes warned him that such a move could succeed only through secret preparations followed by a sudden and concerted blow; otherwise the Jesuits, who were revered by the people, could arouse a troublesome furor throughout the nation and its possessions. On Aranda's suggestion sealed messages, signed by the King, were sent out early in 1767 to officials everywhere in the empire, with orders, on pain of death, to open them only on March 31 in Spain, on April 2 in the colonies. On March 31 the Spanish Jesuits awoke to find their houses and colleges surrounded by troops, and themselves placed under arrest. They were ordered to depart peaceably, taking only such possessions as they could carry with them; all other Jesuit property was confiscated by the state. Each of the exiles was granted a small pension, which was to be discontinued if any Jesuit protested the expulsion. They were taken in carriages under military escort to the nearest port, and shipped to Italy. Charles sent word to Clement XIII that he was transporting them "to the ecclesiastical territories, in order that they may remain under the wise and immediate direction of his Holiness. . . . I request your Holiness not to regard this resolution otherwise than as an indispensable civil precaution, which I have adopted only after mature examination and profound reflection."[41]

When the first vessel, bearing six hundred Jesuits, sought to deposit them at Civitavecchia, Cardinal Torrigiani, papal secretary, refused to let them land, arguing that Italy could not so suddenly take care of so many refugees.[42] For weeks the ship roamed the Mediterranean seeking some hospitable port, while its desperate passengers suffered from weather, hunger, and disease. Finally they were allowed to debark in Corsica; and later, in manageable groups, they were absorbed into the Papal States. Meanwhile the Jesuits experienced similar banishment from Naples, Parma, Spanish America, and the Philippines. Clement XIII appealed to Charles III to revoke edicts whose suddenness and cruelty must shock all Christendom. Charles replied: "To spare the world a great scandal I shall ever preserve, as a secret in my heart, the abominable plot that necessitated this rigor. Your Holiness ought to believe my word: the safety of my life exacts of me a profound silence."[43]

The King never fully revealed the evidence upon which he had based his decrees. The details are so controverted and obscure that judgment is baffled. D'Alembert, no friend of the Jesuits, questioned the method of their banishment. On May 4, 1767, he wrote to Voltaire:

> What do you think of the edict of Charles III, so abruptly expelling the Jesuits? Persuaded as I am that he had good and sufficient reasons, do you not think that he ought to have made them known, and not shut them up in his "royal heart"? Do you not think he ought to have allowed the Jesuits to justify themselves, especially since everyone is sure they could not? Do you not think, too, that it would be very unjust to make them all die of starvation if a single lay brother, who perhaps is cutting cabbage in the kitchen, should say a word, one way or the other, in their favor? . . . Does it not seem to you that he could act with more common sense in carrying out what, after all, is a reasonable matter?[44]

Was the expulsion popular? A year after its completion, on the festival of St. Charles, the King showed himself to the people from the balcony of his palace. When, following custom, he asked what gift they desired of him, they cried out "with one voice" that the Jesuits should be allowed to return, and to wear the habit of the secular clergy. Charles refused, and banished the

Archbishop of Toledo on charge of having instigated the suspiciously con-cordant petition.[45] When, in 1769, the Pope asked the bishops of Spain for their judgment on the expulsion of the Jesuits, forty-two bishops approved, six opposed, eight gave no opinion.[46] Probably the secular clergy were con-tent to be relieved of Jesuit competition. The Augustinian friars of Spain approved the expulsion, and later supported the demand of Charles III that the Society of Jesus be completely dissolved.[47]

No such summary action could be taken with the Inquisition. Far more deeply than the Society of Jesus it was mortised in the awe and tradition of the people, who ascribed to it the preservation of morals and the purity of their faith—even of their blood. When Charles III came to the throne the Inquisition held the mind of Spain by a severe and watchful censorship. Any book suspected of religious heresy or moral deviation was submitted to *calificadores*—qualifiers, or examiners; if they thought it dangerous they sent their recommendations to the Consejo de la Inquisición; this could decree the suppression of the book and the punishment of the author. Periodically the Inquisition published an Index of prohibited books; to own or read one of these without ecclesiastical permission was a crime that only the Inquisition could forgive, and for which the offender could be excommunicated. Priests were required, especially in Lent, to ask all penitents whether they had, or knew anyone who had, a prohibited book. Any person failing to report a violation of the Index was considered as guilty as the violator, and no ties of family or friendship could excuse him.[48]

Charles's ministers here accomplished only minor reforms. In 1768 the Inquisitorial censorship was checked by requiring that all edicts prohibiting books should secure royal approval before being put into effect. In 1770 the King ordered the Inquisition's tribunal to concern itself only with heresy and apostasy, and to imprison no one whose guilt had not been conclusively established. In 1784 he ruled that proceedings of the Inquisition regarding grandees, cabinet ministers, and royal servants must be submitted to him for review. He appointed Inquisitor generals who showed a more liberal attitude toward diversities of thought.[49]

These modest measures had some effect, for in 1782 the Inquisitor General sadly reported that fear of ecclesiastical censure for reading forbidden books was "nearly extinct."[50] In general the agents of the Inquisition, after 1770, were milder, its penalties more humane, than before. Toleration was granted to Protestants under Charles III, and in 1779 to Moslems, though not to Jews.[51] There were four autos-da-fé during the reign of Charles III, the last in 1780 at Seville, of an old woman accused of witchcraft; and this execution aroused such criticism throughout Europe[52] that the way was prepared for the suppression of the Spanish Inquisition in 1813.

Nevertheless even under Charles III freedom of thought, if expressed, was still legally punishable with death. In 1768 Pablo Olavide was denounced to the Inquisition as having pornographic paintings in his Madrid home—per-haps some copies of Boucher's nudes, for Olavide had traveled in France, even to Ferney. A more serious charge was laid against him in 1774—that in the model villages established by him in Sierra Morena he had allowed no monasteries, and had forbidden the clergy to say Mass on weekdays, or beg for alms. The Inquisition notified the King that these and other offenses had been proved by the testimony of eighty witnesses. In 1778 Olavide was summoned to trial; he was accused of upholding the Copernican astronomy, and of corresponding with Voltaire and Rousseau. He abjured his errors, was "reconciled" with the Church, suffered confiscation of all his property, and was sentenced to confinement in a monastery for eight years. In 1780 his health collapsed, and he was allowed to take the waters at a spa in Catalonia. He escaped to France, and received a hero's welcome from his philosophic friends in Paris. But after some years of exile he grew unbearably lonesome for his Spanish haunts. He composed a pious work, *The Gospel Triumphant, or The Philosopher Converted*, and the Inquisition permitted his return.[53]

We note that the trial of Olavide occurred after the fall of Aranda from his place at the head of the Consejo de Castilla. In his final years of power Aranda founded new schools, taught by secular clergy, to supply the void left by the Jesuits; and he reformed the currency by replacing debased coins with money of good quality and superior design (1770). However, his sense of his superior enlightenment made him in time irritable, overbearing, and presumptuous. After making the power of the king absolute, he sought to limit it by increasing the authority of the ministers. He lost perspective and measure, and dreamed of bringing Spain, in one generation, out of its contented Catholicity into the stream of French philosophy. He expressed too boldly his heretical ideas, even to his confessor. Though many of the secular clergy supported some of his ecclesiastical reforms as beneficial to the Church,[54] he frightened many more by disclosing his hope of completely disbanding the Inquisition.[55] He became so unpopular that he did not dare go out of his palace without a bodyguard. He complained so often of the burdens of office that at last Charles took him at his word and sent him as ambassador to France (1773–87). There he predicted that the English colonies in America, which were beginning their revolt, would in time become one of the great powers of the world.[56]

3. The New Economy

Three able men dominated the ministry after Aranda's departure. José Monino, Conde de Floridablanca, succeeded Grimaldi as secretary of state for foreign affairs (1776), and dominated the cabinet till 1792. Like Aranda, but in less degree, he felt the influence of the *philosophes*. He guided the King in measures for improving agriculture, commerce, education, science, and art; but the French Revolution frightened him into conservatism, and he led Spain into the first coalition against Revolutionary France (1792). Pedro de Campomanes presided over the Council of Castile for five years, and was the prime mover in economic reform. Gaspar Melchor de Jovellanos, "the most eminent Spaniard of his age,"[57] came into public view as a humane and incorruptible judge in Seville (1767) and Madrid (1778). Most of his activity in the central government followed 1789, but he contributed powerfully to economic policy under Charles III with his *Informe sobre un proyecto de ley agraria* (1787); this proposal for a revision of agricultural law, written with almost Ciceronian elegance, gave him a European reputation. These three men, with Aranda, were the fathers of the Spanish Enlightenment and the new economy. On the whole, in the judgment of an English scholar, their "result for good rivals that achieved in an equally short time in any other country; and in the history of Spain there is certainly no period which can compare with the reign of Charles III."[58]

The obstacles to reform in Spain were as great in economy as in religion. The concentration of inalienable ownership in titled families or ecclesiastical corporations, and the monopoly of wool production by the Mesta seemed to be insurmountable barriers to economic change. Millions of Spaniards took pride in indolence, and showed no shame in begging; change was distrusted as a threat to idleness.* Money was hoarded in palace coffers and church treasuries instead of being invested in commerce or industry. The expulsion of Moors, Jews, and Moriscos had removed many sources of agricultural betterment and commercial development. Difficulties of internal communication and transport left the interior a century behind Barcelona, Seville, and Madrid.

Despite these deterrents, in Madrid and other centers men of good will —nobles, priests, and commoners, without distinction of sex—formed Sociedades Económicas de los Amigos del País to study and promote education, science, industry, commerce, and art. They founded schools and libraries, translated foreign treatises, offered prizes for essays and ideas, and raised money for progressive economic undertakings and experiments. Acknowledging the influence of French physiocrats and Adam Smith, they condemned the national accumulation of gold as a monument to stagnation, and one of them asserted: "The nation that has the most gold is the poorest, . . . as Spain has shown."[60] Jovellanos hailed "the science of civil economy" as "the true science of the state."[61] Economic treatises multiplied. Campomanes' *Discurso sobre el fomento de la industria popular* inspired thousands, including the King.

Charles began by importing grain and seed for regions where agriculture had decayed. He urged towns to lease their uncultivated common lands to peasants at the lowest practical rent. Floridablanca, using crown revenues from vacant ecclesiastical benefices, established in Valencia and Málaga *montes píos* (pious funds) for lending money to farmers at low interest. To check deforestation and erosion, Charles ordered all communes to plant, each year, a fixed number of trees; hence came that annual celebration of "Arbor Day" which was still, in both hemispheres, a wholesome custom in our youth. He encouraged the disregard of old entails, discouraged new ones, and thereby facilitated the breakup of large estates into peasant properties.

---

* A law of Aragon prescribed that every hidalgo should supply each of his sons with a pension, since "it would not be seemly for a nobleman to work."[59]

The privileges of the Mesta sheep monopoly were sharply reduced; large tracts of land formerly reserved by it for pasturage were opened to cultivation. Foreign colonists were brought in to people sparsely inhabited areas; so, in the Sierra Morena region of southwestern Spain, hitherto abandoned to robbers and wild beasts, Olavide created (1767 f.) forty-four villages and eleven towns of French or German immigrants; these settlements became famous for their prosperity. Extensive canals were dug to connect rivers and irrigate large tracts of formerly arid land. A network of new roads, which for a time were the best in Europe,[62] bound the villages and the towns in a quickened facility of communication, transport, and trade.

Governmental aid went to industry. To remove the stigma traditionally attached to manual labor, a royal decree declared that craft occupations were compatible with noble rank, and that craftsmen were henceforth eligible to governmental posts. Model factories were established: for textiles at Guadalajara and Segovia; for hats at San Fernando; for silks at Talavera; for porcelain at Buen Retiro; for glass at San Ildefonso; for glass, cabinetry, and tapestry at Madrid. Royal edicts favored the development of large-scale capitalistic production, especially in the textile industry. Guadalajara in 1780 had eight hundred looms employing four thousand weavers; one company at Barcelona managed sixty factories with 2,162 cotton-weaving looms; Valencia had four thousand looms weaving silk, and, favored by its facilities for export, was cutting into the silk trade of Lyons. By 1792 Barcelona had eighty thousand weavers, and ranked second only to the English Midlands in the production of cotton cloth.

Seville and Cadíz had long enjoyed a state-protected monopoly of commerce with Spain's possessions in the New World; Charles III ended this privilege, and allowed various ports to trade with the colonies; and he negotiated a treaty with Turkey (1782) that opened Moslem harbors to Spanish goods. The results were beneficial to all parties. Spanish America grew rapidly in wealth; Spain's income from America rose eight hundred per cent under Charles III; her export trade was tripled.[63]

The expanding activities of the government required enlarged revenues. These were raised in some measure by state monopolies in the sale of brandy, tobacco, playing cards, gunpowder, lead, mercury, sulfur, and salt. At the outset of the reign there were sales taxes of fifteen per cent in Catalonia, fourteen per cent in Castile. Jovellanos aptly described sales taxes: "They surprise their prey . . . at its birth, pursue and nip it as it circulates, and never lose sight of it or let it escape, until the moment of its consumption."[64] Under Charles the sales tax in Catalonia was abolished, and in Castile it was reduced to two, three, or four per cent.[65] A moderate graduated tax was laid upon incomes. To secure additional funds by putting the savings of the people to work, Francisco de Cabarrús persuaded the Treasury to issue interest-bearing government bonds. When these fell to seventy-eight per cent of their par value, he founded (1782) the first national bank of Spain, the Banco de San Carlos, which redeemed the bonds at par and restored the financial credit of the state.

The result of statesmanship and enterprise was a substantial rise in the prosperity of the nation as a whole. The middle classes profited most, for it was their organizations that remade the Spanish economy. At Madrid 375 businessmen composed five great merchant guilds—the Cinco Gremios Mayores—which controlled most of the trade of the capital; we may judge their wealth from the fact that in 1776 they lent thirty million reales to the government.[66]

Generally the government favored this rise of the business class as indispensable to freeing Spain from economic and political dependence upon states with a more advanced economy. Here, as there, the growing proletariat had little share in the new affluence. Wages rose, especially in Catalonia, where the well-to-do complained that servants were hard to find and hard to keep;[67] but, by and large, prices rose faster than wages, and the "working classes" were as poor at the end of the reign as at the beginning. An Englishman traveling in Valencia in 1787 remarked the contrast between "the opulence of . . . merchants, manufacturers, ecclesiastics, the military, or gentlemen of landed property," and the "poverty, wretchedness, and rags" visible "in every street."[68] So the middle classes welcomed the Luces—the Enlightenment coming in from France and England—while their employees, crowding the churches and kissing the shrines, comforted themselves with divine grace and hopes of paradise.

The cities expanded under the new economy. The great maritime centers —Barcelona, Valencia, Seville, Cadíz—had populations ranging from 80,000 to 100,000 (1800). Madrid in 1797 had 167,607, plus 30,000 foreigners. When Charles III came to the throne the city had the reputation of being the dirtiest capital in Europe. In the poorer quarters people still emptied their garbage into the streets, relying upon wind or rain to distribute it; when Charles forbade this they denounced him as a tyrant. "The Spaniards," he said, "are children, who cry when they are washed."[69] Nevertheless his agents established a system of garbage-collection and sewage, and scavengers were organized to gather offal for fertilizer.[70] An effort to suppress mendicancy failed; the people refused to let the police arrest beggars—especially the blind ones, who had formed themselves into a powerful guild.

Year by year Charles improved his capital. Water was led from the mountains into seven hundred fountains, from which 720 water carriers laboriously delivered it to the houses of the city. The streets were lighted by oil lamps from nightfall to midnight during six months of autumn and winter. Most streets were narrow and tortuous, following old and devious paths and hiding from the summer sun; but some fine avenues were laid out, and the people enjoyed spacious parks and shady promenades. Especially popular was the Paseo del Prado, or Meadow Walk, cooled with fountains and trees, and favored for amorous reconnaissance and rendezvous. There, in 1785, Juan de Villanueva began to build the Museo del Prado. And there, almost any day, four hundred carriages drove by, and, any evening, thirty thousand Madrilenos gathered. They were forbidden to sing ribald songs, or bathe nude in the fountains, or play music after midnight; but they enjoyed the melodious cries of women selling *naranjas, limas*, and *avellanas*—oranges, limes, and hazelnuts. At the end of the eighteenth century, said travelers, the spectacle visible daily on the Prado equaled that which in other cities of that period could be seen only on Sundays and holidays.[71] Madrid became then, as it has again become in our time, one of the most beautiful cities in Europe.

Charles III was not as successful in foreign policy as in domestic affairs. The revolt of the English colonies in America seemed to offer a chance to avenge the losses suffered by Spain in the Seven Years' War; Aranda urged Charles to help the revolutionists; the King secretly sent the rebels a million livres (June, 1776). Attacks by English corsairs upon Spanish shipping finally led Spain to declare war (June 23, 1779). A Spanish force recaptured Minorca, but an attempt to take Gibraltar failed. An invasion of England was prepared, but was frustrated by "Protestant" storms. In the Peace of Versailles Spain (1783) withdrew its demand for Gibraltar, but regained Florida.

The failure to restore Spain's territorial integrity saddened the King's final years. The wars had consumed much of the wealth which the new economy had produced. His brilliant ministers had never overcome two powerful forces of conservatism—the grandees with their vast estates, and the clergy with their vested interest in the simplicity of the people. Charles himself had seldom wavered in his basic fidelity to the Church. His people never admired him so much as when, meeting a religious procession, he gave his coach to the prelate who was carrying the Host, and then joined the retinue on foot. His religious devotion won the affection which had been withheld from him, as a stranger from Italy, in the first decade of his reign. When he died (December 14, 1788), after fifty-four years of rule in Naples and Spain, there were many who reckoned him, if not the greatest, certainly the most beneficent king that Spain had ever had. His kindly nature shone out when, on his deathbed, he was asked by the attending bishop had he yet pardoned all his enemies. "How should I wait for this pass before forgiving them?" he asked. "They were all forgiven the moment after the offense."[72]

VI. THE SPANISH CHARACTER

What sort of people were they, these Spaniards of the eighteenth century? By all reports their morals were good, compared with their peers in England or France. Their intense religion, their courage and sense of honor, their family coherence and discipline provided strong correctives to their sexual sensitivity and their pugnacious pride, even while sanctioning a passionate chauvinism of race and faith. Sexual selection promoted courage, for Spanish women, desiring protection, gave their most intoxicating smiles to those men who dared the bulls in the arena or the streets, or who quickly resented and avenged an insult, or who returned with glory from the wars.

Sexual morality had softened with the influx of French ideas and ways. Girls were closely guarded, and parental consent (after 1766) was a legal requisite for marriage; but after marriage the women in the larger cities indulged in flirtations. The *cortejo* or *cicisbeo*—courtier or attendant cavalier—became a necessary appendage to a woman of fashion, and adultery increased.[73] One small group, the *majos* and *majas*, constituted a unique aspect of Spanish life. The *majos* were men of the lower class who dressed like dandies, wore long capes, long hair, and broad-rimmed hats, smoked big cigars, were always ready for a fight, and lived a Bohemian life financed as often as possible by their *majas*—their mistresses. Their sexual unions paid no attention to law; often the *maja* had a husband who supported her while she supported her *majo*. Half the world knows the *maja*, garbed or not, from Goya's brush.

Social morality was relatively high. Political and commercial corruption existed, but not on the scale known in France or England; a French traveler reported that "Spanish probity is proverbial, and it shines conspicuously in commercial relations."[74] The word of a Spanish gentleman was moral tender from Lisbon to St. Petersburg. Friendship in Spain was often more lasting than love. Charity was plentiful. In Madrid alone religious institutions daily distributed thirty thousand bowls of nourishing soup to the poor.[75] Many new hospitals and almshouses were established, many old ones were enlarged or improved. Almost all Spaniards were generous and humane, except to heretics and bulls.

Bullfights rivaled religion, sex, honor, and the family as objects of Spanish devotion. Like the gladiatorial games of ancient Rome, they were defended on two grounds: courage had to be developed in men, and bulls had to die before being eaten. Charles III forbade these contests, but they were resumed soon after his death. Skillful and riskful toreadors were the idols of all classes. Each had his following; the Duchess of Alba favored Costillares, the Duchess of Osuna favored Romero, and these factions divided Madrid as Gluck and Piccini divided Paris. Men and women wagered their earnings on the fate of the bulls, and on almost everything else. Gambling was illegal but universal; even private homes held gambling soirees, and the hostesses pocketed the fees.

Genteel male dress gradually abandoned the somber black garb and stiff collar of an earlier generation for the French habit of colored coat, long vest of satin or silk, knee breeches, silk stockings, buckled shoes, all crowned with a wig and a three-cornered hat. Usually the Spanish woman made a sacred mystery of her charms by swathing them in lace bodices and long—sometimes hoop—skirts, and using mantilla veils to hide eyes in whose dark depths some Spaniard would gladly sink his soul. But whereas in the seventeenth century a lady rarely allowed her feet to be seen by a man, now her skirts were shortened to a few inches above the floor, and the formerly heelless slippers were displaced by sharp-pointed high-heeled shoes. Preachers warned that such indecent exposure of female feet added dangerous fuel to the already combustible male. The women smiled, adorned their shoes, flashed their skirts, and waved their fans, even on winter days. Isabella Farnese had an armory of 1,626 fans, some of them painted by artists of national renown.

Social life was restrained in everything but the dance. The evening assemblies avoided serious discussion, preferring games, the dance, and gallantry. Dancing was a major passion in Spain, and sprouted varieties that became famous in Europe. The fandango was danced to a triple measure with castanets; the *seguidilla* was performed by two or four couples, with castanets and usually with song; its derivative, the bolero, took form toward 1780, and soon acquired a mad popularity. In the *contradanza* a line of men faced a line of women in alternating approach and retreat, as if symbolizing the tactics of the eternal war between woman and man; or four couples formed and enclosed a square in the stately *contradanza cuadrada*—the quadrille. Masquerade balls sometimes drew 3,500 eager dancers, and in Carnival time they danced till dawn.

These dances made motion a living poetry and a sexual stimulus. "It was said that a Spanish woman dancing the *seguidilla* was so seductive that even a pope and the whole College of Cardinals would be swept off their dignity."[76] Casanova himself found something to learn in Spain:

> About midnight the wildest and maddest of dances began. . . . It was the fandango, which I fondly supposed I had often seen, but which [here] was far beyond my wildest imaginings. . . . In Italy and France the dancers are careful not to make the gestures which render this the most voluptuous of dances. Each couple, man and woman, make only three steps, then, keeping time to the music with their castanets, they throw themselves into a variety of lascivious attitudes; the whole of love from its birth to its end, from its first sigh to its last ecstasy, is set forth. In my excitement I cried aloud.[77]

He marveled that the Inquisition allowed so provocative a dance; he was told that it was "absolutely forbidden, and no one would dare to dance it if the Conde de Aranda had not given permission."

Some of the most popular forms of Spanish music were associated with the dance; so the *cante flamenco*, or gypsy ("Flemish") singing, used a plaintive and sentimental tone with which all gypsy singers accompanied the *seguidilla gitana*. Perhaps these mournful melodies echoed old Moorish airs, or reflected the somber quality of Spanish religion and art, or the irritating inaccessibility of the female form, or the disillusionment following realization. A more joyous strain came in with Italian opera (1703) and Farinelli's arias. The old *castrato*, after trilling through two reigns, lost favor under Charles III, who dethroned him with a line: "Capons are good only to eat."[78] The Italian influence continued with Scarlatti, and triumphed again with Boccherini, who arrived in 1768, dominated the music of the court under Charles III and Charles IV, and remained in Spain till his death (1805).

By a reverse movement Vicente Martín y Solar, after making a name in Spain, successfully produced Italian opera in Florence, Vienna, and St. Petersburg. Antonio Soler's harpsichord sonatas rivaled Scarlatti's; and Don Luis Misón developed the *tonada*, or vocal solo, into the *tonadillo* as an intermezzo of song between the acts of a play. In 1799 a royal order ended the reign of Italian music in Spain by forbidding the performance of any piece not written in Castilian language and presented by Spanish artists.[79]

We cannot sum up the Spanish character in one homogeneous mold. The Spanish soul varies with the scenery from state to state, and the *afrancesados*, or Frenchified Spaniards, who gathered in Madrid, were quite another type than those natives who had been mortised and tenoned in Spanish ways. But if we set aside exotic minorities, we may recognize in the Spanish people a character indigenous and unique. The Spaniard was proud, but with a silent force that took little from chauvinism or nationality; it was a pride of individuality, a resolute sense of solitary struggle against earthly injury, personal insult, or eternal damnation. To such a spirit the external world could seem of secondary moment, not worth bothering about or toiling for; nothing mattered but the fate of the soul in the conflict with man and in the search for God. How trivial, then, were the problems of politics, the race for money, the exaltation of fame or place! Even the triumphs of war had no glory unless they were victories over the enemies of the faith. Rooted in that faith, the Spaniard could face life with a stoic tranquillity, a fatalism that waited quietly for eventual Paradise.

VII. THE SPANISH MIND

When Louis XIV accepted the offer of the last Hapsburg King of Spain to bequeath his crown to a grandson of the Grand Monarque, a Spanish ambassador at Versailles exclaimed joyfully, "Now there are no more Pyrenees!" But those gloomy masses stood their ground as an obstinate barrier to French *lumières*, and as a symbol of the resistance that would meet the attempt of a dedicated few to Europeanize the Spanish mind.

Campomanes startled the old with a *Discurso sobre la educación popular de los artesanos y su fomento* (1774–76), which made a wider extension of popular education an indispensable base for national vitality and growth. Some high ecclesiastics and great landowners saw no sense in disturbing the people with unnecessary knowledge that might lead to religious heresy and social revolt. Undeterred, Jovellanos labored to spread faith in education. "Numerous are the streams that lead to social prosperity," he wrote, "but all spring from the same source, and that source is public education."[80] He hoped that education would teach men to reason, that reason would free them from superstition and intolerance, and that science, developed by such men, would use the resources of nature for the conquest of disease and poverty. Some noble ladies took up the challenge, and formed a Junta de Damas to finance primary schools. Charles III spent considerable sums in establishing free elementary schools. Private individuals joined in founding academies for the study of language, literature, history, art, law, science, or medicine.

The expulsion of the Jesuits compelled and facilitated the remolding of secondary schools. Charles ordered an expansion of science courses in these colleges, a modernization of their textbooks, and the admission of laymen to their faculties. He endowed colleges, and gave pensions to outstanding teachers.[81] The universities were advised to admit Newton to their courses in physics, and Descartes and Leibniz into their courses in philosophy. The University of Salamanca rejected the advice on the ground that "the principles of Newton . . . and Cartesio do not resemble the revealed truth as much as do those of Aristotle";[82] but most Spanish universities accepted the royal directive. The University of Valencia, with 2,400 students, was now (1784) the largest and most progressive educational center in Spain. Several religious orders adopted *filosofía moderna* in their colleges. The general of the Discalced Carmelites urged Carmelite teachers to read Plato, Aristotle, Cicero, Francis Bacon, Descartes, Newton, Leibniz, Locke, Wolff, Condillac; here was no regimen for saints. One chapter of the Augustinian Friars studied Hobbes, another studied Helvétius. Such studies were always followed by refutations, but many an ardent soul has lost his faith in refuting its enemies.

One remarkable monk had "modernized" while Charles III was still a youth. Though spending the last forty-seven years (1717–64) of his life in a Benedictine monastery at Oviedo, Benito Jerónimo Feijóo y Montenegro managed to study Bacon, Descartes, Galileo, Pascal, Gassendi, Newton, and Leibniz; and he saw with wonder and shame how Spain, since Cervantes, had been isolated from the main currents of European thought. From his cell he sent forth, between 1726 and 1739, a series of eight volumes which he called *Teatro crítico*—not dramatic criticism, but a critical examination of ideas. He attacked the logic and philosophy then taught in Spain; lauded Bacon's plea for inductive science; summarized the findings of scientists in many fields; ridiculed magic, divination, bogus miracles, medical ignorance, and popular superstitions; laid down rules of historical credibility that ruthlessly punctured fond national legends; demanded an extension of education to all classes; and advocated a freer and more public life for women in education and society.

A swarm of enemies gathered around his books, impugning his patriotism and denouncing his audacities. The Inquisition summoned him before its tribunal, but it could find no explicit heresy in him or his work. In 1742 he resumed his campaign with the first of five volumes entitled *Cartas eruditas y curiosas* (*Learned and Inquiring Letters*). He wrote a good style, recognizing every author's moral obligation to be clear; and the public so relished his instruction and his courage that fifteen editions of the *Teatro* and the *Cartas* were required by 1786. He could not banish superstition from Spain; witches, ghosts, and demons still peopled the air and frightened the mind; but a beginning had been made, and it is to the credit of his order that this had been done by a monk who remained unmolested in his modest cell until his death at eighty-eight (1764).

It was another cleric who wrote the most famous prose work of eighteenth-century Spain. Just as the Benedictines saw that no harm should come to Feijóo, so the Jesuits protected one of their priests whose chief production was a satire of sermons. José Francisco de Isla was himself an eloquent preacher, but he was first amused, then disturbed, by the oratorical tricks, the literary conceits, the histrionics and buffoonery with which some preachers caught the attention and pennies of the people in churches and public squares. In 1758 he made high fun of these evangelists in a novel called *Historia del famoso predicador Fray Gerundio*. Brother Gerund, said Father Isla,

> always began his sermons with some proverb, some pothouse witticism, or some strange fragment which, taken from its context, would seem at first blush to be an inconsequence, a blasphemy, or an impiety, until at last, having kept his audience waiting a moment in wonder, he finished the clause, and came out with an explanation that reduced the whole to a sort of miserable trifling. Thus, preaching one day on the mystery of the Trinity, he began his sermon by saying, "I deny that God exists a Unity in essence and a Trinity in person," and then stopped short for an instant. The hearers, of course, looked around, . . . wondering what would be the end of this heretical blasphemy. At length, when the preacher thought he had fairly caught them, he went on: "Thus say the Ebionite, the Marcionite, the Arian, the Manichean, the Socinian; but I prove it against them all from the Scriptures, the Councils, and the Fathers."[83]

Within a day of its publication eight hundred copies of *Fray Gerundio* were sold. The preaching friars assailed it as encouraging disrespect of the clergy. Isla was summoned before the Inquisition, and his book was condemned (1760), but he himself was not punished. Meanwhile he joined his fellow Jesuits in exile, and on the road suffered an attack of paralysis. He spent his declining years at Bologna, living on the pittance allowed him by the Spanish government.

Almost every Spaniard who could write wrote poetry. At a poetic joust in 1727 there were 150 competitors. Jovellanos added poetry and drama to his activities as jurist, educator, and statesman. His home in Madrid became a meeting place for men of letters. He composed satires in the manner of Juvenal, rebuking the corruption he had found in government and law; and, like any city dweller, he sang the joys of rural peace. — Nicolás Fernández de Moratín composed an epic canto on the exploits of Cortez; we are told that this is "the noblest poem of its class produced in Spain during the eighteenth century."[84] The gay and gracious verses of Diego González, an Augustinian friar, were more popular than the didactic *Four Ages of Man* which he dedicated to Jovellanos. — Don Tomás de Iriarte y Oropesa also indulged a didactic bent in his poem *On Music;* better were his *Fables* (1782), which chastised the foibles of pundits and earned him a reputation that still survives. He translated tragedies by Voltaire and comedies by Molière; he made fun of the monks "who hold sway over the heavens and two thirds of Spain"; he was prosecuted by the Inquisition, recanted, and died of syphilis at forty-one (1791).[85]

In 1780 the Spanish Academy offered an award for an eclogue celebrating pastoral life. Iriarte won second prize and never forgave the victor, for Juan Meléndez Valdés went on to become the leading Spanish poet of the age. Juan wooed Jovellanos, and through him obtained the chair of humanities at Salamanca (1781); there he won first the students, then the faculty, to a more adventurous curriculum, even to reading Locke and Montesquieu. Between classes he wrote a volume of lyrics and pastoral poetry—vivid evocations of natural scenery in verses of such delicacy and finish as Spain had not read for more than a century. The continuing favor of Jovellanos raised Meléndez to the judiciary at Saragossa and to the chancery court at Valladolid, and his poetry suffered from his politics. When Jovellanos was exiled (1798) Meléndez was banished, too. He turned his pen to denouncing the French invaders of Spain, and Joseph Bonaparte especially; but in 1808 he returned to Madrid, accepted office under Joseph Bonaparte, and shocked Spain with poetic flatteries of his foreign masters. In the war of liberation that deposed Joseph the poet's house was sacked by French soldiers, he himself was attacked by an angry mob, and he fled for his life from Spain. Before crossing the Bidassoa into France he kissed the last spot of Spanish earth (1813). Four years later he died in obscurity and poverty in Montpellier.

Spain should have had good dramatists in this age, for the Bourbon kings were well disposed toward the theater. Three factors made for its decline: the strong preference of Isabella Farnese for opera and of Philip V for Farinelli; the consequent dependence of the theater upon the general public, whose applause went most to farces, miracles, legends, and verbal conceits; and the effort of the more serious dramatists to imprison their plays within the "Aristotelian unities" of action, place, and time. The most popular playwright of the century was Ramón Francisco de la Cruz, who wrote some four hundred little farces satirizing the manners, ideas, and speech of the middle and lower classes, but portraying the sins and follies of the populace with a forgiving sympathy. Jovellanos, the *uomo universale* of Spain, put his hand to comedy, and won both the audience and the critics with his *Delinquente honrado* (1773)—*The Honored Criminal:* a Spanish gentleman, after repeatedly refusing to fight a duel, finally takes up a persistent challenge, kills his opponent in a fair fight, and is condemned to death by a judge who turns out to be his father. Always a reformer, Jovellanos aimed with his play to obtain a mitigation of the law that made dueling a capital crime.

The campaign for the Aristotelian unities was led by the poet Nicolás Fernández de Moratín, and was carried on to success by his son Leandro. The early poems of this youth pleased Jovellanos, who secured a berth for him with the Spanish embassy in Paris. There he made friends with Goldoni, who turned him to writing plays. Fortune lavished gifts upon "Moratín the Younger"; he was sent at public expense to study the theaters in Germany, Italy, and England; and on his return to Spain he was given a sinecure that allowed him time for literary work. His first comedy was offered to a Madrid theater in 1786, but its presentation was delayed for four years while managers and actors debated whether a play obeying the rules of Aristotle and French drama could win a Spanish audience. Its success was moderate. Moratín took the offensive; in his *Comedia nueva* (1792) he made such fun of the popular comedies that the audience thereafter accepted dramas that studied character and illuminated life. Moratín was acclaimed as the Spanish Molière, and dominated the stage of Madrid until the French invasion of 1808. His French sympathies and liberal politics led him, like Meléndez and

Goya, to co-operate with the government of Joseph Bonaparte. When Joseph fell, Moratín narrowly escaped imprisonment. He sought refuge in France, and died in Paris in 1828—the same year in which the self-exiled Goya died in Bordeaux.

VIII. SPANISH ART

What could be expected of it after the ravaging of Spain in the long War of the Spanish Succession? Invading armies pillaged the churches, rifled the tombs, burned the pictures, and stabled their horses in venerated shrines. And after the war a new invasion came; through half a century Spanish art submitted to French or Italian domination; and when, in 1752, the Academy of San Fernando was formed to guide and help young artists, it labored to impress upon them the principles of a neoclassicism completely uncongenial to the Spanish soul.

Baroque struggled violently to preserve itself, and in architecture and sculpture it had its way. It triumphed in the towers that Fernando de Cases y Nova added (1738) to the cathedral of Santiago de Compostela, and in the north front by Ventura Rodríguez (1764) for that same monument to Spain's patron St. James. One of the legends dear to the people told how a statue of the Virgin on a pillar in Saragossa had come to life and had spoken to St. James; on that site Spanish piety built the Church of the Virgen del Pilar; and for that church Rodríguez designed the Templete, a chapel of marble and silver to house the Virgin's image.

Two famous palaces were raised in the reign of Philip V. Near Segovia he bought the grounds and grange of a monastery; he engaged Filippo Iuvara of Turin to erect there the Palace of San Ildefonso (1719 f.); he surrounded the buildings with gardens and twenty-six fountains rivaling those of Versailles. The ensemble took the name of La Granja, and cost the people 45,000,000 crowns. It had hardly been finished when, on Christmas Eve of 1734, fire destroyed the Alcázar, which had been the royal residence in Madrid since the Emperor Charles V. Philip moved to Buen Retiro, where Philip IV had built a palace in 1631; this remained the chief royal seat for thirty years.

To replace the Alcázar Iuvara planned a *palacio real*—apartments, offices, council rooms, chapel, library, theater, and gardens—which would have surpassed in grandeur any royal residence then known; the model alone contained enough wood to build a house. Before he could begin construction Iuvara died (1736). Isabella Farnese rejected his design as impossibly expensive, and his successor, Giovanni Battista Sacchetti of Turin, raised (1737–64) the royal palace that stands in Madrid today—470 feet long, 470 feet wide, 100 feet high. Here the style of the late Renaissance replaced baroque: the façade was of Doric and Ionic columns, and was crowned by a balustrade pointed with colossal statues of Spain's early kings. When Napoleon escorted his brother Joseph to reign in this palace he said, as they mounted the superb stairway, "You will be better lodged than I."[86] Charles III moved into this immensity in 1764.

Under French and Italian influences Spanish sculpture lost something of its wooden severity, and dowered its seraphim with laughter and a saint or two with grace. Subjects were nearly always religious, for the Church paid best. So the Archbishop of Toledo spent 200,000 ducats for the *Transparente* which Narciso Tomé raised (1721) behind the cathedral choir: a complex of marble angels floating on marble clouds; an opening in the ambulatory, making the marble luminous, gave the altar screen its name. The old realism survived in the *Christ Scourged*[87] of Luis Carmona—a figure in wood, horrible with welts and bloody wounds. Lovelier are the statues of Faith, Hope, and Charity which Francisco Vergara the Younger carved for the cathedrals of Cuença (1759); Ceán-Bermúdez, the Vasari of Spain, ranked these among the finest products of Spanish art.

The great name in the Hispanic sculpture of the eighteenth century was Francisco Zarcillo y Alcáraz. His father and teacher, a sculptor in Capua, died when Francisco was twenty, leaving him the main support of a mother, a sister, and six brothers. Too poor to pay for models, Francisco invited passers-by, even beggars, to share his meal and pose for him; so, perhaps, he found the figures for his masterpiece, *The Last Supper*, now in the Ermita de Jesús in Murcia. With the aid of his sister Inés, who drew and modeled, his brother José, who carved details, and his priest brother Patricio, who colored the figures and the drapes, Francisco in his seventy-four years produced 1,792 statues or statuettes, some with such tasteless devices as an embroidered velvet robe on a figure of Christ, some so moving in their simple piety that Madrid offered him rich commissions to decorate the royal palace. He preferred to remain in his native Murcia, which in 1781 gave him a sumptuous funeral.

Spanish painting in the eighteenth century labored under a double foreign incubus, from which it did not recover until Goya broke all shackles with his impetuous and unprecedented art. First came a French wave, with Jean Ranc, René and Michel-Ange Houasse, and Louis-Michel Vanloo. The last became court painter to Philip V, and painted an immense canvas of the entire royal family, wigs, hoops, and all.[88] Then a flock of lively Italians—Vanvitelli, Amigoni, Corrado . . .

Giambattista Tiepolo and his sons reached Madrid in June, 1762. On the ceiling of the throne room in the new royal palace they painted a vast fresco, *The Apotheosis of Spain*, celebrating the history, power, virtues, piety and provinces of the Spanish monarchy: symbolical mythological figures poised in air, nereids, tritons, zephyrs, winged genii, chubby *putti*, virtues and vices flying through the luminous void, and Spain herself enthroned amid her possessions, and glorified with all the attributes of good government. On the ceiling of the guardroom Tiepolo represented *Aeneas Conducted to the Temple of Immortality by Venus;* and on the ceiling of the Queen's antechamber he portrayed again *The Triumph of the Spanish Monarchy.* In

1766 Charles commissioned Tiepolo to paint seven altarpieces for the Church of San Pasquale at Aranjuez; one of these, still brilliant in the Prado, used the face of a Spanish beauty to represent *The Immaculate Conception of the Virgin.* The King's confessor, Padre Joaquín de Electa, condemned the paganism and crudities of Tiepolo's work as alien to the spirit of Spain. Tiepolo repented, and painted a powerful *Deposition from the Cross*[89]—a meditation on death brightened by angels promising resurrection. These efforts exhausted the old Titan; he died in Madrid in 1770, aged seventy-four. Shortly afterward the Aranjuez altarpieces were removed, and Anton Raphael Mengs was commissioned to replace them.

Mengs had come to Madrid in 1761. He was then thirty-three, strong, confident, masterful. Charles III, who had never felt at ease on Tiepolo's fluorescent clouds, saw in the enterprising German just the man to organize the artwork for the palace. In 1764 Mengs was made director of the San Fernando Academy, and he ruled Spanish painting during his stays in Spain. He misinterpreted the classic style into a bloodless, lifeless immobility, enraging both old Tiepolo and young Goya. But he fought beneficently to end the extravagance of baroque decoration and the fantasies of rococo imagination. Art, said Mengs, should seek first a "natural style," by imitating nature faithfully; only then should it aim at the "sublime style" of the Greeks. How was sublimity to be achieved? By eliminating the imperfect and irrelevant; by combining partial perfections, variously found, into ideal forms conceived by a disciplined imagination, shunning all excess.

Mengs began his work by depicting the deities of Olympus on the ceiling of the King's bedchamber. Similar pictures decorated the bedroom of the Queen. Perhaps perceiving that their Majesties did not quite follow him to Olympus, Mengs produced for the royal oratory an altarpiece, *The Nativity of Our Lord* and a *Descent from the Cross.* He worked hard, ate little, grew irritable, lost his health, thought Rome would restore it; Charles gave him a leave of absence, which Mengs extended to four years. In his second Spanish sojourn (1773–77) he added more frescoes to the royal palaces in Madrid and Aranjuez. His health again gave way, and he begged permission to retire to Rome. The good King granted it, and a continuing pension of three thousand crowns per year.

But were there no native artists then painting in Spain? There were many, but our interest, waning with distance and time, has left them in the murky limbo of fading fame. There was Luis Meléndez, who almost equaled Chardin in still lifes (*bodegones, fruteras*); the Prado has forty of them, the Boston Museum has an appetizing example, but the Louvre outdoes them all with a wonderful self-portrait. And Luis Paret y Alcázar, who rivaled Canaletto in picturing city scenes, as in his *Puerta del Sol*[90]—the main square of Madrid. And Antonio Viladamat, whom Mengs pronounced the finest Spanish painter of the age. And the kindly, surly, devoted Francisco Bayeu y Subías, who won first prize at the Academy in 1758, designed tapestries for Mengs, and became the friend, enemy, and brother-in-law of Goya.

IX. FRANCISCO DE GOYA Y LUCIENTES

1. Growth

Like all Iberian boys, Francisco took the name of a patron saint, then the name of his father, José Goya, and of his mother, Eugracia Lucientes—lady of grace and light. She was an *hidalga*, hence the *de* that Francisco inserted into his name. He was born on March 30, 1746, in Fuentetodos, an Aragon village of 150 souls and no trees—a stony soil, a hot summer, a cold winter, killing many, making the survivors grim and tough.

Francisco dabbled with brushes, and, in his boyhood, painted for the local church a picture of Nuestra Señora del Pilar, patroness of Aragon. In 1760 the family moved to Saragossa; there the father worked as a gilder, and earned enough to send his boy to study art under José Luzán. With him and Juan Ramírez Goya copied Old Masters, imitated Tiepolo's subtle coloring, and learned enough anatomy to draw forbidden nudes. Story tells of his joining—soon leading—a band of wild youths who defended their parish against another, how in one of the brawls some bravos were killed, and how Francisco, fearing arrest, fled to Madrid.

In December, 1763, he took an examination for admission to the Academy, and failed. Legend describes his riotous life in the capital; we only know that Goya was not in love with laws. He competed again in 1766, and failed. Perhaps these failures were his fortune: he escaped the academic tutelage of Mengs, he studied the work that Tiepolo was doing in Madrid, and he laid the foundations of a unique style pervaded with personality. The legend tells next how he joined a troupe of bullfighters and traveled with them to Rome, at a date unknown. He was always a devotee of toreadors, and once he signed himself "Francisco de los Toros." "I used to be a bullfighter in my youth," he wrote in old age to Moratín; "with sword in hand I feared nothing."[91] Perhaps he meant that he had been one of those venturesome lads who fought bulls in the streets. In any case he reached Italy, for in 1770 he won second prize in a competition at the Academy of Fine Arts in Parma. Legend describes him climbing the dome of St. Peter's, and breaking into a convent to carry off a nun. More likely he was studying the pictures of Magnasco, whose dark coloring, tortured figures, and Inquisition scenes may have moved him more deeply than the calm and classic poses that Mengs had recommended in Spain.

In the fall of 1771 he was back in Saragossa, decorating a chapel in the cathedral, Iglesia Metropolitana della Nuestra Señora del Pilar. This he did well, earning fifteen thousand reales for six months' work; and now he could support a wife. Since propinquity dominates in determining our choice of mates, he married (1773) Josefa Bayeu, who had youth and golden hair and was near at hand. She served as his model, and he painted her portrait many times; that which hangs in the Prado shows her tired with many pregnancies, or saddened by Francisco's digressions from monogamy.[92]

He returned to Madrid (1775). Probably on Bayeu's recommendation, Mengs commissioned him (1776) to paint large canvases as "cartoons" for the Royal Tapestry Factory that Philip V had founded in emulation of the Gobelins. Now, risking a serious repulse, Goya made a decision that shaped his career. Ignoring Mengs's predilection for classical mythology and heroic history, he portrayed in massive line and vivid color the people of his own kind and time—their labor and loves, their fairs and festivals, their bullfights and kite-flying, their markets, picnics, and games; and to this realism he added, venturesomely, things he had imagined but never seen. Mengs rose to the occasion: he did not condemn this transcending of academic traditions; he felt the pulse of life in the new style, and gave the rebel more commissions. In fifteen years Goya produced forty-five cartoons as the staple of his work, while moving with growing confidence into other fields. Now he could eat and drink in comfort. "I have twelve to thirteen thousand reales a year," he wrote to his friend Zapater.

A spirochete intruded upon this prosperity. We do not know the origin of Goya's syphilis; we know that he was seriously ill in April, 1777.[93] He recovered gradually, but we may suspect that the ailment had some influence on the pessimism in his art, perhaps on his loss of hearing in 1793. He was well enough in 1778 to take part in a project of Charles III to spread abroad, through prints, the treasures of Spanish art. For this purpose Goya made copies of eighteen paintings by Velázquez; from these copies he made etchings; it was a new skill for him, and his burin was for a while unsure and crude; but from that beginning he grew to be one of the greatest etchers since Rembrandt. He was allowed to present his copies in person to the King, and in 1780 he was enrolled as one of the court painters. Now at last he was received into the Academy. About 1785 he made his famous portrait of Charles III, showing him in hunting costume, dressed to kill, but aged, weary, toothless, bowlegged, bent; here, as usual, Goya sacrificed favor to truth.

His father having died, Goya brought his mother and brother Camilo to live with him, Josefa, and the children. To support this enlarged household he accepted a variety of commissions: to paint a fresco in the Church of San Francisco el Grande, devotional pictures for the Calatrava College at Salamanca, and genre scenes for the country house of the Duke of Osuna; and to execute portraits as the most lucrative branch of his profession. He made several of Osuna;[94] one of the Duke and his family—the children as stiff as dollars; and a three-quarter length of the Duchess of Osuna[95]—a miracle of oils transfigured into silk and lace.

Perhaps Goya was happy in 1784. In that year Javier was born, the only one of his children who would survive him. The frescoes in San Francisco el Grande were ceremoniously unveiled, and were hailed as the finest painting of that age; the King and all the court were present, and joined in the praise. About 1787 Goya painted the portrait of the Marquesa de Pontejos, which is now one of the prize possessions of the National Gallery at Washington. A year later he returned to nature in La Pradera de San Isidro[96]—a field crowded with picnickers celebrating the feast of Madrid's great patron saint by riding, strolling, sitting, eating, drinking, singing, dancing on the grassy shores of the Manzanares. It is only a sketch, but it is a chef-d'oeuvre.

When Charles died (1788) Goya was in his forty-third year, and thought himself old. In the previous December he had written to Zapater: "I have become old, with so many wrinkles in my face that you could no longer recognize me if it were not for my flat nose and sunken eyes."[97] He could hardly foresee that he had forty years more of life in him, and that his wildest adventures and most distinguished work lay in his future. He had developed slowly; now romance and revolution would compel him to quicken his pace or be submerged. He rose with events, and became the greatest artist of his time.

2. Romance

He was kept busy in 1789 making portraits of the new King and Queen for their formal entry into Madrid on September 21. Felipe, eldest son of Charles III, had been barred from the succession as an imbecile; the crown passed to the second son, whom an unsympathetic historian described as only "semi-imbecile."[98] Charles IV was simple and unsuspecting, and so good as almost to invite wickedness. Presuming himself, as second son, excluded from the succession, he had taken to a life of hunting, eating, and parentage. Now, plump and malleable, he submitted amiably to his wife, María Luisa of Parma; he ignored—or was ignorant of—her adulteries, and promoted her lover, Manuel de Godoy, to head the ministry (1792–97).

The new Queen had played with liberal ideas before her accession, and Charles IV in his first year encouraged Floridablanca, Jovellanos, and Campomanes (all of whom Goya portrayed) to continue their program of reforms. But the fall of the Bastille frightened Charles IV and Floridablanca into a political reaction that turned the government back to full co-operation with the Church as the strongest bulwark of monarchy. Many of the progressive measures enacted under Charles III were allowed to lapse; the Inquisition recaptured some of its powers; the importation of French literature was stopped; all newspapers except the official *Diario de Madrid* were suppressed; Jovellanos, Campomanes, and Aranda were banished from the court. The people rejoiced in the triumph of their cherished faith. In 1793 Spain joined in the war of the monarchical powers against revolutionary France.

Amid this turmoil Goya prospered. In April, 1789, he was named *pintor de cámara*—painter to the chamber. When Josefa fell ill and the doctor prescribed sea air, Goya took her to Valencia (1790), where he was feted as Spain's new Velázquez. Apparently he was in demand from one end of Spain to another, for in 1792 we find him in Cádiz as the guest of Sebastián Martínez. On his way back, at Seville, he was stricken with dizziness and partial paralysis; he returned to his friend in Cádiz, and fretted through a lengthy convalescence.

What was this illness? Bayeu spoke of it vaguely as "of the most terrible nature," and doubted that Goya would ever recover.[99] Goya's loyal friend Zapater wrote in March, 1793: "Goya has been brought to this pass by his lack of reflection, but he is to be commiserated with all the pity that his affliction demands."[100] Many students have interpreted the disease as an aftermath of syphilis,[101] but the latest medical analysis rejects this view and diagnoses it as inflammation of the nerves in the labyrinth of the ear.[102] Whatever the cause, Goya, returning to Madrid in July, 1793, was stone deaf, and remained so till his death. In February, 1794, Jovellanos noted in his diary: "I wrote to Goya, who answered that as a result of his apoplexy he was not even capable of writing."[103] But the paralysis gradually disappeared, and by 1795 Goya was strong enough to fall in love.

Teresa Cayetana María del Pilar was the thirteenth duchess of the famous Alba line. As her father had imbibed French philosophy, she was brought up on libertarian lines, with an education that gave her an alert intellect and an undisciplined will. At thirteen she married the nineteen-year-old Don José de Toledo Osorio, Duke of Alba. Frail and sickly, the Duke for the most part kept to his home and absorbed himself in music. Goya portrayed him at the harpsichord confronting a Haydn score. The Duchess was haughty, beautiful, and sensual; a French traveler remarked that "she has not a hair on her head that does not provoke desire";[104] and she satisfied her own desires without restriction of morals, expense, or class. She took into her household a half-wit, a one-eyed monk, and a little Negress who became her especial pet. Generosity hid in her audacities; she may have taken to Goya because he was deaf and unhappy, as well as because he could immortalize her with his brush.

He must have seen her many times before she stood for her portrait by him, for she fluttered in and out of the court, keeping gossip busy with her flirtations and her bold hostility to the Queen. His first dated picture of her shows her in full length, her sharp, thin features shrouded in a mass of black hair, her right hand pointing to something on the ground; looking, clearly we read the inscription: "*A la duquesa de Alba Fco de Goya 1795*";[105] there is here a suggestion of friendship already established. This is not one of Goya's masterpieces. Much better is the portrait that he painted, in this year, of Francisco Bayeu, who had just passed away. In November Goya succeeded him as director of the school of painting in the Academy.

The Duke of Alba died in June, 1796. The Duchess retired for a brief period of mourning to her country estate at Sanlúcar, between Seville and Cádiz. It is not certain that Goya accompanied her; we only know that he was absent from Madrid from October, 1796, till April, 1797, and that he recorded in two notebooks some of the things he had seen in Sanlúcar. Most of the drawings show the Duchess: receiving guests, petting her Negro girl, tearing her own hair in a rage, taking her siesta (while the maid removes the chamber vessel),[106] fainting in a promenade, or flirting with one or another of Goya's rivals for her caressing hands. The sketches show his rising jealousy, and picture also another woman—emerging naked from the bath, lying half dressed on the bed, or adjusting the garter on a shapely leg; perhaps Goya, like the Duchess, indulged in tangents to the curve of love. Yet it was probably in Sanlúcar that he painted his proudest picture of her[107]—dressed as a saucy *maja* in a black-and-yellow costume, with a sash of scarlet and gold about her tiny waist, and a black mantilla over her head; her right hand (itself a masterpiece of painting) carries two rings, one bearing the name "Alba," the other "Goya"; her index finger points to his name, and the date 1797, traced in the sandy soil at her feet. He always refused to sell this portrait.

The bloom of the romance had blown away by the time Goya returned to Madrid. Some of his *Capricho* drawings (1797?) accuse her of wanton surrender to an indecent variety of males. Godoy accused her of seducing the Minister of War, and wrote to the Queen that "the Alba and all her supporters ought to be buried in a huge pit."[108] When the Duchess died (July 23, 1803), age forty, Madrid gossiped that she had been poisoned. Sympathy went out to her because she had left much of her huge fortune to her servants; also she bequeathed an annuity of 3,600 reales to Goya's son Javier. The King ordered an inquiry into her death—and put Godoy at its head. The physician and some attendants of the Duchess were imprisoned; her will was annulled; her servants were deprived of their legacies; the Queen was soon wearing Alba's most beautiful jewels.[109]

3. Zenith

Goya had resigned in 1797 as director of painting at the Academy. He was too busy now to teach. In 1798 he was chosen to decorate the dome and tympanums of the Church of San Antonio de la Florida; and though he troubled the clergy by giving his angels voluptuous limbs, nearly all agreed that he had transferred to those saintly spaces, in a fury of inspiration, the life and blood of Madrid's streets. On October 31, 1799, he was appointed "First Painter to the Court," with a salary of fifty thousand reales per year. He made in 1800 the most famous of all his paintings: *Charles IV and His Family*[110]—a merciless revelation of royal imbecility; we shudder to think how this collection of swollen bodies and stunted souls would have looked without their glamorous raiment—a virtuosity of radiance rarely surpassed in the history of art. We are told that the victims expressed complete satisfaction with the work.[111]

In a corner of that picture Goya painted himself. We must forgive the egotism of his many self-portraits; some of them, doubtless, were experimental studies made with a mirror, like an actor practicing facial expression before a glass; and two of them are magnificent. The best of them (Plate 1 of the *Caprichos*) shows him at fifty, deaf but proud, with a pugnacious chin, sensual lips, enormous nose, sly and surly eyes, black hair growing over his ears and almost to his chin, and, to top it all, a lordly silk hat rising over his massive head like a challenge to all the fortuitous nobles of the world. Nineteen years later, after surviving a revolution, he discarded the hat, opened his shirt at the neck, and showed himself in a more amiable mood, still proud, but too confident of himself to stoop to challenges.[112]

Portraiture was his forte. Though his contemporaries knew that he would not flatter them, they eagerly submitted to the verdict of an art that they hoped would carry them down, for fame or shame, through centuries. We know of three hundred nobles and eighty-eight members of the royal family who sat for him; two hundred of these portraits survive. One of the best is of Ferdinand Guillemardet, the French ambassador; it was brought to Paris by the sitter, was acquired by the Louvre in 1865, and played a part in stirring up Goya's fame in France. Among Goya's pictures of children the finest is that of Don Manuel Osorio de Zuñiga, now in the Metropolitan Museum of Art in New York; here Goya touched Velázquez. He rivaled Velázquez again in his gallery of women, running the range from such scarecrows as *The Infanta María Josefa* to the "ravishing" *Señora García*[113] and the aging actress *La Tirana*[114]—beauty waning but replaced with character.

The most fully revealed of Goya's women is the saucy *maja* who, about 1798, posed unadorned for the *Maja Desnuda,* and, provocatively dressed, for *La Maja Vestida;* these companion pictures attract almost as many gazers in the Prado as the *Mona Lisa* in the Louvre. The *Desnuda* and Velázquez' *Rokeby Venus* are among the few nudes in Spanish painting; to depict the nude in Spanish art was punishable by a year in prison, confiscation of goods, and exile. Velázquez ventured it under the protection of Philip IV, Goya under the protection of Godoy, who agreed with Goya in preferring substantial bosoms, slim waists, and swelling hips. Despite legend, Goya's *Maja* did not represent the Duchess of Alba, nor was the *Vestida* painted overnight to replace the *Desnuda* when the angry Duke (in the legend) came with a duel in his eye. But the two pictures were bought by, or given to, the Duchess, and passed at her death into the collection of Godoy.

While Goya was financing his family with portraits he amused himself (1796–97?) with etchings and water colors which he published in 1799 as *Los Caprichos* eighty-three caprices of graver, brush, and angry mind, describing with somber satire and sarcastic captions the manners, morals, and institutions of his time. The most significant of the series is No. 43: a man has fallen asleep at his desk while demons swarm about his head; on the desk is an inscription: *"El sueño de la razón produce monstruos"* (The dream of reason produces monsters). Goya interpreted this to mean "Fantasy abandoned by reason produces monsters; united with reason she is the mother of the arts and the source of their marvels."[115] This was a thrust at the superstitions that darkened the mind of Spain, but it was also a description of half of Goya's art. He was haunted by horrible dreams; the *Caprichos* especially are ghastly with them. There the human form is degraded into a hundred bloated, haggard, crippled, bestial shapes; owls and cats leer at us, wolves and vultures prowl, witches fly through the air, the ground is strewn with skulls and shinbones, and corpses of newborn children newly dead. It is as if the diseased imagination of Hieronymus Bosch had leaped across France and the centuries to enter and disorder Goya's mind.

Was Goya a rationalist? We can only say that he favored reason against superstition. In one of his drawings he showed a young woman, crowned with laurel and holding a scale, chasing black birds with a whip; underneath this Goya wrote: "Divine Reason, do not spare anyone."[116] Another shows monks unfrocking themselves;[117] and upon a monk in prayer he put the face of a lunatic.[118] He pictured *The Tribunal of the Inquisition*[119] as a dismal scene of pitiful victims judged by cold authority. He represented a Jew chained in an Inquisition cell, and wrote the caption: "Zapata, your glory will be everlasting";[120] was this an echo of Voltaire's *Questions of Zapata?* He made twenty-nine plates of Inquisition victims suffering diverse punishments,[121] and at their end he drew a rejoicing figure over the caption "Divine Liberty!"[122] And yet, to the end of his life, he crossed himself piously, invoked Christ and the saints, and headed his letters with a cross; perhaps all these were vestiges of habits formed in youth.

4. Revolution

Was Goya a revolutionist? No. He was not even a republican. There is no sign in his art or his words that he desired the overthrow of the Spanish monarchy. He attached himself and his fortunes to Charles III, to Charles IV, to Godoy, to Joseph Bonaparte, and associated gladly with the nobility and the court. But he had known poverty, he still saw it around him, he was repelled by the destitution of the masses, their consequent ignorance and superstition, and the Church's acceptance of mass poverty as a natural consequence of the nature and inequality of men. Half of his art commemorated the rich, the other half was a cry for justice to the poor, a protest against the barbarism of law, the Inquisition, and war. He was a loyalist in his portraits, a Catholic in his paintings, a rebel in his drawings; there, with an almost savage power, he expressed his hatred of obscurantism, injustice, folly, and cruelty. One drawing represents a man stretched on a rack, with an inscription, "Because he discovered the movement of the earth." Another pictures a woman in the stocks because "she showed sympathy for the Liberal cause."

Who were these Spaniards who called themselves Liberales? They were apparently the first political faction to use that name. They meant by it to signalize their desire for liberty—of the mind from censorship, of the body from degradation, of the soul from tyranny. They had received gratefully the Luces coming in from the French Enlightenment. They welcomed the entry of a French force into Spain (1807); indeed, half of the population welcomed it as an army of liberation; no protest was heard when Charles IV resigned and his son Ferdinand VII was enthroned under the protection of Murat's soldiery. Goya painted a portrait of the new ruler.

But the mood of the people, and of Goya, changed when Napoleon summoned Charles IV and Ferdinand VII to Bayonne, deposed both of them, exiled one to Italy, the other to France, and made his brother Joseph king of Spain. An angry crowd gathered before the royal palace; Murat ordered his soldiers to clear the square; the crowd fled, but reassembled, twenty thousand strong, in the Plaza Mayor. When French and Mameluke troops marched toward the plaza they were fired on from windows and arcades; infuriated, they entered houses, killing indiscriminately. Troops and crowd entered into an all-day battle, the famous Dos de Mayo (May 2, 1808); hundreds of men and women fell. From some nearby vantage Goya saw part of the massacre.[123] On May 3 thirty of the prisoners taken by the soldiers were executed by a firing squad, and every Spaniard found with a gun in his hands was put to death. Nearly all Spain was now in revolt against the French. A "War of Liberation" spread from province to province, disgracing both sides with bestial ferocities. Goya saw some of these, and was haunted by their memory till his death. In 1811, fearing the worst, he made his will. In 1812 Josefa died. In 1813 Wellington took Madrid; Ferdinand VII was again king.

Goya celebrated the triumph of Spain by painting two of his most famous pictures (1814).[124] One, *Dos de Mayo*, was his reconstruction of what he had seen, heard, or imagined of the battle between the populace of Madrid and the French and Mameluke troops. He placed the Mamelukes in the center, for it was their participation that stirred the hottest resentment in Spanish memory. We need not ask if the picture is accurate history; it is brilliant and powerful art, from the gradations of gleaming colors on the horse of the falling Mameluke to the faces of men terrified and brutalized by the choice between killing and being killed. Even more vivid is the companion picture, *The Shooting of the Third of May*—a squad of French riflemen executing Spanish prisoners; nothing in Goya is more impressive than the contrast of terror and defiance in the central figure of that massacre.

Still a pensioned *pintor de cámara*, but no longer a favorite at the court, Goya, widowed, silenced, and deaf, retired into the world of his art. Perhaps in 1812 he made the most powerful of his engravings, *The Colossus*[125]—a Hercules with the face of Caliban, seated on the edge of the earth, a Mars resting after triumphant war. Ever since 1810 he had been drawing little sketches which he later engraved and printed, and to which he gave the title *The Fatal Consequences of Spain's Bloody War with Bonaparte, and other Caprichos*. He did not dare publish these eighty-five drawings; he bequeathed them to his son, whose son sold them to the Academy of San Fernando, which published them in 1863 as *Los Desastres de la Guerra*.

These sketches are not usual battle scenes, which disguise killing as heroism and glory; they are moments of terror and cruelty in which the frail restraints of civilization are forgotten in the ecstasy of conflict and the intoxication of blood. Here are houses on fire, collapsing upon their inmates; women rushing to the battle with stones or pikes or guns; women raped; men tied to posts before firing squads; men shorn of a leg, an arm, or a head; a soldier cutting off a man's genitals;[126] corpses impaled upon the sharp stumps or limbs of trees; dead women still clutching their infants at their breast; children gazing in horror at the slaughter of their parents; dead men cast in heaps into pits; vultures feasting upon the human dead. Under these pictures Goya added sardonic captions: "This is what you were born for";[127]

"This I saw";[128] "It happened like this";[129] "To bury the dead and be silent."[130] At the end Goya expressed his despair and his hope: No. 79 is a woman dying amid gravediggers and priests, and is captioned "Truth dies"; but No. 80 shows her radiating light, and asks, "Will she rise again?"

5. Decrescendo

In February, 1819, he bought a country house on the other side of the Manzanares. It was shaded by trees, and though he could not hear the music of the brook that bordered it, he could feel the lesson of its placid continuance. The neighbors called his home La Quinta del Sordo, the House of the Deaf. As Javier had married and made a separate household, Goya took with him Doña Leocadia Weiss, who served him as mistress and housekeeper. She was a lusty shrew, but Goya was immune to her eloquence. She brought with her two children—a boy, Guillermo, and a lively little girl, María del Rosario, who became the solace of the artist's declining life.

He badly needed so wholesome a stimulus, for his mind was on the edge of lunacy. Only so can we understand the *pinturas negras* with which he covered many walls of the house that was his asylum. As if reflecting the darkness of his mind, he painted chiefly in black and white; and as if faithful to the vagueness of his visions, he gave no certain contours to the forms, but used rough daubs to quickly fix upon the walls the fleeting images of a dream. On one of the long side walls he represented *The Pilgrimage of San Isidro*—the same festival that he had painted joyfully in 1788, thirty-one years before; but now it was a gloomy panorama of bestial and drunken fanatics. On the opposite wall he gathered even more horrible figures in a *Sabbath of Witches* awesomely worshiping a huge black goat as their Satan and commanding god. At the farther end of the room rose the most hideous form in the history of art, *Saturn Devouring His Offspring*—a giant crunching a naked child, having eaten the head and one arm, and now gorging himself on the other, splashing blood;[131] perhaps it is an insane symbol of insane nations consuming their children in war. These are the visions of a man who is obsessed with macabre imaginings, and madly paints them to drive them out of himself and immobilize them on the wall.

In 1823 Leocadia, whose Freemason activities had made her fear arrest, fled to Bordeaux with her children. Goya, left alone with the madness that he had painted on his walls, decided to follow them. But if he went without royal permission he would forfeit the official salary that he was receiving as *pintor de cámara*. He asked for several months' leave to take the waters at Plombières; it was granted. He deeded the Quinta del Sordo to his grandson Mariano, and in June, 1824, he made his way to Bordeaux, Leocadia, and María of the Rosary.

As he neared death his love for his grandson Mariano became his dominant passion. He settled an annuity on the boy, and offered to pay expenses if Javier would bring Mariano to Bordeaux. Javier could not come, but he sent his wife and son. When they arrived Goya embraced them with such emotion that he broke down and had to take to his bed. He wrote to his son: "My dear Javier, I only want to tell you that all this joy has been too much for me. . . . May God grant that you can come and fetch them, and then my cup of happiness will be full."[132] The next morning his voice was gone, and half his body was paralyzed. He lingered for thirteen days, impatiently awaiting Javier, in vain. He died on April 16, 1828. In 1899 his remains were brought from Bordeaux to Madrid and were interred before the altar of the Church of San Antonio de la Florida, where, 101 years before, he had painted under the dome the pains and griefs, the joys and loves, of Spanish life.

CHAPTER XII

Vale, Italia

1760–89

I. FAREWELL TOUR

IF we indulge ourselves in one more look at Italy we shall find her, even
in this seeming siesta, warm with life: Turin nursing Alfieri, Lucca
publishing Diderot's *Encyclopédie*, Florence flowering again under Grand
Duke Leopold, Milan reforming law with Beccaria, Pavia and Bologna
thrilling with the experiments of Volta and Galvani, Venice suffering Casanova, Naples challenging the papacy, Rome caught in the tragedy of the
Jesuits, and a hundred breeding grounds of music exporting opera and virtuosi to tame the savage transalpine breast. We shall meet in Italy a hundred
thousand foreigners coming to study her treasures and bask in her sun.
There, in this age, Goethe, choked with Weimar dignitaries, came to renew
his youth and discipline his Muse.

Goethe's first impression, as he came down from the Alps into Venezia
Tridentina (September, 1786), was of the mild and luminous air, which
"gave exquisite enjoyment to mere existence, even to poverty."[1] And next,
the uncaged life: "the inhabitants are always out of doors, and, in their
lightheartedness, think of nothing" but to live. He thought that the fruitful
soil must readily provide for the modest wants of these simple people; yet
the poverty, and the lack of sanitation in the smaller towns, dismayed him.

> When I asked the waiter for a certain place he pointed down into the court-
> yard, "*qui abasso puo servire*." "*Dove?*" I asked. "*Da per tutto, dove vuol,*" was
> the friendly reply. . . . Forecourts and colonnades are all soiled with filth, for
> things are done in the most natural manner.[2]

Sensory adaptation gradually reconciled him.

Venice was enjoying her amiable decay. About 1778 Carlo Gozzi described with righteous exaggeration what seemed to him a general dissolution of morality:

> The spectacle of women turned into men, men turned into women, and both
> men and women turned into monkeys; all of them immersed . . . in the whirli-
> gig of fashion; corrupting and seducing one another with the eagerness of
> hounds on the scent, vying in their lusts and ruinous extravagance, . . . burn-
> ing incense . . . to Priapus.[3]

In 1797 he blamed the collapse on philosophy:

> Religion, that salutary curb on human passion, has . . . become a laughing-
> stock. I am bound to believe that the gallows benefit society, being an instru-

ment for punishing crime and deterring would-be criminals. But our newfangled philosophers have denounced the gallows as a tyrannical prejudice, and
by so doing they have multiplied murders on the highway, robberies and acts
of violence, a hundredfold. . . .

It was pronounced a musty and barbarous prejudice to keep women at home
for the supervision of their sons and daughters, . . . their domestic service
and economy. At once the women poured forth, storming like Bacchanals,
screaming, "Liberty! liberty!" The streets swarmed with them. . . . Meanwhile they abandoned their vapory brains to fashions, frivolous inventions,
. . . amusements, amours, coquetries, and all sorts of nonsense. . . . The husbands had not the courage to oppose this ruin of their honor, their substance,
their families. They were afraid of being pilloried with that dreadful word
prejudice. . . . Good morals, modesty, and chastity received the name of
prejudice. . . . When all the so-called prejudices had been put to flight, . . .
many great and remarkable blessings appeared: . . . irreligion, respect and
reverence annulled, justice overturned, . . . criminals encouraged and bewept,
heated imaginations, sharpened senses, animalism, indulgence in all lusts and
passions, imperious luxury, . . . bankruptcies, . . . adulteries.[4]

But of course the basic causes of decay were economic and military;
Venice no longer had the wealth to defend her former power. By contrast
her rival, Austria, had grown so strong in manpower that she commanded
all land approaches to the lagoons, and fought some of her campaigns on the
soil of the neutral but helpless republic.

On March 9, 1789, Lodovico Manin was elected to head the government
—the last of the 120 doges who had presided over Venice in an impressive
continuity since 697. He was a man of great riches and little character, but
poverty and courage would not have prevented his tragedy. Four months
later the Bastille fell; the religion of liberty captured the imagination of
France; and when the religion came with the legions of Napoleon it swept
nearly all Italy under its banner and ecstasy. On the ground that Austrian
forces had used Venetian territory, and on the charge that Venice had
secretly aided his enemies, the victorious Corsican, backed by eighty thousand troops, imposed upon the Queen of the Adriatic a provisional government dictated by himself (May 12, 1797). On that day Doge Manin, resigning, gave his cap of state to an attendant, and bade him "take it away;
we shall not want it again."[5] A few days later he died. On May 16 French
troops occupied the city. On October 17 Bonaparte signed at Campoformio
a treaty that transferred Venice and nearly all her territorial possessions to
Austria in exchange for Austrian concessions to France in Belgium and on
the left bank of the Rhine. It was exactly eleven hundred years since the
first doge had been elected to rule and defend the lagoons.

Parma was a Spanish protectorate, but its Duke, Don Felipe, son of Philip
V and Isabella Farnese, married Louise Elisabeth, daughter of Louis XV; he
adopted her expensive habits, and made his court a miniature Versailles.
Parma became a center of culture, gaily mingling cosmopolitan ways. "It
seemed to me," said Casanova, "that I was no longer in Italy, for everything
had the air of belonging to the other side of the Alps. I heard only French

and Spanish spoken by the passers-by."[6] An enlightened minister, Guillaume du Tillot, gave the duchy stimulating reforms. Here were made some of the finest textiles, crystals, and faïence.

Milan now experienced an industrial expansion modestly prefiguring its economic pre-eminence in the Italy of today. Austrian rule gave loose rein to local ability and enterprise. Count Karl Joseph von Firmian, governor of Lombardy, co-operated with native leaders in improving administration, and reduced the oppressive power of feudal barons and municipal oligarchs. A group of economic liberals led by Pietro Verri, Cesare Bonesana di Beccaria, and Giovanni Carli adopted the principles of the physiocrats, abolished taxes on internal trade, ended the farming of taxes, and spread the burden by taxing ecclesiastical property. The textile industry grew till in 1785 it comprised twenty-nine firms, operating 1,384 looms. The land was surveyed, the state financed irrigation projects, the peasants worked with a will. In the twenty-one years between 1749 and 1770 the population of the duchy rose from 90,000 to 130,000.[7] It was in this period of Milanese exhilaration that the community built the Teatro alla Scala (1776–78), seating 3,600 spectators amid palatial decorations, and offering facilities for music, conversation, eating, playing cards, and sleeping; and, surmounting all, a reservoir of water designed to extinguish any fire. Here Cimarosa and Cherubini now enjoyed resounding victories.

This was the heroic age of Corsica. That mountainous isle was already surfeited with history. The Phocaeans from Asia Minor had established a colony there toward 560 B.C.; they were conquered by the Etruscans, who were conquered by the Carthaginians, who were conquered by the Romans, who were conquered by the Byzantine Greeks, who were conquered by the Franks, who were conquered by the Moslems, who were conquered by the Tuscan Italians, who were conquered by the Pisans, who were conquered by the Genoese (1347). Two thirds of the population, in that century, died from the Black Plague. Under Genoese rule the Corsicans, harassed by pestilence and piratical raids, barred from major offices and taxed beyond bearing, sank into a semisavagery in which violent vendettas were the only honored law. Periodical revolts failed because of internecine feuds and lack of foreign aid. Genoa, fighting for its own life against Austrian armies, appealed to France for help in maintaining order in Corsica; France responded lest the island be taken by the British as a citadel for control of the Mediterranean; French troops occupied Ajaccio and other Corsican strongholds (1739–48). When peace seemed secure the French withdrew, Genoese domination was resumed, and the historic revolt of Paoli began.

Pasquale di Paoli anticipated by a century the exploits of Garibaldi. Lord Chatham called him "one of those men who are no longer to be found but in the pages of Plutarch."[8] Born (1725) the son of a Corsican rebel, he followed his father into exile, studied in Naples under the liberal economist Genovesi, served in the Neapolitan army, returned to Corsica (1755), and was

chosen to lead a rebellion against Genoa. In two years of fighting he succeeded in driving the Genoese from all but some coastal towns. As elected
head of the new republic (1757–68) he proved himself as brilliant in legislation and administration as he had shown himself in the strategy and tactics
of war. He established a democratic constitution, suppressed the vendetta,
abolished the oppressive rights of feudal lords, spread education, and founded
a university at Corte, his capital.

Unable to overcome him, Genoa sold the island to France (May 15, 1768)
for two million francs. Paoli now found himself fighting against repeatedly
reinforced French troops. His secretary and aide at this time was Carlo
Buonaparte, to whom a son Napoleone was born at Ajaccio on August 15,
1769. Overwhelmed by the French at Pontenuovo (May, 1769), Paoli
abandoned the hopeless struggle and took refuge in England; there he received a government pension, was celebrated by Boswell, and numbered
Johnson among his friends. The National Assembly of Revolutionary
France recalled him from exile, acclaimed him as "the hero and martyr of
liberty," and made him governor of Corsica (1791). But the French Convention judged him insufficiently Jacobin; it sent a commission to depose
him; British troops came to his aid, but the British general took control of
the island and sent Paoli back to England (1795). Napoleon dispatched a
French force to expel the British (1796); the islanders welcomed the French
as coming from "the Corsican"; the British withdrew, and Corsica submitted
to France.

Tuscany flourished under the Hapsburg grand dukes who succeeded the
Medici (1738). Since its nominal ruler, Francis of Lorraine, resided in Austria as the husband of Maria Theresa, the government was deputed to a regency under native leaders, who rivaled the Milanese liberals in economic
reforms; seven years before Turgot's similar attempt in France, they established free internal trade in grains (1767). When Francis died (1765) he
was followed as grand duke by his younger son Leopold, who developed
into one of the most enterprising and courageous of the "enlightened despots." He checked corruption in office, improved the judiciary, the administration, and the finances, equalized taxation, abolished torture, confiscation,
and capital punishment, helped the peasantry, drained marshes, ended monopolies, extended free trade and free enterprise, allowed self-government in
the communes, and looked forward to setting up a semidemocratic constitution for the duchy. Goethe was impressed by the comparative cleanliness of
the Tuscan cities, the good condition of roads and bridges, the beauty and
grandeur of the public works.[9] Leopold's brother Joseph, on becoming sole
emperor, supported Leopold in abolishing most feudal privileges in Tuscany,
in closing many monasteries, and in reducing the power of the clergy.

In ecclesiastical reforms Leopold received powerful co-operation from
Scipione de' Ricci, bishop of Pistoia and Prato. A harsh custom in Tuscany
required all dowerless women to take the veil; Ricci joined the Grand Duke
in raising the minimum age for taking the vows, and turning many convents

into schools for girls. Provision was made for secular education by substituting lay for Jesuit schools. Ricci celebrated Mass in Italian, and discouraged superstitions, much to the displeasure of the populace. When it was rumored that he intended to remove as spurious the famous "girdle of the Virgin" at Prato, the people rioted and sacked the episcopal palace. Ricci nevertheless called a diocesan synod, which met at Pistoia in 1786 and proclaimed principles recalling the "Gallican Articles" of 1682: that the temporal power is independent of the spiritual (i.e., the state is independent of the Church); and that the pope is fallible even in matters of faith.

Leopold lived simply, and was liked for his unassuming manners. But as his reign progressed, and the hostility of the orthodox pressed upon him, he grew suspicious and aloof, and employed a multitude of spies to watch not only his enemies but his aides. Joseph advised him from Vienna: "Let them deceive you sometimes, rather than thus torment yourself constantly and in vain."[10] When Leopold left Florence to succeed Joseph as emperor (1790) the forces of reaction triumphed in Tuscany. Ricci was condemned by Pope Pius VI in 1794, and was imprisoned (1799–1805) until he retracted his heresies. The advent of Napoleonic government (1800) restored the liberals to power.

Goethe hurried through Tuscany to Rome. Hear him, writing on November 1, 1786:

> At last I have arrived at this great capital of the world. . . . I have as good as flown over the mountains of the Tirol. . . . My anxiety to reach Rome was so great . . . that to think of stopping anywhere was out of the question. Even in Florence I stayed only three hours. Now, . . . as it would seem, I shall be put at peace for my whole life; for we may almost say that a new life begins when a man once sees with his own eyes all that previously he has but partially heard or read of. All the dreams of my youth I now behold realized before me.

What a dizzy mixture it was, that eighteenth-century Rome, swarming with beggars and nobles, cardinals and *castrati*, bishops and prostitutes, monks and tradesmen, Jesuits and Jews, artists and criminals, *bravi* and saints, and tourists seeking antiquities by day and *cortigiane* by night. Here, within twelve miles of city walls, were pagan amphitheaters and triumphal arches, Renaissance palaces and fountains, three hundred churches and ten thousand priests, 170,000 people, and, around the Vatican citadel of Catholic Christianity, the most turbulent, lawless, and anticlerical rabble in Christendom. Scurrilous pamphlets against the Church were hawked about the streets; buffoons parodied in public squares the most sacred ceremonies of the Mass. Perhaps Winckelmann, a timid and tender soul, exaggerated a bit:

> In the daytime it is pretty quiet in Rome, but at night it is the devil let loose. From the great freedom which prevails here, and from the absence of any sort of police, the brawling, shooting, fireworks, and bonfires in all the streets, last during the whole night. . . . The populace is untamed, and the governor is weary of banishing and hanging.[11]

Even more than Paris, Rome was a cosmopolitan city where artists, students, poets, tourists mingled with prelates and princesses in the salons, the galleries, and the theaters. Here Winckelmann and Mengs were proclaiming the revival of the classic style. And here the harassed, beleaguered popes were struggling to mollify the impoverished populace with bread and benedictions, to hold back ambassadors pressing for the abolition of the Jesuits, and to keep the whole complex edifice of Christianity from crumbling under the advance of science and the assaults of philosophy.

But let us go on, with Goethe, to Naples. He thought he had never seen such *joie de vivre*.

> If in Rome one can readily set oneself to study, here one can do nothing but live. You forget yourself and the world; and to me it is a strange feeling to go about with people who think of nothing but enjoying themselves. . . . Here men know nothing of one another. They scarcely observe that others are also going on their way, side by side with them. They run all day backward and forward in a paradise, without looking about them; and if the neighboring jaws of hell begin to open and to rage, they have recourse to St. Januarius.[12]

Don Carlos, leaving Naples for Spain in 1759, had bequeathed the kingdom of Naples and Sicily to his eight-year-old son Ferdinand IV, with the Marchese di Tanucci as regent. Tanucci continued that war against the Church which he had begun under Carlos. He suppressed many convents and monasteries, and willingly followed the directive of Charles III of Spain to expel the Jesuits. Shortly after midnight of November 3–4, 1767, soldiers arrested all members of the order in the realm, and escorted them, with no possessions but the clothes they wore, to the nearest port or frontier, whence they were deported to the Papal States.

Ferdinand IV, reaching the age of sixteen (1767), ended Tanucci's regency. A year later he married Maria Carolina, pious daughter of Maria Theresa. She soon dominated her husband and led a reaction against Tanucci's anticlerical policies. The Marchese's reforms had strengthened the Neapolitan monarchy against the feudal barons and the Church, but they had done little to mitigate the poverty that left to the populace no hope but in another life.

Sicily followed a similar curve. The erection of the cathedral of Palermo (1782–1802) was of far more moment to the people than the attempt of Domenico di Caraccioli to tame the feudal lords who controlled the land. He had served many years as Neapolitan ambassador in London and Paris, and had listened to Protestants and philosophers. Appointed viceroy of Sicily (1781), he laid heavy taxes upon the great landowners, reduced their feudal rights over their serfs, and ended their privileges of choosing the local magistrates. But when he dared to imprison a prince who protected bandits, and decreed a reduction of two days in the holidays honoring Palermo's patron St. Rosalia, all classes rose against him, and he returned to Naples in defeat (1785).[13] The philosophers had not yet proved that they understood, better than the Church, the needs and nature of man.

II. POPES, KINGS, AND JESUITS

The power of the Catholic Church rested on the natural supernaturalism of mankind, the recognition and sublimation of sensual impulses and pagan survivals, the encouragement of Catholic fertility, and the inculcation of a theology rich in poetry and hope, and useful to moral discipline and social order. In Italy the Church was also the main source of national income, and a valued check upon a people especially superstitious, pagan, and passionate. Superstitions abounded; as late as 1787 witches were burned at Palermo—and refreshments were served to fashionable ladies witnessing the scene.[14] Pagan beliefs, customs, and ceremonies survived with the genial sanction of the Church. "I have arrived at a vivid conviction," wrote Goethe, "that all traces of original Christianity are extinct here" in Rome.[15] There were, however, many real Christians left in Christendom, even in Italy. Conte Caissotti di Chiusano, bishop of Asti, gave up his rich inheritance, lived in voluntary poverty, and traveled only on foot. Bishop Testa of Monreale slept on straw, ate only enough to subsist, kept only 3,000 lire of his revenues for his personal needs, and devoted the remainder to public works and the poor.[16]

The Church responded in some measure to the Enlightenment. The works of Voltaire, Rousseau, Diderot, Helvétius, d'Holbach, La Mettrie, and other freethinkers were of course placed on the Index Expurgatorius, but permission to read them might be obtained from the pope. Monsignor Ventimiglio, bishop (1757–73) of Catania, had in his library full editions of Voltaire, Helvétius, and Rousseau.[17] The Inquisition was abolished in Tuscany and Parma in 1769, in Sicily in 1782, in Rome in 1809. In 1783 a Catholic priest, Tamburini, under the name of his friend Trauttmansdorff, published an essay *On Ecclesiastical and Civil Toleration*, in which he condemned the Inquisition, declared all coercion of conscience to be un-Christian, and advocated toleration of all theologies except atheism.[18]

It was the misfortune of the popes, in this second half of the eighteenth century, that they had to face the demand of Catholic monarchs for the total dissolution of the Society of Jesus. The movement against the Jesuits was part of a contest of power between the triumphant nationalism of the modern state and the internationalism of a papacy weakened by the Reformation, the Enlightenment, and the rise of the business class. The Catholic enemies of the Society did not openly press their chief objection, that it had persistently upheld the authority of the popes as superior to that of kings, but they were keenly resentful that an organization acknowledging no superior except its general and the pope should in effect constitute, within each state, an agent of a foreign power. They acknowledged the learning and piety of the Jesuits, their contributions to science, literature, philosophy, and art, their sedulous and efficient education of Catholic youth, their heroism on foreign missions, their recapture of so much territory once lost to Protestantism. But they charged that the Society had repeatedly interfered in secular affairs, that it had engaged in commerce to reap material gains, that it had inculcated casuistic principles excusing immorality and crime, condoning even the murder of kings, that it had allowed heathen customs and beliefs to survive among its supposed converts in Asia, and that it had offended other religious orders, and many of the secular clergy, by its sharpness in controversy and its contemptuous tone. The ambassadors of the Kings of Portugal, Spain, Naples, and France insisted that the papal charter of the Society be revoked, and that the organization be officially and universally dissolved.

The expulsion of the Jesuits from Portugal in 1759, from France in 1764–67, from Spain and Naples in 1767, had left the Society still operative in Central and North Italy, in the Austro-Hungarian Empire, in Catholic Germany, Silesia, and Poland. On February 7, 1768, they were expelled from the Bourbon duchy of Parma, and were added to the congestion of Jesuit refugees in the states of the Church. Pope Clement XIII protested that Parma was a papal fief; he threatened Duke Ferdinand VI and his ministers with excommunication if the edict of expulsion should be enforced; when they persisted he launched a bull declaring the rank and title of the Duke forfeited and annulled. The Catholic governments of Spain, Naples, and France opened war upon the papacy: Tanucci seized the papal cities of Benevento and Pontecorvo, and France occupied Avignon. On December 10, 1768, the French ambassador at Rome, in the name of France, Naples, and Spain, presented to the Pope a demand for the retraction of the bull against Parma, and for the abolition of the Society of Jesus. The seventy-six-year-old pontiff collapsed under the strain of this ultimatum. He summoned for February 3, 1769, a consistory of prelates and envoys to consider the matter. On February 2 he fell dead through the bursting of a blood vessel in his brain.

The cardinals who were called to choose his successor were divided into two factions: *zelanti* who proposed to defy the kings, and *regalisti* who favored some pacific accommodations. As the Italian cardinals were almost all *zelanti*, and soon gathered in Rome, they tried to open the conclave before the regalist cardinals from France, Spain, and Portugal could arrive. The French ambassador protested, and the conclave was deferred. Meanwhile Lorenzo Ricci, general of the Jesuits, compromised their case by issuing a pamphlet questioning the authority of any pope to abolish the Society.[19] In March Cardinal de Bernis arrived from France, and began to canvass the cardinals with a view to ensuring the election of a pope willing to satisfy their Catholic Majesties. Later rumors[20] that he or others bribed, or otherwise induced, Cardinal Giovanni Ganganelli to promise such action if chosen have been rejected by Catholic[21] and anti-Catholic[22] historians alike. Ganganelli, by common consent, was a man of great learning, devotion, and integrity; however, he belonged to the Franciscan order, which had often been at odds with the Jesuits, both in missions and in theology.[23] On May 19, 1769, he was elected by the unanimous vote of the forty cardinals, and took the name of Clement XIV. He was sixty-three years old.

He found himself at the mercy of the Catholic powers. France and

Naples held on to the papal territory they had seized; Spain and Parma were defiant; Portugal threatened to establish a patriarchate independent of Rome; even Maria Theresa, hitherto fervently loyal to the papacy and the Jesuits, but now losing authority to her freethinker son Joseph II, answered the Pope's appeal for aid by saying that she could not resist the united will of so many potentates. Choiseul, dominating the government of France, instructed Bernis to tell the Pope that "if he does not come to terms he can consider all relations with France at an end."[24] Charles III of Spain had sent a similar ultimatum on April 22. Clement, playing for time, promised Charles soon to "submit to the wisdom and intelligence of your Majesty a plan for the total extinction of the Society."[25] He ordered his aides to consult the archives and summarize the history, achievements, and alleged offenses of the Society of Jesus. He refused to surrender to Choiseul's demand that he decide the issue within two months. He took three years, but finally yielded.

On July 21, 1773, he signed the historic brief *Dominus ac Redemptor Noster*. It began with a long list of religious congregations that had, in the course of time, been suppressed by the Holy See. It noted the many complaints made against the Jesuits, and the many efforts of divers popes to remedy the abuses so alleged. "We have observed with the bitterest grief that these remedies, and others applied afterward, had neither efficacy nor strength to put an end to the troubles, the charges, and the complaints."[26] The brief concluded:

> Having recognized that the Society of Jesus could no longer produce the abundant fruit and the great good for which it was instituted and approved by so many popes, our predecessors, who adorned it with so many most admirable privileges, and seeing that it was almost—and indeed absolutely—impossible for the Church to enjoy a true and solid peace while this order existed, . . . we do hereby, after a mature examination, and of our certain knowledge, and by the plenitude of our Apostolic power, suppress and abolish the Society of Jesus. We nullify and abrogate all and each of its offices, functions, administrations, houses, schools, colleges, retreats, refuges, and other establishments which belong to it in any manner whatever, and in every province, kingdom, or state in which it may be found.[27]

The brief went on to offer pensions to those Jesuits who had not yet taken holy orders, and who wished to return to lay life; it permitted Jesuit priests to join the secular clergy or some religious congregation approved by the Holy See; it allowed "professed" Jesuits, who had taken final and absolute vows, to remain in their former houses provided they dressed like secular priests and submitted to the authority of the local bishop.

For the most part, and excepting a few missionaries in China, the Jesuits took the papal sentence of death for their Society with apparent docility and order. Anonymous pamphlets, however, were printed and circulated in their defense, and Ricci and several assistants were arrested on charges, never proved, that they were in correspondence with opponents of the decree. Ricci died in prison November 24, 1775, aged seventy-two.

Clement XIV survived the edict by little more than a year. Rumors multiplied that in his last months his mind broke down. Physical ills, including scurvy and hemorrhoids, made every day and night a misery to him. A cold contracted in April, 1774, never left him; by the end of August the cardinals were already discussing the succession; and on September 22 Clement died.

After many delays and intrigues the conclave raised to the papacy (February 15, 1775) Giovanni Braschi, who took the name of Pius VI. He was a man of culture rather than a statesman. He collected art, charmed everyone by his kindliness, improved the administration of the Curia, and effected a partial reclamation of the Pontine marshes. He arranged a peaceful *modus vivendi* for the Jesuits with Frederick the Great. In 1793 he joined the coalition against Revolutionary France. In 1796 Napoleon invaded the Papal States; in 1798 the French army entered Rome, proclaimed a republic, and demanded of the Pope a renunciation of all temporal power. He refused, was arrested, and remained in various places and conditions of imprisonment until his death (August 29, 1799). His successor, Pius VII, made the restoration of the Society of Jesus (1814) a part of the victory of the coalition against Napoleon.

III. THE LAW AND BECCARIA

The morals and manners of Italy remained a mixture of violence and indolence, vendetta and love. The fourteen-year-old Mozart wrote from Bologna in 1770, "Italy is a sleepy country";[28] he had not learned the philosophy of siesta. His father, in 1775, was of the opinion that "Italians are rascals all the world over."[29]

Both Mozart and Goethe commented on Italian crime. In Naples, wrote Mozart, "the *lazzaroni* [beggars] have their own captain or head, who draws twenty-five silver ducats from the King each month for nothing more than to keep them in order."[30] "What strikes the stranger most," wrote Goethe, "is the common occurrence of assassination. Today the victim has been an excellent artist—Schwendemann. . . . The assassin with whom he was struggling gave him twenty stabs; and as the watch came up, the villain stabbed himself. This is not generally the fashion here; the murderer usually makes for the nearest church; once there he is quite safe."[31] Every church gave the criminal "sanctuary"—immunity from arrest so long as he remained under its roof.

The law attempted to deter crime rather by severity of punishment than by efficiency of police. Under the laws of the gentle Benedict XIV blasphemy was punished by flogging, and, for a third offense, five years in the galleys. Unlawful entry of a convent at night was a capital crime. The solicitation or public embrace of an honorable woman brought condemnation to the galleys for life. Defamation of character, even if it spoke nothing but the truth, was punishable with death and confiscation of goods. (Pasquinades abounded none the less.) A like penalty was decreed for carrying concealed pistols. These edicts were in many areas evaded by flight to a neighboring state, or by the mercy of a judge, or by sanctuary of a church, but in several instances they were strictly carried out. One man was hanged for pretending that he was a priest, another for stealing an ecclesiastical vestment which he sold for one and a quarter francs; another was beheaded for writing a letter that accused Pope Clement XI of a liaison with Maria Clementina Sobieska.[32] As late as 1762 prisoners were broken on the wheel, bone after bone, or were dragged over the ground at the tail of a prodded horse. We should add, as a brighter side to the picture, that some confraternities raised money to pay the fines and secure the liberation of prisoners. Reform of the law, in both its procedure and its penalties, became a natural part of that humanitarian spirit born from the double parentage of a humanist Enlightenment and a Christian ethic freed from a cruel theology.

It is to the credit of Italy that the most effective appeal for law reform came in this century from a Milanese nobleman. Cesare Bonesana, Marchese di Beccaria, was a product of the Jesuits and the *philosophes*. Though rich enough to be idle, he gave himself with restless devotion to a career of philosophical writing and practical reform. He refrained from attacking the religion of the people, but confronted directly the actual conditions of crime and punishment. He was shocked to see the disease-breeding filth of Milanese jails, and to hear from prisoners how and why they had taken to crime, and how they had been tried. He was dismayed to find flagrant irregularities in procedure, inhuman tortures of suspects and witnesses, arbitrary severities and mercies in judgment, and barbarous cruelties in punishment. About 1761 he joined with Pietro Verri in a society which they called Dei Pugni—"The Fists"—vowed to action as well as thought. In 1764 they started a review, *Il Caffè*, in imitation of Addison's *Spectator*. And in that year Beccaria published his historic *Tratto dei delitti e delle pene* (*Treatise on Crimes and Penalties*).

He modestly announced at the outset that he was following the lead of *The Spirit of Laws* of "the immortal President" of the Bordeaux Parlement. Laws should be based upon reason; their basic reason is not to avenge crime but to preserve social order; they should always aim at "the greatest happiness divided among the greatest number" (*la massima felicità divisa nel maggior numero*);[33] here, twenty-five years before Bentham, was the famous principle of utilitarian ethics. Beccaria, with his customary candor, acknowledged the influence of Helvétius, who had offered the same formula in *De l'Esprit* (1758). (It had already appeared in Francis Hutcheson's *Ideas of Beauty and Virtue*, 1725.) For the good of society, said Beccaria, it would be wiser to widen and deepen education, in the hope of diminishing crime, than to resort to punishments that, by association, may transform an incidental miscreant into a confirmed criminal. Every accused person should have a fair and public trial before competent magistrates pledged to impartiality. Trial should come soon after accusation. Punishment should be proportioned not to the intention of the agent but to the harm done to society. Ferocity of punishment breeds ferocity of character, even in the noncriminal public. Torture should never be used; a guilty man accustomed to pain may bear it well and be supposed innocent, while an innocent man with keener nerves may be driven by it to confess anything and be judged guilty.

Ecclesiastical sanctuary for criminals should no longer be allowed. Capital punishment should be abolished.

The little book went through six editions in eighteen months, and was translated into twenty-two European languages. Beccaria praised the French version by Morellet as superior to the original. Voltaire contributed an anonymous preface to that translation, and repeatedly acknowledged the influence of Beccaria on his own efforts at law reform. Most Italian states soon reformed their penal codes, and nearly all Europe discarded torture by 1789. Catherine was moved by Beccaria as well as Voltaire in abolishing torture in her dominions; Frederick the Great had already ended it in Prussia (1740) except for treason.

In 1768 Beccaria was appointed to a chair of law and economy founded expressly for him in the Palatine College at Milan. In 1790 he was named to a commission for the reform of jurisprudence in Lombardy. His lectures anticipated several basic ideas of Adam Smith and Malthus on the division of labor, the relation between labor and capital, and between population and the food supply. In him the humanism of the Renaissance was reborn as the Enlightenment in Italy.

IV. ADVENTURERS

1. Cagliostro

Giuseppe Balsamo was born to a shopkeeper in Palermo in 1743. He matured early, and was soon an accomplished thief. At thirteen he was entered as a novice in the Monastery of the Benfratelli. There he was assigned to aid the house apothecary, from whose bottles, tubes, and books he learned enough chemistry and alchemy to equip himself for quackery. Required to read the lives of the saints to the friars as they ate, he substituted for the names of the saints those of Palermo's most distinguished prostitutes. Flogged, he decamped, joined the underworld, and studied the art of eating without working. He served as a pimp, a forger, a counterfeiter, a fortune-teller, a magician, and a robber, usually with such concealment of his traces that the police could convict him only of insolence.

Seeing himself uncomfortably suspect, he moved to Messina, crossed to Reggio Calabria, and sampled the opportunities of Naples and Rome. For a while he lived by touching up prints and selling them as his own. He married Lorenza Feliciani, and prospered by selling her body. Taking the name of Marchese de' Pellegrini, he brought his lucrative lady to Venice, Marseilles, Paris, London. He arranged to have his wife discovered in the arms of a rich Quaker; the resultant blackmail supported them for months. He changed his name to Count di Cagliostro, put on whiskers and the uniform of a Prussian colonel, and rechristened his wife Countess Seraphina. He returned to Palermo, was arrested as a forger, but was released on the ominous insistence of his friends, who terrified the law.

As Seraphina's charms were worn with circulation, he put his chemistry to use, concocting and selling drugs guaranteed to flatten wrinkles and set love aflame. Back in England he was accused of stealing a diamond necklace, and spent a spell in jail. He joined the Freemasons, moved to Paris, and set himself up as the Grand Cophta of Egyptian Masonry; he assured a hundred gullibles that he had found the ancient secrets of rejuvenation, which could be obtained through a forty days' course of purges, sweats, root diet, phlebotomy, and theosophy.[34] As soon as he was exposed in one city he went on to another, winning access to moneyed families by his Masonic grip and ring. In St. Petersburg he practiced as a doctor, treated the poor gratis, and was received by Potemkin; but Catherine the Great's physician, a canny Scot, analyzed some of the doctor's elixirs, and found them worthless; Cagliostro was given a day to pack and depart. In Warsaw he was exposed by another physician in a booklet, *Cagliostro démasqué* (1780), but before it could catch up with him he was off to Vienna, Frankfurt, Strasbourg. There he charmed Cardinal Prince Louis-René-Édouard de Rohan, who placed in his palace a bust of the Grand Cophta inscribed "The divine Cagliostro." The Cardinal brought him to Paris, and the great impostor was unwittingly involved in the Affair of the Diamond Necklace. When this hoax was exposed Cagliostro was sent to the Bastille; he was soon liberated as innocent, but was ordered to leave France (1786). He found a new clientele in London. Meanwhile Goethe visited Cagliostro's mother in Sicily, and assured her that her famous son had been acquitted and was safe.[35]*

From London, where doubters had multiplied, the Count and Countess moved to Basel, Turin, Rovereto, Trent, everywhere suspected and expelled. Seraphina begged to be taken to Rome to pray at her mother's grave; the Count agreed. In Rome they tried to set up a lodge of his Egyptian Freemasonry; the Inquisition arrested them (December 29, 1789); they confessed their charlatanry; Cagliostro was sentenced to life imprisonment, and ended his days in the Castle of San Leo near Pesaro in 1795, aged fifty-two. He too was part of the picture of the Illuminated Century.

2. Casanova

Giovanni Jacopo Casanova added the lordly "de Seingalt" to his name by a random plucking of the alphabet, as a useful honorific in overwhelming nuns and braving the governments of Europe. Born to two actors in Venice in 1725, he gave early promise of mental alacrity. He was apprenticed to the law, and claimed to have received the doctorate at the University of Padua when he was sixteen.[36] At every step in his engaging *Memoirs* we must beware of his imagination, but he tells his story with such self-damning candor that we may believe him though we know he lies.

While at Padua he made his first conquest—Bettina, "a pretty girl of thirteen," sister of his tutor the good priest Gozzi. When she fell ill of smallpox Casanova nursed her and caught the disease; by his own account his acts of

---

* Goethe was fascinated by Cagliostro's career, and made it the subject of a middling play, *Der Grosskophta.*

kindness equaled his amours. In his old age, going to Padua for the last time, "I found her old, ill and poor, and she died in my arms."[37] Nearly all his sweethearts are represented as loving him until his death.

Despite his law degree he suffered from a humiliating poverty. His father was dead, his mother was acting in cities as far away as St. Petersburg, and usually forgot him. He earned some bread by fiddling in taverns and streets. But he was strong as well as handsome and brave. When (1746) the Venetian Senator Zuan Bragadino suffered a stroke while descending a stairway, Jacopo caught him in his arms and saved him from a precipitate fall; thereafter the Senator protected him in a dozen scrapes, and gave him funds to visit France, Germany, and Austria. At Lyons he joined the Freemasons; at Paris "I became a Companion, then a Master, of the order." (We note with some shock that "in my time no one in France knew how to overcharge."[38])

In 1753 he returned to Venice, and soon caught the attention of the government by peddling occult wisdom. A year later an official inquisitor reported on him to the Senate:

> He has insinuated himself into the good graces of the noble Zuan Bragadino, . . . and has fleeced him grievously. . . . Benedetto Pisano tells me that Casanova is by way of being a cabalistic philosopher, and, by false reasoning cleverly adapted to the minds he works on, contrives to get his livelihood. . . . He has made . . . Bragadino believe that he can evoke the angel of light for his benefit.[39]

Furthermore (the report continues) Casanova had sent to his friends compositions that revealed him as an impious freethinker. Casanova tells us: "A certain Mme. Memno took it into her head that I was teaching her son the precepts of atheism."[40]

> The things I was accused of concerned the Holy Office, and the Holy Office is a ferocious beast with whom it is dangerous to meddle. There were certain circumstances . . . which made it difficult for them to shut me up in the ecclesiastical prisons of the Inquisition, and because of this it was finally decided that the State Inquisition should deal with me.[41]

Bragadino advised him to leave Venice; Casanova refused. The next morning he was arrested, his papers were confiscated, and he was confined without trial in I Piombi, "the Leads"—a name given to the Venetian state prison from the plates on its roof.

> When night came it was impossible for me to close my eyes, for three reasons: first, the rats; second, the terrible din made by the clock of St. Mark's, which sounded as if it were in my room; and third, the thousands of fleas which invaded my body, bit and stung me, poisoning my blood to such an extent that I suffered from spasmodic constrictions amounting to convulsions.[42]

He was sentenced to five years, but after fifteen months of incarceration he escaped (1757), by a complication of devices, risks, and terrors whose narrative became part of his stock in trade in a dozen lands.

Arrived a second time in Paris, he fought a duel with the young Comte Nicolas de La Tour d'Auvergne, wounded him, healed him with a "magic" ointment, won his friendship, and was introduced by him to a rich aunt,

Mme. d'Urfé, who devoutly believed in occult powers, and hoped through them to change her sex. Casanova played upon her credulity, and found in it a secret means of opulence. "I cannot, now that I am old, look back upon this chapter of my life without blushing";[43] but it lasted through a dozen chapters of his book. He added to his income by cheating at cards, by organizing a lottery for the French government, and by obtaining a loan for France from the United Provinces. En route from Paris to Brussels "I read Helvétius' *De l'Esprit* all the way."[44] (He was to offer to conservatives a persuasive example of the *libertin* [freethinker] becoming a libertine—though the sequence was probably the reverse.) At every stop he picked a mistress; at many stops he found a former mistress; now and then he stumbled upon his own unpremeditated progeny.

He visited Rousseau at Montmorency, and Voltaire at Ferney (1760); we have already enjoyed part of that tête-à-tête. If we may believe Casanova, he took the occasion to reprove Voltaire for exposing the absurdities of the popular mythology:

> CASANOVA: Suppose you do succeed in destroying superstition, with what will you replace it?
>
> VOLTAIRE: I like that! When I have delivered humanity from a ferocious monster that devours it, you ask what shall I put in its place?
>
> CASANOVA: Superstition does not devour humanity; it is, on the contrary, necessary to its existence.
>
> VOLTAIRE: Necessary to its existence! That is a horrible blasphemy. I love mankind; I would like to see it, as I am, free and happy. Superstition and liberty cannot go hand in hand. Do you think that slavery makes for happiness?
>
> CASANOVA: What you want, then, is the supremacy of the people?
>
> VOLTAIRE: God forbid! The masses must have a king to govern them.
>
> CASANOVA: In that case superstition is necessary, for the people would never give a mere man the right to rule them. . . .
>
> VOLTAIRE: I want a sovereign ruling a free people, and bound to them by reciprocal conditions, which should prevent any inclination to despotism on his part.
>
> CASANOVA: Addison says that such a sovereign . . . is impossible. I agree with Hobbes: between two evils one must choose the lesser. A nation freed from superstition would be a nation of philosophers, and philosophers do not know how to obey. There is no happiness for a people that is not crushed, kept down and held in leash.
>
> VOLTAIRE: Horrible! And you are of the people! . . .
>
> CASANOVA: Your master passion is love of humanity. This love blinds you. Love humanity, but love it as it is. Humanity is not susceptible to the benefits you wish to shower upon it; these would only make it more wretched and perverse. . . .
>
> VOLTAIRE: I am sorry you have such a bad opinion of your fellow creatures.[45]

Wherever he went, Casanova made his way into some aristocratic homes, for many of the European nobility were Freemasons, or Rosicrucians, or addicts of occult lore. He not only claimed esoteric knowledge in these fields, but in addition had a good figure, a distinguished (though not handsome) face, a command of languages, a seductive self-assurance, a fund of stories and wit, and a mysterious ability to win at cards or in casino games. Everywhere he was sooner or later escorted to jail or the frontier. Now and then he had to fight a duel, but, like a nation in its histories, he never lost.

At last he succumbed to longing for his native land. He was free to travel anywhere in Italy except Venice. He repeatedly applied for permission to come back; it was finally granted, and in 1775 he was in Venice again. He was employed by the government as a spy; his reports were discarded as containing too much philosophy and too little information; he was dismissed. Relapsing into his youthful ways, he wrote a satire on the patrician Grimaldi; he was told to leave Venice or face another stay in the Leads. He fled to Vienna (1782), to Spa, and to Paris.

There he met a Count von Waldstein, who took a fancy to him and invited him to serve as his librarian in the Castle of Dux in Bohemia. Casanova's arts of love and magic and sleight-of-hand had reached the point of diminishing returns; he accepted the post at a thousand florins per year. Arrived and installed, he was grieved to find that he was considered a servant, and dined in the servants' hall. At Dux he spent his final fourteen years. There he wrote his *Histoire de ma vie*, "principally to palliate the deadly dullness which is killing me in this dull Bohemia. . . . By writing ten or twelve hours a day I have prevented black sorrow from eating up my poor heart and destroying my reason."[46] He professed absolute veracity in his narrative, and in many cases it gibes well enough with history; often, however, we find no verification of his account. Perhaps his memory declined while his imagination grew. We can only say that his book is one of the most fascinating relics of the eighteenth century.

Casanova lived long enough to mourn the death of the Old Regime.

> O my dear, my beautiful France!—where, in those days, things went so well, despite *lettres de cachet*, despite the *corvée* and the misery of the people! . . . Dear France, what have you become today? The people is your sovereign, the people, most brutal and tyrannical of all rulers.[47]

And so, on his last day, June 4, 1798, he ended his career in timely piety. "I have lived a philosopher, and I die a Christian."[48] He had mistaken sensualism for philosophy, and Pascal's wager for Christianity.

V. WINCKELMANN

By contrast let us look at an idealist.

The most influential figure in the art history of this age was not an artist, but a scholar whose mature life was dedicated to the history of art, and whose strange death moved the soul of literate Europe. He was born on December 9, 1717, at Stendal in Brandenburg. His cobbler father hoped he would be a cobbler, but Johann wished to study Latin. He paid for his early education by singing. Eager and industrious, he advanced rapidly. He tutored less able pupils, and bought books and food. When his teacher went blind Johann read to him, and devoured his master's library. He learned Latin and Greek thoroughly, but he had no interest in modern foreign languages. Hearing that the library of the late Johann Albert Fabricius, a famous classical scholar, was to be sold at auction, he walked 178 miles from Berlin to Hamburg, bought Greek and Latin classics, and carried them on his shoulders back to Berlin.[49] In 1738 he entered the University of Halle as a theological student; he did not care for theology, but he seized the opportunity to study Hebrew. After graduating he lived by tutoring. He read twice completely Bayle's *Dictionnaire historique et critique*, presumably with some effect upon his religious faith. In one year he read the *Iliad* and the *Odyssey* thrice through in Greek.

In 1743 he accepted an invitation to be associate director of a school at Seehausen in Altmark, at a salary of 250 thalers per year. During the day he taught "children with scabby heads their A B C, whilst I . . . was ardently longing to attain to a knowledge of the beautiful, and was repeating similes from Homer."[50] In the evening he tutored for his lodging and meals, then he studied the classics till midnight, slept till four, studied the classics again, then went wearily to teach. He gladly accepted a call from Count von Bünau to be assistant librarian in the château at Nötheniz, near Dresden, for lodging and fifty to eighty thalers a year (1748). There he reveled in one of the most extensive book collections of the time.

Among those who used this library was Cardinal Archinto, papal nuncio at the court of the Elector of Saxony. He was impressed by Winckelmann's learning and enthusiasm, his emaciation and pallor. "You should go to Italy," he told him. Johann replied that such a trip was the deepest desire of his heart, but beyond his means. Invited to visit the nuncio in Dresden, Winckelmann went several times. He was delighted by the erudition and the courtesy of the Jesuits he met in the nuncio's home. Cardinal Passionei, who had 300,000 volumes in Rome, offered him the post of librarian there, for board and seventy ducats; however, the post could be filled only by a Catholic. Winckelmann agreed to conversion. As he had already expressed his belief that "after death you have nothing to dread, nothing to hope,"[51] he found no theological, only social, difficulties in making the change. To a friend who reproached him he wrote: "It is the love of knowledge, and that alone, which can induce me to listen to the proposal that has been made to me."[52] *

On July 11, 1754, in the chapel of the nuncio at Dresden, he professed his new faith, and arrangements were made for his journey to Rome. For various reasons he remained for another year in Dresden, living and studying with the painter-sculptor-etcher Adam Oesen. In May, 1755, he published in a

---

* *Cf.* Pater, in his classic essay on Winckelmann: "He may have had a sense of a certain antique and as it were pagan grandeur in the Roman Catholic religion. Turning from the crabbed Protestantism which had been the ennui of his youth, he might reflect that while Rome had reconciled itself to the Renaissance, the Protestant principle in art had cut off Germany from the supreme tradition of beauty."[53] And Goethe wrote in a little book on Winckelmann (1804): "The pagan temper radiates from all of his actions and writings. . . . His remoteness from every Christian way of thinking, indeed his very aversion to this way of thinking, must be kept in mind when we attempt to pass judgment on his so-called change of religion. The parties into which the Christian religion is divided were to him a matter of utter indifference."[54] "Pagan" need not mean atheist; Winckelmann repeatedly affirmed his belief in God, but in "the God of all tongues, nations, and sects."[55]

limited edition of fifty copies his first book, *Gedanken über die Nachahmung der griechischen Werke in Mahlerei und Bildhauerkunst (Thoughts on the Imitation of Greek Works in Painting and Sculpture)*. Besides describing the antiques that had been gathered in Dresden, he contended that the Greek understanding of nature was superior to the modern, and that this was the secret of Hellenic pre-eminence in art. He concluded that "the only way for us to become great, indeed to become inimitably great, . . . is through imitation of the ancients";[56] and he thought that of all modern artists Raphael had done this best. This little volume marked the beginning of the neoclassic movement in modern art. It was well received; Klopstock and Gottsched joined in praising both its erudition and its style. Father Rauch, confessor to Frederick Augustus, secured for Winckelmann, from the Elector-King, a pension of two hundred thalers for each of the next two years, and provided him with eighty ducats for the trip to Rome. At last, on September 20, 1755, Winckelmann set out for Italy, in the company of a young Jesuit. He was already thirty-seven years old.

Arrived in Rome, he had trouble at the customshouse, which confiscated several volumes of Voltaire from his baggage; these were returned to him later. He found lodging with five painters in a house on the Pincian Hill—sanctified by the shades of Nicolas Poussin and Claude Lorrain. He met Mengs, who helped him in a hundred ways. Cardinal Passionei gave him the freedom of his library, but Winckelmann, wishing to explore the art of Rome, refused as yet any regular employment. He obtained permission for repeated visits to the Belvedere of the Vatican; he spent hours before the *Apollo*, the *Torso*, and the *Laocoön;* in contemplation of these sculptures his ideas took clearer form. He visited Tivoli, Frascati, and other suburbs containing ancient remains. His knowledge of classical art won him the friendship of Cardinal Alessandro Albani. Cardinal Archinto gave him an apartment in the Palazzo della Cancelleria—the Papal Chancellery; in return Winckelmann reorganized the palace library. Now he was almost ecstatically happy. "God owed me this," he said; "in my youth I suffered too much."[57] And to a friend in Germany he wrote as a hundred distinguished visitors were writing:

> All is naught, compared with Rome! Formerly I thought that I had thoroughly studied everything, and behold, when I came hither, I perceived that I knew nothing. Here I have become smaller than when I came out of school to the Bünau library. If you wish to learn to know men, here is the place; here are heads of infinite talent, men of high endowments, beauties of the lofty character which the Greeks have given to their figures. . . . As the freedom enjoyed in other states is only a shadow compared with that of Rome—which probably strikes you as a paradox—so there is also in this place a different mode of thinking. Rome is, I believe, the high school of the world; and I too have been tried and refined.[58]

In October, 1757, armed with letters of introduction, he left Rome for Naples. There he lived in a monastery, but he dined with men like Tanucci and Galiani. He visited cities redolent with classic history—Pozzuoli, Baia, Misenum, Cumae—and stood in wonder before the stately temples of Paestum.

In May, 1758, he returned to Rome laden with antiquarian lore. In that month he was called to Florence to catalogue and describe the enormous collection of gems, casts, engravings, maps, and manuscripts left by Baron Philip von Stosch. The task occupied him for nearly a year, and almost ruined his health. Meanwhile Archinto died, and Frederick the Great ravaged Saxony; Winckelmann lost his apartment in the Cancelleria, and his pension from the unfortunate Elector-King. Albani came to his rescue by offering him four rooms and ten scudi per month to take care of his library. The Cardinal himself was a fervent antiquarian; every Sunday he drove out with Winckelmann to hunt antiquities.

Winckelmann added to his reputation by issuing scholarly monographs: *On Grace in Works of Art, Remarks upon the Architecture of the Ancients, Description of the Torso in the Belvedere, The Study of Works of Art.* In 1760 he tried to arrange a trip to Greece with Lady Orford, sister-in-law of Horace Walpole; the plan fell through. "Nothing in the world have I so ardently desired as this," he wrote. "Willingly would I allow one of my fingers to be cut off; indeed, I would make myself a priest of Cybele could I but see this land under such an opportunity."[59] The priests of Cybele had to be eunuchs, but this did not prevent Winckelmann from denouncing an old ordinance of the Roman government requiring the private parts of the *Apollo*, the *Laocoön*, and other statues in the Belvedere to be covered by metal aprons; "there has hardly ever been in Rome," he declared, "so asinine a regulation."

The sense of beauty was so dominant in him that it almost annulled any consciousness of sex. If he felt an aesthetic preference it favored the beauty of the virile male figure rather than the frail and transitory loveliness of woman. The muscular *Torso of Hercules* seems to have moved him more than the soft and rounded contours of the *Venus de' Medici*. He had a good word to say for hermaphrodites—at least for the one in the Villa Borghese.[60] He protested, "I have never been an enemy of the other sex, but my mode of life has removed me from all intercourse with it. I might have married, and probably should have done so, if I had revisited my native land, but now I scarcely think of it."[61] In Seehausen his friendship with his pupil Lamprecht had taken the place of feminine attachments; in Rome he lived with ecclesiastics, and seldom met young women. "For a long time," we are told, "there dined with him, on Saturdays, a young Roman, slender, fair, and tall, with whom he talked of love."[62] He "caused a portrait to be painted of a beautiful *castrato*."[63] He dedicated to the youthful Baron Friedrich Reinhold von Berg a *Treatise on the Capability of the Feeling for Beauty;* "readers found in it, and in the letters to Berg, the language not of friendship but of love; and such it actually is."[64]

In 1762 and 1764 he visited Naples again. His *Letter on the Antiquities of Herculaneum* (1762) and his *Account of the Latest Herculanean Discoveries* (1764) gave European scholars the first orderly and scientific information about the treasures excavated there and at Pompeii. He was now recognized as the supreme authority on ancient classical art. In 1763 he received an office in the Vatican as "antiquarian to the Apostolic Chamber." Finally, in 1764, he published the massive volumes that he had been writing and illustrating for seven years past: *Geschichte der Kunst des Alterthums* (*History of Ancient Art*).

Despite its long and painstaking preparation it contained many errors, two of which were cruel hoaxes. His friend Mengs had foisted upon him, as faithful reproductions of antique paintings, two drawings born of Mengs's imagination; Winckelmann listed these paintings, used the engravings, and dedicated the entire work to Mengs. The translations that soon appeared in French and Italian carried nearly all the errors, to Winckelmann's mortification. "We are wiser today than we were yesterday," he wrote to some friends. "Would to God I could show you my *History of Art* entirely remodeled and considerably enlarged! I had not yet learned to write when I took it in hand: the thoughts were not yet sufficiently linked together; there is wanting, in many cases, the transition from what precedes to what follows—in which the greatest art consists."[65] And yet the book had accomplished a very difficult task—to write well about art. His intense devotion to his subject lifted him to style.

He addressed himself literally to the history of art rather than the much easier history of artists. After a hurried survey of Egyptian, Phoenician, Jewish, Persian, and Etruscan art Winckelmann let all his enthusiasm loose in 450 pages on the classical art of the Greeks. In some final chapters he discussed Greek art under the Romans. Always his emphasis was on the Greeks, for he was convinced that they had found the highest forms of beauty: in the refinement of line rather than in brilliance of color, in the representation of types rather than individuals, in the normality and nobility of the figure, in the restraint of emotional expression, in the serenity of aspect, in the repose of features even in action, and above all in the harmonious proportion and relation of differentiated parts in a logically unified whole. Greek art, to Winckelmann, was the Age of Reason in form.

He connected the superiority of Greek art with the high regard that the Greeks paid to excellence of form in either sex. "Beauty was an excellence that led to fame, for we find that the Greek histories make mention of those who were distinguished for it,"[66] as histories now record great statesmen, poets, and philosophers. There were beauty contests, as well as athletic contests, among the Greeks. Winckelmann thought that political freedom, and Greek leadership of the Mediterranean world before the Peloponnesian War, led to a synthesis of grandeur with beauty, and produced the "grand style" (*hohe, grosse Stil*) in Pheidias, Polycleitus, and Myron. In the next stage the "grand" gave way to the "beautiful" style, or "style of grace"; Pheidias gave way to Praxiteles, and decline began. Freedom in art was part of Greek freedom; artists were liberated from rigid rules, and dared to create ideal forms not found in nature. They imitated nature only in details; the whole was a composite of perfections found only in part in any natural object. Winckelmann was a romantic preaching classic form.

His book was accepted throughout Europe as an event in the history of literature and art. Frederick the Great sent him an invitation (1765) to come to Berlin as superintendent of the royal library and cabinet of antiquities.

Winckelmann agreed to come for two thousand thalers per year; Frederick offered one thousand; Winckelmann stood his ground, and recalled the story of the *castrato* who demanded a fat sum for his songs; Frederick complained that he asked more than his best general cost him; "*Eh bene,*" said the *castrato,* "*faccia cantare il suo generale!*" (Very well, then; let him make his general sing!).[67]

In 1765 Winckelmann revisited Naples, this time in company with John Wilkes, who had made Europe resound with his defiance of Parliament and George III. After gathering more data he returned to Rome and completed his second major work, *Monumenti antichi inediti* (1767). His prelate friends had complained of his writing the *History* in German, which was not yet a major medium of scholarship; now he pleased them by using Italian, and the happy author, seated between two cardinals, had the ecstasy of reading a part of his book at Castel Gandolfo to Clement XIII and a numerous assembly of notables. However, he was accused of having heretical books and making heretical remarks,[68] and he never obtained from the papacy the post which he felt he deserved.

Perhaps in hope that he might there secure the means of seeing Greece, he decided to visit Germany (1768). But he had so immersed himself in classic art and Italian ways that he took no pleasure in his native land; he ignored its scenery and resented its baroque architecture and ornament; "Let us return to Rome," he repeated a hundred times to his traveling companion.[69] He was received with honors in Munich, where he was presented a beautiful antique gem. At Vienna Maria Theresa gave him costly medallions, and both the Empress and Prince von Kaunitz invited him to settle there; but on May 28, after hardly a month's absence, he turned back to Italy.

At Trieste he was delayed while waiting for a ship that would take him to Ancona. During these days he developed acquaintance with another traveler, Francesco Arcangeli. They took walks together, and occupied adjoining rooms in the hotel. Soon Winckelmann showed him the medallions he had received in Vienna; he did not, so far as we know, show his gold-filled purse. On the morning of June 8, 1768, Arcangeli entered Winckelmann's room, found him seated at a table, and threw a noose around his neck. Winckelmann rose and fought; Arcangeli stabbed him five times and fled. A physician bandaged the wounds but pronounced them fatal. Winckelmann received the last sacrament, made his will, expressed a desire to see and forgive his assailant, and died at four o'clock in the afternoon. Trieste commemorates him with a handsome monument.

Arcangeli was captured on June 14. He confessed, and on June 18 he was sentenced: "For the crime of murder, done by you on the body of Johann Winckelmann, . . . the Imperial Criminal Court has decreed that you . . . shall be broken alive on the wheel, from the head to the feet, until your soul depart from your body." On July 20 it was so done.

The limitations of Winckelmann were bound up with geography. Because he never realized his hope of visiting Greece under conditions that would have allowed extensive study of classic remains, he thought of Greek art in terms of Greco-Roman art as found in the museums, collections, and palaces of Germany and Italy, and in the relics of Herculaneum and Pompeii. His predilection for sculpture over painting, for the representation of types rather than individuals, for tranquillity as against the expression of emotion, for proportion and symmetry, for imitation of the ancients as against originality and experiment: all this placed upon the creative impulses in art severe restraints that resulted in the Romantic reaction against the cold rigidity of classical forms. His concentration on Greece and Rome blinded him to the rights and possibilities of other styles; like Louis XIV, he thought that the genre paintings of the Netherlands were grotesqueries.

Even so, his achievement was remarkable. He stirred the whole European realm of art, literature, and history with his exaltation of Greece. He went beyond the semiclassicism of Renaissance Italy and Louis XIV's France to classic art itself. He aroused the modern mind to the clean and placid perfection of Greek sculpture. He turned the chaos of a thousand marbles, bronzes, paintings, gems, and coins into a scientific archaeology. His influence on the best spirits of the next generation was immense. He inspired Lessing, if only to opposition; he shared in maturing Herder and Goethe; and perhaps without the afflatus that rose from Winckelmann Byron would not have crowned his poetry with death in Greece. The ardent Hellenist helped to form the neoclassic principles of Mengs and Thorwaldsen, and the neoclassic painting of Jacques-Louis David. "Winckelmann," said Hegel, "is to be regarded as one of those who, in the sphere of art, have known how to initiate a new organ for the human spirit."[70]

VI. THE ARTISTS

Italy hardly needed Winckelmann's exhortations, for she honored her gods, and her accumulated art served in each generation as a school of discipline for a thousand artists from a dozen lands. Carlo Marchionni designed the palatial Villa Albani (1758), into which Cardinal Albani, guided by Winckelmann, gathered a world-famous collection of antique sculptures— still rich after many rapes. (Napoleon stole 294 of the pieces for France; hence, perhaps, an Italian saying of those days, *Non tutti francesi sono latroni, ma Buona Parte*—not all Frenchmen are thieves, but a good part of them are.)

Venice produced nearly all the leading Italian painters of these years, and three of them inherited already famous names. Alessandro Longhi, son of Pietro, illustrated the genius of his people with some delicate portraits, including two of Goldoni.[71] We have seen Domenico Tiepolo accompanying his father to Augsburg and Madrid, and modestly offering his specialty to the common stock. In the guest house of the Villa Valmarana he struck out for himself with genre scenes from rural life; *Peasants Reposing* is an idyl of dropped tools and restful ease. After his father's death in Spain Domenico returned to Venice, and gave his own style of humorous realism free rein.[72]

Francesco Guardi, brother-in-law to Giambattista Tiepolo, learned painting from his father, his brother, and Canaletto. He missed acclaim in his generation, but his *vedute* caught critical eyes by seizing and conveying subtleties of light, and moods of atmosphere, which may have given some hints to French Impressionists. He did not wait for Constable's caution, "Remember that light and shade never stand still."[73] Perhaps his favorite hour was twilight, when lines were blurred, colors merged, and shadows were dim, as in *Gondola on the Lagoon.*[74] Venetian skies and waters seemed designed to offer such misty, melting views. Sometimes, we are told, Guardi carried his studio into a gondola, and moved on the minor canals to catch unhackneyed scenes. He painted the human figures carelessly, as if he felt that they were evanescent minutiae beside the solid architecture and the changing yet persistent sea and sky. But he could picture men too, crowding the Piazzetta in some gala *Festival*,[75] or moving in stately dress in the great *Sala dei Filarmonici.*[76] In their lifetime his brother Giovanni was rated the better painter, and Canaletto greater than either; today Francesco Guardi promises to outlive them both.

Anton Raphael Mengs returned from Spain in 1768, and was soon lord of the studios in Rome. Hardly anyone questioned his supremacy among contemporary artists. Crowned heads angled for his brush, sometimes in vain. Winckelmann called him the Raphael of his age, praised his deadly *Parnassus* as a masterpiece before which "even Raphael would have bowed his head,"[77] and injected into the *History of Ancient Art* a superlative estimate of his friend.[78]

The best of Mengs's paintings in this period is his self-portrait (1773?).[79] It shows him still vigorous, handsome, black-haired, proud at forty-five. After a second stay in Spain Mengs returned (1777) to spend his declining years in Italy. He continued to prosper, but the death of his wife (1778) broke his once buoyant spirit. A variety of ailments weakened him, and his resort to quack doctors and miraculous cures completed his physical ruin. He died in 1779 at the age of fifty-one. His disciples raised to his memory a cenotaph in the Pantheon, beside the monument to Raphael. Today there is no critic so poor to do him reverence.

VII. *I MUSICI*

Church music had declined with the growing secularization of life, and had suffered infection from operatic forms. Instrumental music was prospering, partly through the improvement of the pianoforte, but still more with the increasing popularity of the violin. Virtuosi like Pugnani, Viotti, and Nardini conquered Europe with a bow. Muzio Clementi, who went from Italy to live for twenty years in England, toured the Continent as organist and pianist, competed with Mozart in Vienna, and may have profited from Mozart's comment that his playing was too mechanical. He was the most successful piano teacher of the eighteenth century, and he established the nineteenth-century style of piano technique with his famous series of exercises and studies, *Gradus ad Parnassum*—steps to the home of the Muses from whom music took its name. Gaetano Pugnani inherited his master Tartini's violin artistry, and passed it on to his pupil Giovanni Battista Viotti, who traversed Europe triumphantly. Viotti's Violin Concerto in A Minor can still be enjoyed by our old-fashioned ears.

Like so many Italians, Luigi Boccherini left a land crowded with musicians to seek an audience abroad. From 1768 till his death in 1805 he charmed Spain with his cello as Farinelli had charmed it with his voice and Scarlatti with his harpsichord. For a generation his instrumental compositions rivaled those of Mozart in international acclaim; Frederick William II of Prussia, himself a cellist, preferred Boccherini's quartets to Mozart's.[80] In his sixty-two years he composed ninety-five string quartets, fifty-four trios, twelve piano quintets, twenty symphonies, five concertos for the cello, two oratorios, and some religious music. Half the world knows his "Minuet"—a movement from one of his quintets; but all the world should know his Concerto in B Flat for violoncello and orchestra.

Europe surrendered without a struggle (again excepting Paris) to the *bel canto* of Italy. From a dozen cities of the Magic Boot prima donnas like Caterina Gabrielli and *castrati* like Gasparo Pacchierotti poured across the Alps to Vienna, Munich, Leipzig, Dresden, Berlin, St. Petersburg, Hamburg, Brussels, London, Paris, and Madrid. Pacchierotti was among the last of the famous emasculates; for a generation he rivaled Farinelli's career. He held London captive for four years; his acclaim there still echoes in Fanny Burney's *Diary*,[81] and in her father's *General History of Music*.[82]

Italian composers and conductors followed the singers. Pietro Guglielmi wrote two hundred operas, and moved from Naples to Dresden to Brunswick to London to conduct them. Another Neapolitan, Niccolò Piccini, has come down to us disfigured by his unwilling contest with Gluck in Paris; but Galiani described him as *un très honnête homme*—a thoroughly honorable man.[83] His *opere buffe* were for a decade the rage of Naples and Rome; even the *Serva padrona* of Pergolesi won no such popularity as Piccini's *La cecchina* (1760). Jommelli, Pergolesi, Leo, and Galuppi had set to music Metastasio's *Olimpiade*; Piccini did likewise, and, by common consent, excelled them all. In 1776 he accepted a call to Paris; the wild war that ensued there must wait its geographical turn; through it all Piccini carried himself with complete courtesy, remaining friends with his rivals Gluck and Sacchini even though their partisans threatened his life.[84] When the Revolution drowned out this *opera buffa* Piccini returned to Naples. There he was placed under house arrest for four years because of sympathy with France; his operas were hooted from the stage, and he lived in a poverty disgraceful to his country. After Napoleon's conquest of Italy he was again invited to Paris (1798); the First Consul gave him a modest sinecure, but a paralytic stroke broke him down in body and spirit, and he died in Paris in 1800.

Antonio Sacchini was born to a fisherman at Pozzuoli, and was being trained to succeed his father when Francesco Durante heard him sing, and carried him off to Naples as pupil and protégé. His *Semiramide* was so well received at the Teatro Argentino in Rome that he remained with that theater for seven years as its composer of operas. After a stay in Venice he set off to conquer Munich, Stuttgart, . . . and London (1772). His operas were applauded there, but hostile cabals damaged his popularity, and his dissolute habits ruined his health. Moving to Paris, he produced his masterpiece, *Oedipe a Colone* (1786), which held the boards of the Opéra through 583 representations in the next fifty-seven years; we can still hear it, now and then, on the air. He adopted several of Gluck's reforms; he abandoned the Italian style of making an opera a patchwork of arias; in *Oedipe* the story controls the arias, and the choruses, inspired by Handel's oratorios, lend grandeur to both the music and the theme.

The melodious conquest went on with Antonio Salieri, foe of Mozart and friend of the young Beethoven. Born near Verona, he was sent at the age of sixteen to Vienna (1766); eight years later Joseph II appointed him composer to the court, and in 1788 *Kapellmeister*. In this post he preferred other composers to Mozart, but the story that this opposition caused Mozart's collapse is a myth.[85] After Mozart's death Salieri befriended the son and promoted his musical development. Beethoven submitted several compositions to Salieri, and accepted his suggestions with unwonted humility.

"The most radiant star in the Italian operatic firmament during the second half of the eighteenth century"[86] was Giovanni Paisiello. Son of a veterinary surgeon at Taranto, his voice so impressed his Jesuit teachers there that they persuaded his father to send him to Durante's conservatory in Naples (1754). When he took to composing operas he found the Neapolitan audiences so enamored of Piccini that he accepted an invitation from Catherine the Great. In St. Petersburg he wrote (1782) *Il barbiere di Siviglia*; it had so lasting a success throughout Europe that when Rossini offered in Rome (February 5, 1816) an opera on the same subject it was damned by the public as an ungentlemanly intrusion upon territory sacred to Paisiello, who was still alive. On his way back from Russia in 1784, Paisiello stopped long enough in Vienna to write twelve "symphonies" for Joseph II, and to produce an opera, *Il re Teodoro*, which soon won Europe-wide acceptance. Then he returned to Naples as *maestro di cappella* to Ferdinand IV. Napoleon persuaded Ferdinand to "lend" him Paisiello; when the composer arrived in Paris (1802) he was received with a magnificence that made him many enemies. In 1804 he returned to Naples under the patronage of Joseph Bonaparte and Murat.

We should note, in passing, how patiently these Italians prepared their careers. Paisiello studied for nine years at Durante's Conservatorio di San Onofrio; Cimarosa studied for eleven years in the Conservatorio di Santa Maria di Loreto, and later at Naples. After long tutelage under Sacchini, Piccini, and others, Domenico Cimarosa produced his first opera, *Le stravaganze del conte*. Soon his operas were heard in Vienna, Dresden, Paris, and London. In 1787 he took his turn at St. Petersburg, where he delighted the polyandrous Empress with *Cleopatra*. Invited by Leopold II to succeed Salieri as *Kapellmeister* at Vienna, he produced there his most celebrated opera, *Il matrimonio segreto* (1792). It so pleased the Emperor that at its close he ordered supper to be served to all those present, and then commanded a repetition of the whole.[87] In 1793 he was called back to Naples as *maestro di cappella* for Ferdinand IV. When the King was deposed by a French Revolutionary army (1799) Cimarosa hailed the event with enthusiasm; when Ferdinand was restored Cimarosa was condemned to death. The sentence was commuted to exile. The composer set out for St. Petersburg, but died on the way at Venice (1801). He left, in addition to many cantatas, Masses, and oratorios, some sixty-six operas, which were far more applauded than Mozart's, and which even now must be reckoned second only to Mozart's in the *opere buffe* of the eighteenth century.

If melody is the heart of music, Italian music is supreme. The Germans had preferred polyphonic harmony to a simple melodic line; in this sense Italy won another victory over Germany when the German Mozart subordinated polyphony to melody. But the Italians gave melody so dominant a place that their operas tended to be a succession of tuneful arias rather than musical dramas such as the first Italian opera composers (c. 1600) had had in mind in their attempt to rival the dramatic art of the Greeks. In Italian opera the significance of the action, and often of the words, was lost in the glory of the song; this was beautiful, but if, as we used to think, art is the replacement of chaos with order to reveal significance, opera, in Italian hands, had fallen short of its highest possibilities. Some Italians, like Jommelli and Traëtta, acknowledged this, and strove to mold the music and the play into a united whole; but that achievement had to await, for its clearest form, the operas of Gluck. So, in the pendulum of life, the Italian conquest of Europe with melody ended when, in 1774, Gluck produced at Paris an *Iphigénie en Aulide* which subordinated the music to the play. But the conflict between melody and drama went on; Wagner won a battle for drama, Verdi captured new trophies for melody. May neither side win.

VIII. ALFIERI

There were no Dantes in this age, but there was Parini in verse, Filangieri in prose, and Alfieri in drama, prose, and poetry.

Giuseppe Parini struggled up from penury, lived by copying manuscripts, and entered print (1752) with a small volume of *versi sciolti*—blank verse. He took holy orders as a means of eating, and even then had to earn his bread by tutoring; there was a plethora of priests in Italy. His poverty sharpened his pen to satire. Contemplating the idleness and pomp of many Italian nobles, he conceived the idea of describing a typical day in such a blueblood's life. In 1763 he issued the first part as *Il mattino* (*Morning*); two years later he added *Il mezzogiorno* (*Noon*); he completed, but never lived to publish, *Il vespro* (*Evening*) and *La notte* (*Night*); together they formed a substantial satire, which he called *Il giorno* (*The Day*). Count von Firmian showed real nobility by appointing the poet-priest editor of the Milan *Gazzetta*, and professor of belles-lettres in the Scuola Palatina. Parini welcomed the French Revolution, and was rewarded by Napoleon with a place on the municipal council of Milan. The odes that he composed between 1757 and 1795 are among the minor classics of Italian literature. We get a faint echo of him in translation, as in this sonnet, written as a lover rather than a priest:

> Benignant Sleep, that, on soft pinion sped,
>   Dost wing through darkling night thy noiseless way,
>   And fleeting multitudes of dreams display
> To weariness reposed on quiet bed:
> Go where my Phillis doth her gentle head
>   And blooming cheek on peaceful pillow lay;
>   And, while the body sleeps, her soul affray
> With dismal shape from thy enchantment bred;
>   So like unto mine own that form be made—
> Pallor so dim disfiguring its face—
>   That she may waken by compassion swayed.
> If this thou wilt accomplish of thy grace,
>   A double wreath of poppies I will braid,
> And silently upon thine altar place.[88]

To this posy let us add, as a flower from the Italian Enlightenment, a passage from Gaetano Filangieri's *La scienza della legislazione* (1780–85), inspired by Beccaria and Voltaire:

> The philosopher should not be the inventor of systems but the apostle of truth. . . . So long as the evils that affect humanity are still uncured; so long as error and prejudice are allowed to perpetuate them; so long as the truth is limited to the few and the privileged, and concealed from the greater part of the human species and from the kings; so long will it remain the duty of the philosopher to preach the truth, to sustain it, to promote it, and to illuminate it. Even if the lights he scatters are not useful in his own century and people, they will surely be useful in another country and century. Citizen of every place and every age, the philosopher has the world for his country, the earth for his school, and posterity will be his disciples.[89]

The age was summed up in Alfieri: the revolt against superstition, the exaltation of pagan heroes, the denunciation of tyranny, the acclaim of the French Revolution, the revulsion from its excesses, and the cry for Italian freedom—all added to a romance of illicit love and noble fidelity. He recorded this passionate career in *Vita di Vittorio Alfieri . . . scritta da esso* —his life "written by himself," and continued to within five months of his death. It is one of the great autobiographies, as revealing as Rousseau's *Confessions*. It begins disarmingly: "Speaking—and, still more, writing—of oneself is beyond all doubt the offspring of the great love one has for oneself." Thereafter there is no mask of modesty, and no sign of dishonesty.

> I was born in the city of Asti in Piedmont January 17, 1749, of noble, opulent, and respectable parents. I notice these circumstances as fortunate ones for the following reasons. Noble birth was of great service to me, . . . for it enabled me, without incurring the imputation of base or invidious motives, to disparage nobility for its own sake, to unveil its follies, its abuses, and its crimes. . . . Opulence made me incorruptible, and free to serve only the truth.[90]

His father died when Vittorio was an infant; his mother married again. The boy retired into himself, brooded, meditated suicide at the age of eight, but could not hit upon any comfortable way. An uncle took charge of him, and sent him, aged nine, to be educated at the Academy of Turin. There he was served and bullied by a valet. His teachers tried to break his will as the first stage in making a man of him, but their tyranny inflamed his pride and his longing for liberty. "The class in philosophy . . . was something to send one to sleep standing upright."[91] The death of his uncle left him, aged fourteen, master of a large fortune.

Having secured the consent of the King of Sardinia as a prerequisite to foreign travel, he set out in 1766 on a three-year tour of Europe. He fell in love with sundry women, French literature, and the English constitution. The reading of Montesquieu, Voltaire, and Rousseau destroyed his inherited theology, and began his hatred of the Roman Church—though he had only recently kissed the foot of Clement XIII, "a fine old man of venerable majesty."[92] In The Hague he became desperately enamored of a married woman; she smiled and went away; again he contemplated suicide; this was the age of Werther, and suicide was in the air. Again finding the idea more attractive in prospect than in execution, he returned to Piedmont, but was so unhappy in an atmosphere of political and religious conformity that he resumed his travels (1769).

Now he went through Germany, Denmark, and Sweden—where, he tells us, he liked the scenery, the people, and even the winter. Then to Russia, which he despised, seeing in Catherine the Great only a crowned criminal; he refused to be presented to her. He enjoyed Frederick's Prussia no better; he hurried on to bravely republican Holland, and to an England that was trying to teach George III to keep out of the government. He cuckolded an Englishman, fought a duel, was wounded. He caught syphilis in Spain,[93] and returned to Turin (1772) to be cured.

In 1774 he was sufficiently recovered to undertake his second great romance, with a woman nine years his senior. They quarreled and parted, and he cleansed her from his dreams by writing a play, *Cleopatra*; what could be more dramatic than two triumvirs, a queen, a battle, and an asp? The piece was produced at Turin June 16, 1775, "amid applause, for two successive nights"; then he withdrew it for alterations. He itched now "with a very noble and elevated passion for fame." He reread Plutarch and the Italian classics, and studied Latin again to delve into Seneca's tragedies; in these readings he found themes and form for his dramas. He would restore ancient heroes and virtues as Winckelmann had restored ancient art.

Meanwhile (1777) he was writing his treatise *Della tirannide*, but it contained such hot indictments of state and Church that he could not think of publishing it; it came to print only in 1787. An almost religious fervor animated it:

> Not pressing poverty, . . . not the slavish idleness in which Italy lies prostrate, no, these were not the reasons which directed my mind to the true lofty honor of assailing false empires with my pen. A fierce god, a god unknown, has ever been at my back scourging me on since my earliest years. . . . My free

> spirit can never find peace or truce unless I pen harsh pages for the destruction of tyrants.[94]

He defined tyrants as

> all those who by force or fraud—or even by the will of the people or the nobles —obtain the absolute reins of government, and believe themselves to be, or are, above the law. . . . Tyranny is the name that must be applied . . . to any government in which he who is charged with the execution of the laws may make, destroy, break, interpret, hinder, or suspend them with assurance of impunity.[95]

Alfieri considered tyrannical all European governments except the Dutch Republic and the constitutional monarchies of England and Sweden. Influenced by Machiavelli, he idealized the Roman Republic, and hoped that revolution would soon establish republics in Europe. He thought the best thing any minister of a tyrant could do would be to encourage him to such excesses of tyranny as would drive the people to revolt.[96] In its first years a revolution is justified in using violence to prevent the revival of the tyranny:

> As political, like religious, opinions can never be completely changed without the use of much violence, so every new government is at first unfortunately compelled to be cruelly stern, sometimes even unjust, so as to convince, or possibly coerce, those who neither desire, understand, love, nor consent to innovations.[97]

Though he himself was a noble as Conte di Cortemilia, Alfieri condemned hereditary aristocracy as a form or instrument of tyranny. He applied the same condemnation to all organized religions of authority. He admitted that "Christianity has contributed no little to softening universal customs," but he noted "many acts of stupid and ignorant ferocity" in Christian rulers "from Constantine to Charles V."[98] In general,

> the Christian religion is almost incompatible with freedom. . . . The pope, the Inquisition, purgatory, confession, indissoluble marriage, and the celibacy of priests—these are the six rings of the sacred chain which binds the profane one [the state] so much more tightly that it becomes ever heavier and more unbreakable.[99]

Alfieri so hated tyranny that he advised against having children, or ever marrying, in a despotic state. Instead of children, but with comparable Italian fertility, he produced fourteen tragedies between 1775 and 1783, all in blank verse, all classical in structure and form, all excoriating tyranny with declamatory passion, and enthroning liberty as nobler than life. So in *La congiura dei Pazzi* his sympathy was with the attempt of the conspirators to overthrow Lorenzo and Giuliano de' Medici; in *Bruto primo* and *Bruto secondo* he gave short shrift to Tarquin and Caesar; in *Filippo* he was all for Carlos against the King of Spain; in *Maria Stuarda*, however, he found more tyranny in the Scottish chieftains than in the Catholic Queen. Criticized for bending history to his thesis, he defended himself:

> More than one malicious tongue will be heard to say . . . that I never depict anything but tyrants, in too many pages devoid of sweetness; that my blood-red pen, dipped in venom, always strikes a single and monotonous note; and

that my surly Muse rouses no man from evil servitude, but makes many laugh. These complaints will not divert my spirit from so sublime a purpose, nor deter my art, though weak and inadequate to so great a need. Nor will my words ever be scattered to the winds if true men are born after us who will hold liberty vital to life.[100]

Only next to his passion for freedom was his love for the Countess of Albany. Daughter of Gustavus Adolphus, Prince of Stolberg-Gedern, she married (1774) Prince Charles Edward Stuart, the Young Pretender, who now called himself the Count of Albany. Once so gallant as Bonnie Prince Charlie, he had taken to drink and mistresses to forget his defeats. The marriage, arranged by the French court, proved childless and unhappy. Apparently the Countess herself was not without fault. Alfieri met her in 1777, pitied her, loved her. To be near her, free to help her and follow her fortunes without the irksome necessity of securing royal permission for every move across the frontier, he gave up his citizenship in Piedmont, transferred most of his fortune and estate to his sister, and moved to Florence (1778). He was now twenty-nine years old.

The Countess returned his love with a discreet delicacy that observed all public decorum. In 1780, when her husband's drunken violence endangered her life, she retired to a convent, and later to the home of her brother-in-law in Rome. "I remained in Florence like an abandoned orphan," wrote Alfieri, "and it was then that I became fully convinced . . . that without her I did not so much as half exist; for I found myself almost completely incapable of doing any good work."[101] Soon he went to Rome, where he was allowed to see his inamorata now and then; but the brother-in-law, under priestly guidance, opposed his efforts to secure an annulment of her marriage. (Hence his Miltonic plea for divorce in *Della tirannide*.[102]) Finally the brother-in-law forbade him any further visit to the Countess. He left Rome, and tried to distract himself with travel and with horses—which were his "third love," next to the Muses and "my lady." In 1784 she won a legal separation. She moved to Colmar in Alsace; there Alfieri joined her, and thenceforth they lived in unwedded union until the death of the husband allowed them to marry. Alfieri wrote of his love with an ecstasy that recalled Dante's *Vita nuova*:

> This, my fourth and last fever of love, was . . . quite different from those of my first three liaisons. In those I had not found myself agitated by any passion of intellect counterbalancing, and commingled with, the passion of the heart. This had indeed less impetuosity and fervor, but proved more lasting and more deeply felt. The strength of my passion was such that it . . . dominated my every emotion and thought, and it will never henceforth be extinguished in me but with life itself. It was clear to me . . . that in her I had found a true woman, for instead of her proving, like all ordinary women, an obstacle to attainment of literary fame—one who set up occupations of utility and cheapened . . . one's thoughts—I found in her, for every good action, both encouragement and comfort and good example. Recognizing and appreciating a treasure so unique, I gave myself to her with utter abandon. Certainly I was not wrong, for now, more than twelve years later, . . . my passion for her increases in proportion as those transitory charms (which are not her enduring

self) by time's decree fade away. But concentrated upon her, my mind is elevated, softened, and with every day made better; and as regards hers I am bold
to say that the same is true, and that from me she may draw support and
strength.[103]

So spurred on, he wrote more tragedies, some comedies, and occasional
poetry. He had already composed five odes entitled "America libera." In
1788 the lovers moved to Paris, where Alfieri supervised the publication of
his works by Beaumarchais' press at Kehl on the Rhine. When the Bastille
fell Alfieri, all fiery for freedom, hailed the Revolution as the dawn of a
happier age for the world. But soon the excesses of the Revolution disgusted
a soul whose conception of liberty was aristocratic, demanding freedom from
mobs and majorities as well as from popes and kings. On August 18, 1792,
he and the Countess left Paris with such possessions as they could take in two
carriages. They were stopped at the city gates by a crowd that questioned
their right to leave. Alfieri "jumped out of the coach amongst the mob,
brandishing all my seven passports, and started in shouting and making a
row, . . . which is always the way to get the better of Frenchmen."[104] They
drove on to Calais and Brussels; there they learned that the Revolutionary
authorities in Paris had ordered the arrest of the Countess. They hurried on
to Italy, and settled in Florence. Now Alfieri composed his *Misogallo*, hot
with hatred of France and its "crowd of ill-begotten slaves."[105]

In 1799 the French Revolutionary army captured Florence. Alfieri and
the Countess took refuge in a suburban villa until the invaders departed. The
excitement of these years weakened and aged him; ending his autobiography
in 1802, aged fifty-three, he spoke of himself as already old. After bequeathing all his goods to the Countess, he died at Florence on October 7, 1803,
and was buried in the Church of Santa Croce. There in 1810 the Countess
raised to him a massive monument by Canova; she posed for the figure of
Italy mourning over the tomb. She joined her lover there in 1824.

Italy honors Alfieri as Il Vate d'Italia, prophet of the Risorgimento that
freed her from alien and ecclesiastical rule. His dramas, though strident and
monotone, were an invigorating advance upon the sentimental tragedies that
had been offered to the Italian stage before him. From his *Filippo,* his *Saul,*
his *Mirra* the soul of Italy prepared for Mazzini and Garibaldi. His *Della
tirannide* was not confined to foreign publication at Kehl (1787) and Paris
(1800); it was printed in Milan (1800) and other Italian cities in 1802,
1803, 1805, 1809, 1848, 1849, 1860; it became for Italy what Paine's *Rights
of Man* (1791) had been for France, England, and America. Alfieri was the
beginning of the Romantic movement in Italy, a Byron before Byron,
preaching the emancipation of minds and states. After him Italy *had* to be
free.

CHAPTER XIII

The Enlightenment in Austria

1756–90

I. THE NEW EMPIRE

STRICTLY, *Austria* designates a nation; loosely it may stand for the empire of which Austria was the head. Formally, till 1806, this was the Holy Roman Empire, which had included Germany, Bohemia, Poland, Hungary, and parts of Italy and France. But nationalistic aims had so weakened Imperial allegiance that what now (1756) survived was really an Austro-Hungarian Empire, embracing Austria, Styria, Carinthia, Carniola, the Tirol, Hungary, Bohemia, the Catholic archbishoprics of Cologne, Trier, and Mainz, diverse and varying parts of Italy, and, since 1713, the formerly Spanish, now Austrian, Netherlands—approximately the Belgium of today.

Hungary, with a population of some five million souls, was proudly feudal. Four fifths of the soil were owned by Magyar nobles, and were tilled by serfs; taxes fell only upon the peasants and the German or Slav burghers of the towns. The new empire had had its legal birth in 1687, when the Hungarian nobles renounced their ancient right of electing their king, and acknowledged the Hapsburg emperors as their sovereigns. Maria Theresa, following Bourbon strategy, invited the leading Hungarian magnates to her court, gave them offices, titles, and ribbons, and lulled them into accepting Imperial law for their domains, and Vienna for their capital. In generous response the Empress commissioned Lukas von Hildebrandt to draw up plans for governmental buildings in Buda; the work was begun in 1769, and was renewed in 1894, giving the old capital one of the most impressive royal structures in the world. Rivaling the Queen, rich Hungarian nobles built lordly châteaux along the Danube or in their mountain retreats; so Prince Pál Esterházy built a family seat at Eisenstadt (1663–72), and Prince Miklós József Esterházy built in Renaissance style, some thirty miles away, the new Schloss Esterházy (1764–66). Here were 126 guest rooms, two great halls for receptions and balls, a rich collection of art, and, nearby, a library of 7,500 volumes, and a theater with four hundred seats. Around the palace a vast swamp was transformed into gardens decorated with grottoes, temples, and statuary, with hothouses, orangeries, and game preserves. Said a French traveler: "There is no place—perhaps excepting Versailles—that equals this castle in splendor." Here came painters, sculptors, actors, singers, virtuosi; here, for a full generation, Haydn conducted, composed, and longed for a larger world.

Bohemia, which is now the Czech part of Czechoslovakia, did not fare so well under Maria Theresa's rule. It had withdrawn from history after the Thirty Years' War, its national spirit broken by foreign rule, and by a Catholic creed imposed upon a people that had once known Jan Hus and Jerome of Prague. Its eight million inhabitants suffered the wounds of war in the repeated conflicts between Prussia and Austria, and its historic capital changed hands again and again as its alien Queen passed from defeat to victory to defeat. Bohemia had to content itself with an independence of culture and taste; it developed its own composers, like Georg Benda, and Prague distinguished itself by giving a hearty reception to the première of Mozart's *Don Giovanni* (1787), which Vienna later damned with faint applause.

In the Austrian Netherlands the struggle of local dignitaries to retain their traditional authority was more successful than in Bohemia; it was to cloud with tragedy the last days of the "revolutionary Emperor." Those seven provinces—Brabant (which included Brussels, Antwerp, and Louvain), Luxembourg, Limburg, Flanders, Hainaut, Namur, and Gelders—had an ancient and prestigious history, and the nobles who ruled their four million souls were jealous of the privileges that had survived so many centuries of trial. "Society" displayed its fashions, gambled its gains, and sometimes drank the waters, as well as the wines, at Spa in the neighboring episcopate of Liége. The flower of that society in this age was Prince Charles-Joseph de Ligne, whom Brussels gave to the world in 1735. He was tutored by several abbés, "only one of whom believed in God"; he himself was "devout for a fortnight"[1] in this strongly Catholic country. He fought with distinction in the Seven Years' War, served Joseph II as counselor and intimate friend, joined the Russian army in 1787, accompanied Catherine the Great in her "progress" to the Crimea, built himself a luxurious château and art gallery near Brussels, wrote thirty-four volumes of *Mélanges*, impressed even the French with the perfection of his manners, and amused the cosmopolitan circles of Europe with his philosophic wit.*

It was this complex empire, stretching from the Carpathians to the Rhine, which for forty years submitted to one of the great women of history.

II. MARIA THERESA

We have seen her in war; there she yielded only to Frederick and Pitt in military statesmanship, in scope of view and pertinacity of purpose, in courage confronting defeat. Said Frederick in 1752: "Except the Queen of Hungary and the King of Sardinia [Charles Emmanuel I], whose genius triumphed over a bad education, all the princes of Europe are only illustrious imbeciles."[3] Elizabeth I of England before her, and Catherine II of Russia after her, excelled her in the art of rule; no other queens. Frederick thought her "ambitious and vengeful,"[4] but did he expect her to seek no redress for his rape of Silesia? The Goncourts saw in her "a good average brain with a

* "Mme. de Lucchesini . . . was able to listen, which is not as easy as many think, and no fool ever knew how to do it."[2]

loving heart, an exalted sense of duty, astonishing powers of work, an imposing presence and exceptional charm; . . . a true mother of her people."[5] She was the soul of kindness to all who did not attack her empire or her faith; note her warm reception of the Mozart family in 1768.[6] She was a good mother to her children; her letters to them are models of tenderness and wise counsel; had Joseph listened to her he might not have died a failure; had Marie Antoinette followed her advice she might have escaped the guillotine.

Maria Theresa was not an "enlightened despot." She was no despot; Voltaire thought "she established her reign in all hearts by an affability and popularity which few of her ancestors had ever possessed; she banished form and restraint from her court; . . . she never refused audience to anyone, and no person ever departed from her presence dissatisfied."[7] She was far from enlightened in Voltaire's sense; she issued intolerant decrees against Jews and Protestants, and remained a devout Catholic to the end. She saw with tremors the infiltration of religious skepticism into Vienna from London and Paris; she tried to stem the tide by a fervent censorship of books and periodicals, and she forbade the teaching of English "because of the dangerous character of this language in respect of its corrupting religious and ethical principles."[8]

And yet she was not untouched by the anticlericalism of her councilors and her son. They pointed out that the territorial and other wealth of the clergy was rapidly increasing through priestly suggestions that moribund patients might expiate their sins and propitiate God by bequeathing property to the Church; at this rate the Church—already a state within a state—must soon be master of the government. Convents and monasteries were multiplying, removing men and women from active life, and excluding more and more property from taxation. Young women were being induced to take conventual vows before they were old enough to realize the significance of these lifelong dedications. Education was so completely controlled by the clergy that every growing mind was being molded into giving its supreme allegiance to the Church rather than to the state. The Empress so far yielded to these arguments as to order some substantial reforms. She forbade the presence of ecclesiastics at the making of wills. She reduced the number of religious establishments, and ordered the taxation of all religious property. No vows were to be taken by persons under twenty-one years of age. Churches and convents were no longer to afford asylum to criminals by "right of sanctuary." No papal brief was to be recognized in the Austrian realm until it had received Imperial consent. The Inquisition was subjected to governmental supervision, and was in effect suppressed. Education was reorganized under the direction of Gerhard van Swieten (the Queen's physician) and Abbot Franz Rautenstrauch; in many professorships Jesuits were replaced by laymen;[9] the University of Vienna was brought under laic administration and state control; the curriculum there and elsewhere was revised to widen instruction in science and history.[10] So the pious Empress anticipated in some measure the ecclesiastical reforms of her skeptical son.

She was a model of morality in an age when the courts of Christendom rivaled Constantinople in polygamy. The Church might have used her as an argument for orthodoxy, except that Augustus III, the Catholic King of Poland, and Louis XV of France were the most avid pluralists of all. The Viennese aristocracy did not follow her example. Count Arco fled to Switzerland with his mistress; Countess Esterházy eloped to France with Count von der Schulenburg; Prince von Kaunitz took his current mistress with him in his coach, and when the Empress remonstrated he told her, "Madame, I have come here to speak about your affairs, not mine."[11] Maria Theresa looked with disgust upon this laxity, and issued Draconic decrees to enforce the Sixth Commandment among the people. She ordered that women's skirts should be lengthened at the bottom and blouses at the top.[12] She organized a corps of Chastity Commissioners empowered to arrest any woman suspected of prostitution. Casanova complained that "the bigotry and narrow-mindedness of the Empress made life difficult, especially for foreigners."[13]

A great part of her success as a ruler was due to her able ministers. She accepted their lead and earned their devotion. Prince von Kaunitz, despite the failure of his "reversal of alliances," remained in charge of foreign affairs, and served the Empire well for forty years. Ludwig Haugwitz transformed internal administration, and Rudolf Chotek reorganized the economy. These three men did for Austria what Richelieu and Colbert had done for France; in effect they created a new state, immeasurably stronger than the disordered realm that Maria Theresa had inherited.

Haugwitz began by rebuilding the Imperial army. He believed that this had collapsed in the face of Prussian discipline because it was composed of independent units raised and commanded by semi-independent nobles; he proposed and created a standing army of 108,000 men under unified training and central control. To finance this force he recommended that nobles and clergy, as well as commoners, be taxed; nobles and clergy protested; the Empress braved their wrath and laid upon them a property and an income tax. Frederick praised his enemy as an administrator: "She put her finances in such order as her predecessors had never attained, and not only recouped by good management what she had lost by ceding provinces to the Kings of Prussia and Sardinia, but she considerably augmented her revenue."[14] Haugwitz went on to co-ordinate the law, to free the judiciary from domination by the nobles, and to bring the feudal lords under control by the central government. A new and unified legal code, the Theresianische Halsgerichtsordnung, was proclaimed in 1768.

Meanwhile Chotek strove to invigorate the sluggish economy. Industry was hampered by monopolies that favored nobles, and by guild regulations which remained in force till 1774; nevertheless Linz had woolen mills with a total of 26,000 employees, Vienna excelled in glass and porcelain, and Bohemia led the Empire in metallurgical operations. Both Austria and Hungary had productive mines; Galicia had great salt deposits, and Hungary mined seven million gulden' worth of gold per year. Chotek protected these industries with tariffs, for Austria, frequently at war, had to be made self-sufficient in necessary goods; free trade, like democracy, is a luxury of security and peace.

Even so, the Empire remained agricultural and feudal. Like Frederick, the Empress, facing war, dared not risk social disruption by attacking the entrenched nobility. She gave a good example by abolishing serfdom on her own lands, and she imposed upon the haughty magnates of Hungary a decree empowering the peasant to move, marry, and bring up his children as he liked, and to appeal from his lord to the county court.[15] Despite these mitigations the peasantry in Hungary and Bohemia was almost as poor as in Russia. In Vienna the lower class lived in traditional poverty, amid lordly palaces, elaborate operas, and magnificent churches dispensing hope.

Vienna was beginning to rival Paris and its environs in royal splendor. Schönbrunn ("Beautiful Spring"), just outside the city, included 495 acres of gardens, laid out (1753–75) in emulation of Versailles, with straight towering hedges, fanciful grottoes, symmetrical ponds, lovely statues by Donner and Beyer, a "Menagerie," a botanical garden, and, on a hill in the background, a "Gloriette" built in 1775 by Johann von Hohenberg—a colonnaded arcade in chaste Romanesque. The Schönbrunn palace itself, an immense congeries of 1,441 rooms, had been designed by Johann Bernhard Fischer von Erlach in 1695, but had been left unfinished in 1705; Maria Theresa engaged Niccolo Pacassi to remodel it; work was resumed in 1744, and was completed in the year of the Empress' death (1780). Within was a Great Gallery 141 feet long, with a rococo ceiling painted by Gregorio Guglielmi (1761). Schönbrunn housed the court from spring till fall.

The court numbered now some 2,400 souls. Two hundred and fifty stewards and grooms were needed to care for the horses and carriages. Altogether the maintenance of the palace and its grounds cost 4,300,000 gulden per year.[16] The Empress herself practiced economy, and excused the splendor of her palace as necessary to the histrionics of royal rule. She offset the luxury of her court with the extent of her charities. A generation later Mme. de Staël reported of Austria: "The charitable elements there are regulated with great order and liberality; private and public beneficence is directed with a fine spirit of justice . . . Everything in this country bears the mark of a parental, wise, and religious government."[17]

Despite poverty there was hardly any begging, and relatively little crime.[18] The people found their simple pleasures in exchanging visits, rubbing elbows in the squares, cooling their heat in shady parks, promenading on the tree-lined Hauptallee of the Prater, picnicking in the countryside, or, at their lowest, thrilling to ferocious fights arranged between famished animals. Prettier were the dances, and, above all, the formal minuet; in this the man and the woman rarely touched each other, every movement was governed by tradition and rule, and was performed with restraint and grace. Music was so large a part of Viennese life that it commands a chapter to itself.

By comparison literature was mediocre and immature. Austria, sacerdotally controlled, had no share in the Sturm und Drang movement that excited Germany. Maria Theresa was no patron of learning or belles-lettres. There were no literary salons in Vienna, no mingling of authors, artists, and philosophers with women, nobles, and statesmen as in France. It was a static society, with the charm and comfort of old and calculable ways, saved from the turmoil of revolution but missing the zest of challenging ideas. The Viennese newspapers, carefully censored, were dull impediments to thought, perhaps excepting the *Wiener Zeitung*, founded in 1780. The Viennese theaters were given to opera for the aristocracy and the court, or to coarse comedies for the general public. Leopold Mozart wrote that "the Viennese public, as a whole, has no love of anything serious or sensible; they cannot even understand it; and their theaters furnish abundant proof that nothing but utter trash, such as dances, burlesques, harlequinades, ghost tricks, and devil's antics will go down with them."[19] But Papa Mozart had been disappointed with Vienna's reception of his son.

Over this medley of actors, musicians, populace, serfs, barons, courtiers, and ecclesiastics the great Empress ruled with maternal watchfulness and solicitude. Her consort, Francis of Lorraine, had been crowned emperor in 1745, but his talents inclined him to business rather than government. He organized manufactures, provided the Austrian armies with uniforms, horses, and arms, sold flour and provender to Frederick while Frederick was at war with Austria (1756),[20] and left the management of the Empire to his wife. Matrimonially, however, he insisted on his rights, and the Empress, loving him despite his adulteries,[21] bore him sixteen children. She brought them up with love and severity, scolded them frequently, and gave them such doses of morality and wisdom that Marie Antoinette was glad to escape to Versailles, and Joseph flirted with philosophy. She plotted skillfully to secure cozy berths for her other offspring: she made her daughter Maria Carolina queen of Naples, her son Leopold grand duke of Tuscany, her son Ferdinand governor of Lombardy. She devoted herself to preparing her eldest son, Joseph, for the formidable responsibilities that she would bequeath to him; and she watched with anxiety his development through education and marriage, through the storms of philosophy and the bereavements of love, to the time when, in a transport of affection and humility, she raised him up, aged twenty-four, to sit beside her on the Imperial throne.

III. JOSEPH GROWING: 1741–65

She had entrusted his education to the Jesuits, but, anticipating Rousseau, she had asked that he be taught as if he were amusing himself.[22] When he was four years old she complained that "my Joseph can't obey";[23] obedience was not amusing. "He has already a high conception of his station," reported the Prussian ambassador when Joseph was six. Maria Theresa resorted to discipline and enforced piety, but the boy found religious observances irksome, and resented the importance attached to the supernatural world; this one, being in part his patrimony, sufficed. He soon tired of orthodoxy, and discovered the fascination of Voltaire. Otherwise he cared little for literature, but he took eagerly to science, economics, history, and international law. He never outgrew his boyhood haughtiness and pride, but he developed into a handsome and alert youth, whose faults did not yet alienate him from his mother. On his travels he wrote to her letters of warm filial tenderness.

At the age of twenty he was made a member of the Staatsrath, or State Council. Soon (1761) he drew up, and submitted to his mother, a paper outlining his ideas on political and religious reform; these remained the essence of his policies to the end of his life. He advised the Empress to extend religious toleration, to reduce the power of the Church, to relieve the peasantry of feudal burdens, and to allow greater freedom in the movement of goods and ideas.[24] He asked her to spend less on the court and its ceremonies, and more on the army. Every member of the government should work for his salary, and the nobles should be taxed like anybody else.[25]

Meanwhile he was learning another side of life. Louis XV, as part of the reversal of alliances, had offered his granddaughter Isabella of Parma as a fit bride for the Archduke. Joseph seemed fortunate: Isabella was eighteen, beautiful, and of good character except for a turn to melancholy. In June, 1760, she came across the Alps in a caravan drawn by three hundred horses; the marriage was celebrated with a sumptuous feast, and Joseph was happy to have so fair a creature in his arms. But Isabella took to heart the theology she had learned; dowered with all the gifts of life, she found no joy in them, but longed for death. "Death is beneficent," she wrote to her sister in 1763. "Never have I thought of it more than now. Everything arouses in me the desire to die soon. God knows my wish to desert a life which insults Him every day. . . . If it were permitted to kill oneself I would already have done it."[26] In November, 1763, she was stricken with smallpox; she gave no encouragement to the physicians who tried to cure her; in five days she was dead. Joseph, who loved her deeply, never recovered from this blow.

A few months later he was taken by his father to Frankfurt-am-Main to be crowned King of the Romans—the traditional step to the Imperial throne. There, March 26, 1764 (young Goethe in the crowd), he was elected, and on April 3 he was crowned. He did not enjoy the prolonged ritual, the religious services, the orations; he complained, in a letter to his mother, of the "trash and idiocies which we had to listen to all day. . . . It costs me great efforts to refrain from telling these gentlemen to their faces how idiotically they act and talk." Through it all he kept thinking of the wife he had lost. "With my heart full of pain I must appear as if enraptured. . . . I love solitude, . . . and yet I must live among people. . . . I have to chatter all day and say pretty nothings."[27] He must have concealed his feelings well, for his brother Leopold reported that "our King of the Romans is always charming, always in good humor, gay, gracious, and polite, and he wins all hearts."[28]

On his return to Vienna he was informed that he must marry again; the orderly continuity of the government seemed to require the continuity of the Hapsburg family. Kaunitz chose a wife for him, Josepha of Bavaria, for Kaunitz was hoping to add Bavaria to the Austrian realm. Joseph signed the proposal of marriage that Kaunitz had composed for him, sent it off, and wrote to the Duke of Parma (father of Isabella) a description of Josepha as "a small squat figure without the charm of youth; pimples and red spots on her face; . . . repulsive teeth. . . . Judge for yourself what this decision has cost me. . . . Have pity on me, and do not fail in your love for a son who, although he has another wife, has eternally buried in his heart the image of his adored."[29] Joseph and Josepha were married early in 1765. She tried to be a good wife, but he abstained from her publicly and privately. She suffered in silence, and died of smallpox in 1767. Joseph refused to marry again. Now, with a tragic mixture of coldness and devotion, of idealism and arrogance, he gave the remainder of his life to government.

IV. MOTHER AND SON: 1765–80

When the Emperor Francis I died (August 18, 1765) Maria Theresa was for a time broken in body and mind. She joined his mistress in mourning him; "My dear Princess," she said, "we have both lost much."[30] She cut off her hair, gave away her wardrobe, discarded all jewelry, and wore mourning till her death. She turned the government over to Joseph, and spoke of retiring to a convent; then, fearful that her impetuous heir should prove unfit to rule, she returned to public affairs, and signed on November 17 an official declaration of co-regency. She kept supreme authority over the internal affairs of Austria, Hungary, and Bohemia; Joseph, as emperor, was to have charge of foreign affairs and the army, and, less fully, of administration and finance; but in foreign affairs he accepted the guidance of Kaunitz, and in all fields his decisions were subject to review by the Empress. His eagerness for power was tempered by his respect and love for his mother. When (1767) she nearly died of smallpox he seldom left her side, and astonished the court with the depth of his anxiety and grief. These three attacks of the disease upon the royal family at last persuaded the Austrian physicians to introduce inoculation.

The loving son troubled his mother with the urgency of his ideas for reform. In November, 1765, he sent to the Council of State a memorandum that must have startled its readers:

> To retain more able men capable of serving the state, I shall decree—whatever the Pope and all the monks in the world may say—that none of my subjects shall embrace an ecclesiastical career before . . . the age of twenty-five. The sad results, for both sexes, often caused by early vows should convince us of the utility of this arrangement, quite apart from reasons of state. . . .
> Religious toleration, a mild censorship, no prosecution for morals, and no espionage in private affairs should be maxims of government. . . . Religion and morals are unquestionably among the principal objects of a sovereign, but his zeal should not extend to correcting and converting foreigners. In faith and morals violence is unavailing; conviction is needed. As for the censorship, we should be very careful about what is printed and sold, but to search pockets and trunks, especially of a foreigner, is an excess of zeal. It would be easy to prove that, despite the now vigorous censorship, every prohibited book is now avail-

> able at Vienna, and everyone, attracted by the veto, can buy it at double the
> price. . . .
>   Industry and commerce are to be prompted through the prohibition of all
> foreign goods except spices, through the abolition of monopolies, the establish-
> ment of schools of commerce, and an end to the notion that the pursuit of busi-
> ness is incompatible with aristocracy. . . .
>   Liberty of marriage should be introduced, even of what we now call *mésal-
> liances*. Neither the divine law nor the law of nature forbids it. Only prejudice
> makes us believe that I am worth more because my grandfather was a count, or
> because I possess a parchment signed by Charles V. From our parents we in-
> herit only physical existence; thus king, count, bourgeois, peasant, it is exactly
> the same.[31]

Maria Theresa and the councilors must have smelled the breath of Voltaire
or the *Encyclopédie* in these proposals. The young Emperor had to proceed
slowly, but he advanced. He transferred to the Treasury twenty million
gulden—in cash, shares, and property—bequeathed him in his father's will,
and he refunded the national debt at a charge of only four instead of six per
cent. He sold the hunting preserves of the late Emperor, and ordered the
slaughter of the wild boars that had served as targets for the hunters and
as destroyers of peasant crops. Over the protests of nobles, but with the
approval of his mother, he opened the Prater and other parks to the public.[32]

In 1769 he shocked Empress and court by going to Neisse, in Silesia, and
spending three days (August 25–27) in friendly discussion with Austria's
most hated enemy, Frederick the Great. He had taken from the King of
Prussia the conception of a monarch as "the first servant of the state." He
admired Frederick's subordination of Church to state, and toleration of religious varieties; he envied the Prussian military organization and law reform.
Both men felt that it was time to sink their differences in a protective accord
against the rising strength of Russia. Joseph wrote to his mother: "After
supper . . . we smoked, and talked about Voltaire."[33] The King, now fifty-
seven, formed no high opinion of the Emperor, now twenty-eight. "The
young prince," he wrote, "affected a frankness which suited him well. . . .
He is desirous of learning, but he has had no patience to instruct himself. His
exalted position makes him superficial. . . . Boundless ambition devours
him. . . . He has enough taste to read Voltaire and appreciate his merits."[34]

The alarming success of Catherine II in Russia led Kaunitz to arrange a
second conference with Frederick. King, Emperor, and Prince met at Neustadt, in Moravia, September 3–7, 1770. Joseph must have developed considerably during the year, for Frederick now wrote to Voltaire: "Brought up in
a bigoted court, the Emperor has discarded superstition; reared in splendor,
he has adopted simple manners; fed with incense, he is modest; eager for
glory, he sacrifices his ambitions to filial duty."[35]

These two meetings were part of Joseph's education in politics. He added
to it by visiting his dominions and examining their problems and possibilities
at first hand. He went not as an emperor but as a common traveler, on horseback. He avoided ceremonies, and put up at inns instead of châteaux. Visiting Hungary in 1764 and 1768, he noted the extreme poverty of the serfs,

and was shocked by seeing, in a field, the corpses of children who had died of hunger. In 1771–72 he saw similar conditions in Bohemia and Moravia; everywhere he heard reports, or saw evidence, of brutal landlords and starving serfs. "The internal situation," he wrote, "is incredible and indescribable; it is heartbreaking."[36] Returning to Vienna, he fumed at the trifling improvements contemplated by the Empress's councilors. "Petty reforms will not do," he said; "the whole must be transformed." He proposed, as a first step, to take over some ecclesiastical lands in Bohemia and build upon them schools, asylums, and hospitals. After much argument he persuaded the Council to issue (1774) an "Urbarian Law" reducing and regulating the amount of serf labor (which the Bohemians called *robota*) due to a feudal lord. The lords of Bohemia and Hungary resisted; the Bohemian serfs rose in disorderly revolt, and were put down by the military. Maria Theresa blamed her son for the turmoil. To her agent in Paris, Mercy d'Argentau, she wrote:

> The Emperor, who pushes his popularity too far, has on his various trips talked too much . . . about religious liberty and peasant emancipation. All this has caused confusion in all our German provinces. . . . It is not only the Bohemian peasant that is to be feared, but also the Moravian, the Styrian, the Austrian; even in our section they dare indulge in the greatest impertinences.[37]

The strain between son and mother increased when (1772) Joseph joined Frederick and Catherine II in the first partition of Poland. She protested against this rape of a friendly (and Catholic) nation; she wept when Joseph and Kaunitz prevailed upon her to add her signature to the agreement, which gave a sector of Poland to Austria. Frederick commented cynically, *"Elle pleure, mais elle prend"* (She weeps, but she takes).[38] Her regret was sincere, as we see from her letter to her son Ferdinand: "How often did I strive to dissociate myself from an action which sullies the whole of my reign! God grant that I shall not be held responsible for it in another world. It weighs upon my heart, tortures my brain, and embitters my days."[39]

She contemplated the character of her son with fear and love. "He likes respect and obedience, regards opposition as distasteful and almost intolerable, . . . and is often inconsiderate. . . . His great and growing vivacity results in a vehement desire to get his way in every detail. . . . My son has a good heart." Once she reproached him bitterly:

> When I am dead I flatter myself that I will live on in your heart, so that the family and the state will not lose by my death. . . . Your imitation [of Frederick] is not flattering. This hero, . . . this conqueror—does he have a single friend? . . . What a life, when there is no humanity! No matter what your talents may be, it is not possible that you have already experienced everything. Beware of falling into spitefulness! Your heart is not yet evil, but it will become so. It is time to no longer take pleasure in all these bon mots, these clever conversations whose only aim is to ridicule others. . . . You are an intellectual coquet. You are only a thoughtless imitator where you think you are an independent thinker.[40]

Joseph revealed his side of the situation in a letter to Leopold:

> Our uncertainties here have reached a pitch you cannot imagine. Tasks accumulate daily, and nothing is done. Every day till five or six, except for a quarter hour for a solitary meal, I am at work; yet nothing happens. Trifling causes, intrigues of which I have long been the dupe, block the way, and meanwhile everything goes to the devil. I make you a present of my position as eldest son.[41]

He scorned the men who had grown old in the service of his mother. Only Kaunitz supported him, but with irritating caution.

The aging Empress heard with trepidation the revolutionary ideas of her son. She told him frankly:

> Among your fundamental principles the most important are: (1) the free exercise of religion, which no Catholic prince can permit without heavy responsibility; (2) the destruction of the nobility [by ending serfdom] . . . ; and (3) the so frequently repeated [advocacy of] liberty in everything. . . . I am too old to accommodate myself to such ideas, and pray to God that my successor will never try them. . . . Toleration, indifferentism, are precisely the means to undermine everything. . . . Without a dominant religion what restraint is there? None. Neither the gallows nor the wheel. . . . I speak politically, not as a Christian. Nothing is so necessary and beneficial as religion. Would you allow everyone to act according to his fancy? If there were no fixed worship, no subjection to the Church, where would we be? Fist law would be the result. . . . I only wish that when I die I can join my ancestors with the consolation that my son will be as great, as religious, as his forefathers, and that he will give up his false arguments, the evil books, and the contact with those who have seduced his spirit at the expense of everything that is precious and sacred, only to establish an imaginary freedom which could . . . only lead to universal destruction.[42]

But if there was one thing Joseph was eager for it was freedom of religion. He may not have been an atheist, as some have thought,[43] but he had been deeply affected by the literature of France. Already in 1763 a group of Austrian intellectuals had formed an Aufklärungspartei, or Party of Enlightenment.[44] In 1772 Gyorgy Bessenyei, of Hungary, published in Vienna a play echoing the ideas of Voltaire; he accepted conversion to Catholicism to please Maria Theresa, but he returned to rationalism after her death.[45] Joseph doubtless knew the remarkable book, *De statu ecclesiae et legitima potestate romani pontificis* (1763), in which a prominent Catholic bishop, under the pseudonym of Febronius, had reasserted the supremacy of general councils over the popes, and the right of each national church to govern itself. The young Emperor saw in the entrenched wealth of the Austrian Church a principal obstacle to economic development, and in the ecclesiastical control of education the main barrier to the maturing of the Austrian mind. In January, 1770, he wrote to Choiseul:

> As regards your plan for getting rid of the Jesuits, you have my complete approval. Don't count too much on my mother; a close attachment to the Jesuits is hereditary in the Hapsburg family. . . . However, you have a friend in Kaunitz, and he does what he likes with the Empress.[46]

Joseph seems to have used his influence in Rome to bring Clement XIV to the final step, and he was well pleased by the papal abolition of the order (1773).[47]

Maria Theresa would have been shocked to see, from her son's letters, how far he had strayed into the camp of the *philosophes*. She did her best to prevent the dissolution of the Society of Jesus, but Kaunitz persuaded her to yield to the view of all the other Catholic powers. "I am disconsolate and in despair about the Jesuits," she wrote to a friend. "I have loved and honored them all my life, and have never seen anything in them but what was edifying."[48] She delayed enforcement of the papal bull by appointing a commission to study it. The Austrian Jesuits had time to remove their cash, valuables, and papers from the country. Jesuit property was confiscated, but the Empress saw to it that the members of the order received pensions, clothing, and diverse gifts.

Joseph's obvious satisfaction over the suppression of the Jesuits widened the gap between mother and son. In December, 1773, he broke under the strain, and begged her to release him from all share in the government. She was dismayed by so startling a proposal, and wrote him a touching appeal for reconciliation:

> I must admit that my abilities, face, hearing, and skill are rapidly deteriorating, and that the weakness which I have dreaded all my life—indecision—is now accompanied by discouragement and lack of faithful servitors. The alienation of yourself and Kaunitz, the death of my loyal advisers, the irreligion, the deterioration of morals, the jargon that everybody uses, and which I do not understand—all this is enough to overwhelm me. I offer you my whole confidence, and ask you to call attention to any mistakes I may make. . . . Help a mother who . . . lives in loneliness, and who will die when she sees all her efforts and sorrows gone to waste. Tell me what you wish and I will do it.[49]

He was reconciled, and for a time the woman who had once fought Frederick to a standstill agreed to co-operate with Frederick's admirer and pupil. Together they applied the confiscated property of the Jesuits to educational reform. In 1774 they issued an "Allgemeine Schulordnung" which effected a basic reorganization of both primary and secondary schools. Grade schools provided compulsory education for all children; they admitted Protestants and Jews as students and teachers, gave religious instruction in each faith to its adherents, but placed control in the hands of state officials; these *Volk-schulen* soon came to be ranked as the best in Europe. Normal schools were established to train teachers; *Hauptschulen* specialized in science and technology, and *Gymnasien* taught Latin and the humanities. The University of Vienna was devoted largely to law, political science, and administration, and served as a nursery for the civil service. Control of education by the Church was replaced by equally rigorous control by the state.

Collaboration of mother and son went on to abolish torture (1776). But the entente was shattered by the events of the following year. Joseph had long thought of visiting Paris—not to see the *philosophes* and bask in the salons, but to study the resources, army, and government of France, to see Marie Antoinette, and to strengthen the ties that so loosely bound the ancient enemies in their frail entente. When Louis XV died, and France seemed about to fall apart, Joseph wrote to Leopold: "I am anxious for my sister;

she will have a difficult part to play."[50] He arrived in Paris April 18, 1777, and courted privacy by pretending to be Count von Falkenstein. He advised the gay young Queen to abandon extravagance, frivolity, and rouge; she listened impatiently. He tried and failed to win Louis XVI to a secret alliance for checking the expansion of Russia.[51] He moved quickly about the capital, and "in a few days he learned more about it than Louis XVI would learn in all his life."[52] He visited the Hôtel-Dieu and did not conceal his astonishment at the inhuman mismanagement of that hospital. The people of Paris were charmed, and the courtiers at Versailles were alarmed, to find the loftiest monarch in Europe dressed like a simple citizen, speaking French like a Frenchman, and meeting all classes with the most unassuming manners. Of literary lights he sought out especially Rousseau and Buffon. He joined a soiree at Mme. Necker's, and met Gibbon, Marmontel, and the Marquise du Deffand; it is a credit to him that he was more embarrassed by her poise and fame than she by his exalted state; blindness is a leveler, for dignities are half composed of garb. He attended a session of the Parlement of Paris and a sitting of the French Academy. The *philosophes* felt that here at last was the enlightened ruler whom they had hoped for as the agent of a peaceful revolution. — After a month in Paris Joseph left for a tour of the provinces, traveling north to Normandy, then along the west coast to Bayonne, then to Toulouse, Montpellier, and Marseilles, then up the Rhone to Lyons and east to Geneva. He passed through Ferney without visiting Voltaire; he did not wish to offend his mother, or too openly ally himself with a man who seemed a devil incarnate to the people of Austria and the King of France.

He was anxious to appease his mother, for during his absence some ten thousand Moravians had abandoned Catholicism for Protestantism, and Maria Theresa—or the Council of State—had reacted to this catastrophe with measures recalling the anti-Huguenot dragonnades under Louis XIV. The leaders of the movement were arrested, Protestant assemblies were dispersed; persistent converts were drafted into the army and assigned to hard labor, and their women were sent to workhouses. When Joseph returned to Vienna he protested to his mother: "To reconvert those people you make soldiers of them, send them to the mines, or use them for public works. . . . I must positively declare . . . that whoever is responsible for this order is the most infamous of your servants, who deserves only my contempt, for he is both a fool and shortsighted."[53] The Empress answered that not she but the Council of State had issued the decrees; however, she did not retract them. A delegation of Moravian Protestants came to see Joseph; Maria Theresa ordered their arrest. The crisis between mother and son was reaching an impasse when Kaunitz persuaded her to withdraw the decrees. The persecutions were stopped; the converts were allowed to practice their new worship provided it was done quietly in their homes. The conflict of the generations paused.

It was resumed when, on December 30, 1777, Maximilian Joseph, elector of Bavaria, died childless after a long and prosperous reign. In the contest for the succession to his power the Elector Palatine, Charles Theodore (Karl Theodor), was supported by Joseph II, on condition of ceding a part of

Bavaria to Austria; and Charles, duke of Zweibrücken, was supported by Frederick the Great, who announced that he would resist any acquisition of Bavarian territory by Austria. The Empress warned her son against challenging the yet invincible King of Prussia. Joseph ignored her advice, Kaunitz upheld him, and an Austrian force was sent into Bavaria. Frederick directed his troops to enter Bohemia and take Prague unless the Austrians evacuated Bavaria. Joseph led his main army to the defense of Prague; the hostile hosts approached each other, and another Austro-Prussian war seemed about to shed fratricidal blood. Frederick, violating precedents and expectations, avoided battle, content to let his soldiers consume Bohemia's crops; and Joseph, knowing Frederick's reputation as a general, hesitated to attack. He had hoped that France would come to his aid, and he dispatched pleas to Marie Antoinette. Louis XVI sent him fifteen million livres, but could do no more, for France had signed (February 6, 1778) an alliance with the revolting American colonies, and had to be prepared for war with England. Joseph fretted in camp, while hemorrhoids agitated him at one end, and an enormous boil at the other.

Maria Theresa, with a last flurry of will, took matters into her own hands, and secretly sent Frederick an offer of peace (July 12). Frederick agreed to negotiate; Joseph submitted to his mother; Louis of France and Catherine of Russia mediated. The Treaty of Teschen (May 13, 1779) solaced Joseph with thirty-four square miles of Bavaria, but allotted all the rest of that electorate to Charles Theodore, so uniting Bavaria and the Palatinate; Prussia was to receive Bayreuth and Ansbach at the death of their childless ruler. Everyone claimed victory.

This third crisis between the aging Frederick and the aging Empress exhausted her life. She was only sixty-three in 1780, but she was stout and asthmatic, and two wars, sixteen pregnancies, and incessant worry had weakened her heart. In November she was caught in a heavy rain while driving in an open carriage; she developed a bad cough, but insisted on spending the next day at her desk, working; she had once remarked, "I reproach myself for the time I consume in sleep."[54] Finding it almost impossible to breathe while lying down, she spent her final illness in a chair. Joseph summoned his brothers and sisters to her side, and attended her lovingly. The doctors abandoned hope for her, and she resigned herself to the last sacrament. In her final hours she rose and stumbled from her chair to her bed. Joseph tried to make her comfortable, saying, "Your Majesty lies in a bad position." She answered, "Yes, but good enough to die in." She died on November 29, 1780.

V. THE ENLIGHTENED DESPOT: 1780–90

After sincerely mourning a mother whose greatness he now realized, Joseph felt free to be himself, and to put into operation his burgeoning ideas for reform. He was absolute monarch over Austria, Hungary, Bohemia, and the Southern Netherlands; his brother Leopold obeyed him in Tuscany, his sister

Marie Antoinette would serve him in France. He felt deeply the opportunities that had come to him at the zenith of his life and power.

What was he like? Forty years old, still in the prime of life, he was quite handsome when he covered his bald head with a wig. He had an alert, almost feverishly active mind, abreast of his time, but insufficiently steadied by a knowledge of history and human character. Always feeling the stinginess of time, he erred only through haste, rarely through ill-will. Many stories tell of his sensitivity to the misfortunes of others, of his readiness to remedy remediable wrongs.[55] He made himself as accessible to the people as his tasks allowed. He lived simply, dressed like any sergeant, and shunned the purple robes of kings. He was as free from mistresses as Frederick, and had no "Greek friends"; his work was his absorbing love. Like Frederick, he worked harder than any of his aides. He had prepared himself conscientiously for his responsibilities; he had traveled not for amusement and display, but for observation and study; he had examined the industries, arts, charities, hospitals, courts, naval and military establishments of many countries; he had looked with his own eyes at the peoples, classes, and problems of his realm. Now he resolved, so far as one man could, to realize the dreams of the philosophers. "Since I have come to the throne, and wear the foremost diadem in the world, I have made philosophy the lawgiver of my empire."[56] Philosophers everywhere in Europe looked at the great enterprise with eager expectations.

The first difficulty was to find aides who would share his dream. Those whom he had inherited were nearly all of the upper classes whose privileges would be clipped by his reforms. Kaunitz and van Swieten supported him; two privy councilors, Qualtenburg and Gebler, and two professors in the University of Vienna, Martini and Sonnenfels, encouraged him; but below these men were bureaucrats mortised in habit, comfortable in tradition, and automatically resisting change. Joseph, too hurried to be courteous, treated these servitors as servants, confused them with a cloud of orders, asked them to report on any serious fault in their associates,[57] clogged them with questionnaires, and demanded of them labor as unremitting as his own. He promised them, and their widows, pensions after ten years of service; they thanked him, resented his methods, and nursed their pride. Joseph's confidence in the justice of his aims led him to impatient intolerance of criticism or debate. He wrote to Choiseul (now in easeful retirement): "Live happier than I can be. I have hardly known happiness, and before I complete the course that I have set out for myself I shall be an old man."[58] He never lived to be old.

He put aside all thought of democracy. His people, he felt, were unprepared for political judgment; with a few exceptions they would adopt whatever opinions were handed down to them by their masters or their priests. Even a constitutional monarchy appeared unpromising; a parliament like England's would be a closed society of landlords and bishops defying any basic change. Joseph took it for granted that only an absolute monarchy could break the cake of custom and the chains of dogma and protect the simple weak from the clever strong. So he took up every problem personally, and issued directives covering every phase of life. To promote compliance with his orders he set up a system of espionage that soured his benefactions.

It was part of his absolutism to raise by conscription a large standing army independent of territorial magnates, manned by universal conscription, and hardened by Prussian discipline. That army, he hoped, would give strength to his voice in international affairs, and would keep Frederick at a distance; perhaps (for our philosopher was somewhat acquisitive) it would enable him to absorb Bavaria and drive the Turks from the adjoining Balkans. He named a commission of jurists to reform and codify the laws; after six years of labor it published a new civil code of judicial procedure. Penalties were lightened, and capital punishment was abolished. (In contemporary England a hundred crimes were still considered capital.) Magic, witchcraft, and apostasy were no longer punishable by law. Dueling was forbidden; to kill in a duel was classified as murder. Marriage was made a civil contract; marriages between Christians and non-Christians became legal; divorce could be obtained from the civil authority. Magistrates were to be appointed only after specific training and after passing difficult examinations. Many ecclesiastical courts were abolished. All persons were to be held equal before the law. Aristocrats were shocked when one of their number was exposed in a pillory and another was sentenced to sweep the streets.

Serfdom was abolished by a series of decrees, 1781–85. The right to change residence or occupation, to own property, and to marry by mutual consent was guaranteed to all, and special attorneys were provided to protect the peasants in their new liberties. The barons lost criminal jurisdiction over their tenants, but, lest baronial manors remain unproductive, the lords could require some customary services from their former serfs.

Convinced that guild regulations hampered economic development, Joseph encouraged capitalist industry, but he opposed the multiplication of machines for fear "it would deprive thousands of their livelihood."[59] He exempted industrial workers from conscription, but they grumbled at his reduction of workless holydays. He elevated merchants, manufacturers, and bankers to aristocratic titles and national honors. He abolished or reduced internal tolls, but retained high protective tariffs on imports. Domestic manufacturers, so shielded from foreign competition, raised prices and produced shoddy goods.[60] Resenting the tariffs, Prussia, Saxony, and Turkey closed their gates to the products of the Empire; the Elbe, the Oder, and the Danube lost some of their trade. Joseph tried to increase overland traffic with Adriatic ports by cutting a new road, the Via Josephina, through the Carniolan Alps; he set up an East India Company, and hoped to develop commerce with the Orient, Africa, and America through the free ports of Fiume and Trieste. In 1784 he negotiated a commercial treaty with Turkey, but three years later his war with Turkey closed the Danube's exits to the Black Sea, and the Danubian merchants followed one another into bankruptcy.

To promote the circulation of capital he removed from the statutes the old prohibition of interest, legalized loans at five per cent, and raised a Jewish banker to the baronetcy. He offered state loans and temporary monopolies to new enterprises. He adopted the physiocratic idea of a single tax falling only upon land, varying with location and fertility, and paid by landowners great or small. The proposal required a survey of all the lands of the Empire; this was carried out at a cost of 120,000,000 gulden, paid by the proprietors. The new law decreed that the peasant was to keep seventy per cent of his produce or income, give twelve per cent to the state, and divide the remainder between feudal dues and ecclesiastical tithes; previously he had paid thirty-four per cent to the state, twenty-nine per cent to the landlord, and ten per cent to the Church, keeping only twenty-seven per cent for himself.[61] The nobles protested that this new division would ruin them; in Hungary they rose in revolt.

The population of Austria, Hungary, and Bohemia rose from 18,700,000 in 1780 to 21,000,000 in 1790.[62] A contemporary reported that brick cottages were replacing the old rural hovels, and that brick was replacing wood in urban housing.[63] Poverty remained, but an Imperial rescript of 1781 established *Armeninstitute* (Institutes for the Poor) where any person unable to earn a living could claim support without sacrificing his self-respect.

Though Joseph was officially "Vicar of Christ," "Advocate of the Christian Church," and "Protector of Palestine . . . and the Catholic Faith," he set about, soon after his rise to absolute power, to reduce the role of the Church in his "hereditary" lands—i.e., Austria, Hungary, and Bohemia. On October 12, 1781, he issued an Edict of Toleration: Protestants and Greek Orthodox were to be free to have their own temples, schools, and conventions, to own property, enter the professions, and hold political or military offices. The Emperor exhorted the people to "forbear all occasions of dispute relative to matters of faith, . . . and to treat affectionately and kindly those who are of a different communion."[64] In a directive to van Swieten Joseph frankly revealed the sources of his inspiration: "Intolerance is banished from my Empire, [which can be] happy that it has not made victims like Calas and Sirven. . . . Toleration is the effect of the propagation of the enlightenment [*les lumières*] which has now spread through all Europe. It is based on philosophy, and on the great men who have established it. . . . It is philosophy alone that governments must follow."[65]

There were limits to this toleration, as there had been in Voltaire's *Treatise on Toleration* (1763). Some councilors warned Joseph that if all restraint were removed there would be a rank growth of wild creeds, even of outright atheism, and that this would eventuate in warring sects, social disorder, and the breakdown of all authority. So when he was told that several hundred Bohemians had publicly declared themselves deists (1783), he ordered that any man so professing "should, without further investigation, be given twenty-four lashes on his buttocks with a leather whip, and then be sent home," and that this operation was to be repeated as often as such public profession was renewed.[66] Some persisting deists were transported to military colonies. We shall see later how far Joseph went in his efforts to liberate the Jews.

One result of the Edict of Toleration was a rapid rise in the number of professing Protestants in the realm, from 74,000 in 1781 to 157,000 in 1786.

Free thought grew, but remained confined to private circles. The Free-masons, who had long been established in Austria, organized in Vienna (1781) a lodge which was joined by many prominent citizens, and (despite its implicit deism) was protected by the Emperor himself. "The aim of the society," said one member, "was to give effect to that freedom of conscience and thought so happily fostered by the government, and to combat super-stition and fanaticism in the . . . monkish orders, which are the main sup-ports of these evils."[67] Masonic lodges multiplied to the number of eight in Vienna alone; it became fashionable to belong; Masonic emblems were worn by both sexes; Mozart wrote music for Masonic ceremonies. In time Joseph suspected the lodges of political conspiracy; in 1785 he ordered the Viennese lodges to merge into two, and allowed only one lodge in each provincial capital.

Joseph appointed a commission to revise the laws of censorship, and in 1782 he promulgated its results in a new code. Books systematically attack-ing Christianity, or containing "immoral utterances and unclean obscenities," were prohibited; but so too were books "containing fabulous miracles, ap-paritions, revelations, and such things, which would lead the common man to superstition, [and] arouse disgust in scholars."[68] Criticisms and lampoons were allowed, even if they assailed the Emperor, but they must bear the au-thor's real name, and were subject to the law of libel. Books listed in the Roman Index Librorum Prohibitorum were to be open to the use of scholars in libraries. Scientific works were to be entirely exempt from censorship; so were learned works, provided some recognized authority vouched for their scholarly character. Books in a foreign language might be imported and sold without hindrance. Academic freedom was enlarged. When fourteen stu-dents at the University of Innsbruck denounced their teacher to the au-thorities for contending that the world was older than six thousand years, Joseph handled the matter summarily: "The fourteen students should be dismissed, for heads so poor as theirs cannot profit from education."[69] — The new regulations elicited indignant protests from the hierarchy; Joseph re-sponded by allowing Vienna complete liberty of publication (1787). Even before this liberation the Viennese printers took advantage of the lax en-forcement of the 1782 code: pamphlets, books, and magazines flooded Aus-tria with semiobscenities, "revelations" of nuns, and attacks upon the Catho-lic Church, or upon Christianity itself.

Joseph felt that he should also regulate ecclesiastical affairs. On November 29, 1781, he issued a decree that closed a great number of monasteries and nunneries, such as "neither operate schools, nor care for the sick, nor engage in studies." Of 2,163 religious houses in the German dominions (Austria, Styria, Carinthia, Carniola) 413 were closed; of their 65,000 inmates 27,000 were freed with pensions; and a similar reduction was effected in Bohemia and Hungary. "The monarchy," said Joseph "is too poor and backward to allow itself the luxury of supporting the idle."[70] The wealth of the disman-tled institutions—amounting to some sixty million gulden—was declared a patrimony of the people, and was confiscated by the state. The surviving monasteries were declared ineligible to inherit property. The mendicant orders were commanded to cease begging, and were forbidden to take novices. Religious brotherhoods were abolished. All ecclesiastical possessions were to be registered with the government, which prohibited their sale, alienation, or exchange.

Joseph proceeded to bring the Catholic episcopate under state control. New bishops were required to take an oath of obedience to the secular authorities. No papal regulation or decree was to be valid in Austria without the government's permission. The papal bulls of 1362 and 1713, condemning heretics or Jansenists, were to be ignored. On the other hand Joseph organized new parishes, built new churches, and provided stipends to support candidates for the priesthood. He opened new seminaries, and prescribed for them a curriculum stressing science and secular knowledge as well as theology and liturgy.

These measures aroused the Catholic clergy throughout Europe. Many prelates begged Joseph to rescind his anticlerical decrees; unheeded, they threatened him with hell; he smiled and kept his course. Finally the Pope himself, Pius VI, handsome, cultured, kindly, vain, took the unusual step of leaving Italy (February 27, 1782), crossed the Apennines and the Alps in winter, and arrived in Vienna (March 22) resolved to make a personal plea to the Emperor; this was the first time since 1414 that a pope had set foot on German soil. Joseph, with his fellow skeptic Kaunitz, went out from the city to escort the pontiff to the apartments that had been used by Maria Theresa. During the Pope's stay in Vienna immense crowds gathered almost daily before the royal palace to seek the papal blessings. Joseph later described them:

> All the passages and stairs of the court were crammed with people; despite redoubled sentries it was impossible to protect oneself from all the things they brought him to be blessed: scapularies, rosaries, images. And for the benedictions which he gave seven times daily from the balcony he had a throng of people so great that one can form no idea of it unless one has seen it; it is no exaggeration to say that at one time there were at least sixty thousand souls. That was a most beautiful spectacle; peasants and their wives and children came from twenty leagues around. Yesterday a woman was crushed right beneath my window.[71]

Joseph was moved less by the Pope's eloquent exhortations than by this evidence of religion's power on the human mind; nevertheless he continued to close monasteries, even while Pius was his guest.[72] The Pope warned him prophetically: "If you persevere in your projects, destructive of the faith and the laws of the Church, the hand of the Lord will fall heavily upon you; it will check you in the course of your career, it will dig under you an abyss where you will be engulfed in the flower of your life, and will put an end to the reign which you could have made glorious."[73] After a month of honors and failure Pius returned sadly to Rome. Shortly afterward the Emperor appointed as archbishop of Milan a Visconti unacceptable to the Curia; the Pope refused confirmation, and Church and Empire neared a break. Joseph was not ready for so drastic a step. He hurried to Rome (December, 1782),

visited Pius, professed piety, and won papal consent to the appointment of
bishops—even in Lombardy—by the state. Prince and prelate parted amicably.
Joseph scattered thirty thousand scudi among the Roman mob, and was
hailed with grateful cries of "*Viva nostro Imperatore!*"

Back in Vienna, he continued his one-man Reformation. Having defied
the Pope like Luther (with whom many Protestants gratefully compared
him), and having attacked the monasteries like Henry VIII, he proceeded
like Calvin to cleanse churches by ordering the removal of votive tablets and
most statuary, and by stopping the touching of pictures, the kissing of relics,
the distribution of amulets . . . He regulated the length and number of religious services, the clothing of the Virgin, the character of church music; the
litanies were hereafter to be recited in German, not Latin. Pilgrimages and
processions were to require the consent of the secular authorities; ultimately
only one procession was allowed—for Corpus Christi Day; the people were
officially informed that they need not kneel in the streets before a procession,
even if it carried a consecrated Host; it was enough to doff their hats. University professors were told that they need no longer swear belief in the
immaculate conception of the Virgin.

No one could question the humanity of Joseph's aims. The wealth taken
from dispensable monasteries was set apart for the support of schools, hospitals, and charities, for pensions to displaced monks and nuns, and for supplementary payment to poor parish priests. The Emperor issued a long series
of ordinances for the promotion of education. All communities containing
a hundred children of school age were required to maintain elementary
schools; elementary education was made compulsory and universal. Schools
for girls were provided by convents or the state. Universities were supported
at Vienna, Prague, Lemberg, Pest, and Louvain; those at Innsbruck, Brünn,
Graz, and Freiburg were made into *lycées* to teach medicine, law, or practical arts. Medical schools were established, including the "Josephinum" at
Vienna, for military medicine and surgery. Vienna began to be one of the
most advanced medical centers in the world.

VI. THE EMPEROR AND THE EMPIRE

The difficulty of Joseph's revolutionary enterprise was doubled by the
diversity of his realm. He knew Austria well, but, despite arduous travels,
he had not realized how deeply entrenched were the Hungarian magnates in
the economic and political life of their nation, and how the patriotism of the
Hungarian masses could outweigh class interests. On acceding to power he had
refused to follow tradition and go to Pressburg to be crowned king of Hungary, for in that ceremony he would be required to swear allegiance to
the Hungarian constitution, which sanctioned the feudal structures of society. He had offended every Hungarian by ordering the crown of Hungary's patron St. Stephen to be removed from Buda to Vienna (1784). He
had replaced Latin with German, not Magyar, as the language of law and

instruction in Hungary. He had angered Hungarian businessmen by imped-ing with tariffs the export of their products into Austria. He had shocked the Catholic Church by interfering with traditional rituals, and by allowing Hungarian Protestant communities to multiply from 272 to 758 in one year (1783–84). Hungary fell into a turmoil of conflicting classes, nationalities, languages, and faiths.

In 1784 the peasants of Wallachia (between the Danube and the Transyl-vanian Alps) broke out in a violent Jacquerie against their feudal lords, set fire to 182 baronial châteaux and sixty villages, slaughtered four thousand Hun-garians,[74] and announced that they were doing all this with the blessing of the Emperor. Joseph sympathized with their resentment of long oppression,[75] but he was seeking to end feudalism peaceably by legislation, and could not allow the peasants to rush matters by arson and murder. He sent troops to put down the insurrection; 150 leaders were executed, and the rebellion halted. The nobles blamed him for the uprising, the peasants blamed him for its fail-ure. The stage was set for national revolt against the Emperor in 1787.

In November, 1780, Joseph came in person to study the problems of the Austrian Netherlands. He visited Namur, Mons, Courtrai, Ypres, Dunkirk, Ostend, Bruges, Ghent, Audenaarde, Antwerp, Malines, Louvain, Brussels. He made a side trip into the United Netherlands—to Rotterdam, The Hague, Leiden, Haarlem, Amsterdam, Utrecht, and Spa (where he dined with the *philosophe* Raynal). He was struck by the contrast between the prosperity of Holland and the relative stagnation of the Belgian economy. He at-tributed this to the activity and opportunities of Dutch businessmen, and to the closing of the River Scheldt to oceanic trade by the Treaty of Münster (1648). He returned to Brussels, and entered into conferences seeking to im-prove commerce, administration, finance, and law. In January, 1781, he ap-pointed his sister Maria Christina and her husband, Duke Albert of Saxe-Teschen, governors of the Austrian Netherlands.

Now for the first time he perceived how opposed to his reforms were the traditional privileges of the upper classes in this historic land. One province, Brabant, had a charter of liberties dating back to the thirteenth century, and known as the Joyeuse Entrée; any ruler entering Brussels was expected to swear fidelity to this charter, and one clause declared that if the sovereign violated any article his Flemish subjects would have the right to refuse him all service and obedience. Another clause required the sovereign to maintain the Catholic Church in all its existing privileges, possessions, and powers, and to enforce all the decisions of the Council of Trent. Similar constitutions were cherished by the patricians and clergy in the other provinces. Joseph resolved not to allow these traditions to defy his reforms. After a brief visit to Paris (July, 1781) he returned to Vienna.

In November he began to apply to these provinces his Edict of Toleration. He made the Belgian monasteries independent of the pope, closed several of them, and confiscated their revenues. The bishops of Brussels, Antwerp, and Malines protested; Joseph passed on to extend to "Belgium" his regulations on votive tablets, processions, and ritual. He withdrew control of the schools from the bishops, saying that "the children of Levi should no longer have a monopoly on the human mind."[76] He abrogated the exclusive privileges long enjoyed by the University of Louvain. He established there a new seminary free from episcopal dominance, and ordered that all Belgian candidates for the priesthood should study for five years in this institution.[77] Eager to improve provincial government, he replaced (January, 1787) the provincial Estates, or assemblies, and the old aristocratic privy councils, with a single Council of General Administration under a plenipotentiary appointed by the emperor; and he substituted a unified and secular judiciary for the existing feudal, territorial, and ecclesiastical courts. All persons, of whatever class, were declared equal before the law.

The nobles and many bourgeois joined the clergy in resisting these measures. Their hostility was not appeased by the futile efforts that Joseph made to reopen the Scheldt to oceanic commerce; Holland refused to permit it, and France, despite the pleas of Marie Antoinette, joined in the refusal. In January, 1787, the Estates of Brabant notified Joseph that changes in the existing constitution of the province could not be made without the consent of the Estates; in effect they informed him that his rule in the Austrian Netherlands must be a constitutional, not an absolute, monarchy. He ignored the declaration, and ordered the enforcement of his decrees. The Estates refused to vote taxes unless attention was paid to their remonstrances. Agitation flared into such widespread violence that Maria Christina promised annulment of the hated reforms (May 31, 1787).

Where was the Emperor during this turmoil? He was flirting diplomatically with Catherine II, believing that an entente with Russia would isolate Prussia and strengthen Austria against the Turks. Even before the death of his mother Joseph had visited the Czarina at Mogilev (June 7, 1780), and thence he had gone on to Moscow and St. Petersburg. In May, 1781, Austria and Russia signed an alliance that pledged each to come to the aid of the other in case of attack.

Thinking that this agreement would immobilize the septuagenarian Frederick, Joseph again (1784) offered the Austrian Netherlands to Elector Charles Theodore in exchange for Bavaria. The Elector was tempted, but Frederick roused all his energies to foil the plan. He stirred up revolt against the Emperor in Hungary and Belgium; he induced the Duke of Zweibrücken —heir to Bavaria—to oppose the exchange; he sent agents to convince the German princes that their independence was threatened by Austrian expansion; and he succeeded in organizing (July 23, 1785) Prussia, Saxony, Hanover, Brunswick, Mainz, Hesse-Cassel, Baden, Saxe-Weimar, Gotha, Mecklenburg, Ansbach, and Anhalt into a Fürstenbund, or League of Princes, pledged to resist any expansion of Austria at the expense of a German state. Joseph again appealed to his sister at Versailles; Marie Antoinette used her charm on Louis XVI to win his support for her brother; Vergennes, foreign minister, cautioned Louis against consent; Joseph confessed himself defeated by the old fox who had been the idol of his youth. When, in August, 1786, he received news of Frederick's death, he expressed a double grief: "As a soldier I regret the passing of a great man who has been epoch-making in the art of war. As a citizen I regret that his death has come thirty years too late."[78]

Now the Emperor's only hope of extending his realm lay in joining Catherine in a campaign to divide between them the European possessions of Turkey. When the Empress of Russia set out in January, 1787, to visit and awe her new conquests in the south, she invited Joseph to meet her en route and accompany her to the Crimea. He went, but did not at once agree to her proposal for a united crusade. "What I want," he said, "is Silesia, and war with Turkey will not give me that."[79] Nevertheless, when Turkey declared war against Russia (August 15, 1787) Joseph's hand was forced; his alliance with Catherine required him to help her in a "defensive" war; besides, now that Turkey was so critically engaged, Austria had a chance to regain Serbia and Bosnia, perhaps even a port on the Black Sea. So, in February, 1788, Joseph sent his soldiers to war, and told them to take Belgrade.

But meanwhile the Swedes seized the opportunity to send a force against St. Petersburg. Catherine summoned troops from the south to defend her capital. The Turks, relieved of Russian pressure, concentrated their power against the Austrians. Joseph, going to lead his army, saw it weakened by apathy, desertion, and disease; he ordered a retreat, and returned to Vienna in despair and disgrace. He turned over the command to Laudon, a hero of the Seven Years' War; the old Marshal redeemed Austrian arms by capturing Belgrade (1789). Sweden's sortie against Russia having failed, Catherine's soldiers swarmed backward to the south, and survived in slightly superior number in competitive holocausts with the Turks. Joseph was rejoicing in the prospect of long-awaited martial glory when Prussia, England, Sweden, and Holland, fearing Russian aggrandizement, intervened to help the Turks. Suddenly Joseph found nearly all of Protestant Europe united and arming against him. Once more he appealed to France, but France, in 1789, was busy with revolution. Prussia, under Frederick William II, signed an alliance with Turkey (January, 1790), and sent agents to foment revolt against the Emperor in Hungary and the Austrian Netherlands.

Hungary welcomed these machinations, for it was in open rebellion against Joseph's edicts of conscription, taxation, language change, and religious reform. In 1786 Emerich Malongei called upon the Hungarians to elect their own king. In 1788 Remigius Franyó organized a plot to make Frederick William king of Hungary; Counts Esterházy and Károlyi betrayed the plot to the Emperor, and Franyó was sentenced to sixty years' imprisonment. In 1789 the Hungarian Estates appealed to Prussia to free Hungary from Austria. When news of the French Revolution reached Hungary the country rang with cries for independence. Joseph, who felt death in his veins, had no more strength to maintain his stand. His brother Leopold urged him to yield. In January, 1790, he announced:

> We have decided to restore the administration of the Kingdom [of Hungary]
> . . . to the status of 1780. . . . We instituted [the reforms] out of zeal for the
> common good, and in the hope that you, taught by experience, would find
> them pleasing. Now we have convinced ourselves that you prefer the old order.
> . . . But it is our will that our Edict of Toleration, . . . as well as that con-
> cerning the serfs, their treatment and their relation to the seigneurs, remain in
> force.[80]

In February the crown of St. Stephen was carried back to Buda, and was acclaimed with public rejoicing at every stop on the way. The revolt died
down.

The revolt in the Austrian Netherlands went full course, for there it felt
the heat of the revolutionary movement in neighboring France. Joseph refused to confirm the promise his sister had given to the Estates of Brabant
that the reforms they resented would be annulled; he ordered their enforcement, and bade his soldiers fire upon any crowds resisting them. It was so
done; six rioters were killed in Brussels (January 22, 1788), an unknown
number in Antwerp and Louvain. A Brussels lawyer, Henri van den Noot,
summoned the people to arm themselves and enroll as volunteers in an army
of independence. The appeal was actively supported by the clergy; an anomalous inspiration was added by news that the Bastille had fallen; soon ten
thousand "Patriots," ably led, were in the field. On October 24 a manifesto
of "the Brabantine people" announced the deposition of Joseph II as their
ruler. On October 26 a force of Patriots defeated the Austrian soldiery.
Town after town was occupied by the insurgents. On January 11, 1790, the
seven provinces declared their independence, and proclaimed the Republic
of the United States of Belgium, taking the name of the Belgic tribes that
had troubled Caesar eighteen centuries before. England, Holland, and Prussia were happy to recognize the new government. Joseph appealed to France
for help, but France herself was busy deposing her King. All the old world
that Joseph had known seemed to be falling apart. And death was calling
him.

VII. *ATRA MORS*

The bitterness of those final months was complete. Hungary and Belgium
were in revolt, the Turks were advancing, his army was mutinous, his own
people, the Austrians, who once had loved him, had turned against him as the
violator of their sacred customs and beliefs. The priests denounced him as an
infidel, the nobles hated him for freeing their serfs, the peasants cried out for
more land; the urban poor were near starvation; all classes cursed the high
taxes and prices caused by the war. On January 30, 1790, in full surrender,
Joseph rescinded all reforms decreed since the death of Maria Theresa, except the abolition of serfdom.

Why had he failed? He had accepted in full faith and generous trust the
thesis of the *philosophes* that a monarch of good education and good will

would be the best instrument of enlightenment and reform. He had a good education, but his good will was tarnished by love of power, and ultimately his eagerness to be a conqueror overcame his zeal for putting philosophy on the throne. He lacked the philosopher's capacity for doubt; he took for granted the wisdom of his means as well as of his ends. He tried to reform too many evils at once, and too hurriedly; the people could not absorb the bewildering multiplicity of his decrees. He commanded faster than he could convince; he sought to achieve in a decade what required a century of education and economic change. Basically it was the people who failed him. They were too deeply rooted in their privileges and prejudices, in their customs and creeds, to give him the understanding and support without which, in such challenging reforms, his absolutism was impotent. They preferred their churches, priests, and tithes to his taxes, spies, and wars. They could not put their trust in a man who laughed at their beloved legends, badgered their bishops, and humiliated their Pope.

Through all those exacting years since 1765 his body had rebelled against his will. His stomach could not digest his pace; repeatedly and in vain it cautioned him to rest. The Prince de Ligne warned him that he was killing himself; he knew it, but "what can I do?" he said; "I am killing myself because I cannot rouse up others to work."[81] His lungs were bad, his voice was feeble and hollow; he had varicose veins, running eyes, erysipelas, hemorrhoids . . . He exposed himself to all kinds of weather in the war with the Turks; like thousands of his troops he contracted quartan fever. Sometimes he could hardly breathe; "my heart palpitates at the slightest movement."[82] In the spring of 1789 he began to vomit blood—"almost three ounces at once," he wrote to Leopold. In June he had violent pains in the kidneys. "I observe the strictest diet; I eat neither meat nor vegetables nor dairy products; soup and rice are my nourishment."[83] He developed an anal abscess; this and his hemorrhoids had to be lanced. He developed dropsy. He summoned Leopold to come and take over the government. "I do not regret leaving the throne," he said; "all that grieves me is to have so few people happy."[84] To the Prince de Ligne he wrote: "Your country has killed me. The taking of Ghent was my agony; the loss of Brussels is my death. . . . Go to the Low Countries; bring them back to their sovereign. If you cannot do this, stay there. Do not sacrifice your interests to me. You have children."[85] He made his will, leaving generous gifts to his servants, and to "the five ladies who bore my society."[86] He composed his own epitaph: "Here lies Joseph, who could succeed in nothing."[87] He received with resignation the last sacrament of the Catholic Church. He begged for death, and on February 20, 1790, it was given him. He was forty-eight years old. Vienna rejoiced at his passing, and Hungary gave thanks to God.

Was he a failure? In war, unquestionably. Despite Laudon's victories Leopold II (1790–92) found it advisable to make peace with Turkey (August 4, 1791) on the basis of the *status quo ante*. Unable to pacify the Hungarian barons, Leopold revoked the grant of freedom to the serfs. In Bohemia and

Austria most of the reforms were preserved. The toleration edicts were not repealed; the closed monasteries were not restored; the Church remained subject to the laws of the state. The economic legislation had freed and stimulated commerce and industry. Austria passed without violent revolution from a medieval to a modern state, and shared in the diverse cultural vitality of the nineteenth century.

"Deeply convinced of the integrity of my intentions," Joseph had written to Kaunitz, "I hope that when I am dead posterity—more favorable, more impartial, and therefore juster than my contemporaries—will examine my actions and goals before judging me."[88] It has taken posterity a long time to do this, but it has learned at last, while deploring his autocracy and haste, to recognize in him the bravest and most thoroughgoing, as well as the least judicious, of the "enlightened despots." After the reaction under Metternich had passed away, the reforms of Joseph II were one by one restored, and the revolutionaries of 1848 laid a wreath of grateful acknowledgment upon his tomb.

CHAPTER XIV

Music Reformed

W E do not readily think of the embattled Joseph II as a musician. Yet we are told that he received a "thorough musical education," had a fine bass voice, heard a concert almost daily, and was "a skillful player from score" on the violoncello, the viola, and the clavier.[1] Many nobles were musicians, many more were patrons of music. The middle classes followed suit; every household had a harpsichord; everyone learned to play some instrument. Trios and quartets were performed in the streets; open-air concerts were given in the parks and, on St. John's Day, from illuminated boats on the Danube Canal. Opera flourished at the court and in the National Opera Theater founded by Joseph II in 1778.

Vienna rose to its early-nineteenth-century sovereignty as the musical capital of Europe because in the late eighteenth century it brought together the rival musical traditions of Germany and Italy. From Germany came polyphony, from Italy melody. From Germany came the *Singspiel*—a mixture of comic drama, spoken dialogue, incidental music, and popular songs; from Italy came *opera buffa;* at Vienna the two forms coalesced, as in Mozart's *The Abduction from the Seraglio.* Generally the Italian influence overcame the German in Vienna; Italy conquered Austria with arias, as Austria conquered North Italy with arms. In Vienna *opera seria* was chiefly Italian until Gluck came, and Gluck was formed on Italian music.

I. CHRISTOPH WILLIBALD GLUCK: 1714–87

He was born at Erasbach, in the Upper Palatinate, to a Catholic forester who in 1717 moved the family to Neuschloss in Bohemia. In the Jesuit school at Komotau Christoph received instruction in religion, Latin, the classics, singing, violin, organ, and harpsichord. Moving to Prague in 1732, he took lessons on the violoncello, and supported himself by singing in churches, playing the violin at dances, and giving concerts in nearby towns.

Every clever boy in Bohemia gravitated to Prague, and some still cleverer found a way to Vienna. Gluck's way was to secure a place in the orchestra of Prince Ferdinand von Lobkowitz. In Vienna he heard Italian operas, and felt the magnetism of Italy. Prince Francesco Melzi liked his playing, and invited him to Milan (1737). Gluck studied composition under Sammartini, and became devoted to Italian styles. His early operas (1741–45) followed Italian methods, and he conducted their premières in Italy. These successes won him an invitation to compose and produce an opera for the Haymarket Theatre in London.

There he presented *La caduta de' giganti* (1746). It was dismissed with faint praise, and gruff old Handel said that Gluck knew "no more counterpoint than mein cook";[2] but the cook was a good basso and Gluck's fame was not to rest on counterpoint. Burney met Gluck, and described him as "of a temper as fierce as Handel's. . . . He was horribly scarred by smallpox, . . . and he had an ugly scowl."[3] Perhaps to balance his budget Gluck announced to the public that he would give "a concerto on twenty-six drinking glasses tuned [by filling them to different levels] with spring water, accompanied with the whole band [orchestra], being a new instrument of his own invention, upon which he performs whatever may be done on a violin or harpsichord." Such a "glass harmonica," or "musical glasses," had been introduced in Dublin two years before. Gluck evoked the notes by stroking the rims of the glasses with moistened fingers. The performance (April 23, 1746) appealed to the curious, and was repeated a week later.

Saddened with this success, Gluck left London December 26 for Paris. There he studied the operas of Rameau, who had moved toward reform by integrating the music and the ballet with the action. In September he conducted operas at Hamburg, had a liaison with an Italian singer, and contracted syphilis. He recovered so slowly that when he went to Copenhagen (November 24) he was unable to conduct. He returned to Vienna, and married Marianne Pergia (September 15, 1750), daughter of a rich merchant. Her dowry made him financially secure; he took a house in Vienna, and disappeared into a long rest.

In September, 1754, Count Marcello Durazzo engaged him as *Kapellmeister* at two thousand florins per year to compose for the court. Durazzo had tired of conventional Italian opera, and collaborated with Gluck in a musical drama, *L'innocenza giustificata*, in which the story was no mere scaffolding for music, and the music no mere assemblage of arias, but the music reflected the action, and the arias—even the choruses—entered with some logic into the plot. The première (December 8, 1755) was therefore the herald and first product of the reform that history associates with Gluck's name. We have seen elsewhere the contributions made by Benedetto Marcello, Jommelli, and Traëtta to this development, and the appeal made by Rousseau, Voltaire and the Encyclopedists for a closer union of drama and music. Metastasio had helped by proudly insisting that the music should be servant to the poetry.[4] Winckelmann's passion for restoring Greek ideals in art may have affected Gluck, and composers knew that Italian opera had begun as an attempt to revive the classic drama, in which the music was subordinated to the play. Meanwhile Jean-Georges Noverre (1760) pleaded for an elevation of the ballet from mere rhythmic prancing to dramatic pantomimes that would express "the passions, manners, customs, ceremonies, and costumes of all the peoples on earth."[5] By the mysterious alchemy of genius Gluck wove all these elements into a new operatic form.

One secret of success is to seize a propitious chance. What was it that brought Gluck to abandon the librettos of Metastasio and take Raniero da Calzabigi as the poet for *Orfeo ed Euridice?* The two men had been born in the same year, 1714, but far apart—Calzabigi in Livorno. After some adventures in love and finance he came to Paris, published there an edition of Metastasio's *Poeste drammatiche* (1755), and prefaced it with a "Dissertazione" expressing his hope for a new kind of opera—"a delightful whole resulting from the interplay of a large chorus, the dance, and a scenic action where poetry and music are united in a masterly way."[6] Moving to Vienna, he interested Durazzo with his ideas on opera; the Count invited him to write a libretto; Calzabigi composed *Orfeo ed Euridice;* Durazzo offered the poem to Gluck, who saw in the simple and unified plot a theme that could elicit all his powers.

The result was presented to Vienna on October 5, 1762. For the role of Orpheus Gluck was able to secure the leading *castrato* contralto of the time, Gaetano Guadagni. The story was as old as opera; a dozen librettists had used it between 1600 and 1761; the audience could follow the action without understanding Italian. The music dispensed with unaccompanied recitatives, *da capo* arias, and decorative flourishes; otherwise it followed the Italian style, but it rose to lyric heights of a purity seldom attained before or since. The despondent cry of Orpheus after losing his beloved a second time to death—"Che farò senz' Euridice?"—is still the loveliest aria in opera; on hearing this, and the threnody of the flute in the "Dance of the Blessed Spirits," we wonder that the stormy Bohemian could have found such delicacy in his soul.

Orfeo was not enthusiastically received in Vienna, but Maria Theresa was deeply moved by it, and sent Gluck a snuffbox stuffed with ducats. Soon he was chosen to teach singing to the Archduchess Maria Antonia. Meanwhile he and Calzabigi worked on what some have rated their most perfect opera, *Alceste*. In a preface to the published form, written for Gluck by Calzabigi, the composer declared the principles of his operatic reform:

> When I undertook to write the music for *Alceste* I resolved to divest it entirely of all those abuses . . . which have so long disfigured Italian opera. . . . I have striven to restrict music to its true office of serving poetry by means of expression, and by following the situations of the story, without interrupting the action or stifling it with useless superfluity of comments. . . . I did not think it my duty to pass quickly over the second section of an aria—of which the words are perhaps the most impassioned and important—in order to repeat regularly . . . those of the first part. . . . I have felt that the overture should apprize the spectators of the nature of the action that is to be represented, and to form, so to speak, its argument; . . . that the orchestral instruments should be introduced in proportion to the interest and intensity of the words, and not leave that sharp contrast between the aria and the recitative in the dialogue, . . . [which] wantonly disturbs the force and heat of the action. . . . I believed that my greatest labor should be devoted to seeking a beautiful simplicity.[7]

In short, the music was to serve and intensify the drama, and not make the drama a mere scaffolding for vocal or orchestral displays. Gluck put the matter extremely by saying that he was "trying to forget that I am a musician";[8] he was to be one person with the librettist in composing a *dramma per musica*. — The story of *Alceste* is a bit beyond belief, but Gluck redeemed it with a somber overture that prefigured and led into the tragic action; with scenes of touching sentiment between Alceste and her children; with her invocation to the underworld gods in the aria "Divinités du Styx"; with majestic chorales and spectacular ensembles. The Viennese audience gave the opera sixty hearings between its première, December 16, 1767, and 1779. The critics, however, found many faults in it, and the singers complained that it gave them insufficient scope to display their art.

Poet and composer tried again with *Paride ed Elena* (November 30, 1770). Calzabigi took the plot from Ovid, who had made the story of Paris and Helen a personal romance instead of an international tragedy. The work received twenty performances in Vienna, one in Naples, none elsewhere. Calzabigi assumed the blame for the comparative failure, and renounced the writing of librettos. Gluck sought other soil for his seed. A friend in the French embassy at Vienna, François du Rollet, suggested that Paris audiences might welcome the compliment of a French opera by a German composer. Following suggestions by Diderot and Algarotti that Racine's *Iphigénie* offered an ideal subject for an opera, Du Rollet molded the play into a libretto, and submitted this to Gluck. The composer found the material perfectly suited to his taste, and at once set to work.

To pave the way to Paris Du Rollet addressed to the director of the Opéra a letter—printed in the *Mercure de France* for August 1, 1772—telling how indignant "Monsieur Glouch" was at the idea that the French language did not lend itself to music, and how he proposed to prove the opposite with *Iphigénie en Aulide*. Gluck softened the expected ire of Rousseau (then living quietly in Paris) by sending the *Mercure* a letter (February 1, 1773) expressing his hope that he might consult with Rousseau about "the means I have in view to produce a music fit for all the nations, and to let the ridiculous distinctions of national music disappear."[9] To complete this masterpiece of advertising, Marie Antoinette, remembering her old teacher, used her influence at the Opéra. The manager agreed to produce *Iphigénie;* Gluck came to Paris, and put singers and orchestra through such arduous and disciplined rehearsals as they had rarely experienced before. Sophie Arnould, the reigning diva, proved so intractable that Gluck threatened to abandon the project; Joseph Legros seemed too weakened by illness to play the mighty Achilles; Gaetan Vestris, the current god of the dance, wanted half the opera to be ballet.[10] Gluck tore at his hair, or his wig, persisted, and triumphed. The première (April 19, 1774) was the musical sensation of the year. We can feel the agitation of the ebullient capital in a letter of Marie Antoinette to her sister Maria Christina in Brussels:

> A great triumph, my dear Christine! I am carried away with it, and people can no longer talk of anything else. All heads are fermenting as a result of this event; . . . there are dissensions and quarrels as though it were . . . some religious dispute. At court, though I publicly expressed myself in favor of this inspired work, there are partisanships and debates of a particular liveliness; and in the city it seems to be worse still.[11]

Rousseau repaid Gluck's advances by announcing that "Monsieur Gluck's opera had overturned all his ideas; he was now convinced that the French language could agree as well as any other with a music powerful, touching, and sensitive."[12] The overture was so startlingly beautiful that the first night's audience demanded its repetition. The arias were criticized as too many, interrupting the drama, but they were marked by a complex depth of feeling characteristic of Gluck's music; of one of them, Agamemnon's "Au faîte des grandeurs," Abbé Arnaud exclaimed, "With such an air one might found a religion."[13]

Gluck now rivaled the dying Louis XV as the talk of Paris. His burly figure, his rubicund face and massive nose were pointed out wherever he went, and his imperious temper became the subject of a hundred anecdotes. Greuze painted his portrait, showing the jovial good nature behind the lines of strife and strain. He ate like Dr. Johnson, and drank only less than Boswell. He made no pretense about scorning money, and joined readily in appreciation of his work. He treated courtiers and commoners alike—as inferiors; he expected noble lords to hand him his wig, his coat, his cane; and when a prince was introduced to him, and Gluck kept his seat, he explained, "The custom in Germany is to rise only for people one respects."[14]

The director of the Opéra had warned him that if *Iphigénie en Aulide* was accepted, Gluck would have to write five more operas in quick order, since *Iphigénie* would drive all other operas from the stage. This did not frighten Gluck, who had a way of conscripting parts of his older compositions to squeeze them into new ones. He had *Orfeo ed Euridice* translated into French; and since no good contralto was available, he rewrote the part of Orpheus for the tenor Legros. Sophie Arnould, become tractable, played Eurydice. The Paris première was a heartening success. Marie Antoinette, now Queen of France, awarded a pension of six thousand francs to *"mon cher Gluck."*[15] He returned to Vienna with his head in the stars.

In March, 1776, he was back in Paris with a French version of *Alceste*, which was produced to mild applause on April 23. Gluck, inured to success, reacted to this setback with angry pride: *"Alceste* is not the kind of work to give momentary pleasure, or to please because it is new. Time does not exist for it; and I claim that it will give equal pleasure two hundred years hence if the French language does not change."[16] In June he retreated to Vienna, and soon thereafter he began to put to music Marmontel's revision of Quinault's libretto *Roland*.

Now began the most famous contest in operatic history. For meanwhile the management of the Opéra had commissioned Niccolò Piccini of Naples to set to music the same libretto, and to come to Paris and produce it. He came (December 31, 1776). Informed of this commission, Gluck sent to Du Rollet (now in Paris) a letter of Olympian wrath:

> I have just received your letter . . . exhorting me to continue my work on the words of the opera *Roland*. This is no longer feasible, for when I heard that the management of the Opéra, not unaware that I was doing *Roland*, had given the same work to M. Piccini to do, I burned as much of it as I had already done, which perhaps was not worth much. . . . I am no longer the man to enter into competition, and M. Piccini would have too great an advantage over me, since—his personal merit apart, which is assuredly very great—he would

have that of novelty. . . . I am sure that a certain politician of my acquaintance will offer dinner and supper to three quarters of Paris in order to win him proselytes.[17]

For reasons not now clear this letter, obviously private, was published in the *Année littéraire* for February, 1777. It became, unintentionally, a declaration of war.

Gluck reached Paris May 29 with a new opera, *Armide*. The rival composers met at a dinner; they embraced, and conversed amicably. Piccini had come to France with no notion that he was to be a pawn in a mess of partisan intrigue and operatic salesmanship; he himself warmly admired Gluck's work. Despite the friendliness of the protagonists the war went on in salons and cafés, in streets and homes; "no door was opened to a visitor," reported Charles Burney, "without the question being asked, previous to admission, *'Monsieur, estes vous Picciniste ou Gluckiste?'* "[18] Marmontel, d'Alembert, and Laharpe led in acclaiming Piccini and the Italian style; the Abbé Arnaud defended Gluck in a *Profession de foi en musique;* Rousseau, who had begun the war with his pro-Italian *Lettre sur la musique française* (1753), supported Gluck.

Armide was produced on September 23, 1777. Subject and music were reversions to modes established before Gluck's reform; the story was from Tasso, exalting the Christian Rinaldo and the pagan Armida; the music was Lully restored with romantic tenderness; the ballet was Noverre *in excelsis*. The audience liked the mixture; it gave the opera a good reception; but the *Piccinistes* condemned *Armide* as a refurbishing of Lully and Rameau. They waited anxiously for their standard-bearer's *Roland*. Piccini dedicated it to Marie Antoinette with apologies: "Transplanted, isolated, in a country where all was new to me, intimidated in my work by a thousand difficulties, I needed all my courage, and my courage forsook me."[19] At times he was on the verge of abandoning the contest and returning to Italy. He persevered, and had the comfort of a successful première (January 27, 1778). The two victories seemed to cancel each other, and the public war went on. Mme. Vigée-Lebrun saw it at first hand. "The usual battlefield was the garden of the Palais-Royal. There the partisans of Gluck and Piccini quarreled so violently that many a duel resulted."[20]

Gluck returned to Vienna in March, stopping at Ferney to see Voltaire. He took home with him two librettos: one by Nicolas-François Guillard based on the *Iphigenia in Tauris* of Euripides, the other by Baron Jean-Baptiste de Tschoudi on the Echo and Narcissus theme. He worked on both books, and by the fall of 1778 he felt ready for another battle. So in November we find him in Paris again; and on May 18, 1779, he presented at the Opéra what most students consider his greatest composition, *Iphigénie en Tauride*. It is a somber story, and much of the music is monotonously plaintive; at times we tire of Iphigenia's high-keyed laments. But when the performance is over, and the incantation of the music and the lines has stilled our skeptic reason, we realize that we have experienced a profound and powerful drama. A contemporary remarked that there were many fine passages in it. "There is only one," said Abbé Arnaud, "—the entire work."[21] The first night's audience gave the piece a wild ovation.

Gluck challenged the gods by hurrying to offer his other piece, *Écho et Narcisse* (September 21, 1779). It failed, and the maestro left Paris in a huff (October), declaring that he had had enough of France, and would write no more operas. If he had remained he could have heard another *Iphigénie en Tauride*, produced by Piccini after two years of labor. The première (January 23, 1781) was well received, but on the second night Mlle. Laguerre, who sang the title role, was so obviously drunk that Sophie Arnould destroyed the performance by calling it *Iphigénie en Champagne*.[22] This contretemps ended the operatic war; Piccini handsomely admitted defeat.

Gluck, in Vienna, dreamed of other victories. On February 10, 1780, he wrote to Goethe's Duke Karl August of Saxe-Weimar: "I have grown very old, and have squandered the best powers of my mind upon the French nation, nevertheless I feel an inward impulse to write something for my own country."[23] Now he put some odes of Klopstock to music that prepared for the finest lieder. In April, 1781, he suffered a stroke, but he was comforted by Vienna's reception of *Iphigenie in Tauris* and the revival of *Orfeo* and *Alceste*. On November 15, 1787, while entertaining friends, he drank at one gulp a glass of strong liquor, which had been forbidden him. He fell into convulsions, and died within four hours. Piccini, in Naples, tried in vain to raise funds for annual concerts in his rival's memory.[24] Italy, pursuing melody, ignored Gluck's reforms; Mozart followed the Italians, and must have been shocked at the idea of making music the servant of poetry. But Herder, coming at the end of this creative era, and looking back upon it with limited knowledge of Bach, Haydn, and Mozart, called Gluck the greatest composer of the century.[25]

II. JOSEPH HAYDN: 1732–1809

It is easier to love Haydn, for here was a man who quarreled with no one but his wife, hailed his competitors as his friends, suffused his music with gaiety, and was constitutionally incapable of tragedy.

He had no advantages of birth. His father was a wagonmaker and house painter at Rohrau, a little town on the Austro-Hungarian frontier. His mother had been cook for the counts of Harrach. Both parents were of Slavic-Croatian, not German, stock, and many of Haydn's melodies echo Croatian songs. He was the second of twelve children, of whom six died in infancy. He was baptized Franz Josef Haydn; however, it was customary to call children by their second name.

Aged six, he was sent to live with a relative, Johann Matthias Franck, who kept a school in Hainburg. There his day began with classes from seven to ten, then Mass, then home for dinner, then classes from twelve to three, then instruction in music. He was trained to piety, and never lost it. His mother longed to make him a priest, and she was deeply grieved when he chose the hazardous life of a musician. Franck encouraged the boy's predilection for music, taught him all that was in his own range, and held him to a severe regimen of study. In old age Haydn recalled and forgave: "I shall be grateful to that man as long as I live for keeping me so hard at work, though I used to get more floggings than food."[26] After two years with Franck, Joseph was taken to Vienna by Georg Reutter, *Kapellmeister* at St. Stephen's; Reutter thought his "weak, sweet voice" could find some modest place in a choir. So, at the age of eight, the timid-eager lad went to live in the Kantorei, or Singers' School, adjoining the stately cathedral. There he received lessons in arithmetic, writing, Latin, religion, singing, and violin. He sang in the cathedral and in the Imperial Chapel, but he was so poorly fed that he welcomed calls to sing in private homes, where he could fill his stomach besides singing his songs.

In 1745 his brother Michael, five years his junior, joined him in the Kantorei. About this time Joseph's voice began to break. He was invited to keep his soprano by having himself castrated, but his parents refused consent. Reutter kept him as long as possible; then, in 1748, Joseph, now sixteen, found himself free and penniless, and with no grace of person to win fortune's smile. His face was pitted with smallpox, his nose was outstanding, his legs were too short for his body, his dress was shabby, his gait awkward, his manner shy. He was not yet skilled in any instrument, but he was already turning over compositions in his head.

A fellow chorister offered him an attic room, and Anton Buchholz lent him 150 florins, which honest Haydn later repaid. He had to fetch water up to his garret every day, but he secured an old clavier, took pupils, and survived. On most days he worked sixteen hours, sometimes more. He played the violin in a church; he played the organ in the private chapel of Count Haugwitz, minister to Maria Theresa; he sang tenor, now and then, in St. Stephen's. The famous Metastasio had an apartment in the same building; he secured Haydn as music teacher for the daughter of a friend; through Metastasio Haydn met Porpora; Haydn agreed to serve this prince of singing masters in any capacity, in return for instruction in composition. He received the precious lessons, cleaned the maestro's shoes, coat, and wig, and provided clavier accompaniment for Porpora and pupils. Said Haydn in retrospect: "Young people can learn from my example that something can come out of nothing. What I am is all the result of the direst need."[27]

Through his new friends he became acquainted with Gluck and Dittersdorf, and several members of the nobility. Karl Joseph von Fürnberg took him (1755) for a long stay at his country house, Weinzierl, near Melk; there Haydn found an orchestra of eight pieces, and some leisure to compose. Now he wrote his first quartets. To the sonata structure of three movements, which he adopted from Karl Philipp Emanuel Bach, he added a minuet, scored the four movements for four pieces, and gave the instrumental quartet its modern form. He returned to Vienna in 1756, attracted distinguished pupils like the Countess von Thun, and (1759) accepted the post of *Musikdirektor* for Count Maximilian von Morzin, whose private orchestra of twelve to sixteen pieces played at Vienna in winter and, in summer, in the Count's villa at Lukavec in Bohemia. For this ensemble Haydn wrote his first symphony (1759).

As he was now earning two hundred florins per year, with board and lodging, he thought he could risk the gamble of marriage. Among his pupils were two daughters of a wigmaker; he fell in love with the younger one, but she became a nun, and the father prevailed upon Haydn to marry the sister, Maria Anna (1760). She was thirty-one, he twenty-eight. She proved to be quarrelsome, bigoted, wasteful and barren. "She doesn't care a straw," said Haydn, "whether her husband is an artist or a cobbler."[28] He began to look at other women.

The audience in Morzin's home occasionally included Prince Pál Anton Esterházy. When Morzin disbanded his orchestra the Prince engaged Haydn (1761) as assistant music director for his country seat at Eisenstadt in Hungary. The contract called for four hundred florins per year with a seat at the officers' table; and "it is especially observed that when the orchestra shall be summoned to perform before company, the . . . musicians shall appear in uniform, . . . in white stockings, white linen, and . . . a queue or a tiewig."[29] At Eisenstadt the *Kapellmeister*, Gregor Werner, busied himself with church music; Haydn prepared concerts and composed music for them. He had under him fourteen musicians, seven singers, and a chorus chosen from the servants of the Prince. The small size of the orchestra, and the character of the audience, shared in determining the light and amiable quality of the music written by Haydn for the Esterházy family. His genial spirit made him popular with the musicians; they called him "Papa Haydn" soon after his coming to Eisenstadt, though he was then only twenty-nine.[30] For them he composed sonatas, trios, quartets, concertos, songs, cantatas, and some thirty symphonies. Many of these compositions, though by contract they belonged to the Prince, were published or circulated in manuscript, in Vienna, Leipzig, Amsterdam, Paris, and London, and gave Haydn, by 1766, an international reputation.

When Pál Anton died (March 18, 1762) he was succeeded, as head of the Esterházy family, by his brother Miklós József, who loved music almost as much as his diamond-studded uniform. He played well on the viola di bordone (a variant of the viola da gamba), and was a kindly master to Haydn in the nearly thirty years of their association. Said Haydn: "My Prince was always satisfied with my works. I not only had the encouragement of constant approval, but as conductor of an orchestra I could make experiments, observe what produced an effect and what weakened it, and was thus in a position to improve, alter, . . . and be as bold as I pleased. I was cut off from the world, there was no one to confuse or torment me, and I was forced to become original."[31]

Werner died on March 5, 1766, and Haydn became *Kapellmeister*. Soon afterward the household moved into the new palace—the Schloss Esterházy —which Miklós had built at the southern end of the Neusiedler See in northwestern Hungary. The Prince was so fond of this place that he lived there from early spring through autumn; in winter he removed, sometimes with his musicians, to Vienna. The players and singers resented this rural isolation, especially since they were separated, for three seasons of the year, from their wives and children; but they were well paid, and dared not complain. Once, to hint to Miklós that his musicians were longing for a leave of absence, Haydn composed the *Farewell Symphony* (No. 5), in which, toward the end, one instrument after another disappeared from the score, the musician put out his candle, took up his music and his instrument, and left the stage. The Prince saw the point, and arranged for an early departure of the troupe to Vienna.

Haydn, by exception, was allowed to have his wife with him at Esterháza, but he did not appreciate the privilege. In 1779 he fell in love with Luigia Polzelli, a mediocre singer who had been engaged for Esterháza along with her violinist husband Antonio. Haydn seems to have felt that since the Catholic Church did not allow him to divorce his troublesome wife, it should, in mercy, permit him a diversion or two; and he made little effort to conceal his liaison. Antonio was too old and ill to make effective protest, and knew that he was kept on the rolls only because the *Kapellmeister* relished Luigia. She had come to Esterháza with a two-year-old son; in 1783 she bore another boy, whom gossip credited to Papa Haydn; he took both the boys to his heart, and helped them throughout his life.

During those busy years at Esterháza Haydn, lacking outside stimulus and competition, developed slowly as a composer. He produced nothing memorable till he was thirty-two—an age at which Mozart had completed his *oeuvre* except for *The Magic Flute* and the *Requiem*. Haydn's finest works came after he was fifty: his first major symphony when he was nearly sixty, *The Creation* when he was sixty-six. He wrote several operas for performance at Esterháza, but when Prague invited him to present an opera there, in a series that was to include *The Marriage of Figaro* and *Don Giovanni*, he demurred in a letter of noble modesty (December, 1787):

> You desire an *opera buffa* from me. . . . If you intend to stage it at Prague I cannot oblige you. My operas are inseparable from the company for which I wrote them, and would never produce their calculated effect apart from their native surroundings. It would be quite another matter if I had the honor of being commissioned to write a new opera for your theater. Even then, however, it would be a risk to put myself in competition with the great Mozart. If I could only inspire every lover of music, especially among the great, with feelings as deep, and comprehension as clear, as my own, in listening to the inimitable works of Mozart, then surely the nations would contend for the possession of such a jewel within their borders. Prague must strive to retain this treasure within her grasp, but not without fitting reward. The want of this often saddens the life of a great genius, and offers small encouragement for further efforts and future times. I feel indignant that Mozart has not yet been engaged at any imperial or royal court. Pardon my wandering from the subject; Mozart is a man very dear to me.[32]

Haydn himself was longing for some court where his talent might more widely spread its wings, but he had to be content with royal compliments.

Gifts arrived from Ferdinand IV of Naples, Frederick William II of Prussia, and the Grand Duchess Maria Feodorovna of Russia. In 1781 Charles III of Spain sent him a golden snuffbox set with diamonds, and the Spanish ambassador at Vienna traveled to Esterháza to present the little treasure in person. Perhaps Boccherini, then settled in Madrid, had a hand in this, for he so zealously adopted Haydn's style that he was nicknamed "Haydn's wife."[33] When the cathedral chapter at Cadíz decided to commission a musical setting for the "Seven Last Words of Our Saviour" it applied to Haydn, who responded with an oratorio (1785) that was soon performed in many lands—in the United States as early as 1791. In 1784 a Paris producer asked for six symphonies; Haydn obliged with six *Paris Symphonies*. Several invitations came to him to conduct concerts in London. Haydn felt bound to Esterháza by loyalty as well as contract, but his private letters revealed his increasing eagerness for a larger stage.

On September 28, 1790, Prince Miklós József died. The new Prince, Anton Esterházy, cared little for music; he dismissed nearly all the musicians, but kept Haydn nominally in his service, gave him a yearly pension of fourteen hundred florins, and allowed him to live wherever he pleased. Haydn almost precipitately moved to Vienna. Several proposals were now made to him, most urgently from Johann Peter Salomon, who announced, "I have come from London to fetch you; we shall conclude our accord tomorrow." He offered £300 for a new opera, £300 more for six symphonies, £200 more for their copyright, £200 more for twenty concerts in England, £200 more for a concert to be given there for Haydn's benefit—£1,200 in all. Haydn knew no English, and dreaded the Channel crossing. Mozart begged him not to take on such labors and risks: "Oh, Papa, you have had no education for the wide world, and you speak so few languages!" Haydn answered, "But my language is understood all over the world."[34] He sold the house Prince Miklós József had given him in Eisenstadt, provided for his wife and his mistress, and set off on the great adventure. He spent with Mozart the final days before departure. Mozart wept to see him go; "I'm afraid, Papa, that this will be our last farewell."

Haydn and Salomon left Vienna December 15, 1790, and reached London January 1, 1791. His first concert (March 11) was a triumph. The *Morning Chronicle* ended its report by saying: "We cannot suppress our very anxious hope that the first musical genius of the age may be induced by our liberal welcome to take up his residence in England."[35] All the concerts went well, and on May 16 a benefit concert gladdened Haydn with £350. In that month he attended the Handel Commemoration Concert in Westminster Abbey and heard the *Messiah;* he was so impressed that he wept, saying, humbly, "Handel, the master of us all."[36] Burney suggested that Oxford give the new Handel an honorary degree; it was offered; Haydn went up to the university in July, became a doctor of music, and conducted there his Symphony in G Major (No. 92); he had composed it three years before, but henceforth history knew it as the *Oxford Symphony*. Its lovely slow movement recalls the old English ballad "Lord Randall."

Having had a view of the English countryside as a divine transfiguration of seed and rain, Haydn, after returning to London, gladly accepted invitations to country houses. There and in the city he won many friends by his cheerful readiness to play and sing at private gatherings. He took advanced pupils to teach them composition. One of these was a comely and wealthy widow, Johanna Schroeter. Though he was sixty the aura of his fame went to her head, and she tendered him her love. He said later, "In all likelihood I should have married her if I had been single."[37] Meanwhile his wife importuned him to come home. In a letter to Luigia Polzelli he grumbled: "My wife, that infernal beast, wrote me so many things that I was forced to answer that I was never coming back."[38]

Despite three women on his conscience and his purse, he worked hard and now composed six (Nos. 93–98) of his twelve *London Symphonies*. They show a remarkable development from his productions at Eisenstadt and Esterháza. Perhaps Mozart's symphonies had stimulated him, or he had been put on his mettle by the reception given him in England, or hearing Handel had stirred in him depths untouched by his quiet environment in the Hungarian hills, or his love affairs had moved him to tender sentiments as well as simple joy. He found it difficult to leave England, but he was under contract with Prince Anton Esterházy, who now insisted that Haydn return to share in the festivities prepared for the coronation of the Emperor Francis II. So, toward the end of June, 1792, he braved the Channel again, passed from Calais to Brussels to Bonn, met Beethoven (then twenty-two), attended the coronation at Frankfurt, and reached Vienna July 29.

No newspaper mentioned his return, no concerts were arranged for him, the court ignored him. Mozart would have welcomed him, but Mozart was no more. Haydn wrote to the widow, offered gratis lessons to Mozart's son, and urged publishers to print more of Mozart's music. He went to live with his wife in the house which is now preserved as a Haydn museum (Haydngasse 19). The wife wished him to put the property in her name; he refused. His quarrels with her were intensified. Beethoven came in December, 1792, to study with him. The two geniuses did not harmonize: Beethoven was proud and domineering; Haydn called him "that great Mogul,"[39] and was too absorbed in his own work to correct his pupil's exercises conscientiously. Beethoven secretly found another teacher, but continued to take lessons from Haydn. "I have learned nothing from him," said the young Titan;[40] however, many of his early pieces follow Haydn's style, and some were dedicated to the old master.

Appreciation of Haydn grew in Austria, and at Rohrau, in 1792, Count von Harrach set up a monument to the town's now famous son. But the memory of triumphs and friendships in England was still warm, and when Salomon offered him a second engagement in London, with a commission to write six new symphonies, the composer readily agreed. He left Vienna on January 19, 1794, and reached London on February 4. This stay of eighteen months in England was as heartening a success as the first. The second set of *London Symphonies* (Nos. 99–104) was well received, a benefit concert netted Haydn £400, pupils paid him a guinea per lesson, and Mrs. Schroeter lived nearby. He was again a favorite with the aristocracy; both the King and the King's enemy, the Prince of Wales, received him; the Queen offered him a residence at Windsor for the summer if he would remain in England for another season. He excused himself on the ground that the new Prince Esterházy was summoning him, and he could not so long absent himself from his wife (!). Prince Anton had died; his successor, Prince Miklós II, wished to restore orchestral performances at Eisenstadt. So, his trunks packed and his pockets full, Haydn left London August 15, 1795, and made his way home.

After a visit to his own statue at Rohrau, he reported to Miklós II at Eisenstadt, and organized music for various occasions there. Except for summer and autumn, however, he lived in his own house on the outskirts of Vienna. In the years 1796-97 Napoleon was driving the Austrians before him in Italy, and the rise of revolutionary sentiment in Austria threatened the Hapsburg monarchy. Haydn recalled how the emotion aroused by the singing of "God Save the King" had strengthened the Hanoverian dynasty in England; might not a national anthem do likewise for Emperor Francis II? His friend Baron Gottfried van Swieten (son of Maria Theresa's physician) suggested this to Count von Saurau, minister of the interior; Saurau appointed Leopold Haschka to compose a text; the poet responded with "*Gott erhalte Franz den Kaiser, unsern guten Kaiser Franz!*" Haydn adapted to these words the tune of an old Croat song, and the result was a simple but stirring anthem. It was first publicly sung on the Emperor's birthday, February 12, 1797, in all the principal theaters of the Austro-Hungarian realm. It continued, with some change of words, to be the Austrian national hymn until 1938. Haydn developed the melody, with variations, into the second movement of his string quartet Opus 76, No. 3.

Still under the spell of Handel, Haydn tried next to rival the *Messiah*. Salomon had offered him a libretto compiled from Milton's *Paradise Lost*; van Swieten translated the libretto into German, and Haydn composed his massive oratorio *Die Schöpfung. The Creation* was performed before an invited audience in the palace of Prince von Schwarzenberg April 29-30, 1798. So great a crowd gathered outside the palace that fifty mounted police (we are assured) were needed to keep order.[41] The Prince financed a public performance in the National Theater March 19, 1799, and gave all the proceeds (four thousand florins) to the composer. The auditors greeted the music with almost religious fervor; soon the oratorio was heard in almost every major city in Christendom. The Catholic Church condemned the composition as too lighthearted for so august a theme, and Schiller agreed with Beethoven in ridiculing Haydn's mimicry of Eden's animals; but Goethe acclaimed the work, and in Prussia it was more frequently performed in the nineteenth century than any other choral composition.

Van Swieten offered another libretto, adapted from James Thomson's *The Seasons*. Haydn labored over it for nearly two years (1799-1801), at much cost to his health; *The Seasons*, he said, "has broken my back." The première

(April 24, 1801) was well received, but the piece aroused no wide or lasting enthusiasm. After conducting *The Seven Last Words of Christ* for a hospital benefit, Haydn retired from active life.

His wife had died on March 20, 1800, but he was now too old to enjoy his freedom, though not too old to enjoy his fame. He was recognized as the dean of composers; a dozen cities voted him honors; famous musicians— Cherubini, the Webers, Ignaz Pleyel, Hummel—came to pay him homage. Nevertheless rheumatism, dizziness, and other ailments left him melancholy, irritable, and fearfully pious. Camille Pleyel, visiting him in 1805, found him "holding a rosary in his hands, and I believe he passes almost the whole day in prayer. He says always that his end is near. . . . We did not stay long, for we saw that he wished to pray."[42] In that year a false report spread that Haydn had died. Cherubini wrote a cantata on his death, and Paris planned a memorial concert with Mozart's *Requiem*; then word came that the old man was still alive. When Haydn heard of this he remarked, "I would have traveled to Paris to conduct the *Requiem* myself."[43]

He made his last public appearance on March 27, 1809, when *The Creation* was sung at the University of Vienna to celebrate his approaching seventy-sixth birthday. Prince Esterházy sent his carriage to take the invalid to the concert; Haydn was borne in an armchair into the hall amid an audience of nobles and celebrities; princesses wrapped their shawls around his shivering body; Beethoven knelt and kissed his hand. Emotion overcame the old composer; he had to be taken home in the intermission.

On May 12, 1809, Napoleon's artillery began to bombard Vienna. A cannonball fell near Haydn's house, shaking it and the inmates, but Haydn assured them, "Children, don't be frightened; where Haydn is no harm can come to you." It proved true except for himself; the bombardment shattered his nervous system. When the French took the city Napoleon ordered a guard of honor to be placed before the composer's home. A French officer, entering, sang an aria from *The Creation* in "so manly and sublime a style" that Haydn embraced him. On May 31 he died, aged seventy-seven. All the major cities of Europe held services in his memory.

Haydn's historic achievement was in the development of musical forms. He gave the orchestra a new vitality by balancing the strings with wind and percussion instruments. Building upon the work of Sammartini, Stamitz, and Karl Philipp Emanuel Bach, he established the structure of the sonata as the exposition, elaboration, and recapitulation of contrasted themes. He prepared the *divertimento* for Mozart as less formal than the suite, and better adapted for social gatherings. He gave the string quartet its classic configuration by extending it to four movements, and by giving the first movement "sonata form." Here his successors had to use the same number and quality of instruments that Haydn had employed, and he achieved in several instances a cheerful and tender loveliness to which some of us return with relief from the laborious involutions of Beethoven's later quartets.

Nine or ten of the 104 Haydn symphonies still live. The names they bear were not his choice, but were applied by commentators or editors. We have noted elsewhere the evolution of the sinfonia (i.e., assembled sounds) from the overture through the experiments of Sammartini and Stamitz; many others preceded Haydn in molding the structure of the "classic" symphony; and when he emerged from Esterháza into a wider world he was not too old to learn from Mozart how to fill out the structure with significance and feeling. The *Oxford Symphony* marks his rise to greater amplitude and power, and the *London Symphonies* show him in his fullest symphonic reach. No. 101 (the *Clock Symphony*) is delightful, and No. 104 is quite up to Mozart.

Generally we perceive in his music a kindly, gracious nature which may never have felt the depths of grief or love, and which had been compelled to produce too rapidly to permit the maturing of concept, theme, or phrase. Haydn was too happy to be profoundly great, and spoke too often to say much. And yet there is a treasure of pure and placid delight in these playful scores; here, as he put it, "the weary and worn, or the man burdened with affairs, may enjoy some solace and refreshment."[44]

Haydn fell out of fashion soon after his death. His works reflected a stable feudal world, and an environment of aristocratic security and ease; they were too gay and self-content to satisfy a century of revolutions, crises, and romantic ecstasies and despair. He came back into favor when Brahms praised him and Debussy wrote *Homage à Haydn* (1909). Men then realized that though the Raphael and the Michelangelo of music who followed him poured deeper thought with subtler mastery into their compositions, they were able to do this because Haydn and his predecessors had molded the forms to receive their gold. "I know that God has bestowed a talent upon me," Haydn said, "and I thank Him for it. I think I have done my duty, and been of use; . . . let others do the same."[45]

CHAPTER XV

Mozart

I. THE WONDERFUL BOY: 1756–66

SALZBURG, like Prague and Pressburg and Esterháza, was a musical outpost of Vienna. It had its own character, partly from the salt mines that explain its name, partly from its environing mountains and its bisecting Salzach River, partly from having grown up around the monastery and episcopal see founded there about A.D. 700 by St. Rupert of Worms. The archbishop had been made an Imperial prince in 1278, and from that time till 1802 he was the civic as well as the ecclesiastical ruler of the city. In 1731–32 some thirty thousand Protestants had been forced to migrate, leaving Salzburg thoroughly and theocratically Catholic. Otherwise the archiepiscopal rule rested lightly on an orthodox population which, assured of eternal certainties, devoted itself to epidermal contacts and other worldly joys. Sigismund von Schrattenbach, archbishop during Mozart's youth, was especially genial and kindly, except to heretics.

To this lovely town Leopold Mozart had come in 1737, aged eighteen, from his native Augsburg, presumably to study theology and become a priest. But he lost his heart to music, served for three years as musician and valet in a patrician's home, and in 1743 became fourth violinist in the Archbishop's orchestra. When he married Anna Maria Pertl (1747) he and she were rated the handsomest couple in Salzburg. He composed concertos, Masses, symphonies, and wrote a long-honored textbook of violin technique. In 1757 he was appointed court composer to the Archbishop. Of his seven children only two survived childhood: Maria Anna (Marianna, "Nannerl"), born 1751, and Wolfgang Amadeus, born January 27, 1756. (The boy's full name—soliciting the intercession of several saints—was Joannes Chrysostomus Wolfgangus Theophilus Mozart; Theophilus was translated from Greek into Latin as Amadeus, Lover of God.) Leopold was a good husband and father, devoted and industrious. His letters to his son are warm with love, and not wanting in wisdom. The Mozart home—allowing for a little obscenity—was a haven of mutual affection, parental piety, childish pranks, and music without end.

Every German child was expected to become in some measure, on some instrument, a musician. Leopold taught his children music with their ABC's. Marianna was already at eleven a virtuoso at the clavichord. Wolfgang, stimulated by her lead, took eagerly to the clavier: at three he picked out chords; at four he played several pieces from memory; at five he invented compositions which the father put on paper as they were played. Leopold refrained, at some cost, from taking other pupils, wishing to give full attention to his children. He did not send "Wolf" to school, for he proposed to be his teacher in everything. Presumably some German discipline was used, but not much was needed in this case; the boy would of his own accord remain at the keyboard for hours on end till forced away.[1] Years later Leopold wrote to him:

> Both as a child and as a boy you were serious rather than childlike; and when you were at the clavier, or otherwise engaged with music, you would not suffer the least joking to go on with you. Your very countenance was so serious that many observant persons prophesied your early death, on the ground of your precocious talent and earnest mien.[2]

In January, 1762, while Germany was still torn with war, Leopold took daughter and son to Munich to display their artistry before the Elector Maximilian Joseph; and in September he led them to Vienna. They were invited to Schönbrunn; Maria Theresa and Francis I were delighted with the children; Wolfgang leaped into the Empress' lap, hugged and kissed her; challenged by the Emperor, he played the violin with one finger, and played the clavichord unerringly though the keys were covered with a cloth. Romping with the princesses, Wolfgang stumbled and fell; the Archduchess Maria Antonia, seven years old, picked him up and comforted him. "You are good," he said, and gratefully added, "I will marry you."[3] A dozen aristocrats opened their homes to the Mozarts, marveled at the music they heard, and rewarded the trio with money and gifts. Then the boy was bedded for a fortnight with scarlet fever—the first of many illnesses that were to mar his travels. In January, 1763, the troupe returned to Salzburg.

The indulgent Archbishop overlooked the fact that Leopold had exceeded his leave of absence; indeed, he promoted him to be *Vize-Kapellmeister*. But on June 9, forfeiting further promotion, Leopold took to the road again, this time with his wife, to show his brood to Europe; after all, they could not remain child prodigies forever. At Mainz the children gave two concerts, at Frankfurt four; sixty years later Goethe recalled that he had heard one of these, and how he had marveled at "the little man with wig and sword"—for so Leopold had accoutered his son. Wolfgang was exploited by his father as almost a circus wonder. An announcement in a Frankfurt newspaper of August 30, 1763, promised that in the concert of that evening

> the little girl, who is in her twelfth year, will play the most difficult compositions of the greatest masters; the boy, who is not yet seven, will perform on the clavichord or harpsichord; he will also play a concerto for the violin, and will accompany symphonies on the clavier, the keyboard being covered with a cloth, with as much facility as if he could see the keys. He will instantly name all notes played at a distance, whether singly or in chords, on the clavier or on any other instrument—bell, glass, or clock. He will finally, both on the harpsichord and the organ, improvise as long as may be desired, and in any key.[4]

Such demands upon the boy's talents may have done some damage to his health or nerves, but he seems to have enjoyed the applause as much as his father enjoyed the florins.

They played at Coblenz, were disappointed at Bonn and Cologne, but had a concert at Aachen. At Brussels they expected that the governor-general,

Prince Charles of Lorraine, would honor their performance with his presence, but he was busy. Leopold angrily reported:

> We have now been nearly three weeks in Brussels . . . and nothing has happened. . . . His Highness does nothing but hunt, gobble, and swill, and we may in the end discover that he has no money. . . . I own that we have received sundry presents here, but we do not wish to convert them into cash. . . . What with snuffboxes and leather cases and such-like gewgaws, we shall soon be able to open a stall.[5]

The Prince finally agreed to attend; a concert was given, florins were collected, and the troupe encoached for Paris.

On November 15, 1763, they arrived in Paris after tumbling three days on rough and rutted roads. They had letters of introduction to many notables, but none proved so valuable as the one to Melchior Grimm. He arranged to have the Mozarts received by Mme. de Pompadour, by the royal family, finally by Louis XV and Queen Marie Leszczinska. Now the most lordly homes were opened to the visitors, private and public concerts went off well, and Grimm wrote enthusiastically to his clientele:

> True miracles are rare, but how wonderful it is when we have the opportunity to see one! A Salzburg Kapellmeister by the name of Mozart has just come here with two of the prettiest children in the world. His daughter, aged eleven, plays the piano in the most brilliant fashion, performs the longest and most difficult pieces with astounding precision. Her brother, who will be seven next February, is such an extraordinary phenomenon that you can hardly believe what you see with your own eyes. . . . His hands are hardly big enough to take a sixth. . . . He improvises for an hour, yielding himself to the inspiration of his genius, with a wealth of delightful ideas. . . . The most consummate Kapellmeister cannot possibly have so deep a knowledge of harmony and modulation as this child. . . . It is nothing for him to decipher whatever you put before him. He writes and composes with marvelous ease, and does not find it necessary to go to the piano and look for his chords. I wrote out a minuet for him and asked him to put a bass to it. He seized a pen, and without going to the piano he wrote the bass. . . . The child will turn my head if I listen to him much more. . . . What a pity that so little is understood of music in this country![6]

After many triumphs in Paris the family departed for Calais (April 10, 1764). In London they were received by George III. For four hours, on May 19, before King and court, Wolfgang played Handel and Bach and other masters at sight; he accompanied Queen Charlotte's singing, and improvised a new melody to the bass of a Handel aria. Johann Christian Bach, who had settled in London in 1762, placed the boy on his knee and played a sonata with him, each playing a bar in turn, "with so much precision that no one would have suspected two performers."[7] Bach began a fugue, Wolfgang pursued it, again as if the two geniuses were one. Thereafter, for several years, Mozart's compositions showed the influence of Johann Christian Bach. On June 5 the children gave a concert which gladdened Leopold with a hundred guineas net. But the father was afflicted with severe inflammation of the throat, and the family retired to Chelsea for seven weeks' rest, during which Wolfgang, now eight, composed two symphonies (K. 16 and 19).

On July 24, 1765, they left London for Holland, but at Lille both father and son took sick, and the tour was halted for a month, though Archbishop von Schrattenbach had long ago called for Leopold's return. They reached The Hague on September 11, but on the next day Marianna fell ill in her turn, and soon worsened so that on October 21 she received the last sacrament. On September 30 Wolfgang gave a concert without his sister's aid. She had scarcely recovered when he was seized with a fever, and the family had to live in costly idleness till January, 1766. On January 29 and February 26 they gave concerts at Amsterdam; now for the first time a Mozart symphony (K. 22) was publicly performed. During these months the boy composed furiously. In May they returned to Paris, where much of their baggage had been left; Grimm secured comfortable lodgings for them; they again performed at Versailles and in public; not till July 9 did they tear themselves away from the fascinating capital.

They dallied at Dijon as guests of the Prince de Condé; they spent four weeks at Lyons, three at Geneva, one in Lausanne, another in Bern, two in Zurich, twelve days at Donaueschingen; then brief stops at Biberach, Ulm, and Augsburg; a longer stay at Munich, where Wolfgang again took sick. At last, toward the end of November, 1766, after an absence of three and a half years, the family regained Salzburg. The old Archbishop forgave them, and they could now appreciate the comforts of home. All seemed well, but Mozart was never quite healthy again.

II. ADOLESCENCE: 1766–77

Leopold was an unrelenting taskmaster. He put his son through a hard course of instruction in counterpoint, thorough bass, and such other elements of composition as had come down to him from German and Italian music. When the Archbishop heard that Wolfgang composed, he wondered was not the father co-operating. To settle the question he invited the boy to stay with him for a week; he isolated him from all outside help, gave him paper, pencil, and harpsichord, and bade him compose part of an oratorio on the First Commandment. At the close of the week Mozart presented the result; the Archbishop was told that it merited praise; he commissioned his *Konzertmeister*, Michael (brother of Joseph) Haydn, to compose a second part, and his organist to compose a third; the whole was performed at the archiepiscopal court on March 12, 1767, and was judged worthy of repetition on April 2. Mozart's part is now included as No. 35 in Köchel's catalogue.*

Learning that the Archduchess Maria Josepha was soon to marry King Ferdinand of Naples, Leopold thought the ceremonies to be held at the Imperial court would offer a new opportunity for his children. On September 11, 1767, the family left for Vienna. They were admitted to the court, with

* This was originally issued at Leipzig in 1862 as *Chronologisch-thematisches Verzeichniss sämmtlicher Tonwerke W. A. Mozarts*. We use the revision by Alfred Einstein in *Mozart, His Character and His Work* (London, 1957), 473-83.

the result that both Wolfgang and Marianna caught smallpox from the bride. The unhappy parents took their prodigies to Olmütz in Moravia, where Count Podstatsky gave them shelter and care. Mozart was blind for nine days. On January 10, 1768, the family was back in Vienna; both the Empress and Joseph II received them cordially, but the court was mourning the death of the bride, and concerts were out of the question.

After a long and unprofitable absence the family returned to Salzburg (January 5, 1769). Mozart continued his studies with his father, but toward the end of the year Leopold decided that he had taught the boy all that he could, and that what Wolfgang needed now was acquaintance with the musical life of Italy. Having secured letters of introduction to Italian *maestri* from Johann Hasse and others, father and son set out on December 13, 1769, leaving Marianna and mother to keep a footing in Salzburg. On the next evening Mozart gave a concert at Innsbruck; he played at sight an unfamiliar concerto placed before him as a test of his skill; the local press acclaimed his "extraordinary musical attainments."[8] At Milan they met Sammartini, Hasse, and Piccini, and Count von Firmian secured for Wolfgang a commission for an opera; this meant a hundred ducats for the family coffers. At Bologna they heard the still marvelous voice of Farinelli, who had returned from his triumphs in Spain, and they arranged with Padre Martini that Wolfgang should return to take the tests for the coveted diploma of the Accademia Filarmonica. At Florence, at the court of the Grand Duke Leopold, Mozart played the harpsichord to Nardini's violin. Then father and son hurried on to Rome for the Holy Week music.

They arrived on April 11, 1770, in a storm of thunder and lightning, so that Leopold could report that they had been "received like grand people with a discharge of artillery."[9] They were just in time to go to the Sistine Chapel and hear the "Miserere" of Gregorio Allegri, which was sung there annually. Copies of this famous chorale, written for four, five, or nine parts, were hard to get; Mozart listened to it twice and wrote it out from memory. They stayed four weeks in Rome, giving concerts in the homes of the civil or ecclesiastical nobility. On May 8 they undertook the journey to Naples; robbers made the road perilous; the Mozarts traveled with four Augustinian monks to secure divine protection or an emergency viaticum. Naples held them for a full month, for the aristocracy, from Tanucci downward, invited them to soirees and placed lordly equipages at their disposal. When Wolfgang played at the Conservatorio della Pietà the superstitious audience ascribed his prowess to some magic in the ring he wore; they were amazed when, having discarded the ring, he played as brilliantly as before.

After enjoying Rome again they crossed the Apennines to worship the Virgin in her Santa Casa at Loretto; then they turned north to spend three months at Bologna. Almost daily Mozart received instruction from Padre Martini in the arcana of composition. Then he took the test for admission to the Accademia Filarmonica: he was given a piece of Gregorian plain chant, to which, while he was shut up alone in a room, he was required to add three upper parts in *stile osservato*—strict traditional style. He failed, but the good padre corrected his work, and the revised form was accepted by the jury "in view of the special circumstances"—presumably Mozart's youth.

On October 18 father and son were in Milan. There Wolfgang had his first triumph as a composer, but after hard work and much tribulation. The subject for his commissioned opera was *Mitridate, re di Ponto;* the libretto was taken from Racine. The fourteen-year-old youth toiled so hard in composing, playing, and rewriting that his fingers ached; his enthusiasm became a fever, and his father had to restrict his hours of work and cool his agitation with an occasional walk. Mozart felt that this, his first *opera seria*, was a far more critical test than that antiquarian trial at Bologna; his career as an operatic composer might depend upon the outcome. Now, though not much inclined to piety, he begged his mother and sister to pray for the success of this venture, "so that we may all live happily together again."[10] At last, when he was near exhaustion with rehearsals, the opera was presented to the public (December 26, 1770); the composer conducted, and his triumph was complete. Every important aria was received with wild applause, some with cries of "*Evviva il maestro! Evviva il maestrino!*" The opera was repeated twenty times. "We see by this," wrote the proud and pious father, "how the power of God works in us when we do not bury the talents that He has graciously bestowed upon us."[11]

Now they could go home with their heads high. On March 28, 1771, they reached Salzburg. They had hardly arrived when they received a request from Count von Firmian, in the name of the Empress, that Wolfgang write a serenata or cantata, and come to Milan in October to conduct it as part of the ceremonies that were to celebrate the marriage of Archduke Ferdinand to the Princess of Modena. Archbishop Sigismund consented to another absence of Leopold from his duties; and on August 13 *pater et filius* set out again for Italy. Arrived in Milan, they found that Hasse was there, preparing an opera for the same ceremonies; perhaps without intending it so, the managers had arranged a battle of genius between the most renowned living composer of Italian opera, who was in his seventy-third year, and the fifteen-year-old lad who had barely tried his operatic wings. Hasse's *Ruggiero* was performed to great applause on October 16. On the next day Mozart's cantata, *Ascanio in Alba,* was sung under his baton, and "the applause was extraordinary." "I am sorry," wrote Leopold to his wife, "that Wolfgang's serenata should have so entirely eclipsed Hasse's opera."[12] Hasse was generous; he joined in the praise of Mozart, and made a famous prophecy: "*Questo ragazzo ci farà dimenticar tutti*" (This boy will throw us all into oblivion).[13]

Father and son returned to Salzburg (December 11, 1771). Five days later the good Sigismund died. His successor as archbishop, Hieronymus von Paula, Count von Colloredo, was a man of intellectual culture, an admirer of Rousseau and Voltaire, an enlightened despot eager to carry out the reforms that Joseph II was preparing. But even more than Joseph he was despotic as well as enlightened, demanding discipline and obedience, and intolerant of opposition. For his ceremonial installation on April 29, 1772, he asked nothing less than an opera from Mozart. The now famous youth responded hastily with *Il sogno di Scipione* (*The Dream of Scipio*); it served its turn and is forgotten. Colloredo forgave it, and appointed Wolfgang concertmaster with a yearly salary of 150 florins. The youth busied himself for some months with composing symphonies, quartets, and religious music, but also he worked on an opera, *Lucio Silla*, which Milan had ordered for 1773.

By November 4, 1772, Leopold and his moneymaker were again in the Lombard capital, and soon Wolf was laboring to find compromises between his musical ideas and the caprices and capacities of the singers. The prima donna began by being imperious and hard to satisfy; the *maestrino* was patient with her; she ended by loving him, and declared herself "enchanted by the incomparable way Mozart had served her."[14] The première (February 26, 1772) was not so certain a success as *Mitridate* two years before; the tenor fell ill during rehearsals, and had to be replaced by a singer with no stage experience; nevertheless the opera bore nineteen repetitions. The music was difficult; the arias were strung too high with passion; perhaps some strain of Germany's Sturm und Drang had made here an incongruous entry into Italian opera.[15] In exchange, Mozart brought back with him the *bel canto* clarity of Italian song, and his naturally happy spirit was further brightened by Italian skies and plein-air life. He learned in Italy that *opera buffa*, as he heard it in the works of Piccini and Paisiello, could be high art; he studied the form, and in *Figaro* and *Don Giovanni* he perfected it. To his alert mind and ears every experience was education.

March 13, 1773, saw *père et fils* again in Salzburg. The new Archbishop was not as tolerant of their long absences as Sigismund had been. He saw no reason for rewarding Leopold with promotion, and treated Wolfgang as merely one of his household retinue. He expected the Mozarts to supply his choir and his orchestra with music prompt, new, and good; and for two years they labored to satisfy him. But Leopold wondered how he could support his family without additional tours, and Wolfgang, accustomed to applause, could not adjust himself to being a musical servant. Besides, he wanted to write operas, and Salzburg had too small a stage, too small a choir, orchestra, and audience, to let the bright fledgling flap his expanding wings.

The clouds broke for a while when Elector Maximilian Joseph of Bavaria commissioned Mozart to write an *opera buffa* for the Munich Carnival of 1775, and secured the Archbishop's consent to a leave of absence for the composer and his father. They left Salzburg on December 6, 1774. Wolfgang suffered from the severe cold, which brought on a toothache more severe than either music or philosophy could mitigate. But the première of *La finta giardiniera* (*The Pretended Garden Girl*), January 13, 1775, led Christian Schubart, a prominent composer, to predict: "If Mozart does not turn out to be a hothouse plant [too rapidly developed by intensive domestic care], he will undoubtedly be one of the greatest composers that ever lived."[16] His head swirling with success, Mozart returned to Salzburg to serve what he felt to be an unworthy vassalage.

The Archbishop ordered a music drama to celebrate the expected visit of

Maria Theresa's youngest son, the Archduke Maximilian; Mozart took an old libretto by Metastasio and composed *Il re pastore* (*The Shepherd King*). It was performed on April 23, 1775. The story is silly, the music is excellent; excerpts from it still show up in the concert repertoire. Meanwhile Mozart was pouring forth sonatas, symphonies, concertos, serenades, Masses; and some of the compositions of these unhappy years—e.g., the Piano Concerto in E Flat (K. 271) and the Serenade in B (K. 250)—are among his enduring masterpieces. The Archbishop, however, told him that he knew nothing of the composer's art, and should go to study at the Naples Conservatory.[17]

Unable to bear the situation longer, Leopold asked permission to take his son on a tour; Colloredo refused, saying he would not have members of his staff go on "begging expeditions." When Leopold asked again the Archbishop dismissed him and his son from their employment. Wolfgang rejoiced, but his father was frightened at the prospect of being flung, aged fifty-six, upon the indiscriminate world. The Archbishop relented and reinstated him, but would not hear of any absence from his work. Who now would go with Wolfgang upon the extensive foray that had been planned? Mozart was twenty-one, just the age for sexual adventure and marital imprisonment; more than ever he needed guidance. So it was decided that his mother should accompany him. Marianna, trying to forget that she too had been a genius, remained to give her father the most loving care. On September 23, 1777, mother and son left Salzburg to conquer Germany and France.

III. MUSIC AND MARRIAGE: 1777–78

From Munich, on September 26, Mozart wrote to his father a paean of liberation: "I am in my very best spirits, for my head has been as light as a feather ever since I got away from all that humbug; and what is more, I have become fatter."[18] That letter must have crossed one from Leopold, whose emotion may remind us again that the events of history were written upon human flesh:

> After you both had left, I walked up our steps very wearily, and threw myself down on a chair. When we said good-by I made great efforts to retain myself in order not to make our parting too painful, and in the rush and flurry I forgot to give my son a father's blessing. I ran to the window and sent my blessing after you, but I did not see you. . . . Nannerl wept bitterly. . . . She and I send greetings to Mamma, and we kiss you and her millions of times.[19]

Munich taught Wolfgang that he was no longer a prodigy, but just one musician in a land where the supply of composers and performers was outrunning the demand. He had hoped to secure a good place in the Elector's musical retinue, but all places were filled. Mother and son passed on to Augsburg, where they wore themselves out with visiting, at Leopold's urging, the friends of Leopold's youth; but the survivors were now mostly fat and stodgy, and Wolfgang found no interest in them except with a merry cousin, Maria Anna Thekla Mozart, whom he was to immortalize with obscenities.

More to his purpose was Johann Andreas Stein, maker of pianofortes; here for the first time Mozart, who had hitherto used the harpsichord, began to appreciate the possibilities of the new instrument; by the time he reached Paris he had made his transition to the piano. At a concert in Augsburg he played both the piano and the violin, to great applause but little profit.

On October 26 mother and son moved on to Mannheim. There Mozart enjoyed the company and stimulus of skilled musicians, but the Elector Karl Theodor could find no opening for him, and rewarded his performance at court with only a gold watch. Mozart wrote to his father: "Ten carolins would have suited me better. . . . What one needs on a journey is money; and, let me tell you, I now have five watches. . . . I am seriously thinking of having a watch pocket on each leg of my trousers; when I visit some great lord I shall wear both watches, . . . so that it will not occur to him to give me another."[20] Leopold advised him to hurry on to Paris, where Grimm and Mme. d'Épinay would help him; but Wolfgang persuaded his mother that the trip would be too arduous for her in the winter months. Assuming that they were soon leaving for Paris, Leopold warned Wolfgang to beware of the women and the musicians there, and reminded him that he was now the financial hope of the family. Leopold had gone into debt for seven hundred gulden; he was taking pupils in his old age,

> and that, too, in a town where this heavy work is wretchedly paid. . . . Our future depends upon your abundant good sense. . . . I know that you love me, not merely as your father, but also as your truest and surest friend; and that you understand and realize that our happiness and unhappiness, and, what is more, my long life or my speedy death, are, . . . apart from God, in your hands. If I have read you aright, I have nothing but joy to expect from you, and this alone must console me when I am robbed by your absence of a father's delight in hearing you, seeing you, and folding you in my arms. . . . From my heart I give you my paternal blessing.[21]

To one of Leopold's letters (February 9, 1778) "Nannerl," now twenty-six, dowerless and facing spinsterhood, added a note that rounds out the picture of this loving family:

> Papa never leaves me room enough to write to Mamma and yourself. . . . I beg her not to forget me. . . . I wish you a pleasant journey to Paris, and the best of health. I do hope, however, that I shall be able to embrace you soon. God alone knows when that will happen. We are both longing for you to make your fortune, for that, I know for certain, will mean happiness for us all. I kiss Mamma's hands and embrace you, and trust that you will always remember us and think of us. But you must do so only when you have time, say for a quarter of an hour when you are neither composing nor teaching.[22]

It was in this mood of great expectations and loving trust that Leopold received a letter written by Wolfgang on February 4, announcing the arrival of Cupid. Among the minor musicians at Mannheim was Fridolin Weber, who was blessed and burdened with a wife, five daughters, and a son. Frau Weber was casting nets to snare husbands, especially for the oldest daughter, Josefa, nineteen and nervously nubile. Mozart, however, fancied Aloysia, sixteen, whose angelic voice and swelling charms made her a young musician's dream. He hardly noticed Constanze, fourteen, who was to be his wife. For Aloysia he composed some of his tenderest songs. When she sang them he forgot his own ambitions, and thought of accompanying her—and Josefa and their father—to Italy, where she could get vocal instruction and operatic opportunities, while he would help to support them by giving concerts and writing operas. All this the brave young lover explained to his father:

> I have become so fond of this unfortunate family that my dearest wish is to make them happy. . . . My advice is that they should go to Italy. So now I should like you to write to our good friend Lugiati, and the sooner the better, and inquire what are the highest terms given to a prima donna in Verona. . . . As far as Aloysia's singing is concerned, I would wager my life that she will bring me renown. . . . If our plan succeeds, we—Herr Weber, his two daughters, and I—will have the honor of visiting my dear sister for a fortnight on our way through Salzburg. . . . I will gladly write an opera for Verona for fifty zecchini ($650?), if only in order that she may make her name. . . . The eldest daughter will be very useful to us, for we could have our own ménage, as she can cook. Apropos, you must not be too much surprised when you learn that I have only forty-two gulden left out of seventy-seven. This is merely the result of my delight at being again in the company of honest and like-minded people. . . .
>
> Send me an answer soon. Do not forget how much I desire to write operas. I envy anyone who is composing one. I could really weep for vexation when I hear . . . an aria. But Italian, not German; seria, not buffa! . . . I have now written all that is weighing on my heart. My mother is quite satisfied with my ideas. . . . The thought of helping a poor family, without injury to myself, delights my very soul. I kiss your hands a thousand times and remain until death your most obedient son.[23]

Leopold replied on February 11:

> My dear son! I have read your letter of the 4th with amazement and horror. . . . For the whole night I have been unable to sleep. . . . Merciful God! . . . Those happy moments are gone when, as a child or a boy, you never went to bed without standing on a chair and singing to me, . . . and kissing me again and again on the tip of my nose, and telling me that when I grew old you would put me in a glass case and protect me from every breath of air, so that you might always have me with you and honor me. Listen to me, therefore, in patience! . . .

He went on to say that he had hoped Wolfgang would defer marriage until he had made a secure place for himself in the musical world; then he would get a good wife, bring up a fine family, help his parents and his sister. But now, infatuated with a young siren, this son forgets his parents, and thinks only of following a girl to Italy, as part of her entourage. What incredible nonsense!

> Off with you to Paris! and that soon! Find your place among great people. Aut Caesar aut nihil! . . . From Paris the name and fame of a man of great talent resounds through the whole world. There the nobility treat men of genius with the greatest deference, esteem, and courtesy; there you will see a refined manner of life, which forms an astonishing contrast to the coarseness of our German courtiers and their ladies; and there you may become proficient in the French tongue.[24]

Mozart answered humbly that he had not taken very seriously the plan to escort the Webers to Italy. He said a tearful goodbye to the Webers, and promised to see them on his way home. On March 14, 1778, he and his mother set off in the public coach for Paris.

IV. IN PARIS: 1778

They arrived on March 23, just in time to be engulfed in the apotheosis of Voltaire. They took simple lodgings, and Mozart ran about seeking commissions. Grimm and Mme d'Épinay bestirred themselves to draw some attention to the youth whom Paris had acclaimed as a prodigy fourteen years before. Versailles offered him the post of court organist at two thousand livres for six months' service per year; Leopold advised him to take it; Grimm opposed; Mozart refused it as too poorly paid, and perhaps as uncongenial to his talent. Many homes were opened to him if he would play the piano for a meal, but even to get to those homes required an expensive cab ride through muddy streets. One noble, the Duc de Guines, looked promising; for him and his daughter Mozart composed the glorious Concerto in C for flute and harp (K. 299), and he gave the young lady lessons in composition at a good fee; but soon she married, and the Duke paid only three louis d'or ($75?) for a concerto that should have laid Paris at Mozart's feet. For the first time in his life Mozart lost courage. "I am tolerably well," he wrote to his father on May 29, "but I often wonder whether life is worth living." His spirits revived when Le Gros, director of the Concerts Spirituels, engaged him to write a symphony (K. 297). It was performed on June 18 with success.

Then, on July 3, his mother died. She had begun by enjoying her vacation from Salzburg and housewifery; soon she was longing to return to her home and the daily tasks and contacts that had given substance and significance to her life. The nine days' trip to Paris in a jolting coach and jarring company and drenching rain had broken her health; and the failure of her son to find a berth in Paris had cast a gloom over her usually buoyant spirit. Day after day she had sat solitary amid strange surroundings and unintelligible words, while her son went to pupils, concerts, operas . . . Now, seeing her fade quietly away, Mozart spent the last weeks at her side, caring for her tenderly, and hardly believing that she could die so soon.

Mme. d'Épinay offered him a room in her home with Grimm, a place at her table, and the use of her piano. He did not quite harmonize with Grimm so near; Grimm idolized Voltaire, Mozart despised him, and was shocked at the assumption of his hosts and their friends that Christianity was a myth useful in social control. Grimm wanted him to accept small commissions as a road to larger ones, and to play gratis for influential families; Mozart felt that such procedure would sap his strength, which he preferred to give to composing. Grimm thought him indolent, and so informed Leopold, who agreed.[25] The situation was made worse by Mozart's repeated borrowing from Grimm, to a total of fifteen louis dor ($375?). Grimm told him that repayment could be indefinitely postponed; it was.[26]

The situation was resolved by a letter (August 31, 1778) from Mozart *père* that Archbishop Colloredo had offered to make the father *Kapellmeister* if Wolfgang would serve as organist and concertmaster, each to receive five hundred florins per year; moreover, "the Archbishop has declared himself prepared to let you travel where you will if you want to write an opera." As irresistible bait Leopold added that Aloysia Weber would probably be invited to join the Salzburg choir, in which case "she must stay with us."[27] Mozart replied (September 11): "When I read your letter I trembled with joy, for I felt myself already in your embrace. It is true, as you will acknowledge, that it is not much of a prospect for me; but when I look forward to seeing you, and embracing my very dear sister, I think of no other prospect."

On September 26 he took the coach to Nancy. At Strasbourg he earned a few louis d'or with arduous concerts to almost empty houses. He dallied at Mannheim, hoping to be appointed conductor of German opera; this too failed. He went on to Munich, dreaming of Aloysia Weber. But she had found a place in the Elector's choir, perhaps in his heart; she received Mozart with a calm that showed no desire to be his bride. He composed and sang a bitter song, and resigned himself to Salzburg.

V. SALZBURG AND VIENNA: 1779–82

He reached home in mid-January, and was welcomed with festivities saddened by the now keenly realized death of the mother. Soon he was in harness as organist and concertmaster, and soon he was fretting. He later recalled:

> In Salzburg work was a burden to me, and I could hardly ever settle down to it. Why? Because I was never happy. . . . In Salzburg—for me at least—there is not a farthing's worth of entertainment. I refuse to associate with a good many people there—and most of the others do not think me good enough. Besides, there is no stimulus for my talent. When I play, or when any of my compositions is performed, it is just as if the audience were all tables and chairs. If only there were even a tolerably good theater in Salzburg![28]

He longed to write operas, and gladly accepted the request of Elector Karl Theodor to compose one for the next Munich festival. He began work on *Idomeneo, re di Creta*, in October, 1780; in November he went to Munich for rehearsals; on January 29, 1781, the opera was produced with success, despite its unusual length. Mozart remained six weeks more in Munich, relishing its social life, until a summons came from Archbishop Colloredo to join him in Vienna. There he had the pleasure of living in the same palace with his employer, but he ate with the servants. "The two valets sit at the head of the table, and I have the honor to be placed above the cooks."[29] This was the custom of the time in the homes of the nobility; Haydn bore it with silent resentment, Mozart rebelled against it ever more audibly. He was pleased to have his music and his talent displayed in the homes of the Archbishop's friends, but he fumed when Colloredo refused most of his requests to let him accept outside engagements that might have brought him added income and wider fame. "When I think of leaving Vienna without at least a thousand florins in my pocket, my heart sinks within me."[30]

He made up his mind to quit Colloredo's service. On May 2, 1781, he went to live as a lodger with the Webers, who had moved to Vienna. When the Archbishop sent him instructions to return to Salzburg, he replied that he could not leave till May 12. An interview followed, in which the Archbishop (as Mozart reported to his father)

> called me the most opprobrious names—oh, I really cannot bring myself to write you all! At last, when my blood was boiling, I could hold out no longer, and said, "Then your Serene Highness is not satisfied with me?" "What! do you mean to threaten me, you rascal, you villain? There is the door; I will have nothing more to do with such a wretched fellow!" At last I said, "Neither will I with you." "Then be off!" As I went I said, "Let it be so, then; tomorrow you shall hear from me by letter." Tell me, dear father, should I not have had to say this sooner or later? . . .
>
> Write to me privately that you are pleased—for indeed you may be so—and find fault with me heartily in public, so that no blame may attach to you. But if the Archbishop offers you the least impertinence, come to me at once in Vienna. We can all three live on my earnings.[31]

Leopold was plunged into another crisis. His own position seemed imperiled, and it was not for some time yet that he would receive reassurances from Colloredo. He was alarmed at the news that his son was rooming with the Webers. The father of that family was now dead; Aloysia had married the actor Joseph Lange; but the widow had another daughter, Constanze, waiting for a husband. Was this another blind alley for Wolfgang? Leopold begged him to apologize to the Archbishop, and come home. Mozart now for the first time refused to obey his father. "To please you, my dear father, I would renounce my happiness, my health, and life itself, but my honor comes before all with me, and so it must be with you. My dearest, best of fathers, demand of me what you will, only not that."[32] On June 2 he sent Leopold thirty ducats as an earnest of future aid.

Three times he went to the Archbishop's Vienna residence to submit his formal resignation. Colloredo's chamberlain refused to transmit it, and on the third occasion he "threw him [Mozart] out of the antechamber and gave him a kick in the behind"—so Mozart described the scene in his letter of June 9.[33] To appease his father he left the Weber home and took other lodgings. He assured Leopold that he had only "had fun" with Constanze: "if I had to marry all those with whom I have jested, I should have two hundred wives at least."[34] However, on December 15 he informed his father that Constanze was so sweet, so simple and domestic, that he wished to marry her.

> You are horrified at the idea? But I entreat you, dearest, most beloved father, to listen to me. . . . The voice of nature speaks as loud in me as in others—louder, perhaps, than in many a big, strong lout of a fellow. I simply cannot live as most young men do in these days. In the first place, I have too much religion; in the second place I have too much love of my neighbor and too high a feeling of honor to seduce an innocent girl; and in the third place I have too much

horror and disgust, too much dread and fear of diseases, and too much care for my health, to fool about with whores. So I can swear that I have never had relations of that sort with any woman. . . . I stake my life on the truth of what I have told you. . . .

But who is the object of my love? . . . Surely not one of the Webers? Yes, . . . Constanze, . . . the kindest-hearted, the cleverest, the best of them all. . . . Tell me whether I could wish myself a better wife. . . . All that I desire is to have a small assured income (of which, thank God, I have good hopes), and then I shall never cease entreating you to allow me to save this poor girl and to make myself and her—and, if I may say so, all of us—very happy. For surely you are happy when I am? And you are to enjoy one half of *my fixed income.* . . . Please take pity on your son![35]

Leopold did not know what to believe. He used every effort to dissuade his almost penniless son from marriage, but Mozart felt that after twenty-six years of filial obedience it was time for him to have his own way, to lead his own life. Through seven months he pleaded in vain for parental consent; finally, on August 4, 1782, he married without it. On August 5 it came. Now Mozart was free to discover how far one could support a family by composing the most varied assemblage of superb music in man's history.

VI. THE COMPOSER

He had reason for confidence, for he had already won reputation as a pianist, had acquired some paying pupils, and had produced successful operas. Just a month after leaving the Archbishop's service he received from Count Orsini-Rosenberg, director of court theaters for Joseph II, a commission to compose a *Singspiel*—a spoken drama interspersed with songs. The result was presented on July 16, 1782, in the presence of the Emperor, as *Die Entführung aus dem Serail* (*The Abduction from the Seraglio*). A hostile clique condemned it, but nearly all the audience was won over by the vivacious arias that adorned an aged theme: a Christian beauty captured by pirates, sold to a Turkish harem, and rescued by her Christian lover after incredible intrigues. Joseph II commented on the music, "Too beautiful for our ears, my dear Mozart, and far too many notes"; to which the reckless composer answered, "Exactly as many, your Majesty, as are needed."[36] The operetta was repeated thirty-three times in Vienna in its first six years. Gluck praised it, though he perceived that it quite ignored his "reform" of the opera; he admired the instrumental compositions of the impetuous youth, and invited him to dinner.

Mozart took inspiration rather from Italy than from Germany; he preferred melody and simple harmony to complex and erudite polyphony. Only in his final decade did he feel strong influences from Handel and Johann Sebastian Bach. In 1782 he joined the musicians who, under the aegis of Baron Gottfried van Swieten, gave concerts, chiefly of Handel and Bach, in the National Library or in van Swieten's home. In 1774 the Baron had brought from Berlin to Vienna *The Art of the Fugue, The Well-tempered Clavichord*, and other works of J. S. Bach. He deprecated Italian music as amateurish; real music, he thought, required strict attention to fugue, polyphony, and counterpoint. Mozart, though he never allowed structure, rule, or form to be an end in itself, profited from van Swieten's counsel and concerts, and carefully studied Handel and the major Bachs. After 1787 he conducted Handel concerts in Vienna, and took some liberties in adjusting Handel's scores to Viennese orchestras. In his later instrumental music he wedded Italian melody and German polyphony in a harmonious union.

A glance at Köchel's catalogue of Mozart's compositions is an impressive experience. Here are listed 626 works—the largest body of music left by any composer except Haydn, all produced in a life of thirty-six years, and including masterpieces in every form: 77 sonatas, 8 trios, 29 quartets, 5 quintets, 51 concertos, 96 divertimenti, dances or serenades, 52 symphonies, 90 arias or songs, 60 religious compositions, 22 operas. If some of those near Mozart thought him indolent, it may have been because they did not quite realize that the labor of the spirit can exhaust the flesh, and that without intervals of lethargy genius would slip into insanity. His father told him, "Procrastination is your besetting sin,"[37] and in many cases Mozart waited till almost the last hour before putting to paper the music that had been taking form in his head. "I am, so to speak, steeped in music," he said; "it is in my mind the whole day, and I love to dream, to study, to reflect on it."[38] His wife reported, "He was always strumming upon something—his hat, his watch fob, the table, the chair, as if they were the keyboard."[39] Sometimes he carried on this silent composition even while apparently listening to an opera. He kept scraps of music paper in his pockets, or, when traveling, in the side pocket of the carriage; on these he made fragmentary notes; usually he carried a leather case to receive such *obiter scripta*. When he was ready to compose he sat not at a keyboard but at a table; he "wrote music like letters," said Constanze, "and never tried a movement until it was finished." Or he would sit at the piano for hours on end, improvising, leaving his musical fancy seemingly free, but half unconsciously subjecting it to some recognizable structure—sonata form, aria, fugue . . . Musicians enjoyed Mozart's improvisations because they could detect, with esoteric delight, the order hidden behind the apparently whimsical strains. Niemetschek said in old age, "If I dared to pray for one more earthly joy it would be that I might hear Mozart improvise."[40]

Mozart could play almost any music at sight, because he had seen certain combinations and sequences of notes so often that he could read them as one note, and his habituated fingers played them as one musical phrase or idea, just as a practiced reader takes in a line as if it were a word, or a paragraph as if it were a line. Mozart's trained memory was allied with this capacity to perceive aggregates, to feel the logic that compelled the part to indicate the whole. In later years he could play almost any one of his concertos by heart. At Prague he wrote the drum and trumpet parts of the second finale in *Don Giovanni* without having at hand the score for the other instruments; he had kept that complex music in his memory. Once he wrote down only the violin part of a sonata for piano and violin; the next day, without a rehearsal, Regina Strinasacchi played the violin part at a concert, and Mozart played the piano part purely from the memory of his conception, without having had time to set it down upon paper.[41] Probably no other man in history was ever so absorbed in music.

We think of Mozart's sonatas as rather slight and playful, hardly in a class with Beethoven's passionate and powerful pronouncements in the same genre; this may be because they were written for pupils of limited legerdemain, or for harpsichords of minor resonance, or for a piano that had no means of continuing a note.[42] The favorite of our childhood, the Sonata in A (K. 331), with its engaging "Minuetto" and its "Rondo alla Turca," is still (1778) in harpsichord style.

Mozart did not at first care for chamber music, but in 1773 he came upon Haydn's early quartets, envied their contrapuntal excellence, and imitated them with something short of success in the six quartets that he composed in that year. In 1781 Haydn published another series; Mozart was again stirred to rivalry, and issued (1782-85) six quartets (K. 387, 421, 428, 458, 464–65) that are now universally recognized as among the supreme examples of their kind. Performers complained that they were abominably difficult; critics especially condemned the sixth for its clashing dissonances and its turbulent mixture of major and minor keys. An Italian musician returned the score to the publisher as obviously full of gross mistakes, and one purchaser, when he found that the discords were deliberate, tore up the sheets in a rage. Yet it was after playing the fourth, fifth, and sixth of these quartets with Mozart, Dittersdorf, and others that Haydn said to Leopold Mozart, "Before God, and as an honest man, I tell you that your son is the greatest composer known to me either in person or by name. He has taste, and, what is more, the most profound knowledge of composition."[43] When the six quartets were published (1785) Mozart dedicated them to Haydn with a letter that shines out even in a brilliant correspondence:

> A father who had decided to send his sons out into the great world thought it his duty to entrust them to the protection and guidance of a man who was very celebrated at the time, and who, moreover, happened to be his best friend. In like manner I send my six sons to you, most celebrated and very dear friend. They are indeed the fruit of a long and laborious study; but the hope which many friends have given me that their toil will be in some degree rewarded, . . . flatters me with the thought that these children may one day prove a source of consolation to me.
>
> During your last stay in this capital you . . . expressed to me your approval of these compositions. Your good opinion encourages me to offer them to you, and leads me to hope that you will not consider them unworthy of your favor. Please then receive them kindly, and be to them a father, guide, and friend. From this moment I surrender to you all my rights over them. I entreat you, however, to be indulgent to those faults which may have escaped their composer's partial eye, and, in spite of them, to continue your generous friendship towards one who so highly appreciates it.[44]

Mozart had a particular fondness for his quintets. He thought his Quintet in E Flat for piano, oboe, clarinet, horn, and bassoon (K. 452) "the best work I have ever composed,"[45] but that was before he had written his major operas. "Eine kleine Nachtmusik" was originally (1787) composed as a quintet, but it was soon taken up by small orchestras, and is now classed among Mozart's serenades. He valued, as "rather carefully" written, the Serenade in E Flat (K. 375), with which he himself was serenaded one evening in 1781, but musicians rank above it the Serenade in C Minor (K. 388)—which is as somber as the *Pathétiques* of Beethoven and Tchaikowsky.

Having discovered the orchestra, Mozart turned it to a hundred experiments: overtures, nocturnes, suites, cassations (variants of the suite), dances, *divertimenti*. The last were usually intended to serve a passing purpose rather than to echo in the halls of history; they are not to be weighed but enjoyed. Even so, Divertimenti No. 15 (K. 287) and No. 17 (K. 334) are substantial works, more delightful than most of the symphonies.

For his symphonies Mozart, like Haydn, used a "band" of thirty-five pieces; hence they fail to convey their full worth to ears accustomed to the multiplied sonority of twentieth-century orchestras. Pundits praise No. 25 (K. 183) as "impassioned"[46] and "a miracle of impetuous expression,"[47] but the earliest Mozart symphony of note is the *Paris* (No. 31, K. 297), which Mozart adapted to the French taste for refinement and charm. The *Haffner Symphony* (No. 35, K. 385) was originally composed in haste to grace the festivities planned by Sigismund Haffner, former burgomaster of Salzburg, for the wedding of his daughter (1782); Mozart later added parts for flute and clarinet, and presented it at Vienna (March 3, 1783) at a concert attended by Joseph II. The Emperor "gave me great applause," and twenty-five ducats.[48] In this and No. 36, written at Linz in November, 1783, Mozart still kept to the form and stamp—always pleasant, seldom profound—that Haydn had laid upon the symphony; in both cases the slow movement comes most gratefully to aging ears. We must speak more respectfully of No. 38, which Mozart composed for Prague in 1786; here the first movement pleases the musician with its structural logic and contrapuntal skill, and the andante, adding contemplation to melody, has stirred experts to speak of its "undying perfection"[49] and its "enchanted world."[50]

By common consent the greatest of Mozart's symphonies are the three that he poured forth in a torrent of inspiration in the summer of 1788—at a time of depressing poverty and mounting debts. The first is dated June 26, the second July 25, the third August 10—three births in three months. So far as we know, none of them was ever played in his lifetime; he never heard them; they remained in that mysterious realm in which black spots on a sheet were for the composer "ditties of no sound"—notes and harmonies heard only by the mind. The third, misnamed the *Jupiter* (No. 41 in C, K. 551), is usually accounted the best; Schumann equated it with Shakespeare and Beethoven,[51] but it does not lend itself to amateur appreciation. No. 40 in G Minor (K. 550) begins with a vigor that presages the *Eroica*, and it proceeds to a development that has led commentators—struggling in vain to express music in words—to read into it a *Lear* or *Macbeth* of personal tragedy;[52] yet to simpler ears it seems almost naïvely joyous. To the same ears the most satisfying of the symphonies is No. 39 in E Flat (K. 543). It is not burdened with woe, nor is it tortured with technique; it is melody and harmony flowing in a placid stream; it is such music as might please the gods on a rural holiday from celestial chores.

The *sinfonia concertante* is a cross between the symphony and the concerto; it grew out of the *concerto grosso* by opposing two or more instruments to the orchestra in a dialogue between melody and accompaniment. Mozart raised the form to its apex in the Sinfonia Concertante in E Flat (K. 364) for flute, violin, and viola (1779); this is as fine as any of his symphonies.

All the concertos are delightful, for in them the solo passages help the untrained ear to follow themes and strains that in the symphonies may be obscured by technical elaboration or contrapuntal play. Debate is interesting, and all the more so when, as in the form of the concerto as proposed by Karl Philipp Emanuel Bach and developed by Mozart, the contest is of one against all—*solo contra tutti*. Since Mozart relished such harmonious confrontations, he wrote most of his concertos for the piano, for in these he played the solo part himself, usually adding, toward the end of the first movement, a cadenza that allowed him to frolic and shine as a virtuoso.

He first touched excellence in this form with Piano Concerto No. 9 in E Flat (K. 271). The earliest of his still popular concertos is No. 20 in D Minor (K. 466), famous for its almost childlike "Romanze"; in this slow movement, we might say, the Romantic movement in music began. Whether through laziness or distractions, Mozart did not complete the score of this concerto till an hour before the time appointed for its performance (February 11, 1785); copies reached the players just before the recital, allowing no time for practice or rehearsal; yet the performance went so well, and Mozart played his part so expertly, that many repetitions were called for in the ensuing years.

Mozart offered noble music for other solo instruments. Perhaps the melodious Concerto in A for clarinet (K. 622) comes over the air more frequently than any other of his compositions. In his merry youth (1774) he had great fun with a Concerto in B Flat for the bassoon. The horn concertos were bubbles gaily blown upon the score—which sometimes bore humorous directions for the performer: "*da bravo!*," "*coraggio!*," "*bestia!*," "*ohimè!*"—for Mozart was familiar with more wind instruments than one. Then the Concerto for Flute and Harp (K. 299) lifts us to the stars.

In 1775 Mozart, aged nineteen, composed five violin concertos, all of them beautiful, three of them still in living repertoires. No. 3 in G (K. 216) has an adagio that sent an Einstein into ecstasy,[53] No. 4 in D is one of music's masterpieces, and No. 5 in A has an andante cantabile that rivals the miracle of a woman's voice.

Little wonder that Mozart produced, especially in the years of his love for Aloysia Weber, some of the most delectable airs in all the literature of song. They are not full-blown lieder, such as found their ripe development in Schubert and Brahms; they are simpler and shorter, often adorning silly words; but when Mozart found a real poem, like Goethe's "Das Veilchen," he rose to the peak of the form (K. 476). A violet, trembling with joy at the approach of a pretty shepherdess, thinks how sweet it would be to lie upon her breast; but as she walks along, gaily singing, she crushes it unseen under her foot.[54] Was this a memory of the cruel Aloysia? For her Mozart had written one of his tenderest arias—"Non so d'onde viene." But he attached little importance to such isolated songs; he kept the secret resources of his vocal art for the arias in his operas and his compositions for the Church.

His religious music was rarely heard outside Salzburg, for the Catholic Church frowned upon the operatic qualities apparently expected by the archbishops whom Mozart served. High Mass in Salzburg was sung to an accompaniment of organ, strings, trumpets, trombones, and drums, and passages of merriment broke out in the most solemn places in Mozart's Masses. Yet the religious spirit must surely be moved by the motets "Adoramus Te" (K. 327) and "Santa Maria Mater Dei" (K. 341b); and the most hauntingly beautiful strain in all of Mozart appears in the "Laudate Dominum" in the fourth of the "Vesperae solennes di confessore" (K. 339).[55]

All in all, Mozart's music is the voice of an aristocratic age that had not heard the Bastille fall, and of a Catholic culture undisturbed in its faith, free to enjoy the charms of life without the restless search to find new content for an emptied dream. In its lighter aspects this music harmonizes with the elegance of rococo ornament, with the pictorial romances of Watteau, the calmly floating Olympus of Tiepolo, the smiles and robes and pottery of Mme. de Pompadour. It is, by and large, serene music, touched now and then by suffering and anger, but raising neither a humble prayer nor a Promethean challenge to the gods. Mozart began his work in childhood, and a childlike quality lurked in his compositions until it dawned upon him that the Requiem which he was writing for a stranger was his own.

VII. SPIRIT AND FLESH

Mozart was not physically attractive. He was short, his head was too large for his body, his nose was too large for his face, his upper lip overlapped the lower, his bushy brows darkened his restless eyes; only his abounding blond hair impressed. In later years he sought to offset the shortcomings of his stature and features by splendid dress: shirt of lace, blue coat with tails, gold buttons, knee breeches, and silver buckles on his shoes.[56] Only when he performed at the piano was his physique forgotten; then his eyes burned with intense concentration, and every muscle of his body subordinated itself to the play of his mind and hands.

As a boy he was modest, good-natured, trustful, loving; but his early fame, and an almost daily diet of applause, developed some faults in his character. "My son," Leopold warned him (1778), "you are hot-tempered and impulsive, . . . much too ready to retort in a bantering tone to the first challenge."[57] Mozart admitted this and more. "If anyone offends me," he wrote, "I must revenge myself; unless I revenge myself with interest, I consider I have only repaid my enemy and not corrected him."[58] And he yielded to no one in appreciating his genius. "Prince Kaunitz told the Archduke that people like myself come into the world only once in a hundred years."[59]

A sense of humor prevailed in his letters, and appeared in his music, till his dying year. Usually it was harmlessly playful; sometimes it became sharp satire; occasionally, in youth, it ran to obscenity. He passed through a stage of fascination with defecation. When he was twenty-one he wrote to his cousin Maria Anna Thekla Mozart nineteen letters of incredible vulgarity.[60] A letter to his mother celebrated flatulence in prose and verse.[61] She was not squeamish, for in a letter to her husband she counseled him, "Keep well, my love; into your mouth your arse you'll shove."[62] Apparently such fundamental phrases were standard procedure in the Mozart family and their circle; they were probably an heirloom from a lustier generation. They did not prevent Mozart from writing to his parents and his sister letters of the tenderest affection.

He was, on his own word, a virgin bridegroom. Was he a faithful husband? His wife accused him of "servant gallantries."[63] According to his devoted biographer:

> Rumor was busy among the public and in the press, and magnified solitary instances of weakness on his part into distinguishing features of his character. He was credited with intrigues with every pupil he had, and with every singer for whom he wrote a song; it was considered witty to designate him as the natural prototype of Don Juan.[64]

The frequent confinements of his wife, her repeated trips to health resorts, his own absence from her on concert tours, his sensitivity to all the charms of women, his association with bewitching singers and uninhibited actresses, created a situation in which some adventure was well-nigh inevitable. Constanze related how he had confessed such an "indiscretion" to her, and why she forgave him—"he was so good it was impossible to be angry with him"; but her sister reports violent outbreaks now and then.[65] Mozart seems to have been very fond of his wife; he bore patiently her deficiencies as a housewife, and wrote to her, during their separations, letters of almost childish endearment.[66]

He was not a success socially. He judged some rivals harshly. "Clementi's sonatas are worthless. . . . He is a charlatan, like all Italians."[67] "Yesterday I was fortunate enough to hear Herr Freyhold play a concerto of his own wretched composition. I found very little to admire."[68] On the other hand, he praised the quartets recently published by Ignaz Pleyel, though they competed with his own. His father reproached him for getting himself disliked because of his arrogance;[69] Mozart denied the arrogance, but it cannot be denied that he had very few friends among Viennese musicians, and that his proud spirit raised obstacles to his advancement. In Austria and Germany a musician's fate depended upon the aristocracy, and Mozart refused to give precedence to birth over genius.

He suffered another handicap in having never gone to school or university. His father had allowed him no time for general education. Mozart had among his few books some volumes of poetry by Gessner, Wieland, and Gellert, but he seems to have used them chiefly as a source of possible librettos. He cared little for art or literature. He was in Paris when Voltaire died; he could not understand why the city had made such a fuss over the old rebel's visit and death. "That godless rascal Voltaire," he wrote to his father, "has pegged out like a dog, like a beast! That is his reward."[70] He imbibed some anticlericalism from his Masonic confrères, but he took part, candle in hand, in a Corpus Christi procession.[71]

Perhaps it was the simplicity of his mind that made him lovable despite his faults. Those who were not his rivals in music found him sociable, cheerful, kind, and usually serene. "All my life," his sister-in-law Sophie Weber wrote, "I have never seen Mozart in a temper, still less angry";[72] but there were contrary reports. He was the life of many a party, always willing to play, always ready for a joke or a game. He liked bowling, billiards, and the dance; at times he seemed prouder of his dancing than of his music.[73] If he was not generous to his competitors, he was almost thoughtlessly liberal to everybody else. Beggars were seldom repulsed by him. A piano tuner repeatedly borrowed from him and failed to repay. Mozart talked frankly about his high regard for money, but that was because he had so little time or inclination to think of it that he often had none. Thrown upon his own moneymaking resources, and called upon to support a family by competing with a hundred jealous musicians, he neglected his finances, allowed his earnings to slip unheeded through his fingers, and fell into despondent destitution just when, in his last three symphonies and his last three operas, he was writing the finest music of his time.

VIII. APOGEE: 1782–87

He began his free-lance career in Vienna with heartening success. He was well paid for the lessons he gave; each of his concerts in 1782–84 brought him some five hundred gulden.[74] Only seventy of his compositions were published in his lifetime, but he was reasonably paid. The publisher Artarin gave him a hundred ducats for the six quartets dedicated to Haydn—a handsome sum for those days.[75] Another publisher, Hoffmeister, lost money by printing Mozart's piano quartets in G Minor (K. 478) and E Flat (K. 493); the musicians found them too difficult (they are now considered easy), and Hoffmeister warned Mozart, "Write more popularly, or else I can neither print nor pay for anything more of yours."[76] Mozart received the usual fee, a hundred ducats, for his operas; for *Don Giovanni* he was paid 225 ducats plus the proceeds of a benefit concert. He had in these years "a very good income."[77] His father, visiting him in 1785, reported: "If my son has no debts to pay, I think that he can now lodge two thousand gulden in the bank."[78]

But Mozart did not put those gulden in the bank. He spent them on current expenses, entertainment, good clothes, and in meeting the needs of mendicant friends. For these and more obscure reasons he fell into debt at the height of the demand for his services and his compositions. As early as February 15, 1783, he wrote to the Baroness von Waldstädten that one of his creditors had threatened to "bring an action against me. . . . At the moment I cannot pay—not even half the sum! . . . I entreat your Ladyship, for Heaven's sake, to help me keep my honor and my good name."[79] He was temporarily relieved by the success of a concert given for his benefit in March, which brought in sixteen hundred gulden. Out of this he sent a gift to his father.

In May, 1783, he moved to a good house at No. 244 in the Judenplatz. There his first child was born (June 17)—"a fine, sturdy boy, as round as a ball." This event, and the gift, softened paternal resentment of the marriage; Wolfgang and Constanze took advantage of the thaw to visit Leopold and Nannerl in Salzburg, leaving the infant in Vienna with a nurse. On August 19 the child died. Its parents remained in Salzburg, for Mozart had arranged for the performance there of his Mass in C Minor, in which Constanze was to sing. Wolfgang and Constanze outstayed their welcome, for Leopold had to count every penny, and thought three months were too long a visit. On their way back to Vienna they stopped at Linz, where Count von Thun commissioned Mozart to write a symphony.

Home again, he worked hard, teaching composing, performing, conducting. In two months (February 26 to April 3, 1784) he gave three concerts and played in nineteen others.[80] In December he joined one of the seven Freemason lodges in Vienna; he enjoyed their meetings, and readily consented to write music for their festivals. In February his father, mollified by the birth of another son to Constanze, came for a long visit. And in 1785 Lorenzo da Ponte entered Mozart's life.

This Lorenzo had almost as adventurous a life as his friend Casanova. He had begun life in 1749 as the son of a tanner in the ghetto of Ceneda. When he was fourteen Emmanuele Conegliano and two brothers were taken by their father to Lorenzo da Ponte, bishop of Ceneda, to be baptized into the Catholic Church. Emmanuele adopted the bishop's name, became a priest, had an affair at Venice with a married woman, was banished, moved to Dresden, then to Vienna, and was engaged in 1783 as poet and librettist to the National Theater.

Mozart suggested to him the possibility of making an opera libretto out of Beaumarchais' recent comedy *Le Mariage de Figaro*. This had been translated into German with a view to staging it in Vienna, but Joseph II forbade it as containing revolutionary sentiments that would scandalize his court. Could the Emperor, who was himself quite a revolutionary, be persuaded to allow an opera judiciously abstracted from the play? Ponte admired Mozart's music; he was to speak of him later as one who, "although endowed with talents surpassing those of any composer, past, present, or future, had not been able as yet, owing to the intrigues of his enemies, to utilize his divine genius in Vienna."[81] He eliminated the radical overtones of Beaumarchais' drama, and transformed the remainder into an Italian libretto rivaling the best of Metastasio.

The story of *Le nozze di Figaro* was the old maze of disguises, surprises, and recognitions, and the clever hoodwinking of masters by servants: all familiar in comedy since Menander and Plautus. Mozart took readily to the theme, and composed the music almost as fast as the libretto took form; both were completed in six weeks. On April 29, 1786, Mozart wrote the overture; on May 1 the première went off triumphantly. Part of the success may have been due to the jovial, stentorian basso, Francesco Benucci, who sang the part of Figaro; more must have been due to the vivacity and fitness of the music, and to such arias as Cherubino's plaintive "Voi che sapete" and the Countess' intense yet restrained appeal to the god of love in "Porgi amor." So many encores were demanded that the performance took twice the usual time; and at the end Mozart was repeatedly called to the stage.

The income from the production of *Figaro* in Vienna and Prague should have kept Mozart solvent for a year had it not been for his extravagance, and the illnesses and pregnancies of his wife. In April, 1787, they moved to a less expensive house, Landstrasse 224. A month later Leopold died, leaving his son a thousand gulden.

Prague commissioned another opera. Ponte suggested for a subject the sexual escapades of Don Juan. Tirso de Molina had put the legendary Don on the stage at Madrid in 1630 as *El burlador de Sevilla* (*The Deceiver of Seville*); Molière had told the story in Paris as *Le Festin de pierre* (*The Feast of Stone*, 1665); Goldoni had presented it in Venice as *Don Giovanni Tenorio* (1736); Vincente Righini had staged *Il convitato di pietra* in Vienna in 1777; and at Venice, in this very year 1787, Giuseppe Gazzaniga had produced, under the same title, an opera from which Ponte stole many lines, including the jaunty catalogue of Giovanni's sins.

The "greatest of all operas" (as Rossini called it) had its première at Prague on October 29, 1787. Mozart and Constanze went up to the Bohemian capital for the event; they were feted so fully that he deferred the composition of the overture till the eve of the première; then, at midnight, "after spending the merriest evening imaginable,"[82] he composed a piece which is almost Wagnerian in foreshadowing the tragic and comic elements of the play. The score reached the orchestra just in time for the performance.[83] The Vienna *Zeitung* reported: "On Monday Kapellmeister Mozart's long-expected opera, *Don Giovanni*, was performed . . . Musicians and connoisseurs are agreed that such a performance has never before been witnessed in Prague. Herr Mozart himself conducted, and his appearance in the orchestra was the signal for cheers, which were renewed at his exit."[84]

On November 12 the happy couple were back in Vienna. Gluck died three days later, and Joseph II appointed Mozart to succeed him as *Kammermusikus*—chamber musician— to the court. After much trouble with the singers *Don Giovanni* was produced in Vienna on May 7, 1788, to scanty applause. Mozart and Ponte made further alterations, but the opera never attained in Vienna the success it had in Prague, Mannheim, Hamburg . . .

A Berlin critic complained that the *dramma giocoso* was an offense against morals, but he added: "If ever a nation might be proud of one of its children, Germany may be proud of Mozart, the composer of this opera."[85] Nine years later Goethe wrote to Schiller: "Your hopes for opera are richly fulfilled in *Don Giovanni*",[86] and he mourned that Mozart had not lived to write the music for Faust.

IX. NADIR: 1788–90

The proceeds from *Don Giovanni* were soon used up, and Mozart's modest salary hardly paid for food. He took some pupils, but teaching was an exhausting, time-consuming task. He moved to cheaper quarters in suburban Währingerstrasse; debts multiplied nevertheless. He borrowed wherever he could—chiefly from a kindly merchant and fellow Mason, Michael Puchberg. To him Mozart wrote in June, 1788:

> I still owe you eight ducats. Apart from the fact that at the moment I am not in a position to pay you back this sum, my confidence in you is so boundless that I dare implore you to help me out with a hundred gulden until next week, when my concerts in the Casino are to begin. By that time I shall certainly have received my subscription money, and shall then be able quite easily to pay you back 136 gulden with my warmest thanks.[87]

Puchberg sent the hundred gulden. Encouraged, Mozart appealed to him (June 17) for a loan of "one or two thousand gulden for a year or two at a suitable rate of interest." He had left unpaid the arrears of rent at his former home; the landlord threatened to have him jailed; Mozart borrowed to pay him. Apparently Puchberg sent less than was asked, for the desperate composer made further appeals in June and July. It was in those harassed months that Mozart composed the three "Great Symphonies."

He welcomed an invitation from Prince Karl von Lichnowsky to ride with him to Berlin. For that trip he borrowed a hundred gulden from Franz Hofdemel. Prince and pauper left Vienna April 8, 1789. At Dresden Mozart played before Elector Frederick Augustus, and received a hundred ducats. At Leipzig he gave a public performance on Bach's organ, and was stirred by the Thomasschule choir's singing of Bach's motet "Singet dem Herrn." At Potsdam and Berlin (April 28 to May 28) he played for Frederick William II, and received a gift of seven hundred florins, with commissions for six quartets and six sonatas. But his gains were spent with mysterious celerity; an unverified rumor ascribed part of the outlet to a liaison with a Berlin singer, Henriette Baronius.[88] On May 23 he wrote to Constanze: "As regards my return, you will have to look forward to me more than to the money."[89] He reached home June 4, 1789.

Constanze, pregnant again, needed doctors and medicines and an expensive trip to take the waters at Baden-bei-Wien. Mozart again turned to Puchberg:

> Great God! I would not wish my worst enemy to be in my present position. If you, most beloved friend and brother [Mason] forsake me, we are altogether lost—both my unfortunate and blameless self and my poor sick wife and chil-

dren. . . . All depends . . . upon whether you will lend me another five hundred gulden. Until my affairs are settled, I undertake to pay back ten gulden a month; and then I shall pay back the whole sum. . . . Oh, God! I can hardly bring myself to dispatch this letter, and yet I must!—For God's sake forgive me, only forgive me![90]

Puchberg sent him 150 gulden, most of which went to pay Constanze's bills at Baden. On November 16, at home, she gave birth to a daughter, who died the same day. Joseph II helped by commissioning Mozart and Ponte to write a *dramma giocoso* on an old theme (used by Marivaux in *Le Jeu de l'amour et du hasard*, 1730): two men disguise themselves to test the fidelity of their fiancées; they find them pliable, but forgive them on the ground that *"così fan tutte"*—"so do all" women; thence the opera's name. It was hardly a subject fit for Mozart's tragic mood (except that Constanze had flirted a bit at Baden), but he provided for the clever and witty libretto music that is the very embodiment of cleverness and wit; seldom has nonsense been so glorified. It had a moderately successful première on January 26, 1790, and four repetitions in a month, bringing Mozart a hundred ducats. Then Joseph II died (February 20), and the Vienna theaters were closed till April 12.

Mozart hoped that the new Emperor would find work for him, but Leopold II ignored him. He ignored Ponte too, who went off to England and America, and ended (1838) as a teacher of Italian in what is now Columbia University in New York.[91] Mozart made further appeals to Puchberg (December 29, 1789, January 20, February 20, April 1, 8, and 23, 1790), never in vain, but seldom receiving all that he asked. Early in May he pleaded for six hundred gulden to pay rent due; Puchberg sent a hundred. He confessed to Puchberg on May 17, "I am obliged to resort to moneylenders"; in that letter he numbered his pupils as only two, and asked his friend "to spread the news that I am willing to give lessons."[92] However, he was too nervous and impatient to be a good teacher. Sometimes he failed to keep appointments with his pupils; sometimes he played billiards with them instead of giving a lesson.[93] But when he found a student of promising talent he gave himself unreservedly; so he gladly and successfully taught Johann Hummel, who came to him (1787) at the age of eight and became a famous pianist in the next generation.

Serious illnesses added pains to Mozart's griefs. One physician diagnosed his ailments as "excretory pyelitis with pyonephritis, latent focal lesions of the kidneys, tending inescapably toward eventual total nephritic insufficiency"[94]—i.e., a disabling pus-forming inflammation of the kidneys. "I am absolutely wretched today," he wrote to Puchberg on August 14, 1790. "I could not sleep at all last night because of pain. . . . Picture to yourself my condition—ill, and consumed with worries and anxieties. . . . Can you not help me with a trifle? The smallest sum would be very welcome." Puchberg sent him ten gulden.

Despite his physical condition Mozart undertook a desperate expedient to support his family. Leopold II was to be crowned at Frankfurt October 9, 1790. Seventeen court musicians were in the Emperor's retinue, but Mozart was not invited. He went nevertheless, accompanied by Franz Hofer, his violinist brother-in-law. To defray the expense he pawned the family's silver plate. At Frankfurt on October 15 he played and conducted his Piano Concerto in D (K. 537), which he had composed three years before, but which the whim of history has named the "Coronation Concerto"—hardly among his best. "It was a splendid success," he wrote to his wife, "from the point of view of honor and glory, but a failure as far as money was concerned."[95] He returned to Vienna having earned little more than his expenses. In November he moved to cheaper lodgings at Rauhensteingasse 70, where he was to die.

X. REQUIEM: 1791

He was kept alive for another year by three commissions coming in crowded succession. In May, 1791, Emanuel Schikaneder, who produced German operas and plays in a suburban theater, offered him the sketch of a libretto about a magic flute, and appealed to his brother Mason to provide the music. Mozart agreed. When Constanze, pregnant once more, went to Baden-bei-Wien in June, he accepted Schikaneder's invitation to spend his days in a garden house near the theater, where he could compose *Die Zauberflöte* under the manager's prodding. In the evenings he joined Schikaneder in the night life of the town. "Folly and dissipation," Jahn tells us, "were the inevitable accompaniments of such an existence, and these soon reached the public ear, . . . covering his name for several months with an amount of obloquy beyond what he deserved."[96] Amid these relaxations Mozart found time to drive to Baden (eleven miles from Vienna) to visit his wife, who on July 26 gave birth to Wolfgang Mozart II.

In that month a request came from an anonymous stranger, offering a hundred ducats for a Requiem Mass to be secretly composed and to be transmitted to him without any public acknowledgment of its authorship. Mozart turned from the merriment of *The Magic Flute* to the theme of death, when, in August, he received a commission from Prague for an opera, *La clemenza di Tito*, to be performed there at the approaching coronation of Leopold II as king of Bohemia. He had barely a month to set Metastasio's old libretto to new music. He worked at it in shaky coaches and noisy inns while journeying to Prague with his wife. The opera was sung on September 6 to mild applause. Mozart had tears in his eyes as he left the one city that had befriended him, and as he realized that the Emperor had witnessed his failure. His only consolations were the two hundred ducats' fee and the later news that the repetition of the opera at Prague on September 30 was a complete success.

On that day he conducted from the piano the première of *Die Zauberflöte*. The story was in part a fairy tale, in part an exaltation of Masonic initiation ritual. Mozart gave his best art to the composition, though he kept most of the arias to a simple melodic line congenial to his middle-class audience. He lavished coloratura pyrotechnics on the Queen of the Night, but privately he laughed at coloratura singing as "cut-up noodles."[97] The March of the

Priests, opening the second act, is Masonic music; the aria of the high priest, "In diesen heiligen Hallen"—"In these holy halls we know nothing of revenge, and love for their fellow men is the guiding rule of the initiated"—is the claim of Freemasonry to have restored that brotherhood of man which Christianity had once preached. (Goethe compared *The Magic Flute* to Part II of *Faust*, which also preached brotherhood; and, himself a Mason, he spoke of the opera as having "a higher meaning which will not escape the initiated."[98] The first performance had an uncertain success, and the critics were shocked by the mixture of fugues and fun;[99] soon, however, *The Magic Flute* became the most popular of Mozart's operas, and of all operas before Wagner and Verdi; it was repeated a hundred times within fourteen months of its première.

This last triumph came when Mozart already felt the hand of death touching him. As if to accentuate the irony, a group of Hungarian nobles now assured him an annual subscription of a thousand florins, and an Amsterdam publisher offered him a still larger sum for the exclusive right to print some of his work. In September he received an invitation from Ponte to come to London; he replied: "I would gladly follow your advice, but how can I? . . . My condition tells me that my hour strikes; I am about to give up my life. The end has come before I could prove my talent. Yet life was beautiful."[100]

In his final months he gave his failing strength to the *Requiem*. For several weeks he worked at it feverishly. When his wife sought to turn him to less gloomy concerns he told her, "I am writing this Requiem for myself; it will serve for my funeral service."[101] He composed the Kyrie and parts of the Dies Irae, the Tuba Mirum, the Rex Tremendae, the Recordare, the Confutatis, the Lacrimosa, the Domine, and the Hostias; these fragments were left unrevised, and reveal the disordered state of a mind facing collapse. Franz Xaver Süssmayr completed the *Requiem* remarkably well.

In November Mozart's hands and feet began to swell painfully, and partial paralysis set in. He had to take to his bed. On those evenings when *The Magic Flute* was performed he laid his watch beside him and followed each act in imagination, sometimes humming the arias. On his last day he asked for the score of the *Requiem;* he sang the alto part, Mme. Schack sang the soprano, Franz Hofer the tenor, Herr Gerl the bass; when they came to the Lacrimosa, Mozart wept. He predicted that he would die that night. A priest administered the last sacrament. Toward evening Mozart lost consciousness, but shortly after midnight he opened his eyes; then he turned his face to the wall, and soon suffered no more (December 5, 1791).

Neither his wife nor his friends could give him a fitting funeral. The body was blessed in St. Stephen's Church on December 6, and was buried in the churchyard of St. Mark's. No grave had been bought; the corpse was lowered into a common vault made to receive fifteen or twenty paupers. No cross or stone marked the place, and when, a few days later, the widow came there to pray, no one could tell her the spot that covered Mozart's remains.

BOOK IV

ISLAM AND THE SLAVIC EAST
1715–96

CHAPTER XVI

Islam

1715–96

I. THE TURKS

IN the eighteenth century Christianity was caught between Voltaire and
Mohammed—between the Enlightenment and Islam. Though the Moslem world had lost military power since Sobieski's repulse of the Turks from
Vienna in 1683, it still dominated Morocco, Algeria, Tunisia, Libya, Egypt,
Arabia, Palestine, Syria, Persia, Asia Minor, the Crimea, South Russia, Bessarabia, Moldavia, Wallachia (Romania), Bulgaria, Serbia (Yugoslavia),
Montenegro, Bosnia, Dalmatia, Greece, Crete, the Aegean Isles, and Turkey. All these except Persia were part of the immense empire of the OttomanTurks. On the Dalmatian coast they touched the Adriatic and faced the
Papal States; on the Bosporus they controlled the sole naval outlet from the
Black Sea, and could at will block the Russians from the Mediterranean.

Crossing from Hungarian territory into Moslem lands, one would at first
note little difference between Christian and Mohammedan civilization. Here
too the simple and pious poor tilled the soil under the overlordship of the
clever and skeptical rich. But beyond the Bosporus the economic landscape
changed: hardly fifteen per cent of the terrain had come under cultivation;
the rest was desert, or mountains permitting only mining or pasturage; there
the characteristic figure was the Bedouin, black and parched with the sun,
and wrapping himself complexly against the sand and the heat. The coastal
cities or incidental towns hummed with trade and handicrafts, but life
seemed more leisurely than in Christian centers; women stayed at home, or
walked in stately dignity under their burdens and behind their veils, and the
men moved unhurried along the streets. Industry was nearly all manual,
and the craftsman's shop was a frontal annex to his home; he smoked and
chatted as he worked, and sometimes shared his coffee (*qahveh*) and his pipe
with a lingering customer.

By and large the common Turk was so satisfied with his civilization that he
had not for centuries tolerated any significant change. As in Roman Catholic
doctrine, tradition was as sacred as sacred scripture. Religion was more
powerful and pervasive in Islam than in Christendom; the Koran was the
law as well as the gospel, and the theologians were the official interpreters of
the law. The pilgrimage to Mecca annually led its moving drama over the
desert and along the dusty roads. But in the upper classes the rationalist
heresies voiced by the eighth-century Mutazilites, and continued through
the Age of Faith by Moslem poets and philosophers, received a wide and
secret assent. From Constantinople in 1719 Lady Mary Wortley Montagu
reported:

> The effendis (that is to say, the learned) . . . have no more faith in the inspiration of Mohammed than in the infallibility of the pope. They make a frank profession of deism among themselves, or to those they can trust, and never speak of their law [the dictates of the Koran and the traditions] but as a politic institution, fit now to be observed by wise men, however at first introduced by politicians and enthusiasts.[1]

The Sunni and Shi'a sects divided Islam, as Catholicism and Protestantism divided Western Christianity; and in the eighteenth century a new sect was founded by Mohammad ibn-Abd-al-Wahab, a sheik of the Nejd—that central plateau which we now know as Saudi Arabia. The Wahabites were the Puritans of Islam: they condemned the worship of saints, destroyed the tombs and shrines of saints and martyrs, denounced the wearing of silk and the use of tobacco, and defended the right of each individual to interpret the Koran for himself.[2] In all the sects superstitions were popular; religious impostors and bogus miracles found ready credence; and by most Moslems the realm of magic was considered as real as the world of sand and sun.[3]

Education was dominated by the clergy, who held that good citizens or loyal tribesmen could be more surely made by disciplining character than by liberating intellect. The clergy had won the battle against the scientists, philosophers, and historians who had prospered in medieval Islam; astronomy had relapsed into astrology, chemistry into alchemy, medicine into magic, history into myth. But in many Moslems a wordless wisdom took the place of education and erudition. As the wise and eloquent Doughty wrote: "The Arabs and Turks, whose books are men's faces, . . . and whose glosses are the common saws and thousand old sapient proverbs of their oriental world, touch near the truth of human things. They are old men in policy in their youth, and have little later to unlearn."[4] Wortley Montagu, in a letter of 1717, assured Addison that "the men of consideration among the Turks appear in their conversation as civilized as any I have met with in Italy."[5] Wisdom has no nationality.

Poets have always abounded in Islam. The awesome deserts, the encompassing sky, and the infinity of stars on cloudless nights stirred the imagination, as well as religious faith, with the sense of mystery, and the blood idealized with impeded desire the charms that women wisely enhanced with concealment and modesty. In 1774 Sir William Jones, in *Commentaries on Arabic Poetry*, revealed to alert minds in Western Europe the popularity, elegance, and passion of poetry in Islam. Greatest of Ottoman poets in the eighteenth century was Nedim, who sang in the time of Sultan Ahmed III (1703–30):

> Love distraught, my heart and soul are gone for naught, . . .
> All my patience and endurance spent. . . .
> Once I bared her lovely bosom, whereupon did calm and peace
> Forth from my breast take flight. . . .
> Paynim [pagan] mole, paynim tresses, paynim eyes, . . .
> All her cruel beauty's kingdom forms a heathenness, I swear.
> Kisses on her neck and kisses on her bosom promised she.
> Woe is me, for now the Paynim rues the troth she pledged while-ere.

Such the winsome grace wherewith she showed her locks from 'neath her fez;
Whatsoever wight beheld her, gazed bewildered then and there. . . .
Ruthless, 'tis for thee that all men weep and wail in drear despair. . . .
Sweeter than all the perfumes, brighter than all dyes, thy dainty frame;
One would deem some fragrant rose had in her bosom nurtured thee. . . .
Holding in one hand a rose, in one a cup, thou comest, sweet;
Ah, I know not which of these—rose, cup, or thee—to take to me.
Lo, there springs a jetting fountain from the Stream of Life, methought,
When thou madest me that lovely lissom shape of thine to see.[6]

Women had to take what advantage they could of their lissom shapes, for once their lilies and roses faded they were lost in the recesses of the *harim*. This term was applied not only to the wives and concubines of the husband but to all the females of his household. Seclusion was still their lot in the eighteenth century; they might go out, but (after 1754) they had then to veil all but their alluring eyes, and no male but father, brother, husband and son might enter their apartment. Even after death this separation of the sexes was supposed to remain: saved women would have their own Elysium, apart from the men; saved men would go to another Paradise, where they would be entertained by houris—heavenly nymphs periodically revirginized. Adultery by women was severely punished, and was rare; Arabs swore by "the honor of my women" as their securest oath.[7] Lady Mary reported that the Turkish women whom she had been allowed to meet did not resent their separation from the men. Some of them she thought as fair in face and figure, and as refined in manners, as "our most celebrated English beauties."[8] Admitted to one of the many public baths, she discovered that women could be beautiful even without clothing. She was especially charmed by the ladies in a bathing establishment at Adrianople. They invited her to undress and bathe with them; she begged to be excused. "They being all so earnest in persuading me, I was at last forced to open my shirt and show them my stays; which satisfied them very well, for I saw they believed I was so locked up in that machine that it was not in my power to open it; which contrivance they attributed to my husband"; and one of them remarked, "See how cruelly the poor English ladies are used by their husbands."[9]

The Turks were proud of their public baths, and generally considered themselves a more cleanly people than the Christian infidels. Many persons in the upper and middle classes went to a "Turkish bath" twice a week, more of them once a week. There they sat in a steam room until they had sweated abundantly; then an attendant manipulated every joint, massaged the flesh, rubbed it with a coarse cloth, washed it; we do not hear much about arthritis in Turkey. Some other diseases flourished, especially ophthalmia; sand and flies infected the eyes. But the Turks, as we have seen, taught Europe to inoculate for smallpox.

They had no doubt that their civilization excelled that of Christendom. They admitted that slavery was more widespread in Islam, but they saw no real difference between slaves in Turkey and serfs or servants in the Christian world, and Lady Mary and etymology agreed with them. They were as zealous as we in the love and care of flowers; they too, as in Constantinople under Ahmed III (1703-30), had feverish competitions in cultivating tulips; apparently it was the Turks who, through Venice and Vienna and the Netherlands, introduced to Christian Europe the tulip, the Oriental hyacinth, and the garden ranunculus, as well as the chestnut and mimosa trees.[10]

Art in Turkey was now in decline, as in most Christian lands. The Turks considered themselves superior in pottery, textiles, rugs, decorations, even in architecture. They had inherited the art of endowing abstract painting with logic, communication, and significance. They gloried in the splendor of their faïence (as on the Fountain of Ahmed III in Constantinople), the unfading gleam of their tiles, the strength and delicacy of their weaves, the sturdy brilliance of their rugs. Anatolia and the Caucasus were noted in this age for the lustrous pile and strict geometrical design of their carpets, especially of their prayer rugs, whose columns and pointed arches kept the bent worshiper facing the mihrab that indicated, in each mosque, the direction of Mecca. And the Turks preferred their domed and tiled and minaretted mosques to the spires and arches and gloomy grandeur of Gothic cathedrals. Even in this declining age they raised the majestic mosques of Nuri-Osmanieh (1748) and Laleli-Jamissi (1765), and Ahmed III brought the style of the Alhambra to the palace that he built in 1729. Constantinople, despite its tangled streets and noisome slums, was probably the most impressive, as well as the largest, of European capitals; its population of two million souls[11] was double that of London, three times that of Paris, eight times that of Rome.[12] When Lady Mary looked out upon the city and the port from the palace of the British ambassador, she thought they constituted "perhaps, all together, the most beautiful prospect in the world."[13]

Over this Ottoman Empire, from the Euphrates to the Atlantic, reigned the sultans of the decline. We have considered elsewhere[14] the causes of that decline: the movement of Asia-bound West-European commerce around Africa by sea instead of overland through Egypt or western Asia; the destruction or neglect of the irrigation canals; the expansion of the empire to distances too great for effective central rule; the consequent independence of the pashas and the separatism of the provinces; the deterioration of the central government through corruption, incompetence, and sloth; the repeated rebellions of Janissaries repudiating the discipline that had made them strong; the domination of life and thought by a fatalistic and unprogressive religion; and the lassitude of sultans who preferred the arms of women to those of war.

Ahmed III began his reign by allowing the Janissaries to dictate his choice of a grand vizier. It was this vizier who, when he led 200,000 Turks against the 38,000 troops of Peter the Great at the River Prut, accepted a bribe of 230,000 rubles to let the cornered Czar escape (July 21, 1711). When Venice incited the Montenegrins to revolt, Turkey declared war against Venice (1715), and completed the conquest of Crete and Greece. When Austria intervened, Turkey declared war against Austria (1716); but Eugene of Savoy defeated the Turks at Peterwardein, and compelled the Sultan, by the

Treaty of Passarowitz (1718), to evacuate Hungary, to cede Belgrade and parts of Wallachia to Austria, and to surrender to Venice certain strongholds in Albania and Dalmatia. An attempt to balance these losses by raids on Persia brought more reverses; a mob led by a bath attendant killed the Vizier Ibrahim Pasha, and forced Ahmed to abdicate (1730).

His nephew, Mahmud I (r. 1730-54), renewed the struggle with the West to determine by war the flow of taxes and the doctrines of theology. One Turkish army took Ochakov and Kilburun from Russia, another recovered Belgrade from Austria. But the military decline of Turkey was resumed under Mustafa III (1757-74). In 1762 Bulgaria declared itself independent. In 1769 Turkey opened war with Russia to prevent the spread of Russian power in Poland; so began the long conflict in which the armies of Catherine the Great inflicted fatal repulses upon the Turks. After Mustafa's death his brother Abdul-Hamid I (1774-89) signed the humiliating Treaty of Kuchuk Kainarji (1774), which finished Turkish influence in Poland, South Russia, Moldavia, and Wallachia, and Turkish control of the Black Sea. Abdul-Hamid renewed the war in 1787, suffered disastrous routs, and died of grief. Turkey had to wait for Kemal Pasha to end two centuries of chaos and make it a modern state.

II. AFRICAN ISLAM

The Turks, after conquering Arabic Egypt (1517), delegated its government to pashas and viceroys. The Mamelukes, who had ruled Egypt since 1250, were allowed to retain local power as the beys of the twelve sanjaks into which the country was divided. While the pashas lost their vigor in luxury, the beys trained their soldiers to personal loyalty, and soon challenged the authority of the hated viceroys. The most enterprising of these local rulers was 'Ali Bey, who in boyhood had been sold as a slave. In 1766 he deposed the pasha; in 1769 he declared Egypt independent. Feverish with success, he led his Mameluke troops to the conquest of Arabia, captured Mecca, and took the titles of Sultan of Egypt and Khakan of the Two Seas (the Red and the Mediterranean). In 1771 he sent abu'l-Ahahab with thirty thousand men to conquer Syria; abu'l-Ahahab conquered, but then allied himself with the Porte, and led his army back into Egypt. 'Ali fled to Acre, organized another army, met the forces of abu'l-Ahahab and the Turks, fought till he was disabled by wounds, was captured, and died within a week (1773). Egypt became again a province of the Ottoman Empire.

Beneath such oscillations of power and ecstasies of homicide the ships and caravans of trade, the industry of craftsmen, the annual overflow of the Nile, and the labor of fellaheen in the fertile mud, maintained in Egypt an economy whose profits went to a minority dowered by nature or circumstance with ability or place. The toil and yield of fields and seas fed the cities—here, above all, Alexandria, one of the greatest ports, and Cairo, one of the most populous capitals, of the eighteenth-century world. The streets were narrow to obstruct the sun, and were made picturesque by latticed windows and balconies from which the women of the harem could look unseen upon the life below. The larger streets hummed with handicrafts that defied capitalistic intrusion or machine production. In Islam every industry was an art, and the quality of the product took the place of quantity. The poor made beautiful things for the rich, but they never sold their pride.

Three hundred mosques supported the poor of Cairo with hope, and adorned it with massive domes, shady porticos, and stately minarets. One mosque, El Azhar, was also the mother university of Islam; to it came two or three thousand students, from as far east as Malaysia and as far west as Morocco, to learn Koranic grammar, rhetoric, theology, ethics, and law. The graduates of universities constituted the ulema, or body of scholars, from whom were chosen the teachers and judges. It was a regimen made for a rigorous orthodoxy in religion, morals, and politics.

So morals hardly changed from century to century. Puberty came earlier than in the north; many girls married at twelve or thirteen, some at ten; to be unmarried at sixteen was a disgrace. Only the rich could afford the polygamy that Koranic law allowed. A cuckolded husband was not only permitted by law, but was encouraged by public opinion, to put the offending wife to death.[15] Islamic theology, like the Christian, considered woman a main source of evil, which could be controlled only by her strict subordination. Children grew up in the discipline of the harem; they learned to love their mother and to fear and honor their father; nearly all of them developed self-restraint and courtesy.[16] Good manners prevailed in all classes, along with a certain ease and grace of motion probably derived from the women, who may have derived it from carrying burdens on their heads. The climate forbade haste, and sanctioned indolence.

Polygamy did not prevent prostitution, for prostitutes could provide the excitation that familiarity had allayed. The courtesans of Egypt specialized in lascivious dances; some ancient monuments reveal the antiquity of this lure. Every large town allotted to prostitutes a special quarter where they might practice their arts without fear of the law. As in all civilizations, women skilled in erotic dances were engaged to vibrate before male assemblies, and in some cases women also took pleasure in witnessing such performances.[17]

Music served both love and war; in either case it aroused attack and soothed defeat. Professional musicians, of either sex, could be engaged to provide entertainment. "I have heard the most celebrated musicians in Cairo," said Edward Lane in 1833, "and have been more charmed with their songs . . . than with any other music that I have ever enjoyed."[18] The favorite instrument was the *kemengeh*, a kind of emaciated viol, with two strings of horsehair over a sounding box made of a cocoanut shell partly cut open between center and top, and covered with fish skin tightly stretched. The performer sat cross-legged, rested the pointed end of the instrument upon the ground, and stroked the strings with a bow of horsehair and ash. Or the artist sat with a large *chanoon*, or zither, on his lap, and plucked the strings with horn plectra attached to the forefingers. The ancient lute now took the form of a guitar (the *co'd*). Add a flute, a mandolin, and a tambourine, and the ensemble would provide an orchestra whose strains might suit a civilized taste better than the primitive music that now agitates Occidental gatherings.

The "Barbary States," or lands of the allegedly barbarous Berbers—Tripoli, Tunisia, Algeria, Morocco—entered history in the eighteenth century chiefly through the exploits of their corsairs or the assassination of their beys or deys. These governments, by sending occasional "presents" to the sultans at Constantinople, maintained virtual independence. The people lived predominantly by agriculture or piracy; the ransoms paid for Christian captives were a substantial part of the national income; the corsair captains, however, were mostly Christians.[19] The arts maintained a precarious existence, but the Moroccan builders kept enough skill to blazon with radiant blue and green tiles the lordly "Bab-Mansur" that was added as a gateway in 1732 to the immense seventeenth-century palace-mosque of Mulai Ismail at Meknes, then the seat of the Moroccan sultans. Mulai Ismail, in a reign of fifty-five years (1672-1727), established order, begot hundreds of children, and thought his achievements warranted him in asking for his harem a daughter of Louis XIV.[20] It is difficult for us to appreciate ways of life much different from our own, but it is helpful to remember the remark of the Moroccan traveler who, on returning from a visit to Europe, exclaimed, "What a comfort to be getting back to civilization!"[21]

III. PERSIA: 1722–89

A Persian would have expressed similar relief on returning to his native land after a sojourn in Christendom, or even in Ottoman Islam. Until the fall of the Safavid dynasty (1736) an educated Persian would probably have ranked Iranian civilization as superior to any contemporary culture except possibly the Chinese. He would have deprecated Christianity as a reversion to popular polytheism. He might have admitted the superiority of Christendom in science, commerce, and war, but he would have preferred art to science and handicrafts to mechanized industry.

The eighteenth was a bitter century for Persia. Conquered by Afghans from the southeast, harassed by slave-gathering raids from the Uzbeks in the northeast, attacked by Russian depredations in the north, repeatedly overrun by vast Turkish armies in the west, impoverished by the taxgathering tyranny of its own spectacular Nadir Shah, and dismembered by the brutal conflict of rival families for the Persian throne—how could Iran continue, in this turbulence, the great traditions of Persian literature and art?

In the sixteenth century the land now called Afghanistan was divided by three governments: Kabul under Indian rule, Balkh under the Uzbeks, and Herat and Kandahar under the Persians. In 1706-08 the Afghans of Kanda-

har rose under Mir (Amir) Vais and expelled the Persians. His son Mir Mahmud invaded Persia, deposed the Safavid ruler Husein, and made himself
shah. Religion strengthened his arms, for the Afghans followed the Sunni,
or orthodox, form of Mohammedanism, and considered the Shi'a Persians
to be damned infidels. Mahmud put to death in hot blood three thousand of
Husein's bodyguard, three hundred Persian nobles, and some two hundred
children suspected of resenting the murder of their fathers. After a long rest
Mahmud in one day (February 7, 1725) slaughtered all the surviving members of the royal family except Husein and two of his younger children.
Then Mahmud went insane, and was killed, aged twenty-seven, by his cousin Ashraf (April 22, 1725), who proclaimed himself shah. So began the
bloodletting that devitalized Persia in that century.

Tahmasp, son of Husein, appealed to Russia and Turkey for help; they
responded by agreeing to partition Persia between them (1725). A Turkish
army entered Persia and took Hamadan, Kazvin, and Maragha, but was defeated by Ashraf near Kermanshah. The Turkish troops lacked fervor; why,
they asked, should they fight their fellow Sunnis, the Afghans, to restore the
heretical Shi'a Safavids? The Turks made peace with Ashraf, but retained
the provinces they had conquered (1727).

Ashraf now seemed secure, but a year later his usurped and alien power
was challenged by the rise of an obscure Persian who swept in a few years
through a military career as brilliant and bloody as any in history. Nadir Kuli
(i.e., "Slave of the Wonderful"—i.e., of Allah) was born in a tent in north-
eastern Iran (1686). He helped his father to tend their flocks of sheep and
goats; he had no schooling but a hard and adventurous life. When he was
eighteen, and had succeeded his dead father as head of the family, he and his
mother were carried off by Uzbek raiders to Khiva and were sold as slaves.
The mother died in bondage, but Nadir escaped, became the head of a robber band, captured Kalat, Nishapur, and Meshed, declared himself and these
cities loyal to Shah Tahmasp, and undertook to drive the Afghans out of
Persia and restore Tahmasp to the Persian throne. He accomplished this in
swift campaigns (1729–30); Tahmasp was reinstated, and made Nadir "sultan" of Khurasan, Seistan, Kerman, and Mazanderan.

The victorious general soon set out to recover the provinces that Turkey
had seized. By decisively defeating the Turks at Hamadan (1731) he brought
Iraq and Azerbaijan under Persian rule. Hearing of a rebellion in Khurasan,
he raised the siege of Erivan and marched fourteen hundred miles across
Iraq and Iran to invest Herat—a march that dwarfs the famous crossings of
Germany by Frederick the Great in the Seven Years' War. Meanwhile
Tahmasp in person took the field against the Turks, lost all that Nadir had
won, and ceded Georgia and Armenia to Turkey on promise of Turkish
help against Russia (1732). Nadir rushed back from the east, denounced the
treaty, deposed and imprisoned Tahmasp, set up Tahmasp's six-month-old
son as Shah Abbas III, proclaimed himself regent, and sent Turkey a declaration of war.

Having raised, by persuasion or conscription, an army of eighty thousand
men, he marched against the Turks. Near Samarra he encountered a vast

Turkish force led by Topal Osman, who, maimed in both legs, commanded from a litter. Nadir twice had horses shot under him; his standard-bearer fled, thinking him slain; an Arab contingent on whose aid he had relied turned against him; the Persian rout was complete (July 18, 1733). He assembled the remnants at Hamadan, recruited, armed, and fed new thousands, marched again to meet the Turks, and overwhelmed them at Leilan in a holocaust in which Topal Osman was killed. Another revolt having broken out in southeastern Persia, Nadir again crossed from west to east, and overcame the rebel leader, who committed suicide. Marching back across Persia and Iraq, he met eighty thousand Turks at Baghavand (1735), and so thoroughly defeated them that Turkey signed a peace ceding Tiflis, Gandzha, and Erivan to Persia.

Nadir had not forgotten that Peter the Great had attacked Persia in 1722–23, appropriating the Caspian provinces of Gilan, Astarabad, and Mazanderan, and the cities of Derbent and Baku. Russia, busy on other fronts, had restored the three provinces to Persia (1732). Now (1735) Nadir threatened that unless Russia withdrew from Derbent and Baku he would ally himself with Turkey against Russia. The two cities were surrendered, and Nadir entered Isfahan as the triumphant rebuilder of Persian power. When the child Abbas III died (1736), ending the Safavid dynasty, Nadir wedded reality to form, and made himself Nadir Shah.

Believing that the religious differences between Turkey and Persia made for repeated wars, he declared that henceforth Persia would abandon its Shi'a heresy and accept the orthodoxy of Sunni Islam. When the head of the Shi'a sect condemned this move Nadir had him strangled as quietly as possible. He confiscated the religious endowments of Kazvin to meet the expenses of his army, saying that Persia owed more to its army than to its religion.[22] Then, lonesome for war, he appointed his son Riza Kuli regent, and led 100,000 men to the conquest of Afghanistan and India.

For a year he besieged Kandahar. When it surrendered (1738) he treated its defenders so leniently that a troop of Afghans enlisted under his standard and remained faithful to him till his death. He marched on to Kabul, the key to the Khyber Pass; there the captured booty enabled him to keep his army in good spirits. Mohammed Shah, Mogul emperor of India, had refused to believe a Persian invasion possible; one of his governors had killed Nadir's envoy; now Nadir crossed the Himalayas, took Peshawar, crossed the Indus, and advanced to within sixty miles of Delhi before Mohammed's army resisted him. On the plain of Karnal the immense hordes met in battle (1739); the Indians relied on their elephants, the Persians attacked these patient animals with fireballs; the elephants turned and fled, throwing the Indian army into disorder; ten thousand Indians were slain, more were captured; Mohammed Shah came as a suppliant for mercy "to our heavenly presence," Nadir reported.[23] The victor exacted from him the surrender of Delhi and of nearly all its portable wealth, amounting to £87,500,000, and including the famous Peacock Throne, which had been made (1628–35) for Shah Jehan at the zenith of Mogul power. A riot among the populace killed some of Nadir's soldiers; he avenged them by allowing his army to massacre

100,000 natives in seven hours. He apologized for this by giving his son Nasrulla in marriage to Mohammed's daughter. Then he marched unimpeded back to Persia, having established himself as the greatest conqueror since Timur.

It was his fatality that if he disbanded his army it might create havoc and rebellion; if he kept it in force it would have to be clothed and fed; his conclusion was that war would be cheaper than peace if the war could be fought on foreign soil. Whom should he attack next? He remembered the Uzbek raids on northeast Persia, and his own enslavement, and his mother's death in slavery. In 1740 he led his troops into Uzbekistan. The Emir of Bokhara had no force or stomach to dispute Nadir's advance; he submitted, paid a huge indemnity, and agreed that the River Oxus should, as of old, be the boundary between Uzbekistan and Persia. The Khan of Khiva had put Nadir's emissary to death; Nadir slew the Khan, and released thousands of Persian and Russian slaves (1740).

Nadir was all soldier, with no mind left for statesmanship. Peace became for him an intolerable bore. His spoils made him avaricious instead of generous. Enriched by Indian treasure, he declared a three years' moratorium on taxes in Persia; then he changed his mind and ordered the accustomed payments; his tax collectors impoverished Persia as if it had been a conquered land. He suspected his son of plotting to depose him; he had him blinded. "It is not my eyes that you have put out," said Riza Kuli, "but the eyes of Persia."[24] The Persians began to hate their savior, as the Russians had learned to hate Peter the Great. The religious leaders roused against him the resentment of a nation offended in its religious faith. He tried to suppress the rising rebellion by wholesale executions; he built pyramids from the skulls of the victims. On June 20, 1747, four members of his own bodyguard entered his tent and attacked him; he killed two of them; the others cut him down. All Persia breathed a sigh of relief.

After him the country fell into worse disorder than under the Afghan domination. Several provincial khans claimed the throne; a contest of assassination ensued. Ahmed Khan Durani contented himself with founding the modern kingdom of Afghanistan; Shah Rukh—handsome, amiable, humane—was blinded shortly after his accession, and retired to rule Khurasan till 1796. Karim Khan emerged victorious from the contest, and established (1750) the Zand dynasty, which held power till 1794. Karim made Shiraz his capital, adorned it with handsome buildings, and gave South Persia twenty-nine years of moderate order and peace. Upon his death the scramble for power took again the form of civil war, and chaos was restored.

With the overthrow of the Safavid dynasty by the Afghans, Persia ended the last of her great periods in art, and only some minor productions graced this century. The Madrasa-i-Shah-Husein (1714) at Isfahan, a college for training scholars and lawyers, was described by Lord Curzon as "one of the stateliest ruins in Persia";[25] Sir Percy Sykes marveled at its "exquisite tiles . . . and lovely stenciling."[26] The tilemakers were still the ablest in the world, but the impoverishment of the upper classes by protracted wars destroyed the market for excellence, and compelled the potters to lower their art into an industry. Splendid book covers were made of lacquered papier mâché. Textile workers produced brocades and embroidery of consummate finesse. Persian rugs, though they had seen their last supremacy under Shah Abbas I, were still woven for the fortunate of many nations. Especially at Joshagan, Herat, Kerman, and Shiraz, the weavers produced carpets that "suffer only by comparison with their classical predecessors."[27]

The Afghan conquest broke the heart of Persian poetry, and left it almost voiceless through the ensuing servitude. Lutf 'Ali Beg Adar, about 1750, compiled a biographical dictionary of Persian poets, concluding with sixty contemporaries; despite this apparent abundance, he deplored what seemed to him the dearth of good writers in his time, and ascribed it to the prevalent chaos and misery, "which have reached such a point that no one has the heart to read poetry, let alone compose it."[28] Typical was the experience of Shaykh 'Ali Hazin, who wrote four *diwans* (collections) of verse, but was caught in the siege of Isfahan by the Afghans; all the dwellers in his household died then except himself; he recovered, fled from the ruins of the once beautiful city, and spent the last thirty-three years of his life in India. In his *Memoirs* (1742) he commemorated a hundred Persian poets of his time. Accounted greatest of these was Sayyid Ahmad Hatif of Isfahan; probably the most praised of his poems was an ecstatic reaffirmation of faith in God despite doubt and desolation:

> In the church I said to a Christian charmer of hearts, "O thou in whose net the heart is held captive!
> O thou to the warp of whose girdle each hair tip of mine is separately bound!
> How long wilt thou miss the way to the Divine Unity? How long wilt thou impose upon the One the shame of the Trinity?
> How can it be right to name the One True God "Father, Son, and Holy Ghost"?
> She parted her sweet lips and said to me, while with sweet laughter she poured sugar from her lips:
> "If thou art aware of the secret of the Divine Unity, do not cast upon me the stigma of infidelity!
> In three mirrors the Eternal Beauty casts a ray from His effulgent countenance." . . .
> Whilst we were so speaking, this chant rose up beside us from the church bell:
> "He is One and there is naught but He;
> There is no God save Him alone!" . . .
>
> In the heart of each atom which thou cleavest thou wilt behold a sun in the midst.
> If thou givest whatever thou hast to love, may I be accounted an infidel if thou shouldst suffer a grain of loss! . . .
> Thou wilt pass beyond the narrow straits of dimensions, and wilt behold the spacious realms of the Placeless;
> Thou shalt hear what ear hath not heard, and shalt see what eye hath not seen;
> Until they shall bring thee to a place where, of the world and its people, thou shalt behold One alone.
> To that One thou shalt give love with heart and soul, until with the eye of certainty thou shalt clearly see that
> "He is One and there is naught but he;
> There is no God save Him alone!"[29]

CHAPTER XVII

Russian Interlude

1725-62

I. WORK AND RULE

FREDERICK the Great wrote, about 1776: "Of all the neighbors of Prussia, Russia merits most attention, as being the most dangerous; it is powerful and near. Those who in the future will govern Prussia will, like me, be forced to cultivate the friendship of these barbarians."[1]

Always, in thinking of Russia, we must remember its size. Under Catherine II it included Esthonia, Livonia, Finland (in part), European Russia, the northern Caucasus, and Siberia. Its area expanded from 687,000 to 913,000 square kilometers in the eighteenth century; its population grew from thirteen millions in 1722 to thirty-six millions in 1790.[2] Voltaire in 1747 estimated the population of France or Germany to be slightly greater than that of Russia, but he noted that Russia was three times larger than either of those states. Time and Russian loins would fill those vast spaces.

In 1722, 97.7 per cent of the Russian population was rural; in 1790, still 96.4 per cent; so slow was industrialization. In 1762 all but ten per cent of the people were peasants, and 52.4 per cent of these were serfs.[3] Half of the land was owned by some 100,000 nobles, most of the rest by the state or the Russian Orthodox Church, some by semifree peasants still owing services and obedience to local lords. A landlord's wealth was reckoned by the number of his serfs; so Count Peter Cheremetyev was 140,000 serfs rich.[4] The 992,000 serfs of the Church were a main part of her wealth, and 2,800,000 serfs tilled the lands of the Crown in 1762.[5]

The noble provided military leadership and economic organization; he was usually exempt from military service, but often offered it in hopes of favors from the government. He had judiciary rights over his serfs, he could punish them, sell them, or banish them to Siberia; normally, however, he allowed his peasants to govern their internal affairs through their village assembly, or mir. He was obliged by law to provide seed for his serfs, and to maintain them through periods of dearth. A serf might achieve freedom by buying it from his owner or by enlisting in the army; but this required his owner's consent. Free peasants could buy and own serfs; some of these freemen, called *kulaki* (fists), dominated village affairs, lent money at usurious rates, and exceeded the lords in exploitation and severity.[6] Master and man alike were a tough breed, strong in frame and arm and hand; they were engaged together in the conquest of the soil, and the discipline of the seasons lay heavy upon them both. Sometimes the hardships were beyond bearing. Repeatedly we hear of serfs in great number deserting their farms and losing themselves in Poland or the Urals or the Caucasus; thousands of them died on the way, thousands were hunted and captured by soldiery. Every now and then peasants rose in armed revolt against masters and government, and gave desperate battle to the troops. Always they were defeated, and the survivors crept back to their tasks of fertilizing the women with their seed and the soil with their blood.

Some serfs were trained to arts and crafts, and supplied nearly all the needs of their masters. At a feast given to Catherine II (the Comte de Ségur tells us) the poet and the composer of the opera, the architect who had built the auditorium, the painter who decorated it, the actors and actresses in the drama, the dancers in the ballet, and the musicians in the orchestra were all serfs of Count Cheremetyev.[7] In the long winter the peasants made the clothing and the tools they would need in the coming year. Town industry was slow in developing, partly because every home was a shop, and partly because difficulties of transportation usually limited the market to the producer's vicinity. The government encouraged industrial enterprises by offering monopolies to favorites, sometimes by providing capital, and it approved participation by nobles in industry and trade. An incipient capitalism appeared in mining, metallurgy, and munitions, and in factory production of textiles, lumber, sugar, and glass. Entrepreneurs were permitted to buy serfs to man their factories; such "possessional peasants," however, were bound not to the owner but to the enterprise; a governmental decree of 1736 required them, and their descendants, to remain in their respective factories until officially permitted to leave. In many cases they lived in barracks, often isolated from their families.[8] Hours of labor ran from eleven to fifteen per day for men, with an hour for lunch. Wages ranged from four to eight rubles per day for men, from two to three rubles for women; but some employers gave their workers food and lodging, and paid their taxes for them. After 1734 "free"—non-serf—labor increased in the factories, as giving more stimulus to the workers and more profits to the employer. Labor was too cheap to favor the invention or application of machinery; but in 1748 Pulzunov used a steam engine in his ironworks in the Urals.[9]

Between the nobles and the peasants a small and politically powerless middle class slowly took form. In 1725 some three per cent of the population were merchants: tradesmen in the villages and towns and at the fairs; importers of tea and silk from China, of sugar, coffee, spices, and drugs from overseas, and of the finer textiles, pottery, and paper from Western Europe; exporters of timber, turpentine, pitch, tallow, flax, and hemp. Caravans moved to China via Siberian or Caspian routes; ships went out from Riga, Revel, Narva, and St. Petersburg. Probably more traffic went on the rivers and canals than on the roads or the sea.

At the center of that internal commerce was Moscow. Physically it was the largest city in Europe, with long, broad streets, 484 churches, a hundred palaces, thousands of hovels, and a population of 277,535 in 1780;[10] here Russians, Frenchmen, Germans, Greeks, Italians, English, Dutch, and Asiatics talked their own languages and freely worshiped their own gods. St. Petersburg was the citadel of government, of a Frenchified aristocracy, of literature and art; Moscow was the hub of religion and commerce, of a half-Oriental, still-medieval life, and of a jealously and conscientiously Slavic patriotism. These were the rival foci around which Russian civilization revolved, sometimes tearing the nation in two like a dividing cell, sometimes making it the tense complexity that would, before the end of the century, become the terror and arbiter of Europe.

It was impossible that a people so used up and brutalized by the conflict with nature, so lacking in facilities of communication or in security of life, with so little opportunity for education and so little time for thought, should enjoy, except in the isolated villages, the privileges and perils of democracy. Some form of feudalism was inevitable in the economy, some mode of monarchy in central rule. It was to be expected that the monarchy would be subject to frequent overturns by noble factions controlling their own military support; that the monarchy should seek to make itself absolute; and that it should depend upon religion to help its soldiery, police, and judiciary to maintain social stability and internal peace.

Corruption clogged every avenue of administration. Even the wealthy nobles who surrounded the throne were amenable to "gifts." "If there be a Russian proof against flattery," said the almost contemporary Castéra, "there is not one who can resist the temptation of gold."[11] Nobles controlled the palace guard that made and unmade "sovereigns"; they formed a caste of officers in the army; they manned the Senate which, under Elizabeth, made the laws; they headed the *collegia*, or ministries, that ruled over foreign relations, the courts, industry, commerce, and finance; they appointed the clerks who carried on the bureaucracy; they guided the ruler's choice of the governors who managed the "guberniyas" into which the empire was divided, and (after 1761) they chose the *voevodi* who governed the provinces. Over all branches of the government loomed the mostly middle-class Fiscal, a federal bureau of intelligence, authorized to discover and punish peculation; but, despite its large use of informers, it found itself foiled, for if the monarch had dismissed every official guilty of venality the machinery of the state would have stopped. The tax collectors had such sticky fingers that scarcely a third of their gleanings reached the treasury.[12]

II. RELIGION AND CULTURE

Religion was especially strong in Russia, for poverty was bitter, and merchants of hope found many purchasers. Skepticism was confined to an upper class that could read French, and Freemasonry had many converts there.[13] But the rural, and most of the urban, population lived in a supernatural world of fearful piety, surrounded by devils, crossing themselves a dozen times a day, imploring the intercession of saints, worshiping relics, awed by miracles, trembling over portents, prostrating themselves before holy images, and moaning somber hymns from stentorian breasts. Church bells were immense and powerful; Boris Godunov had set up one of 288,000 pounds, but the Empress Anna Ivanovna outrang him by having one cast of 432,000 pounds.[14] The churches were filled; the ritual was more solemn here, and the prayers were more ecstatic, than in half-pagan papal Rome. The Russian priests—each of them *a papa*, or pope—wore awesome beards and flowing hair, and dark robes reaching to their feet (for legs are an impediment to dignity). They seldom mingled with the aristocracy or the court, but lived in modest simplicity, celibate in their monasteries or married in their rectories. Abbots and priors governed the monks, abbesses the nuns; the secular clergy submitted to bishops, these to archbishops, these to provincial metropolitans, these to the patriarch in Moscow; and the Church as a whole acknowledged the secular sovereign as its head. Outside the Church were dozens of religious sects, rivaling one another in mysticism, piety, and hate.

Religion served to transmit a moral code that barely availed to create order amid the strong natural impulses of a primitive people. The nobles of the court adopted the morals, manners, and language of the French aristocracy; their marriages were transactions in realty, and were alleviated with lovers and mistresses. The women of the court were better educated than the men, but in moments of passion they could erupt in hot words and murderous violence. Among the people language was coarse, violence was frequent, and cruelty corresponded with the strength of the frame and the thickness of the skin. Everyone gambled and drank according to his means, and stole according to his station,[15] but everyone was charitable, and huts exceeded palaces in hospitality. Brutality and kindness were universal.

Dress varied from the fashions of Paris at the court to the fur caps, sheepskins, and thick mittens of the peasantry; from the silk stockings of the noble to the woolen bands that encased the legs and the feet of the serf. In summer the common people might bathe nude in the streams, sex ignored. Russian baths, like the Turkish, were heroic but popular. Otherwise hygiene was occasional, sanitation primitive. Nobles shaved; commoners, despite the ukases of Peter the Great, kept their beards.

Nearly every home had a balalaika, and St. Petersburg, under Elizabeth and Catherine II, had opera imported from Italy and France. Here came famous composers and conductors, and the finest singers and virtuosi of the age. Musical education was well financed, and justified itself in the outburst of musical genius in the second half of the nineteenth century. From all Russia promising male voices were sent to the leading churches to be trained. As the Greek rite allowed no instruments in choirs, the voices had free play, and attained such depths of unison and harmony as were hardly equaled elsewhere in the world. Boys took the soprano parts, but it was the bassos that astonished many a foreigner with their nether reach, and their range of feeling from whispers of tenderness to waves of guttural power.

Who composed this moving music for Russia's choirs? Mostly obscure monks, unknelled and unknown. Two stand out in the eighteenth century. Sozonovich Berezovsky was a Ukrainian lad whose voice seemed designed for the adoration of God. Catherine II sent him to Italy at state expense to get the best musical education; he lived for years at Bologna, and under

Padre Martini he learned the art of composition. Returning to Russia, he wrote religious music that combined Russian intensity with Italian elegance. His efforts to reform the singing of the choirs met with orthodox resistance; he fell into morbid melancholy, and killed himself at the age of thirty-two (1777).[16] Still more famous was Dmitri Bortniansky. When only seven years old he was admitted to the Court Church Choir; the Empress Elizabeth commissioned Galuppi to tutor him; when Galuppi returned to Italy Catherine II sent Dmitri with him to Venice; thence he passed to Padre Martini, and then to Rome and Naples, where he composed music in the Italian style. In 1779 he returned to Russia; he was soon appointed director of the Court Church Choir, and he kept this post till his death (1825). For the choir he composed a Greek Mass, and settings in four and eight parts for forty-five Psalms. It was due especially to his training that the choir reached the excellence which made it one of the wonders of the musical world. In 1901 St. Petersburg celebrated with pomp the 150th anniversary of his birth.

French influence dominated Russian art, but the leading figure was an Italian, Francesco (or Bartolomeo) Rastrelli. His father, Carlo, had been called to Russia by Peter the Great (1715), and had cast in bronze an equestrian statue of Peter, and a full-length figure of the Empress Anna Ivanovna. The son inherited the Louis Quinze Style that Carlo had brought from France; he added to it some inspiration from the baroque masterpieces of Balthasar Neumann and Fischer von Erlach in Germany and Austria; and he adapted these influences so harmoniously with Russian needs and styles that he became the architectural favorite of Czarina Elizabeth. Almost every Russian building of artistic note from 1741 to 1765 was designed by him or his aides. On the left bank of the Neva he raised (1732-54) the Winter Palace, which was burned down in 1837 but was conjecturally restored on the original plan: a monstrous mass of windows and columns in three layers, topped by statues and battlements. More to Elizabeth's taste was the Palace of Tsarskoe Selo (i.e., the Czar's village), on a hill fifteen miles south of St. Petersburg. At its left he built a church; in the interior of the palace a ceremonial stairway led to a Grande Galerie which was illuminated by immense windows during the day and by fifty-six chandeliers at night; at the farther end were the throne room and the apartments of the Empress. A Chinese Room paid the usual homage of the eighteenth century to Chinese art; an Amber Room was paneled with plaques of amber, given to Peter the Great by Frederick William I in exchange for fifty-five tall grenadiers; and a picture gallery housed some of the imperial collections. The interior was mostly in rococo decoration, which an English traveler described as a "mixture of barbarism and magnificence."[17] Catherine II, who was chaste if only in her taste, had the golden ornaments of the façade removed.

Literature developed more slowly than art. The paucity of readers gave it little encouragement, censorship by Church and state cramped expression, and the Russian language had not yet refined itself, in grammar or vocabulary, into a literary vehicle. And yet, even before the accession of Elizabeth (1742), three writers left their names on the face of history. Vasili Tatishchev was a man of action and thought, a traveler and historian, a diplomat and philosopher, loving Russia but opening his mind eagerly to economic and intellectual developments in the West. He was one of several promising youths whom Peter sent abroad for intellectual insemination. He came back with dangerous ideas: he had read, directly or in summaries, Bacon, Descartes, Locke, Grotius, and Bayle; his Orthodox faith had withered, and he supported religion only as an aide to government.[18] He served Peter in dangerous campaigns, became governor of Astrakhan, and was accused of peculation.[19] In his wanderings he gathered a store of geographical, ethnological, and historical data, which he used in a *History of Russia*. The book offended the clergy; no one dared print it till the early and liberal years of Catherine II's reign (1768–74).

Prince Antioch Cantemir continued the revolt against theology. Son of a Moldavian *hospodar* (governor), he was brought to Russia in his third year, learned to speak six languages, served in embassies to London and Paris, met Montesquieu and Maupertuis, and, returning, wrote satires of those "Pan-Slavic" patriots who opposed the contamination of Russian life with Western ideas. Here is a bit of his poem "To My Mind":

> Immature mind, fruit of recent studies, be quiet, urge not the pen into my hands. . . . Many easy paths lead in our days to honors; the least acceptable is the one the nine barefoot sisters [the Muses] have laid out. . . . You have to toil and moil there, and while you labor people avoid you as a pestilence, rail at you, loathe you. . . . "Who pores over books becomes an atheist"; thus Crito grumbles, his rosary in his hands, . . . and bids me see how dangerous is the seed of learning that is cast among us: our children, . . . to the horror of the Church, have begun to read the Bible; they discuss all, want to know the cause of all, and put little faith in the clergy; . . . they place no candles before the images, they observe no feasts. . . .
>
> O Mind, I advise you to be dumber than a dumpling. . . . Complain not of your obscurity. . . . If gracious Wisdom has taught you anything, . . . explain it not to others.[20]

Kantemir offended further by translating Fontenelle's *Entretiens sur la pluralité des mondes*. The book was denounced as Copernican, heretical, blasphemous, but Kantemir foiled his persecutors by dying at thirty-six (1744). Not till 1762 did his satires find a publisher.

Under Czarina Elizabeth Russian literature began to assert itself as something more than an echo of the French. Mikhail Lomonosov felt rather the German influence; having studied at Marburg and Freiburg, he married a *Fräulein*, and brought with her to St. Petersburg a heavy load of science. He became the lion of the Academy, adept in everything, even in drinking.[21] He refused to specialize; he became a metallurgist, geologist, chemist, electrician, astronomer, economist, geographer, historian, philologist, orator; Pushkin called him "the first Russian university."[22] Amid all this he was a poet.

His chief rival for the applause of the intelligentsia was Alexis Sumarokov, who published a volume of odes by himself and by Lomonosov to display the latter's inferiority. [The difference was negligible.] The real distinction of Sumarokov was his establishment of a Russian national theater (1756). For it he wrote plays echoing those of Racine and Voltaire. Elizabeth compelled the courtiers to attend; but as they paid no admission, Sumarokov complained that his salary of five thousand rubles per year did not suffice to keep both his theater and himself alive. "What was once seen at Athens, what is now to be seen in Paris, is also seen in Russia, by my care. . . . In Germany a crowd of poets has not produced what I have succeeded in doing by my own efforts."[23] In 1760 he tired of his labors and moved to Moscow, but there his flair for quarreling soon left him moneyless. He appealed to Catherine II to send him abroad at state expense, and assured her: "If Europe were described by such a pen as mine, an outlay of 300,000 rubles would seem small."[24] Catherine bore with him till he died of drink (1777).

Let us enliven our pages with the romance of a princess. Natalia Borisovna Dolgorukaya was the daughter of Count and Field Marshal Boris Cheremetyev, comrade in arms of Peter the Great. At the age of fifteen (1729), "radiantly beautiful," and "one of the greatest heiresses in Russia,"[25] she was betrothed to Vasili Lukich Dolgoruki, the prime favorite of Czar Peter II. Before they could be married Peter died, and his successor banished Vasili to Siberia. Natalia insisted on marrying him and following him into exile. She lived with him for eight years in Tobolsk, and bore him two children. In 1739 he was put to death. After three more years of exile she was allowed to return to European Russia. Having completed the education of her children, she entered a convent at Kiev. There, at the request of her son Mikhail, she composed her *Memoirs* (1768), which her poet grandson, Prince Ivan Mikhailovich Dolgoruki, published in 1810. Three Russian poets have celebrated her memory, and Russia honors her as the type of the many Russian women who ennobled revolution with their heroism and constancy.

All in all, Russian civilization was a mixture of unavoidable discipline and callous exploitation, of piety and violence, of prayer and profanity, of music and vulgarity, of fidelity and cruelty, of servile obsequiousness and indomitable bravery. These people could not develop the virtues of peace because they had to fight, through long winters and long winter nights, a bitter war against the arctic winds that crossed unhindered over their frozen plains. They had never known the Renaissance or the Reformation, and so—except in their artificial capital—they were still imprisoned in medieval swaddling clothes. They comforted themselves with pride of race and surety of faith: not yet a territorial nationalism, but a fierce conviction that while the West was damning itself with science, wealth, paganism, and unbelief, "Holy Russia" remained loyal to the Christianity of the patriarchs, was more endeared to Christ, and would someday rule and redeem the world.

III. RUSSIAN POLITICS: 1725–41

Between Peter the Great and Elizaveta Petrovna Russian history is a dreary and confusing record of intrigue and palace revolutions; here, if anywhere, we may with a good conscience save space and time. Nevertheless, some elements of the mélange must be noted if we are to understand the position, character, and conduct of Catherine the Great.

The natural heir to the throne in 1725 was Piotr Alexeevich, the ten-year-old boy of Peter's slain son Alexis. But Peter's widow, who could neither read nor write, persuaded the palace guard (by paying their long-overdue wages) that he had designated her as his successor; and with their support she proclaimed herself (February 27, 1725) Catherine I, Empress of All the Russias. This lesser Catherine then took to drink and adultery, achieved stupor every evening, retired regularly by 5 A.M., and left the government to her former lover Prince Alexander Danilovich Menshikov and a Supreme Council. Count Andrei Ostermann, of German birth, took charge of foreign affairs and directed Russia into friendship with Germany and Austria and hostility to France. Following the plans of Peter I, Catherine married her daughter Anna Petrovna to Karl Friedrich, duke of Holstein-Gottorp; the couple went to live in Kiel, where Anna bore the future Peter III. Catherine herself, exhausted with pleasure, died May 6, 1727, having nominated as her heir that same Piotr Alexeevich whose throne she had usurped.

Peter II was still only twelve; Menshikov continued to govern, and used his power to feather his nest. A group of nobles, led by the brothers Ivan and Vasili Lukich Dolgoruki, overthrew Menshikov and banished him to Siberia, where he died in 1729. A year later Peter II was carried off by smallpox, and the male branch of the Romanov dynasty ended. It was this contretemps that allowed Russia to be ruled for sixty-six years by three women who rivaled or exceeded, in executive capacity and political results, most contemporary kings, and outpaced all of them but Louis XV in sexual promiscuity.

The first of these czarinas was Anna Ivanovna, the thirty-five-year-old daughter of Ivan Alexeevich, the feeble-minded brother of Peter the Great. The Council chose her because she had acquired a protective reputation for humility and obedience. Dominated by the Dolgorukis and the Golitsyns, the Council drew up "Conditions" which they sent to Anna, then in Kurland, as prerequisite to her confirmation as empress. She signed (January 28, 1730). But neither the army nor the clergy wished to replace autocracy with oligarchy. A delegation of the palace guard went out to meet Anna, and petitioned her to take absolute power. Emboldened by their arms, she tore up the "Conditions" in the presence of the court.

Distrusting the Russian nobles, Anna brought in from Kurland the Germans who had pleased her there. Ernst von Bühren, or Biron, who had been her lover, became the head of her government; Ostermann was restored to foreign affairs; Count Christoff von Münnich reorganized the army; Löwenwolde, Korff, and Keyserling helped to give the new regime some German efficiency. Taxes were collected with careful rigor; education was extended and improved; an instructed civil service was prepared. With similar effectiveness the new administration imprisoned, banished, or executed the Dolgorukis and the Golitsyns.

Satisfied with two lovers (Biron and Löwenwolde), Anna lived a relatively regular life, rose at eight, gave three hours to government, and smiled approval as her Germans expanded Russian power. An army under Münnich invaded Poland, deposed the French-oriented Stanislas Leszczyński, enthroned the Saxon Augustus III, and took the first step toward binding Poland to Russia. France countered by urging Turkey to attack Russia; the Sultan demurred, being busy on his Persian front; Russia thought it a good time to declare war against Turkey; so began (1735) sixty years of conflict for control of the Black Sea. Anna's diplomats explained that the Turks, or their dependents in South Russia, held the outlets of the five great rivers—Dniester, Bug, Dnieper, Don, Kuban—which were the main channels of south-bound Russian commerce; that the semibarbarous Moslem tribes inhabiting the lower basins of these streams were a standing threat to the Christians of Russia; that the northern shores of the Black Sea were a natural and necessary part of Russia; and that a great and growing nation like Russia should no longer be blocked from free access to the Black Sea and the Mediterranean. This remained the theme song of Russia through the remainder of the century, and beyond.

The first objective was the Crimea, the almost-island that stood as a Turkish stronghold on the northern front of the Black Sea. To take that peninsula was the goal of Münnich's campaign in 1736. His chief foes were space and disease. He had to cross 330 miles of wilderness in which not one town could provide food or medicine for his 57,000 troops; eighty thousand wagons had to accompany them in a long line subject at any point and moment to attack by Tatar tribes. With brilliant generalship Münnich in twenty-nine days took Perekop, Koslov, and Bakhchisarai (the Crimean capital); but in that month dysentery and other ailments spread such misery and mutiny among his men that he had to abandon his conquests and retreat into the Ukraine. Meanwhile another of Anna's generals took Azov, which controlled the mouth of the Don.

Münnich marched south again in April, 1737, with seventy thousand men, and captured Ochakov, near the mouth of the Bug. In June Austria joined in attacking the Turks, but its campaign so miscarried that it signed a separate peace; and Russia, suddenly left to face the full Turkish army, and expecting war with Sweden, signed (September 18, 1739) a peace that restored to the Turks almost all that had been won in three campaigns. This treaty was celebrated in St. Petersburg as a splendid triumph, which had cost only a hundred thousand lives.

Anna survived the war by a year. Shortly before her death (October 17, 1740) she named as heir to the throne the eight-week-old Ivan VI, son of her German-born niece Anna Leopoldovna and Prince Anton Ulrich of Brunswick, Biron to be regent till Ivan reached seventeen. But Münnich and Ostermann had now had enough of Biron; they joined with Ulrich and Leopoldovna to send him to Siberia (November 9, 1740). Anna Leopoldovna became regent, with Münnich as "first minister." Fearing the total domination of Russia by Teutons, the French and Swedish ambassadors aroused and financed a revolt of the Russian nobles. They chose as their secret candidate for the throne Elizaveta Petrovna, daughter of Peter the Great and Catherine I.

Elizabeth, as we shall call her, was thirty-two years old, but was at the height of her beauty, courage, and vivacity. She loved athletics and violent exercise, but also she was fond of amorous delight, and entertained a succession of gallants. She had little education, wrote Russian with difficulty, spoke French well. She seems to have had no thought of gracing the throne until Anna Leopoldovna and Ostermann set her aside in favor of foreigners. When the Regent ordered the St. Petersburg regiments to Finland, and the soldiers grumbled at facing a winter war, Elizabeth seized the opportunity; she put on military garb, went to the barracks at 2 A.M. December 6, 1741, and appealed to the soldiers to support her. At the head of a regiment she sledged over the snow to the Winter Palace, awakened the Regent, and sent both her and the baby Czar to prison. When the city awoke it found that it had a new ruler, a thoroughly Russian Empress, a daughter of the great Peter. Russia and France rejoiced.

IV. ELIZABETH PETROVNA: 1741–62

It is difficult to make her out through the mists of time and prejudice. Catherine II, meeting her in 1744, was "struck by her beauty and the majesty of her bearing. . . . In spite of being very stout, she was not in the least disfigured by her size, nor embarrassed in her movements, . . . though she wore an immense hoop when she dressed up."[26] She was privately skeptical to the verge of atheism;[27] publicly she was zealously orthodox. A French observer noted her "pronounced taste for liquor,"[28] but we must remember that Russia is cold and vodka warms. She refused marriage, fearing that it would divide her power and multiply disputes; some say that she secretly married Alexis Razumovsky; if so, he was merely *primus inter pares*. She was vain, loved finery, had fifteen thousand dresses, heaps of stockings, 2,500 pairs of shoes;[29] some of these she used as missiles in argument. She could upbraid her servants and courtiers in the language of a sergeant. She sanctioned some cruel punishments, but she was basically kind.[30] She abolished the death penalty except for treason (1744); torture was allowed only in the gravest trials; flogging remained, but Elizabeth felt that some way had to be found to discourage the criminals who made the highways and city streets unsafe at night. She was both restless and indolent. She had a keen natural intelligence, and gave her country as good a government as the condition of Russian education, morals, manners, and economy allowed.

Having banished Ostermann and Münnich to Siberia, she restored the Senate to administrative leadership, and entrusted foreign affairs to Alexei Petrovich Bestuzhev-Ryumin. Catherine II described him as "a great intriguer, suspicious, firm and intrepid in his principles, an implacable enemy, but the true friend of her friends."[31] He was fond of money, as those usually are who know that their high state invites a fall. When England sought to bribe him it estimated his integrity as costing 100,000 crowns.[32] We do not know if the purchase went through, but Bestuzhev generally took an English line; this, however, was a natural retort to French support of Sweden and Turkey against Russia. Frederick the Great in his turn offered Bestuzhev 100,000 crowns if he would ally Russia with Prussia; the offer was refused;[33] instead, Bestuzhev allied Russia with Austria (1745) and England (1755). When England followed this by an alliance with Prussia (January 16, 1756), Bestuzhev's house of chancelleries fell apart, and Elizabeth henceforth ignored his advice. A new ministry bound Russia to the Franco-Austrian "reversal of alliances," and the Seven Years' War was on.

We have seen—far back!—how the Russian general Apraksin defeated the Prussians at Gross-Jägersdorf (1757), and then withdrew his army into Poland. The French and Austrian ambassadors convinced Elizabeth that Bestuzhev had ordered Apraksin's retreat and was conspiring to depose her. She ordered the arrest of both the Chancellor and the general (1758). Apraksin died in jail. Bestuzhev denied both charges, and later knowledge has cleared him. His foes wished to torture him into confession; Elizabeth forbade this. Mikhail Vorontsov replaced Bestuzhev as chancellor.

Amid the balls, gambling, intrigues, jealousies, and hatreds of the court, Elizabeth encouraged her aides to advance Russian civilization. Her young favorite Ivan Shuvalov opened a university at Moscow, established primary and secondary schools, sent students abroad for graduate study in medicine, and imported French architects, sculptors, and painters for the Academy of Arts (Akademia Iskustv) which he set up in the capital (1758). He corresponded with Voltaire, and induced him to write a *History of the Russian Empire under Peter the Great* (1757). His brother Piotr Shuvalov helped the economy by removing tolls on internal trade. Meanwhile, however, to console the Pan-Slavists, Elizabeth allowed religious intolerance to grow; she closed some mosques in the Tatar regions, and banished 35,000 Jews.

Her proudest achievement was that her armies and generals repeatedly defeated Frederick II, stopped the Prussian advance, and were on the point of crushing him when her physical decline weakened her power to hold the Franco-Austro-Russian alliance together. As early as 1755 the British ambassador reported: "The health of the Empress is bad; she is affected with spitting of blood, shortness of breath, constant coughing, swollen legs, and water on the chest; yet she danced a minuet with me."[34] Now she paid heavily for having preferred promiscuity to marriage. Childless, she had long sought someone of royal blood who could face the external and internal problems of Russia, and, inexplicably, her choice had fallen upon Karl Friedrich Ulrich, son of her sister Anna Petrovna and of Karl Friedrich, duke of Holstein-Gottorp. It was the greatest error of her reign, but she redeemed it by her choice for his mate.

V. PETER AND CATHERINE: 1743–61

Piotr Feodorovich, as Elizabeth renamed her heir, was born at Kiel in 1728. As grandson of both Peter I and Charles XII, he was eligible to both the

Russian and the Swedish thrones. Of feeble health, he was kept at home till he was seven; then, by a sudden change, he was assigned to the Holstein Guards, and was raised to be a soldier. He became a sergeant at nine, marched proudly in field parades, and learned the language and morals of army officers. At eleven he was given a German tutor who brought him up unforgettably in the Lutheran faith, and disciplined him into neurosis. Browbeaten by this pedagogue, he shrank into timidity and secrecy, took to cunning and deceit,[35] became "permanently irritable, stubborn, quarrelsome."[36] Rousseau might have cited him as illustrating the notion that man is good by nature but is deformed by a bad environment; Peter had a kind heart, and a longing to do the right, as we shall see by his royal decrees; but he was ruined by being cast for parts he was not fitted to play. Catherine II, meeting him when he was eleven, described him as "good-looking, well-mannered, courteous," and she "felt no repugnance at the idea" of becoming his wife.[37]

In 1743 Elizabeth had him brought to Russia, made him grand duke, converted him, apparently, to the Orthodox faith, and tried to train him for rule. But she "stood aghast" at the inadequacy of his education and the instability of his character. At St. Petersburg he added drunkenness to his other faults. Elizabeth hoped that before she herself died this strange youth, if mated to a healthy and intelligent woman, might beget a competent future czar. With that lack of ethnic prejudice which marked the European aristocracies even during the rise of nationalistic states, Elizabeth looked outside Russia and chose an undistinguished princess from one of the smallest German principalities. The wily Frederick II had recommended this choice, hoping to have a friendly German czarina in a Russia already fearsome to Germany.

At this point we are confronted by the memoirs of Catherine the Great. There is no doubt of their authenticity; they were not printed till 1859, but the French manuscript, in Catherine's own hand, is preserved in the national archives in Moscow. Are they trustworthy? By and large the story they tell is confirmed by other sources.[38] Their fault is not mendacity but partiality; they are a tale told well with wit and verve, but they are in part an apologia for having dethroned her husband, and for bearing with such equanimity the news that he had been killed.

She was born in Stettin, Pomerania, April 21, 1729, and was christened Sophia Augusta Frederika after three of her aunts. Her mother was Princess Johanna Elisabeth of Holstein-Gottorp; through her Catherine was a cousin to Peter. Her father was Christian August, prince of Anhalt-Zerbst in central Germany, a major general in Frederick's army. Both parents were disappointed by the birth of a girl; the mother mourned as if it had been a miscarriage. Catherine atoned for her sex by developing the virility of a general and the statesmanship of an emperor, all the while remaining the most sought and found mistress in Europe.

She had a variety of childhood sicknesses, one so severe that it left her apparently deformed for life, "the backbone running zigzag," the "right shoulder much higher than the left"; she now "assumed the shape of the letter

Z." The local hangman, who had become a specialist in dislocations, encased her in a corset "which I never removed day or night except when changing my underclothes"; and "after eighteen months I began to show signs of straightening out."[39] She was so often told that she was ugly that she determined to develop intelligence as a substitute for beauty; she was another case of a felt defect stimulating compensatory powers. Her ugliness disappeared as puberty rounded out her angles into curves. Despite her tribulations she was of "a happy disposition," and of such natural vivacity "as needed to be restrained."[40]

She was educated by tutors, especially by a Lutheran clergyman who suffered from her questions. Was it not unfair, she asked, "that Titus, Marcus Aurelius, and all the great men of antiquity, virtuous though they might be, should have been damned because they did not know about Revelation?" She argued so well that her teacher proposed to flog her, but a governess intervened. She especially wanted to know what that chaos had been like which, according to Genesis, had preceded the Creation. "His replies never seemed to satisfy me," and "we both lost our tempers." He was still further harassed by her insistence on his explaining "just what was circumcision?"[41] Her other teachers and the governess were French, so that she learned that language well; she read Corneille, Racine, and Molière, and was clearly ready for Voltaire. She became one of the best-educated women of her time.

News of this bright princess reached the Empress Elizabeth, eager for a girl who might give Peter intelligence by osmosis. On January 1, 1744, an invitation came to Sophia's mother to come with her for a visit to the Russian court. The parents hesitated; Russia seemed dangerously unstable and primitive; but Sophia, surmising that she was being considered as a wife for the Grand Duke, pleaded for an affirmative reply. On January 12 they began the long and difficult journey through Berlin, Stettin, East Prussia, Riga, and St. Petersburg to Moscow. At Berlin Frederick entertained them, and took a fancy to Sophia, "asking me a thousand questions, and talking about opera, comedy, poetry, dancing, everything, in short, that one could possibly imagine in conversing with a girl of fourteen."[42] At Stettin "my father tenderly took leave of me, and this was the last time I saw him; I cried bitterly." Mother and daughter, with a lavish entourage, reached Moscow on February 9, after a sleigh ride of fifty-two hours from St. Petersburg.

That evening she met Peter for the second time, and again was favorably impressed, until he confided to her that he was a convinced Lutheran, and was in love with one of the ladies in waiting at the court.[43] She noticed that his German accent and manners were distasteful to the Russians; for her part she resolved to learn Russian thoroughly, and to accept the Orthodox faith *in toto*. She felt "little more than indifference" toward Peter, but "I was not indifferent to the Russian crown." She was given three teachers—for the language, for the religion, and for Russian dances. She studied so earnestly— once getting out of bed in the middle of the night to study her lessons—that on February 22 she was bedded with pleurisy. "I remained between life and death for twenty-seven days, during which I was bled sixteen times, sometimes four times a day."[44] Her mother lost favor at court by asking that a Lutheran clergyman be summoned; Sophia won many hearts by asking for a Greek priest. At last, on April 21, she was able to appear in public. "I had become as thin as a skeleton; . . . my face and features were drawn, my hair was falling out, and I was totally pale."[45] The Empress sent her a pot of rouge.

On June 28 Sophia underwent, with impressive piety, the ceremony of conversion to the Orthodox faith. Now to her existing names were added Ekaterina Alexeevna; henceforth she was Catherine. The next morning, in the great cathedral, Ouspenski Sobor, she was formally betrothed to Grand Duke Peter. All who saw her were pleased with her tactful modesty; even Peter began to love her. After fourteen months of apprenticeship they were married, August 21, 1745, at St. Petersburg. On October 10 Catherine's mother left for home.

Peter was now seventeen, his wife sixteen. She was beautiful and he was plain, having suffered from smallpox in their betrothal year. She was intellectually avid and alert; he "displayed," said Soloviev, "every symptom of mental backwardness, and resembled a grown-up child."[46] He played with dolls and marionettes and toy soldiers; he was so fond of dogs that he kept several of them in his apartment; Catherine was not clear which was worse, their barking or their stench.[47] He did not improve the situation by playing his violin. His taste for liquor increased; "from 1753 he got drunk almost daily."[48] The Empress Elizabeth often reproved him for his faults, but she did not add example to precept. She was more disturbed by his unconcealed dislike of Russia, which he called "an accursed land";[49] by his scorn of the Orthodox Church and clergy; above all, by his idolatry of Frederick the Great, even when Russia and Prussia were in deadly war. He surrounded himself with a "Holsteiner Guard" of soldiers nearly all German; in his pleasure house at Oranienbaum he dressed his attendants in German uniforms, and put them through Prussian drills. When the Russian generals Fermor and Saltykov defeated the Prussians in 1759 they refrained from pursuing their victories for fear of offending Peter,[50] who might at any moment become czar.

The marriage became almost a conflict of cultures, for Catherine was furthering her education by studying the literature of France. It seems incredible that this young woman, in her unhappy years as grand duchess, read Plato, Plutarch, Tacitus, Bayle, Voltaire, Diderot, and Montesquieu, whose *Spirit of Laws*, she said, should be "the breviary of every sovereign of common sense."[51] Such books must have finished Catherine's religious beliefs—though she continued assiduously her observation of the Orthodox ritual; and they gave her that conception of "enlightened despotism" which Frederick had imbibed from Voltaire a generation before.

Meanwhile (if we may believe her firsthand report) "the marriage between me and the Grand Duke had not been consummated."[52] Castéra, who in 1800 wrote a well-informed and hostile biography of Catherine, thought that "Peter had a defect which, though easy to remove, seemed so much the more cruel; the violence of his love, his reiterated efforts, could not accomplish the consummation of his marriage"[53]—a remarkable parallel with Louis XVI and Marie Antoinette. Perhaps the distaste that Catherine, during their long betrothal, had come to feel for Peter had become evident to him, and made him psychologically impotent. He soon turned to other women, and took a succession of mistresses, who hoped to replace Catherine as grand duchess. In her account these first years of marriage were years of misery for her. One day (according to Horace Walpole), when the Empress asked her why no issue had come of her union, she replied that none should be expected—which in effect announced her husband's impotence. "Elizabeth replied that the state demanded successors, and left the Grand Duchess to procure them by whose assistance she pleased. A son and a daughter were the fruits of her obedience."[54] Mme. Maria Choglokova, appointed by Elizabeth to be lady in waiting to Catherine, explained to the Grand Duchess (according to the Grand Duchess) that there were important exceptions to the rule of marital fidelity; she promised to keep the secret if Catherine took a lover;[55] and "there can be little doubt that this shameful suggestion came not from the lady in waiting, but from the Empress herself."[56] We must see these matters in the perspective of a Russian court long accustomed to polyandrous queens, a French court inured to polygynous kings, and a Saxon-Polish court with the 150 children of Augustus III.

Did Catherine follow these exemplars to excess? After her accession, yes. Before her accession she seems to have limited herself stoically to three lovers. First—some six years after marriage—came Sergei Saltykov, a lusty young officer. Catherine explains her response:

> If I may venture to be frank, . . . I combined, with the mind and temperament of a man, the attractions of a lovable woman. I pray to be forgiven for this description, which is justified by its truthfulness. . . . I was attractive; consequently one half of the road to temptation was already covered, and it is only human in such situations that one should not stop halfway. . . . One cannot hold one's heart in one's hand, forcing it or releasing it, tightening or relaxing one's grasp at will.[57]

In 1751 she became pregnant, but had a miscarriage; and this painful experience was repeated in 1753. In 1754 she gave birth to the future Emperor Paul I. Elizabeth rejoiced, gave Catherine a present of 100,000 rubles, and sent Saltykov to safe obscurity in Stockholm and Dresden, where, Catherine tells us, he was "frivolous with all the women he met."[58] Peter drank more, and took fresh mistresses, finally settling down with Elizaveta Vorontsova, niece of the new Chancellor. Catherine quarreled with him, and made public fun of him and his friends.[59] In 1756 she accepted the attentions of a handsome Pole, twenty-four years old, Count Stanislas Poniatowski, who had come to St. Petersburg as attaché to Sir Charles Hanbury-Williams, the British ambassador. Stanislas' autobiography describes her in 1755:

> She was five-and-twenty years old; . . . she was at that perfect moment which is generally, for women who have beauty, the most beautiful. She had black hair, a dazzlingly white skin, long black eyelashes, a Grecian nose, a

mouth that seemed made for kisses, perfect hands and arms, a slim figure rather tall than short, an extremely active bearing, yet full of nobility. The sound of her voice was pleasant, and her laugh was as merry as her disposition.[60]

Gazing at her, he "forgot that there was a Siberia." This was the most deeply felt of her many loves, and his; long after she had taken other suitors her heart remained with Poniatowski, and he never quite recovered from his infatuation, however sorely tried by her policies. When she went to stay with Peter at Oranienbaum, Stanislas risked his life by secretly visiting her there. He was detected, and Peter gave orders that he be hanged. Catherine interceded with Peter's mistress, who, softened by a gift, appeased the Grand Duke. Finally, in a burst of good nature, Peter not only forgave Poniatowski but called Catherine to join her lover, and entered with them and Elizaveta Vorontsova into an amiable *ménage à quatre*, with many gay suppers together.[61]

On December 9, 1758, Catherine gave birth to a daughter. The court generally believed that Poniatowski was the father,[62] but Peter took the credit, accepted congratulations, and organized festivities to celebrate his achievement;[63] however, the child died four months later. The Empress had Poniatowski recalled to Poland, and Catherine was briefly loveless. But she was charmed by the adventures, in love and war, of Grigori Grigorievich Orlov, aide-de-camp to Piotr Shuvalov. Orlov had made a reputation by keeping to his post in the battle of Zorndorf despite three wounds. He had the build of an athlete and "the face of an angel";[64] but his only morality was to win power and women by any available means. Shuvalov had a mistress, Princess Elena Kurakin, one of the fairest and loosest beauties of the court; Orlov won her away from his superior; Shuvalov vowed to kill him, but died before attending to the matter. Catherine admired Orlov's courage, and noted that in the guards he had four brothers all tall and strong; these five warriors would be useful in an emergency. She arranged a meeting with Grigori, then another, and another; soon she displaced Kurakin. By July, 1761, she was pregnant; in April, 1762, she gave birth, as secretly as possible, to Orlov's son, who was brought up as Alexis Bobrinsky.

In December, 1761, it became apparent that the Empress was entering upon her final illness. Attempts were made to bring Catherine into a plot to prevent the accession of Peter; she was warned that Peter, as czar, would cast her aside and make Elizaveta Vorontsova his wife and queen; but Catherine refused to join in the plot. On January 5, 1762 (N.S.), the Empress Elizabeth died, and Peter, without open opposition, mounted the throne.

VI. PETER III: 1762

He astonished everyone by the generosity of his measures. The good nature that had been blurred by coarse and thoughtless manners came to the fore in a burst of gratitude for his peaceful accession to power. He pardoned enemies, he retained most of Elizabeth's ministers, and he tried to be kind to

Catherine. In the royal palace he allowed her comfortable quarters at one end, housed himself at the other, and assigned to his mistress the intermediate rooms; it was a mortal affront, of course, but Catherine was secretly pleased to be at a distance from him. He provided her with an ample allowance, and paid her extensive debts without inquiring into their origin.[65] In official ceremonies he gave her equal standing with himself, sometimes yielded her precedence.[66]

He recalled from exile the men and women whom previous rulers had sent to Siberia; now Münnich returned, aged eighty-two, to be welcomed by thirty-two grandsons; Peter restored him to his rank as field marshal; Münnich vowed to serve him to the end, and did. The happy Emperor freed the nobles from the obligation that Peter the Great had laid upon them to give many years of their lives to the state; they proposed to build a statue of him in gold; he bade them use the metal more sensibly.[67] A decree of February 21 abolished the universally hated secret police, and forbade arrest on political charges until these had been reviewed and sanctioned by the Senate. On June 25 Peter issued a ukase that adultery should henceforth be exempt from official censure, "since in that matter even Christ had not condemned";[68] the court was delighted. Merchants were pleased by a lowering of export dues; the price of salt was reduced; the buying of serfs for factory labor was stopped. Old Believers, who had fled from Russia to avoid persecution under Elizabeth, were invited to return and enjoy religious freedom. The clergy, however, was incensed by decrees of February 16 and March 21 nationalizing all the lands of the Church, and making all Orthodox clergymen salaried employees of the government. The serfs on these secularized domains were freed, and serfs on the estates of the nobility expected that they too would soon be freed. Amid all these reforms—suggested to him by various ministers—Peter continued to drink heavily.

The most startling of his measures, and the one that gave him the greatest happiness, was his termination of the war with Prussia. Even before his accession he had done much to help Frederick, secretly transmitting to him the military plans of Elizabeth's Council; now he boasted of having done this.[69] On May 5 he bound Russia with Prussia in defensive and offensive alliance. He instructed the commander of the Russian forces then with the Austrian army to put them at the service of "the King my master."[70] He donned a Prussian uniform, and ordered the local soldiery to do the same; he established Prussian discipline in the army; he organized military exercises every day for his court, and compelled every male courtier to participate regardless of age and gout.[71] He gave his own "Holsteiner Guard" precedence over the proud regiments of the capital.

The Russian army was not averse to peace, but it was shocked by Russia's precipitate desertion of her French and Austrian allies, and her surrender of all terrain won from Prussia during the war. It was alarmed when Peter announced that he proposed to send a Russian host against Denmark to recover that duchy of Schleswig which Denmark had taken from the dukes of Holstein, who included Peter's father. The troops made it clear that they would refuse to fight such a war; when Peter asked Kirill Razumovsky to lead an army to Denmark, the general answered, "Your Majesty must first give me another army to force mine to advance."[72]

Suddenly, despite his brave and remarkable reforms, Peter found himself unpopular. The army hated him as a traitor, the clergy hated him as a Lutheran or worse, the unfreed serfs clamored for emancipation, and the court ridiculed him as a fool. Upon all this came the general suspicion that he intended to divorce Catherine and marry his mistress.[73] "That young woman" (according to Castéra), "destitute of everything like address, but stupidly proud, . . . had the art of obtaining from the Czar—sometimes by flattery, sometimes by chiding, and sometimes even by beating him—a renewal of the promise he had made her, . . . to marry her and place her, instead of Catherine, upon the throne of Russia."[74] As power and liquor went more and more to his head, he treated Catherine harshly, even to publicly calling her a fool.[75] The Baron de Breteuil wrote to Choiseul: "The Empress [Catherine] is in the cruelest state, and is treated with the utmost contempt. . . . I should not be surprised, knowing her courage and violence, if this were to drive her to some extremity . . . Some of her friends are doing their best to pacify her, but they would risk everything for her if she required it."[76]

St. Petersburg and its environs were full of Catherine's partisans. She was popular with the army, the court, and the populace. Next to her ladies in waiting and Grigori Orlov, her closest intimate in these critical days was Ekaterina Romanovna, Princess Dashkova. This bold and enterprising lady was only nineteen years old, but, as niece to Chancellor Vorontsov and sister to Peter's mistress, she was already prominent in the affairs of the court. Peter, in his simplicity or his cups, had revealed to her his intention to depose Catherine and enthrone Elizaveta Vorontsova.[77] Dashkova carried the news to Catherine, and begged her to join in a plot to put Peter aside. But Catherine had already organized a conspiracy with Nikita Panin, tutor to her son Paul, and Kirill Razumovsky, hetman of the Ukraine, and Nikolai Korff, head of the police, and the Orlov brothers, and P. B. Passek, an officer in a local regiment.

On June 14 Peter ordered Catherine's arrest; he canceled the order, but bade her retire to Peterhof, twelve miles west of the capital. Peter himself withdrew to Oranienbaum with his mistress. He left instructions that the army should prepare to sail for Denmark, and promised to join it in July. On June 27 Lieutenant Passek was arrested for making derogatory speeches against the Emperor. Fearing that he would be tortured into confessing the plot, Grigori and Alexei Orlov decided that they must act at once. Early on the twenty-eighth Alexei rode in haste to Peterhof, roused Catherine from her sleep, and persuaded her to ride back with him to St. Petersburg. On the way they stopped at the barracks of the Ismailovsky Regiment; the soldiers were summoned by a drum roll; Catherine appealed to them to save her from the threats of the Emperor; they swore to protect her; "they rushed to kiss my hands and feet, the hem of my dress, calling me their savior" (so Catherine wrote to Poniatowski[78])—for they knew that she would not send them to

Denmark. Escorted by two regiments and the Orlovs, she proceeded to the Kazan Cathedral, where she was proclaimed autocrat of Russia. The Preobrazhensky Regiment joined her there, and begged her to "forgive us for being the last to come."[79] The Horse Guards fell in, and fourteen thousand troops accompanied her to the Winter Palace; there the Church Synod and the Senate officially announced the dethronement of Peter and the accession of Catherine. Some high dignitaries protested, but the army frightened them into swearing allegiance to the Empress.

She donned the uniform of a captain of the Horse Guards, and rode at the head of her troops to Peterhof. Peter had come there that morning to see her; informed of the revolt, he fled to Kronstadt; Münnich offered to go with him to Pomerania and organize an army to restore him; Peter, unable to decide, returned to Oranienbaum. When Catherine's forces approached he spent a day in pleas for a compromise; then, on June 29 (O. S.), he signed his abdication; "he allowed himself to be overthrown," said Frederick, "as a child lets himself be sent to bed."[80] He was imprisoned at Ropsha, fifteen miles from St. Petersburg. He begged Catherine to let him keep his Negro servant, his lapdog, his violin, and his mistress. He was allowed all but the last. Elizaveta Vorontsova was banished to Moscow, and disappeared from history.

CHAPTER XVIII

Catherine the Great

1762–96

I. THE AUTOCRAT

CATHERINE was victorious, but exposed to all the hazards of a chaotic change. To reward the soldiers who had escorted her to power, she ordered the drinking establishments of the capital to supply them with beer and vodka free of charge; the result was a general drunkenness that for a time almost dissolved the military basis of her power. At midnight of June 29–30 Catherine, who was having her first sleep in forty-eight hours, was awakened by an officer who told her, "Our men are terribly drunk. A hussar has shouted to them, 'To arms! Thirty thousand Prussians are coming to take away our mother [Catherine]!' So they have armed themselves, and are coming here to see how you really are." Catherine dressed, went out, denied the rumor about the Prussians, and persuaded her warriors to go to bed.[1]

Her son Paul, now eight years old, endangered her. Panin, many nobles, and most of the clergy felt that legitimacy required the coronation of Paul as emperor, with Catherine as regent. She feared that this would put the government in the hands of an aristocratic oligarchy, which would seek to depose or dominate her. She officially declared Paul heir to the throne, but his supporters continued their agitation; and the son grew up to hate his mother as having cheated him of the crown.

As news of the *coup d'état* spread through Russia it became evident that public opinion outside the capital was hostile to Catherine. The capital had known Peter's faults at first hand, and generally agreed that he was unfit to rule; but the Russian people outside St. Petersburg knew him chiefly through the liberal measures that had given some nobility to his reign. The populace of Moscow, too distant to feel Catherine's charm, remained sullenly opposed to her accession. When Catherine took Paul to Moscow (the stronghold of orthodoxy), Paul was fervently applauded, Catherine was coolly received. Many provincial regiments denounced the Petersburg soldiery as usurpers of national power.

We do not know if the wide sympathy for Peter was a factor in his death. Broken in spirit, the fallen Czar sent humble petitions to his wife to "have pity on me, and give me my only consolation"—his mistress—and to let him return to his relatives in Holstein. Instead of receiving such comfort he was confined to a single room, and was always under surveillance. Alexei Orlov, chief of those who guarded him, played cards with him, and lent him money.[2] On July 6, 1762 (N. S.), Alexei rode in haste to St. Petersburg and informed

Catherine that Peter had quarreled with him and other attendants, and in the ensuing scuffle had died. As to the mode of his death history has only rumors, none confirmed: that he was poisoned or strangled,[3] that he was fatally beaten,[4] that he died of "inflammation of the bowels and apoplexy";[5] "the details of the murder," the latest historian concludes, "were never fully revealed, and the part played in it by Catherine remains uncertain."[6] It is improbable that Catherine ordered the deed,[7] but she punished no one for it, concealed it from the public for a day, went through two days of visible weeping, and then reconciled herself to the *fait accompli*. Nearly all Europe held her guilty of murder, but Frederick the Great, who had so much to lose by Peter's dethronement, exonerated her: "The Empress was quite ignorant of this crime, and she heard of it with a despair which was not feigned, for she justly foresaw the judgment that everybody passes upon her today."[8] Voltaire agreed with Frederick. Catherine's son Paul, after reading the private papers left by his mother at her death, concluded that Alexei had killed Peter without any order or request from Catherine.[9]

The event created, as well as solved, problems for Catherine: it inspired a succession of conspiracies to depose her, and left her harassed and imperiled amid the administrative chaos that surrounded her. She later wrote of this period: "The Senate remained lethargic and deaf to the affairs of state. The seats of legislation had reached a degree of corruption and disintegration that made them scarcely recognizable."[10] Russia had just emerged from a victorious but costly war; the treasury owed thirteen million rubles, and was running a deficit of seven million rubles per year; the condition of the fisc had been signalized by the refusal of Dutch bankers to lend Russia money. The pay of the troops was many months in arrears. The army was so disorganized that Catherine feared at any moment an invasion of the Ukraine by the Tatars of South Russia. The court was agitated with plots and counterplots, with dread of losing, or hope of gaining, offices of profit or power. Shortly after Peter's fall, the Prussian ambassador considered it "certain that the reign of the Empress Catherine is not to be more than a brief episode in the history of the world."[11] This was wishful thinking, for Frederick deplored the death of his worshipful ally, and Catherine was annulling Peter's orders to help Frederick.

The Empress sought to quiet ecclesiastical opposition by deferring the operation of Peter's ukases for the secularization of Church lands. She warmed the ardor of her partisans with rich rewards; Grigori Orlov received fifty thousand rubles, and access to the royal bed. Bestuzhev was recalled from exile and restored to comfort but not to office. Those who had opposed her were treated leniently. Münnich made his submission, was readily forgiven, and was appointed governor of Esthonia and Livonia. These measures may have helped to keep her on her slippery seat, but the chief factors were her own courage and intelligence. Seventeen years as the neglected wife of the heir to the throne had taught her, against her youthful vivacity, a degree of patience, prudence, self-control, and statesmanly dissimulation. Now, defying Panin's advice, and suspicious of the Senate's loyalty, integrity, and competence, she decided to center all rule in herself, and to face the absolute monarchs of Europe with an absolutism that would rival Frederick's combination of militarism with philosophy. She took no husband. Since the nobility controlled the Senate, the choice was between the autocracy of the sovereign and the fragmentary absolutism of feudal lords—precisely the choice faced by Richelieu in seventeenth-century France.

Catherine surrounded herself with able men, and won their loyalty, frequently their love. She made them work hard, but she paid them well, perhaps too well; the splendor and luxury of her court became a major drain upon the revenues. It was a heterogeneous court, rooted in barbarism, veneered with French culture, and ruled by a German woman superior to her aides in education and intellect. Her lavish rewards for exceptional service begot emulation without checking corruption. Many members of her entourage took bribes from foreign governments; some achieved impartiality by accepting bribes from opposite sides. In 1762 Catherine issued to the nation a remarkable confession:

> We consider it as our essential and necessary duty to declare to the people, with true bitterness of heart, that we have for a long time heard, and now in manifest deeds see, to what degree corruption has progressed in our Empire, so that there is hardly an office in the government in which . . . justice is not attacked by the infection of this pest. If anyone asks for place, he must pay for it; if a man has to defend himself against calumny, it is with money; if anyone wishes falsely to accuse his neighbor, he can by gifts insure the success of his wicked designs.[12]

Of the conspiracies that multiplied around her, some aimed to replace her with Ivan VI. Deposed by the *coup d'état* of December, 1741, he had now suffered twenty-one years of imprisonment. In September, 1762, Voltaire voiced apprehension that "Ivan may overthrow our benefactress";[13] and he wrote, "I am afraid that our dear Empress will be killed."[14] Catherine visited Ivan, and found him "a human derelict reduced to idiocy by long years of incarceration."[15] She left orders with his guards that if any attempt, not authorized by herself, should be made to release him, they should put Ivan to death rather than surrender him. At midnight of July 5–6, 1764, an army officer, Vasili Mirovich, appeared at the prison with a paper purporting to be an order of the Senate that Ivan should be turned over to him. Supported by several soldiers, he knocked at the door of the cell in which two guards slept with Ivan, and demanded entrance. Refused, he ordered cannon to be brought up to demolish the door. Hearing this, the guards slew Ivan. Mirovich was arrested; a document found on him declared that Catherine had been deposed, and that Ivan VI was henceforth czar. At his trial he refused to reveal the names of his accomplices. He was put to death. Public opinion generally accused Catherine of murdering Ivan.[16]

Conspiracies continued. In 1768 an officer named Choglokov, asserting that he had been commissioned by God to avenge the death of Peter III, armed himself with a long dagger, found entry to the royal palace, and hid himself at the turn of a passage where Catherine usually passed. Grigori

Orlov heard of the plot, and arrested Choglokov, who proudly confessed his intent to kill the Empress. He was banished to Siberia.

II. THE LOVER

Surrounded by nobles whom she could not trust, and harassed by intrigues that disordered administration, Catherine invented a new form of rule by making her successive lovers the executives of the government. Each of her lovers was, during his ascendancy, her prime minister; she added her person to the emoluments of the office, but she exacted competent service in return. "Of all places in the government," wrote Masson (one of Catherine's many French enemies), "there was not one of which the duties were so scrupulously fulfilled. . . . Nor, perhaps, was there any post in which the Empress displayed more choice and discernment. I believe no instance occurred of its having been filled by a person incapable of it."[17] It would be a mistake to think of Catherine as a debauchee; she observed all the external amenities, never indulged in risqué conversation, never allowed it in her presence.[18] To most of her lovers she gave a faithful—to some a tender—attachment; her letters to Potemkin are almost girlishly devoted, and the death of Lanskoi afflicted her with a desolating grief.

She approached with both art and science the task of choosing a new favorite. She watched for men who combined political with physical capacity; she invited a prospect to dinner, sampled his manners and mind; if he passed this scrutiny she had him examined by the court physician; if he survived this test she appointed him her aide-de-camp, gave him a succulent salary, and admitted him to her bed. Being quite devoid of religious belief, she allowed no Christian ethic to interfere with her unique manner of choosing ministers. She explained to Nikolai Saltykov: "I am serving the Empire in educating competent youths."[19] The treasury paid heavily for these favorites—though probably much less than France paid for the mistresses and concubines of Louis XV. Castéra reckoned that the five Orlovs received seventeen million rubles, Potemkin fifty million, Lanskoi 7,260,000. Some of this outlay came back to Russia in effective service; Potemkin, the most pampered of her lovers, added lucrative territory to the empire.

But why did she change her paramours so often, taking twenty-one in forty years? Because some failed in one or the other of their double duties; some died; some proved unfaithful; some were needed in distant posts. One, Rimsky-Korsakov, she surprised in her own apartments in the arms of her maid of honor; Catherine merely dismissed him; another, Mamonov, left her for a younger mate; the Empress resigned him without revenge.[20] "It is a very remarkable feature in the character of Catherine," said Masson, "that none of her favorites incurred her hatred or her vengeance, though several of them offended her, and their quitting their office did not depend upon herself. No one [of them] was ever seen to be punished. . . . In this respect Catherine appears superior to all other women."[21]

After the accession Grigori Orlov retained his ascendancy for ten years. Catherine amorously extolled him:

> Count Grigori has the mind of an eagle. I have never met a man who has a finer grasp of any matter that he undertakes or even that is suggested to him. . . . His honesty is proof against any assault. . . . It is a pity that education has had no chance to improve his qualities and talents, which are indeed supreme, but which his haphazard life has allowed to lie fallow.[22]

"This one," she wrote elsewhere, "would have remained [her lover and favorite] forever had he not been the first to tire."[23] Grigori labored for the emancipation of the serfs, proposed the liberation of Christians from the Ottoman yoke, served capably during the wars, offended the court by pride and insolence, and played truant from Catherine's arms. He was banished in 1772 to wealth and comfort on his estates. His brother Alexei became grand admiral, led the Russian fleet to victory over the Turks, remained in favor throughout the reign, and lived to lead his regiments against Napoleon.

Grigori was succeeded as favorite by an obscure Adonis, Alexis Vassil-chik, whom a court faction foisted upon Catherine to divert her mind from the banished Orlov, but she found him politically and otherwise inept and replaced him (1774) with Grigori Alexandrovich Potemkin. He was an officer in the Horse Guards, whose uniform she had donned (1762) to lead them against Peter. Noticing that her sword lacked the tassel proudly worn by the Guards, Potemkin tore his from the hilt, rode boldly out of the ranks, and presented the decoration to her; she accepted it, forgave his audacity, admired his handsome face and muscular frame. His father, a retired colonel in the lesser nobility, had destined him for the priesthood; Potemkin received considerable education in history, classics, and theology, and distinguished himself at the University of Moscow. But he found army life more suitable than a seminary to his wild and imaginative temperament. Of course he was hypnotized by Catherine's union of beauty and power; "when she enters an unlit room," he said, "she lights it up."[24] In the war of 1768 he led his cavalry regiment with such reckless courage that Catherine sent him a personal commendation. Back in St. Petersburg, he fretted with jealousy of the Orlovs and Vassilchik. He quarreled with the Orlovs, and in a brawl with them he lost an eye.[25] To get the Empress out of his mind—or to get himself into hers —he left the court, isolated himself in a suburb, studied theology, let his hair and beard grow, and declared that he would become a monk. Catherine took pity on him, sent him word that she had a high regard for him, and invited him to return. He cut his beard, trimmed his hair, donned his military uniform, appeared at court, and thrilled to imperial smiles. When Catherine found Vassilchik inadequate she opened her arms to Potemkin, then twenty-four, at the peak of his masculine vigor and dashing charm. Soon she was as infatuated with him as he with her. She showered favors, rubles, land, serfs, upon him, and when he was absent she sent him billets-doux quite innocent of majesty.

> How odd it is! Everything I used to laugh at has now happened to me, for my love for you has made me blind. Sentiments that I thought idiotic, exag-

gerated, and scarcely natural I am now experiencing myself. I can't keep my silly eyes off you. . . .

We can meet only during the next three days, for then comes the first week of Lent, which is reserved for prayers and fasting, and . . . it would be a great sin to meet. The mere thought of this separation makes me cry.[26]

He proposed marriage to her; some historians believe they were secretly wed; in several letters she calls him "my beloved husband," and speaks of herself as "your wife"[27]—though we must never conclude to reality from words. He seems to have tired of her, perhaps because of her unchecked fondness; the call of adventure proved stronger than the invitation to assault a citadel already won. His influence over her remained so great that most of the favorites who succeeded him did so only after his approval had been secured.

It was so with Piotr Zavadovsky, who basked in her boudoir from 1776 to 1777; with Simon Zorich (1777–78), and Ivan Rimsky-Korsakov (1778–80). Not until she took Alexis Lanskoi (1780) did she have again an affair of the heart. He was not only handsome and accomplished, he was a man of poetic sensibility and humane beneficence, an intelligent friend to letters and arts. "Everybody seemed to share the Sovereign's predilection for him."[28] Suddenly he was seized with unbearable pain in the bowels; the court suspected Potemkin of having poisoned him; despite all medical aid and Catherine's devoted care, he died, breathing his last breath in her arms. She passed three days in seclusion and grief. We hear the woman behind the ruler—the heart behind history—in her letter of July 2, 1784:

I thought I should die of irreparable loss. . . . I had hoped that he would be the support of my old age. He was attentive, he learned much, he had acquired all my tastes. He was a young man whom I was bringing up, and who was grateful, kind, and good. . . . Lanskoi is no more, . . . and my room, so pleasant before, has become an empty den, in which I can just drag myself about like a shadow. . . . I cannot look upon a human face without my voice choking. . . . I cannot sleep or eat. . . . I know not what will become of me.[29]

For a year she denied herself a lover; then she yielded to Alexis Ermolov (1785–86), who so displeased Potemkin that he was quickly replaced by Alexis Mamonov. Alexis soon tired of his fifty-seven-year-old mistress; he asked permission to marry Princess Sherbatov; Catherine gave the couple a court marriage, and sent them off loaded with presents (1789).[30] The last on the list was Platon Zubov (1789–96), a lieutenant in the Horse Guards, muscular and mannerly. Catherine was grateful for his services; she took upon herself the care of his education, and ended by treating him as a son. He stayed with her till her death.

III. THE PHILOSOPHER

Between love and war, statesmanship and diplomacy, this astonishing woman found time for philosophy. We get a measure of the high repute won by the French *philosophes* when we see the two ablest rulers of the eighteenth century proud to correspond with them, and competing for their praise.

Long before her accession Catherine had relished the style, wit, and irreverencies of Voltaire, and had dreamed of becoming the "enlightened despot" of his dreams. She must have liked Diderot too, for in September, 1762, she offered to print the *Encyclopédie* in St. Petersburg if the French government continued to outlaw it. Only one letter survives of those that she wrote to Voltaire before 1765; it replied to some lines that he had sent her in October, 1763:

> For the first time I regret that I am not a poet, and that I must answer your verses in prose. But I may tell you that since 1746 I have been under the greatest obligations to you. Before that period I read nothing but romances, but by chance your works fell into my hands, and ever since then I have never ceased to read them, and have had no desire for books less well written than yours, or less instructive. . . . So I return continually to the creator of my taste as to my deepest amusement. Assuredly, monsieur, if I have any knowledge I owe it to you. I am now reading the *Essai sur l'histoire générale*, and I should like to learn every page of it by heart.[31]

Throughout her life, or till their deaths, Catherine corresponded with Voltaire, Diderot, d'Alembert, Mme. Geoffrin, Grimm, and many more French notables. She contributed to the funds Voltaire raised for the Calas and the Sirvens. We have seen how she ordered large shipments of watches from Ferney, and of stockings knitted by Voltaire's workers, sometimes (if we may believe the old fox) by Voltaire himself. It was a feather in his skullcap that crowned heads should so honor him, and he repaid Catherine by becoming her press agent in France. He exonerated her from complicity in the death of Peter III; "I know," he wrote, "that Catherine is reproached with some bagatelle about her husband; but these are family matters in which I do not mix."[32] He pleaded with his friends to support him in supporting Catherine; so to d'Argental:

> I have another favor to ask of you; it is for my Catherine. We must establish her reputation in Paris among worthy people. I have strong reasons for believing that MM. the Dukes of Praslin and Choiseul do not regard her as the most scrupulous woman in the world. Nevertheless I know . . . that she had no part in the death of that drunkard of hers. . . . Besides, he was the greatest fool that ever occupied a throne. . . . We are under obligations to Catherine for having had the courage to dethrone her husband, for she reigns with wisdom and with glory, and we ought to bless a crowned head who makes religious toleration universal through 135 degrees of longitude. . . . Say, then, much good for Catherine, I pray you.[33]

Mme. du Deffand thought this exculpation of the Empress quite shameful; Mme. de Choiseul and Horace Walpole denounced it.[34] Praslin and Choiseul, who were directing the foreign relations of France, could not be expected to admire an Empress who was opposing French influence in Poland and defying it in Turkey. Voltaire himself had occasional doubts; when he learned that Ivan VI had been slain, he admitted sadly that "we must moderate a little our enthusiasm" for Catherine.[35] But soon he was praising her legislative

program, her patronage of the arts, her campaign for religious liberty in
Poland; now (May 18, 1767) he gave her the title of "Semiramis of the
North." When she went to war with Turkey he interrupted his attack upon
l'infâme (the Catholic Church) to applaud her crusade to save Christians
from Mohammedans.

Diderot was equally fascinated by beauty on the throne, and with substantial reasons. When Catherine heard that he was planning to sell his
library in order to raise a dowry for his daughter, she instructed her Paris
agent to buy it at whatever price Diderot should ask; he asked and received
sixteen thousand livres. Then she requested Diderot to keep the books till his
death, and to be their custodian for her at a salary of a thousand livres per
year; moreover, she paid his salary twenty-five years in advance. Diderot
overnight became a rich man and a defender of Catherine. When she invited
him to visit her he could hardly refuse. "Once in a lifetime," he said, "one
must see such a woman."[36]

Having arranged the finances of his wife and daughter, he set out, aged
sixty (June 3, 1773), on the long, rough journey to St. Petersburg. He dallied
two months in The Hague, sipping fame; proceeded via Dresden and Leipzig; carefully avoiding Berlin and Frederick, about whom he had made some
barbed remarks. Twice on the trip he fell violently sick of colic. He reached
St. Petersburg on October 9, and was received by the Czarina on the tenth.
"Nobody knows better than she," he reported, "the art of putting everyone
at his ease."[37] She invited him to speak frankly, "as man to man." He did, and
gestured in his accustomed way, driving points home by slapping the imperial
thighs. "Your Diderot," Catherine wrote to Mme. Geoffrin, "is an extraordinary man. I emerge from interviews with him with my thighs bruised and
quite black. I have been obliged to put a table between us to protect myself
and my members."[38]

For a while he tried, like Voltaire with Frederick, to play the diplomat,
and turn Russia from alliance with Austria and Prussia to alliance with
France;[39] she soon diverted him to topics nearer to his trade. He told her in
some detail how Russia could be transformed into Utopia; she listened gaily,
but remained skeptical. Later she recalled these conversations in a letter to
Comte Louis-Philippe de Ségur:

> I talked much and frequently with him, but with more curiosity than profit.
> If I had believed him everything would have been turned upside down in my
> kingdom; legislation, administration, finance—all would have been turned topsy-
> turvy to make room for impractical theories. . . . Then, speaking openly to
> him, I said: "Monsieur Diderot, I have listened with the greatest pleasure to all
> that your brilliant intellect has inspired. With all your high principles one
> would make fine books, but very bad business. . . . You work only upon
> paper, which endures all things; . . . but I, poor Empress as I am, work on the
> human skin, which is irritable and ticklish to a different degree." . . . There-
> after he talked only about literature.[40]

When she came upon some notes that he had made "On the Instructions of
her Imperial Majesty . . . for the Drawing up of Laws," she described

them (after his death) as "veritable babble, in which one could find neither knowledge of realities nor prudence, nor insight."[41] Nevertheless she enjoyed his vivacious conversation, and talked with him almost every day during his long stay.*

After five months of ecstasy in her friendship, and discomfort at her court, Diderot turned homeward. Catherine ordered a special carriage built for him, in which he could recline at ease. She asked him what gifts she should send him; he answered, None, but he reminded her that she had not yet kept her promise to reimburse him for the expenses of his trip; he calculated these at fifteen hundred rubles, she gave him three thousand and a costly ring, and assigned an officer to accompany him to The Hague. On his return to Paris he eulogized her gratefully.

Catherine made no approaches to Rousseau, who was painfully antipodal to her in temper and ideas. But she cultivated Melchior Grimm, for she knew that his *Correspondance littéraire* reached influential Europeans. He took the first step by offering (1764) to send her his periodical letters; she agreed, and paid him fifteen hundred rubles per year. He first saw her when he went to St. Petersburg (1773) in the retinue of the Prince of Hesse-Darmstadt to attend the marriage of the Prince's sister to Grand Duke Paul. Catherine found him much more realistic than Diderot, and very usefully informed on all aspects of that Parisian world which fascinated her with its literature, philosophy, art, women, and salons. She invited him to chat with her almost every day during the winter of 1773–74. About these meetings she wrote to Voltaire: "M. Grimm's conversation is a delight to me; but we have so many things to say to each other that thus far our interviews have been marked by more eagerness than order or sequence." In the ardor of these conversations she had repeatedly to remind herself that (as she put it) she must return to her *gagne-pain*—earn her bread by attending to the business of government.[43] Grimm came back to Paris dripping with enthusiasm for Catherine as "the nourishment of my soul, the consolation of my heart, the pride of my mind, the joy of Russia, and the hope of Europe."[44] He visited St. Petersburg again in 1776, and saw her almost daily for a year. She begged him to remain and supervise the reorganization of education in Russia, but he became lonesome for Paris and Mme. d'Épinay. Catherine was not jealous; when she learned that Mme. d'Épinay was in financial straits she sent her, with delicate indirectness, enough to meet her wants.[45] From 1777 Grimm served as Catherine's agent in France for art purchases and confidential missions. His friendship for her lasted untroubled till her end.

What were the results of this flirtation between autocracy and philosophy? Insofar as she cultivated the *philosophes* as her press agents in France, the political effect was nil; French policy, and consequently French historians, remained bitterly hostile to a Russia that was balking French aims in Eastern Europe. But her admiration for the heroes of the French Enlightenment was sincere, having begun long before her accession to power; if it had been an

* The story that Euler confused Diderot before the Russian court with an imaginary algebraic proof of God's existence is probably apocryphal.[42]

affectation it would not have borne such long confrontations with Diderot and Grimm. Her liaison with French thought helped to Europeanize literate Russia, and to modify the Western view of Russia as a colossal brute. Many Russians followed Catherine's lead, corresponded with French writers, and felt the influence of French culture, manners, and art. A growing number of Russians visited Paris, and though many spent their time in sexual adventures, many frequented the salons, the museums, and the court, read French literature and philosophy, and brought back with them ideas that shared in preparing the outburst of Russian literature in the nineteenth century.

IV. THE STATESMAN

We can hardly doubt the good intentions of Catherine in the early years of her reign.

In her copy of Fénelon's *Télémaque* were found these resolutions:

> Study mankind, learn to use men without surrendering to them unreservedly. Search for true merit, be it at the other end of the world, for usually it is modest and retiring.
>
> Do not allow yourself to become the prey of flatterers; make them understand that you care neither for praise nor for obsequiousness. Have confidence in those who have the courage to contradict you, . . . and who place more value on your reputation than on your favor.
>
> Be polite, humane, accessible, compassionate, and liberal-minded. Do not let your grandeur prevent you from condescending with kindness toward the small, and putting yourself in their place. See that this kindness, however, does not weaken your authority nor diminish their respect. . . . Reject all artificiality. Do not allow the world to contaminate you to the point of making you lose the ancient principles of honor and virtue. . . .
>
> I swear by Providence to stamp these words into my heart.[46]

She informed herself assiduously on every relevant subject, and wrote detailed instructions on a thousand topics from army training and industrial operations to the toilette of her court and the production of operas and plays. Said one of her earliest and least friendly biographers:

> Ambition extinguished not in Catherine's soul an ardent relish for pleasure. But she knew how to renounce pleasure, and to make the transition to employments the most serious, and application the most indefatigable to the affairs of government. She assisted at all the deliberations of the Council, read the dispatches of her ambassadors, and dictated, or indicated . . . the answers to be returned. She entrusted her ministers with only the details of business, and still kept her eye on the execution.[47]

The task of governing her vast area was made almost impossible by the number (ten thousand), diversity, contradictions, and chaos of existing laws. Hoping to play Justinian to Russia, and to consolidate her power, Catherine, on December 14, 1766, summoned to Moscow administrative agents and legal experts from every part of the empire, to undertake a thorough revision and codification of Russian law. In preparation for their coming she personally prepared a *Nakaz*, or *Instructions*, describing the principles upon which the new code should be formed. These reflected her reading of Montesquieu, Beccaria, Blackstone, and Voltaire. She began by declaring that Russia must be thought of as a European state, and should have a constitution based upon "European principles." This did not, in her understanding, mean a "constitutional government" subordinating the sovereign to a legislature chosen by the people; the educational level of Russia would not permit even so limited an electoral franchise as existed in Britain. It meant a government in which the ruler, though ultimately the sole source of law, ruled in obedience to law. Catherine upheld the feudal system—i.e., the system of mutual loyalty and services between peasant and vassal, vassal and liege lord, lord and sovereign—as indispensable to economic, political, and military order in the Russia of 1766 (a land of communities almost isolated from one another, and from the center of government, by difficulties of communication and transport); but she urged that the rights of masters over their serfs should be defined and limited by law, that serfs should be allowed to own property, and that the trial and punishment of serfs should be transferred from the feudal lord to a public magistrate responsible to a provincial court responsible to the sovereign.[48] All trial should be open, torture should not be used, capital punishment should be abolished in law as well as in fact. Religious worship should be free; "amongst so many different creeds the most injurious error would be intolerance."[49] The *Nakaz*, before being printed, was submitted by her to her advisers; they warned her that any sudden change from existing custom would plunge Russia into disorder; and she allowed them to modify her proposals, especially those for the gradual emancipation of the serfs.[50]

Even as so bowdlerized the *Instructions*, published in Holland in 1767, stirred the European intelligentsia to enthusiastic praise. The Empress sent a copy direct to Voltaire, who made his usual obeisance. "Madame, last night I received one of the guarantees of your immortality—your code in a German translation. Today I have begun to translate it into French. It will appear in Chinese, in every tongue; it will be a gospel for all mankind."[51] And he added in later letters: "Legislators have the first place in the temple of glory; conquerors come behind them. . . . I regard the *Instructions* as the finest monument of the century."[52] The French government forbade the sale of the *Instructions* in France.

The modified *Nakaz* was presented to the "Committee for Drafting a New Code," which met on August 10, 1767. It was composed of 564 members elected by various groups: 161 from the nobility, 208 from the towns, 79 from the free peasantry, 54 from the Cossacks, 34 from non-Russian tribes (Christian or not), and 28 from the government. The clergy was not represented as a class, and the serfs were not represented at all. In some ways the Committee corresponded to the States-General that was to meet in Paris in 1789; and, as in that more famous assembly, the delegates brought to the government lists of grievances and proposals for reform from their constituents. These documents were transmitted to the Empress, and they offered her and her aides a valuable survey of the condition of the realm.

The Committee was empowered not to pass laws, but to advise the sovereign on the state and needs of each class or district, and to offer suggestions for legislation. The delegates were guaranteed freedom of speech and inviolability of person. Some of them proposed the emancipation of all serfs, some asked that the right to own serfs be more widely extended. In December, 1767, the Committee recessed; in February, 1768, it moved to St. Petersburg; altogether it held 203 sessions; on December 18, 1768, it was adjourned *sine die* because the outbreak of war with Turkey called many delegates to the front. The task of drafting proposed legislation was deputed to subcommittees, some of which continued to meet till 1775; but no code of laws was formulated. Catherine was not altogether displeased with this inconclusive result. "The Committee," she said, ". . . has given me light and knowledge for all the Empire. I know now what is necessary, and with what I should occupy myself. It has elaborated all parts of the law, and has distributed the affairs under heads. I should have done more had it not been for the war with Turkey, but a unity hitherto unknown in the principles and methods of discussion has been introduced."[53] Meanwhile she had shown the nobles on how broad a base her power rested. The Committee, before adjourning, proposed to confer upon her the appellation "Great"; she refused, but consented to be called "Mother of the Country."

Two of Catherine's recommendations became law: the abolition of torture and the establishment of religious toleration. This was widely extended: it allowed the Roman Catholic Church to compete with the Greek Orthodox; it protected the Jesuits even after the dissolution of their order by Pope Clement XIV (1773); it permitted the Volga Tatars to rebuild their mosques. Catherine admitted the Jews into Russia, but she subjected them to special taxes, and (possibly for their safety) confined them to specific areas. She left the Raskolniki—religious dissenters—free to practice their rites unhindered; "we have indeed," she wrote to Voltaire, "fanatics who, as they are no longer persecuted by others, burn themselves; but if those of other countries did the same, no great harm would result."[54]

The *philosophes* were especially pleased by Catherine's subordination of the Russian Church to the state. Some of them complained that she still attended religious services (so did Voltaire); the older of them recognized that her attendance was indispensable to retaining the allegiance of the people. By a decree of February 26, 1764, she turned into state property all the lands of the Church. The salaries of the Orthodox clergy were henceforth paid by the state—so ensuring their support of the government. Many monasteries and nunneries were closed; those that remained were forbidden to accept more than a prescribed number of novices, and the legal age for taking vows was raised. The surplus revenues from ecclesiastical institutions were applied to the foundation of schools, asylums, and hospitals.[55]

Both the clergy and the nobility opposed the extension of popular education, fearing that the spread of knowledge among the masses would lead to heresy, unbelief, and factionalism, and would imperil social order. Here, as elsewhere, Catherine began with liberal aspirations. She appealed to Grimm:

> Listen a moment, my philosophical friends: you would be charming, ador-
> able, if you would have the charity to map out a plan for young people, from
> ABC to university. . . . I, who have not studied and lived in Paris, have neither
> knowledge nor insight in the matter. . . . I am very much concerned about an
> idea for a university and its management, a *gymnasium* [secondary school]
> and an elementary school. . . . Until you accede to my request I shall hunt
> through the *Encyclopédie*. Oh, I shall be certain to draw out what I want![56]

Meanwhile she was moved by the pedagogical enthusiasm of Ivan Betsky,
who had traveled in Sweden, Germany, Holland, Italy, and France, had
frequented the salon of Mme. Geoffrin, had studied the *Encyclopédie*, and
had met Rousseau. In 1763 she organized at Moscow a school for foundlings,
which by 1796 had graduated forty thousand students; in 1764 a school for
boys was opened in St. Petersburg, and in 1765 a school for girls; in 1764
the Smolny Monastery was transformed into the Smolny Institute for girls
of the nobility—an echo of Mme. de Maintenon's St.-Cyr; Catherine was the
first Russian ruler to do anything for the education of women. Baffled by
the dearth of qualified teachers, she sent Russian students to study pedagogy
in England, Germany, Austria, and Italy. A teachers' college was founded
in 1786.

She admired Joseph II's reforms of education in Austria, and asked him to
lend her someone familiar with his procedure. He sent her Theodor Yankovich, who drew up for her a plan which she promulgated as a "Statute of
Popular Schools" (August 5, 1786). An elementary school was established
in the chief town of each county, and a high school in each of the principal
cities of twenty-six provinces. These schools were open to all children of any
class; corporal punishment was not allowed in them; teachers and textbooks
were provided by the state. The project was largely frustrated by the reluctance of the parents to send their children to school rather than use them for
labor at home. In the ten years between their foundation and Catherine's
death the "popular schools" grew slowly from forty to 316; the teachers from
136 to 744; the pupils from 4,398 to 17,341. In 1796 Russia was still far behind the West in public instruction.

Higher education was scantily provided by the University of Moscow,
and by special academies. A School of Commerce was founded in 1772, an
Academy of Mines in 1773. The old Academy of Sciences was enlarged and
was provided with ample funds. In 1783, on urging by Princess Dashkova,
and under her presidency, a Russian Academy was organized for the improvement of the language, the encouragement of literature, and the study
of history; it issued translations, published periodicals, and compiled a dictionary which appeared in six installments between 1789 and 1799.

Appalled by the high death rate in Russia, and the primitive character of
public sanitation and personal hygiene, Catherine brought in foreign physicians, established a College of Pharmacy at Moscow, and provided funds for
the production of surgical instruments. She opened in Moscow three new
hospitals, a foundling asylum, and an insane asylum, and in St. Petersburg
three new hospitals, including a "Secret Hospital" for venereal diseases.[57] In

1768 she introduced into Russia inoculation for smallpox, and quieted public fears by serving, aged forty, as the second Russian subject of the treatment; soon Catherine reported to Voltaire that "more people had been inoculated here in one month than in Vienna in a year."[58] (In 1772 Naples had its first inoculation, and in 1774 Louis XV, *un*inoculated, died of smallpox.)

V. THE ECONOMIST

One of Catherine's basic measures (1765) provided for a survey of all Russian land. The operation met with much resistance from landlords; by the end of the reign it had covered twenty out of fifty provinces, but it was not completed till the middle of the nineteenth century. As it proceeded the Empress realized with discouraging clarity how the economy of Russia rested upon the organization of agriculture by a feudal system of lords and serfs. In 1766 she offered a prize of a thousand ducats for the best essay on the emancipation of the serfs. The winner was Béardé de l'Abbaye of Aix-la-Chapelle, who argued that "the whole universe demands of sovereigns that they should emancipate the peasants," and predicted that agricultural production would be immensely increased by "making the farmers the owners of the land they cultivate."[59] The noble landowners, however, warned Catherine that unless the peasant was bound to the land and his landlord he would migrate to the towns or, more irresponsibly, from village to village, creating chaos, disrupting production, and interfering with the conscription of sturdy peasant sons for the army or the fleet.

The puzzled Czarina proceeded cautiously, for the nobles had the money and the arms to overthrow her, and in such an attempt they could rely upon the support of a clergy resenting the loss of their lands and their serfs. She feared the disorder that might come from a wholesale movement of liberated peasants to towns unprepared to house or feed or employ them. She made moves toward emancipation. She renewed the edict of Peter III forbidding the purchase of serfs for factory labor, and she required employers to pay their workers in cash and to maintain conditions of work as determined by the officials of the town or the mir;[60] even so, the status of industrial serfs remained one of heartless and stupefying slavery. Catherine forbade serfdom in the towns that she founded,[61] and, on their payment of a small fee, she freed the serfs on lands taken over from the Church.[62] These improvements, however, were outweighed by her repeated grants of state lands to men who had served her well as generals, statesmen, or lovers; in this way over 800,000 free peasants became serfs. The proportion of serfs in the rural population rose from 52.4 per cent at the outset of the reign to 55.5 per cent at its close, and the number of serfs rose from 7,600,000 to 20,000,000.[63] By her "Letters of Grace to the Nobility" (1785) Catherine completed her surrender to the nobles: she reaffirmed their exemption from the poll tax, corporal punishment, and military service, and their right to be tried only by their peers, to mine their lands, to own industrial enterprises, and to travel abroad at will. She forbade the landlords to be tyrannical or cruel, but she nullified this prohibition by forbidding the serfs to send her their complaints.

The peasants, so silenced, resorted to flight, rebellion, or assassination. Between 1760 and 1769 thirty landlords were killed by their peasants; between 1762 and 1773 there were forty peasant revolts.[64] These were quickly suppressed until a rebel leader arose who knew how to turn resentment into organization, and peasant arms into victories. Emelyan Pugachev was a Don Cossack who had fought in Russian ranks against the Prussians and the Turks. He asked for discharge, was refused, deserted, was captured, deserted again, and accepted the life of an outlaw. In November, 1772, encouraged by discontented monks, he proclaimed that he was Peter III, who had miraculously survived all attempts to kill him. He attracted peasants and brigands to his standard, until he felt strong enough to declare open rebellion against the usurper Catherine (September, 1773). Cossacks of the Urals, the Volga, and the Don; thousands of men who had been condemned to force-labor in the mines and smelters of the Urals; hundreds of Old Believers eager to overthrow the Orthodox Church; local Tatar, Kirghiz, and Bashkir tribes who had not forgiven Elizabeth's dragooning of them into Christianity; serfs who had fled from their masters, and prisoners who had escaped from jail: these flocked to Pugachev's standard, until he had twenty thousand men under his command. They moved triumphantly from town to town, defeated the forces sent against them by local governors, captured important cities like Kazan and Saratov; they conscripted supplies, killed landlords, forced reluctant peasants to join them, and marched up the Volga basin toward Moscow. Pugachev announced that there he would place not himself but Grand Duke Paul on the throne. But—probably with grim humor —he called his peasant wife queen, and named his chief lieutenants after Catherine's: Count Orlov, Count Panin, Count Vorontsov.

Catherine at first made fun of "*le marquis* Pugachev," but when she learned that the rebels had taken Kazan, she sent a substantial force under General Piotr Ivanovich Panin to suppress the rebellion. The nobles, seeing the whole feudal structure endangered, came to her aid; soon General Alexander Vasilievich Suvorov joined Panin with cavalry freed by peace with the Turks; the insurgents were thrown into disorder by their encounter with disciplined troops under imperial officers; they retreated from one position to another, exhausted their provisions, and began to starve. Some of their leaders, hoping to earn bread and pardon, made Pugachev their prisoner and delivered him to the victors. He was brought to Moscow in an iron cage, was tried in the Kremlin, was beheaded and then quartered, and his head was exhibited on a pole in four sections of the city, *pour décourager les autres*. Five of his captains were executed, others were knouted this side of death, and were sent to Siberia. One result of the revolt was to strengthen the alliance of the Empress with the nobility.

In some measure she challenged the nobility by favoring the growth of a business class. Convinced by the arguments of the physiocrats, she established free trade in agricultural products (1762), later in everything; she put an end

(1775) to government-sanctioned monopolies by ruling that any man should be free to undertake and operate an industrial enterprise. The growth of a middle class was retarded by the predominance of cottage and manorial industry, and the participation of nobles in industrial and commercial ventures. Factories multiplied from 984 to 3,161 during Catherine's reign, but these were mostly small shops employing only a few workers. Urban population increased from 328,000 in 1724 to 1,300,000 in 1796—still less than four per cent of the population.[65]

The busy Empress, with only grudging support from her noble entourage, did what she could to promote commerce. Roads were terrible, but rivers were many, and canals bound them into a beneficent web. Under Catherine a canal was begun between the Volga and the Neva to join the Baltic with the Caspian Sea, and she planned another to join the Caspian and Black Seas.[66] By negotiation or by war she secured the unhindered passage of Russian commerce into the Black Sea and thence into the Mediterranean. She prodded her diplomats to arrange trade treaties with England (1766), Poland (1775), Denmark (1782), Turkey (1783), Austria (1785), and France (1787). Foreign commerce grew from 21,000,000 rubles in 1762 to 96,000,-000 in 1796.[67]

In such figures we must allow for the currency inflation with which governments pay for their wars. To finance her campaigns against Turkey Catherine borrowed, at home and abroad, 130,000,000 rubles; she issued paper money far beyond any gold collateral; during her reign the ruble lost thirty-two per cent of its value. In the same period, despite a rise of revenues from 17,000,000 to 78,000,000 rubles, the national debt rose to 215,000,-000.[68] Most of this was due to the wars that broke the power of Turkey, and carried the borders of Russia to the Black Sea.

VI. THE WARRIOR

Like any philosopher, Catherine had begun with pacific aims. She announced that the internal problems of the empire would absorb her attention, and that she would, if unmolested, avoid all conflict with foreign powers. She confirmed Peter III's peace with Prussia, and ended his war with Denmark. She rejected in 1762 the temptation to conquer Kurland or to interfere in Poland; "I have people enough to make happy," she said, "and that little corner of the earth will add nothing to my comfort."[69] She reduced the army, neglected the arsenals, and sought to negotiate with Turkey a treaty of perpetual peace.

But the more she studied the map, the more fault she found with the boundaries of Russia. On the east the empire was well protected by the Urals, the Caspian Sea, and the weakness of China. On the north it was protected by ice. But on the west Sweden held part of Finland, from which at any moment an attack might be expected from a nation still resenting its losses to Peter the Great; and Poland and Prussia barred the way into "Europe" and Europeanization. On the south the Tatars, under a Moslem and Turkish-controlled khan, barred the way to the Black Sea. What abortions of history had given Russia such geography, such anomalous boundaries? Old General Münnich, new general Grigori Orlov, whispered to her how much more rational it would be if the Black Sea were the southern boundary, and how sweet it would be if Russia could take Constantinople and control the Bosporus. Nikita Panin, her foreign minister from 1763 to 1780, pondered ways of promoting Russia's influence in Poland and preventing that defenseless land from falling under Prussian domination.

Catherine was moved by their arguments. And she itched to give her adopted country a place in politics commensurate with its place on the map. Within a year of her accession she sallied forth upon a foreign policy that aimed at nothing less than to make Russia the pivotal power on the Continent. "I tell you," she wrote to Count Keyserling, her ambassador at Warsaw, "that my aim is to be joined in bonds of friendship with all the powers, in armed alliance, so that I may always be able to range myself on the side of the oppressed, and so become the arbiter of Europe."[70]

At times she came close to her goal. By taking Russia out of the Seven Years' War she in effect decided that Continent-wide conflict in favor of Frederick. In 1764 she signed with Frederick a treaty that presaged the dismemberment of Poland. She took advantage of Denmark's need of Russian support against Sweden to dominate the foreign policy of the Danes. In 1779 she served as arbiter between Frederick and Joseph at the Peace of Teschen, and became protectress of the German Imperial Constitution. In 1780 she bound Denmark, Sweden, Prussia, Austria, and Portugal with Russia in a "League of Armed Neutrality" to protect neutral shipping in the war of England with the American colonies: neutral ships were to be free from attack by either combatant unless they carried munitions of war; and a blockade, to be legal and respected, must be real, and no mere paper declaration.

Long before that second reversal of alliances the irrepressible conflict had begun for control of the Black Sea. Catherine's first Turkish war originated as a strange by-product of her invasion of Poland. She had sent troops there to help the non-Catholics in their struggle for equal rights with the Catholic majority; the Catholics moved a papal nuncio to explain to Turkey that now was an opportune time for Turkey to attack Russia; France seconded the suggestion, and urged Sweden and the Khan of the Crimea to join in the attack.[71] Voltaire mourned for his endangered Empress. "That a nuncio enlists the Turks in his crusade against you," he wrote to her, "is worthy of an Italian farce: Mustafa the worthy ally of the Pope!"—the situation almost persuaded him to be a Christian. Indeed, in a letter of November, 1768, he proposed to Catherine a holy war against the infidels:

> You force the Poles to be tolerant and happy despite the nuncio, and you seem to be having trouble with the Mussulmen. If they wage war on you, perhaps Peter the Great's idea of making Constantinople the capital of the Russian Empire may take shape. . . . I think that if ever the Turks are expelled from Europe it will be by the Russians. . . . It is not enough to humiliate them; they must be sent back forever.[72]

Sweden refused to share in the assault upon Russia, but the Crimean Tatars ravaged the newly settled Russian colony of Novaya Serbia (January, 1769). A Turkish army of 100,000 men advanced toward Podolia to join the army of the Polish Confederation. Catherine refused to withdraw her forces from Poland. She sent thirty thousand men under Alexander Golitsyn and Piotr Rumiantsev to repulse the Tatars and check the Turks; told that these were too numerous, she replied, "The Romans did not concern themselves with the number of their enemies; they only asked, 'Where are they?' "[73] The Tatars were driven back; Azov and Taganrog, at the mouth of the Don, were taken; seventeen thousand Russians defeated 150,000 Turks at Kagul (1770); Rumiantsev advanced as far as Bucharest, where he was received with joy by the Orthodox population. In 1771 Vasili Mikhailovich Dolgoruki overran the Crimea and put an end to Turkish rule there. Even more spectacular was the exploit of Alexei Orlov, who led a Russian fleet through the English Channel, the Atlantic, and the Mediterranean, defeated the Turkish navy off Chios, and annihilated it at Chesmé (July, 1770); but the damage to his own ships was too severe to let him follow up his victories.

Some other events were less comforting to Catherine. A plague broke out in the Russian army along the Danube and spread back to Moscow, where, in the summer of 1770, it took a thousand lives a day. She knew that Frederick looked askance at the extension of her realm and power; that Joseph II was disturbed by the advance of Russia to the Austrian frontier in the Balkans; that France was leaving no stone unturned to strengthen her Turkish ally; that England would vigorously oppose Russian control of the Bosporus; and that Sweden was merely awaiting her opportunity. Catherine invited the Turks to a conference; they came, but balked at her insistence on the independence of the Crimea; and in 1773 the war was resumed.

In January, 1774, Mustafa III died; his successor decided that Turkey had reached a condition of chaos and exhaustion that threatened her existence as a European state. By the Peace of Kuchuk Kainarji (in Romania), July 21, 1774, Turkey recognized the independence of the Crimea (which remained under Tatar rule), ceded Azov, Kerch, Yenikale, and Kilburun (at the mouth of the Dnieper) to Russia, opened the Black Sea, the Bosporus, and the Dardanelles to Russian shipping, paid Russia a war indemnity of 4,500,-000 rubles, granted amnesty to Christians involved in insurrections against their Turkish governors, and acknowledged the right of Russia to protect Christians in Turkey. Altogether, this was one of the most advantageous treaties ever made by Russia.[74] Russia was now a Black Sea power; the Crimea and the other Tatar regions in South Russia were left open to early Russian conquest, and the skeptical Empress could pose as the defender of the faith. Drunk with success, Catherine dreamed of liberating—i.e., conquering— Greece, and crowning her grandson Constantine at Constantinople as head of a new empire. She gladdened Voltaire's aging heart with visions of Olympic Games restored; "we will have the ancient Greek tragedies enacted by Grecian players in the theater of [Dionysius at] Athens." Then, mindful of armies and treasury exhausted, she added: "I must practice moderation, and say that peace is better than the finest war in the world."[75]

She was now replacing Frederick as the most famous sovereign in Europe; everyone marveled at her resolute pursuit of her aims, and the awesome extension of her power. Joseph II of Austria, who had so long bowed to the genius of Frederick, traveled to Mogilev, and thence all the way to St. Petersburg, to meet the Czarina and solicit her alliance. In May, 1781, she signed with Joseph a pact for united action in Poland and against Turkey.

Meanwhile Potemkin was making a name for himself in the south. He organized, equipped, and fed a new army of 300,000 men, built a Black Sea fleet, with harbors at Sevastopol and Odessa and an arsenal at Kherson, colonized the sparsely settled regions of South Russia, founded towns and villages, established manufactures, and supplied the colonists with cattle, tools, and seed—all with a view to having bases of supplies in a campaign to add the Crimea to Catherine's crown, and perhaps win a crown for himself. The Tatars of the Crimea quarreled and divided; Potemkin softened their leaders with bribes; when, at last, he invaded the peninsula (December, 1782), he found only negligible resistance, and on April 8, 1783, over Turkey's futile protests, the Crimea was absorbed into the Russian realm. Potemkin was made field marshal, president of the College of War, Prince of Tauris, and governor general of the Crimea. The Empress added a *pourboire* of 100,000 rubles; Potemkin used them on mistresses, liquor, and food.

Catherine too thought it time for relaxation. She combined pleasure with business by arranging a stately "progress" over land and water to inspect her conquests and impress their people—and all Europe—with the wealth and splendor of her court. On January 2, 1787, muffled in furs, she left the Winter Palace and began the long journey in a *berline*, or coach, large enough to contain—besides her now spacious self—her current favorite Mamonov, her chief lady in waiting, a lapdog, and a small library. She was followed by fourteen carriages and 170 sleighs, bearing the ambassadors of Austria, Britain, and France—Cobenzl, Fitzherbert, and the Comte de Ségur—plus the Prince de Ligne and an army of officials, courtiers, musicians, and servants. Potemkin had gone some days in advance to prepare the route, to light it by hundreds of torches, and to arrange for each evening's meals and sleeping quarters for all. At major towns the cortege rested for one or two days while the Czarina met the local dignitaries, surveyed conditions, asked questions, distributed censure or reward. Every town on the route, warned and instructed by Potemkin, was on its best behavior, washed and dressed as never before, happy for a day.

At Kiev Potemkin superintended the transfer of the mobile court to eighty-seven vessels which he had equipped and adorned. On these the imperial horde moved down the Dnieper. Along the river Catherine saw the "Potemkin villages" which the clever Prince of Tauris had primed and polished for her pleasure, and perhaps to impress the diplomats with the prosperity of Russia. Some of the prosperity had been improvised by Potemkin, some of it was real. "That he constructed sham villages along the banks, and marshaled the peasantry to create the illusion of progress was the fantastic invention of a Saxon diplomatist."[76] The Prince de Ligne made several excursions ashore to see behind the façades; he reported that while Potemkin had used some legerdemain, he (Ligne) had been impressed by the "superb estab-lishments in their infancy, growing manufactures, villages with regular streets lined by trees."[77] Catherine herself was probably not deceived, but she may have concluded, as Ségur did, that even if half the prosperity and neatness of those towns was a passing show, the actuality of Sevastopol—town, forts, and port, built on Crimean shores in two years—was enough to merit Potemkin praise. The Prince de Ligne, who had known almost everyone of account in Europe, called him "the most extraordinary man I have ever met."[78]

At Kaniov Stanislas Poniatowski, king of Poland, came to offer his homage to the woman who had given him her love and his throne. Farther down the Dnieper, at Kaidaky, Joseph II joined the procession, which thence went ov-erland to Kherson and into the Crimea. There the Empress, the Emperor, and the Governor General fondled their dreams of driving the Turks from Eu-rope: Catherine of capturing Constantinople, Joseph of absorbing the Bal-kans, Potemkin of making himself king of Dacia (Romania). England and Prussia advised Sultan Abdul-Hamid to strike at the Russians while they were off guard, with their military preparations incomplete.[79] The insolence of the Russian ambassador at Constantinople provided an additional stimulus; the Sultan jailed him, declared a holy war, and demanded the restoration of Cri-mea as the price of peace. In August, 1787, the main Turkish army crossed the Danube and marched into the Ukraine.

Potemkin had celebrated too soon; Russia was not yet prepared for the ultimate test; he advised the Empress to surrender the Crimea. She reproved him for his unwonted timidity; she ordered him, Suvorov, and Rumiantsev to marshal all their available forces and go forth to meet the invaders; she her-self retreated to St. Petersburg. Suvorov routed the Turks at Kilburun, and Potemkin besieged Ochakov, which commanded the outlets of both the Dniester and the Bug. While jihad and crusade came face to face in South Russia, Sweden decided that now at last the time had come to recapture her lost provinces. Encouraged by England and Prussia,[80] Gustavus III renewed an old alliance with the Turks, and demanded of Catherine the return of Fin-land and Karelia to Sweden, and of the Crimea to Turkey. Of that war we may speak later; it is enough to say here that on July 9, 1799, a Swedish fleet decisively defeated the Russians in the Baltic; the roar of Swedish cannon could be heard from the Winter Palace; Catherine thought of evacuating her capital. Soon, however, her agents persuaded Sweden to peace (August 15, 1790).

Now she was free to concentrate forces against the Turks, and Austria joined Russia in the war. Potemkin ended the siege of Ochakov by ordering his men to attack at whatever price; the victory cost the Russians eight thou-sand lives; and the fury of battle ended in indiscriminate massacre (Decem-ber 17, 1788). Potemkin went on to take Bender, the Austrians captured Bel-grade, Suvorov routed the Turks at Rimnik (September 22, 1789). Turkey seemed doomed.

The Western powers felt that the situation called for united action against Catherine if the strategic Bosporus was not to fall into her hands and make

Russia the master of Europe. Frederick the Great having died (1786), his successor, Frederick William II, saw with dismay the movement of Russia toward Constantinople, and of Austria into the Balkans; between Russia and Austria so strengthened, Prussia would be at their mercy. On January 31, 1790, he bound his government with the Porte in a pact that committed him to declare war upon both Russia and Austria in the spring, and not to lay down arms till all Turkey's lost territory had been restored.

The political tide seemed to be turning against Catherine. Revolt in the Austrian Netherlands and disorder in Hungary weakened Joseph II; he died on February 20, 1790, and his successor signed an armistice with the Turks. England and Prussia again urged Catherine to make peace on the basis of restoring all terrain won in the war; she refused; the capture of Ochakov had cleared Russian access to the Black Sea; she would not surrender that vital gain. Moreover, her generals were moving from victory to victory, culminating in the capture of Izmail (December 22, 1790) by Suvorov and Potemkin; in taking that Turkish stronghold on the Danube the Russians lost ten thousand men, the Turks thirty thousand. After that feast of blood Potemkin, exhausted, relapsed into luxurious indolence and shameless incest with his nieces; and on October 15, 1791, he died on a road near Jassy. Catherine fainted three times on the day that she heard of his death.

In March, 1791, William Pitt the Younger proposed to Parliament that an ultimatum be dispatched to Russia requiring her to return to Turkey all territory taken in the present conflict, and he prepared to send a British fleet into the Baltic as a promise of war. Catherine made no reply, and Parliament, hearing British merchants mourn the loss of Russian trade, dissuaded Pitt from his enterprise. Turkey, exhausted, gave up the struggle, and signed at Jassy (January 9, 1792) a treaty that confirmed Russia's control of the Crimea and the basins of the Dniester and the Bug. Catherine had not reached Constantinople, but she had risen to the zenith of her career as the most powerful ruler in Europe, and the most remarkable woman of her century.

VII. THE WOMAN

Was she a woman, or a monster? We have seen that at the beginning of her reign she was physically attractive; by 1780 she had grown stout, but this merely added weight to her majesty. The Prince de Ligne (who was among the first to call her "the Great"[81]) described her gallantly:

> She still [in 1780] looked well. One saw that she had been beautiful rather than pretty. . . . It needed no Lavater to read on her forehead, as in a book, genius, justice, courage, depth, equanimity, sweetness, calm, and decision. Her fine bust had been acquired at the expense of her waist, once so terribly thin; but people generally grow fat in Russia. . . . One never noticed that she was short.[82]

Castéra, writing shortly after her death, pictured her as modestly dressed in a green robe. "Her hair, lightly powdered, floated over her shoulders, and was surmounted by a small cap covered with diamonds. In the last years of her life she put on a great deal of rouge, for she still had pretensions not to allow the traces of time to appear on her face; and it is probable that only these pretensions were the cause of her living in the utmost temperance."[83]

She was vain, visibly conscious of her accomplishments and her power. "Vanity is her idol," Joseph II told Kaunitz; "luck and exaggerated compliments have spoiled her."[84] Frederick the Great thought that if Catherine were corresponding with God she would claim at least equal rank.[85] Yet she talked with Diderot as "man to man," and begged Falconet to omit compliments. She was as amiable (barring a few possible murders and the sanctified slaughters of war) as Charles II of England and Henry IV of France. She daily threw from her windows bread for the thousands of birds that came regularly to her to be fed.[86] In the ending years of her reign she indulged now and then in fits of rage unbefitting omnipotence, but she took care not to give an order or sign a paper in these volcanic moods; soon she grew ashamed of such outbursts, and schooled herself to self-control. As to her courage Europe discarded all doubt.

She was unquestionably and imperturbably sensual, but her amours offend us less than the Parc aux Cerfs of Louis XV. Like all the rulers of her time she subordinated morality to politics, and suppressed personal feelings when these impeded the aggrandizement of her state. Where there was no such conflict she had all the tenderness of a woman, loving children, gamboling with them, teaching them, making toys for them. On her tours she was always careful that drivers and servants were properly fed.[87] Among the papers found on her table after her death was an epitaph she had composed for herself: "She forgave easily, and hated no one. Tolerant, understanding, of a gay disposition, she had a republican spirit and a kind heart."[88]

She was not kind to her first son; partly because Paul had been taken from her soon after birth, and had been brought up by Panin and others under Elizabeth's supervision; partly because the conspiracies to unseat her sometimes proposed to make him emperor with a regency; partly because Paul long suspected his mother as Peter's murderer; and also because Paul "was always brooding over the theft of his rights" to succeed his presumptive father on the throne. But Catherine took to her heart Paul's charming sons Alexander and Constantine, personally attended to their education, tried to alienate them from their father, and schemed to have Alexander, not Paul, inherit her crown.[89] Paul, happily mated with a second wife, looked with manifest disgust upon the concatenation of paramours that amused his mother and drained the revenues of the state.

Mentally Catherine surpassed all her favorites. She indulged their greed, but rarely allowed them to determine her policy. She absorbed French literature to a point where she could correspond with its leaders as one *philosophe* to another; indeed, her letters to Voltaire excelled his in good sense, and rivaled them in grace and wit. Her correspondence was almost as voluminous as Voltaire's, though written in the interstices of court intrigues, domestic insurrections, critical diplomacy, and map-remaking wars. Her conversation kept Diderot on his toes, and moved Grimm to ecstasy: "One must have seen, at those moments, this singular head, composed of genius and grace, to form an idea of the fire that swayed her, the shafts that she let fly, the sallies that pressed . . . one upon another . . . Had it only been in my power to take down these conversations literally, the whole world would have possessed a precious and perhaps unique fragment in the history of the human mind."[90] There was, however, a hurried confusion and instability in the torrent of her ideas; she plunged too quickly into projects that she had not thought through, and she was sometimes defeated by the urgency of events and the multiplicity of her tasks. Even so, the result was immense.

It seems incredible that in a career of such political and military excitement Catherine found time to write poems, chronicles, memoirs, plays, opera librettos, magazine articles, fairy tales, a scientific treatise on Siberia, a history of the Roman emperors, and extensive *Notes on Russian History*. In 1769–70 she edited anonymously a satirical journal to which she was the chief contributor. One of her sketches described a religious hypocrite who attended Mass every day, lit candles before holy images, and mumbled prayers intermittently, but cheated tradesmen, maligned neighbors, beat servants, denounced current immorality, and mourned the good old days.[91] Catherine's fairy tale *Prince Khlor* told of a youth who went through perilous adventures to find a fabled rose without thorns, only to discover in the end that there was no such rose but virtue; this story became a classic in Russian literature, and was translated into many languages. Two of her plays were historical tragedies imitating Shakespeare; most of them were unpretentious comedies ridiculing charlatans, dupes, misers, mystics, spendthrifts, Cagliostro, Freemasons, religious fanatics; these pieces lacked subtlety but they pleased the audiences, though Catherine concealed her authorship. On the curtain of the theater that she built in the Hermitage she placed an inscription, *Ridendo castigat mores*—"He chastizes manners with laughter"; this well expressed the aim of her comedies. *Oleg*, the best of her dramas, was a remarkable succession of scenes from Russian history, enlivened by seven hundred performers in dances, ballets, and Olympic games. Most of Catherine's literary work was revised by secretaries, for she never mastered Russian spelling or grammar, and she did not take herself too seriously as an authoress; but literature took courage from the imperial example, and gave a final and tarnished glory to her reign.

VIII. LITERATURE

Russia was becoming aware of its intellectual immaturity. A host of authors humbly copied foreign models, or translated works that had won fame in France, England, or Germany. Catherine allowed five thousand rubles from her privy purse to further this exotic flow; she herself translated Marmontel's *Bélisaire*. With Russian enthusiasm for vast enterprises, Rachmaninov, a landowner in Tambov, translated the works of Voltaire, and Verevkin, director of the College of Kazan, turned into Russian the *Encyclopédie* of Diderot. Others translated the plays of Shakespeare, the Greek and Latin classics, the *Gerusalemme liberata* of Tasso . . .

Gavril Romanovich Derzhavin was the most successful poet of the reign. Born lowly in eastern Orenburg, with Tatar blood in his veins, he served for ten years in the Preobrazhensky Regiment, saw Catherine's ride to power, took part as an officer in suppressing Pugachev's revolt, and worked his way up to a seat in the Senate. Noting that the Empress had used the name Felitza for a benevolent princess in *Prince Khlor,* Derzhavin, in a famous ode (1782), gave the same name to "the godlike Queen of the Kirghiz-Kazakh horde," and begged this sultana to "teach me how to find the rose without thorns, . . . how to live pleasantly but justly."[92] When the poet apostrophized Felitza as one "from whose pen flows bliss to all mortals," he was obviously extolling Catherine. When he reproved himself for "sleeping till noon, smoking tobacco, drinking coffee, . . . and making the world tremble with my looks," or indulging in "sumptuous feasts at a table sparkling with silver and gold," all the court knew that this was a hit at Potemkin. Derzhavin rose to raptures in praising the "Empress" Felitza, who "creates light from darkness," injures no one, treats small faults forgivingly, lets people speak freely, "writes fables for the instruction" of her people, and "teaches the alphabet to Khlor" (grandson Alexander). And the poet concluded: "I pray the great prophet that I may touch the dust of your feet, that I may enjoy the sweet stream of your words and your look. I entreat the heavenly powers to extend their sapphire wings and invisibly guard you, . . . that the renown of your deeds may shine in posterity like the stars in the sky."[93] Derzhavin protested that he wished no reward for bringing so much honey, but Catherine promoted him, and soon he was so close to her that he could see her faults; he wrote no more lauds. He turned to a higher throne and indited an "Ode to the Deity," congratulating Him on being "three-in-one," and on keeping the heavens in such good order. At times he descended to metaphysics, and echoed Descartes' proof of God's existence: "Surely I am, hence Thou too art."[94] This ode remained for half a century unrivaled in popularity until Pushkin came.

Denis Ivanovich von Visin startled the capital with two lively comedies: *The Brigadier* and *The Minor.* The success of the latter was so complete that Potemkin advised the author to "die now, or never write again"—i.e., anything further would dim his fame.[95] Visin rejected the advice and saw its implied prophecy come true. In his later years he traveled in Western Europe and sent home some excellent letters, one of which contained a proud prediction: "We [the Russians] are beginning; they [the French] are ending."[96]

The most interesting figure in the literature of Catherine's reign was Nikolai Ivanovich Novikov. Dismissed from the University of Moscow for laziness and backwardness, he developed into a man of incessant intellectual activity. At the age of twenty-five (1769), in St. Petersburg, he edited a magazine, *The Drone,* impishly so called to counter Sumarokov's periodical, *The Industrious Bee.* In lively style Novikov attacked the corruption prevalent in the government; he assailed the Voltairean irreligion of the upper classes as destructive of morals and character; he lauded by contrast what he supposed to have been the unquestioning faith and exemplary morals of the Russians before Peter the Great. "It is as if the old Russian rulers had foreseen that, through the introduction of arts and sciences, the most precious treasure of the Russians—their morality—would be irretrievably lost";[97] here too Rousseau was at war with Voltaire. Catherine gave *The Drone* some sour looks, and it ceased publication in 1770. In 1775 Novikov joined the Freemasons, who in Russia were turning to mysticism, Pietism, and Rosicrucian fancies while their brothers in France were playing with revolution. In 1779 he moved to Moscow, took charge of the university press, and published more books in three years than had come from that press in twenty-four. Financed by a friend, he acquired additional presses, formed a publishing house, opened bookstores throughout Russia, and scattered broadcast his gospel of religion and reform. He established schools, hospitals, and dispensaries, and model housing for workingmen.

When the French Revolution turned Catherine from an enlightened into a frightened despot, she feared that Novikov was subverting the existing order. She directed Platon, the Metropolitan of Moscow, to examine Novikov's ideas. The prelate reported: "I implore the all-merciful God that there may be, not only in the flock entrusted to me by God and you but throughout the world, such Christians as Novikov."[98] Suspicious nevertheless, the Empress ordered Novikov's imprisonment in the fortress of Schlüsselburg (1792). There he remained till Catherine's death. Released by Paul I, he retired to his estate of Tikhvin, and passed his remaining years in works of piety and charity.

A worse fate fell to Alexander Nikolaevich Radishchev. Sent by Catherine to the University of Leipzig, he picked up some works of the *philosophes*, and was especially moved by Rousseau's *Social Contract* and Raynal's exposure of European brutality in colonial exploitation and the slave trade. He returned to St. Petersburg fired with social ideals. Put in charge of the customshouse, he learned English to deal with British merchants, took up English literature, and was especially influenced by Sterne's *Sentimental Journey*. In 1790 he published one of the classics of Russian literature, *Journey from St. Petersburg to Moscow*. It professed orthodoxy, but denounced the impositions of priests upon popular credulity; it accepted monarchy but justified revolt against a ruler who violated the "social contract" by overriding the law. It described the dismemberment of families by conscription, and the abuse of serfs by masters; at one place, said Radishchev, he had been told of a landlord who had violated sixty peasant maidens. He denounced censorship, and pleaded for freedom of the press. He did not advocate revolution, but he asked for a merciful understanding of its advocates. He appealed to the nobles and the government to end serfdom. "Let yourselves be softened, you hardhearted ones; break the fetters of your brethren, open the dungeons of slavery. The peasant who gives us health and life has a right to control the land which he tills."[99]

Strange to say, the book was passed by the censor. But Catherine in 1790 was fearful that her people might imitate the French Revolution. She made note to punish the violator of sixty virgins, but she ordered Radishchev to be tried for treason. Passages were found in his book about the storming of fortresses and the uprising of soldiers against a cruel czar; and there were eulogies of the English for resisting an unjust king. The Senate condemned the author to death; the Empress commuted this to ten years in Siberia. Emperor Paul I allowed Radishchev to return from exile (1796); Alexander I invited him to St. Petersburg (1801). There, a year later, thinking, without reason, that he was to be banished again, he killed himself. His fate and that of Novikov are among the many blots on a brilliant reign.

IX. ART

Catherine did a little more for art than for literature, for art appealed only to the upper classes, and sounded no tocsin of revolt. Popular music, however, was unwittingly revolutionary, for nearly all of it consisted of sad songs, in a minor key and with plaintive accompaniment, telling not only of hearts broken in love but of lives worn out with toil. The nobles rarely heard those songs, but they enjoyed the Italian operas that were brought to St. Petersburg by Galuppi, Paisiello, Salieri, and Cimarosa, all paid by the state. Catherine herself did not care much for opera. "In music," she said, "I can recognize no tones but those of my nine dogs, who in turn share the honor of being in my room, and whose individual voices I can recognize from a distance."[100]

She confessed, too, that she had no understanding of art. She did what she could to develop such understanding in Russia. She provided the funds with which Betsky set into actual functioning (1764) the Academy of Arts that had been organized under Elizabeth (1757). She bought acknowledged masterpieces abroad, and displayed them in her galleries; so she gave 180,000 rubles for the collection of Count von Brühl in Dresden, £40,000 for the collection of Sir Robert Walpole at Houghton Hall, 440,000 francs for Choiseul's collection, and 460,000 for Crozat's. Without knowing it, she made fine bargains, for these gleanings included eleven hundred pieces by Raphael, Poussin, Vandyck, Rembrandt, and other perennials, whose value has grown with the advance of time and the retreat of currency. Through Grimm and Diderot (whose *Salons* she followed carefully) she gave commissions to French artists—Vernet, Chardin, Houdon. She had life-size copies made of Raphael's frescoes in the Vatican, and built a special gallery for them in the Hermitage.

She gave few commissions to native artists, for to her French taste there was little of lasting worth in the Russian art of her time. However, she provided funds for the education and support of students in the Academy of Arts, and sent several of them to study in Western Europe. From that Academy came the history painter Anton Losenko and the portrait painters Dmitri Levitsky and Vladimir Borovikovsky. After five years in Paris and three in Rome, Losenko returned to St. Petersburg (1769) to teach in the

Academy. He made a stir with *Vladimir before Rogneda*, but—perhaps too burdened with academic duties—he failed to produce the masterpieces expected of him, and death took him at thirty-six (1773). — Catherine employed Levitsky to portray some of the young women who were studying at the Smolny Institute; the result is a testimony to their beauty. His portrait of Catherine concealed her amplitude under flowing robes. She sat also for Mme. Vigée-Lebrun, who was one of many French artists whom she invited to give Gallic grace to Russian art.

The greatest of her imported artists was Falconet. He came in 1766, and stayed twelve years. Catherine asked him to design, and cast in bronze, an equestrian statue of Peter the Great. He had brought with him a young woman, Marie-Anne Collot, who modeled the colossal head. Falconet dared the laws of physics by representing the horse as springing into the air, with only its hind feet touching terra firma—an immense boulder brought from Karelia to symbolize the massive resistance that Peter had overcome; to secure equilibrium Falconet showed a brass serpent—symbol of envy—biting the horse's tail. This chef-d'oeuvre kept its poise while St. Petersburg changed into Petrograd and then into Leningrad. Falconet took longer with this work than Catherine had expected; she lost interest in it, and neglected the sculptor, who returned to Paris disappointed with her, Russia, and life.

In 1758 Nicolas-François Gillet came from France to teach sculpture at the Academy. Three of his pupils achieved excellence in Catherine's reign: Chubin, Kozlovsky, and Shchedrin. Chubin was commissioned by Potemkin to carve a *Catherine II* for the rotunda of the Taurida Palace; experts called it "lifeless and cold";[101] so too seems the statue Chubin made of Potemkin. Kozlovsky achieved similar rigidity in his tomb for Marshal Suvorov, and even in his *Cupid*. Shchedrin's main work was done under Alexander I: to 1812 belongs the *Caryatids Holding Up the Celestial Sphere*—woman bears the world. Ivan Petrovich Martos specialized in funerary monuments; cemeteries in St. Petersburg were peopled with his *pleurants;* "he made marble weep." Native sculpture lagged except in imitation of foreign styles. Orthodox churches excluded statuary, and the nobles were content with such artists as they found among their serfs.

But architecture flourished under Catherine, for she was resolved to leave her mark upon her capital. "Great buildings," she said, "declare the greatness of a reign no less eloquently than great actions."[102] "You know," she wrote in 1779, "that the mania for building is stronger with us than ever, and no earthquake ever demolished as many structures as we have set up. . . . This mania is an infernal thing; it runs away with money, and the more one builds, the more one wants to build; it is a disease, like drunkenness."[103] Though she told Falconet, "I can't even draw," she had her own mind in art, or a mind influenced by the Roman excavations at Herculaneum and the books of Caylus and Winckelmann. She turned her back upon the ornate baroque and flowery rococo that had reigned under Elizabeth, and cast her vote for the chaster neoclassic style. Some contemporaries credited her with providing explicit instructions and preliminary sketches for her architects.[104]

Finding no native artists who could realize her conceptions, she called to

Western Europe for men who had inherited the classical tradition. So came Jean-Baptiste Vallin de La Mothe, who built for her on the Neva the Palace of the Academy of Arts (1765–72)—a Renaissance façade of coated bricks and classic portico, and, within, a majestic semicircular stairway leading to a rotunda under a dome. As an adjunct to the Winter Palace Vallin built the famous Hermitage, which Catherine thought of as a refuge from court etiquette, but which became her art gallery, and is now one of the principal museums of the world. Catherine described it to Grimm in 1790 as "my little retreat, so situated that to go there and back from my room is just three thousand paces. There I walk about amid a quantity of things that I love and delight in, and those winter walks are what keep me in health."[105]

From France, too, came the Scot Charles Cameron, who had studied classic ornament there. Catherine was delighted with the brilliance and delicacy with which he adorned—with silver, lacquer, glass, jasper, agate, and polychrome marble—the private apartment that she reserved for herself, her lovers, and her dogs in the Grand Palace at Tsarskoe Selo. "I have never seen the equal of these newly decorated rooms," she wrote; "during the last nine weeks I have never tired of contemplating them."[106] Around this palace she had a park designed in the "natural" and "English" style, which she described in a letter to Voltaire: "I now madly love the *jardins à l'anglaise*, the short lines, the curved lines, the gently graded slopes, the pools and lakes. . . . I have a profound aversion to straight lines; in a word, Anglomania dominates my plantomania."[107] For her son Paul and his lovely second wife Cameron built in Pavlovsk (another suburb of the capital) a palace in Italian villa style; here the Grand Duke and Maria Feodorovna housed the art collected in their West-European tours.

From Italy came Antonio Rinaldi, who raised two luxurious mansions as gifts from Catherine to Grigori Orlov: the Marble Palace on the Neva, and, near Tsarskoe Selo, the Gatchina Palace, which became the favorite residence of Paul I. And from Italy came Giacomo Quarenghi, who had been fascinated by the Greek temples at Paestum and the masterpieces of Palladio in Vicenza. In 1780 he submitted to Catherine, through Grimm, plans and models for various structures that he hoped to build. Catherine was attracted, and from that date till 1815 Quarenghi raised, in or near St. Petersburg, a profusion of buildings in classic style: the theater of the Hermitage, the Smolny Institute (which he added to the Smolny Monastery of Rastrelli), the Bank of the Empire, the Chapel of the Malta Order, the English Palace at Peterhof, and the Alexander Palace at Tsarskoe Selo. This was designed for Catherine's grandson the future Alexander I, who moved into it in 1793, two years after its completion. "It is one of the masterpieces of eighteenth-century architecture."[108] *

But were there no Russian architects fit to spend Catherine's rubles? Yes. Hoping to leave a monument to her memory at Moscow, she commissioned

---

* It was the favorite residence of Czar Nicholas II; from it he fled to Siberia and death in 1917. The Soviets transformed it into a museum. It was severely damaged in the Second World War, but has been restored.

Vasili Bazhenev to design a stone Kremlin to replace the brick Kremlin of Ivan the Great. Bazhenev conceived an immensity that would have dwarfed Versailles; those who saw the wooden model—which itself cost sixty thousand rubles—marveled at its architectural excellence. But the foundations laid for it sank as the soil subsided through the action of the Moscow River, and Catherine withdrew from the enterprise. However, she found funds that enabled Ivan Starov to build, on the left bank of the Neva, the Taurida Palace; this splendor she presented to Potemkin to commemorate his conquest of the Crimea.

Whatever the cost of her buildings, Catherine achieved her object. The contemporary Masson wrote: "A Frenchman, after winding along the inhospitable shores of Prussia and traversing the wild and uncultivated plains of Livonia, is struck with astonishment and rapture at finding again, in the midst of a vast desert, a large and magnificent city, in which the society, amusements, arts and luxuries abound which he had supposed to exist nowhere but in Paris."[109] And the Prince de Ligne, after seeing nearly all Europe, concluded that "in spite of Catherine's shortcomings her public and private edifices make St. Petersburg the finest city in the world."[110] The flesh and blood of ten million peasants had been turned into brick and stone.

X. JOURNEY'S END

Catherine, like rulers throughout the ages, would have explained that since men must die in any case, why should not genius be employed by statesmen to direct those harassed lives and certain deaths to making the country strong and its cities great? Years of power, the challenges of revolt and war, the fluctuations of victory and defeat, had accustomed her to bear unflinchingly the sufferings of others, and to turn aside from the exploitation of the weak by the strong as beyond her means to cure.

Disturbed by a dozen conspiracies to unseat her, and frightened by Pugachev's revolt, she was terrified by the French Revolution. She bore with it complacently when it promised to be only the overthrow of an idle aristocracy and an incompetent government; but when a Paris mob forced Louis XVI and Marie Antoinette to leave Versailles and live in the Tuileries amid an unchained populace—when the Constituent Assembly declared itself supreme, and Louis consented to be merely its executive officer—Catherine shuddered at the encouragement so given to those who sought similar action in Russia. She allowed the clergy to forbid the publication of her once beloved Voltaire's works (1789);[111] she herself soon proscribed all French publications; she had the busts of Voltaire removed from her chambers to a lumber room (1792).[112] She banished the idealistic Radishchev (1790), imprisoned the public-spirited Novikov (1792), and established an inquisitorial censorship over literature and plays. When Louis XVI and Marie Antoinette were guillotined (1793) she broke off all relations with the French government, and urged the European monarchies to form a coalition against France.

She herself did not join in that coalition; she used it to keep the Western powers busy while she completed her absorption of Poland. "Many of my enterprises are unfinished," she told one of her diplomats; "the courts of Berlin and Vienna must be occupied so as to leave us unfettered."[113]

Some vestiges of her early liberalism survived till 1793. In that year a courtier reported to her that Frédéric-César de Laharpe, who had been tutoring her grandsons, was an unregenerate republican. She sent for him and told him of the report; he answered: "Your Majesty knew, before entrusting me with the education of the Grand Dukes, that I was a Swiss, and therefore a republican." He asked her to examine his pupils, and from their conduct judge his work. But she already knew how well he had taught them. "Monsieur," she said, "be a Jacobin, a republican, or what you please; I believe you are an honest man, and that is enough for me. Stay with my grandchildren, retain my complete confidence, and instruct them with your wonted zeal."[114]

Amid the turmoil she took her last lover (1789). Platon Zubov was twenty-five, she was sixty-one. She wrote to her *amant-en-titre*, Potemkin: "I have returned to life like a fly that the cold had benumbed."[115] Her new "pupil" proposed a three-pronged attack upon Turkey: a Russian army under his twenty-four-year-old brother Valerian was to cross the Caucasus into Persia and shut off all overland trade between Turkey and the East; another army, under Suvorov, was to go through the Balkans to besiege Constantinople; and Russia's new Black Sea Fleet, led by the Empress herself, was to capture control of the Bosporus. After years of preparation this epic enterprise was begun (1796); Derbent and Baku were taken; and Catherine looked forward to victories that would complete her program and crown her career.

On the morning of November 17, 1796, she seemed as gay as ever. After breakfast she retired to her room. As time passed and she did not reappear, her female attendants knocked at the door. Receiving no answer, they entered. They found the Empress stretched out on the floor, the victim of the rupture of an artery in the brain. She was twice bled, and for a moment recovered consciousness, but she could not speak. At ten o'clock that evening she died.

Her enemies felt that she had not deserved so merciful a death. They never forgave her the contradictions between her liberal professions and her absolutist rule, her intolerance of opposition, her failure to carry out her proposed reform of Russian law, her surrender to the nobility in her extension of serfdom. Families impoverished by high taxes, or mourning the loss of sons in her wars, did not thank her for her victories. But the people as a whole applauded her for expanding Russia to wider and safer boundaries. She had added 200,000 square miles to Russia's area, had opened new ports to Russia's trade, had raised the population from nineteen to thirty-six million souls. She had been unscrupulous in her diplomacy—perhaps, in her absorption of Poland, a little more so than most other rulers of that time.

Her greatest achievement lay in carrying on the efforts of Peter the Great to bring Russia into Western civilization. Whereas Peter had thought of this chiefly in terms of technology, Catherine thought of it principally in terms of culture; by the force and courage of her personality she drew the literate classes of Russia out of the Middle Ages into the orbit of modern thought in literature, philosophy, science, and art. She was ahead of her Christian compeers (excepting the un-Christian Frederick II) in establishing religious toleration. A French historian compared her favorably with Le Grand Monarque:

> The generosity of Catherine, the splendor of her reign, the magnificence of her court, her institutions, her monuments, her wars, were precisely to Russia what the age of Louis XIV was to Europe; but, considered individually, Catherine was greater than this Prince. The French formed the glory of Louis; Catherine formed that of the Russians. She had not, like him, the advantage of reigning over a polished people; nor was she surrounded from infancy by great and accomplished characters.[116]

In the estimate of an English historian Catherine was "the only woman ruler who has surpassed England's Elizabeth in ability, and equaled her in the enduring significance of her work."[117] "She was," said a German historian, "every inch a 'political being,' unmatched by anyone of her sex in modern history, and yet at the same time a thorough woman and a great lady."[118] We may apply to her the magnanimous principle laid down by Goethe: her faults were an infection from her time, but her virtues were her own.

CHAPTER XIX

The Rape of Poland

1715–95

I. POLISH PANORAMA: 1715–64

GEOGRAPHY, race, religion, and politics were the natural enemies of Poland. The country was as large as France, extending in 1715 from the Oder in the west almost to Smolensk and Kiev in the east; but it had no natural boundary—no mountains or broad river—on either front to protect it from invasion; it was named from *pole*, a plain. It had only one outlet to the sea—at Danzig; and the Vistula that found its exit there was no defense against adjacent Prussia. The nation had no ethnic unity: the Polish majority of its 6,500,000 souls (1715) was in intermittent strife with German, Jewish, Lithuanian, and Russian minorities; here the Teutons and the Slavs came face to face in spontaneous hostility. There was no religious unity: the Roman Catholic majority ruled and oppressed the "Dissidents"—themselves contentiously divided between Protestants, Greek Orthodox, and Jews. There was no political unity, for the jealously sovereign power lay in a Sejm, or Diet, composed exclusively of nobles each of whom had, through the *liberum veto*, the authority to nullify any proposal of all the rest, and at will bring any session, any elected Diet, to an end. The king was chosen by the Diet, and was subject to "conventions" signed by him as a condition of his election; he could pursue no long-term policy with any assurance of transmitting his crown or receiving steady support. The nobles demanded such limitless power over legislation because each wished to be completely free in ruling his lands and his serfs. But limitation is the essence of liberty, for as soon as liberty is complete it dies in anarchy. The history of Poland after Jan Sobieski was a chronicle of anarchy.

Nearly all the soil was tilled by serfs in a feudal subjection from which there was no appeal. The master was sometimes kind, but he was always absolute. His serfs not only owed him such part of their produce as he might demand; they were required also to give him gratis two or three days of work each week on his manor. Fortunately the well-watered land was fertile, and the peasants had enough to eat, but Coxe described them as "poorer, humbler, and more miserable than any people we have yet observed on our travels."[1] Their local masters were the lower nobility, or gentry (szlachta*), and these squires in turn were subject to some hundred magnates owning or controlling immense areas. The gentry held most of the executive offices in

---

* English readers may pronounce Polish *c* usually as *ts*; *cz* as *ch*; *sz* as *sh*; and *w* as *v*.

the state, and theoretically they dominated the Sejm; actually Polish politics was a strife of magnates or their families, manipulating szlachta groups by economic influence or direct bribery.[2]

In Poland the family still retained its primitive priority over the state. The Radziwills, the Potockis, the Czartoryskis were severally united by a sentiment of family solidarity more intense than any national bond; here patriotism was literally reverence for the father, and above all for the oldest father. The family was strong as an institution because it was the unit of economic production and moral discipline; there was no economic individualism scattering the sons over the country; normally the son remained on the patrimonial estate, subject to paternal command as long as the father lived; the family flourished through that same unity of authority whose absence weakened the state. All the wealth of the family was under centralized patriarchal control; in many cases it grew from year to year through the reinvested profits of exploitation and exportation, and in several cases it exceeded the wealth of the king. Twenty Polish families in the eighteenth century spent, each of them, over 200,000 livres per year on their households.[3] Powerful families called their homes courts, with retainers, private armies, numerous servants, and semiroyal displays; so Prince Karol Radziwill, whose estate was half as large as Ireland, gave in 1789 a feast to four thousand guests at a cost of a million marks.[4]

The most famous of Polish families—so well-known that it was called "the Family"—was the Czartoryskis. It had held princely rank since the fifteenth century, and was related to the house of Jagiello, which had ruled Poland from 1384 to 1572. Prince Kasimierz Czartoryski (d. 1741), vice-chancellor of Lithuania, married Isabella Morstin, who brought a further infusion of French culture into the family. By her he had three children of note: (1) Fryderyk Michal Czartoryski, who became grand chancellor of Lithuania; (2) Alexander Augustus Czartoryski, who became Prince Palatine of "Red Russia"; and (3) Konstantia, who married Stanislas Poniatowski I, and bore to him Stanislas Poniatowski II, the most tragic figure in Polish history.

It was an added distinction of the Czartoryskis that their liberalism grew with their wealth. They had long been known for their humane treatment of their serfs; "if I had been born a serf," said a contemporary, "I should wish to be the serf of Prince [Alexander] Augustus Czartoryski."[5] They organized schools for children, supplied them with textbooks, built chapels, hospitals, model cottages. To their estate and mansion in Pulawy (near Lublin) they brought teachers and scholars who trained promising youths, from any class, for the service of the state. Politically the Family opposed the *liberum veto* as making effective government impossible. Against them were ranged many families which felt that the veto was their sole protection against a centralized autocracy. Strongest of these were the Potockis, led by Prince Felix Potocki, who could ride thirty miles in one direction without leaving his land—three million acres in the Ukraine.

Industry and commerce, which in the sixteenth century had shared in making Poland great and its towns prosperous, had been retarded by the hostility of the landowners and their obedient Diet. Many towns were wholly within the private property of a magnate who, fearing the rise of an independent middle class, favored agriculture against industry. The competition of serf handicrafts on the manors had depressed the artisans of the towns. "The ruin of the cities," wrote Antoni Potocki in 1744, "is so evident that with the single exception of Warsaw the first ones in the country can well be compared to dens of robbers."[6] Grass grew in the streets of Lvov, some city squares had become open fields, and Cracow, formerly one of the great cultural centers of Europe, had declined to a population of nine thousand, and its famous university to six hundred students.[7]

The decay of the towns was due in part to the Catholic reconquest of Poland. Many of the displaced Protestants had been merchants or artisans; their diminution in all but western Poland (where many Germans remained) left the Polish scene to the landlords; and these were either Roman Catholics or, in the east, Greek Orthodox or Uniates (Catholics using the Eastern ritual but acknowledging the pope of Rome). The Dissidents—Protestants, Greek Orthodox, and Jews, numbering eight per cent of the population—were excluded from public office and the Diet; all suits against them were tried before completely Catholic courts.[8] Religious hostility reached the point where, in 1724, in predominantly Protestant Toruń (Thorn), the populace, infuriated by the behavior of a Jesuit student, desecrated the Host and trampled upon an image of the Virgin. Nine of the raiders were put to death. The Protestants of Poland appealed to Prussia, the Greek Orthodox appealed to Russia; Prussia and Russia offered protection, from which they progressed to invasion and partition.

Polish morals resembled the German at table and the French in bed. The peasants were inured to monogamy by care of the soil and their brood, but in the capital it was made difficult by the beauty and the "seductive manners"[9] of the women, who did not allow their superior education to interfere with their charm. The ladies of Warsaw, we are told, were sexually as lax as those of Paris.[10] Poniatowski assures us that he was a virgin till twenty-two,[11] but he adds that such continence was exceptional in his class. — Drunkenness was endemic, and made no class distinctions. Among the peasants it gave periodic amnesia from poverty, hardship, or cold; among the nobles it solaced isolation and ennui; and in all ranks the males looked upon it as not a vice but an accomplishment. Pan Komarczewski was honored because he could empty a bucket of champagne at one draft without losing his head or his feet; Poniatowski was warned that he would never be popular unless he got drunk twice a week.[12] Hospitality was universal, but it was judged by the amount of food and drink provided for the guests. Sometimes a magnate mortgaged a town to pay for a banquet.

The literate Poles colored the scene with their dress. The peasant, in summer, made shift with shirt and knee breeches of coarse linen, without stockings or shoes, and in winter he bundled himself up with no care for color and no time for art; but the gentry, numbering some 725,000, wore boots, sword, plumed hat, a colored robe of silk or lace, and, around the waist, a broad sash of patterned fabrics in rich hues. This proudly national garb had come up from Islam through the contact of the Lithuanians with Turks in the Ukraine; it reflected the occasional alliance of Poland with Turkey against Austria or Russia; and perhaps it expressed an Asiatic element in Polish manners and character.

Culturally Poland, from 1697 to 1763, was retarded by the indifference of its Saxon kings to Slavic literature and art, and by two devastating wars. The Catholic Church was not only the chief patron of the arts, it was also the dispenser of education and the main repository of learning and literature. It carefully quarantined Poland from the movement of science and philosophy in the West, but within its limits it spread and cultivated knowledge. Józef Zaluski, bishop of Kiev, gathered 200,000 volumes at Warsaw into one of the greatest libraries of the age; in 1748 he opened it to the public and presented it to the nation; meanwhile he himself lived frugally, and sacrificed himself in the struggle to preserve Poland's independence.

It was he who turned the eager young priest Stanislas Konarski to the study of history and law. In 1731 Konarski issued the first of four volumes—*Volumina legum*—which codified Polish legislation from Casimir the Great to his own time. These and other researches revealed to Konarski how tragically Poland had fallen from her Renaissance flowering. Convinced that regeneration could come only from the top, he established in Warsaw (1740) a Collegium Nobilium, where pedigreed youths could receive an education not only in mathematics and the classic languages and literatures (which the Jesuits taught well) but also in the natural sciences and modern languages. It was an heroic task, for he had neither money nor textbooks, neither teachers nor students; yet after fifteen years of labor he had made his College of Nobles a famous and honored institution, one of the sources of the cultural revival under Poniatowski, and of the enlightened constitution of 1791. He appealed for a reform of the Polish language, seeking to rid it of Latin phrases and flowering rhetoric; the nation protested, still it learned. Konarski crowned his work by publishing (1760–63) the most important political treatise of the century in Poland, innocently entitled *On the Effective Conduct of Debates;* however containing a blast against the *liberum veto.* Again there were many protests, but after 1764 no Diet was dissolved by the *liberum veto.* It was with Konarski's aid that Poniatowski began the reform of the Polish constitution.

Before that brilliant and fitful resurrection Poland suffered sixty-seven years of disorder, disgrace, and decline under Saxon kings.

II. THE SAXON KINGS: 1697–1763

Other pages[13] have told how the Polish Diet passed over the son of the great Sobieski to give the crown of Poland to Frederick Augustus, Elector of Saxony, who embraced Catholicism overnight to become Augustus II (the "Strong") of Poland; how Charles XII of Sweden replaced him with Stanislas Leszczyński (1704), and how the defeat of Charles at Poltawa (1709) allowed Augustus to regain his throne. He enjoyed few of the legislative powers of an eighteenth-century monarch, but all the sexual privileges of royalty. Failing to rule Poland, he turned his love back to Saxony, beautified Dresden, filled himself with beer, and depleted himself with mistresses; he added insult to injury by taking only one of these from the Polish belles. Toward the end of his reign he planned to partition Poland among Austria, Prussia, and Saxony, but he died (February 1, 1733) before effecting this deviltry. On his deathbed he said, "My whole life was one ceaseless sin."[14] *In morte veritas.*

In the interregnum that ensued during the assembling of an electoral Diet, French emissaries lavished livres to win deputies to the restoration of Leszczyński. Since his deposition Stanislas had lived in peace and hope in Alsace. In 1725 his daughter Marie had become queen of France by marrying Louis XV; now Louis expected his father-in-law, if enthroned, to follow the French policy of aligning Poland with Prussia and Turkey in a cordon around Austria. Feeling that such an alliance would weaken Russia in her inevitable conflicts with Turkey and Prussia, the Russian government dispatched rubles to Warsaw to prevent the election of Leszczyński. The livres outweighed the rubles, and on September 10, 1733, Leszczyński became King Stanislas I of Poland.

A minority refused to recognize his election, and put themselves under the protection of a Russian army that advanced to the Vistula and proclaimed the Saxon Elector as King Augustus III of Poland (October 6). So began the War of the Polish Succession, and the first decisive interference of Russia in Polish affairs. Stanislas looked for a Polish army to defend him; none existed except on paper; he fled to Danzig and appealed to France for aid. The French government was then led by Cardinal Fleury, who had no stomach for a war with distant Russia; he sent a detachment of 2,400 soldiers; the Russians, with twelve thousand men, overwhelmed it. Stanislas escaped from Danzig and retired to Lorraine. In January, 1736, he signed his abdication; in July Augustus III was acknowledged king.

But he was no more fit than Leszczyński to guide a nation which had chaos built into its constitution. For a time he co-operated with the Czartoryskis in attempts to end the *liberum veto;* the Potocki repeatedly used the veto to preserve it; Augustus gave up, comforted himself in Dresden, and rarely visited Poland. Corruption continued and flourished; unable to stop it, the King shared in it, selling offices to the highest bidder. Magnates controlled the courts and the armed forces; they negotiated directly with foreign powers, and received subsidies from them.[15] France, Austria, Prussia, Russia maneuvered to see which could profit most from the imminent dissolution of the Polish state.

Before and after the death of Augustus III (October 5, 1763), the competition to name and rule his successor ran through every device of diplomacy to the brink of war. The Potockis pleaded for a standing army of 100,000 to protect Poland from foreign domination. The Czartoryskis resigned themselves to a Russian protectorate, and negotiated with Catherine II. Russia claimed the right to protect the Greek Orthodox minority in Poland, and stretched its memory to recall that the eastern Polish provinces had been taken from Russia by St. Vladimir (956?–1015) eight hundred years before. France favored the son of Augustus III to succeed him; if Russia mastered Poland the whole structure of French foreign policy in the East would collapse. Frederick the Great, who had just concluded seven years of bitter war against France and Austria, needed the friendship of Catherine, by whose permission he had escaped disaster; he agreed to support her candidate for the Polish crown; moreover, he signed with her (April 11, 1764) a treaty secretly binding both of them to oppose any changes in the constitution of either Poland or Sweden, lest an increase in the royal power should make one or both of these countries dangerously strong; they proposed to defend chaos in the name of liberty. The Czartoryskis were appeased by Catherine's promise to curtail the *liberum veto* after stability had been restored, and by her choice of a Czartoryski protégé as her candidate for the throne. On September 7, 1764, by the unanimous vote of a Diet convinced by rubles and a Russian army only three miles away, Stanislas Poniatowski was chosen king.

III. PONIATOWSKI

He was born to Stanislas Poniatowski the elder, governor of Cracow, and to Konstantia Czartoryski, January 17, 1732. "I was brought up very strictly," he told Mme. Geoffrin, "by a mother the like of whom you will scarce find anywhere nowadays, while my father only preached to me by his example."[16] At the age of sixteen he began extensive travels. In 1753 he captivated Mme. Geoffrin, her salon, and nearly all Paris by his figure, his manners, and his youth. A few years later, following a fashion of the time, he composed a self-portrait that accorded fairly with the facts:

> I should be content with my figure if only I were an inch taller, . . . and my nose less hooked, and my mouth a little smaller. With these reservations I believe that my face is noble and expressive, my figure not without distinction. . . . My shortsightedness often makes me look awkward, but only for an instant. Indeed I am rather apt to offend by the opposite extreme—too haughty a demeanor. An excellent education enables me to conceal my mental and bodily defects, so that many people perhaps expect more from me than I can readily give. I have wit enough to take part in any conversation, but not enough to converse long and frequently. However, my natural sympathy and amiability often come to my assistance. I have a natural penchant toward art. . . . My indolence prevents me from going as far as I should like to go in the arts and sciences. I work either overmuch or not at all. I can judge very well of affairs, . . . but I am very much in need of good counsel to carry out any plan of my own. I am very impressionable, but far more affected by sorrow than by joy. I am the first to be depressed. . . . When I love I love too passionately. . . . I am not vindictive. Though in the first moment of irritation I may long to avenge myself upon my enemies, I am never able to carry out my desire; compassion always comes between.[17]

To see—and express—himself so well suggests that Poniatowski was born to think and write rather than to plan and do. He had met Montesquieu and read Voltaire; he had acquired the intellectual polish and subtlety of French society along with a degree of that "sensibility" which was finding expression in Rousseau. He was extremely sensitive to women, and felt that what they gave him, in body and soul, was beyond price. Rumor said that in Paris he was arrested for debt, and was released after an hour's imprisonment upon payment of 100,000 livres by Mme. Geoffrin.[18]

After five months in Paris, and having learned English, he went to England, attended some sessions of Parliament, and aspired to remold the Polish situation in the image of England as interpreted by Montesquieu. Back from his travels (1754), he was appointed high steward of Lithuania. A year later he accompanied Sir Charles Hanbury-Williams to Russia, with results already noted. He returned home in 1756, but went to St. Petersburg in 1757 as Polish ambassador. He shared in the intrigue against Elizabeth in 1758, and was forced to leave Russia at short notice. Catherine mourned his departure, but when she supported him for the throne of Poland it was not because she still loved him, but because (she said) he had less right than any other candidate, and should therefore be all the more grateful.[19] As for himself, he never quite recovered from that exciting liaison; he remembered Catherine before she had been hardened by power, and that fascination survived even when she made him her tool in the subjection of his people.

Two days after his election he sent the news to Mme. Geoffrin:

> MY DEAR MAMA: It seems to me that I have greater pleasure in calling you by that name since the day before yesterday. [His own mother was now dead.] In all our history there has never been an election so tranquil and so unanimous. . . . All the principal ladies of the kingdom were present on the Field of Election amid the squadrons of the nobility. . . . I had the satisfaction of being proclaimed by the voices of all the women as well as by those of all the men. . . . Why were you not there? You would have named your son.[20]

We have seen how "Mama" braved the roads of Europe to visit her "son" in his palace at Warsaw (1766). Having no realistic conception of the gap between French and Polish civilization, she longed to have him pull Poland up a century in a year; her advice became troublesome, and strained Poniatowski's filial devotion; he was relieved when she left, though he soothed her with compliments and a picture of himself set in diamonds. She kept the picture and sent back the diamonds. Once away, her love for him returned to full fervor, and she wrote to him from Vienna affirming for him "an affection which is a necessity of my life."[21]

Stanislas did his best. He gave himself dutifully, in these first years, to the chores of government. He attended daily the deliberations of his ministers, and worked till late at night on problems which he undertook in conscientious detail. He succeeded in good measure in training a civil-service corps of unusual competence and startling integrity.[22] He made himself easily accessible, and charmed all by his amiability, not all by his enthusiasm for reform. But his energy was diluted by a sense of his dependence upon Catherine, even upon the Russian troops that she had left in Poland as a guarantee of his security and obedience. Her ambassador, Count Otto von Stackelberg, watched over him lest he forget his Russian strings.

He was surrounded by enemies far and near. The Polish nobility was divided into two factions: one, led by the Potockis, agitated for independence before reform, and wished to check the royal power by keeping the aristocracy strong; the other, under the Czartoryskis, asked for reform first, arguing that in its present disorder Poland was too weak to throw off the Russian protectorate. The Czartoryskis were hesitant in the support of Poniatowski, for they deplored his extravagances and his mistresses. The Diet allowed him 2,200,000 thalers per year, and raised this, by 1786, to 6,143,000 gulden—one third of the government's revenue. He spent more than this allowance, having borrowed from banks at home and abroad. Twice the state paid his debts; yet in 1790 he still owed 11,500,000 gulden.[23] Like Catherine, he aspired to make his reign memorable for fine buildings; he divided himself and his retinue between two costly palaces; he gave expensive entertainments, and lavished gifts upon artists, writers, and women.

His attractiveness was costly. Thirty-two at his accession, handsome, cultured, generous, and unmarried, he gathered about him a swarm of belles eager for his hand and his purse. Several who could not marry him were glad to share his bed, and some Parisian actresses joined in amusing the King. The Czartoryskis protested; he confessed his sins and continued them. Finally one mistress, Pani Grabowska, led him to the altar in a secret marriage. Thereafter his sexual life was under strict surveillance, and he could give more attention to government, literature, and the arts.

He took a personal interest in the works and the lives of the artists and authors of the time. Like Catherine, he collected pictures, statuary, and books, built a gallery and a library, and gave prominence, in the latter, to a statue of Voltaire. He found work for native artists, and brought in others from France, Italy, and Germany. Piranesi and Canova could not come, but they executed works for him in Italy. He transformed half the royal palace into a school of art, and provided funds to enable promising young artists to study abroad. He established near Warsaw a porcelain industry whose products ranked with those of Meissen and Sèvres. He inspired well-to-do Poles —Adam Czartoryski, Elizabeth Lubomirska, Helen Radziwill, and others—to collect art, to commission artists, and, in building and decorating their palaces, to replace the rococo of the Saxon period with variations of the neoclassical style. He himself favored a mixture of baroque and classical; in this style Domenico Merlini designed the Lazienki Palace on the outskirts of Warsaw. Meanwhile foreign painters were training a new generation of Polish artists, who came to maturity after Polish liberty had disappeared.

The first moves toward that catastrophe were the obstacles placed by Frederick the Great in the path of Poland's self-reform. Thus far (1767) Catherine seems to have had no intention to dismember a Poland so obviously subject to Russian influence; partition would enlarge Prussia into a much more formidable barrier than Slavic Poland could be to Russian participation in the affairs and culture of Western Europe. She was content to demand the admission of the Dissidents to full civil rights. But Frederick wanted more. He could never reconcile himself to the fact that West Prussia, predominantly German and Protestant, was subject to Polish and Catholic rule. Hence some partition of Poland was with him an unforgettable objective. Any strengthening of Poland, political or military, would hinder his aims; therefore his agents supported the *liberum veto*, opposed the formation of a Polish national army, and welcomed the quarrels of Catholics and Dissidents as offering a ground for invasion.

The intolerance of the Roman Catholic hierarchy co-operated with Frederick's schemes. It resisted every attempt to admit the Dissidents to civil rights. In "White Russia"—which was then a part of Poland, and included Minsk—the Roman Catholic authorities took two hundred churches from their Greek Orthodox congregations and gave them to the Uniates; the Orthodox communities were forbidden to repair their old churches and to build new ones. In many cases children were separated from their parents to be brought up in the Roman obedience. Orthodox priests were ill-treated, and some were put to death.[24] Poniatowski, child of the *philosophes*, favored toleration,[25] but he knew that the Diet would fight, with force if necessary, any move to admit non–Roman Catholics to its membership; and he felt that such proposals should be deferred until some modification of the *liberum veto* could strengthen his hand. Frederick and Catherine replied that they were asking no more of Poland than they themselves were granting to their own religious minorities. To the Diet that met in October and November, 1766, Prussia, Russia, Denmark, and Great Britain presented a petition that their coreligionists in Poland should receive full civil rights.

Aroused by the eloquence of Bishop Kajetan Soltyk of Cracow, the deputies rose to their feet in anger and demanded not only the rejection of the petition, but the prosecution of its Polish supporters as traitors to Poland and God.[26] A member who tried to defend the petition narrowly escaped death.[27] Poniatowski sought to quiet the assembly by issuing (November, 1766) a pamphlet called *Considerations of a Good Citizen*, calling upon all Poles for national unity, and warning them that a divided nation invited conquest. At the same time he begged the Polish ambassador at St. Petersburg to detach Russia from the petitioning powers. "If this [petition] be persisted in," he wrote, "I can see nothing but a St. Bartholomew's Eve [Massacre] for the Dissidents, and a harvest of Ravaillacs [assassins] for myself. . . . The Empress would make of my royal mantle a robe of Nessus. I shall have to choose between renouncing her friendship and being an enemy to my country." Catherine answered, through Nikolai Repnin, her ambassador at Warsaw: "I cannot conceive how the King can fancy himself a traitor to his country by simply supporting the demands of equity."[28] She was too far from Poland, in space and education, to feel the consuming heat of Polish passion and pride. When a group of Protestant nobles formed a confederacy at Thorn, and a Czartoryski faction formed a confederacy at Radom, Catherine bade Repnin offer them the protection of Russia. Under this pretext he brought eighty thousand Russian troops to the Polish border, and some of them into Warsaw itself.

The Diet reconvened in October, 1767. Bishops Zaluski and Soltyk exhorted the deputies to stand firm against any change in the constitution. Going over Poniatowski's head, Repnin arrested the bishops and two laymen on the charge of having insulted the Empress, and had them transported to Kaluga, ninety miles southwest of Moscow. The Diet protested; Repnin announced that if further opposed he would deport not four but forty magnates. On February 24, 1768, the Diet surrendered to threats of war and signed with Russia a treaty accepting all of Catherine's demands: full freedom of religious worship, and eligibility to the Diet and public office, were granted to the Dissidents; suits between Catholics and Dissidents were to be tried before mixed courts. The Diet, Catherine, and Frederick were pleased that the treaty confirmed the *liberum veto*, with some exceptions for economic legislation. The Diet humbly accepted Catherine as the protectress of this new constitution. In return she guaranteed the territorial integrity of Poland so long as this entente continued. She rejoiced that she had not only given Poland a greater degree of religious liberty than even England enjoyed, but had foiled Frederick's plan for partition. Poniatowski received the congratulations of the philosophers and the scorn of his people.

IV. THE FIRST PARTITION: 1768–72

Polish patriots and priests agreed with Frederick in not accepting the situation. The Roman Catholic clergy forcefully condemned the surrender of Poland's autonomy to a Russian infidel. Adam Krasiński, bishop of Kamieniec, and Józef Pulaski (father of the Casimir Pulaski who fought for America) roused the Poles, by sermons and pamphlets, to reassert their political freedom and religious dictatorship. Within a week after the surrender of the Diet to Repnin a group of Poles formed (February 29, 1768) the Confederation of Bar—a town on the Dniester in the Polish Ukraine. The magnates who financed the movement were inspired by hatred of Catherine and the King; the "imbecile mass," as Frederick called their followers, burned with zeal for the one true faith; and this ardor was voiced by poets lamenting, in somber threnodies, the humiliation of Poland and the "apostasy" of its King. Arms and funds were sent to the patriots by Turkey and Austria, and Dumouriez came from France to organize them into fighting units. Poles who wished to restore the Saxon dynasty entered the movement, which soon spread to scattered points throughout the land; "All Poland is on fire," Repnin reported to Catherine. Poniatowski thought of joining the Confederation, but the hotheads in it frightened him away by demanding his deposition, if not his death.[29] If we may believe Voltaire,[30] thirty confederates took an oath at Częstochowa:

> We, excited by a holy and religious zeal, having resolved to avenge the Deity, religion, and our country, outraged by Stanislas Augustus, a despiser of

laws both divine and human, a favorer of atheists and heretics, do promise and swear, before the sacred and miraculous image of the Mother of God, to extirpate from the face of the earth him who dishonors her by trampling upon religion. . . . So help us God!

Repnin ordered Russian troops to suppress the rebellion. They drove the confederates over the Turkish border, and burned a Turkish town; Turkey declared war upon Russia (1768), and demanded Russian evacuation and liberation of Poland. Cossacks took advantage of the turmoil to invade the Polish Ukraine, killing landlords, Jewish stewards, Roman Catholic or Protestant peasants in an orgy of indiscriminate slaughter; in one town they slew sixteen thousand men, women, and children. The confederates retaliated by murdering all available Russians and Dissidents, so that Protestants and Jews suffered double jeopardy. Altogether in those years (1768–70), fifty thousand inhabitants of Poland died by massacre or war.[31]

All sides now began to talk of partition. The confederates were charged by their enemies with having agreed to divide Poland between themselves and their allies.[32] In February, 1769, Frederick sent to St. Petersburg a proposal for dividing Poland among Russia, Prussia, and Austria; Catherine replied that if Prussia and Austria would help Russia to expel the Turks from Europe, she would consent to Prussian appropriation of that part of Poland which separated mainland Prussia from East Prussia—the remainder of Poland to be under a Russian protectorate;[33] Frederick demurred. Choiseul, for France, suggested to Austria that it should seize Polish territory adjoining Hungary: Austria thought it a good idea in a good time, and in April, 1769, it occupied the Polish province of Spiż, which had been mortgaged to Poland by Hungary in 1412 and had never been redeemed.[34] In 1770 the Turks, then at war as a defender of Poland, proposed to Austria a partition of Poland between Austria and Turkey.[35]

While these negotiations were proceeding, the Western powers resigned themselves to the partitioning of Poland as the fated result of her political chaos, her religious animosities, and her military impotence; "the catastrophe was recognized as inevitable by every Continental statesman."[36] But the anti-Confederation Poles at this time sent a member of the Diet to ask the socialist *philosophe* Mably and the *antiphilosophe* Rousseau to draw up tentative constitutions for a new Poland. Mably submitted his recommendations in 1770–71; Rousseau finished his *Constitution of Poland* in April, 1772—two months after the first partition treaty had been signed.

The Confederation of Bar had some moments of ecstasy before its collapse. In March, 1770, from the Turkish city of Varna, it proclaimed the deposition of Poniatowski. On November 3, 1771, some confederates intercepted him as he was leaving the house of an uncle at night, overpowered his escort, shot one of them dead, dragged the King out of his carriage, cut his head with a saber blow, and abducted him from the capital. In the forest of Bielny they were attacked by a patrol; in the melee Poniatowski escaped, and communicated with the Royal Guards, who came and escorted him, disheveled and bloody, back to his palace at five o'clock in the morning. All chances of reconciliation between the government and the Confederation disappeared. Poniatowski fell back upon Russian aid, and the Confederation was suppressed, leaving a remnant in Turkey—the Crescent protecting the Cross (1772).[37]

Meanwhile the advance of Russia's armies to the Black Sea and the Danube disturbed both Prussia and Austria. Neither Frederick II nor Joseph II took pleasure in contemplating Russian control of the Black Sea, much less of Constantinople. By treaties of 1764 and 1766 Prussia had pledged help to Russia if Russia should be attacked; Turkey was formally the aggressor in the Russo-Turkish war of 1768; Prussia was now endangering its solvency by sending subsidies to Russia. Austria, resenting the entry of Russian forces into Wallachia, was threatening to ally itself with Turkey against Russia; in that case Russia would expect Prussia to attack Austria. But Frederick had had enough of war. He had fought two wars to take and hold Silesia; why risk it now? He preferred diplomacy. Perhaps the three powers could be appeased with servings of Polish soil? As things were going, with the Russian ambassador the real ruler of Poland, it was only a matter of time till Russia would completely absorb the country, under whatever phrase. Was it still possible to prevent this? Yes, if Catherine would consent to take only eastern Poland, to let Frederick take western Poland, and to withdraw from the Danube. Would a share in the spoils moderate Joseph's belligerency?

In January, 1771, Prince Henry, Frederick's brother, proposed the plan to the Russian diplomats at St. Petersburg. Panin objected that Russia had guaranteed the territorial integrity of Poland; he was reminded that this guarantee was conditional upon Poland's adherence to her new constitution and her alliance with Russia, and this adherence had ceased when so many deputies joined the rebellious Confederation of Bar. Even so, Catherine was reluctant. Why give Frederick a part of Poland when she might soon take all? Why strengthen Prussia with additional territory, resources, Baltic ports, and more six-foot troops? But she did not want to fight Frederick; he had 180,000 men in arms; she preferred to have him keep Joseph from uniting with Turkey against Russia. Her present goal was not Poland but the Black Sea. On January 8, 1771, almost casually at a party, she indicated to Henry her tentative consent to Frederick's scheme.

A year passed before negotiation could settle the division of the spoils. Frederick wanted Danzig; Catherine objected; so did Britain, whose Baltic commerce anchored on that port. Meanwhile Austria mobilized, and secretly allied itself with Turkey. On February 17, 1772, Frederick and Catherine signed a "convention" for the partition of Poland. Catherine softened Joseph by renouncing all Russian claims to Wallachia and Moldavia; and the failure of the 1771 harvest had made it impossible for him to feed his troops. On the other hand, Maria Theresa was using all her tears to keep her son from joining in the rape. Frederick and Catherine forced his hand by beginning actual seizure of their self-assigned terrain. On August 5, 1772, Joseph added his signature to the partition pact.

The treaty, after invoking the Blessed Trinity, agreed to let Poland keep two thirds of her soil and one third of her population. Austria took southern Poland between Volhynia and the Carpathians, with Galicia and western Podolia—27,000 square miles, 2,700,000 souls. Russia took "White Russia" (eastern Poland to the Dvina and the Dnieper)—36,000 square miles, 1,800,-000 souls. Prussia took "West Prussia," excepting Danzig and Thorn—13,000 square miles, 600,000 souls. Frederick took the smallest share, but he had bound the conspirators to peace, and had "sewed together," as he put it, West Prussia and East Prussia with Brandenburg. After all, said the patriotic Treitschke, this was merely restoring to Germany "the stronghold of the . . . Teutonic Order, the lovely Weichsal Valley, which in days of yore the German knights had wrested from the barbarians."[38] Frederick reminded Europe that the population of West Prussia was predominantly German and Protestant, and Catherine pointed out that the region she had taken was peopled almost entirely by Russian-speaking Greek Catholics.[39]

The three powers soon occupied their shares with troops. Poniatowski appealed to the Western powers to prevent the partition; they were too busy; France was expecting war with England, and hesitated to oppose her ally Austria; England faced incipient revolt in America, with danger from France and Spain; George III advised Poniatowski to pray to God.[40] The partitioning powers demanded that a Diet be called to confirm the new geography; Poniatowski temporized for a year; finally he summoned a Diet to meet at Grodno. Many nobles and prelates refused to attend; some who came and protested were sent to Siberia; others accepted bribes; the rump Diet changed itself into a confederation (in which majority rule was permitted by Polish law), and signed the treaty ceding the expropriated territories (September 18, 1773). Poniatowski, like Maria Theresa, wept and signed.

Western Europe accepted the first partition as the only alternative to the complete absorption of Poland by Russia. Some diplomats, we are told, "were startled by the moderation of the partners, who took only a third when the whole was theirs for the asking."[41] The *philosophes* rejoiced that an intolerant Poland had been chastened by their enlightened despots; Voltaire hailed the partition as an historic repulse of *l'infâme*.[42] It was, of course, the triumph of organized power over reactionary impotence.

V. THE POLISH ENLIGHTENMENT: 1773–91

Poniatowski had to choose now between Russia and Prussia as his protector and master. He chose Russia, for it was farther away, and only Russia could prevent Frederick from taking Danzig and Thorn. Catherine was anxious to prevent the further aggrandizement of Prussia, whose army was the greatest obstacle to Russian aggrandizement in the West. She ordered her ambassador in Warsaw to help Poniatowski in every way consonant with Russian interests, and she sent to the King the proposals that Panin had drawn up for a more workable Polish constitution. It retained elective monarchy and the *liberum veto*, but it increased the royal power by establishing, under his presidency and as his executive arm, a Permanent Council of thirty-six members, divided into ministries of police, justice, finance, foreign affairs, and war; and it provided for a regular army of thirty thousand men. The nobles feared that such an army would endanger their domination of the King; they reduced the figure to eighteen thousand; but, with this and some minor exceptions, the Diet of 1775 ratified the new constitution, and Poniatowski could now proceed to restore some health to the nation.

Corruption continued but anarchy diminished, guerrilla bands were overcome, and the national economy grew. Rivers were deepened for large vessels, canals were dug between rivers, and a "Royal Canal," completed in 1783, connected the Baltic with the Black Sea. Between 1715 and 1773 the population of Poland grew from 6,500,000 to 7,500,000, and the state revenue was doubled. A system of national schools was established, textbooks were prepared and provided, the universities of Cracow and Wilno were re-endowed and revitalized, and teachers' colleges were established and financed by the state. Poniatowski liked to surround himself with poets, journalists, and philosophers. "The King," reported Coxe, "gives a dinner every Thursday to the men of letters who are most conspicuous for learning and abilities, and his Majesty himself presides at table,"[43] leading the discussion of books and ideas. He took three authors to live with him, and quietly added to the income of others.[44] Thousands of Poles, while making their courteous obeisance to the Church—even while serving as its priests—read Locke, Montesquieu, Voltaire, Diderot, d'Alembert, and Rousseau. The foundations were laid of the Polish, or Stanislavian, Enlightenment.

Adam Naruszewicz, a Jesuit, caught the ear of the King by his poems; he was raised to a bishopric, but continued to indite lyrics to nature; his "Hymn to the Sun" and his "Four Seasons" still endear him to those who can read him in the original. His *Satires* used a popular vocabulary sometimes Rabelaisian or profane. Stanislas asked him to write a readable but scholarly history of Poland; Naruszewicz gave nine years to the task, and in six volumes (1780–86) produced a work remarkable for its discriminate documentation. He lost heart after the second partition, fell into melancholy, and survived the final partition by only a year.[45]

The outstanding Polish writer of the period was Ignacy Krasicki. In his travels he won the friendship of Voltaire and Diderot.[46] He became a priest, ultimately an archbishop, but Stanislas urged him to give rein to his poetic gifts. In a mock-heroic *Mousiad* (1775) he satirized the wars of his time as battles between rats and mice; in *Monomachia* (1778) he made fun of monastic disputes—the deadly weapons being theological tomes. Turning to prose, he told, in *The Adventures of Mr. Nicholas Find-Out* (1776), how a young Polish noble, equipped with all fashionable attainments and sentiments, and wrecked on a strange island, discovered how men and women, though in a "state of nature," could be industrious and virtuous. Having followed the lead of Homer, Swift, and Defoe in these works, Krasicki took up the style of Addison, and produced a series of genre pictures, *Pan Podstoli* (1778 f.), describing the life of a model gentleman and citizen. In *Fables and Parables*

(1779) he challenged Phaedrus and La Fontaine, and struck with trenchant irony at the dishonesty and brutality that flourished about him. His final advice was Horatian: seek a quiet corner, and let happiness come by stealth.[47]

Although the influence of the French Enlightenment upon Naruszewicz and Krasicki was sacerdotally subdued, it appeared decisively in Stanislas Trembecki, who never mentioned religion except with hostility. His poetry idolized nature, but not in those pleasant aspects that most often stir sentiment; he liked rather her wilder phases—her mad profusion of plants and animals, her storms and torrents, the strife of life with life, of eaten with eater; his fables took their form from La Fontaine but their spirit from Lucretius. The power, subtlety, and finish of his verse won him a high place in this literary flowering. Poniatowski supported him through all his trials, and when the King was deposed the poet accompanied him into exile, and stayed with him till death.

There was much religious poetry, for religion was the ultimate consolation of the Poles in their personal and national misfortunes. Franciszek Karpiński's "Morning Song," "Evening Song," and "Christ Is Being Born" are literature as well as piety. Franciszek Kniaźnin passed readily between those ancient enemies, religion and sex: on the verge of ordination he discovered Anacreon and love; he published *Erotica* (1770), pursued worldly happiness, returned to religion, and died insane. The attempt to reconcile opposites may lead to madness as well as to philosophy.

In the drama the dominant figure was Wojciecz Boguslawski, whom his countrymen honor as "the father of the Polish theater"; we might call him the Garrick of Poland, but the Poles would call Garrick the Boguslawski of England. He was apparently the first Pole who gave his entire career to the stage—as actor, dramatist, and producer, as director of permanent theaters in Warsaw and Lvov, and as manager of companies that spread an appreciation of the drama throughout the provinces and over the frontiers. He presented Shakespeare and Sheridan in translation, and himself wrote comedies some of which still hold the Polish stage. The best play of this period was *The Deputy's Return*, by Julian Ursyn Niemcewicz, himself a deputy; here the two sides of the political crisis were dramatically pictured in the devotion of a reform deputy to a girl whose parents defend the privileges of the magnates and the ways of the past.

Last and greatest of the Polish *illuminés* was Hugo Kollontaj. His education infected him with the ideas of the *philosophes*, but he concealed his heresies sufficiently to secure a comfortable canonry at Cracow. Poniatowski appointed him (1773) to an Education Committee, for which Kollontaj, aged twenty-three, drew up a program of educational reform quite up to the best of its time. At twenty-seven he was entrusted with the reorganization of Cracow University; he carried this through in a few years, and then remained as rector. In *Letters of an Anonymous Writer to the President of the Diet* (1788–89), and in *The Political Law of the Polish Nation* (1790), he offered proposals which became the basis of the constitution of 1791.

Prodded by its poets and publicists, Poland struggled to transform itself into an effective and defensible state. An opportunity came when, to the

"Four Years' Diet" of 1788–92, Frederick II's successor, Frederick William II, offered an alliance that pledged protection by the powerful Prussian army against any foreign interference. Russia was busy with war against both Turkey and Sweden; now Poland might deliver itself from its long subservience to Catherine, and from such depredations as Russian soldiers had committed on Polish soil during the last twenty-five years. Over Poniatowski's protests the Diet dissolved his Permanent Council, voted to raise, subject to the Diet, an army of 100,000 men, and ordered Russian troops to leave Poland at once (May, 1789). Catherine, needing all her forces elsewhere, made no resistance, but vowed revenge. On March 29, 1790, the Diet signed alliance with Prussia.

By this time Poniatowski too was intoxicated with the air of freedom. Throwing off his allegiance to Catherine, he took the lead in drafting a new constitution. Its terms made the monarchy hereditary, but assured the succession, after the childless Poniatowski's death, to the house of Saxony. The executive powers of the Crown were to be enlarged by giving the king a suspensive veto—i.e., the right to prevent a measure passed by one Diet from becoming law until reaffirmed by the next. The king was to appoint his ministers and the bishops, and to have command of the army. A small number of burghers and other townsmen were to be elected as deputies. The Diet was to consist of two chambers: a House of Deputies, which alone could originate laws; and a Senate—composed of bishops, provincial governors, and the king's ministers—whose consent was to be necessary to any law. The *liberum veto* was to be replaced by majority rule. Roman Catholicism was to be recognized as the prevailing religion of the nation, and apostasy from it was made a crime; but otherwise freedom of worship was guaranteed to all. Serfdom remained, but peasants might now appeal from the patrimonial to a provincial or national court. The influence of the constitution adopted by the United States of America (1787–88) was evident in these recommendations; Poles who had fought for the American colonies had prepared the mind of Poniatowski, and he had not forgotten his reading of Locke, Montesquieu, and the *philosophes*.

To ensure the ratification of his proposals Poniatowski resorted to a ruse. Many members of the Diet went home for the Easter holydays of 1791; the King summoned it to reconvene on May 3, too soon to let distant members return to Warsaw for the reopening; those nearby deputies who arrived on time were mostly liberals who could be depended upon to support the new constitution. It was offered to them in the royal palace as soon as they convened; it was received with wild acclaim, and was ratified by a large majority. That day, May 3, 1791, was proudly remembered by patriotic Poles, and was celebrated in Polish literature, art, and song.

VI. DISMEMBERMENT: 1792–95

All the powers except Russia recognized the new constitution. Edmund Burke called it "the noblest benefit received by any nation at any time," and declared that Stanislas II had earned a place among the greatest kings and statesmen in history;[48] but this enthusiasm may have reflected England's pleasure at Catherine's defeat.

The Empress concealed for a time her hostility to the new Poland. But she did not forgive the expeditious expulsion of her troops, nor the replacement of Russian with Prussian influence in Polish affairs. When the Peace of Jassy (January 9, 1792) ended her war with Turkey, and the involvement of Prussia and Austria in war against Revolutionary France (April, 1792) freed her from fear of her former accomplices, she looked around for another opening into Poland.

It was provided for her by conservative Poles. They quite agreed with Catherine that Poniatowski's constitution had been approved by a Diet so hastily assembled that many nobles had been unable to attend. Felix Potocki and other magnates were furious at the abandonment of that *liberum veto* which had insured their power against any central authority, and they were unwilling to surrender their right to elect—and therefore dominate—the king. Refusing to take an oath of loyalty to the new charter, Potocki led a group of nobles to St. Petersburg and asked the Empress to help them restore the older constitution (of 1775) which she had promised to protect. She answered that she did not care to interfere in Poland at the request of a few individuals, but that she would consider an appeal from a substantial organized Polish minority. Informed of these negotiations, Frederick William II, involved against France and unwilling to wage war against Russia, informed the Polish government (May 4, 1792) that if it intended to defend its new constitution by force of arms, it must not expect support from Prussia.[49] Potocki returned to Poland, formed (May 14, 1792) in a little town of the Ukraine the Confederation of Targowica, and invited to his standard all those who wished to restore the old constitution. His followers called themselves Republicans, condemned the alliance of Poland with Prussia, praised Catherine, and begged for her blessing and her troops.

She sent both, and, so strengthened, the confederates marched toward Warsaw. Their propaganda for "freedom" made some impression, for several towns received them as liberators; and at Teresapol (September 5) Potocki was hailed as in effect the new king of Poland. Poniatowski called upon the Diet to give him all powers needed for defense. It appointed him dictator, summoned all adult male Poles to military service, and adjourned. Stanislas made his nephew, the twenty-nine-year-old Prince Józef Poniatowski, commander in chief of the army, which he found untrained and miserably equipped. Józef ordered all detachments of the army to join him at Lubar on the River Slucz; but many had been surrounded by Russian forces, and could not come, and those that came were too weak to withstand the Russian advance. The young commander withdrew to Polonne, his center of supplies, in an orderly retreat made possible by the valiant rear-guard action of Thaddeus Kosciusko, who had fought for the colonies in America, and was already, at forty-six, old in the honors of patriotism and war.

On June 17, 1792, the Poles encountered a major Russian army at Zielence, and defeated it in the first pitched battle won by Poland since Sobieski's days. Here again Kosciusko proved his skill, by seizing a hill from which his artillery commanded the field; and Józef, hitherto distrusted by subordinates twice his age, won their respect by leading his reserves in person to force the retreat of the Russians. The report of this victory rejoiced Poniatowski, but was almost outweighed by news that Prince Ludwig of Württemberg, a Prussian-army commander in charge of the Polish forces in Lithuania, had deserted his post, leaving his troops in such disarray that on June 12 the Russians easily captured Wilno, the Lithuanian capital.

Józef's army remained the sole defense of Poland. Its supplies were so low that some of its regiments fasted for twenty-four hours, and only a dozen charges of ammunition were left in the artillery. The Prince ordered retreat to Dubno; accused of cowardice, he took a stand at Dubienka (July 18), and with 12,500 men fought 28,000 Russians to a draw. He fell back in good order to Kurow, where he awaited the reinforcements and supplies that had been promised him by the King.

But Stanislas had given up. The refusal of Frederick William II to honor the terms of the Prusso-Polish alliance, the treachery of Prince Ludwig, the hundreds of desertions from the army that he had collected at Praga, had been too much for his never very valiant spirit. He sent a personal appeal to Catherine for some honorable terms; her reply (July 23) was an ultimatum requiring him to join the Confederation of Targowica, and to restore the constitution of 1775. He was shocked by her uncompromising tone; was this the same woman who had once responded to his reckless love?

It was his tenderness that now dominated him. He had thought of resisting, of arming himself and going to the front to lead a forlorn defense; but his wife, his sister, and his niece wept so copiously at the thought of his death and their own desolation that the King promised he would yield. And, after all, of what use would resistance be? Now that no help—now that attacks on the undefended western front—could be expected from Prussia, how could Poland stand against Russia? Had he not striven to dissuade the Diet from flouting Catherine and risking all on the promises of Prussia? Had he not pleaded for a large army properly equipped, and had not the Diet, after voting the men, refused the funds? Even if the existing Polish army won a victory or two over the Russians, could not Catherine, surfeited with soldiers by peace with Turkey, send wave after wave of disciplined and well-armed troops against his scattered and disorganized remnants? Why sacrifice more lives, and surrender half of Poland to devastation, when surrender would be the end in any case?

The new Russian ambassador, Yakov Sievers, sent to his sister a sympathetic picture of Poniatowski in this hour of physical and spiritual collapse:

> The King is still [at sixty] a handsome man who wears well, though his face
> is pale, but one can see that a dark veil has been drawn over his soul. He speaks
> well, and even eloquently, and is courteous and attentive always and to every-
> one. He is lodged badly, slighted, despised, and betrayed; and yet he is the
> most amiable of men. Leaving his high position out of the question, and re-

garding him simply from the personal point of view, I may say that his good qualities outweigh his bad ones. Certainly, after Louis XVI, he is the most unfortunate of monarchs. He loves his kinsfolk most tenderly, and it is just these very people who have been the cause of all his misfortunes.[50]

On July 24, 1792, Poniatowski read the Russian ultimatum to his privy councilors, and advised them to trust to Catherine's magnanimity. Many councilors protested against such simplicity. One of them, Malachowski, offered to raise within an hour 100,000 gulden for defense, and urged that even if Warsaw had to be abandoned, the Polish troops could retreat to Cracow and raise a new army in the populous south. Poniatowski's motion to surrender was defeated in the Council by a vote of twenty to seven. By his authority as dictator he overruled them, and ordered his nephew to make no further resistance. Józef replied that instead of such capitulation the King should hasten to the front with what forces he could gather, and fight to the end. When Stanislas insisted that the army must join the Confederation, all the officers but one sent in their resignations, and Józef returned to his former home in Vienna. On August 5 a Russian army occupied Praga. In October Józef sent a plea to his uncle to abdicate before every shred of honor had gone. In November Potocki, with the advance guard of the Confederation, made a triumphal entry into Warsaw, and lectured Poniatowski on the duties of a king. But Potocki's victory was soon seen to be a calamity, for in January, 1793, Prussian troops entered Poland, and then moved on to occupy Danzig and Thorn, without Potocki's Russian allies raising a musket to prevent them. It became clear that Russia and Prussia had agreed to partition Poland again.

Catherine and Frederick William had signed such an agreement on January 23, but they kept it secret till February 28. Potocki appealed to Poles of all parties to rise in defense of Poland; they laughed at him; Józef denounced him as the betrayer of his country, and challenged him to single combat; Stanislas forbade the duel.

By the second partition Russia took 89,000 square miles of eastern Poland, with 3,000,000 population, including Wilno and Minsk; Prussia took 23,000 square miles of western Poland, with 1,000,000 population, including Danzig and Thorn; Poland retained 80,000 square miles and 4,000,000 souls—approximately one half of what had been left to her in 1773. Austria had no share in this second spoliation, but was mollified by Russo-Prussian promises to aid her in acquiring Bavaria. The Western powers, still absorbed in the struggle with Revolutionary France, took no action against this second rape, which Catherine explained to them as made necessary by the development of revolutionary agitation in Warsaw, endangering all monarchies.

To give the theft a garb of legality she ordered Poniatowski to summon a Diet to meet at Grodno, and bade him come there in person to sign an alliance with Russia. At first he declined to go, but when she offered to pay his debts—which now amounted to 1,566,000 ducats—he accepted this added humiliation for the sake of his creditors. The Russian ambassador was supplied with funds to bribe a sufficient number of deputies to attend the Diet, and he found it easy to corrupt several members of the King's suite to report every word and action of their master. This "Last Diet" (June 17 to November 24, 1793) was persuaded to sign a treaty with Russia, but it refused for months to ratify the second partition. Told that they would not be allowed to leave the hall till they had signed, the members still refused, and sat in silence for twelve hours. Then the marshal put the question to a vote, and, hearing no answer, declared that silence was consent (September 25). The residue of Poland became again a Russian protectorate; the constitution of 1775 was restored.

If one man could redeem the nation it was Kosciusko. Financed by the Czartoryskis, he went to Paris (January, 1793), and besought the help of France for a Poland warmly sympathetic with the French Revolution. He promised that if help came the Polish peasants would rise against serfdom, the townsmen against the nobility; Poniatowski would abdicate in favor of a republic, and a Polish army would support France in its war with Prussia.[51] The French leaders welcomed his proposals, but the outbreak of war with England (February, 1793), and the invasion of France by the Allies, ended all chance of aid to Poland.

During Kosciusko's absence some burghers, Freemasons, and army officers raised a new Polish army (March, 1794). Kosciusko hurried from Dresden to Cracow to join it; he was appointed commander in chief with dictatorial powers; he ordered every five houses in Poland to send him a foot soldier, every fifty houses a cavalryman, and bade these recruits to bring whatever weapons they could muster, even pikes and scythes. On April 4, with four thousand regulars and two thousand peasant recruits, Kosciusko attacked a force of seven thousand Russians at Raclawice, near Cracow, and defeated it partly by his generalship, partly by the effectiveness of the peasants' scythes.

On hearing of this victory the radical, or "Jacobin," element in Warsaw organized an insurrection. Middle-class leaders hesitantly joined it. On April 17 these rebels attacked the Russian garrison of 7,500 men, slew many of them, and defeated a Prussian contingent of 1,650 troops; the occupation forces fled, and for a moment Warsaw was under Polish control. A similar uprising freed Wilno (April 23), hanged the Grand Hetman of Lithuania, and regained parts of Poland almost to Minsk. On May 7 Kosciusko promised liberation to the serfs, and guaranteed ownership of the lands they tilled. So many volunteers and conscripts came to his standard that by June of 1794 he commanded 150,000 men, only 80,000 of them properly equipped.

Against them came wave after wave of disciplined Russian or Prussian troops. On June 6 an allied army of 26,000 surprised the Poles near Szczekociny; Kosciusko had time to bring up only 14,000 men. He was beaten with heavy losses; he sought death in battle, but it evaded him; the Polish remnant retired to Warsaw. On June 15 the Prussians took Cracow; on August 11 the Russians recaptured Wilno; on September 19 a Polish army of 5,500 men was annihilated at Teresapol by a Russian force of 12,500 seasoned soldiers under Suvorov; on October 10 Kosciusko himself, with 7,000 Poles, was overwhelmed by 13,000 Russians at Maciejowice; he was seriously wounded and was taken prisoner. He did not, as legend supposed, utter the despairing cry *"Finis Poloniae!,"* but that defeat was the end of the heroic revolt.

Suvorov, uniting various Russian armies, stormed the entrenched camp of the Poles at Praga, and his battle-crazed troops slaughtered not only the defenders but the civilian population of the town. Poniatowski surrendered Warsaw to avoid a greater massacre. Suvorov dispatched Kosciusko and other rebel leaders to imprisonment at St. Petersburg, and sent the King to Grodno to await the pleasure of the Empress. There, on November 25, 1795, he signed his abdication. He appealed to Catherine to let some part of Poland survive, but she determined to solve the Polish question by putting an end, as she thought, to the Polish nation. After fifteen months of dispute Russia, Prussia, and Austria signed the Third Partition Treaty (January 26, 1797). Russia took Kurland, Lithuania, and western Podolia and Volhynia—181,000 square miles; Austria took "Little Poland," with Cracow and Ludlin—45,000 square miles; Prussia received the remainder, with Warsaw—57,000 square miles. By all three partitions Russia absorbed some 6,000,000 of Poland's 12,-200,000 souls (1797), Austria 3,700,000, Prussia 2,500,000.

Thousands of Poles fled from their country; aliens received the confiscated properties. Poniatowski remained in Grodno, playing at botany and writing memoirs. After Catherine's death Paul I invited him to St. Petersburg and assigned him the Marble Palace and 100,000 ducats a year. There he died, February 12, 1798, in his sixty-sixth year. Kosciusko was freed by Emperor Paul in 1796, returned to America, then to France, and continued his efforts for Polish liberation till his death (1817). Józef Poniatowski escaped to Vienna, joined in Napoleon's campaign against Russia, was wounded at Smolensk, fought valiantly at Leipzig, was made a marshal in the French army, and died in 1813, honored even by his enemies. Poland ceased to be a state, but continued to be a people and a civilization, sullied by religious persecution, but distinguished by great poets, novelists, musicians, artists, and scientists, and never abandoning the resolve to rise again.

BOOK V

THE PROTESTANT NORTH

1756–89

CHAPTER XX

Frederick's Germany

1756–86

I. FREDERICK VICTORIOUS

WHO was this ogre, internationally feared and admired, who had stolen Silesia, defeated half of Europe united against him, laughed at religion, snubbed marriage, given lessons in philosophy to Voltaire, and torn off a limb from Poland if only to keep Russia from absorbing it all?

He looked more like a ghost than an ogre when he returned, sad and victorious, from the Seven Years' War and entered Berlin (March 30, 1763) amid the plaudits of a destitute populace. "I return to a city," he wrote to d'Argens, "where I shall know only the walls, where I shall find none of my acquaintances, where an immense task awaits me, where I shall before long leave my bones in a place of refuge troubled by neither war nor calamities nor the villainy of man."[1] His skin was parched and wrinkled, his blue-gray eyes were somber and swollen, his face was lined with battle and bitterness; only the nose had retained its pristine majesty. He thought that he could not long survive the drain made by the protracted war upon his resources of body, mind, and will, but his temperate habits preserved him for twenty-three years more. He ate and drank sparingly, and knew no luxury; he lived and dressed in his Potsdam New Palace as if he were still in camp. He grudged the time given to the care of his person; in his later years he gave up shaving, merely clipping his beard now and then with scissors; and gossip said that he did not often wash.[2]

The war completed that hardening of his character which had begun as a defense against his father's cruelty. He looked on with stoic calm as condemned soldiers ran the gauntlet thirty-six times.[3] He harassed his officials and generals with secret spies, sudden intrusions, abusive language, stinted pay, and such detailed commands as stifled initiative and interest. He never won the love of his brother Prince Henry, who served him so effectively and loyally in diplomacy and war. He had some women friends, but they feared rather than loved him, and none of them was admitted to his inner circle. He respected the silent suffering of his neglected Queen, and on his return from the war he surprised her with a present of 25,000 thalers; but it is doubtful if he ever shared her bed. She learned to love him nevertheless, seeing him heroic in adversity and devoted in government; she spoke of him as "our dear King," "this dear Prince whom I love and adore."[4] He had no children, but he was deeply attached to his dogs; usually two of them slept in his room at night, probably as a guard; sometimes he took one of them into his bed to warm him with animal heat. When the last of his favorite dogs died he "wept all day long."[5] He was suspected of homosexuality,[6] but of this we have only surmise.

Beneath his martial carapace there were elements of tenderness which he rarely exposed to public view. He wept abundantly over the death of his mother, and he repaid with sincere affection the devotion of his sister Wilhelmine. He spread little inconspicuous kindnesses among his nieces. He laughed at Rousseau's sentiment, but he forgave his hostility and offered him asylum when the Christian world cast him out. He passed from the stern drilling of his troops to blowing melodies from his flute. He composed sonatas, concertos, and symphonies which he shared in performing before his court. The learned Burney heard him there, and reported that he played with "great precision, a clean and uniform attack, brilliant fingering, a pure and simple taste, a great neatness of execution, and equal perfection in all his pieces"; Burney adds, however, that "in some of the difficult passages . . . his Majesty was obliged, against the rules, to take a breath in order to finish the passage."[7]* In later years his increasing shortness of breath, and the loss of several front teeth, compelled him to give up flute playing, but he resumed study of the clavier.

Next to music, his favorite diversion was philosophy. He liked to have a philosopher or two at his table to flay the parsons and stir the generals. He held his own in exchanges with Voltaire, and remained a skeptic when most of the *philosophes* developed dogmas and fantasies. He was the first avowedly agnostic ruler of modern times, but he made no public attack upon religion. He thought that "we have sufficient degrees of probability to reach the certainty that *post mortem nihil est*,"[9] but he rejected the determinism of d'Holbach, insisting (like a man who was will incarnate) that the mind acts creatively upon sensations, and that our impulses can, through education, be controlled by reason.[10] His favorite philosophers were "my friend Lucretius, . . . my good Emperor Marcus Aurelius"; nothing of any importance, he thought, had been added to them.[11]

He agreed with Voltaire in believing that the "masses" bred too fast, and worked too hard, to allow time for real education. Disillusionment with their theology would only incline them to political violence. "The Enlightenment," said Frederick, "is a light from heaven for those who stand on the heights, and a destructive firebrand for the masses";[12] here was a history of the September Massacres of 1792 and the Terror of 1793 before the French Revolution had begun. And to Voltaire in April, 1759: "Let us admit the truth: philosophy and the arts are diffused amongst only a few; the great masses . . . remain as nature made them, malevolent animals."[13] He called mankind (half in humor) *"diese verdammte Rasse"*—this damned race—and laughed at utopias of benevolence and peace:

> Superstition, self-interest, vengeance, treason, ingratitude, will produce
> bloody and tragic scenes until the end of time, because we are governed by

---

* In 1889 Breitkopf and Härtel published 120 compositions by Frederick the Great. Several are available on records. His Sinfonia in D for Two Flutes and Orchestra was revived in Berlin in 1928 and in New York in 1929.[8]

passions and very rarely by reason. There will always be wars, lawsuits, devastations, plagues, earthquakes, bankruptcies. . . . Since this is so, I presume it must be necessary. . . . But it seems to me that if this universe had been made by a benevolent being, he should have made us happier than we are. . . . The human mind is weak; more than three fourths of mankind are made for subjection to the most absurd fanaticism. Fear of the Devil and of hell fascinates their eyes, and they detest the wise man who tries to enlighten them. . . . In vain do I seek in them that image of God which the theologians assert they bear upon them. Every man has a wild beast in him; few can restrain it; most men let loose the bridle when not restrained by terror of the law.[14]

Frederick concluded that to allow governments to be dominated by the majority would be disastrous. A democracy, to survive, must be, like other governments, a minority persuading a majority to let itself be led by a minority. Frederick thought like Napoleon that "among nations and in revolutions aristocracy always exists."[15] He believed that an hereditary aristocracy would develop a sense of honor and loyalty, and a willingness to serve the state at great personal cost, which could not be expected of bourgeois geniuses formed in the race for wealth. So, after the war, he replaced with *Junker* most of the middle-class officers who had risen in the army.[16] But since these proud nobles could be a source of fragmentation and chaos, and an instrument of exploitation, the state should be protected against division, and the commonalty from class injustice, by a monarch wielding absolute power.

Frederick liked to picture himself as the servant of the state and the people. This may have been a rationalization of his will to power, but he lived up to the claim. The state became for him the Supreme Being, to which he would sacrifice himself and others; and the demands of that service overrode, in his view, the code of individual morality; the Ten Commandments stop at the royal doors. All governments agreed with this *Realpolitik*, and some monarchs accepted the view of kingship as a sacred service. Frederick had the latter notion through contact with Voltaire; and through contact with Frederick the *philosophes* developed their *thèse royale*—that the best hope for reform and progress lay in the enlightenment of kings.

So, despite his wars, he became the idol of the French philosophers, and softened the hostility even of the virtuous Rousseau. D'Alembert long refused Frederick's invitations, but did not withhold his praise. "The philosophers and men of letters in every land," he wrote to Frederick, "have long looked upon you, Sire, as their leader and their model."[17] The cautious mathematician at last succumbed to repeated calls, and spent two months with Frederick at Potsdam in 1763. Intimacy (and a pension) did not diminish d'Alembert's admiration. He was delighted with the King's disregard of etiquette, and with his remarks—not only on war and government, but also on literature and philosophy; this, he told Julie de Lespinasse, was finer converse than one could then hear in France.[18] When, in 1776, d'Alembert was desolate over Julie's death, Frederick sent him a letter which shows the ogre in a wise and tender vein:

I am sorry for the misfortune which has befallen you. . . . The wounds of the heart are the most sensitive of all, and . . . nothing but time can heal them. . . . I have, to my misery, had only too much experience of the suffering caused by such losses. The best remedy is to put compulsion upon oneself in order to divert one's mind. . . . You should choose some geometrical investigation which demands constant application. . . . Cicero, to console himself for the death of his dear Tullia, threw himself into composition. . . . At your age and mine we should be the more readily consoled because we shall not long delay to join the objects of our regrets.[19]

He urged d'Alembert to come again to Potsdam. "We will philosophize together concerning the nothingness of life, . . . concerning the vanity of stoicism. . . . I will feel as happy in allaying your grief as if I had won a battle." Here was, if not quite a philosopher king, at least a king who loved philosophers.

This no longer applied to Voltaire. Their quarrels in Berlin and Potsdam, and the arrest of Voltaire in Frankfurt, had left wounds deeper than grief. The philosopher remained bitter longer than the King. He told the Prince de Ligne that Frederick was "incapable of gratitude, and never had any except for the horse on which he ran away at the battle of Mollwitz."[20] The correspondence between these two most brilliant men of the century reopened when Voltaire wrote to dissuade the desperate warrior from suicide. Soon they were exchanging reproaches and compliments. Voltaire reminded Frederick of the indignities which the philosopher and his niece had suffered at the hands of the King's agents; Frederick answered: "If you had not had to do with a man madly enamored of your fine genius, you would not have gotten off so well. . . . Consider all that as done with, and never let me hear again of that wearisome niece."[21] But then the King stroked the philosophic ego bewitchingly:

> Do you want sweet things? Very good; I will tell you some truths. I esteem in you the finest genius that the ages have borne; I admire your poetry, I love your prose. . . . Never has an author before you had a touch so keen, a taste so sure and delicate. . . . You are charming in conversation; you know how to amuse and instruct at the same time. You are the most seductive being that I know. . . . All depends for a man upon the time when he comes into the world. Though I came too late, I do not regret it, for *I have seen Voltaire,* . . . and he writes to me.[22]

The King supported with substantial contributions Voltaire's campaigns for the Calas and the Sirvens, and applauded the war against *l'infâme,* but he did not share the *philosophes'* trust in the enlightenment of mankind. In the race between reason and superstition he predicted the victory of superstition. So, to Voltaire, September 13, 1766:

> Your missionaries will open the eyes of a few young people. . . . But how many fools there are in the world who do not think! . . . Believe me, if the philosophers founded a government, within half a century the people would create new superstitions. . . . The object of adoration may change, like your French fashions; [but] what does it matter whether people prostrate themselves before a piece of unleavened bread, before the ox Apis, before the Ark of the Covenant, or before a statue? The choice is not worth the trouble; the superstition is the same, and reason gains nothing.[23]

Having accepted religion as a human need, Frederick made his peace with it, and protected all its peaceful forms with full toleration. In conquered

Silesia he left Catholicism undisturbed, except that he opened to all faiths the University of Breslau, which had previously admitted only Catholics. He welcomed, as valuable teachers, the Jesuits who, expelled by Catholic kings, sought refuge under his agnostic rule. He protected as well Mohammedans, Jews, and atheists; and in his reign and realm Kant practiced that freedom of speech and teaching and writing which was so sharply rebuked and ended after Frederick's death. Under this toleration most forms of religion declined in Prussia. In 1780 there was one ecclesiastic per thousand population in Berlin; in Munich there were thirty.[24] Frederick thought that toleration would soon put an end to Catholicism. "It will take a miracle to restore the Catholic Church," he wrote to Voltaire in 1767; "it has been struck by a terrible apoplexy; and you will yet have the consolation of burying it and writing its epitaph."[25] The most thorough of skeptics had forgotten for a moment to be skeptical of skepticism.

II. REBUILDING PRUSSIA

No ruler in history ever worked so hard at his trade, except perhaps his pupil Joseph II of Austria. Frederick disciplined himself as he did his troops, rising usually at five, sometimes at four, working till seven, breakfasting, conferring with his aides till eleven, reviewing his palace guard, dining at twelve-thirty with ministers and ambassadors, working till five, and only then relaxing into music, literature, and conversation. The "midnight" suppers, after the war, began at half past nine, and were over at twelve. He allowed no family ties to distract him, no court ceremonies to burden him, no religious holidays to interrupt his toil. He watched the work of his ministers, dictated almost every move of policy, kept an eye on the treasury; and over all the government he established a Fiscal, or bureau of accounts, empowered to examine any department at any time, and instructed to report any suspicion of irregularity. He punished malfeasance or incompetence so rigorously that official corruption, which flourished everywhere else in Europe, almost disappeared from Prussia.

He prided himself on this, and on the rapid recovery of his devastated country. He began with domestic economies that earned him gibes from the extravagant courts of defeated Austria and France. The royal household was as frugally managed as a tradesman's home. His wardrobe was a soldier's uniform, three old coats, waistcoats soiled with snuff, and one ceremonial robe that lasted him all his life. He dismissed his father's retinue of huntsmen and hunting dogs; this warrior preferred poetry to the hunt. He built no navy, sought no colonies. His bureaucrats were poorly paid, and he provided with like parsimony for the modest court that he maintained at Berlin—while he stayed in Potsdam. Yet the Earl of Chesterfield judged it "the politest, the most shining, the most useful court in Europe for a young fellow to be at," and added, "You will see the arts and wisdom of government better in that country now [1752] than in any other in Europe."[26] Twenty years later, however, Lord Malmesbury, the British minister to Prussia, perhaps with a view to consoling London, reported that there was "in that capital [Berlin] neither an honest man nor a chaste woman."[27]

Frederick checked his parsimony when national defense was concerned. By persuasion and conscription he soon restored his army to its prewar strength; only with that weapon in hand could he maintain the territorial integrity of Prussia against the ambitions of Joseph II and Catherine II. That army, too, had to buttress the laws that gave order and stability to Prussian life. Organized central force, he felt, was the only alternative to disorganized and disruptive force in private hands. He hoped that obedience through fear of force would grow into obedience through habituation to law—which was force reduced to rules and hiding its claws.

He renewed his behest to jurists to codify into one system of law—an "Allgemeine Preussische Landrecht"—the divers and contradictory legislation of many provinces and generations; this task, interrupted by the death of Samuel von Cocceji (1755) and by the war, was resumed by Chancellor Johann von Carmer and Privy Councilor K. G. Svarez, and was completed in 1791. The new code took feudalism and serfdom for granted, but within those limitations it sought to protect the individual against private or public oppression or injustice. It abolished superfluous courts, reduced and quickened legal procedure, moderated penalties, and raised the requirements for appointment to magistracies. No sentence of death could be executed without sanction by the king, and appeal to the king was open to all. He won a reputation for impartial justice, and Prussian courts were soon acknowledged to be the most honest and efficient in Europe.[28]

In 1763 Frederick issued a "Generallandschulreglement" confirming and extending the compulsory education proclaimed by his father in 1716–17. Every child in Prussia, from his fifth to his fourteenth year, was to attend school. It was characteristic of Frederick that Latin was dropped from the elementary curriculum, that old soldiers were appointed as schoolmasters, and that most learning was by semimilitary drill.[29] The King added: "It is a good thing that the schoolmasters in the country teach the youngsters religion and morals. . . . It is enough for the people in the country to learn only a little reading and writing. . . . Instruction must be planned . . . to keep them in the villages and not to influence them to leave."[30]

Economic reconstruction received priority in time and money. Using at first the funds that had been collected for another, now unneeded, campaign, Frederick financed the rebuilding of towns and villages, the distribution of food to hungry communities, the provision of seed for new sowings; he dispersed among the farms sixty thousand horses that could be spared from the army. Altogether 20,389,000 thalers were spent in public relief.[31] War-ravaged Silesia was excused from taxes for six months; eight thousand houses were built there in three years; a land bank advanced money to Silesian farmers on easy terms. Credit societies were established at various centers to encourage agricultural expansion. The marshy area along the lower Oder was drained, providing cultivable land for fifty thousand men. Agents were sent abroad to invite immigrants; 300,000 came.[32]

As serfdom bound the peasant to his lord, there was not in Prussia that freedom to move to the towns which, in England, made possible the rapid development of industry. Frederick worked in a hundred ways to overcome this handicap. He lent money on easy terms to entrepreneurs; he permitted temporary monopolies; he imported workmen; he opened technical schools; he set up a porcelain factory in Berlin. He strove to establish a silk industry, but the mulberry trees languished in the northern cold. He promoted vigorous mining in Silesia, which was rich in minerals. On September 5, 1777, he wrote to Voltaire as one businessman to another: "I am returning from Silesia, with which I am well content. . . . We have sold to foreigners 5,000,000 crowns' worth of linen, 1,200,000 crowns' worth of cloth. . . . A much simpler process than that of Réaumur has been discovered for making iron into steel."[33]

To facilitate trade the King abolished internal tolls, widened harbors, dug canals, and built thirty thousand miles of new roads. Foreign trade was held back by high duties on imports and by embargoes on the export of strategic goods; international chaos compelled the protection of home industry to ensure industrial adequacy in war. Nevertheless Berlin grew as the hub of trade as well as government: in 1721 it had 60,000 population; in 1777 it had 140,000;[34] it was preparing to be the capital of Germany.

To finance this amalgam of feudalism, capitalism, socialism, and autocracy Frederick drew from his people in taxation almost as much as he returned to them in social order, subsidies, and public works. He kept for the state a monopoly on salt, sugar, tobacco, and (after 1781) coffee, and he owned a third of the arable land.[35] He taxed everything, even street singers, and brought in Helvétius to devise an inescapable system of taxgathering. "The new projects of excise [taxation]," wrote an English ambassador, "have really alienated the affections of the people from their sovereign."[36] At his death Frederick left in the treasury 51,000,000 thalers—two and a half times the annual revenue of the state.

Mirabeau *fils*, having made three visits to Berlin, published in 1788 a devastating analysis *De la Monarchie prussienne sous Frédéric le Grand*. Inheriting from his father the free-enterprise principles of the physiocrats, he condemned the Frederician regime as a police state, a bureaucracy choking all initiative and invading every privacy. Frederick might have replied that in the chaotic condition of Prussia after the Seven Years' War *laissez-faire* would have annulled his victory with economic anarchy. Direction was imperative; he was the only one who could effectively command; and he knew no other form of command than that of a general to his troops. He saved Prussia from defeat and collapse, and paid by losing the love of his people. He realized this result, and comforted himself with righteousness:

> Mankind move if you urge them on, and stop as soon as you leave off driving them. . . . Men read little, and have no desire to learn how anything can be managed differently. As for me, who never did them anything but good, they think that I want to put a knife to their throats, so soon as there is any question of introducing a useful improvement, or, indeed, any change at all. In

such cases I have relied on my honest purpose and my good conscience, and on the information in my possession, and have calmly pursued my way.[37]

His will prevailed. Prussia, even in his lifetime, grew rich and strong. Population doubled, education spread, religious intolerance hid its head. It is true that this new order depended upon enlightened despotism, and that when, after Frederick's death, the despotism remained without the enlightenment, the national structure was weakened and collapsed at Jena before a will as strong as Frederick's own. But the Napoleonic edifice too, depending upon one will and brain, collapsed; and in the long run it was Frederick's distant heir and beneficiary Bismarck who chastened the France of Napoleon's heir, and made from Prussia and a hundred principalities a united and powerful Germany.

III. THE PRINCIPALITIES

We remind ourselves again that in the eighteenth century Germany was not a nation but a loose federation of nearly independent states, which formally accepted the "Holy Roman" emperor at Vienna as their head, and sent representatives occasionally to a Reichstag, or Imperial Diet, whose chief functions were to hear speeches, suffer ceremonies, and elect an emperor. The states had a common language, literature, and art, but differed in manners, dress, coinage, and creed. There were some advantages in this political fragmentation: the multiplicity of princely courts favored a stimulating diversity of cultures; the armies were small, instead of being united for the terror of Europe; and a considerable degree of tolerance in religion, custom, and law was forced upon state, church, and people by the ease of emigration. Theoretically the power of each prince was absolute, for the Protestant faith sanctioned the "divine right of kings." Frederick, who recognized no divine right but that of his army, satirized "most small princes, particularly German ones," who "ruin themselves by reckless extravagance, misled by the illusion of their imagined greatness. . . . The youngest son of the youngest son of an appanaged dynasty imagines he is of the same stamp as Louis XIV. He builds his Versailles, keeps mistresses, and has an army . . . strong enough to fight . . . a battle on the stage of Verona."[38]

The most important of the principalities was Saxony. Its age of art and glory ended when Elector Frederick Augustus II allied himself with Maria Theresa against Frederick the Great; the merciless King bombarded and ruined Dresden in 1760; the Elector fled to Poland as its Augustus III, and died in 1763. His grandson Frederick Augustus III inherited the electorate at the age of thirteen, earned the name of "Der Gerechte" (The Just), made Saxony a kingdom (1806), and through many vicissitudes kept his throne till his death (1827).

Karl Eugen, duke of Württemberg, comes into our story chiefly as the friend and enemy of Schiller. He taxed his subjects with inexhaustible ingenuity, sold ten thousand of his troops to France, and maintained what Casanova thought "the most brilliant court in Europe,"[39] with a French theater, Italian opera, and a concatenation of concubines. More important to our narrative is Karl August, reigning duke of Saxe-Weimar from 1775 to 1828; but we shall see him to better advantage surrounded by the stars who brightened his reign—Wieland, Herder, Goethe, and Schiller. He was one of several minor "enlightened despots" who in this age, feeling the influence of Voltaire and the example of Frederick, contributed to the awakening of Germany. The archbishops who ruled Münster, Cologne, Trier, Mainz, and Würzburg-Bamberg fell in line by multiplying schools and hospitals, checking court extravagance, softening class distinctions, reforming prisons, extending poor relief, and bettering the conditions of industry and trade. "It is not easy," wrote Edmund Burke, "to find or to conceive governments more mild and indulgent than these church sovereignties."[40]

Class distinctions, however, were emphasized in most of the German states, as part of the technique of social control. Nobles, clergy, army officers, professional men, merchants, and peasants constituted separate classes; and within every category there were grades each of which stiffened itself with scorn of the next beneath. Marriage outside one's class was almost unthinkable, but some merchants and financiers bought nobility. The nobles held a monopoly of the higher posts in the army and the government, and many of them earned their privileges by bravery or competence; but many were parasites, composed of uniforms, competing for social precedence at the court, and following French fashions in language, philosophy, and mistresses.

It is to the credit of the princes, prelates, and nobles of western Germany that by 1780 they had freed their peasants from serfdom, and on terms that made possible a wide spread of rural prosperity. Reinhold Lenz thought the peasants finer human beings—simpler, heartier, more elemental—than the penny-counting tradesmen or the prancing young aristocrats.[41] Heinrich Jung's autobiography (1777) idealized village life in its daily labor as well as its seasonal festivals; Herder found the folk songs of the peasantry to be truer and profounder than the poetry of the books; and Goethe, in his *Dichtung und Wahrheit*, described the vintage celebration as "pervading a whole district with jubilation," fireworks, song, and wine.[42] This was one side of the German scene; the other was hard labor, high taxes, women old at thirty, illiterate children dressed in rags and begging in the streets. "At one station," Eva König told Lessing in 1770, "there crowded around me . . . eighty beggars; . . . in Munich whole families ran after me, exclaiming that surely one would not let them starve."[43]

In the eighteenth century the family was more important than the state or the school. The German home was the source and center of moral discipline, social order, and economic activity. There the child learned to obey a stern father, take refuge with a loving mother, and share at an early age in the diverse and formative tasks that filled the day. Schiller's "Song of the Bell" gave an ideal picture of "the housewife so modest, . . . wisely governing the circle of the family, training the girls, restraining the boys, and using all spare moments to ply the loom."[44] The wife was subject to the husband, but she was the idol of her children. Outside the home, except at the courts, men usually excluded women from their social life, and so their conversation tended to be either dull or profane. At the courts there were many women of culture and fine manners; some, Eckermann thought, "write an excellent style, and surpass, in that respect, many of our most celebrated authors."[45] As in France, so in Germany, the women of the upper classes had to learn swooning as part of their technique, and a readiness for sentiment melting into tears.

Court morals followed French models in drinking, gambling, adultery, and divorce. Titled ladies, according to Mme. de Staël, changed husbands "with as little difficulty as if they were arranging the incidents of a drama," and with "little bitterness of spirit."[46] The princes set the pace for immorality by selling their soldiers to foreign rulers; so the Landgrave of Hesse-Cassel built an elegant palace, and maintained a sumptuous court, from the proceeds of his *Soldatenhandel*—commerce in soldiery. Altogether, during the American Revolution, German princes sold—or, as they put it, "lent"—thirty thousand troops to England for some £500,000; 12,500 of these men never returned.[47] Outside of Prussia the Germans of the eighteenth century—recalling the horrors of the seventeenth—showed little inclination to war. Apparently "national character" can change from one century to another.

Religion in Germany was more subordinate to the state than in Catholic lands. Divided into sects, it had no awesome pontiff to co-ordinate its doctrine, strategy and defense; its leaders were appointed by the prince, its income depended upon his will. In the middle and lower classes it was a strong faith; only the nobles, the intellectuals, and a few clergymen were affected by the waves of unbelief that swept in from England and France. The Rhine region was mostly Catholic, but it was there that this period saw the rise of a movement boldly challenging the authority of the popes.

In 1763 Johann Nikolaus von Hontheim, auxiliary bishop of Trier, published, under the pseudonym Justinus Febronius, a treatise *De Statu Ecclesiae et legitima Potestate romani Pontificis* (*On the State of the Church, and the Legitimate Power of the Roman Pontiff*). The book was translated into German, French, Italian, Spanish, and Portuguese, and made a stir throughout Western Europe. "Febronius" accepted the primacy of the pope, but only as one of honor and executive administration; the pope is not infallible; appeal should be possible from his decision to a general council, which should have the ultimate legislative authority in the Church. The author distrusted the secret conservative influence of the Roman Curia, and suggested that the excessive centralization of ecclesiastical power had produced the Reformation; decentralization might ease the return of Protestants to the Catholic Church. In matters of human, not divine, law secular princes were entitled to refuse obedience to the papacy; if necessary, they might rightfully separate their national churches from Rome. The Pope condemned the book (February, 1764), but it became "the breviary of the governments."[48] We have seen its influence on Joseph II.

The archbishops of Cologne, Trier, Mainz, and Salzburg favored the views of "Febronius"; they wished to be independent of the pope as the other principalities were of the emperor. On September 25, 1786, they issued the "Punctation [preliminary statement] of Ems" (near Coblenz), which, if it had been put into effect, would have created a new Reformation:

> The pope is and remains the highest authority in the Church, . . . but those [papal] privileges which do not spring from the first Christian centuries but are based on the false Isadoran Decretals, and are disadvantageous to the bishops, . . . can no longer be considered valid; they belong among the usurpations of the Roman Curia; and the bishops are entitled (since peaceful protests are of no avail) themselves to maintain their lawful rights under the protection of the Roman-German Emperor. There should no longer be any appeals [from the bishops] to Rome. . . . The [religious] orders should take no directions from foreign superiors, nor attend general councils outside Germany. No contributions should be sent to Rome. . . . Vacant benefices should be filled not by Rome but by a regular election of native candidates. . . . A German national council should regulate these and other matters.[49]

The German bishops, fearing the financial power of the Curia, gave no support to this declaration; moreover, they hesitated to replace the distant overlordship of Rome with the immediate and less evadable authority of the German princes. The incipient revolt collapsed; Hontheim retracted (1788); the archbishops withdrew their "punctation" (1789), and all was as before.

IV. THE GERMAN ENLIGHTENMENT

Not quite. Education, except in the ecclesiastical principalities, had passed from church to state control. University professors were appointed and paid (with shameful parsimony) by the government, and held the status of public officials. Although all teachers and students were required to subscribe to the religion of the prince, the faculties, until 1789, enjoyed a growing measure of academic freedom. German replaced Latin as the language of instruction. Courses in science and philosophy multiplied, and philosophy was spaciously defined (at the University of Königsberg in Kant's day) as "the ability to think, and to investigate the nature of things without prejudices or sectarianism."[50] Karl von Zedlitz, the devoted Minister of Education under Frederick the Great, asked Kant to suggest means of "holding back the students in the universities from the bread-and-butter studies, and making them understand that their modicum of law, even their theology and medicine, will be much more easily acquired and safely applied if they are in possession of philosophical knowledge."[51]

Many poor students obtained public or private aid for a university education; pleasant is Eckermann's story of how he was helped by kind neighbors at every step of his development.[52] There were no class distinctions in the student body.[53] Any graduate was allowed to lecture under university auspices, for whatever fees he could collect from his auditors; Kant began his professorial career in this way; and such competition from new teachers kept old pundits on their toes. Mme. de Staël judged the twenty-four German universities to be "the most learned in Europe. In no country, not even England, are there so many means of instruction, or of bringing one's capacities to perfection. . . . Since the Reformation the Protestant universities have been incontestably superior to the Catholic; and the literary glory of Germany depends upon these institutions."[54]

Educational reform was in the air. Johann Basedow, inspired by reading Rousseau, issued in 1774 a four-volume *Elementarwerke*, which outlined a plan for teaching children through direct acquaintance with nature. They were to acquire health and vigor through games and physical exercises; they were to receive much of their instruction outdoors instead of being tied to desks; they were to learn languages not through grammar and rote but through naming objects and actions encountered in the day's experience; they were to learn morals by forming and regulating their own social groups; and they were to prepare for life by learning a trade. Religion was to enter into the curriculum, but not as pervasively as before; Basedow openly doubted the Trinity.[55] He established at Dessau (1774) a sample Philanthropinum, which produced pupils whose "sauciness and pertness, omniscience and arrogance"[56] scandalized their elders; but this "progressive education" harmonized with the Enlightenment, and spread rapidly throughout Germany.

Experiments in education were part of the intellectual ferment that agitated the country between the Seven Years' War and the French Revolution. Books, newspapers, magazines, circulating libraries, reading clubs, multiplied enthusiastically. A dozen literary movements sprouted, each with its ideology, journal, and protagonists. The first German daily, *Die Leipziger Zeitung*, had begun in 1660; by 1784 there were 217 daily or weekly newspapers in Germany. In 1751 Lessing began to edit the literary section of the *Vossische Zeitung* in Berlin; in 1772 Merck, Goethe, and Herder issued *Die Frankfurter gelehrte Anzeigen*, or *Frankfurt Literary News;* in 1773–89 Wieland made *Der teutsche Merkur* the most influential literary review in Germany. There were three thousand German authors in 1773, six thousand in 1787; Leipzig alone had 133. Many of these were part-time writers; Lessing was probably the first German who, through many years, made a living by literature. Almost all authors were poor, for copyright protected them only in their own principality; pirated editions severely limited the earnings of author and publisher alike. Goethe lost money on *Götz von Berlichingen*, and made little on *Werther*, the greatest literary success of that generation.

The outburst of German literature is among the major events of the second half of the eighteenth century. D'Alembert, writing from Potsdam in 1763, found nothing worthy of report in German publications;[57] by 1790 Germany rivaled, perhaps surpassed, France in contemporary literary genius. We have noted Frederick's scorn of the German language as raucous and coarse and poisoned with consonants; yet Frederick himself, by his dramatic repulse of so many enemies, inspired Germany with a national pride that encouraged German writers to use their own language and stand up before the Voltaires and the Rousseaus. By 1763 German had refined itself into a literary language, and was ready to voice the German Enlightenment.

This Aufklärung was no virgin birth. It was the painful product of English deism coupled with French free thought on the ground prepared by the moderate rationalism of Christian von Wolff. The major deistic blasts of Toland, Tindal, Collins, Whiston, and Woolston had by 1743 been translated into German, and by 1755 Grimm's *Correspondance* was disseminating the latest French ideas among the German elite. Already in 1756 there were enough freethinkers in Germany to allow the publication of a *Freidenkerlexikon*. In 1763–64 Basedow issued his *Philalethie* (*Love of Truth*), which rejected any divine revelation other than that of nature itself. In 1759 Christoph Friedrich Nikolai, a Berlin bookseller, began *Briefe die neueste Literatur betreffend;* enriched with articles by Lessing, Herder, and Moses Mendelssohn, these *Letters concerning the Latest Literature* continued till 1765 to be a literary beacon of the Aufklärung, warring against extravagance in literature and authority in religion.

Freemasonry shared in the movement. The first lodge of *Freimaurer* was founded at Hamburg in 1733; other lodges followed; members included Frederick the Great, Dukes Ferdinand of Brunswick and Karl August of Saxe-Weimar, Lessing, Wieland, Herder, Klopstock, Goethe, Kleist. Generally these groups favored deism, but avoided open criticism of orthodox belief. In 1776 Adam Weishaupt, professor of canon law at Ingolstadt, organized a kindred secret society, which he called Perfektibilisten, but which later took on the old name of Illuminati. Its ex-Jesuit founder, following the model of the Society of Jesus, divided its associates into grades of initiation, and pledged them to obey their leaders in a campaign to "unite all men capable of independent thought," make man "a masterpiece of reason, and thus attain the highest perfection in the art of government."[58] In 1784 Karl Theodor, elector of Bavaria, outlawed all secret societies, and the Order of the Illuminati suffered an early death.

Even the clergy were touched by the "Clearing Up." Johann Semler, professor of theology at Halle, applied higher criticism to the Bible: he argued (precisely contrary to Bishop Warburton) that the Old Testament could not be inspired by God, since, except in its final phase, it ignored immortality; he suggested that Christianity had been deflected from the teachings of Christ by the theology of St. Paul, who had never seen Christ; and he advised theologians to consider Christianity as a transient form of the effort of man to achieve a moral life. When Karl Bahrdt and others of his pupils rejected all of Christian dogma except belief in God, Semler returned to orthodoxy, and held his chair of theology from 1752 to 1791. Bahrdt described Jesus as simply a great teacher, "like Moses, Confucius, Socrates, Semler, Luther, and myself."[59] Johann Eberhard also equated Socrates with Christ; he was expelled from the Lutheran ministry, but Frederick made him professor of philosophy at Halle. Another clergyman, W. A. Teller, reduced Christianity to deism, and invited into his congregation anyone, including Jews, who believed in God.[60] Johann Schulz, a Lutheran pastor, denied the divinity of

Jesus, and reduced God to the "sufficient ground of the world";[61] he was dismissed from the ministry in 1792.

These vocal heretics were a small minority; perhaps silent heretics were many. Because so many clergymen offered a welcome to reason, because religion was much stronger in Germany than in England or France, and because the philosophy of Wolff had provided the universities with a compromise between rationalism and religion, the German Enlightenment did not take an extreme form. It sought not to destroy religion, but to free it from the myths, absurdities, and sacerdotalism that in France made Catholicism so pleasing to the people and so irritating to the philosophers. Following Rousseau rather than Voltaire, German rationalists recognized the profound appeal that religion makes to the emotional elements in man; and the German nobility, less openly skeptical than the French, supported religion as an aid to morals and government. The Romantic movement checked the advance of rationalism, and prevented Lessing from being to Germany what Voltaire had been to France.

V. GOTTHOLD LESSING: 1729–81

His great-grandfather was burgomaster of a small town in Saxony; his grandfather was for twenty-four years burgomaster of Kamenz, and wrote a plea for religious toleration; his father was the head Lutheran pastor in Kamenz, and wrote a catechism which Lessing learned by heart. His mother was the daughter of the preacher to whose pastorate his father had succeeded. It was natural for her to intend him for the ministry, and for him, sated with piety, to rebel.

His early education, at home and in a grammar school at Meissen, was a mixture of German discipline and classic literature, of Lutheran theology and Latin comedy. "Theophrastus, Plautus, and Terence were my world, which I studied with delight."[62] At seventeen he was sent to Leipzig on a scholarship. He found the town more interesting than the university; he sowed some wild oats, fell in love with the theater and an actress, was allowed behind the scenes, learned the machinery of the stage. At nineteen he wrote a play, and managed to get it produced. Hearing of this sin, the mother wept, the father angrily summoned him home. He smiled them out of their grief, and talked them into paying his debts. His sister, coming upon his poems, found them wondrously improper, and burned them; he threw snow into her bosom to cool her zeal. He was sent back to Leipzig to study philosophy and become a professor; he found philosophy deadly, incurred incurable debts, and fled to Berlin (1748).

There he lived as a literary journeyman, writing reviews, making translations, and joining with Christlob Mylius in editing a short-lived magazine of the theater. By the age of nineteen he was an addict of free thought. He read Spinoza and found him, despite geometry, irresistible. He composed a drama (1749?), *Der Freigeist* (*The Free Spirit*); it contrasted Theophan, a kindly young clergyman, with Adrast, a harsh and raucous freethinker and something of a rogue; here Christianity had much the better of the argument. But about this time Lessing wrote to his father: "The Christian faith is not something which one should accept on trust from one's parents."[63] Now he composed another play, *Die Juden*, discussing the intermarriage of Christian and Jew: a rich and honorable Hebrew, named simply "The Traveler," saves the lives of a Christian noble and his daughter; the nobleman, as reward, offers him his daughter in marriage, but withdraws the offer when the Jew reveals his race; the Jew agrees that the marriage would be unhappy. It was not until five years later (1754) that Lessing, over a game of chess, made the acquaintance of Moses Mendelssohn, who seemed to him to embody the virtues that he had ascribed to "Der Reisende."

Early in 1751 Voltaire, or his secretary, engaged Lessing to translate into German some material which the expatriate philosopher wished to use in a suit against Abraham Hirsch. The secretary allowed Lessing to borrow part of a manuscript of Voltaire's *Le Siècle de Louis XIV*. Later in that year Lessing went to Wittenberg, and took the manuscript with him. Fearing that this uncorrected copy might be used for a pirated edition, Voltaire sent Lessing a politely urgent request for the return of the sheets. Lessing complied, but resented the urgent tone; and this may have colored his subsequent hostility to Voltaire's works and character.

Lessing received the master's degree at the University of Wittenberg in 1752. Back in Berlin, he contributed to various periodicals articles of such positive thought and pungent style that by 1753 he had won an audience large enough to pardon his publishing, at the age of twenty-four, a six-volume collected edition of his work. These included a new play, *Miss Sara Sampson*, which was a milestone in the history of the German stage. Till this time the German theater had presented native comedies, but rarely a native tragedy. Lessing urged his fellow playwrights to turn from French to English models, and to write their own tragic dramas. He praised Diderot for defending the comedy of sentiment and the middle-class tragedy, but it was from England—from George Lillo's *The London Merchant* (1731) and Samuel Richardson's *Clarissa* (1748)—that he took his inspiration for *Miss Sara Sampson*.

The play was performed at Frankfurt-an-der-Oder in 1755, and was well received. It had all the elements of drama: it began with a seduction, ended with a suicide, and connected them with a river of tears. The villain Mellefont (Honeyface) is Richardson's Lovelace; he is a hardened hand at defloration, but deprecates monogamy; he promises marriage to Sara, elopes with her, sleeps with her, then postpones marriage; a former mistress tries to win him back, fails, poisons Sara; Sara's father arrives, ready to forgive everything and accept Mellefont as his son, only to find his daughter dying; Mellefont, quite out of character, kills himself, as if to exemplify Lessing's quip that in tragic dramas the protagonists die of nothing but the fifth act.[64]

He thought that now he could butter his bread by writing for the stage; and as Berlin had no theater he moved to Leipzig (1755). Then the Seven

Years' War broke out, the theater was closed, the book trade languished, Lessing was penniless. He moved back to Berlin, and contributed to Nikolai's *Briefe die neueste Literatur betreffend* articles that marked a new height in German literary criticism. "Rules," said his Letter XIX, "are what the masters of the art choose to observe." In 1760 the Austro-Russian army invaded Berlin; Lessing fled to Breslau as secretary to a Prussian general. During his five years there he haunted taverns, gambled, studied Spinoza, the Christian Fathers, and Winckelmann, and wrote *Laokoon.* In 1765 he returned to Berlin, and in 1766 he sent his most famous book to the press.

Laokoon, oder Über die Grenzen der Malerei und Poesie (Laocoön, or On the Boundaries between Painting and Poetry) derived its immediate stimulus from Winckelmann's *Thoughts on the Imitation of Greek Works in Painting and Sculpture* (1755). When Lessing had written half of his manuscript Winckelmann's *History of Ancient Art* (1764) reached him; he interrupted his essay and wrote: *"The History of Art* by Herr Winc' lmann has appeared. I will not venture a step further without having read this work."[65] He took as his starting point Winckelmann's conception of classic Greek art as characterized by serene dignity and grandeur, and he accepted Winckelmann's claim that the *Laocoön* statuary group in the Vatican Gallery preserved these qualities despite mortal pain. (Laocoön, priest of Apollo at Troy, suspected that there were Greeks in the "Trojan horse," and hurled a spear at it; the goddess Athena, favoring the Greeks, persuaded Poseidon to send up from the sea two huge serpents that twined themselves murderously around the priest and his two sons.) Winckelmann supposed that the *Laocoön*—now reckoned as a work of Rhodian sculptors in the last century before Christ—belonged to the classic age of Pheidias. Why Winckelmann, who had seen and studied the work, ascribed calm grandeur to the distorted features of the priest is a mystery; Lessing accepted the description because he had never seen the statue.[66] He agreed that the sculptor had moderated the expression of pain; he proceeded to inquire into the reason for this artistic restraint; and he proposed to derive it from the inherent and proper limitations of plastic art.

He quoted the dictum of the Greek poet Simonides that "painting is silent poetry, and poetry is eloquent painting."[67] But, he added, the two must keep within their natural bounds: painting and sculpture should describe objects in space, and not try to tell a story; poetry should narrate events in time, and not try to describe objects in space. Detailed description should be left to the plastic arts; when it occurs in poetry, as in Thomson's *The Seasons* or Haller's *Die Alpen,* it interrupts the narrative and obscures the events. "To oppose this false taste, and to counteract these unfounded opinions, is the principal object of the following observations."[68] Lessing soon forgot this purpose, and lost himself in a detailed discussion of Winckelmann's *History.* Here he was without experience or competence, and his exaltation of ideal beauty as the object of art had a sterilizing effect upon German painting. He confused painting with sculpture, applying to both of them the norms proper chiefly to sculpture, and so encouraging the cold formality of Anton Raphael Mengs.

But his influence on German poetry was a blessing; he freed it from long descriptions, scholastic didacticism, and tedious detail, and guided it to action and feeling. Goethe gratefully acknowledged the liberating effect of the *Laocoön*.

Lessing found himself more at home when (April, 1767) he moved to Hamburg as playwright and dramatic critic at eight hundred thalers per year. There he produced his new play, *Minna von Barnhelm*. Its hero, Major Tellheim, returning with honors from the war to his estates, wins betrothal to the wealthy and lovely Minna. A turn of fortune and hostile intrigues reduce him to poverty; he withdraws from his engagement as being no longer a fit husband for the heiress to a great fortune. He disappears; she pursues him and begs him to marry her; he refuses. Perceiving his reason, she contrives a hoax whereby she becomes attractively penniless; now the major offers himself as a mate. Suddenly two messengers enter, one announcing that Minna, the other that Tellheim, has been restored to affluence. Everybody rejoices, and even the servants are precipitated into marriage. The dialogue is sprightly, the characters are improbable, the plot is absurd—but nearly all plots are absurd.

On the same day (April 22, 1767) that saw the opening of the National Theater at Hamburg Lessing issued the prospectus of his *Hamburgische Dramaturgie*. Periodically, in the next two years, these essays commented on the plays produced in Germany, and on the theory of drama in the philosophers. He agreed with Aristotle in judging drama to be the highest species of poetry, and he accepted with reckless inconsistency the rules laid down in the *Poetics:* "I do not hesitate to confess . . . that I deem it as infallible as the *Elements* of Euclid"[69] (who has ceased to be infallible). Yet he implored his countrymen to abandon their subserviency to Corneille, Racine, and Voltaire, and to study the art of drama as revealed in Shakespeare (who ignored Aristotle's rules). He felt that the French drama was too formal to effect that catharsis of the emotions which Aristotle had found in the Greek drama; Shakespeare, he thought, had accomplished this purge better in *Lear*, *Othello*, and *Hamlet* by the intensity of the action and the force and beauty of his language. Forgetting Desdemona's handkerchief, Lessing stressed the need of probability: the good dramatist will avoid dependence upon coincidences and trivialities, and he will so build up each character that the events will follow inevitably from the nature of the persons involved. The dramatists of the Sturm-und-Drang period agreed to take Shakespeare as a model, and gladly liberated the German drama from the French. The nationalist spirit, rising with the victories of Frederick and the defeat of France, inspired and seconded Lessing's appeal, and Shakespeare dominated the German stage for almost a century.

The Hamburg experiment collapsed because the actors quarreled among themselves and concurred only in resenting Lessing's critiques. Friedrich Schröder complained: "Lessing was never able to devote his attention to an entire performance; he would go away and come back, talk with acquaintances, or give himself up to thought; and from traits which excited his passing pleasure he would form a picture that belonged rather to his own mind than to the reality."[70] This perceptive judgment well described Lessing's wayward life and mind.

Shall we stop him here in mid-career and look at him? He was of medium height, proudly erect, strong and supple through regular exercise; with fine features, dark-blue eyes, and light-brown hair that kept its color till his death. He was warm in his friendships, hot in his enmities. He was never so happy as in controversy, and then he dealt wounds with a sharp pen. "Let a critic," he wrote, ". . . first seek out someone with whom he can quarrel. Thus he will gradually get into a subject, and the rest will follow as a matter of course. I frankly admit that I have selected primarily the French authors for this purpose, and among them particularly M. de Voltaire"[71]—which was brave enough. He was a brilliant but reckless talker, quick in repartee. He had ideas about everything, and they were too many and forceful to let him give them order, consistency, or full effect. He enjoyed the pursuit of truth more than the dangerous delusion of having found it. Hence his most re-nowned remark:

> Not the truth of which a man is—or believes himself to be—possessed, but the sincere effort he has made to reach it, makes the worth of a man. For not through the possession, but through the investigation, of truth does he develop those energies in which alone consists his ever-growing perfection. Possession makes the mind stagnant, indolent, proud. If God held enclosed in His right hand all truth, and in His left hand simply the ever-moving impulse toward truth, although with the condition that I should eternally err, and said to me, "Choose!," I should humbly bow before His left hand, and say, "Father, give! Pure truth is for Thee alone."[72]

Two precious friendships remained from the Hamburg fiasco. One was with Elise Reimarus, daughter of Hermann Reimarus, who was professor of Oriental languages in the Hamburg Academy. She made her home a center for the most cultivated society in the city; Lessing joined her circle, and Mendelssohn and Jacobi came when they were in town; we shall see the vital part that this association played in Lessing's history. Still more intimate was his attachment with Eva König. Wife of a silk merchant, mother of four children, she was, Lessing tells us, "bright and animated, gifted with womanly tact and graciousness," and "still had some of the freshness and charm of youth."[73] She too gathered about her a salon of cultured friends, of whom Lessing was *facile princeps*. When her husband left for Venice in 1769 he said to Lessing, "I commend my family to you." It was hardly a provident ar-rangement, for the dramatist had no asset but genius, and owed a thousand thalers. And in October of that year he accepted an invitation from Prince Karl Wilhelm Ferdinand of Brunswick to take charge of the ducal library at Wolfenbüttel. This town had declined to some six thousand souls since the removal (1753) of the reigning Duke's residence to Brunswick, seven miles away, but Casanova reckoned the collection of books and manuscripts to be "the third greatest library in the world."[74] Lessing was to receive six hundred thalers a year, with two assistants and a servant, and free residence in the old ducal palace. In May, 1770, he settled in his new home.

He was not a successful librarian; still he pleased his employer by discovering, amid the manuscripts, a famous but lost treatise by Berengar of Tours (998–1088), questioning transubstantiation. In his now sedentary life he missed the strife and stimulus of Hamburg and Berlin; poring over bad print in poor light weakened his eyes and brought on headaches; his health began to fail. He consoled himself by writing another drama, *Emilia Galotti,* which expressed his resentment of aristocratic privileges and morals. Emilia is the daughter of an ardent republican; their sovereign, the Prince of Guastalla, desires her, has her fiancé murdered, and abducts her to his palace; the father finds her, and, at her insistence, stabs her to death; then he surrenders himself to the Prince's court and is condemned to die, while the Prince continues his career only momentarily disturbed. The passion and eloquence of the play redeemed its finale; it became a favorite tragedy on the German stage; Goethe dated from its première (1772) the resurrection of German literature. Some critics hailed Lessing as a German Shakespeare.

In April, 1775, Lessing went to Italy as cicerone to Prince Leopold of Brunswick. For eight months he enjoyed Milan, Venice, Bologna, Modena, Parma, Piacenza, Pavia, Turin, Corsica, Rome; there he was presented to Pope Pius VI, and may have seen, belatedly, the *Laocoön.* By February, 1776, he was again at Wolfenbüttel. He thought of resigning, but was persuaded to stay by an increase of two hundred thalers in his salary, and by receiving a hundred louis d'or per year as adviser to the Mannheim theater. Now, aged forty-seven, he proposed to the widowed Eva König that she become his wife and bring her children with her. She came, and they were married (October 8, 1776). For a year they experienced a quiet happiness. On Christmas Eve, 1777, she gave birth to a child, who died the next day. Sixteen days later the mother died, too. Lessing lost his savor for life.

Controversy sustained him. On March 1, 1768, Hermann Reimarus passed away, leaving his wife a voluminous manuscript which he had never dared to print. We have said a word elsewhere[75] about this "Schutzschrift für die vernünftigen Verehrer Gottes" (Apology for the Rational Worshipers of God). Lessing had seen some of this remarkable work; he asked Frau Reimarus to let him publish parts of it; she agreed. As librarian he had authority to publish any manuscript in the collection. He deposited the "Schutzschrift" in the library, and then published a part of it in 1774 as *The Toleration of Deists, . . . by an Anonymous Writer.* It made no stir. But the supernatural experts were aroused by the second portion of Reimarus' manuscript, which Lessing issued in 1777 as *Something More from the Papers of the Anonymous Writer, concerning Revelation.* It argued that no revelation addressed to a single people could win universal acceptance in a world of so many diverse races and faiths; only a minority of humanity had yet, after seventeen hundred years, heard of the Judaeo-Christian Bible; consequently it could not be accepted as God's revelation to mankind. A final fragment, *The Aims of Jesus and His Disciples* (1778), presented Jesus not as the Son of God but as a fervent mystic who shared the view of some Jews that the world as then known would soon end, and be followed by the establishment of God's kingdom on earth; the Apostles (said Reimarus) so understood him, for they hoped to be appointed to thrones in this coming kingdom. When the dream collapsed with Jesus' despairing cry on the Cross—"My God, my God, why hast Thou forsaken me?"—the Apostles (Reimarus supposed) invented the fable of his resurrection to conceal his defeat, and pictured him as the rewarding and avenging judge of the world.

The shocked theologians attacked these "Wolfenbüttel Fragments" in over thirty articles in the German press. Johann Melchior Goeze, chief Hamburg pastor, charged Lessing with secretly agreeing with the "Anonymous Writer"; this hypocrite, he urged, should be punished by both Church and state. Milder opponents reproved Lessing for publishing in intelligible German doubts that should have been expressed, if at all, in Latin to an esoteric few. Lessing replied in eleven pamphlets (1778) that rivaled Pascal's *Lettres provinciales* in gay sarcasm and deadly wit. "No head was safe from him," said Heine; "many a skull he struck off from pure wantonness, and then he was mischievous enough to hold it up to the public to show that it was empty."[76] Lessing reminded his assailants that freedom of judgment and discussion was a vital element in the program of the Reformation; moreover, the people had a right to all available knowledge; otherwise one Roman pope would be preferable to a hundred Protestant prophets. After all (he argued), the worth of Christianity will remain even if the Bible be a human document and its miracles mere pious fables or natural events. — The ducal government confiscated the Wolfenbüttel Fragments and the Reimarus manuscript, and ordered Lessing to publish nothing further without the approval of the Brunswick censor.

Silenced in his pulpit, Lessing turned to the stage, and wrote his finest play. Made insolvent again by the expenses involved in the sickness and death of his wife, he borrowed three hundred thalers from a Hamburg Jew to provide the leisure to finish *Nathan der Weise*. He placed the action in Jerusalem during the Fourth Crusade. Nathan is a pious Jewish merchant whose wife and seven sons are slaughtered by Christians demoralized through years of war. Three days later a friar brings him a Christian infant whose mother has just died, and whose father, recently slain in battle, has on several occasions saved Nathan from death. Nathan names the child Recha, brings her up as his daughter, and teaches her only those religious doctrines on which Jews, Christians, and Moslems are agreed.

Eighteen years later, while Nathan is away on business, his house burns down; Recha is rescued by a young Knight Templar who disappears without identifying himself; Recha thinks him a miraculous angel. Nathan, returning, searches for the rescuer to reward him, is insulted by him as a Jew, but persuades him to come and receive Recha's gratitude. He comes, falls in love with her and she with him; but when he learns that she was of Christian birth and is not being reared as a Christian, he wonders is he not bound by his knightly oath to report the matter to the Christian Patriarch of Jerusalem. He describes his problem to the Patriarch without naming individuals; the Patriarch guesses they are Nathan and Recha, and vows to have Nathan put to death. He sends a friar to spy on the Jew. But this is the same friar who brought Recha to Nathan eighteen years before; he has observed, through these years, the kindly wisdom of the merchant; he tells him of his danger, and deplores the religious animosity that has made men so murderous.

Saladin, now governor of Jerusalem, is in financial straits. He sends for Nathan, hoping to arrange a loan. Nathan comes, senses Saladin's need, and offers the loan before being asked. The Sultan, knowing Nathan's reputation for wisdom, inquires which of the three religions he considers best. Nathan answers with a judicious variation of the story that Boccaccio had ascribed to the Alexandrian Jew Melchizedek: A precious ring is passed down from generation to generation to designate the legitimate heir of a rich estate. But in one of these generations the father loves his three sons with such equal fervor that he has three similar rings made, and privately gives one to each son. After his death the sons dispute as to which ring is the original and only true one; they bring the matter to court where it is still undecided. The loving father was God; the three rings are Judaism, Christianity, and Islam; history has not yet decided which creed is the true law of God. Nathan gives a new turn to the tale: the original ring was supposed to make its wearer virtuous; but as none of the three sons is more virtuous than other men, it is likely that the original ring was lost; each ring—each faith—is true only insofar as it makes its wearer virtuous. Saladin so admires Nathan's answer that he rises and embraces him. — Shortly after this philosophical parley an Arabic manuscript turns up which shows that the Templar and Recha are children of the same father. They mourn that they cannot marry, but rejoice that they may now love each other as brother and sister, blessed by Nathan the Jew and Saladin the Mohammedan.

Was Nathan modeled on Moses Mendelssohn? There are resemblances between the two, as we shall see in a later chapter; and, despite many differences, it is probable that Lessing found in his friend much to inspire his idealization of the merchant of Jerusalem. Perhaps Lessing, in his eagerness to preach toleration, painted the Jew and the Moslem with more sympathy than the Christian; the Templar is, in his first meeting with Nathan, fanatically harsh, and the Patriarch (Lessing's memory of Goeze?) hardly does justice to the kindly and enlightened bishops who were then governing Trier, Mainz, and Cologne. The Christian public of Germany repudiated the play as unfair when it was published in 1779; several of Lessing's friends joined in the criticism. *Nathan the Wise* did not reach the stage till 1783, and on the third night the house was empty. In 1801 a version prepared by Schiller and Goethe was well received at Weimar, and thereafter the play remained for a century a favorite in German theaters.

A year before his death Lessing issued his final appeal for understanding. He couched it in religious terms, as if to mollify resistance and provide a bridge from old ideas to new. In some aspects the essay *The Education of the Human Race* (*Die Erziehung des Menschengeschlects*, 1780) justifies the old ideas; then we perceive that the apology is a plea for the Enlightenment. All history may be viewed as a divine revelation, as a gradual education of mankind. Every great religion was a stage in that step-by-step illumination; it was not, as some Frenchmen had supposed, a trick imposed upon credulous people by self-seeking priests; it was a world theory intended to civilize humanity, to inculcate virtue, decency, and social unity. In one stage (the Old Testament) religion sought to make men virtuous by promising them worldly goods in a long life; in another stage (the New Testament) it sought to overcome the discouraging discrepancy between virtue and earthly success by promising rewards after death; in both cases the appeal was adjusted to the limited understanding of the people at the time. Each religion contained a precious kernel of truth, which may have owed its acceptance to the coating of error that sweetened it. If, around the basic beliefs, theologians developed dogmas hard to understand, like original sin and the Trinity, these doctrines too were symbols of truth and instruments of education: God may be conceived as one power with many aspects and meanings; and sin is original in the sense that we are all born with a tendency to resist moral and social laws.[77] But supernatural Christianity is only a step in the evolution of the human mind; a higher stage comes when the race learns to reason, and when men grow strong and clear enough to do the right because it is seen to be right and reasonable, rather than for material or heavenly rewards. That stage has been reached by some individuals; it has not yet come to the race, but "it will come! It will assuredly come, . . . the time of a new, eternal Gospel!"[78] Just as the average individual recapitulates in his growth the intellectual and moral development of the race, so the race slowly passes through the intellectual and moral development of the superior individual. To put it Pythagoreanly, each of us is reborn and reborn until his education —his adjustment to reason— is complete.

What were Lessing's final views on religion? He accepted it as an immense aid to morality, but he resented it as a system of dogmas demanding acceptance on pain of sin, punishment, and social obloquy. He thought of God as the inner spirit of reality, causing development and itself developing; he thought of Christ as the most ideal of men, but only metaphorically an incarnation of this God; and he hoped for a time when all theology would have disappeared from Christianity, and only the sublime ethic of patient kindness and universal brotherhood would remain. In the draft of a letter to Mendelssohn he declared his adherence to Spinoza's view that body and mind are the outside and inside of one reality, two attributes of one substance identical with God. "The orthodox conceptions of deity," he told Jacobi, "no longer exist for me; I cannot endure them. *Hen kai pan*—One and All! I know of nothing else."[79] In 1780 Jacobi, visiting him at Wolfenbüttel, asked him for help in refuting Spinoza, and was shocked by Lessing's reply: "There is no other philosophy but Spinoza's. . . . If I were to call myself after someone, I know of no other name."[80]

Lessing's heresies, and his occasional truculence in controversy, left him lonely in his final years. He had a few friends in Brunswick, with whom, now and then, he came to chat and play chess. His wife's children lived with him in Wolfenbüttel; he devoted entirely to them the little legacy she had left. But his adversaries denounced him throughout Germany as a monstrous atheist. He defied them, and dared to oppose the man who paid his salary: when Karl Wilhelm Ferdinand, now (1780) duke of Brunswick, threw into prison a young Jew who had incurred his displeasure, Lessing visited the youth in jail, and later took him into his house to win back health.

His own health was gone. His eyesight was now so dim that he could hardly read. He suffered from asthma, weakening of the lungs, hardening of the arteries. On February 3, 1781, on a visit to Brunswick, he experienced a severe asthmatic attack, and vomited blood. He instructed his friends: "When you see me about to die, call a notary; I will declare before him that I die in none of the prevailing religions."[81] On February 15, as he lay in bed, some friends gathered in the next room. Suddenly the door of his room opened; Lessing appeared, bent and weak, and raised his cap in greeting; then he sank to the floor in an apoplectic stroke. A theological journal announced that at his death Satan bore him away to hell as another Faust who had sold his soul.[82] He left so little money that the Duke had to pay for his funeral.

He was the herald of Germany's greatest literary age. In the year of his passing Kant published the epochal *Critique of Pure Reason*, and Schiller published his first play. Goethe looked up to Lessing as the great liberator, the father of the German Enlightenment. "In life," said Goethe to Lessing's shade, "we honored you as one of the gods; now that you are dead your spirit reigns over all souls."

VI. THE ROMANTIC REACTION

Goethe spoke for a small minority; the great majority of the German people clung to their Christian heritage, and they hailed as divinely inspired the poet who sang their faith. Six years after Handel stirred at least Ireland with the heavenly strains of *Messiah*, Friedrich Gottlieb Klopstock won the heart of Germany with the first fervent cantos of *Der Messias* (1748–73).

Born in 1724, Klopstock antedated Lessing by five years, survived him by twenty-two. Lessing, the son of a clergyman, became a freethinker; Klopstock, the son of a lawyer, took as a main mission of his life the composition of an epic poem on the life of Christ. He was so aflame with his theme that he published the first three cantos when still a lad of twenty-four. These unrhymed hexameters won so grateful an audience that when, a year later, he proposed to his cousin, letters came to her from various parts of Germany urging her to accept him; she refused. But Frederick V of Denmark, on the recommendation of his minister Johann von Bernstorff, invited Klopstock to come and live at the Danish court and finish his epic at four hundred thalers a year. On his way to Copenhagen the poet took kindly to a Hamburg admirer, Margareta Moller; in 1754 he married her; in 1758 she died, breaking his heart and darkening his verse. He commemorated her in the fifteenth canto of *The Messiah,* and in some of the most moving of his odes. He stayed in Copenhagen twenty years, fell from favor when Bernstorff was dismissed, returned to Hamburg, and in 1773 published the final cantos of his massive poem.

It began with an invocation echoing Milton; then through twenty cantos it told the sacred story from the meditations of Christ on the Mount of Olives to his ascension into heaven. After taking almost as long to write his epic as Jesus had taken to live it, Klopstock concluded with a grateful Te Deum:

> Lo, I have reached my goal! The stirring thought
> Thrills through my spirit. Thine all-powerful arm,
> My Lord, my God, alone hath guided me
> By more than one dark grave, ere I might reach
> That distant goal! Thou, Lord, hast healed me still,
> Hast shed fresh courage o'er my sinking heart,
> Which held with death its near companionship;
> And if I gazed on terrors, their dark shapes
> Soon disappeared, for thou protectedst me!
> Swiftly they vanished. — Savior, I have sung
> Thy Covenant of Mercy. I have trod
> My fearful path! My hope hath been in Thee![83]

The Messiah was welcomed by orthodox Germany as the best poetry yet written in the German language. Goethe tells of a Frankfurt councilor who read the first ten cantos "every year in Passion Week, and thus refreshed himself for the entire year." As for himself, Goethe could enjoy the epic only by "discarding certain requirements which an advancing cultivation does not willingly abandon."[84] Klopstock poured his piety so profusely into his verse that his poem became a succession of lyrics and Bachian chorales rather than the fluent narrative that an epic should be; and we find it difficult to follow a lyric flight through twenty cantos and twenty-five years.

As Voltaire generated his opposite in Rousseau, so Lessing, by his skepticism, rationalism, and intellectualism, made Germany feel the need of writers who would, in contrast, recognize the place and rights of feeling, sentiment, imagination, mystery, romance, and the supernatural in human life. In some Germans of this period, especially women, the cult of *Empfindsamkeit* (sensibility) became a religion as well as a fashion. Darmstadt had a "Circle of Sensitives" whose members made a principle and ritual of sentiment and emotional expression. Rousseau was the Messiah of these spirits. His influence in Germany was far greater than Voltaire's; Herder and Schiller acknowledged him as a fountainhead; Kant's *Critique of Practical Reason* was suffused with Rousseau; Goethe began with Rousseau ("*Gefühl ist Alles*"), went on to Voltaire ("*Gedenke zu leben!*"), and ended by knocking their heads together. From England, meanwhile, came the poets of feeling, James Thomson, William Collins, Edward Young, and the novelists of feeling, Richardson and Sterne. The *Reliques* of Percy and the "Ossianic" poems of Macpherson aroused interest in medieval poetry, mystery, and romance; Klopstock and Heinrich von Gerstenberg brought to life the pre-Christian mythology of Scandinavia and Germany.

Johann Georg Hamann, before 1781, was the *Kapellmeister* of the revolt against reason. Born, like Kant, in cloudy Königsberg, strongly imbued by his father with religious feeling, educated in the university, he labored in poverty as a tutor, and found solace in a Protestant faith resilient to all the blows of the Enlightenment. Reason, he contended, is only a part of man, lately developed and not fundamental; instinct, intuition, feeling, are deeper; and a true philosophy will base itself upon the whole nature and gamut of man. Language originated not as a product of reason but as a gift of God for the expression of feeling. Poetry is deeper than prose. Great literature is written not by knowledge and observance of rules and reasons, but by that indefinable quality called genius, which, guided by feeling, overleaps all rules.

Friedrich Jacobi agreed with Hamann and Rousseau. Spinoza's philosophy, he said, is perfectly logical if you accept logic, but it is false because logic never reaches the heart of reality, which is revealed only to feeling and faith. God's existence cannot be proved by reason, but feeling knows that without belief in God the life of man is a tragic and hopeless futility.

With this exaltation of feeling and poetry, the Teutonic soul was primed for such flights of imaginative literature as made the second half of the eighteenth century in Germany recall the fervor and fertility of Elizabethan England. Magazines of poetry multiplied, suffering their usual brief tenure of life. Johann Heinrich Voss, besides translating Homer, Virgil, and Shakespeare, wrote a tender novel in verse, *Luise* (1783–95), which won the heart of Germany and stirred Goethe to rivalry. Salomon Gessner gained an international audience with his delicate lyrics and prose pastorals. Matthias Claudius touched a hundred thousand mothers with idyllic songs of domesticity, like his "Wiegenlied bei Mondenschein zu singen" (Lullaby to Sing by the Light of the Moon):

So schlafe nun, du Kleine!	Sleep now, my little girl!
Was weinest du?	Why do you cry?
Sanft ist im Mondenscheine	Soft in the moonlight,
Und süss die Ruh.	And sweet, is rest.
Auch kommt der Schlaf geschwinder,	Then sooner comes sleep,
Und sonder Müh.	And without pain.
Der Mond freut sich der Kinder,	The moon rejoices in children,
Und liebet sie.	And loves you.[85]

Gottfried Bürger had all the qualities of a romantic genius. Son of a pastor, he was sent to Halle and Göttingen to study law, but his dissolute life led to his withdrawal from college. In 1773 he won universal absolution of his sins by his ballad "Lenore." Lenore's lover goes off with Frederick's army to the siege of Prague. Each morning she starts up from her dreams and asks, "Wilhelm, are you faithless, or dead? How long will you tarry?" The war ends; the troops return; wives and mothers and children greet them with joy and thanks to God.

Sie frug den Zug wohl auf und ab	She questioned all in that parade,
Und frug nach allen Namen,	And begged of each his name,
Doch keiner war der Kundschaft gab	But there was none who gave her word,
Von allen, so da kamen.	None of all who came.
Als nun das Heer vorüber war,	And when the soldiers all were gone
Zerraufte sie ihr Rabenhaar,	She tore her raven hair,
Und warf sich hin zur Erde	And threw herself upon the ground
Mit wütiger Gebärde.	In throes of wild despair.

Her mother tells her that "what God does is well done"; Lenore answers that this is a delusion, and she begs for death. The mother talks to her of heaven and hell; Lenore replies that heaven is to be with Wilhelm, hell is to be without him. All day long she raves. At night a rider draws up at her door, gives no name, bids her come with him and be his bride. She rides behind him on his black horse, rides all through the night. They come to a cemetery; ghosts dance around them. Suddenly the horseman turns into a corpse; Lenore finds herself clinging to a skeleton. While she hovers between life and death spirits wail these words:

Geduld, Geduld! Wenn's Herz auch bricht!	Patience, patience! Even when the heart breaks!
Mit Gott im Himmel hadre nicht.	With God in heaven quarrel not.
Des Leibes bist du ledig;	Of your body you are shorn;
Gott sei der Seele gnädig!	God have mercy on your soul![86]

VII. STURM UND DRANG

From the piety of Klopstock and the tenderness of Gessner the Romantic movement surged on to the irreverent individualism, the "storming and striving" of German youth in the ecstasy of moral and social revolt. The stiff aristocracy of the courts, the fading dogmas of the preachers, the dreary money-grubbing of the business class, the dulling routine of bureaucrats, the pompous pedantry of pundits—all aroused the resentment of young Germans conscious of ability and deprived of place. They listened to Rousseau's cry for naturalness and freedom, but took no stock in his apotheosis of the "general will." They agreed with him in rejecting materialism, rationalism, and determinism, and with Lessing in preferring the lusty irregularity of Shakespeare to the cramping classicism of Corneille and Racine. They relished Voltaire's wit, but thought they found a desert where he had passed. They were thrilled by the rebellion of the American colonies against England. "We wished the Americans all success," Goethe recalled; "the names of Franklin and Washington began to shine and sparkle in the firmament of politics and war."[87] These *Stürmer und Dränger* felt the intoxication of physical adolescence and mental awakening, and bemoaned the incubus of the old upon the young, of the state upon the soul. They were all for originality, for direct experience and unhindered expression, and some of them believed that their genius exempted them from the law. They felt that time was on their side, that the near future would see their victory. "Oh," exclaimed Goethe, "that was a good time when Merck and I were young!"[88]

Some rebels expressed their philosophy by defying the conventions of dress and replacing them with conventions of their own; so Christoph Kaufmann went about with head uncovered, hair uncombed, and shirt open to the navel.[89] But this was exceptional; most of the protagonists, barring a suicide or two, avoided such inverted sartorial display; and some of them were well-to-do. Goethe himself was one of the progenitors of Sturm und Drang with his play *Götz von Berlichingen* (1773); and in the following year his *Werther* became the triumphant standard of Romanticism; Schiller joined the movement with *Die Räuber* (1781); but these complex and evolving spirits soon left the campaign to more impassioned and weakly-rooted youths.

Johann Merck was one of the founding fathers. To all appearances he was sane and strong; he had gone through university, was *persona grata* at the court of Hesse-Darmstadt, became paymaster general of the army, and had a reputation for both sharp intelligence and practical ability. Goethe, meeting him in 1771, was favorably impressed, and shared with him and Herder in maintaining a critical review, the *Frankfurter gelehrte Anzeigen;* hence the rebels were at first called "Frankfurters."[90] Familiar with business and politics, traveling through Germany and into Russia, Merck saw and satirized the vanities of wealth, the tedium of courts, and the exploitation of the peasantry. Finding himself powerless to reform these conditions, he became bitter and cynical. Goethe called him "Mephistopheles Merck," and took himself and Merck as part models for the protagonists in *Faust.* Reverses in business and misery in marriage unsettled Merck's mind. He sank into debt, from which the Duke of Saxe-Weimar, at Goethe's request, rescued him. He fell a prey to persistent melancholy, and killed himself at the age of fifty (1791).

Even more tragic was the career of Reinhold Lenz. Son of a Lutheran pastor in Livonia, his weak nerves and excitable temperament were affected in childhood by stress on the doctrines of sin and hell.[91] He was helped for a time by hearing Kant's lectures in Königsberg; Kant introduced him to Rousseau's writings, and soon Lenz spoke of *La Nouvelle Héloïse* as the best book ever printed in France. At Strasbourg he met Goethe, was fascinated by his positive character, imitated him in thought and style, wrote lyrics so much like Goethe's that they were included in some editions of Goethe's works. He went on to Sesenheim, fell in love (after Goethe) with Friederike Brion, and composed fervent poems in her praise. He assured her that unless she returned his love he would kill himself; she did not and he did not. He moved to Weimar, was befriended by Goethe, envied Goethe's success, mocked Goethe's relation with Charlotte von Stein, and was invited by the Duke to leave the duchy. He had considerable talent as poet and dramatist. One of his plays, *Die Soldaten,* sharply satirized class distinctions and bourgeois life; its central character is a middle-class girl who, aspiring in vain to marry an officer, becomes a prostitute and solicits her unrecognized father in the streets. Himself too unstable to find a firm footing in life, Lenz wandered from post to post and failure to failure, suffered spells of madness, repeatedly tried suicide, and died insane (1792).

Maximilian von Klinger was the cleverest of the *Stürmer.* He denounced the world and rose to high place in it; he indulged in violent speech in his plays, and became curator of the University of Dorpat; he enjoyed all the oats and follies of youth and lived to be seventy-nine. It was of him that Goethe wrote the perceptive line, "In girls we love what they are, but in young men what they promise to be." Klinger's most famous play, *Sturm und Drang* (1776), written at the age of twenty-four, gave its name and mood to the movement. It showed European rebels expatriating themselves to America in the hope of finding free outlets for their individualities; its language was that of passion run wild; its gospel was that of genius liberated from all rules. Klinger served in the Austrian and Russian armies, married a natural daughter of Catherine the Great, subsided into a professorship, and congealed into a pillar of the state.

Wilhelm Heinse capped *Sturm und Drang* with a novel, *Ardinghello* (1787), which united anarchism, nihilism, communism, fascism, amoralism, and will to power in a revel of sensuality and crime. Crime is not crime, says the hero, if it is brave; the only real crime is weakness; the truest virtues are strength and courage of body and will. Life is the manifestation of elemental instincts, and we miss the mark if we brand these as immoral. So Ardinghello seduces and murders at opportunity or whim, and sees in his unshackled passions nature's highest law. He describes the exploits of Hannibal, honors him as a superman, and asks: "What are millions of men—who all their lives have not had a single hour like his—compared with this one man?"[92] He founds a communistic society with communism of women, woman suffrage, and the worship of the elements as the only religion.

In the confused whirlwind of Sturm und Drang some dominating ideas gave the movement character and influence. Most of its leaders came from the middle class, and began their revolt as a protest against the privileges of birth, the insolence of office, and the luxury of prelates feasting on peasants' tithes. They all agreed in commiserating the lot, and idealizing the character, of the peasant, serf or free. They challenged women to discard their fashions and farthingales, their sentiment and swooning and submissive piety, and summoned them to come and share the exciting life of the emancipated mind and the roaming male. They redefined religion as a divine afflatus in a soul whose genius is part of the creative urge and mystery of the world. They identified nature with God, and concluded that to be natural was to be divine. They took the medieval legend of Faust as a symbol for the intellectual hunger and burning ambition that breaks through all barriers of tradition, convention, morals, or laws. So "Maler Müller," long before Goethe, wrote a drama, *Fausts Leben*, "because I early recognized him as a great fellow . . . who feels all his power, feels the bridle that fate has put upon him, and tries to throw it off, who has the courage to hurl everything down that steps in his way."[93]

The enthusiasm and exaggerations of Sturm und Drang marked it as an expression of intellectual adolescence, the voice of a minority condemned to grow up and simmer down. The movement won no popular support, for tradition and the people have always supported each other. Finding themselves without a base in the structure of German life, the Stormers made their peace with the princes, and, like the *philosophes*, trusted that enlightened rulers would lead the way to intellectual liberation and social reform. Herder, Goethe, and Schiller touched the movement in their youth, withdrew from the consuming fire, clipped their claws and folded their wings, and gratefully accepted the protection of Weimar's genial dukes.

VIII. THE ARTISTS

The Germans of this age were quite equal to the French and Italians in art. They took baroque from Italy and rococo from France, but they gave Winckelmann and Mengs to Italy, and their expatriates David Roentgen, "Jean" Riesener, and Adam Weisweiler were preferred to French cabinet-makers by French kings and queens; so Louis XVI paid eighty thousand livres for a *secrétaire* by Roentgen.[94] The *Residenz* at Munich, Frederick's Neues Palais at Potsdam, and the homes of well-to-do Germans were crowded with massive furniture elaborately carved, until, at the end of this age, a lighter style came in from England's Chippendale and Sheraton. — The Meissen factories had been injured in the war, but Nymphenburg, Ludwigsburg, Potsdam, and other centers carried on the arts of porcelain and faïence. German shelves, mantels, tables, and desks smiled with jolly, graceful dancing, singing, kissing figurines.

On a larger scale there was admirable statuary. Martin Klauer made a bust of Goethe in the early Weimar days—eager, bright-eyed, confident.[95] Martin's son Ludwig did not do so well with Schiller;[96] better is the *Schiller* now in a square at Stuttgart, by Johann von Dannecker. Supreme in German sculpture in this age was Johann Gottfried Schadow, who became court sculptor at Berlin in 1788. In 1791 he made a head of Frederick; in 1793 he carved him in full length; in 1816 he cast in bronze a smaller *Frederick*[97]—an unforgettable masterpiece. He cast the bronze *Quadriga of Victory* for the Brandenburg Gate, and achieved an almost classical loveliness in the marble group of Crown Princess Luise and her sister Friederike.

Germany had so many painters that she could afford to surrender a dozen of them to Italy and still have good ones left. Tischbeins were so numerous in the brotherhood of the brush that we can confuse them with ease. Johann Heinrich Tischbein, painter to the court of Hesse-Cassel, made a fine portrait of Lessing. His nephew Johann Friedrich Tischbein painted in Cassel, Rome, Naples, Paris, Vienna, The Hague, Dessau, Leipzig, and St. Petersburg, and made a charming group of the children of Duke Karl August of Saxe-Weimar. Johann Heinrich Wilhelm Tischbein lived in Italy 1787–99, painted a famous picture, *Goethe in the Roman Campagna*, and returned to be court painter to the Duke of Oldenburg.

One source of the German *Drang nach Italien* was Adam Friedrich Oeser, sculptor, painter, etcher, teacher, champion of art reform on classic lines; Winckelmann lived with him for a time in Dresden, criticized his drawing, admired his character, and said, "He knows as much as one can know outside of Italy."[98] In 1764 Oeser was made director of the art academy at Leipzig; Goethe visited him there, and caught the Italian fever.

Of those artists who remained in Germany Daniel Chodowiecki led the list, and he was a Pole. Born in Danzig, left an orphan, he learned to support himself by drawings, engravings, and paintings. In 1743 he moved to Berlin, and became German in all but name. He told the life of Christ in superb miniatures which gave him a national reputation; then, in a more Voltairean mood, he painted *Jean Calas and His Family*. His drawings were in such demand that for years hardly any major work of literature was published in Prussia without illustrations from his hand. In the finest of his etchings he sketched his own household: himself at work, his wife proudly surveying her five children, the walls covered with art. With a red crayon he drew the figure of Lotte Kestner, whom Goethe loved and lost. In his work there is a grace of line and a tenderness of feeling that distinguish him from Hogarth, to whom he was often compared because of his many pictures of common life; but he rightly deprecated such a correlation. Often he was inspired by Watteau; *A Gathering in the Zoological Garden*[99] has Watteau's flair for the open air and the entrancing swirl of feminine robes.

Anton Graff left a portrait of Chodowiecki[100]—all smiles and curls and avoirdupois—and a portrait of himself[101] looking up from his work but dressed as for a ball. He put more spirit into his lovely portrait of his wife,[102] caught the pride of the actress Korona Schröter,[103] and glorified with golden raiment the overflowing form of Frau Hofrat Böhme.[104]

Last of the line in this half century was Asmus Jakob Carstens, who absorbed Winckelmann's gospel in letter and spirit, and completed the classic revival in German painting. Born in Schleswig, schooled in Copenhagen and Italy, he worked chiefly in Lübeck and Berlin; but he went back to Italy in 1792, and feasted on the remains of ancient sculpture and architecture. He did not know that time had washed away the color from Greek art, leaving only line; so, like Mengs, he reduced his brush to a pencil, and aimed only at perfect form. He was disturbed by the physical imperfections of the models who posed in the studios; he decided to trust to his imagination; and he delighted in picturing Greek gods, and scenes from Greek mythology, as he and Winckelmann conceived them. From these he passed to illustrating Dante and Shakespeare. Always his passion for line and form missed color and life; and even when he achieved an almost Michelangelesque vision of godlike figures, as in *The Birth of Light*,[105] we can only praise him for remembering the Sistine Chapel's paintings as accurately as Mozart remembered its music. Rome returned his affection, and gave his work (1795) one of the most extensive and celebrated exhibitions that any modern artist had ever received. There, three years later, he died, still only forty-four years old. Art, like sex, can be a consuming fire.

The neoclassic mood dominated the architectural embellishment of Potsdam and Berlin under Frederick the Great. He had begun the Neues Palais in 1755; he did not let the war deter him from the project. Three architects —Büring, Gontard, and Manger—shared in designing it; they mingled classic with baroque in an imposing edifice that recalled the palaces of ancient Rome; and in the interior decoration they rivaled the finest specimens of French rococo. The Französische Kirche, or French Church, in Berlin had a classic portico; Gontard and his pupil Georg Unger added a classic tower (1780–85). Unger augmented the majesty of Berlin with a Königliche Bibliothek, or Royal Library, in 1774–80. The Brandenburger Tor, or Brandenburg Gate, raised by Karl Langhans in 1788–91, was frankly modeled on the Propylaea of the Acropolis; it barely survived the Second World War, but lost the famous *Quadriga*, the four-horse chariot with which Schadow had crowned it.

Other German cities were minting monuments to house princes, nobles, and cadavers. Frederick's sister Wilhelmine beautified Bayreuth with a palace of charming rococo (1744–73). At Cassel Simon-Louis du Ry designed (1769 f.) the sumptuous dance hall and Blue Room in the *Schloss* of the Landgrave of Hesse-Cassel. On the Rhine near Düsseldorf Nikolaus von Pigage built the lordly Schloss Benrath (1755–69); and near Ludwigsburg Philippe de La Guépière raised the pretty Palace of Monrepos (1762–64).

IX. AFTER BACH

Germany was blessed and excited with music beyond any other nation but Italy. A family without musical instruments was an abnormality. Schools taught music almost on a par with religion and reading. Church music was in decline because science and philosophy, cities and industry, were secularizing minds; the great Lutheran hymns still resounded, but song was passing from church choirs to lieder, *Singspiele*, and opera. Johann Peter Schulz opened a new era in song with his *Lieder im Volkston* (1782); henceforth Germany enjoyed an unquestioned leadership in this application of music to lyric poetry.

The mechanical improvement of the piano stimulated the spread of concerts and the rise of instrumental virtuosi. Performers like Johann Schobert, Abt Vogler, and Johann Hummel conquered a dozen cities. On March 10, 1789, Hummel, then eleven years old, gave a piano recital at Dresden; he did not know that Mozart was to be in the audience; during the concert he saw and recognized his former teacher; as soon as his piece was finished he made his way through the applauding assemblage and embraced Mozart with warm expressions of homage and joy.[106] Abt (i.e., Abbot) Vogler won his title by being ordained as a priest (1773); at Mannheim he was both court chaplain and music director. As a writer on music he was one of the most original and influential of the century; as a virtuoso on the organ he won the jealousy of Mozart; as a teacher he formed Weber and Meyerbeer; as a papal legate he made Mannheim laugh by wearing blue stockings, carrying his breviary with his music, and sometimes keeping his audience waiting while he finished his prayers.

Mannheim's orchestra was now a group of seventy-six select musicians, ably led by Christian Cannabich as teacher, conductor, and solo violinist. Famous was Lord Fordyce's remark that Germany stood at the head of the nations for two reasons: the Prussian army and the Mannheim orchestra. Only less renowned was the Gewandhaus orchestra in Leipzig. Concerts were gigantic—three or four, sometimes six, concertos on one program; and they were everywhere—in theaters, churches, universities, palaces, taverns, and parks. The symphony now competed with the concerto in the orchestral repertoire; by 1770—even before Haydn—it was accepted as the highest form of instrumental music.[107]

Half the famous composers of this period came from the strong heart and loins of Johann Sebastian Bach. By his first wife he had seven children, of whom two, Wilhelm Friedemann and Karl Philipp Emanuel, achieved international celebrity. By his second wife he had thirteen children, of whom two, Johann Christoph Friedrich and Johann Christian, became prominent in music. Johann Christoph Friedrich begot a minor composer, Wilhelm Friedrich Ernst Bach, so that Johann Sebastian gave the world five men who secured a place in music history. A distant relative, Johann Ernst Bach, studied with the master at Leipzig, became *Kapellmeister* at Weimar, and left several compositions to oblivion.

Wilhelm Friedemann Bach was born at Weimar. The first part of his father's *Wohltemperirte Klavier* was written for his instruction. He progressed rapidly, and was already a composer at sixteen. At twenty-three he was appointed organist at the Sophienkirche in Dresden; and as his duties there were light, he wrote several sonatas, concertos, and symphonies. He rose in stipend and fame by being chosen (1746) organist at the Liebfrauenkirche in Halle. There he remained eighteen years; so he came to be called the "Halle Bach." He loved drink only next to music; he resigned in 1764, and for twenty years he drifted from town to town, living literally from hand to mouth by giving recitals and taking pupils. In 1774 he settled in Berlin, where he died in poverty in 1784.

Karl Philipp Emanuel Bach was lefthanded, and so had to confine his musical performance to the organ and the piano. In 1734, aged twenty, he entered the University of Frankfurt; there he enjoyed the friendship of Georg Philipp Telemann, who had been one of his godfathers and had given him part of his name. In 1737 he played some of his compositions before an audience that included Frederick William I of Prussia. Knowing that Crown Prince Frederick loved music, he went to Rheinsberg and presented himself, with no immediate result; but in 1740 Frederick, now king, appointed him cembalist in the chapel orchestra at Potsdam. He found it irritating to accompany Frederick's temperamental flute and to accept his royal authority in music. After sixteen years of service in the orchestra he retired to specialize in teaching. His *Versuch über die wahre Art das Klavier zu spielen* (1753 f.) marked the beginning of modern pianoforte technique; Haydn formed his piano artistry on this manual, and because of it Mozart said of this "Berlin Bach": "He is the father, we are his boys (*Buben*); those of us who know anything correctly have learned from him, and any [student] who does not confess this is a rascal [*Lump*]."[108] In his compositions Emanuel consciously diverged from his father's contrapuntal style to a simpler homophonic treatment and melodic line. In 1767 he accepted the post of director of church music at Hamburg; there he spent the remaining twenty-one years of his life. In 1795 Haydn came to Hamburg to see him, only to find that the greatest of Johann Sebastian's sons was seven years dead.

Johann Christoph Friedrich Bach, after studying with his father and at the University of Leipzig, became at eighteen (1750) *Kammermusikus* at Bückeburg to Wilhelm, Count of Schaumburg-Lippe; at twenty-six he was *Konzertmeister*. The great event in his twenty-eight years at this court was the coming of Herder (1771) as preacher; Herder provided him with inspiring texts for oratorios, cantatas, and songs. Johann Christoph followed his father's methods and spirit, and was lost in the changefulness of time.

In contrast, the youngest son, Johann Christian Bach, gave his musical allegiance to Italy. Only fifteen when his father died, he was sent to Berlin, where his half-brother Wilhelm Friedemann gave him support and instruction. At nineteen he went to Bologna, where Conte Cavaliere Agostino Litta paid for his studies under Padre Martini. The youth was so charmed by Italian life and Catholic music that he became a convert, and for six years devoted his compositions chiefly to the Church. In 1760 he was made organist in the Milan cathedral, and became the "Milan Bach." Meanwhile Italian opera had aroused his ambition to excel in secular as well as ecclesiastical music; he produced operas at Turin and Naples (1761), and his Milan employers complained that the *galanterie* of these compositions discorded with his position in the cathedral. Johann Christian changed his foot of earth to London (1762), where his operas had unusually long runs. Soon he was appointed music master to Queen Charlotte Sophia. He welcomed the seven-year-old Mozart to London in 1764, and frolicked with him at the piano. The boy loved the now fully accomplished musician, and took many hints from him in composing sonatas, operas, and symphonies. In 1778 Bach went to Paris to present his *Amadis des Gaules;* there he again met Mozart, and the youth of twenty-two was as delighted with him as he had been fifteen years before. "He is an honest man, and does people justice," Wolfgang wrote to his father; "I love him from my heart."[109]

All in all, this Bach dynasty, from the Veit Bach who died in 1619 to the Wilhelm Friedrich Ernst Bach who died in 1845, is the most remarkable in cultural history. Of some sixty Bachs known by name among the relatives of Johann Sebastian, fifty-three were professional musicians; eight of his ancestors and five of his progeny were of sufficient caliber to warrant special articles in a dictionary of music.[110] Several of the sons won greater fame and reputation in their lifetimes than Johann Sebastian had enjoyed. Not that they monopolized musical fame; the executants, as usual, received the greater acclaim when alive, and were sooner forgotten when dead; and composers like Karl Friedrich Fasch and Christian Friedrich Schubart rivaled Bach's sons in renown.

Looking back upon this second half of the eighteenth century we perceive some special lines of musical evolution. The growing range and power of the piano freed music from subservience to words, and encouraged instrumental compositions. The widened audience for concerts, and the lessening of ecclesiastical dominance, led composers away from the polyphony of Johann Sebastian Bach to the more easily appreciated harmonies of his successors. The influence of Italian opera made for melody even in instrumental pieces, while, by a contrasting movement, the lieder gave a new complexity to song.

The revolt against Italian opera culminated in Gluck, who proposed to sub-ordinate music to drama, but rather ennobled drama with music; by another avenue the revolt developed the *Singspiel*, which reached its peak in *The Magic Flute*. The *concerto grosso* passed into the concerto for one solo instrument and orchestra; the sonata, in Karl Philipp Emanuel Bach and Haydn, took its classic form, and the quartet evolved into the symphony. Everything was prepared for Beethoven.

X. DER ALTE FRITZ

Over all this varied life of politics, religion, industry, amusement, music, art, science, philosophy, philanthropy, and sin loomed the aging hero whom Germany called Der Alte Fritz—not loving him, but honoring him as the most amazing Teuton of his time. Not content with ruling his kingdom and his orchestra, he envied Voltaire's pen, and longed to be lauded as a poet and historian. He bequeathed to posterity thirty volumes of writings: seven of history, six of poetry, three of military treatises, two of philosophy, twelve of correspondence; all in French. His poems were mostly of the "fugitive" kind, and have escaped remembrance. He was one of the leading historians of the age. Early in his reign he wrote the history of his ancestors —*Mémoires pour servir à l'histoire de la maison de Brandebourg* (1751). Like most historians, he claimed impartiality: "I have risen above all preju-dice; I have regarded princes, kings, relatives, as ordinary men";[111] but he rose to rapture when describing Frederick William, the Great Elector.

His literary masterpiece was *L'Histoire de mon temps*, recording his own rule. He began it soon after the close of the First Silesian War (1740–42), and continued it at intervals till late in life. Probably under the influence of Voltaire—though writing much of this book before the appearance of Vol-taire's *Le Siècle de Louis XIV* and *L'Essai sur les moeurs*—Frederick in-cluded the history of science, philosophy, literature, and art. He apologized for spending space on "imbeciles clothed in purple, charlatans crowned with a tiara. . . . But to follow the discovery of new truths, to grasp the causes of change in morals and manners, to study the processes by which the dark-ness of barbarism has been lifted from the minds of men—these, surely, are subjects worthy to occupy all thinking men."[112] He praised Hobbes, Locke, and the deists in England, Thomasius and Wolff in Germany, Fontenelle and Voltaire in France. "These great men and their disciples struck a mortal blow at religion. Men began to examine what they had stupidly adored; reason overthrew superstition. . . . Deism, the simple worship of the Su-preme Being, gained many followers."[113] Despising the French government but loving French literature, Frederick rated Voltaire's *Henriade* above the *Iliad*, and Racine above Sophocles; he equaled Boileau with Horace, and Bossuet with Demosthenes. He laughed at the language and literature, praised the architecture, of Germany. He labored to excuse his invasion of Silesia: a statesman, he felt, may violate the Ten Commandments if the vital interests of his state require it; "it is better that the sovereign should break his word than that the people should perish"[114]—which he hoped we would believe had been the danger to Prussia in 1740. He admitted making many mistakes as a general, but he thought it unnecessary to record his flight at Mollwitz. All in all, these two volumes rank with the best historical writing of modern Europe before Gibbon.

Hardly had the Seven Years' War been concluded when Frederick set himself to writing his *Histoire de la guerre de Sept Ans*. Like Caesar he aspired to be the best historian of his own campaigns, and like Caesar he avoided embarrassment by speaking of himself in the third person. Again, and perhaps with better reason, he sought to justify the bold initiative with which he had opened hostilities. He lauded his great enemy, Maria Theresa, in all that concerned her domestic government, but in foreign relations he condemned her as "this proud woman" who, "devoured by ambition, wished to reach the goal of glory by every path."[115] Amid his fairly impartial record of the campaigns, he stopped to mourn the death of his mother in 1757 and of his sister in 1758; the page in which he described Wilhelmine is an oasis of love in a waste of war.

He concluded that history is an excellent teacher, with few pupils. "It is in the nature of man that no one learns from experience. The follies of the fathers are lost on their children; each generation has to commit its own."[116] "Whoever reads history with application will perceive that the same scenes are often repeated, and that one need only change the names of the actors."[117] And even if we could learn, we should still be subject to unpredictable chance. "These *Memoirs* convince me more and more that to write history is to compile the follies of men and the strokes of fortune. Everything turns on these two articles."[118]

Twice (1752, 1768) in a *Last Testament*, he tried to convey some of the lessons of his own experience to his heirs. He urged them to study the aims and resources of the various states, and the methods available for protecting and developing Prussia. He followed his father in stressing the need of keeping the army in good order. He cautioned his successors against spending beyond revenue; he predicted political trouble for fiscally reckless France; and he advised that revenues be increased not by imposing new taxes but by stimulating the productivity of the economy. All religions should be protected if they kept the peace—though "all religions, when one looks into them, rest on a system of fable more or less absurd."[119] The royal power should be absolute, but the king should consider himself the first servant of the state. Since Prussia was endangered by her smallness amid large states like Russia, France, and the Austro-Hungarian Empire, the king should seize upon any opportunity to enlarge and unify Prussia—preferably by conquest of Saxony, Polish Prussia, and Swedish Pomerania. "The first concern of a prince is to maintain himself; the second is to extend his territory. This demands suppleness and resource. . . . The way to hide secret ambitions is to profess pacific sentiments till the favorable moment arrives. This has been the method of all great statesmen."[120]

The king should prepare his successor for government; he should have him educated by enlightened men, not by ecclesiastics, for these will stuff him with superstitions calculated to make him a docile tool of the church.[121] Such an education produces a mediocre mind soon crushed by the responsibilities of state. "That is what I have seen, and if I except the Queen of Hungary [Maria Theresa] and the King of Sardinia [Charles Emmanuel I], all the princes of Europe are merely illustrious imbeciles."[122] This was written when Elizabeth ruled Russia; the *Testament* of 1768 was more polite, for Catherine had already shown her mettle; now Frederick prophesied that Russia would be the most dangerous power in Europe.[123]

As he aged he began to wonder if his nephew and presumptive heir— Frederick William II—was fit to inherit the government. "I labor for you," he wrote, "but one must think of keeping what I make; if you are idle and indolent, what I have accumulated with so much trouble will melt away in your hands."[124] And in 1782, still more pessimistic, he wrote: "If, after my death, my nephew goes soft, . . . within two years there will no longer be a Prussia."[125] The prediction was verified at Jena in 1806, not so much because Frederick William II was soft, but because Napoleon was hard.

Frederick himself, in his final decade, became unendurably hard. He curbed much of the freedom that he had allowed to the press before 1756. "Your Berlin freedom," Lessing wrote to Nikolai in 1769, "reduces itself . . . to the freedom to bring to market as many absurdities against religion as you like. . . . But let someone . . . raise his voice on behalf of subjects, and against exploitation and despotism, . . . and you will soon discover which is the most servile land in Europe today."[126] Herder hated his native Prussia, and Winckelmann turned in "horror" from that "despotic land."[127] When Goethe visited Berlin in 1778 he was surprised by the unpopularity of the King. Yet the people reverenced Frederick as an old man who through forty-five years had not missed a day of service to the state.

War and peace alike had worn him out. His attacks of gout and asthma, of colic and hemorrhoids, had increased in frequency and severity, and his predilection for heavy meals and highly spiced foods intensified his ailments. On August 22–25, 1778, near Breslau, he reviewed his Silesian army. On the twenty-fourth, dressed only in his usual uniform, he sat on his horse for six hours in a heavy rain; he returned to his quarters drenched and shivering; he was never well again. In June, 1786, he summoned Dr. Zimmermann from Hanover. He balked at the drugs prescribed for him, and preferred lively conversations about literature and history; to keep him quiet Zimmermann prescribed Gibbon's *Decline and Fall of the Roman Empire*.[128] Dropsy was added to his troubles, and incisions made to reduce the swellings developed gangrene. Pneumonia completed the siege, and on August 17, 1786, Frederick died, aged seventy-four. He had asked to be buried in the garden of Sanssouci near the graves of his dogs and his favorite horse; this parting edict on humanity was ignored, and he was interred beside his father in the Garrison Church at Potsdam. When Napoleon, after defeating the Prussians at Jena, came and stood before Frederick's tomb, he said to his generals, "If he were alive we should not be here."[129]

CHAPTER XXI

Kant

1724–1804

I. PROLEGOMENA

IF Frederick the Great had not lived we might never have had Immanuel Kant. The *Critique of Pure Reason* and *Religion within the Limits of Reason Alone* were made possible by Frederick's skepticism and toleration; within two years after Frederick's death Kant was silenced by the Prussian government.

Like Frederick, Kant was a child of the Enlightenment, and—despite all his strategic wavering—held by reason to the end; but also, like Rousseau, he was part of the Romantic movement, laboring to reconcile reason with feeling, philosophy with religion, morality with revolt. He received an infusion of Pietism from his parents, and crossed it with the rationalism of Christian von Wolff; he absorbed the heresies of the *philosophes*, and crossed them with the "Profession of Faith of the Savoyard Vicar" in *Émile*; he inherited the subtle psychology of Locke, Leibniz, Berkeley, and Hume, and used it in an attempt to save science from Hume and religion from Voltaire. He ordered his life with bourgeois regularity, and hailed the French Revolution. Isolated in East Prussia, he felt and summed up all the mental currents of his time.

He was born in Königsberg (April 22, 1724), far from clarity-loving France and misty with the sea. Some doubt has been cast upon the Scottish origin of the family, but Kant himself tells us that his grandfather, "at the end of the last . . . century (I know not for what cause) emigrated from Scotland to Prussia."[1] His father, Johann Georg Cant, married Anna Reuter; Immanuel (i.e., God with us) was the fourth of their eleven children. He took his Christian name from the saint of his birth day; he changed his surname from Cant to Kant to prevent the Germans from pronouncing it "Tsant."[2] All the family was brought up in the Pietist sect, which, like English Methodism, stressed faith, repentance, and immediate appeal to God, as against the orthodox Lutheran worship in church with a mediating priest.

A Pietist preacher had established at Königsberg a Collegium Fredericianum; Immanuel attended this from his eighth to his sixteenth year. The school day began at 5:30 A.M. with a half hour of prayer; every class hour ended with prayer; an hour every morning was devoted to religious instruction, with emphasis on the fires of hell; history was taught chiefly from the Old Testament, Greek solely from the New. Sunday was given largely to religious devotions. It was an education that produced virtue in some of its graduates, hypocrisy in others, and perhaps a somber spirit in most. Kant later resented this heavy dose of piety and terror; fear and trembling, he said, overcame him when he recalled those days.[3]

In 1740 he moved on to the University of Königsberg. Here his favorite teacher was Martin Knutzen, who, though a Pietist, introduced Kant to the "rationalism" of Wolff. Knutzen had read the English deists; he condemned them but he discussed them, and he left some deistic doubts in at least one pupil. When, after six years at the university, Kant was invited to enter the Lutheran ministry, he refused despite the promise of early advancement to a comfortable post.[4] Instead, for nine years, he lived in poverty, tutoring in private families, and continuing to study. His interest till 1770 was rather in science than in theology. Lucretius was one of his favorite authors.[5]

In 1755 Kant received the doctoral degree, and was allowed to lecture in the university as a *Privatdozent*, or private teacher, recompensed only by such fees as his students chose to pay. He continued in that insecure status for fifteen years. Twice in that long novitiate his applications for a professorship were rejected. He remained poor, moving from one boardinghouse to another, never daring to marry, never having a home of his own till he was fifty-nine.[6] He lectured on a wide variety of topics, probably to attract a greater range of students, and he had to make himself clear in order to survive. Kant as a teacher must have been quite different from Kant the author, so famous for obscurity. Herder, who was one of his pupils (1762–64), described him thirty years later with grateful memory:

> I have had the good fortune to know a philosopher who was my teacher. In the prime of life he possessed the joyous courage of youth, and this also, as I believe, attended him to extreme old age. His open, thoughtful brow was the seat of untroubled cheerfulness and joy, his conversation was full of ideas and most suggestive. He had at his service jest, witticism, and humorous fancy, and his lectures were at once instructive and most entertaining. With the same spirit in which he criticized Leibniz, Wolff, Baumgarten, . . . and Hume, he investigated the natural laws of Newton, Kepler, and the physicists. In the same way he took up the writings of Rousseau. . . . No cabal or sect, no prejudice or reverence for a name, had the slightest influence with him in opposition to the extension and promotion of truth. He encouraged and gently compelled his hearers to think for themselves; despotism was foreign to his disposition. This man, whom I name with the greatest gratitude and reverence, is Immanuel Kant; his image stands before me, and is dear to me.[7]

If we were to remember Kant chiefly by his work before his fifty-seventh year (1781), we should think of him as rather a scientist than a philosopher —though these two terms were not yet separate. His first published work, *Gedanken von der wahren Schätzung der lebendigen Kräfte* (*Thoughts on the True Evaluation of Dynamic Forces*, 1747), is a learned discussion of whether the force of a body in motion is to be measured (as Descartes and Euler held) by mv, the mass times the velocity, or (as Leibniz held) by mv^2, the mass times the square of the velocity; a remarkable performance for a lad of twenty-three. Seven years later came an essay on whether the time of the earth's daily rotation is altered by the ebb and flow of the tides. In the same year Kant published *Die Frage, ob die Welt veralte* (*The Question*

Whether the Earth Is Aging); here we have our modern solicitude over the sun's daily loss of energy and the future congealing of our earth.

In a brilliant treatise of 1755, *Allgemeine Naturgeschichte und Theorie des Himmels*, the venturesome youth of thirty-one offered "a general history of nature and theory of the heavens." It was published anonymously and was dedicated to Frederick the Great; perhaps Kant feared trouble from the theologians and hoped for protection from the King. He reduced all the operations of earth and sky to mechanical laws, but argued that the result, by its co-ordination and beauty, proved the existence of a supreme intelligence. To explain the origin of the solar system Kant proposed his "nebular hypothesis":

> I assume that all the material of our solar system . . . was, at the beginning of all things, decomposed into its primary elements, and filled the whole space . . . in which the bodies formed out of it now revolve. . . . In space so filled, a universal repose could last only a moment. . . . The scattered elements of a denser kind, by their attractive force, gather from . . . around them all the matter of less specific gravity; these elements themselves, together with the material which they have united with them, collect in those points where particles of a still denser kind are found; these in like manner join still denser particles, and so on. . . .
> But nature has other forces, . . . by which these particles repel one another, and which, by their conflict with attractions, bring forth that movement which is, as it were, the lasting life of nature. . . . This force of repulsion is manifested in the elasticity of vapors, the effluence of strong-smelling bodies, and the diffusion of all spirituous matters. It is by this force that the elements, which may be falling to the point that attracts them, are turned sideways . . . from their movement in a straight line; and their perpendicular fall thereby issues in a circular movement around the center to which they are falling.[8]

Kant believed that all the stars had been gathered—or were being gathered —into such systems of planets and suns; and he added a significant phrase: *"Die Schöpfung ist niemals vollendet"*—creation is never complete; it is ever going on.[9]

This nebular hypothesis of 1755, as well as its emendation by Laplace (1796), is as rich in difficulties as most subsequent theories of origins; yet in the judgment of a famous living astronomer, "Kant's treatise on cosmogony was, I believe, the finest objective summary of science up to that time."[10] For us the significance of the essay is in its indication that Kant was no mystic metaphysician but a man fascinated by science, and struggling to reconcile scientific method with religious belief. This is the essence of his labors to the end.

In 1756, stirred like Voltaire to the depths of his philosophy by the Lisbon disaster of 1755, Kant published three essays on earthquakes, and one on a theory of winds. In 1757 he issued an "Outline and Announcement of a Course of Lectures on Physical Geography"; and in 1758, a "New Doctrine of Motion and Rest." Then, his interest widening, he sent to the press short treatises on optimism (1759), the syllogism (1762), and "diseases of the head" (1764)—here suggesting that the increasing division of labor might by monotonous repetitions produce insanity. In 1763 he moved into theology with a treatise, *The Only Possible Ground for Proving the Existence of God*; obviously he was uncomfortable over the tottering of his religious faith. In 1764, eight years after Burke's similar disquisition, he offered *Observations on the Feeling of the Beautiful and the Sublime*.

At times he thought of extending his evolutionary cosmogony to biology; he was familiar with the idea that new forms had evolved from older ones through changes in the conditions of life;[11] and he accepted the view that the human anatomy was originally adapted to four-legged locomotion.[12] Yet he drew back from a fully mechanistic biology. "I also have at times steered into the gulf, assuming here blind natural mechanics as the ground of explanation, and I believed I could discover a passage to the simple and natural conception. But I constantly made shipwreck of reason, and I have therefore preferred to venture upon the boundless ocean of ideas."[13] Rudolph Raspe (author of *Baron Münchausen's Travels*) had recently discovered, and had in 1765 published, Leibniz' long-lost *Nouveaux Essais sur l'entendement humain*; Kant could read this in French; it shared in turning him toward epistemology. He did not quite abandon his interest in science; as late as 1785 he composed an essay *On Volcanoes in the Moon*. But the internal conflict between his scientific studies and his inherited theology impelled him to seek a reconciliation in philosophy.

Probably his new direction was caused in part by the offer (1770) of a professorship in logic and metaphysics. The salary was small for a man of forty-six—167 thalers per year, rising slowly to 225 in 1786; incidental services as "senator" and "senior of the faculty" raised this in 1789 to 726 thalers. Custom required a newly appointed professor to deliver in Latin an inaugural discourse. Kant chose a difficult subject—*De Mundi sensibilis et intelligibilis Forma et Principiis* (*On the Form and Principles of the Sensible and Intelligible World*). Kant used the Scholastic terminology that still prevailed in the German universities. By "sensible world" he meant the world as perceived by the senses; he would later call this also the phenomenal world, or world of appearances. By "intelligible world" he meant the world as conceived by the intellect or reason; this he would later call the "noumenal," or thinkable, world. We seek to understand the sensible world by applying to it the subjective concepts of space and time through mathematics and the sciences; we seek to understand the conceivable world by going beyond the senses, through intellect and metaphysics, to the supersensual sources and causes of the sensible world. Here Kant already laid down his basic theses: that space and time are not objective or sensible objects, but are forms of perception inherent in the nature and structure of the mind; and that the mind is no passive recipient and product of sensations, but is an active agent—with inherent modes and laws of operation—for transforming sensations into ideas.

Kant considered this seminal dissertation as "the text on which something further is to be said in the following work." This statement, in a letter of 1771 to Marcus Herz, shows that the philosopher was already planning the

Kritik der reinen Vernunft. After twelve years of work on that immense treatise he gave it to the world in 1781, dedicated to Karl von Zedlitz, minister of education and ecclesiastical affairs under Frederick the Great. Zedlitz, like the King, was a child of the Aufklärung, and supported the freedom of the press. His protection would be precious if the theologians should perceive, behind Kant's esoteric vocabulary and apparently orthodox conclusions, one of the most destructive analyses that the Christian theology has ever received.

II. *CRITIQUE OF PURE REASON,* 1781

If the world finds this book difficult, it may be because of Kant's method of work. He wrote to Moses Mendelssohn (August 16, 1783) that though the volume was "the result of reflection which occupied me for at least twelve years, I brought it to completion in the greatest haste within four or five months, giving the closest attention to the contents, but with little thought of the exposition, or of rendering it easy of comprehension by the reader—a decision which I have never regretted, since otherwise, had I longer delayed and sought to give it a more popular form, the work would probably never have been completed at all."[14] Clarity takes time, and Kant was not sure that he had the time. He deliberately omitted illustrative examples lest they swell his book; "these are necessary only from a popular point of view, and this work can never be made suitable for popular consumption."[15] So he wrote for the trade, and trusted to others to dilute him into digestibility. Though Christian von Wolff had preceded him in writing philosophy in German, that language was still crude in phrasing shades of thought, and it had not established a technical terminology. At almost every step Kant had to invent a German translation of a Latin term, and in many cases even Latin lacked terms for the distinctions and subtleties he wished to express. He confused his readers by giving new meanings to old words, and sometimes forgetting his redefinitions. The first hundred pages are tolerably clear; the rest is a philosophical conflagration in which the untutored reader will see nothing but smoke.

The title itself needed clarification. Who could have known that *Kritik der reinen Vernunft* meant a critical and judicial examination of reason as independent of experience? *Kritik* meant not only analysis and exposition, it also meant judgment, as in its Greek parent *krinein,* to judge. Kant proposed to describe sensation, perception, idea, and reason, and to set, for each of these, its proper bounds and jurisdiction. Further, he hoped to show that reason can give us knowledge independently of any confirmatory experience, as when we know that six times six equals thirty-six, or that an effect must have a cause. These are examples of "pure reason"—i.e., of a priori knowledge—i.e., of knowledge requiring no experiential proof. "The faculty of knowledge from a priori principles may be called pure reason, and the general investigation of its possibility and bounds [constitutes] the critique of pure reason."[16] Kant believed that such an investigation would involve all the problems of metaphysics, and he was confident that "there is not a single metaphysical problem which has not been solved, or for the solution of which the key at least has not been supplied" in this *Critique*.[17] He thought that his only danger was "not that of being refuted, but of not being understood."[18]

What had drawn him into so heroic an adventure? One might have supposed that the exaltation of reason by the French Enlightenment—the assumption of the *philosophes* that faith must submit to reason—and the havoc so inflicted upon Christian theology, had been the provocative cause of Kant's determination to study the origin, operation, and limits of reason. That motive played its part, as stated in Kant's preface to the second edition;[19] but that same preface made it clear that his chosen enemy was all "dogmatism" whatever—i.e., all systems of thought, orthodox or heretical, evolved by an unscrutinized reason. He named as "the greatest of all dogmatical philosophers" Christian von Wolff, who had undertaken to prove the doctrines of Christianity, and the philosophy of Leibniz, by reason alone. All attempts to demonstrate the truth or falsity of religion by pure reason were, to Kant, forms of dogmatism; and he condemned as "the dogmatism of metaphysics" any system of science or philosophy or theology that had not first submitted to a critical examination of reason itself.

He accused his own thinking, till 1770, as guilty of such dogmatism. From such unscrutinized speculations, he tells us, he was awakened by reading Hume—probably the *Enquiry concerning the Human Understanding*, of which a German translation had appeared in 1755. Hume had argued that all reasoning depended upon the notion of cause; that in actual experience we perceive not causation but only sequence; and that therefore all science, philosophy, and theology rest on an idea—cause—which turns out to be an intellectual supposition, not a perceived reality. "I freely admit," wrote Kant, "it was David Hume's remark that first, many years ago, interrupted my dogmatic slumber and gave a completely different direction to my inquiries in the field of speculative philosophy."[20] How could the concept of cause be rescued from the lowly status of uncertain supposition in which Hume had left it? Only, said Kant, by showing that it is a priori, independent of experience, one of those categories, or forms of thought, which, though not necessarily innate, are part of the inherent structure of the mind.* So he set himself to overcome both the dogmatism of Wolff and the skepticism of Hume by a criticism—a critical examination—that would at once describe, delimit, and restore the authority of reason. These three stages—dogmatism, skepticism, criticism—were, in Kant's view, the three ascending phases in the evolution of modern philosophy.

Loving definitions, distinctions, and classifications, using long words to shorten speech, Kant divided all knowledge into empirical (dependent upon

---

* In a letter to Garve, 1798, Kant gave a later explanation of his "awakening": "The antinomies of pure reason [the difficulties involved in either believing or disbelieving in God, free will, or immortality] . . . first aroused me from my dogmatic slumber and drove me to a critique of reason."[21]

experience) and transcendental (independent of, and therefore transcending, experience). He agreed that all knowledge *begins* with experience, in the sense that some sensation must precede and arouse the operations of thought; but he believed that the moment experience begins it is molded by the structure of the mind through its inherent forms of "intuition" (perception) or conception. The inherent forms of "intuition" are the universal forms that experience takes in our outward sensation as space, and in our inward sensibility as time.

Likewise there are inherent forms of conception or thought, which are independent of experience and mold it; Kant called them categories, and divided them with fond and suspicious symmetry into four triplets: three categories of quantity—unity, plurality, and totality; three categories of quality—reality, negation, and limitation; three twin categories of relation—substance and quality, cause and effect, activity and passivity; and three twin categories of modality—possibility and impossibility, existence and nonexistence, necessity and contingency. Every perception falls into one or more of these basic forms or molds of thought. Perception is sensation interpreted by the inherent forms of space and time; knowledge is perception transformed by the categories into a judgment or an idea. Experience is not a passive acceptance of objective impressions upon our senses; it is the product of the mind actively working upon the raw material of sensation.

Kant tried to counter Hume's skepticism of causation by making the cause-and-effect relation not an objective reality but an intrinsic form of thought; as such it is independent of experience, and is not subject to the uncertainty of empirical ideas. Yet it is a necessary part of all experience, since we cannot understand experience without it. Hence "the concept of cause involves the character of necessity, which no experience can yield."[22] Kant supposed that by this *léger-de-plume* he had saved science from that humiliating limita tion to probability to which Hume had condemned it. Indeed, he argued, it is the human mind, and not nature, that establishes the universal "laws of nature," by endowing some of our generalizations—like those of mathematics—with qualities of universality and necessity not objectively perceived. "We ourselves introduce that order and regularity in the appearance which we entitle 'nature.' We could never find them in appearances had we not ourselves, by the nature of our own mind, originally set them there."[23] The "laws of nature" are not objective entities but mental constructs useful in handling experience.

All knowledge takes the form of ideas. In this sense the idealist is right: the world, *for us*, is merely our ideas. Since we know matter only as and through ideas, materialism is logically impossible, for it attempts to reduce the directly known (ideas) to the unknown or indirectly known. But the idealist is wrong if he believes that nothing *exists* except our ideas; for we know that ideas can be produced by sensations, and we cannot explain all sensations without assuming, for many of them, an external cause. As our knowledge is limited to phenomena or appearances—i.e., to the form the external cause takes *after* being molded by our modes of perception and conception—we can never know the objective nature of that external cause;[24] it must remain for us a mysterious *Ding-an-sich,* a thing-in-itself, a "noumenon" conceived but never perceived. The external world exists, but in its ultimate reality it is unknowable.[25]

The soul too is real but unknowable. We never perceive it as an entity additional to the mental states that we perceive; it too is a noumenon, necessarily conceived as the reality behind the individual self, the moral sense, and the forms and processes of the mind. The sense of self mingles with every mental state, and provides continuity and personal identity. The consciousness of self ("apperception") is the most intimate of all our experiences; and by no feat of the imagination can we conceive it as material.[26] It seems impossible that an immaterial soul should act upon—and be acted upon by—a material body; but we may believe that the unknowable reality behind matter "may not, after all, be so different in character" from that inner thing-in-itself which is the soul.[27]

We cannot prove by pure or theoretical reason (as Wolff tried to do) that the individual soul is immortal, or that the will is free, or that God exists; but neither can we by pure reason disprove these beliefs (as some skeptics thought to do). Reason and the categories are equipped to deal only with phenomena or appearances, external or internal; we cannot apply them to the thing-in-itself—the reality behind sensations or the soul behind ideas. When we try to prove or disprove the dogmas of faith we fall into "paralogisms" (fallacies) or "antinomies"—inherent contradictions. We end in equal absurdities if we hold that the world had or had not a beginning; that the will is or is not free; or that a necessary or supreme being does or does not exist. Kant expressed with unwonted eloquence the argument from design,[28] but he concluded that "the utmost that the argument can prove is an *architect* . . . who is always very much hampered by the adaptability of the material in which he works, not a *creator* . . . to whose idea everything is subject."[29]

And yet how can we rest content with so baffling a conclusion—that free will, immortality, and God can be neither proved nor disproved by pure reason? There is (Kant urges) something in us deeper than reason, and that is our irrefutable consciousness that consciousness, mind, and soul are not material, and that the will is in some measure, however mysteriously and illogically, free; and we cannot be long content to think of the world as a senseless sequence of evolution and dissolution without moral significance or inherent mind. How can we justify our will to believe? Partly (says Kant) by the intellectual usefulness of belief—by its offering us some guidance in the interpretation of phenomena, as well as some philosophical sanity and religious peace.

> The things of the world must be viewed *as if* they received their existence from a highest intelligence. The idea [of God] is thus really a heuristic, not an ostensive, concept [it is an assumption helpful to discovery and understanding, but it is not a demonstration]. . . . In the domain of theology we must view everything *as if* the sum of all appearances (the sensible world itself) had a single, highest, and all-sufficient ground beyond itself—namely, a self-subsistent,

original, creative reason. For it is in the light of this idea of a creative reason that we so guide the empirical employment of *our* reason as to secure its greatest possible extension. . . . The only determinate concept which the purely speculative reason gives us of God is, in the strictest sense, *deistic;* that is, reason does not determine the objective validity of such a concept, but yields only the idea of something which is the ground of the highest and necessary unit of all empirical reality.[30]

But a more imperative reason for religious belief, in Kant's view, is that such belief is indispensable to morality. "If there is no primordial being distinct from the world, if the world is . . . without an Author, if our will is not free, if the soul is . . . perishable like matter, then *moral* ideas and principles lose all validity."[31] If moral character and social order are not to depend entirely on fear of the law, we must support religious belief, if only as a regulative principle; we must act *as if we knew* that there is a God, that our souls are immortal, that our wills are free.[32] Moreover, as an aid to thought and morals, "we are justified in representing the cause of the world in terms of a subtle anthropomorphism (without which we could not think anything whatever in regard to it), namely, as a being that has understanding, feelings of pleasure and displeasure, and desires and volitions corresponding to these."[33]

So the famous *Critique* concludes, leaving opposite schools of thought comforted and displeased. The skeptics could argue that Kant had justified agnosticism, and could scorn his reinstatement of God as a supplement to the police. The buffeted theologians reproached him for admitting so much to the infidels, and rejoiced that religion had apparently survived its perilous passage through Kant's labyrinthine mind. In 1786 Karl Reinhold described the turmoil:

> The *Critique of Pure Reason* has been proclaimed by the dogmatists as the attempt of a skeptic who undermines the certainty of all knowledge; by the skeptics as a piece of arrogant presumption that undertakes to erect a new form of dogmatism upon the ruins of previous systems; by the supernaturalists as a subtly plotted artifice to displace the historical foundations of religion, and to establish naturalism without polemic; by the naturalists as a new prop for the dying philosophy of faith; by the materialists as an idealistic contradiction of the reality of matter; by the spiritualists as an unjustifiable limitation of all knowledge to the corporeal world, concealed under the name of the domain of experience . . .[34]

Almost all these schools of thought attacked the book, giving it fame if only as a *succès de scandale*. Even its difficulty exalted it, making it a challenge that every up-to-date mind had to meet. Soon the *sesquipedalia verba* of Kant were in every learned mouth.

He could not understand why his critics could not understand him. Had he not defined every basic term over and over again? (Yes, and how variously!) In 1783 he answered the attacks by rephrasing the *Critique* in what he thought was a simpler form; and he defiantly entitled his rejoinder *Prolegomena to Every Future Metaphysic That Will Be Able to Appear as*

Science. Before his *Critique*, he claimed, there had been no real metaphysics at all, for no system had prefaced itself with a critical scrutiny of its instrument—reason. If some readers could not understand the *Kritik*, that might be because they were not quite up to it; "in such a case one should apply one's mental gifts to another object"; after all, "there is no need for everybody to study metaphysics."[35] The old professor had humor and pride, and temper too. As it proceeded, the *Prolegomena* became as difficult as the *Critique*.

The controversy continued under the tolerant regime of Frederick the Great. Kant had written in the *Critique* some eloquent passages on the nobility of reason, and its right to freedom of expression.[36] In 1784, still relying on protection by Frederick and Zedlitz, he published an essay entitled *Was ist Aufklärung?* He defined the Enlightenment as freedom and independence of thought, and took as his motto and counsel *Sapere aude*—"Dare to know." He regretted that intellectual liberation was so retarded by the conservatism of the majority. "If we ask whether we live in an enlightened [*aufgeklärt*] age, the answer is no"; we live only "in an age of enlightening" (*Aufklärung*). He hailed Frederick as the embodiment and protector of the German Enlightenment, as the one monarch who had told his subjects, "Reason as you will."[37]

This may have been written in the hope that Frederick's successor would keep to the policy of toleration. But Frederick William II (1786–97) was more interested in the power of the state than in the freedom of the mind. When a second edition of the *Critique of Pure Reason* was prepared (1787) Kant modified some passages, and tried to soften his heresies with an apologetic preface: "I have found it necessary to deny knowledge [of things in themselves] in order to make room for faith. . . . Criticism alone can sever the root of materialism, fatalism, atheism, freethinking, fanaticism, and superstition."[38] He had reason for caution. On July 9, 1788, Johann Christian von Wöllner, "minister for the Lutheran Department," issued a *Religionsedikt* which explicitly rejected religious toleration as responsible for the loosening of morals, and threatened with expulsion from their pulpits or chairs all preachers or teachers who deviated from orthodox Christianity. It was in this atmosphere of reaction that Kant published his second *Critique*.

III. *CRITIQUE OF PRACTICAL REASON*, 1788

Since the first *Critique* had argued that pure reason could not prove the freedom of the will, and since, in Kant's view, morality required such freedom, the operations of reason seemed to have left morality, like theology, without a rational basis. Worse yet, the Enlightenment had sapped the religious foundation of morals by questioning the existence of a rewarding and punishing God. How could civilization survive if these traditional supports of morality collapsed? Kant felt that he himself, as an avowed disciple of the Aufklärung, was obligated to find some rational ground for a moral code. In a preliminary essay, *Fundamental Principles of the Metaphysics of Morals*

(*Grundlegung zur Metaphysik der Sitten*, 1785), he rejected the attempt of freethinkers to base morality upon the experience of the individual or the race; such an a posteriori derivation would deprive moral principles of that universality and absoluteness which, in his judgment, a sound ethic required. With characteristic self-confidence he announced: "It is clear that all moral conceptions have their seat and origin completely a priori in the reason."[39] His second major work, *Kritik der praktischen Vernunft*, proposed to find and elucidate that seat and origin. It would analyze the a priori elements in morality as the first *Critique* had analyzed the a priori elements in knowledge.

Every individual (Kant argues) has a conscience, a sense of duty, a consciousness of a commanding moral law. "Two things fill the mind with ever new and increasing admiration and awe . . . . : the starry heavens above, and the moral law within."[40] This moral consciousness often conflicts with our sensual desires, but we recognize that it is a higher element in us than the pursuit of pleasure. It is not the product of experience, it is a part of our inherent psychological structure, like the categories; it is an internal tribunal present in every person in every race.[41] And it is absolute; it commands us unconditionally, without exception or excuse, to do the right for its own sake, as an end in itself, not as a means to happiness or reward or some other good. Its imperative is categorical.

That categorical imperative takes two forms. "Act so that the maxim of thy will can always hold good as a principle of universal legislation"; act in such a way that if all others should act like you, everything would be well; this [variation of the Golden Rule] is the "fundamental law of the pure practical reason,"[42] and is "the formula of an absolutely good will."[43] In a second formulation, "So act as to treat humanity, whether in thine own person or in that of any other, in every case as an end, never only as a means,"[44] Kant proclaimed a principle more revolutionary than anything in the American or French declaration of the rights of man.

The sense of moral obligation is additional evidence for some freedom of the will. How could we have this consciousness of duty if we were not free to do or not to do, if our actions were merely links in an unbreakable chain of mechanical cause and effect? Without free will personality is meaningless; if personality is meaningless, so is life; and if life is meaningless, so is the universe.[45] Kant recognizes the apparently inescapable logic of determinism; and how can a free choice intervene in an objective world which (he confesses) is apparently governed by mechanical laws?[46] His reply is a masterpiece of obscurity. Mechanical law, he reminds us, is a mental construct, a scheme which the mind, through its category of causality, imposes upon the world of space and time as a device for dealing with it consistently. Since we have limited the categories to the world of phenomena, and since we have admitted that we do not know the nature of the noumenal world—the thing-in-itself behind the phenomena—we cannot assume that the laws which we construct for the phenomena hold also for the ultimate reality. And as we have admitted that we know, in ourselves, only the phenomenal self—only the world of perceptions and ideas—and do not know the nature of the inner and noumenal soul, we cannot assume that the laws of cause and effect that seem to govern the actions of our bodies (including our brains) apply also to the volitions of the ultimate spiritual reality behind our mental processes. Behind the mechanisms of the phenomenal world of space and of ideas in time there may be freedom in the spaceless and timeless noumenal world of ultimate outer or inner reality. Our actions and ideas are determined once they enter the world of perceivable physical or mental events; they may still be free in their origin in the unperceivable soul; "in this way freedom and nature . . . can exist together."[47] We cannot prove this, but we may legitimately assume it as implied by the imperative character of our moral sense; our moral life would die without it.

After all (says Kant), why should we not give primacy to the practical over the speculative reason? Science, which seems to reduce us to automata, is ultimately a speculation—a gamble on the permanent validity of conclusions and methods that are always changing. We are justified in feeling that the will in man is more basic than the intellect; the intellect is an instrument forged *by the will* for dealing with the external and mechanical world; it should not be the master of the personality that uses it.[48]

But if the moral sense warrants us in assuming a measure of free will, it also warrants us in believing in the immortality of the soul. For our moral sense urges us on to a perfection that is repeatedly frustrated by our sensual impulses; we cannot achieve this perfection in our short earthly life; we must assume, if there is any justice in the world, that we shall be granted, for our moral fulfillment, a continued life after death. If this also assumes that a just God exists, this too is warranted by practical reason. Earthly happiness does not always accord with virtue; we feel that somewhere the balance between virtue and happiness will be restored; and this is possible only by supposing that there is a deity who will effect this reconciliation. "Accordingly the existence of a cause of all nature, distinct from nature itself, and containing the principle of . . . the exact harmony of happiness with morality, is also postulated" by the practical reason.[49]

Kant inverted the usual procedure: instead of deriving the moral sense and code from God (as the theologians had done), he deduced God from the moral sense. We must conceive our duties not as "arbitrary ordinances of a foreign will, but as essential laws of every free will in itself"; however, since that will and God both belong to the noumenal world, we should accept these duties as divine commands. "We shall not look upon [moral] actions as obligatory because they are commands of God, but we shall regard them as divine commands because we have an inward obligation to them."[50]

If all this will-ful thinking is slightly obscure, it may be because Kant was not very enthusiastic about his attempt to reconcile Voltaire with Rousseau. The *Critique of Pure Reason* had gone even further than Voltaire in confessing that pure reason cannot prove free will, immortality, or God. But Kant had found in Rousseau's doctrines—of the weakness of reason, the primacy of feeling, and the derivation of religion from man's moral sense—a possible escape from agnosticism, moral disintegration, and Wöllner's police.

He thought that Rousseau had awakened him from "dogmatic slumber" in ethics as Hume had done in metaphysics.[51] The first *Critique* belonged to the Aufklärung; the second belonged to the Romantic movement; the attempt to combine both was one of the subtlest performances in the history of philosophy. Heine credited the attempt to solicitude for popular needs: the professor saw his faithful servant Lampe weeping over the death of God; "then Immanuel Kant had compassion, and showed himself not only a great philosopher but also a good man, and half kindly, half ironically he said: 'Old Lampe must have a God, or he cannot be happy; . . . for my part the practical reason may, then, guarantee the existence of God.' "[52]

IV. *CRITIQUE OF JUDGMENT,* 1790

Kant himself must have been dissatisfied with his arguments, for in a *Kritik der Urteilskraft* he returned to the problem of mechanism versus free will, and advanced to the conflict between mechanism and design; to which he added complex dissertations on beauty, sublimity, genius, and art. It is not an appetizing brew.

Urteilskraft—the power of judgment—"is in general the faculty of thinking the particular as contained in the universal"; it is the act of bringing an object, idea, or event under a class, or principle, or law. The first *Critique* had tried to bring all ideas under the a priori universal categories; the second had sought to bring all ethical concepts under a universal a priori moral sense; the third undertook to find a priori principles for our aesthetic judgments—of order, beauty, or sublimity in nature or art.[53] "I venture to hope that the difficulty of unraveling a problem so involved in its nature may serve as an excuse for a certain amount of hardly avoidable obscurity in its solution."[54]

"Dogmatic" philosophy had attempted to find an objective element in beauty; Kant feels that here, especially, the subjective element is pre-eminent. Nothing is beautiful or sublime but feeling makes it so. We ascribe beauty to any object the contemplation of which gives us disinterested pleasure—i.e., a pleasure free from all personal desire; so we derive aesthetic, but no other, satisfaction from a sunset, a Raphael, a cathedral, a flower, a concerto, or a song. But why do certain objects or experiences give us this disinterested pleasure? Probably because we see in them a union of parts functioning successfully in a harmonious whole. In the case of the sublime we are pleased by grandeur or power that does not threaten us; so we feel sublimity in the sky or the sea, but not if their turbulence endangers us.

Our appreciation of beauty or sublimity is increased by accepting teleology—i.e., by recognizing in organisms an inherent adaptation of parts to the needs of the whole, and by feeling in nature a divine wisdom behind the coordination and harmony, the grandeur and power. And yet science aims at just the opposite—to show that all objective nature operates through mechanical laws, without submission to any external design. How can we reconcile these two approaches to nature? By accepting both mechanism and teleology insofar as they help us as "heuristic" principles—as assumptions that facilitate understanding or research. The mechanical principle helps us most in investigating inorganic substances; the teleological principle serves best in studying organisms. In these there are powers of growth and reproduction that baffle mechanical explanation; there is a visible adaptation of parts to the purposes of the organ or the organism, as of the claws for grasping and of the eyes for sight. It would be wise to recognize that neither mechanism nor design can be shown to be universally true. In a sense science itself is teleological, since it assumes an intelligible order, regularity, and unity in nature, *as if* a divine mind had organized it and sustains it.[55]

Kant acknowledged many difficulties in viewing man and the world as products of divine design.

> The first thing that would have to be expressly arranged in a system ordered with a view to a final whole of natural beings on the earth would be their habitat—the soil or element on or in which they are intended to thrive. But a more intimate knowledge of the nature of this basic condition of all organic production shows no trace of any causes but those acting altogether without design, and in fact tending toward destruction rather than calculated to promote genesis of forms, order, and ends. Land and sea not only contain memorials of mighty primeval disasters that have overtaken them and all their brood of living forms, but their entire structure—the strata of the land and the coast lines of the sea—has all the appearances of being the outcome of the wild and all-subduing forces of a nature working in a state of chaos.[56]

And yet again, if we abandon all notion of design in nature we take all moral meaning out of life; life becomes a silly succession of painful births and agonizing deaths, in which, for the individual, the nation, and the race, nothing is certain except defeat. We must believe in some divine design if only to maintain our sanity. And since teleology proves merely a struggling artificer instead of a divine and omnipotent benevolence, we must rest our faith in life upon a moral sense that has no warrant except through belief in a just God. With that creed we may believe—though we cannot prove—that the just man is the final end of creation, the noblest product of the grand and mysterious design.[57]

V. RELIGION AND REASON, 1793

Kant was never content with his hesitant *as if* theology. In 1791, in a little book *On the Failure of All Philosophical Attempts at Theodicy*, he repeated that "our reason is altogether incapable of giving insight into the relation between the world . . . and the highest Wisdom." He added a caution, perhaps to himself: "The philosopher should not play the part of a special pleader in this matter; he should not defend any cause whose justice he is unable to grasp, and which he cannot prove by means of the modes of thought peculiar to philosophy."[58]

He returned to the problem again in a series of essays which brought him into open defiance of the Prussian government. The first of them, "On Radical Evil," was printed in the *Berliner Monatsschrift* for April, 1792. The censor allowed its publication on the ground that "only deep-thinking scholars read the writings of Kant,"[59] but he refused to allow the second essay, "On the Contest between the Good and Evil Principles for the Control of Man." Kant resorted to a stratagem. German universities had the privilege of sanctioning books and articles for publication; Kant submitted the second, third, and fourth essays to the philosophical faculty at the University of Jena (then controlled by Goethe and Duke Karl August of Saxe-Weimar, and having Schiller on its staff); the faculty gave its imprimatur; and with this all four essays were printed at Königsberg in 1793 under the title *Die Religion innerhalb der Grenzen der blossen Vernunft* (*Religion within the Limits of Reason Alone*).

The first lines announce the pervading theme: "So far as morality is based upon the conception of man as a free agent, who, just because he is free, blinds himself through his reason to unconditioned laws, it stands in need neither of the idea of another Being over him for him to apprehend his duty, nor of an incentive, other than the law itself, for him to do it. . . . Hence for its own sake morality does not need religion at all."[60] Kant promises obedience to the authorities, and admits the need of censorship, but he urges that censorship "shall create no disturbance in the field of the sciences."[61] The invasion of science by theology, as in the case of Galileo, "might arrest all the endeavors of human reason. . . . Philosophical theology . . . must have complete freedom so far as its science reaches."[62]

Kant derives the problems of morality from man's twofold inheritance of good and evil tendencies. "That a corrupt propensity must indeed be rooted in man need not be formally proved in view of the multitude of crying examples which experience . . . puts before our eyes."[63] He does not agree with Rousseau that man is born good or was good in a "state of nature," but he concurs with him in condemning the "vices of culture and civilization" as "the most offensive of all."[64] "Indeed, it is still a question whether we should not be happier in an uncivilized condition . . . than we are in the present state of society"[65] with all its exploitation, hypocrisy, moral disorder, and wholesale homicide in war. If we wish to know the real nature of man we need only observe the behavior of states.

How did the "radical evil in human nature" begin? Not through "original sin"; "surely of all the explanations of the spread and propagation of this evil through all members and generations of our race, the most inept is that which describes it as descending to us as an inheritance from our first parents."[66] Probably the "evil" propensities were strongly rooted in man by their necessity to his survival in primitive conditions; only in civilization—in organized society—do they become vices; and there they require not suppression but control.[67] "Natural inclinations, *considered in themselves*, are *good*, that is, not a matter for reproach; and not only is it futile to want to exterminate them, but to do so would be harmful and blameworthy. Rather let them be tamed, and instead of clashing with one another they can be brought into that harmony in a wholeness which is called happiness."[68]

Moral good is also innate, as evidenced by the universal moral sense; but it is at first only a need, which must be developed by moral instruction and arduous discipline. The best religion is not one that excels in the careful observance of ritual worship but rather one that most influences men toward a moral life.[69] A religion of reason bases itself not upon a divine revelation, but upon a sense of duty interpreted as the divinest element in man.[70] Religion may legitimately organize itself into a church,[71] it may seek to define its creed through sacred scriptures, it may rightly worship Christ as the most Godlike of men, it may promise heaven and threaten hell,[72] and "no religion can be conceived which involves no belief in a future life."[73] But it should not be necessary for a Christian to affirm faith in miracles, or the divinity of Christ, or the atonement, by Christ's crucifixion, for the sins of mankind, or the predestination of souls to heaven or hell by divine grace given with no regard to good or evil works.[74] It is "necessary carefully to inculcate some forms of prayer in children (who still stand in need of the letter)";[75] but petitional "prayer . . . as a means of [winning divine] grace is a superstitious illusion."[76]

When a church becomes an institution for compelling belief or worship; when it assumes to itself the sole right to interpret Scripture and define morality; when it forms a priesthood claiming exclusive approaches to God and divine grace; when it makes its worship a magic ritual possessing miraculous powers; when it becomes an arm of the government and an agent of intellectual tyranny; when it seeks to dominate the state and to use secular rulers as tools of ecclesiastical ambition—then the free mind will rise against such a church, and will seek outside of it that "pure religion of reason" which is the pursuit of the moral life.[77]

This last major work of Kant was marked with the vacillation and obfuscation natural to a man who had no passion for imprisonment. There is much scholastic verbiage in it, some wondrous logic-chopping and fantastic theology. The wonder remains that a man of sixty-nine should still display such vigor of thought and speech, and such courage in combat with the united powers of church and state. The conflict between the philosopher and the King came to a head when (October 1, 1794) Frederick William II sent him the following "order in council."

> Our Most High Person has for a long time observed with great displeasure how you misuse your philosophy to undermine and debase many of the most important and fundamental doctrines of the Holy Scriptures and Christianity; how, namely, you have done this in your book, *Religion within the Limits of Reason Alone.* . . . We demand of you immediately a most conscientious answer, and expect that in the future, toward the avoidance of our highest disfavor, you will give no such cause for offense, but rather, in accord with your duty, employ your talents and authority so that our paternal purpose may be more and more attained. If you continue to resist you may certainly expect unpleasant consequences to yourself.[78]

Kant gave a propitiatory reply. He pointed out that his writings were addressed only to scholars and theologians, whose freedom of thought should be preserved in the interest of the government itself. His book had admitted the inadequacy of reason to judge the final mysteries of religious faith. He concluded with a pledge of obedience: "I hereby, as your Majesty's most faithful servant, solemnly declare that henceforth I will entirely refrain from all public statements on religion, both natural and revealed, either in lectures or in writings." When the King died (1797) Kant felt released from his promise; moreover, Frederick William III dismissed Wöllner (1797), abolished the censorship, and repealed the *Religionsedikt* of 1788. After the battle Kant summed up its issues in a booklet, *Der Streit der Fakultäten* (*The Conflict of the Faculties*, 1798), in which he repeated his claim that academic freedom was indispensable to the intellectual growth of a society. Essentially the little professor in a far-off corner of the world had won his battle against a state having the strongest army in Europe. That state was soon to collapse, but by 1800 Kant's books were the most influential in the intellectual life of Germany.

VI. THE REFORMER

He retired from lecturing in 1797 (aged seventy-three), but till 1798 he continued to issue essays on vital themes. Despite his isolation he kept in touch with world affairs. When the Congress of Basel assembled in 1795 to arrange peace among Germany, Spain, and France, Kant took the occasion (as the Abbé de Saint-Pierre had done with the Congress of Utrecht in 1713) to publish a brochure *Zum ewigen Frieden* (*On Perpetual Peace*).

He began modestly by describing "eternal peace" as a fit motto for a cemetery, and assuring statesmen that he did not expect them to take him as anything more than a "scholastic pedant who can bring no danger to the state."[79] Then, setting aside as temporizing trivia the articles of peace signed at Basel, he drew up, as a committee of one, "six preliminary articles" outlining the conditions prerequisite to a lasting peace. Article I outlawed all secret reservations or addenda to a treaty. Article II forbade the absorption or domination of any independent state by another. Article III called for the gradual elimination of standing armies. Article IV held that no state might "interfere by force with the constitution of another." Article VI required that no state at war with any other should "permit such acts of hostility as would make mutual trust, in case of a future peace, impossible, such as the employment of assassins or poisoners, . . . and the instigation of rebellion in the enemy state."

Since no durable peace can be made between states that acknowledge no limits to their sovereignty, persistent efforts must be made to develop an international order and so provide a legal substitute for war. So Kant drew up some "definite articles" for a lasting peace. First, "the constitution of every state must be republican." Monarchies and aristocracies tend to frequent wars, because the ruler and the nobles are usually protected from loss to their lives and property in war, and so engage in it too readily as "the sport of kings"; in a republic "it rests with the citizens to determine whether war shall be declared or not," and they will bear the consequences; hence "it is not likely that the citizens of a state [a republic] would ever enter on so costly a game."[80] Second, "all international right must be grounded upon a federation of free states."[81] This should not be a superstate; "indeed, war is not so incurably bad as the deadness of a universal monarchy."[82] Each people should determine its own government, but the separate states (at least of Europe) should unite in a confederation empowered to govern their external relations. The ideal never to be abandoned is the practice by states of the same moral code that they require of their citizens. Could such a venture possibly produce more evil than the perpetual practice of international deceit and violence? In the end, Kant hoped, Machiavelli would be proved wrong; there need be no contradiction between morality and politics; only "morals can cut the knot which politics cannot unloose."[83]

Kant obviously had delusions about republics (which have joined in the most terrible wars of all); but we should note that by "republic" he meant constitutional government rather than a complete democracy. He distrusted the wild impulses of unchained men,[84] and feared universal suffrage as the empowerment of unlettered majorities over progressive minorities and nonconforming individuals.[85] But he resented hereditary privilege, class arrogance, and the serfdom encompassing Königsberg. He welcomed the American Revolution, which, as he saw it, was creating a federation of independent states along the lines that he had proposed for Europe. He followed the French Revolution with almost youthful enthusiasm, even after the September Massacres and the Terror.

But, like nearly all followers of the Enlightenment, he put more faith in education than in revolution. Here, as in so many fields, he felt the influence of Rousseau and the Romantic movement. "We must allow the child from his earliest years perfect liberty in every respect, . . . provided that . . . he does not interfere with the liberty of others."[86] Soon he hedged on this perfect liberty; some measure of discipline, he admitted, is necessary in the formation of character; "neglect of discipline is a greater evil than neglect of culture, for this last can be remedied later in life."[87] Work is the best discipline, and should be required at all stages of education. Moral education is indispensable, and should begin early. Since human nature contains the seed of both good and evil, all moral progress depends upon weeding out the evil and cultivating the good. This should be done not through rewards and punishments, but by stressing the concept of duty.

Education by the state is no better than education by the church; the state will seek to make obedient, pliable, patriotic citizens. It would be better to leave education to private schools led by enlightened scholars and public-spirited citizens;[88] hence Kant applauded the principles and schools of Johann Basedow. He deplored the nationalistic bias of state schools and textbooks, and hoped for a time when all subjects would be treated impartially. In 1784 he published an essay, *Ideen zu einer allgemeinen Geschichte in weltbürgerlicher Absicht* (*Ideas for a Universal History from a Cosmopolitan Standpoint*); it sketched the progress of mankind from superstition to enlightenment, allowed only a minor role to religion, and called for historians who would rise above nationalism.

Like the *philosophes*, he warmed his heart with faith in progress, moral as well as intellectual. In 1793 he chided Moses Mendelssohn for saying that every advance is canceled by retrogression.

> Many proofs may be given that the human race on the whole, and especially in our own as compared with all preceding times, has made considerable advances morally for the better. Temporary checks do not prove anything against this. The cry of the continually increasing degradation in the race arises just from this, that when one stands on a higher step of morality he sees further before him, and his judgment on what men are, as compared with what they ought to be, is more strict.[89]

As Kant entered his last decade (1794) his early optimism suffered darkening, perhaps because of reaction in Prussia and the coalition of the powers against Revolutionary France. He retired into himself, and secretly wrote that gloomy *Opus postumum* which was to be his last testament to mankind.

VII. POSTHUMOUS

Physically he was one of the smallest men of his time—just a little above five feet in height, and made still shorter by a forward curvature of the spine. His lungs were weak, his stomach ailed; he survived only by a regular and abstemious regimen. It was characteristic of him that at seventy he wrote an essay "On the Power of the Mind to Master the Feeling of Illness by Force of Resolution." He stressed the wisdom of breathing through the nose; one could avoid many colds, and other mishaps, by keeping his mouth shut.[90] So, in his daily walks, he walked alone, shunning conversation. He went to bed punctually at ten, rose at five, and in thirty years (he assures us) never overslept.[91] Twice he thought of marriage, twice he retreated. But he was not unsociable; usually he invited one or two guests, most often his pupils—never any woman—to share his dinner at 1 P.M. He was a professor of geography, but rarely moved outside Königsberg; he never saw a mountain, and probably—near though it was—never saw the sea.[92] He was sustained through poverty and censorship by a pride that only outwardly yielded to any authority other than his own reason. He was generous, but he was severe in his judgments, and lacked that sense of humor which should save philosophy from taking itself too seriously. His moral sense rose at times to an ethical pedantry that held all pleasures suspect until they had proved themselves virtuous.

He cared so little for organized religion that he attended church only when his academic functions required it.[93] He seems never to have prayed in his mature life.[94] Herder reported that Kant's students based their religious skepticism on Kant's teaching.[95] "It is indeed true," Kant wrote to Mendelssohn, "that I think many things with the clearest conviction, and to my great satisfaction, which I never have the courage to say, but I never say anything that I do not think."[96]

Till his last years he strove to improve his work. In 1798 he told a friend: "The task with which I now busy myself has to do with the transition from the metaphysical basis of the natural sciences to physics. This problem must be solved, or otherwise here is a gap in the system of critical philosophy."[97] But in that letter he described himself as "incapacitated for intellectual work." He entered into a long period of physical decline, accumulating ailments, and the loneliness of unmarried old age. He died on February 12, 1804. He was buried in the Königsberg cathedral, in what is now known as the Stoa Kantiana; and over his grave were inscribed his words, "The starry heavens above me; the moral law within me."

At his death he left a confused mass of writings which were published as his *Opus postumum* in 1882–84. In one of these he described the "thing-in-itself"—the unknowable substratum behind phenomena and ideas—as "not a real thing, . . . not an existing reality, but merely a principle . . . of the synthetic a priori knowledge of the manifold sense-intuition."[98] He named it a *Gedankending*, a thing existing only in our thought. And he applied the same skepticism to the idea of God:

> God is *not a substance existing outside me*, but merely a moral relation within me. . . . The categorical imperative does not assume a substance issuing its commands from on high, conceived therefore as outside me, but is a commandment or a prohibition of my own reason. . . . The categorical imperative represents human duties as divine commandments not in the historical sense, as if [a divine being] had given commands to men, but in the sense that reason . . . has power to command with the authority and in the guise of a divine person. . . . The Idea of such a being, before whom all bend the knee, etc., arises out of the categorical imperative, and not vice versa. . . . The *Ens Summum* [Supreme Being] is an *ens rationis* [a creation of reason], . . . not a substance outside me.[99]

So the Kantian philosophy, to which Christianity clung so long, in Germany and later in England, as the last, best hope of theism, ended in a bleak conception of God as a useful fiction developed by the human mind to explain the apparent absoluteness of moral commands.

Kant's successors, not knowing his *Opus postumum*, acclaimed him as the savior of Christianity, the German hero who had slain Voltaire; and they magnified his achievement until his influence exceeded that of any other modern philosopher. One disciple, Karl Reinhold, predicted that within a century Kant's reputation would rival that of Christ.[100] All Protestant Germans (except Goethe) accepted Kant's claim that he had effected a "Copernical revolution" in psychology: that instead of having the mind (the sun) revolve around the object (the earth) he had made the object (things) revolve around—and depend upon—the mind. The human ego was flattered by being told that its intrinsic modes of perception were the determining constituents of the phenomenal world. Fichte concluded (even before Kant died) that the external world is a creation of the mind, and Schopenhauer, accepting Kant's analysis, began his massive treatise *The World as Will and Idea* with the announcement "The world is my idea"—which rather surprised Mme. de Staël.

Idealists rejoiced that Kant had made materialism logically impossible by showing mind to be the only reality directly known to us. Mystics were happy that Kant had restricted science to phenomena, had barred it from the noumenal and really real world, and had left this shady realm (whose existence he secretly denied) as the private park of theologians and philosophers. Metaphysics, which the *philosophes* had banished from philosophy, was reinstated as the judge of all science; and Jean Paul Richter, conceding mastery of the sea to Britain, and of the land to France, assigned to Germany the mastery of the air. Fichte, Schelling, and Hegel built metaphysical castles upon the transcendental idealism of Kant; and even Schopenhauer's masterpiece took its start from Kant's emphasis upon the primacy of the will. "See," said Schiller, "how a single rich man has given a living to a number of beggars."[101]

German literature, too, soon felt Kant's influence, for the philosophy of one age is likely to be the literature of the next. Schiller buried himself for a while in Kant's tomes, wrote a letter of homage to their author, and, in his prose essays, achieved an almost Kantian obscurity. Obscurity became a fashion in German writing, a coat of arms attesting membership in the ancient order of web weavers. "On the whole," said Goethe, "philosophical speculation is an injury to the Germans, as it tends to make their style vague, difficult, and obscure. The stronger their attachment to certain philosophical schools, the worse they write."[102]

One would not readily think of Kant as romantic, but his learned-hazy passages on beauty and sublimity became one of the founts of the Romantic movement. Schiller's lectures at Jena, and his *Letters on the Aesthetic Education of Mankind* (1795)—milestones in that movement—grew out of studying Kant's *Critique of Judgment*. The subjectivist interpretation of Kant's theory of knowledge gave a philosophical basis to the romantic individualism that flaunted its flag in Sturm und Drang. The Kantian literary influence crossed to England, and affected Coleridge and Carlyle; it crossed to New England and gave a name to the Transcendentalist movement of Emerson and Thoreau.[103] The bent little professor of geography shook the world as he trod the "Philosopher's Walk" in Königsberg. Certainly he offered to philosophy and psychology the most painstaking analysis of the knowledge process that history has ever known.

CHAPTER XXII

Roads to Weimar

1733-87

I. THE ATHENS OF GERMANY

WHY did the supreme age of German literature make Weimar its home? Germany had no one capital to concentrate her culture, as France and England had, and no concentrated wealth to finance it. Berlin and Leipzig had been weakened—Dresden had been almost destroyed—by the Seven Years' War; Hamburg gave its money first to opera, then to the theater. In 1774 Weimar, capital of the duchy of Saxe-Weimar-Eisenach, was a quiet little town of some 6,200 souls; even after it had become famous Goethe spoke of it as "this small capital, which, as people jokingly say, has ten thousand poets and a few inhabitants."[1] Was its glory made by great individuals?

From 1758 to 1775 Weimar was governed by a niece of Frederick the Great, the vivacious Dowager Duchess Anna Amalie, who, at the age of nineteen, had been widowed by the death of Duke Konstantin, and had become regent for their one-year-old son Karl August. It was she who opened a door between government and literature by inviting Wieland to come and tutor her sons (1772). She was one of several cultivated women who, under her lead, and till her death in 1807, stimulated poets, dramatists, and historians with sex and praise. After 1776 she made her home a salon, and there—though all spoke French as well—she encouraged the use of German as a language of literature.

In 1775 the Weimar court included some twenty-two persons and their servitors. The poet Count Christian zu Stolberg found a pleasant informality there in that year of Goethe's arrival. "The old Duchess [then thirty-six] is the very personification of good sense, and yet most agreeable and natural. The Duke is a wonderful lad and full of promise; so is his brother. And many excellent people."[2] In 1787 Schiller described "the Weimar ladies" as "very sensitive; there is scarcely one of them that has not had an *affaire de coeur*. They all strive to make conquests. . . . A quiet, scarcely perceptible government allows everyone to live, and to bask in the air and sunshine. If one is disposed to gaiety, every opportunity is offered."[3]

Karl August assumed the government of the duchy on September 3, 1775, at the age of eighteen. Shortly thereafter, having pensioned his mistress,[4] he took a wife, Princess Luise of Hesse-Darmstadt, and captured Goethe on the way. He hunted with fury, drove his carriage wildly through the quiet town, and passed hurriedly from woman to woman; but his impetuosity was checked by an intellect that slowly matured into good judgment. He studied and fostered agriculture and industry, cultivated the sciences, helped litera-ture, and labored for the good of his principality and its people. Hear Mme. de Staël, who toured Germany in 1803:

> Of all the German principalities there is none that makes us feel more than Weimar the advantages of a small state, when its sovereign is a man of strong understanding, and is capable of endeavoring to please all classes of his subjects without losing anything in their obedience. . . . The military talents of the Duke are universally respected, and his lively and reflective conversation con-tinually brings to our recollection that he was formed by the great Frederick. It is by his own and his mother's reputation that the most distinguished men of learning have been attracted to Weimar. Germany, for the first time, has a literary metropolis.[5]

II. WIELAND: 1733–75

Christoph Martin Wieland is the least known, but perhaps the most lov-able, of the four men who made Weimar's fame. Almost all the influences of the time played upon him and tuned his lyre in their turn. Son of a pastor in Oberholzheim (near Biberach in Württemberg), he was nurtured in piety and theology. When he discovered poetry, he made the virtuous Klopstock his ideal, and then turned to Voltaire for relief. At nearby Warthausen he found the extensive library of Count von Stadion; he plunged into French and English literature, and sloughed off so much theology that in a romance, *Don Sylvio von Rosalva* (1764), he held up his boyhood faith to ridicule. He published prose translations of twenty plays by Shakespeare (1762–66), thereby giving Germany for the first time a view of Shakespeare as a whole, and providing German playwrights with an escape from the classic formula of French drama. Meanwhile Winckelmann and others were spreading the Hellenic gospel; Wieland made his own version of it, adopted a light epi-curean tone in *Komische Erzählungen* (*Comic Tales*, 1765), and made a fictitious Greek the protagonist of his main prose work, *Geschichte des Aga-thon* (1766–67). Lessing called it "the only novel for thinking men."[6]

In its wandering pages Wieland (aged thirty-three) proposed to expound his philosophy of life, exemplified in the physical and intellectual adventures of an Athenian of the Periclean age. "Our plan," said the preface, "required that our hero should be represented in a variety of trials," whose effect would be to educate a man in integrity and wisdom without the use of religious incentives or supports.[7] Agathon (i.e., Good), young and handsome, resists the attempt of a Delphic priestess to seduce him; instead he develops for the simple maiden Psyche (Soul) a pure though passionate love. He enters poli-tics, becomes disgusted by the factionalism of parties, denounces the voters for their lack of principle, and is banished from Athens. Wandering in the mountains of Greece, he comes upon a band of Thracian women who are celebrating the feast of Bacchus with wild and sensual dances. They mistake Agathon for Bacchus, and almost stifle him with their embraces; he is rescued by a pirate band, which sells him as a slave in Smyrna to Hippias, a Sophist

of the fifth century B.C. Wieland expounds the philosophy of the Sophists
with indignation:

> The wisdom of which the Sophists made a profession was in quality, as well
> as in effect, the exact opposite of that professed by Socrates. The Sophists
> taught the art of exciting other men's passions [through oratory]; Socrates in-
> culcated the art of controlling one's own. The former showed how to appear
> wise and virtuous, the latter how to be so. The former encouraged the youth of
> Athens to assume control of the state; the latter pointed out to them that it
> would take half their lifetime to learn how to rule themselves. The Socratic
> philosophy took pride in going without riches; the philosophy of the Sophists
> knew how to acquire them. It was complaisant, prepossessing, versatile; it
> glorified the great, . . . dallied with women, and flattered everybody who
> paid for it. It was everywhere at home, a favorite at court, in the boudoir, with
> the aristocracy, even with the priesthood, while Socrates' doctrines . . . would
> be pronounced unprofitable by the busy, insipid by the idle, and dangerous
> by the devout.[8]

Hippias, as Wieland pictures him, embodies all the ideas and vices of the
Sophists. He is a philosopher, but he has seen to it that he is also a millionaire.
He resolves to bring the upright Agathon to an epicurean way of thought and
life. The wisest policy, he argues, is to pursue pleasant sensations, and "all
pleasures are in reality sensual."[9] He laughs at those who deny themselves
mundane joys to gain heavenly delights that may never materialize. "Who
has ever seen those gods, and those spiritual beings, whose existence it [re-
ligion] asserts?" All that is a trick the priests play upon us.[10] Agathon condemns this philosophy as ignoring the spiritual element in man and the needs
of social order. Hippias introduces him to the rich and lovely Danae, encourages her to seduce him, and conceals from him Danae's hetaera past. She
dances, and the grace of her body, added to the charm of her conversation
and the music of her voice, leads Agathon to offer her his full but virtuous
love. Danae spoils Hippias' plot by returning Agathon's love in kind. She, who
had passed through many arms, finds a new experience and happiness in Agathon's devotion. Tired of soulless loves, she aspires to begin with Agathon a
new and purer life. She buys him from Hippias, frees him, and invites him
to share her wealth. Hippias, in revenge, reveals to Agathon Danae's career
as a courtesan. Agathon takes ship to Syracuse.

There he gains such repute for wisdom and integrity that he becomes
chief minister to the dictator Dionysius. By this time he has surrendered some
of his idealism:

> He did not now have as highflown conceptions of human nature as before.
> Or, rather, he had come to know the infinite distance between the metaphysi-
> cal man, of whom one thinks or dreams in speculative solitude, or the natural
> man as he proceeds in crude simplicity from the hands of the universal mother,
> and the artificial man whom society, laws, opinions, needs, dependence, and
> continual struggle of his desires with his circumstances, of his own advantage
> with the advantage of others, and the consequent necessity of continual dis-
> simulation and masking of his true intentions, have falsified, degraded, distorted,
> and disguised, in a thousand unnatural and deceptive forms. He was no longer
> the youthful enthusiast who imagined that it would be as easy to carry out a

great undertaking as to conceive it. He had learned how little one ought to expect from others, how little one ought to count on their co-operation, and (what is most important) how little one ought to trust oneself. . . . He had learned that the most perfect plan is often the worst [and] that in the moral world, as in the material, nothing moves in a straight line; in short, that life is like a voyage, where the pilot must adapt his course to wind and weather, where he is never sure that he will not be delayed or drifted aside by contrary currents; and that everything depends upon this: amid a thousand deviations from one's course, yet to hold one's mind unbendingly fixed upon the port of destination.[11]

Agathon serves Syracuse well and accomplishes some reforms, but a court cabal deposes him, and he retires to Tarentum. There he is welcomed by his father's old friend the Pythagorean philosopher and scientist Archytas (fl. 400–365 B.C.), who realizes Plato's dream of a philosopher-king. There Agathon finds his youthful love Psyche, but, alas, she is married to Archytas' son, and turns out to be Agathon's sister. However (with the magic wand of a novelist) Danae is brought from Smyrna to Tarentum; she has abandoned her epicurean ways to live in a demure modesty. Agathon, realizing that he had sinned in deserting her, begs her forgiveness; she embraces him, but refuses marriage; she has resolved to atone for the meandering morals of her past by living her remaining years in continence. The story ends with Agathon incredibly content with sisters.

The book has a hundred faults. The structure is loose, the coincidences are lazy evasions of artistry; the style is agreeable but diffuse; in many paragraphs the subject avoids the predicate until it is forgotten; a critic greeted the author's birthday by wishing him a life as long as his sentences. Even so, *The History of Agathon* is one of the major works of the Frederician age. Its conclusions indicated that Wieland had reconciled himself with the world, and could now be trusted to teach and tame stormy and stressful youths. In 1769 he was made professor of philosophy at Erfurt. Thence, three years later, he issued *Der goldene Spiegel* (*The Golden Mirror*), which expressed his ideas on education. Anna Amalie was charmed; she invited him to try his pedagogy on her sons. He came, and spent the rest of his life in Weimar. In 1773 he founded *Der teutsche Merkur* (*The German Herald*), which under his leadership was for a generation (1773-89) the most influential literary review in Germany. He was the intellectual star of Weimar till Goethe came; and when, in 1775, the dashing young author of *Werther* took the city by storm, Wieland welcomed him without jealousy, and was to remain his friend for thirty-six years.

III. GOETHE PROMETHEUS: 1749-75

1. Growth

From the time when he trod the streets of Frankfurt-am-Main as consciously the grandson of its mayor, to his septuagenarian years when his casual conversation made the renown of his Boswell Eckermann, Johann

Wolfgang von Goethe ran a full gamut of experience, absorbing all that life, love, and letters could give him, and returning it gratefully in wisdom and art.

Frankfurt was a "free city," dominated by merchants and fairs, but also the imperially designated seat for the coronation of German kings and Holy Roman emperors. In 1749 it contained 33,000 souls, nearly all pious, well-behaved, and *gemütlich*. Goethe's birthplace was a substantial four-story house (destroyed by fire in 1944, rebuilt in 1951). His father, Johann Kaspar Goethe, was the son of a prosperous tailor and innkeeper; he ruined his political career by pride and arrogance, and retired from the practice of law to a life of amateur scholarship in his elegant library. In 1748 he married Katharina Elisabeth, daughter of Johann Wolfgang Textor, *Schultheiss* or *Bürgermeister* of Frankfurt. Her son never forgot that through her he belonged to the untitled patriciate that had ruled the city for generations. When he was seventy-eight he told Eckermann, "We Frankfurt patricians always considered ourselves equal to the nobility; and when I held in my hands the diploma of nobility [granted him in 1782], I had nothing more, in my own opinion, than I had possessed long ago."[12] He felt that "*nur die Lumpe sind bescheiden*"—only rascals are modest.[13]

He was the eldest of six children, of whom only he and his sister Cornelia survived childhood; in those days much parentage was love's labor lost. It was not a happy household; the mother was of a kindly nature, inclined to humor and poetry, but the father was a pedantic disciplinarian who alienated his offspring by the harshness and impatience of his temper. "With my father," Goethe recalled, "there could be no pleasant relation."[14] From him, as well as from experience as a privy councilor, Goethe may have derived something of the stiffness that showed in his later life. From his mother he may have taken his poetic spirit and his love of the drama. She built a marionette theater in her home; her son never recovered from its fascination.

The children received their first education from their father, then from tutors. Wolfgang acquired a reading knowledge of Latin, Greek, and English, some Hebrew, and the ability to speak French and Italian. He learned to play the harpsichord and the violoncello, to sketch and paint, to ride and fence and dance. But he took life as his best teacher. He explored all quarters of Frankfurt, including the Judengasse; he ogled the pretty Jewish girls, visited a Jewish school, attended a circumcision, formed some notion of Jewish holydays.[15] The Frankfurt fairs, by bringing into the city exotic faces and goods, added to his education; so did the French officers in the Goethe home during the Seven Years' War. In 1764 the fifteen-year-old boy saw the coronation of Joseph II as King of the Romans; he sucked in every bit of it, and spent twenty pages describing it in his autobiography.[16]

At fourteen he had the first of the many love affairs that engendered half of his poetry. He had already won a reputation for his facility in writing verses. Some boys with whom he occasionally mingled asked him to compose a poetic letter in the style of a girl to a youth; he did so well that they had it delivered to a lovelorn member of the group as coming from the object of his devotion. This lad wished to answer in kind but lacked wit and rhymes; would Goethe compose a reply for him? Goethe consented, and in gratitude the lover paid the expenses of an outing for the group to a suburban inn. The waitress there was a lass in her teens, called Margarete—Gretchen for short; Goethe gave that name to the heroine of *Faust*. Perhaps because of the romances he had read and the letters he had written, he was in a mood to appreciate the charm of girlhood. "The first propensities to love in an uncorrupted youth," he wrote at sixty, "take altogether a spiritual direction. Nature seems to desire that one sex may by the senses perceive goodness and beauty in the other. And so, by the sight of this girl, and by my strong inclination for her, a new world of the beautiful and the excellent was revealed to me."[17] He never lost that world; one woman after another stirred his sensitive spirit, almost always with reverence as well as desire; at the age of seventy-three he fell in love with a girl of seventeen.

For a while he was too awed to speak to the charmer. "I went to church for love of her, and . . . during the long Protestant service I gazed my fill at her."[18] He saw her again at her inn, seated, like another Gretchen, at a spinning wheel. Now she took the initiative, and gaily signed the second love letter that he had fabricated as from a girl. Then one of the group, whom Goethe had recommended to his grandfather, was caught falsifying bonds and wills; Wolfgang's parents forbade him further association with those boys; Gretchen moved to a distant town, and Goethe never saw her again. He was much put out when he learned that she had said, "I always treated him as a child."[19]

He was quite content now (1765) to leave Frankfurt and study law at the University of Leipzig. Like any eager youth he read widely outside of his assigned subjects. He had already, in his father's library, browsed in Bayle's *Dictionnaire historique et critique*, with much damage to his religious faith; "and as soon as I reached Leipzig I tried to free myself altogether from my connection with the church."[20] For a time he delved into mysticism, alchemy, even magic; this too entered *Faust*. He tried his hand at etching and woodcuts, studied the picture collection at Dresden, frequently visited the painter Oeser in Leipzig. Through Oeser he became acquainted with the writings of Winckelmann; through these, and Lessing's *Laokoon*, he received his first infusions of reverence for the classic style. He and other students were preparing a hearty reception for Winckelmann at Leipzig when the news came that Winckelmann had been murdered in Trieste (1768).

The sense of beauty was predominant in his approach to the world. In religion he liked only its colorful and dramatic sacraments. He did not care for philosophy as written by philosophers, except Spinoza; he shuddered at logic and fled from Kant. He loved drama, wrote a worthless one at Leipzig, and composed poetry almost every day, even while listening to lectures on law. The poems which he published as *Das Leipziger Liederbuch* are in the style of Anacreon, playful, sometimes erotic:

> Yet I'm content, and full of joy,
> If she'll but grant her smile so sweet,

> Or if at table she'll employ,
> To pillow hers, her lover's feet;
> Give me the apple that she bit,
> The glass, from which she drank, bestow,
> And, when my kiss so orders it,
> Her bosom, veiled till then, will show.[21]

Was this merely wishful thinking? Apparently not. He had found in Leipzig a pretty head—Annette Schönkopf—who was willing to enter at least the vestibule of love. She was the daughter of a wine merchant who served a midday meal to students; Goethe ate there frequently, and fell in desire with her. She returned his ardor with judicious reserve, and allowed other men to be attentive to her; he grew jealous, and took to spying on her; they quarreled and made up, quarreled and made up, quarreled and parted. Even in these ecstasies he reminded himself that he was the grandson of a *Bürgermeister*, and that he had in him a daimon—the urge and drive of an omnivorous genius that demanded freedom for its full development to its own imperative destiny. Annette accepted another suitor.

Goethe counted this a defeat, and tried to forget it in dissipation. "I had lost her really, and the frenzy with which I revenged my fault upon myself by assaulting in various frantic ways my physical nature, in order to inflict some hurt on my moral nature, contributed very much to the bodily maladies under which I lost some of the best years of my life."[22] He sank into melancholy, suffered from nervous indigestion, developed a painful tumor in the neck, and woke up one night with an almost fatal hemorrhage. He left Leipzig without taking his degree, and returned to Frankfurt (September, 1768) to face paternal reproofs and maternal love.

During his long convalescence he made the acquaintance of Susanne von Klettenberg, an ailing, kindly Moravian Pietist. "Her serenity and peace of mind never left her; she looked upon her sickness as a necessary element of her transient earthly existence."[23] He described her, years later, with sympathy and skill in the "Confessions of a Beautiful Soul" which he inserted into *Wilhelm Meisters Lehrjahre*, but he recorded very debonairly her claims that his nervousness and melancholy were due to his failure to reconcile himself to God.

> Now I had believed, from my youth upward, that I stood on very good terms with my God—nay, I even fancied . . . that he might be in arrears to me, as I was daring enough to think that I had something to forgive him. This presumption was grounded on my infinite good will, to which, it seemed to me, he should have given better assistance. It may be imagined how often I got into disputes on this subject with my friends, which, however, always terminated in the friendliest way.[24]

Nevertheless he experienced stray moments of piety, even to attending some sessions of the Moravian Brethren; but he was repelled by the "mediocre intelligence" of these simple people,[25] and soon returned to his casual combination of pantheistic faith and rationalistic doubt.

In April, 1770, he departed for Strasbourg, hoping to get his law degree. A fellow student described him (then twenty-one) as "a handsome figure,

with a magnificent forehead and great, flashing eyes," but added, "All would
not be smooth sailing with this young man, for he seemed to have a wild and
unsettled air."[26] Perhaps his long illness had unnerved him; his "daimon" was
too unsettling to let him gain stability; but what youth with fire coursing in
his blood can enjoy repose? When he stood before the great cathedral he
hailed it patriotically as not Catholic but "German architecture, *our* architecture, for the Italians can boast of none like it, still less the French."[27] (He
had not yet seen Italy or France.) "Alone I climbed to the highest peak of
the tower, . . . and ventured at that elevation to step out on a platform
which measured scarcely a square yard. . . . I inflicted this terror and torture upon myself so many times until the experience became a matter of
indifference to me."[28] One of his professors noted that "Herr Goethe behaved
himself in a way which caused him to be regarded as a meretricious pretender to scholarship, a frantic opponent of all religious teaching . . . It
was the well-nigh universal opinion that he had a slate loose in the upper
story."[29]

A dozen new experiences served to feed his flame. He met Herder several
times during the latter's stay in Strasbourg. Herder, five years older, dominated these encounters; Goethe, in a modest interlude, called himself a
"planet" revolving around Herder's sun. He was disturbed by Herder's dictatorial tendency, but was stimulated by him to read old ballads, Macpherson's "Ossian," and (in Wieland's translation) Shakespeare. But also he read
Voltaire, Rousseau, and Diderot. Besides pursuing his work in law, he took
courses in chemistry, anatomy, obstetrics . . . And he continued his study
of women.

He felt their charm with all the keen sensitivity of a poet, all the electric
incandescence of youth. Forty-seven years later he told Eckermann that he
believed in a mysterious magnetic effect of one person upon another, and
most of all through difference of sex.[30] He was stirred by the light and
prancing walk of girls, by the music of their voices and laughter, by the
color and rustle of their dress; and he envied the intimacy of the flower they
sometimes wore in their corsage or their hair. One after another of these
magic creatures called to his blood, grew in his imagination, and moved his
pen. There had already been Gretchen and Annette; soon there would be
Lotte and Lili and Charlotte; later Minna and Ulrike. But now, at Sesenheim
(near Strasbourg), there was the most appealing of them all, Friederike
Brion.

She was the younger daughter (nineteen in 1771) of the town pastor,
whom Goethe compared to Goldsmith's virtuous Vicar of Wakefield. The
pages about Friederike in Goethe's autobiography are the finest prose he
ever wrote.[31] Several times he rode out from Strasbourg to enjoy the unspoiled simplicity of this rural family. He took Friederike for long walks,
for she was most at home in the open air. She fell in love with him, and gave
him all that he asked. "In a lonely place in the forest we embraced each other
with deep emotion, and gave each other the most faithful assurance that each
loved the other from the bottom of the heart."[32] Soon he was confessing to a

friend that "one is not happier by a hair's breadth by attaining the object of his wishes."

Meanwhile he was writing, in Latin, his doctoral thesis, which affirmed (like "Febronius") the right of the state to be independent of the church. It won the approval of the university faculty; he passed the examinations, and on August 6, 1771, he received his degree as a licentiate at law. The time had come to leave Strasbourg. He rode out to Sesenheim to say goodbye to Friederike. "When from my horse I reached her my hand, the tears stood in her eyes, and I felt very uneasy. . . . Having at last escaped the excitement of a farewell, I, in a quiet and peaceful journey, pretty well regained my self-possession."[33] Remorse came later. "Gretchen had been taken away from me; Annette had left me; now for the first time I was guilty. I had wounded the most lovely heart to its very depths; and the period of a gloomy repentance—with the absence of a refreshing love, to which I had become accustomed—was most agonizing."[34] It is sadly self-centered; but which of us, in the trial and error of love, has not wounded one or two hearts before winning one? Friederike died unmarried, April 3, 1813.

2. Götz *and* Werther

In Frankfurt the new licentiate grudgingly practiced law. He visited Darmstadt occasionally, and felt the influence of its cult of sentiment. He was now in a strong reaction against France, against French drama and its rigid rules, even against Voltaire. More and more he relished Shakespeare, who had put the nature of man, lawful or lawless, upon the stage. In this mood, and in the exuberant vigor of youth, he was ripe for Sturm und Drang. He sympathized with its rejection of authority, its exaltation of instinct over intellect, of the heroic individual over the tradition-imprisoned masses. And so, in 1772–73, he wrote *Götz von Berlichingen.*

It was a remarkable performance for a lad of twenty-three: a drama uniting war, love, and treachery in a story warm with zeal for liberty, exuding vitality, and holding the interest from beginning to end. Götz was a knight whose right hand had been shot off in battle when he was twenty-four (1504); an iron hand had been attached to his arm, and with it he wielded his sword as lethally as before. Refusing to acknowledge any overlord but the Emperor, he became one of those "robber barons" who, in the name of freedom, claimed full authority on their lands, even to pillaging wayfarers and waging private war. In 1495 Emperor Maximilian I had issued an edict against private wars, under the double penalty of ban by the Empire and excommunication by the Church. Götz of the Iron Hand rejected the ban as contravening traditional rights, and the play turned at first on the struggle between the rebel knight and the Prince-Bishop of Bamberg. Goethe, loving women much more than war, let the center of interest pass to Adelaide von Walldorf, whose beauty and wealth fired a dozen men with reckless passion. For her Adelbert von Weislingen, another "free" knight, broke his alliance with Götz and his troth with Götz's sister Maria, and went over to the Bishop. Perhaps in Weislingen's vacillating love Goethe remembered his own unfaithfulness. He sent a copy of the play to Friederike by a friend, saying, "Poor Friederike will feel somewhat consoled when she sees that the faithless lover is poisoned."[35]

The author colored history to suit his drama; Gottfried von Berlichingen was not so noble and magnanimous as Goethe's Götz; but such emendations are poetic licenses, like tortured rhymes. Forgivable, too, is the rough, wild speech which Goethe ascribed to his hero as echoing virility. When the play was produced in Berlin (1774) Frederick the Great condemned it as a "detestable imitation" of the "barbarism" that he, like Voltaire, saw in Shakespeare, and he called upon German dramatists to seek their models in France. Herder at first agreed with Frederick, and told Goethe, "Shakespeare has ruined you";[36] but he sent the published version to his friends with high praise: "You have hours of enchantment before you. There is an uncommon degree of authentic German power, depth, and sincerity in the piece, though now and then it is merely an intellectual exercise."[37] The younger generation hailed Götz as the supreme expression of Sturm und Drang. German readers were glad to hear of medieval knights, symbols of the mighty German character. Protestants relished the echoes of Luther in "Brother Martin," who complains that his vows of poverty, chastity, and obedience are unnatural, who describes woman as "the glory and crown of creation," welcomes wine as "rejoicing the heart of man," and overturns an old adage by saying that "joyousness is the mother of every virtue."[38] Even Goethe's father, who had to help him with his law and regarded him as a deterioration of the paternal stock, admitted that perhaps there was something in the lad after all.

In May, 1772, the young advocate had to go on legal business to Wetzlar, seat of the Imperial Appellate Court. Not at all absorbed in law, he wandered through fields, woods, and boudoirs, drawing, writing, absorbing. In Wetzlar he met Karl Wilhelm Jerusalem, poet and mystic, and Georg Christian Kestner, a notary whom Goethe described as "distinguished by a calm and equable demeanor, clearness of view, . . . serene and tireless activity,"[39] and so confident of advancement that he was already engaged to marry. Kestner described Goethe magnanimously:

> Twenty-three years old, the only son of a very wealthy father. According to his father's intention he was to practice law at the court here; according to his own he was to study Homer and Pindar and whatever else his genius, his taste, and his heart should inspire. . . . Indeed, he has true genius, and is a man of character. He possesses an imagination of extraordinary vividness, and expresses himself in images and similes . . . His feelings are violent, but he is usually master of them. His convictions are noble. He is quite free from prejudice, and acts as he likes without caring whether it pleases others, or is the fashion, or is permissible. All compulsion is hateful to him. He loves children, and can play with them for hours. . . . He is a quite remarkable man.[40]

On June 9, 1772, at a country dance, Goethe met Kestner's betrothed, Charlotte Buff. The next day he visited her, and found a new charm in womanhood. "Lotte," then twenty, was the eldest sister in a family of eleven. The mother was dead, the father was busy earning a living; Lotte served as mother to the brood. She not only had the bright gaiety of a healthy girl, she had also the attractiveness of a young woman who, simply but neatly dressed, performed the duties of her place with competence, affection, and good cheer. Goethe soon fell in love with her, for he could not remain long without some feminine image warming his imagination. Kestner saw the situation, but, sure of his possession, showed an amiable tolerance. Goethe allowed himself almost the privileges of a rival wooer, but Lotte always checked him, and reminded him that she was engaged. Finally he asked her to choose between them; she did, and Goethe, his pride only momentarily shaken, left Wetzlar the next day (September 11). Kestner remained his loyal friend till death.

Before returning to Frankfurt Goethe stopped at Ehrenbreitstein on the Rhine, the home of Georg and Sophie von La Roche. Sophie had two daughters, "of whom the eldest," Maximiliane, "soon particularly attracted me. . . . It is a very pleasant sensation when a new passion begins to stir in us before the old one is quite extinct. Thus, when the sun is setting, one likes to see the moon rise on the opposite side."[41] Maximiliane, however, married Peter Brentano, and bore a lively daughter Bettina, who fell in love with Goethe thirty-five years later. Goethe resigned himself to Frankfurt and law. Not quite, for at times he thought of suicide.

> Among a considerable collection of weapons I possessed a handsome, well-polished dagger. This I laid every night by my bed, and before extinguishing the candle I tried whether I could succeed in plunging the sharp point a couple of inches deep into my heart. Since I could never succeed in this, I at last laughed myself out of the notion, threw off all hypochondriacal fancies, and resolved to live.
> To be able to do this with cheerfulness I was obliged to solve a literary problem, by which all that I had felt . . . should be reduced to words. For this purpose I collected the elements which had been at work in me for a few years; I rendered present to my mind the cases which had most affected and tormented me; but nothing would come to a definite form. I lacked an event, a fable, in which they could be seen as a whole.[42]

A fellow advocate at Wetzlar provided the amalgamating event. On October 30, 1772, Wilhelm Jerusalem, having borrowed a pistol from Kestner, killed himself in despair over his love for the wife of a friend. "All at once, [when] I heard the news of Jerusalem's death," Goethe recalled, ". . . the plan of *Werther* was formed, and the whole ran together from all sides."[43] Perhaps so, but it was not until fifteen months later that he began to write the book. Meanwhile he carried on with Maximiliane Brentano—who had moved with her husband to Frankfurt—a flirtation so persistent that the husband protested, and Goethe withdrew.

A variety of abortive literary projects distracted him. He dallied with the idea of retelling the story of the Wandering Jew; he planned to have him visit Spinoza, and to show that Satan, to all appearances, was triumphing over Christ in Christendom;[44] but he wrote only ten pages of *Der ewige Jude*. He composed some satires on Jacobi, Wieland, Herder, Lenz, and Lavater, but managed to win their friendship nevertheless. He contributed to Lavater's

Physiognomische Fragmente, and allowed him to physiognomize his head, with flattering results: "Intelligence is here, with sensibility to kindle it," judged the Swiss. "Observe the energetic brow, . . . the eye so swiftly penetrating, searching, enamored, . . . and the nose, in itself enough to proclaim the poet. . . . With the virile chin, the well-opened vigorous ear—who could question the genius in this head?"[45]—and who could live up to such a cephalogram? Jacobi thought it could be done, for, after visiting Goethe in July, 1773, he described him in a letter to Wieland as "from head to toe all genius; a man possessed, who is destined to act according to the dictates of the individual spirit."[46]

At last, in February, 1774, Goethe wrote the book that gave him a European renown—*Die Leiden des jungen Werthers.* He had thought of it so long, had so long rehearsed it in brooding and fancy, that now he dashed it off, he tells us, "in four weeks. . . . I isolated myself completely, I forbade the visits of my friends."[47] Fifty years later he said to Eckermann, "That was a creation which I, like the pelican, fed with the blood of my own heart."[48] He killed Werther to give himself peace.

He was inspired in making the book brief. He used the letter form, partly in imitation of Richardson's *Clarissa* and Rousseau's *Julie,* partly because it lent itself to the expression and analysis of emotion, and perhaps because in that form he could use some of the letters he had written from Wetzlar to his sister Cornelia or to his friend Merck. He shocked Charlotte and Kestner by giving her actual name, Lotte, to the object of a love obviously describing Goethe's passion for Kestner's bride. Kestner became "Albert," and was favorably portrayed. Even the meeting at the dance, and the morrow's visit, were in the story as they had been in fact. "Since that day sun, moon, and stars can go calmly about their business, but I am conscious neither of day nor of night, and the whole world around me is fading away. . . . I have no more prayers to say except to her."[49] Werther is not quite Goethe: he is more sentimental, more given to tears and gushing words and self-commiseration. In order to lead the narrative to its tragic denouement, Werther had to be changed from Goethe to Wilhelm Jerusalem. The final touches echo history: Werther, like Jerusalem, borrows Albert's pistol for his suicide, and Lessing's *Emilia Galotti* lies on his desk as he dies. "No clergyman escorted him" to his grave.

The Sorrows of the Young Werther (1774) was an event in the history of literature and of Germany. It expressed and promoted the romantic element in Sturm und Drang, as *Götz von Berlichingen* had expressed the heroic. Rebellious youth acclaimed it with praise and imitation; some dressed in blue coat and buff vest like Werther, some wept like Werther; some committed suicide as the only fashionable thing to do. Kestner protested at the invasion of his privacy, but was soon appeased, and we are not told that Charlotte complained when Goethe told her, "Your name is uttered in reverence by thousands of adoring lips."[50] The German clergy did not join in the applause. A Hamburg preacher denounced *Werther* as an apology for suicide; Pastor Goeze, Lessing's enemy, blasted the book, and Lessing condemned it for its sentimentality and lack of classic restraint.[51] At a public dinner the Reverend J. C. Hasenkampf censured Goethe to his face for "that wicked piece of writing," and added, "May God improve your perverse heart!" Goethe deflated him with a soft answer: "Remember me in your prayers."[52] Meanwhile the little book swept through Europe in a dozen translations, three in France in three years; now for the first time France admitted that Germany had a literature.

3. The Young Atheist

The clergy had some excuse for worrying about Goethe, for he was in this stage openly hostile to the Christian Church. "He reveres the Christian religion," Kestner wrote in 1772, "but not in the form our theologians give it. . . . He does not go to church, nor to Communion, and he rarely prays."[53] Goethe was especially averse to the Christian emphasis on sin and contrition;[54] he preferred to sin without remorse. He wrote to Herder (about 1774): "If only the whole teaching of Christ were not such bilge that I, as a human being, a poor limited creature of desires and needs, am infuriated by it!"[55] He planned a drama on Prometheus as a symbol of man defying the gods; he wrote little more than a prologue, which shocked Jacobi and pleased Lessing. What remains of it is the most radical of Goethe's antireligious outbursts. Prometheus speaks:

> Cover thy heaven, Zeus, with cloudy mist,
> And disport yourself—like a child who cuts off thistle heads—
> On oaks and mountain peaks!
> My earth you must still let stand,
> And my cottage, which you did not build,
> And my hearth, whose glow you envy me.
>
> I know nothing poorer under the sun than you, O gods!
> You nourish your majesty with difficulty
> From sacrifices and votive prayers,
> And it would starve,
> Were not children and beggars such hopeful fools.
>
> When I was but a child, and knew not what to think,
> My erring eyes turned to the sun,
> As if there might be an ear to hear my plaint,
> A heart like mine
> To pity a troubled soul.
>
> Who helped me against the Titans' insolence?
> Who rescued me from death, from slavery?
> Has not my own holy, glowing heart
> Accomplished all this by itself, but, young and good,
> And deceived, gives thanks to that Sleeping One up there?
>
> Honor thee? Why?
> Have you ever lightened the sorrows of the heavy-laden?
> Have you ever dried the tears of the anguish-stricken?
> Have I not been molded into a man
> By almighty Time and everlasting Fate—
> My masters and yours? . . .

> Here sit I, forming men after my image,
> A race that may be like me,
> To grieve and weep, to enjoy and be glad,
> And to disdain you, as I do.

From this nadir of proud atheism Goethe moved slowly to the gentler pantheism of Spinoza. Lavater reported that "Goethe told us many things about Spinoza and his writings. . . . He had been an extremely just, upright, poor man. . . . All modern deists had drawn primarily from him. . . . His correspondence, Goethe added, was the most interesting in the whole world as concerned uprightness and love of humanity."[56] Forty-two years later Goethe told Karl Zelter that the writers who had most influenced him were Shakespeare, Spinoza, and Linnaeus.[57] On June 9, 1785, he acknowledged the receipt of Jacobi's book *On the Teachings of Spinoza;* his discussion of Jacobi's interpretation reveals considerable study of the Jewish philosopher-saint. "Spinoza," he wrote, "does not demonstrate the existence of God; he demonstrates that existence [the matter-mind reality] *is* God. Let others call him an atheist on this account; I am inclined to call him and praise him as most godly, and even most Christian. . . . I receive from him the most wholesome influences upon my thinking and acting."[58] In his autobiography Goethe remarked on his reply to Jacobi:

> Happily I had already prepared myself, . . . having in some degree appropriated the thoughts and mind of an extraordinary man. . . . This mind, which had worked upon me so decisively, and was destined to affect so deeply my whole mode of thought, was Spinoza. After looking through the world in vain to find a means of development for my strange nature, I at last fell upon the *Ethics* of this philosopher. . . . I found in it a sedative for my passions; and a free, wide view over the sensible and moral world seemed to open before me. . . . I was never so presumptuous as to think that I understood perfectly a man who . . . raised himself, through mathematical and rabbinical studies, to the highest reach of thought, and whose name, even at this day, seems to mark the limit of all speculative efforts.[59]

He gave added warmth to his Spinozistic pantheism by the intensity with which he loved nature. It was not merely that he found delight in bright fields, or mystic woods, or plants and flowers multiplying with such exuberant diversity; he also loved nature's sterner moods, and liked to fight his way through wind or rain or snow, and up to perilous mountaintops. He spoke of nature as a mother from whose breast he sucked the sap and zest of life. In a prose-poem rhapsody, *Die Natur* (1780), he expressed with religious feeling his humble surrender to, his happy absorption in, the generative and destructive forces that envelop man.

> Nature! By her we are surrounded and encompassed—unable to step out of her, and unable to enter deeper into her. She receives us, unsolicited and unwarned, into the circle of her dance, and hurries along with us, till we are exhausted, and drop out of her arms. . . .
> She creates ever new forms; what now is, was never before; what was, comes not again; all is new, and yet always the old. . . .
> She seems to have contrived everything for individuality, but cares nothing

for individuals. She is ever building, ever destroying, and her workshop is in-accessible . . .

She has thought, and is constantly meditating; not as a man, but as nature. She has an all-embracing mind of her own; no one can penetrate it. . . .

She lets every child tinker with her, every fool pass judgment on her; thou-sands stumble over her and see nothing; she has her joy in all. . . .

She is kindly. I praise her with all her works. She is wise and quiet. One can tear no explanation from her, extort from her no gift which she gives not of her own free will. . . .

She has placed me here, she will lead me away. I trust myself to her. She may do as she likes with me. She will not hate her work.[60]

In December, 1774, Duke Karl August stopped at Frankfurt en route to seek a bride at Karlsruhe. He had read and admired *Götz von Berlichingen;* he invited the author to meet him. Goethe came and made a favorable impres-sion; the Duke wondered might not this handsome and mannerly genius be an ornament of the Weimar court. He had to hurry on, but asked Goethe to meet him again on his return from Karlsruhe.

Goethe spoke often of destiny, too little of chance. He might have an-swered that it was destiny, not chance, that brought him to the Duke, and that it turned him from the loveliness of Lili Schönemann to Weimar's un-known perils and opportunities. Lili was the only daughter of a rich mer-chant in Frankfurt. Goethe, now a social lion, was invited to a reception in her home. She performed brilliantly at the piano; Goethe leaned over a corner of it and drank in her sixteen-year-old charms as she played. "I was sensible of feeling an attractive power of the gentlest kind. . . . We grew into the habit of seeing each other. . . . We were now necessary to each other. . . . An irresistible longing dominated me"[61]—so rapidly can that famous fever rise, blown up by a poet's sensitivity. Before he quite realized what it meant, he was officially engaged (April, 1775). Then Lili, thinking him securely captured, coquetted with others. Goethe saw and fumed.

Just at this time two friends, Counts Christian and Friedrich zu Stolberg, came to Frankfurt on their way to Switzerland. They suggested that Goethe join them. His father urged him to go, and to continue on into Italy. "With some intimation, but without leavetaking, I separated myself from Lili."[62] He started out in May, 1775; at Karlsruhe he met the Duke again, and was definitely invited to Weimar. He went on to Zurich, where he met Lavater and Bodmer. He climbed St. Gotthard, and looked longingly at Italy. Then the image of Lili regained ascendancy; he left his companions, turned home-ward, and in September had Lili in his arms. But, back in his room, he felt again his old dread of marriage as imprisonment and stagnation. Lili resented his vacillation; they agreed to break off their betrothal; in 1776 she married Bernhard von Türckheim.

The Duke, briefly at Frankfurt on his way back from Karlsruhe, offered to send a coach to take Goethe to Weimar. Goethe consented, made his arrangements, and waited for the appointed day. The coach did not come. Had he been played with and deceived? After some days of fretful delay, he started out for Italy. But at Heidelberg the promised coach caught up with him; the Duke's emissary made explanations and apologies; Goethe accepted them. On November 7, 1775, he reached Weimar, aged twenty-six, torn as always between Eros and Destiny, longing for woman, but resolved to be great.

IV. HERDER: 1744–76

Hardly a month after Goethe's arrival at Weimar he passed on to the Duke, with warm approval, Wieland's suggestion that the vacant post of *Generalsuperintendent* of the clergy and the schools of the duchy be offered to Johann Gottfried Herder. The Duke agreed.

Born at Mohrungen in East Prussia (August 25, 1744), Herder was, by geography and Baltic mists, akin to Immanuel Kant. His father was a poor schoolmaster and Pietist cantor, so that the boy had all the uses of adversity. From the age of five he suffered from a fistula in the right eye. Soon required to add to the family income, he left school to become secretary and servant to Sebastian Trescho, who made a good living by writing handbooks of piety. Trescho had a library, which Johann consumed. At eighteen he was sent to Königsberg to have the fistula removed, and to study medicine at the university. The operation failed, and the dissection classes so upset the youth's stomach that he turned from medicine to theology.

He formed a friendship with Hamann, who taught him English, using *Hamlet* as a text; Herder learned almost all the play by heart. He attended Kant's lectures on geography, astronomy, and Wolff's philosophy; Kant liked him so much that he excused him from the fees charged for the courses. Herder supported himself by translating and tutoring, and from the age of twenty to twenty-five he taught in the cathedral school at Riga. At twenty-one he was ordained a Lutheran minister; at twenty-two he became a Freemason;[60] at twenty-three he was appointed adjutant pastor in two churches near Riga. He broke into print at twenty-two with a volume *Über die neuere deutsche Litteratur*; he added a second and third tome to it a year later; Kant, Lessing, Nikolai, and Lavater were impressed by the young author's learning, and they commended his appeal for a national literature liberated from foreign tutelage.

Herder anticipated the Werther fashion by falling hopelessly in love with a married woman; he suffered so severe a physical and mental depression that he was given a leave of absence with promise of re-employment at a better salary on his return. He borrowed money, left Riga (May 23, 1769), and never saw it again. He went by ship to Nantes, stayed there four months, and passed to Paris. He met Diderot and d'Alembert, but he was never won to the French Enlightenment.

His bent was aesthetic rather than intellectual. In Paris he began to collect primitive poetry, and found in it more delight than in the classic literature of France. He read Macpherson's "Ossian" in a German translation, and pronounced these skillful imitations superior to most modern English verse after Shakespeare. He began in 1769 those essays in artistic and literary criticism which he called *Wäldchen* (groves); three volumes of these he published in his lifetime as *Kritische Wälder* (*Critical Woods*). In February, 1770, he spent fourteen days in fruitful contact with Lessing at Hamburg. Then he joined the Prince of Holstein-Gottorp as tutor and companion, and traveled with him through western Germany. In Cassel he met Rudolph Raspe, professor of archaeology and soon to be author of *Baron Münchausen's Narrative of His Marvelous Travels and Campaigns in Russia* (1785). Raspe had called the attention of Germany to Thomas Percy's *Reliques of Ancient English Poetry* in the year of its appearance (1765). Herder was strengthened in his belief that poets should abandon the Winckelmann-Lessing call for imitation of Greek classics, and should rather cling to the popular sources of their nation's traditions in folk poetry and ballad history.

Passing with the Prince to Darmstadt, Herder met its "Circle of Sensitives," took kindly to their exaltation of sentiment, and especially appreciated the sentiments of Caroline Flachsland, the orphaned sister-in-law of Privy Councilor Andreas von Hesse. He was invited to preach in a local church. She heard him and was moved; they walked in the woods; they touched hands and he was moved. He proposed. She warned him that she lived on the charity of her sister, and could bring him no dowry; he replied that he was heavily in debt, had only the dimmest prospects, and was committed to accompany the Prince. They pledged each other no formal troth, but agreed to love each other by mail. On April 27, 1770, his party left for Mannheim.

When it reached Strasbourg Herder, though he longed to see Italy, left the Prince. The fistula in his lachrymal gland blocked the tear duct to the nostril, causing constant pain. Dr. Lobstein, professor of gynecology at the university, promised that an operation would clear up the matter in three weeks. Herder submitted, without anesthetics, to repeated drilling of a channel through the bone to the nasal passage. Infection set in, and for almost six months Herder was confined to his hotel room, discouraged by the failure of the operation, and gloomy with doubts of his future. It was in this mood of suffering and pessimism that he met Goethe (September 4, 1770). "I was able to be present at the operation," Goethe recalled, "and to be serviceable in many ways."[64] He was inspired by Herder's view that poetry arose instinctively among the people, not from "a few refined and cultivated men."[65] When Herder left, his funds quite exhausted, Goethe "borrowed a sum of money for him," which Herder later repaid.

Reluctantly he accepted an invitation from Count Wilhelm zu Lippe, ruler of the little principality of Schaumburg-Lippe, in northwest Germany, to serve him as court preacher and consistory president in his modest capital, Bückeburg. In April, 1771, Herder left Strasbourg, visited Caroline at Darmstadt and Goethe at Frankfurt, and reached Bückeburg on the twenty-eighth. He found the Count an "enlightened despot" of a rigid disciplinarian cast. The town was provincial in everything but music, which was well supplied by Johann Christoph Friedrich Bach. Herder resigned himself to isolation from the mainstream of German thought; but the books that he issued from his foot of earth powerfully affected that stream, and shared in forming the literary ideas of Sturm und Drang. He assured German authors that if they were to seek their inspiration in the roots of the nation and the life of the people they would in time outshine all that the French had done. In philosophy and science this prediction was verified.

His *Abhandlung über den Ursprung der Sprache* (*Treatise on the Origin of Language*, 1772) won the prize that had been offered by the Berlin Academy in 1770. While sincerely professing piety, Herder rejected the notion that language was a special creation of God; it was a human creation, naturally resulting from the processes of sensation and thought. Originally, he suggested, language and poetry were one as expressions of emotion, and verbs, expressing action, were the first "part of speech." — Another volume, *Auch eine Philosophie der Geschichte* (*One More Philosophy of History*, 1774), presented history as "the natural philosophy of successive events." Each civilization was a biological entity, a plant with its own birth, youth, maturity, decline, and death; it should be studied from the standpoint of its own time, without moral prepossessions based on another environment and age. Like the Romantics in general, Herder admired the Middle Ages as the age of imagination and feeling, of popular poetry and art, of rural simplicity and peace; by contrast, post-Reformation Europe was the worship of the state, of money, urban luxury, artificiality, and vice. He criticized the Enlightenment as the idolatry of reason, and compared it unfavorably with the classic cultures of Greece and Rome. In all the historic process Herder, like Bossuet, saw the hand of God, but sometimes the eloquent pastor forgot his theology, and thought that "the general change of the world was guided far less by man than by a blind fate."[66]

His loneliness moved him, despite his meager income, to ask Caroline and her brother-in-law might he come and make her his wife. They consented, and the lovers were married at Darmstadt on May 2, 1773. They returned to Bückeburg, and Herder borrowed money to make his rectory a pleasant home for his mate. She gave him a lifelong service and devotion. Through her a coolness that had developed between Herder and Goethe was ended, and when Goethe found himself in a position to recommend the pastor to a more remunerative post, he was happy to do it. On October 1, 1776, Herder and Caroline arrived in Weimar, and moved into the house that Goethe had prepared for them. Now only one member had yet to come of the quadrumvirate that was to make Weimar's fame.

V. SCHILLER'S *WANDERJAHRE*: 1759–87

Johann Christoph Friedrich Schiller was born on November 10, 1759, at Marbach in Württemberg. His mother was the daughter of the landlord of the Lion Inn. The father was a surgeon—later a captain—in the army of Duke Karl Eugen; he moved about with his regiment, but his wife stayed mostly in Lorch or Ludwigsburg. In those towns Friedrich received his education. His parents intended him for the ministry, but were persuaded by the Duke to send him, aged fourteen, to the Karlsschule at Ludwigsburg (later at Stuttgart), where the sons of officers were prepared for law, medicine, or an army career. The discipline was rigorously military; the studies were uncongenial to a lad almost femininely sensitive. Schiller reacted by imbibing all the rebel ideas that he could find, and pouring them (1779–80) into *Die Räuber* (*The Robbers*), a drama that surpassed *Götz von Berlichingen* as an expression of Sturm und Drang.

In 1780 Schiller was graduated in medicine, and became surgeon to a regiment at Stuttgart. His salary was slight; he lived in one room with Lieutenant Kapf; they prepared their own meals, chiefly of sausage, potatoes, and lettuce, and, on gala occasions, wine. He tried hard to be a man in the soldier's sense of battle, beer, and bordellos; he visited the prostitutes who attended the camp;[67] but he had no taste for vulgarity, for he idealized women as sacred mysteries to be approached with trembling reverence. His landlady, Luise Vischer, was a thirty-year-old widow, but when she played the harpsichord "my spirit left its mortal clay,"[68] and he wished he could be "fixed forever to thy lips, . . . thy breath to drink,"[69]—a novel way of suicide.

He tried in vain to find a publisher for *The Robbers;* failing, he saved and borrowed, and paid for its printing himself (1781). Its success astonished even the twenty-two-year-old author. Carlyle thought it marked "an era in the Literature of the World;"[70] but respectable Germany was shocked to find that the play left hardly any aspect of current civilization undamned. Schiller's preface pointed out that the denouement showed the grandeur of conscience and the wickedness of revolt.

Karl Moor, elder son of the aging Count Maximilian von Moor, is especially beloved by his father for his idealism and generosity, and is therefore envied and hated by his brother Franz. Karl goes off to the University of Leipzig, and imbibes the rebellious sentiments that were seething in the youth of Western Europe. Dunned for his debts, he denounces the heartless money-grubbers who "damn the Sadducee who fails to come to church regularly, although their own devotion consists in reckoning up their usurious gains at the very altar."[71] He loses all faith in the existing social order, joins a robber band, becomes its captain, pledges to be loyal to it till death, and comforts his conscience by playing Robin Hood. One of the band describes him:

> He does not commit murder, as we do, for the sake of plunder, and as to money . . . he seems not to care a straw for it; his third of the booty, which belongs to him of right, he gives to orphans, or to support promising youths at college. But should he happen to get into his clutches a country squire who grinds his peasants like cattle, or some gold-laced villain who warps the law to his own purposes, . . . or any other chap of that kidney—then, my boy, he is in his element, and rages like a very devil.[72]

Karl denounces the clergy as sycophants of power and secret worshipers of Mammon; "the best of them would betray the whole Trinity for ten shekels."[73]

Meanwhile Franz arranges that a false message should announce to the Count that Karl is dead. Franz becomes heir to the estate, and offers marriage to Amelia, who loves Karl alive or dead. Franz poisons his father, and quiets his qualms with atheism: "It has not yet been proved that there is an eye above this earth to take account of what passes on it. . . . There is no God."[74] Karl hears of his brother's crimes, leads his band to the paternal castle, besieges Franz, who prays desperately to God for help, and, none coming, kills himself. Amelia offers herself to Karl if he will leave his life of robbery; he longs to do so, but his followers remind him of his pledge to remain with them till death. He respects his pledge and turns away from Amelia; she begs him to kill her; he accommodates her; then, having arranged that a poor workingman should receive the reward for capturing him, he gives himself up to the law and the gallows.

All this, of course, is nonsense. The characters and events are incredible, the style is bombastic, the speeches unbearable, the conception of woman romantically ideal. But it is powerful nonsense. There is in nearly all of us a secret sympathy with those who defy the law; we too sometimes feel ourselves "squeezed into stays" by the thousands of laws and ordinances that bind or mulct us; we are so accustomed to the benefits of law that we take them for granted; we have no natural sympathy with the police until lawlessness makes us its victim. So the printed play found fervent readers and applause, and the complaints of preachers and lawmakers that Schiller had idealized crime did not deter a reviewer from hailing Schiller as promising to be a German Shakespeare,[75] nor producers from proposing to stage the play.

Baron Wolfgang Heribert von Dalberg offered to present it in the Nationaltheater at Mannheim if Schiller would provide a happier ending. He did: Moor marries Amelia instead of killing her. Without asking permission of Duke Karl Eugen, his military commander, Schiller slipped away from Stuttgart to attend the première on January 13, 1782. People came from Worms, Darmstadt, Frankfurt, and elsewhere to see the performance; August Iffland, one of the finest actors of that generation, played Karl; the audience shouted and sobbed its approval; no other German drama had ever received such an ovation;[76] it was a high-water mark in Sturm und Drang. After the play Schiller was feted by the actors and courted by a Mannheim publisher; he found it hard to return to Stuttgart and resume his life as regimental surgeon. In May he escaped again to Mannheim to see another performance of *The Robbers*, and to discuss with Dalberg plans for a second drama. Back again with his regiment, he received a reproof from the Duke, and was forbidden to write any more plays.

He could not accept such a prohibition. On September 22, 1782, accompanied by a friend, Andreas Streicher, he fled to Mannheim. He offered Dalberg a new play—*Die Verschwörung des Fiesko zu Genua* (*The Conspiracy of Fiesko at Genoa*). He read it to the actors; they pronounced it a sad decline from *The Robbers*; Dalberg thought he might produce the play if Schiller revised it; Schiller spent weeks on this task; Dalberg rejected the result. Schiller found himself penniless. Streicher spent, in supporting him, the money he had saved to study music in Hamburg. When this ran out, Schiller welcomed an invitation to stay in Bauerbach in a cottage owned by Frau Henrietta von Wolzogen. There he wrote a third play, *Kabale und Liebe (Intrigue and Love)*, and fell in love with Fräulein Lotte von Wolzogen, aged sixteen. She preferred a rival. Meanwhile *Fiesko*, published, had a good sale. Dalberg repented, and sent Schiller an invitation to be resident playwright for the Mannheim theater at three hundred florins per year. He agreed (July, 1783).

Despite many unpaid debts, and one serious illness, Schiller, modestly lodged in Mannheim, had a year of precarious bliss. *Fiesko* received its première January 11, 1784; the incredibly happy ending which Dalberg had insisted upon spoiled it, and the play aroused no enthusiasm. But *Kabale und Liebe* was better constructed, had fewer orations, and showed a growing sense of the theater; some have pronounced it, from the theatrical point of view, the best of all German tragedies.[77] After the initial performance (April 15, 1784) the audience gave it such tumultuous applause that Schiller rose from his seat in a box and bowed.

His happiness was extreme and brief. He was not temperamentally fit to deal with actors, who were almost as high-strung as himself; he judged their acting strictly, and reproved them for not accurately memorizing their lines.[78] He was unable to finish a third play, *Don Carlos*, by the stipulated time. When his contract as *Theaterdichter* neared expiration in September, 1784, Dalberg refused to renew it. Schiller had saved nothing, and was again faced with destitution and impatient creditors.

About this time he published some letters, *Philosophische Briefe*, which indicate that religious doubts were added to his economic embarrassments. He could not accept the old theology, and yet his poetic spirit was revolted by such materialistic atheism as d'Holbach had expressed in *Système de la nature* (1770). He could no longer pray, but he envied those who could, and he described with a sense of great loss the comfort that religion was bringing to thousands of souls in suffering, grief, and the nearness of death.[79] He kept his faith in free will, immortality, and an unknowable God, basing all, like Kant, on the moral consciousness. And he expressed memorably the ethic of Christ: "When I hate, I take something from myself; when I love, I become richer by what I love. To pardon is to receive a property that has been lost. Misanthropy is a protracted suicide."[80]

Amid these complications Christian Gottfried Körner brought into Schiller's life one of the finest friendships in literary history. In June, 1784, he sent to Schiller from Leipzig a letter of warm admiration, accompanied by portraits of himself, his fiancée Minna Stock, her sister Dora, and Dora's fiancé Ludwig Huber, and a wallet that Minna had embroidered. Körner had been born in 1756 (three years before Schiller) to the pastor of that same Thomaskirche where Bach a generation earlier had conducted so much enduring music. The youth became a licentiate in law at the age of twenty-one, and was now counselor to the Upper Consistory in Dresden. Schiller, pressed with troubles, delayed reply till December 7. Körner answered:

"We offer you our friendship without reserve. Come to us as soon as possible."[81]

Schiller hesitated. He had made friendships in Mannheim, and had had several amours, especially (1784) with Charlotte von Kalb, who had been married only a year before. At Darmstadt, in December, 1784, he met Duke Karl August of Saxe-Weimar, read to him the first act of *Don Carlos*, and received the title of *Rat*, or honorary councilor; but no offer came of a place in the Weimar firmament. He decided to accept Körner's invitation to Leipzig. On February 10, 1785, he sent to his unknown admirer an emotional appeal that shows him near the breaking point:

> While half of Mannheim is rushing to the theater . . . I fly to you, dearest friends. . . . Since your last letter the thought has never left me that we were meant for each other. Do not misjudge my friendship because it may seem somewhat hasty. Nature waives ceremony in favor of certain beings. Noble souls are held together by a delicate thread which often proves lasting. . . .
> If you will make allowances for a man who cherishes great ideas and has performed only small acts; who as yet can only surmise from his follies that Nature has destined him for something; who demands unbounded love and yet knows not what he can offer in return; but who can love something beyond himself, and has no greater torment than the thought that he is very far from being what he desires to be; if a man of this stamp may aspire to your friendship ours will be eternal, for I am that man. Perhaps you will love Schiller; even should your esteem for the poet have declined.

This letter was interrupted, but was resumed on February 22.

> I cannot remain any longer in Mannheim. . . . I must visit Leipzig, and make your acquaintance. My soul thirsts for new food—for better men—for friendship, affection, and love. I must be near you, and, by your conversation and company, freshness will be breathed into my wounded spirit. . . . You must give me new life, and I shall become more than I ever was before. I shall be happy—I never yet was happy. . . . Will you welcome me?[82]

Körner answered on March 3, "We will welcome you with open arms"; and he paid G. J. Göschen, a Leipzig publisher, to send Schiller an advance payment for future essays.[83] When the poet reached Leipzig (March 17, 1785) Körner was absent in Dresden, but his fiancée, her sister, and Huber revived Schiller with food and solicitous hospitality. Göschen took to him at once. "I cannot describe to you," he wrote, "how grateful and accommodating Schiller is when given critical advice, and how much he labors at his own moral development."[84]

Körner met Schiller for the first time at Leipzig on July 1, and then returned to Dresden. "Heaven brought us together in a wonderful manner," Schiller wrote to him, "and our friendship is a miracle." But he added that he was again approaching bankruptcy.[85] Körner sent him money, assurance, and advice:

> Should you be in want of more, write to me, and by return post I will send you any amount . . . If I were ever so rich, and could . . . place you above ever wanting the necessaries of life, still I would not dare do it. I know that you are capable of earning wherewith to provide for all your wants as soon

as you put your hand to the work. But allow me at least for one year to place you above the necessity of working. I can spare it without being worse off myself; and you can repay me, if you like, at your own convenience.[86]

Körner's generosity was all the more remarkable since he was preparing for marriage. The wedding took place at Dresden on August 7, 1785. In September Schiller joined them, and he lived with them, or at their expense, till July 20, 1787. It was about this time—perhaps amid the happiness of the newlyweds—that he composed his most famous poem, *An die Freude*, the *Ode to Joy* that became the crown of the Ninth Symphony. Everyone knows Beethoven's stirring melody, but few of us, outside of Germany, know Schiller's words. They began with a call to universal love, and ended with a summons to revolution:

Freude, schöner Götterfunken	Joy of flame celestial fashioned,
Tochter aus Elysium,	Daughter of Elysium,
Wir betreten feuertrunken	By that holy fire impassioned
Himmlische, dein Heiligtum.	To thy sanctuary we come.
Deine Zauber binden wieder	Thine the spells that reunited
Was die Mode streng gesteilt,	Those estranged by custom dread;
Alle Menschen werden Brüder	Every man or brother plighted
Wo dein sanfter Flügel weilt.	Where thy gentle wings are spread.
Chorus: Seid umschlungen, Millionen!	*Chorus:* Millions in our arms we gather;
Diesen Kuss der ganzen Welt!	To the world our kiss is sent!
Brüder—überm Sternenzelt	Past the starry firmament,
Muss ein lieber Vater wohnen.	Brothers, dwells a loving Father.
Wem der grosse Wurf gelungen	Who that height of bliss has provèd
Eines Freundes Freund zu sein,	Once a friend of friends to be,
Wer ein holdes Weib errungen,	Who has won a maid beloved,
Mische seinen Jubel ein!	Join us in our jubilee.
Ja—wer auch nur eine Seele	Whoso holds a heart in keeping—
Sein nennt auf dem Erdenrund,	One in all the world his own—
Und wer's nie gekonnt, der stehle	Who has failed, let him with weeping
Weinend sich aus diesem Bund.	From our fellowship be gone.
Chorus: Was den grossen Ring be-	*Chorus:* All the mighty globe con-
wohnet,	taineth
Huldige der Sympathie!	Homage to Compassion pay!
Zu den Sternen leitet sie	To the stars she leads the way
Wo der Unbekannte thronet. . . .	Where the unknown Godhead reign-eth. . . .
Festen Mut in schweren Leiden	Hearts in direst need unquailing,
Hilfe wo die Unschuld weint.	Aid to innocence in woe;
Ewigkeit geschwornen Eiden,	Troth eternally unfailing,
Wahrheit gegen Freund und Feind,	Loyalty to friend and foe!
Männerstolz vor Königsthronen,	Fronting kings, and manly spirit,
Brüder, gält es Gut und Blut;	Though it cost us wealth and blood!
Dem Verdienste seine Kronen,	Crowns to naught save noblest merit,
Untergang der Lügenbrut!	Death to all the Liars' brood!
Chorus: Schliesst den heilgen Zirkel	*Chorus:* Close the holy circle. Ever
dichter,	
Schwört bei diesem goldnen Wein,	Swear it by the wine of gold!
Dem Gelübde treu zu sein,	Swear these sacred vows to hold,
Schwört es bei dem Sternenrichter!	Swear it by the stars' Lawgiver!

For two years Körner supported Schiller, hoping that the poet would beat into presentable shape the drama that was to portray the conflict between Philip II and his son Carlos. But Schiller dallied so long with the play that he lost the mood in which he had begun it; perhaps more reading of history had altered his view of Philip; in any case, he changed the plot out of unity and sequence. Meanwhile (February, 1787) he fell in love with Henrietta von Arnim, and love letters consumed his ink, while Henrietta shopped for a richer suitor. Körner persuaded Schiller to isolate himself in a suburb until he had finished his play. At last it was complete (June, 1787), and the Hamburg theater offered to produce it. Schiller's spirits and pride revived; perhaps now he might be judged worthy to join the galaxy of literary lights that shone around Duke Karl August. Körner, relieved, agreed that there was no future for the poet in Dresden. Besides, Charlotte von Kalb was in Weimar, husbandless and beckoning. On July 20, after many farewells, Schiller drove out from Dresden into a new life. On the morrow he was in Weimar, and the great circle was complete.

CHAPTER XXIII

Weimar in Flower

1775–1805

I. WIELAND SEQUEL: 1775–1813

MOZART, seeing Wieland at Mannheim in 1777, described his face as "frightfully ugly, covered with pockmarks, and he had a long nose; . . . aside from that he is . . . a most gifted fellow. . . . People stare at him as if he had dropped from heaven."[1] The stormy petrels of Sturm und Drang disliked him because he laughed at their rebel ecstasies, but Weimar liked him because he sweetened his satires with grace and a general absolution for mankind, and because he bore with good humor the repeated irruption of new stars in the literary sky where he could have claimed priority. Goethe's autobiography commemorated him gratefully.[2] Schiller at first encounter thought him vain and melancholy; but "the footing on which he at once placed himself toward me shows confidence, love, and esteem."[3] "We will shortly open our hearts to each other," said the older to the younger poet; "we will assist each other in turn";[4] and he proved faithful to this promise. "Wieland and I draw daily closer together. . . . He never omits an occasion for saying a kind word."[5]

Wieland competed successfully with the newcomers by issuing in 1780 a poetic romance, *Oberon*, about a knight who is rescued from a hundred fairies, and from the quagmire charms of an overheated queen, by the magic wand of the prince of fairies. When Goethe had to sit for a portrait, and wished to remain quiet for an hour, he asked Wieland to read parts of the epic to him. "Never," Wieland reported, "have I seen anyone so happy over the work of another as Goethe was."[6] John Quincy Adams translated the poem while he was United States minister to Prussia in 1797–1801, and James Planché took from it the libretto for Weber's opera (1826).

The March, 1798, number of Wieland's *Neue teutsche Merkur* contained an article—presumably by Wieland—which remarkably presaged coming events. It noted the chaos into which France had fallen since 1789; it recommended the appointment of a dictator, as in the crises of republican Rome; and it nominated young Bonaparte, then having trouble in Egypt, as clearly fitted for the task. When Napoleon had in effect conquered Germany he met Wieland in Weimar and in Erfurt (1808), talked with him about Greek and Roman history and literature, and honored him, among German authors, as second only to Goethe.[7]

On January 25, 1813, Goethe wrote in his diary, "Wieland buried today," and sent the news to a friend at Karlsbad: "Our good Wieland has left us.

. . . On September 3 we still quite festively celebrated his eightieth birthday. There was a beautiful balance of tranquillity and activity in his life. With a remarkable deliberateness, without any impassioned striving or crying, he contributed an infinite amount to the intellectual culture of the nation."[8]

II. HERDER AND HISTORY: 1777–1803

"I have just left Herder," Schiller wrote in July, 1787. ". . . His conversation is brilliant, his language warm and powerful; but his feelings are swayed by love and hate."[9]

Herder's duties at Weimar were multifarious, and allowed him little time for writing. As chaplain to the Duke he performed the baptisms, confirmations, marriages, and funerals of the ducal family and the court. As *Generalsuperintendent* of the duchy he supervised clerical conduct and appointments, attended consistory meetings, and preached sermons as orthodox as his private doubts would permit. The schools of the duchy were under his management, and became a model for all Germany. These responsibilities, added to his fistula and general ill-health, made him irritable, and gave his conversation, now and then, what Goethe called a "vicious bite."[10] For three years (1780–83) he and Goethe avoided each other; the Duke resented some of Herder's sermons ("After such a sermon," said Goethe, "there's nothing left for a prince but to abdicate"[11]); and the amiable Wieland remarked, in 1777, "I'd like to have a dozen pyramids between Herder and me."[12] Weimar learned to make clinical allowances for its Dean Swift, and his pleasant wife Caroline counteracted some of his bite. On August 28, 1783, Goethe took advantage of this being the birthday of himself and Herder's eldest son to invite the Herders to dinner; councilor and *Generalsuperintendent* were reconciled, and Goethe wrote that "the wretched clouds that so long separated us have been dispelled, and, I am convinced, forever."[13] A month later he added: "I know no one of a nobler heart or a more liberal spirit";[14] and Schiller noted in 1787, "Herder is a passionate admirer of Goethe—he almost idolizes him."[15] In time Wieland and Herder became understanding friends,[16] and in the salon of Anna Amalie it was these two, rather than Goethe or Schiller, who led the conversation and won the Dowager Duchess's heart.[17]

Amid his administrative chores Herder pursued primitive poetry, gathered specimens from a dozen nations, and from Orpheus to Ossian, and published them in an anthology, *Volkslieder* (1778), which became a fountainhead of the Romantic movement in Germany. While Goethe was preparing a return to classical ideals, forms, and styles, and to restraint of emotion by intellect, Herder counseled a reaction against eighteenth-century rationalism and seventeenth-century formalism to medieval faith, legends, lays, and ways.

In 1778 the Bavarian Academy offered a prize for the best essay "On the Effects of Poetry upon the Customs and Morals of the Nations." Herder's contribution was crowned, and was published by the Academy in 1781. It traced what the author considered the deterioration of poetry, among the Hebrews, the Greeks, and the North Europeans, from an early bardic expression of popular history, feelings, and ideas, in free and flowing rhythms, into a "refined" and scholastic exercise, counting syllables, wrenching rhymes, venerating rules, and losing the vitality of the people in the deadening artificialities of city life. The Renaissance, Herder held, had taken literature away from the people and imprisoned it in courts, and printing had replaced the living minstrel with the book. In another essay, "On the Spirit of Hebrew Poetry" (1783), Herder, who had made himself a good Hebraist, proposed that the Book of Genesis should be read as poetry, not as science; and he suggested that such poetry could convey as much truth through symbolism as science does through "fact."

His religious faith struggled to maintain itself despite his wide reading in science and history. In his first year at Weimar he was suspected of being an atheist, a freethinker, a Socinian, an "enthusiast" (mystic).[18] He had read the Wolfenbüttel Fragments of Reimarus as published by Lessing, and was sufficiently impressed to doubt the divinity of Christ.[19] He was not an atheist, but he accepted Spinoza's pantheism. He told Jacobi in 1784, "I do not recognize an extramundane God."[20] He followed Lessing in studying and defending Spinoza; "I must confess that this philosophy makes me very happy."[21] He devoted to Spinoza the opening chapters of *Gott, einige Gespräche* (*God, Some Conversations*, 1787); in this treatise God lost personal form and became the energy and spirit of the universe, unknowable except in the order of the world and the spiritual consciousness of man.[22] However, in tracts addressed to the clergy Herder accepted the supernatural quality of Christ's miracles, and the immortality of the soul.[23]

He brought the scattered elements of his philosophy into a comparatively ordered whole in a massive masterpiece which he modestly entitled *Ideen zur Philosophie der Geschichte der Menschheit* (*Ideas for a Philosophy of the History of Mankind*), one of the epochal, seminal books of the eighteenth century. It appeared in four parts in 1784, 1785, 1787, and 1791. That so vast an undertaking should have neared completion amid Herder's official responsibilities is evidence of a strong character and a good wife. So Herder wrote to Hamann, May 10, 1784: "In my whole life I have not written any work with so many troubles and exhaustions from within, and so many disturbances from without, as I have this one; so that if my wife, who is the real *autor autoris* [author of the author] of my writings—and Goethe, who accidentally got to see Book I—had not incessantly encouraged me and urged me on, everything would have remained in the Hades of the unborn."[24]

Part I begins with a frankly secular story of "creation," based on current astronomy and geology, and making no use of the Bible except as poetry. Life did not evolve from matter, for matter itself is alive. Body and mind are not separate and opposed substances, they are two forms of one force, and every cell in every organism contains, in some degree, both forms. There is no external design visible in nature, but there is an internal design—the mysterious and "perfect determination" of each seed to develop into a specific organism with all its own complex and characteristic parts. Herder does not derive man from lower animals, but he sees him as a member of the animal kingdom, fighting like other organisms for sustenance and survival. Man became man by taking erect stature, which developed in him a sensory system based upon sight and hearing rather than upon smell and taste; forefeet became hands, free for grasping, *manipulation*, com*prehens*ion, thought. The highest product of God or nature is the conscious mind acting with reason and freedom, and destined to immortality.

Part II of the *Ideen* starts with the assumption that man is by nature good; it renews the argument for the relative excellence and happiness of primitive societies, and deprecates the Kantian—later Hegelian—notion that the state is the goal of human development. Herder despised the state as he knew it. "In great states," he wrote, "hundreds must go hungry so that *one* can strut and wallow in luxury; tens of thousands are oppressed and driven to death so that *one* crowned fool or wise man can carry out his fancy."[25]

In Part III Herder praised Athens for its comparative democracy, which allowed culture to spread into many strata of the population. Rome, building its wealth on conquest and slavery, developed a narrow culture that left the people in poverty and ignorance. In all this history Herder saw no Providence; it was too evil to be divine. God, being one with nature, lets matters take their course according to natural law and human stupidity. Nevertheless, by the very struggle for existence, some progress emerges from the chaos; mutual aid, social order, morals, and law are developed as means of survival, and man moves slowly toward a humane humanity. Not that there is a continuous line of progress; this cannot be, for each national culture is a unique entity, with its own inherent character, its own language, religion, moral code, literature, and art; and, like any organism, each culture, barring accidents, tends to grow to its natural maximum, after which it declines and dies. There is no guarantee that later cultures will excel earlier ones, but the contributions of each culture are better transmitted to its successors, and so the human heritage grows.

Part IV lauds Christianity as the mother of Western civilization. The medieval papacy served a good purpose in checking the despotism of rulers and the individualism of states; the Scholastic philosophers, though they wove meaningless webs with ponderous words, sharpened the terms and tools of reason; and the medieval universities gathered, preserved, and transmitted much of Greek and Roman culture, something even of Arabic and Persian science and philosophy. So the intellectual community grew too numerous and subtle for the custodians of power; the cake of custom was broken, and the modern mind declared itself free.

Between the third and fourth installments of the *Ideen* Herder realized his long-deferred hope of seeing Italy. Johann Friedrich Hugo von Dalberg, Catholic privy councilor to the Archbishop-Elector of Trier, invited Herder to accompany him on a grand tour, all expenses paid. The Duke of Saxe-Weimar—and Caroline—gave him leave of absence, and Herder left Weimar

August 7, 1788. When he joined Dalberg in Augsburg he found that Dalberg's mistress was an important member of the party. Her presence and her demands shared with ill-health in souring the trip for Herder. In October Anna Amalie arrived in Rome; Herder left Dalberg and joined her entourage. He liked Angelica Kauffmann too much for Caroline's liking, and Caroline's letters spoke too often and fondly of Goethe. Herder, having heard of Goethe's life in Rome, resumed his bite: "My journey here," he wrote, "has unfortunately made Goethe's selfish existence, which is inwardly altogether unconcerned about others, clearer to me than I could desire. He can't help it, so let him be."[26]

He returned to Weimar July 9, 1789. Five days later the Bastille fell, and Herder changed his writing plans. He completed Part IV of the *Ideen*, then put the book aside, and, instead, wrote *Briefe zur Beförderung der Humanität* (*Letters for the Advancement of Humanity*, 1793–97). He began with cautiously approving the French Revolution; he welcomed the collapse of French feudalism, and shed no tears over the secularization of the Catholic Church in France.[27] When the Duke and Goethe went off to face the French at Valmy, and came back sore with defeat, Herder suppressed those early *Briefe*, and devoted the remainder to praise of geniuses safely dead.

In his old age he lost none of his relish for intellectual combat. He countered Kant's criticism of the *Ideen* with an incisive attack upon the *Critique of Pure Reason*. He called that book a monstrous jugglery of words with metaphysical phantoms, like "synthetic judgments a priori"; he denied the subjectivity of space and time; and he accused Kant of bringing back into psychology the "faculties" into which the Scholastic philosophers had allegedly divided the mind. He suggested, prophetically, that philosophy might make a new approach through a logical analysis of language—for reasoning is internal speech.

Goethe largely agreed with Herder's criticism of Kant, but this did not protect him from an occasional bite. When the two were staying under the same roof at Jena in 1803 Goethe read, to a gathering that included Herder, some parts of his new drama, *Die natürliche Tochter*. Herder praised the play to others, but when the author asked for his opinion he could not resist a pun about the boy that Goethe's mistress had borne him: "I like your natural son better than your *Natural Daughter*." Goethe did not appreciate the wit. The two men never saw each other again. Herder retired into the seclusion of his Weimar home, and died there December 18, 1803—two years before Schiller, ten before Wieland, twenty-nine before Goethe. Duke Karl August, who had often been offended by him, had him buried with high honors in the Church of Sts. Peter and Paul.

III. GOETHE COUNCILOR: 1775–86

Goethe was welcomed to Weimar by all but the politicians. "I must tell you," wrote Wieland to Lavater, November 13, 1775, "that Goethe has been with us since Tuesday last, and that within three days I have conceived so deep an affection for this magnificent person—I so thoroughly see into him, feel and understand him—as you can far better imagine than I can describe."[28] In that same month a member of the court wrote to Goethe's parents: "Conceive of your son as the most intimate friend of our dear Duke, . . . loved to adoration, too, by all the good ladies hereabout."[29]

But there were clouds. The Duke relished wild hunts and drinking; Goethe at first accompanied him in both; Klopstock publicly charged the poet with corrupting a virtuous prince. Luise feared that Goethe would alienate her husband from her; actually he used his influence to bring the Duke back to the Duchess despite the fact that the marriage had not been one of love. Some officials distrusted Goethe as a Sturm und Drang radical with pagan beliefs and romantic dreams. Several gladiators of that movement—Lenz, Klinger, and more—rushed to Weimar, introduced themselves as Goethe's friends, and clamored for plums. When Goethe took a fancy to a garden house—outside the city gate but near the ducal castle—Karl August lost Goethe some public good will by evicting the tenants so that Goethe might move in (April 21, 1776). There the poet found relief from court etiquette, and learned to grow vegetables and flowers. For three years he lived there all the year round, then only in the summer till 1782, when he moved to a spacious mansion in the town to attend to his mounting duties as a member of the government.

The Duke had thought of him as a poet, and had invited him to Weimar as a literary ornament to his court. But he perceived that the twenty-six-year-old author of a rebel play and a tearful romance was becoming a man of practical judgment. He appointed Goethe to a Bureau of Works, and asked him to look into the condition and operation of the mines at Ilmenau. Goethe did this with such assiduity and intelligence that Karl August determined to add him to the Privy Council that administered the duchy. A senior member protested against this sudden infusion of poetry, and threatened to resign. The Duke and the Dowager appeased him, and on June 11, 1776, Goethe became *Geheimer Legationsrat*—privy councilor of legation—at an annual salary of twelve hundred thalers. He reduced his attentions to the ladies. "For long now," Wieland informed Merck on June 24, "from the moment that he decided to devote himself to the Duke and the Duke's affairs, he has behaved with faultless wisdom and with worldly circumspection."[30] In 1778 Goethe was advanced to the then peaceful post of minister of war, and in 1799 to full membership in the Privy Council. He attempted some reforms, but found himself thwarted by vested interests at the top and public apathy below; soon he himself was a complete conservative. In 1781 he was made president of the Ducal Chamber. In 1782 he was given by Joseph II a patent of nobility, and became *von* Goethe. "In those days," he told Eckermann forty-five years later, "I felt so satisfied with myself that if I had been made a prince I should not have thought the change so very remarkable."[31]

Interwoven with his political career was the most lasting, intense, and poignant love affair in his life. Hear Dr. Johann Zimmermann's quite un-medical description of one of his patients in November, 1775:

> The Baroness von Stein, wife of the Chamberlain and Master of the Horse, has extraordinarily large black eyes of the highest beauty. Her voice is gentle and repressed. No one can fail to mark on her face . . . seriousness, gentleness, kindliness, . . . virtue, and profound sensibility. The manners of the court, which she possesses to perfection, have been transformed in her case into rare and high simplicity. She is very pious, with a touching and almost ecstatic elevation of soul. From her exquisite carriage and her almost professional skill in dancing one would hardly infer the tranquil moonlight . . . which fills her heart with peace. She is thirty-three years old. She has several children, and weak nerves. Her cheeks are red, her hair quite black, her complexion . . . of an Italian hue.[32]

Born in 1742, Charlotte von Schardt had married Baron Josias Gottlob von Stein in 1764. By 1772 she had borne seven children, of whom four were now dead. When Goethe met her she was still ailing from repeated pregnancies, and her sense of frailty entered into the modesty and diffidence of her character. Goethe idealized her, for he had the blood of a youth and the imagination of a poet, accustomed and commissioned to embellish reality; yet he did not exceed her physician in glorifying her. She was something new in his rosary of women: she was an aristocrat, in whom fine manners seemed inborn, and Goethe saw her as enshrined in nobility. It was one result of their relationship that she transmitted to him the manners of her class, and schooled him in self-possession, ease, moderation, and courtesy. She was grateful for his love as restoring her interest in life, but she accepted it as a woman of breeding receives the adoration of a youth seven years younger than herself—as the growth pains of an eager spirit seeking experience and fulfillment.

It was not love at first sight; six weeks after joining the Weimar circle he was still writing verses about "lovely Lili" Schönemann.[33] But on December 29, 1775, Dr. Zimmermann remarked Goethe's awakening to "new virtues and beauties in Charlotte." By January 15 he was trying to resist the incipient enthrallment; "I am glad to get away and wean myself from you," he told her; by January 28 he had quite surrendered. "Dear Angel," he wrote to her, "I'm not coming to the court. I feel too happy to stand the crowd. . . . Suffer me to love you as I do." And on February 23: "I must tell you, O you chosen among women, that you have placed a love in my heart which makes me joyful."[34]

She wrote many letters in return, but from this first period only one survives. "I had so detached myself from the world, but now it grows dear to me again, dear through you. My heart reproaches me; I feel that I torment both myself and you. Six months ago I was so ready to die, and I am ready no longer."[35] He was in ecstasy. "There is no explanation for what this woman does to me," he told Wieland, ". . . unless you accept the theory of transmigration. Oh, yes, once we were man and wife!"[36] He took the matrimonial privilege of quarreling and making up. Charlotte to Zimmermann, May, 1776: "He stormed away from me a week ago, and then returned with overflowing love. . . . What will he end by making of me?"[37] Apparently she insisted upon their love remaining Platonic, and he was too passionate to leave it so. "If I am not to live with you," he told her, "your love avails me no more than that of others who are absent."[38] But on the next day: "Forgive me for making you suffer. I'll try hereafter to bear it alone."[39]

He was desolate when she went to far-north Pyrmont for a cure, but when she returned she visited him at Ilmenau (August 5–6, 1776). On August 8 he wrote: "Your presence has had a wondrous effect upon me. . . . When I think that you were here in my cave with me, and that I held your hand, while you leaned over me . . . Your relationship to me is both sacred and strange. . . . There are no words for it, and the eyes of men cannot perceive it."[40] Almost five years after their first meeting he was still warm. So, on September 12, 1780, lonely in Zillbach: "Whenever I awake from my dreams, I find that I still love you and long for you. Tonight, as we were riding along and saw the lit windows of a house ahead, I thought: If only she were there to be our hostess. This is a rotten hole, and yet, if I could live quietly here all winter long with you, I'd like it very well."[41] And on March 12, 1781:

> My soul has so grown into yours that, as you know, I am inseparably tied to you, and neither height nor depth can part us. I wish there were some vow or sacrament which would bind me to you visibly and according to some law. How precious that would be! And surely my novitiate was long enough for me to take all due thought . . . The Jews have cords which they bind about their arms in the act of prayer. Thus I bind about my arm your dear cord when I address my prayer to you, and desire you to impart to me your goodness, wisdom, moderation, and patience.

Some have interpreted the expired "novitiate," or period of probation, as indicating Charlotte's physical surrender;[42] and yet he wrote to her, six years later: "Dear Lotte, you do not know what violence I have done to myself, and still do, and how the thought that I do not possess you . . . exhausts and consumes me."[43] If consummation came the secret was well kept. Baron von Stein, who did not die till 1793, bore with the liaison with the courtesy of an eighteenth-century gentleman. Occasionally Goethe ended his letters with "Regards to Stein."[44]

He had learned to love her children too, feeling more and more keenly the lack of his own. In the spring of 1783 he persuaded her to allow her ten-year-old boy, Fritz, to stay with him for extended visits, even to accompany him on long trips. One of her letters to Fritz (September, 1783) shows her maternal side, and the human hearts behind the dehumanized façade of history:

> I am so glad that you don't forget me out in the beautiful world, and that you write me in tolerably, though not very well-formed, letters. Since you're staying much longer than I expected, I'm afraid that your clothes won't be looking very well. If they get soiled, and you too, tell Privy Councilor Goethe just to throw my dear little Fritz into the water. . . . Try to appreciate your good luck, and do your best to please the Councilor by your behavior. Your father wishes to be remembered to you.[45]

By 1785 Goethe's passion had subsided into long silences. In May, 1786, Charlotte complained that "Goethe thinks a great deal and says nothing."[46] She was now forty-four, he was thirty-seven, and was retiring into himself. Often he went to Jena to get away from the Weimar court and seek rejuvenation among students. He had always refreshed himself with nature, climbing the Brocken (a 3,747-foot peak in the Harz Mountains, long associated with the Faust legend), and traveling with the Duke in Switzerland (September, 1779, to January, 1780). Sometimes, in retrospect, he felt that "during the first ten years of my official and court life at Weimar I scarcely accomplished anything"[47] in the way of literature or science. But it was good that the poet had been crossed with the administrator, and that the half-spoiled youth and faithless lover had been disciplined by the responsibilities of office and the deferment of amorous victory. He made use of every experience, and grew with every defeat. "The best thing about me is that deep inner stillness in which I live and grow, despite the world, and through which I gain what the world can never take from me."[48] Nothing was lost on him; everything found expression somewhere in his works; finally he was all the best of intellectual Germany fused into an integrated whole.

Two of his greatest poems belong to this period: the marriage of philosophy and religion, poetry and prose, in *Die Natur*; and the most perfect of his lyrics—the second of those called "Wanderers Nachtlied"—which he carved on the walls of a hunting lodge on September 7, 1780,[49] perhaps in a mood of restless longing:

Über allen Gipfeln	O'er all the hilltops
Ist Ruh;	Is quiet now;
In allen Wipfeln	In all the treetops
Spürest du	Hearest thou
Kaum einen Hauch;	Hardly a breath;
Die Vögelein schweigen im Walde.	The birds are asleep in the trees.
Warte nur! Balde	Wait: soon like these
Ruhest du auch.	Thou too shalt rest.[50]

Another of Goethe's famous lyrics belongs to this stage of his development: the somber "Erlkönig" which Schubert put to music. When has the child's sense of mystic beings pervading nature been more vividly expressed than in this swift fantasy of the dying child who sees the "king of the elves" coming to snatch it from the arms of its father?

Now, too, Goethe wrote in prose three dramas: *Egmont* (1775), *Iphigenie auf Tauris* (1779), and *Torquato Tasso* (1780)—fruit enough for five political years. *Egmont* was not produced till 1788. *Iphigenie* was presented at the Weimar theater on April 6, 1779 (six weeks before the première of Gluck's opera of the same name); but it was so transformed, as well as versified, during Goethe's stay in Rome that it will be better viewed as a product of Goethe's classic phase. *Tasso* also was remodeled and versified in Italy, but it belongs here as part of Goethe's enchantment with Charlotte von Stein. On April 19, 1781, he wrote to her: "All that Tasso says is addressed to you."[51] Taking him at his word, she identified herself with Leonora, Goethe with Tasso, and Karl August with the Duke of Ferrara.

Goethe readily accepted the legend that Tasso's mental breakdown at the Ferrara court was intensified, if not brought on, by an unhappy love affair with a sister of Alfonso II (r. 1559–97)[52] He doubtless had himself in mind when he described the working of Tasso's poetic mind:

> His eye scarce lingers on this earthly scene;
> To nature's harmony his ear is tuned.
> What history offers, and what life presents,
> His bosom promptly and with joy receives.
> The widely scattered is by him combined,
> And his quick feeling animates the dead. . . .
> Thus, moving in his own enchanted sphere,
> The wondrous man doth still allure us on
> To wander with him and partake his joy.
> Though seeming to approach us, he remains
> Remote as ever; and perchance his eye,
> Resting on us, sees spirits in our place.[53]

And Leonora, the stately princess who accepts the poet's love but bids him restrain his ardor within protocol, may well be Charlotte von Stein holding Goethe's passion this side of adultery. Tasso proclaims—and here both poets speak—

> Whatever in my song doth reach the heart
> And find an echo there, I owe to one,
> And one alone! No image undefined
> Hovered before my soul, approaching now
> In radiant glory, to retire again.
> I have myself, with mine own eyes, beheld
> The type of every virtue, every grace.[54]

Duke Alfonso resembles Karl August in patience with the poet's tantrums, amours, and reveries, and, like him, mourns the poet's delay in finishing a promised masterpiece:

> After each slow advance he leaves his task;
> He ever changeth, and can ne'er conclude[55]—

which well describes Goethe's piecemeal composition, and his procrastination with *Wilhelm Meister* and *Faust*. Another princess praises Alfonso–Karl August for giving Tasso-Goethe a chance to mature by contact with affairs: and here rise famous lines:

> *Es bildet ein Talent sich in der Stille;*
> *Sich ein Charakter in dem Strom der Welt.*

"Talent forms itself in quiet; character takes form in the stream of the world."[56] But the correlation between the two poets fades at the end: Tasso shows none of Goethe's capacity for swimming in the worldly stream; he sinks into his realm of dreams, throws caution and proportion to the winds, clasps the startled princess in his arms, and goes insane when she removes herself from his embrace and his life. Perhaps Goethe felt that he had skirted that precipice.

He often thought of Italy as an escape from a situation that threatened his mind. About this time, in the first form of *Wilhelm Meister*, he composed for Mignon a song of longing that fitted his own hopes rather than Mignon's:

> Kennst du das Land, wo die Zitronen blühn,
> Im dunken Laub die Gold-Orangen glühn,
> Ein sanfter Wind vom blauen Himmel weht,
> Die Myrte still und hoch der Lorbeer steht:
> Kennst du es wohl? Dahin! Dahin!
> Möcht ich mit dir, O mein Geliebte, ziehn!*

Weimar was beautiful, but it was not warm. And the cares of office rasped the poet's soul; " 'tis a bitter way of earning one's bread to have to try to establish harmony among the discords of the world."[57] Court life wearied him; "I have nothing in common with these people, nor they with me."[58] He had been partly estranged from the Duke, unable to keep the ducal pace of hunting and wenching. His one great love had been worn thin by time and quarrels. He felt that he had to break away from these many bonds, to seek a new orientation and perspective. He asked the Duke for a leave of absence. The Duke consented, and agreed to continue Goethe's salary. To raise additional funds Goethe sold to Göschen of Leipzig the right to publish an edition of his collected works. Only 602 sets were bought; Göschen lost 1,720 thalers in the enterprise.

On September 1, 1786, Goethe wrote to Charlotte from Karlsbad:

> Now a final farewell. I want to repeat to you that I love you dearly . . . and that your assurance that you are again taking pleasure in my love renews the joy of my life. I have borne much in silence hitherto, but I have desired nothing more intensely than that our relationship might take a form over which no circumstance could have power. If that cannot be, I would not dwell where you are, but rather be alone in that world into which I now go forth.[59]

IV. GOETHE IN ITALY: 1786–88

He traveled under a pseudonym, "M. Jean-Philippe Möller," for he wished to be freed from the inconveniences of fame. He was thirty-seven years old, but he came with even more than the bright expectancy of youth, and much better prepared, knowing something of Italy's history and art. On September 18 he wrote to Herder, "I hope to return a newborn person," and to Karl August, "I hope to bring back a thoroughly cleansed and far better equipped human being." To these and other friends he sent "Letters from Italy" that still have in them the *allegrezza* of Italian life. He prefaced them with the old motto *Auch in Arkadien*—he too was now in Arcady. We have seen elsewhere how grateful he was for the sunshine; "I believe in God again!" he cried out as he entered Italy.[60] But he loved the Italian people too, their open faces and hearts, the naturalness of their lives, the passion and jollity of their speech. Being a scientist as well as a poet, he made note of

---

* "Know you the land where the lemon trees bloom, where the golden oranges glow in the dark foliage, where a soft wind blows from the blue sky, and the quiet myrtle and the lofty bay tree stand: do you know it well? There, there would I go with you, O my beloved!"

meteorological peculiarities, geological formations, mineral specimens, varieties of animals and plants; he liked even the lizards that darted over the rocks.

He was so eager to reach Rome that he passed hurriedly through Venezia, Lombardy, and Tuscany. But he stopped long enough in Vicenza to feel the classic simplicity and power of Palladio's architecture. He strongly reaffirmed his antipathy to Gothic: "from all taste for those . . . tobacco-pipe shafts, our little steeple-crowned towers and foliated terminals, . . . I am now, thank God, set free forever! . . . Palladio has opened the road for me to every . . . art."[61] Through that road he went back to Vitruvius, whom he studied in an edition by Galiani, our witty friend from Naples and Paris. The classical style now became a passion with him, coloring his works and thought, re-forming some past productions, like *Iphigenie* and *Tasso*, into classic mold and line. In Venice the baroque palaces seemed immodestly garish, too femininely elegant; and even from the Renaissance façades he turned to the relics of classic architecture and statuary in the museums. But his warm blood responded to the color and pride of Veronese and Titian.

In Ferrara he sought in vain the palace where Tasso had been confined. After three days in Bologna and only three hours in Florence, he rushed on through Perugia and Terni and Città di Castello, and on October 29, 1786, he rode through the Porta del Popolo into Rome. Now he felt a passing moment of modesty. "All roads are open to me, because I walk in a spirit of humility."[62]

Not yet master of spoken Italian, he sought out the German colony, and especially the artists, for he aspired to learn at least the elements of drawing, painting, and sculpture. Angelica Kauffmann admired his enthusiasm and good looks; she painted a portrait of him, stressing his black hair, lofty forehead, and clear eyes. He formed an intimate friendship with Johann Heinrich Wilhelm Tischbein, who handed him down to us, in the famous *Goethe in der Campagna*,[63] reclining at ease as if he had conquered Arcady. Long before coming to Italy Goethe had corresponded with this painter; they met for the first time on November 3, when they converged in the Piazza San Pietro; the poet recognized the artist, and introduced himself simply: "I am Goethe."[64] Tischbein described him in a letter to Lavater:

> I found him to be quite what I had expected. The only thing that surprised me was the gravity and tranquillity of one of such vivid sensibility, and also that he is able to be at ease and at home in all circumstances. What pleases me still more is the simplicity of his life. All he asked me to provide for him was a little room where he could sleep and work without interruption; and the very simplest fare. . . . Now he sits in that little room and works at his *Iphigenie* from early in the morning till nine o'clock. Then he goes out to study the great works of art.[65]

Tischbein often guided him in these explorations, had drawings made for him, and secured for him copies of the more famous paintings; Goethe himself made sketches of what he especially wished to recall. He tried his hand at sculpture, and modeled a head of Hercules. He admitted that he had no talent for the plastic arts, but he felt that these experiments gave him a better sense of form, and helped him to visualize what he wished to describe.[66] He pored over Winckelmann's *History of Ancient Art*; "Here on the spot I find it highly valuable. . . . Now at last my mind can rise to the greatest and purest creations of art with calm consideration."[67] "The history of the whole world attaches itself to this spot, and I reckon a . . . true new birth since the day I entered Rome. . . . I think I am changed to the very marrow."[68] Meanwhile he seems to have enjoyed the living art provided by the "dainty" models who posed in the studios.[69] His stay in Rome completed that de-romantification which had begun with the responsibilities of office. Now the lawlessness of *Götz* and the tears of *Werther* seemed to the maturing Goethe signs of an unbalanced mind; "romanticism is a disease," he said; "classicism is health."[70] There was something romantic in his new enthusiasm for classic marbles, columns, capitals, and pediments, and the pure lines of Greek statuary. "If we really want a pattern, we must always return to the ancient Greeks, in whose works the beauty of mankind is constantly represented."[71] Like Winckelmann, Goethe saw only the "Apollonian" side of Greek civilization and art—the exaltation of form and restraint; he now almost ignored that "Dionysian" ecstasy which so warmly colored Greek character, religion, and life, and which, in Goethe himself, had spoken through his "daimon" and his loves.

It was in this classic rapture that he rewrote *Iphigenie auf Tauris* in verse (1787), resolved to rival Racine, even Euripides himself. Still cherishing the embers of the fire that Charlotte von Stein had ignited in him, he poured into the speeches of the Greek princess something of the tenderness and self-control of the German baroness. He told the old story well, with all its complications of mythology and genealogy; he intensified the drama by portraying the Scythian king favorably; and he dared to change the ending to accord with the idea—rare among the Greeks—that one has moral obligations even to "barbarians." Only those who can read German fluently can appreciate Goethe's performance; yet Hippolyte Taine, a Frenchman, a supreme critic, and presumably familiar with Racine's dramas, said: "I place no modern work above Goethe's *Iphigenie auf Tauris*."[72]

The memories of Charlotte in this play, and still more in *Torquato Tasso*, which he rewrote in Rome, revived his feeling for her. She had been deeply wounded by his sudden flight to Italy, and by his leaving her boy in charge of a servant; she at once took Fritz back, and demanded the return of all the letters she had written to Goethe. He wrote apologetically from Rome (December 8, 13, and 20, 1786); she sent him (December 18) a note of "bittersweet" reproof; he answered (December 23): "I cannot express to you how it pierces my heart that you are ill, and ill through my fault. Forgive me. I myself fought with death and life, and no tongue can speak the things that went on within me." Finally she relented. "Now," he wrote on February 1, 1787, "I can go to work in a happier mood, since I have a letter from you in which you say that you love and take delight in my letters."

In that month he and Tischbein went to Naples. He ascended Vesuvius twice; on his second attempt a minor eruption covered his head and shoulders with ashes. He reveled in the classic ruins at Pompeii, and marveled at the simple majesty of the Greek temples at Paestum. Returning to Rome, he took ship to Palermo, went on to study the classic temples at Segeste and Girgenti (Agrigento), stood in the Greek theater at Taormina, and was back in Rome in June. More and more in love with "the most remarkable city in the whole world,"[73] he persuaded Duke Karl August to continue his salary to the end of 1787. When that extension expired, he slowly reconciled himself to the North. He left Rome on April 25, 1788, traveled leisurely through Florence, Milan, and Como, and reached Weimar on June 18. Every day he wondered how the Duke, the court, and Charlotte would receive a Goethe who felt himself transformed.

V. GOETHE WAITING: 1788–94

With the absent poet's consent the Duke had appointed a new president of the Council; now, at his own request, Goethe was relieved of all official duties except as minister of education, and henceforth he served the Council only in an advisory capacity. The Duke was kind, but he had taken other intimates, and he did not like the semirepublican sentiments of the rewritten *Egmont*. The reading public had almost forgotten Goethe; it had taken up a new poet called Schiller, and had enthusiastically applauded a play, *The Robbers*, full of that Sturm-und-Drang rebelliousness and violence which now seemed absurd and immature to a poet ready to preach classic order and restraint. Charlotte von Stein received him coldly; she resented his long absence, his leisurely return, his persistent rapture about Italy; and perhaps she had heard of those models in Rome. Their first meeting after his arrival was "utterly false in tone," she wrote, "and nothing but boredom was exchanged between us."[74] She left for a stay in Kochberg, and Goethe was free to think of Christiane Vulpius.

She came into his life on July 12, 1788, bearing a message from her brother. She was twenty-three years old, and worked in a factory making artificial flowers. Goethe was struck with her fresh spirit, her simple mind, her budding womanhood. He invited her to his garden house as his housekeeper, and soon made her his mistress. She had no education, and "cannot understand poetry at all," said Goethe,[75] but she yielded herself trustfully, and gave him the physical fulfillment that Charlotte had apparently refused. In November, 1789, when she was nearing motherhood, he took her into his Weimar home, and openly made her his wife in all but name. Charlotte and the court were shocked at his crossing class lines and his failure to veil the illicit relation; this reaction caused him and Christiane much grief; but the Duke, an old hand with mistresses, served as godfather to the child that was born on Christmas Day, 1789, and Herder, stern but forgiving, christened it August.

Goethe, so often a lover but only now a father, found much happiness in "the little man" and *"das kleine Weib,"* the little woman. She kept house for him, she listened to him lovingly even when she did not understand him, and she gave him health. "Since she first crossed this threshold," he told a friend, "I have had nothing but joy of her."[76] Her only fault in his eyes was that she loved wine even more than he did, and that it sometimes led her to almost uncontrolled merriment. She frequented the theater, and went to many dances while Goethe stayed home and celebrated her in his *Römische Elegien* (1789–90), written in the manner of Propertius and with the morals of Catullus. There is nothing mournful about these "Roman elegies"; they get their names from their "elegiac" meter of alternating hexameters and pentameters; and they concern not Rome but a merry widow through whose disguise we see Christiane herself.

> All that thy sacred walls, eternal Rome, hold within them
> Teemeth with life; but to *me* all is still silent and dead.
> Oh, who will whisper unto me?—when shall I see at the casement
> That one beauteous form, which, while it scorcheth, revives? . . .
> Do not repent, mine own love, that thou so soon didst surrender!
> Trust me; I deem thee not bold; reverence only I feel. . . .
> Alexander and Caesar and Henry and Frederick, the mighty,
> On me would gladly bestow half of the glory they earned,
> Could I but grant unto them one night on the couch where I'm lying;
> But they by Orcus' night sternly, alas, are held down.
> Therefore rejoice, O thou living one, blest in thy love-lighted homestead,
> Ere the dark Lethe's sad wave wetteth thy fugitive foot.[77]

That pretty widow may have been a Roman memory, but the warmth of these lines came from Christiane. After all, was he not studying art?

> Yet it is studious too with sensitive hand
> To mark her bosom's lovely curves, and let
> Wise fingers glide down the smooth thigh, for thus
> I master the antique sculptor's craft, reflect,
> Compare, and apprehend to come and see
> With feeling eye, and feel with seeing hand.[78]

The Weimar ladies were not pleased by this cheapening exposure of their charms, and the stately Charlotte mourned the degeneration of her Galahad. Even Karl August was a bit disturbed, but was soon appeased. When the Dowager Duchess was returning from Italy he sent Goethe to Venice to escort her home. His stay there (March to June, 1790) was protracted uncomfortably; he longed for Christiane, and vented his irritation with Italian shopkeepers and hygiene in *Venezianische Epigramme*—the least attractive of his works.

On his return from Venice he found that the French Revolution was arousing the youth of Germany to ecstasy, and the rulers to fear. Many of his friends, including Wieland and Herder, were applauding the overthrow of monarchical absolutism in France. Goethe, perceiving that all thrones were threatened, took his stand beside the Duke, and counseled caution; so many people, he said, were "running about with bellows in their hands, when, it seems to me, they had better be looking for cold-water jugs" to control the fire.[79] He obeyed the order of Karl August to accompany him in the campaign of the First Coalition against France. He was present at the battle of Valmy (September 20, 1792), stood calmly under fire, and shared in the defeat. A German officer recorded in his diary that when the poet-councilor was asked to comment on the event, he answered, "From today and from this place begins a new epoch in the history of the world"[80]; we have no confirmation of this story. In any case, back in Weimar, Goethe wrote vigorously against the Revolution, which was entering the period (1792–94) of its excesses and savagery.

These developments confirmed in Goethe the natural turn of the maturing mind from a zest for liberty to a love of order. As any fool can be original, so Goethe felt that "any fool can live arbitrarily,"[81] safely violating customs or laws because others observe them. He had no enthusiasm for democracy; if ever such a system should actually be practiced it would be the sovereignty of simplicity, ignorance, superstition, and barbarity. He was kindly and generous within his sphere, and spent part of his income in secret charities,[82] but he shrank from the crowd. In the presence of multitudes or strangers he withdrew proudly and timidly within himself, and found his only happiness in his home. In these unsettling years (1790–94) he fell into a somber torpor from which he was aroused by the touch of Schiller's ardent youth and the competition of his pen.

VI. SCHILLER WAITING: 1787–94

When Schiller reached Weimar Goethe was in Italy. The almost penniless poet admitted jealousy of the absent councilor. "While he is painting in Italy, the Toms, Dicks, and Harrys are sweating for him like beasts of burden. He is squandering a salary of 1,800 thalers there, and here they have to work double tides for half the money."[83] On August 12, 1787, he wrote more favorably:

> Goethe is spoken of here by many with a sort of devotion, and is even more loved and admired as a man than as an author. Herder says he has a most clear judgment, great depth of feeling, and the purest sentiments. . . . According to Herder, Goethe is free from all spirit of intrigue; he has never done harm to anyone. . . . In his political transactions he acts openly and boldly. . . . Herder says that as a man of affairs Goethe is more deserving of admiration than as a poet, . . . that he has a mind large enough for anything.[84]

The Duke was away when Schiller came, but Anna Amalie and Charlotte von Stein received him cordially. Wieland told him that he "was wanting in polish, clearness, and taste,"[85] and offered to polish him; soon the eager poet was contributing to Wieland's *Teutsche Merkur*. He found more intimate entertainment with Charlotte von Kalb, who, like the other Charlotte, had a broad-minded husband. "People begin to whisper pretty loudly here about my connection with Charlotte. . . . Herr von Kalb has written to me. He comes here at the end of September, and his arrival will greatly influence my arrangements. His friendship for me remains unchanged, which is astonishing, for he loves his wife, and is aware of my intimacy with her. . . . But he can never for one moment doubt her fidelity. . . . He still remains the honest, goodhearted fellow he always was."[86]

On August 27, 1787, *Don Carlos* had its première in Hamburg. Schiller was too fond of Weimar to attend. This, his first play in verse, was both praised and condemned as a surrender to the style of French tragedy, but it lacked the dramatic unity required by Aristotelian rules. It began with the conflict between Philip II and his son for the love of Elizabeth of Valois; then, mid-play, the center of interest shifted to the struggle of the Netherlands to free themselves from Spanish suzerainty and Alva's cruelty. Schiller tried to give an impartial portrait of Philip, and Protestant readers applauded the appeal of Marquis Posa to the King:

> Your Majesty,
> I lately passed through Flanders and Brabant—
> So many rich and blooming provinces,
> Filled with a valiant, great, and honest people!
> To be the father of a race like this
> I thought must be divine indeed! And then
> I stumbled on a heap of burned men's bones! . . .
> Restore us all you have deprived us of,
> And, generous and strong, let happiness
> Flow from your horn of plenty; let man's mind
> Ripen in your vast empire, . . . and become
> Amidst a thousand kings a king indeed! . . .
> Let every subject be what once he was—
> The end and object of the monarch's care,
> Bound by no duty save a brother's love.[87]

Despite the success of *Don Carlos*, Schiller for a long time abandoned drama. In 1786 he had written to Körner: "History has with each successive day new attractions for me. . . . I wish I had studied nothing else for ten years together; I think I should have been another sort of being. Do you think there is yet time to make up for what I have lost?"[88] He could not support himself, much less a family, on the proceeds of occasional plays that even after an applauded première might wither to an early death. Perhaps some successful work of history would give him sufficient reputation as a scholar to win a professorship in the University of Jena. There he would be only fourteen miles from Weimar, and still within the jurisdiction and bounty of the Duke.

So, after finishing *Don Carlos*, he gave his pen to a *Geschichte des Abfalls der Vereinigten Niederlande* (*History of the Fall of the United Netherlands*). As Schiller could not read Dutch, he relied on secondary authorities, from whose narratives he put together a compilation of no lasting worth. Körner criticized Volume I (1788) with his usual honesty: "The present work, with all its talent, does not bear the stamp of that genius of which you are capable."[89] Schiller abandoned the Netherlands; no second volume came.

On July 18, 1788, Goethe returned from Italy, and in September met Schiller in suburban Rudolstadt. Schiller reported to Körner: "The high idea I had conceived of him is not lessened in the slightest degree, . . . but I doubt if we shall ever draw very close to each other. . . . He is so far ahead of me . . . that we cannot meet on the road. His whole life from the very beginning has run in a direction contrary to mine. His world is not my world. On some points our notions are diametrically opposed."[90] And indeed the two poets seemed providentially designed to dislike each other. Goethe, thirty-nine, had arrived and matured; Schiller, twenty-nine, was climbing and experimenting; only in proud egotism did they agree. The younger man was of the people, poor, writing semirevolutionary lines; the other was rich, a man of rank and state, a privy councilor deprecating revolution. Schiller was just emerging from Sturm und Drang; he was the voice of feeling, sentiment, freedom, romance; Goethe, wooing Greece, was all for reason, restraint, order, and the classic style. In any case, it is not natural for authors to like one another; they are reaching for the same prize.

When they returned to Weimar, Goethe and Schiller lived only a short walk from each other, but they did not communicate. Matters were worsened by the appearance of Schiller's hostile review of Goethe's *Egmont.* Goethe decided that "little Athens" was not large enough to contain both of them. In December, 1788, he recommended Schiller for a chair in history at Jena. Schiller gladly accepted, and called on Goethe to thank him, but in February, 1789, he wrote to Körner:

> It would make me unhappy to be a great deal in Goethe's society. He never warms even toward his best friends; nothing attaches him. I verily believe he is an egotist of the first water. He possesses the talent of putting men under an obligation to him by small as well as great acts of courtesy, but he always manages to remain free himself. . . . I look upon him as the personification of a well calculated system of unbounded selfishness. Men should not tolerate such a being near them. He is hateful to me for this reason, though I cannot do otherwise than admire his mind, and think nobly of him. He has aroused in me a curious mixture of hatred and love.[91]

On May 11, 1789, Schiller took up his duties at Jena, and on May 26 he delivered his "inaugural address" on "What Is, and to What End Does One Study, Universal History?" Admission being free, the audience proved far too large for the room assigned, and the professor moved with his auditors in a gay stampede to a hall at the other end of town. This lecture was highly praised; "the students gave me a serenade that night, and three rounds of cheers";[92] but enrollment for the course—for which admission was charged—was small, and Schiller's scholastic income was meager.

He added to it by writing. In 1789–91 he brought out, in three installments, *Geschichte des Dreissigjährigen Krieges* (*History of the Thirty Years' War*). Here he was at home at least with the language, though again he was too harassed to go to the primary sources, and his predilection for judging and philosophizing colored and halted the tale. Nevertheless Wieland hailed the work as indicating Schiller's "capacity for rising to a level with Hume, Robertson, and Gibbon."[93] Seven thousand copies of Volume I were sold in its first year.

Schiller now felt that he could indulge his longing for a home, and for a woman to give him love and care. He had had a brief glimpse of Charlotte and Caroline von Lengefeld at Mannheim in 1784. He saw them again at Rudolstadt in 1787; "Lotte" was living there with her mother, and Caroline, unhappily married, was living next door. "Both, without being pretty," Schiller wrote to Körner,[94] "are interesting, and please me exceedingly. They are well read in the literature of the day, and give proofs of a highly finished education. They are good performers on the piano." Frau von Lengefeld frowned upon the idea of her daughter marrying an impecunious poet, but Karl August gave him a small pension of two hundred thalers, and the Duke of Saxe-Meiningen secured him a patent of nobility. He warned Lotte that he had many faults; she told him she had noticed them, but added: "Love is loving people as we find them, and, if they have weaknesses, accepting them with a loving heart."[95] They were married on February 22, 1790, and took a modest home in Jena. Lotte brought her own income of two hundred thalers a year, gave him four children, and proved, through all his tribulations, a patient and tender wife. "My heart swims in happiness," he wrote, "and my mind draws fresh strength and vigor."[96]

He worked hard, preparing two lectures a week, writing articles, poems, and history. For months he labored fourteen hours a day.[97] In January, 1791, he suffered two spells of "catarrhal fever," involving gastric pains and expectoration of blood. For eight days he lay in bed, his stomach rejecting all food. Students helped Lotte to care for him, and "vied with one another as to who should sit up with me at night. . . . The Duke sent me half a dozen of old Madeira, which, with some Hungarian wine, has done me good service."[98] In May he was attacked by "a fearful spasm, with symptoms of suffocation, so that I could not but think that my last moment had come. . . . I took farewell of my loved ones, and thought to pass away any minute. . . . Strong doses of opium, camphor, and musk, and the application of blisters, relieved me most."[99]

A false report of his death alarmed his friends, and reached even to Copenhagen. There—on suggestions from Karl Reinhold and Jens Baggesen—two Danish noblemen, Duke Friedrich Christian of Holstein-Augustenburg and Count Ernst von Schimmelmann, offered Schiller an annual gift of a thousand thalers for three years. He received it gratefully. The university excused him from teaching, but he lectured to a small private circle. Part of his new leisure he gave, at Reinhold's urging, to the study of Kant's philosophy, which he accepted almost completely, to Goethe's amusement and Herder's disgust, and perhaps with some detriment to Schiller's poetry.

Now (1793) he sent forth his long essay *On Grace and Dignity*, which began the romantic cultivation of *die schöne Seele*. "A beautiful soul" he defined as one in which "reason and the senses, duty and inclination, are in harmony, and are outwardly expressed in grace."[100] The Copenhagen donors must have been alarmed to receive, as some return for their gift, a little volume entitled *Briefe über die ästhetische Erziehung des Menschen* (*Letters on the Aesthetic Education of Mankind*, 1793–94). Starting with Kant's conception of the sense of beauty as a disinterested contemplation of harmonious forms, Schiller argued (with Shaftesbury) that "the feeling developed by the beautiful refines manners," and the aesthetic sense becomes one with morality. – It is a consolation to read, in this pronouncement from Weimar's halcyon days, that Schiller (like Goethe) thought his generation decadent, sunk in "profound moral degradation."[101]

When he turned back from philosophy to poetry he found it difficult to recapture "that boldness and living fire I formerly possessed; . . . critical discussion has spoiled me."[102] But he insisted that "the poet is the only authentic human being; the best philosopher is a mere caricature compared with him";[103] and he exalted to the plane of celestial inspiration the function of the poet to teach and raise mankind. In a long ode, *Die Künstler* (*The Artists*, 1789), he described poets and artists as guiding mankind to the union of beauty with morality and truth. In another poem, *Die Götter Griechenlands* (*The Gods of Greece*, 1788) he lauded the Greeks for their aesthetic sensibility and artistic creations, and argued, with cautious obscurity, that the world had become gloomy and ugly since the replacement of Hellenism by Christianity. He was already falling under Goethe's spell, as Goethe had fallen under Winckelmann's.

Probably in both Schiller and Goethe the romantification of Hellas was an escape from Christianity. Despite some pious passages Schiller, as well as Goethe, belonged to the Aufklärung; he accepted the eighteenth-century faith in salvation by human reason rather than by divine grace. He retained a deistic belief in God—personal only in poetry—and a misty immortality. He rejected all churches, Protestant as well as Catholic. He could not bear sermons, even Herder's. In an epigram entitled "Mein Glaube" (My Faith) he wrote two famous lines:

> *Welche Religion ich bekenne? Keine von allen*
> *Die du mir nennst. Und warum keine? Aus Religion.*

–"Which religion do I acknowledge? None of all those that you name to me. And why none? Because of religion."[104] He wrote to Goethe, July 9, 1796: "A healthy and beautiful nature—as you yourself say—requires no moral code, no law for its nature, no political metaphysics. You might as well have added that it requires no godhead, no idea of immortality wherewith to support and maintain itself." Nevertheless there were factors of imagination and tenderness in him that drew him back toward Christianity:

> I find that Christianity virtually contains the first elements of what is highest and noblest; and its various outward forms seem distasteful and repulsive to us only because they are misrepresentations of the highest. . . . No sufficient emphasis has been placed upon what this religion can be to a beautiful mind, or rather what a beautiful mind can make of it. . . . This explains why this religion is so successful with feminine natures, and why it is that only in women is it at all supportable.[105]

Schiller was not, like Goethe, physically built for thorough paganism. His face was handsome but pale, his frame tall but thin and frail. He distrusted the diurnal vacillations of the weather, and preferred to sit in his room smoking and taking snuff. He contrasted himself with Goethe as idea versus nature, imagination versus intellect, sentiment versus objective thought.[106] He was at once timid and proud, shrinking from hostility but always fighting back; occasionally irritable and impatient,[107] perhaps because aware that his time was running out; often critical of others, sometimes envious.[108] He had a tendency to moralize about everything, and to take a high idealistic tone. It is a relief to find him enjoying the eroticism of Diderot's *Les Bijoux indiscrets*.[109] He analyzed his own talent well in an early letter to Goethe:

> The poetic mind generally got the better of me when I ought to have philosophized, and my philosophical mind when I wished to poetize. Even now it often happens that imagination intrudes upon my abstractions, and cold reason upon my poetical productions. If I could obtain such mastery over these two powers as to assign to each its limits [as Goethe did], I might yet look forward to a happy fate. But, alas, just when I have begun to know and to use my moral energies rightly, illness seizes me, and threatens to undermine my physical powers.[110]

His ailment returned with fury in December, 1793; he recovered, but the sense that he could not be cured, and must expect recurrent seizures, darkened his mood. On December 10 he wrote to Körner: "I struggle against this with all the force of my mind, . . . but I am always driven back. . . . The uncertainty of my prospects; . . . doubts of my own genius, which is not sustained and encouraged by contact with others; the total absence of that intellectual conversation which has become a necessity to me": these were the mental accompaniments of his physical trials. He looked with longing, from Jena to Weimar, to the enviably healthy Goethe, that *mens sana in corpore sano;* there, Schiller felt, was the man who could give him stimulus and support, if only the ice between them would melt, if only that fourteen-mile barrier would fall away!

VII. SCHILLER AND GOETHE: 1794–1805

It fell for a moment when, in June, 1794, both men attended in Jena a session of the Society for Natural History. Encountering Goethe as they left the hall, Schiller remarked that the biological specimens exhibited at the conference lacked life, and could offer no real help to understanding nature. Goethe emphatically agreed, and the conversation kept them together till they reached Schiller's home. "The talk induced me to go in" with him, Goethe later recalled. "I expounded to him . . . *The Metamorphosis of Plants*"—a treatise in which Goethe had argued that all plants were variations of one primitive type, the *Urpflanze*, and that nearly all parts of a plant were variations or developments of the leaf. "He heard . . . all this with much interest and distinct apprehension; but when I had done he shook his head and said, 'This is not experiment, it is an idea' "; i.e., it was a theory not yet verified by observation or test. The comment nettled Goethe, but he saw that Schiller had a mind of his own, and his respect for him grew. Schiller's wife, "whom I had loved and valued since her childhood, did her best to strengthen our reciprocal understanding."[111]

In May of 1794 Schiller had signed a contract to edit a literary monthly to be called *Die Horen.* (The Horae, in Greek mythology, were the goddesses of the seasons.) He hoped to enlist as contributors Kant, Fichte, Klopstock, Herder, Jacobi, Baggesen, Körner, Reinhold, Wilhelm von Humboldt, August Wilhelm von Schlegel, and—best catch of all—Goethe. On June 3 he sent to Weimar a letter addressed to "Hochwohlgeborener Herr, Hochzuverehrender Herr Geheimer Rat" (High and Wellborn Sir, Highly Honored Sir Privy Councilor) a prospectus of the proposed magazine, and added: "The enclosed paper expresses the wish of a number of men, whose esteem for you is unbounded, that you would honor the periodical with contributions from your pen, in regard to the value of which there can be but one voice among us. We feel, your Excellency, that your consent to support this undertaking will be a guarantee of its success."[112] Goethe replied that he would gladly contribute, and was "certain that a closer connection with the sterling men who form your committee will arouse to new life much that is now stagnant within me."[113]

So began a correspondence that is among the treasures of literary history, and a friendship whose exchange of respect and aid, lasting for eleven years —till Schiller's death—should enter into our estimate of mankind. Perhaps the most revealing of the 999 extant letters is the fourth (August 23, 1794), in which Schiller, after several meetings with Goethe, analyzed with both courtesy and candor, both modesty and pride, the differences between their minds:

> My recent conversations with you have put the whole store of my ideas in motion. . . . Many things about which I could not come to a right understanding with myself have received new and unexpected light from the contemplation I have had of your mind (for so I call the general impression of your ideas upon me). I needed the *object*, the body, to several of my speculative ideas, and you have put me on the track for finding it. Your calm and clear way of looking at things keeps you from getting lost in the side roads into which speculation, as well as arbitrary imagination . . . are so apt to lead me astray. Your correct intuition grasps all things, and that far more perfectly than what is laboriously sought for by analysis. . . . Minds like yours seldom know how far they have penetrated, and how little cause they have to borrow from philosophy, which in fact can only learn from them. . . . Although I have done so at a distance, I have long watched the course which your mind has pursued. . . . You seek for the necessary in nature, but . . . you look at nature as a whole when seeking to get light thrown on her individual parts; you look for the explanation of the individual in the totality of all her various manifestations.[114]

Goethe's answer (August 27) cleverly avoided an analysis of Schiller's mind:

For my birthday, which occurred this week, I could have received no more agreeable gift than your letter, in which, with a friendly hand, you sum up my existence, and in which, by your sympathy, you encourage me to a more assiduous and active use of my powers. . . . It will be a pleasure to unfold to you at leisure what your conversation has been to me; how I too regard those days as an epoch in my life; for it seems to me that after so unexpected a meeting we cannot but wander on in life together.

Goethe followed this up (September 4) with an invitation to Schiller to come and spend some days with him in Weimar. "You could take up any kind of work you like without being disturbed. We would converse together at convenient hours, . . . and I think we would not part without some profit. You should live exactly as you like, and as much as possible as if you were in your own home." Schiller readily accepted, but warned Goethe that "the asthmatic spasms from which I suffer oblige me to stay in bed all morning, since they leave me no peace at night." So, from September 14 to 28, Schiller was Goethe's guest, almost his patient. The older man took tender care of the ailing poet, guarded him against annoyance, gave him dietetic counsel, taught him to love fresh air. Back in Jena, Schiller wrote (September 29): "I find myself at home again, but my thoughts are still in Weimar. It will take me a long time to unravel all the ideas which you have awakened in me." Then (October 8), with characteristic eagerness, he urged: "It seems to me necessary that we should come at once to some clear understanding about our ideas of the beautiful."

There followed three months of preparation for the first number of *Die Horen*. This appeared on January 24, 1795; the second, on March 1; the rest monthly for three years. Goethe reported from Weimar (March 18): "People are running after it, snatching the numbers from one another's hands; we could not want more for a beginning." On April 10 Schiller informed Goethe: "Kant has written me a very friendly letter, but begs for a delay in sending his contributions. . . . I am glad we have induced the old bird to join us." Goethe asked that his own pieces be unsigned, for they included several of his *Roman Elegies*, and he knew that their lusty sensuality would seem unbecoming in a privy councilor.

In the rash enthusiasm of success Schiller persuaded Goethe to join him in another periodical, *Der Musenalmanach*, which appeared yearly from 1796 to 1800. The liveliest pieces in this were the *Xenien* that the two poets wrote on the model of Martial's *Xenia*—epigrams written as gifts to guests. Schiller described the project to Körner: "The whole affair consists in a conglomeration of epigrams, of which each is a single couplet. They are chiefly wild and impish satires, especially against authors and their works, interspersed here and there by sudden flashes of poetical or philosophical ideas. There will be no less than six hundred of such monodistichs."[115] Goethe had suggested this plan as a way to strike back at their critics, to make fun of pompous authors and bourgeois tastes, and to stir the German reading public to a keener interest in literature; they would send these "gifts" into the camp of the Philistines "like foxes with burning tails."[116] The epigrams were unsigned, and some of them were the joint product of the two conspirators. Since many of these burning tails were directed at authors or controversies now forgotten, time has extinguished their fire; but one of them, by Goethe, especially merits remembrance:

> *Immer strebe zum Ganzen, und kannst du selber kein Ganzes*
> *Werden, als dienendes Glied schliess an ein Ganzes dich an!*

—"Always strive for the whole, and if you yourself cannot become a whole, tie yourself to some whole as a serving part." Another distich, usually credited to Schiller, extends the thought:

> *Vor dem Tod erschrickst du? Du wünschest unsterblich zu leben?*
> *Leb' im Ganzen! Wenn du lange dahin bist, es bleibt.*

—"You are frightened by death? You wish to live undying? Live in the Whole! When you are long gone hence, it will remain." The satirical part of the *Xenien* brought counterattacks, which made Schiller suffer and Goethe laugh. Goethe advised Schiller to let his work be his sole reply. "After our mad venture with the *Xenien*, we must take pains to work only on great and dignified works of art, and shame all our adversaries by transforming our Protean natures into noble forms."[117]

It was done. In these years of their developing friendship Goethe and Schiller wrote some of their finest poems: Goethe "The Bride of Corinth" and "The God and the Bayadere"; Schiller "The Walk" (1795), "The Cranes of Ibycus" (1797), and "The Song of the Bell" (1800). Schiller added a major essay *Über naive und sentimentalische Dichtung* (1795), and Goethe sent forth *Wilhelm Meisters Lehrjahre* (1796).

By "naïve and sentimental poetry" Schiller meant poetry born of objective perception versus poetry developed by reflective feeling; secretly he was comparing Goethe and Schiller. The "naïve" poet is not simple or superficial or deluded; he is one who is so readily adjusted to the external world that he feels no opposition between himself and nature, but approaches reality through direct and unhesitating intuition; Schiller cites Homer and Shakespeare as examples. As civilization becomes more complex and artificial, poetry loses this objective immediacy and subjective harmony; conflict enters the soul, and the poet has to recapture through imagination and feeling —as an ideal remembered or hoped for—this concord and union of the self with the world; poetry becomes reflective, clouded with thought.[118] Schiller believed that most Greek poetry was of the naïve or direct sort, and most modern poetry the result of discord, disunity, and doubt. The ideal poet is he who will fuse both the simple and the reflective approaches in one vision and poetic form. Goethe later pointed out that this essay became a fountainhead of the debate between classical and Romantic literature and art.

The embryology of *Wilhelm Meisters Lehrjahre* illustrates Goethe's method of creation. He conceived the story in 1777, completed Book I in 1778, put it aside, and did not finish Book II until July, 1782. He worked on Book III until November of that year, and on Book IV till November, 1783;

Books V and VI dragged along for three years more. He called these six books "Wilhelm Meisters theatralische Sendung," and read parts of them to friends; then he laid them aside. He took up the tale again in 1791 on the urging of Herder and Anna Amalie; added two books by June, 1794; submitted the growing manuscript to Schiller, who sent back criticisms, suggestions, and encouragement as the pages came; it was almost a picture of a midwife assisting at a long-overdue birth. At last, in 1796, the whole was delivered to the press. No wonder the final product was slightly deformed, weak in structure, adipose and confused, excellent only in parts and in its mirroring of Goethe's uncertain wandering amid conflicting interests and vague ideals. That decisiveness and self-confidence which Schiller ascribed to him were the proud concealment of internal vacillation and strife.

Lehrjahre—"learning years"—expressed the period of apprenticeship in the German guilds; through that time of tutelage Wilhelm became *Meister*, master; so the meandering theme of the novel is Wilhelm's slow and painful apprenticeship in the guild of life. Because of the puppet shows Goethe had loved as a child, and his continuing interest in the theater, he tied the tale to a troupe of actors passing through a dozen towns and a hundred vicissitudes as lessons in living and pictures of German ways. Faithful to his own unfaithfulness, he made his hero enter upon the scene by deserting his mistress Marianne. Wilhelm is not an alluring character. He lets himself be carried from one situation or idea to another by the whim of circumstance or the power of personality; it is the woman who takes the initiative in his love affairs. Born a bourgeois, he flounders in admiration for men of noble birth, and humbly hopes that these will someday recognize the aristocracy of the mind. Philine is more attractive: a pretty actress who waltzes lightly from love to love, but graces her erotic tourism with a contagious gaiety and an absolving unconsciousness of sin. Unique is little Mignon, who follows her old father dutifully as he strums his harp in penny-gathering peregrinations. Goethe describes her as speaking "very broken German,"[119] but puts into her mouth that perfect song, "Kennst du das Land." She falls in adolescent love with Wilhelm, who loves her as a child, and she dies in grief when she sees him in Theresa's arms. Ambroise Thomas plucked her out of these eight hundred pages to make of her a sad and delightful opera (1866).

Schiller praised the calm serenity of the style in *Wilhelm Meisters Lehrjahre*, and the truth to life in the description of a wandering troupe; but he pointed out contradictions in chronology, psychological improbabilities, offenses against taste, and faults in characterization and design.[120] He proposed changes in the plot, and gave his ideas as to how the story should end.[121] Goethe assured him, "I shall certainly comply with your just wishes as far as I possibly can";[122] but he confessed to Eckermann, thirty-three years later, that it was all he could do to protect his novel from Schiller's influence.[123] Other critics were less friendly; one described the book as a brothel on tour; and Charlotte von Stein complained that "when Goethe deals with lofty emotions he always flings some dirt at them, as if to deprive human nature of any pretensions to the divine."[124] The novel did not deserve these indiscriminate censures; it has many pleasant pages, and can still carry the interest of readers freed from the tumult of the world.

On March 23, 1796, Schiller went again to Weimar as Goethe's guest. There they worked together for the theater. Goethe was a strict manager, chose the plays to be presented, and trained the actors. "All that was morbid, weak, lachrymose, or sentimental, as well as all that was frightful, horrible, or offensive to decorum, was utterly excluded."[125] The audience was usually confined to the court, except when some students were invited from Jena. August von Schlegel remarked, acidly: "Germany has two national theaters —Vienna, with a public of fifty thousand, and Weimar, with a public of fifty."[126]

Schiller returned to Jena April 12, stimulated by his renewed contact with the stage to revert from history, philosophy, and incidental poetry to the drama. He had long thought of writing a play on Wallenstein; Goethe urged him to proceed with it. In November Goethe went to Jena, and lived for some time in daily communication with Schiller. Back in Weimar, Goethe wrote: "Do not fail to make use of your best hours, so as to get on with your tragedy, that we may begin to discuss it."[127]

While Schiller worked on *Wallenstein*, Goethe, stirred to rivalry by the success of Johann Heinrich Voss's verse idyl of German life and sentiment, *Luise* (1795), tried his hand at this favorite genre, and published in 1798 *Hermann und Dorothea*. Hermann is the strong and healthy, shy and quiet son of a bilious father and tender mother, who keep the Golden Inn and an extensive farm in a village near the Rhine. They learn that hundreds of refugees are approaching from a frontier town captured by the French; the family make up parcels of clothing and food, which Hermann conveys to the refugees. He finds among them a lass with "swelling bosom" and "neatly shaped ankles,"[128] who is serving them with aid and comfort. He falls in love with her, and, after due tribulations, brings her home to his parents as his bride. The story is told in fluent hexameters; vignettes of rural life give color to the tale; calls for the expulsion of the French invaders pleased patriotic Germans who had found *Iphigenie auf Tauris* and *Torquato Tasso* foreign and recondite; and the little epic gave new popularity to an author who, since *Werther*, had had few readers outside the Saxe-Weimar duchy.

Schiller's star was in the ascendant from 1798 to 1800. On November 28, 1796, he wrote to Körner: "I am still brooding seriously over *Wallenstein*, but the unfortunate work is still before me, shapeless and endless." He began it in prose, put it aside, then started it again in verse. The material was partly familiar to him from his studies for his *History of the Thirty Years' War*, but it was so abundant, so complex in characters and events, that he abandoned the attempt to compress it into five acts. He decided to preface the drama with a one-act prologue called *Wallensteins Lager* (*Wallenstein's Camp*), and to divide the remainder into two plays. *Die Piccolomini* expounded the plot to depose the rebellious general, and set it off with a fiery love affair between Wallenstein's daughter and the son of a leader in the plot. The final and essential drama would be *Wallensteins Tod*.

When Goethe read the prologue he was so struck by the realistic portrayal of an army camp, and the clever preparation for later developments, that he insisted on staging *Wallensteins Lager* in the Weimar theater (October 12, 1798) before *Die Piccolomini* was complete; perhaps it was a subtle way of keeping the poet to his task. Early in 1799 Schiller went to Weimar to stage *Die Piccolomini*; it had its première on January 30, and was well received; he returned to Jena and worked feverishly on *The Death of Wallenstein*. A letter of March 19, 1799, reveals the mood of a writer emerging from the ardor of creation: "I have long dreaded the moment when I should be rid of my work, much as I wished that moment would come; and in fact I feel my present freedom to be worse than the state of bondage that I have been in heretofore. The mass which has hitherto drawn and held me to it has now gone, and I feel as if I were hanging indefinitely in empty space."

Excitement enough came with the rehearsals and première (April 20, 1799) of *Wallensteins Tod*. Its success was complete; even the highly critical Weimar audience felt that it had witnessed a masterpiece of dramatic presentation. Schiller had now reached the peak of his development. He had shortened the speeches and intensified the action; he had drawn all the leading characters with vitality and power; he had brought all the threads of the plot together in the tragic denouement—the ignominious death of a great man ruined by limitless ambition and pride. Schiller felt that he could now stand on an equality with Goethe;[129] and in the field of drama he was justified. Probably at Goethe's suggestion, the Duke added two hundred thalers to Schiller's pension, and invited him to reside in Weimar. On December 3, 1799, the family moved to a house so close to Goethe's that for a time the two poets saw each other every day.[130]

Meanwhile, carried onward by his triumph, Schiller had flung himself into another play. "Thank God!" he wrote to Körner on May 8, 1799, "I have already hit upon a new subject for a tragedy." For his *Maria Stuart* he studied the historical background, but he laid no claim to writing history; he proposed to write a play using history as material and background. He rearranged events and chronology for dramatic consistency and effect; he stressed the unpleasant elements in Elizabeth's character, and made Mary an almost immaculate heroine; and he brought the two queens face to face in a dramatic confrontation. History knows of no such meeting, but the scene is one of the most powerful in the literature of the stage. When it was presented at Weimar, June 14, 1800, Schiller was again exalted with success. By July he was at work on *Die Jungfrau von Orleans*. Here too he revised history to his purpose: in place of burning the Maid he pictured Joan as escaping from her English captors, rushing into battle to rescue her king, and dying in victory on the field. The première at Leipzig (September 18, 1801) was the greatest triumph that Schiller ever had.

Was Goethe jealous of his friend's sudden rise to ascendancy on the German stage? He rejoiced over it, and twenty-eight years later he still judged *Wallensteins Tod* "so great that there is nothing else like it of the kind."[131] However, he did not rank his rival as high in poetry as in drama; he felt that

Schiller had clouded his poetry with philosophy, and had never quite mastered the music of verse.[132] When some admirers of Schiller wished to stage a tribute to him in the Weimar theater, Goethe forbade it as too ostentatious.[133] In July, 1800, he went to Jena for seclusion and study, while Schiller remained in Weimar; but on November 23 Schiller still spoke in terms of friendship unimpaired. He ranked Goethe as "the most gifted man since Shakespeare. . . . In the six years of our intimacy no slightest doubt of his integrity ever arose. He possessed the highest veracity and sense of honor, and the deepest earnestness in the pursuit of what is right and good."[134] "I wish," he added, "that I could justify Goethe as warmly in respect of his domestic relations! . . . Through false notions of what constitutes domestic happiness, and through an unhappy fear of marriage, he has slipped into an entanglement which oppresses him and makes him wretched in his very home, and which he is too weak and softhearted to shake off. This is his only vulnerable spot." Schiller's wife, like the other ladies of Weimar, would not receive Christiane in her home, and Schiller rarely mentioned Christiane in his extant communications with Goethe.

Despite these flaws in the friendship of the *Dioskuren*, as they were sometimes called, it at least proved that a classic and a Romantic genius might live in harmony. They sent messages to each other almost every day; they frequently had supper together; Goethe often put his carriage at Schiller's disposal; he sent to Schiller "a portion of the order which my wine merchant has just delivered."[135] "Let us have a walk together toward evening," Goethe wrote on April 20, 1801; and on June 11; "Farewell; give my kind greetings to your dear wife, and gladden me, on my return [from Göttingen], by showing me some fruits of your industry"; and on June 28, 1802: "A key to my garden and garden house will be given you; I want you to have as good a time there as possible." Twenty-two years after Schiller's death Goethe said to Eckermann, "It was fortunate for me . . . that I found Schiller; for, different as our natures were, our tendencies were still toward one point, which made our connection so intimate that one really could not live without the other."[136]

In the final years of their alliance each was handicapped by disease. For the first three months of 1801 Goethe suffered from nervousness, sleeplessness, violent influenza, and abscesses that for a time closed his eyes. At one stage he was unconscious for so long that Weimar expected his death. On January 12 Charlotte von Stein wrote to her son Fritz: "I did not know that my former friend Goethe was still so dear to me, and that a serious illness, which overcame him nine days ago, would so shake me to the very core."[137] She took Christiane's boy, August, into her home for a while to ease the burdens that Goethe's sickness had laid upon his mistress, who tended him tirelessly. His recovery was slow and painful. "It is hard," he wrote to Charlotte, "to find the way back."[138]

In 1802 Schiller, now prosperous from the rising proceeds of his acted and published plays, bought a home in Weimar for 7,200 gulden, and Goethe, then in Jena, helped him to sell the house he had lived in there. On March 17,

1803, Schiller produced *Die Braut von Messina*, a self-confessed[139] attempt to rival Sophocles' *Oedipus* by portraying, with a divided chorus, the strife of two brothers in love with a woman who turns out to be their sister. The play did not please. Goethe experienced a similar setback when, in 1803, he staged *Die natürliche Tochter*.

Among the spectators at a performance of *The Natural Daughter* was a brilliant and volatile lady, Germaine Necker, Mme. de Staël, who was gathering material for her book *De l'Allemagne*. She saw Schiller for the first time in December, 1803,

> in the salon of the Duke and Duchess of Weimar, in a society as enlightened as it is exalted. He read French very well, but he had never spoken it. I maintained with some warmth the superiority of our dramatic system over that of all others; he did not refuse to enter the lists with me, without feeling any uneasiness from the difficulty and slowness with which he expressed himself in French. . . . I soon discovered so many ideas through the impediment of his words, I was so struck with the simplicity of his character, . . . I found him so modest, . . . so animated, that I vowed him, from that moment, a friendship full of admiration.[140]

Schiller prepared Goethe for her: "She represents the intellectual culture of France in its purity. . . . The only trouble with her is her quite extraordinary volubility. One has to turn oneself into one concentrated organ of hearing in order to follow her."[141] He brought her to Goethe on December 24. Goethe reported: "A most interesting hour. I didn't get a chance to say a word. She speaks well, but far too much." Her own report was identical except for a slight change: she said that Goethe had talked so much that she had not had a chance to speak one syllable.[142] Her book served as a revelation to France of Germany as "the native land of thought." "It is impossible," she wrote, "that the German writers, the best-informed and the most reflecting men in Europe, should not deserve a moment's attention to be bestowed upon their literature and their philosophy."[143]

Resolved to win back the audience that had rejected *The Bride of Messina*, Schiller, at Goethe's suggestion, chose for his next drama the popular story of William Tell. He was soon on fire with the theme. "After he had gathered all necessary material," Goethe recalled in 1820, "he sat down to work and . . . did not get up from his chair until the play was finished. If weariness overcame him he laid his head on his arm and slept a while. So soon as he awoke he asked . . . for strong black coffee to keep himself awake. So the play was written in six weeks."[144]

Schiller accepted as history the legend of a William Tell who had led the revolt of the Swiss against Austria in 1308. The revolt was real; so was Gessler, the hated Austrian bailiff. Gessler, in the legend, promised Tell full pardon if he proved his famed prowess with bow and arrow by shooting an apple from his boy's head. Tell placed two arrows in his belt; with the first he shot the apple; Gessler asked for what he had intended the second; Tell answered, "For you if the first should strike my son." The play was acclaimed at Weimar on March 17, 1804, and soon thereafter everywhere;

Switzerland adopted it as part of its national lore. Published, the play sold seven thousand copies in a few weeks. Schiller was now more famous than Goethe.

But he had less than a year of life left to him. In July, 1804, he had so violent an attack of colic that his doctor feared for his death and Schiller hoped for it. He recovered slowly, and began another play, *Demetrius* (the "false Dmitri" of Russian history). On April 28, 1805, he saw Goethe for the last time; from that meeting Goethe returned to his home and himself fell seriously ill with colic. On the twenty-ninth Schiller's final sickness began. Heinrich Voss reported: "His eyes were sunk deep in his head, and every nerve twitched convulsively."[145] The unhealthy tensions of literary effort, the inflammation of his bowels, and the decay of his lungs joined to destroy him. "Schiller never drank much," said Goethe later; "he was very temperate, but in such hours of bodily weakness he was obliged to stimulate his powers with spirituous liquors."[146] On May 9 Schiller met death with a strange calm: he bade farewell to his wife, his four children, and his friends; then he fell asleep, and did not wake again. An autopsy showed the left lung completely destroyed by tuberculosis, the heart degenerated, the liver, the kidney, and the intestines all diseased. The doctor told the Duke: "Under the circumstances we cannot help wondering how the poor man could have lived so long."[147]

Goethe was so ill at the time that no one dared tell him of Schiller's death. On May 10 Christiane's sobbing revealed it to him. "I thought I was losing my own life," he wrote to Zelter, "and instead I lost a friend who was the very half of my existence."[148] With what remained he came to his own fulfillment.

CHAPTER XXIV

Goethe Nestor

1805-32

I. GOETHE AND NAPOLEON

SHALL we, honoring our stated limits, leave Goethe suspended at this point, with *Faust* on his pen and wisdom in his age, or shall we, burdening space and risking time, pursue this ever-evolving Olympian to his end? *Die ewige Weisheit zieht uns hinan:* timeless wisdom draws us on.[1]

On October 14, 1806, Napoleon defeated the Prussians at Jena. Duke Karl August, allied with Prussia, had led his own little army against the French in that battle. The routed survivors, and then the hungry victors, entered Weimar, sacked the stores, and quartered themselves in private homes. Sixteen Alsatian troops took over Goethe's house; Christiane gave them food, drink, and beds. That night two other soldiers, intoxicated, forced their way in, and, finding no more beds available on the lower floor, ran upstairs into Goethe's room, brandished their swords in his face, and demanded accommodations. Christiane placed herself between these soldiers and her mate, persuaded them to leave, and then bolted the door. On the fifteenth Bonaparte reached Weimar and restored order; instructions were issued that "the distinguished scholar" was not to be disturbed, and that "all measures should be taken to protect the great Goethe and his home."[2] Marshals Lannes, Ney, and Augereau stayed with him for a while, and then left with apologies and compliments. Goethe thanked Christiane for her bravery, and said to her, "God willing, we shall be man and wife." On October 19 they were married. His good mother, who had borne lovingly with all his faults, and modestly with all his honors, sent them renewed blessings. She died on September 12, 1808, and Goethe inherited half of her estate.

In October, 1808, Napoleon presided over a meeting of six sovereigns and forty-three princes at Erfurt, and remade the map of Germany. Duke Karl August attended, taking Goethe in his retinue. Bonaparte asked Goethe to visit him on October 2; the poet came, and spent an hour with the conqueror, Talleyrand, two generals, and Friedrich von Müller, a Weimar magistrate. Napoleon complimented him on his vigor (Goethe was then fifty-nine), inquired about his family, and launched into a spirited critique of *Werther.* He condemned current dramas that emphasized fate. "Why talk about fate? Politics are fate. . . . *Qu'en dit Monsieur Goet?*—What does Monsieur Goethe say about it?" We do not know Goethe's reply, but Müller reported that as Goethe was leaving the room Napoleon remarked to his generals, "*Voilà un homme!*" (Behold a man!)[3]

On October 6 Napoleon returned to Weimar, taking with him a company of actors from Paris, the great Talma among them. They played, in Goethe's theater, Voltaire's *La Mort de César*. After the performance the Emperor took Goethe aside and discussed tragedy. "The serious drama," he said, "could very well be a school for princes as well as for the people, for in certain ways it is above history. . . . *You* ought to portray the death of Caesar more magnificently than Voltaire has done, and show how happy Caesar [Napoleon] would have made the world if the people had only granted him time in which to carry out his lofty plans." And a little later: "You must come to Paris! I make this definite request of you! You will there obtain a larger view of the world, and you will find a wealth of themes for your poetry."[4] — When Napoleon passed through Weimar again, after his disastrous retreat from Moscow, he asked the French ambassador to convey his greetings to Goethe.

The poet felt that in Bonaparte he had met, as he expressed it, "the greatest mind the world has ever seen."[5] He quite approved Napoleon's rule of Germany; after all (Goethe had written in 1807), there was no Germany, only a farrago of petty states, and the Holy Roman Empire had ceased to exist in 1806; it seemed good to Goethe that Europe should be united, especially under so brilliant a head as Bonaparte's. He did not rejoice over Napoleon's defeat at Waterloo, though his Duke again led the Weimar regiments against the French. His culture and concern were too universal to let him feel much patriotic glow; and he could not find it in him, though often asked to do so, to write songs of nationalistic fervor. In his eightieth year he said to Eckermann:

> How could I write songs of hatred when I felt no hate? And, between ourselves, I never hated the French, although I thanked God when we were rid of them. How could I, to whom the only significant things are civilization [*Kultur*] and barbarism, hate a nation which is among the most cultivated in the world, and to which I owe a great part of my own culture? In any case this business of hatred between nations is a curious thing. You will always find it most powerful and barbarous on the lowest levels of civilization. But there exists a level at which it wholly disappears, and where one stands, so to speak, above the nations, and feels the weal or woe of a neighboring people as though it were one's own. This level was appropriate to my nature; I had reached it long before my sixtieth year.[6]

Would that there had been, in every major state, a million such "good Europeans"!

II. *FAUST:* PART I

Goethe did not accept Napoleon's invitation to move to Paris or to write about Caesar; he had long nurtured in his mind and his manuscripts a subject that moved him more deeply than even the most majestic political career: the struggle of the soul toward understanding and beauty, the defeat of the soul by the brevity of beauty and the elusiveness of truth, and the peace obtainable by the soul through narrowing the goal and broadening the self. But how to vision all this in a modern parable and dramatic form? For fifty-eight years Goethe tried.

He had learned the story of Faust[7] in his childhood through chapbooks and puppet shows, and he had seen pictures of Faust and the Devil on the walls of Auerbach's cellar in Leipzig. He himself, in youth, had meddled with magic and alchemy. His own restless search for understanding went into his conception of Faust; his reading of Voltaire and his contact with Herder's sarcasms went into Mephistopheles; the Gretchen whom he had loved in Frankfurt, and the Friederike Brion whom he had deserted in Sesenheim, gave name and form to Margaret.

How deeply the story of Faust moved Goethe, how varied the forms it took in his thought, shows in the fact that he began to write the play in 1773, and did not finish it till 1831. Of his meeting with Herder in 1771 he wrote in his autobiography:

> I most carefully concealed from him my interest in certain subjects which had rooted themselves in me, and were, little by little, molding themselves into poetic form. These were Götz von Berlichingen and Faust. . . . The significant puppet show of the latter resounded and vibrated, many-toned, within me. I too had wandered about in all sorts of science, and had early enough been led to see its vanity. I had, moreover, tried all sorts of ways in real life, and had always returned unsatisfied and troubled. Now these things, as well as many others, I carried about with me, and delighted myself with them in solitary hours, but without writing anything down.[8]

On September 17, 1775, he told a correspondent: "I felt fresh this morning, and wrote a scene of my *Faust*."[9] Later in that month Johann Zimmermann asked him how the play was progressing. "He brought in a bag filled with a thousand fragments of paper, and threw it on the table. 'There,' he said, 'is my *Faust*.' "[10] When he went to Weimar (November, 1775) the first form of the drama was complete.[11] Dissatisfied with it, he put it aside; this *Urfaust*, or *Original Faust*, never reached print till 1887, when a manuscript copy made by Fräulein von Göchhausen was found in Weimar.[12] Through fifteen more years he revised and expanded it. Finally he published it (1790) as *Faust, ein Fragment*, which now runs to sixty-three pages;[13] this was the first printed form of the most famous play since *Hamlet*.

Still discontent with it, Goethe dropped the theme till 1797. On June 22 he wrote to Schiller: "I have determined to take up my *Faust* again, . . . breaking up what has been printed, arranging it in large masses, . . . and further preparing the development. . . . I only wish that you would be so good as to think the matter over on one of your sleepless nights, and tell me what you would demand of the whole, and to interpret my dreams to me like a true prophet." Schiller replied the next day: "The duality of human nature, and the unsuccessful endeavor to unite in man the godlike and the physical, is never lost sight of. . . . The nature of the subject will force you to treat it philosophically, and the imagination will have to accommodate itself to serve a rational idea." Goethe's imagination was too rich, his vividly remembered experiences too many; he inserted many of them into the *Frag-*

ment, doubling its size, and in 1808 he gave the world what we now call *Faust*, Part I.

Before letting his puppet say a word, he prefixed to the drama a tender *Zueignung*—dedication—to his dead friends; and a droll "Prologue in the Theater" between manager, playwright, and jester; and a "Prologue in Heaven" wherein God bets Mephistopheles that Faust cannot be permanently won to sin. Then at last Faust speaks, in simplest doggerel:

Habe nun, ach! Philosophie,	I have studied, alas, philosophy,
Juristerei und Medizin,	Jurisprudence, and medicine too,
Und leider auch Theologie	And, saddest of all, theology,
Durchaus studiert, mit heissem Be- *mühn.*	With ardent labor, through and through.
Da steh ich nun, ich armer Tor!	And here I stick, as wise, poor fool,
Und bin so klug als wie zuvor.	As when my steps first turned to school.
Heisse Magister, heisse Doktor gar,	Master they style me, nay, Doctor forsooth,
Und ziehe schon an die zehen Jahr	And nigh ten years, over rough and smooth
Herauf, herab, und quer und krumm	And up and down, and acrook and across,
Meine Schüler an der Nase herum,	I lead my pupils by the nose,
Und sehe dass wir nichts wissen kön- *nen.*	And know that in truth we can know naught.[14]

This four-foot meter, handed down from Hans Sachs's playlets, proved to be just the rippling rhythm for a drama that chastened philosophy with fun.

Faust, of course, is Goethe, even to being a man of sixty years; and, like Goethe, he was still, at sixty, thrilled by feminine loveliness and grace. His double aspiration for wisdom and beauty was the soul of Goethe; it challenged the avenging gods by its presumption, but it was noble. Faust and Goethe said Yea to life, spiritual and sensual, philosophical and gay. By contrast, Mephistopheles (who is not Satan but only Satan's philosopher) is the devil of denial and doubt, to whom all aspiration is nonsense, all beauty a skeleton wearing skin. In many moments Goethe was this mocking spirit too, or he could not have given him such wit and life. At times Mephistopheles seems to be the voice of experience, of realism and reason checking the romantic desires and delusions of Faust; indeed, Goethe told Eckermann, "the character of Mephistopheles is . . . a living result of an extensive acquaintance with the world."[15]

Faust does not sell his soul unconditionally; he agrees to go to hell only if Mephistopheles shows him a pleasure so durably satisfying that he will be glad to stay with it forever:

> If ever on the bed of sloth I loll contented ever,
> Then with that moment end my race! . . .
> Should I to any moment say,
> "Tarry a while, you are so fair!"*
> Then may you into fetters cast me;
> Then will I gladly go down there.

---

* *Verweile doch, du bist so schön!*

On this condition Faust signs the compact with his blood, and cries reck-lessly, "Our glowing passions in a sensual sea now will we quench!"[16]

So Mephistopheles takes him to Margaret—"Gretchen." Faust finds in her all the charm of that simplicity which departs with knowledge and returns with wisdom. He woos her with jewels and philosophy:

MARGARET. Tell me, how is't with thy religion, pray?
           Thou art a good and kindly man,
           And yet, I think, small heed thereto dost pay.
FAUST.   Enough, dear child! I love thee, thou dost feel.
           For those I love my blood and life I'd spill,
           Nor of his faith, his church, would any man bereave.
MARGARET. That is not right! We must believe! . . .
           Dost thou believe in God?
FAUST.   What man can say, my dearest,
           "I believe in God"? . . .
MARGARET. Then thou believest not?
FAUST.   Thou winsome angel-face, mishear me not!
           Who can name Him? Who thus proclaim him?
           I believe Him?
           Who that has feeling, his bosom steeling,
           Can say, "I believe Him not"?
           The All-embracing, the All-sustaining;
           Clasps and sustains He not
           Thee, me, Himself?
           Springs not the vault of heaven above us?
           Lieth not earth, firm-'stablished, 'neath our feet? . . .
           Great though it be, fill thou therefrom thine heart,
           And when in the feeling wholly blest thou art,
           Call it then what thou wilt!
           Call it Bliss, Heart, Love, God!
           I have no name for it.
           Feeling is all [Gefühl ist alles]!
           Name is but sound and smoke
           Clouding the glow of heaven. . . .
MARGARET. It seemeth fair in these words of thine,
           But yet . . . thou hast no Christianity.
FAUST.   Dear child![17]

She is moved not by his cloudy pantheism but by the fine figure and raiment with which Mephistopheles' magic has endowed his restored youth. She sings at her spinning wheel a song of wistful longing:

Meine Ruh ist hin,	My peace is fled,
Mein Herz ist schwer,	My heart is sore,
Ich finde sie nimmer	I shall find it never,
Und nimmermehr. . . .	And nevermore. . . .
Nach ihm nur schau ich	Him only I watch for,
Zum Fenster hinaus,	The window near;
Nach ihm nur geh ich	Him only I look for
Aus dem Haus.	When forth I fare.
Sein hoher Gang,	His lofty gait,
Sein' edle Gestalt,	His lordly guise,
Seines Mundes Lächeln,	The smile of his lips,

Seiner Augen Gewalt. . . .	The might of his eyes. . . .
Mein Busen drängt	My bosom yearns
Sich nach ihm hin.	For him, for him.
Ach, dürft ich fassen	Ah, could I clasp him
Und halten ihn,	And cling to him,
Und küssen ihn,	And kiss him, as fain
So wie ich wollt,	I would, then I,
An seinen Küssen	Faint with his kisses,
Vergehen sollt!	Should swoon and die![18]

All the Western world knows the rest of the story, if only through Gounod. Margaret, in order to kiss and swoon unchaperoned, gives her mother a sleeping potion, from which the mother never wakes. Faust kills Margaret's brother Valentine in a duel, and then disappears; Margaret, in shame and grief, kills her fatherless child; she is arrested and condemned to death. Faust visits her in her dungeon and begs her to escape with him; she embraces him, but refuses to leave her cell. Mephistopheles draws Faust away, while a voice from heaven cries, "She is redeemed."

Only slowly did the reading public realize that this *Faust* of 1808 was the finest drama and the finest poetry that Germany had yet produced. But some alert few recognized it at once as fit to stand among the peaks of the world's literature. Friedrich Schlegel compared Goethe with Dante, Jean Paul Richter equaled him with Shakespeare; Wieland gave him in the realm of poetry the same sovereignty that Napoleon then held in government and war.[19]

III. NESTOR IN LOVE

In the years 1818–21 Goethe had two soul-stirring romances, not counting Bettina Brentano. On April 23, 1807, Bettina, twenty-two, came to the aging poet with a letter of introduction from Wieland. She was the granddaughter of Sophie von La Roche, who had loved Wieland, and she was the daughter of Maximiliane Brentano, who had flirted with Goethe; she felt that she had a primogenital lien on Goethe's heart. Soon after entering his room she flung herself into his arms. He accepted her as a child, and thereafter corresponded with her in that sense; but he enclosed with his letters the latest love poems he had written, and though they were not addressed to her she treated them as declarations of passion, and gave them that color in the *Goethes Briefwechsel mit einem Kinde* (*Goethe's Correspondence with a Child*) which she published in 1835.

Most of the poems had been inspired by Wilhelmine Herzlieb. Minna, as Goethe soon called her, was the daughter of a Jena bookseller. He had known her as a child, but in 1808 she was nineteen, modest, tender, and blooming. She hung on every word that he spoke, and mourned that age and status forbade her to love and possess him. He perceived her feeling, responded to it, wrote sonnets to her, punning on her name as a loving heart; but he recalled that he had only recently made Christiane his wife. He seems

to have had Minna in mind when he portrayed the shy, highstrung, affectionate Ottilie of the *Elective Affinities* (1809).

This remarkable novel—*Die Wahlverwandtschaften*—is, as its author
thought,[20] his best work of prose fiction, far better organized and more com-
pactly told than either of the Wilhelm Meister circumambulations. Note
Goethe's words to Eckermann (February 9, 1829): "In the whole of the
Elective Affinities there is not a line which I myself did not actually live, and
there is far more behind the text than anyone can assimilate at a single reading." Indeed, the fault of the book is that there is too much Goethe in it, too
much philosophizing put into unlikely mouths. (He makes the girl Ottilie
keep a diary in which he deposits some of his maturest *obiter cogitata*, such
as, "Against great excellence in another there is no way of defending ourselves except love."[21]) But it is because there is so much of Goethe in this
book that it is warm with life and rich in thought: because the Charlotte of
the story is again Charlotte von Stein, tempted, but refusing, to be unfaithful
to her husband; because the Captain is Goethe in love with his friend's wife;
because Edward, the fifty-year-old husband infatuated with Ottilie, is
Goethe drawn to Minna Herzlieb; and because the novel is Goethe's attempt
to analyze his own erotic sensitivity.

He here proposed to think of sexual attraction in chemical terms. He may
have taken his title from the *Elective Affinities* published by the great Swedish chemist Torbern Olof Bergman in 1775. The Captain describes to Edward and Charlotte the attractions, repulsions, and combinations of material
particles: "You ought yourselves to see these substances—which seem so
dead and are yet so full of energy and force—at work before your eyes. Now
they seek each other out, . . . seize, crush, devour, destroy one another,
and then suddenly they reappear . . . in fresh, renovated, unexpected
forms."[22] So, when Edward invites his friend the Captain, and Charlotte invites her niece Ottilie, to stay with them for long visits, the Captain falls in
love with Charlotte, and Edward falls in love with Ottilie. When Edward
has intercourse with his wife he thinks of Ottilie, and Charlotte thinks of the
Captain, in a kind of psychological adultery. The offspring looks strangely
like Ottilie, and Ottilie takes to the child as if her own. Then, apparently by
accident, she lets it drown; in remorse she starves herself to death. Edward
dies of a broken heart; the Captain disappears; Charlotte survives, spiritually
dead. A town philosopher concludes: "Marriage is the beginning and end
of all civilization. It tames the savage, and gives to the most cultivated their
best opportunity for gentleness. It should be indissoluble, for it brings so
much happiness that its incidental tribulations count for nothing in the
scale."[23] Four pages later, however, one character suggests trial marriage, in
which the contract is for only five years at a time.

In 1810 we find Goethe at Karlsbad taking the waters and flirting with
young women, while Christiane, four years married, remained at home,
flirting with young men. The sixty-one-year-old poet won the passionate
love of a darkly beautiful Jewess, Marianne von Eybenberg; then he fled
from her with blond Silvie von Ziegesar. In a poem addressed to Silvie he

called her "daughter, mistress, darling, white, and slim."[24] Christiane sent him appeals for fidelity:

> And have Bettina and that Frau von Eybenberg arrived in Karlsbad yet? They say here that Silvie and the Gotters are to be there, too. So what will you do, between all your flirtations? Rather too many! But you won't forget your oldest one, will you? Think of me a little, too, now and then. I mean to trust you absolutely, whatever people may say. For you are the only one, you know, who thinks of me at all.[25]

He sent her little gifts.

He found time almost every day to compose some poetry or prose. About 1809 he began to write his autobiography. He called it *Aus meinem Leben Dichtung und Wahrheit* (*Fiction and Truth from My Life*). The title handsomely admitted that he might now and then, intentionally or not, have mingled imagination with reality. He touched only lightly and delicately on his love for Charlotte Buff, but told more fully of his romance with Friederike Brion; both of these women still lived. He analyzed well and generously many friends of his youth—Lenz, Basedow, Merck, Herder, Jacobi, Lavater. Of himself he spoke modestly; his private notes complained that the autobiographer is expected to confess his faults but not to reveal his virtues.[26] The book is the history of a mind rather than of a life; incidents in it are few, reflections abound. It is his greatest book of prose.

In 1811 he received from Beethoven a letter of admiration, with the *Overture to Egmont*. Poet and composer met at Teplitz in July, 1812; Beethoven played for Goethe, and took walks with him. If we may trust the novelist August Frankl, "wherever they went, the people on the promenade respectfully made way for them and saluted them. Goethe, annoyed by these constant interruptions, said, 'What a nuisance! I can never avoid this sort of thing!' With a smile, Beethoven answered, 'Don't let it bother your Excellency; the homage is probably meant for me.'" Goethe wrote to Zelter (September 2, 1812): "Beethoven's talent astonished me; his personality, alas, is wholly ungovernable. He is not wrong . . . in finding the world detestable, but this attitude renders it more enjoyable neither to him nor to others. Much of it is to be excused on the deplorable ground that he is losing his hearing."[27] Beethoven's comment on Goethe: "What patience the great man has had with me! What good he has done me!" But "the court atmosphere suits him too well."[28]

Court appearances and conduct were part of Goethe's official life, for he was still active in administration. His home life had lost its charm: August, twenty-two in 1812, was an unsalvageable mediocrity, and Christiane was fat and taking to drink. She had some excuse, for his flirtations continued. During his visits to Frankfurt he often stayed at the suburban villa of Johann von Willemer, and admired Willemer's wife, Marianne. In the summer of 1815 he spent almost four weeks with them. Marianne was thirty-one, but she was in the fullness of womanly beauty. She sang Goethe's lyrics and Mozart's arias enchantingly, wrote excellent verse, and exchanged with Goethe a series of poems in imitation of Hafiz, Firdausi, and other Persian bards. (Hafiz had been translated into German in 1812.) Some of the poems are frankly sensual and tell of mutual joy in physical embraces, but this license may be merely poetic. The three met again in September at Heidelberg; the two poets took long walks together, and Goethe wrote Marianne's name in Arabic letters in the dust around the castle fountain. They never saw each other again after that day, but they corresponded through the seventeen remaining years of his life. Willemer seems to have cherished his wife all the more for having charmed so famous a man, and for answering Goethe's verse with poems scarcely inferior to his own. Goethe included hers with his in the *Westöstlicher Diwan* (*West-Eastern Book of Many Leaves*) that he published in 1819.

While this correspondence was proceeding in prose and rhyme, Christiane died (June 6, 1816). Goethe noted in his diary: "Her death struggle was dreadful. . . . Emptiness and deathly silence within and around me."[29] A profound depression clouded these years. When Charlotte Kestner, the lost beloved of his youth, now the sixty-four-year-old wife of the successful Councilor Kestner of Hanover, visited him with her daughter (September 25, 1816), no emotion seemed to stir in him, and all his talk was courteous triviality. But in 1817 his son August, interrupting a career of dissipation, married Ottilie von Pogwisch; Goethe invited them to live with him; Ottilie brought the gaiety of youth into the household, and soon gave the aging poet grandchildren who made his heart beat again.

Ulrike von Levetzow helped. She was one of the three daughters of Amalie von Levetzow, whom Goethe had known in Karlsbad. At Marienbad in August, 1821, he met Ulrike, who later recalled: "As I had been for some years in a French boarding school at Strasbourg, and was only seventeen, I had never heard of Goethe, and had no idea that he was a famous man and a great poet. So I wasn't at all shy with the friendly old gentleman. . . . The very next morning he asked me to take a walk with him. . . . He took me along on his walk nearly every morning."[30] He returned to Marienbad in 1822, and "all that summer Goethe was very friendly to me." A year later they met in Karlsbad, and soon they stirred the gossip of the spa. By this time the poet had decided that his love was more than paternal. Duke Karl August urged Ulrike to marry Goethe; if she would do this a fine house would be given to her family in Weimar, and after the poet's death she would receive a pension of ten thousand thalers a year.[31] Mother and daughter refused. Goethe returned desolate to Weimar, and drowned his disappointment in ink. Ulrike lived to be ninety-five.

In that year 1821 which led Goethe to Ulrike, Karl Zelter, music director at Jena, brought to him in Weimar a twelve-year-old pupil, Felix Mendelssohn. Zelter had opened Goethe's soul to the world of music, and had even taught him to compose. Now the skill of the young pianist astonished and gladdened the old poet, who insisted on having him stay with him for several days. "Every morning," Felix wrote on November 6, "the author of *Faust* and *Werther* kisses me. In the afternoon I play for him for about two hours, partly fugues of Bach, partly my improvisations." On November 8

Goethe held a reception to introduce Felix to Weimar society. On November 10 Felix wrote: "Every afternoon he opens the piano and says, 'I have not heard you at all today. Come, make a little noise for me!' Then he sits down next to me and listens. You have no idea how kind and affectionate he is." When Zelter wished to take Felix back to Jena, Goethe persuaded him to let his pupil remain a few days more. "Now," wrote the happy boy, "gratitude to Goethe rose on all sides, and the girls and I kissed his lips and hands. Ottilie von Pogwisch threw her arms around his neck; and since she is very pretty, and he flirts with her all the time, the effect was excellent."[32] There are happy moments in history behind the drama of tragedy, and beneath the notice of historians.

IV. THE SCIENTIST

Let us go back to his younger years, when, with alert attention and omnivorous interest, he had begun his lifelong pursuit of science. Few of us have known that Goethe devoted more time to scientific investigation and compositions than to all his poetry and prose combined.[33] He had studied medicine and physics at Leipzig, chemistry at Strasbourg; he took up anatomy in 1781; and for years he wandered about Thuringia gathering mineral and botanical specimens and observing geological formations. In his travels he noted not merely men, women, and art, but also fauna and flora, optical and meteorological phenomena. He took a leading part in establishing laboratories in Jena. He rejoiced or grieved as intensively over his victories or defeats in science as over his successes or failures in literature.

He did something about the weather. He organized meteorological observation stations in the duchy of Saxe-Weimar, helped to set up others throughout Germany,[34] and prepared instructions for them. He wrote essays on "The Theory of Weather" and "The Causes of Barometric Fluctuations." He persuaded Duke Karl August to begin the collections that formed the core of the Museum of Mineralogy at Jena. After studying the geological strata at Ilmenau he argued that they confirmed Abraham Werner's theory that all the rocky formations on the earth's crust were the result of the slow action of water. (This "Neptunist" theory has had to be combined with the "Vulcanist" theory of change by violent action.) He was among the first to suggest that the age of strata might be judged from the fossils imbedded in them, and to defend the view that the great boulders now erratically distributed in high places had been swept up there by surges of ice coming down from the Arctic Zone.[35]

In 1791–92 Goethe published in two volumes *Beiträge zur Optik* (*Contributions to Optics*). "My purpose," he wrote, "has been to assemble all that is known in this field, and to undertake all the experiments myself, varying them as much as possible, making them easier to follow, and keeping them within the scope of the ordinary person."[36] During the years from 1790 to 1810 he made numberless experiments to explain color; the Goethe

Museum at Weimar still preserves the instruments he used. The result appeared in 1810 in two large volumes of text, and one of plates, entitled *Zur Farbenlehre* (*On the Theory of Color*); this was his major work as a scientist.

He studied colors as due not only to the chemical composition of objects but to the structure and operation of the eye. He analyzed the adaptation of the retina to darkness and light, the physiology of color blindness, the phenomena of color shadows and afterimages, the effects of color contrasts and combinations in sensation and in art. He mistakenly thought of green as a blend of yellow and blue. (They do blend so on the artist's palette, but when the blue and yellow of the color spectrum combine they yield gray and white.) He repeated many of the experiments described in Newton's *Opticks* (1704), found in several cases results different from those there reported, and ended by accusing Newton of incompetence and occasional deceit.[37] He opposed Newton's view that white is a composition of colors, and held that their combination regularly produced not white but gray. — Neither his contemporaries nor his successors in the field of optics accepted his conclusions. They praised his experiments and discarded many of his theories. In 1815 Arthur Schopenhauer, who admired Goethe as a poet and as a philosopher, sent him an essay ably defending Newton's conception of white as a composition of colors; the old man never forgave him. The general rejection of the *Farbenlehre* added to the gloom of his final years.

A man so sensitive to color as Goethe was could not but be fascinated by the world of plants. At Padua in 1786 he was thrilled by the botanical gardens; here was a richer and more varied collection than he had ever seen. He saw how different the plants of the south were from those of the north, and he resolved to study the influence of environment upon the form and growth of plants. Nor had he ever felt so deeply the mysterious and overwhelming capacity of nature to develop each form, with its unique pattern of structure, texture, color, and line, out of apparently simple and similar seeds. What fertility, and what originality! But were there some common elements in all the diversity of individuals, and in all the evolution of organs and parts? The idea came to him that these genera, species, and varieties were variations of a basic archetype; that all these plants, for example, were formed on some fundamental and original—even if imaginary—model, an *Urpflanze*, or First Plant, the mother of them all. "The same law" or theory, he wrote to Herder, "will be applicable to all that lives"—i.e., to animals as well as plants; they too are variations on one structural theme.[38] And as the individual organism, with all its uniqueness, is an imitation of a primal archetype, so the parts of an organism may be variations of one fundamental form. Goethe noticed in Padua a palmetto whose leaves were in diverse stages of development; he studied the visible transitions from the simplest leaf to the complete, majestic fan; and he conceived the idea that all the structures of a plant—except the axis, or stem—were variations and stages of the leaf.*

---

* Caspar Friedrich Wolff had come to the same conclusion in 1768.

After his return to Weimar Goethe published his theory in an eighty-six-page book entitled *An Attempt by J. W. von Goethe, Privy Councilor of the Duchy of Saxe-Weimar, to Explain the Metamorphosis of Plants* (1790). Botanists laughed at it as the dreams of a poet, and advised the poet to stick to his trade.[39] He took them at their word, and rephrased his views in a poem, "The Metamorphosis of Plants." Gradually the theory accumulated evidence and supporters. In 1830 Étienne Geoffroy Saint-Hilaire presented Goethe's essay to the French Academy of Sciences as a work of careful research and creative imagination confirmed by the progress of botany.[40]

Applying his theory to anatomy, Goethe suggested (1790) that the skull is a variation and continuation of the vertebrae, enclosing the brain as the spine encloses the spinal cord. There is no agreement today on this conception. One definite and brilliant achievement is credited to Goethe in anatomy —the demonstration of an intermaxillary bone in man. (This is the bone, between the maxillae, or jaw bones, that carries the upper incisor teeth.) The anatomists had recognized such a bone in animals, but had questioned its existence in man; Goethe's discovery narrowed the structural difference between man and the ape. Hear the poet proclaim his success in a letter from Jena to Charlotte von Stein, March 27, 1784—the lover and the scientist all compact: "A few lines to my Lotte by way of saying good morning. . . . I have been granted a delightful satisfaction. I have made an anatomical discovery that is at once beautiful and important. You shall have your share in it, but do not say a word about it."[41] He announced his finding in a manuscript monograph sent to divers scientists in 1784 and entitled "Versuch, aus der vergleichenden Knochenlehre, dass der Zwischenknochen der oberen Kinnlade dem Menschen mit den übrigen Thieren gemein sei" (An Attempt, Based on Comparative Osteology, to Show That the Intermaxillary Bone in the Upper Jaw is Common to Man and the Higher Animals). This was "the first treatise ever written that can be properly described as lying in the field of comparative anatomy, and thus it is a milestone in the history of this science."[42] (The French anatomist Félix Vicq d'Azyr published the same discovery in the same year 1784.)

In his essay Goethe wrote: "Man is very closely akin to the brute creation. . . . Every creature is only a tone, a modification, in a mighty harmony."[43] Like many scientists and philosophers before him, he thought of man as part of the animal kingdom, and wrote a poem, "The Metamorphosis of Animals." But he was not an evolutionist in the Darwinian sense. Following Linnaeus, he assumed the fixity of species; so his *Urpflanze* was not an actual primitive plant from which all plants had evolved, but only a general type of which all plants were modifications. Goethe did not, like his contemporaries Lamarck and Erasmus Darwin, think of species evolving from other species by the environmental selection of favorable variations.

Was Goethe a real scientist? Not in the professional sense; he was a zealous and enlightened amateur, a scientist between poems, novels, amours, artistic experiments, and administrative chores. He used extensive equipment, collected a large library of science, made useful observations and careful experiments; Helmholtz testified to the factual accuracy of the objective processes and experiments that Goethe described.[44] He avoided teleological explanations. But he was not accepted as a scientist by professionals, for these looked upon him as a dilettante who depended too trustfully upon intuition and hypothesis. He passed too quickly from one subject or investigation to another, touching each at some special point, and achieving nowhere, except in optics and the theory of color, a survey of the field. But there was something ideal and heroic in his divergent and polymorphous persistence. Said Eckermann in 1825: "Goethe will be eighty years old in a few years, but he is not tired of inquiries and experiments. He is always on the track of some great synthesis."[45] And perhaps the poet was right in thinking that the chief aim of science should not be to equip old desires with new tools, but to enlarge wisdom with knowledge for the enlightenment of desire.

V. THE PHILOSOPHER

As in science, so in philosophy he was a lover, not a professor—though it was he who secured the appointment of Fichte, Schelling, and Hegel to chairs of philosophy at Jena. He had very little interest in the debates of the schools, but he was endlessly concerned with the interpretation of nature and the meaning of life. As he became older he grew through science and poetry into a sage. He found illumination about the whole from every object, moment, and part: *"Alles Vergängliche ist nur ein Gleichnis"*—everything transient is but a symbol.[46] The *Sprüche in Prosa*, or incidental apothegms, which he left unprinted at his death, ooze wisdom on every page.

He offered no system of logic, but he suggested, pragmatically, that "that alone is true which is fruitful,"[47] and that "in the beginning was [not the word but] the deed" (*Im Anfang war die That*[48]); we find truth in action rather than in thought; thought should be an instrument, not a substitute, for action. He did not take to Kant as Schiller did; he acknowledged that the ultimate nature of reality is beyond our ken, but he did not feel that this committed him to orthodoxy; on the contrary, he recommended ignoring the unknowable; "the unfathomable is of no practical value"; the perceived world is enough for our lives.[49] He had no epistomological qualms about admitting the existence of an external world. After reading Kant and Schelling he wrote to Schiller: "I willingly concede that it is not nature [in itself] that we perceive, but that nature is comprehended by us merely according to certain forms and faculties of our mind. . . . But the appropriateness [adjustment] of our organic natures to the outer world . . . [indicates] a *determination from without, a relation toward things*."[50] "Many people resist acknowledging reality, only because they would collapse if they accepted it."[51]

But Goethe rejected materialism as well as subjectivist idealism. D'Holbach's *Système de la nature* "appeared to us [students at Strasbourg] so dark,

. . . so deathlike, that we found it a trouble to endure its presence, and shuddered at it as at a specter."[52] That was in youth, but in old age he felt likewise, writing to Knebel, April 8, 1812:

> A man who does not grasp the fact, nor rise to the vision, that spirit and matter, soul and body, thought and extension, . . . are the necessary twin ingredients of the universe, and will forever be; and that these two have equal rights, and may therefore be considered in their togetherness as the representatives of God: he who has not grasped this might as well employ his days with the idle gossip of the world.

This, of course, is Spinoza, and Goethe usually follows Spinoza into determinism—"We belong to the laws of nature, even when we rebel against them";[53] but at times he inclines to agree with Kant that "our lives, like the universe to which we belong, are mysteriously composed of freedom and necessity."[54] He felt a force of destiny working in him—of qualities compelling and determining his development; but he co-operated with it, like some free agent serving a cause that moves and includes him.

His religion was an adoration of nature, and a desire to collaborate with her creative forces—her multiform productivity and her obstinate perseverance; however, he took long to acquire her patience. He vaguely personified Nature, seeing mind and will in her, but a mind quite unlike ours, and a will indifferently neutral as between men and fleas. Nature has no moral feelings in our sense of the obligation of the part to co-operate with the whole, for she *is* the whole. In the poem "Das Göttliche" (1782) Goethe described nature as without feeling or mercy. She destroys as exuberantly as she makes. "All your ideals shall not prevent me [Goethe] from being genuine, and good and bad, like Nature."[55] Her only ethic is, Live and make live. Goethe recognized the need many souls have for supernatural support, but he felt no such need until his final years. "He has religion [enough] who has art or science; who has not art or science needs religion."[56] "As a poet and artist I am a polytheist [personifying the separate forces of nature], while in my role as scientist I incline to pantheism [seeing one God in everything]."[57]

"Resolutely pagan" in religion and morals, he had no sense of sin, felt no need of a god dying to atone for him,[58] and resented all talk of the cross. He wrote to Lavater, August 9, 1782: "I am no anti-Christian, no un-Christian, but very decidedly a non-Christian. . . . You accept the Gospel, as it stands, as divine truth. Well, no audible voice from heaven would convince me that a woman bears a child without a man, and that a dead man arises from the grave. I regard all these as blasphemies against God and his revelation of himself in nature."[59] Lavater pressed him (Goethe tells us), and "at last came out with the hard dilemma, 'Either Christian or atheist!' Upon this I declared that if he would not leave me my own Christianity as I had hitherto cherished it, I could readily decide for atheism, especially as I saw that nobody knew precisely what either term meant."[60] Goethe thought that "the Christian religion is an abortive political revolution that turned moral."[61] There are in literature "a thousand pages as beautiful and useful" as in the

Gospels.[62] "Yet I regard all four Gospels as quite genuine, for in them is evident the reflected splendor of the sublime power which emanated from the person of Christ and his nature, which was as divine as ever the divine has appeared on earth. . . . I bow before him as a divine manifestation of the highest principle of morality."[63] But he proposed to worship the sun as much as Christ, as equally a manifestation of divine power.[64] He admired Luther, and praised the Reformation for breaking the shackles of tradition, but he regretted its relapse into dogma.[65] He suspected that Protestantism would suffer for lack of inspiring, habit-forming ceremonies, and he thought Catholicism wise and beneficent in symbolizing spiritual relations and developments with impressive sacraments.[66]

Goethe's views on immortality were a function of his years. On February 2, 1789, he wrote to Friedrich zu Stolberg: "For my own part I cling more or less to the teachings of Lucretius, and confine myself and all my hopes to this life." But on February 25, 1824, he told Eckermann: "I would by no means dispense with the happiness of believing in a future existence; and indeed I would say, with Lorenzo de' Medici, that those who hope for no other life are dead even in this one"; and on February 4, 1825: "I hold the firm conviction that our spirit is something altogether indestructible."[67] He read Swedenborg, accepted the conception of a spirit sphere,[68] and played with hopes of transmigration. He studied the Cabala and Pico della Mirandola, and even drew an occasional horoscope.[69] More and more, as he aged, he admitted the rights of faith:

> Strictly speaking, I can have no knowledge of God except such as I derive from the limited vision of my sensory perceptions on this single planet. Such knowledge is a fragment of a fragment. I do not admit that this limitation, which is applicable to our observation of nature, need be applicable in the exercise of faith. The contrary is the case. It may well be that our knowledge, necessarily imperfect, demands supplementation and perfecting through an act of faith.[70]

In 1820 he regretted that he had written the rebellious *Prometheus* in his youth, for the young radicals of the day were quoting it against him.[71] He turned away from Fichte when Fichte was accused of atheism.[72] "It is our duty," he now held, "to tell others no more than they are able to receive. Man grasps only what is to his measure."[73]

Like his views of religion, his conception of morality changed with age. Bouncing with youthful energy and pride, he had interpreted life as purely a theater for self-development and display. "This craving to raise as high as possible the pyramid of my life, the base of which has been given and established for me, outweighs all else, and scarcely permits of a moment's relapse."[74] We have seen him hurting some tender souls in this process. As he matured through political office he perceived that human life is a co-operative process; that the individual survives by mutual aid, and that self-seeking actions, though still the basic force, must be limited by the needs of the group. Faust, in Part I, is individualism incarnate; in Part II he finds "salvation," health of soul, through working for the general good. Wilhelm Meister in the *Lehrjahre* seeks to educate and develop himself, though by nature and training he often aids his fellow men; in the *Wanderjahre* he seeks to further the happiness of the community. Goethe balked at the behest to love one's enemies, but he defined nobility nobly in one of his greatest poems:

Edel sei der Mensch,	Let man be noble,
Hülfreich und gut.	Helpful and good.
Denn das allein	For that alone
Unterscheidet ihn	Marks him off
Von allen Wesen	From all beings
Die wir kennen . . .	That we know. . . .
Denn unfühlend	Quite unfeeling
Ist die Natur:	Is Nature:
Es leuchtet die Sonne	The sun shines
Ueber Bös' und Gute,	Upon the base and the good;
Und dem Verbrecher	And upon the lawbreaker
Glänzen, wie dem Besten,	Gleam, as upon the best,
Der Mond und die Sterne.	The moon and the stars.
Wind und Ströme,	Winds and streams,
Donner und Hagel,	Thunder and hail,
Rauschen ihren Weg,	Roar on their way,
Und ergreifen	And snatch up
Vorübereilend,	And sweep before them
Einen und den Andern. . . .	One after another. . . .
Nach ewigen, ehrnen,	By eternal, ironclad
Grossen Gesetzen	Great laws
Müssen wir Alle	Must we all,
Unseres Daseins	Of our existence,
Kreise vollenden.	Fulfill the round.
Nur allein der Mensch	But man alone
Vermag das Unmögliche;	Can do the impossible;
Er unterscheidet,	He distinguishes,
Wählet und richtet;	Chooses, and judges;
Er kann dem Augenblick	He can to the fleeting moment
Dauer verleihen.	Give duration.
Er allein darf	He alone can
Den Guten lohnen,	Reward the good,
Den Bösen strafen,	Punish the bad,
Heilen und retten,	Heal and save.
Alles Irrende, Schweifende	And to the erring and straying
Nützlich verbinden. . . .	Bring wise counsel.
Der edle Mensch	Let the noble man
Sei hülfreich und gut.	Be helpful and good.

To become noble one must beware of debasing influences, and "all is influence except ourselves."[75] "Never mind studying contemporaries and those who strive with you; study the great men of the past, whose works have maintained their value and stature for centuries. A truly gifted man will naturally so incline, and the desire to delve into the great precursors is the very mark of a higher endowment."[76] Reverence libraries as the heritage left by these men. "Contemplating a library, one feels as though in the presence of vast capital silently yielding incalculable interest."[77] But intellect without character is far worse than character without intellect; "anything

that liberates the mind without giving us dominion over ourselves is pernicious."[78] Plan your living—*gedenke zu leben!*—but seek a balance between
thought and action; thought without action is a disease. "To know and practice a craft lends greater culture than half-knowledge a hundred times
over."[79] "No blessing is equal to the blessings of work."[80] Above all, be a
whole or join a whole. "Only mankind is the true man, and the individual
can be joyous and happy only when he has the courage to feel himself in
the whole."[81]

So the young man who inherited comfort and security, and set the Strasbourg students laughing at his rich and fancy dress, learned, through the
philosophers, the saints, and the experience of life, to think kindly of the
poor, and to wish that the fortunate would share their wealth more generously. Nobles should be taxed in proportion to their income, and should let
their dependents benefit from "the advantages which expanding knowledge
and prosperity are bringing."[82] Even after attaining European fame, Goethe
felt the bourgeois' envy of noble birth. "In Germany no one except a nobleman has an opportunity for acquiring a well-rounded . . . personal culture."[83] He observed all the usual obeisances in his behavior toward his superiors. Everyone knows the story of Goethe and Beethoven at Teplitz,
July, 1812; but its sole source is the unreliable Bettina Brentano von Arnim,
who claimed to be quoting Beethoven's account:

> Kings and princes can indeed bestow titles and orders, but they cannot make
> great men, who therefore must be held in respect. When two come together,
> such as Goethe and I, then these highborn gentlemen must observe what it is
> that counts for great with such as we. Yesterday we met the whole Imperial
> Family [of Austria], and Goethe disengaged himself from my arm in order to
> stand aside. I pressed my hat down on my head and went through the thickest
> of the crowd with my arms hanging at my sides. Princes and courtiers drew
> up in a double line; the Duke of Weimar took off his hat to me, and the Em-
> press greeted me first. Much to my amusement I saw the procession file by
> Goethe, who stood at one side, bowing with his hat in his hand. I took him
> roundly to task for it afterward.[84]

Our reaction to this story will vary with our age. Goethe felt than an
aristocracy functioning actively and with public spirit provided the best
government then possible in Europe, and deserved the respect required for
social order and control. Abuses should be reformed, but without violence
or precipitancy; revolutions cost more than they are worth, and usually
end where they began. So Mephistopheles to Faust:

> Alack! Away! Forbear of yonder squabble
> 'Twixt tyranny and slavery to babble!
> It irks me. Scarce 'tis ended when *de novo*
> With the whole farce they start *ab ovo*.[85]

And so Goethe to Eckermann in 1824: "It is quite true that I was no friend
of the French Revolution. Its horrors were too immediate, . . . while its
beneficial effects were not yet visible. . . . But I was just as little a friend
of the arbitrary rule that had preceded it. I was convinced even then that

no revolution is the fault of the people, but always the fault of the government."[86] He welcomed Napoleon as a boon to order in France and Europe
after a decade of convulsions. He distrusted democracy, for "nothing is
worse than active ignorance";[87] and "it is unthinkable that wisdom should
ever be popular."[88]

He laughed at the oscillation of power between parties. "In politics, as
on a sickbed, men toss from side to side in the hope of lying more com-
fortably."[89] He opposed freedom of the press on the ground that it subjected
society and government to perpetual disturbance by immature and irresponsible writers. The cry for freedom seemed to him, in his declining years, to
be merely the hunger of the unplaced for power and plums. "The sole object is for power, influence, and fortune to pass from one hand to the next.
Freedom is the whispered password of secret conspirators, the clamorous
battle cry of the avowed revolutionary, indeed the slogan of despotism itself
as it leads its subjugated masses forward against the foe, promising surcease
from external oppression for all time."[90]

Goethe fulfilled to the maximum the obligation of the old to serve as a
brake upon the energy of the young.

VI. *FAUST*: PART II

He poured his aging philosophy into Part II of *Faust*. At the end of Part I
he had left his alter ego, broken and desolate, in the power of Mephistopheles—desire punished for its excess. But could that be all, and the sum of
wisdom? Faust had not quite lost his wager; the Devil had not yet found for
him any delight that could calm his striving and fill his life. Was there anywhere such a fulfillment? Through twenty-four years Goethe struggled to
find for the story a continuation and a culmination that should contain or
symbolize the conclusions of his thought, and should give to his hero a
noble and inspiring end.

At last, aged seventy-eight, he faced the task. On May 24, 1827, he wrote
to Zelter, who had grown old with him and was to die with him: "I want
quietly to confess to you that . . . I have gone to work at *Faust* again. . . .
Tell no one." The dramatic finale of Byron in the Greek War of Liberation
had stirred Goethe; now he could make Byron, as Euphorion [Well-Being],
son of Faust and Helen, represent the healing of the torn and questioning
modern mind through union with the calm beauty of classic Greece. He
labored in the morning hours, achieving at best a page a day, until, in August of 1831, seven months before his death, he announced to Eckermann
that the consuming task was complete—fifty-nine years after its first conception. "The happiest man," he had written, "is he who is able to integrate the
end of his life with its beginning."[91] And now he said: "Whatever of life
remains to me I can regard henceforth as a gift; and it does not really matter
whether I accomplish anything more or not."[92]

Only in the assurance of eighty years can one take time to read all of

Faust, Part II, today. From the opening scene, in which Faust, awaking in spring fields, describes the sunrise with no word-worn eloquence, the action repeatedly stops for lyric paeans to nature's beauty or grandeur or terror; it is well done, but too often; Goethe, preaching classic restraint, here sins against "nothing too much." He poured into the drama almost everything that cluttered his teeming memory: Greek and German mythologies, Leda and the swan, Helen and her train, witches and knights and fairies and gnomes, griffins and pygmies, dryads and sirens, dissertations on "Neptunian" geology, long speeches by heralds, flower girls, garden nymphs, woodcutters, punchinellos, drunkards, pages, seneschals, wardens, a charioteer and a sphinx, an astrologer and an emperor, fauns and philosophers, the cranes of Ibycus, and a "little man" (homunculus) chemically created by Faust's pupil Wagner. The farrago is more confusing than a tropical jungle, for it adds the supernatural to the natural, and endows everything with oratory or song.

What a comfort it is when, in Act III, Helen appears, still miraculously *dia gynaikon*—goddess among women—conquering men with the grace of her movement or the glance of her eyes. The story takes on new force, and the chorus rises to a Sophoclean tone, when Helen hears that Menelaus, as punishment for "beauty insolently bold," has ordered her and her attendant women to be surrendered to the lusts of a "barbarian" horde invading Hellas from the north. Their leader is Faust himself, transformed by Mephistophelean art into a medieval knight, handsome in figure, face, and garb. Goethe reaches the apex of his dramatic art as he describes the meeting of Helen and Faust—classic Greece confronting medieval Germany. Let these two unite!—this is the burden of the tale. Faust, enthralled like all men, lays at Helen's feet all the wealth and power that magic and war have given him. She yields herself to his entreaties; after all, this was hardly a fate worse than death. But Menelaus approaches with his army and interrupts their bliss; Faust turns in a trice from love to war, calls his men to arms, and leads them to the conquest of Sparta (a memory of the "Franks" conquering the Morea in the thirteenth century).

The scene changes; years have flown by; Euphorion is a happy youth, gladdening Faust and Helen with "caresses, playful banter, sportive calls,"[93] leaping recklessly from cliff to cliff, gently cautioned by his parents, dancing wildly with nymphs entranced by his charm (Byron in Italy?); he seizes one of them rapturously, only to have her burst into flame in his arms. Hearing with welcome the tocsin of war, he rushes off, falls from a precipice, and, dying, summons his mother to join him in the nether world.

> HELEN [*to Faust*].   Woe is me! An ancient adage proves on me its truth—
> That fortune weds with Beauty never abidingly.
> Asunder rent the bond of life is, as of love,
> And, both bewailing, anguished, I say farewell,
> Upon thy bosom casting me yet once again.
> Receive, Persephone, the child and me.
> (*She embraces Faust; her corporeal part vanishes; robes and veil remain in his arms.*)

So ends the third and finest act of this second *Faust*. This was the part that Goethe wrote first, which he called *Helena,* and which for a time he thought of as a separate and finished whole; he might have done well to leave it so. Here, by some heroic draft upon his surviving powers, Goethe rose for the last time to the peak of his poetry, mingling drama with music as in Periclean days, and raising to life and blood the figures of a complex allegory for the healing of the modern mind.

From that height *Faust II* slips down to a war between an emperor and a contender for the Holy Roman throne. Faust and Mephistopheles, using their magic arts, win the war for the emperor; Faust asks and receives, as reward, great stretches of the Empire's northern coast, with such land as he can wrest from the sea. In Act V Faust, a hundred years old, is master of a vast domain, but not yet of himself. The cottage of a peasant couple, Philemon and Baucis, obstructs the view from his mansion; he offers them a better home elsewhere; they refuse; he asks Mephistopheles and his agents to drive them out; meeting resistance, they set fire to the cottage; the old couple die of fright. Faust is soon haunted by visions of avenging Furies—gray hags named Want, Guilt, Care, Need, and Death. Care breathes into his face and blinds him. A partly unselfish thought raises him out of despair: he orders Mephistopheles and his devils to dike the sea, drain the swamps, and build, on the new land, a thousand homes amid green fields; he visions this reclaimed terrain, and feels that if he could "with a free people stand on a free soil," he would at last say to such a moment, "Tarry a while, thou art so fair."[94] He hears the sounds of picks and spades, and thinks that his grand design is progressing; actually the devils are digging his grave. Exhausted, he falls dying to the ground; Mephistopheles gloats over him as a horde of devils prepares to take Faust's soul to hell; but a host of angels swoops down from heaven, and while Mephistopheles is distracted with admiration of their legs they "bear aloft the mortal remains of Faust." In heaven Faust, new-clothed in a transfigured body, is greeted by a glorified Gretchen, who begs the Virgin Mother: "Grant me to teach him!" The Virgin bids her lead him upward, and a Chorus Mysticus ends the play:

Alles Vergängliche	Everything transitory
Ist nur ein Gleichnis;	Is only a symbol;
Das Unzulängliche	The ever unfinished
Hier wirds Ereignis;	Here is completed;
Das Unbeschreibliche	The indescribable
Hier ist es getan;	Is here accomplished;
Das Ewig-Weibliche	The eternal womanly
Zieht uns hinan.	Draws us upward and on.

VII. FULFILLMENT: 1825–32

In 1823 Johann Peter Eckermann, aged thirty-one, became Goethe's secretary, and began to note the old man's conversation for posterity. The resultant *Gespräche mit Goethe* (three volumes, 1836–48)—partly revised by Goethe—contains more wisdom than is to be found in most philosophers.

In September, 1825, Weimar celebrated the semicentennial of Karl August's accession. Goethe attended the ceremony. The Duke grasped his hand, and murmured to him, "Together to the last breath."[95] On November 7 the court celebrated the fiftieth anniversary of Goethe's coming to Weimar, and the Duke sent him a letter which was also made a public proclamation:

> With profound pleasure I would mark the fiftieth return of this day as the jubilee not only of the premier servant of my state but of the friend of my youth, who has accompanied me through all the mutability of life with unchanged affection, loyalty, and steadfastness. I owe the happy outcome of my most important undertakings to his circumspect counsel, his ever-living sympathy and beneficent service. To have attached him permanently to myself I regard as one of the highest ornaments of my reign.[96]

Now came those sadly aging years when friend after friend disappears. On August 26, 1826, two days before Goethe's seventy-seventh birthday, Charlotte von Stein, eighty-four years old, sent her last known letter to her lover of half a century before: "All my best wishes and blessings on this day. May the guardian angels in the heavenly parliament command that all that is good or beautiful be granted to you, my very dear friend. I continue to remain yours in hope and without fear, while I beg of you for myself your freely given kindness during the brief span that remains to me."[97] She died on January 6, 1827. Hearing of it, Goethe wept. On June 15, 1828, the Duke died, and Weimar knew that its golden age was ending. Goethe prepared for his turn by working feverishly on *Faust*. But he was not next in line. His only surviving child, August, after forty years of failure, twenty of dissipation, died in Rome, October 27, 1830. A post-mortem showed a liver five times the normal size. When the news was brought to Goethe he said, "*Non ignoravi me mortalem genuisse*—I was not unaware that I had begotten a mortal."[98] "I tried to absorb myself in work," he wrote; "I forced myself to continue Volume IV of *Poetry and Truth*."[99]

At eighty he began to narrow his interests. In 1829 he stopped reading newspapers. "I can't begin to tell you," he wrote to Zelter, "the time I have gained, and the things I have accomplished, during the six weeks that I have left all French and German papers unopened."[100] "Fortunate is he whose world lies in his home."[101] He enjoyed love and care from August's widow, Ottilie, and he took delight in her children. Sometimes, however, he withdrew even from them, and sought full privacy, praising solitude as the nurse and test of a well-furnished mind.

His face now showed its eighty years: deep wrinkles across the forehead and around the mouth; silver hair receding; eyes quiet and wondering; but his stature was erect and his health was good. He prided himself on having avoided coffee and tobacco, both of which he condemned as poisons. He was vain of his looks and his books, honestly relished praise, gave it frugally. When, in 1830, a young poet sent him a volume of verse, Goethe acknowledged it caustically: "I have glanced through your little book. Since, however, in an epidemic of cholera, one must protect oneself against weakening influences, I have laid it aside."[102] Mediocrity offended him. He grew more and more irritable as the years threw him back into himself, and he admitted as much: "Everyone who, judging by my work, considered me amiable, found himself greatly deceived when he came in contact with a man of coldness and reserve."[103] Visitors described him as slow to thaw, a bit formal and stiff, perhaps out of embarrassment, or grudging time taken from his tasks. Yet many of his letters show tenderness and consideration.

He was now famous throughout Europe. Carlyle acclaimed him, long before Goethe's death, as one of the great figures in world literature. Byron dedicated *Werner* to him; Berlioz dedicated *The Damnation of Faust* to "Monseigneur Goethe"; kings sent him gifts. But in Germany his reading public was small, the critics were hostile, his rivals belittled him as a pompous councilor affecting to be a poet and a scientist. Lessing condemned *Götz* and *Werther* as romantic trash; Klopstock scorned *Hermann und Dorothea* as commonplace, and *Iphigenie* as a "stiff" imitation of the Greeks. Goethe reacted with repeated expressions of contempt for Germany—for its climate, scenery, history, language, and mind. He complained that he had "to write in German, and thereby . . . squandered life and art on the worst material."[104] He told his friends that "these fools of Germans" had quite deserved their defeat by Napoleon at Jena,[105] and Germany had the laugh on him when the allies overcame Bonaparte at Waterloo.

Detached from the main (Romantic) stream of literature in his old age, he consoled himself with deepened contempt of the world and man. "Viewed from the heights of reason, all life looks like some malignant disease, and the world like a madhouse."[106] "A few days ago," he wrote to Zelter on March 26, 1816, "I came upon a copy of the first edition of *Werther*, and that long-silenced song began to rise again. It was hard for me to understand how a man could endure the world for forty years when he had seen its absurdity even in his youth."[107] And he looked for no substantial betterment in the future. "Men exist only to trouble and kill one another; so was it, so is it, so will it ever be."[108] Like most of us after sixty, he thought that the new generation was degenerate. "The incredible arrogance in which the young are growing up will show its results in a few years in the greatest follies. . . . Yet much is stirring that in after years may be cause for rejoicing."[109]

On March 15, 1832, he caught a cold while out driving. On the eighteenth he seemed recovered, but on the twentieth the infection had sunk into his chest, catarrhal fever consumed him, and his face was distorted with pain. On the twenty-second he noted that spring had begun; "perhaps this will help me to get well." The room had been darkened to ease his eyes; he protested, "Let in more light." Still oppressed by the gloom, he ordered his valet, "Open the blind of the other window, so that more light may come in." These were apparently his last words. He had asked Ottilie, "Little woman, give me your little paw." He died in her arms and holding her hand, at noon, March 22, 1832, aged eighty-two years and seven months.[110]

Eckermann saw the corpse on the next day.

The body lay naked, wrapped only in a white sheet. . . . The valet drew aside the sheet, and I was astonished at the godlike magnificence of the limbs. The breast was powerful, broad, and arched; the arms and thighs were full, and softly muscular; the feet were elegant, and of the most perfect shape; nowhere on the whole body was there a trace either of fat or of leanness or decay. A perfect man lay in great beauty before me; and the rapture which the sight caused me made me forget for a moment that the immortal spirit had left this abode.[111]

So ended a great age, from Frederick's somber triumph in 1763 through Lessing and Kant, Wieland and Herder, to Schiller and Goethe. Not since Luther had the German mind been so active, so various, so rich in independent thought. It was no disaster for Germany that it was not an expanding empire like Britain's, absorbed in conquest and trade; nor a centralized monarchy like the French, falling apart through the failure of government; nor a despotism like Russia's, gorging itself with land or stupefying itself with holy water. Politically, Germany was not yet born, but in literature she was challenging, and in philosophy she was leading, the Western world.

CHAPTER XXV

The Jews

1715-89

I. THE STRUGGLE FOR EXISTENCE

"The Jews," said Rousseau,

> afford an astonishing spectacle. The laws of Solon, Numa, and Lycurgus are dead; those of Moses, much more ancient, continue to live. Athens, Sparta, and Rome have perished and left no offspring on the earth. But Zion, destroyed, has not lost her children; they are preserved, they multiply, they spread throughout the world. . . . They mingle with all peoples, yet are not confused with them; they have no rulers, yet they are always a people. . . . What must have been the force of a legislator capable of effecting such marvels! Of all the systems of legislation now known to us, only this one has undergone all tests, has always been steadfast.[1]

Perhaps the Mosaic Code owed its survival not so much to its inherent wisdom as to its service in maintaining order and stability in communities living dangerously amid hostile creeds and alien laws. In the Dispersion the synagogue had to be both church and government, and the rabbis held their people together through all vicissitudes by giving the sanction of a proud religious faith to a code that regulated every phase of Jewish life. The Pentateuch became the constitution—the Talmud became the supreme court—of an invisible state stronger even than human hate.

Anti-Semitism lost some of its religious bases as orthodoxy declined. An enlightened minority saw the absurdity and cruelty of punishing an entire people, generation after generation, for the ancient sin of a handful of individuals collected on his way from Temple to court by an old priest who resented the admiration given to Christ by the great majority of those who knew of him. Careful readers of the Gospels remembered that Jesus had always remained loyal to Judaism even while critical of its pious hypocrites. Those who had learned some history were aware that almost every people in Christendom had at one time or another persecuted heretics, not by one crucifixion but by wholesale massacre, inquisitions, or pogroms.

Voltaire knew all this.[2] He repeatedly denounced the Christian persecution of the Jews. His epic *Henriade* spoke of

> Madrid's and Lisbon's horrid fires,
> The yearly portion of unhappy Jews
> By priestly judges doomed to temporal flames
> For thinking their forefathers' faith the best.

He praised the Jews' "sober and regular way of life, their abstinence, their toil." He recognized that European Jews had taken to trade because, prohibited from owning land, they had been "unable to establish themselves permanently"—securely—"in any country."[3] Yet Voltaire became violently anti-Semitic. He had unfortunate dealings with Jewish financiers. When he went to England he carried letters of exchange on the London banker Medina, who meanwhile went bankrupt owing Voltaire twenty thousand francs.[4] In Berlin, as we have seen, he employed Abraham Hirsch to buy depreciated bonds in Saxony, planning to import them (illegally, as Hirsch warned him) into Prussia and there have them redeemed at a sixty-five-percent profit.[5] Philosopher and financier quarreled, went to court, and ended with mutual hate. In his *Essai sur les moeurs* Voltaire let himself go; he described the ancient Hebrews as "a petty nation, a brigand people, atrocious, abominable, whose law is the law of savages, and whose history is a tissue of crimes against humanity."[6] A Catholic priest protested that this was a ridiculously savage indictment.[7] Isaac Pinto, a learned Portuguese Jew, published in 1762 *Reflections* criticizing the anti-Semitic passages in the article "The Jews" in the *Dictionnaire philosophique*; Voltaire admitted that he had been "wrong to attribute to a whole nation the vices of some individuals," and promised to alter the offending passages in future printings; but this slipped his mind.[8] French writers in general sided against Voltaire in this matter.[9] Rousseau spoke of the Jews with understanding sympathy.[10]

The Jews in France had no civil rights before the Revolution, but they developed some thriving communities and influential leaders. One of these bought a seigniory that included Amiens; he exercised his feudal right to appoint the canons of the cathedral; the bishop protested; the Parlement of Paris upheld the Jewish seigneur (1787). The French government gratefully acknowledged the help of Jewish financiers in the wars of the Spanish and Polish successions, and Jews played a large part in reviving the Compagnie des Indes after the collapse of Law's venture in 1720.[11] The Jews of Bordeaux were especially prosperous; their merchants and bankers were known for their integrity and their liberality; but they prided themselves on their Sephardic descent, and succeeded in excluding all Ashkenazi Jews from Bordeaux.

There were no professed Jews in eighteenth-century Spain. In the first years of the Spanish Bourbons some small groups presumed on the supposed enlightenment of Philip V to resume secret observance of Judaic worship; many cases were discovered; the Inquisition, between 1700 and 1720, put to death three Jews in Barcelona, five in Cordova, twenty-three in Toledo, five in Madrid. Enraged by these revelations, the Inquisition flared up in renewed activity; in the 868 cases tried by its tribunals between 1721 and 1727 over eight hundred were for Judaism, and of those condemned seventy-five were burned. Thereafter such instances were extremely rare. In the final years of its career, 1780–1820, the Spanish Inquisition tried some five thousand defendants, of whom only sixteen were accused of Judaism, and ten of these were foreigners.[12] The laws of Spain continued to exclude from civic or military office all persons who could not prove their *limpieza*—the purity of their blood from all tincture of Jewish ancestry. Reformers complained that this requirement denied to the Spanish army and government the services of many able men; and in 1783 Charles III relaxed these laws.[13]

In Portugal the Inquisition burned twenty-seven Jews for refusing to apostatize from Judaism (1717).[14] Antônio da Silva, whom Southey rated the best Portuguese dramatist, came to Lisbon in 1712 from Rio de Janeiro; he and his mother were arrested as Jews in 1726; the mother was burned, the son abjured and was released; apparently he relapsed, for he was burned in 1739, aged thirty-five.[15] The Marquês de Pombal, among his many reforms, ended all legal distinctions between Old and New (converted) Christians (1774).[16]

In Italy Venice led the way in liberating the Jews: in 1772 the Jews of the republic were declared free and equal with the rest of the population. Rome lagged; the ghetto there was the worst in Europe. High fertility, encouraged by the rabbis, increased the poverty and squalor; at one time ten thousand Jews lived in the space of one square kilometer.[17] Annually the Tiber overflowed, covering the ghetto's narrow streets and filling the cellars with pestilential mud. Excluded from most trades, the Roman Jews took to tailoring; in 1700 three fourths of their adult males were tailors,[18] setting a custom that endured till our time. In 1775 Pope Pius VI issued an "Editto sopra gli Ebrei," renewing the old disabilities of the Jews and adding new ones: they must not ride in carriages, nor sing dirges at funerals, nor erect tombstones over their dead.[19] The Jews of Rome had to wait for Napoleon to bring them freedom.

In Austria Maria Theresa felt that piety compelled her to confine the Jews to certain narrow districts, and to exclude them from crafts, office, and the ownership of realty.[20] Her son Joseph, touched by the French Enlightenment, proposed to the Council of State in 1781 a project for "rendering useful to society the large class of Israelites in our hereditary lands" (Austria, Hungary, and Bohemia). They should be encouraged to learn—and, after three years, be required to use—the national language in all legal, political, or business affairs. The Jews were "not to be troubled in any way in the exercise of their ritual or doctrine." They should be invited to take up agriculture, to enter industry and business, to practice the arts—but they still could not become masters in the guilds, for this required an oath of Christian belief. All humiliating distinctions, and all constraints hitherto imposed upon the Jews, were to be abrogated, "as well as all external marks whatever." The Council of State and the provincial administrators objected to the program as too broad and sudden for public acceptance. Joseph compromised by issuing on January 2, 1782, a "Toleranzpatent" for the Jews of Vienna and Lower Austria: they received the right to send their children to state schools and colleges, and to enjoy economic liberty except as to owning real estate; however, they must not maintain a separate communal organization, they should not build synagogues in the capital, and they were forbidden to reside in certain towns—perhaps because anti-Semitism there was dangerously keen. Joseph counseled his Christian subjects to respect the persons and rights of Jews as their fellow men; any insult or violence offered to a Jew "will be sternly punished," and there must be no compulsory conversions. Soon the Emperor issued similar edicts for Bohemia, Moravia, and Austrian Silesia. He appreciated Jewish contributions to his treasury; he raised several Jews to the nobility, and employed several as state financiers.[21]

But his reforms, reported the French envoy at Vienna, "arouse a universal cry of disapproval; . . . the great facilities accorded to the Jews are considered as assuring ruin to the state."[22] Christian merchants deplored the new competition, and priests condemned the edicts as tolerating open heresy. Some rabbis objected to Jewish children attending state schools, fearing that these would lure Jewish youth from Judaism. Joseph persisted, and a year before his death he extended the Patent of Toleration to Galicia; there one town, Brody, had so many Jews (eighteen thousand) that the Emperor called it the modern Jerusalem. By the time Joseph died (1790) Vienna had accustomed itself to the new dispensation, and the ground was prepared for the brilliant Judaeo-Christian culture of Vienna in the nineteenth century.

By and large the Jews fared better in Islam than in Christendom. With presumably some exaggeration Lady Mary Wortley Montagu described their condition in the Turkey of 1717:

> The Jews . . . are in incredible power in this country. They have many privileges above all the natural Turks themselves, . . . being judged by their own laws. They have drawn the whole trade of the Empire into their hands, partly by the firm union among themselves, partly by the idle temper and want of industry of the Turk. Every pasha has his Jew, who is his *homme d'affaires*. . . . They are the physicians, the stewards, and the interpreters of all the great men. . . . There are many of them vastly rich.[23]

Quite different was the fate of the few Jews who were found in Russia —chiefly in the "border provinces" confronting Poland—on the death of Peter the Great. In 1742 the Empress Elizabeth Petrovna ordered that "from our whole Empire . . . all Jews shall . . . be immediately deported, . . . and shall henceforth under no pretext be admitted into our Empire . . . unless they . . . accept the Christian religion of the Greek persuasion." By 1753 nearly 35,000 Jews had been expelled.[24] Some Russian businessmen pleaded with the Empress to relax the edict, arguing that the expulsion had depressed the economy of the provinces by deflecting trade from these to Poland and Germany; Elizabeth refused to relax.

When Catherine II acceded she wished to let the Jews re-enter, but felt too insecure on her throne to face the opposition of the clergy. The first partition of Poland, however, brought the problem to a new phase: what was to be done with the 27,000 Jews long established in that part of Poland which Russia had now acquired? Catherine declared (1772) that "the Jewish communities residing in the cities and territories now incorporated into the Russian Empire will be left in the enjoyment of all those liberties which they possess at present."[25] A large measure of self-government was allowed to these Polish Jews, and they were made eligible to municipal office; however, they were forbidden to emigrate from the "Pale of Settlement" (the formerly Polish provinces) into the Russian interior. In 1791 the Jews were permitted to settle in the provinces of Kherson, Taurida, and Ekaterinoslav, as a means of rapidly populating these recently conquered regions and making them easier to defend. Meanwhile the economic anti-Semitism of most Russian businessmen, and the religious anti-Semitism of the Russian commonalty, made life difficult and dangerous for the Jews in the empire.

In 1766 there were 621,000 Jews in Poland.[26] Protective "privileges" granted them by previous rulers were ratified by Augustus II and Augustus III, but these Saxons, busy with two realms and two faiths (not to mention their mistresses), had little time to counter the racial hostility of the Polish populace. The government laid extra taxes upon the Jews, the gentry sought to reduce them to serfdom, and the local administrators made them pay heavily for protection from mob violence. The priests denounced the Jews for "stubbornly clinging to irreligion"; an ecclesiastical synod in 1720 demanded that the government forbid "the building of new synagogues and the repair of old ones"; a synod of 1733 repeated the medieval maxim that the only reason for tolerating the Jews was that they might serve as a "reminder of the tortures of Christ, and be an example, by their enslaved and miserable condition, of the just chastisement inflicted by God upon infidels."[27]

In 1716 a converted Hebrew, Serafinovich, published an *Exposure of the Jewish Ceremonies*, in which he charged the Jews with using the blood of Christians for various magical purposes: to smear the doors of Christians, to mix in the matzoth eaten at Passover, to soak a cloth containing an incantation designed to protect a house or bring business success. . . The Jews challenged Serafinovich to defend his allegations, and assembled a board of rabbis and bishops to hear him; he did not appear, but republished his book.[28] Repeatedly the Jews were accused of killing children to get Christian blood; Polish Jews were summoned to trial on such charges in 1710, 1724, 1736, 1747, 1748, 1753, 1756, 1759, 1760; in many cases they were tortured, in some cases to death; some were flayed alive; some died slowly by impalement.[29] The terrorized Jews appealed to Pope Benedict XIV to stop these accusations; the evidence pro and con was laid before Cardinal Campanelli; after receiving a report from the papal nuncio in Warsaw, he issued a memorandum to the effect that in none of the cases had guilt been proved. The Roman tribunal of the Inquisition supported the Cardinal's memorandum. The nuncio informed the Polish government (1763) that "the Holy See, having investigated all the foundations of this aberration—that the Jews need human blood for the preparation of their unleavened bread," had concluded that "there was no evidence whatever testifying to the correctness of that prejudice."[30] Pope Innocent IV had made a similar pronouncement in 1247. The aberration persisted.

Fear of massacre was a frequent element in the life of the Polish Jew. In 1734, 1750, and 1768 bands of Cossacks and Russian Orthodox peasants, organized as *haidamacks* (rioters), ravaged many towns and villages in the provinces of Kiev, Volhynia, and Podolia, pillaging estates and slaying Jews. In 1768 the raiders carried a "golden charter" falsely ascribed to Catherine II, inviting them "to exterminate the Poles and the Jews, the desecrators of our holy religion"; in one town, Uman, they slaughtered twenty thousand Poles and Jews. Catherine sent a Russian army to co-operate with Polish forces to suppress the raiders.[31]

In Germany the Jews were relatively safe and prosperous, though they suffered various disabilities in economic and political life. Special taxes were levied upon them in most of the principalities.[32] The law allowed only a limited number of Jews to live in Berlin, but the law was loosely enforced, and the Berlin community grew in number and wealth; similar Jewish settlements existed in Hamburg and Frankfurt. Over a thousand Jewish merchants attended the Leipzig fair in 1789.[33] German rulers, even Catholic prince-bishops, employed Jews to manage their finances or provision their armies. Joseph Oppenheimer (1692?–1738), known as "Jew Süss," served in these and other capacities the Elector Palatine at Mannheim and Karl Alexander, duke of Württemberg. His skill and industry enriched him and the Duke, and earned him many enemies. Accused of malfeasance at the mint, he was exonerated by a board of investigators, and was raised to membership in the Duke's Privy Council, where he soon became the dominant power. He invented new taxes, established royal monopolies, and apparently accepted bribes—which he divided with the Duke.[34] When the Duke proposed that all church moneys should be deposited in a central state bank, the Protestant clergy joined with the nobility in opposition to the Duke and his minister. On March 3, 1737, the Duke suddenly died; army and civil leaders arrested Oppenheimer and all Stuttgart Jews. Oppenheimer was tried and convicted; on February 3, 1738, he was strangled, and his corpse was suspended in a cage in a public square.[35]

We have noted Goethe's sallies into the Judengasse in Frankfurt. One of the oldest families there took its later name, Rothschild, from the red shield that distinguished its dwelling. In 1755, on the death of his parents, Meyer Amschel of the Rot Schild became head of the family at the age of eleven. The numerous states of Germany, each with its independent coinage, made money changing a frequent necessity for travelers; Meyer learned in his boyhood the interstate monetary equivalents, and earned a small fee for each exchange. As a side interest he studied numismatics and collected rare coins; he guided another collector, Prince Wilhelm of Hanau, and secured from him the title of "crown agent," which helped him in his Frankfurt business. He married in 1770, and thereafter begot five sons, who later developed branches of the Rothschild firm in Vienna, Naples, Paris, and London. Meyer earned a reputation for judgment, integrity, and reliability. When Wilhelm of Hanau succeeded his father as landgrave of Hesse-Cassel, more court business came to Meyer Amschel, so that by 1790 he had a yearly income of three thousand gulden—six hundred more than that of Goethe's prosperous father.[36] The family wealth grew rapidly during the French Revolutionary Wars; Meyer engaged in provisioning armies, and was entrusted with the concealment, sometimes the investment, of princely fortunes.

The Jews continued to enjoy a relative freedom in the Netherlands and Scandinavia. The Amsterdam congregation flourished. In Denmark ghettos were unknown; the Jews moved about freely, and mixed marriages were allowed. Altona, a commercial city across the Elbe from Hamburg but then belonging to Denmark, had one of the most prosperous Jewish communities in Europe. In Sweden Gustavus III protected the Jews in the peaceful practice of their religion.

Many Jews, fleeing from persecution in Poland or Bohemia, found refuge in England. Their number there rose from 6,000 in 1734 to 26,000 in 1800, of whom London had 20,000. Their poverty was extreme, but they took care of their own poor, and maintained their own hospitals.[37] Jew-baiting was a popular sport; it declined when the Jews took up boxing and one of their number became the national pugilistic champion.[38] The requirement of a Christian oath excluded Jews from civil or military office. Sampson Gideon, having accepted conversion, became one of the governors of the Bank of England. In 1745, when the Young Pretender was advancing upon London with a Scottish army pledged to depose George II and restore the Stuarts, and the public, losing confidence in the security of the government, fell into panic and threatened a run on the bank, Gideon led the Jewish merchants and magnates to the rescue; they poured their private funds into the bank, and bound themselves to accept the notes of the bank at face value in their commercial transactions; the bank met its obligations, confidence was restored, the Pretender was repulsed.[39]

The Whig ministry expressed its appreciation by introducing into Parliament (1753) a bill offering naturalization and citizenship to all foreign-born Jews who had resided in England or Ireland for three years. (Jews born there were naturalized by birth.[40]) The lords and the bishops approved the bill; the Commons passed it ninety-six to fifty-five. But the British public, which knew, or understood, little of the role which the Jews had played in saving the bank, rose overwhelmingly against the measure. Protests came to Parliament from almost every town in Britain; pulpits and taverns united in their condemnation; merchants complained that Jewish commercial competition would become intolerable; the bishops who had voted for the bill were insulted in the streets; old legends of ritual murder of Christians by Jews were revived; hundreds of hostile pamphlets, ballads, caricatures, and lampoons were circulated; women decorated their dresses and bosoms with crosses, and wore ribands bearing the motto "No Jews, Christianity Forever."[41] The Whig leaders, fearing defeat in the coming election, secured repeal of the law (1754).

II. THE MYSTIC SOLACE

From their earthly sufferings many Jews, especially in Poland, retreated into supernatural consolations. Some ruined their eyes studying the Talmud; some lost their wits in the Cabala; some "Sabbataians," despite the apostasy and death of the false Messiah, Sabbatai Zevi, still believed in his divinity, and abandoned Talmudic Judaism for heretical hopes and rites. Jankiew Leibowicz, who came to be known by the name the Turks gave him, Jacob Frank, persuaded hundreds of Polish Jews to accept him as a reincarnation of Zevi; he taught them a doctrine akin to the amiable Christian heresy that conceived the Trinity as composed of God the Father, Mary the Mother, and the Messiah their Son; finally he led his followers into the Catholic Church (1759).

The lowly state of Polish Judaism was in some measure redeemed by the Hasidic movement. The founder of this "doctrine of piety" was Israel ben Eliezer, known as Baal Shem-Tob ("Master of the Good Name"), and, for short, from his initials, Besht. He wandered from place to place as a teacher of children; he lived in cheerful poverty, prayed rapturously, and made "miraculous" cures with mountain herbs. He asked his followers to pay less attention to synagogue rites and Talmudic lore, to approach God directly in humble but intimate communion, to see and love God in all forms and manifestations of nature, in rocks and trees as well as in good fortune and pain; he bade them enjoy life in the present instead of mourning the sins and miseries of the past. Sometimes his simple sayings resembled those of Christ. "A father complained to the Besht that his son had forsaken God, and asked, Rabbi, what shall I do? The Besht answered, 'Love him more than ever.' "[42]

In some ways the Hasidic movement in Poland corresponded to the Moravian Brethren, the German Pietists, and the English Methodists; it agreed with these in bringing religion out of the temple and into the heart; but it rejected asceticism and gloom, and bade its adherents dance, enjoy the embraces of their spouses, and even, now and then, drink to the brim of ecstasy.

When Baal Shem-Tob died (1760) his flock was shepherded, and sometimes fleeced,[43] by a succession of Zaddikim ("Righteous Men"). Orthodox Talmudists, led by the scholarly but fanatical Elijah ben Solomon of Wilna, fought the Hasidim with exhortations and excommunications, but their number increased as Poland died (1772–92), and by the end of the century they claimed 100,000 souls.[44]

A life so harassed on earth, and souls so fixed in heaven, could not contribute much to secular literature, science, or philosophy. Almost everywhere the Jews were excluded from the universities by the oath of Christian faith required of all students. Their Mosaic Code barred them from the practice of pictorial art, and dulled their appreciation. Writing in a Hebrew understood only by a small minority, or in a Yiddish which had not yet become a literary language, they had little stimulus to produce any literature beyond religious commentaries or popular trivialities. One memorable contribution they made to practical arts in this fallow age: Jacob Rodrigue Péreire of Bordeaux invented a sign language for the deaf and dumb, earning the praise of Diderot, d'Alembert, Rousseau, and Buffon. And one Jewish poet illuminated the gloom.

Moses Chayim Luzzatto was born in Italy (1707), of parents rich enough to give him a good education. He derived from the Latin poets, and from

Italian poets like Guarini, such skill in poetic meters that he was able to give to his Hebrew verse a fluent ryhthm and delicate charm hardly known in that language since Jehuda Halevy. In his seventeenth year he composed a drama on Samson and the Philistines. Then he took to studying the Zohar, Bible of the Cabala; his imagination was caught by its mystic fancies; he turned some of them into poetry, and they turned his head with the notion that he was divinely inspired. He wrote a second Zohar, and announced that he was the Messiah promised to the Jews. The rabbis of Venice excommunicated him (1734); he fled to Frankfurt-am-Main, where the rabbis made him promise to renounce his messianic illusions; he moved to Amsterdam, where the Jewish community welcomed him; he supported himself, like Spinoza, by polishing lenses; and he resumed his cabalistic studies. In 1743 he composed a Hebrew drama, *La-Yesharim Tehilla* (*Glory to the Virtuous*), which, despite the abstractions used as *dramatis personae*, earned lauds from those competent to judge. Popular Ignorance, maintained by Craft and Deceit, generates Folly, which repeatedly frustrates Wisdom, and deprives Merit of its crown, until Reason and Patience at last overcome Deceit by revealing Truth; however, by Truth Luzzatto meant the Cabala. In 1744 he went to Palestine, hoping to be acclaimed as the Messiah, but he died at Acre of plague (1747), aged thirty-nine. He was the last eloquent voice of Judaic medievalism, just as

III. MOSES MENDELSSOHN

was the first major voice of a Judaism emerging from protective isolation into contact with modern thought.

Friend and opponent of Kant, friend and inspirer of Lessing, the grandfather of Felix Mendelssohn was one of the noblest figures of the eighteenth century. His father, Menahem Mendel, was a clerk and teacher in a Jewish school at Dessau. Born there on September 6, 1729, the "third Moses" grew up with such a passion for study that he suffered a lasting curvature of the spine. At fourteen he was sent to Berlin for further study of the Talmud; there he followed almost literally the Talmudic command "Eat bread with salt, drink water by measure, sleep on the hard earth, live a life of privations, and busy thyself with the Law."[45] For seven years he contented himself with a garret room, marked his weekly loaf of bread with lines for his daily allowance,[46] and earned a pittance by copying documents in his elegant hand. In Berlin he pored over the works of Maimonides, found courage in the career of that "second Moses," and learned from him and life to control his pride to modesty and cool his hot temper to gentleness and courtesy. His Berlin associates taught him Latin, mathematics, and logic; he read Locke in a Latin translation, passed on to Leibniz and Wolff, and was soon enamored of philosophy. He learned to write German with a smooth clarity rare in the literature of his country in his time.

His poverty ended when, aged twenty-one, he became tutor in the family of Isaac Bernhard, who owned a silk plant in Berlin. Four years later he was made bookkeeper, then a traveling agent of the firm, finally a partner. He kept this business relation actively to the end of his life, for he was resolved not to be dependent upon the popularity and monetary returns of his books. Probably in 1754 he met Lessing, apparently in a game of chess; so began a friendship that endured, despite philosophical differences, till Lessing's death. On October 16, 1754, Lessing wrote to another friend: "Mendelssohn is a man of five-and-twenty, who, without any [university] education, has acquired great attainments in languages, mathematics, philosophy, and poetry. I foresee in him an honor to our nation if he is allowed to come to maturity by his co-religionists. . . . His candor and his philosophical spirit cause me to regard him, in anticipation, as a second Spinoza."[47] For his part Mendelssohn said that a friendly word or look from Lessing banished from his mind all grief or gloom.[48]

In 1755 Lessing arranged the publication of Mendelssohn's *Philosophische Gespräche*, which expounded and defended both Spinoza and Leibniz. In the same year the two friends collaborated in an essay, *Pope ein Metaphysiker!*, in which they argued that the English poet had had no philosophy of his own, but had merely versified Liebniz. Also in 1755 Mendelssohn published *Briefe über die Empfindungen* (*Letters on the Feelings*); this anticipated Kant's view that the sense of beauty is quite independent of desire. These publications won the young Jew full welcome into the not quite "serene brotherhood of philosophes" in Berlin. Through Lessing he met Friedrich Nikolai; he and Nikolai studied Greek together, and soon he was reading Plato in the original. He helped Nikolai to establish the *Bibliothek der Schönen Wissenschaften und der Freien Künste* (*Library of Belles-Lettres and Fine Arts*), and contributed to this and other periodicals articles that strongly influenced current ideas in the criticism of literature and art.

Mendelssohn now felt sufficiently secure to set up a home of his own. In 1762, thirty-three years old, he married Fromet Gugenheim, twenty-five. Both had reached the age of reason, and the union brought them much happiness. On their honeymoon he began work in competition for a prize offered by the Berlin Academy for the best essay on "Whether the Metaphysical Sciences Are Susceptible of Such Evidence as the Mathematical." Among other contestants was Immanuel Kant. Mendelssohn's contribution won (1763), bringing him fifty ducats and international renown.

One of the contestants was Thomas Abt, a professor in Frankfurt-am-Oder. In a long correspondence with Mendelssohn he expressed doubts as to the immortality of the soul, and mourned that the loss of that belief might undermine the moral code and deprive misfortune of its last consolation. Partly as a result of this exchange, Mendelssohn composed his most famous work: *Phaidon, oder Über die Unsterblichkeit der Seele*. Like its Platonic exemplar, it was cast in dialogue form and popular style. The soul of man (ran the argument) is clearly different from matter; we may therefore believe that it does not share the body's fate; and if we believe in God we can hardly suppose that he would deceive us by implanting in our minds a hope

without basis in truth. Moreover [as Kant was to hold] the soul has a natural drive toward self-perfection; this cannot be attained in our lifetime;
God must surely allow the soul to survive the death of the body. "Without
God, Providence, and immortality," Mendelssohn felt, "all the goods of life
would lose their worth in my eyes, and our earthly life would be . . . like
wandering in wind and weather without the consoling prospect of finding
cover and protection at night."[49] The demonstrations were fragile, but the
style of the work delighted many readers; the charm of Plato's dialogues
seemed to have been recaptured; indeed, "the German Plato" became another name for Mendelssohn. The little book ran through fifteen editions,
and was translated into nearly all European languages as well as Hebrew; it
was, in its time, the most widely read nonfiction book in Germany. Herder
and Goethe joined in its praise. Lavater visited the author, examined his head
and face, and announced that every bump and line revealed the soul of Socrates.[50]

Christians of diverse sects applauded the eloquent Jew, and two Benedictine friars asked for his spiritual counsel. But in 1769 Lavater, who was as
ardent a theologian as he was a phrenologist, caused a flurry by making a
public appeal to Mendelssohn to become a Christian. Mendelssohn replied in
Schreiben an den Herrn Diaconus Lavater (1770). He admitted defects in
Judaism and Jewish life, but pointed out that such abuses develop in every
religion in the course of its history; he asked Lavater to consider the hardships suffered by the Jews in Christendom, and added: "He who knows the
state in which we now are, and has a humane heart, will understand more
than I can express"; and he concluded: "Of the essentials of my faith I am
so firmly . . . assured that I call God to witness that I will adhere to my
fundamental creed as long as my soul does not assume another nature."[51]
Lavater was moved, and humbly apologized for having issued his appeal.[52]
But a swarm of pamphleteers denounced Mendelssohn as an infidel, and some
orthodox Jews condemned him for admitting that abuses had crept into Jewish religious usages.[53] For a time the controversy generated more discussion
than national politics or the decline of Frederick's health.

Mendelssohn's own health suffered from the turmoil; for several months
in 1771 he had to refrain from all mental activity. On recovering his strength
he devoted more of his time than before to the relief of his co-religionists.
When some cantons in Switzerland were preparing further restrictions
against the Jews he asked Lavater to interfere; Lavater did, with good effect. When the Dresden authorities planned to expel several hundred Jews
Mendelssohn used his friendship with a local official to secure an accom-
modation.[54] He began in 1778 to publish his German translation of the
Pentateuch; issued in 1783, this aroused another storm. To write some of
the commentaries on the text Mendelssohn had engaged Herz Homberg,
who was associated with Berlin Jews quite estranged from the synagogue.
Several rabbis banned the translation, but it found its way into the Jewish
communities; young Jews learned German from it, and the next generation
of Jews moved into active participation in German intellectual life. Mean-

while (1779) Lessing published his drama *Nathan der Weise*, which hundreds of readers interpreted as an exaltation of his Jewish friend.

Now at the height of his fame and influence Mendelssohn persuaded Marcus Herz to translate into German that *Vindication of the Jews* which Manasseh ben Israel had addressed to the English people in 1656. To the translation he added a preface on "The Salvation of the Jews" (1782), in which he pleaded with the rabbis to abandon their right of excommunication. He followed this in 1783 with an eloquent work called *Jerusalem, oder Über religiöse Macht und Judenthum* (*On Religious Authority and Judaism*), in which he reaffirmed his Judaic faith, called upon the Jews to come out of the ghetto and take their part in Western culture, urged the separation of church and state, condemned any compulsion of belief, and proposed that states be judged by the degree in which they relied on persuasion rather than force. Kant, now too at his zenith, wrote to the author a letter that deserves a place in the annals of friendship:

> I consider this book the herald of a great reform, which will affect not alone your people but also others. You have succeeded in combining your religion with such a degree of freedom of conscience as was never imagined possible. . . . You have, at the same time, so clearly and thoroughly demonstrated the necessity of unlimited freedom of conscience in every religion, that ultimately our [Lutheran] Church will also be led to consider how to remove from its midst everything that disturbs or oppresses conscience.[55]

The book was attacked by orthodox leaders Christian or Jewish, but it contributed immensely to the liberation and Westernization of the Jews.

In 1783 Mendelssohn was only fifty-four, but he had always been frail in physique and health, and he felt that he had not much longer to live. In his final years he delivered to his children and some friends lectures defining his religious creed; these were published in 1785 as *Morgenstunden, oder Vorlesungen über das Dasein Gottes* (*Morning Hours, or Lectures on the Existence of God*). In his last year he was shocked to learn, from a book by Jacobi, that his dear friend Lessing, now dead, had long adhered to Spinoza's pantheism. He could not believe it. He wrote a passionate defense of Lessing—*An die Freunde Lessings*. While taking the manuscript to the publishers he caught a cold; and in the course of that sickness he died of an apoplectic stroke, January 4, 1786. Christians joined with Jews in erecting a statue to him in Dessau, the city of his birth.

He was one of the most influential figures of his generation. Inspired by his writings and his successful crossing of religious frontiers, young Jews came out of the ghetto, and soon made their mark in literature, science, and philosophy. Marcus Herz went to the University of Königsberg as a medical student; he took several of Kant's courses, and became the great epistemolog's assistant and friend; it was he who, reading the *Critique of Pure Reason* in manuscript, stopped halfway for fear that if he continued he would go insane. Back in Berlin, he developed a large practice as a physician, and gave lectures in physics and philosophy to audiences of Christians and Jews. His wife, Henrietta, beautiful and accomplished, opened a salon which, at the turn of the century, was a leading rendezvous of intellectual Berlin; there came Wilhelm von Humboldt, Schleiermacher, Friedrich Schlegel, Mirabeau *fils* . . . The resultant mixture of ideas might not have pleased Mendelssohn. Several of his children became converts to Christianity. Two of his daughters joined Henrietta Herz and others in a "Tugenbund," or Band of Virtue, which honored "elective affinities" above marital fidelity. Henrietta carried on a liaison with Schleiermacher; Dorothea Mendelssohn left her husband to be the mistress and then loyal wife of Friedrich Schlegel, and ended as a Roman Catholic; Henrietta Mendelssohn also accepted the Roman creed; and Abraham Mendelssohn caused his children, including Felix, to be baptized as Lutherans; the orthodox rabbis claimed that their fears had been justified. These were incidental results of the new freedom; the more lasting aspects of Mendelssohn's influence appeared in the intellectual, social, and political liberation of the Jews.

IV. TOWARD FREEDOM

Intellectually, the liberation took at this time the form of the Haskalah—a word which meant wisdom, but which came in this context to signify the Jewish Enlightenment, the revolt of a rising number of Jews against rabbinical and Talmudic domination, and their resolve to enter actively into the stream of modern thought. These rebels learned German, and some of them, especially in the families of merchants or financiers, learned French; they read German freethinkers like Lessing, Kant, Wieland, Herder, Schiller, and Goethe, and many of them delved into Voltaire, Rousseau, Diderot, Helvétius, and d'Holbach. A division arose between liberal Jews, eager for modernity, and conservative Jews who felt that devotion to the Talmud and the synagogue was the only way to preserve the religious, ethnical, and ethical integrity of the Jewish people.

The Haskalah movement spread from Germany southward into Galicia and Austria, eastward into Bohemia, Poland, and Russia. In Austria it was accelerated by Joseph II's Toleranzpatent, which invited the Jews to enter non-Jewish schools. When conservative rabbis opposed this, Naphtali Wessely, a Jewish poet of Hamburg, pleaded with them, in an eloquent Hebrew manifesto, to sanction the participation of Jews in secular education; he urged the younger generation to replace Yiddish with Hebrew and German, and to study science and philosophy as well as the Bible and the Talmud. His views were rejected by the rabbis of Austria; they were accepted by Jewish leaders in Trieste, Venice, Ferrara, and Prague. From that time to ours the Jews have contributed to science, philosophy, literature, music, and law far beyond their proportion in the population.

Intellectual and economic developments promoted Jewish emancipation. Catholic scholars like Richard Simon made rabbinical learning known to Christian students of the Bible, and the Protestant theologian Jacques Basnage wrote a friendly *History of the Religion of the Jews* (1707). The growth of commerce and finance brought Christians and Jews into contacts that sometimes stimulated, but often reduced, racial hostility. Jewish financiers played helpful and patriotic roles in several governments.

Christian voices now rose to propose an end to religious persecution. In 1781 Christian Wilhelm Dohm, a friend of Mendelssohn, published at his suggestion the epochal tract *Über die bürgerliche Verbesserung der Juden in Deutschland* (*On the Civil Betterment of the Jews in Germany*). The occasion for it was a plea sent to Mendelssohn by Alsatian Jews, asking him to formulate a protest against their disabilities. Dohm undertook the task, and enlarged it into a general appeal for Jewish liberation. He described in impressive detail the handicaps suffered by the Hebrews in Europe, and pointed out what a loss it was to Western civilization that it made so little use of the intellectual gifts of the Jews. "These principles of exclusion, equally opposed to humanity and politics, bear the stamp of the Dark Ages, and are unworthy of the enlightenment of our times."[56] Dohm proposed that the Jews be admitted to full freedom of worship, to educational institutions, to all occupations, and to all civil rights except, for the present, eligibility to office, for which they were not yet prepared.

His treatise aroused comment in many countries. Some opponents charged him with having sold his pen to the Jews, but several Protestant clergymen came to his defense. Johannes von Müller, the Swiss historian, supported him, and asked that the works of Maimonides be translated into German or French. The Toleration Patent of 1782 in Austria and the political emancipation of the Jews in the United States (1783) gave impetus to the liberation movement. The French government responded meagerly by removing (1784) personal taxes that had burdened the Jews. The Marquis de Mirabeau shared with Malesherbes in securing this relief; and his son, the Comte de Mirabeau, helped with his essay *On Mendelssohn and the Political Reform of the Jews* (1787). The Abbé Henri Grégoire advanced the matter with a prize-winning essay, *Sur la régénération physique, morale, et politique des Juifs* (1789).

Final political emancipation came only with the Revolution. The Declaration of the Rights of Man proclaimed by the National Assembly (August 27, 1789) implied it, and on September 27, 1791, the Constituent Assembly voted full civil rights to all the Jews of France. The armies of the Revolution or of Napoleon brought freedom to the Jews of Holland in 1796, of Venice in 1797, of Mainz in 1798, of Rome in 1810, of Frankfurt in 1811. For the Jews the Middle Ages had at last come to an end.

CHAPTER XXVI

From Geneva to Stockholm

I. THE SWISS: 1754–98

THOSE of us who have enjoyed peace amid the scenic paradise of Switzerland, and inspiration in the courage and integrity of its people, find it difficult to realize that beneath the calm character, patient husbandry, and steady industry that Europe admired then, and does now, there lay the natural conflicts of race against race, language against language, creed against creed, canton against canton, class against class. On their modest scale the Swiss had very nearly realized the ideal pictured by the Abbé de Saint Pierre and dreamed of by Rousseau and Kant: a confederation of states independent in their internal affairs but pledged to united action in their relations with the surrounding world. In 1760 the Helvetic Union (Helvetische Gesellschaft) was formed to promote national rather than cantonal dedication, and to unite the scattered movements for political reform.

Voltaire, living close by, estimated the population of Switzerland in 1767 at 720,000.[1] Most of them tilled the soil or trained the vine, terracing the slopes almost to the mountaintops. The textile industry was growing, especially in the province of St. Gallen and the canton of Zurich; other manufacturing centers were taking form in Glarus, Bern, and Basel; and Geneva and Neuchâtel were the great centers of watchmaking. Agents spreading over Europe from London to Constantinople (which had eighty-eight of them) developed for Geneva an export trade that rapidly enriched the city on the Rhone. Banks multiplied, for the Swiss financiers had won an international reputation for fidelity.

As everywhere, the majority of abilities was contained in a minority of men, and led to a concentration of wealth. Generally the cantons were ruled by oligarchies, which behaved like any ruling class. The patricians were generous patrons of literature, science, and art, but they resisted every move to extend the franchise. Gibbon, dwelling in Lausanne, accused the Bernese oligarchy of discouraging industry in their dependent provinces, and of keeping down the standard of living there, on the principle that "poor and obedient subjects are preferable to rich and recalcitrant ones."[2] Societies for the abolition of economic or political privilege were repeatedly organized, but were kept in check by state and church allied.[3] Class war agitated Geneva, on and off, throughout the eighteenth century. Relative peace prevailed there from 1737 to 1762, but the burning of *Émile* by the municipal council (1762) set off an agitation for widening the franchise. Rousseau and Voltaire both aided this movement, and after much controversy the patriciate yielded to the middle classes a minor share in the government.

This left quite voteless three fourths of the population—the *natifs*, persons

born in Geneva but of non-native parents. These were excluded also from
most of the professions, from military office, and from mastership in the
guilds; and they were forbidden to address petitions to the Grand Conseil
and the Petit Conseil that ruled the republic. But they were heavily taxed.
On April 4, 1766, a delegation of *natifs* went to Ferney and asked Voltaire
to help them secure the franchise. He told them:

> My friends, you constitute the most numerous class of an independent, indus-
> trious community, and you are in slavery. You ask only to be able to enjoy
> your natural advantages. It is just that you be accorded so moderate a request.
> I shall serve you with all the influence I have; . . . and if you are forced to
> leave a country which prospers through your labor, I shall be able to serve and
> protect you elsewhere.[4]

Aristocracy and bourgeoisie united to resist the appeal of the *natifs*, and
all that Voltaire could do was to welcome into his industrial colony as many
of the discontented artisans as came to him (1768). In 1782 the *natifs* rose
in a revolt that overthrew the patriciate and established a representative government. But the aristocrats appealed to France, Bern, and Sardinia; these
powers intervened, the rebellion was put down, the oligarchy was restored.
The *natifs* had to wait for the French Revolution to bring them freedom.

The cantons produced in this third of a century some personages of international renown. Johann Heinrich Pestalozzi was one of those rare individuals who take the New Testament as a guide to conduct. He agreed with
Rousseau that civilization had corrupted man, but he felt that reform could
come not through new laws and institutions, but through the remaking of human conduct by education. All through his life he welcomed children, especially the poor and, above all, the homeless; he gave them shelter and schooling, and in their instruction he applied the libertarian principles of Rousseau's
Émile, along with some ideas of his own. He expounded his views in one of
the most widely read books of that generation. The heroine of *Lionhard und
Gertrud* (1781–87) reforms an entire village by trying to deal with people
as Christ would have done, and by educating her children with patient consideration of their natural impulses and aptitudes. Pestalozzi proposed to give
the children as much freedom as the rights of others would permit. Early
education should begin by example, and should teach by objects, the senses,
and experience rather than by words, ideas, or rote. Pestalozzi practiced his
methods in various Swiss schools, chiefly at Yverdon. There Talleyrand,
Mme. de Staël, and others visited him, and thence his theories spread through
Europe. Goethe, however, complained that Pestalozzi's schools were forming insolent, arrogant, and undisciplined individualists.[5]

Angelica Kauffmann, born in the Grisons canton, rivaled Mme. Vigée-
Lebrun as the most renowned woman artist of their time. Even at the age of
twelve, besides being a good musician, she painted so well that bishops and
nobles sat to her for their portraits. At the age of thirteen (1754) she was
taken by her father to Italy, where she continued her studies and was everywhere feted for her accomplishments and her personal charm. Invited to
England in 1766, she made a stir by her portrayal of Garrick. Sir Joshua

Reynolds became very fond of "Miss Angel," painted her portrait, and was painted in turn. She joined in the establishment of the Royal Academy of Arts, which in 1773 appointed her, with others, to decorate St. Paul's. In 1781 she retired to Rome, where (1788) she numbered Goethe among her devoted friends. She died there in 1807; her funeral, arranged by Canova, was one of the events of the age; the entire art community followed her to her tomb.

The outstanding Swiss of the generation after Rousseau was Johann Kaspar Lavater. Born at Zurich in 1741, he became a Protestant pastor, and retained throughout his life the most fervent attachment to orthodox Christianity. We have seen his attempts to convert Goethe and Mendelssohn. But he was not dogmatic; he maintained friendships across religious and national boundaries, and all who knew him respected him; many loved him.[6] He wrote works of mystical piety, expounded the Book of Revelations fancifully, believed in the miraculous powers of prayer and Cagliostro, and gave his wife hypnotic treatments on prescriptions by Mesmer. His most characteristic claim was that character can be judged from the features of the face and the contours of the head. He interested Goethe and Herder in his views, and they contributed articles to his book *Physiognomische Fragmente* (1775–78). He studied the looks, heads, and figures of prominent individuals, and correlated cranial and facial features with specific qualities of mind and character. His analyses and conclusions were widely accepted but are now generally rejected; his general principle, that psychological qualities share (with air, environment, diet, occupation, etc.) in molding the body and the face, retains a substantial measure of truth. Every face is an autobiography.

Lavater was part of a Swiss efflorescence which included Rousseau, the poet and scientist Albrecht von Haller, the poet and painter Salomon Gessner, the historian Johannes von Müller, and Horace de Saussure, who started the sport of mountain climbing by scaling Mont Blanc in 1787 after twenty-seven years of trying. Meanwhile the cantons felt the winds of revolution blowing across the border from France. In 1797 Frédéric César de Laharpe, who had tutored the grandchildren of Catherine the Great, joined with Peter Ochs, a guild merchant of Basel, in calling upon the French Revolutionary government to help them establish a democratic republic in Switzerland. Local revolts in Bern and Vaud (January, 1798) paved the way; a French army crossed the frontier on January 28; most of the Swiss population welcomed it as a liberator from oligarchy; on March 19 the "One and Indivisible Helvetic Republic" was proclaimed, abolishing all privileges of canton, class, or person, and making all Swiss equal before the law. Zurich resisted longest, and in the turmoil that ensued honest old Lavater was shot (1799). He died in 1801 as the slow effect of the wound.

II. THE DUTCH: 1715–95

Everybody liked the Dutch. The Danish dramatist Holberg, who visited the United Provinces ("Holland") and "Belgium" in 1704, enthused especially over their canals, whose boats, he said, "transport me from one place to another" in dulcet peace, and "enable me to spend every night in a town of considerable size, so that of an evening I have been able to go to the opera or the theater directly upon arrival."[7] Twelve years later Lady Mary Wortley Montagu was similarly pleased:

> The whole country [Holland] appears a large garden; the roads all well paved, shaded on each side with rows of trees, and bordered with large canals full of boats passing and repassing. . . . All the streets [in Rotterdam] . . . so neatly kept that . . . I walked almost all over town yesterday, *incognita,* in my slippers, without receiving one spot of dirt; and you may see the Dutch maids washing the pavement . . . with more application than ours do our bedchambers. . . . The merchants' ships come [on the canals] to the very doors of the houses. The shops and warehouses are of a surprising neatness and magnificence, filled with an incredible quantity of fine merchandise.[8]

But these rosy reports described Holland before she had felt the economic effects of her victory over Louis XIV in the War of the Spanish Succession. Then she had bled her men and money close to exhaustion; her public debt was enormous; much of her carrying trade had been lost to her military allies but commercial competitors—and to Germany. The dividends of the Dutch East India Company fell from forty per cent in 1715 to twelve and a half per cent in 1737, those of the Dutch West India Company from five per cent in 1700 to two per cent in 1740.[9] The Seven Years' War brought further damage. The bankers of Amsterdam grew rich on high interest loans to the warring powers, but the peace of 1763 ended this boon, and many Dutch banks failed, leaving every major business harmed. Boswell, in Holland in 1763, reported "many of the principal towns sadly decayed. . . . You meet with multitudes of poor creatures who are starving in idleness."[10] Taxes were raised, leading to the emigration of capital and sturdy human stock; now Dutch and German colonists mingled their blood in South Africa, slowly forming the Boers.

Recovery came through Dutch character, industry, and integrity. A calm, strong, frugal people tilled the land, oiled their windmills, tended their cows, cleaned their dairies, and produced delectable malodorous cheeses; Holland led Europe in scientific farming.[11] Delft recaptured its market for porcelain. The Dutch and Jewish bankers of Amsterdam regained their reputation for reliability and resourcefulness; they lent at low interest and risk, received lucrative contracts to pay and provision troops; governments and business applied to Amsterdam for loans, and rarely went away empty; through nearly all that turbulent century the bourse in Amsterdam was the financial center of the Western world. Said Adam Smith about 1775: "The province of Holland, . . . in proportion to the extent of its territory and the number of its people, is a richer country than England."[12]

What most impressed Voltaire in 1725[13] was the almost peaceful cohabitation of diverse faiths. Here were orthodox Catholics and Jansenist Catholics (had not Jansen himself been Dutch?), Arminian free-will Protestants and Calvinist predestination Protestants, Anabaptists and Socinians, Moravian Brethren and Jews, and a sprinkling of freethinkers basking in the French Enlightenment.[14] Most of the magistrates were Protestant, but they "regularly took money from the Catholics," says a Dutch historian, "for conniving at their religious exercises, and allowing them to hold office."[15] The Catholics were now a third of the three million population. The upper classes, acquainted through commerce with a dozen faiths, were skeptical of them all, and did not allow them to interfere with gambling, drinking, gourmandizing, and some discreet adultery in Gallic style.[16]

French was the language of the cultured. Schools were numerous, and the University of Leiden was famous for its courses in medicine, which remembered the great Boerhaave. Nearly all towns had art societies, libraries, and "chambers of rhetoric" with periodic contests in poetry. Dutch art dealers had a European reputation for their treasures and frauds.[17] The great age of Dutch painting had ended with Hobbema (d. 1709), but Cornelis Troost was at least an echo of its glory. Perhaps the most brilliant product of Dutch art in this age was glass delicately stippled, or engraved with diamond points.[18] Amsterdam was a nest of publishers, some of them gentlemen, some pirates. Creative activity in literature sank to a low level in the first half of the eighteenth century; but toward 1780 a revival of letters nourished a real poet, Willem Bilderdijk.

One of Boswell's friends told him that he would find the Dutch "happy in their own dullness";[19] but Boswell reported from Utrecht: "We have brilliant assemblies twice a week, and private parties almost every evening. . . . There are so many beautiful and amiable ladies in our circle that a quire of paper could not contain their praises."[20] The most fascinating pages in Boswell's Holland jottings are those that describe his hesitant romance with "Zélide," or "Belle de Zuylen"—i.e., Isabella van Tuyll. She belonged to an old and distinguished family; her father, "lord of Zuilen and Westbroek," was one of the governors of Utrecht province. She received more education than she could hold, became proudly heterodox, and flouted conventions, morals, religion, and rank, but she charmed any number of men with her beauty, gaiety, and exciting candor. She shrank from genteel and dutiful marriage. "If I had neither father nor mother I would not get married. . . . I should be well pleased with a husband who would take me as his mistress; I should say to him, 'Do not look upon faithfulness as a duty. You should have none but the rights and jealousies of a lover.' "[21] To which Boswell, the most assiduous fornicator in Europe, replied, "Fie, my Zélide, what fancies are these?" She persisted: "I would prefer being my lover's laundress, and living in a garret, to the arid freedom and good manners of our great families."[22]

Zélide passed through a succession of love affairs that left her single and permanently scarred. Already at twenty-four she was quieting her nerves with opium. At thirty (1771) she married Saint-Hyacinthe de Charrière, a Swiss tutor, and went to live with him near Lausanne. Finding him intellectually inadequate, she fell in love in her forties with a man ten years younger than herself; he used her and left her. She sought catharsis in writing a novel,

Caliste (1785–88), which sent Sainte-Beuve into raptures. At forty-seven, in Paris, she met Benjamin Constant, aged twenty, and seduced him with her mind (1787). "Mme. de Charrière," he wrote, "had so original and lively a manner of looking at life, so deep a contempt for prejudice, so powerful an intellect, and so vigorous and disdainful a superiority over the common run of men, that, . . . bizarre and arrogant like her, I discovered in her conversation a pleasure I had not known before. . . . We became intoxicated with our scorn of the human race."[23] This went on till 1794, when Benjamin found a fresh intoxication with Mme. de Staël. Zélide retired into a bitter seclusion, and died at sixty-five, having created and exhausted the emptiness of life.

She could have found food for pessimism in the political history of the United Provinces in the eighteenth century. After the death of William III (1702) the government was monopolized by an oligarchy of business leaders devoted to taxation, nepotism, and intrigue. "The citizens," complained a Dutch writer in 1737, "are shut out of the administration, . . . and no advice or vote is asked in affairs of state."[24] The military incompetence of this regime was exposed when Holland entered the War of the Austrian Succession (1743): a French army invaded Holland, and met with little resistance; many towns surrendered without argument; Maréchal de Noailles reported, "We have to do with some very obliging people."[25] Not all; most of the citizens cried out for a martial leader to save the country, as William III had done in 1672; his collateral descendant William IV, Prince of Orange, was made stadholder of the seven provinces, captain of the army, admiral of the navy (May 3, 1747); in October these offices were made hereditary in his family; in effect monarchy was restored. But the fourth William was too much of a Christian to be a good general; he was unable to re-establish discipline in the army; defeat followed defeat; and in the Treaty of Aix-la-Chapelle (1748) Holland was lucky to survive territorially intact but again economically desolate. William died of erysipelas at forty (1751); his widow, Princess Anne, served as regent till her death (1759); Prince Ludwig Ernst of Brunswick-Wolfenbüttel ruled sternly but ably till William V came of age (1766).

In the war between England and the American colonies Holland protested British interference with Dutch shipping, and joined Russia in the "Armed Neutrality" of 1780; England declared war, and captured nearly all Dutch shipping. In the Treaty of Paris (1783) the interests of Holland were almost ignored; she surrendered Negapatam (in south India) to England, and allowed the English free navigation through the Moluccas. Holland ceased to play a part among the powers.

These disasters destroyed the popularity of William V. Moreover, the success of the revolt in America stimulated democratic ideas in the Netherlands, and led to the rise of a party of "Patriots" hostile to the ruling family. Through every change of government the moneyed minority had so absorbed the declining wealth of the nation that many men turned to begging, and many women to prostitution, in once flourishing and orderly towns. In 1783 companies of "free shooters" were secretly formed in Amsterdam and

The Hague to prepare revolution. In 1787 the Patriots seized power, but William V was restored by armed intervention from Prussia. The French Revolution revived the ardor of the Patriots; they invited France to come to their aid. In 1794 French troops invaded Holland; the Dutch army was overwhelmed; William V fled to England; and the Dutch revolutionists joined with the French in organizing the Batavian Republic (1795–1806). In 1815 the son of William V restored the house of Orange-Nassau to power as King William I. His descendants reign in the Netherlands today (1967).

III. THE DANES: 1715–97

The first official census of Denmark (1769) reckoned its population at 825,000 souls, with another 727,600 in Norway, which remained till 1814 under the Danish kings. Nearly all the peasants in Norway owned their lands, and were as proud as Vikings. In Denmark half the peasantry were serfs, and the other half were subject to feudal dues. The kings labored to check this feudalism, but they were financially dependent upon the magnates, and serfdom continued till 1787. In this regime little encouragement was given to commerce or industry; no significant middle class developed; and the opening of the Kiel Canal (1783) benefited English and Dutch traders rather than the Danes. In 1792 Denmark was the first European power to abolish the slave trade in its dominions.

As the nobles ruled the state, so the Lutheran Church ruled the pulpit, the press, and, hopefully, the mind. A severe censorship, maintained from 1537 to 1849, outlawed all print or speech not in accord with Lutheran orthodoxy, and many nontheological books, like Goethe's *Werther*, were proscribed as imperiling public morality. The development of literature was further hampered by the use of German at court, Latin at the universities, and French in belles-lettres—of which there was almost none. To have inaugurated Danish literature by writing in the vernacular, and to have brought some rays of the Enlightenment into Denmark, were among the accomplishments of the most brilliant Dane of the eighteenth century.

Norway as well as Denmark can claim Ludvig von Holberg, for he was born in Bergen (December 3, 1684). After studying at the local Latin school, he crossed the water to enter the University of Copenhagen. Soon his funds ran short; he returned to Norway and served as tutor in the family of a country parson. Having saved sixty thalers, he set out to see the world. In 1704 he was in Holland; in 1706–8 he was educating himself in the libraries of Oxford. Back in Copenhagen, he gave lectures which brought him little more than self-instruction; meanwhile he lived by tutoring, and fed on ambition. In 1714 the university appointed him to a professorship, without pay, but a private gift enabled him to wander through Italy and France for two years, mostly on foot. Returning from this grandest of grand tours, he was made professor of metaphysics, which he hated, then of Latin and rhetoric, at last (1730) of history and geography, which he loved.

In his leisure moments he created Danish literature. Till his time there had been, in Danish, hardly anything but ballads, farces, hymns, and works of popular piety. Holberg produced a small library of poems, satires, novels, and treatises in Danish on politics, law, history, science, and philosophy. Only Voltaire rivaled him in versatility. Like Voltaire he used laughter as a scourge of pompous professors worshiping the classics, lawyers hobbling justice with technicalities, clergymen scrambling for money and place, physicians easing patients into eternity. Nearly all these pillars of society were pilloried in his first major work, a mock epic, *Peder Paars* (1719). Some great Danes felt the sting, and urged King Frederick IV to suppress the book as offensive to morals and making fun of priests; the King had the first canto read to him, and judged it "a harmless, amusing work"; but the royal council informed Holberg that it would have been better if the poem had never been written.[26]

So he turned to the stage. In 1720 a French actor, Étienne Capion, opened in Copenhagen the first Danish theater. Finding no Danish plays meriting production, he imported dramas from France and Germany. He saw from *Peder Paars* that Holberg had the materials and talent for comedy; he appealed to him to provide the new theater with vernacular plays; within a year Holberg composed five, within eight years twenty, and all so rich in pictures of local mores that his great successor, Adam Oehlenschläger, said of him: "He knew how to paint the bourgeois life of his Copenhagen so faithfully that if this city were to be swallowed up, and if after two hundred years the comedies of Holberg were rediscovered, one would be able to reconstruct the epoch from them, just as from Pompeii and Herculaneum we know the times of ancient Rome."[27]

Holberg took forms and ideas from Plautus, Terence, Molière, and the Commedia dell' Arte, which he had seen in Italy. Some of his comedies are one-act trivialities that have lost their thrust, like *Sganarel's Journey to the Land of the Philosophers*;[28] some still have force, like *Jeppe of the Hill*, from which we learn that peasants, when they acquire power, are more brutal than their lords. Some are full-length plays, like *Rasmus Montanus*; this is a rollicking satire of scholastic pedantry, theological dogmatism, and popular ignorance, with a sly touch of rural candor, as when Lisbed, hearing that her fiancé is returning from university, tells her father, "Then my dream has come true. . . . I dreamed that I slept with him last night."[29] Despite these lively comedies, the Copenhagen theater closed in 1727 for lack of public support. The final performance was Holberg's *The Funeral of Danish Comedy*.

He had shocked his university confreres by writing for the stage; now he mollified them with historical works presenting to Danish readers the results of West-European scholarship. *A Description of Denmark and Norway* (1729), *A History of Denmark* (1732–35), a *Universal Church History* (1727–47), and *A History of the Jews* were compilations, but they were well done. From these labors Holberg sought relief in his masterpiece—*Nicolai Klimii Iter subterraneum* (1741). He wrote it in Latin prose to reach a European audience; it did, but through translations: Jens Baggesen turned it into Danish, in which it ran through three editions; in German it had ten, in Swedish, Dutch, and English, three, in French and Russian two, in Hungarian one. It was this *Subterranean Journey of Niels Klim* that made Holberg the Swift as well as the Voltaire of Denmark.

The noises from a cave rouse Niels's curiosity; he resolves to investigate; his friends lower him by a rope, which breaks; "with amazing velocity I was hurried down into the abyss."[30] Within the crust of the earth he finds an open space or firmament, containing a sun, its planets, and many stars. Falling toward one of these planets, he becomes its satellite, and revolves around it helplessly; but he catches hold of an eagle and is carried with it to make a soft landing on the planet Potu ("Utop[ia]" reversed). Here the trees are the ruling species, rich in sapient sap; unfortunately "that very tree which I climbed upon . . . was the wife of the sheriff."[31] Potu has some excellent laws. People who "dispute publicly about the qualities and essence of the Supreme Being are looked upon as slightly insane"; they are treated by bloodletting to reduce their fever, and then are kept in confinement until they "emerge from this delirium."[32] Mothers in Potu nurse their infants—twenty-one years before Rousseau's appeal to maternal breasts. In the province of Cocklecu (Cuckoldy) the women govern the state, the men keep house or become prostitutes, the Queen has a harem of three hundred handsome youths. The philosophers in Cocklecu spend their time trying to get to the sun, and pay little attention to earthly affairs. In the province of Mikolac all the people are atheists, and "do whatever evil they can conceal from the police."[33] Niels comes upon a book entitled *Tanian's Journey to the Superterranean World*, which describes Europe and its strange customs: heads covered with enormous wigs, hats worn under the arm (as among the nobles of France), "little cakes or wafers that are carried about the streets, and which the priests say are gods; the very men who baked them . . . will take their oaths that these wafers created the world."[34]

The *Iter subterraneum* contained some satires of Christian dogma, and called for freedom of worship for all sects; but it recommended belief in God, heaven, and hell as necessary supports for a moral code continually battered by the demands of the ego and the flesh.[35] King Frederick V made the reformed reformer a baron in 1747; Holberg had the pleasure of rebellion in his youth and of acceptance in old age, which ended in 1754. He remains to this day the dominating figure in the literature of Denmark.

Some would give that place rather to Johannes Ewald, whose career matched those of Byron, Keats, and Shelley in adventure, suffering, and brevity. Born in Copenhagen in 1743, son of a Lutheran minister, he rebelled against his puritanic elders, fell in love at sixteen with Arense Hulegaard, abandoned a theological career as too tardy in its rewards, enlisted in the Prussian and then the Austrian army, resolved to win the wealth and glory that would make Arense his bride. But privations and disease destroyed his health; he returned to Copenhagen and theology; Arense married a prompter fortune, and Ewald poured out his heart in poetry and prose. He wrote the first original Danish tragedy, *Rolf Krage* (1770), and reached the zenith of Danish poetry in the eighteenth century with *Balder's Death* (1773), an heroic drama in verse. His work brought him hardly enough bread to live on; he retired to rural solitude, nursed a succession of ailments, and was at last revived by a pension from the government. He rewarded it with a play, *The Fishers* (1779), containing the patriotic ballad "King Christian Stood by the Lofty Mast," which became the favorite national song of the Danes.[36] It was Ewald's call to glory and his farewell to life; he died after a long and painful illness in 1781, aged thirty-eight. Scandinavians rank him as "one of the greatest lyric poets of the North, perhaps the very greatest."[37]

As the eighteenth century progressed, the political history of Denmark became part of the unending modern drama between tradition and experiment. Christian VI (r. 1730–46) mingled the opposed forces. He and his ministers advanced economic development by importing weavers and spinners to establish a textile industry, by forming national companies to trade with Asia and America, and by opening the Bank of Copenhagen (1736). They brought Greenland under the Danish crown (1744). They spread primary and secondary schools, and founded academies for the promotion of letters and learning. However, they renewed an old ordinance requiring Sunday attendance at Lutheran services; they closed all theaters and dance halls, banished actors, forbade masquerades.

Christian's son Frederick V (r. 1746–66) allowed these laws to stand, but softened them by his genial spirit and sensual life. In 1751 he secured from Hanover Johann Hartwig Ernst von Bernstorff, who, as chief minister, raised the honesty and competence of administration, restored the army and navy, kept them out of the Seven Years' War, and stirred the still waters of Danish culture by importing professors, poets, artists, and scientists; we have seen Klopstock accepting such an invitation. In 1767 Count von Bernstorff crowned his pacific foreign policy by persuading Catherine the Great to sign an agreement releasing Holstein-Gottorp to Denmark.

Frederick V, worn out with pleasure, died at forty-three (1766). His son Christian VII (r. 1766–1808) was hurried into marriage at the age of seventeen with Caroline Matilda, sister of England's George III; she brightened the social life of the capital, but her half-insane husband neglected her for a life of profligacy, and Caroline slipped into a tragic amour with the court physician, Johann Friedrich Struensee. Son of a theology professor at Halle, Struensee studied medicine there, and, like most physicians, lost his religious faith. He owed his influence with the King to his skill in treating the clinical results of royal amours, and with the Queen to his success in bringing Christian VII sufficiently to her bed to beget an heir. As the King's mind sank into apathetic gloom, the Queen's power in the government grew; and as she allowed her physician to direct her policies as well as to enjoy her favors, he became (1770) the real ruler of the state. Orders went out from the royal palace signed by Struensee in the name of the *non-compos-mentis* King. Bernstorff was dismissed, and retired peacefully to his estates in Germany.

Struensee had read the *philosophes*, and on their principles he proposed to remodel Danish life. He abolished the abuses of noble privilege, ended censorship of the press, established schools, cleansed the civil service of corruption and jobbery, emancipated the serfs, forbade judicial torture, proclaimed toleration for all religions, encouraged literature and art, reformed the law and the courts, the police, the university, the finances, municipal sanitation . . . To reduce the public debt he canceled many pensions, and appropriated the revenues of pious foundations to public ends.

The nobles plotted his fall, and used the freedom of the press to sap his popularity. Pious Danes resented religious toleration as atheism, and spoke of Struensee as a foreigner whose sole source of authority was the bed of the Queen. On January 17, 1772, a group of army officers persuaded the King that Struensee and the Queen were planning to kill him. He signed an order for their arrest. Caroline was deported to Hamlet's Castle of Kronborg; Struensee was cast into a dungeon, and, after five weeks of suffering, confessed adultery with the Queen. On April 28, 1772, he was hacked to pieces on a scaffold in the presence of an approving multitude. Caroline, on the insistence of George III, was allowed to retire to Celle in Hanover, where she died on May 10, 1775, aged twenty-four.

The successful conspirators raised to power Ove Guldberg, tutor of Prince Frederick. During twelve years of rule Guldberg led a patriotic reaction against foreign influence in government, language, and education, opened office to commoners, restored serfdom, judicial torture, the supremacy of the Lutheran Church, and the religious orientation of the university. Count von Bernstorff's nephew and protégé Andreas Peter von Bernstorff was put in charge of foreign affairs. When Prince Frederick made himself regent (1784) Guldberg was dismissed; Andreas von Bernstorff became chief minister, and remained so till his death. Under his prudent guidance serfdom was again abolished (1787), the slave trade was ended in Danish dominions, economic enterprise was freed. When Bernstorff died (1797) Denmark had been set firmly on the road to that peaceful prosperity which made her the envy of the world.

IV. THE SWEDES

1. Politics: 1718–71

The dramatic career of Charles XII had been a tragedy for Sweden. His aims had consulted his thirst for glory rather than the resources of his country. The Swedish people had borne with him valiantly while he exhausted their manpower and their wealth, but they had known, long before he died, that he was doomed to fail. By the Treaties of Stockholm (1719–20) Sweden yielded the duchies of Bremen and Verden to Hanover, and the larger part of Pomerania to Prussia. By the Peace of Nystad (1721) she surrendered Livonia, Esthonia, Ingermanland, and east Karelia to Russia. Sweden's power on the mainland was ended, and she was compelled to withdraw into a peninsula rich in minerals and national character, but demanding arduous labor and persistent skill as the price of life.

The defeat of Charles weakened the monarchy, and allowed the nobles to regain control of the government. The constitution of 1720 gave dominant power to a Riksdag, or Diet, made up of four "estates": a *Riddarhus*, or House of Nobles, composed of the heads of all noble families; a House of Priests—the bishops plus some fifty delegates elected by and from the parish clergy; a House of Burgesses—some ninety delegates representing the administrative officials and business leaders of the towns; and a House of Peasants —approximately a hundred delegates chosen by and from the free landowning farmers. Each estate sat separately, and no measure could become law unless three estates approved; in effect the peasant estate had no legislative power except by consent of two other estates. During the meetings of the Riksdag a "Secret Committee" of fifty nobles, twenty-five priests, and twenty-five burgesses prepared all bills, chose the ministers, and controlled foreign policy. The nobles were free from taxation, and had exclusive right to the higher offices in the state.[38] When the Riksdag was not in session the government was led by a Råd (Council) of sixteen or twenty-four men chosen by the Riksdag and responsible to it. The king presided over this Council and could cast two votes; otherwise he had no lawmaking power. Russia, Prussia, and Denmark collaborated to support this constitution, on the ground that it favored a policy of peace and checked the martial propensities of strong kings.

The monarchy ceased to be hereditary, became elective. At the death of Charles XII (November 30, 1718) the throne would have passed by heredity to Karl Friedrich, duke of Holstein-Gottorp, a son of Charles's eldest sister; but the Riksdag, assembling in January, 1719, for the first time in twenty years, gave the crown to Ulrika Eleanora, another sister of Charles, on her agreement to renounce the royal absolutism that her brother had exercised. Even so, she proved hard to manage, and in 1720 she was persuaded to abdicate in favor of her husband, Landgrave Frederick I of Hesse-Cassel, who now became King Frederick I of Sweden. Under the prudent guidance of Count Arvid Bernhard Horn as chancellor, Sweden was allowed eighteen years of peace in which to recover from the wounds of war.

Proud Swedes ridiculed his pacifism, and called his partisans "Nightcaps" —"Caps" for short—implying that they were dotards sleeping while Sweden fell behind in the parade of the powers. Against these a party of "Hats" was formed by Count Carl Gyllenborg, Karl Tessin, and others; this captured the Riksdag in 1738, and Gyllenborg replaced Horn. Resolved to restore Sweden to her former place among the powers, he renewed the lapsed alliance with France, which sent her subsidies in return for opposition to the aims of Russia; and in 1741 the government declared war against Russia, hoping to regain those Baltic provinces which had been lost to Peter the Great. But neither the army nor the navy had been sufficiently prepared; the navy was incapacitated by disease, and the army yielded all Finland to the Russian advance. Czarina Elizabeth, anxious to win Sweden's support, agreed to restore most of Finland if her cousin, Adolphus Frederick of Holstein-Gottorp, was named heir to the Swedish throne. On these terms the Peace of Åbo ended the war (1743). When Frederick I died (1751) Adolphus Frederick became king.

The estates soon taught him that he was king in name only. They disputed his right to name new peers, or to choose the members of his household; they threatened to dispense with his signature if he objected to signing certain measures or documents. The King was docile, but he had a proud and commanding consort, Louisa Ulrika, sister of Frederick the Great. King and Queen attempted a revolt against the power of the estates. It failed; its agents were tortured and beheaded; the King was spared because the people loved him. Louisa Ulrika consoled and distinguished herself by becoming Queen of Letters: she befriended Linnaeus, and gathered about her a circle of poets and artists through whom she spread the ideas of the French Enlightenment. The Riksdag appointed a new tutor for her ten-year-old son, with instructions to inform the future Gustavus III that in free states kings exist only on sufferance; that they are invested with splendor and dignity "more for the honor of the realm than for the sake of the person who may happen to occupy the chief place in the pageant," and that "as the glare and glitter of a court" might mislead them into delusions of grandeur, they would do well to visit the huts of the peasantry now and then, and see the poverty that pays for the royal pomp.[39]

On February 12, 1771, Adolphus Frederick died, and the Council summoned Gustavus III to come from Paris and accept the forms of royalty.

2. *Gustavus III*

He was the most attractive king since Henry IV of France. Handsome and gay, loving women, the arts, and power, he flashed through Swedish history like an electric charge, bringing to action all the vital elements in the nation's life. He had been well educated by Karl Tessin, and had been spoiled by his fond mother. He was intellectually precocious and keen, well endowed with imagination and aesthetic sense, restless with ambition and pride; it is not easy to be a humble prince. His mother transmitted to him her love of French literature; he read Voltaire avidly, sent him homage, learned the *Henriade* by heart. The Swedish ambassador at Paris forwarded to him each volume of the *Encyclopédie* as it appeared. He studied history with attention and fascination; he was thrilled by the careers of Gustavus Vasa, Gustavus Adolphus, Charles XII; after reading of these men he could not bear to be a do-nothing king. In 1766, without consulting him, and without the consent of his parents, the Council married him to Princess Sophia Magdalena, daughter of Denmark's Frederick V. She was shy, gentle, pious, and thought the theater a place of sin; he was skeptical, loved the drama, and never forgave the Council for projecting him into this uncongenial marriage. The Council appeased him for a time by a handsome grant for a trip to France (1770–71).

He stopped at Copenhagen, Hamburg, and Brunswick, but Paris was his goal. He braved the anger of Louis XV by calling upon the banished Choiseul, and he violated the conventions by visiting Mme. du Barry in her château at Louveciennes. He met Rousseau, d'Alembert, Marmontel, and Grimm, but was disillusioned; "I have made the acquaintance of all the philosophers," he wrote to his mother, "and find their books much more agreeable than their persons."[40] He shone as a northern star at the salons of Mmes. Geoffrin, du Deffand, de Lespinasse, d'Épinay, and Necker. Amid his triumphs he received word that he had become king of Sweden. He did not hurry back; he stayed in Paris long enough to secure large subsidies for Sweden from the almost bankrupt government of France, and 300,000 livres for his own use in managing the Riksdag. On his way home he stopped to see Frederick the Great, who warned him that Prussia would defend—if necessary by arms—that Swedish constitution which so strictly limited the powers of the king.

Gustavus reached Stockholm on June 6. On the fourteenth he opened his first Riksdag with amiable words strangely like those with which another hampered king, George III, had opened his first Parliament in 1760. "Born and bred among you, I have learned from my tenderest youth to love my country, and I hold it the highest privilege to have been born a Swede, and the greatest honor to be the first citizen of a free people."[41] His eloquence and patriotism won a warm response from the nation, but it left the politicians unmoved. The Caps, friends of the constitution and Russia, and financed by forty thousand pounds from Catherine II, won a majority in three of the four estates. Gustavus countered by borrowing 200,000 pounds from Dutch bankers to buy the election of his nominee as marshal of the Riksdag. But he had still to be crowned, and the Cap-controlled estates revised the coronation oath to pledge the king to abide by the decision of "a majority of the estates," and to base all preferments on merit alone. Gustavus resisted for half a year this move toward democracy; then (March, 1772) he signed it. Secretly he resolved to overthrow this ungracious constitution as soon as opportunity came.

He prepared his ground by establishing popularity. He made himself accessible to all; he "bestowed favors as if receiving them"; he sent no one away discontent. Several army leaders agreed with him that only a strong central government, untrammeled by a venal Riksdag, could save Sweden from domination by Russia and Prussia—which at this very time (August 5, 1772) were partitioning Poland. Vergennes, the French ambassador, contributed 500,000 ducats to the expenses of the coup. On August 18 Gustavus arranged that army officers should meet him at the arsenal the next morning. Two hundred came; he asked them to join him in overthrowing a regime of corruption and instability fostered by Sweden's enemies; all but one agreed to follow him. The exception, Governor-General Rudbeck, rode through the streets of Stockholm calling upon the people to protect their freedom; they remained apathetic, for they admired Gustavus, and had no love for a Riksdag that, in their view, covered an oligarchy of nobles and businessmen with democratic forms. The young King (now twenty-six) led the officers to the barracks of the Stockholm Guards; to these he spoke so persuasively that they pledged him their support. He seemed to be repeating, step by step, the procedure by which Catherine II had reached power in Russia ten years before.

When the Riksdag met on August 21 it found its Rikssaal surrounded by grenadiers, and the hall itself held by troops. Gustavus, in a speech that made history, reproved the estates for having debased themselves with party quarrels and foreign bribery, and he ordered read to them the new constitution that his aides had prepared. It retained a limited monarchy, but widened the powers of the king; it gave him control of the army, navy, and foreign relations; he alone could appoint and depose ministers; the Riksdag was to assemble only at his call, and he could dismiss it at will; it could discuss only such measures as he laid before it, but no measure could become law without the Riksdag's consent, and it would retain control of the purse through the Bank of Sweden and the right to tax. The king was not to engage in a war of offense without the Riksdag's concurrence. Judges were to be named by the king and be then irremovable; and the right of habeas corpus would protect all arrested persons from the delays of the law. Gustavus asked the delegates to accept this constitution; the bayonets convinced them; they accepted, and swore loyalty. The King thanked the Riksdag and dismissed it, promising to recall it within six years. The Hats and Caps parties disappeared. The *coup d'état* was effected with bloodless expedition, and apparently to the satisfaction of the people; they "hailed Gustavus as their liberator, and loaded him with blessings; . . . men embraced one another with tears of joy."[42] France rejoiced, Russia and Prussia threatened war to restore the old constitution. Gustavus stood his ground; Catherine and Frederick retreated, lest war should endanger their Polish spoils.

In the ensuing decade Gustavus behaved as a constitutional monarch—i.e., subject to constituted law. He carried out beneficent reforms, and earned a place among the "enlightened despots" of the century. Voltaire hailed him as "the worthy heir of the great name of Gustavus."[43] Turgot, frustrated in France, had the satisfaction of seeing his economic policies succeed in Sweden, where free trade was legalized in grains, and industry was released from the cramping regulations of the guilds. Commerce was stimulated by the organization of free ports on the Baltic and free market towns in the interior. Mirabeau *père* was asked for advice on improving agriculture; Lemercier de la Rivière was commissioned to draw up a plan for public education.[44] Gustavus sent to Voltaire a copy of the ordinance guaranteeing freedom of the press (1774), and wrote: "It is you that humanity has to thank for the destruction of those obstacles which ignorance and fanaticism have opposed to its progress."[45] He reformed the law and the judiciary, abolished torture, reduced penalties, and stabilized the currency. He lowered the taxes of the peasantry. He reorganized the army and the fleet. Ending the Lutheran monopoly on Swedish piety, he granted toleration to all Christian sects and, in three major cities, to Jews. When he summoned the Riksdag in 1778, his first six years of rule were approved by it without a single dissenting voice.

Gustavus wrote to a friend: "I have reached the happiest stage of my career. My people are convinced that I desire nothing but to promote their welfare and establish their freedom."[46]

3. The Swedish Enlightenment

Amid this activity of legislation and administration, the King contributed with all his heart to the magnificent outburst of literature and science that put Sweden fully abreast of European intellectual developments in the eighteenth century. This was the age of Linnaeus in botany, of Scheele and Bergman in chemistry; we have elsewhere paid them honor. But perhaps we should have included under science one of the most remarkable Swedes of the age, Emanuel Swedenborg, for it was as a scientist that he first earned fame. He did original work in physics, astronomy, geology, paleontology, mineralogy, physiology, and psychology. He improved the air pump by using mercury; he gave good accounts of magnetism and phosphorescence; he proposed a nebular hypothesis long before Kant and Laplace; he anticipated modern research on the ductless glands. He showed, 150 years before any other scientist, that the motion of the brain is synchronous with the respiration rather than with the pulse. He localized in the cortex of the brain the higher operations of the mind, and assigned to specific parts of the brain the control of specific parts of the body.[47] He addressed the House of Nobles on the decimal system, the reform of the currency, the balance of trade. All his genius seemed directed to science. But when he concluded that his studies were leading him to a mechanistic theory of mind and life, and that this theory led to atheism, he reacted strongly away from science toward religion. In 1745 he began to have visions of heaven and hell; he came to trust these visions literally, and he described them in his treatise *Heaven and Its Wonders and Hell.* He informed his thousands of readers that in heaven they would not be disembodied spirits but real flesh-and-blood men and women, enjoying the physical as well as the spiritual delights of love. He did not preach, nor did he found a sect; but his influence spread throughout Europe, affecting Wesley, William Blake, Coleridge, Carlyle, Emerson, and Browning; and finally (1788) his followers formed the "New Jerusalem Church."

Despite his opposition Sweden gave its mind more and more to the Enlightenment. The import or translation of French and English works rapidly produced a secularization of culture and a refinement of literary taste and forms. Under Gustavus III and his mother the new liberalism found wide acceptance in the middle and upper classes, even among the higher clergy, who began to preach toleration and a simple deistic creed.[48] Everywhere the watchwords were *reason, progress, science, liberty,* and *the good life here on earth.* Linnaeus and others organized the Swedish Royal Academy of Sciences in 1739; Karl Tessin founded the Royal Academy of Fine Arts in 1733. A Royal Academy of Belles-Lettres had had a brief existence under Queen Louisa Ulrika; Gustavus revived it (1784) with a rich endowment, and directed it to award yearly a medal worth twenty ducats for the best Swedish work in history, poetry, or philosophy; he himself won the first award with his panegyric of Lennart Torstenson, the most brilliant of Gustavus Adolphus' generals. In 1786 the King established (to use his own words) "a new academy for the cultivation of our own language, on the model of the Académie Française. It is to be called the Swedish Academy, and will consist of eighteen members." This and the Academy of Belles-Lettres were provided with funds for pensions to Swedish scholars and authors.[49] Gustavus personally helped men of letters, of science, or of music; he made them feel that his bounty was their due; he gave them new social status by inviting them to his court; and he stimulated them by his competition.

There had been drama in Sweden before him, especially under encouragement by his mother, but it had been provided by French actors presenting French plays. Gustavus dismissed the alien troupe, and called upon native talent to produce plays for a really Swedish theater. He himself collaborated with Johan Willander in writing an opera, *Thetis och Pelée*; this had its première on January 18, 1773, and ran for twenty-eight nights. Then for eight years the King gave himself to politics. In 1781 he took up the pen again, and composed a series of plays which still rank high in Swedish literature. The first of them, *Gustaf Adolfs Adelmod* (*Gustavus Adolphus' Magnanimity*, 1782) marked the beginning of the Swedish drama. The King took his subjects from historical records, and taught his people the history of their country as Shakespeare had taught the English. In 1782, at state expense, a superb theater was built for both drama and music. Gustavus wrote his plays in prose, had them versified by Johan Kellgren, and had native or foreign composers put them to music; so his plays became operas. The best results of this collaboration were *Gustaf Adolf och Ebba Brahe*, celebrating the great commander's love story, and *Gustaf Vasa*, which told how the first Gustavus had freed Sweden from Danish domination.

With such royal leadership, and three universities (Uppsala, Åbo, and Lund), Sweden moved into its own Enlightenment. Olof von Dalin provided an Addisonian prelude by writing anonymously, and periodically publishing (1733–34), *Den svenska Argus*, discussing everything except politics, in the genial style of the *Spectator*. Nearly every reader was pleased. The Riksdag voted a reward to the author, who forthwith came out of hiding. Queen Louisa Ulrika made him court poet and tutor to the future Gustavus III. This fettered and dulled his Muse, but it allowed him time and money to write his chef-d'oeuvre, *Svea Rikes Historia*, the first critical history of the Swedish realm.

The most interesting figure in the new Pléiade was a woman, Hedvig Nordenflycht, the Sappho, Aspasia, and Charlotte Brontë of Sweden. She alarmed her puritan parents by reading plays and poetry; they punished her, she persisted, and wrote verses so charming that they resigned themselves to the scandal. But they compelled her to marry the overseer of their estate, who was wise and ugly; "I loved to listen to him as a philosopher, but the sight of him as a lover was unendurable."[50] She learned to love him, only to have him die in her arms after three years of marriage. A handsome young clergyman ended her mourning by courting her; she became his wife, and enjoyed "the most blissful life that any mortal can have in this imperfect world"; but he died within a year, and Hedvig went almost insane with grief. She isolated herself in a cottage on a small island, and voiced her sorrow in poems that were so well received that she moved to Stockholm and issued annually (1744–50) *Aphorisms for Women, by a Shepherdess of the North*. Her home became a salon for the social and intellectual elite. Young poets like Fredrik Gyllenborg and Gustaf Creutz followed her in adopting the classic French style and in espousing the Enlightenment. In 1758, aged forty, she fell in love with Johan Fischerström, twenty-three; he confessed that he loved another, but when he saw Hedvig desolate he proposed marriage to her. She refused the sacrifice, and to simplify matters she tried to drown herself. She was rescued, but she died three days later. *Shepherdess of the North* is still a classic in the literature of Sweden.

Creutz followed her romantic flight with an exquisite cycle of songs, *Atis och Camilla* (1762), which remained for many years the most admired poem in the language. Camilla, as a priestess of Diana, is vowed to chastity; Atis, a hunter, sees her, longs for her, wanders through the woods in despair. Camilla too is stirred, and asks Diana, "Is not nature's law as holy as your decree?" She comes upon a wounded hart; she tends and comforts it; it licks her hand; Atis begs similar privileges; she rebukes him; he jumps from a high cliff, seeking death; Cupid breaks his fall; Camilla tends him and accepts his embrace; a serpent buries its fang in her alabaster breast; she dies in Atis' arms. Atis sucks the poison from her wound, and nears death. Diana relents, revives them both, and releases Camilla from her virgin vows; all is well. This idyl was acclaimed by literate Sweden and by Voltaire, but Creutz turned to politics and became chancellor of Sweden.

If Hedvig Nordenflycht was the Sappho of Sweden, Karl Bellmann was its Robert Burns. Brought up in comfort and piety, he learned to prefer the jolly songs of the taverns to the somber hymns of his home. In the taverns the realities of life and feeling were revealed with little concern for convention and propriety; there each soul was bared by liquor, and let truth come out between fancy and wrath. The most tragic figure in this human wreckage was Jan Fredman, once clockmaker to the court, now trying to forget in drink the failure of his marriage; and the gayest was Maria Kiellström, queen of the lower depths. Bellmann sang their songs with them, composed songs about them, sang these before them to music composed by himself. Some of his songs were a bit loose, and Kellgren, the uncrowned poet laureate of the age, reproved him; but when Bellmann prepared *Fredmans Epistlar* for the press (1790), Kellgren chaperoned these verse letters with an enthusiastic preface, and the volume received an award from the Swedish Royal Academy. Gustavus III heard Bellmann gladly, called him "the Anacreon of the North," and gave him a sinecure in the government. The assassination of the King (1792) left the poet without income; he sank into poverty, was imprisoned for debt, was released by friends. Dying of consumption at the age of fifty-five, he insisted on a last visit to his favorite tavern; there he sang till his voice failed him. He died soon afterward, February 11, 1795. Some rank him as "the most original of all Swedish poets," and "by all odds the greatest in the circle of poets" that honored this reign.[51]

But the man whom his contemporaries recognized as second only to the King in the intellectual life of the time was Johan Henrik Kellgren. Son of a clergyman, he discarded the Christian creed, marched with the French Enlightenment, and welcomed all the pleasures of life with a minimum of remorse. His earliest book, *Mina Löjen* (*My Laughter*) was an extended ode to joy, erotic joys included; Kellgren hailed laughter as "the one divine, distinguishing mark of humanity," and invited it to accompany him to the end of his days.[52] In 1778, aged twenty-seven, he joined with Karl Peter Lenngren in founding the *Stockholmsposten*; for seventeen years his lively pen made this journal the dominant voice in Swedish intellectual life; in its pages the French Enlightenment held full sway, the classic style was honored as the supreme norm of excellence, German romanticism was laughed out of court, and Kellgren's mistresses were exalted in poems that scandalized the conservatives of the hinterland. The assassination of his beloved King took the heart out of the poet's hedonistic philosophy. In 1795 one of his amours ran out of control and deepened into love. Kellgren began to acknowledge the rights of romance, idealism, and religion; he retracted his condemnation of Shakespeare and Goethe, and he thought that, after all, the fear of God might be the beginning of wisdom. However, when he died (1795), aged only forty-four, he asked that no bells be tolled for him;[53] he was, at the end, again a son of Voltaire.

A charming aspect of his character was his willingness to open the columns of the *Posten* to opponents of his views. The most vigorous of them was Thomas Thorild, who declared war on the Enlightenment as the immature idolatry of superficial reason. At the age of twenty-two Thorild startled Stockholm with *Passionerna* (*The Passions*), which, he said, "contains the full force of my philosophy and all the splendor of my imagination—unrhymed, ecstatic, marvelous." He declared that "his whole life was consecrated to . . . revealing nature and reforming the world."[54] Around him gathered a group of literary rebels who fed their fires with Sturm und Drang, ranked Klopstock above Goethe, Shakespeare above Racine, Rousseau above Voltaire. Failing to win Gustavus III to these views, Thorild migrated to England (1788), nourished his soul with James Thomson, Edward Young, and Samuel Richardson, and joined the radicals who favored the French Revolution. In 1790 he returned to Sweden and published political propaganda that stirred the government to banish him. After two years in Germany he was readmitted into Sweden, and subsided into a professorial chair.

There were several other stars in this literary firmament. Carl Gustaf af Leopold pleased the King with the classic form and courtly tone of his verse. Bengt Lidner, like Thorild, preferred romance. He was expelled from the University of Lund because of his escapades (1776); continued his studies and irregularities at Rostock; was put on a ship bound for the East Indies, escaped from it, returned to Sweden, and attracted the attention of Gustavus with a volume of poetic fables. He was appointed secretary to Count Creutz in the embassy at Paris; there he studied women more than politics, and was sent home, where he died in poverty at the age of thirty-five (1793). He redeemed his life by three volumes hot with Byronic fire. — And there was modest Anna Maria Lenngren, wife of Kellgren's collaborator on the *Stockholmsposten*. To that periodical she contributed verse that won her a special commendation by the Swedish Royal Academy. But she did not let her Muse interfere with her household chores, and in a poem addressed to an imaginary daughter she counseled her to avoid politics and society and content herself with the tasks and joys of the home.

Was there, in Swedish art, any movement answering to the literature and the drama? Hardly. Karl Gustaf of Tessin decorated in rococo (c. 1750) the royal palace that his father, Nicodemus Tessin, had built in 1693–97, and he gathered a rich collection of paintings and statuary, which is now part of the Stockholm National Museum. Johan Tobias Sergel carved a *Venus* and a *Drunken Faun* in classic style, and commemorated in marble the robust features of Johan Pasch. The Pasch family included four painters: Lorenz the Elder, his brother Johan, his sister Ulrica, and Lorenz the Younger; each of these painted royalty and nobility. They were a modest part in the brilliant Enlightenment that graced this reign.

4. Assassination

It was the King himself who brought the bright flowering to a tragic end. The American Revolution, so powerfully aided by France, seemed to him a threat to all monarchies; he called the colonists "rebellious subjects," and vowed that he would never recognize them as a nation until the King of England had absolved them from their oath of allegiance.[55] More and more in his final decade he strengthened the royal power, surrounded it with ceremony and etiquette, and replaced able aides of independent mind with servitors who obeyed his wishes without hesitation or dissent. He began to restrict the freedom that he had given to the press. Finding his wife dull, he indulged in flirtations[56] that shocked public opinion, which expected the kings of Sweden to give the nation a model of marital affection and fidelity. He alienated the people by establishing a governmental monopoly in the distillation of liquor; the peasants, accustomed to distill their own, evaded the monopoly by a hundred expedients. He spent increasingly on the army and navy, and was visibly preparing for war with Russia. When he assembled his second Riksdag (May 6, 1786) he found no longer, in the estates, the approval that the Riksdag of 1778 had given to his measures; almost all of his proposals were rejected, or were amended to futility, and he was compelled to surrender the government's liquor monopoly. On July 5 he dismissed the Riksdag, and resolved to rule without its consent.

That consent, by the constitution of 1772, was necessary for any war but one of defense, and Gustavus was meditating an attack upon Russia. Why? He knew that Russia and Denmark had signed (August 12, 1774) a secret treaty for united action against Sweden. He visited Catherine II at St. Petersburg in 1777, but their mutual pretenses of friendship deceived neither the hostess nor her guest. As Russian victories against Turkey mounted, Gustavus feared that if nothing were done to end them the Empress would soon direct her immense armies westward in the hope of subjecting Sweden to her will as she had done with Poland. Was there any way of frustrating that design? Only, the King felt, by aiding Turkey with a flank attack upon St. Petersburg. The Sultan helped him decide by offering Sweden a subsidy of a million piasters annually for the next ten years if she would join in the effort to check Catherine. Perhaps now Sweden could recover what she had surrendered to Peter the Great in 1721. In 1785 Gustavus began to prepare his army and navy for war. In 1788 he sent to Russia an ultimatum demanding the restoration of Karelia and Livonia to Sweden, and of the Crimea to Turkey. On June 24 he embarked for Finland. On July 2, at Helsingfors, he took charge of his assembled forces, and began to drive toward St. Petersburg.

Everything went wrong. The fleet was stopped by a Russian flotilla in an indecisive battle off the island of Hogland (July 17). In the army 113 officers mutinied, charging that the King had violated his pledge to make no offensive war without the Riksdag's consent; they sent an emissary to Catherine offering to place themselves under her protection and to cooperate with her in making both Swedish and Russian Finland an independent state. Meanwhile Denmark dispatched an army to attack Göteborg, the richest city in Sweden. Gustavus accepted this invasion as a challenge that would arouse the spirit of his people; he appealed to the nation, and especially to the rugged peasants of the mining districts called the Dales, to give him a new and more loyal army; he went in person, dressed in the Dalesmen's characteristic garb, to address them from that same churchyard, in the village of Mora, where Gustavus Vasa had asked for their aid in 1521. The people responded; volunteer regiments were formed in a hundred towns. In September the King, fighting for his political life, rode 250 miles in forty-eight hours, made his way into Göteborg, and inspired the garrison to continue its defense against twelve thousand besieging Danes. Fortune turned in his favor. Prussia, unwilling to let Sweden fall subject to Russia, threatened war upon Denmark; the Danes withdrew from Swedish soil. Gustavus returned in triumph to his capital.

Now, emboldened by a new army dedicated to him, he summoned the Riksdag to assemble on January 26, 1789. Of 950 men in the House of Nobles, seven hundred supported the mutinous officers, but the other houses—clergy, burgesses, and peasants—were overwhelmingly for the King. Gustavus declared political war against the nobles by submitting to the Riksdag an "Act of Unity and Security" which ended many privileges of the aristocracy, opened nearly all offices to commoners, and gave the King full monarchical powers over legislation, administration, war, and peace. The three lower estates accepted the act, the Riddarhus rejected it as unconstitutional. Gustavus arrested twenty-one nobles, including Count Fredrik Axel von Fersen and Baron Karl Fredrik von Pechlin—one honorable and ineffective, the other clever and treacherous. But the power of the purse still remained with the Riksdag, and appropriations required the consent of all four chambers. The three lower orders voted the King, for as long as he might consider necessary, the funds he asked for continuing the war against Russia; the House of Nobles refused to vote supplies beyond two years. On April 17 Gustavus entered the Riddarhus, took the chair, and put to the nobles the question of accepting the decision of the three other houses. The noes preponderated, but the King announced that his proposal had won. He thanked the nobles for their gracious support, and withdrew, having risked assassination by the infuriated magnates.

He now felt free to prosecute the war. During the remainder of 1789 he rebuilt the army and the fleet. On July 9, 1790, his navy met the Russian in the Svensksund part of the Gulf of Finland, and won the most decisive victory in Sweden's naval history; the Russians lost fifty-three ships and 9,500 men. Catherine II, still busy with the Turks, was ready for peace; by the Treaty of Värälä (August 15, 1790) she agreed to end her efforts to control the politics of Sweden, and prewar boundaries were restored. On October 19, 1791, Gustavus persuaded her to sign with him a defensive alliance which pledged her to send Sweden 300,000 rubles per year.

Doubtless their common fear of the French Revolution turned the old foes to this new partnership. Gustavus remembered gratefully that France had been Sweden's faithful friend through 250 years, and that Louis XV and Louis XVI had supported him with 38,300,000 livres between 1772 and 1789. He proposed a League of Princes to invade France and restore the monarchy to power; he sent Hans Axel von Fersen (son of his enemy Count von Fersen) to arrange the flight of Louis XVI from Paris; he himself went to Aix-la-Chapelle to lead the allied army; and he offered asylum in his camp to the French émigrés. Catherine gave money but no men, Leopold II refused to co-operate, and Gustavus returned to Stockholm to protect his throne.

The nobles whose political supremacy he had ended were not reconciled to defeat. They looked upon Gustavus' absolute rule as a plain violation of the constitution that he had sworn to support. Jakob Ankarström brooded over the fall of his class. "I bethought me much if perchance there was any fair means of getting the King to rule his land and people according to law and benevolence, but every argument was against me. . . . 'Twere better to venture one's life for the commonweal." In 1790 he was tried for sedition. "This misfortune . . . knit my resolve rather to die than live a wretched life, so that my otherwise sensitive and affectionate heart became altogether callous as regards this horrible deed."[57] Pechlin, Count Karl Horn, and others joined in the conspiracy to kill the King.

On March 16, 1792, a date ominously recalling Caesar, Gustavus received a letter warning him not to attend a masquerade ball scheduled for that night in the French Theater. He went half masked, but the decorations on his breast revealed his rank. Ankarström recognized him, shot him, and fled. Gustavus was carried to a coach and led through an excited crowd to the royal palace. He was bleeding dangerously, but he jokingly remarked that he resembled a pope borne in procession through Rome. Within three hours of the attack Ankarström was arrested; within a few days, all the ringleaders. Horn confessed that the plot had had a hundred accomplices. The populace cried out for their execution; Gustavus recommended clemency. Ankarström was scourged, beheaded, and quartered, Gustavus lingered for ten days; then, told that he had only a few hours of life left to him, he dictated documents for a regency to govern the country and the capital. He died on March 26, 1792, aged forty-five. Nearly all the nation mourned him, for it had learned to love him despite his faults, and it realized that under his lead Sweden had lived through one of the most glorious ages in her history.

BOOK VI

JOHNSON'S ENGLAND

1756–89

CHAPTER XXVII

The Industrial Revolution

I. CAUSES

WHY did the Industrial Revolution come to England first? Because England had won great wars on the Continent while keeping its own soil free from war's devastation; because it had secured command of the seas and had thereby acquired colonies that provided raw materials and needed manufactured goods; because its armies, fleets, and growing population offered an expanding market for industrial products; because the guilds could not meet these widening demands; because the profits of far-flung commerce accumulated capital seeking new avenues of investment; because England allowed its nobles—and their fortunes—to engage in commerce and industry; because the progressive displacement of tillage by pasturage drove peasants from the fields to the towns, where they added to the labor force available for factories; because science in England was directed by men of a practical bent, while on the Continent it was predominantly devoted to abstract research; and because England had a constitutional government sensitive to business interests, and vaguely aware that priority in the Industrial Revolution would make England for over a century the political leader of the Western world.

British command of the seas had begun with the defeat of the Spanish Armada; it had been extended by victories over Holland in the Anglo-Dutch wars, and over France in the War of the Spanish Succession; and the Seven Years' War had made oceanic commerce almost a British monopoly. An invincible navy made the English Channel a protective moat for "this fortress built by Nature . . . against infection and the hand of war."[1] The English economy was not only spared the ravages of soldiery, it was nourished and stimulated by the needs of British and allied armies on the Continent; hence the special expansion of the textile and metallurgical industries, and the call for machines to accelerate, and for factories to multiply, production.

Command of the seas facilitated the conquest of colonies. Canada and the richest parts of India fell to England as fruit of the Seven Years' War. Voyages like those of Captain Cook (1768–76) secured for the British Empire islands strategically useful in war and trade. Rodney's victory over de Grasse (1782) confirmed British dominion over Jamaica, Barbados, and the Bahamas. New Zealand was acquired in 1787, Australia in 1788. Colonial and other overseas trade gave British industry a foreign market unrivaled in the eighteenth century. Commerce with the English settlements in North America employed 1,078 vessels and 29,000 seamen.[2] London, Bristol, Liverpool, and Glasgow flourished as chief ports for this Atlantic trade. The colonies took manufactured articles and sent back food, tobacco, spices, tea, silk, cotton, raw materials, gold, silver, and precious stones. Parliament restricted with high tariffs the import of foreign manufactures, and discouraged the development of colonial or Irish industries competitive with those of Britain. No internal tolls (such as those that hampered domestic trade in France) impeded the movement of goods through England, Scotland, and Wales; these lands constituted the largest free-trade area in Western Europe. The upper and middle classes enjoyed the highest prosperity, and a purchasing power that was an added stimulus to industrial production.

The guilds were not competent to meet the demands of expanding markets at home and abroad. They had been instituted chiefly to supply the needs of a municipality and its environs; they were shackled by old regulations that discouraged invention, competition, and enterprise; they were not equipped to procure raw materials from distant sources, or to acquire capital for enlarged production, or to calculate, obtain, or fill orders from abroad. Gradually the guild master was replaced by "projectors" (entrepreneurs) who knew how to raise money, to anticipate or create demand, to secure raw materials, and to organize machines and men to produce for markets in every quarter of the globe.

The money was provided by the profits of commerce or finance, by the spoils of war and privateers, by the mining or import of gold or silver, by the great fortunes made in the slave trade or the colonies. Englishmen went out poor, some came back rich. As early as 1744 there were fifteen men who, returning from the West Indies, had money enough to buy election to Parliament;[3] and by 1780 the "nabobs" who had acquired riches in India were a power in the House of Commons. Much of this exotic pelf was available for investment. And whereas in France the nobles were forbidden, in England they were permitted, to engage in commerce or industry; and wealth rooted in land grew through investment in business enterprise; so the Duke of Bridgewater risked his patrimony in mining coal. Thousands of Britons were depositing their savings in banks, which lent at low rates of interest. Moneylenders were everywhere. Bankers had discovered that the easiest way to make money is to handle other people's money. There were twenty banks in London in 1750, fifty in 1770, seventy in 1800.[4] Burke reckoned twelve banks outside of London in 1750; in 1793 there were four hundred.[5] Paper money added to the fertilizing pollen; in 1750 it was two per cent of the currency; in 1800 it was ten per cent.[6] Hoarded money ventured into investment as commerce and industry announced their rising dividends.

The multiplying shops and factories needed men. The natural supply of labor was augmented by the rising number of rural families that could no longer make a living on the farm. The flourishing wool industry demanded wool; more and more land was withdrawn from tillage and given to pasturage; sheep replaced men; Goldsmith's Auburn was not the only deserted village in Britain. Between 1702 and 1760 there had been 246 acts of Parliament authorizing the removal of four hundred acres from planting; between

1760 and 1810 there were 2,438 such acts, affecting nearly five million acres.[7] As agricultural machinery improved, small holdings became undesirable, because they could not use or pay for the new machines; thousands of farmers sold their land and became hired hands on large-scale farms or in rural mills or in the towns. The large farms, with better methods, organization, and machines, produced more per acre than the farms of the past, but they almost wiped out the yeomen, or peasant proprietors, who had been the economic, military, and moral backbone of England. Meanwhile immigration from Ireland and the Continent added to the men, women, and children who competed for jobs in the factories.

Science played only a modest part in the economic transformation of eighteenth-century England. The researches of Stephen Hales on gases, of Joseph Black on heat and steam, helped Watt to improve the steam engine. The Royal Society of London was composed mostly of practical men, who favored studies that promised industrial application. The British Parliament too had a mind for material considerations; though it was dominated by landowners, several of these took a hand in commerce or industry, and most of the members were amenable to the pleas and gifts of businessmen for relaxing the restrictions that earlier governments had laid upon the economy. The advocates of free enterprise and free trade—and of wages and prices left free to rise or fall with the laws of supply and demand—won the support of several parliamentary leaders, and the legal barriers to the spread of commerce and manufactures were slowly broken down. All the conditions prerequisite to English priority in the Industrial Revolution were fulfilled.

II. COMPONENTS

The material elements of the Industrial Revolution were iron, coal, transportation, machinery, power, and factories. Nature played its part by providing England with iron, coal, and liquid roads. But iron as it came from the mines was permeated with impurities, from which it had to be freed by smelting—melting or fusing with fire. Coal too was alloyed with impurities; these were removed by heating or "cooking" coal till it became coke. Iron ore heated and purified to diverse degrees by burning coke became wrought iron, cast iron, or steel.

To increase the heat Abraham Darby built (1754 f.) blast furnaces in which extra air was supplied to the fire from a pair of bellows worked by a water wheel. In 1760 John Smeaton replaced the bellows with a compressed-air pump driven partly by water, partly by steam; the constant high-pressure blast raised the production of industrial iron from twelve tons to forty tons per furnace per day.[8] Iron became cheap enough to be used in hundreds of new ways; so, in 1763, Richard Reynolds built the first known railway—iron tracks that enabled cars to replace pack horses in transporting coal and ore.

Now began an age of famous ironmasters who dominated the industrial scene and made great fortunes by using iron for purposes that seemed quite alien to that metal. So John Wilkinson and Abraham Darby II spanned the River Severn with the first iron bridge (1779). Wilkinson amused England by proposing an iron ship; some said he had lost his mind; but, relying upon principles established by Archimedes, he put together with metal sheets the first iron vessel known to history (1787). Businessmen came from abroad to see and study the great works set up by Wilkinson, Richard Crawshay, or Anthony Bacon. Birmingham, close to extensive deposits of coal and iron, became the leading center of England's iron industry. From such shops new tools and machines, stronger, more durable and reliable, were poured into Britain's shops and factories.

Coal and iron were heavy, costly to convey except by water. A richly indented coastline allowed maritime transport to reach many major cities of Britain. To bring materials and products to towns distant from the coast and navigable streams a revolution in transportation had to be effected. The movement of goods overland was still difficult despite the network of turn-pikes built between 1751 and 1771. (They took their name from the pike-studded turnstiles that obstructed passage until toll was paid.)[9] These toll roads doubled the speed of transit and quickened internal trade. Pack horses were superseded by horse-drawn carts, and travel by horseback gave way to stage coaches. The turnpikes, however, were left to private enterprise for their maintenance, and rapidly deteriorated.

So commercial traffic still preferred the waterways. Streams were dredged to bear heavy vessels, and rivers and towns were bound with one another by canals. James Brindley, without formal or technical education, grew from a letterless millwright into the most remarkable canal engineer of the time, solving by his mechanical bent the problems of carrying canals through locks and tunnels and over aqueducts. In 1759–61 he built a canal that brought to Manchester the coal from the mines of the Duke of Bridgewater at Worsley; this cut in half the cost of coal at Manchester, and played a principal part in making that city an industrial metropolis. One of the most picturesque sights in eighteenth-century England was a ship moving along the Brindley-Bridgewater canal carried by an aqueduct ninety-nine feet high over the River Irwell at Barton. In 1766 Brindley began the Grand Trunk Canal, which, by connecting the Rivers Trent and Mersey, opened a water route across mid-England from the Irish to the North Sea. Other canals bound the Trent with the Thames, and Manchester with Liverpool. In a period of thirty years hundreds of new canals greatly reduced the cost of commercial traffic in Britain.

Given materials, fuels, and transportation, the Industrial Revolution had next to multiply goods. The demand for machines to accelerate production was greatest in textiles. People wanted to be clothed, and soldiers and lasses had to be hypnotized with uniforms. Cotton was entering England in rapidly rising amounts—three million pounds in 1753, thirty-two million in 1789;[10] hand labor could not process this into finished goods in time to meet demand. The division of labor that had developed in the clothing trades suggested and promoted the invention of machines.

John Kay had begun the mechanization of weaving by his "flying shuttle" (1733), and Lewis Paul had mechanized spinning by a system of rollers (1738). In 1765 James Hargreaves of Blackburn, Lancashire, changed the position of the spinning wheel from vertical to horizontal, placed one wheel on top of another, turned eight of them by one pulley and belt, and wove eight threads at once; he added more power to more spindles until his "spinning jenny" (Jenny was his wife) wove eighty threads at a time. Hand spinners feared that this contraption would throw them out of work and food; they broke up Hargreaves' machines; he fled for his life to Nottingham, where a shortage of labor allowed his jennies to be installed. By 1788 there were twenty thousand of them in Britain, and the spinning wheel was on its way to becoming a romantic ornament.

In 1769 Richard Arkwright, using the suggestions of various mechanics, developed a "water frame" by which water power moved cotton fibers between a succession of rollers that pulled and stretched the fibers into tighter, harder yarn. About 1774 Samuel Crompton combined Hargreaves' jenny and Arkwright's rollers into a hybrid machine which English wit called "Crompton's mule": an alternate backward and forward motion of the rotating spindles stretched, twisted, and wound the thread, giving it greater fineness and strength; this procedure remained till our time the principle of the most complex textile machinery. The jenny and the water frame had been made of wood; the mule, after 1783, used metal rollers and wheels, and became sturdy enough to bear the speed and strain of power operation.

Power looms worked by cranks and weights had been used in Germany and France, but in 1787 Edmund Cartwright built at Doncaster a small factory in which twenty looms were operated by animal motion. In 1789 he replaced this power plant by a steam engine. Two years later he joined with some Manchester friends to set up a large factory in which four hundred looms were run by steam. Here too the workers rebelled; they burned the factory to the ground and threatened to kill the promoters. In the ensuing decade many power looms were built, rioters smashed some of them, some survived and multiplied; the machines won.

England had been helped to industry through water power from numerous streams fed by abundant rain. So, in the eighteenth century, mills were erected not so much in the towns as in the countryside, along streams that could be dammed to create waterfalls of sufficient force to turn great wheels. At this point a poet might wonder had it not been better if steam had never replaced water as a motive force, and industry, instead of being congregated in cities, had been mingled with agriculture in the rural scene. But the more effective and profitable method of production displaces the less, and the steam engine (which also, till lately, had a romantic glow) promised to produce or transport more goods and gold than the world had ever seen before.

The steam engine was the culmination, not quite a product, of the Industrial Revolution. Not to go back to Hero of Alexandria (A.D. 200?), Denis Papin described all the components and principles of a practical steam engine in 1690. Thomas Savery built a steam-driven pump in 1698. Thomas Newcomen developed this (1708–12) into a machine in which steam generated by heated water was condensed by a jet of cold water, and the alternation of atmospheric pressure drove a piston up and down; this "atmospheric engine" remained the standard until James Watt transformed it into a true steam engine in 1765.

Unlike most inventors of that time, Watt was a student as well as a practical man. His grandfather was a teacher of mathematics; his father was an architect, shipbuilder, and magistrate in the borough of Greenock in southwest Scotland. James had no college education, but he had creative curiosity and a mechanical bent. Half the world knows the story that an aunt reproved him: "I never saw such an idle boy as you are: . . . for the last hour you have not spoken one word, but you have taken off the lid of that kettle, and put it on again, and, holding now a cap and now a silver spoon over the steam, watching how it rises from the spout, and catching and counting the drops."[11] This has the odor of legend. However, an extant manuscript in James Watt's hand describes an experiment in which "the straight end of a pipe was fixed on the spout of a Tea Kettle"; and another manuscript reads: "I took a bent glass tube and inverted it into the nose of a tea kettle, the other end being immersed in cold water."[12]

At the age of twenty (1756) Watt tried to set up in Glasgow as a maker of scientific instruments. The city guilds refused him a license on the ground that he had not completed the full term of apprenticeship, but the University of Glasgow gave him a workshop within its grounds. He attended the chemistry lectures of Joseph Black, won his friendship and aid, and was especially interested in Black's theory of latent heat.[13] He learned German, French, and Italian to read foreign books, including metaphysics and poetry. Sir James Robison, who knew him at that time (1758), was struck by Watt's varied knowledge, and said, "I saw a workman and expected no more; I found a philosopher."[14]

In 1763 the university asked him to repair a model of Newcomen's engine used in a physics course. He was surprised to find that three fourths of the heat supplied to the machine were wasted: after each stroke of the piston the cylinder lost heat through the use of cold water to condense the new supply of steam entering the cylinder; so much energy was lost that most manufacturers had judged the machine unprofitable. Watt proposed to condense the steam in a separate container, whose low temperature would not affect the cylinder in which the piston moved. This "condenser" increased by some three hundred per cent the efficiency of the machine in the proportion of fuel used to work done. Moreover, in Watt's reconstruction, the piston was moved by the expansion of steam, not of air; he had made a true steam engine.

The passage from plans and models to practical application consumed twelve years of Watt's life. To make successive samples and improvements of his engine he borrowed over a thousand pounds, chiefly from Joseph Black, who never lost faith in him. John Smeaton, himself an inventor and engineer, predicted that Watt's engine could "never be brought into general use because of the difficulty of getting its parts manufactured with sufficient precision."[15] In 1765 Watt married, and had to earn more money; he put aside his invention and took to surveying and engineering, drawing up plans for harbors, bridges, and canals. Meanwhile Black introduced him to John Roebuck, who was looking for a more effective engine than Newcomen's for pumping water from the coal mines that supplied fuel for his ironworks at Carron. In 1767 he agreed to pay Watt's debts and provide capital for building engines to Watt's specifications, in return for two thirds of the profits from installations or sales. To protect their investment Watt in 1769 asked Parliament for a patent that would give him sole right to produce his engine; it was granted him till 1783. He and Roebuck set up an engine near Edinburgh, but poor workmanship by the smiths made it a failure; in some cases the cylinders made for Watt were an eighth of an inch greater in diameter at one end than at the other.

Pressed by reverses, Roebuck sold his share of the partnership to Matthew Boulton (1773). Now began an alliance notable in the history of friendship as well as of industry. Boulton was no mere moneymaker; he was so interested in improving his modes and mechanisms of production that in achieving this he lost a fortune. In 1760, aged thirty-two, he married a rich woman and might have retired on her income; instead he built at Soho, near Birmingham, one of England's most extensive industrial plants, manufacturing a great variety of metal articles from shoe buckles to chandeliers. To operate the machines in the five buildings of his factory he had relied on water power. He proposed now to try steam power. He knew that Watt had shown the inefficiency of the Newcomen engine, and that Watt's engine had failed because of inaccurately bored cylinders. He took a calculated risk that this defect could be overcome. In 1774 he moved Watt's engine to Soho; in 1775 Watt followed it. Parliament extended the patent from 1783 to 1800.

In 1775 ironmaster Wilkinson invented a hollow cylindrical boring bar that enabled Boulton and Watt to produce engines of unprecedented power and competence. Soon the new firm was selling engines to manufacturers and mine owners throughout Britain. Boswell visited Soho in 1776, and reported:

> Mr. Hector was so good as to accompany me to see the great works of Mr. Boulton. . . . I wished Johnson had been with us, for it was a scene which I should have been glad to contemplate by his light. The vastness and the contrivances of some of the machinery would have "matched his mighty mind." I shall never forget Mr. Boulton's expression to me: "I sell here, Sir, what all the world desires to have—POWER." He had about seven hundred people at work. I contemplated him as an *iron chieftain*, and he seemed to be a father to his tribe.[16]

Watt's engines were still unsatisfactory, and he constantly labored to improve them. In 1781 he patented a device by which the reciprocal motion of the piston was converted into rotating motion, thereby adapting the engine for driving ordinary machinery. In 1782 he patented a double-acting engine, in which both ends of the cylinder received impulses from the boiler and the condenser. In 1788 he patented a "fly-ball governor" that adjusted the flow of steam to promote uniform speed in the engine. During these experimental years other inventors were making competitive engines, and it was not till 1783 that Watt's sales paid off his debts and began to bring in gains. When his patent expired he retired from active work, and the firm of Boulton and Watt was carried on by their sons. Watt amused himself with minor inventions, and lived into a cheerful old age, dying in 1819 at the age of eighty-three.

There were many other inventions in this exuberant age, when, as Dean Tucker said, "almost every master manufacturer hath a new invention of his own, and is daily improving on those of others."[17] Watt himself developed a duplicating process by using a glutinous ink and pressing the written or printed page against a moistened sheet of thin paper (1780). One of his employees, William Murdock, applied Watt's engine to traction, and built a model locomotive that traveled eight miles an hour (1784). Murdock shared with Philippe Lebon of France the distinction of using coal gas for illumination; he so lighted the exterior of the Soho factory (1798). The central view of the English economy at the end of the eighteenth century is one of the steam engine leading and quickening the pace, harnessing itself to machines in a hundred industries, luring textile works from water to steam power (1785 f.), changing the countryside, invading the towns, darkening the sky with coal dust and fumes, and hiding in the bowels of ships to give new force to England's mastery of the seas.

Two other elements were needed to make the revolution complete: factories and capital. The components—fuel, power, materials, machines, and men—could co-operate best when brought together in one building or plant, in one organization and discipline, under one head. There had been factories before; now, as the widened market called for regular and large-scale production, they multiplied in number and size, and "the factory system" became one name for the new order in industry. And as industrial machinery and plants became more costly, the men and institutions that could collect or furnish capital rose to power, the banks surmounted the factories, and the entire complex took the name of capitalism—an economy dominated by the providers of capital. Now, with every stimulus to invention and competition, with enterprise increasingly freed from guild restrictions and legislative barriers, the Industrial Revolution was ready to remake the face and sky and soul of Britain.

III. CONDITIONS

Both employer and employee had to change their habits, skills, and relations. The employer, dealing with ever more men, and in a faster turnover, lost intimacy with them, and had to think of them not as acquaintances engaged in a common task, but as particles in a process that would be judged by profits alone. Most artisans, before 1760, worked in guild shops or at home, where the hours of labor were not inflexible, and intervals of rest might be allowed; and in an earlier age there had been holydays in which all gainful labor was forbidden by the Church. We must not idealize the condition of the common man before the Industrial Revolution; nevertheless we may say that the hardships to which he was subjected were such as had tradition, habituation, and in many cases the open air to soften them. As industrialization advanced, the hardships of the employee were mitigated by shorter hours, higher wages, and wider access to the increasing flow of goods from the machines. But the half century of transition from craft and home to factory, after 1760, was for the laborers of England one of inhuman subjection sometimes worse than slavery.

Most factories in that period required twelve to fourteen hours of work per day six days a week.[18] Employers argued that the laborer had to be kept for long hours because he could not be relied upon to report regularly: many workers drank too heavily on Sunday to come in on Monday; some others, after working for four days, stayed home the next three. Adam Smith explained that "excessive application during four days of the week is frequently the real cause of the idleness of the other three"; he warned that prolongation or high speed of work might lead to physical or mental breakdown; and he added that "the man who works so moderately as to be able to work constantly not only preserves his health the longest, but in the course of the year, executes the greatest quantity of work."[19]

Real wages, of course, can be estimated only in connection with prices. In 1770 a four-pound loaf of bread in Nottingham cost about sixpence, a pound of cheese or pork fourpence, a pound of butter sevenpence. Adam Smith, toward 1773, calculated the average wage of London workers at 10 shillings, in smaller centers 7 shillings, in Edinburgh 5 shillings.[20] Arthur Young, about 1770, reported the weekly wages of English industrial workers as varying geographically from six shillings sixpence to 11 shillings. Wages were evidently much lower in relation to prices than now, but some employers added fuel or rent to the wages, and some employees gave part of their time to agricultural work. After 1793, when England began her long war with Revolutionary France, prices rose much faster than wages, and poverty became desperate.

Many eighteenth-century economists recommended low wages as a stimulus to steady work. Even Arthur Young, who was disturbed by the poverty that he saw in some districts of France, declared: "Everyone but an idiot knows that the lower classes must be kept poor, or they will never be industrious."[21] Or, as one J. Smith put it:

> It is a fact well known to those who are conversant in this matter, that scarcity, to a certain degree, promotes industry, and that the manufacturer [i.e., manual worker] who can subsist on three days' work, will be idle and drunk the remainder of the week. . . . Upon the whole we can fairly aver that a reduction of wages in the woolen manufacture would be a national blessing, and no real injury to the poor. By this means we might keep our trade, uphold our rents [revenues], and reform the people into the bargain.[22]

Women and children were employed in the factories, usually for unskilled operations. Some skilled women weavers made as much as their men, but the usual earnings of factory women averaged three shillings sixpence—rarely more than half the wage of men.[23] Textile mills alone, in 1788, employed 59,000 women and 48,000 children.[24] Sir Robert Peel had over a thousand children in his Lancashire factories.[25] Child labor was no new practice in Europe; it had been taken for granted on the farms and in domestic industry. Since universal education was frowned upon by conservatives as leading to a surplus of scholars and a dearth of manual laborers, very few Englishmen in the eighteenth century saw any evil in children going to work instead of to school. When machines were simple enough to be tended by children, factory owners welcomed boys and girls five years old or more. Parish authorities, resenting the cost of supporting orphans or pauper children, gladly farmed them out to industrialists, sometimes in lots of fifty, eighty, or a hundred; in several cases they stipulated that the employer should take one idiot to every twenty children.[26] The usual working day for child laborers was from ten to fourteen hours. They were often housed in groups, and in some factories they worked in twelve-hour shifts, so that the machines rarely stopped and the beds were seldom unoccupied. Discipline was maintained by blows or kicks. Disease found defenseless victims in these factory apprentices; many were deformed by their labor, or were maimed by accidents; some killed themselves. A few men were delicate enough to condemn such child labor; however, it diminished not because men became more humane but because machines became more complex.

Children, women, and men were subjected in the factories to conditions and disciplines not known to them before. The buildings were often of hasty or flimsy construction, assuring many accidents and much disease. Rules were severe, and violations of them were punished by fines that might forfeit the wages of a day.[27] Employers argued that the proper care of the machinery, the necessity of co-ordinating different operations, and the lax habits of a population not accustomed to regularity or speed required a rigorous discipline if confusion and waste were not to cancel profits and to price the product out of the market at home or abroad. The discipline was endured because an unemployed artisan faced hunger and cold for himself and his family, and the employee knew that the unemployed were eager for his job. Hence it was to the advantage of the employer to have a pool of unemployment from which to take replacements for workers disabled, dissatisfied, or dismissed. Even the well-behaved and competent employee faced dismissal when "overproduction" saturated the available market beyond its buying power, or when peace put an end to the blessed willingness of armies to order more and more goods and to destroy them as rapidly as possible.

Under the guild system the workers were protected by guild or municipal ordinances, but in the new industrialism they had little protection by the law, or none at all. The propaganda of the physiocrats for leaving the economy free from regulation had made headway in England as in France; the employers convinced Parliament that they could not continue their operations, or meet foreign competition, unless wages were governed by the laws of supply and demand. In village mills the justices of the peace retained some control over wages; in the factories, after 1757, they had none.[28] The upper and middle classes saw no reason for interfering with the captains of industry; the swelling flood of exports was conquering new markets for British trade; and Englishmen who could pay were pleased with the abundance of manufactured goods.

But the workers did not share in this prosperity. Despite the multiplication of goods by the machines they tended, they themselves remained as poor in 1800 as they had been a century before.[29] They no longer owned the tools of their trade, they had little part in designing the product, they took no profit from the widening of the market they fed. They added to their poverty by continuing the high fertility that had paid living dividends on the farm; they found in drink and sex their chief consolation, and their women were still rated by the number of children they bore. Pauperism spread; the expenditure for poor relief rose from £600,000 in 1742 to £2,000,000 in 1784.[30] The growth of housing could not keep up with the immigration or multiplication of industrial workers; these had often to live in tumble-down dwellings that crowded one another in dismal and narrow streets. Some laborers lived in cellars, whose dampness added to the causes of disease. By 1800 all the larger towns had developed slums in which living conditions were worse than anything known in the previous history of England.

The workers tried to better their lot by riots, strikes, and organization. They attacked the inventions that threatened them with unemployment or drudgery. Parliament in 1769 made the destruction of machinery a capital crime.[31] Nevertheless in 1779 the workers in Lancashire factories formed themselves into a mob that grew from five hundred to eight thousand men; they collected firearms and ammunition, melted their pewter dishes to make bullets, and swore to demolish every machine in England. At Bolton they completely wrecked a factory and its equipment; at Altham they took by storm the textile factory of Robert Peel (father of Sir Robert the minister), and smashed its costly equipment. They were on their way to attack the plant of Arkwright at Cromford when troops sent from Liverpool came up with them, whereupon they fled in a rout. Some of them were caught and were sentenced to be hanged. The justices of the peace explained that "destroying machines in this country would only be the means of transferring them to other countries, . . . to the detriment of the trade of Britain."[32] An anonymous "Friend of the Poor" bade the workers be more patient: "All improvements by machines do at first produce some difficulties to some particular persons. . . . Was not the first effect of the printing press to deprive many copyists of their occupation?"[33]

The law forbade the formation of labor unions for collective bargaining; however, "journeymen's associations" existed, some dating from the seventeenth century. In the eighteenth they were numerous, especially among textile workers. They were primarily social clubs or mutual-benefit societies, but as the century advanced they became more aggressive; and sometimes, when Parliament rejected their petitions, they organized strikes. In 1767–68, for example, there were strikes of sailors, weavers, hatters, tailors, glass grinders; and several of these walkouts were accompanied by armed violence on both sides.[34] Adam Smith summarized the results to 1776:

> It is not difficult to foresee which of the two parties must, upon all ordinary occasions, have the advantage in the dispute, and force the other into compliance with their terms. The masters, being fewer in number, can combine much more easily, and the law . . . does not prohibit their combinations, while it prohibits those of the workmen. We have no acts of Parliament against combining to lower the price [wages] of work, but many against combining to raise it. In all such disputes the masters can hold out much longer. . . . Many workmen could not subsist a week, few could subsist a month, and scarce any a year, without employment.[35]

The employers had their way, both in the factories and in Parliament; in 1799 the Commons declared illegal any associations aiming to secure higher wages, to alter the hours of work, or to decrease the quantity of work required of the workers. Employees entering into such combinations were punishable by imprisonment, and informers against such men were to be indemnified.[36] The triumph of the employers was complete.

IV. CONSEQUENCES

The results of the Industrial Revolution were almost everything that followed in England, barring literature and art; they could not be adequately described without writing a history of the last two centuries. We must note merely the peaks of the continuing and unfinished process of change.

1. The transformation of industry itself by the proliferation of inventions and machines—a process so manifold that our present ways of producing and distributing goods differ more from those of 1800 than these did from the methods prevalent two thousand years before.

2. The passage of the economy from regulated guilds and home industry to a regime of capital investment and free enterprise. Adam Smith was the British voice of the new system; Pitt II gave it governmental sanction in 1796.

3. The industrialization of agriculture—the replacement of small farms by large tracts of land capitalistically managed, using machinery, chemistry, and mechanical power on a large scale to grow food and fibers for a national or an international market—goes on today. The family-tilled farm joins the guild among the casualties of the Industrial Revolution.

4. The stimulation, application, and diffusion of science. The primary encouragement was to practical research, but studies in pure science led to immense practical results; so abstract research too was financed, and science became the distinctive feature of modern, as religion had been of medieval, life.

5. The Industrial Revolution (and not Napoleon, as Pitt II expected) re-

made the map of the world by assuring for 150 years the British control of the seas and the most profitable colonies. It furthered imperialism by leading England—and, later, other industrial states—to conquer foreign areas which could provide raw materials, markets, or facilities for commerce or war. It compelled agricultural nations to industrialize and militarize themselves in order to obtain or maintain their freedom; and it created economic, political, or military interrelations that made independence imaginary and interdependence real.

6. It changed England in character and culture by multiplying its population, industrializing half of it, shifting it northward and westward to towns near deposits of coal or iron, or near waterways or the sea; so grew Leeds, Sheffield, Newcastle, Manchester, Birmingham, Liverpool, Bristol . . . The Industrial Revolution transformed large expanses of England, and of other industrialized countries, into blotches of land fuming with factories, choking with gases and dust; and it deposited its human slag into reeking and hopeless slums.

7. It mechanized, extended, and depersonalized war, and vastly improved man's ability to destroy or kill.

8. It compelled better and faster communication and transportation. Thereby it made possible greater industrial combinations, and the government of larger areas from one capital.

9. It generated democracy by raising the business class to predominant wealth, and, in gradual consequence, to political supremacy. To effect and protect this epochal shift of power, the new class enlisted the support of an increasing segment of the masses, confident that these could be kept in line by control of the means of information and indoctrination. Despite this control, the people of industrial states became the best-informed publics in modern history.

10. Since the developing Industrial Revolution required ever more education in workers and managers, the new class financed schools, libraries, and universities on a scale hardly dreamed of before. The aim was to train technical intelligence; the by-product was an unprecedented extension of secular intelligence.

11. The new economy spread goods and comforts among a far greater proportion of the population than any previous system, for it could sustain its ever-rising productivity only by ever-widening purchasing power in the people.

12. It sharpened the urban mind, but dulled the aesthetic sense; many cities became depressingly ugly, and at last art itself renounced the pursuit of beauty. The dethronement of the aristocracy removed a repository and court of standards and tastes, and lowered the level of literature and art.

13. The Industrial Revolution raised the importance and status of economics, and led to the economic interpretation of history. It habituated men to think in terms of physical cause and effect, and led to mechanistic theories in biology—the attempt to explain all the processes of life as mechanical operations.

14. These developments in science, and similar tendencies in philosophy, combined with urban conditions and expanding wealth to weaken religious belief.

15. The Industrial Revolution transformed morality. It did not change the nature of man, but it gave new powers and opportunities to old instincts primitively useful, socially troublesome. It emphasized the profit motive to a point where it seemed to encourage and intensify the natural selfishness of man. The unsocial instincts had been checked by parental authority, by moral instruction in the schools, and by religious indoctrination. The Industrial Revolution weakened all these checks. In the agricultural regime the family was the unit of economic production as well as of racial continuance and social order; it worked together on the land under the discipline of the parents and the seasons; it taught co-operation and molded character. Industrialism made the individual and the company the units of production; the parents and the family lost the economic basis of their authority and moral function. As child labor became unprofitable in the cities, children ceased to be economic assets; birth control spread, most among the more intelligent, least among the less, with unexpected results to ethnic relations and theocratic power. As family limitation, and mechanical devices, freed woman from maternal cares and domestic chores, she was drawn into factories and offices; emancipation was industrialization. As the sons took longer to reach economic self-support, the lengthened interval between biological and economic maturity made premarital continence more difficult, and broke down the moral code that early economic maturity, early marriage, and religious sanctions had made possible on the farm. Industrial societies found themselves drifting in an amoral interregnum between a moral code that was dying and a new one still unformed.

The Industrial Revolution is still proceeding, and it is beyond the capacity of one mind to comprehend it in all its facets, or to pass moral judgment upon its results. It has begotten new quantities and varieties of crime, and it has inspired scientists with all the heroic dedication of missionaries and nuns. It has produced ugly buildings, dismal streets, and squalid slums, but these were not derived from its essence, which is to replace human labor with mechanical power. It is already attacking its own evils, for it has found that slums cost more than education, and that the reduction of poverty enriches the rich. Functional architecture and mechanical excellence—as in a bridge—can produce a beauty that mates science with art. Beauty becomes profitable, and industrial design takes its place among the arts and embellishments of life.

CHAPTER XXVIII

The Political Drama

1756–92

I. THE POLITICAL STRUCTURE

THE Industrial Revolution was the most basic process, the political struggle was the most exciting drama, of the second half of the eighteenth century in England. Now the giants of English oratory—Chatham, Burke, Fox, and Sheridan—made the House of Commons the stage of bitter and momentous conflicts between Parliament and the king, between Parliament and the people, between England and America, between the conscience of England and the English rulers of India, and between England and the French Revolution. The political structure was the frame and machinery of the play.

The government of Great Britain was a constitutional monarchy in the sense that the king implicitly agreed to rule according to existing laws and traditional usages, and to make no new laws without the consent of Parliament. The constitution was an accumulation of precedents, not a document, with two exceptions. One was the Magna Carta signed by King John in 1215. The other arose when the Westminster Convention in 1689, offering the crown of England to William of Orange and Mary his wife, accompanied the offer with an "Act Declaring the Rights and Liberties of the Subject, and Settling the Succession of the Crown." This "Bill of Rights," as brevity called it, asserted that the "power of suspending of laws or the execution of laws by regal authority without consent of Parliament is illegal"; that "levying money for or to the use of the Crown, by pretense of prerogative, without grant of Parliament . . . is illegal"; and it added: "Having therefore an entire confidence that . . . the Prince of Orange will . . . preserve them [the Parliament] from the violation of their rights which they have here asserted, and from all other attempts upon their religion, rights and liberties, the . . . Lords Spiritual and Temporal and Commons . . . do resolve that William and Mary, Prince and Princess of Orange, be and be declared King and Queen of England, France and Ireland." In accepting the throne William III and Mary II implicitly accepted the limitations which the proud and powerful aristocracy of England, by this declaration, placed upon the authority of the king. When, by a later "Act of Settlement" (1701), and on certain conditions, Parliament offered the throne to the Hanoverian "Princess Sophia and the heirs of her body being Protestants," it assumed that she and those heirs, by accepting the crown, agreed to a Bill of Rights that took from them all power to make laws except by consent of Parliament. While nearly all other European states were, till 1789, ruled by absolute monarchs who made and unmade laws, England had a constitutional government that was praised by philosophers and envied by half the world.

The census of 1801[1] estimated the population of Great Britain at nine million souls, divided into the following classes:

1. At the top, 287 temporal (secular) peers and peeresses, as heads of families totaling some 7,175 persons. Within this class there were ranks in descending order: princes of the [royal] blood, dukes, marquesses, earls, viscounts, and barons. These titles carried down generation after generation to the eldest son.

2. Twenty-six bishops—the "spiritual lords." These, with the 287 temporal lords, were entitled to sit in the House of Lords. Together these 313 families constituted the nobility proper; to all of them except dukes and princes the appellation "lord" could be properly applied. A less formal and nontransmissible nobility could be acquired by appointment to the higher offices in the administration, the army or the navy; but usually these appointments went to persons already ennobled.

3. Some 540 baronets, and their wives, entitled to prefix "Sir" and "Lady" to their Christian names, and to transmit these titles.

4. Some 350 knights, and their wives, entitled to the same prefixes, but not to transmit them.

5. Some six thousand (e)squires—the "gentry," or most numerous class of landowners. The baronets, knights, and squires, and their wives, constituted the "lesser nobility," and were generally included with their superiors in the "aristocracy."

6. Some twenty thousand "gentlemen" or "ladies" living on income without manual work, having a coat of arms, and assumed to be of "gentle" birth—i.e., born in the *gens*, or group of old and accepted families.

7. Below all these came the remainder of the population: the lower clergy, civil servants, businessmen, farmers, shopkeepers, artisans, laborers, soldiers, and sailors; also some 1,040,000 "paupers" receiving public relief, and about 222,000 "vagrants, gypsies, rogues, thieves, swindlers, counterfeiters of base money, in or out of prison, and common prostitutes."[2]

The aristocracy, with only occasional resistance, dominated the government by its wealth (the 287 peers received twenty-nine per cent of the national income in 1801[3]), by its prominence in high civil or military posts, by the prestige of ancient rank, and by its control of parliamentary elections and legislation. Electorally, England was divided into forty counties (rural districts) and 203 boroughs (townships). Excluded from the franchise were women, paupers, convicted criminals, Roman Catholics, Quakers, Jews, agnostics, and others who could not swear allegiance to the authority and doctrines of the Church of England. In the counties only those Protestant landowners who paid forty shillings annual tax were entitled to vote for Parliament; these totaled about 160,000. As voting was public, very few voters dared support any candidate other than the one nominated by the principal landlords of the county; hence relatively few voters bothered to vote, and many elections were decided by arrangement among the leaders without any balloting at all. The major landowners thought it only just that, having so much at stake in the conduct of the government and the fate of the nation, their representation in Parliament should be proportionate to their property; and most of the lesser landlords agreed.

The boroughs displayed a confusing variety of electoral patterns. In the city of Westminster (now central London) there were about nine thousand voters; in the city of London as then constituted there were six thousand; in Bristol, five thousand; only twenty-two boroughs had more than a thousand.[4] In twelve boroughs all adult males could vote; in most of the others only property holders; in several the candidates were chosen by the municipal "corporation"—which has been defined as "an urban oligarchy of attorneys, merchants, brokers, and brewers entrenched in a self-electing corporation which had by royal charter exclusive control over the town's property."[5] Some of these corporations gave their vote to the candidate(s) whose sponsor(s) paid the highest price. In 1761 the borough of Sudbury openly advertised its vote for sale; and in the following election the corporation of Oxford formally offered to re-elect its M.P.s if they would pay the corporation's debts.[6] In some boroughs the privilege of choosing the candidate belonged by custom to specific individuals or families not necessarily residing there; so Lord Camelford boasted that if he wished he could elect his Negro butler to Parliament.[7] Such "pocket boroughs" were sometimes sold like merchandise; Lord Egremont bought Midhurst for £40,000.[8] In some "rotten boroughs" a handful of voters could send one or more representatives to Parliament, while the city of London returned only four. Even when the franchise was almost universal the election was usually determined by bribery, by violence, or by keeping a refractory voter too intoxicated to vote.[9] By various means 111 "patrons" controlled the elections in 205 boroughs.[10] There were some 85,000 voters in the boroughs, 160,000 in the counties—245,000 in all.

From such varied elections came the 558 members of the House of Commons in 1761. Scotland sent forty-five, the counties of England and Wales ninety-four, the boroughs 415, the two universities two each. The House of Lords then contained 224 peers, temporal or spiritual. "Parliamentary privilege" included the right of Parliament to pass on bills proposed for legislation; to levy taxes and thereby hold the "power of the purse"; to judge the credentials of persons claiming admission to it; to penalize—with imprisonment if it so wished—any injury to its members or any disobedience to its rules; and to enjoy full freedom of speech, including immunity from punishment for words uttered in Parliament.

The division of members into Tories or Whigs had by 1761 lost nearly all significance; the real division was between supporters and opponents of the current "government," or ministry, or of the king. By and large the Tories protected the landed interest; the Whigs were willing now and then to consider the desires of the business class; otherwise both Tories and Whigs were equally conservative. Neither party legislated for the benefit of the masses.

No bill could become law unless approved by both houses of Parliament and signed by the king. He possessed the "royal prerogative"—i.e., powers, privileges, and immunities accorded him by English custom and law. He had military powers: he was supreme commander of the army and navy; he could declare war, but needed parliamentary appropriations to wage it; he could negotiate treaties and make peace. He had some legislative rights: he could withhold assent from a bill passed by Parliament—but it could bring him to terms by its power of the purse, and so he never exercised that right after 1714; he could add to the laws by proclamation or by orders in council, but he could not alter the common law, or create a new offense; for the colonies he could legislate as he pleased. He had executive powers: he alone could summon, prorogue, or dissolve Parliament; he appointed the ministers who directed policy and administration. Part of the furor in the first decades (1760–82) of George III's sixty-year reign concerned the extent of the royal prerogative in choosing ministers and determining policy.

The right of the king to legislate was narrowly limited, and the measures proposed to Parliament by his ministers could be made into law only by persuading both houses of Parliament to accept them. This was done by political bargains, by the promise or withholding of posts or pensions, or by bribery. (In 1770 over 190 members of the House of Commons held appointive places in the administration.) The pounds and plums required for these operations were mostly supplied by the king's "civil list"—an account of his expenses for himself and his family (the "privy purse"), for his houses and servants, for salaries paid by him, and for pensions awarded. Parliament allowed George III £800,000 annually for this civil list; he often exceeded this in his outlays; in 1769 Parliament added £513,511, and in 1777 £618,-340, to pay the royal debts. Part of the king's money was used to buy votes in parliamentary elections;[11] part was used to buy votes in Parliament itself. Funds voted by Parliament for secret service were in many cases remitted to Parliament in bribes. When we add to this royal traffic the money spent in elections or legislation by "nabobs" returning to England with wealth gleaned in India, or by businessmen seeking governmental contracts or escape from governmental interference, we get a picture of political corruption hardly rivaled west of the Oder, and unpleasantly instructive on the nature of man.

Some minor details of the British system should be noted. Taxes were levied upon all landowners, great or small; perhaps this entered into the respect that the commonalty paid to the peerage. No standing army—only a militia—was allowed by Parliament; this was a minor factor in England's superior prosperity at a time when France was supporting a permanent army of 180,000 men, Prussia 190,000, Russia 224,000. In wartime, however, the armed forces were rigorously recruited by enlistment and impressment; the violations of personal liberty by this custom, and the brutalizing cruelties of army and navy life, were dark shadows on the English scene.

Blackstone felt (c. 1765) that the political structure of England was the best the nature and education of men permitted at that time. He quoted the classical opinion that the best form of government would be one that combined monarchy, aristocracy, and democracy, and he found all these "well and happily united" in the British constitution.

> For as with us the executive power of the laws is lodged in a single person, they have all the advantages of strength and dispatch that are to be found in the most absolute monarchy; and as the legislature of the kingdom is entrusted to three distinct powers entirely independent of each other; first the king; secondly, the lords spiritual and temporal, which is an aristocratical assembly of persons selected for their piety, their birth, their wisdom, their valor, or their property; and thirdly, the House of Commons, freely chosen by the people among themselves, which makes it a kind of democracy; as this aggregate body, activated by different springs and attentive to different interests, . . . has the supreme disposal of everything, there can no inconvenience be attempted by either of the three branches but will be withstood by the other two; each branch being armed with a negative power sufficient to repel any innovation which it shall think inexpedient or dangerous. Here, then, is lodged the sovereignty of the British constitution, and lodged as beneficially as is possible for society.[12]

We may smile at the patriotic conservatism of an eminent jurist viewing the matter from a comfortable eminence; but very probably his judgment would have been ratified by ninety per cent of the English people under George III.

II. THE PROTAGONISTS

The persons of the drama were among the most famous in English history. At the top was George III, who held the throne for the fateful years (1760–1820) that saw England through the American and French Revolutions and the Napoleonic Wars. He was the first of the Hanoverian monarchs to be born in England, to think of himself as an Englishman, and to take an absorbing interest in English affairs. He was the grandson of George II, and son of the unruly Frederick Louis, Prince of Wales, who had died in 1751. The future George III was then twelve years old. His mother, Princess Augusta of Saxe-Gotha, frightened by the "ill-educated and vicious young people of quality"[13] whom she met, kept him in quarantine from such company, and brought him up—one of nine children—in an aseptic isolation from the games, joys, turmoil, and thought of his peers and his time. He grew up timid, lethargic, pious, poorly educated, and unhappy. "If I ever have a son," he told his censorious mother, "I will not make him so unhappy as you make me."[14] She transmitted to him her scorn of his grandfather for having tolerated the supremacy of Parliament; repeatedly she bade him, "George, be a king!"—recapture active leadership of the government. A tradition often questioned credits the youth with being influenced by Bolingbroke's *Idea of a Patriot King* (1749), which exhorted rulers "to govern as well as to reign," and (while "letting Parliament retain the powers it possessed") to initiate measures for improving English life.[15] One of George's teachers, Lord Waldegrave, described him in 1758 as "strictly honest, but wants that frank and open behavior which makes honesty ami-

able. . . . He does not want resolution, but it is mixed with too much obstinacy. . . . He has a kind of unhappiness in his temper, which . . . will be a
source of frequent anxiety."[16] These qualities remained with him to the end
of his sanity.

After the death of George's father the widow formed a close friendship
with John Stuart, Earl of Bute, groom of the stole in the princely household.
Bute was thirty-eight in 1751, and was already fifteen years married to Mary
Wortley Montagu, daughter of the famous Lady Mary of that name. In the
last years before George became king he accepted Bute as his chief preceptor and confidant. He admired the Scot's learning and integrity, gratefully
received his advice, and was encouraged by him to prepare for aggressive
leadership in government. When the royal youth thought of proposing marriage to the fifteen-year-old beauty Lady Sarah Lennox, he yielded sadly
but affectionately to Bute's admonition that he must marry some foreign
princess who would help to cement a useful political alliance. "I surrender
my future into your hands," he wrote, "and will keep my thoughts even
from the dear object of my love, grieve in silence, and never trouble you
more with this unhappy tale; for if I must either lose my friend or my love I
will give up the latter, for I esteem your friendship above every earthly
joy."[17] George took Bute with him when he ascended the throne.

His reign was one of the most calamitous in England's history, and he
shared in the blame. Yet he himself was emphatically a Christian and usually a gentleman. He accepted the theology of the Anglican Church, observed its rites with unostentatious devotion, and rebuked a court preacher
who praised him in a sermon. He imitated his political enemies in the use of
bribery, and bettered their instruction, but he was a paragon of virtue in
his private life. In a generation noted for sexual license he gave to England
an example of husbandly fidelity that quietly contrasted with the adulteries
of his predecessors and the irregularities of his brothers and sons. He was the
soul of kindness in everything but religion and politics. Though lavish in
gifts, he was a man of simple habits and tastes. He forbade gambling at his
court. He toiled resolutely at government, attending to minute details, and
sending messages of instruction to his aides and ministers a dozen times a day.
He was no somber Puritan: he liked the theater, music, and the dance. He
was not wanting in courage: he fought his political foes tenaciously for
half a century; he faced a violent mob bravely in 1780, and kept his com-
posure in two attempts upon his life. He frankly recognized the defects of
his education; to the end he remained relatively innocent of literature, science, and philosophy. If he was a bit weak in the mind it may have been due
to some quirk in the genes or some negligence in his teachers, as well as to
the thousand strains that hedge a king.

One of George's faults was a suspicious jealousy of ability and independence. He could never forgive William Pitt I for conscious pre-eminence
in political vision and understanding, penetration of judgment, force and eloquence of speech. We have seen elsewhere[18] the career of this extraordinary

man from his entry into Parliament (1735) to his triumph in the Seven Years' War. He could be arrogant and obstinate—far more so than George III; he felt himself to be the proper custodian of the empire that had been created under his leadership, and when the king in name met the king in deed there followed a duel for the throne. Pitt was personally honest, untouched by the bribery that flourished around him, but he thought of politics purely in terms of national power, and allowed no sentiment of humanity to divert his resolve to make England supreme. He was called "the Great Commoner" because he was the greatest man in the House of Commons, not because he thought of improving the lot of the commonalty; however, he rose to defend Americans and the people of India against oppression by Englishmen. Like the King he resented criticism, and was "unapt to forget or to forgive."[19] He would not serve the King unless he could rule him; he resigned from the ministry (1761) when George III insisted on violating England's compact with Frederick and making a separate peace with France. If in the end he was defeated it was by no other foe than gout.

Pitt's influence on English politics was matched by Edmund Burke's influence on English thought. Pitt disappeared from the scene in 1778; Burke appeared on it in 1761, and held the attention of educated England, intermittently, till 1794. The fact that he was born in Dublin (1729), the son of an attorney, may have handicapped him in his struggle for political office and power; he was not an Englishman except by adoption, and not a member of any aristocracy except that of the mind. The fact that his mother and sister were Catholics must have entered into his lifelong sympathy for the Catholics of Ireland and England, and his persistent emphasis upon religion as an indispensable bulwark of morality and the state. He received his formal education at a Quaker school in Ballitore, and at Trinity College, Dublin. He learned enough Latin to admire Cicero's orations and to make them the foundation of his own forensic style.

In 1750 he passed to England to study law at the Middle Temple. Later he praised law as "a science which does more to quicken and invigorate the understanding than all the other kinds of learning put together," but he thought it "not apt, except in persons very happily born, to open and to liberalize the mind exactly in the same proportion."[20] About 1775 his father withdrew Edmund's allowance on the ground that he was neglecting his legal studies for other pursuits. Apparently Edmund had developed a taste for literature, and was frequenting the theaters and the debating clubs of London. A legend arose that he fell in love with the famous actress Peg Woffington. He wrote to a friend in 1757: "I have broken all rules; I have neglected all decorum"; and he described his "manner of life" as "chequered with various designs; sometimes in London, sometimes in remote parts of the country, sometimes in France, and shortly, please God, to be in America." Otherwise we know nothing about Burke in those experimental years, except that in 1756, in uncertain sequence, he published two remarkable books, and married.

One book was entitled *A Vindication of Natural Society, or a View of the Miseries and Evils Arising to Mankind from Every Species of Artificial Society. A Letter to Lord ——. By a late Noble Writer.* The essay, some forty-five pages long, is on its face a vigorous condemnation of all government, far more anarchistic than Rousseau's *Discourse on the Origin of Inequality,* which had appeared only a year before. Burke defined "natural society" as "society founded in natural appetites and instincts, and not in any positive institution."[21] "The development of laws was a degeneration."[22] History is a record of butchery, treachery, and war;[23] and "political society is justly charged with much the greater part of this destruction."[24] All governments follow the Machiavellian principles, reject all moral restraints, and give the citizens a demoralizing example of greed, deceit, robbery, and homicide.[25] Democracy in Athens and Rome brought no cure for the evils of government, for it soon became dictatorship through the ability of demagogues to win admiration from gullible majorities. Law is injustice codified; it protects the idle rich against the exploited poor,[26] and adds a new evil—lawyers.[27] "Political society has made the many the property of the few."[28] Look at the condition of the miners of England, and consider whether such misery could have existed in a natural society—i.e., before the making of laws. — Should we nevertheless accept the state, like the religion that upholds it, as being made necessary by the nature of man? Not at all.

> If we are resolved to submit our reason and our liberty to civil usurpation, we have nothing to do but to conform as quietly as we can to the vulgar [popular] notions which are connected with this, and take up the theology of the vulgar as well as their politics. But if we think this necessity rather imaginary than real, we shall renounce their dreams of society together with their visions of religion, and vindicate ourselves into perfect liberty.[29]

This has the bold ring and angry sincerity of a young radical, a youth religious in spirit but rejecting the established theology, and sensitive to the poverty and degradation that he had seen in England; a talent conscious of itself but as yet without place and standing in the stream of the world. Every alert youngster passes through this stage on his way to position, possessions, and such frightened conservatism as we shall find in Burke's *Reflections on the Revolution in France.* We note that the author of the *Vindication* covered his tracks with anonymity, even to playing dead. Nearly all readers, including William Warburton and the Earl of Chesterfield, understood the tract as a genuine attack upon current evils,[30] and many ascribed it to Viscount Bolingbroke, who, having died in 1751, was "a late Noble Writer." Nine years after publishing the essay Burke ran for election to Parliament. Fearing that his youthful ebullition would be held against him, he reprinted it in 1765 with a preface that said in part: "The design of the following little piece was to show that . . . the same [literary] engines which were employed for the destruction of religion might be employed with equal success for the subversion of government."[31] Most biographers of Burke have accepted this explanation as sincere; we cannot join them, but we can understand the effort of a political candidate to protect himself against popular prejudice. Which of us would have a future if his past were known?

Just as eloquent as the *Vindication*, and much subtler, was Burke's other publication in 1756: *A Philosophical Enquiry into the Origin of the Sublime and Beautiful;* to which in a second edition he added *A Discourse on Taste.* We must admire the courage of the twenty-seven-year-old youth who pursued these elusive subjects a full decade before Lessing's *Laokoon.* He may have taken a lead from the opening of Book II of Lucretius' *De rerum natura:* "Pleasant it is, when the winds are troubling the waters in a mighty sea, to witness from the land another's great toil; not because it is a delight to behold anyone's tribulation, but because it is sweet to see from what evils you yourself are free." So Burke wrote: "The passions which belong to self-preservation turn on pain and danger; they are simply painful when their causes immediately affect us; they are delightful when we have an idea of pain and danger without being actually in such circumstances. . . . Whatever excites this delight I call sublime." Secondarily, "all works of great labor, expense, and magnificence are sublime, . . . and all buildings of very great richness and splendor, . . . for in contemplating them the mind applies the ideas of the greatness of exertion necessary to produce such works, to the works themselves."[32] Gloom, darkness, mystery help to arouse a sense of sublimity; hence the care of medieval builders to let only dim and filtered light enter their cathedrals. Romantic fiction, as in Horace Walpole's *Castle of Otranto* (1764) or Ann Radcliffe's *Mysteries of Udolpho* (1794), profited from these ideas.

"Beauty," said Burke, "is a name I shall apply to all such qualities in things as induce in us a sense of affection and tenderness, or some other passion the most nearly resembling these."[33] He rejected the classical reduction of these qualities to harmony, unity, proportion, and symmetry; we all agree that the swan is beautiful, though its long neck and short tail are quite disproportionate to its body. Usually the beautiful is small (and thereby contrasts with the sublime). "I do not now recollect anything beautiful that is not smooth";[34] a broken or rugged surface, a sharp angle or sudden projection, will disturb us and limit our pleasure even in objects otherwise beautiful. "An air of robustness and strength is very prejudicial to beauty. An appearance of *delicacy*, and even of *fragility*, is almost essential to it."[35] Color adds to beauty, especially if it is varied and bright, but not glaring or strong. — Strange to say, Burke did not ask whether a woman is beautiful because she is small, smooth, delicate, and colorful, or whether these qualities seem beautiful because they remind us of woman, who is beautiful because she is desired.

In any case June Nugent was desirable, and Burke married her in this fecund year 1756. She was the daughter of an Irish physician; she was a Catholic, but she soon conformed to the Anglican worship. Her mild and gentle disposition soothed her husband's irascible temperament.

The impression made by the style, if not the arguments, of the *Vindication* and the *Enquiry* opened doors to Burke. The Marquis of Rockingham engaged him as secretary, despite the Duke of Newcastle's warning that

Burke was a wild Irishman, a Jacobite, a secret papist and Jesuit.[36] Late in 1765 Burke was elected to Parliament from the borough of Wendover through the influence of Lord Verney, "who owned it."[37] In the House of Commons the new member acquired the reputation of an eloquent, yet not persuasive, orator. His voice was harsh, his accent Hibernian, his gestures awkward, his jests occasionally coarse, his denunciations unduly passionate. Only in reading him did men perceive that he was creating literature as he spoke—by his command of the English language, his luminous descriptions, his range of knowledge and illustrations, his ability to bring philosophic perspective to the issues of the day. Perhaps these qualities were handicaps in the House. Some hearers, Goldsmith tells us, "loved to see him wind into his subject like a serpent,"[38] but many others were impatient with his excessive detail, his digressions into theory, his ornate declamations, his massive periodic sentences, his flights into literary elegance; they wanted practical considerations and immediate relevance; they praised his diction, but ignored his advice. So, when Boswell said that Burke was like a hawk, Johnson countered, "Yes, sir, but he catches nothing."[39] Almost to the end of his career he defended policies unpalatable to the people, the ministry, and the King. "I know," he said, "that the road I take is not the road to preferment."[40]

Apparently, during the years of his climb, he read much and judiciously. One contemporary described him as an encyclopedia, from whose stores everyone received instruction. Fox paid him an unmeasured compliment: "If he [Fox] were to put all the political information which he had learned from books, all which he had gained from science, and all which any knowledge of the world and its affairs had taught him, into one scale, and the improvement which he had derived from his right honorable friend's instruction and conversation were placed in the other, he should be at a loss to decide to which to give the preference."[41] Johnson, who usually administered praise in small doses, agreed with Fox: "You could not stand five minutes with that man beneath a shed while it rained, but you must be convinced you had been standing with the greatest man you had ever yet seen."[42]

Burke joined the Johnson-Reynolds circle about 1758. He rarely entered into debate with the invincible debater, probably fearing his own temper as well as Johnson's; but when he did, the Great Cham drew in his horns. When Johnson was sick, and someone mentioned Burke, the Doctor cried out, "That fellow calls forth all my powers; were I to see Burke now it would kill me."[43] Yet the two men agreed on almost all basic questions of politics, morals, and religion. They accepted the aristocratic rule of Britain, though both were commoners; they scorned democracy as the enthronement of mediocrity; they defended orthodox Christianity and the Established Church as irreplaceable bastions of morality and order. Only the revolt of the American colonies divided them. Johnson called himself a Tory, and denounced Whigs as criminals and fools; Burke called himself a Whig, and gave a stronger, better-reasoned defense of Tory principles than any other man in English history.

He seemed at times to uphold the most questionable elements of the existing order. He opposed changes in the rules for the election of members or the enactment of laws. He thought "rotten" or "pocket" boroughs forgivable, since they sent good men like himself to Parliament. Instead of widening the suffrage he would, "by lessening the number, add to the weight and independency, of our voters."[44] Nevertheless he espoused a hundred liberal causes. He advocated freedom of trade before Adam Smith, and attacked the slave trade before Wilberforce. He advised removing the political disabilities of Catholics, and supported the petition of the Dissenters for full civil rights. He tried to soften the barbarous severity of the penal code, and the handicaps of a soldier's life. He vindicated the freedom of the press though he himself had felt its sting. He stood up for Ireland, America, India in the face of chauvinistic majorities. He championed Parliament against the King with a candor and audacity that forfeited all chance of political office. We may debate his views and his motives, but we can never doubt his courage.

The last crusade of Burke's career—against the French Revolution—cost him the friendship of a man whom he had long admired and loved. Charles James Fox returned his affection and shared with him the dangers of battle in a dozen causes, but differed from him in almost every quality of mind and character except humanity and bravery. Burke was Irish, poor, conservative, religious, moral; Fox was English, rich, radical, and kept only so much religion as comported with gambling, drinking, mistresses, and the French Revolution. He was the third but favorite son of Henry Fox, who inherited one fortune, squandered it, married another, accumulated a third as paymaster of the forces, helped Bute to buy M.P.s, was rewarded by being created Baron Holland, and was denounced as "the public defaulter of unaccounted millions."[45] His wife, Caroline Lennox, was granddaughter of Charles II by Louise de Kéroualle, so that Charles James had in his veins the diluted blood of a rakish Stuart king and a Frenchwoman of complaisant morals. His very names were Stuart memories, and must have grated on Hanoverian ears.

Lady Holland tried to bring up her sons to integrity and responsibility, but Lord Holland indulged Charles in every humor, and inverted old maxims for him: "Never do today what you can put off till tomorrow, nor ever do yourself what you can get anyone else to do for you."[46] When the boy was barely fourteen his father took him from Eton College for a tour of Continental casinos and spas, and allowed him five guineas per night for play. The youth returned to Eton a confirmed gambler, and kept this up at Oxford. He found time to read much, both in classical and in English literature, but he left Oxford after two years to spend two years in travel. He learned French and Italian, lost £16,000 in Naples, visited Voltaire at Ferney, and received from him a list of books to enlighten him on Christian theology.[47] In 1768 the father bought a borough for him, and Charles took a seat in Parliament at the age of nineteen. This was quite illegal, but so many members were impressed by the youth's personal charm and presumptive wealth that no protest made itself heard. Two years later, through his father's influence, he was made a lord of the admiralty in the ministry of Lord North. In 1774 the father, the mother, and an elder son died, and Charles became the master of a large fortune.

His physical appearance in his mature years was as careless as his morals. His stockings were loosely tied, his coat and waistcoat were rumpled, his shirt was open at the neck, his face was puffed and ruddy with food and drink, and his swelling paunch, when he sat, threatened to tumble over his knees. When he fought a duel with William Adam he rejected the advice of his second to assume the customary sideways stance, for he said, "I am as thick one way as the other."[48] He took no pains to conceal his faults. It was common gossip that he proved to be an amiable victim of sharpers. Once (Gibbon tells us) he played for twenty-two hours at a sitting, and lost in that time £200,000. Fox remarked that the greatest pleasure in life, next to winning, was losing.[49] He kept a stable of racing horses, bet heavily on them, and (we are asked to believe) won more on them than he lost.[50]

Sometimes he was as careless of his political principles as of his morals and his dress; more than once he let his personal interests or animosity determine his course. He tended to indolence, and did not prepare his parliamentary speeches or measures with that care and study which distinguished Burke. He had few graces as an orator, and sought none; his addresses were often formless and repetitious, sometimes shocking the grammarians; he "threw himself into the middle of his sentences," said the scholar Richard Porson, "and left it to God Almighty to get him out again."[51] But he was gifted with such quickness of mind and power of memory that he became, by general consent, the ablest debater in the House. "Charles Fox," wrote Horace Walpole, "has tumbled old Saturn [Chatham] from the throne of oratory."[52]

Fox's contemporaries were lenient with his faults since these were so widely shared, and they almost unanimously testified to his virtues. Through most of his life after 1774 he followed liberal causes at reckless sacrifice of preferment and popularity. Burke, who scorned vice, nevertheless loved Fox because he saw that Fox was unselfishly devoted to social justice and human liberty. "He is a man made to be loved," said Burke, "of the most artless, open, candid, and benevolent disposition; disinterested in the extreme, of a temper mild and placable to a fault, without one drop of gall in his whole constitution."[53] Gibbon agreed: "Perhaps no human being was ever more perfectly exempt from the taint of malevolence, vanity, or falsehood."[54] Only George III was immune to that spontaneous charm.

Bound with Burke and Fox in leading the liberal factor of the Whigs was a second Irishman, Richard Brinsley Sheridan. His grandfather, Thomas Sheridan I, published translations from Greek and Latin, and an *Art of Punning* which may have infected the grandson. The father, Thomas Sheridan II, was by some ranked second only to Garrick as actor and theatrical manager. He married Frances Chamberlaine, a successful playwright and novelist. He received degrees from Dublin, Oxford, and Cambridge; lectured at Cambridge on education; was instrumental in getting Johnson a royal pension, and got one for himself. He wrote an entertaining *Life of Swift*, and dared to publish a *General Dictionary of the English Language* (1780) only twenty-five years after Johnson's. He helped his son manage Drury Lane Theatre, and saw him rise in romance, literature, and Parliament.

So Richard had wit and drama in his milieu, if not in his blood. Born in Dublin (1751), he was sent to Harrow at the age of eleven, stayed there six years, and acquired a good classical education; at twenty he echoed his grandfather by publishing translations from the Greek. In that year 1771, while living at Bath with his parents, he fell into raptures over the lovely face and voice of Elizabeth Ann Linley, seventeen, who sang in the concerts presented by her father, composer Thomas Linley. Those who have seen any of Gainsborough's portraits of her[55] will understand that Richard had no alternative but rapture. Neither had she, if we may believe his sister, who thought him irresistibly handsome and lovable. "His cheeks had the glow of health; his eyes the finest in the world. . . . A tender and affectionate heart. . . . The same playful fancy, the same sterling and innoxious wit, that was shown afterwards in his writings, cheered and delighted the family circle. I admired—I almost adored—him. I would most willingly have sacrificed my life for him."[56]

Elizabeth Ann had many suitors, including Richard's elder brother Charles. One of them, Major Mathews, rich but married, annoyed her to such aggravation that she took laudanum to kill herself. She recovered, but lost all desire for life until Richard's devotion revived her spirits. Mathews threatened to force her; half in fear, half in love, she eloped with Sheridan to France, married him (1772), and then took refuge in a convent near Lille while Richard returned to England to conciliate his father and hers. He fought two duels with Mathews; victor in the first, he spared Mathews' life; drunk in the second, he disarmed his adversary, allowed the duel to degenerate into a wrestling match, and returned to Bath smeared with blood, wine, and mud. His father disowned him, but Thomas Linley brought Elizabeth Ann back from France, and sanctioned her marriage (1773).

Too proud to let his wife support him by public singing, Richard, twenty-two, undertook to make a fortune by writing plays. On January 17, 1775, his first comedy, *The Rivals*, was produced at Covent Garden. It was poorly acted and poorly received; Sheridan secured a better actor for the leading role, and a second performance (January 28) began a series of dramatic successes that brought Sheridan fame and wealth. Soon all London was talking about Sir Anthony Absolute, Sir Lucius O'Trigger, and Miss Lydia Languish, and was imitating Mrs. Malaprop's mangling of words ("Forget this fellow, illiterate him quite from your memory",[57] "as headstrong as an allegory on the banks of the Nile.").[58] Sheridan had a mint of sallies in his brain, scattering them on every page, dowering lackeys with wit, and making fools talk like philosophers. Critics complained that the characters were not always consistent with their speech, and that the wit, crackling in every scene, bubbling in almost every mouth, dulled its point by excess; no matter; audiences relished the merriment, and relish it to this day.

Even greater was the success of *The Duenna*, which had its première at Covent Garden on November 2, 1775; it ran for seventy-five nights in its first season, breaking the record of sixty-three nights set by *The Beggar's Opera* in 1728. David Garrick, at the Drury Lane Theatre, was alarmed by this lively competition, but could find no better riposte than to revive *The Discovery*, a play by Sheridan's lately deceased mother. Flushed with success, Sheridan offered to buy Garrick's half share of the Drury Lane; Garrick, feeling his years, agreed for £35,000; Sheridan persuaded his father-in-law and a friend to contribute £10,000 each; he himself invested £1,300 in cash; the remainder he raised on a loan (1776). Two years later he gathered together another £35,000, took ownership of the theater with his partners, and assumed the management.

Many thought that his confidence had overreached itself, but Sheridan went on to another triumph by producing (May 8, 1777) *The School for Scandal*, the greatest dramatic success of the century. The author's father, who had been pouting ever since Richard's elopement five years before, was now reconciled with his son. After these victories there was a pause in Sheridan's ascent. The offerings at the Drury Lane proved unpopular, and the specter of bankruptcy frightened the partners. Sheridan saved the situation with a farce, *The Critic*, a satire of tragic dramas and dramatic pundits. However, his wonted dilatoriness intervened, and two days before the scheduled opening he had not yet written the final scene. By some ruse his father-in-law and others lured him to a room in the theater, gave him paper, pen, ink, and wine, bade him finish the play, and locked him in. He emerged with the desired denouement; it was rehearsed and found adequate; the première (October 29, 1779) was another smile of fortune for the ebullient Irishman.

He looked around for new worlds to conquer, and decided to enter Parliament. He paid the burgesses of Stafford five guineas for their vote, and in 1780 he took his seat in the House of Commons as an ardent liberal. He shared with Fox and Burke in prosecuting Warren Hastings, and in one brilliant day outshone them both. Meanwhile he lived with his accomplished wife in happiness and luxury, famed for his conversation, his wit, his exuberance, his kindness, and his debts. Lord Byron summed up the marvel: "Whatsoever Sheridan has done, or chooses to do, has been par excellence, always the *best* of its kind. He has written the best comedy, the best drama, . . . the best farce, . . . the best address [a *Monologue on Garrick*], and, to crown all, delivered the very best oration . . . ever conceived or heard in this country."[59] And he had won and kept the love of the loveliest woman in England.

Sheridan was all romance; it is hard to picture him in the same world and generation as William Pitt II, who recognized only reality, stood above sentiment, and ruled without eloquence. He was born (1759) at the height of his father's career; his mother was sister to George Grenville, chief minister 1763–65; he was nursed on politics, and grew up in the odor of Parliament. Frail and sickly in childhood, he was kept from the rigors and socializing contacts of "public" school; he was tutored at home under the careful super-vision of his father, who taught him elocution by making him recite Shake-speare or Milton every day. By the age of ten he was a classical scholar and had written a tragedy. At fourteen he was sent to Cambridge, soon fell ill, returned home; a year later he went again, and, being a peer's son, he was graduated as Master of Arts in 1776 without examination. He studied law at Lincoln's Inn, practiced law briefly, and was projected into Parliament at the age of twenty-one from a pocket borough controlled by Sir James Lowther. His maiden speech so well supported Burke's proposal for economic reforms that Burke called him "not a chip of the old block but the old block itself."[60]

Being a second son, he was allowed only £300 a year, with occasional help from his mother and uncles; these conditions encouraged a stoic sim-plicity in his conduct and character. He avoided marriage, having pledged himself indivisibly to the pursuit of power. He took no pleasure in gambling or the theater. Though he later used liquor in excess to dull his nerves after the tumult of politics, he earned a reputation for purity of life and incor-ruptibility of purpose; he could buy, but he could not be bought. He never sought wealth, and seldom made concessions to friendship; only an intimate few discovered, behind his cold aloofness and self-control, a friendly gaiety, even at times an affectionate tenderness.

Early in 1782, when Lord North's ministry was about to resign, "the boy," as some members condescendingly called Pitt, included in one of his speeches a rather unusual announcement: "For myself, I could not expect to form part of a new administration; but were my doing so within my reach, I feel myself bound to declare that I never would accept a subordinate posi-tion";[61] that is, he would accept no place lower than the six or seven seats that constituted what came to be called the cabinet. When the new ministry offered to appoint him vice-treasurer of Ireland at £5,000 a year, he de-clined, and continued to live on his £300. He was confident of advance-ment, and hoped to win it on his own merits; he worked hard, and became the best-informed man in the House on domestic politics, industry, and finance. A year after his proud pronouncement the King turned to him not merely to join but to head the government. No man before him had ever been chief minister at the age of twenty-four; and few ministers have left a deeper mark on English history.

III. THE KING VERSUS PARLIAMENT

George II completed his reign of thirty-three years with a decided distaste for English politics. "I am sick to death of all this foolish stuff, and wish with all my heart that the Devil may take all your bishops, and the Devil take your ministers, and the Devil take your Parliament, and the Devil take the whole island, provided I can get out of it and go to Hanover."[62] He found peace on October 25, 1760, and was buried in Westminster Abbey.

The accession of George III on the day of his grandfather's death was welcomed enthusiastically by nearly all Englishmen except a few who still hankered after the Stuarts. He was twenty-two, handsome, industrious, and modest. (He was the first English king since Henry VI to omit in his title a claim to the sovereignty over France.) In his first address to Parliament he added, to the text prepared for him by his ministers, words that neither of his Hanoverian predecessors could have spoken: "Born and educated in this country, I glory in the name of Briton." "The young King," wrote Horace Walpole, "has all the appearance of being amiable. There is great grace to temper much dignity, and extreme good nature, which breaks out on all occasions."[63] He added to his popularity by the proclamation that he issued on October 31 "for the encouragement of piety and virtue, and for preventing and punishing of vice, profaneness, and immorality." In 1761 he married Princess Charlotte Sophia of Mecklenburg-Strelitz; adjusting himself to her charmlessness, he begot fifteen children by her, and found no time for adultery. This was unprecedented for a Hanoverian king.

He did not like the Seven Years' War, then four years old, and felt that some adjustment could be made with France. William Pitt I, secretary of state for the Southern Department, and the dominant figure in the ministry of the Duke of Newcastle, insisted on continuing the war until France should be weakened beyond any likelihood of her challenging the empire that had been created by British victories in Canada and India; moreover, he urged, no peace should be made except in concert with England's ally, Frederick the Great. In March, 1761, the Earl of Bute was made secretary of state for the Northern Department, and proceeded with the plan for a separate peace. Pitt resisted in vain, and on October 5 he resigned. George mollified him with a pension of £3,000 for himself and his heir, and a peerage for his wife, who became Baroness of Chatham. Pitt (till 1766) refused a peerage for himself, since this would have excluded him from his favorite battlefield, the House of Commons. As he had spoken of pensions with scorn, he was severely criticized for accepting these emoluments, but they were less than he had earned, and others who had earned far less received far more.

On May 26, 1762, the Duke of Newcastle gave up his post after forty-five years of prominence in politics. Three days later Bute succeeded him as chief minister. Now the purposes of the young King took form and drive. He and Bute considered it part of the royal prerogative to determine the major lines of policy, especially in foreign affairs. Furthermore, he was eager to break the hold which a few rich families had taken on the government. In 1761 an old Whig, William Pulteney, Earl of Bath, in an anonymous pamphlet, urged the King not to be content with the "shadow of royalty," but to use his "legal prerogatives" to check the "illegal claims of factious oligarchy."[64]

The majority in the House of Commons held that the King should choose his ministers from the acknowledged leaders of the party or faction victorious in the elections; George insisted on his legal right to choose his ministers regardless of party, with no restrictions except his responsibility to the nation.[65] The Whigs had engineered the accession of the Hanoverian Elector to the throne of England; some Tories had negotiated with the exiled Stuarts; inevitably the first two Georges had taken only Whigs into their government; most of the Tories had retired to their estates. But in 1760 they accepted the new dynasty, and came in considerable number to offer their homage to the British-born King. George welcomed them, and saw no reason why he should not appoint able Tories, as well as able Whigs, to office. The Whigs protested that if the King were free to choose ministers and determine policy without responsibility to Parliament, the "Bill of Rights" of 1689 would be violated, the authority of the King would remount to the level claimed by Charles I, and the revolutions of 1642 and 1688 would be nullified. The party system had its faults, but (the leaders argued) it was indispensable to responsible government; it offered to each ministry an opposition that watched it, criticized it, and (when the electors so desired) could replace it with men equipped to alter the direction of policy without disturbing the stability of the state. So the lines formed for the first major conflict of powers in the new reign.

Bute bore the brunt of the battle. Criticism mostly spared the King, but not his mother; lampoons accused her of being Bute's mistress; this calumny roused the King to uncompromising wrath. Bute concluded a separate peace with France, and to force Frederick's acquiescence he ended England's subsidies to Prussia; Frederick called him a scoundrel, and fought on. The English people, though glad to have the war ended, denounced the peace as too lenient to defeated France; Pitt fulminated against it, and predicted that France, with her navy left intact, would soon resume war on England—which she did in 1778. The House of Commons ratified the treaty, 319 to 65. George's mother rejoiced that the royal will had prevailed; "Now," she said, "my son is really King of England."[66]

Hitherto the new sovereign had enjoyed a reputation for integrity. But when he saw that the Whigs were buying parliamentary votes, and were engaging journalists to attack his policies, he resolved to better the instruction. He used his funds and his power of patronage to induce authors like Smollett to defend the aims and actions of the ministry. Perhaps Bute had such services in view when, in July, 1762, he persuaded the King to give a pension to Samuel Johnson, and he was not disappointed. But no partisan of the minister could offset the clever diatribes of John Wilkes, the savage satires of Charles Churchill, or the anonymous vituperation of "Junius." "Libels on the court, exceeding in audacity and rancor any that had been published for many years, now appeared daily, in both prose and verse."[67]

Parliament took the King's money and gave him votes, but it disliked his chief minister as a Scot who had not risen to power through long service to some party in the House. Feeling against Scotland ran high in an England that still remembered the Scottish invasion of 1745. Moreover, Bute had given political plums to his countrymen: he had made Robert Adam court architect and Allan Ramsay court painter (ignoring Reynolds); he had pensioned John Home, the Scottish playwright, while refusing a professorship to Thomas Gray. The London populace expressed its feelings by hanging or burning a jackboot (as a pun for Bute), and by attacking the minister's carriage; he had to hide his face when he attended the theater. A tax on cider alienated the rural population, and left Bute the most unpopular minister in English history. Unable to breast the torrent, broken in health and spirits, and realizing his unfitness for the agitation and intrigues of politics, Bute resigned (April 8, 1763), after less than a year as chief minister to the King.

His successor, George Grenville, suffered three misfortunes: he was attacked in the press by the invincible John Wilkes (1763 f.); he put through Parliament (March, 1765) the Stamp Act that began the alienation of the American colonies; and George III had his first fit of insanity. The failure and resignation of Bute had broken the King's nerves and resolution; his marriage had brought him no happiness; and Grenville was painfully independent, almost domineering. George soon recovered, but he no longer felt strong enough to resist the Whig oligarchy that controlled most of Parliament and the press. He compromised by inviting a Whig, the Marquis of Rockingham, to form a new ministry.

Perhaps on suggestions from his secretary, Edmund Burke, the Marquis in a year put through Parliament several mollifying measures. The cider tax was abolished or modified; the stamp tax was repealed; a treaty with Russia furthered trade; the agitation over Wilkes was subdued; and apparently no bribery was used to advance this legislation. The King resented the repeal of the tax, and the concessions to Wilkes. On July 12, 1766, he dismissed the Rockingham ministry, offered a peerage to Pitt, and asked him to take charge of the government. Pitt agreed.

But the "Great Commoner" had lost his health, almost his mind. Now he sacrificed what remained of his popularity by accepting ennoblement as Earl of Chatham, thereby abandoning his place in the House. He had some excuse: he felt too weak to bear the tensions and conflicts of the Commons; in the Lords he would have more leisure and less strain. He took a relatively quiet post as lord of the privy seal, and allowed his friend, the Duke of Grafton, to fill the nominally pre-eminent post as first lord of the treasury. His colleagues, however, noted that he determined policy without consulting them, or over their opposition, and many were relieved when he went to Bath to seek some easing of his gout. He achieved this, but with drugs that disordered his mind. When he returned to London he was in no condition to attend to politics. In October, 1768, he resigned, and Grafton became chief minister.

It was in this period of political anarchy (1766–68) that a group known as "the King's Friends" associated themselves to further the aims of the King. They guided George in his distribution of favors for political support, and used every means to elect candidates, and advance ministers, pledged to the royal views. When Grafton enmeshed himself in difficulties and blunders they compounded his confusion until he resigned (January 27, 1770). On February 10 they achieved their greatest victory when Frederick North (known to us as Lord North, though he fell heir to this title only in 1790) began his twelve years of service as first lord of the treasury.

North was a weak, but not a bad, man. It was his sense of loyalty and pity that kept him in office and earned him so unpleasant a place in history. Born to fortune as son of the Earl of Guilford, he received all the advantages of education and association, entered the House of Commons at the age of twenty-two, and kept his seat there for nearly forty years. He made many friends by his modesty, kindliness, affability, and humor.* But he followed the conservative side too consistently to please anyone but the King. He supported the Stamp Act, the expulsion of Wilkes, and (until its last stages) the war with America. He defended the policies of George III even when he doubted their wisdom; he considered himself the agent of the King, not of the Parliament, much less of the people, and he seems to have been sincere in his conviction that the sovereign had the legal right to choose ministers and direct policy. Through North, and his tact in managing the House of Commons—and through the use of funds voted by Parliament—George III for a decade ruled England. Through his agents he bought seats and votes, sold pensions and posts, subsidized journalists, and tried to shackle the press. It is a measure of his courage and his obstinacy that it took a combination of John Wilkes, "Junius," Burke, Fox, Sheridan, Franklin, and Washington to defeat him.

IV. PARLIAMENT VERSUS THE PEOPLE

We read in Gibbon's *Journal* under September 23, 1762:

> Colonel Wilkes dined with us. . . . I scarcely ever met with a better companion. He has inexhaustible spirits, infinite wit and humor, and a great deal of knowledge, but is a thorough profligate in principle as in practice. His character is infamous, his life strained with every vice, and his conversation full of blasphemy and bawdy. These morals he glories in—for shame is a weakness he has long since surmounted. He told us himself that in this time of public dissension he was resolved to make his fortune.[69]

This was the view of a conservative who voted with the government in all his eight years as a member of the House of Commons, and who could not readily sympathize with a confessed and colorful enemy of Parliament and the King. Wilkes, however, would have admitted most of the indictment. He had discarded the ethics as well as the theology of Christianity, and enjoyed flaunting his hedonism in the face of M.P.s who shared his morals but were alarmed by his candor.

John Wilkes was the son of a malt distiller in Clerkenwell, north London. He received a good education at Oxford and Leiden, enough to surprise Johnson with his knowledge of the classics and his "manners of a gentleman."[70] At twenty he married "a lady half as old again as myself," but "of a large fortune."[71] She was a Dissenter given to a solemn piety; he took to

---

* When one speaker complained that North slept through the oration, North replied that it was unjust to complain of his taking a remedy which the honorable gentleman himself had supplied. When an irate member demanded his head he answered that he would gladly surrender it provided he did not have to accept the member's head in exchange.[68]

drink and mistresses. About 1757 he joined Sir Francis Dashwood, Bubb Dodington, George Selwyn, the poet Charles Churchill, and the fourth Earl of Sandwich in a "Hell-Fire Club" that met in the old Cistercian Abbey of Medmenham on the banks of the Thames near Marlow. There, as "the Mad Monks of Medmenham," they caricatured Roman Catholic rites by celebrating a "Black Mass" to Satan, and indulging their profane and Priapean bent.[72]

Through the influence of his associates, and by the expenditure of £7,000, Wilkes was elected M.P. for Aylesbury (1757). He attached himself at first to the elder Pitt, and, after 1760, to the foes of Bute. As Bute was subsidizing Smollett's journal *The Briton*, Wilkes, aided by Churchill, began in June, 1762, a counter weekly, *The North Briton*, which gained a wide readership through the verve and wit of its style, and the virulence of its attacks upon the ministry. In one number he denied at length—i.e., he spread—the rumor that Bute had made a mistress of the King's mother. In No. 45 (April 23, 1763) he inveighed against Bute for violating England's agreement with Prussia by concluding a separate peace with France, and for pretending, in a "speech from the throne" presented by the minister in the name of the King, that this treaty had the sanction of Frederick the Great.

> This week has given the public the most abandoned instance of ministerial effrontery ever attempted . . . on mankind. The *minister's speech* of last Tuesday is not to be paralleled in the annals of this country. I am in doubt whether the imposition is greater on the sovereign or on the nation. Every friend of his country must lament that a prince of so many great and amiable qualities . . . can be brought to give the sanction of his sacred name to the most odious measures, and to the most unjustifiable public declarations. . . . I am sure all foreigners, especially the King of Prussia, will hold the minister in contempt and abhorrence. He had made our sovereign declare: "My expectations have been fully answered by the happy effects which the several allies of my crown have derived from the Definitive Treaty. The powers at war with my good brother the King of Prussia have been induced to agree to such terms of accommodation as that great prince has approved." The infamous fallacy of this whole sentence is apparent to all mankind, for it is known that the King of Prussia . . . was basely deserted by the Scottish prime minister of England. . . . As to the "entire approbation" of Parliament which is so vainly boasted of, the world knows how that was obtained. The large debt on the *Civil List* . . . shows pretty clearly the transactions of the winter.[73]

Though Wilkes had interpreted the "King's speech" as really Bute's, George III took the article as a personal affront, and ordered Lords Halifax and Egremont, then secretaries of state, to arrest all persons involved in the publication of *The North Briton*'s No. 45. They issued a general warrant—i.e., one not naming the persons to be apprehended; and on its vague terms forty-nine persons were imprisoned, including Wilkes (April 30, 1763), despite his claim of immunity as a member of Parliament. Williams, printer of the journal, was put in the pillory, but a crowd cheered him as a martyr and raised £200 for his relief. Wilkes applied to the Court of Common Pleas for a writ of habeas corpus, obtained it, argued his case, and won from Chief Justice Charles Pratt (a friend of Pitt) an order for his release on the ground that his arrest violated parliamentary privilege. Wilkes sued Halifax and others for illegal arrest and property injury, and obtained £5,000 in damages. Pratt's condemnation of general warrants ended an abuse almost as obnoxious to Britons as *lettres de cachet* to the French.

Tempting fate, Wilkes collaborated with Thomas Potter (son of the Archbishop of Canterbury) in composing an *Essay on Woman* as a poetic parody of Pope's *Essay on Man*. It was a medley of obscenity and blasphemy, equipped with learned notes in the same key, ascribed to Bishop William Warburton, who had added notes to Pope's poem. The little piece was printed by Wilkes's press in his own home; it was not published, but thirteen copies were struck off for a few friends. The King's ministers secured the proof sheets, and persuaded the Earl of Sandwich to read them to the House of Lords. The Earl did (November 15), to the amusement of the peers, who knew his reputation for profligacy. Walpole tells us that they "could not keep their countenance"[74] as Sandwich proceeded, but they agreed that the poem was "a scandalous, obscene, and impious libel," and asked the King to prosecute Wilkes for blasphemy. When Sandwich told Wilkes that he would die either on the gallows or from venereal disease, Wilkes answered, "That depends, my Lord, on whether I embrace your principles or your mistress."[75]

On that same November 15 Wilkes rose in the Commons to enter a complaint of breach of privilege in his arrest. He was voted down, and Parliament ordered the hangman to publicly burn No. 45 of *The North Briton*. On the seventeenth Samuel Martin, who had been abused in that issue, challenged Wilkes to a duel. They met in Hyde Park; Wilkes was seriously wounded, and was bedded for a month. The people of London condemned Martin as a hired assassin; they rioted when the hangman tried to burn No. 45; "Wilkes and liberty!" and "Number Forty-five" became watchwords of a rising popular rebellion against both King and Parliament.[76] After a frenzied Scot tried to kill him, Wilkes left for France (December 26). On January 19, 1764, he was formally expelled from Parliament. On February 21 he was judged guilty, in the Court of King's Bench, for reprinting No. 45 and for printing the *Essay on Woman;* he was summoned to appear for sentencing; he did not come, and on November 1 he was declared an outlaw.

For four years Wilkes wandered in France and Italy, fearing life imprisonment if he returned to England. In Rome he saw much of Winckelmann; in Naples he met Boswell, who found him interesting company. "His lively and energetic sallies on moral questions gave to my spirits a not unpleasant agitation."[77] On the way back to Paris Wilkes visited Voltaire at Ferney, and charmed the wittiest man in Europe with his wit.

The return of the liberals to power under Rockingham and Grafton led Wilkes to hope for a pardon. He received private assurances that he would not be molested if he remained quiet. He returned to England (1768), and announced his candidacy for Parliament from London. Losing that contest, he sought election from Middlesex, and received a substantial plurality after a riotous campaign; that county, largely urbanized (it now includes north-west London), was known for its radical leanings and its hostility to the rising capitalism. On April 20 Wilkes submitted to the court, expecting to have his sentence of outlawry annulled; it was, but he was condemned to a fine of £1,000 and imprisonment for twenty-two months. An angry crowd rescued him from the officers and bore him in triumph through the streets of London. Having escaped from his admirers, he gave himself up to jail in St. George's Fields. A mob assembled there on May 10 and proposed to free him again. Soldiers fired upon the rioters; five were killed, fifteen wounded.

On February 4, 1769, the House of Commons again expelled him; Middlesex again elected him (February 16); he was again expelled; Middlesex again elected him (April 13), this time by a vote of 1,143 to 296 for Henry Luttrell; Parliament gave the seat to Luttrell on the ground that Wilkes, having been expelled from Parliament, was legally disqualified during the tenure of that Parliament. Luttrell was attacked as he left the House; he did not dare appear on the streets.[78] Seventeen counties and many boroughs sent up addresses to the throne, complaining that the rights of freeholders to choose their representatives in the House of Commons had been flagrantly violated. The King, who had vigorously supported the expulsions, ignored the petitions, whereupon one member, Colonel Isaac Barré, said in Parliament that disregard of petitions "might teach the people to think of assassination."[79]* John Horne Tooke, a young parson who had surrendered his faith to the charm of Voltaire, unfrocked himself and declared, after the repeated disbarments of Wilkes, that he would dye his (ministerial) black coat red.

Tooke led in organizing the Society of Supporters of the Bill of Rights (1769), whose immediate purpose was to free Wilkes from jail, pay his debts, and restore him to Parliament. In public meetings it agitated for the dissolution of the current Parliament as irreclaimably corrupt, and as unresponsive to the general will; it called for annual Parliaments elected by universal adult male suffrage, and for the responsibility of ministries to Parliament in their policies and expenditures.[80] Every candidate for Parliament should take oath never to accept any form of bribe, nor any post or pension or other emolument from the Crown; and every member must defend the views of his constituents even if contrary to his own. The grievances of Ireland should be redressed, and the American colonies should alone have the right to tax their people.[81]

In July, 1769, William Beckford, as lord mayor of London, and the city's "livery," or uniformed officials, presented to the King an address censuring the conduct of his ministers as subverting the constitution on which the house of Hanover had been given the throne of England. On March 14, 1770, they sent up to the King a remonstrance that used the language of revolution: "Under the secret and malign influence which, through each successive administration, has defeated every good and suggested every bad intention, the majority of the House of Commons have deprived your people

---

* The city of Wilkes-Barre, in Pennsylvania, was named for Wilkes and Barré, who strongly supported the cause of the colonies in Parliament.

of their dearest rights. They have done a deed more ruinous in its consequences than the levying of ship money by Charles I, or the pensioning power assumed by James II."[82] It appealed to the King to restore "constitutional government, . . . remove those evil ministers forever from your councils,"[83] and dissolve the present Parliament. The infuriated monarch, laying his hand on his sword, exclaimed, "Sooner than yield to a dissolution, I will have recourse to this."[84] London, rather than Paris, seemed near to revolution in 1770.

Into this fiery vortex of politics "Junius" dropped the most incendiary letters in the history of England. He kept his identity so secret, even from his publishers, that to this day no one knows who he was, though most guesses name Sir Philip Francis, whom we shall meet as the unrelenting foe of Warren Hastings. The author had already signed some letters "Lucius," some "Brutus"; now he took the middle name of that Lucius Junius Brutus who, according to Livy, had deposed a king (c. 510 B.C.) and founded the Roman Republic. The virile command of English in these letters indicates that "Junius" had the education, if not the manners, of a gentleman. He was probably a man of means, for he took no money for the letters, whose force and sting profitably enlarged the circulation of *The Public Advertiser*, in which they appeared from November 21, 1768, to January 21, 1772.

In a "Dedication to the English Nation," which he prefixed to the collected *Letters of Junius* (1772), the author proclaimed his purpose to "assert the freedom of election, and vindicate your exclusive right to choose your representatives." He took as his starting point the repeated disbarment of Wilkes, and the arrest, by a general warrant, of everybody connected with *The North Briton*'s No. 45. "The liberty of the press is the Palladium of all the civil, political, and religious rights of an Englishman; and the right of juries . . . is an essential part of our constitution." From this standpoint the author reviewed the foundations of the British government. "The power of the King, Lords, and Commons is not an arbitrary power. They are the trustees, not the owners, of the estate. The fee simple is in us. . . . I am persuaded you will not leave it to the choice of seven hundred persons, notoriously corrupted by the Crown, whether seven million of their equals shall be freemen or slaves."[85]

Junius proceeded to charge the administration of Grafton (1768–70) with selling offices and corrupting Parliament by favors and bribes. Here the attack became direct, and rose to such heat as to suggest a resolve to avenge some personal injury or affront.

> Come forward, thou virtuous minister, and tell the world by what interest Mr. Hine has been recommended to so extraordinary a mark of his Majesty's favor; what was the price of the patent he has bought? . . . You are basely setting up the royal patronage to auction. . . . Do you think it possible such enormities should escape without impeachment? It is indeed highly your interest to maintain the present House of Commons. Having sold the nation in gross, they will undoubtedly protect you in the detail, for while they patronize your crimes, they feel for their own.[86]

The attack continued long after Grafton had resigned, as in the letter of June 22, 1771:

> I cannot, with any decent appearance of propriety, call you the meanest and the basest fellow in the Kingdom. I protest, my Lord, I do not think you so. You will have a dangerous rival in that kind of fame . . . as long as there is one man living who thinks you worthy of his confidence, and fit to be trusted with any share in his government.

This seemed to name George III himself as "the basest fellow in the Kingdom." Already, in Letter xxxv, Junius had proposed to attack the King "with dignity and firmness, but not with respect": "Sir, it is the misfortune of your life . . . that you should never have been acquainted with the language of truth until you heard it in the complaints of your people. It is not, however, too late to correct the error of your education." Junius advised George to dismiss his Tory ministers, and to allow Wilkes to hold the seat to which he had been elected. "The Prince, while he plumes himself upon the security of his title to the crown, should remember that as it was acquired by one revolution, it may be lost by another."[87]

Henry Woodfall, who published this letter in *The Public Advertiser*, was arrested on a charge of seditious libel. The jury, reflecting the feelings of the middle class, refused to convict him, and he was released on payment of costs. Junius had now reached the apex of his temerity and power. But the King stood his ground, and strengthened his position by giving the chief ministry to the amiable and immovable Lord North. Junius continued his letters till 1772, and then left the field. We note that in 1772 Sir Philip Francis left the War Office (of whose affairs Junius had shown intimate knowledge), and departed for India.

The letters belong to the literary as well as the political history of England, for they are a living example of the style to which many British statesmen could rise, or stoop, when passion inflamed—and anonymity protected—them. Here is sterling English alloyed with abuse, but the abuse itself is often a masterpiece of subtle thrust or piercing epigram. There is no mercy here, no generosity, no thought that the accuser's own party shared in sin and guilt with the accused. We sympathize with Sir William Draper, who, answering Junius' letter of January 21, 1769, wrote: "The kingdom swarms with such numbers of felonious robbers of private character and virtue that no honest man is safe, especially as these cowardly base assassins stab in the dark, without having the courage to sign their real names to their malevolent, wicked productions."[88]

The passage of the British press to ever greater freedom and influence was marked by another conflict in these years. Toward 1768 some newspapers began to print reports of the major speeches delivered in Parliament. Most of these reports were partisan and inaccurate, some were imaginary, some were scurrilous. In February, 1771, Colonel George Onslow complained to the House of Commons that a journal had referred to him as "the little scoundrel" and "that paltry insignificant insect." On March 12 the House ordered the arrest of the printers. They resisted, arrested their would-be captors, and brought them before two aldermen (one of whom was Wilkes) and the Lord Mayor, Brass Crosby. The latter voided the attempted apprehension of the printers on the ground that the charters of the city forbade the arrest of a Londoner except on warrant issued by a city magistrate. The Lord Mayor was committed to the Tower by order of Parliament, but the populace rose in his support, attacked the carriages of M.P.s, threatened the ministers, hissed the King, and invaded the House of Commons. The Lord Mayor was released, and was acclaimed by an immense crowd. Newspapers resumed their reports of parliamentary debates; Parliament ceased to prosecute the printers. In 1774 Luke Hansard, with the consent of Parliament, began to publish with promptness and accuracy the *Journals of the House of Commons,* and he continued these till his death in 1828.

This historic victory of the British press affected the character of parliamentary debates, and contributed to make the second half of the eighteenth century the golden age of English eloquence. Orators became more cautious, perhaps more dramatic, when they felt that they were being heard throughout the British Isles. Some advance toward democracy was inevitable now that political information and intelligence were more widely spread. The business class, the intellectual community, and the rising radicals found in the press a voice that became increasingly bold and effective, until it subdued monarchy itself. Electors could know now how well their representatives had defended them and their interests in the making and unmaking of laws. Corruption continued, but diminished, for it could be more openly exposed. The press became a third force that could sometimes hold the balance between classes in the nation or parties in Parliament. Men who could buy or control newspapers became as powerful as ministers.

The new freedom, like most liberties, was frequently abused. Sometimes it became the instrument of aims more selfish and partisan, of opposition coarser and more violent, than any that had appeared in Parliament; then it deserved the name that Chatham gave it—"a chartered libertine."[89] In its turn it had to be chastened by a fourth voice, public opinion, of which, however, the press was partly the source, often the seducer, sometimes the voice. Armed with broader knowledge, untitled men and women began to speak out on the policies and methods of the government; they gathered in public meetings, and their debates occasionally rivaled those of Parliament in influence on history. Now money as well as birth could claim the right to rule; and occasionally, between the combatants, the people would be heard.

Wilkes was released from jail on April 17, 1770. Many houses were illuminated as for a festival, and the Lord Mayor displayed before his Mansion House a sign bearing the word LIBERTY in letters three feet high.[90] Soon Wilkes was elected alderman, then lord mayor, and in 1774 he was again sent to Parliament by Middlesex. Now the Commons did not dare refuse him his seat, and he kept it through all elections till 1790. He led a small group of "radicals" in Parliament, who urged parliamentary reform and the enfranchisement of the "lower orders."

> Every free agent in this kingdom should, in my wish, be represented in Parliament. The mean and insignificant boroughs, so emphatically styled the *rotten part of our constitution*, should be lopped off, and the rich, populous trading towns—Birmingham, Manchester, Sheffield, Leeds, and others—be permitted to send deputies to the great council of the nation. . . . I wish, Sir, an English Parliament to speak the free, unbiased sense of the body of the English people.[91]

Parliament waited fifty-six years to accept these reforms.

Wilkes refused to stand for re-election in 1790, and retired into private life. He died in 1797, aged seventy, as poor as he was born, for he had been scrupulously honest in all his offices.[92]

V. ENGLAND VERSUS AMERICA

In 1750 the population of the English colonies in North America was approximately 1,750,000; the population of England and Wales was some 6,140,000.[93] As the rate of growth in the colonies was much higher than in the mother country, it was only a matter of time when the offspring would rebel against the parent. Montesquieu had predicted this in 1730, even to specifying that the break would be caused by British restrictions on American trade. The Marquis d'Argenson, about 1747, foretold that the colonies would rise against England, form a republic, and become one of the great powers. Vergennes, soon after England had taken Canada from France in the Seven Years' War, told an English traveler: "England will soon repent of having removed the only check that could keep her colonies in awe. They stand no longer in need of her protection. She will call upon them to contribute to the burdens they have helped to bring upon her, and they will answer by striking off all dependence."[94]

The British Crown claimed authority to veto laws passed by the colonial assemblies. It did not often use that power; but when the Assembly of South Carolina, "sensible of the great social and political danger arising from the enormous multiplication of Negroes in the colony," passed a law imposing a heavy duty upon the importation of slaves, the law was rescinded by the Crown, for "the slave trade was one of the most lucrative branches of English commerce."[95] In economic matters Parliament assumed the right to legislate for all the British Empire, and usually its acts favored the motherland at the expense of the colonies. Its aim was to make America a source of articles not readily produced in England, and a market for British manufactured goods.[96] It discouraged the growth of colonial industries that would compete with England's. It forbade the colonists to manufacture cloth, hats, leather wares, or iron products;[97] so the Earl of Chatham, otherwise so friendly to the colonies, declared that he would not allow a single nail to be made in America without the permission of Parliament.[98] The colonies were forbidden to set up steel furnaces or rolling mills.

Many checks were put upon American merchants. They could ship goods only in British vessels; they could sell tobacco, cotton, silk, coffee, sugar, rice, and many other articles only to British dominions; they could import goods from the European Continent only after these had first been landed in England, had paid a port duty, and had been transferred to British vessels. To protect the export of English woolens to American colonies, colonial merchants were prohibited from selling colonial woolens outside the colony that had produced them.[99] A heavy tax was laid by Parliament (1733) upon American imports of sugar or molasses from any but British sources. The colonists, especially in Massachusetts, evaded some of these regulations by smuggling, and by secret selling of American products to foreign nations, even to the French during the Seven Years' War. Of 1,500,000 pounds of tea imported yearly into the American colonies, only some ten per cent conformed to the requirement of passing through English ports.[100] Much of the whiskey produced by the sixty-three distilleries of Massachusetts in 1750 used sugar and molasses smuggled in from the French West Indies.[101]

In justification of the restrictions, the British pointed out that other European nations, to protect or reward their own people, laid similar restraints upon their colonies; that many American products enjoyed a virtual monopoly of the English market through their exemption from import dues; and that England deserved some economic return for the cost of the protection which her navy gave to colonial shipping, and which her armies gave to the colonists against the French and the Indians in America. The expulsion of French power from Canada, and of Spanish power from Florida, had freed the English from dangers that had long troubled them. England felt warranted in asking America to help her pay off the enormous debt— £140,-000,000—which Great Britain had incurred in the Seven Years' War. The colonists replied that they had furnished twenty thousand troops for that war, and had themselves incurred a debt of £2,500,000.

In any case England decided to tax the colonies. In March, 1765, Grenville proposed to Parliament that all colonial legal documents, all bills, diplomas, playing cards, bonds, deeds, mortgages, insurance policies, and newspapers be required to bear a stamp for which a fee would have to be paid to the British government. Patrick Henry in Virginia, Samuel Adams in Massachusetts, advised rejection of the tax on the ground that by tradition—Magna Carta, the Great Rebellion against Charles I, the "Bill of Rights"—Englishmen could justly be taxed only with their consent or the consent of their authorized representatives. How, then, could English colonials be taxed by a Parliament in which they had no representation? Britons answered that difficulties of travel and communication made American representation in Parliament impracticable; and they pointed out that millions of adult Englishmen had for centuries loyally accepted taxation by Parliament though they had had no vote in electing it; they felt what Americans should feel—that they were virtually represented in Parliament, because its members considered themselves as representing the whole British Empire.

The colonists were not convinced. Since Parliament had retained the power of taxing as the fulcrum of control over the king, so the colonies defended their exclusive right to tax themselves as the only alternative to financial oppression by men whom they had never seen, and who had never touched American soil. Lawyers evaded the requirement to use stamped documents; some newspapers carried a death's head where the stamp should have appeared; Americans began to boycott British goods; merchants canceled orders for British products, and some refused payment of their debts to England till the Stamp Act should be repealed.[102] Colonial maidens pledged themselves to accept no suitors who would not denounce the Stamp Act.[103] Popular resentment rose to the pitch of rioting in several cities; in New York the governor (appointed by the King) was hanged in effigy; in Boston the home of the lieutenant governor, Thomas Hutchinson, was burned down; the distributors of the stamps were forced, under threat of hanging, to resign their offices. Feeling the boycott, British merchants called for a repeal of the act; petitions were sent to the government from London, Bristol, Liverpool, and other cities, stating that without repeal many English manufacturers would be ruined; already thousands of workers had been dismissed because of lack of orders from America. Perhaps it was in recognition of these appeals that Pitt, after a long illness, made a dramatic return to Parliament, and declared (January 14, 1766), "It is my opinion that this kingdom has no right to lay a tax upon the colonies." He ridiculed the "idea that the colonies are *virtually* represented in the House." When George Grenville interrupted and implied that Pitt was encouraging sedition, Pitt answered defiantly, "I rejoice that America has resisted."[104]

On March 18 Lord Rockingham persuaded Parliament to repeal the stamp tax. To appease "the King's Friends" he added to the repeal a "declaratory act" reaffirming the authority of the king, with the consent of Parliament, to make laws binding on the colonies, and the authority of Parliament to tax the British colonies. The Americans accepted the repeal, and ignored the declaratory act. Reconciliation now seemed possible. But in July the Rockingham ministry fell, and in the Grafton ministry that followed it the Chancellor of the Exchequer, Charles Townshend, renewed the attempt to make the colonies pay for the administrative and military forces needed to protect them against internal disorder or external attack. On May 13, 1767, he proposed to Parliament that new duties be laid upon glass, lead, paper, and tea imported into America. The revenue from these imposts was to be used by the King to pay the salaries of the governors and judges appointed by him for America; any surplus would be directed to maintain the British troops there. Parliament approved. Townshend died a few months later.

The Americans resisted the new duties as disguised taxation. They had kept the royal troops and governors under control by making them largely dependent for their sustenance upon funds voted by the colonial assemblies; to surrender this power of the purse to the King would be to yield the direction of the American government to royal authority. The assemblies united in urging a renewed boycott of British goods. Efforts to collect the new duties were violently resisted. Lord North sought a compromise by canceling all the Townshend imposts except for a threepence-per-pound duty on tea. The colonies relaxed their boycott, but resolved to drink only such tea as had been smuggled in. When three ships of the East India Company tried to land 298 chests of tea at Boston, half a hundred irate colonials, disguised as Mohawk Indians, boarded the vessels, overpowered the crews, and emptied the cargoes into the sea (December 16, 1773). Riots in other American ports frustrated further efforts to bring in the company's tea.

The rest of the story belongs mostly to America, but the part played in it by British statesmen, orators, writers, and public opinion forms a vital element in the history of England. Just as in America a numerous and active minority called for loyalty to the mother country and its government, so in England, while the public generally supported the martial measures of Lord North's ministry, a minority, represented in Parliament by Chatham, Burke, Fox, Horace Walpole, and Wilkes, labored for peace on terms favorable to America. Some saw in this division of English opinion a revival of the opposition between Royalists and Parliamentarians in 1642. The Anglican Church fully supported the war against the colonies; so did the Methodists, following Wesley's lead; but many other Dissenters regretted the conflict, for they remembered that a majority of the colonists had come from Dissenting groups. Gibbon agreed with Johnson in condemning the colonies, but David Hume, nearing death, warned Britain that the attempt to coerce America would lead to disaster.[105] The business interests veered to support of the King as war orders brought them profits. War, Burke mourned, "is indeed become a substitute for commerce. . . . Great orders for provisions and stores of all kinds . . . keep up the spirits of the mercantile world, and induce them to consider the American war not so much their calamity as their resource."[106]

The liberals feared that the war would strengthen the Tories against the Whigs, and the King against Parliament; one liberal, the Duke of Richmond, thought of moving to France to escape royal despotism.[107] George III gave some excuse for such fears. He took full charge of the war, even of its military details; Lord North and the other ministers, often against their private judgment, obeyed the royal lead. The King felt that if the Americans succeeded England would face revolt in other colonies, and would finally be confined to its island. The Earl of Chatham, however, warned Parliament that the forcible suppression of America would be a victory for the principles of Charles I and James II. On November 20, 1777, when British armies had suffered many defeats in America, and France was sending subsidies to the colonies, Chatham, coming to the House of Lords as if from the grave, heard with mounting impatience the ministerial "address from the throne," and rose to make one of the greatest speeches in the records of British eloquence. Here history and literature unite:

> I rise, my lords, to declare my sentiments on this most solemn and serious subject. . . . I cannot concur in a blind and servile address which approves, and endeavors to sanctify, the monstrous measures that have heaped disgrace and misfortune upon us—that have brought ruin to our doors. This, my lords,

is a perilous and tremendous moment! It is not a time for adulation. The smoothness of flattery cannot now avail. . . . It is now necessary to instruct the throne in the language of truth. . . . This, my lords, is our duty; it is the proper function of this noble assembly, sitting upon our honors in this House, the hereditary council of the Crown. And who is the minister—where is the minister—that has dared to suggest to the throne the contrary, unconstitutional language this day delivered from it? The accustomed language from the throne has been application to Parliament for advice. . . . But on this day, and in this extreme momentous exigency, no reliance is reposed on our constitutional counsels, no advice is asked from the sober and enlightened care of Parliament, but the Crown, from itself and by itself, declares an unalterable determination to pursue measures . . . dictated and forced upon us, . . . which have reduced this late flourishing Empire to ruin and contempt. "But yesterday, and England might have stood against the world; now none so poor to do her reverence." . . .

My lords, you cannot conquer America. . . . You may swell every expense and every effort still more extravagantly; pile and accumulate every assistance you can buy or borrow; traffic and barter with every little pitiful German prince that sells and sends his subjects to the shambles . . .; your efforts are forever vain and impotent—doubly so from this mercenary aid on which you rely, for it irritates, to an incurable resentment, the minds of your enemies. . . . If I were an American, as I am an Englishman, while a foreign troop was landed in my country, I never would lay down my arms—never—never—never![108]

Burke used all his powers of reasoning in the effort to dissuade Parliament and the ministry from a policy of force against America. From 1774 to 1780 he represented in Parliament the city of Bristol, whose merchants at first opposed war with America;[109] he was also at this time a salaried agent of the state of New York.[110] He did not, like Chatham, deny the right of Parliament to tax the colonies, and he did not support the appeal of the colonists to abstract theories of "natural right." He brought the question down to where hardheaded men of action could understand him: Was it practical to tax America? In his speech on American taxation (April 19, 1774) he condemned not only the Townshend Acts but the threepence tax on tea; he warned that if taxes were added to the industrial and commercial restrictions already laid upon America the colonists would persist in a revolt that would break up the nascent British Empire and tarnish the prestige of the Parliament.

Beaten on this issue, he renewed, on March 22, 1775, his plea for conciliation. He pointed out that trade with America had grown tenfold between 1704 and 1772,[111] and he asked was it wise to disrupt, perhaps sacrifice, that commerce with war. He feared that war with the colonies would leave England open to attack by a foreign enemy; this happened in 1778. He agreed that American representation in Parliament was made impracticable by the sea; *opposuit natura*; he asked only that England rely not upon taxation but upon voluntary grants from the colonial assemblies; such grants might well exceed the proceeds of direct taxation after the costs of forcible collection had been deducted.[112]

His motion to this effect was rejected 270 to 78, but he had the solace of winning to his cause the eloquence and skill of Charles James Fox; so began a friendship cemented by the American Revolution and sundered by the French. Gibbon called Fox's speech of October 31, 1776, the most masterly that he had ever heard, and Horace Walpole declared it "one of his [Fox's] finest and most animated orations."[113] Walpole ranged himself on the side of conciliation; he deplored the collapse of British statesmanship under Lord North; and on September 11, 1775, he wrote to Horace Mann:

> The Parliament is to meet on the 20th of next month and vote 26,000 seamen. What a paragraph of blood is there! With what torments must liberty be preserved in America! In England what can save it? Oh, mad, mad England! What frenzy, to throw away its treasures, lay waste its empire of wealth, and sacrifice its freedom, that its prince may be the arbitrary lord of boundless deserts in America, and of an impoverished, depopulated, and thence insignificant island in Europe![114]

Not the fervor of Chatham, Burke, and Fox, but the victories and diplomacies of the colonies persuaded the English people, and then their government, to thoughts of peace. Burgoyne's surrender at Saratoga (October 17, 1777) was the turning point; for the first time England appreciated Chatham's warning, "You cannot conquer America." When France recognized the "United States of America," and joined in war against England (February 6, 1778), the judgment of French statesmen confirmed Chatham's, and the weight of French arms and of a restored French navy was added to the burden borne by the British nation. Lord North himself lost heart, and begged permission to resign; the King, loading him with gifts, bade him stay on.

Many prominent Englishmen now felt that only a government led by the Earl of Chatham could win the colonies back from the French alliance to union with England. But George would not hear of it. "I solemnly declare," he told North, "that nothing shall bring me to treat personally with Lord Chatham."[115] The Earl came to the House of Lords for the last time on April 7, 1778, supported by crutches and his son William, his face ghastly with the nearness of death, his voice so weak as to be barely heard. Again he counseled conciliation, but stood out "against the dismemberment of this ancient and most noble monarchy" by a grant of independence to America.[116] The Duke of Richmond answered that only by such a grant could America be won away from France. Chatham tried to rise and speak again, but he collapsed in an apoplectic fit. He died on May 11, 1778. Parliament voted him a public funeral, with a tomb and monument in Westminster Abbey. He was, by general consent, the greatest Englishman of his time.

Events hurried to complete the catastrophe that he had predicted. In June, 1779, Spain joined France in war against England; it laid siege to Gibraltar, and sent its fleet to share in the attack upon British shipping. In August a combined flotilla of sixty French and Spanish vessels entered the English Channel; England feverishly prepared to resist invasion; sickness disabled the hostile fleet and compelled it to retire to Brest. In March, 1780, Russia, Denmark, and Sweden united in a "Declaration of Armed Neutrality," which vowed to resist England's practice of boarding neutral vessels in search of enemy goods; soon other neutrals signed the declaration. English search of Dutch vessels continued; it found evidence of secret agreements between the city of Amsterdam and an American negotiator. England demanded the punishment of the Amsterdam officials; the Dutch government refused; England declared war (December, 1780). Now almost all the Baltic and Atlantic states were allied against the England that only recently had ruled the seas.

The mood of Parliament reflected the multiplication of disasters. Resentment was mounting against the King's frustration of his minister's desire to end the war. On April 6, 1780, John Dunning had offered to the House of Commons a motion declaring "that the influence of the Crown has increased, is increasing, and ought to be diminished"; the motion was approved by a vote of 233 to 215. On January 23, 1781, the younger Pitt took his seat in the House; in his second speech he denounced the war with America as "most accursed, wicked, barbarous, cruel, unnatural, unjust, and diabolical."[117] Fox joyfully welcomed Pitt to the ranks of the opposition, not foreseeing that this youth was soon to be his strongest foe.

On October 19, 1781, Lord Cornwallis surrendered to Washington at Yorktown. "Oh, God, it is all over!" exclaimed Lord North, but the King insisted that the war must go on. In February and March, 1782, news came that Minorca had been taken by the Spaniards, and several West Indian islands by the French. Public meetings throughout England clamored for peace. North's majority in the Commons fell to twenty-two, to nineteen, to one—on a motion "that the House could no longer repose confidence in the present ministers" (March 15, 1782); this set an historic precedent for Parliament's procedure in forcing a change of ministry. On March 18 North wrote to George III a letter telling him, in effect, that both the royal policy toward America and the attempt to establish the supremacy of the king over Parliament had failed.

> Your Majesty is well apprized that in this country the Prince on the throne cannot, with prudence, oppose the deliberate resolution of the House of Commons. . . . The Parliament have uttered their sentiments, and their sentiments, whether just or erroneous, must ultimately prevail. Your Majesty . . . can lose no honor if you yield.[118]

On March 20, 1782, after twelve years of patient service and submission, Lord North resigned. George III, his spirit broken, wrote a letter of abdication, but did not send it. He accepted a ministry of triumphant liberals: Rockingham, the Earl of Shelburne, Charles James Fox, Burke, and Sheridan. When Rockingham died (July 1), Shelburne succeeded him as first lord of the treasury. Fox, Burke, and Sheridan, disliking Shelburne, resigned. Shelburne proceeded to arrange a treaty of peace (Paris, November 30, 1782; Paris and Versailles, January 20 and September 3, 1783) that surrendered Minorca and Florida to Spain, and Senegal to France, and acknowledged not only the independence of the American colonies but their right to all the territory between the Alleghenies, Florida, the Mississippi, and the Great Lakes.

The English people had been eager for peace, but they resented the cession of so much terrain to the colonies. Criticism of Shelburne reached such bitterness that he submitted his resignation (February 24, 1783). As the quarrel between Shelburne and Fox had divided the liberal Whigs into factions neither of which was strong enough to control Parliament, Fox agreed to form a coalition ministry with his old enemy Lord North. Burke again became paymaster of the forces. Sheridan, who was always in debt, was made secretary of the treasury. Both Fox and Burke had for some time been studying the behavior of Englishmen in India, and that country now replaced America as the most urgent problem in British politics.

VI. ENGLAND AND INDIA

The British East India Company had been reorganized in 1709 as the "United Company of Merchants of England trading to the East Indies." Its charter from the British government entitled it to a monopoly of British trade with India. It was managed by a chairman and twenty-four directors annually elected by a "Court of Proprietors" in which every holder of £500 or more of stock had one vote. In India the company became a military as well as a commercial organization, and fought Dutch, French, and native armies for pieces of the crumbling empire of the Moguls. It was in one of these wars that Siraj-ud-daula, the Nawab (Viceroy) of Bengal, captured Calcutta from the company, and imprisoned 146 Europeans in the "Black Hole of Calcutta"—a room eighteen by fourteen feet, with only two small windows; 123 of the prisoners died overnight (June 20–21, 1756) from heat or asphyxiation.

Robert Clive, governor of Fort St. David, led a small force to recapture Calcutta for the company. He joined in the plot of Mir Jafar, a noble at Siraj-ud-daula's court, to overthrow the Viceroy; with nine hundred European and 2,300 native troops he defeated fifty thousand men at Plassey (June 23, 1757); Siraj-ud-daula was put to death, and Mir Jafar was set up in his place as nawab of Bengal. Clive entered the capital, Murshidabab, as a conqueror. It seemed to him equal to London in size and perhaps superior in wealth. In the Nawab's treasury he saw an incredible accumulation of rupees, jewels, gold, silver, and other riches. Invited to name his reward for enthroning Mir Jafar, he asked £160,000 for himself, £500,000 for his army and navy, £24,000 for each member of the company's governing board, and £1,000,000 as indemnity for damage to the company's property in Calcutta. It was to this occasion that Clive referred when he told the House of Commons that he marveled at his own moderation.[119] He received a total of £200,000 as presents from Mir Jafar,[120] and was acknowledged as British governor of Bengal. The company, by paying a yearly rental of £27,000 to Mir Jafar, was recognized as supreme landlord of 882 square miles around Calcutta. In 1759, in return for aid in suppressing a rebellion, Mir Jafar agreed to remit to Clive annually the rental paid by the company.

Secure from competition, the company exploited with scant mercy the natives subject to its rule. Armed with superior weapons, it made Indian rulers pay heavily for British protection. Far from supervision by the British government, and immune to the Ten Commandments east of Suez, its senior officials made huge profits in trade, and returned to England as nabobs capable of buying, without serious injury to their capital, a pocket borough or a member of Parliament.

Clive came home to England in 1760, aged thirty-five, expecting to enjoy fame and wealth. He bought enough boroughs to command a bloc in the Commons, and was himself elected from Shrewsbury. Some directors of the East India Company, feeling that he had stolen beyond his years, attacked him for using forged documents in dealing with Siraj-ud-daula and Mir Jafar; but when word reached London that native revolts, official venality, and administrative incompetence were endangering the position of the company in India, Clive was hurried back to Calcutta (1765) as governor of Bengal. There he labored to stem corruption among his aides, mutiny among his troops, and recurrent uprisings of native rulers against the company. On August 12, 1765, he persuaded the helpless Mogul Shah Alam to give the company full financial control of the provinces of Bengal, Behar, and Orissa, with a population of thirty million souls and an annual revenue of £4,000,-000. This, and Clive's victory at Plassey, created the British Empire in India.

His health shattered by two years of strife, Clive returned to England in January, 1767. The attack upon him by company directors was renewed, and was seconded by officials whose extortions he had checked. News of a great famine in India, and of native attacks upon company strongholds, shared in causing a panic in which prominent Englishmen suffered severe losses. In 1772 two parliamentary committees investigated Indian affairs, and revealed such exactions and cruelties that Horace Walpole cried out: "We have outdone the Spaniards in Peru! We have murdered, deposed, plundered, usurped. Nay, what think you of the famine in Bengal, in which three millions perished, being caused by a monopoly of provisions by the servants of the East India Company?"[121] In 1773 one of the investigating committees called upon Clive to account to the House of Commons for his methods and gains in India. He admitted nearly all the facts, defended them as warranted by local customs and the necessities of the situation, and added that when the members came to judge of his honor they should not forget their own. The House voted, 155 to 95, that he had received £234,000 during his first administration of Bengal, but that he "did at the same time render great and meritorious services to his country."[122] A year later, aged forty-nine, Clive killed himself (November 22, 1774).

In 1773 Lord North put through Parliament a regulatory act that advanced a loan of £1,400,000 to the company to save it [and its parliamentary shareholders] from bankruptcy, and brought all company-ruled territory in India under the presidency of Bengal, which in turn would be responsible to the British government. Warren Hastings was appointed governor of Bengal.

He had risen to this position from lowly origins. His mother died in giving him birth; his father went off to adventure and death in the West Indies. An uncle sent the boy to Westminster School, but in 1749 the uncle died, and Warren, aged seventeen, sailed to seek fortune in India. He enrolled as a volunteer under Clive, shared in the recapture of Calcutta, showed diligence and ability in administration, and was appointed to the council governing company affairs in Bengal. In 1764 he returned to England. Four years later the directors persuaded him to join the Council of Madras. On his way to India he met Baron Imhof and his wife, Marion, who became Hastings' mistress and then his wife. He did well in Madras, and in 1774 he began his turbulent rule as governor of Bengal.

He worked hard, but his methods were dictatorial, and some of his measures provided material for attacks upon him by Sir Philip Francis in the Bengal Council, as later by Burke in Parliament. When Maratha tribes restored Shah Alam to the Mogul throne at Delhi, and he made over to them those districts of Kora and Allahabad which Clive had assigned to him, Hastings sold the districts to the Nawab of Oudh for fifty lacs of rupes ($20,-000,000?), and assigned company troops to help the Nawab recover the region. He allowed the Nawab to use company troops to invade and appropriate the territory of Rohilkhand, whose chief (said the Nawab) owed him money; the company received a large sum for these soldiers. Hastings' action clearly violated orders given him by the directors;[123] however, those directors reckoned the worth of a governor by the money he sent back to England.

An Indian official, Nuncomar, accused Hastings of accepting a bribe. Francis and other councilors credited the charge, and alleged that there was "no species of peculation from which the Honorable Governor has thought it reasonable to abstain."[124] Nuncomar was arrested on a charge of forgery, was convicted, and was put to death (1775). Hastings was suspected of having influenced the chief justice, Sir Elijah Impey (formerly a fellow student at Winchester), to exact an unusually severe penalty. In 1780 Hastings promoted Impey to an additional post bringing £6,500 a year. Mutual recrimination between Hastings and Francis led to a duel in which Francis was seriously wounded.

Haidar Ali, maharajah of Mysore, thought the quarrels between Hastings and his council offered an opportunity for expelling the company from India. Supported by the French, he attacked company strongholds, and won some alarming victories (1780). Hastings sent troops and money from Bengal to oppose him; Haidar Ali died (1782), but his son Tipu Sahib carried on the war till his final defeat in 1792. Probably it was to finance these campaigns that Hastings resorted to money-raising schemes that led to his impeachment.

He demanded from Chait Singh, rajah of Benares, a war subsidy additional to the revenue which that district annually paid to the company. The Rajah pleaded inability to comply. Hastings led a small force to Benares (1781), deposed Chait Singh, and exacted double the revenue from Chait's successor. — The Nawab of Oudh, remiss in his payments to the company, explained that he could make these payments if the company would help him compel his mother and grandmother, the begums (princesses) of Oudh, to release to him some of the £2,000,000 left them by the Nawab's father. The mother had already yielded him a large sum on his promise to ask for no more; the company, over Hastings' protest, made a like promise. Hastings advised the Nawab to ignore the promise. He sent company troops to Fyzabad; by torture and near-starvation they forced the eunuch servitors of the princesses to surrender the treasure (1781). Out of this the Nawab paid his dues to the company.[125]

Meanwhile Sir Philip Francis, having recovered from his wounds, returned to England (1781), and expounded to the directors and to his friends in Parliament what he considered to be the crimes of Hastings. In 1782 the House of Commons censured Hastings and other company agents as having "in sundry instances acted in a manner repugnant to the honor and policy of the nation," and ordered the directors to recall them. The directors issued such an order, but the Court of Proprietors countermanded it, probably because the Mysore revolt was continuing.

In November, 1783, Charles James Fox, as secretary of state for foreign affairs in the coalition ministry, offered Parliament an "India Reform Bill" that would have put the East India Company under control of commissioners appointed by the ministry. Critics moaned that the bill would give the Fox-Burke Whigs a rich well of patronage. It passed the House, but the King sent word to the Lords that he would consider as his enemy any man who voted for the measure; they voted against it, 95 to 76. The Commons filed a formal protest that this royal interference with legislation was a scandalous breach of parliamentary privilege. The King, claiming that the coalition ministry had lost the confidence of Parliament, dismissed it (December 18, 1783), and invited William Pitt, aged twenty-four, to form a new government. Believing that he could win a national election, George III dissolved the Parliament (March 23, 1784), and ordered his agents to spread the royal wishes and plums among the electorate to insure the return of a conservative majority. The Parliament that assembled on May 18 was overwhelmingly for Pitt and the King.

Pitt was a master of political administration and management. His meticulous devotion to his task, his detailed knowledge of affairs, his habit of careful reflection and prudent judgment gave him a superiority which nearly all his fellow ministers soon conceded. Now for the first time since Robert Walpole (for whom his son had used the term in 1773[126]), England had a "prime" minister, for no important action was taken by Pitt's colleagues without his consent. In effect he established "cabinet government"—the assembled deliberation and united responsibility of the leading ministers under one leadership. Though Pitt had assumed office as favoring the royal authority, his hard work and wide information gradually raised him to a position where he guided rather than followed the King. After George III's second seizure (1788) it was Pitt who ruled England.

His special acquaintance with business and finance enabled him to restore a treasury dangerously burdened by two major wars in one generation. Pitt had read Adam Smith; he listened to merchants and manufacturers; he reduced import dues, negotiated a treaty of lowered tariffs with France (1786), and delighted industrial leaders by declaring that manufacturers should in general be free from taxes. He made up for this by taxing consumption: ribbons, gauzes, gloves, hats, candles, couches, salt, wine, bricks, tiles, paper, windows; many houses boarded up some windows to reduce the tax.[127] By 1788 the budget was balanced, and England had escaped the governmental bankruptcy that was leading France to revolution.

Before the election Pitt had introduced his "First India Bill," which had been defeated. Now he offered a second bill: a Board of Control appointed by the King was to manage the political relations of the East India Company, while commercial relations and patronage were left in company hands, subject to royal veto. The bill was passed (August 9, 1784), and governed British-Indian affairs till 1858.

Fox and Burke considered this arrangement a shameful surrender to a company notorious for corruption and crime. Burke had special reasons for dissatisfaction. His patron Lord Verney, his brother Richard Burke, and his relative William Burke had invested in the East India Company, and had suffered heavy losses in the fluctuations of its stock.[128] When William Burke went to India Edmund recommended him to Sir Philip Francis as one whom he loved tenderly; William was made a paymaster, and proved "as corrupt as any."[129] Francis, back in England, gave Burke and Fox his version of Hastings' administration; he was one source of Burke's remarkable knowledge of Indian affairs. The attack upon Hastings by the liberal Whigs was presumably motivated in part by desire to discredit and overthrow Pitt's ministry.[130]

In January, 1785, Hastings resigned, and returned to England. He hoped that his long years of administration, his restoration of the company to solvency, and his rescue of British power in Madras and Bombay would be rewarded with a pension, if not with a peerage. In the spring of 1786 Burke asked the House of Commons for the official records of Hastings' rule in India. Some were refused, some were given him by the ministers. In April he laid before the House a bill of charges against the ex-governor of Bengal. Hastings read to the House a detailed reply. In June Burke presented charges relating to the Rohilkhand war, and asked for the impeachment of Hastings; the Commons refused to prosecute. On June 13 Fox told the story of Chait Singh, and asked for impeachment. Pitt surprised his cabinet by voting with Fox and Burke; many of his party followed his lead, which may have been designed to dissociate the ministry from Hastings' fate. The motion to impeach was carried 119 to 79.

The prorogation of Parliament and the pressure of other issues interrupted the drama, but it was resumed with éclat on February 7, 1787, when Sheridan made what Fox and Burke and Pitt called the best speech ever heard in the House of Commons.[131] (Sheridan was offered £1,000 for a corrected copy of the address; he never found time to do this, and we know it only from subdued summaries.) With all the art of a man born to the theater, and all the fervor of a romantic spirit, Sheridan recounted the spoliation of the begums of Oudh. After speaking for over five hours, he demanded that Hastings be impeached. Again Pitt voted for the prosecution; the motion was carried, 175 to 68. On February 8 the House appointed a committee of twenty—with Burke, Fox, and Sheridan at their head—to prepare the articles of impeachment. These were presented, and on May 9 the House ordered "Mr. Burke, in the name of the House of Commons, . . . to go to the bar of the House of Lords and impeach Warren Hastings, Esquire, . . . of high crimes and misdemeanors." Hastings was arrested and brought before the peers, but was released on bail.

After a long delay the trial began, February 13, 1788, in Westminster Hall. All lovers of literature will recall Macaulay's gorgeous description[132] of that historic assemblage: the lords sitting in ermine and gold as the high court of the realm; before them Hastings, pale and ill, aged fifty-three, height five feet six inches, weight 122 pounds; the judges under their great ear-lapping wigs; the family of the King; the members of the House of Commons; the galleries crowded with ambassadors, princesses, and duchesses; Mrs. Siddons in her stately beauty; Sir Joshua Reynolds amid so many notables whom he had portrayed; and on one side the committee, now called the "managers," ready to present the case for impeachment. Clerks read the charges and Hastings' reply. For four days, in the most powerful speech of his career, Burke laid upon the accused an overwhelming mass of accusations. Then, on February 15, he made the historic hall ring with his passionate demand:

> I impeach Warren Hastings, Esquire, of high crimes and misdemeanors.
> I impeach him in the name of the Commons of Great Britain, . . . whose Parliamentary trust he has betrayed. . . .
> I impeach him in the name of the people of India, whose laws, rights, and liberties he has subverted, whose properties he has destroyed, whose country he has laid waste and desolate.
> I impeach him in the name, and by the virtue, of those eternal laws of justice which he has violated.
> I impeach him in the name of human nature itself, which he has cruelly outraged, injured, and oppressed in both sexes, in every age, rank, situation, and condition of life.[133]

With a hundred interruptions the trial proceeded, as Burke, Fox, Sheridan, and others told the story of Hastings' administration. When it became known that at noon on June 3 Sheridan would present the evidence concerning the begums of Oudh, the streets leading to Westminster Hall were crowded from eight in the morning with persons, many of high rank, anxious to find admittance. Some who had secured cards of admission sold them for fifty guineas ($1,500?) each. Sheridan understood that a dramatic performance was expected of him; he gave it. He spoke at four sittings; on the final day (June 13, 1788), after holding the floor for five hours, he sank exhausted into the arms of Burke, who embraced him. Gibbon, who was in the gallery, described Sheridan as "a good actor," and remarked how well the orator looked when the historian called upon him the next morning.[134]

That speech was the climax of the trial. Each of the score of charges required investigation; the lords took their time, and may have dallied to let the effect of eloquence wear off, and let interest in the case be diverted to other events. These came. In October, 1788, King George went mad, quite seriously mad, borne down by the stress of the trial and the misconduct of his son. George Augustus Frederick, Prince of Wales, was fat, good-natured, generous, wasteful, and amorous. He had maintained a succession of mistresses, and had accumulated debts which his father or the nation paid. In 1785 he had privately married Mrs. Maria Anne Fitzherbert, a devout Roman Catholic, already twice widowed, and six years older than the Prince. The Whigs, led by Fox, proposed to set up a regency under the Prince, who sat up through two nights waiting for the King to be declared incompetent. George III confused matters by having lucid intervals, in which he talked of Garrick and Johnson, sang snatches of Handel, and played the flute. In March, 1789, he recovered, shed his strait jacket, and resumed the forms of rule.

The French Revolution provided another diversion from the trial. Burke gave up the chase of Hastings and ran to the aid of Marie Antoinette. The immoderation of his speeches ended the remains of his popularity; he complained that the members of Parliament slipped away when he began to speak. Most of the press was hostile to him; he charged that £20,000 had been used in buying journalists to attack him and defend Hastings; and unquestionably a large part of Hastings' fortune had been so spent.[135] It must have been no surprise to Burke when, at last, eight years after the impeachment, the House of Lords acquitted Hastings (1795). The general feeling was that the verdict was just: the accused had in many respects been guilty, but he had saved India for England, and had been punished by a trial that had broken his health and his hopes and had left him tarnished in reputation and ruined in purse.

Hastings survived all his accusers. The East India Company rescued him from insolvency by voting him a gift of £90,000. He bought back his family's ancestral estate at Daylesford, restored it, and lived in Oriental luxury. In 1813, aged eighty-one, he was asked to testify on Indian affairs before the House of Commons; he was received there with acclamation and reverence, his services remembered, his sins washed away by time. Four years later he passed away, and of his tumultuous generation only one remained—the blind and imbecile King.

VII. ENGLAND AND THE FRENCH REVOLUTION

After almost exhausting himself in his war against the East India Company, Burke took on the French Revolution as his personal enemy, and in the course of this new campaign he made a major contribution to political philosophy.

He had predicted the Revolution twenty years before its coming. "Under such extreme straitness and distraction labors the whole of French finances, so far does their charge outrun their supply in every particular, that no man, . . . who has considered their affairs with any degree of attention or information, but must hourly look for some extraordinary convulsion in that whole system; the effect of which on France, and even on all Europe, it is difficult to conjecture."[136] In 1773 he visited France; at Versailles he saw Marie Antoinette, then dauphine; he never forgot that vision of youthful beauty, happiness, and pride. He formed a favorable opinion of the French nobility, and still more of the French clergy. He was shocked by the anti-Catholic, often antireligious, propaganda of the *philosophes,* and on his return to England he warned his countrymen against atheism as "the most horrid and cruel blow that can be offered to civil society."[137]

When the Revolution came he was alarmed by the acclaim it received from his friend Fox, who hailed the fall of the Bastille as "the greatest event that ever happened in the world, and . . . the best."[138] Radical ideas stemming from the campaigns of Wilkes and the Society of Supporters of the Bill of Rights had slowly spread in England. One obscure writer, in 1761, proposed communism as a cure for all social ills except overpopulation, which, he feared, might cancel all attempts to relieve poverty.[139] A Society for Commemorating the Revolution (of 1688) had been formed in 1788; its membership included prominent clergymen and peers. At its meeting on November 4, 1789, it was so stirred by a Unitarian preacher, Richard Price, that it sent an address of congratulations to the National Assembly at Paris, expressing the hope that "the glorious example given in France" might "encourage other nations to assert the inalienable rights of mankind."[140] The message was signed by the third Earl Stanhope, president of the society and brother-in-law of William Pitt.

That sermon and that message aroused Burke to fear and wrath. He was now sixty years old, and had reached the right to be conservative. He was religious, and owned a large estate. The French Revolution seemed to him not only "the most astonishing that has hitherto happened in the world,"[141] but the most outrageous attack upon religion, property, order, and law. On February 9, 1790, he told the House of Commons that if any friend of his should concur in any measures tending to introduce into England such democracy as was taking form in France, he would renounce that friendship, however long established and dearly cherished. Fox soothed the orator with his famous compliment to Burke as his best educator; the break between the two was postponed.

In November, 1790, Burke published *Reflections on the Revolution in France*, in the form of a letter (365 pages long) to "a gentleman in Paris." Leader of the liberals during the American Revolution, Burke was now the hero of conservative England; George III expressed his delight with his old enemy. The book became the bible of courts and aristocracies; Catherine the Great, once the friend and darling of the *philosophes*, sent her congratulations to the man who had set out to dethrone them.[142]

Burke began with a reference to Dr. Price and the Society for Commemorating the Revolution. He deplored the entry of clergymen into political discussions; their business was to guide souls to Christian charity, not to political reform. He had no trust in the universal male suffrage that Price pleaded for; he thought the majority would be a worse tyrant than a king, and that democracy would degenerate into mob rule. Wisdom lies not in numbers but in experience. Nature knows nothing of equality. Political equality is a "monstrous fiction, which, by inspiring false ideas and vain expectations into men destined to travel in the obscure walks of laborious life, serves only to aggravate that real inequality, which it never can remove."[143] Aristocracy is inevitable; and the older it is, the better it will fulfill its function of silently establishing that social order without which there can be no stability, no security, and no liberty.[144] Hereditary monarchy is good because it gives to government a unity and continuity without which the legal and social relations of the citizens would fall into a hectic and chaotic flux. Religion is good, because it helps to chain those unsocial impulses which run like subterranean fire beneath the surface of civilization, and which can be controlled only by the constant co-operation of state and church, law and creed, fear and reverence. Those French philosophers who undermined religious belief in the educated ranks of their people were foolishly loosing the reins that had kept men from becoming beasts.

Burke was revolted by the triumph of the mob at Versailles over "a mild and lawful monarch," treating him with "more fury, outrage, and insult than ever any people" raised "against the most illegal usurper and the most sanguinary tyrant."[145] Here came the famous page that thrilled our youth:

> It is now sixteen or seventeen years since I saw the Queen of France, then the Dauphiness, at Versailles; and surely never lighted on this orb, which she hardly seemed to touch, a more delightful vision. I saw her just above the horizon, decorating and cheering the elevated sphere she just began to move in —glittering like the morning star, full of life, and splendor, and joy. Oh, what a revolution! and what a heart must I have to contemplate without emotion that elevation and that fall!* Little did I dream, when she added titles of veneration to those of enthusiastic, distant, respectful love, that she should ever be obliged to carry the sharp antidote against disgrace concealed in that bosom; little did I dream that I should have lived to see such disasters fallen upon her in a nation of gallant men, in a nation of men of honor, and of cavaliers. I thought ten thousand swords must have leaped from their scabbards to avenge even a look that threatened her with insult. But the age of chivalry is gone. That of sophisters, economists, and calculators has succeeded, and the glory of Europe is extinguished forever.[146]

Sir Philip Francis laughed at all this as romantic moonshine, and assured Burke that the Queen of France was a Messalina and a jade.[147] So thought many patriotic Englishmen; Horace Walpole, however, affirmed that Burke had pictured Marie Antoinette "exactly as she appeared to me the first time I saw her when Dauphiness."[148]

---

* I.e., the compulsion laid upon Louis XVI and Marie Antoinette, by the mob at Versailles, to march back with it to Paris and to live under popular surveillance in the Tuileries (Oct. 5–6, 1789).

As the Revolution proceeded Burke continued his attack with a *Letter to a Member of the National Assembly* (January, 1791). In this he suggested that the governments of Europe should unite to check the revolt, and to restore the King of France to his traditional power. Fox was alarmed at this proposal, and in the House of Commons, on May 6, the friends who had fought shoulder to shoulder in so many campaigns came to a dramatic parting of the ways. Fox reiterated his praise of the Revolution. Burke rose in protest. "It is indiscreet," he said, "at any period, but especially at my time of life, to provoke enemies, or give my friends occasion to desert me. Yet if my firm and steady adherence to the British constitution place me in such a dilemma I am ready to risk it." Fox assured him that no severance of friendship was involved in their differences. "Yes, yes," answered Burke, "there is a loss of friends. I know the price of my conduct. . . . Our friendship is at an end."[149] He never spoke to Fox again, except formally in their constrained union in the Hastings trial.

In his writings on the French Revolution Burke gave a classical expression to a conservative philosophy. Its first principle is to distrust the reasoning of an individual, however brilliant, if it conflicts with the traditions of the race. Just as a child cannot understand the reasons for parental cautions and prohibitions, so the individual, who is a child compared with the race, cannot always understand the reasons for customs, conventions, and laws that embody the experience of many generations. Civilization would be impossible "if the practice of all moral duties, and the foundations of society, rested upon having their reasons made clear and demonstrative to every individual."[150] Even "prejudices" have their use; they prejudge present problems on the basis of past experience.

So the second element of conservatism is "prescription": a tradition or an institution should be doubly reverenced and rarely changed if it is *already written* or embodied in the order of the society or the structure of the government. Private property is an example of prescription and of the apparent irrationality of wisdom: it seems unreasonable that one family should own so much, another so little, and even more unreasonable that the owner should be allowed to transmit his property to successors who have not lifted a hand to earn it; yet experience has found that men in general will not bestir themselves to work and study, or to laborious and expensive preparation, unless they may call the results of their efforts their own property, to be transmitted, in large measure, as they desire; and experience has shown that the possession of property is the best guarantee for the prudence of legislation and the continuity of the state.

A state is not merely an association of persons in a given space at a given moment; it is an association of individuals through extensive time. "Society is indeed a contract, . . . a partnership not only between those who are living, but between those who are living, those who are dead, and those who are to be born";[151] that continuity is our country. In this triune whole a present majority may be a minority in time; and the legislator must consider the rights of the past (through "prescription") and of the future as well as those of the living present. Politics is, or should be, the art of adjusting the aims of clashing minorities with the good of the continuing group. Moreover, there are no absolute rights; these are metaphysical abstractions unknown to nature; there are only desires, powers, and circumstances; and "circumstances give to every political principle its distinguishing color and discriminating effect."[152] Expediency is sometimes more important than rights. "Politics ought to be adjusted not to [abstract] human reasonings but to human nature, of which the reason is but a part, and by no means the greatest part."[153] "We must make use of existing materials."[154]

All these considerations are illustrated by religion. The doctrines, myths, and ceremonies of a religion may not conform to our present individual reason, but this may be of minor moment if they comport with the past, present, and presumed future needs of society. Experience dictates that the passions of men can be controlled only by the teachings and observances of religion. "If we should uncover our nakedness [release our instincts] by throwing off that Christian religion which has been . . . one great source of civilization amongst us, . . . we are apprehensive (being well aware that the mind will not endure a void) that some uncouth, pernicious, and degrading superstition might take place of it."[155]

Many Englishmen rejected Burke's conservatism as a cult of stagnation,[156] and Thomas Paine answered him vigorously in *The Rights of Man* (1791–92). But the England of Burke's old age generally welcomed his ancestor worship. As the French Revolution went on to the September Massacres, the execution of the King and the Queen, and the Reign of Terror, the great majority of Britons felt that Burke had well predicted the results of revolt and irreligion; and for a full century England, though eliminating her rotten boroughs and widening her suffrage, kept resolutely to its constitution of king, aristocracy, Established Church, and a Parliament thinking in terms of imperial powers rather than of popular rights. After the Revolution France returned from Rousseau to Montesquieu, and Joseph de Maistre rephrased Burke for the repentant French.

Burke continued to the end his campaign for a holy war, and he rejoiced when France declared war on Great Britain (1793). George III wished to reward his old enemy for recent services with a peerage, and with that title of Lord Beaconsfield which Disraeli later graced; Burke refused, but accepted a pension of £2,500 (1794). When talk arose of negotiations with France, he issued four *Letters on a Regicide Peace* (1797 f.), passionately demanding that the war go on. Only death cooled his fire (July 8, 1797). Fox proposed that he be buried in Westminster Abbey, but Burke had left instructions that he should have a private funeral and be interred in the little church at Beaconsfield. Macaulay thought him the greatest Englishman since Milton—which may have slighted Chatham; and Lord Morley more prudently called him "the greatest master of civil wisdom in our tongue"[157] —which may have slighted Locke. In any case Burke was what conservatives had longed for in vain throughout the Age of Reason—a man who could defend custom as brilliantly as Voltaire had defended reason.

VIII. THE HEROES RETIRE

As the French Revolution advanced, Charles James Fox found himself in a diminishing minority in Parliament and in the country. Many of his allies were won to the view that England must join Prussia and Austria in fighting France. After the execution of Louis XVI Fox himself turned against the Revolution, but he still opposed entry into the war. When war came nevertheless, he consoled himself by drinking, by reading the classics, and by marrying (1795) his (and Lord Cavendish's, Lord Derby's, and Lord Cholmondeley's) former mistress, Mrs. Elizabeth Armstead, who paid his debts.[158] He welcomed the Peace of Amiens (1802), traveled in France, was acclaimed there with civic and popular honors, and was received by Napoleon as a patriot of civilization. In 1806 he served as foreign secretary in a "Ministry of All the Talents"; he labored to keep the peace with France, and decisively supported Wilberforce's campaign against the slave trade. When he learned of a plot to assassinate Napoleon he sent the Emperor a warning through Talleyrand. Had Fox's health not broken down, he might have found a means of reconciling Bonaparte's ambition with England's security. But in July, 1806, he was disabled by dropsy. A succession of painful operations failed to stay the progress of the disease; he made his peace with the Established Church, and on September 13 he died, mourned by his friends and his enemies, and even by the King. He was the most widely loved man of his time.

The younger Pitt, prematurely old, preceded him to the Abbey's vaults. He too found that he could bear the pace of political life only through the occasional amnesia of drink. The precarious sanity of George III was a constant problem; any serious conflict of views between King and minister might throw the crowned head out of balance and bring in a regency by the Prince of Wales, who would sack Pitt and call in Fox. So Pitt abandoned his plans for political reform, and withdrew his opposition to the slave trade, when he found that on these, as on many other matters, George was fretfully resolved to perpetuate the past. Pitt concentrated his genius on economic legislation, in which he served the rising middle class. Much to his distaste, he led England in war against what he called "a nation of atheists."[159] He did not do well as a war minister. Fearing a French invasion of Ireland, he tried to appease the Irish with a program of parliamentary union and Catholic emancipation; the King balked, and Pitt resigned (1801). He returned (1804) to head his second ministry; Napoleon proved too much for him; and when the news came of the French victory at Austerlitz (December 2, 1805), which made Napoleon master of the Continent, Pitt broke down in body and spirit. Seeing a large map of Europe, he bade a friend, "Roll up that map; it will not be wanted these ten years."[160] He died January 23, 1806, honorably poor, and only forty-six years old.

Life took longer to destroy Sheridan. He had joined with Burke and Fox in the defense of America and the battle of Hastings; he supported Fox in applauding the French Revolution. Meanwhile that wife whose charm and gentle nature were favorite themes among his friends, and who had put her beauty on the hustings to help him win a seat in Parliament, died of tuberculosis in her thirty-eighth year (1792). Sheridan broke down. "I have seen him," said an acquaintance, "night after night cry like a child."[161] He found some consolation in the daughter she had borne him; but she died in the same year. During those months of grief he faced the task of rebuilding the Drury Lane Theatre, which had become too old and weak for safety; and to finance this operation he incurred heavy liabilities. He had accustomed himself to luxurious living, which his income could not maintain; he borrowed to continue that style. When his creditors came to dun him he treated them like lords, entertained them with liquor, courtesy, and wit, and sent them away in a humor that almost forgot his debts. He remained active in Parliament till 1812, when he failed of re-election. As a member of the House he had been immune to arrest; now his creditors closed in upon him, appropriated his books, his pictures, his jewels; finally they were about to carry him off to jail when his physician warned them that Sheridan might die on the way. He succumbed on July 7, 1816, in his sixty-fifth year. He was rich again in his funeral, for seven lords and one bishop bore him to the Abbey.

The half-mad King survived them all, survived even the triumph of England at Waterloo, though he knew it not. By 1783 he recognized that he had failed in his attempt to make the ministers responsible to him rather than to Parliament. The long struggles with the House of Commons, with America, and with France proved too much for him, and in 1801, 1804, and 1810 he relapsed into insanity. In his old age the people came to recognize his courage and his sincerity, and the popularity that had been denied him in his days of strife came to him at last, tinged with pity for a man who had seen England suffer so many defeats and was not permitted to witness her victory. The death of his favorite daughter, Amelia (1810), completed his divorce from reality; in 1811 he became incurably insane as well as blind, and he remained in seclusion, under guard, till his death (January 29, 1820).

CHAPTER XXIX

The English People

1756-89

I. ENGLISH WAYS

SO much for the government; let us now consider the people.

First, look at their figures. Doubtless Reynolds idealized them, showing us mostly the titled fortunate, and glorifying their corpulence with the robes and insignia of dignity. But hear Goethe on the Englishmen he saw in Weimar: "What fine, handsome people they are!"—and he worried lest these confident young Britishers, bearing empire in their stride, would disenchant German girls with German men.[1] Several of these youths kept their figures into later years, but many of them, as they passed from the playgrounds of their schools to the pleasures of the table, swelled in paunch and jowls, blossomed like a red, red rose, and fought in the still of the night the gout they had fed in the jovial day. Some Elizabethan robustness had been lost in Restoration roistering. English women, by contrast, were more beautiful than ever, at least on the easels: refined features, flowered and ribboned hair, mysteries in silk, poems of stately grace.

Sartorial class distinctions were disappearing on the streets as a new plenty of cotton clothing issued from the multiplying mills, but on formal occasions they remained; Lord Derwentwater rode to his execution in a scarlet coat and waistcoat laced with gold.[2] Wigs were waning, and they vanished when Pitt II taxed the powder that deodorized them; they survived on doctors, judges, barristers, and Samuel Johnson; most men were now content with their own hair, gathered at the back of the neck in a ribboned queue. About 1785 some men extended their breeches from knees to calves; in 1793, inspired by the triumphant French sans-culottes, they let them reach the ankle, and modern man was born. Women still laced their bosoms to the verge of suffocation, but the hoopskirt was losing fashion and breadth, and dresses were assuming those flowing lines that fascinated our youth.

Cleanliness was next to godliness in rarity, for water was a luxury. Rivers were lovely but usually polluted; the Thames was a drainage canal.[3] Most London houses had water piped into them three times a week for three shillings per quarter;[4] some had mechanical toilets; a few had bathrooms with running water. Most privies (whose current name was "Jerichos") were extramural, built over open pits that sent their seepage through the soil to wells from which much of the drinking water came.[5] Nevertheless public sanitation was improving; hospitals were multiplying; infantile mortality fell from seventy-four per hundred births in 1749 to forty-one in 1809.[6]

No one drank water if he could get something safer. Beer was considered a food, necessary for any vigorous work; wine was a favorite medicine, whiskey was a portable stove, and drunkenness was a venial sin, if not a necessary part of social conformity. "I remember," said Dr. Johnson, "when all the decent people in Lichfield got drunk every night, and were not the worse thought of."[7] Pitt II came drunk to the House of Commons, and Lord Cornwallis went drunk to the opera.[8] Some hackney coachmen added to their incomes by cruising the streets at late hours, picking up gentlemen who were "as drunk as a lord," and delivering them to their homes. Drunkenness declined as the century advanced; tea took up some of the task of warming the vitals and loosing the tongue. Tea imports rose from a hundred pounds in 1668 to fourteen million pounds in 1786.[9] The coffeehouses now served more tea than coffee.

Meals were hearty, bloody, and immense. Dinner came about four in the afternoon for the upper classes, and was progressively deferred till six as the century declined. A hurried man might ease his hunger with a sandwich. This contraption took its name from the fourth Earl of Sandwich, who, not to interrupt his gambling with dinner, ate two slices of bread divided by meat. Vegetables were eaten under protest. "Smoking has gone out [of fashion]," Johnson told Boswell in 1773; but tobacco was taken in the form of snuff. Opium was widely used as a sedative or a cure.

At table the Englishman could drink himself into loquacity, and then the conversation might rival that of the Paris salons in wit and excel it in substance. One day (April 9, 1778), as Johnson, Gibbon, Boswell, Allan Ramsay, and other friends gathered in the home of Sir Joshua Reynolds, the Doctor remarked: "I question if in Paris such a company as is sitting around this table could be got together in less than half a year."[10] Aristocratic gatherings preferred wit to learning, and Selwyn to Johnson. George Selwyn was the Oscar Wilde of the eighteenth century. He had been expelled from Oxford (1745) because "he did impiously affect to personate the Blessed Saviour, and did ridicule the institution of the Holy Sacrament,"[11] but this did not prevent him from getting several lucrative sinecures in the administration, or from sitting and sleeping in the House of Commons from 1747 to 1780. He had a host of friends, but never married. He had a passion for executions, but skipped that of a namesake of Charles James Fox, a political enemy for whom he hopefully awaited a Tyburn elevation—"I make a point of never attending rehearsals."[12] He and Horace Walpole were intimate friends for sixty-three years, without a cloud or a woman between them.

Those who did not enjoy executions could choose among a hundred other amusements, from whist or bird-watching to horse races or prize fights. Cricket was now the national game. The poor squandered their wages in taverns, the rich gambled their fortunes in clubs or in private homes; so Walpole, at Lady Hertford's, "lost fifty-six guineas before I could say an Ave Maria."[13] James Gillray, in famous caricatures, called such hostesses "Faro's daughters."[14] To take losses calmly was a prime requisite of an English gentleman, even if he ended by blowing out his brains.

It was a man's world, legally, socially, and morally. Men took most of their social pleasures with other men; not till 1770 was a club organized for bisexual membership. Men discouraged intellect in women, and then complained that women were incapable of intellectual conversation. Some women, nevertheless, managed to develop intellects. Mrs. Elizabeth Carter learned to speak Latin, French, Italian, and German, studied Hebrew, Portuguese, and Arabic, and translated Epictetus with a Greek scholarship that drew Johnson's praise. She protested against the reluctance of men to discuss ideas with women, and she was one of those ladies who made the "blue-stockings" the talk of literate London.

The name was first given to the mixed gatherings at the home of Mrs. Elizabeth Vesey in Hertford Street, Mayfair. At these evening assemblies card playing was banned and discussion of literature was encouraged. Meeting, one day, Benjamin Stillingfleet, who had a momentary reputation as poet, botanist, and philosopher, Mrs. Vesey invited him to her next "rout." He excused himself on the ground that he had no clothes fit for a party. He was wearing blue hose. "Don't mind dress," she told him; "come in your blue stockings." He came. "Such was the excellence of his conversation," Boswell relates, "that . . . it used to be said, 'we do nothing without the blue stockings'; and thus by degrees the title was established,"[15] and Mrs. Vesey's group came to be called the Bas Bleu Society. There came Garrick and Walpole, and there one evening Johnson awed all with pontifical discourse.

But "the Queen of the Blues," as Johnson called her, was Elizabeth Robinson Montagu. She was married to Edward Montagu, grandson of the first Earl of Sandwich and relative of Edward Wortley Montagu, husband of the volatile Lady Mary whom we celebrated in pages gone by.[16] Elizabeth was a wit, a scholar, an author; her essay *The Writings and Genius of Shakespeare* (1769) indignantly defended the national bard against the strictures of Voltaire. She was rich, and could afford to entertain in style. She made the Chinese Room in her Berkeley Square home the favorite center of London's intellect and beauty; there came Reynolds, Johnson, Burke, Goldsmith, Garrick, Horace Walpole, Fanny Burney, Hannah More; there artists met lawyers, prelates met philosophers, poets met ambassadors. Mrs. Montagu's "excellent cook" put them all in good humor, but no liquor was served, and intoxication was taboo. She played Maecenas to budding authors, and scattered bounty. Other London ladies—Mrs. Thrale, Mrs. Boscawen, Mrs. Monckton—opened their homes to talent and charm. London society became bisexual, and began to rival Paris in the fame and genius of its salons.

II. ENGLISH MORALS

"In every society," said Adam Smith, "where the distinction of ranks has once been completely established, there have always been two different schemes or systems of morality current at the same time; of which one may be called the strict or austere, the other the liberal, or, if you will, the loose system. The former is generally admired and revered by the common people, the latter . . . more esteemed and adopted by what are called people of fashion."[17] John Wesley, who belonged to the austere class, described English morality in 1757 as a medley of smuggling, false oaths, political corruption, drunkenness, gambling, cheating in business, chicanery in the courts, servility in the clergy, worldliness among Quakers, and private embezzlement of charitable funds.[18] It is an old refrain.

Then, as now, sexual differentiation was far from complete. Some women tried to be men, and almost succeeded; we hear of cases where women disguised themselves as men and maintained the deception till death; some joined the army or navy as men, drank, smoked, and swore like men, fought in battle, and bore flogging manfully.[19] Toward 1772 "Macaronis" became prominent on London streets; they were young men who wore their hair in long curls, dressed in rich materials and striking colors, and "wenched without passion"; Selwyn described them as "a kind of animal neither male nor female, but of the neuter gender."[20] Homosexualism had its brothels, though homosexual acts, if detected and proved, were punishable with death.

The double standard flourished. A thousand bordellos served tumescent men, but those men branded female unchastity as a crime for which only death could atone. So the gentle Goldsmith:

> When lovely woman stoops to folly
> And finds too late that men betray,—
> What charm can soothe her melancholy,
> What art can wash her guilt away?
> The only art her guilt to cover,
> To hide her shame from every eye,
> To give repentance to her lover
> And wring his bosom, is—to die.[21]

Early marriage was advised as a preventive of such calamities. The law allowed girls to marry at twelve, boys at fourteen. Most women of the educated classes married young, and deferred their deviations; but then the double standard checked them. Hear Johnson on adultery (1768):

> Confusion of progeny constitutes the essence of the crime, and therefore the woman who breaks her marriage vows is much more criminal than a man who does it. A man, to be sure, is criminal in the sight of God, but he does not do his wife a very material injury if he does not insult her; if, for instance, from mere wantonness of appetite, he steals privately to her chambermaid. Sir, a wife ought not greatly to resent this. I would not receive home a daughter who had run away from her husband on that account. A wife should study to reclaim her husband by more attention to please him. Sir, a man will not, once in a hundred instances, leave his wife and go to a harlot, if his wife has not been negligent of pleasing.[22]

In Boswell's own circle it was taken as quite ordinary that men should occasionally go to a prostitute. In the aristocracy—even in the royal family—adultery was widespread. The Duke of Grafton, while chief minister, lived openly with Nancy Parsons, and took her to the opera in the face of the

Queen.[23] Divorce was rare; it could not be obtained except by act of Parliament, and as this cost "several thousand pounds," it was a luxury of the rich; only 132 such grants were recorded in the years 1670–1800.[24] It was generally supposed that the morals of the commonalty were better than those of the aristocracy, but Johnson thought otherwise (1778): "There is as much fornication and adultery amongst farmers as amongst noblemen," and "so far as I have observed, the higher in rank, the richer ladies are, they are the better instructed, and the more virtuous."[25] The literature of the day, as in Fielding and Burns, pictured the peasant as celebrating almost every week-end with a carouse, spending half his pay in taverns, and some on tarts. Each class sinned according to its ways and means.

The poor fought one another with fists and cudgels, the rich with pistols and swords. Dueling was a point of honor in the nobility; Fox fought Adam, Shelburne fought Fullerton, Pitt II fought Tierney; it was difficult to get through a titled life without at least one puncture. Many stories attest the *sang-froid* of British gentlemen in these encounters. Lord Shelburne, having received a wound in the groin, assured his anxious seconds, "I don't think Lady Shelburne will be the worse for it."[26]

Worse than the looseness of sexual morals was the brutality of industrial exploitation: the merciless consumption of human life in the grasp for profits; the use of children six years of age in factories or as chimneysweeps; the reduction of thousands of men and women to such destitution that they sold themselves into payless bondage for passage to America; the governmental protection of the slave trade as a precious source of England's wealth . . .

From Liverpool, Bristol, and London—as from Holland and France—merchants sailed to Africa, bought and captured Negroes, shipped them to the West Indies, sold them there, and returned to Europe with lucrative cargoes of sugar, tobacco, or rum. By 1776 English traders had carried three million slaves to America; add 250,000 who died in passage and were thrown into the sea. The British government granted an annual subsidy of £10,000 to the African Company and its successor, the Regulated Company, toward the maintenance of their forts and posts in Africa, on the ground that they were "the most beneficial to this island of all the Companies that were ever formed by our merchants."[27] George III (1770) forbade the governor of Virginia "to assent to any law by which the importations of slaves should be in any respect prohibited or obstructed."[28] In 1771 there were in England about fourteen thousand Negroes, who had been brought in by their colonial masters, or had escaped from them; some were used as domestic servants with no right to wages;[29] some were sold at public auction, as in Liverpool in 1766.[30] In 1772, however, an English court ruled that a slave automatically became a free man the moment he touched English soil.[31]

Slowly the conscience of England awoke to the contradiction between this traffic and the simplest dictates of religion or morality. The finest spirits in Britain denounced it: George Fox, Daniel Defoe, James Thomson, Richard Steele, Alexander Pope, William Paley, John Wesley, William Cowper,

Francis Hutcheson, William Robertson, Adam Smith, Josiah Wedgwood, Horace Walpole, Samuel Johnson, Edmund Burke, Charles James Fox. The first organized opposition to slavery was by the Quakers in England and America; in 1761 they excluded from their membership all persons engaged in the traffic; in 1783 they formed an association "for the relief and liberation of the Negro slaves in the West Indies, and for the discouragement of the slave trade on the coast of Africa."[32] In 1787 Granville Sharp formed a committee to advance abolition; in 1789 William Wilberforce began his long campaign in the House of Commons to end the English trade in slaves. The merchants repeatedly persuaded the House to defer action; it was not till 1807 that Parliament enacted that no vessel should carry slaves from any port within the British dominions after May 1, 1807, or to any British colony after March 1, 1808.[33]

In political morality England now touched nadir. The rotten-borough system flourished, and the nabobs outbid all other purchasers. Franklin deplored the American war for a peculiar reason: "Why did they not let me go on? If they [the colonies] had given me a fourth of the money they have spent on the war, we should have had our independence without spending a drop of blood. I would have bought all the Parliament, the whole government of Britain."[34] Corruption ruled in the Church, the universities, the judiciary, the civil service, the army and navy, and the councils of the King. Military discipline was more rigorous than in any other European country[35] with the possible exception of Prussia; and when the men were demobilized nothing was done to ease their transition into a useful and law-abiding life.

Social morality hovered between the essential good nature of the individual Englishman and the irresponsible brutality of mobs. Between 1765 and 1780 there were nine major riots, nearly all in London; we shall see an example presently. Crowds ran to a hanging as a holiday, and sometimes bribed the hangman to be especially thorough in flogging a prisoner.[36] The penal code was the severest in Europe. Language in nearly all classes tended to violence and profanity. The press engaged in orgies of vituperation and calumny. Almost everyone gambled, if only in the national lottery, and almost everyone drank to excess.

The faults of the English character were allied to its basic quality—a hearty, lusty vigor. The peasant and the factory laborer expended it in toil, the nation showed it in every crisis but one. Out of that vigor came the voracious appetite, the high spirits, the resort to prostitutes, the brawls in the pubs and the duels in the park, the passion of parliamentary debate, the capacity for suffering silently, the proud claim of every Englishman that his home was his castle, not to be entered except by due process of law. When, in this age, England was defeated, it was by Englishmen who had transplanted to America the English passion for freedom. Mme. du Deffand noted the diversity of individuals in the Englishmen whom she met, and most of whom she never saw. "Each one," she said, "is original; there are no two alike. We [French] are just the opposite; when you have seen one of our courtiers you have seen all."[37] And Horace Walpole agreed: "It is certain that no other country produces so many singular and discriminate characters as England."[38] Look at Reynolds' men: they agree only in their pride of country and class, their ruddy faces, their bold confronting of the world. It was a powerful breed.

III. FAITH AND DOUBT

The English masses remained faithful to their various forms of the Christian creed. The most widely read book, next to the Bible, was *Nelson's Festivals and Fasts*, a guide to the ecclesiastical year.[39] Johnson's *Prayers and Meditations*, published after his death, went through four editions in four years. In the upper classes religion was respected as a social function, an aid to morals, and an arm of government, but it had lost private credence and all power over policy. The bishops were named by the king, and the parsons were appointees and dependents of the squires. The deistic attack on religion had so far subsided that Burke could ask in 1790: "Who, born within the last forty years, has read one word of Collins, and Toland, and Tindal, and Chubb, and Morgan, and that whole race who called themselves Freethinkers?"[40] But if no one rose to answer him it may be because those rebels had won the battle, and educated men shrugged off the old questions as settled and dead. Boswell in 1765 (forgetting the commonalty) described his time as "an age when mankind are so fond of incredulity that they seem to pique themselves in contracting their circle of belief as much as possible."[41] We have seen Selwyn mocking religion at Oxford, and Wilkes at Medmenham Abbey. The younger Pitt, according to Lady Hester Stanhope, "never went to church in his life."[42] And one did not have to believe in order to preach. "There are," Boswell wrote in 1763, "many infidels in orders, who, considering religion merely as a political institution, accept of a benefice as of any civil employment, and contribute their endeavors to keep up the useful delusion."[43] "The forms of orthodoxy, the articles of faith," said Gibbon, "are subscribed with a sigh or a smile by the modern clergy."[44]

Private clubs offered relief from public conformity. Many aristocrats joined one or another of the Freemason lodges. These condemned atheism as stupid, and required of their members a belief in God, but they inculcated toleration of differences on all other doctrines of religion.[45] In the Lunar Society of Birmingham manufacturers like Matthew Boulton, James Watt, and Josiah Wedgwood heard without horror the heresies of Joseph Priestley and Erasmus Darwin.[46] Nevertheless the furor of deism had passed, and nearly all freethinkers accepted a truce by which they would not interfere with the propagation of the faith if the Church allowed some latitude to sin. The English upper classes, with their sense of order and moderation, avoided the reckless radicalism of the French Enlightenment; they recognized the intimate union of religion and government, and were too economical to replace a supernatural morality with an infinitude of police.

Since they were now servants of the state, the Anglican bishops, like the Catholic cardinals, thought themselves entitled to a measure of worldly enjoyment. Cowper satirized in bitter lines[47] the clergymen who scrambled like politicians for richer or additional benefices; but many others led lives of quiet attention to their duties, and several were scholarly and able defenders of the faith. William Paley's *Principles of Moral and Political Philosophy* (1785) displayed a generous spirit of doctrinal latitude and toleration, and his *Evidences of Christianity* (1794) persuasively presented the argument from design. He welcomed into holy orders men of freethinking tendencies so long as they preached the essentials of religion and served as moral leaders in their communities.[48]

Dissenters—Baptists, Presbyterians, and Independents (Puritans)—enjoyed religious toleration provided they adhered to Trinitarian Christianity; but no one could hold political or military office, or enter Oxford or Cambridge, without accepting the Anglican Church and its Thirty-nine Articles. Methodism continued to spread among the lower classes. In 1784 it broke its tenuous ties with the Established Church, but meanwhile it had inspired the "Evangelical movement" in a minority of Anglican clergymen. These men admired Wesley, and agreed with him that the Gospel, or Evangel, should be preached precisely as handed down in the New Testament, with no concessions to rationalist or textual criticism.

England's memory of the Gunpowder Plot, the Great Rebellion, and the reign of James II still kept on the statute books the old laws against Roman Catholics. Most of these laws were no longer enforced, but many disabilities remained. Catholics could not legally buy or inherit land except through a subterfuge and payment of a double tax on their property. They were excluded from the army and navy, from the legal profession, from voting or standing for Parliament, and from all governmental posts. Even so, their number was growing. In 1781 they included seven peers, twenty-two baronets, 150 "gentlemen." Mass was celebrated in private homes, and only two or three arrests for this offense are recorded in the sixty years of George III's reign.

In 1778 Sir George Savile offered Parliament a bill for "Catholic relief," legalizing the purchase and inheritance of land by Catholics, and allowing Catholics to enlist in the armed forces without renouncing their religion. The bill was passed, and met with no serious opposition from the Anglican bishops in the House of Lords. It applied only to England, but in 1779 Lord North moved that it be extended to Scotland. When news of this proposal reached the Lowlands, riots broke out in Edinburgh and Glasgow (January, 1779); several houses inhabited by Catholics were burned to the ground; the shops of Catholic tradesmen were looted and wrecked; the houses of Protestants—like Robertson the historian—who expressed sympathy for the Catholics were likewise attacked, and the outbreak ended only when Edinburgh magistrates announced that the Act for Catholic Relief would not be applied to Scotland.

A Scottish member of Parliament, Lord George Gordon, took up the "No-Popery" cause in England. On May 29, 1780, he presided over a meeting of the "Protestant Association," which planned a mass march to present a petition for repeal of the Relief Act of 1778. On June 2 sixty thousand men, wearing blue cockades, surrounded Parliament House. Many members were mauled on their way in; the carriages of Lords Mansfield, Thurlow, and Stormont were demolished; some noble lords reached their seats wigless, disheveled, and trembling.[49] Gordon and eight of his followers entered the House of Commons; they presented a petition, allegedly bearing 120,000 signatures, calling for repeal, and demanded immediate action as the sole alternative to invasion of the House by the mob. The members resisted. They sent for troops to check the crowd; they locked all doors; a relative of Gordon declared that he would kill him the moment any outsider forced his way into the chamber; then the House voted to adjourn till June 6. Troops arrived and cleared a way for the members to return to their homes. Two Catholic chapels, belonging to Sardinian and Bavarian ministers, were gutted, and their furniture made a bonfire in the streets. The crowd dispersed, but on June 5 rioters looted other foreign chapels, and burned several private homes.

On June 6 the mob regathered, broke into Newgate Gaol, freed the prisoners, captured an arsenal, and marched, armed, through the capital. Nobles barricaded themselves in their homes; Horace Walpole complimented himself on guarding a duchess in his "garrison" in Berkeley Square.[50] On June 7 more houses were looted and burned; distilleries were entered, and thirst was freely quenched; several rioters were cremated as they lay intoxicated in burning buildings. The London magistrates, who alone had legal authority over the municipal guard, refused to order them to fire upon the crowd. George III called out the citizen militia, and bade them shoot whenever the mob used or threatened violence. Alderman John Wilkes earned forgiveness from the King, and lost his popularity with the populace, by mounting a horse and joining with the militia in attempting to disperse the assemblage. The militia, attacked by the rioters, fired upon them, killing twenty-two. The crowd fled.

On June 9 the riot flared again. Houses—whether of Catholics or of Protestants—were pillaged and burned, and firemen were prevented from extinguishing the flames.[51] Troops suppressed the uprising at the cost of 285 men killed and 173 wounded; 135 rioters were arrested, twenty-one were hanged. Gordon was arrested in flight toward Scotland; he proved that he had taken no part in the riots; he was freed. Burke secured the approval of the Commons for reaffirmation of the Act for Catholic Relief in England. An act of 1791 extended legal toleration to Catholic worship and education, but no Catholic church was to have a steeple or a bell.[52]

IV. BLACKSTONE, BENTHAM, AND THE LAW

A learned jurist thought "the publication of Blackstone's *Commentaries* . . . in some ways the most notable event in the history of the law."[53] This is patriotic, but it serves to point the reverential awe with which English-speaking students, till our time, approached the *Commentaries on the Laws of England* which William Blackstone published in four volumes and two thousand pages in 1765–69. Despite or because of its size it was acclaimed as a monument of learning and wisdom; every lord had it in his library, and George III took it to his heart as the apotheosis of kings.

Blackstone was the son of a London tradesman rich enough to send him through Oxford and the Middle Temple to the practice of law. His lectures at Oxford (1753–63) reduced the contradictions and absurdities of the statutes to some order and logic, and expounded the result with clarity and charm. In 1761 he was elected to Parliament; in 1763 he was appointed solicitor general to Queen Charlotte; in 1770 he began service as judge in the Court of Common Pleas. Addicted to study and hating locomotion, he sank into a gentle but premature decomposition, and died in 1780 at the age of fifty-seven.

His *opus maximum* had the virtues of his lectures: logical arrangement, lucid exposition, and a gracious style. Jeremy Bentham, his passionate opponent, praised him as the man who had "taught jurisprudence to speak the language of the scholar and the gentleman, put polish on that rugged science, cleansed her from the dust and cobwebs of the office."[54] Blackstone defined law as "a rule of action dictated by some superior being";[55] he had an ideal and static conception of law as serving in a society the same function that the laws of nature served in the world, and he tended to think of the laws of England as rivaling the laws of gravitation in their majesty and eternity.

He loved England and Christianity just as he found them, and would hardly admit any flaw in either. He was more orthodox than Bishop Warburton, and more royalist than George III. "The King of England is not only the chief, but properly the sole, magistrate of the nation. . . . He may reject what bills, may make what treaties, . . . may pardon what offenses he pleases, unless the Constitution hath expressly, or by evident consequence, laid down some exception or boundary."[56] Blackstone placed the king above Parliament and above the law; the king "is not only incapable of doing wrong, but even of thinking wrong"—by which, however, Blackstone meant that there was no law above the king by which the king could be judged. But he warmed the pride of all England when he defined "the absolute rights of every Englishman: the right of personal security, the right of personal liberty, and the right of private property."[57]

Blackstone's conception of English law as a system permanently valid because ultimately grounded on the Bible as the word of God eminently pleased his time, but it discouraged the growth of English jurisprudence and the reform of penology and prisons; it is to his credit, however, that he applauded the efforts of John Howard to ameliorate the conditions in British jails.[58]

Howard took Christianity not as a system of law but as an appeal to the heart. Appointed sheriff at Bedford (1773), he was appalled by conditions in the local prison. The jailer and his aides received no salary; they lived on fees exacted from the prisoners. No man was released, after serving his term, until he had paid all fees required of him; many men remained incarcerated for months after the court had found them innocent. Traveling from county to county, Howard found similar abuses, or worse. Defaulting debtors and first offenders were thrown in with hardened criminals. Most prisoners wore chains, heavy or light according to the fee they paid. Each prisoner was allowed one- or twopenceworth of bread daily; for additional food he had to pay, or rely on relatives or friends. Three pints of water were allowed to each inmate daily for drinking and washing. No heat was provided in winter, and there was little ventilation in summer. The stench in these dungeons was so strong that it clung to Howard's clothes long after he emerged. "Prison fever" and other diseases killed many prisoners; some died of slow starvation.[59] At Newgate Gaol in London fifteen to twenty men lived in a room twenty-three by twenty-five feet.

In 1774 Howard presented to Parliament his report on fifty prisons visited; the House of Commons passed an act requiring hygienic reforms in the jails, providing salaries for the jailers, and freeing all prisoners against whom the grand jury had failed to find a true bill. In 1775–76 Howard visited Continental prisons. He found those of Holland best equipped and relatively humane; among the worst were those in Hanover, ruled by George III. The publication of Howard's book *The State of the Prisons in England and Wales, . . . and an Account of Some Foreign Prisons* (1777) stirred the sleeping conscience of the nation. Parliament voted funds for two "penitentiary houses," in which an attempt was made to redeem prisoners by individual treatment, supervised labor, and religious instruction. Howard resumed his travels, and reported his findings in new editions of his book. In 1789 he toured Russia; at Kherson he caught camp fever, and died (1790). His efforts for reform produced only modest results. The act of 1774 was ignored by most jailers and justices. Descriptions of London prisons in 1804 and 1817 showed no improvement since Howard's time; "perhaps the condition of things had become worse instead of better."[60] Reform had to wait for Dickens' account of the New Marshalsea Prison in *Little Dorrit* (1855).

Jeremy Bentham's diverse labors for reform in law, government, and education fall mostly after this period, but his *Fragment on Government* (1776) belongs here, as being principally a criticism of Blackstone. He scorned the jurist's worship of tradition; he pointed out that "whatever *now* is established, *once* was innovation";[61] present conservatism is reverence of past radicalism; consequently those who advocate reforms are quite as patriotic as those who tremble at the thought of change. "Under a government of laws, what is the motto of a good citizen? *To obey punctually, to censure freely.*"[62] Bentham rejected Blackstone's view of royal sovereignty; a good government will distribute powers, encourage each of these to check the others, and allow freedom of the press, of peaceable assemblage and opposition. In the last resort, revolution may do less damage to the state than a dulling submission to tyranny.[63] This little book was published in the year of the American Declaration of Independence.

In the same essay Bentham expounded that "greatest-happiness principle" to which John Stuart Mill in 1863 gave the name "utilitarianism." "It is the greatest happiness of the greatest number that is the measure of right and wrong."[64] By this "principle of utility" all moral and political proposals and practices should be judged, for "the business of government is to promote the happiness of society."[65] Bentham derived this "principle of happiness" from Helvétius, Hume, Priestley, and Beccaria,[66] and his general viewpoint was formed from reading the *philosophes*.[67]

In 1780 he wrote, and in 1789 he published, *An Introduction to the Principles of Morals and Legislation*, giving a more detailed and philosophical exposition of his ideas. He reduced all conscious action to the desire for pleasure or the fear of pain, and he defined happiness as "the enjoyment of pleasure, security from pain."[68] This seemed to justify complete selfishness, but Bentham applied the happiness principle to individuals as well as states: did the individual's action make for his greatest happiness? In the long run, he thought, the individual obtains most pleasure or least pain by being just to his fellow men.

Bentham practiced what he preached, for he devoted his life to a long series of reform proposals: universal literate male adult suffrage, secret ballot, annual Parliaments, free trade, public sanitation, the amelioration of prisons, the cleansing of the judiciary, the abolition of the House of Lords, the modernization and codification of the law in terms intelligible to laymen, and the extension of international law (Bentham invented this term[69]). Many of these reforms were effected in the nineteenth century, largely through the efforts of "utilitarians" and "philosophical radicals" like James and John Stuart Mill, David Ricardo, and George Grote.

Bentham was the last voice of the Enlightenment, the bridge between the liberating thought of the eighteenth century and the reforms of the nineteenth. Even more than the *philosophes* he trusted to reason. He remained a bachelor to the end of his life, though he was one of the most lovable of men. When he died (June 6, 1832), aged eighty-four, he willed that his body should be dissected in the presence of his friends. It was, and the skeleton is still preserved in University College, London, wearing Bentham's habitual dress.[70] On the day after his death the historic Reform Bill that embodied many of his proposals was signed by the King.

V. THE THEATER

1. The Performance

This second half of the eighteenth century was rich in theater, poor in drama. It saw some of the finest actors in history, and produced only two dramatists whose works have escaped the Reaper: Sheridan, whom we have already laid to rest, and Goldsmith, who will get a niche of his own under the rubric of literature. Perhaps the dearth of serious plays was cause and effect of the Shakespearean revival, which continued till the end of the century.

The dramatists suffered from the tastes of the audience. There was much discussion of histrionic, little of dramatic, technique and art. The author received, usually as his only material reward, the profits of the third performance, if this arrived; some actors and actresses, however, became as rich as prime ministers. Hired claques could damn a good play with hostile noise, or make a worthless play an exciting success. A run of twenty nights in a season was attained only by the most favored dramas. Performances began at six or six-thirty, and ordinarily included a three-hour play and a farce or a pantomime. Seats cost one to five shillings; there were no reservations except by sending a servant to buy and hold a place till the master or lady came. All seats were backless benches.[71] Some favored spectators sat on the stage, until Garrick ended this abomination (1764). All lighting was by candles in chandeliers, which remained lit throughout the program. Costumes, before 1782, were eighteenth-century English regardless of the play's time or place; Cato, Caesar, and Lear were shown in knee breeches and wigs.

Despite opposition by the clergy, and the competition of opera and circuses, the theater flourished, both in London and in the "provinces." Bath, Bristol, Liverpool, Nottingham, Manchester, Birmingham, York, Edinburgh, and Dublin had good playhouses; some had their own companies; and since the major companies went on tour, nearly every town saw good acting. London was kept on edge by the lively rivalry of two principal theaters. In 1750 both of these played *Romeo and Juliet* nightly for the same two weeks, with Spranger Barry and Susannah Cibber at Covent Garden, and Garrick and Miss Bellamy at Drury Lane. Samuel Foote had his own Little Theatre in the Haymarket, where he specialized in satirical mimicry; his imitations of Garrick were long a misery in David's life.

Never had the English stage seen so many first-class performers. Charles Macklin opened the great age in 1741 with his productions of Shakespeare; he was the first actor to present Shylock as a serious character, though still as a merciless villain. (Not till Henry Irving was Shylock interpreted with some sympathy.) John Philip Kemble closed this century-long revival of Shakespeare. His supreme hours were when he and his sister Sarah played *Macbeth* at Drury Lane in 1785.

Some memorable actresses now graced the stage. Peg Woffington was gifted with stirring beauty of figure and face, but she lived loosely, suffered a paralytic stroke in mid-play (1757), and died prematurely old at forty-six (1760). Kitty Clive stayed with Garrick's company twenty-two years; she astonished London by her exemplary morals; after quitting the stage (1769) she lived sixteen years in a house that Horace Walpole gave her in Twickenham. Mrs. Hannah Pritchard was the foremost tragedienne before Mrs. Siddons surpassed her as Lady Macbeth; she absorbed her life in her acting, and (it was said) never read a book; Johnson called her "an inspired idiot";[72] but she outlasted many belles, acting till within a few months of her death. Mrs. Frances Abington starred as Beatrice, Portia, Ophelia, and Desdemona, but her most famous role was as Lady Teazle in *The School for Scandal*. Mary Robinson acquired her popular name "Perdita" from acting that part so well in *A Winter's Tale;* she served as mistress to the Prince of Wales and lesser lovers, and sat for Reynolds, Gainsborough, and Romney.

The conscious goddess of the stage was Sarah Kemble Siddons. Born to a traveling actor in a hostelry in Wales (1755), she married at eighteen the actor William Siddons, and starred at nineteen in Otway's *Venice Preserved*. Garrick engaged her a year later, but critics pronounced "her powers not equal to a London stage," and Henry Woodward, who played comic parts for Garrick, advised her to go back to country theaters for a while. She did, and for six years she played in provincial towns. Recalled to Drury Lane in 1782, she surprised everyone by her development as an actress. She was the first to adopt in her roles the dress of the period represented. Soon Garrick favored her for Shakespearean roles, and London marveled at the dignity and pathos with which she elevated the part of Lady Macbeth. Her private life won the respect and friendship of eminent contemporaries; Johnson wrote his name on the hem of her robe in Reynolds' picture of her as the Tragic Muse, and was struck by her "great modesty and propriety" when she called on him.[73] Two of her brothers, one of her sisters, and two of her nieces continued the Kemble dynasty in the theater till 1893. Through her and Garrick the social status of actors was raised, even in an England that made class distinctions the soul and machinery of government.

2. Garrick

All who know of Johnson will recall that David Garrick was born in Lichfield (1717), attended Johnson's school at Edial (1736), and accompanied him in their historic migration to London (1737). Seven years younger, he never won Johnson's full friendship, for the older man could not forgive David for being an actor and rich.

On reaching London Garrick joined his brother in importing and selling wine. This involved frequent visits to taverns; there he met actors; their talk fascinated him; he followed some of them to Ipswich, where they let him take minor parts. He learned the histrionic art so rapidly that soon he undertook to play the lead in *Richard III* at an unlicensed theater in Goodman's Fields in the East End of London. He relished that role because he was small, like the hunchback King, and because he enjoyed dying on the stage. His performance was so well received that he abandoned the vintner business, to the shame and chagrin of his Lichfield relatives. But William Pitt the Elder came backstage to compliment him, and Alexander Pope, as crippled as Richard, said to another spectator, "That young man never had his equal, and he will never have a rival."[74] Here was an actor who poured all his body and soul into the part that he played; who became Richard III in face and voice and hands and broken frame and sly mind and evil aims; who did not cease to act his part when others spoke, and with difficulty forgot it when he left the stage. Soon he was the talk of theatergoing London. Aristocracy came to see him; lords dined with him; "there are a dozen dukes a night at Goodman's Fields," wrote Thomas Gray.[75] The Garricks of Lichfield proudly claimed David as their own.

He tried Lear next (March 11, 1742). He failed; he was too active in his movements to portray an octogenarian, and he had not acquired the dignity of a king. The failure chastened him, and proved invaluable. He gave up the part for a while, studied the play, practiced the facial expressions, the feeble gait, the ailing vision, the shrill and plaintive tones of the unhappy Lear. In April he tried again. He was transformed; the audience wept and cheered; Garrick had created another of the roles that for almost a century would recall his name. Everybody applauded but Johnson, who decried acting as mere pantomime, and Horace Walpole, who thought Garrick's expressiveness excessive, and Gray, who mourned the fall from classic restraint to romantic emotionalism and sentiment. Scholars complained that Garrick played not an unadulterated Shakespeare but versions revised and bowdlerized, sometimes by Garrick himself; half the lines of his *Richard III* were written by Colley Cibber,[76] and the last act of his *Hamlet* was changed to provide a tender finale.

In that season 1741–42 Garrick offered eighteen roles—a feat suggesting almost incredible powers of memory and attention. When he performed, the theater was filled; when he was not billed it was half empty. The licensed theaters suffered reduced attendance. By some backstage politics the playhouse in Goodman's Fields was forced to close. Garrick, lost without a stage, signed a contract with the Drury Lane Theatre for 1742–43 at £500—a record salary for an actor. Meanwhile he left for a spring season in Dublin. Handel had just captured that city with his *Messiah* (April 13, 1742); now Garrick and Peg Woffington conquered it with Shakespeare. When they returned to London they set up housekeeping together, and Garrick bought a wedding ring. But she resented his parsimony and he her extravagance. He began to wonder what kind of wife would emerge from Peg's miscellaneous past. He kept the ring, and they parted (1744).

His acting at Drury Lane marked an era in the art. He gave to each role all the force of his energy, and constant care that every motion of his body, every inflection of his voice, should be in character. He made the alarm and terror of Macbeth so vivid that this, more than any other of his roles, remained in the public memory. He replaced the declamation of older tragedians with a more natural speech. He achieved a sensitivity of facial expression that varied with the slightest change of thought or mood in the text. Years later Johnson remarked, "David looks much older than he is, for his face has had double the business of any other man's; it is never at rest."[77] And there was his versatility. He played comic parts with almost all the care and finish that he had given to his Macbeth or Hamlet or Lear.

After five seasons as an actor Garrick signed (April 9, 1747) a contract to divide the management of Drury Lane with James Lacy: Lacy to take charge of business affairs, Garrick to choose the plays and the actors and direct the rehearsals. During his twenty-nine years as manager he produced seventy-five different plays, wrote one himself (in collaboration with George Colman), revised twenty-four of Shakespeare's dramas, composed a great number of prologues, epilogues, and farces, and wrote for the press anonymous articles promoting and praising his work. He appreciated money, and tempered his choice of plays to the greatest happiness of the greatest paying number. He loved applause, as actors and writers must, and he arranged parts to get most of it. His actors thought him tyrannical and stingy, and complained that he underpaid them while he was becoming rich. He established order and discipline among jealous and hypersensitive individuals each of whom verged or brooded on genius. They grumbled, but they were glad to stay, for no other company weathered so well the winds of fortune and the tides of taste.

In 1749 Garrick married Eva Maria Weigel, a Viennese dancer who had come to England as "Mlle. Violette," and had earned plaudits for her performances in opera ballets. She was, and remained, a pious Catholic; Garrick smiled at her belief in the story of St. Ursula and the eleven thousand virgins,[78] but he respected her faith since she lived up to its moral code. She did much, by her devotion, to ease the strain of an actor-manager's life. He lavished his wealth upon her, took her on Continental tours, and bought for her an expensive home in Hampton village. There, and in his London house on Adelphi Terrace, he entertained sumptuously, and many lords and distinguished foreigners were happy to be his guests. There he romped with Fanny Burney, and sheltered Hannah More.

In 1763 he gave up acting except for special occasions. "Now," he said, "I will sit down and read Shakespeare."[79] In 1768 he suggested, planned, and supervised the first Shakespeare festival at Stratford-on-Avon. He continued to manage Drury Lane, but found the tempers and quarrels of the actors ever harder on his aging nerves. Early in 1776 he sold his share of the partnership to Richard Brinsley Sheridan, and on March 7 he announced that he would soon retire. For three months thereafter he gave farewell performances of his favorite roles, and enjoyed such a succession of triumphs as probably no other actor in history has ever known. His departure from the stage caused as much talk in London as the war with America. On June 10, 1776, he closed his theatrical career with a benefit for the Decayed Actors' Fund.

He survived three years more. He died on January 20, 1779, aged sixty-two. On February 1 his corpse was borne to Westminster Abbey by members of Britain's highest nobility, and was deposited in the Poets' Corner at the foot of Shakespeare's monument.

VI. LONDON

Johnson's first view of London (1737) was one of virtuous horror:

> Here malice, rapine, accident, conspire,
> And now a rabble rages, now a fire;
> Their ambush here relentless ruffians lay,
> And here the fell attorney prowls for prey;
> Here falling houses thunder on your head,
> And here a female Atheist talks you dead.*[80]

* Lady Mary Wortley Montagu?

These, of course, were but some aspects of London, chosen to feed the rage of unplaced youth. Three years later Johnson described London as "a city famous for wealth and commerce and plenty, and for every other kind of civility and politeness, but which abounds with such heaps of filth as a savage would look on with amazement."[81] The civic authorities, at that time, left street cleaning to the citizen, who was commanded to keep in neat repair the pavement—or earth—before his house. In 1762 the Westminster Paving Acts arranged for municipal cleaning of streets, collection of rubbish, paving and repair of main thoroughfares, and establishment of an underground sewerage system; soon other sections of London followed suit. Elevated footpaths protected pedestrians, and gutters drained the streets. New streets were laid out in straight lines, houses were built more durably, and the venerable metropolis effused a more genteel odor.

There was no public fire department, but insurance companies maintained private hose brigades to limit their losses. Coal dust and fog sometimes collaborated to blanket the city with a pall so thick that one could not tell friend from foe. When the sky was visible certain streets were bright with colorful shops. On the Strand the largest and richest stores in Europe displayed behind their windows the products of half the world. Not far away were a thousand shops of a hundred crafts, and here and there were potteries, glass factories, smithies, breweries. The noises of artisans and tradesmen, of carriages and horses, of hawkers and street singers, contributed to the din and sense of life. If one wished a quieter scene and cleaner air he could saunter in St. James's Park, or watch fascinating ladies swing their spreading skirts and show their silken shoes on the Mall. In the morning one could buy fresh milk from maids who milked cows on the park green. In the evening he might prowl, like Boswell, for a *fille de joie*, or wait for the night to cover a multitude of sins. Farther west one could ride or drive in Hyde Park. And there were the great amusement resorts: Vauxhall with its colorful crowds, its acres of gardens and arbored walks, and Ranelagh with its spacious tiered Rotunda, where Mozart performed when a child of eight.

The poor had alehouses, the middle and upper classes had clubs, and there were taverns for all. There was the Boar's Head, and the Mitre, where the Great Cham supped, and the Globe, dear to Goldsmith, and the Devil's Tavern, which had entertained famous figures from Jonson to Johnson. There were two Turk's Heads—one a coffee shop on the Strand, the other a tavern in Gerrard Street, which became the home of *The* Club. Women as well as men came to taverns, and some were for sale. In clubs like White's or Almack's (which became Brooks's) the well-to-do could drink and gamble in select privacy. And there were the theaters, with all the excitement of their competition and the radiance of their stars.

Near the theaters were brothels. Preachers complained that "to the said plays and interludes great numbers of mean, idle, and disorderly people do commonly resort, and after the performance is over from thence they go to bawdy houses."[82] Nearly all classes who could afford it patronized prostitutes, and agreed in condoning the habit as unavoidable in the current state of male development. There were some colored courtesans who drew customers even from the nobility; Boswell describes Lord Pembroke as exhausted after a night in "a black bawdy house."[83]

Slums continued. In the lower orders it was not unusual for a family to live in one room of a tenement. The very poor lived in damp, unheated cellars, or in garrets with leaky roofs; some slept on bunks or in doorways or under booths. Johnson told Miss Reynolds that "as he returned to his lodgings about one or two o'clock in the morning he often saw poor children asleep on thresholds and stalls and that he used to put pennies into their hands to buy them a breakfast."[84] A magistrate informed Johnson that in any week over twenty Londoners died of starvation.[85] Now and then epidemics ran through the city. Even so, its population rose from 674,000 in 1700 to 900,-000 in 1800,[86] presumably due to immigration by landless peasants, and to the growth of commerce and industry.

The Thames and its docks were crowded with merchantmen and their cargoes. "The whole surface of the Thames," wrote a contemporary, "is covered with small vessels, barges, boats, and wherries, passing to and fro, and, below the three bridges, such a forest of masts for miles together, that you would think all the ships of the universe were here assembled."[87] Two new bridges were added in this period: Blackfriars and Battersea. Canaletto, coming to London from Venice (1746, 1751), painted magnificent views of city and river; prints from these *vedute* enabled educated Europeans to realize how London had grown to be the chief port of the Christian world.

Never since ancient Rome (excepting Constantinople) had history known so vast and rich and complex a city. In St. James's Palace the King and Queen and their attendants, the court and its ceremonies; in the churches fat prelates mumbling hypnotic formulas, and humble worshipers resting from reality and begging divine aid; in Parliament House the Lords and the Commons playing the game of politics with souls as their pawns; in Mansion House the Lord Mayor and his liveried aides laying down ordinances about chapels and brothels, and wondering how to control the next epidemic or mob; in the barracks soldiers gaming, wenching, and profaning the air; in the shops the tailors curving their spines, plumbers inhaling lead, jewelers, watchmakers, cobblers, hairdressers, vintners, hurrying to meet the demands of ladies and gentlemen; in Grub Street or Fleet Street the hack writers puffing up clients, tumbling ministries, challenging the King; in the prisons men and women dying of infection or graduating to greater crimes; in the tenements and cellars the hungry, the unfortunate, and the defeated multiplying their like eagerly and forever.

With all this both Johnson and his biographer loved London. Boswell admired "the liberty and the whims . . . and curious characters, the immense crowd and hurry and bustle of business and diversion, the great number of public places of entertainment, the noble churches and the superb buildings, . . . the satisfaction of pursuing whatever plan is most agreeable without being known or looked at"[88]—the protective, erosive anonymity of the crowd. And Johnson, relishing and deepening "the full flow of London talk," settled the matter with one authoritative line: "When a man is tired of London he is tired of life."[89]

CHAPTER XXX

The Age of Reynolds

1756–90

I. THE MUSICIANS

THIS England loved great music, but could not produce it.

Appreciation abounded. In Zoffany's picture *The Cowper and Gore Families* we see the part that music played in cultivated homes. We hear of the hundreds of singers and performers that were brought together for the Handel Commemoration Concert in 1784. The *Morning Chronicle* of December 30, 1790, announced, for the ensuing months, a series of "Professional Concerts," another of "Ancient Concerts," "Ladies' Subscription Concerts" for Sunday evenings, oratorios twice a week, and six symphony concerts to be conducted by the composer himself—Joseph Haydn;[1] this rivaled the musical wealth of London today. Just as Venice made choirs from orphans, so the "Charity Children" of St. Paul's Cathedral gave annual performances, of which Haydn wrote, "No music has ever moved me so much in my life."[2] Concerts and light operas were presented in the Ranelagh Rotunda and the Marylebone Gardens. A dozen societies of amateur musicians gave public performances. The English predilection for music was so widely known that a score of virtuosos and composers came to the island —Geminiani, Mozart, Haydn, Johann Christian Bach; and Bach remained.

The taste for serious opera declined in England after Handel's surfeit. Some enthusiasm returned when Giovanni Manzuoli opened the 1764 season in *Ezio;* Burney described his voice as "the most powerful and voluminous soprano that has been heard on our stage since Farinelli."[3] This was apparently the last triumph of Italian opera in England in that century. When the Italian opera house in London was burned down (1789), Horace Walpole rejoiced, and hoped it would never be rebuilt.[4]

If there were now no memorable British composers, there were two eminent historians of music, whose works appeared in the same year, 1776—the *annus mirabile* of *The Decline and Fall of the Roman Empire* and *The Wealth of Nations*, not to speak of the American Declaration of Independence. Sir John Hawkins' five-volume *General History of the Science and Practise of Music* was a work of careful scholarship, and though he himself —attorney and magistrate—was not a musician, his appraisals have stood well amid the flux of critical opinion. Charles Burney was organist at St. Paul's and the most sought-for musical teacher in England. His handsome face and amiable personality, added to his accomplishments, won him the friendship of Johnson, Garrick, Burke, Sheridan, Gibbon, and Reynolds—who made an attractive portrait of him gratis.[5] He traveled through France, Germany, Austria, and Italy to get materials for his *General History of Music*, and spoke with firsthand knowledge of the leading composers who were then alive. About 1780 he reported that "old musicians complain of the extravagance of the young, and these again of the dryness and inelegance of the old."[6]

II. THE ARCHITECTS

English builders now offered a lively contest between Gothic and classical revivals. The grandeur of the old cathedrals, the vestigial splendor of stained glass, the ivied ruins of medieval abbeys in Britain, stirred the imagination to idealize the Middle Ages, and fell in with the developing Romantic reaction against classic couplets, cold columns, and oppressive pediments. Horace Walpole engaged a succession of second-rate architects to rebuild his "Strawberry Hill" at Twickenham in Gothic form and ornament (1748–73); he gave years of finical care to making his home the very palladium of the anti-Palladian style. Year after year he added rooms, until there were twenty-two; one, "the Gallery," housing his art collections, was fifty-six feet long. Too often he used lath and plaster instead of stone; even a first glance reveals a fragility forgivable in interior decoration but unpardonable in external structure. Selwyn called Strawberry Hill "gingerbread Gothic,"[7] and another wit reckoned that Walpole had outlived three sets of crenellated battlements,[8] which had to be repeatedly restored.

Despite these experiments, Palladio and Vitruvius remained the tutelar deities of English architecture in the second as in the first half of the eighteenth century. The classic spirit was reinforced by the excavations at Herculaneum and Pompeii, and it was spread by descriptions of classic ruins in Athens, Palmyra, and Baalbek. Sir William Chambers defended the Palladian view in his *Treatise on Civil Architecture* (1759), and added example to precept by rebuilding Somerset House (1776–86) with a vast façade of Renaissance windows and Corinthian porticoes.

A remarkable family of four brothers, John, Robert, James, and William Adam, came out of Scotland to dominate English architecture in this half century. Robert left the strongest impress upon his time. After studying in the University of Edinburgh he spent three years in Italy, where he met Piranesi and Winckelmann. Noting that the private palaces praised by Vitruvius had disappeared from the Roman scene, and learning that one remained relatively intact, the palace of Diocletian at Spalato (now Split in Yugoslavia), he made his way to that ancient Dalmatian capital, spent five weeks making measurements and drawings, was arrested as a spy, was freed, wrote a book about his researches, and came back to England resolved to use Roman styles in British building. In 1768 he and his brothers leased for ninety-nine years a tract of sloping land between the Strand and the Thames, and erected on it the famous Adelphi Terrace—a district of fine streets and handsome houses on an embankment supported by massive Roman arches and vaults; here some dramatic notables lived, from Garrick to Bernard Shaw. Robert designed also some famous mansions, like Bute's Luton Hoo (i.e., house at Luton, thirty miles north of London). "This," said Johnson, "is one of the places I do not regret having come to see";[9] and he was hard to please.

By and large the classic orders won the battle against the Gothic revival. Many of the great palaces of this age, like Carlton House in London and Harewood House in Yorkshire, were in the neoclassic style. Walpole did not live to see Gothic return in triumph and splendor in the Houses of Parliament (1840–60).

III. WEDGWOOD

The Adam brothers were not content with designing buildings and interiors; they built some of the loveliest furniture of the time. But the great name here is Thomas Chippendale. In 1754, at the age of thirty-six, he published *The Gentleman and Cabinet Maker's Director*, which was to the art of furniture what Reynolds' *Discourses* were to painting. His characteristic products were chairs with slim "ribbon backs" and charming legs. But also he delighted the lords and ladies of George III's reign with cabinets, writing tables, commodes, bookcases, mirrors, tables, and fourposter beds—all elegant, mostly novel, generally frail.

The frailty continued in the work of Chippendale's rival, George Hepplewhite, and their successor, Thomas Sheraton; they seemed converted to Burke's theory that in art, as in life, beauty must be frail. Sheraton carried lightness and grace to their apex. He specialized in satinwood and other beautifully grained products; he polished them patiently, painted them delicately, and sometimes inlaid them with metal ornaments. In his *Cabinet Dictionary* (1802) he listed 252 "master cabinet makers" working in or near London. The upper classes in England now rivaled the French in the refinement of their furniture and interior appointments.

They were giving a lead to the French in designing gardens and parks. Lancelot Brown earned the nickname "Capability" because he was so quick to see the "capabilities" offered by his clients' grounds for fantastic—and expensive—designs; in this spirit he laid out gardens at Blenheim and Kew. The fashion in gardens ran now to the exotic, unexpected, or picturesque. Miniature Gothic temples and Chinese pagodas were used as outdoor ornaments; Sir William Chambers, in decorating the Kew Gardens (1757–62), introduced Gothic shrines, Moorish mosques, and Chinese pagodas. Funerary urns were favorite garden glories, sometimes holding the ashes of departed friends.

The ceramic arts had an almost revolutionary development. England was producing glass as fine as any in Europe.[10] The Chelsea and Derby potteries turned out delightful figures in porcelain, usually in the styles of Sèvres. But the busiest ceramic center was the "Five Towns" in Staffordshire—chiefly Burslem and Stoke-on-Trent. Before Josiah Wedgwood the industry was poor in methods and earnings; the potters were coarse and letterless; when Wesley first preached to them they pelted him with mud; their houses were huts, and their market was restricted by impassable roads. In 1755 a rich deposit of kaolin—hard white clay like that used by the Chinese—was discovered in Cornwall; but that was two hundred miles from the Five Towns.

Wedgwood began at the age of nine (1739) to work at the potter's wheel. He received little schooling, but he read much; and his study of Caylus' *Recueil d'antiquités égyptiennes, étrusques, grecques, romaines, et gauloises* (1752–67) inspired him with ambition to reproduce and rival classic ceramic forms. In 1753 he started his own business at the Ivy House Works, and built around it, near Burslem, a town which he called Etruria. He attacked with the energy of a warrior and the vision of a statesman the conditions that hampered the industry. He arranged better transport for the kaolin of Cornwall to his factories; he campaigned—and helped to pay—for the improvement of roads and the building of canals; he was resolved to open avenues from the Five Towns to the world. Heretofore the English market for fine pottery had been dominated by Meissen, Delft, and Sèvres; Wedgwood captured the domestic, then much of the foreign, trade; by 1763 his potteries were annually exporting 550,000 pieces to the Continent and North America. Catherine the Great ordered a dinner set of a thousand pieces.

By 1785 the Staffordshire potteries were employing fifteen thousand workers. Wedgwood introduced specialization of labor, established factory discipline, paid good wages, built schools and libraries. He insisted on good workmanship; an early biographer described him as stamping about his shops on his wooden leg, and breaking with his own hand any pot that showed the least flaw; usually, in such cases, he chalked on the careless artisan's bench the warning "This won't do for Josiah Wedgwood."[11] He developed precision tools, and bought steam engines to power his machines. As a result of his large-scale production of commercial pottery, pewter went out of general use in England. His output ranged from earthenware pipes for London drains to the most exquisite vessels for Queen Charlotte. He divided his offerings between "Useful" and "Ornamental." For the latter he frankly imitated classic models, as in his luxurious agate vases; but also he developed original forms, especially the famous jasper ware with Greek figures delicately embossed in white on a base of blue.

His interest and enthusiasm ranged far beyond pottery. In experiments to find more satisfactory mixtures of earth and chemicals, and better methods of firing, he invented a pyrometer for measuring high temperatures; this and other researches won him entry into the Royal Society (1783). He was an early member of the Society for the Abolition of Slavery; he designed and made the seal. He campaigned for universal male suffrage and parliamentary reform. He supported the American colonies from the beginning to the end of their revolt. He hailed the French Revolution as promising a happier and more prosperous France.

He had the good sense to employ John Flaxman to provide new and refined designs for his pottery. From this work Flaxman went on to illustrate Homer, Aeschylus, and Dante with drawings based on the art of the Greek vase painters. They are admirable in line, but, lacking body and color, they are as attractive as a woman without flesh. Something of this cold quality was carried into Flaxman's sculpture, as in his monument to Nelson in St. Paul's; but in the marble *Cupid and Marpessa*[12] he achieved full-blooded forms in one of the best imitations of classic statuary. Funerary monuments became his specialty; he raised them to Chatterton at Bristol, to Reynolds in St. Paul's, to Paoli in Westminster Abbey. He served in England the same role as Canova in Italy—the neoclassic attempt to recapture the smooth and voluptuous grace of Praxiteles.

We find less beauty but more life in the portrait busts that Joseph Nollekens made of famous Englishmen. Born in London of Flemish parents, he studied there till he was twenty-three, then went to Rome. He lived and worked there for ten years, selling real and counterfeit antiques.[13] Returning to England, he made so successful a bust of George III that he was soon in general demand. Sterne, Garrick, Fox, Pitt II, and Johnson sat for him, sometimes to their sorrow, for Nollekens carved no compliments. Johnson grumbled that the sculptor had made him look as if he had taken physic.[14]

It was an age of popular engravers. The public was intensely interested in the powerful personalities that trod the political and other stages; prints of their figures and faces were scattered throughout England. James Gillray's caricatures were almost as lethal as the letters of Junius; Fox confessed that such drawings did him "more mischief than the debates in Parliament."[15] Thomas Rowlandson caricatured men as beasts, but also he drew pleasant landscapes, and he amused several generations with his *Tours of Dr. Syntax*. Paul Sandby and Edmund Dayer developed water color to almost finished excellence.

Britons returning from the grand tour brought back prints, engravings, paintings, and other works of art. The appreciation of art spread; artists multiplied, raised their heads, their fees, and their status; some were knighted. The Society for the Encouragement of Art, Manufacture, and Commerce (1754) gave good sums in prizes to native artists, and presented exhibitions. The British Museum opened its collections in 1759. In 1761 a separate Society of Arts began annual displays. Soon it divided into conservatives and innovators. The conservatives formed the Royal Academy of London, with a charter and £5,000 from George III, and made Joshua Reynolds its president for twenty-three years. The great age of English painting began.

IV. JOSHUA REYNOLDS

Richard Wilson led the way. Son of a Welsh clergyman, he came to London at fifteen, and made a living by painting portraits. In 1749 he went to Italy; there and in France he absorbed the heritage of Nicolas Poussin and

Claude Lorrain, and learned to value historical and landscape painting above portraiture. Back in England, he painted landscapes luminous with atmosphere but cluttered with gods, goddesses, and other classic ruins. Especially beautiful is *The Thames at Twickenham*,[16] which catches the spirit of an English summer day—bathers lolling, trees and sailboats hardly moved by the quiet breeze. But the English would not buy landscapes; they wanted portraits to preserve their faces in their prime. Wilson persisted. He lived in poverty in a half-furnished room in Tottenham Court Road, and sweetened his bitterness with alcohol. In 1776 the Royal Academy rescued him by making him its librarian. The death of a brother left him a small property in Wales; he spent his final years there in such obscurity that no journal mentioned his death (1782).

By contrast the career of Reynolds was a lifelong pageant of honors and prosperity. He was fortunate in being born (1723) to a Devonshire clergyman who kept a Latin school and loved books. Among these Joshua found an *Essay on the Whole Art . . . of Painting* (1719) by Jonathan Richardson. This inflamed him with a desire to be a painter, and his sympathetic parents indulged his choice; they sent him to London to study with Thomas Hudson, a Devon man who had married Richardson's daughter and was then the most courted portrait painter in England. In 1746 the father died, and the young artist set up house with his two sisters in what is now Plymouth. In that famous port he met sailors and commanders, painted their portraits, and made precious friendships. When Captain Augustus Keppel was commissioned to take gifts to the Dey of Algiers he offered Joshua free passage to Minorca, for he knew that the youth longed to study in Italy. From Minorca Reynolds made his way to Rome (1750).

He remained in Italy three years, painting and copying. He labored to discover the methods used by Michelangelo and Raphael in achieving line, color, light, shade, texture, depth, expression, and mood. He paid a price, for while copying Raphael in some unheated rooms of the Vatican he caught a cold that apparently damaged his inner ear. Passing to Venice, he studied Titian, Tintoretto, and Veronese, and learned how to endow any sitter with the dignity of a doge. On his way home he stopped for a month in Paris, but he found contemporary French painting too feminine for his taste. After a month in Devon he established himself with his sister Frances in London (1753), and remained there for the rest of his life.

Almost at once he caught attention with another portrait of Captain Keppel[17]—handsome, eager, masterful; here the Vandyck tradition was restored to make portraits as resplendent images of aristocracy. Within two years Reynolds had received 120 sitters, and was recognized as the finest painter in England. His facility was his limitation. He became so absorbed and expert in portraiture that he lacked the time and skill for historical, mythological, or religious pictures. He did well a few, like *The Holy Family* and *The Three Graces*,[18] but his inspiration was not in them. Nor did his patrons want such pictures; they were nearly all Protestants, who discountenanced religious paintings as encouraging idolatry; they loved nature, but as an adjunct to their personalities or their hunts; they wished to see themselves age-less on their walls, impressing themselves upon posterity. So they came to Reynolds, two thousand of them, and they sent him their wives and children, sometimes their dogs. None went away grieved, for Reynolds' amiable imagination could always supply what nature had failed to give.

Never has a generation or a class been so fully preserved as in Reynolds' 630 surviving portraits. Here are the statesmen of that lusty age: Bute in a splendor of color;[19] Burke rather somber for thirty-eight; Fox potbellied, wistful, and noble at forty-four . . . Here are the writers: Walpole, Sterne, Goldsmith[20] looking really like "Poor Poll," Gibbon with those fat cheeks which the Marquise du Deffand, who could see only with her hands, mis-took for "the sitting part of a child,"[21] and Boswell[22] as proud as if he had created Johnson, and Johnson himself, lovingly painted five times, and sitting in 1772 for the best-known of Reynolds' portraits of men.[23] Here are the deities of the stage: Garrick "torn between the rival Muses of Tragedy and Comedy," Mary Robinson as Perdita, Mrs. Abington as the Comic Muse, and Sarah Siddons as the Tragic Muse;[24] an enthusiast paid Reynolds seven hundred guineas ($18,200?) for this proud masterpiece.

Most numerous in this incomparable gallery are the aristocrats who gave social order to an individualistic people, triumphant strategy to foreign pol-icy, and a controlling constitution to the king. See them first in their hand-some youth, like twelve-year-old Thomas Lister—a picture which, as Reyn-old's *Brown Boy*, challenges the *Blue Boy* of Gainsborough. Many of them swelled in the girth when their dangerous days were over, like that same Augustus Keppel who had been so presentable as a captain in 1753, but was so full-filled as an admiral in 1780. Despite such rotundities, and the silk and lace of their investiture, Reynolds succeeded in transforming intangible courage and pride into color and line. Take, as example, the powerful form and personality of Lord Heathfield, bold in British red and holding the key to Gibraltar, which he had invincibly defended against a four-year siege by the Spanish and the French.

And so we come to those *diai gynaikon*, goddesses among women, whom Reynolds found in the wives and daughters of the British aristocracy. Un-married, he was free to love all of them with his eyes and brush, to straighten their noses, refine their features, arrange their luxuriant hair, and transfigure them with such fluffy, flowing raiment as would make Venus long to be clothed. See Lady Elizabeth Keppel, Marchioness of Tavistock, wearing the courtly robes she had worn years ago as bridesmaid to Queen Charlotte; what would she be without those folds of painted silk enveloping legs that, after all, could not be much different from Xanthippe's? Sometimes Reyn-olds tried what he could do with a woman in simple garb; he pictured Mary Bruce, Duchess of Richmond, dressed in a common cloak, and sewing a pattern into a cushion;[25] this is a face that could haunt a philosopher's dreams. Almost as simple in dress and seraphic in profile is Mrs. Bouverie listening to Mrs. Crewe.[26] There was a still profounder beauty in the quiet and gentle face of Emma Gilbert, Countess of Mount Edgcumbe;[27] this lovely portrait was destroyed by enemy action in the Second World War.

Nearly all these women had children, for part of the aristocratic obligation was to maintain the family and the property in undivided continuity. So Reynolds painted Lady Elizabeth Spencer, Countess of Pembroke, with her six-year-old son, Lord Herbert to be;[28] and Mrs. Edward Bouverie with her three-year-old Georgiana;[29] and this daughter, become Duchess of Devonshire (the gay beauty who with kisses bought votes for Fox in his campaign for Parliament), with her three-year-old daughter, another Georgiana, the future Countess of Carlisle.[30]

Finally, and perhaps the most attractive of all, the children themselves, a full gallery of them, nearly all individualized as unduplicable souls, and sympathetically understood in the insecurity and wonderment of youth. The world knows Reynolds' masterpiece in this sector, *The Age of Innocence*,[31] which he painted in 1788, in the last years of his vision; but how soon his understanding of childhood reached an almost mystic intuition can be seen in his indescribably beautiful portrait of Lord Robert Spencer, aged eleven,[32] painted in 1758. Thereafter he painted them at every age: at age one Princess Sophia Matilda; at two years Master Wynn with his lamb; at three Miss Bowles with her dog; at four Master Crewe in a perfect imitation of Henry VIII, and, about the same age, the "Strawberry Girl";[33] at five the Brummell boys William and George ("Beau Brummel" to be); at six Prince William Frederick; at seven Lord George Conway; at eight Lady Caroline Howard; at nine Frederick, Earl of Carlisle; and so on to youth and marriage and children.

Reynolds admitted that he preferred titled sitters; "the slow progression of things naturally makes elegance and refinement the last effect of opulence and power"[34] and only the rich could pay the £300 that he asked for "a whole length with two children."[35] In any case he had struck gold, and soon earned £16,000 a year. In 1760 he bought a house at 17 Leicester Square, then the most select quarter of London; he furnished it luxuriously, collected Old Masters, and took for his studio a chamber as large as a ballroom. He had his own coach, with painted panels and gilded wheels; he asked his sister to drive in it about town, for he believed that such an advertisement of prosperity would bring more.[36] In 1761 he was knighted. He was received everywhere, and himself played host to genius, beauty, and class; he had more literary men at his table than any other man in England.[37] To him Goldsmith dedicated *The Deserted Village*, and Boswell the *Life of Samuel Johnson*. It was Reynolds who in 1764 founded "The Club" to give Johnson a forum of his peers.

He must have loved Johnson, he made so many portraits of him. He made even more of himself. He was not blessed with good looks: his face was florid and scarred by childhood smallpox; his features were blunt, his upper lip had been disfigured by a fall in Minorca. At thirty he pictured himself shading his eyes and trying to pierce a maze of light and shade to catch the soul behind a face.[38] He painted himself at fifty in his doctoral robes,[39] for Oxford had just made him a doctor of civil law. Finest of the series is the portrait in the National Gallery, about 1775; his face is now more refined, but his hair is gray and his hand is cupped to his ear, for he was going deaf.

When the Royal Academy of Arts was founded in 1768 Reynolds was by common consent made its president. For fifteen years he opened its seasons with a discourse to the students. Boswell was among the friends who sat in the front row at the first discourse (January 2, 1769). Many who heard these addresses were surprised at their literary excellence; some thought that Burke or Johnson had written them, but Sir Joshua had learned much from his associations, and had developed a style, as well as a mind, of his own. Naturally, as an Academician, he stressed the importance of study; he deprecated the notion that genius may dispense with schooling and hard work; he derided "this phantom of inspiration," and insisted that "labor is the only price of solid fame."[40] Furthermore, "every opportunity should be taken to discountenance that false and vulgar opinion—that rules are the fetters of genius."[41] There should be three stages in the normal development of an artist: first, tutelage—learning the rules, draftsmanship, coloring, modeling; second, studying those masters who have received the approbation of time; through such studies "those perfections which lie scattered among various masters are now united in one general idea, which is henceforth to regulate the student's taste and enlarge his imagination. . . . The third and last period emancipates the student from subjection to any authority but what he shall himself judge to be supported by reason."[42] Only then should he innovate. "Having well established his judgment and stored his memory, he may now without fear try the power of his imagination. The mind that has been thus disciplined may be indulged in the wildest enthusiasm, and venture to play on the borders of the wildest extravagance."[43]

Hogarth had rejected the Old Masters as "Black Masters," and had advised a realistic portrayal of nature. Reynolds thought that this should be merely a preparation for a more idealistic art. "Nature herself is not to be too closely copied. . . . The wish of the genuine painter must be more extensive: instead of endeavoring to amuse mankind with the minute neatness of his imitations, he must endeavor to improve them by the grandeur of his ideas. . . . [He] must strive for fame by captivating the imagination."[44] Everything in nature is imperfect from the standpoint of beauty, has in it some blemish or defect; the artist learns to eliminate these from his creations; he combines in one ideal the excellences of many deficient forms; "he corrects nature by herself, her imperfect state by her more perfect. . . . This idea of the perfect state of nature, which the artist calls the Ideal Beauty, is the great leading principle by which the works of genius are conducted." To distinguish the faulty from the perfect, the noble from the base, and to school and chasten and exalt the imagination, the artist must enlarge himself with literature and philosophy, and by "the conversation of learned and ingenious men."[45] So Reynolds had done.

In 1782 he suffered a paralytic stroke, from which he partially recovered. For seven years more he continued to paint. Then his left eye clouded, and soon lost its vision; in 1789 the right eye began to fail, and he put down his brush, despondent that almost total blindness was to be added to the semi-deafness which since his twenty-seventh year had forced him to use an ear trumpet. On December 10, 1790, he delivered the last of his discourses. He reaffirmed his faith in the academic and conservative precepts of his earlier addresses, and renewed his counsel to study line before color, and the classic painters before attempting innovation. He ended with a paean to Michelangelo:

> Were I now to begin the world again, I would tread in the steps of that great master; to kiss the hem of his garment, to catch the slightest of his perfections, would be glory and distinction enough for an ambitious man. . . . I reflect, not without vanity, that these discourses bear testimony of my admiration of that truly divine man; and I should desire that the last word which I should pronounce in this Academy, and from this place, might be the name of Michael Angelo.[46]

The repentant portraitist died on February 23, 1792, and nine noblemen were proud to bear his remains to St. Paul's.

V. THOMAS GAINSBOROUGH

Reynolds was a man of the world, ready to make the obeisances required for social acceptance; Gainsborough was a passionate individualist who raged at the sacrifices demanded of his personality and his art as the price of success. His parents were Dissenters; Thomas inherited their independence of spirit without their piety. Stories are told of his playing truant from school in his native Sudbury to roam the countryside, sketching trees and sky, and the cattle grazing in the fields or drinking at a pond. Having by the age of fourteen drawn all the trees in the neighborhood, he obtained permission from his father to go to London and study art. There he studied the women of the town, as we gather from his later advice to a young actor: "Don't run about London streets, fancying you are catching strokes of *nature,* at the hazard of your constitution. It was my first school, and deeply read in petticoats I am; therefore you may allow me to caution you."[47]

Suddenly, still but nineteen, he found himself married to a Scottish girl of sixteen, Margaret Burr. She was, by most accounts, the illegitimate daughter of a duke, but she had an income of £200 a year.[48] In 1748 they settled in Ipswich. He joined a music club there, for he was fond of music, and played several instruments. "I make portraits for a living, landscapes because I love them, and music because I cannot help myself."[49] In the work of the Dutch "landskip" painters he found a reinforcement of his interest in nature. Philip Thicknesse, governor of the nearby Landguard Fort, commissioned him to paint the fort, the neighboring hills, and Harwich; then he advised him to seek a richer and wider clientele in Bath.

Arrived there (1759), Gainsborough sought out the musicians rather than the artists, and soon numbered Johann Christian Bach among his friends. He had the soul and sensitivity of a musician, and in his paintings he turned music into warmth of color and grace of line. Bath had some good collections; now he could study landscapes by Claude Lorrain and Gaspard Poussin, and portraits by Vandyck; he became the inheritor of Vandyck's English manner—portraits that added the highest refinement of art to distinction of personality and elegance of dress.

In Bath he did some of his best work. The Sheridans were living there; Gainsborough painted Richard's lovely young wife.[50] He lavished all his maturing artistry on *The Honorable Mrs. Graham*,[51] whose red robe, in its wrinkles and folds, allowed him to display the most delicate gradations of color and shade. When this portrait was exhibited in the Royal Academy at London (1777) it seemed to many observers to outshine anything that Reynolds had done. About 1770 Gainsborough transfigured Jonathan Buttal, son of an ironmonger, into *The Blue Boy*, for which the Huntington Art Gallery paid $500,000. Reynolds had expressed his conviction that no acceptable portrait could be done in blue; his rising rival met the challenge triumphantly; blue became henceforth a favorite color in English painting.

Now every notable in Bath wished to sit for Gainsborough. But "I'm sick of portraits," he told a friend, "and wish very much to take my viol-da-gamba and walk off to some sweet village, where I can paint landskips and enjoy the fag end of life in quietness and ease."[52] Instead he moved to London (1774) and rented sumptuous rooms in Schomberg House, Pall Mall, at £300 a year; he was not to be outdone by Reynolds' display. He quarreled with the Academy on the hanging of his pictures; for four years (1773–77) he refused to exhibit there; and after 1783 his new work could be seen only at the annual opening of his studio. Art critics began an ungracious war of comparisons between Reynolds and Gainsborough; Reynolds was generally rated superior, but the royal family favored Gainsborough, and he painted them all. Soon half of the blue bloods of England flocked to Schomberg House, seeking the precarious immortality of paint. Now Gainsborough portrayed Sheridan, Burke, Johnson, Franklin, Blackstone, Pitt II, Clive . . . To establish himself, and pay his rent, he had to resign himself to portraiture.

His sitters found him hard to please. One lord put on all his airs as he posed; Gainsborough sent him away unpainted. Garrick's features were so mobile and changeful (for this was half the secret of his superiority as an actor) that the artist could find no expression that lasted long enough to reveal the man. He had the same trouble with Garrick's rival Samuel Foote. "Rot them for a couple of rogues," exclaimed Gainsborough; "they have everybody's face but their own."[53] He found a different difficulty with Mrs. Siddons: "Damn your nose, madam! There's no end to it."[54] He was at his best with women; he felt their sexual attraction strongly, but he sublimated this into a poetry of soft colors and dreamy eyes.

When his expensive establishment allowed him he painted landscapes, for which there was little demand. Often he placed his sitters—or standees—against a rustic scene, as in *Robert Andrews and His Wife* (which brought $364,000 at an auction in 1960). Too busy to go and sketch in the face of living nature, he brought into his studio stumps, weeds, branches, flowers, animals, and arranged them—with dressed-up dolls to serve as people—into a tableau;[55] from these objects, from his memories, and from his imagination, he painted landscapes. There was a certain artificial quality in them, a formalism and regularity seldom found in nature; even so the result conveyed an air of rural fragrance and peace. In his later years he painted some "fancy pictures," in which he made no pretense to realism, but indulged his romantic temper; one of these, *Cottage Girl with Dog and Pitcher*, has all the sentiment of Greuze's *La Cruche cassée* (*The Broken Pitcher*); both were painted in 1785.[56]

Only an artist can measure Gainsborough's worth. In his own time he was ranked below Reynolds; his drawing was criticized as careless, his composition as lacking unity, his figures as improperly posed; but Reynolds himself praised the shimmering brilliance of his rival's coloring. There was a poetry and music to Gainsborough's work that the great portraitist could not warmly understand. Reynolds had a more masculine intellect, and succeeded better in portraying men; Gainsborough was a more romantic spirit, who preferred to paint women and boys. He had missed the classical training that Reynolds had received in Italy, and he lacked the stimulating associations that enriched Reynolds' mind and art. Gainsborough did little reading, had few intellectual interests, shunned the circle of wits that gathered around Johnson. He was generous but impulsive and critical; he could never have listened with patience to Reynolds' lectures or Johnson's decrees. Yet he kept Sheridan's friendship to the end.

As he grew older he turned melancholy, for the romantic spirit, unless it is religious, is helpless in the face of death. In many Gainsborough landscapes a dead tree intrudes itself as a *memento mori* amid rich foliage and lush grass. Probably he surmised that cancer was consuming him, and felt a rising bitterness at the thought of so prolonged an agony. A few days before he died he wrote a letter of reconciliation to Reynolds and asked the older man to visit him. Reynolds came, and the two men, who had not so much quarreled as been the subject of lesser men's disputes, engaged in a friendly chat. When they parted Gainsborough remarked, "Goodbye till we meet in the hereafter, Vandyck in our company."[57] He died on August 2, 1788, in his sixty-first year.

Reynolds joined Sheridan in carrying the body to Kew Churchyard. Four months later Reynolds, in his Fourteenth Discourse, paid him a just tribute. He frankly noted defects as well as excellences in Gainsborough's work, but he added: "If ever this nation should produce genius sufficient to acquire to us the honorable distinction of an English School, the name of Gainsborough will be transmitted to posterity, in the history of art, among the very first of that rising name."[58]

George Romney struggled to reach the popularity of Reynolds and Gainsborough, but his defects of education, health, and character kept him to a more modest role. Without schooling after the age of twelve, he worked in his father's carpentry shop in Lancashire till he was nineteen. His drawings won him instruction in painting from a local wastrel. At twenty-two he fell seriously ill; recovering, he married the nurse; soon restless, he left her to seek his fortune; he saw her only twice in the next thirty-seven years, but he sent her a part of his earnings. He made enough to visit Paris and Rome, where he was influenced by the neoclassical trend. Back in London, he attracted patronage by his ability to clothe his sitters in grace or dignity. One of these was Emma Lyon, the future Lady Hamilton; Romney was so captivated by her beauty that he portrayed her as goddess, Cassandra, Circe, Magdalen, Joan of Arc, and saint. In 1782 he painted a portrait of Lady Sutherland, for which he received £18; it was recently sold for $250,000. In 1799, broken in body and mind, he returned to his wife; she nursed him again, as she had done forty-four years before. He lingered through three years of paralysis, and died in 1802. Through him and Reynolds and Gainsborough England was now, in this half century, in painting as well as in politics and literature, in the full stream of European civilization.

CHAPTER XXXI

England's Neighbors

1756–89

I. GRATTAN'S IRELAND

A^N English traveler, visiting Ireland in 1764, explained why the poor were taking to crime:

> What dread of justice or punishment can be expected from an Irish peasant in a state of wretchedness and extreme penury, in which, if the first man that met him were to knock him on the head and give him an everlasting relief from his distressed and penurious life, he might have reason to think it a friendly and meritorious action? . . . That many of them bear their . . . abject state with patience is to me a sufficient proof of the natural civility of their disposition.[1]

The landlords, who were almost all Protestants, were not the direct or most brutal oppressors of the peasants, who were almost all Catholics; usually the owners lived in England and did not see the blood on the rents exacted by the middlemen to whom they leased their land; it was the middlemen who drew every possible penny from the peasants, until these had to feed on potatoes and dress in rags.

In 1758, because disease was decimating cattle in England, Ireland was allowed for five years to export livestock to Britain. Many acres in Ireland—including common lands formerly used by the tenant farmers—were changed from tillage to grazing or pasturage; the rich were enriched, the poor were further impoverished. They added to their problems by marrying early—"upon the first capacity," as Sir William Petty put it;[2] presumably they hoped that children would soon earn their keep and then help pay the rent. So, despite a high death rate, the population of Ireland grew from 3,191,000 in 1754 to 4,753,000 in 1791.[3]

The industrial picture was brightening. Many Protestants and some Catholics had gone into the production of linens, woolens, cotton goods, silk, or glass. In the final quarter of the century, after Grattan had secured a moderation of British restrictions on Irish manufactures and commerce, a middle class developed which provided economic leverage for liberal politics and cultural growth. Dublin became one of the leading centers of education, music, drama, and architecture in the British Isles. Trinity College was becoming a university, and already had a long roster of distinguished graduates. If Ireland had kept her shining lights at home—Burke, Goldsmith, and Sheridan as well as Swift and Berkeley—she would have shone with the most brilliant nations of the age. After 1766 the lord lieutenant made Dublin his permanent home instead of paying brief visits once a year. Now majestic public buildings rose, and elegant mansions. Dublin's theaters rivaled London's in the excellence of their productions; here Handel's *Messiah* received its first performance and welcome (1742), and Thomas Sheridan staged many successful plays, some of them written by his wife.

Religion, of course, was the pervading issue in Ireland. Dissenters—i.e., Presbyterians, Independents (Puritans), and Baptists—were excluded from office and from Parliament by the Test Act, which required reception of the Sacrament according to the Anglican rite as a precondition to eligibility. The Toleration Act of 1689 was not extended to Ireland. The Presbyterians of Ulster protested in vain against these disabilities; thousands of them emigrated to America, where many of them fought devotedly in the Revolutionary armies.

The population of Ireland was eighty per cent Catholic, but no Catholic could be elected to Parliament. Only a few Catholics owned land. Protestant tenants were given leases for their lives, Catholic tenants for no more than thirty-one years; and they had to pay two thirds of their profits as rent.[4] No Catholic schools were allowed, but the authorities did not enforce the law forbidding the Irish to seek education abroad. Some Catholic students were admitted to Trinity College, but they could not receive a degree. Catholic worship was permitted, but there were no legal means of preparing Catholic priests; candidates for the priesthood, however, might go to seminaries on the Continent. Some of these students adopted the genial manners and liberal views of the hierarchy in France and Italy; returning to Ireland as priests, they were welcomed at the tables of educated Protestants, and helped to soften bigotry on both sides. By the time that Henry Grattan entered the Irish Parliament (1775) the movement for Catholic emancipation had won the support of thousands of Protestants in both England and Ireland.

In 1760 Ireland was governed by a lord lieutenant, or viceroy, appointed by and responsible to the king of England; and by a Parliament dominated in the House of Lords by Anglican bishops, and in the House of Commons by Anglican landowners and governmental placemen, or pensioners. Elections to Parliament were subject to the same system of "rotten" and "pocket" boroughs as in England; a few leading families, known as "the Undertakers," owned the vote of their boroughs as they owned their homes.[5]

Catholic resistance to English rule was sporadic and ineffective. In 1763 bands of Catholics called "Whiteboys"—from the white shirts they wore over their clothes—roamed the countryside, tearing down enclosure fences, crippling cattle, and assaulting the collectors of taxes or tithes; the leaders were caught and hanged, and the rebellion collapsed. The movement for *national* liberation fared better. In 1776 most British troops were taken from Ireland for service in America; at the same time the Irish economy was depressed by cessation of trade with America; to guard against domestic revolt or foreign invasion the Protestants of Ireland formed an army called the Volunteers. These grew in number and power until, by 1780, they were a redoubtable force in politics. It was through support by these forty thousand armed men that Henry Flood and Henry Grattan won their legislative victories.

Both of them were officers in the Volunteers, and both were among the greatest orators in a country which could send Burke and Richard Sheridan to England and still have a store of eloquence left. Flood entered the Irish Parliament in 1759. He led a brave campaign to reduce venality in a House where half the members were indebted to the government. He was defeated by wholesale bribery, and surrendered (1775) by accepting the office of vice-treasurer at a salary of £3,500.

In that year Henry Grattan was elected to the Parliament by a Dublin constituency. He soon took Flood's place as leader of the opposition. He announced an ambitious program: to secure relief to Irish Catholics, to free Dissenters from the Test Act, to end English restrictions on Irish trade, and to establish the independence of the Irish Parliament. He pursued these aims with an energy, devotion, and success that made him the idol of the nation, Catholic or Protestant. In 1778 he secured passage of a bill enabling Catholics to take leases of ninety-nine years, and to inherit land on the same conditions as Protestants. A year later, on his urging, the Test Act was repealed, and full civil rights were assured to Dissenters. He and Flood persuaded the Irish Parliament and the Viceroy that the continuance of British obstructions to Irish trade would lead to revolutionary violence. Lord North, then heading the British government, favored repeal of the restrictions; English manufacturers bombarded him with petitions against repeal; he yielded to them. The Irish began to boycott British goods. The Volunteers assembled before the Irish Parliament House with arms in their hands and cannon labeled "Free Trade or This." The English manufacturers, hurt by the boycott, withdrew their opposition; the English ministry withdrew its veto; the Free Trade Act was passed (1779).

Grattan next pressed for the independence of the Irish Parliament. Early in 1780 he moved that only the king of England, *with the consent of the Parliament of Ireland*, could legislate for Ireland, and that Great Britain and Ireland were united only by the bond of a common sovereign. His motion was defeated. The Volunteers, meeting at Dungannon 25,000 strong (February, 1782), announced that if legislative independence were not granted, their loyalty to England would cease. In March Lord North's aged ministry fell; Rockingham and Fox came into power. Meanwhile Cornwallis had surrendered at Yorktown (1781); France and Spain had joined America in war against England; Britain could not afford to face an Irish revolution at this time. On April 16, 1782, the Irish Parliament, led by Grattan, declared its legislative independence; a month later this was conceded by England. The Irish Parliament voted a grant of £100,000 to Grattan, who was a relatively poor man; he accepted half.

This, of course, was a victory for the Protestants of Ireland, not for the Catholics. When Grattan—strongly supported by the Anglican Bishop Frederick Hervey—went on to campaign for a measure of Catholic emancipation, the best he could do (in what historians call "Grattan's Parliament") was to win the franchise for propertied Catholics (1792); these few received the right to vote but not the right to be elected to Parliament, to municipal office, or to the judiciary. Grattan went to England, secured election to the British Parliament, and there continued his campaign. He died in 1820, nine years before that Parliament passed the Catholic Relief Act, which admitted Catholics to the Irish Parliament. Justice is not only blind, it limps.

II. THE SCOTTISH BACKGROUND

When the Union of 1707 merged Scotland with England through a joint Parliament, London quipped that the whale had swallowed Jonah; when Bute (1762 f.) brought a score of Scots into the British government the wits grumbled that Jonah was swallowing the whale.[6] Politically the whale won: the sixteen Scottish peers and forty-five commoners were engulfed by 108 English peers and 513 commoners. Scotland submitted its foreign policy, and in large measure its economy, to legislation dominated by English money and minds. The two countries did not forget their former enmity: the Scots complained of commercial inequalities between Jonah and the whale, and Samuel Johnson spoke for the whale in biting at Jonah with chauvinistic iteration.

Scotland in 1760 had a population of some 1,250,000 souls. The birth rate was high, but the death rate followed close. Said Adam Smith, toward 1770: "It is not uncommon, I have been told, in the Highlands of Scotland, for a mother who has borne twenty children not to have two alive."[7] The Highland chieftains owned nearly all the land outside the towns, and kept the tenant farmers primitively poor on a rocky soil harassed by summer downpours, and by winter snow from September to May. Rents were repeatedly raised—on one farm from five pounds to £20 in twenty-five years.[8] Many peasants, seeing no escape from poverty at home, emigrated to America; so, said Johnson, "a rapacious chief could make a wilderness of his estate."[9] The landlords pleaded depreciation of the currency as their excuse for raising rents. Conditions were even worse in the coal mines and salt pits, where, until 1775, workers were bound to their jobs as long as they lived.[10]

In the Lowland towns the Industrial Revolution brought prosperity to an expanding and enterprising middle class. Southwest Scotland was dotted with textile factories. Glasgow, through industries and foreign trade, grew from a population of 12,500 in 1707 to eighty thousand in 1800; it had rich suburbs, slum tenements, and a university. In 1768–90 a canal was dug connecting the Rivers Clyde and Forth, so establishing an all-water commercial route between the industrial southwest and the political southeast. Edinburgh —which had some fifty thousand inhabitants in 1740—was the focus of Scotland's government, intellect, and fashion; every well-to-do Scottish family aspired to spend at least a part of the year there; here came Boswell and Burns, here lived Hume and Robertson and Raeburn; here were renowned lawyers like the Erskines, and a prestigious university, and the Royal Society of Edinburgh. And here were the headquarters of Scottish Christianity.

Roman Catholics were few, but enough, as we have seen, to cause trepidation in a land still reverberating with echoes of John Knox. The Episcopal Church had many adherents among the affluent, who liked the bishops and ritual of the Anglican communion. But the allegiance of the great majority went to the Church of Scotland, the Presbyterian Kirk, which rejected bishops, minimized ritual, and accepted in religion and morals no other rule than that of its parish sessions, its district presbyteries, its provincial synods, and its General Assembly. Probably nowhere else in Europe except Spain was a people so thoroughly imbued with theology. The kirk session, composed of elders and minister, could levy fines and inflict penalties for misconduct and heresy; it could sentence fornicators to stand up and be publicly rebuked during the service; Robert Burns and Jean Armour were thus chastened in a kirk session on August 6, 1786. The Calvinist eschatology dominated the common mind, making free thought a danger to life and limb; but a group of "Moderate" clergymen—led by Robert Wallace, Adam Ferguson, and William Robertson—tempered the intolerance of the people sufficiently to allow David Hume a natural death.

Perhaps a hard religion was required to counter the revels of a people so cold that they drank to intoxication, and so poor that their only pleasure lay in sexual pursuit. The career of Burns indicates that the men drank and fornicated despite the Devil and the dominies, and that willing girls were not rare. In the final quarter of the eighteenth century there was a marked decline in religious belief and in adherence to the traditional morality. William Creech, an Edinburgh painter, noted that in 1763 Sunday had been a day of religious devotion; in 1783 "attendance on church was greatly neglected, and particularly by the men"; and at night the streets were noisy with loose and riotous youth. "In 1763 there were five or six brothels; . . . in 1783 the number of brothels had increased twenty-fold, and the women of the town more than a hundred-fold. Every quarter of the city and the suburbs was infected with multitudes of females abandoned to vice."[11] Golf was luring men from church to the links on Sundays, and on weekdays men and women danced (formerly a sin), went to theaters (still a sin), attended horse races, and gambled in taverns and clubs.

The Kirk was the chief source of democracy and education. The congregation chose the elders, and the minister (usually chosen by a "patron") was expected to organize a school in every parish. The hunger for education was intense. Of the four universities, that of St. Andrews was in decay, but claimed to have the best library in Britain. Johnson found the University of Aberdeen flourishing in 1773. The University of Glasgow had on its faculty Joseph Black, physicist, Thomas Reid, philosopher, and Adam Smith, economist, and was sheltering James Watt. Edinburgh University was the youngest of the four, but it was alive with the excitement of the Scottish Enlightenment.

III. THE SCOTTISH ENLIGHTENMENT

Only the growth of trade with England and the world, and the rise of industry in the Lowlands, can explain the outburst of genius that illuminated Scotland between Hume's *Treatise of Human Nature* (1739) and Boswell's *Life of Johnson* (1791). In philosophy Francis Hutcheson, David Hume, and Adam Ferguson; in economics Adam Smith; in literature John Home,[12] Henry Home (Lord Kames), William Robertson, James Macpherson, Robert Burns, James Boswell; in science Joseph Black, James Watt, Nevil Maskelyne, James Hutton, Lord Monboddo;[13] in medicine John and William Hunter:[14] here was a galaxy to rival the stars that shone in England around the Great Bear! Hume, Robertson, and others formed in Edinburgh a "Select Society" for weekly discussions of ideas. These men and their like kept in touch with French rather than English thought, partly because France had for centuries been associated with Scotland, partly because the lingering hostility between Englishmen and Scots impeded the fusion of the two cultures. Hume had a low opinion of the English mind in his time until, in the year of his death, he gratefully acclaimed *The Decline and Fall of the Roman Empire*.

We have already discharged our debt to Hutcheson and Hume.[15] Now we look at Hume's genial enemy, Thomas Reid, who strove to bring philosophy back from idea-listic metaphysics to an acceptance of objective reality. While teaching at Aberdeen and Glasgow he wrote his *Inquiry into the Human Mind on the Principles of Common Sense* (1764). Before publishing it he sent the manuscript to Hume with a courteous letter conveying compliments, and explaining his regret that he had to oppose the older man's skeptical philosophy. Hume replied with characteristic amiability, and bade him publish without fear of reproach.[16]

Reid had formerly yielded to Berkeley's view that we know only ideas, never things; but when Hume, by similar reasoning, contended that we know only mental states, never a "mind" additional to them, Reid felt that such a finical analysis undermined all distinctions between true and false, right and wrong, and all belief in God or immortality. To avoid this debacle, he thought, he had to refute Hume, and to refute Hume he had to reject Berkeley.

So he ridiculed the notion that we know only our sensations and ideas; on the contrary, we know things directly and immediately; it is only "from an excess of refinement" that we analyze our experience of a rose, for example, and reduce it to a bundle of sensations and ideas; the bundle is real, but so is the rose, which maintains an obstinate persistence when our sensations of it cease. Of course the primary qualities—size, shape, solidity, texture, weight, motion, number—belong to the objective world, and are subjectively altered only through subjective illusions; and even the secondary qualities have an objective source insofar as physical or chemical conditions in the object or the environment give rise to the subjective sensations of smell, taste, warmth, brightness, color, or sound.[17]

　Common sense tells us this, but "the principles of common sense" are not the prejudices of unlettered multitudes; they are the instinctive "principles . . . which the constitution of our nature [the sense common to us all] leads us to believe, and which we are under a necessity to take for granted in the common concerns of life."[18] Compared with this universal sense, daily tested and a thousand times confirmed, the airy reasonings of metaphysics are merely a game played in solitary flight from the world; even Hume, as he confessed, abandoned this intellectual game when he left his study.[19] But the same return to common sense restores reality to the mind: it is not only ideas that exist; there is an organism, a mind, a self, that has the ideas. Language itself testifies to this universal belief: every language has a first-person-singular pronoun; it is *I* who feel, remember, think, and love. "It seemed very natural to think that the *Treatise of Human Nature* required an author, a very ingenious one too; but now we learn that it is only a set of ideas which came together and arranged themselves by certain associations and attractions."[20]

　Hume took all this good-naturedly. He could not accept Reid's theological conclusions, but he respected his Christian temper, and perhaps he was secretly relieved to learn that after all, despite Berkeley, the external world existed, and that, despite Hume, Hume was real. The public too was relieved, and bought three editions of Reid's *Inquiry* before he died. Boswell was among the comforted; Reid's book, he tells us, "settled my mind, which had been very uneasy from speculations in the abstruse and skeptical style."[21]

　Art added color to Scotland's Age of Light. The four Adam brothers, who left their mark on English architecture, were Scots. Allan Ramsay (son of the poet Allan Ramsay), failing to win honors in his native Edinburgh, migrated to London (1752), and, after years of labor, became painter-in-ordinary to the King, much to the fury of English artists. He made a good portrait of George III,[22] but a still better one of his own wife.[23] The dislocation of his right arm ended his career as a painter.

　Sir Henry Raeburn was the Reynolds of Scotland. Son of an Edinburgh manufacturer, he taught himself oil painting, and portrayed a widowed heiress to such satisfaction that she married him and dowered him with her fortune. After two years of study in Italy he returned to Edinburgh (1787). Soon he had more patrons than he had time to paint: Robertson, John Home, Dugald Stewart, Walter Scott, and, best of his portraits, Lord Newton—an immense body, a massive head, a character of iron mingled with balm. At opposite poles is the modest loveliness that Raeburn found in his wife.[24] Sometimes he rivaled Reynolds in picturing children, as in the *Drummond Children* in the Metropolitan Museum of Art. Raeburn was knighted in 1822, but died a year later, aged sixty-seven.

　The Scottish Enlightenment excelled in historians. Adam Ferguson shared in founding the study of sociology and social psychology with his *Essay on the History of Civil Society* (1767), which had seven editions in his lifetime. History (Ferguson argued) knows man only as living in groups; to understand him we must see him as a social but competitive creature, composed of gregarious habits and individualistic desires. Character development and social organization are determined by the interplay of these contrary tendencies, and are seldom affected by the ideals of philosophers. Economic rivalry, political oppositions, social inequalities, and war itself are in the nature of man; they will continue; and by and large they advance the progress of mankind.

Ferguson in his day was as famous as Adam Smith, but their friend William Robertson won still wider renown. We recall Wieland's hope that Schiller as historian would "rise to a level with Hume, Robertson, and Gibbon."[25] Horace Walpole asked in 1759: "Can we think that we want writers of history while Mr. Hume and Mr. Robertson are living? . . . Robertson's work is one of the purest style, and of the greatest impartiality, that I have ever read."[26] Gibbon wrote in his *Memoirs:* "The perfect composition, the nervous language, the well-turned periods of Dr. Robertson influenced me to the ambitious hope that I might one day tread in his footsteps";[27] and he was "elated as often as I find myself ranked in the triumvirate of British historians" with Hume and Robertson.[28] He ranked these two with Guicciardini and Machiavelli as the greatest of modern historians, and later called Robertson "the first historian of the present age."[29]

Like Reid, Robertson was a clergyman son of a clergyman. Installed as minister at Gladsmuir at the age of twenty-two (1743), he was elected two years later to the General Assembly of the Kirk. There he became the leader of the Moderates, and protected heretics like Hume. After six years of labor, and careful study of documents and authorities, he issued in 1759 a *History of Scotland during the Reigns of Queen Mary and of James VI until His Accession to the Crown of England;* he modestly ended where Hume's *History of England* had begun. It pleased Scotland by avoiding idolatry of Mary Queen of Scots, and pleased Englishmen with its style—though Johnson was amused to find in it some Johnsonianly cumbrous words. The book went through nine editions in fifty-three years.

But Robertson's masterpiece was his three-volume *History of the Reign of the Emperor Charles V* (1769). We may judge of the reputation that he had won from the price paid him by the publishers, £4,500, as compared with the £600 he had received for the *History of Scotland*. All Europe acclaimed the new book in its various translations. Catherine the Great carried it with her on her long journeys; "I never leave off reading it," she said, "especially the first volume";[30] like all of us she was delighted with the long prologue, which reviewed medieval developments leading to Charles V. The book has been superseded by later research, but no later presentation of the subject can compare with it as a piece of literature. It is pleasant to note that the praise which the book received, considerably greater than that accorded to Hume's *History*, did not cool the friendship of the minister and the heretic.

More famous than either was James Macpherson, who was ranked with Homer by Goethe, and above Homer by Napoleon.[31] In 1760 Macpherson, then twenty-four years old, announced that an epic of some length and splendor existed in scattered Gaelic manuscripts, which he would undertake to collect and translate if he could secure some financial aid. Robertson, Ferguson, and Hugh Blair (eloquent Presbyterian minister of Edinburgh) raised the money; Macpherson and two Gaelic scholars toured the Highlands and the Hebrides, gathering old manuscripts; and in 1762 Macpherson published *Fingal, an Ancient Epic Poem in Six Books, . . . Composed by Ossian, the Son of Fingal, Translated from the Gaelic Language*. A year later he issued another epic, *Temora*, allegedly by Ossian; and in 1765 he published both as *The Works of Ossian*.

Ossian, in Gaelic (Irish and Scottish) legend, was the poet son of the warrior Finn MacCumhail;[32] he lived, we are told, three hundred years, long enough to express his pagan opposition to the new theology brought to Ireland by St. Patrick. Some poems attributed to him were preserved in three fifteenth-century manuscripts, chiefly in *The Book of Lismore*, which James Macgregor compiled in 1512; Macpherson had these manuscripts.[33] *Fingal* told how the young warrior, having defeated Scottish invaders of Ireland, invited them to a feast and a song of peace. The story is vividly told, warmed by the Scots' appreciation of Irish girls. "Thou art snow on the heath," says one warrior to Morna, daughter of King Cormac; "thy hair is the mist of Cromla when it curls on the hill, when it shines to the beam of the west! Thy breasts are two smooth rocks seen from Branno of streams; thy arms like two white pillars in the halls of the great Fingal."[34] We meet other bosoms, less rocky: "white bosom," "high bosom," "heavy bosom";[35] they are a bit distracting; but soon the tale turns from love to the hatreds of war.

Macpherson's *Ossian* made a stir in Scotland, England, France, and Germany. Scots hailed it as a page from their heroic medieval past. England, which in 1765 was welcoming Percy's *Reliques of Ancient English Poetry*, was ripe for the romance of Gaelic legend. Goethe, toward the end of *Werther* (1774), showed his hero reading to Lotte six pages of *Ossian*. These were the story of the tender maiden Daura, as told by her father, Armin: how the wicked Erath lured her out to a rock in the sea by promising that her lover, Armar, would meet her there; how Erath abandoned her on the rock, and no lover came. "She lifted up her voice; she called for her brother and her father: 'Arindal! Armin!' " Arindal rowed out to rescue her, but an arrow well aimed by a hidden enemy slew him. Lover Armar came to the shore, tried to swim out to Daura; "sudden a blast from the hill came over the waves; he sank, and he rose no more." The father, too old and weak to go to her, cried out in horror and despair.

> Alone on the sea-beat rock my daughter was heard to complain. Frequent and loud were her cries. What could her father do? All night I stood on the shore. I saw her by the faint beam of the moon. . . . Loud was the wind; the rain beat hard on the hill. Before morning appeared her voice was weak. It

died away like the evening breeze among the grass of the rocks. Spent with grief she expired.

Gone is my strength in war! fallen my pride among women! When the storms aloft arise, when the north wind lifts the wave on high, I sit by the sounding shore, and look on the fatal rock. Often, by the setting moon, I see the ghosts of my children. . . . Will none of you speak in pity?[36]

Controversy soon arose: was *Ossian* really a translation from old Gaelic ballads, or was it a series of poems by Macpherson and foisted upon a poet who perhaps never lived? Herder and Goethe in Germany, Diderot in France, Hugh Blair and Lord Kames in Scotland, credited Macpherson's claim. But in 1775 Samuel Johnson, in *A Journey to the Western Islands of Scotland*, after some inquiries in the Hebrides (1773), declared of the "Ossianic" poems: "I believe they never existed in any other form but that which we have seen. The editor, or author, never could show the original, nor can it be shown by any other."[37] Macpherson wrote to Johnson that only the Englishman's age protected him from a challenge or a beating. Johnson replied: "I hope I shall never be deterred from detecting what I think a cheat, by the meanness of a ruffian. . . . I thought your book an imposture, I think it an imposture still. . . . Your rage I defy."[38] Hume, Horace Walpole, and others joined in Johnson's doubts. Asked to produce the originals which he claimed to have translated, Macpherson delayed; but at his death he left the manuscripts of Gaelic ballads, some of which he had used in contriving the plot and setting the tone of his poems. Many phrases and names he took from these texts; the two epics, however, were his own composition.[39]

The deception was not so complete or so heinous as Johnson supposed; let us call it poetic license on too grand a scale. Taken in themselves, the two prose-poetry epics warranted some of the admiration they received. They conveyed the beauty and terrors of nature, the fury of hatred, and the zest of war. They were tenderly sentimental, but they had some of the nobility that Sir Thomas Malory had conveyed in *Le Morte d'Arthur* (1470). They rose to fame on the Romantic wave that engulfed the Enlightenment.

IV. ADAM SMITH

Next to Hume, Adam Smith was the greatest figure in the Scottish Enlightenment. His father, controller of the customs at Kirkaldy, died some months before Adam's birth (1723). Almost the only adventure the economist had in his life came when, a child of three years, he was kidnapped by gypsies, who, being pursued, abandoned him beside the road. After some schooling at Kirkaldy, and attending the courses of Hutcheson at Glasgow, Adam went down to Oxford (1740), where he found the teachers as lazy and worthless as Gibbon would describe them in 1752. Smith educated himself by reading, but the college authorities confiscated his copy of Hume's *Treatise of Human Nature* as quite unfit for a Christian youth. One year with the dons was enough; loving his mother better, he returned to Kirkaldy, and continued to absorb books. In 1748 he moved to Edinburgh, where he lectured independently on literature and rhetoric. His discourses impressed influential persons; he was appointed to the chair of logic in the University of Glasgow (1751), and a year later became professor of moral philosophy —which included ethics, jurisprudence, and political economy. In 1759 he published his ethical conclusions in *Theory of Moral Sentiments*, which Buckle, ignoring Aristotle and Spinoza, pronounced "the most important work that has ever been written on this interesting subject."[40]

Smith derived our ethical judgments from our spontaneous disposition to imagine ourselves in the position of others; thereby we echo their emotions, and by this sympathy, or fellow feeling, we are moved to approve or condemn.[41] The moral sense is rooted in our social instincts, or in the mental habits developed by us as members of a group; but it is not inconsistent with self-love. The summit of a man's moral development comes when a man learns to judge himself as he judges others, "to command himself according to the objective principles of equity, natural law, prudence, and justice."[42] Religion is not the source nor the mainstay of our moral sentiments, but these are strongly influenced by belief in the derivation of the moral code from a rewarding and punishing God.[43]

In 1764 Smith, now forty-one, was engaged as tutor and guide to accompany the eighteen-year-old Duke of Buccleuch on a tour of Europe. The fee, £300 a year for life, gave Smith the security and leisure for his masterpiece, which he began to write during an eighteen-month stay in Toulouse. He visited Voltaire at Ferney, and in Paris he met Helvétius and d'Alembert, Quesnay and Turgot. Returning to Scotland in 1766, he lived for the next ten years contentedly with his mother in Kirkaldy, working on his book. The *Inquiry into the Nature and Causes of the Wealth of Nations* appeared in 1776, and was greeted with a letter of praise from Hume, who died shortly thereafter.

Hume himself, in his essays, had helped to form the economic as well as the ethical views of Adam Smith. He had ridiculed the "mercantile system," which favored protective tariffs, trade monopolies, and other governmental measures to ensure an excess of exports over imports, and the accumulation of precious metals as a nation's basic wealth. This policy, said Hume, was like toiling to keep water from seeking its natural level; and he called for liberation of the economy from the "numberless bars . . . and imposts which all nations of Europe, and none more than England, have put upon trade."[44] Of course Smith was acquainted with the campaign of Quesnay and other French physiocrats against the obstructive regulations of industry and trade by guilds and governments, and their demand for a *laissez-faire* policy that would let nature take its course, and all prices and wages find their level in free competition. The revolt then rising in America against British restrictions on colonial trade was part of the background of Smith's thought. If the freedom of trade which he proposed had guided the British government, the year of his book might not have seen the Declaration of Independence.

Smith had some ideas about the strife between Britain and America. He considered the English monopoly of colonial trade to be one of the "mean and malignant expedients of the mercantile system."[45] He proposed that if the colonists refused to be taxed to support the expenses of the British Empire, America should be given its independence without further quarrel. "By thus parting good friends, the natural affection of the colonists to the mother country . . . would quickly revive. It might dispose them . . . to favor us in war as well as in trade, and, instead of turbulent and factious subjects, to become our most faithful . . . and generous allies."[46] And he added: "Such has hitherto been the rapid progress of that country in wealth, population, and improvement, that in the course of little more than a century, perhaps, the produce of America might exceed that of British taxation. The seat of empire would then naturally remove itself to that part of the empire which contributed most to the general defense and support of the whole."[47]

Smith defined the wealth of a nation not as the amount of gold or silver it possessed, but as the land with its improvements and products, and the people with their labor, services, skills, and goods. His thesis was that, with some exceptions, the greatest physical wealth results from the greatest economic liberty. Self-interest is universal, but if we let this powerful motive operate with the greatest economic freedom it will stimulate such industry, enterprise, and competition as will generate more riches than any other system known to history. (This was Mandeville's *Fable of the Bees*[48] worked out in detail.) Smith believed that the laws of the market—especially the law of supply and demand—would harmonize the liberty of the producer with the welfare of the consumer; for if a producer made excessive profits, others would enter the same field, and the mutual competition would keep prices and profits within fair limits. Moreover, the consumer would enjoy a kind of economic democracy: by buying or refusing to buy he would in great measure determine what articles would be produced, what services would be offered, in what quantity and at what price, instead of having all these matters dictated by a government.

Following the physiocrats (but judging the products of labor and the services of trade to be wealth as real as the produce of the land), Smith called for an end to feudal tolls, guild restrictions, governmental economic regulations, and industrial or commercial monopolies, as all limiting that freedom which—by allowing the individual to work, spend, save, buy, and sell at his pleasure—keeps the wheels of production and distribution in motion. The government must *laisser faire*, must let nature—the natural propensities of men—operate freely; it must allow the individual to shift for himself, to find by trial and error the work that he can do, the place that he can fill, in the economic life; it must let him sink or swim.

> According to this system of natural liberty, the sovereign [or the state] has only three duties to attend to: . . . first, the duty of protecting the society from the violence and invasion of other independent societies; secondly, the duty of protecting, as far as possible, every member of the society from the injustice or oppressions of every other member of it, or the duty of establishing

an exact administration of justice; and thirdly, the duty of maintaining certain
public works and public institutions which it can never be for the interest of
any individual, or small number of individuals, to erect or maintain.[49]

Here was the formula of Jeffersonian government, and the outline of a state
that would enable the new capitalism to grow and flourish exceedingly.

There was a loophole in the formula: what if the duty of preventing injustice should imply the obligation to prevent the inhuman usage of the
simple or the weak by the clever or the strong? Smith answered: such injustice can come only through monopolies in restraint of competition or
trade, and his principles called for the suppression of monopolies. We must
rely upon the competition of employers for workers, and of these for jobs,
to regulate wages; all attempts of governments to regulate them are sooner
or later frustrated by the laws of the market. Though labor (and not land,
as the physiocrats held) is the sole source of wealth,[50] it is a commodity, just
like capital, and is subject to the laws of supply and demand. "Whenever the
law has attempted to regulate the wages of workers, it has always been rather
to lower them than to raise them";[51] for "whenever the legislature attempts
to regulate the differences between masters and their workmen, its counselors are always the masters."[52] This was written at a time when English law
allowed employers, but forbade employees, to organize themselves to protect
their economic interests. Smith denounced this partiality of the law, and
foresaw that better wages would be obtained not through governmental regulation but by the organization of labor.[53]

The supposed herald of capitalism almost always took the side of the
workers against the employers. He warned against letting merchants and
manufacturers determine the policy of the government.

> The interest of the dealers, . . . in any particular branch of trade or manu-
> factures, is always in some respects different from, and even opposite to, that
> of the public. . . . The proposal of any new law, or regulation of commerce,
> which comes from this order ought always to be listened to with great pre-
> caution. . . . It comes from an order of men . . . who have generally an in-
> terest to deceive, and even to oppress, the public and who . . . have, upon
> many occasions, both deceived and oppressed it.[54]

Is this Adam Smith or Karl Marx? But Smith defended private property as
an indispensable stimulus to enterprise, and he held that the number of available jobs, and the wages paid, will depend above all upon the accumulation
and application of capital.[55] Nevertheless, he advocated high wages as profitable to employer and employee alike,[56] and urged the abolition of slavery on
the ground that "the work done by free men comes cheaper in the end than
that performed by slaves."[57]

When we consider Smith himself, in his appearance, habits, and character,
we wonder that a man so removed from the processes of agriculture, industry, and trade should have written about these esoteric complexities with
such realism, insight, and audacity. He was as absent-minded as Newton,
and cared little for convention. Usually mannerly and mild, he was capable
of meeting Samuel Johnson's rudeness with a four-word retort that ques-

tioned the Great Cham's legitimacy. After publishing *The Wealth of Nations* he spent two years in London, where he enjoyed the acquaintance of Gibbon, Reynolds, and Burke. In 1778 he—apostle of free trade—was appointed commissioner of customs from Scotland. Thereafter he lived in Edinburgh with his mother, remaining a bachelor to the end. She died in 1784; he followed her in 1790, aged sixty-seven.

His achievement lay not so much in the originality of his thought as in the mastery and co-ordination of data, the wealth of illustrative material, the illuminating application of theory to current conditions, a simple, clear, and persuasive style, and a broad viewpoint that raised economics from a "dismal science" to the level of philosophy. His book was epochal because it summarized and explained—of course it did not produce—the facts and forces that were changing feudalism and mercantilism into capitalism and free enterprise. When Pitt II reduced the duty on tea from 119 to twelve and a half per cent, and tried in general to bring about freer trade, he acknowledged his indebtedness to *The Wealth of Nations*. Lord Rosebery tells how, at a dinner attended by Pitt, the whole company rose when Smith entered, and Pitt said, "We will stand till you are seated, for we are all your scholars."[58] Sir James Murray-Pulteney predicted that Smith's work "would persuade the present generation and govern the next."[59]

V. ROBERT BURNS

"My ancient but ignoble blood," said Scotland's greatest poet, "has crept through scoundrels since the Flood."[60] We shall go no further back than William Burnes, no scoundrel but a hard-working, irascible tenant farmer. In 1757 he married Agnes Brown, who presented him Robert in 1759. Six years later William took lease of a seventy-acre farm at Mount Oliphant; there the multiplying family lived "sparingly" in an isolated house. Robert received tutoring at home and attended a parish school, but from the age of thirteen he worked on the farm. When he was fourteen "a bonnie, sweet, sonsy [jolly] lass initiated me into a certain delicious passion, which, in spite of acid disappointment, ginhorse prudence, and bookworm philosophy, I hold to be the finest of human joys."[61] At fifteen he met a second "angel," and spent feverish nights thinking of her. His brother recalled that Robert's "attachment [to women] became very strong, and he was constantly the victim of some fair enslaver."[62]

In 1777, in a spell of reckless courage, William Burnes leased the Lochlie farm, 130 acres, in Tarbolton, for which he contracted to pay £130 a year. Now Robert, eighteen, the eldest of seven children, became the chief worker, for William, broken by unrewarding toil, was prematurely old. Father and son drew apart as the one narrowed into puritanism and the other eased into a broader code. Despite parental prohibition Robert attended a dancing school; "from that instance of rebellion," the poet recalled, "he took a kind of dislike to me, which I believe was one cause of that dissipation which marked my future years."[63] At the age of twenty-four Robert joined a Freemason lodge. In 1783 the farm was attached for default of rent. Robert and his brother Gilbert pooled their poverty to lease a farm of 118 acres for ninety pounds a year; there for four years they labored, allowing themselves seven pounds each per year for personal expenses; and there they supported their parents, sisters, and brothers. The father died in 1784 of tuberculosis.

In the long winter evenings Robert read many books, including Robertson's histories, Hume's philosophy, and *Paradise Lost*. "Give me a spirit like my favorite hero, Milton's Satan."[64] Resenting the Kirk's censorship of morals, he found no difficulty in discarding its theology and keeping only a vague faith in God and immortality. He laughed at "Orthodox, orthodox, who believe in John Knox," and he suspected that the dominies, between Sundays, were secretly as sinful as himself.[65] In "The Holy Fair" (about a religious revival meeting) he described a succession of preachers flaying sin and brandishing hell, while harlots outside waited confidently for the congregation's patronage.

Burns's dislike for clergymen gained fervor when one of them sent an agent to rebuke and fine him for sleeping unwed with Betty Paton. It became anger when his kindly landlord, Gavin Hamilton, was censured by the kirk session of Mauchline (1785) for repeated absence from church services. Now the poet wrote his sharpest satire, "Holy Willie's Prayer," which ridiculed the Pharisaic virtue of William Fisher, an elder of the Mauchline kirk. Burns pictured him addressing God:

> I bless and praise Thy matchless might,
> When thousands Thou hast left in night,
> That I am here afore thy sight,
>   For gifts an' grace
> A burning and a shining light
>   To a' this place. . . .
>
> O Lord! yestreen, Thou kens, wi' Meg—
> Thy pardon I sincerely beg—
> O! may't never be a livin' plague
>   To my dishonor,
> An' I'll ne'er lift a lawless leg
>   Again upon her.
>
> Besides I farther maun* avow
> Wi' Leezie's lass three times, I trow—
> But Lord, that Friday I was fou†
>   When I cam near her,
> Or else, Thou kens, Thy servant true
>   Wad never steer her. . . .
>
> Lord, mind Gau'n Hamilton's deserts,
> He drinks an' swears, an' plays at cartes,
> Yet hae sae mony takin' arts
>   Wi' great an' sma',

---

* Must.
† Drunk.

> Frae God's ain priest the people's hearts
>   He steals awa'. . . .
>
> Lord, in Thy day of vengeance try him;
> Lord, visit them who did employ him,
> And pass not in Thy mercy by them,
>   Nor hear their pray'r;
> But, for Thy people's sake, destroy them,
>   An' dinna spare.
>
> But, Lord, remember me an' mine
> Wi' mercies temporal an' divine,
> That I for grace an' gear* may shine
>   Excell'd by nane,
> And a' the glory shall be Thine.
>   Amen, Amen!

Burns did not dare publish this poem; it reached print three years after his death.

Meanwhile he was giving the Kirk plenty of reason for reproof. He called himself a "fornicator by profession."[66] Every second maiden stirred him: "charming Chloe, tripping o'er the pearly lawn," Jean Armour, Highland Mary Campbell, Peggy Chalmers, "Clarinda," Jenny Cruikshank, Jenny of Dalry "comin' thro' the rye," "bonnie wee" Deborah Davies, Agnes Fleming, Jeanie Jaffrey, Peggy Kennedy of "bonnie Doon," Jessie Lewars, Jean Lorimer ("Chloris"), Mary Morison, Anna Park, Anna and Polly Stewart, Peggy Thomson—and there were more.[67] Only their bright and laughing eyes and soft hands and bosoms of "driven snaw" reconciled him to the toils and griefs of life. He excused his sexual meandering on the ground that all things in nature change, and why should man be an exception?[68] But he warned women never to trust the promises of a male.[69] We know of five children begotten by him in wedlock, and nine others outside it. "I have a genius for paternity," he said, and he surmised that only emasculation could cure him.[70] As for the reproaches of ministers and the laws of Scotland—

> The Kirk an' State may join an' tell,
>   To do sic things I maunna;†
> The Kirk an' State may gae to hell,
>   And I'll gae to my Anna.[71]

When Betty Paton bore him a child (May 22, 1785) Burns offered to marry her; her parents rejected the offer. He turned to Jean Armour and gave her a written promise of marriage; soon she was pregnant. On June 25, 1786, he appeared before the kirk session and admitted his responsibility; he had (he said) considered himself married to Jean, and would stand by his pledge; but her father refused to let her marry a seventeen-year-old farmer already burdened with an illegitimate child. On July 9, in his pew at church, Burns humbly received public reproof. On August 3 Jean bore twins. On August 6 he and Jean accepted rebuke before the congregation, and were

---

* Wealth.
† To do such things I must not.

"absolved from the scandal." The father swore out a warrant for Burns's arrest; the poet went into hiding, and planned to take ship to Jamaica. The warrant was not executed, and Robert returned to his farm. In that same summer he promised to marry Mary Campbell and take her to America; she died before they could act on the plan; Burns celebrated her in "Highland Mary" and "To Mary in Heaven."[72]

In that prolific year 1786 he published at Kilmarnock, by subscription, his first volume of verse. He omitted poems likely to offend the Kirk or the morals of the folk; he delighted his readers with his Scottish dialect and his descriptions of familiar scenery; he pleased the peasants by raising the details of their life into intelligible verse. Probably no other poet ever expressed such fellow feeling for animals sharing the burden of the farmer's day, or the "silly sheep" bewildered in the driving snow, or the mouse dislodged from his nest by the advancing plow.

> But, mousie, thou art no thy lane*
> In proving foresight may be vain;
> The best laid schemes o' mice and men
> Gang aft a-gley.

Almost as proverbial are the lines that end the poem "To a Louse on Seeing One on a Lady's Bonnet at Church":

> O wad some pow'r the giftie gie us
> To see oursels as ithers see us.[73]

To make sure that his little book would be welcomed, Burns capped it with "The Cotter's Saturday Night": the farmer resting after a week of heavy toil; his wife and children gathering about him, each with a tale of the day; the oldest daughter timidly introducing the shy courter; the happy sharing in the simple fare; the Bible-reading by the father; the united prayer. To this pleasant picture Burns added a patriotic apostrophe to "Scotia, my dear, my native soil!" — Of the 612 copies printed all but three were sold in four weeks, netting Burns twenty pounds.

He had thought of using the proceeds to pay for passage to America; instead he devoted them to a sojourn in Edinburgh. Arriving there on a borrowed horse in November, 1786, he shared a room and bed with another rural youth. Some noisy harlots occupied the floor above them.[74] The favorable reception of his book by Edinburgh reviewers opened doors to him; for a season he was an idol of polite society. Sir Walter Scott described him:

> I was a lad of fifteen in 1786–87 when Burns came first to Edinburgh. . . . I saw him one day at the late venerable Professor Ferguson, where there were several gentlemen of literary reputation. . . . His person was strong and robust; his wanness rustic, not clownish; a sort of dignified plainness and simplicity. . . . His countenance massive, . . . the eye large and of a dark cast, which glowed . . . when he spoke. . . . Among the men, who were the most learned of their time and country, he expressed himself with perfect firmness, but without the least forwardness.[75]

---

* Not alone.

Burns was encouraged to issue an enlarged edition of his poems. To give the new volume added substance he proposed to include one of his major productions, "The Jolly Beggars," which he had not ventured to print in the Kilmarnock volume. It described an assemblage of tramps, paupers, criminals, poets, fiddlers, harlots, and crippled, derelict soldiers in Nancy Gibson's alehouse at Mauchline. Burns put into their mouths the most candid and unrepentant autobiographies, and ended the medley with a drunken chorus:

> A fig for those by law protected!
>   Liberty's a glorious feast!
> Courts for cowards were erected,
>   Churches built to please the priest.[76]

Hugh Blair, scholar and preacher, expressed alarm at the thought of publishing such a snub to the virtues; Burns yielded, and later forgot that he had written the poem;[77] a friend preserved it, and it saw the light in 1799.

The Edinburgh editor sold some three thousand copies, netting Burns £450. He bought a mare and rode out (May 5, 1787) into the Highlands, and then across the Tweed to sample England. On June 9 he visited his relatives at Mossgiel, and called on Jean Armour; she received him warmly, and conceived again. Back in Edinburgh, he met Mrs. Agnes M'Lehose. At seventeen she had married a Glasgow surgeon; at twenty-one (1780) she left him, taking her children with her, and settled down to "frugal decency" in the capital. She invited Burns to her home; he fell in love with her without delay; apparently she did not give herself to him, for he continued to love her. They exchanged letters and poems, his signed "Sylvander," hers "Clarinda." In 1791 she decided to go and rejoin her husband in Jamaica; Burns sent her, as his farewell, some tender lines:

> Ae* fond kiss, and then we sever!
> Ae farewell, and then forever! . . .
> Had we never lov'd sae kindly,
> Had we never lov'd sae blindly,
> Never met nor never parted,
> We had ne'er been brokenhearted.[78]

She found her husband living with a Negro waitress; she returned to Edinburgh.

His passion for her being unfulfilled, Burns sought companionship and revelry with a local club, the Crochallan Fencibles—men pledged to the defense of their city. There wine and women were the *lares et penates,* and bawdy reigned. For them Burns collected old Scots songs, and added some of his own; several of these found anonymous and esoteric publication in 1800 as *The Merry Muses of Caledonia.* Burns's membership in this club, his open scorn of class distinctions,[79] and his frank expression of radical views in religion and politics rapidly ended his welcome in Edinburgh society.

He tried to secure a post as a tax collector; repeatedly put off, he resigned

---

* One.

himself to another venture in farming. In February, 1788, he rented the Ellisland farm, five miles from Dumfries, twelve from Carlyle's Craigenputtock. The owner, who candidly described the soil as "in the most miserable state of exhaustion,"[80] advanced the poet £300 to build a farmhouse and fence the field; Burns was to pay fifty pounds annually for three years, then seventy pounds. Meanwhile Jean Armour gave birth to twins (March 3, 1788), who soon died. Some time before April 28 Burns married her; with her one surviving child of the four she had borne him she came to serve him faithfully as wife and housekeeper at Ellisland. She gave him another child, whom Burns called "my *chef-d'oeuvre* in that species of manufacture, as I look upon 'Tam o'Shanter' to be my standard performance in the political line."[81] In 1790 he became intimate with Anna Park, waitress in a Dumfries tavern; in March, 1791, she bore him a child, which Jean took and brought up with her own.[82]

Life was hard at Ellisland. Nevertheless he continued to write great poetry. There he added two famous stanzas to an old drinking song, "Auld Lang Syne." Burns worked until he too, like his father, broke down. He was glad to be appointed (July 14, 1788) an exciseman, and so to travel about the country gauging casks, examining victualers, chandlers, and tanners, and reporting to the Excise Board in Edinburgh. Despite frequent bouts with John Barleycorn he seems to have satisfied the board. In November, 1791, he sold his farm at a profit, and moved with Jean and the three children to a house in Dumfries.

He offended the respectable folk of the town by frequenting the taverns, and coming home drunk, on many occasions, to patient Jean.[83] He continued to be a great poet; in those five years at Dumfries he composed "Ye banks an' braes o' bonnie Doon," "Scots wha' hae wi' Wallace bled," and "O my luve's like a red, red rose." Finding no mental mate in his wife, he corresponded with—sometimes visited—Mrs. Frances Dunlop, who had in her veins some residue of Wallace's blood; she strove to tame Burns's morals and vocabulary, not always to the benefit of his verse. He appreciated better the five-pound notes she sent him now and then.[84]

He endangered his commission as exciseman by his radical views. He told George III, in fifteen excellent stanzas, to get rid of his corrupt ministers, and advised the Prince of Wales to end his dissipations, and his "rattlin' dice withe Charlie [Fox]," if he wished to inherit the throne.[85] In a letter to the Edinburgh *Courant* he applauded America's Declaration of Independence, and in 1789 he was an "enthusiastic votary" of the French Revolution. In 1795 he sent out a blast against rank distinctions:

> Is there for honest poverty
>   That hings* his head and a' that?
> The coward slave, we pass him by;
>   We dare be poor for a' that!
>   For a' that, an' a' that,
>   Our toils obscure, an' a' that,

---

* Hangs.

> The rank is but the guinea's stamp,
> The man's the gowd* for a' that.
>
> . . . .
>
> The honest man, tho' e'er sae poor,
> Is king o' men for a' that.
>
> Ye see yon birkie† ca'd a lord,
> Wha' struts an' stares, an' a' that;
> Tho' hundreds worship at his word,
> He's but a coof‡ for a' that. . . .
>
> Then let us pray that come it may,
> As come it will for a' that,
> That Sense and Worth, o'er a' the earth,
> Shall bear the gree§ an' a' that.
> For a' that an' a' that,
> It's coming yet, for a' that,
> That man to man the world o'er
> Shall brithers be for a' that.

Complaints were made to the Excise Board that such a radical was no fit man to check chandlers and gauge casks, but the commissioners forgave him for his love and praise of Scotland. The ninety pounds a year his post brought him hardly sufficed to keep him in oats and ale. He continued to roam sexually, and in 1793 Mrs. Maria Ridell, who confessed his "irresistible power of attraction," bore him a child. His repeated intoxication at last weakened his mind and his pride. Like Mozart in this same decade, he sent begging letters to his friends.[86] Stories went around that he had syphilis, and had been found, one bitter morning in January, 1796, lying drunken in the snow.[87] These reports have been criticized as unconfirmed heresy, and Scottish doctors describe Burns's final illness as rheumatic fever impairing the heart.[88] Three days before his death he wrote to his father-in-law: "Do, for Heaven's sake, send Mrs. Armour here immediately. My wife is hourly expecting to be put to bed. Good God! What a situation for her to be in, poor girl, without a friend!"[89] Then he took to his bed, and on July 21, 1796, he died. While he was being buried his wife gave birth to a son. Friends raised a fund to care for her, and she, strong of frame and heart, lived till 1834.

VI. JAMES BOSWELL**

1. The Cub

He had royal blood in him. His father, Alexander Boswell, Laird of Auchinleck in Ayrshire and judge of the Scottish Court of Session, was de-

---

* Gold.   † Fellow.   ‡ Dolt.   § Prize.

** The discovery of Boswell's journals was among the most exciting events in the literary history of our time. He had bequeathed his papers to his heirs, who judged them too scandalous for publication. One bundle, containing the *London Journal*, was found at Fettercairn House, near Aberdeen, in 1930; a larger treasure was ferreted out from the chests and closets

scended from the Earl of Arran, a great-grandson of James II of Scotland. His mother was descended from the third Earl of Lennox, who was grandfather of Lord Darnley, who was father of James VI. James Boswell was born in Edinburgh October 29, 1740. As the eldest of three sons he was heir to the modest estate of Auchinleck (which he pronounced "Affleck"); but, since his father lived till 1782, James had to be discontent with such income as the Laird allowed him. Brother John suffered in 1762 the first of several attacks of insanity. Boswell himself was oppressed with spells of hypochondria, for which his cures were the amnesia of alcohol and the warmth of female forms. His mother taught him the Presbyterian Calvinist creed, which had a warmth of its own. "I shall never forget," he later wrote, "the dismal hours of apprehension that I have endured in my youth from narrow notions of religion, while my mind was lacerated with infernal horror."[90] Throughout his life he oscillated between faith and doubt, piety and venery, and never achieved more than momentary integration or content.

After some tutoring at home, he was sent to the University of Edinburgh, then to Glasgow, where he attended the lectures of Adam Smith and studied law. At Glasgow he met actors and actresses, some of them Catholic. It seemed to him that their religion was more compatible than Calvinism with a jolly life; he liked especially the doctrine of purgatory, which allowed a sinner to be saved after a few aeons of burning. Suddenly James rode off to London (March, 1760), and joined the Roman Church.

His alarmed father sent a plea to the Earl of Eglinton, an Ayrshire neighbor living in London, to take James in hand. The Earl pointed out to the youth that as a Catholic he could never practice law, or enter Parliament, or inherit Auchinleck. James returned to Scotland and the Kirk, and lived under the paternal roof and eye; but, as the judge was busy, his son managed to "catch a Tartar"[91]—the first of his many bouts with venereal disease. Fearing that this reckless youth, on inheriting Auchinleck, would squander the estate in revelry, the father persuaded him, in return for an annuity of £100, to sign a document giving the future management of the property to trustees named by Boswell Senior.

On October 29, 1761, James came of age, and his annuity was doubled. In the following March he impregnated Peggy Doig; in July he passed his bar examination. On November 1, 1762, leaving ten pounds to Peggy, he set out for London. (Her child was born a few days later; Boswell never saw it.) In London he took a comfortable room in Downing Street. By November 25 he "was really unhappy for want of women";[92] but he remembered his infection, and "the surgeons' fees in this city are very high."[93] So he steeled himself to continence "till I got some safe girl, or was liked by some woman of fashion."[94] His impression was that London provided every va-

of Malahide Castle, near Dublin, in 1925–40. Most of the papers were bought by Colonel Ralph Isham, and were acquired from him by Yale University. Professor Frederick A. Pottle edited them for the McGraw-Hill Book Company, which has sole publishing rights. We are grateful for permission received, from editor and publisher, to quote some passages from the journals. Professor Pottle's *James Boswell: The Earlier Years* appeared after this section was written.

riety of courtesan, "from the splendid Madam at fifty guineas a night down to the civil nymph . . . who . . . will resign her engaging person to your honor for a pint of wine and a shilling."[95] He developed a connection with "a handsome actress," Louisa, whose long resistance seemed to attest hygiene. Finally he persuaded her, and achieved quintuple ecstasy; "she declared I was a prodigy."[96] Eight days later he discovered that he had gonorrhea. By February 27 he felt cured; on March 25 he picked up a streetwalker, and "engaged her in armor" (with a prophylactic sheath). On March 27 "I heard service at St. Dunstan's Church." On March 31 "I strolled into the Park and took the first whore I met."[97] During the next four months Boswell's *London Journal* records similar bouts—on Westminster Bridge, in Shakespeare's Head Tavern, in the park, in a tavern on the Strand, in the Temple law courts, in the girl's home.

This, of course, is only one side of the picture of a man, and to group these scattered episodes in one paragraph gives a false impression of Boswell's life and character. The other side of him was his "enthusiastic love of great men."[98] His first catch in this pursuit was Garrick, who sipped Boswell's compliments and took to him readily. But James aimed at the top. In Edinburgh he had heard Thomas Sheridan describe the erudition and meaty conversation of Samuel Johnson. It would be a "kind of glory" to meet this pinnacle of London's literary life.

Chance helped him. On May 16, 1763, Boswell was drinking tea in Thomas Davies' bookshop in Russell Street when "a man of most dreadful appearance" entered. Boswell recognized him from a portrait of Johnson by Reynolds. He begged Davies not to reveal that he came from Scotland; Davies "roguishly" revealed it at once. Johnson did not lose the opportunity to remark that Scotland was a good country to *come from*; Boswell winced. Johnson complained that Garrick had refused him a free ticket for Miss Williams to a current play; Boswell ventured to say, "Sir, I cannot think that Mr. Garrick would grudge such a trifle to you." Johnson bore down on him: "Sir, I have known David Garrick longer than you have done, and I know no right you have to talk to me on the subject." This hardly promised a life-long friendship; Boswell was "stunned" and "mortified"; but after some more conversation "I was satisfied that though there was a roughness in his manner, there was no ill-nature in his disposition."[99]

Eight days later, encouraged by Davies, and fortified by his pachydermatous audacity, Boswell presented himself at Johnson's rooms in the Inner Temple, and was received with kindness if not with charm. On June 25 bear and cub supped together at the Mitre Tavern in Fleet Street. "I was quite proud to think on whom I was with." On July 22 "Mr. Johnson and I had a room at the Turk's Head Coffee-house." "After this," Boswell wrote in his journal, "I shall just mark Mr. Johnson's *memorabilia* as they rise up in my memory."[100] So the great biography began.

When, at his father's urging, Boswell left for the Netherlands (August 6, 1763) to study law, master and man jibed so well that Johnson, aged fifty-three, accompanied Boswell, aged twenty-two, to Harwich to see him off.

2. *Boswell Abroad*

He settled in Utrecht, studied law, learned Dutch and French, and (he tells us) read all of Voltaire's *Essai sur les moeurs*. He suffered at the outset a severe attack of melancholy, upbraided himself as a worthless philanderer, and thought of suicide. He blamed his recent dissipation on his loss of religious faith. "I was once an infidel; I acted accordingly; I am now a Christian gentleman."[101] He drew up an "Inviolable Plan" of self-reform: he would prepare himself for the duties of a Scottish laird; he would "be steady to the Church of England," and cleave to the Christian moral code. "Never talk of yourself," but "reverence thyself. . . . Upon the whole you will be an excellent character."[102]

He regained his interest in life when he was accepted in the homes of the well-to-do Dutch. Now he dressed "in scarlet and gold, . . . white silk stockings, handsome pumps, . . . Barcelona handkerchief, and elegant toothpick case."[103] He fell in love with Isabella van Tuyll, known to her admirers as "Belle de Zuylen," and also as "Zélide"; we have already paid our respects to her as one of many brilliant women in the Holland of those years. But she avoided marriage, and Boswell convinced himself that he had rejected her. He tried Mme. Geelvinck, a pretty widow, but found her "delicious and impregnable."[104] Finally "I determined to take a trip to Amsterdam and have a girl." Arrived there, he "went to a bawdy house. . . . I was hurt to find myself in the sinks of gross debauchery." The next day "I went to a chapel and heard a good sermon. . . . I then strolled through mean brothels in dirty lanes."[105] He regained "the dignity of human nature" on receiving from a friend a letter of introduction to Voltaire.

Having carried out his promise to his father that he would study faithfully at Utrecht, he received paternal permission and funds for the usual grand tour that crowned a young English gentleman's education. He bade farewell to Zélide, sure she had tears of love in her eyes, and on June 18, 1764, he crossed the border into Germany. For almost two years thereafter he and Belle corresponded, exchanging compliments and barbs. From Berlin, July 9, he wrote:

> As you and I, Zélide, are perfectly easy with each other, I must tell you that I am vain enough . . . as to imagine that you really was in love with me. . . . I am too generous not to undeceive you. . . . I would not be married to you to be a king. . . . My wife must be a character directly opposite to my dear Zélide, except in affection, in honesty, and in good humor.[106]

She did not answer. He wrote again on October 1, assuring her that she loved him; she did not answer. He wrote again on December 25:

> Mademoiselle, I am proud, and I shall be proud always. You ought to be flattered by my attachment. I know not if I ought to have been equally flattered by yours. A man who has a heart and mind like mine is rare. A woman with many talents is not so rare. . . . Perhaps you are able to give me an explanation of your conduct toward me.[107]

Her reply deserves a place in the history of woman:

> I received your letter with joy and read it with gratitude. . . . All those expressions of friendship and all those promises of eternal regard and of constantly tender recollection which you have collected [from her past words to him] are acknowledged and renewed by my heart at this moment. . . . You went on repeating . . . that I was in love with you. . . . You would have me admit this, you were determined to hear me say it and say it again. I find this a very strange whim in a man who does not love me and thinks it incumbent upon him (from motives of delicacy) to tell me so in the most express and vigorous terms. . . . I was shocked and saddened to find, in a friend whom I had conceived of as a young and sensible man, the puerile vanity of a fatuous fool.
>
> My dear Boswell, I will not answer for it that never at any moment may my talk, my tone, or my look have kindled with you. If it happened, forget it. . . . But never lose the memory of so many talks when the pair of us were equally lighthearted: I well content in the flattery of your attachment, and you as happy to count me your friend *as if there were something rare about a woman with many talents*. Keep the memory, I say, and be sure that my tenderness, my esteem, I would even say my respect, are yours always.[108]

This letter chastened Boswell transiently; he kept his peace for a year. Then (January 16, 1766) he wrote from Paris to Zélide's father, asking for her hand. "Would it not be a pity if so fortunate an alliance were unrealized?"[109] The father answered that Zélide was considering another offer. A year later Boswell sent her a direct proposal. She replied, "I read your belated endearments with pleasure, with a smile. Well, so you once loved me!"[110]—and she refused his offer.

While this epistolary game was going on, Boswell had sampled many countries and women. In Berlin he saw Frederick on the paradeground, but no nearer. He took to his bed a pregnant chocolate vendor; she seemed a safe port. In Leipzig he met Gellert and Gottsched; at Dresden he visited "the grand gallery of pictures, which I was told is the noblest in Europe."[111] He passed down through Frankfurt, Mainz, Karlsruhe, and Strasbourg into Switzerland. We have already accompanied him on his visits to Rousseau and Voltaire. In those exalted days the aura of genius and the fever of fame subdued the lust of youth.

On January 1, 1765, he left Geneva to cross the Alps. He spent nine exhilarating months in Italy, saw every major city, and sampled feminine wares at every stop. In Rome he sought out Winckelmann, kissed the Pope's slippered foot, prayed in St. Peter's, and caught his favorite disease again. He ascended Vesuvius with John Wilkes. In Venice he shared the same courtesan with Lord Mountstuart (son of the Earl of Bute), and renewed his infection. In a month at Siena he courted Porzia Sansedoni, the mistress of his friend Mountstuart; he urged her not to let any sentiment of fidelity interfere with generosity, for "my Lord is so formed that he is incapable of fidelity himself, and does not expect it of you."[112]

His better side showed in his next exploit. From Livorno he took ship to Corsica (October 11, 1765). Paoli had liberated the island from Genoa in 1757, and was now in the eighth year of his rule of the new state. Boswell reached him at Sollacarò, and presented a letter of introduction from Rousseau. He was at first suspected as a spy, but "I took the liberty to show him a memorial I had drawn up on the advantages to Great Britain from an alliance with Corsica"; thereafter he dined regularly with the General.[113] He took many notes that served him later in writing his *Account of Corsica* (1768). He left the island on November 20, and traveled along the Riviera to Marseilles. There "a tall and decent pimp" secured for him "an honest, safe, and disinterested girl."[114]

From Aix-en-Provence he began to send to *The London Chronicle* news paragraphs to be released in successive issues from January 7, 1766, informing the British public that James Boswell was approaching England with firsthand data on Corsica. Arriving in Paris (January 12), he received word from his father that his mother had died. He undertook to escort Rousseau's Thérèse Levasseur to London; if we may believe him she gave herself to him en route. He dallied in London for three weeks, saw Johnson on several occasions, and finally presented himself to his father in Edinburgh (March 7, 1766). His three years and four months of independence and travel had done something to mature him. It had not weakened his lust nor tempered his vanity, but it had broadened his knowledge and perspective, and had given him a new poise and self-confidence. He was now "Corsican Boswell," a man who had dined with Paoli, and who was writing a book that might stir England to go to the Liberator's aid and make the island a British stronghold in a strategic sea.

3. Boswell at Home

On July 29, 1766, he was admitted to the Scottish bar, and for the next twenty years his life was centered in Edinburgh, with many forays into London and one to Dublin. Helped perhaps by his father's position as a judge, but also by his readiness in debate, he "came into great employment," and "made sixty-five guineas" in his first winter before the courts.[115] An exuberant generosity mingled with his self-esteem; he defended the lowliest criminals, spent his florid eloquence on obviously guilty persons, lost most of his cases, and dissolved his fees in drink. After those sunny months in Italy he felt to his bones the cold of Scotland, for which there seemed no cure but alcohol.

He continued his sexual wandering. He took a Mrs. Dodds as his mistress, but to supplement her services he "lay all night with . . . a common girl," and presently "discovered that some infection had reached me."[116] Three months later, in a vertigo of intoxication, he tells us that he "went to a bawdy house, and passed a whole night in the arms of a whore. She was a fine, strong, spirited girl, a whore worthy of Boswell, if Boswell must have a whore."[117] Another infection. Obviously marriage was the only device that could save him from physical and moral degeneration. He courted Catherine Blair; she rejected him. He fell in love with Mary Ann Boyd, an Irish lass with a Grecian form and a rich father. He followed her to Dublin

(March, 1769), lost his passion on the way, got drunk, went to an Irish prostitute, contracted venereal disease again.[118]

In February, 1768, he sent to the press *An Account of Corsica, The Journal of a Tour to That Island, and Memoirs of Pascal Paoli.* Its plea for British aid to Paoli caught the imagination of England, and prepared public opinion to approve the action of the British government in sending secret arms and supplies to the Corsicans. The book sold ten thousand copies in England; it was translated into four languages, and gave Boswell more fame on the Continent than Johnson enjoyed. On September 7, 1769, the author appeared at the Shakespeare festival in Stratford in the garb of a Corsican chief, with "Corsican Boswell" inscribed on his hat; but, as this was for a masquerade ball, it did not quite deserve the ridicule it received.

His cousin Margaret Montgomerie had accompanied him to Ireland, and had borne humbly with his Irish courtship and revelry. She was two years older than he, and her £1,000 made her no equal match (as Boswell Senior urged) for the heir of Auchinleck, but when he contemplated her patient devotion to him it dawned upon him that she was a good woman and would make a good wife; moreover, his reputation for lechery and drinking had narrowed his choice. The judge himself was contemplating marriage, which would put a stepmother between father and son, and might eat into the estate. Boswell begged his father not to marry; the father persisted; they quarreled; Boswell thought of going to America. On July 20, 1769, he wrote to "Peggy" Montgomerie asking would she marry him and consent to go with him to America and live on his £100 a year and the interest on her £1,000. He warned her that he was subject to periods of melancholy. Her reply (July 22) deserves remembrance:

> I have thought fully, as you desired, and . . . I accept your terms. . . . J. B. with £100 a year is every bit as valuable to me as if possessed of the estate of Auchinleck. . . . Free of ambition, I prefer real happiness to the splendid appearance of it. . . . Be assured, my dear Jamie, you have a friend that would sacrifice everything for you, who never had a wish for wealth till now, to bestow it on the man of her heart.[119]

On November 19 the father married; on November 25 the son. The younger couple set up a separate household, and in 1771 they rented a flat from David Hume. James strove for sobriety, worked hard as an advocate, and rejoiced in the children his wife bore him. Apparently she discouraged his marital approaches during the later months of her repeated pregnancies. On October 27, 1772, he went to a prostitute after having "too much wine."[120] He excused himself by arguing that concubinage was permitted by Scripture. He resumed his drinking, and added gambling. His journal noted, October 5, 1774: "Drank to intoxication." November 3: "Many of us drank from dinner till ten at night." November 4: "Much intoxicated; . . . fell with a good deal of violence." November 8: "Drunk again." November 9: "I was very ill, and could not get up till about two." December 24: "I was very drunk, . . . stayed above an hour with two whores at their lodging in a narrow dirty stair in the Bow. I found my way home about twelve. I had fallen."[121] His wife forgave him, and cared for him in his ill-nesses.

His drinking had many causes: his many failures at the bar, his difficulties with his father, his shame of his infidelities, his awareness that he had not realized the dreams of his vanity, and his distaste for life in Scotland. Almost yearly he ran off to London, partly to plead cases there, partly to savor the conversation of Johnson, Reynolds, Garrick, and Burke. In 1773 he was admitted to "the Club." In the fall of that year he proudly walked the streets of Edinburgh with Dr. Johnson at his side, as a prelude to their tour of the Hebrides.

At first, on these London trips, he remained faithful to his wife, and wrote to her fondly; but by 1775 he had resumed his patronage of promiscuity. He was especially busy toward the end of March, 1776. "When I got into the street the whoring rage came upon me. I thought I would devote a night to it." His devotion continued for several nights. "I thought of my valuable spouse with the highest regard and warmest affection, but had a confused notion that my corporeal connection with whores did not interfere with my love for her."[122] Another venereal infection sobered him transiently.

These exploits, and his subservience to Johnson, earned him scornful comments from men like Horace Walpole, and (posthumously) a lethal lashing by Macaulay,[123] but they did not leave him friendless. "My character as a man of parts and extensive acquaintance makes people fond of my attention."[124] Most Londoners agreed with Boswell that no woman had a right to a whole man. If men like Johnson and Reynolds liked him, and many London homes were open to him, he must have had many amiable traits. These men of discernment knew that he passed from woman to woman, and from idea to idea, like a hasty traveler, scratching many surfaces but never reaching to the heart of the matter, never feeling the bruised soul behind the sacrificial flesh. And he knew it, too. "I have really a little mind with all my pride," he said; "my brilliant qualities are like embroidery upon gauze."[125] "There is an imperfection, a superficialness, in all my notions. I understand nothing clearly, nothing to the bottom. I pick up fragments, but never have in my memory a mass of any size."[126]

It was those fragments, and that memory, that redeemed him. He made amends for his defects by worshiping in others the excellence that he could not achieve for himself; by attending upon them humbly, by remembering their words and deeds, and, at last, with no minor artistry, placing them in an order and a light that made an unrivaled picture of a man and an age. And may we never be disrobed, in body and mind, in secret lust and inde-fatigable vanity, as thoroughly as this man, half lackey and half genius, re-vealed himself for posterity.

CHAPTER XXXII

The Literary Scene

1756–89

I. THE PRESS

IN the background were newspapers, magazines, publishers, circulating libraries, theaters, all multiplying recklessly, bringing to an ever wider public the conflicts of parties and talents. Several journals were now born: *The Literary Magazine* and *The Critical Review* in 1756, *The Public Ledger* in 1760. Johnson's *Rambler* began in 1750; *The Gentleman's Magazine*, which fed Johnson in his struggling years, had begun in 1731, and was to survive till 1922. The London newspapers doubled their number and total circulation in this period. *The Monitor* began in 1755, *The North Briton* in 1761, *The Morning Chronicle* in 1769, *The Morning Herald* in 1780, *The Daily Universal Register* in 1785, becoming *The Times* in 1788. *The Public Advertiser* struck gold in the letters of Junius; its circulation rose from 47,500 to 84,000. Most of the other dailies subsisted on narrow clienteles; so the circulation of *The Times* in 1795 was only 4,800. They were more modest in size than in speech—usually four pages, one of which was given to advertisements. Johnson in 1759 thought that newspaper advertising had reached its limit.

> Advertisements are now so numerous that they are very negligently perused, and it is therefore necessary to gain attention by magnificence of promise, and by eloquence sometimes sublime and sometimes pathetic. . . . The vendor of the beautifying fluid sells a lotion that repels pimples, washes away freckles, smooths the skin, and plumps the flesh. . . . The trade of advertising is now so near perfection that it is not easy to propose any improvement. But as every art ought to be exercised in due subordination to the public good, I cannot but propose it as a moral question to these masters of the public ear, whether they do not sometimes play too wantonly with our passions?[1]

Printers, booksellers, and publishers were still largely confused in one profession. Robert Dodsley had published Pope and Chesterfield, and now printed Walpole and Goldsmith. Thomas Davies had a popular bookshop, where he allowed leisurely browsing, and Johnson and others came there to sample the books and ogle the pretty wife. William Strahan won fame by publishing Johnson's *Dictionary*, Smith's *Wealth of Nations*, and Gibbon's *Decline and Fall of the Roman Empire*—the latter two in the *annus mirabilis* 1776. Oxford established the Clarendon Press in 1781. Booksellers paid well for good books, but could get hacks to prepare articles and compilations for a pittance. Says a bookseller in Henry Brooke's *The Fool of Quality*

(1766): "I can get one of these gentlemen, . . . on whose education more money has been spent than . . . would maintain a decent family to the end of the world—I can get one of them to labor like a hackney horse from morning to night at less wage than I could hire . . . a porter or shoe-boy for three hours."[2] Authors multiplied to saturation of the market, fought desperately for their starveling share, and satirized one another with poisoned ink. Women added to the competition: Mrs. Anna Barbauld, Sarah Fielding, Mrs. Amelia Opie, Mrs. Elizabeth Inchbald, Mrs. Elizabeth Montagu, Fanny Burney, Hannah More. A country parson entered the game and walked away with the prize.

II. LAURENCE STERNE

He was not made for a parson; he was the son of a soldier, and was dragged from post to post for ten years; then and afterward he picked up enough military lore to make Uncle Toby talk like an old general about sieges and forts. His mother he later described as "the daughter of . . . a poor sutler [peddler] who followed the camp in Flanders."[3] However, his great-grandfather had been archbishop of York, and the Sterne family managed to get Laurence to Cambridge on a scholarship. He took his degree there in 1737, but a lung hemorrhage in 1736 foretold a lifelong struggle with tuberculosis. Ordained an Anglican priest (1738), he was given a modest vicarage at Sutton-in-the-Forest, near York. In 1741 he married Elizabeth Lumley, and took her to live with him in his tattered rectory. She entrusted to him her forty pounds a year; he invested some of it in land, and it grew.

Otherwise they were miserable. Both were consumptives, and both were made of nerves. Mrs. Sterne soon concluded that "the largest house in England could not contain them both, on account of their turmoils and disputes."[4] Her cousin, "bluestocking" Elizabeth Montagu, described her as a fretful porcupine, "with whom one could avoid a quarrel only by keeping at a distance."[5] Two children came; one died, the other, Lydia, became conspicuously attached to her mother. Unhappiness increased when Sterne's mother and sister, who had been living in poverty in Ireland, came to York and appealed to him to settle eight pounds a year upon them out of his wife's income. The idea aroused no enthusiasm. Sterne gave his mother some money and begged her to go back to Ireland. She remained in York. When she was arrested for vagrancy Sterne refused to bail her out.

After eighteen years of arduous marriage the vicar felt that any really Christian soul would allow him a little adultery. He fell in love with Catherine Fourmantelle, and swore, "I love you to distraction, and will love you to eternity."[6] His wife accused him of infidelity; he denied it; she came so close to insanity that he put her and Lydia in care of "a lunatic doctor," and continued the liaison.

Amid the tumult he wrote one of the most famous books in English literature. His friends, having read some of the manuscript, begged him to eliminate "gross allusions which could be matter of just offense, especially when coming from a clergyman." Sorrowfully he deleted some 150 pages. The remainder he sent to the press anonymously; it was published in January, 1760, as *The Life and Opinions of Tristram Shandy, Gent.* Enough scandal and whimsical humor remained in the two volumes to make them the literary event of the London year. Far off in Ferney the furor echoed: "A very unaccountable book," Voltaire reported, "and an original one; they run mad about it in England."[7] Hume called it "the best book that has been writ by any Englishman these thirty years, bad as it is."[8] At York, where Sterne's authorship was an open secret and many local figures were recognized in the leading characters, two hundred copies were sold in two days.

It is hard to describe the book, for it has no form or subject, no head or tail. The title is a trick, for the "Gent." who tells the story, and whose "life and opinions" were to be presented, does not get born until page 209 of Volume IV (of the original nine-volume edition). The substance of the tale is what happened, or was said, while he was being conceived, and while he was growing leisurely in the womb. The first page is the best:

> I wish either my father or my mother, or indeed both of them, as they were in duty both equally bound to it, had minded what they were about when they begot me; had they duly considered how much depended upon what they were doing;—that not only the production of a rational Being was concerned in it, but that possibly the happy formation and temperature of his body, perhaps his genius and the very cast of his mind, . . . might take their turn from the humors and dispositions which were then uppermost;—Had they duly weighed and considered all this, and proceeded accordingly, I am verily persuaded I should have made a quite different figure in the world.
>
> "Pray, my Dear," quoth my mother, "have you not forgot to wind up the clock?"—"Good G—!" cried my father, . . . "Did ever woman, since the creation of the world, interrupt a man with such a silly question?"

From that contretemps onward the book consists of digressions. Sterne had no tale to tell, much less that tale of love which is the burden of most fiction; he wished to amuse himself and the reader with whimsical discourse on everything, but in no order; he galloped around the big and little problems of life like a frisky horse in a field. After writing sixty-four chapters he bethought himself that he had given his book no preface; he inserted one at that point; this allowed him to make fun of his critics. He called his method "the most religious, for I begin with writing the first sentence, and trusting to Almighty God for the second,"[9] and to free association for the rest. Rabelais had done something of the sort; Cervantes had allowed Rosinante to lead him from episode to episode; Robert Burton had roamed the world before anatomizing melancholy. But Sterne raised inconsequence to a method, and freed all novelists from the need to have a subject or a plot.

The leisure classes of Britain were delighted to see how much ado could be made about nothing, and how a book could be written in Anglo-Saxon English in the age of Johnson. Lusty Britons welcomed the jolly novelty of a clergyman talking about sex and flatulence, and the slit in Uncle Toby's pants. In March, 1760, Sterne went down to London to sip his success; he was happy to find the two volumes sold out; he took £630 for them and two to come. Even the *Sermons of Mr. Yorick*, published four months after *Tristram*, found ready sale when it was known that Yorick was Sterne. Invitations came to the author from Chesterfield, Reynolds, Rockingham, even Bishop Warburton, who surprised him with fifty guineas, perhaps to escape adorning some satiric page in future volumes. Sterne bought a carriage and team, and drove in merry triumph back to York, where he preached in the great minster. He was presented to a richer parsonage at Coxwold, fifteen miles from York; he took his wife and daughter to live with him there; and there, with inconsequential facility, he wrote Volumes III–IV of *Tristram*.

In December of that year 1760 he went to London to see these volumes through the press. They were adversely reviewed, but the edition was sold out in four months. Now Tristram reached birth by forceps, which deformed his nose; whereupon the author sailed forth on a long discourse on the philosophy of noses, in the style of the most learned pundits. The shape of a child's nose, said one authority, was determined by the softness or hardness of the nursing breast: "by sinking into it, . . . as into so much butter, the nose was comforted, nourished, plumped up, refreshed, refocillated."[10]

After half a year in London Sterne returned to his wife, who told him she had been happier without him. He withdrew into his manuscript, and wrote Volumes V–VI; in these Tristram was almost forgotten, and Uncle Toby and Corporal Trim, with their war memories and toy forts, occupied the stage. In November, 1761, the parson went off again to London, and on the last day of the year he saw V–VI published. They were well received. He flirted with Mrs. Elizabeth Vesey, one of the "bluestockings"; vowed he would give the last rag of his priesthood for a touch of her divine hand;[11] had a lung hemorrhage, and fled to the south of France. He stopped long enough in Paris to attend some dinners at d'Holbach's "synagogue of atheists," where Diderot took a lasting fancy to him. Hearing that his wife was ill, and that Lydia was developing asthma, Sterne invited them to join him in France. All three settled down near Toulouse (July, 1762).

In March, 1764, he left his wife and daughter, with their consent, and returned to Paris, London, and Coxwold. He wrote Volumes VII–VIII of *Tristram*, received advance payment for them, and sent part of the proceeds to Mrs. Sterne. The new volumes appeared in January, 1765, to waning acclaim; the Shandy-Toby vein was running thin. In October Sterne began a tour of eight months in France and Italy. On his way north he joined his family in Burgundy; they asked to remain in France; he paid their expenses and returned to Coxwold (July, 1766). Between hemorrhages he wrote Volume IX. He went to London to see it born (January, 1767), and enjoyed the furor caused by his skirting the brink of sex in describing Uncle Toby's wooing of Mrs. Wadman. Scandalized readers wrote to newspapers and the Archbishop of York, demanding that this shameless parson be unfrocked and evicted; the prelate refused. Sterne meanwhile collected subscriptions, totaling £1,050, for a promised *Sentimental Journey*. He sent more money to his wife, and made love to Elizabeth Draper.

She was the wife of an East India Company official then (March, 1767) stationed in India. She had married him at fourteen, when he was thirty-four. Sterne sent her his books, and proposed to follow them with his hand and his heart. For a while they saw each other daily, and exchanged tender missives. The ten "Letters to Eliza" voice the last sad passion of a man dying of tuberculosis. " 'Tis true, I am ninety-five in constitution, and you but twenty-five; . . . but what I want in youth I will make up in wit and good humor. Not Swift so loved his Stella, Scarron his Maintenon, or Waller his Sacharissa, as I will love and sing thee, my wife elect!"—for "my wife cannot live long."[12] Ten minutes after dispatching this letter he had a severe hemorrhage, and he bled till four in the morning. In April, 1767, Mrs. Draper, summoned by her husband, sailed for India. From April 13 to August 4 Sterne kept a "Journal to Eliza," a "diary of the miserable feelings of a person separated from a Lady for whose society he languished." "I will take thee on any terms, Eliza! I shall be . . . so just, so kind to thee, I will deserve not to be miserable hereafter."[13] In the journal under April 21: "Parted with twelve ounces of blood." A doctor told him he had syphilis; he protested it was "impossible, . . . for I have had no commerce whatever with the sex—not even with my wife, . . . these fifteen years." "We will not reason about it," said the physician, "but you must undergo a course of mercury."[14] Other doctors confirmed the diagnosis; one assured him that "taints of the blood laid dormant twenty years." He yielded, protesting his virtue.

By June he had recovered, and returned to Coxwold. While writing *A Sentimental Journey* he suffered more hemorrhages, and realized that he had not long to live. He went to London, saw the little book published (February, 1768), and for the last time enjoyed the undiminished affection of his friends. As *Tristram* had recalled Rabelais, so the new volume reflected the rising influence of Richardson and Rousseau. But Sterne's virtue was less irrefragable than Richardson's, and his tears less hot and sincere than Rousseau's. Perhaps it was this book, and Henry Mackenzie's *The Man of Feeling* (1771), that made *sentiment* and *sentimental* fashionable words in England. Byron thought that Sterne "preferred whining over a dead ass to relieving a living mother."[15]

While Sterne was enjoying his final triumph in London he caught a cold, which grew into pleurisy. He wrote to a Mrs. James a pitiful letter asking her to care for Lydia if Mrs. Sterne should die. Death came to him on March 18, 1768, in an inn on Old Bond Street, with no friends near. He was fifty-two years old. He had a bit of the mountebank in him, and made himself "a motley to the view"; but we can understand his sensitivity to women, and the strain that an unhappy marriage placed upon a man capable of such subtle perceptions and delicate artistry. He suffered much, gave much, and wrote one of the most peculiar books in all the history of literature.

III. FANNY BURNEY

A woman briefly rivaled his success in fiction. She was born in 1752 to Charles Burney, the future historian of music. She was brought up on notes rather than on letters; till she was eight she could not read;[16] no one dreamed that she would be a writer. Her mother died when Frances was nine. As almost all the musicians who performed in London came to her father's home, and attracted to it a good portion of the elite, Fanny acquired education by listening to words and music. She matured slowly, was shy and plain, and took forty years to find a husband. When her famous novel was published (January, 1778) she was twenty-five, and was so fearful lest it displease her father that she concealed her authorship. *Evelina, or A Young Lady's Entrance into the World*, made a stir. Anonymity aroused curiosity; rumor said a girl of seventeen had written it. Johnson, who had been praised in its preface, praised it, and recommended it to Dr. Burney. Mrs. Thrale complained that it was too short. When Mrs. Thrale learned the secret it spread over London; Fanny became a lioness of society; everybody read her book, and "my kind and most devoted father was so happy in my happiness."[17]

Her art lay in describing, with lingering memory and lively imagination, how the world of London society appeared to an orphaned girl of seventeen who had been brought up by a rural parson not at all like Laurence Sterne. Doubtless Fanny too had thrilled to Garrick's acting, and had felt as Evelina wrote to her guardian: "Such ease! such vivacity in his manner! such grace in his motions! such fire and meaning in his eyes! . . . And when he danced, O, how I envied Clarinda! I almost wished to have jumped on the stage and joined them."[18] London, wearying of its vice, felt cleansed by the fresh wind blowing from these youthful pages.

That once famous novel is dead, but the diary that Fanny kept is still a living part of English literature and history, for it offers a near view of celebrities from Johnson and George III to Herschel and Napoleon. Queen Charlotte made Miss Burney her keeper of the robes (1786), and for the next five years Fanny dressed and undressed her Majesty. The constrained and narrow life nearly stifled the authoress; at last her friends rescued her, and in 1793, youth quite gone, she married a ruined émigré, General d'Arblay. She supported him by her writings and her income; for ten years she lived with him in France and obscurity, isolated by the intensity of the Revolutionary and Napoleonic wars. In 1814 she was allowed to return to England and receive the last blessing of her father, who died at the age of eighty-eight. She herself lived to that age, into quite a different world, which did not realize that the famous Jane Austen (died 1817) had taken her inspiration from the forgotten novels of a forgotten lady who was still alive in 1840.

IV. HORACE WALPOLE

"This world," he said, "is a comedy to those who think, a tragedy to those who feel."[19] So he learned to smile at the world, even to humor his gout. He chronicled his time, but washed his hands of it. He was son of a prime minister, but had no pleasure in politics. He loved women, from Fanny Burney to the grandest duchesses, but he would have none of them for a wife, nor (so far as we know) for a mistress. He studied philosophy, but thought the philosophers the bane and bore of the century. One author he admired without reserve for her fine manners and unaffected art—Mme. de Sévigné; her alone he sought to emulate; and if his letters did not catch her gay charm and grace, they became, far more than hers, a living daily history of an age. Though he called them annals of Bedlam,[20] he wrote them with care, hoping that some of them would give him a nook in man's remembrance; for even a philosopher who is reconciled to decay finds it hard to accept oblivion.

Horatio (so he was baptized in 1717) was the youngest of five children presented to Sir Robert Walpole, the doughty Premier who sacrificed his reputation by preferring peace to war, but hardly hurt it by preferring adultery to monogamy.[21] Perhaps to avenge his first wife, gossipers for a time ascribed Horace's paternity to Carr, Lord Hervey, brother to the effeminate John, Lord Hervey of Ickworth—who accused Sir Robert of attempting to seduce Lady Hervey.[22] These matters are too intricate for present adjudication; we can only say that Horace was brought up with no imputation, by his relatives, of any undue origin. He was treated with busy indifference by the Prime Minister, and (he tells us) was "indulged" with "extreme fondness" by his mother.[23] He was a very handsome boy, and was dressed like a prince, but he was frail and diffident, and as sensitive as a girl. When his mother died (1737) many feared that the twenty-year-old youth would die of grief. Sir Robert comforted him with governmental sinecures that paid for his son's fine clothing, elegant living, and costly collection of art. Horace kept to the end of his life a latent hostility to his father, but always defended his politics.

At ten he was sent to Eton, where he learned Latin and French and formed a friendship with the poet Gray. At seventeen he entered King's College, Cambridge; there he learned Italian, and imbibed deism from Conyers Middleton. At twenty-two, without taking a degree, he set out with Gray on a tour of Italy and France. After some wandering they settled for fifteen months in a Florentine villa as guests of the British chargé d'affaires, Sir Horace Mann. Walpole and Mann never met again, but they corresponded during the next forty-five years (1741–85). At Reggio Emilia Gray and Walpole quarreled, for Horace had paid all the bills, and the poet could not forgive the superior attentions received by the son of the man who was ruling England. In retrospect Horace took the blame: "I was too young, too fond of my own diversions, . . . too much intoxicated by indulgence, vanity, and the insolence of my situation, . . . not to have been inattentive and insensible to the feelings of one I thought below me; of one, I blush to say it, that I knew was obliged to me."[24] They parted; Walpole nearly died of remorse, or quinsy; he arranged for Gray's passage home. They were reconciled in 1745, and most of Gray's poems were printed by Walpole's press at Strawberry Hill. Meanwhile, at Venice, Walpole posed for a lovely pastel portrait by Rosalba Carriera.

Before reaching England (September 12, 1741), Walpole had been elected to Parliament. There he made a modest and futile speech against the opposition that was bringing to an end his father's long and prosperous ministry. He was regularly re-elected till 1767, when he voluntarily withdrew from active politics. Generally he supported the liberal Whig program: he resisted extension of the royal power, recommended a compromise with Wilkes, and denounced slavery (1750) nine years before Wilberforce was born. He opposed the political emancipation of English Catholics on the ground that "papists and liberty are contradictions."[25] He rejected the American case against the Stamp Act,[26] but he defended the claim of the American colonies to freedom, and prophesied that the next zenith of civilization would be in America.[27] "Who but Machiavel," he wrote (1786), "can pretend that we have a shadow of title to a foot of land in India?"[28] He hated war, and when the Montgolfier brothers made their first balloon ascension (1783) he predicted with horror the extension of war to the skies. "I hope," he wrote, "these new mechanic meteors will prove only playthings for the learned or the idle, and not be converted into engines of destruction to the human race, as is so often the case of refinements or discoveries in science."[29]

Finding himself too often on the losing side, he decided to spend most of his time in the country. In 1747 he rented five acres and a small house near Twickenham. Two years later he bought the property, and transformed the building in neo-Gothic style—as we have seen. Into this medievalized castle he gathered a variety of objects distinguished by art or history; soon his home was a museum that required a catalogue. In one room he installed a printing press, where he published in elegant formats thirty-four books, including his own. Chiefly from Strawberry Hill he sent out the 3,601 letters that survive. He had a hundred friends, quarreled with nearly all of them, made up, and was as kind as his delicate irritability would allow. Every day he set out bread and milk for the squirrels who courted him. He guarded his sinecures and angled for more, but when his cousin Henry Conway was dismissed from office Walpole proposed to share his income with him.

He had a thousand faults, which Macaulay meticulously accumulated in a brilliant and ungenerous essay. Walpole was vain, fussy, secretive, capricious, proud of his ancestry, and disgusted with his relatives. His humor tended to satire with sharp teeth. He carried to his grave, and into his histories, his scorn of all who had shared in deposing his father. He was often wildly biased, as in his descriptions of Lady Pomfret[30] or Lady Mary Wortley Montagu.[31] His fragile frame inclined him to be something of a dilettante. If Diderot, in Sainte-Beuve's illuminating phrase, was the most German of all Frenchmen, Walpole was the most French of all Englishmen.

He was fearlessly candid about his uncommon tastes and views; he thought Virgil a bore, and *a fortiori*, Richardson and Sterne; he called Dante "a Methodist in Bedlam."[32] He affected to disdain all authors, and insisted, like Congreve, that he wrote as a gentleman for his own amusement, not as a literary laborer dependent upon the merchandizing of his words. So he wrote to Hume: "You know in England we read their works, but seldom or never take any notice of authors. We think them sufficiently paid if their books sell, and of course leave them to their colleges and obscurity, by which means we are not troubled by their vanity and impertinence. . . . I, who am an author, must own this conduct very sensible; for in truth we are a most useless tribe."[33]

But, as he admitted, he too was an author, vain and voluminous. Bored in his castle, he explored the past as if wishing to sink the roots of his mind into the richest seams. He drew up a *Catalogue of the Royal and Noble Authors of England* (1758) their nobility would excuse their authorship, and first-rate men like Bacon and Clarendon could qualify. He had three hundred copies printed, and gave most of them away; Dodsley risked an edition of two thousand copies; they sold readily, and brought Walpole such fame as must have made him hang his head in shame. He compounded his indignity with five volumes of *Anecdotes of Painting in England* (1762–71), an engaging compilation which won Gibbon's praise.

As if in recreation from such laborious scholarship, Walpole composed a medieval romance, *The Castle of Otranto* (1764), which became the mother of a thousand stories of supernatural wonders and terrors. He combined mystery with history in *Historic Doubts on the Life and Reign of King Richard III*. He contended, like others after him, that Richard had been maligned by tradition and Shakespeare; Hume and Gibbon called his arguments unconvincing; Walpole repeated them till his death. Turning to events of which he had firsthand knowledge, he composed memoirs of the reigns of George II and George III; they are illuminating but partisan. Imprisoned in his prejudices, he took a dark view of his time: "treacherous ministers, mock patriots, complacent parliaments, fallible princes."[34] "I see my country going to ruin, and no man with brains enough to save it";[35] this was written in 1768, when Chatham had just created the British Empire. Fourteen years later, when the King and Lord North seemed to have ruined it, Walpole concluded: "We are totally degenerated in every respect, which I suppose is the case of all falling states";[36] a generation later the little island defeated Napoleon. All mankind seemed to Walpole a menagerie of "pigmy, short-lived, . . . comical animals."[37] He found no comfort in religion. He supported the Established Church, for it upheld the government that paid his sinecures, but he frankly termed himself an infidel.[38] "I begin to think that folly is matter, and cannot be destroyed. Destroy its form, it takes another."[39]

For a while he thought he could find stimulation in France (September, 1765). All doors were opened to him; Mme. du Deffand welcomed him as a replacement for d'Alembert. She was sixty-eight, Walpole was forty-eight, but the interval disappeared as their kindred souls met in an affectionate exchange of despair. She was pleased to find that Walpole agreed with most of what Voltaire said, but would have gone to the stake to prevent him from saying it; for he trembled to think what would happen to Europe's governments if Christianity collapsed. He deprecated Voltaire, but he ridiculed Rousseau. It was on this trip to Paris that he wrote the letter, supposedly from Frederick the Great, inviting Rousseau to come to Berlin and enjoy more persecutions. "The copies have spread like wildfire," and "behold me à la mode!"[40]—he succeeded Hume as the lion of the salons. He learned to love the gay and merciless excitement of Paris, but he was consoled to find "the French ten times more contemptible than we [English] are."[41]

After reaching home (April 22, 1766) he began his long correspondence with Mme. du Deffand. We shall see later how he fretted lest her affection make him ridiculous; yet it was probably to see her again that he revisited Paris in 1767, 1769, 1771, 1775. Her love made him forget his age, but the death of Gray (July 30, 1771) reminded him of his own mortality. He surprised himself by surviving till 1797. He had no financial worries; he had in 1784 an income of £8,000 ($200,000?) a year;[42] and in 1791 he succeeded to the title of Lord Orford. But his gout, which had begun when he was twenty-five, continued to be his tribulation till the end. Sometimes, we are told, accumulations of "chalk" broke out from his fingers.[43] He grew parched and stiff in his final years, and occasionally he had to be carried by his servants from room to room; but he kept on working and writing, and when visitors came they marveled at the bright interest in his eyes, the alertness of his courtesy, the gaiety of his speech, the alacrity and clarity of his mind. Almost every day distinguished people came to see his famous home and varied collection; Hannah More in 1786, Queen Charlotte in 1795.

Yet it was not at Strawberry Hill, but at his town house in Berkeley Square that he passed away, March 2, 1797, in his eightieth year. As if regretting that his memoirs and letters contained so many lines with a sting, he ordered his manuscripts to be locked in a chest not to be opened "till the first Earl of Waldegrave that shall attain the age of thirty-five years shall demand it."[44] So the memoirs came to be published only in or after 1822, when all who might have taken offense would be dead. Some of the letters were published in 1778, more in 1818, 1820, 1840, 1857. . . . All over the English-reading world there are men and women who have read every word of those letters, and who treasure them as among the most delightful legacies of the illuminating century.

V. EDWARD GIBBON

"Good historians," Walpole wrote to one of them, Robertson, "are the most scarce of all writers, and no wonder! A good style is not very common; thorough information is still more rare; and if these meet, what a chance that impartiality should be added to them!"[45] Gibbon did not quite meet the last test, but neither did Tacitus, who alone can stand with him among the supreme historians.

1. Preparation

Gibbon wrote or began six autobiographies, which his literary executor, the first Earl of Sheffield, sewed into remarkably well-knit, but unduly purified, *Memoirs* (1796), sometimes known as his *Autobiography*. Also Gibbon kept a journal, begun in 1761 and continued under diverse titles till January 28, 1763. These prime sources for his development have been judged reasonably accurate, except for his pedigree.

He spent eight pages detailing a distinguished ancestry; cruel genealogists have taken it from him.[46] His grandfather, Edward Gibbon I, was among those directors of the South Sea Company who were arrested for malfeasance after that "Bubble" exploded (1721). Of his estate, which he reckoned at £106,543, all was confiscated except £10,000; on this, the historian tells us, he "erected the edifice of a new fortune . . . not much inferior to the first."[47] He did not approve the marriage of his son, Edward II; hence his will left the major part of his wealth to his daughters, Catherine and Hester. Catherine's daughter married Edward Eliot, who later bought a seat in Parliament for Edward Gibbon III; Hester became a rich devotee of William Law,[48] and long vexed her nephew by her dilatory dying. Edward II was tutored by Law, passed through Winchester School and Cambridge, married Judith Porten, and had seven children, of whom only Edward III survived childhood.

He was born at Putney in Surrey, May 8, 1737. His mother died in 1747 of her seventh pregnancy. The father moved to a rural estate at Buriton, in Hampshire, fifty-eight miles from London, leaving the boy to be cared for by an aunt in the grandfather's house in Putney. There the future scholar made much use of the well-stored library. His frequent illnesses interrupted his progress at Winchester School, but he occupied his convalescent days with eager reading, mostly of history, especially of the Near East. "Mahomet and his Saracens soon fixed my attention; . . . I was led from one book to another, till I had ranged round the circle of Oriental history. Before I was sixteen I had exhausted all that could be learned in English of the Arabs and Persians, the Tartars and Turks."[49] Hence those fascinating chapters on Mohammed and the early caliphs, and the capture of Constantinople.

When, aged fifteen, he was sent to Magdalen College, Oxford, "I arrived with a stock of erudition that might have puzzled a doctor, and a degree of ignorance of which a schoolboy would have been ashamed." He was too sickly to engage in sports, too shy to mingle at ease with other students. He would have been an apt pupil to a competent teacher. But, eager to learn, he found no professor eager to teach. Most of the faculty allowed their scholars to attend the lectures or not, and to spend half their time in "the temptations of idleness."[50] They indulged his "improprieties of conduct, ill-chosen company, late hours, and inconsiderate expense"—even excursions to Bath or London. However, he "was too young and bashful to enjoy, like a manly Oxonian in town, the taverns and bagnios of Covent Garden."[51]

The faculty members were all clergymen, who taught and took for granted the Thirty-nine Articles of the Anglican Church. Gibbon was combative and questioned his teachers. It seemed to him that the Bible and history justified the Catholic Church in its claim to a divine origin. A Catholic acquaintance procured him some unsettling books, chiefly Bossuet's *Exposi-*

tion of the Catholic Doctrine and the *History of the Protestant Variations;* these "achieved my conversion, and I surely fell by a noble hand."[52] With youthful precipitation he confessed to a Catholic priest, and was received into the Church of Rome (June 8, 1753).

He notified his father, and was not surprised to be summoned home, for Oxford accepted no Catholic students, and, according to Blackstone, for a Protestant to be converted to Roman Catholicism was "high treason." The scandalized parent hastily banished the youth to Lausanne, and arranged to have him stay with a Calvinist pastor. There Edward lived at first in a mood of sullen obstinacy. But M. Pavilliard, though not indulgent, was kind, and the boy slowly warmed to him. Moreover, the pastor was a good classical scholar. Gibbon learned to read and write French as readily as English, and acquired an easy familiarity with Latin. Soon he was received into cultured families, whose manners and conversation were a better education than Oxford had given him.

As his French improved he felt the breezes of French rationalism blowing into Lausanne. When only twenty (1757) he attended with delight the plays presented by Voltaire in nearby Monrion. "I sometimes supped with the actors."[53] He met Voltaire, he began to read Voltaire, he read Voltaire's recently published *Essai sur l'histoire générale* (*Essai sur les moeurs*). He pored over Montesquieu's *Esprit des lois* (1748), and the *Considérations sur les causes de la grandeur des Romains et de leur décadence* (1734) became the starting point of the *Decline and Fall.* In any case the influence of the French philosophers, added to his reading of Hume and the English deists, undermined Gibbon's Christianity as well as his Catholicism, and M. Pavilliard's victory for the Reformation was canceled by Gibbon's secret acceptance of the Enlightenment.

It must have been exhilarating to meet, in the same year (1757), both Voltaire and Suzanne Curchod. She was twenty, blond, beautiful, gay, and lived with her Protestant parents at Crassy, four miles from Lausanne. She was the leading spirit in the Société du Printemps—a group of fifteen or twenty young women who met at one another's homes, sang, danced, acted comedies, and flirted judiciously with young men; Gibbon assures us that "their virgin chastity was never sullied by the breath of scandal or suspicion." Let him tell the story.

> In her short visits to some relations at Lausanne the wit, the beauty, and erudition of Mlle. Curchod were the theme of universal applause. The report of such a prodigy awakened my curiosity; I saw and loved. I found her learned without pedantry, lively in conversation, pure in sentiment, and elegant in manners. . . . Her fortune was humble, but her family was respectable. . . . She permitted me to make her two or three visits at her father's house. I passed some happy days there, . . . and her parents honorably encouraged the connection. . . . I indulged my dream of felicity.[54]

Apparently they were formally engaged in November, 1757,[55] but Suzanne's consent was conditional on Gibbon's promise to live in Switzerland.[56]

Meanwhile his father, confident that his son was now a good Protestant, bade him return home and hear the plans that had been made for him. Gibbon was not eager to go back, for the father had taken a second wife; but he obeyed, and reached London May 5, 1758. "I soon discovered that my father would not hear of this strange alliance, and that without his consent I was myself destitute and helpless. After a painful struggle, I yielded to my fate: I sighed as a lover, I obeyed as a son."[57] He conveyed this sigh to Suzanne by a letter of August 24. His father settled upon him an annuity of £300. His stepmother earned his gratitude by bearing no children, and soon he developed an affection for her. He spent a large part of his income on books, and "gradually formed a numerous and select library, the foundation of my works, and the best comfort of my life."[58]

He had begun at Lausanne, he finished at Buriton (where he spent his summers), an *Essai sur l'étude de la littérature*, which was published in London in 1761 and in Geneva in 1762. Written in French, and dealing chiefly with French literature and philosophy, it made no stir in England, but was received on the Continent as a remarkable performance for a youth of twenty-two. It had some significant ideas on the writing of history. "The history of empires is that of the misery of man. The history of knowledge is that of his greatness and happiness. . . . A host of considerations makes the last order of study precious in the eyes of the philosopher."[59] Hence, "if philosophers are not always historians, it is at least desirable that historians should be philosophers."[60] In his *Memoirs* Gibbon added: "From earliest youth I aspired to the character of an historian."[61] He cast about for a subject that would lend itself to philosophy and literature as well as to history. In the eighteenth century history made no pretense to be a science; rather, it longed to be an art. Gibbon felt that it was as a philosopher and an artist that he wished to write history: to deal with large subjects in a large perspective, and to give to the chaos of materials philosophical significance and artistic form.

Suddenly he was called from scholarship to action. During the Seven Years' War England had been repeatedly in danger of invasion from France. To prepare against such an emergency the English gentry formed a militia for defense against invasion or rebellion. Only propertied persons could serve as officers. Gibbon Senior and Junior were commissioned as major and captain in June, 1759. Edward III joined his company in June, 1760, and stayed with it, on and off, till December, 1762, moving from camp to camp. He was ill suited to military life, and "tired of companions who had neither the knowledge of scholars nor the manners of gentlemen."[62] Amid his military career he found his scrotum expanding with fluid. "I was obliged today [September 6, 1762] to consult Mr. Andrews, a surgeon, in relation to a complaint I had neglected for some time; it was a swelling in my left testicle, which threatens being a serious affair."[63] He was bled and physicked, with only temporary relief. This "hydrocele" was to torment him until it caused his death.

On January 25, 1763, he set out upon a Continental tour. He stopped some time in Paris, where he met d'Alembert, Diderot, Raynal, and other luminaries of the Enlightenment. "Four days in a week I had a place . . . at the hospitable tables of Mesdames Geoffrin and Boccage, of the celebrated Helvétius, and of the Baron d'Olbach. . . . Fourteen weeks insensibly stole away; but had I been rich and independent I should have prolonged, and perhaps have fixed, my residence at Paris."[64]

In May, 1763, he reached Lausanne, where he remained almost a year. He saw Mlle. Curchod, but, finding her well courted, he made no attempt to renew his friendship with her. In this second stay in Switzerland, he confesses, "the habits of the militia and the example of my countrymen betrayed me into some riotous intemperance; and before my departure I had deservedly forfeited the public opinion which had been acquired by my better days."[65] He lost substantial sums in gambling. But he continued his studies in preparation for Italy, poring over ancient medals, coins, itineraries, and maps.

In April, 1764, he crossed the Alps. He spent three months in Florence, then went on to Rome. "In the daily labor of eighteen weeks" a Scotch expatriate guided him among the remains of classical antiquity. "It was at Rome, on the fifteenth of October, 1764, as I sat musing amidst the ruins of the Capitol, while the barefooted friars were singing vespers in the Temple of Jupiter, that the idea of writing the decline and fall of the city first started to my mind. But my original plan was circumscribed to the decay of the city rather than of the Empire."[66] He came to think of that fateful disintegration as "the greatest, perhaps, and most awful scene in the history of mankind."[67] After visiting Naples, Padua, Venice, Vicenza, and Verona he returned through Turin and Lyons and Paris ("another happy fortnight") to London (June 25, 1765).

Spending most of his time now at Buriton, he let himself be diverted into beginning, in French, a history of Switzerland. Hume, having seen the manuscript in London, wrote to Gibbon (October 24, 1767) begging him to use English, and predicting that English would soon surpass the French language in spread and influence; moreover, he warned Gibbon that his use of the French tongue had led him "into a style more poetical and figurative and more highly colored, than our language seems to admit of in historical productions."[68] Gibbon later admitted: "My ancient habits . . . encouraged me to write in French for the continent of Europe, but I was conscious myself that my style, above prose and below poetry, degenerated into a verbose and turgid declamation."[69]

The death of his father (November 10, 1770) left him an ample fortune. In October, 1772, he took up permanent residence in London. "No sooner was I settled in my house and library than I undertook the composition of the first volume of my history."[70] He allowed himself many distractions—evenings at White's, attendance at Johnson's "Club," trips to Brighton, Bath, Paris. In 1774 he was elected to Parliament from a "pocket borough" controlled by a relative. He kept silence amid the debates in the House of Commons. "I am still mute," he wrote (February 25, 1775); "it is more tremendous than I imagined; the great speakers fill me with despair, the bad ones with terror";[71] but the "eight sessions that I sat in Parliament were a school of civil prudence, the first and most essential virtue of an historian."[72] Surrounded by the controversy on America, he voted regularly for the policy of the government; he addressed to the French nation a *Mémoire justificatif* (1779) presenting England's case against her revolting colonies; and he received as reward a seat on the Board of Trade and Plantations, bringing him £750 a year. Fox accused him of profiting by the same kind of political corruption which he indicated as one cause of the decline of Rome.[73] The wits said George III had bought Gibbon lest the author record the decline and fall of the British Empire.[74]

2. The Book

After 1772 Gibbon's absorbing concern was his history, and he found it difficult to think seriously about anything else. "Many experiments were made before I could hit the middle tone between a dull chronicle and a rhetorical declamation. Three times did I compose the first chapter, and twice the second and third, before I was tolerably satisfied with their effect."[75] He was resolved to make his history a work of literature.

In 1775 Gibbon offered the manuscript of the first sixteen chapters to a publisher, who refused it as necessitating a prohibitive price. Two other booksellers, Thomas Caldwell and William Strahan, pooled their risks in printing (February 17, 1776) Volume I of *The Decline and Fall of the Roman Empire*. Though it was priced at a guinea ($26.00?), the thousand copies were sold by March 26. A second edition, of fifteen hundred copies, issued on June 3, was exhausted in three days. "My book was on every table, and almost on every toilette."[76] The literary world, usually rent with factional jealousies, united in praising it. William Robertson sent generous compliments; Hume, in this year of his death, wrote to the author a letter which, said Gibbon, "overpaid the labor of ten years."[77] Horace Walpole, on the day after publication, announced to William Mason: "Lo, there is just appeared a truly classic work."

The book began logically and bravely with three scholarly chapters detailing the geographical extent, the military organization, the social structure, and the legal constitution of the Roman Empire at the death of Marcus Aurelius (A.D. 180). The preceding eighty-four years, Gibbon felt, had seen the Empire at its peak of official competence and public content.

> If a man were called upon to fix the period in the history of the world during which the condition of the human race was most happy and prosperous, he would, without hesitation, name that which elapsed from the death of Domitian [96] to the accession of Commodus [180]. The vast extent of the Roman Empire was governed by absolute power, under the guidance of virtue and wisdom. The armies were restrained by the firm but gentle hand of four successive emperors whose characters and authority commanded involuntary respect. The forms of the civil administration were carefully preserved by Nerva, Trajan, Hadrian, and the Antonines, who delighted in the image of liberty, and were pleased with considering themselves as the accountable ministers of the laws.

. . . The labors of these monarchs were overpaid by the . . . honest pride of virtue, and by the exquisite delight of beholding the general happiness of which they were the authors.[78]

But Gibbon recognized the "instability of a happiness which must depend on the character of a single man. The fatal moment was perhaps approaching, when some licentious youth or some jealous tyrant would abuse . . . that absolute power."[79] The "good emperors" had been chosen by adoptive monarchy—each ruler transmitting his authority to a chosen and trained member of his entourage. Marcus Aurelius allowed the imperial power to pass down to his worthless son Commodus; from that accession Gibbon dated the decline.

Gibbon thought that the rise of Christianity had contributed to that decline. Here he abandoned the lead of Montesquieu, who had said nothing like this in his *Greatness and decadence of the Romans;* Gibbon, rather, followed Voltaire. His attitude was thoroughly intellectual; he had no sympathy for mystic rapture or hopeful faith. He expressed his view in a passage that has a Voltairean flavor: "The various modes of worship which prevailed in the Roman world were all considered by the people as equally true, by the philosopher as equally false, and by the magistrate as equally useful. And thus toleration produced religious concord."[80] Gibbon usually avoided any direct expression of hostility to Christianity. There were still laws on the statute books of England making such expression a serious crime; e.g., "if any person educated in the Christian religion shall by writing . . . deny the Christian religion to be true, he shall . . . for the second offense . . . suffer three years' imprisonment without bail."[81] To avoid such inconvenience Gibbon developed subtle suggestion and transparent irony as elements in his style. He carefully pointed out that he would discuss not the primary and supernatural sources of Christianity, but only the secondary and natural factors in its origin and growth. Among these secondary factors he listed "the pure and austere morals of the Christians" in their first century, but he added, as another cause, "the inflexible (and, if we may use the expression, the intolerant) zeal of the Christians."[82] And while he praised "the union and discipline of the Christian republic," he noted that "it gradually formed an independent and increasing state in the heart of the Roman Empire."[83] In general he reduced the early progress of Christianity from a miracle to a natural process; he removed the phenomenon from theology to history.

How had Christianity made for the decline of Rome? First, by sapping the faith of the people in the official religion, and thereby undermining the state which that religion supported and sanctified. [This, of course, was precisely the argument of the theologians against the *philosophes.*] The Roman government distrusted the Christians as forming a secret society hostile to military service, and diverting men from useful employments to concentration on heavenly salvation. (The monks, in Gibbon's judgment, were idlers who found it easier to beg and pray than to work.) Other sects could be tolerated because they were tolerant and did not imperil the unity of the nation; the Christians were the only new sect that denounced all others as vicious and damned, and openly predicted the fall of "Babylon"—i.e., Rome.[84] Gibbon attributed much of this fanaticism to the Judaic origin of Christianity, and he followed Tacitus in denouncing the Jews at various points in his narrative. He proposed to interpret Nero's persecution of the Christians as really a persecution of the Jews;[85] this theory has no supporter today. With more success he followed Voltaire in reducing the number of Christians martyred by the Roman government; he reckoned them to be two thousand at most; and agreed with Voltaire "that the Christians, in the course of their intestine dissensions [since Constantine], have inflicted far greater severities on each other than they have experienced from the zeal of infidels"; and "the Church of Rome defended by violence the empire she had acquired by fraud."[86]

These concluding chapters (xv–xvi) of Volume I aroused many replies accusing Gibbon of inaccuracy, unfairness, or insincerity. Ignoring his critics for the time being, he treated himself to an extended vacation in Paris (May to November, 1777). Suzanne Curchod, become the wife of the banker and finance minister Jacques Necker, invited him to their home. She was now too comfortable to resent his having "sighed as a lover, obeyed as a son"; and M. Necker, so far from being jealous, often left the former lovers alone and went to business or bed. "Could they insult me more cruelly?" Gibbon complained. "What an impertinent security!" Suzanne's daughter, Germaine (the future Mme. de Staël), found him such good company that she (aged eleven) tried her budding arts on him, and offered to marry him so as to keep him in the family.[87] At the Neckers' he met the Emperor Joseph II; at Versailles he was presented to Louis XVI, who was said to have shared in translating Volume I into French. He was feted in the salons, particularly by the Marquise du Deffand, who found him "gentle and polite, . . . superior to nearly all the persons among whom I live," but pronounced his style "declamatory, oratorical," and "in the tone of our professed wits."[88] He rejected an invitation from Benjamin Franklin, with a card saying that though he respected the American envoy as a man and a philosopher, he could not reconcile it with his duty to his King to have any conversation with a revolted subject. Franklin replied that he had such high regard for the historian that if ever Gibbon should consider the decline and fall of the British Empire as a subject, Franklin would be happy to furnish him with some relevant materials.[89]

Back in London, Gibbon prepared a reply to his critics—*A Vindication of Some Passages in the Fifteenth and Sixteenth Chapters of the History of the Decline and Fall of the Roman Empire* (1779). He dealt briefly and courteously with his theological opponents, but he rose to some temper in handling Henry Davies, a youth of twenty-one, who had in 284 pages accused Gibbon of inaccuracies. The historian admitted some mistakes, but denied "willful misrepresentations, gross errors, and servile plagiarisms."[90] The *Vindication* was generally received as a successful rebuttal. Gibbon made no further reply to criticism except casually in the *Memoirs*, but he found place for some conciliatory compliments to Christianity in his later volumes.

His writing was accelerated by the loss of his seat in Parliament (September 1, 1780). Volumes II and III of the *History* were published on March 1, 1781. They were quietly received. The barbarian invasions were an old story, and the long and expert discussions of the heresies that had excited the Christian Church in the fourth and fifth centuries were of no interest to a generation of worldly skeptics. Gibbon had sent an advance copy of Volume II to Horace Walpole; he visited Walpole in Berkeley Square, and was chagrined to be told that "there is so much of the Arians and Eunomians and semi-Pelagians . . . that though you have written the story as well as it could be written, I fear few will have patience to read it." "From that hour to this," Walpole wrote, "I have never seen him, though he used to call once or twice a week."[91] Gibbon later agreed with Walpole.[92]

Volume II recovered life when Constantine came to the front. Gibbon interpreted the famous conversion as an act of statesmanship. The Emperor had perceived that "the operation of the wisest laws is imperfect and precarious. They seldom inspire virtue, they cannot always restrain vice." Amid the chaos of morals, economy, and government in the disrupted Empire, "a prudent magistrate might observe with pleasure the progress of a religion which diffused among the people a pure, benevolent, and universal system of ethics, adapted to every duty and every condition of life, recommended as the will and reason of the supreme Deity, and enforced by the sanction of eternal rewards or punishments."[93] That is, Constantine recognized that the aid of a supernatural religion was a precious aid to morality, social order, and government. Then Gibbon penned 150 eloquent and impartial pages on Julian the Apostate.

He ended Chapter XXXVIII and Volume III with a footnote praising George III's "pure and generous love of science and of mankind." In June, 1781, by the aid of Lord North, Gibbon was re-elected to Parliament, where he resumed his support of the ministry. The fall of Lord North (1782) brought an end to the Board of Trade, and to Gibbon's post therein; "I was stripped of a convenient salary of £750 a year."[94] When North took a place in the coalition ministry (1783), Gibbon applied for another sinecure; he received none. "Without additional income I could not long or prudently maintain the style of expense to which I was accustomed."[95] He calculated that he could afford that style in Lausanne, where his pounds sterling had twice the purchasing power they had in London. He resigned his seat in Parliament, sold all his impersonal effects except his library, and on September 15, 1783, he left London—"its smoke and wealth and noise"—for Lausanne. There he shared a comfortable mansion with his old friend Georges Deyverdun. "Instead of looking on a paved court twelve feet square, I command a boundless prospect of vale, mountain, and water."[96] His two thousand books reached him after some delay, and he proceeded with Volume IV.

He had originally planned to end *The Decline and Fall* with the conquest of Rome in 476. But after publishing Volume III he "began to wish for the daily task, the active pursuit, which gave a value to every book, and an object to every inquiry."[97] He decided to interpret "Roman Empire" to mean the Eastern as well as the Western Empire, and to continue his narrative to the destruction of Byzantine rule through the conquest of Constantinople by the Turks in 1453. So he added a thousand years to his scope, and undertook hundreds of new subjects requiring arduous research.

Volume IV included masterly chapters on Justinian and Belisarius, a chapter on Roman law which won high praise from jurists, and a dreary chapter on the further wars within Christian theology. "I wish," wrote Walpole, "Mr. Gibbon had never heard of Monophysites, Nestorians, or any such fools!"[98] In Volume V Gibbon turned with evident relief to the rise of Mohammed and the Arab conquest of the Eastern Roman Empire, and he lavished upon the Prophet and the martial caliphs all the impartial understanding that had failed him in the case of Christianity. In Volume VI the Crusades gave him another stirring theme, and the capture of Constantinople by Mohammed II provided the climax and crown of his work.

In the final chapter he summarized his labors in a famous sentence: "I have described the triumph of barbarism and religion."[99] Like his unacknowledged teacher, Voltaire, he saw nothing in the Middle Ages but crudity and superstition. He pictured the ruinous state of Rome in 1430, and quoted Poggio's lament, "This spectacle of the world, how it is fallen, how changed, how defaced!"—the destruction or dilapidation of classic monuments and art, the Forum Romanum overgrown with weeds and possessed by cattle and swine. And Gibbon concluded sadly: "It was among the ruins of the Capitol that I first conceived the idea of a work which has amused and exercised near twenty years of my life, and which, however inadequate to my own wishes, I finally deliver to the curiosity and candor of the public." And in his *Memoirs* he recalled that hour of ambivalent deliverance:

> It was on the . . . night of the 27th of June, 1787, between the hours of eleven and twelve, that I wrote the last lines of the last page, in a summer house in my garden. After laying down my pen I took several turns in . . . a covered walk of acacias, which commands a prospect of the country, the lake, and the mountains. . . . I will not dissemble the emotions of joy on the recovery of my freedom, and, perhaps, the establishment of my fame. But my pride was soon humbled, and a sober melancholy was spread over my mind, by the idea that I had taken an everlasting leave of an old and agreeable companion, and that whatever might be the future fate of my History, the life of the historian must be short and precarious.[100]

3. The Man

Gibbon at sixteen was described by M. Pavilliard as "a thin little figure with a large head."[101] Hating exercise and loving food,[102] he soon developed a rotundity of body and face, a portly belly sustained by spindly legs; add red hair curled at the side and tied at the back, gentle cherubic features, a button nose, puffy cheeks, multiple chin, and, above all, a broad, high forehead promising "enterprises of great pith and moment," majesty, and scope. He rivaled Johnson in appetite and Walpole in gout. His scrotum swelled painfully year by year to proportions which his tight breeches set off to disconcerting prominence. Despite his handicaps he was vain of his appearance and his dress, and prefaced Volume II with his portrait by Reynolds. He carried a snuffbox at his waist, and tapped it when nervous or wishing to be heard. He was self-centered, like any man with an absorbing purpose. But he truthfully claimed: "I am endowed with a cheerful temperament, a moderate sensibility [but no sentiment!], and a natural disposition to repose."[103]

In 1775 he was elected to "the Club." He attended frequently but rarely spoke, disliking Johnson's idea of conversation. Johnson commented too audibly on Gibbon's "ugliness";[104] Gibbon called the Great Bear an "oracle," "an unforgiving enemy," "a bigoted though vigorous mind, greedy of every pretext to hate and persecute those who dissent from his creed."[105] Boswell, feeling no mercy for an infidel, described the historian as "an ugly, affected, disgusting fellow," who "poisons our Literary Club for me." Nevertheless Gibbon must have had many friends, for in London he dined out almost every night.

He came from Lausanne to London in August, 1787, to supervise the publication of Volumes IV–VI. They appeared on his fifty-first birthday, May 8, 1788, and brought him £4,000, one of the highest fees paid to an author in the eighteenth century. "The conclusion of my work was generally read, and variously judged. . . . Yet, upon the whole, the *History of the Decline and Fall* seems to have struck root, both at home and abroad, and may, perhaps, a hundred years hence, still continue to be abused."[106] Already Adam Smith ranked him "at the head of the whole literary tribe at present existing in Europe."[107] On June 13, 1788, during the trial of Hastings in Westminster Hall, Gibbon, in the gallery, had the pleasure of hearing Sheridan, in one of his most dramatic addresses, refer to "the luminous pages of Gibbon."[108] According to an unlikely story, Sheridan later claimed to have said "voluminous";[109] but that adjective could hardly be applied to pages, and "luminous" was surely the fitting word.

In July, 1788, Gibbon returned to Lausanne. A year later Deyverdun died, leaving his home to Gibbon for the duration of the historian's life. There, with several servants and an income of £1,200 a year, Gibbon lived at ease, drank much wine, and added to his gout and girth. "From February 9 to July 1, 1790, I was not able to move from my house or chair."[110] To this period belongs the legend that he knelt at the feet of Mme. de Crousaz with a declaration of love, that she bade him rise, and that he could not, being too heavy.[111] The sole source of the story is Mme. de Genlis, whom Sainte-Beuve described as "a woman with a malicious tongue";[112] and her own daughter rejected the tale as due to a confusion of persons.[113]

The French Revolution interfered with Gibbon's tranquillity. Revolutionary sentiments were voiced in the Swiss cantons, and word came of similar agitation in England. He had good reason to fear the collapse of the French monarchy, having invested £1,300 in a French government loan.[114] In 1788, in an unlucky prophecy, he had written of the French monarchy that "it stood founded, as it might seem, on the rock of time, force, and opinion, supported by the triple Aristocracy of the Church, the Nobility, and the Parliaments."[115] He rejoiced when Burke issued *Reflections on the Revolution in France* (1790); he wrote to Lord Sheffield advising against any reform in the British political structure; "if you admit the smallest and most specious change in our parliamentary system, you are lost."[116] Now he deplored the success of the *philosophes* in combating religion; "I have sometimes thought of writing a dialogue of the dead, in which Lucian, Erasmus, and Voltaire should mutually acknowledge the danger of exposing an old superstition to the contempt of the blind and fanatical multitude."[117] He urged some Portuguese leaders not to abandon the Inquisition during this crisis that threatened all thrones.[118]

Partly to escape the French Revolutionary army that was nearing Lausanne, partly to seek English surgery, and proximately to comfort Lord Sheffield on the death of his wife, Gibbon left Lausanne (May 9, 1793) and hurried to England. There he found Sheffield so busy with politics as to have rapidly recovered from his grief; "the patient was cured," Gibbon wrote, "before the arrival of the doctor."[119] The historian himself now submitted to the physicians, for his hydrocele had grown "almost as big as a small child. . . . I crawl about with some labor and much indecency."[120] One operation drained four quarts of "transparent watery liquid" from the affected testicle. But the fluid collected again, and a second tapping drew three quarts. Gibbon was temporarily relieved, and resumed dining out. Once more the hydrocele formed; now it became septic. On January 13, 1794, a third tapping was made. Gibbon seemed to be recovering rapidly; the doctor allowed him meat; Gibbon ate some chicken, and drank three glasses of wine. He was seized with severe gastric pains, which, like Voltaire, he sought to ease with opium. On January 16 he died, aged fifty-six.

4. The Historian

Gibbon was not inspiring in his visible person, character, or career; his greatness was poured into his book, into the grandeur and courage of its conception, the patience and artistry of its composition, the luminous majesty of the whole.

Yes, Sheridan's word was right. Gibbon's style is as luminous as irony would allow, and it shed light wherever it turned, except where prejudice darkened his view. His diction was molded by his Latin and French studies; he found simple Anglo-Saxon words unsuitable to the dignity of his manner, and often he wrote like an orator—Livy sharpened with the satire of Tacitus, Burke brightened with the wit of Pascal. He balanced clauses with the skill and delight of a juggler, but played the game so often that sometimes it neared monotony. If his style seems pompous, it fitted the reach and splendor of his theme—the thousand-year crumbling of the greatest empire the world had ever seen. The venial sins of his style are lost in the masculine march of the narrative, the vigor of the episodes, the revealing portraits and descriptions, the magisterial summations that cover a century in a paragraph, and marry philosophy to history.

Having undertaken so extensive a subject, Gibbon felt justified in narrowing its limits. "Wars, and the administration of public affairs," he said, "are the principal subjects of history."[121] He excluded the history of art, science, and literature; so he had nothing to say about Gothic cathedrals or Moslem mosques, about Arabic science or philosophy; he crowned Petrarch, but passed Dante by. He paid almost no attention to the condition of the lower classes, the rise of industry in medieval Constantinople and Florence. He lost interest in Byzantine history after the death of Heraclius (641). "He failed," in the judgment of Bury, "to bring out the momentous fact that [till] the twelfth century the [Eastern Roman] Empire was the bulwark of Europe against the East; nor did he appreciate its importance in preserving the heritage of Greek civilization."[122] Within his set limits Gibbon achieved greatness by connecting effects with natural causes, and by reducing the immensity of his materials to intelligible order and a guiding perspective of the whole.

His scholarship was immense and detailed. His footnotes are a treasury of learning lightened with wit. He studied the most recondite aspects of classical antiquity, including roads, coins, weights, measures, laws. He made mistakes which specialists have corrected, but the same Bury who pointed out his errors added: "If we take into account the vast range of his work, his accuracy is amazing."[123] He could not (like professional historians confining themselves to a small area of subject, place, and time) burrow into unprinted original sources; to get his work done he restricted himself to printed material, and frankly relied in part on secondary authorities like Ockley's *History of the Saracens* or Tillemont's *Histoire des empereurs* and *Histoire ecclésiastique;* and some of the authorities he relied upon are now rejected as untrustworthy.[124] He declared his sources in honest detail, and thanked them; so, when he passed beyond the time that Tillemont treated, he said in a footnote: "Here I must take leave forever of that incomparable guide."[125]

What conclusions did Gibbon reach from his study of history? Sometimes he followed the *philosophes* in accepting the reality of progress: "We may acquiesce in the pleasing conclusion that every age in the world has increased and still increases the real wealth, the happiness, the knowledge, and perhaps the virtue, of the human race."[126] But in less amiable moments—and perhaps because he had taken war and politics (and theology) as the substance of history—he judged history to be "indeed little more than the register of the crimes, follies, and misfortunes of mankind."* [127] He saw no design in history; events are the outcome of unguided causes; they are the parallelogram of forces of different origin and composite result. In all this kaleidoscope of events human nature seems to remain unchanged. Cruelty, suffering, and injustice have always afflicted mankind, and always will, for they are written in the nature of man. "Man has much more to fear from the passions of his fellow creatures than from the convulsions of the elements."[129]

Child of the Enlightenment, Gibbon longed to be a philosopher, or at

---

* *Cf.* Voltaire: "All history, in short, is little else than a . . . collection of crimes, follies, and misfortunes . . ."[128]

least to write history *en philosophe*. "An enlightened age requires from the historian some tincture of philosophy and criticism."[130] He loved to interrupt his narrative with philosophical comments. But he did not profess to reduce history to laws, or to formulate a "philosophy of history." On some basic questions, however, he took a stand: he confined the influence of climate to the early stages of civilization; he rejected race as a determining factor;[131] and he acknowledged, within limits, the influence of exceptional men. "In human life the most important scenes will depend upon the character of a single actor. . . . An acrimonious humor falling upon a single fiber of one man may prevent or suspend the misery of nations."[132] When the Koreish could have assassinated Mohammed "the lance of an Arab might have changed the history of the world."[133] If Charles Martel had not defeated the Moors at Tours (732) the Moslems might have overrun all Europe; "the interpretation of the Koran would now be taught in the schools of Oxford, and her pupils might demonstrate to a circumcised people the sanctity and truth of the revelation of Mahomet. From such calamities was Christendom delivered by the genius and fortune of one man."[134] However, for maximum influence on his time, the exceptional individual must stand upon some wide support. "The effects of personal valor are so inconsiderable, except in poetry or romance, that victory . . . must depend upon the degree of skill with which the passions of the multitude are combined and guided for the service of a single man."[135]

All in all, *The Decline and Fall of the Roman Empire* may be ranked as the supreme book of the eighteenth century, with Montesquieu's *L'Esprit des lois* as its closest competitor. It was not the most influential; it could not compare in effect upon history with Rousseau's *Social Contract* or Adam Smith's *Wealth of Nations*, or Kant's *Critique of Pure Reason*. But as a work of literary art it was unsurpassed in its time or kind. When we ask how Gibbon came to produce such a masterpiece, we perceive that it was the accidental combination of ambition with money, leisure, and ability; and we wonder how soon such a combination can be expected to recur. Never, said another historian of Rome, Barthold Niebuhr; "Gibbon's work will never be excelled."[136]

VI. CHATTERTON AND COWPER

Who would now suppose that in 1760 the most popular of living English poets was Charles Churchill? Son of a clergyman, and himself ordained an Anglican priest, he took to the pleasures of London, dismissed his wife, rolled up debts, and wrote a once famous poem, *The Rosciad* (1761), which enabled him to pay his debts, to settle an allowance on his wife, and to "set up in glaringly unclerical attire as a man about town."[137] His poem took its name from Quintus Roscius, who had dominated the Roman theater in Caesar's day; it satirized the leading actors of London, and made Garrick wince; one victim "ran about the town like a stricken deer."[138] Churchill joined Wilkes in the ribald rites of Medmenham Abbey, helped him write *The North Briton,* and went to France to share Wilkes's exile; but he died at Boulogne (1764) of a drunken debauch, and "with epicurean indifference."[139]

Another clergyman, Thomas Percy, lived up to his cloth, became bishop of Dromore in Ireland, and made a mark on European literature by rescuing, from the hands of a housemaid who was about to burn it, an old manuscript that provided one source for his *Reliques of Ancient Poetry* (1765). These ballads from medieval Britain appealed to old memories, and encouraged the romantic spirit—so long subdued by rationalism and the classic temper—to express itself in poetry, fiction, and art. Wordsworth dated from these *Reliques* the rise of the Romantic movement in English literature. Macpherson's *Ossian,* Chatterton's poems, Walpole's *Castle of Otranto* and Strawberry Hill, Beckford's *Vathek* and Fonthill Abbey, were varied voices joining in the cry for feeling, mystery, and romance. For a time the Middle Ages captured the modern soul.

Thomas Chatterton began his attempt to medievalize himself by brooding over old parchments which his uncle had found in a Bristol church. Born in that city (1752) soon after his father's death, the sensitive and imaginative boy grew up in a world of his own historic fancies. He studied a dictionary of Anglo-Saxon words, and composed, in what he thought was fifteenth-century language, poems which he pretended to have found in St. Mary Radcliffe Church, and which he ascribed to Thomas Rowley, an imaginary fifteenth-century monk. In 1769, aged seventeen, he sent some of these "Rowley poems" to Horace Walpole—who had himself published *Otranto* as a medieval original five years before. Walpole praised the poems and invited more; Chatterton sent more, and asked for help in finding a publisher, and some remunerative employment in London. Walpole submitted the verses to Thomas Gray and William Mason, both of whom pronounced them forgeries. Walpole wrote to Chatterton that these scholars "were by no means satisfied with the authenticity of his supposed MSS;" and he advised him to put poetry aside until he could support himself. Then Walpole went off to Paris, forgetting to return the poems. Chatterton wrote three times for them; three months passed before they came.[140]

The poet went to London (April, 1770) and took an attic room in Brook Street, Holborn. He contributed pro-Wilkes articles, and some of the Rowley poems, to various periodicals, but was so poorly paid (eightpence per poem) that he could not sustain himself on the proceeds. He tried and failed to secure a post as surgeon's assistant on an African trader. On August 27 he composed a bitter valedictory to the world:

> Farewell, Bristolia's dingy piles of brick,
> Lovers of Mammon, worshipers of trick!
> Ye spurned the boy who gave you antique lays,
> And paid for learning with your empty praise.
> Farewell, ye guzzling aldermanic fools,
> By nature fitted for corruption's tools! . . .

Farewell, my mother!—cease, my anguish'd soul,
Nor let distraction's billows o'er me roll!
Have mercy, Heaven! when here I cease to live,
And this last act of wretchedness forgive.

Then he killed himself by drinking arsenic. He was seventeen years and nine months old. He was buried in a pauper's grave.

His poems now fill two volumes. Had he called them imitations instead of originals he might have been recognized as a genuine poet, for some of the Rowley pieces are as good as most originals of the same genre. When he wrote in his own name he could indite satiric verses almost rivaling Pope's, as in "The Methodist"[141] or—bitterest of all—seventeen lines lashing Walpole as a heartless sycophant.[142] When his surviving manuscripts were published (1777) the editor charged Walpole as partly responsible for the poet's death; Walpole defended himself on the ground that he had felt no obligation to help a persistent impostor.[143] Some warmhearted souls like Goldsmith insisted that the poems were genuine; Johnson laughed at his friend, but said: "This is the most extraordinary young man that has encountered my knowledge. It is wonderful how the whelp has written such things."[144] Shelley briefly commemorated the boy in *Adonais*,[145] and Keats inscribed *Endymion* to his memory.

Chatterton escaped from the rugged realities of Bristol and London via medieval legends and arsenic; William Cowper fled from the London that Johnson loved into rural simplicity, religious faith, and periodic insanity. His grandfather was acquitted of murder and became a judge; his father was an Anglican clergyman; his mother belonged to the same family that had produced John Donne. She died when he was six, leaving him melancholy memories of fond solicitude; fifty-three years later, when a cousin sent him an old picture of her, he recalled, in a tender poem,[146] the efforts she often made to calm the fears that darkened his childhood nights.

From those indulgent hands he passed, in his seventh year, to a boarding school where he became the timid fag of a bully who spared him no humiliating task. He suffered from inflammation of the eyes, and for years he had to be under an oculist's care. In 1741, aged ten, he was sent off to Westminster School in London. At seventeen he began three years' service as clerk in a solicitor's office in Holborn. He was ripe now for romance; as his cousin Theodora Cowper lived nearby, she became the idol of his daydreams. At twenty-one he took quarters in the Middle Temple, and at twenty-three he was admitted to the bar. Disliking law, and timid before courts, he fell into a mood of hypochondria, which was deepened when Theodora's father forbade her any further association with her cousin. Cowper never saw her again, never forgot her, and never married.

In 1763, faced with the necessity to appear before the House of Lords, he broke down, became deranged, and tried to kill himself. Friends sent him to an asylum at St. Albans. After eighteen months he was released, and took to an almost solitary life at Huntingdon, near Cambridge; now, he said, he "desired no other communion than with God and Jesus Christ."[147] He accepted the Calvinist creed literally, and thought much of salvation and damnation. By some happy chance he fell in with a local family whose religion brought peace and kindness rather than fear: the Reverend Morley Unwin, his wife Mary, his son William, and his daughter Susannah. Cowper compared the father with Parson Adams in Fielding's *Joseph Andrews;* he saw a second mother in Mrs. Unwin, who was seven years his senior. She and the daughter treated him as son and brother, and gave him delicate feminine attentions that almost made him love life again. They invited him to live with them; he did (1765), and found healing in their simple life.

This bliss was suddenly ended when the father was killed by a fall from a horse. The widow and her daughter, taking Cowper with them, moved to Olney in Buckinghamshire, to be near the famous evangelical preacher John Newton. He persuaded Cowper to join him in visiting the sick and writing hymns. One of these "Olney Hymns" contained famous lines:

> God moves in a mysterious way
>   His wonders to perform;
> He plants his footsteps in the sea,
>   And rides upon the storm.[148]

But Newton's hellfire sermons, which had "thrown more than one of his parishioners off their balance," intensified rather than allayed the poet's theological fears.[149] "God," said Cowper, "is always formidable to me but when I see Him disarmed of His sting by having sheathed it in the body of Christ Jesus."[150] He proposed to Mrs. Unwin, but a second attack of insanity (1773) prevented the marriage; he recovered after three years of loving care. In 1779 Newton left Olney, and Cowper's piety took a milder turn.

Other women helped Mary Unwin to keep the poet in contact with earthly things. Lady Austin, widowed but merry, gave up her London house, moved to Olney, associated with the Unwins, and brought gaiety where there had been too long a concentration on the occasional tragedies of life. It was she who told Cowper the story which he turned into "The Diverting History of John Gilpin"[151] and his wild unwilling ride. A friend of the family sent the rollicking ballad to a newspaper; an actor who had succeeded Garrick at the Drury Lane Theatre recited it there; it became the talk of London, and Cowper had his first taste of renown. He had never taken himself seriously as a poet; now Lady Austin urged him to write some substantial work. But on what subject? On anything, she answered; and, pointing to a sofa, she assigned him the task of celebrating it in verse. Pleased to be commanded by a charming woman, Cowper wrote *The Task.* Published in 1785, it found welcome among people who were tired of war and politics and city strife.

It would be a real task to write or read six "books" about a sofa unless one had the morals of Crébillon *fils;*[152] Cowper was sane enough to use it only as a starting post. After making it the climax in a humorous history of chairs, he slipped into his favorite subject, which might be summed up in the poem's most famous line: "God made the country, and man made the town."[153] The poet admitted that art and eloquence flourished in London; he praised Reynolds and Chatham, and marveled at the science that "measures an atom and now girds the world";[154] but he reproached the "queen of cities" for punishing some small thefts with death while lavishing honors on "peculators of the public gold."

> Oh for a lodge in some vast wilderness,
> Some boundless contiguity of shade,
> Where rumor of oppression and deceit,
> Of unsuccessful or successful war,
> Might never reach me more! My ear is pain'd,
> My soul is sick, with every day's report
> Of wrong and outrage with which earth is filled.[155]

He was horrified by the traffic in slaves; his was one of the first English voices to denounce the man who

> finds his fellow guilty of a skin
> Not colored like his own; and having power
> To enforce the wrong, . . .
> Dooms and devotes him as his lawful prey. . . .
> Then what is man? And what man, seeing this,
> And having human feelings, does not blush,
> And hang his head, to think himself a man?[156]

And yet, he concluded, "England, with all thy faults I love thee still."[157]

He felt that these faults would be mitigated if England would return to religion and a rural life. "I was a stricken deer that left the herd"—i.e., he had left London, where "prostitutes elbow us aside"—and had found healing in faith and nature. Come to the countryside! See the River Ouse, "slow winding through a level plain"; the placid cattle, the peasant cottage and its sturdy family, the village spire pointing grief and hope; hear the splash of waterfalls, and the morning converse of the birds. In the country every season has its joy; the spring rains are a blessing, and the winter snow is clean. How pleasant it is to tramp through the snow and then gather about the evening fire!

Cowper wrote little of value after *The Task*. In 1786 he removed to nearby Weston Underwood; there he had another half year of insanity. In 1792 Mrs. Unwin suffered a paralytic stroke; for three years she lingered as a helpless invalid; Cowper nursed her as she had nursed him, and in her last month he wrote his lines "To Mary Unwin":

> Thy silver locks, once auburn bright,
> Are still more lovely in my sight
> Than golden beams of orient light,
>   My Mary![158]

In 1794, overcome with care, and with work on his unsuccessful translation of Homer, he again went mad, and tried to destroy himself. He recovered, and was relieved from financial distress by a governmental pension of £ 300. But on December 17, 1796, Mary Unwin died, and Cowper felt quite lost and desolate, though he had found a new friend in Theodora's sister, Lady Harriet Cowper Hesketh. His final days were obsessed with religious fears. He died on April 25, 1800, aged sixty-eight.

He belonged to the Romantic movement in literature, and to the evangelical movement in religion. He ended the reign of Pope in poetry, and prepared for Wordsworth; he brought into poetry a naturalness of form and a sincerity of feeling that stopped the torrent of artificial couplets which the Augustan Age had let loose upon England. His religion was a curse to him in its picture of a vengeful God and an unforgiving hell; yet it may have been religion, as well as maternal instincts, that led those kindly women to care for this "stricken deer" through all his griefs and darkenings.

VII. OLIVER GOLDSMITH

"Poor Poll" too had his tragedies, but they were not deepened by a sadistic creed, and were relieved by triumphs in prose and poetry and on the stage.

His father was a humble Anglican curate in an Irish village, who, by adding tillage to theology, earned forty pounds a year. When Oliver was two years old (1730) the curate was made rector of Kilkenny West, and the family moved into a house on a main road near Lissoy, which later renamed itself Auburn in confidence that Goldsmith had had it in mind when he wrote *The Deserted Village*.

Oliver went through a succession of elementary schools, and remembered best a quartermaster turned schoolmaster, who could never forget his wars, but also told absorbing tales of fairies, banshees, and ghosts. At the age of nine the boy nearly died of smallpox, which further disfigured one of the least beautiful faces ever given to a lovable soul. At fifteen he entered Trinity College in Dublin as a sizar, or working student, wearing a distinguishing costume, performing menial services, and harassed by a tyrannical tutor. He ran away to Cork, planning to find passage to America, but his older brother Henry overtook him and beguiled him back to college. Oliver did well with the classics, but proved impervious to science; however, he managed to get his bachelor's degree.

He applied for admission to minor ecclesiastical orders, but astonished the bishop by appearing in scarlet breeches. Rejected, he became a tutor, quarreled with his pupil, and again headed for Cork and America. An uncle intervened by advancing him fifty pounds to go to London; Oliver lost it all in a gambling house. His relatives were dismayed by his shiftless incompetence, but were charmed by his gaiety, flute, and songs. A fund was raised to finance his study of medicine in Edinburgh, then in Leiden. He made some progress, but left Leiden without a degree. At Paris (he tells us) he attended the chemical lectures of Rouelle. Then he set out leisurely (1755), walking through France, Germany, Switzerland, and north Italy, playing his flute at country dances, earning haphazard meals, receiving alms at monastery gates.[159] In January, 1756, he returned to England.

He practiced medicine in London, corrected proofs for Samuel Richardson, taught school in Surrey, then settled down in London as a hack writer, doing odd literary jobs and contributing to magazines. He wrote in four weeks a *Life of Voltaire*. In 1759 he persuaded Dodsley to publish a superficial *Enquiry into the State of Polite Learning in Europe*. Its comments on theatrical managers gave lasting offense to Garrick. It argued that ages of creative literature tend to be followed by ages of criticism, which deduce rules from the practice of creators, and tend to cramp the style and imagination of new poets. Goldsmith thought that Europe was in such a state in 1759.

A year later he wrote for Newbery's *Public Ledger* some "Chinese Letters," which were republished in 1762 as *The Citizen of the World*. The scheme was old: to imagine an Oriental traveler reporting with amusement and horror the ways of Europeans. So Lien Chi Altangi, in letters to a friend at home, describes Europe as a disorderly theater of avarice, ambition, and intrigue. Goldsmith issued the book anonymously, but the denizens of Fleet Street recognized his style in the simple language, lively descriptions, and amiable tone. Feeling his fame, he moved to better quarters at No. 6 Wine Office Court. Having complimented Johnson in the "Chinese Letters," he ventured to invite the lexicographer (who lived just across the way) to supper. Johnson came, and their long friendship began (May 31, 1761).

One day in October, 1762, Johnson received an urgent message from Goldsmith, asking for help. He sent a guinea, came shortly afterward, and found that Goldsmith was about to be arrested for failure to pay his rent. He asked his friend had he nothing of value to pawn or sell. Goldsmith gave him a manuscript entitled *The Vicar of Wakefield*. Johnson (according to Johnson's account[160]) bade the landlady wait, brought the novel to John Newbery, a bookseller, sold it for £60, and took the money to Goldsmith, who paid his rent and celebrated with a bottle of wine. The bookseller kept the manuscript unpublished for four years.

In December, 1764, Goldsmith sent forth his first major poem, *The Traveller, or A Prospect of Society*. He retraced his Continental wanderings, described the faults and virtues of each land, and noted that each country thought itself the best. He gloried in the power of England (which had just won the Seven Years' War), and described the M.P.s:

> Pride in their port, defiance in their eye,
> I see the lords of human kind pass by;

but he warned that avarice was tarnishing British rule, that selfish enclosures were impoverishing the peasantry and driving England's sturdiest sons to America. He had shown the manuscript to Johnson, who contributed nine lines, chiefly toward the end, belittling the influence of politics on the individual's happiness, and lauding domestic joys.

The success of the poem surprised all but Johnson, who helped it by proclaiming, "There has not been so fine a poem since Pope's time"[161]—which slighted Gray. The publisher made a handsome profit on repeated editions, but yielded only twenty guineas to the author. Goldsmith moved to better rooms in the Temple; he bought a new outfit, with purple breeches, scarlet cloak, a wig, and a cane, and resumed with this dignity the practice of medicine. The experiment did not prosper, and the success of *The Vicar of Wakefield* brought him back to literature.

The bookseller who had bought the manuscript from Johnson felt that the fresh fame of Goldsmith would carry the strange novel to acceptance. It appeared in a small edition on March 27, 1766; this was sold out in two months, and a second edition in three months more; but not till 1774 did the sales repay the publisher's investment. As early as 1770 Herder recommended it to Goethe, who rated it "one of the best novels ever written."[162] Walter Scott agreed.[163] Washington Irving marveled that a bachelor homeless since his childhood could draw "the most amiable picture of domestic virtue and all the endearments of the married state."[164] Perhaps it was Goldsmith's exclusion from family life that made him idealize the home, his unwilling bachelordom that made him idealize young womanhood, and his anonymous amours that made him exalt feminine chastity as more precious than life. His fond memories of his father and his brother furnished the portrait of Dr. Primrose, who, as "a priest, an husbandman, and the father of a family, . . . unites in himself the three greatest characters on earth."[165] His own wanderings reappeared in son George, who, like Goldsmith, had ended his travels as a hack writer in London. The story is incredible and charming.

The proceeds from *The Traveller* and *The Vicar of Wakefield* were soon spent, for Goldsmith was a sieve for currency, and always lived in the future. He looked with envy upon the fame and fortune that might come from a successful play. He set his pen to the difficult genre, called the result *The Good-Natured Man*, and offered it to Garrick. David tried to forget the derogatory remarks that Goldsmith had made about him; he agreed to produce the play. However, it laughed at sentimental comedies, and these were Garrick's moneymakers. He proposed changes, Goldsmith rejected them; Garrick advanced the author forty pounds, but dallied so long that the reckless author turned the manuscript over to Garrick's rival, George Colman, who managed the Covent Garden Theatre. Colman's actors disparaged the play; Johnson gave it all his support, attended rehearsals, wrote the prologue. The drama had its première on January 29, 1768; it ran ten nights, and was then withdrawn as only a moderate success; even so it netted the author £500.

Flush for a year, Goldsmith, against Johnson's advice, moved to a handsome apartment in Brick Court, and fitted it so well that he had to return to hack writing to meet his bills. Now he turned out popular histories of Rome, Greece, England, and a *History of Animated Nature*—all of them poor in scholarship but enriched with gracious prose. When someone asked why he wrote such books, he answered that they enabled him to eat, while poetry let him starve. Nevertheless, on May 26, 1770, he sent forth his masterpiece, *The Deserted Village*, for which he received a hundred guineas—a fair price at that time for a poem only seventeen pages long. It sold out four editions in three months.

Its theme was the desertion of the countryside by farmers who had lost their lands through enclosures. It pictured

> Sweet Auburn! loveliest village of the plain,
> Where health and plenty cheered the laboring swain;

it lent all the rosy colors of Goldsmith's urban imagination to the peasant prosperity that (he presumed) had preceded the enclosures. He described the rural scenes, the diverse flowers, "the sheltered cot, the cultivated farm," the village sports and dances, the "bashful virgin" and the pimpled youth, and the happy families where piety and virtue reigned. Again he saw his father ministering at Kilkenny West:

> A man he was to all the country dear,
> And passing rich with forty pounds a year—

enough to let him feed the vagrant, save the spendthrift, house the broken soldier, visit the sick, and comfort the dying.

> At church, with meek and unaffected grace,
> His looks adorned the venerable place;
> Truth from his lips prevailed with double sway,
> And fools who came to scoff remained to pray.

That schoolmaster who had disciplined the poet's boyhood was transformed in recollection into a teacher "stern to view":

> Yet he was kind, or if severe in aught,
> The love he bore to learning was in fault; . . .
> In arguing, too, the parson owned his skill,
> For e'en though vanquished he could argue still; . . .
> With words of learned length and thundering sound
> Amazed the gazing rustics ranged around;
> And still they gazed, and still the wonder grew,
> That one small head could carry all he knew.

This paradise had been ruined, Goldsmith thought, by enclosures; the peasant farm had been turned to pasturage, the peasant families had fled to the towns or the colonies, and the rural fount of honest virtue was drying up.

> Ill fares the land, to hastening ills a prey,
> Where wealth accumulates and men decay.

Having written the best poem of that generation, Goldsmith now returned to drama. In 1771 he offered to Colman a new comedy, *She Stoops to Conquer*. Colman dallied as Garrick had done, until Johnson intervened and almost commanded the manager to stage the play. Garrick, reconciled, wrote the prologue. After tribulations that almost broke the author's spirit, the piece was produced, March 15, 1773. Johnson, Reynolds, and other friends attended the première and led the applause; Goldsmith himself wandered meanwhile in St. James's Park, until someone found him and assured him that his play was a great success. It had a long run; the benefit nights brought Goldsmith a year of prosperity.

He had now raised himself to a place second only to Johnson among the English writers of the day, and even to foreign fame. He was a leading figure in the Club, and dared to differ from Johnson frequently. When there was talk about animal fables he remarked that it was especially difficult to make fishes talk like fishes; and "this," he told Johnson, "is not so easy as you seem to think; for if you were to make little fishes talk they would all talk like whales."[166] The Great Bear sometimes clawed him cruelly, but loved him none the less, and the affection was returned despite Goldsmith's envy of Johnson's conversational mastery. He himself had never put his learning in order; he could not draw on it readily or aptly; he "wrote like an angel," said Garrick, "and talked like poor Poll."[167] Boswell tended to belittle Goldsmith, but many contemporaries—Reynolds, Burke, Wilkes, Percy—protested against this as unjust.[168] It was observed that Goldsmith often spoke well in gatherings where Johnson was not present.[169]

His accent, his manners, and his appearance were against him. He had never lost his Irish brogue. He dressed too carelessly, and sometimes he sported incongruous polychrome finery. He was vain of his accomplishments, and did not admit Johnson's superiority to him as a writer. He was five feet five inches tall, and resented Johnson's height and bulk. His good nature shone through his homely face. Reynolds' portrait did not idealize him; here were thick lips, a receding forehead, an advancing nose, and worried eyes. Caricaturists like Henry Bunbury widened Oliver's mouth and prolonged his nose; the *London Packet* described him as an orangutan;[170] a hundred stories traveled the town about his blunders of speech and action, and his secret love for pretty Mary Horneck.

His friends knew that his faults were on the surface, concealing a spirit of good will, affection, and almost ruinous generosity. Even Boswell described him as "the most generous-hearted man that exists; and now that he has had a large supply of gold by his comedy, all the needy draw upon him."[171] When he had no more money to give he borrowed to meet the demands of the poor who applied to him.[172] He appealed to Garrick (whose forty pounds had not been repaid) to advance him sixty pounds on the promise of another play; Garrick sent the sum. Goldsmith owed £2,000 at his death. "Was ever poet," Johnson asked, "so trusted before?"[173]

In 1774, as he was about to leave for one of the several clubs to which he belonged, he was stricken with fever. He insisted on prescribing for himself, forgetting Beauclerk's advice that he should prescribe only for his enemies; he took a patent medicine, and grew worse. A doctor was called, too late to save him. He died on April 4, only forty-five years old. A crowd of mourners gathered about the corpse, simple men and women who had almost lived on his charity. He was buried in the churchyard of the Temple, but his friends insisted that some memorial to him should be set up in the Abbey. Nollekens carved the monument, Johnson wrote the epitaph. Better would have been the poet's own lines in *The Good-Natured Man:* "Life at the greatest and best is but a forward child, that must be humored and coaxed a little till it falls asleep, and then all the care is over."[174]

CHAPTER XXXIII

Samuel Johnson

1709–84

I. DEFORMATIVE YEARS: 1709–46

HE was unique and yet typical; unlike any Englishman of his time, yet summarizing John Bull in body and soul; surpassed in every literary field (except lexicography) by his contemporaries, yet dominating them for a generation, reigning over them without raising anything but his voice.

Let us record briefly the blows that beat him into his peculiar form. He was the first child born to Michael Johnson, bookseller, printer, and stationer in Lichfield, 118 miles from London. The mother, nee Sarah Ford, was of slightly genteel stock. She was thirty-seven when, in 1706, she married Michael, who was fifty.

Samuel was a sickly child, so weak at birth that he was baptized at once, lest, dying unchristened, he should, by the laws of theology, be lodged forever in Limbo, the gloomy vestibule of hell. He soon showed signs of scrofula. When he was thirty months old his mother, though pregnant with her second son, took him on the long ride to London to be "touched for the king's evil" by Queen Anne. The Queen did her best, but the disease cost Johnson the use of one eye and one ear, and shared with other tribulations in disfiguring his face.[1] Nevertheless he grew strong in muscle and frame; and his strength as well as his bulk supported that absolutism which, as Goldsmith complained, turned the republic of letters into a monarchy. Samuel thought that he had inherited from his father the "vile melancholy which has made me mad all my life, at least not sober."[2] Perhaps, as in Cowper's case, his hypochondria had a religious as well as a physical basis; Johnson's mother was a firm Calvinist, who thought that eternal damnation was just around the corner. Samuel suffered from fear of hell to the day of his death.

From his father he derived his Tory politics, Jacobite leanings, and a passion for books. He read eagerly in his father's store; later he told Boswell, "I knew almost as much at eighteen as I do now."[3] After some elementary instruction he passed on to Lichfield grammar school, where the headmaster was "so brutal that no man who had been educated by him sent his son to the same school";[4] however, when asked in after years how he had acquired so good a command of Latin, he answered: "My master whipt me very well. Without that, Sir, I should have done nothing."[5] In old age he deplored the obsolescence of the rod. "There is now less flogging in our great schools than formerly, but then less is learned there, so that what the boys get at one end they lose at the other."[6]

In 1728 his parents found means to send him to Oxford. There he devoured the Greek and Latin classics, and harassed his teachers by insubor-
dination. In December, 1729, he hurried back to Lichfield, perhaps because
parental funds ran out, or because his hypochondria had come so close to
madness that he needed medical treatment. He received this at Birmingham;
then, instead of returning to Oxford, he helped in his father's shop. When
the father died (December, 1731) Samuel went to work as assistant teacher
in a school at Market Bosworth. Soon tiring of this, he moved to Birmingham, lived with a bookseller, and made five guineas by translating a book
about Abyssinia; this was a distant source of *Rasselas*. In 1734 he returned
to Lichfield, where his mother and brother were carrying on the store. On
July 9, 1735, two months short of twenty-six, he married Elizabeth Porter,
a widow of forty-eight with three children and £700. With her money he
opened a boarding school at nearby Edial. David Garrick, a Lichfield boy,
was one of his pupils, but there were not enough to reconcile him to pedagogy. Authorship was fermenting in him. He wrote a drama, *Irene*, and
sent word to Edward Cave, editor of *The Gentleman's Magazine*, explaining how that periodical could be improved. On March 2, 1737, he rode off
to London, with David Garrick and one horse, to sell his tragedy and carve
out a place for himself in the cruel world.

His appearance was against him. He was thin and tall, but with a large
bony frame that made him a mass of angles. His face was blotched with
scrofula and was frequently agitated by a convulsive twitch; his body was
subject to alarming starts; his conversation was illustrated by odd gesticula-
tions. One bookseller to whom he applied for work advised him to "get a
porter's knot and carry trunks."[7] Apparently he received some encouragement from Cave, for in July he went back to Lichfield, and brought his wife
to London.

He was not without subtlety. When Cave was attacked in the press Johnson wrote a poem in his defense and sent it to him; Cave published it, gave
him literary commissions, and joined Dodsley in issuing (May, 1738) Johnson's *London*, for which they gave him ten guineas. The poem frankly imitated Juvenal's Third Satire, and therefore emphasized the lamentable aspects of the city that the author soon learned to love; it was also an attack
upon the administration of Robert Walpole, whom Johnson later described
as "the best minister this country ever had."[8] The poem was in part the angry
blast of a country youth who, after a year in London, was still uncertain of
tomorrow's food; hence the famous line "Slow rises worth, by poverty depressed."[9]

In those days of struggle Johnson turned his pen to every genre. He wrote
Lives of Eminent Persons (1740), and various articles for *The Gentleman's
Magazine*, including imaginary reports of parliamentary debates. Since reporting of the debates was as yet forbidden, Cave hit on the expedient of
pretending that his magazine was merely recording debates in the "Senate
of Magna Lilliputia." In 1741 Johnson took over this task. From general in-

formation as to the course of discussion in Parliament he composed speeches which he ascribed to characters whose names were anagrams for the main contenders in the House.[10] The debates bore such an air of verisimilitude that many readers took them as verbatim reports, and Johnson had to warn Smollett (who was writing a history of England) not to rely on them as factual. Once, hearing praise of a speech ascribed to Chatham, Johnson remarked, "That speech I wrote in a garret in Exeter Street."[11] When someone commended the impartiality of his reports, he confessed: "I saved appearances tolerably well, but I took care that the Whig dogs should not have the best of it."[12]

How was he paid for his work? He once called Cave a "penurious paymaster," but he frequently professed affection for his memory. Between August 2, 1738, and April 21, 1739, Cave paid him forty-nine pounds; and in 1744 Johnson estimated fifty pounds a year as "undoubtedly more than the necessities of life require."[13] However, Johnson has been traditionally described as living in dire poverty in London in those years. Boswell believed that "Johnson and Savage were sometimes in such extreme indigence that they could not pay for a lodging, so that they wandered whole nights in the streets";[14] and Macaulay assumed that those months of penury habituated Johnson to slovenliness of dress and a "ravenous greediness" in eating.[15]

Richard Savage claimed, unconvincingly, to be the son of an earl, but he had become a wastrel when Johnson met him in 1737. They roamed the streets because they loved taverns more than their rooms. Boswell mentions "with all possible respect and delicacy" that Johnson's

> conduct after he came to London, and had associated with Savage and others, was not so strictly virtuous, in one respect, as when he was a younger man. It was well known that his amorous inclinations were uncommonly strong and impetuous. He owned to many of his friends that he used to take women of the town to taverns, and hear them relate their history.—In short, it must not be concealed that, like many other good and pious men [did Boswell have Boswell in mind?], . . . Johnson was not free from propensities which were ever "warring against the law of his mind"—and that in his combats with them he was sometimes overcome.[16]

Savage left London in July, 1739, and died in a debtor's prison in 1743. A year later Johnson issued *The Life of Richard Savage*, which Henry Fielding called "as just and well written a piece as, of its kind, I ever saw."[17] It presaged (and was later included in) the *Lives of the Poets*. It was published anonymously, but literary London soon discovered Johnson's authorship. The booksellers began to think of him as the man to compile a dictionary of the English language.

II. THE DICTIONARY: 1746–55

Hume had written in 1741: "We have no dictionary of our language, and scarcely a tolerable grammar."[18] He was mistaken, for Nathaniel Bailey had published *An Universal Etymological English Dictionary* in 1721, and this had had predecessors semi-lexicographical. The proposal for a new dictionary was apparently made by Robert Dodsley in the presence of Johnson, who said, "I believe I shall not undertake it."[19] But when other booksellers joined Dodsley in offering Johnson £1,575 if he would assume the obligation, he signed the contract, June 18, 1746.

After much rumination he drew up a thirty-four-page *Plan for a Dictionary of the English Language*, and had it printed. He sent this to several persons, among them Lord Chesterfield, then secretary of state, with some hopeful praise of the Earl's excellence in English and other departments. Chesterfield invited him to call. Johnson did; the Earl gave him ten pounds and a word of encouragement. Later Johnson called again, was kept waiting an hour, left in anger, and abandoned the idea of dedicating his work to Chesterfield.

He went to his task leisurely, then more diligently, for his fee was meted out to him in installments. When he reached the word *lexicographer* he defined it as "a writer of dictionaries, a harmless drudge . . ." He had hoped to finish in three years; he took nine. In 1749 he moved to Gough Square, off Fleet Street. He hired—and himself paid for—five or six secretaries, and set them to work in a third-floor room. He read the recognized English authors of the century from 1558 to 1660—from the accession of Elizabeth I to that of Charles II; he believed that the English language had in that period reached its highest excellence, and he proposed to take that Elizabethan-Jacobean speech as a standard by which to establish good usage. He drew a line under each sentence that he proposed to quote as illustrating the use of a word, and noted in the margin the first letter of the word to be defined. His aides were instructed to copy each marked sentence on a separate slip, and insert this at its alphabetical place in Bailey's dictionary, which served as a starting point and guide.

During these nine years he took many holidays from definitions. Sometimes he found it easier to write a poem than to define a word. On January 9, 1749, he issued a twelve-page poem, *The Vanity of Human Wishes*. Like the *London* of a decade earlier, it was in form an imitation of Juvenal, but it spoke with a power that was his own. He still resented his poverty, and Chesterfield's neglect:

> There mark what ills the scholar's life assail—
> Toil, envy, want, the patron, and the gaol.

How vain are the warrior's victories! See Charles XII of Sweden:

> He left the name, at which the world grew pale,
> To point a moral, or adorn a tale.[20]

How foolish, then, to pray for long life when we see the vanity, deceptions, and pains of old age: the mind wandering in repeated anecdotes, fortune shaking with every day's events, children scheming for a legacy and mourning death's delay, while "unnumbered maladies the joints invade, lay siege to life, and press the dire blockade."[21] From vain hopes and sure decay there is only one escape: prayer, and faith in a redeeming, rewarding God.

Yet this pessimist had happy moments. On February 6, 1749, Garrick staged *Irene*. It was a great event for Johnson; he washed himself, bound his paunch in a scarlet waistcoat trimmed with gold lace, flourished a hat likewise adorned, and watched his friend play Mohammed II to Mrs. Cibber's Irene. The tragedy ran for nine nights, and brought Johnson £200; it was never revived, but Dodsley gave him another £100 for the copyright. He was now (1749) sufficiently famous and opulent to found a club: not *The* Club, which came fifteen years later, but the "Ivy Lane Club," so named from the street where, at the King's Head Tavern, Johnson, Hawkins, and seven others met on Tuesday evenings to eat beefsteak and to barter prejudices. "Thither," said Johnson, "I constantly resorted."[22]

Every Tuesday and Friday from March 21, 1750, to March 14, 1752, he wrote a little essay published by Cave as *The Rambler*, for which he received four guineas a week. The essays sold fewer than five hundred copies, and Cave lost money on the venture, but when they were collected into a book they achieved twelve editions before Johnson's death. Shall we confess that the only numbers that we found interesting are 170 and 171,[23] in which Johnson made a prostitute point a moral and adorn her tale? Critics complained that the style and vocabulary were too sesquipedalianly Latinesque; but Boswell, between sins, found comfort in Johnson's exhortations to piety.[24]

Johnson was under special strain in those years, for his mind was fatigued by definitions, and his spirits were depressed by the deterioration of his wife. "Tetty" calmed the pains of age and solitude with alcohol and opium. Often she kept Johnson from her bed.[25] He rarely took her with him when he dined out. Dr. Taylor, who knew both of them intimately, said she "was the plague of Johnson's life, was abominably drunken and despicable in every way, and Johnson frequently complained . . . of his situation with such a wife."[26] Her death (March 28, 1752) made him forget her faults, and he developed a post-mortem uxoriousness that amused his friends. He extolled her virtues, lamented his loneliness, and hoped she would intercede for him with Christ.[27] "He told me," Boswell recalled, "that he generally went abroad at four in the afternoon, and seldom came home till two in the morning. . . . His place of frequent resort was the Mitre Tavern in Fleet Street, where he loved to sit up late."[28]

To be alone was terror. So Johnson, after his wife's death, took into his Gough Square home (1752) Anna Williams, a Welsh poetess who was losing her sight. An operation to cure her failed, and she became completely blind. Except for short intervals she stayed with Johnson till her death (1783), superintending the household and the kitchen, and carving the roast —and judging the fullness of cups with no other guide than her fingers. To care for his more intimate needs Johnson (1753) took a Negro servant, Frank Barber, who remained with him twenty-nine years. Johnson sent him to school, labored to have him learn Latin and Greek, and left him a substantial legacy. To complete the establishment Johnson invited a derelict doctor,

Robert Levett, to live with him (1760). The three formed a quarrelsome ménage, but Johnson was thankful for their company.

In January, 1755, he sent the final sheets of the *Dictionary* to the printer, who thanked God that he was nearly finished with such a job and such a man. News of the approaching publication reached Chesterfield, who hoped for a dedication. He tried to atone for his former invisibility by writing, for a magazine, two articles hailing the expected work, and praising Johnson as one whom he would be glad to accept as dictator of good English usage. The proud author sent the Earl (February 7, 1755) a letter which Carlyle described as "that far-famed Blast of Doom proclaiming that patronage should be no more":

MY LORD:

I have been lately informed, by the proprietor of *The World*, that two papers, in which my Dictionary is recommended to the Publick, were written by your Lordship. To be so distinguished is an honor, which, being little accustomed to favors from the great, I know not well how to receive, or in what terms to acknowledge. . . .

Seven years, my Lord, have now passed since I waited in your outward room, or was repulsed from your door; during which time I have been pushing on my work through difficulties, of which it is useless to complain, and have brought it, at last, to the verge of publication, without one act of assistance, one word of encouragement, or one smile of favor. Such treatment I did not expect, for I never had a Patron before. . . .

Is not a Patron, my Lord, one who looks with unconcern on a man struggling for life in the water, and, when he has reached ground, encumbers him with help? The notice which you have been pleased to take of my labors, had it been early, had been kind; but it has been delayed till I am indifferent, and cannot enjoy it; till I am solitary, and cannot impart it; till I am known, and do not want it. I hope it is no very cynical asperity not to confess obligations where no benefit has been received, or to be unwilling that the Publick should consider me as owing that to a Patron, which Providence has enabled me to do for myself.

Having carried on my work thus far with so little obligation to any favorer of learning, I shall not be disappointed though I should conclude it, if less be possible, with less. For I have been long wakened from that dream of hope in which I once boasted myself, with so much exaltation,

My Lord,

Your Lordship's most humble,
Most obedient servant,
SAM. JOHNSON[29]

Chesterfield's only comment on the letter was that it was "very well written." And indeed it is a masterpiece of eighteenth-century prose, quite free from the Latin derivatives that had sometimes clogged and burdened Johnson's style. Its author must have felt and pondered it deeply, for he recited it to Boswell from memory twenty-six years later.[30] It was not published till after Johnson's death. Presumably his resentment discolored his condemnation of Chesterfield's *Letters to His Son*—that "they teach the morals of a whore, and the manners of a dancing master."[31]

Johnson went up to Oxford early in 1755, partly to consult the libraries, but also to suggest to his friend Thomas Warton that it would help float the *Dictionary* if its author could put a degree after his name. Warton managed it, and in March Johnson was made an honorary Master of Arts. So at last the *Dictionary* was published, in two large folio volumes of almost 2,300 pages, priced at four pounds ten. In ending the preface Johnson proclaimed that

> the *English Dictionary* was written with little assistance of the learned, and without any patronage of the great; not in the soft obscurities of retirement, or under the shelter of academic bowers, but amid inconvenience and distraction, in sickness and in sorrow; and it may repress the triumph of malignant criticism to observe, that if our language is not here fully displayed, I have only failed in an attempt which no human powers have hitherto completed. . . . I have protracted my work till most of those whom I wished to please have sunk into the grave, and success and miscarriage are empty sounds; I therefore dismiss it with frigid tranquillity, having little to fear or hope from censure or praise.

The critics could not be expected to realize that Johnson's *Dictionary* marked a crest and watershed in the English literature of the eighteenth century, as the *Encyclopédie* (1751–72) of Diderot and d'Alembert marked a crest and turning point in the literature of France. Much fun was made of incidental defects in Johnson's work. Among the forty thousand entries there were oddities like *gentilitious* and *sygilate* (which are respectfully preserved by Webster). There were angry definitions like that of *pension:* "An allowance made to anyone without an equivalent. In England it is generally understood to mean pay given to a state hireling for treason to his country." Or *excise:* "a hateful tax on commodities." There were personal quirks, as in the definition of *oats:* "a grain which in England is generally given to horses, but in Scotland supports the people"—which was quite true. Boswell asked Johnson "if civilization was a word; he said No, but civility was."[32] Many of Johnson's etymologies are now rejected; he had much Latin and less Greek, but was poorly acquainted with modern languages; he admitted frankly that etymology was his weak point.[33] He defined *pastern* as "the knee of a horse" (it is part of a horse's foot); when a lady asked him how he came to make such a mistake he answered, "Ignorance, madam, pure ignorance."[34] In so large a work, whose every page gave a dozen openings to error, he could not escape missteps.

Johnson's achievement was appreciated abroad. The French Academy sent him a copy of its *Dictionnaire*, and the Accademia della Crusca of Florence sent him its *Vocabolario*.[35] The *Dictionary* sold well enough to please the booksellers, who paid Johnson to prepare an abbreviated edition. The larger form remained standard until Noah Webster replaced it in 1828. It placed Johnson at the head of English authors in his time; he actually acquired, except for aristocrats like Horace Walpole, a dictatorship over English letters. The reign of the "Great Cham of Literature" began.*

---

* *Cham* meant *khan*. The phrase was apparently first used by Smollett in a letter to Wilkes, March 16, 1759.

III. THE CHARMED CIRCLE

However, he was not above being arrested for debt. He had spent his payment for the *Dictionary* as fast as it came. On March 16, 1756, he wrote to Samuel Richardson: "Sir, I am obliged to entreat your assistance. I am now under arrest for five pounds eighteen shillings. . . . If you will be so good as to send me this sum, I will gratefully repay you, and add it to all former obligations."[36] Richardson sent six guineas. He earned his bread at this time by writing magazine articles, by composing sermons at two guineas for less articulate clergymen, by taking advance subscriptions to his promised edition of Shakespeare, and by contributing to *The Universal Chronicle* a weekly essay (April 15, 1758, to April 5, 1760) under the name of "The Idler." These were in a lighter vein than *The Rambler*, but still too grave and ponderous for those who must run as they read. One denounced vivisection; another exposed debtors' prisons; No. 5 lamented the separation of soldiers from their wives, and proposed squads of "Lady Hussars," who would handle commissary and nursing, and otherwise comfort their men.

In January, 1759, he learned that his ninety-year-old mother, whom he had not seen in twenty-two years, was nearing death. He borrowed money from a printer, and sent her six guineas in a tender letter. She died on January 23. To pay for her funeral and her debts he wrote in the evenings of one week (so he told Reynolds) *The History of Rasselas, Prince of Abyssinia*. He sent it to the printer part by part, and received £100 for it. On its publication in April the critics hailed it as a classic, and contrasted it patriotically with Voltaire's *Candide*, which appeared almost at the same time and dealt with the same problem—Can life bring happiness? Johnson did not delay his answer: "Ye who listen with phantoms of hope, who expect that old age will perform the promises of youth, and that the deficiencies of the present day will be supplied by the morrow; attend to the history of Rasselas."[37]

It was the custom of Abyssinian kings (Johnson tells us) to confine the heir to the throne to a pleasant and fertile valley until the time came for his accession. Everything was supplied him: a palace, good food, animal pets, intelligent companions. But in his twenty-sixth year Rasselas wearies of these delights. He misses not only liberty but struggle. "I should be happy if I had something to pursue." He ponders how he may escape this peaceful valley to see how other men seek and find happiness.

A skillful mechanic proposes to build a flying machine that will lift the Prince and himself above the encircling mountains to freedom. He explains:

> He that can swim needs not despair to fly; to swim is to fly in a grosser fluid, and to fly is to swim in a subtler. We are only to proportion our power of resistance to the different density of matter through which we pass. You will be necessarily upborne by the air if you can renew any impulse upon it faster than the air can recede from the pressure. . . . The labor of rising from the ground will be great, . . . but as we mount higher, the earth's attraction, and the body's gravity, will be gradually diminished till we arrive at a region where the man will float in the air without any tendency to fall.

Rasselas encourages the mechanic, who agrees to make a plane, "but only on this condition, that the art shall not be divulged, and that you shall not require me to make wings for any but ourselves." "Why," asks the Prince, "should you envy others so great an advantage?" "If men were all virtuous," the mechanic replies, "I should with great alacrity teach them to fly. But what would be the security of the good if the bad could at pleasure invade them from the sky?" He builds a plane, tries to fly, and falls into a lake, from which the Prince rescues him.[38]

Rasselas likes better to talk with Imlac the philosopher, who has seen many lands and men. They find a cave that leads to a passage into the outer world; they escape from their paradise, with the Prince's sister Nekayah and her maid. Armed with jewels as universal currency, they visit Cairo, join its pleasures, and tire of them. They hear a Stoic philosopher discourse on the conquest of passions; a few days later they find him wild with grief over his daughter's death. Having read pastoral poetry, they presume that shepherds must be happy; but they discover that the hearts of these men are "cankered with discontent" and with "malevolence toward those that are placed above them."[39] They come upon a hermit, and learn that he secretly longs for the delights of the city. They inquire into domestic felicity, and find every home darkened with discord and "the rude collisions of contrary desires."[40] They explore the Pyramids and judge them the summit of folly. They learn about the happy life of scholars and scientists; they meet a famous astronomer, who tells them that "integrity without knowledge is weak and useless, and knowledge without integrity is dangerous and dreadful";[41] but the astronomer goes mad. They conclude that no way of life on earth leads to happiness, and Imlac comforts them with a discourse on the immortality of the soul. They resolve to return to Abyssinia and accept the vicissitudes of life calmly in the confidence of a blessed resurrection.

It is an old story in one of its finest incarnations. What amazes us is the graceful flow and clarity of the style, far removed from the ponderous vocabulary of Johnson's essays, and even of his conversation. It seemed impossible that the learned lexicographer had written this simple tale, and quite incredible that he had turned out these 141 pages in seven days.

Meanwhile he had moved again, from Gough Square to Staple Inn (March 23, 1759); soon he would move to Gray's Inn, then to Inner Temple Lane. These changes were probably motivated by economy; but in July, 1762, Johnson was suddenly lifted into relative affluence by a pension of £300 a year granted him by George III on the advice of Lord Bute. Why this beneficence fell upon a man who had persistently opposed the Hanoverian dynasty, had belabored the Scots at every turn, and had described a pension as "pay given to a state hireling for treason to his country," has been the subject of many mystery stories. Johnson's enemies charged him with preferring money to principle, and assumed that Bute was looking for a mighty pen to answer Wilkes, Churchill, and others who were denigrating him with ink. Johnson claimed that he had accepted the pension on the explicit understanding, twice confirmed by Bute, that he would not be asked to write in support of the government.[42] He confided to Boswell that "the pleasure of cursing the House of Hanover, and drinking King James's health, was amply overbalanced by £300 a year."[43] In any case he earned the pension many times over, not so much by the political tracts of later years, but by enriching English literature with pen and speech, with wisdom and cleansing wit.

He had enough friends to afford a scattering of enemies. "Friendship," he said, "is the cordial drop to make the nauseous draft of life go down."[44] In almost every gathering that he attended he became the center of conversation, not so much because he forced his way to it, but because he was the most individual personality in the literary circles of London, and could be relied upon to say something whenever he spoke. It was Reynolds who suggested the formation of "the Club," which Boswell later called "the Literary Club"; Johnson seconded the motion, and on April 16, 1764, the new group began its Monday-evening meetings at the Turk's Head in Gerrard Street, Soho. The original members were Reynolds, Johnson, Burke, Goldsmith, Christopher Nugent, Topham Beauclerk, Bennet Langton, Anthony Chamier, and Sir John Hawkins. Others were added later by vote of the Club: Gibbon, Garrick, Sheridan, Fox, Adam Smith, Dr. Burney . . .

Boswell did not win admission till 1773, partly, it may be, because he was only occasionally in London. During the twenty-one years between his meeting with Johnson and Johnson's death, he spent no more than two years and a few weeks within reach of his idol. The unconcealed warmth of his admiration, and Johnson's awareness that Boswell was planning a biography of him, made the older man forgive the Scot's almost sycophantic idolatry. A good talker and a good listener make a happy couple. Johnson had no high regard for Boswell's brains. When "Bozzy," as he called him, remarked that the wine he had drunk in the course of their conversation had given him a headache, Johnson corrected him: "Nay, sir, it was not the wine that made your head ache, but the *sense* that I put into it." "What, sir," Boswell exclaimed, "will sense make the head ache?" "Yes, sir, when it is not used to it."[45] (There are passages in the *Life* where Boswell seems to be talking better sense than Johnson.) Praising Pope's *Dunciad*, Johnson noted that it had given some dunces a lasting fame, and continued his fun: "It was worth while being a dunce then. Ah, sir, hadst thou lived in those days!"[46] But the aging bear soon learned to like his cub. "There are few people whom I take so much to as you," he told him in 1763.[47] "Boswell," he said, "never left a house without leaving a wish for his return."[48] In 1775 Boswell was given a room in Johnson's lodgings to sleep in when the conversation had kept him late.[49]

On March 31, 1772, he wrote in his journal: "I have constant plan to write the life of Mr. Johnson. I have not told him of it yet, nor do I know if I should tell him." But Johnson knew of it by April, 1773, if not sooner.[50] Others knew of it, and resented Boswell's way of raising controversial questions with the evident aim of drawing the old master out and getting some new gem for the biography. The inquisitive Scot boasted that "the fountain was at times locked up till I opened the spring."[51] The Johnson that we know and relish might never have taken form without the stimulus of Boswell's fond provocation and tireless pursuit. How different is the Johnson that we find in Hawkins' *Life*, or even in the lively *Anecdotes* of Mrs. Thrale!

It was in January, 1765, that Johnson began with the Thrales an association that played a larger part in his life than his friendship for Boswell. Henry Thrale was a brewer, son of a brewer. He had received a good education, had traveled, and was to certify his status by being elected to Parliament. In 1763 he married Hester Lynch Salusbury, a Welsh girl only five feet tall but vivacious and intelligent. Henry, twelve years her senior, absorbed himself in his business, but attended to his wife sufficiently to make her pregnant annually between 1764 and 1778, and to convey to her his venereal infection.[52] She bore him twelve children, of whom eight died in infancy. She solaced herself with literature, and when her husband brought home with him the famous Samuel Johnson, she used all her feminine arts and graces to attach him to the family. Soon he was dining with the Thrales every Thursday in their Southwark home; and from 1766 onward he usually spent the summer with them in their country villa at Streatham in Surrey. With Johnson as a center, Mrs. Thrale made her home a salon, to which came Reynolds, Goldsmith, Garrick, Burke, the Burneys, and finally and jealously Boswell—for he learned that Mrs. Thrale was gathering notes about her lion's looks and ways and words. So the *Life* was to have a rival.

IV. URSUS MAJOR

What was the Great Bear like? Boswell, after their first meeting (1763) wrote: "Mr. Johnson is a man of a most dreadful appearance. . . . A very big man, troubled with sore eyes, the palsy [a nervous tic] and the king's evil. He is very slovenly in his dress, and speaks with a most uncouth voice."[53] Mrs. Thrale described him in his later years: "His stature was remarkably high, and his limbs exceedingly large. . . . His features strongly marked, his countenance particularly rugged. . . . His sight was near, and otherwise imperfect; yet his eyes . . . were so wild, so piercing, and at times so fierce, that fear was, I believe, the first emotion in the eyes of all his beholders."[54]

He deplored as "a waste of time" the hours spent in sitting for a portrait; however, he did this ten times for Reynolds, and once for a bust by Nollekens. In 1756 Sir Joshua showed him as already stout and indolent;[55] in 1770 he painted him in profile and made him look like Goldsmith;[56] in 1772 the most famous of the portraits delivered him to posterity as a man of ungainly bulk, enormous wig, large full face, lowering brows over puzzled eyes, massive nose, thick lips, and double chin. His wig was repeatedly dislodged by convulsive movements of his head, shoulders, and hands.[57] He was careless in his dress; "fine clothes," he told Boswell, "are good only as they supply the want of other means of procuring respect."[58] Not until he became a guest of the Thrales did he bother much about personal hygiene.

He ate voraciously, having much space to fill, and perhaps recalling hungry years. Boswell reported:

> I never knew any man who relished good eating more than he did. When at table he was totally absorbed in the business of the moment; his looks seemed riveted to his plate; nor would he, unless when in very high company, say one word, or pay the least attention to what was said by others, till he had satisfied his appetite; which was so fierce . . . that the veins of his forehead swelled, and generally a strong perspiration was visible.[59]

He ate fish with his fingers, "because I am shortsighted, and afraid of bones."[60] He could hardly bear the sight of vegetables. In his heartier days he "loved to exhilarate himself with wine, but was never intoxicated but once."[61] When Mrs. Williams denounced drunkenness, saying, "I wonder what pleasure men can take in making beasts of themselves," Johnson retorted, "I wonder, madam, that you have not penetration enough to see the strong inducement to this excess, for he who makes a beast of himself gets rid of the pain of being a man."[62] But drinking, he said, "does not improve conversation; it alters the mind so that you are pleased with any conversation."[63] In later life he shunned all liquor, and contented himself with chocolate, lemonade, and countless cups of tea. He never smoked. "It is a shocking thing, blowing smoke out of our mouths into other people's mouths, eyes, and noses, and having the same thing done to us." He explained the habit of smoking as "preserving the mind from utter vacuity."[64]

His boorish manners were partly a relic of his days and nights in the lower depths, partly the result of physical irritations and mental fears. He was strong, and proud of it; he could knock down a bookseller with little fear of retaliation; he could pick up and throw aside a man who had dared to occupy a chair that Johnson had temporarily vacated; he mounted a horse and joined Thrale in a fifty-mile cross-country foxhunt. But he had difficulty in carrying his own weight. "When he walked the streets, what with the constant roll of his head, and the concomitant motion of his body, he appeared to make his way by that motion, independent of his feet."[65] When he rode "he had no command or direction of his horse, but was carried as if in a balloon."[66]

He suffered, after 1776, from asthma, gout, and dropsy. These and other physical difficulties must have intensified his melancholy, which at times so depressed him that "I would consent to have a limb amputated to recover my spirits."[67] He would not believe that any man was happy; of one who claimed to be so he said, "It is all cant; the dog knows he is miserable all the time."[68] A physician having told him that hypochondria sometimes led to insanity, Johnson feared that he would go insane.[69] "Of the uncertainties of our present state," he made Imlac say in *Rasselas*, "the most dreadful and alarming is the uncertain continuance of reason."[70]

Being nearsighted, he found little pleasure in the beauty of women, nature, or art.[71] He thought sculpture was overrated. "The value of statuary is owing to its difficulty. You would not value the finest head cut upon a carrot."[72] He tried to learn some musical instrument, "but I never made out a tune." "Pray, sir," he asked, "who is this Bach? Is he a piper?"[73]—referring to Johann Christian Bach, then (1771) the most famous pianist in England. He felt that music was being spoiled by digital acrobatics. Hearing a violinist praised because the feats he performed were so difficult, Johnson exclaimed, "Difficult—I wish it had been impossible."[74]

So vigorous a man must have found it troublesome to deal with the sexual fancies that agitate even the normal mind. When he attended the première of *Irene*, and was brought by Garrick into the "greenroom" where the players waited between scenes, he rejected a suggestion that he repeat this visit. "No, David, I will never come back. For the white bubbies and the silk stockings of your actresses excite my genitals."[75] Boswell was astonished to hear him say, one day in the Hebrides, "I have often thought that if I kept a seraglio . . ."[76]

In general his faults were more obvious than his virtues, which were quite as real. We might justly invert Horace Walpole's comment that "though he was good-natured at bottom he was very ill-natured at top."[77] Goldsmith said the same thing more graciously: "Johnson has a roughness in his manner, but no man alive has a more tender heart. He has nothing of the bear but the skin."[78] Untidy, indolent, superstitious, rude, dogmatic, proud, he was also kind, humane, generous, quick to ask forgiveness and to forgive. Mrs. Thrale reckoned that Johnson gave away £200 of his £300 pension;[79] and she added:

> He nursed whole nests of people in his house. . . . Commonly spending the middle of the week at our house, he kept his numerous family in Fleet Street upon a settled allowance, but returned to them every Saturday to give them three good dinners, and his company, before he came back to us on the Monday night—treating them with the same, or perhaps more ceremonious civility than he would have done by as many people of fashion.[80]

He wrote prefaces, dedications, sermons, even legal opinions, for others, often gratis. He labored by word and pen to save Dr. William Dodd from the gallows. Seeing a prostitute lying in the street he (then seventy-five) took her on his back, carried her to his rooms, cared for her till she was well, and "endeavored to put her in a virtuous way of living."[81] George Steevens, who collaborated with him in editing Shakespeare, said: "Could the many bounties he studiously concealed, the many acts of humanity he performed in private, be displayed with equal circumstantiality [as his frailties], his defects would be so far lost in the blaze of his virtues that the latter only would be regarded."[82]

In the last nineteen years of his life he wrote only one substantial book—*Lives of the Poets;* otherwise he substituted the tongue for the pen. He described himself as "a man who loves to fold his legs and have out his talk."[83] If we leave eating aside, he lived most when he was talking to an intelligent company. He had gathered, by observation and reading, an extraordinary fund and range of knowledge about human affairs; he carried much of it in his lumber room of memory, and he welcomed a chance to unburden himself. Yet he seldom initiated any serious discussion; he spoke up only when someone raised a subject or a challenge. He was always tempted to oppose what another had said; he was ready to defend any proposition or its opposite; he relished debate, knowing himself invincible; and he was resolved to win the argument, even if truth should perish beneath his blows. He knew that this was not the finest kind of conversation, but he was sure that it was the most interesting. In the heat and zest of the conflict he found little place for courtesy. "He spared none of us," said Boswell.[84] To one disputant: "I have found you an argument, but I am not obliged to find you an understanding."[85] "There is no arguing with Johnson," said Goldsmith; "for if his pistol misses fire he knocks you down with the butt."[86] "When I called upon Dr. Johnson next morning," Boswell relates, "I found him highly satisfied with his colloquial powers the preceding evening. 'Well (said he), we had a good talk.' *Boswell.* 'Yes, Sir, you tossed and gored several persons.' "[87] Thomas Sheridan called him a bully,[88] and Gibbon called him a bigot.[89] Lord Monboddo called him "the most invidious and malignant man I have ever known, who praised no author or book that other people praised [he praised Fanny Burney's *Evelina*], and . . . could not with any patience hear any other person draw the attention of the company for ever so short a time."[90] Horace Walpole, secure in his sinecures, shuddered at thought of him, and summed him up as seen by the son of a Whig prime minister:

> With a lumber of learning and some strong points, Johnson was an odious and mean character. By principle a Jacobite, arrogant, self-sufficient, and overbearing. . . . He had prostituted his pen to party even in a dictionary, and had afterwards, for a pension, contradicted his own definitions. His manners were sordid, supercilious, and brutal, his style ridiculously bombastic and vicious, and in one word, with all the pedantry he had all the gigantic littleness of a country schoolmaster. . . . What will posterity think of us when it reads what an idol we adored?[91]

Ideally, of course, the best conversation is in a small unhurried group where all are informed and courteous; or, as Johnson put it in an amiable interlude: "That is the happiest conversation where there is no competition, no vanity, but a calm quiet interchange of sentiments";[92] but when did he have that experience? "Treating your adversary with respect," he told Boswell, presumably with a twinkle in his eyes, "is giving him an advantage to which he is not entitled."[93] We who never felt his butt forgive him all those blows and insults and prejudices because his wit and humor and penetration, his preference of realities to pretenses, of candor to cant, and his capacity for concentrating wisdom in a phrase, make him one of the most dominating characters in English history.

V. THE CONSERVATIVE MIND

Shall we give him the floor? He had something interesting to say on almost everything under the sun. He thought life a misfortune which no one would want to repeat, and which most people "supported with impatience and quitted with reluctance."[94] When Lady McLeod asked him "if no man was naturally good," he answered, "No, madam, no more than a wolf."[95] "Men are evidently . . . so corrupt that all the laws of heaven and earth are insufficient to restrain them from crimes."[96] "Men hate more sturdily than they love; and if I have said something to hurt a man once, I shall not get the better of this by saying many things to please him."[97]

He did not often discuss economics. He denounced the exploitation of colonial peoples,[98] and strongly condemned slavery; once, at Oxford, he astonished some professors by proposing a toast to "the insurrection of the Negroes in the West Indies."[99] However, he thought that "raising the wages of day laborers is wrong; for it does not make them live better, but [said the Idler] only makes them idler, and idleness is a very bad thing for human nature."[100] Like Blackstone, he upheld the sanctity of property rights; and like his antipodes, Voltaire, he defended luxury as giving work to the poor, instead of corroding them with charity.[101] He anticipated Adam Smith in advocating free enterprise.[102] But the multiplication of merchants irritated him. "I am afraid the increase of commerce, and the incessant struggle for riches which commerce excites, gives no prospect of an end speedily to be expected of artifice and fraud. . . . Violence gives way to cunning."[103] He made no pretense of despising money, having suffered from its lack, and he thought that "no man but a blockhead ever wrote except for money"[104] —which underestimated vanity.

He felt (recall the lines he added to Goldsmith's *Traveller*) that we exaggerate the importance of politics. "I would not give half a crown to live under one form of government rather than another."[105] Hence "most schemes of political improvement are very laughable things."[106] Yet he had been hot against the "Whig dogs," and it took a pension to reconcile him to the Hanoverians. He called patriotism "the last refuge of a scoundrel,"[107] but he defended with patriotic warmth the right of Britain to the Falkland Islands (1771), and he had an almost chauvinistic scorn of the Scots and the French.

He quite anticipated, in 1763, Burke's apologia for conservatism. "Human experience, which is constantly contradicting theory, is the great test of truth. A system built on the discoveries of a great many minds is always of more strength than what is produced by the mere workings of any one mind."[108] After 1762 he was quite content with the status quo. He praised the British government as "approaching nearer to perfection than anything that experience has shown us, or history related."[109] He admired aristocracy and class distinctions and privileges as necessary for social order and prudent legislation.[110] "I am a friend to subordination. It is most conducive to the happiness of society. . . . Submission is the duty of the ignorant, and content the virtue of the poor."[111] He mourned, like every generation, that

> subordination is sadly broken down in this age. No man now has the same authority which his father had—except a gaoler. No master has it over his servants; it is diminished in our colleges, nay, in our grammar schools. . . . There are many causes, the chief of which is, I think, the great increase of money. . . . Gold and silver destroy feudal subordination. But, besides, there is a gen-

eral relaxation of reverence. No son now depends upon his father, as in former times. . . . My hope is that as anarchy produces tyranny, this extreme relaxation will produce *freni strictio* [a tightening of the reins].[112]

Contemplating the London populace, Johnson judged that democracy would be a disaster. He laughed at liberty and equality as impracticable shibboleths.[113] "So far is it from being true that men are naturally equal, that no two people can be half an hour together but one shall acquire an evident superiority over the other."[114] In 1770 he wrote a pamphlet, *The False Alarm*, condemning radicalism, and justifying the exclusion of Wilkes from Parliament.

In another pamphlet, *The Patriot* (1774), Johnson renewed his attack on Wilkes, and moved on to what Boswell called "an attempt to reduce our fellow subjects in America to unconditional submission."[115] In earlier writings Johnson had spoken with occasional impartiality on the American colonies. These had been "snatched upon no very just principles of policy," largely because other European states were snatching too much,[116] and England wished to protect herself from a France and a Spain made dangerously strong by absorbing America. He had praised the French colonists for treating the Indians humanely and intermarrying with them, and he had condemned the British colonists for defrauding the Indians and oppressing the Negroes.[117] But when the colonists talked of liberty, justice, and natural rights, Johnson scorned their claims as specious cant, and asked, "How is it that we hear the loudest yelps for liberty among the drivers of Negroes?"[118] He stated the case against the emancipation of the colonies in a powerful brochure, *Taxation No Tyranny* (1775). This was apparently written at the request of the ministry, for Johnson complained (says Boswell) that his pension had been given him "as a literary character," and now he had been "applied by the administration to write political pamphlets."[119]

By accepting the protection of Great Britain (Johnson argued) the colonists had implicitly recognized the right of the British government to tax them. Taxation, to be just, did not require the direct representation of the taxed persons in the government; half the population of England was without representatives in Parliament, and yet it accepted taxation as a fair return for the social order and legal protection provided by the government. Hawkins, who had supplied Johnson with arguments,[120] thought that *Taxation No Tyranny* "has never received an answer,"[121] but Boswell, remembering Corsica, took the American side, deplored the "extreme violence" of Johnson's pen, and said: "That this pamphlet was written at the desire of those who were then in power I have no doubt; and indeed he owned to me that it had been revised and curtailed by some of them."[122] One passage deleted by the ministry predicted that the Americans would, "in a century and a quarter, be more than equal to the inhabitants of [Western] Europe."[123]

There were some liberal elements in his political philosophy. He preferred Fox to Pitt II, and was induced to dine with Wilkes, who overcame Johnson's political principles by helping him to some fine veal.[124] And in one passage the old Tory flirted with revolution:

> When we consider in abstracted speculation the unequal distribution of the pleasures of life, . . . when it is apparent that many want the necessaries of nature, and many more the comforts and conveniences of life; that the idle live at ease by the fatigues of the diligent, and the luxurious are pampered with delicacies untasted by those who supply them; . . . when the greater number must always want [lack] what the smaller are enjoying and squandering without use; it seems impossible to conceive that the peace of society can long subsist; it were natural to expect that no man would be left long in possession of super-fluous enjoyments while such numbers are destitute of real necessaries.[125]

His conservatism returned to full force when he spoke of religion. After a youthful year of skepticism[126] he gave increasingly ardent support to the doctrines and privileges of the Established Church. Sometimes he inclined to Catholicism: he liked the idea of purgatory, and when he heard that an Anglican clergyman had been converted to the Roman Church he said, "God bless him!"[127] "He defended the Inquisition," Boswell tells us, "and maintained that false doctrine should be checked on its first appearance; that the civil power should unite with the Church in punishing those who dare to attack the established religion, and that such only were punished by the Inquisition."[128] He hated Dissenters, and applauded the expulsion of Methodists from Oxford.[129] He refused to speak to a lady who left the Established Church to join the Quakers.[130] He reproved Boswell for his mild friendship with the "atheist" Hume. When Adam Smith assured him that Hume led an exemplary life, Johnson cried out, "You lie!" To which Smith retorted, "You are a son of a bitch."[131] Johnson felt that religion was indispensable to social order and morality, and that only the hope of a happy immortality could reconcile one to the tribulations of earthly life. He believed in angels and devils, and thought that "we are all to reside hereafter either in the regions of horror or bliss."[132] He accepted the reality of witches and ghosts; he believed that his dead wife had appeared to him.[133]

He did not care for science; he praised Socrates for trying to turn investigation from the stars to man.[134] He abhorred vivisection. He took no interest in exploration; the discovery of unknown lands would only lead to "conquest and robbery."[135] He thought philosophy was an intellectual labyrinth leading either to religious doubt or to metaphysical nonsense. So he refuted Berkeley's idealism by kicking a stone, and defended free will by telling Boswell, "We *know* our will is free, and there's an end on 't. . . . All theory is against the freedom of the will, all experience for it."[136]

He rejected with disgust the whole philosophy of the French Enlightenment. He denied the right of an individual mind, however brilliant, to sit in judgment on institutions that the trial-and-error experience of the race had built up to protect social order against the unsocial impulses of men. He felt that the Catholic Church, with all its faults, was performing a vital function in preserving French civilization, and he condemned as shallow fools the *philosophes* who were weakening the religious supports of the moral code. Voltaire and Rousseau seemed to him two varieties of imbecile: Voltaire an intellectual fool, Rousseau a sentimental fool; but the difference between them was so slight that it was "difficult to settle the proportion of iniquity between them."[137] He reproved Boswell for courting Rousseau in Switzerland, and deplored the hospitality that England was offering the author of *Émile* (1766). "Rousseau, Sir, is a very bad man. I would sooner sign a sentence for his transportation than that of any felon who has gone from the Old Bailey these many years. Yes, Sir, I should like to have him work in the plantations."[138]

Johnson was not as conservative as his opinions. He gaily broke a hundred conventions in conduct, speech, and dress. He was not a prig; he laughed at the Puritans, he favored dancing, cardplaying, the theater. However, he condemned Fielding's *Tom Jones*, and was shocked to hear that prim Hannah More had read it.[139] He was afraid of sensuality in literature because he had difficulty in suppressing his own sensual impulses and imagination. One would have supposed from his doctrines that he had not enjoyed life, but we can see in Boswell that he relished "the full tide of human existence." He pronounced life painful and worthless, but, like most of us, he prolonged it as much as he could, and faced with angry reluctance his declining years.

VI. AUTUMN: 1763–80

In 1765 he moved from the Inner Temple to a three-story house at No. 7 Johnson's Court in Fleet Street; it was named after an earlier resident. There Boswell found him on returning from the Continent. In July he was given the honorary degree of Doctor of Laws by the University of Dublin; now for the first time he was Dr. Johnson, but he never attached the title to his name.[140]

In October, 1765, he issued in eight volumes his edition of Shakespeare, eight years later than he had promised it to his subscribers. He dared to point out faults, absurdities, and childish verbal conceits in the Bard; he censured him for having no moral purpose; he thought that Shakespeare had left "perhaps not one play which, if it were now exhibited as the work of a contemporary writer, would be heard to the conclusion."[141] But he praised the poet for subordinating the love interest in the greater dramas, and for making his protagonists not heroes but men; and he vigorously defended, against Voltaire, Shakespeare's neglect of the unities of time and place.[142] Critics challenged many of his comments and corrections; the edition was superseded by Edmund Malone's in 1790; but Malone acknowledged that his own edition was based on Johnson's, and he overvalued Johnson's preface as "perhaps the finest composition in our language."[143]

In 1767, while visiting Buckingham Palace, Johnson came upon George III; they exchanged compliments. Meanwhile the friendship with Boswell warmed to such a degree that in 1773 Johnson accepted his admirer's invitation to join him in a tour of the Hebrides. It was a brave undertaking for a man of sixty-four. It began with a long and arduous stagecoach ride from London to Edinburgh. There he met Robertson, but refused to meet Hume. On August 18 he and Boswell and a servant started north in a post chaise along the east coast to Aberdeen; thence they struck across the rugged High-lands through Banff to Inverness, and then mostly on horseback through Anoch to Glenelg on the west coast. There they took a boat to the island of Skye, which they toured rather thoroughly from September 2 to October 3. They encountered many hardships, which Johnson took with glum courage; he slept upon hay in barns, evaded vermin, clambered over rocks, and rode with precarious dignity on ponies hardly larger than himself. At one stop a lady of the Macdonald clan sat on his knee and kissed him. "Do it again," he said, "and let us see who will tire first."[144] On October 3 the party left by open boat for a forty-mile ride to the island of Coll and thence to the island of Mull. They crossed back to the mainland on October 22, and then traveled through Argyllshire via Dumbarton and Glasgow to Auchinleck (November 2). There Johnson met Boswell's father, who entertained him honorably, though lamenting his anti-Scot prejudices; they had a debate so violent that Boswell refused to record it. Boswell Senior afterward dubbed Johnson "Ursa Major," which the son gracefully interpreted as meaning not Great Bear but "a constellation of genius and learning."[145] The travelers reached Edinburgh November 9, eighty-three days after leaving it. Looking back upon their hardships, they "heartily laughed at the ravings of those absurd visionaries who have attempted to persuade us of the specious advantages of a state of nature." Johnson left Edinburgh November 22, and reached London on the twenty-sixth. In 1775 he published *A Journey to the Western Islands of Scotland*; it was not as racy as even the bowdlerized account that Boswell issued in 1785 as *A Journal of a Tour to the Hebrides with Samuel Johnson*, for philosophy is less interesting than biography; but some passages[146] have a placid beauty that reveal Johnson again as a master of English prose.

On April 1, 1775, Oxford finally came around to giving Johnson the honorary degree of Doctor of Civil Law. In March, 1776, he moved for the last time, to No. 8 Bolt Court, taking his motley family with him. In a strange mood of exuberance he wrote to the Lord Chamberlain (April 11, 1776) asking for an apartment in Hampton Court Palace: "I hope that to a man who has had the honor of vindicating his Majesty's government, a retreat in one of his houses may not be improperly or unworthily allowed."[147] The Lord Chamberlain regretted that there was a surfeit of applicants.

One more achievement remained. Forty London booksellers joined in preparing a many-volumed edition of the English poets, and asked Johnson to introduce each poet with a biography. They let him name his terms; he required £200; had he "asked one thousand, or even fifteen hundred guineas," said Malone, "the booksellers, who knew the value of his name, would doubtless have readily given it."[148] Johnson had thought of writing "little lives"; he forgot that one of the laws of composition is that a pen in motion, like matter in Newton's first law, continues in motion unless it is compelled to change that state by forces impressed upon it from without. Of the minor poets he wrote with laudable brevity, but with Milton, Addison, and Pope he let himself go, and wrote essays—of sixty, forty-two, 102 pages—that are among the finest specimens of literary criticism in the English language.

His view of Milton was colored by his dislike of the Puritans, their politics, and their regicide. He read Milton's prose as well as his verse, and called him "an acrimonious and surly republican."[149] The essay on Pope (which in the original edition ran to 373 pages) was the last blow struck for the classic style in English poetry, by the greatest inheritor of that style in English prose. He, who knew Greek well, supposed that Pope's translation of the *Iliad* had improved upon Homer. He praised Gray's "Elegy," but dismissed the odes as cluttered with mythological machinery. When the ten volumes of *The Lives of the Poets* were published (1779–81), some readers were shocked by Johnson's unorthodox but pontifical judgments, his insensitivity to the subtler graces of poetry, his tendency to rate and berate poets according to the moral tendency of their poems and their lives. Walpole declared, "Dr. Johnson has indubitably neither taste nor ear nor criterion of judgment but his old woman's prejudices,"[150] and laughed at "this weight on stilts," who "seems to have read the ancients with no view but of pilfering polysyllables."[151] Why, then, are these *Lives* more widely and fondly read than any other product of Johnson's pen? Perhaps because of those very prejudices and the candor of their expression. He made literary criticism a living force, and almost raised the dead with his chastisements.

VII. RELEASE: 1781–84

There is a secret pride in surviving our contemporaries, but we are punished with loneliness. The death of Henry Thrale (April 4, 1781) was the beginning of the end for Johnson. He served as one of four executors of the brewer's will, but thereafter his visits to the Thrale family lessened. Long before her husband's death Mrs. Thrale had begun to weary of the strains put upon her by Johnson's need for attentions and attentive ears. Thrale had kept his captive bear in reasonably good behavior, but (the widow complained), "when there was nobody to restrain his [Johnson's] dislikes it was extremely difficult to find anybody with whom he could converse without living always on the verge of a quarrel. . . . Such accidents occurred too often, and I was forced . . . to retire to Bath, where I knew Mr. Johnson would not follow me."[152]

The *Morning Post* made matters worse by announcing that a treaty of marriage between Johnson and Mrs. Thrale was "on tap."[153] Boswell composed a burlesque "Ode by Samuel Johnson to Mrs. Thrale upon Their Supposed Approaching Nuptials."[154] But in 1782 Johnson was seventy-three and Mrs. Thrale was forty-one. It was not of her own will that she had married Thrale; he had often neglected her, and she had never learned to love him. Now she claimed a right to love and be loved, and to find a mate for the second half of her life. She was at an age when a woman urgently longs for some physical and understanding companionship. Even before her husband's death she had developed a fondness for Gabriel Piozzi, who was giving music lessons to her daughters. Born in Italy, he had taken up residence in England in 1776, and was now about forty-two years old. When she first met him, at a party given by Dr. Burney, she mimicked his mannerisms as he per-formed at the piano. But his elegant manners, his amiable temper, and his musical accomplishments made him a relieving contrast to Johnson. Now that she was free she abandoned herself to romance. She confessed to her four surviving daughters her desire for remarriage. They were alarmed; re-marriage would affect their financial expectations; marriage to a musician —worse yet, a Roman Catholic—would hurt their social standing. They pleaded with their mother to reconsider; she tried and failed. Piozzi behaved like a gentleman: he went off to Italy (April, 1783), and stayed away almost a year. When he returned (March, 1784) and found Mrs. Thrale still eager, he yielded. The daughters refused their consent, and moved to Brighton.

On June 30 Mrs. Thrale sent Johnson an announcement that she and Piozzi were to be married. He replied (July 2, 1784):

MADAM:
   If I interpret your letter aright, you are ignominiously married; if it is yet undone, let us once more talk together. If you have abandoned your children and your religion, God forgive your wickedness; if you have forfeited your fame [reputation] and your country, may your folly do no further mischief. If the last act is yet to do, I, who have loved you, esteemed you, reverenced you, and served you, I who long thought you the first of womankind, entreat that, before your fate is irrevocable, I may once more see you.
   I was, I once was, Madam, most truly yours,
                                           SAM. JOHNSON[155]

Mrs. Thrale resented the word "ignominious" as a slur on her fiancé. She an-swered Johnson on July 4: "Till you have changed your opinion of Mr. Piozzi let us converse no more." She married Piozzi on July 23. All Lon-don agreed with Johnson in condemning her. On November 11 Johnson told Fanny Burney, "I never speak of her, and I desire never to hear of her more."[156]

These events must have taken a toll of Johnson's failing vitality. He found it increasingly difficult to sleep, and resorted to opium to ease his pains and quiet his nerves. On January 16, 1782, his "doctor in ordinary," Robert Levett, died; whose turn would it be next? Johnson had always feared death; now this and his belief in hell made his final years a mixture of heavy dinners and theological terrors. "I am afraid I may be one of those who shall be damned," he told Dr. William Adams, master of Pembroke College; and when Adams asked what he meant by "damned" he cried out, "Sent to hell, sir, and punished everlastingly."[157] Boswell could not help contrasting the calm with which the unbelieving Hume had approached his end.[158]

On June 17, 1783, Johnson suffered a mild stroke—"a confusion and indis-tinctness in my head, which lasted, I suppose, half a minute. . . . My speech was taken from me. I had no pain."[159] A week later he was well enough to dine at the Club, and in July he astonished his intimates by making excur-sions to Rochester and Salisbury. "What a man am I," he exclaimed to Haw-kins, "who have got the better of three diseases—the palsy, the gout, and the asthma—and can now enjoy the conversation of my friends!"[160] But on September 6 Mrs. Williams died, and his loneliness became intolerable. Finding the Club insufficient—for several of the old members (Goldsmith, Garrick, Beauclerk) were dead, and some of the new ones were distasteful to him— he founded (December, 1783) the "Evening Club," which met at an alehouse in Essex Street; there any decent person, by paying threepence, might come in and hear him talk, three nights a week. He invited Reynolds to join; Sir Joshua refused. Hawkins and others thought the new club a "degradation of those powers which had given delight" to more august persons.[161]

On June 3, 1784, he was well enough to journey with Boswell to Lichfield and Oxford. Returning to London, Boswell persuaded Reynolds and other friends to ask the Chancellor to provide money whereby Johnson might be enabled to take a trip to Italy for his health; Johnson said he would prefer a doubling of his pension. The Chancellor refused. On July 2 Boswell left for Scotland. He never saw Johnson again.

The asthma that had been overcome returned, and dropsy was added. "My breath is very short," he wrote to Boswell in November, 1784, "and the water is now increasing upon me."[162] Reynolds, Burke, Langton, Fanny Burney, and others came to bid him a last goodbye. He wrote his will; he left £2,000, of which £1,500 were bequeathed to his Negro servant.[163] Several doctors treated him, refusing any fee. He begged them to lance his legs more deeply; they would not; when they were gone he plunged lancets or scissors deep into his calves, hoping to release more water and reduce the painful swelling; some water came, but also ten ounces of blood. That evening, December 13, 1784, he died. A week later he was buried in Westminster Abbey.

He was the strangest figure in literary history, stranger even than Scarron or Pope. It is at first acquaintance hard to like him; he covered his tenderness with brutality, and the coarseness of his manners rivaled the propriety of his books. No one received so much adulation and gave so little praise. But the older we become, the more wisdom we find in his words. He surrounded his wisdom with platitudes, but he elevated platitudes to epigrams by the force or color of his speech. We might compare him with Socrates, who also talked at the slightest provocation, and is remembered for his spoken words. Both were stimulating gadflies, but Socrates asked questions and gave no answers, Johnson asked no questions and answered all. Socrates was certain about nothing, Johnson was certain about everything. Both appealed to science to leave the stars alone and study man. Socrates faced death like a philosopher and with a smile; Johnson faced it with religious tremors rivaling his enervating pains.

No one now idealizes him. We can understand why the English aristocracy—excepting Langton and Beauclerk—avoided him and ignored his pontificate. We realize what a John Bull he would have been in the china shop of the nobility, or amid the precious bric-a-brac of Strawberry Hill. He was not designed for beauty, but he served to frighten some of us out of cant, hypocrisy, and gush, and to make us look at ourselves with fewer delusions about the nature of man or the ecstasies of freedom. There must have been something lovable in a man to whom Reynolds and Burke and Goldsmith could listen through a thousand and one nights, and something fascinating in one who could inspire a great biography, and fill its twelve hundred pages with enduring life.

VIII. BOSWELL *MORITURUS*

When the Great Bear was dead the literary flock swarmed about him to draw some sustenance from his corpse. Boswell himself did not hurry; he worked for seven years on the *Life;* but he issued in 1785 his *Journal of a Tour to the Hebrides with Samuel Johnson;* it reached a third edition in one year. Hester Thrale Piozzi had gathered material about Johnson's words and ways; now, from these *Thraliana*, she compiled *Anecdotes of the Late Samuel Johnson, LL.D., during the Last Twenty Years of His Life* (1786). The little book presented a less amiable picture of her guest than she had drawn day by day in her diary; doubtless the final letters of Johnson had left a lasting wound.

Next in the arena—barring a dozen entries now forgotten—was *The Life of Samuel Johnson*, published in five sumptuous volumes by Sir John Hawkins in 1787. Hawkins had had sufficient success as an attorney to be knighted (1772), and sufficient learning to write a good *History of Music* (1776). He joined with Johnson in organizing the Ivy Lane Club (1749), and was one of the original members of "the Club." He left this after an argument with Burke, which caused Johnson to dub him "an unclubbable man"; but Johnson remained his friend, often sought his advice, and appointed him one of the executors of his will. Soon after Johnson's death a group of booksellers asked Hawkins to edit an edition of the Doctor's works, and to introduce it with a biography. This was criticized as revealing Johnson's faults without mercy, and Boswell later questioned its accuracy; but "the charges against it cannot be sustained in a fair hearing."[164] Nearly all the faults ascribed to Johnson by Hawkins were noted by other contemporaries.

Mrs. Piozzi returned to the feast with *Letters to and from the Late Samuel Johnson* (1788), all fascinating, for Johnson's letters (except the last one to his lost lady) were far more humane than his speech. Meanwhile Boswell was laboring patiently, between lawsuits and carouses, on what he was resolved to make an incomparable biography. He had begun to make memoranda of Johnson's conversation soon after their first meeting (1763); he planned the *Life* as early as 1772; so lengthy and laborious was this gestation. He rarely took notes on the spot, and he could not write shorthand; but he made it a principle to jot down, on returning to his room, his memory of what had happened or had been said. He began writing *The Life of Samuel Johnson* in London on July 9, 1786. He ran about the city seeking data from Johnson's surviving friends. Edmund Malone, the Shakespearean scholar, helped him to sort out his huge chaos of notes, and buttressed his courage when Boswell, broken down by dissipation, grief, and the death of his wife, seemed about to abandon himself to women and drink. Boswell wrote in 1789: "You cannot imagine what labor, what perplexity, what vexation I have endured in arranging a prodigious multiplicity of materials, in supplying omissions, in searching for papers buried in different masses, and all this besides the exertion of composing and polishing. Many a time have I thought of giving it up."[165] He took from William Mason's *Life and Letters of Gray* (1774) the idea of interspersing his hero's letters with the story. He deliberately accumulated details, feeling that these would add up to a full and vivid picture. The fragments were woven into a chronological narrative and a consistent whole.

Was he accurate? He claimed to be. "I am so nice in recording him that every trifle must be authentic."[166] Where we can check his report of Johnson's words with other accounts it seems factually correct, though not verbatim. A comparison of his *Notebook* with the *Life* shows that Boswell turned his own summary of Johnson's speech into direct quotation, which he sometimes expanded, sometimes compressed, sometimes improved,[167] sometimes purified, elongating certain four-letter words to respectable proportions. Occasionally he omitted facts unfavorable to himself.[168] He did not claim to have told the whole truth about Johnson,[169] but when Hannah More begged him "to mitigate some of Johnson's asperities," he replied that he "would not cut off Johnson's claws, nor make a tiger a cat to please anybody."[170] Actually he revealed his master's faults as fully as others had done, but in a large perspective that reduced their prominence. He tried to show as much of the complete man as affection and decency would permit. "I am absolutely certain," he said, "that my mode of biography, which gives not only a *history* of Johnson's *visible* progress through the world, and of his publication, but a *view* of his mind in his letters and conversations, is the most perfect that can be conceived, and will be *more* of a *Life* than any work that has ever yet appeared."[171]

At last it came from the press, in two large volumes, in May, 1791. It was not at once recognized as a unique treasury. Many persons resented Boswell's reporting of their private conversation, not always admirable: Lady Diana Beauclerk was able to read how Johnson had called her a whore; Reynolds saw where Johnson had reproved him for drinking too much; Burke learned that Johnson had questioned his political integrity and had thought him capable of picking up a prostitute; Mrs. Piozzi and Mrs. Elizabeth Montagu winced. "Dr. Blagden," wrote Horace Walpole, "says justly that it is a new kind of libel, by which you may abuse anybody by saying some dead person said so and so of somebody alive."[172] Others found the detail excessive, many letters trivial, some pages dull. Only gradually did England realize that Boswell had achieved a masterpiece, and had given some nobility to his life.

His father had died in 1782, leaving him Laird of Auchinleck with an income of £1,600 a year. He proved to be a kindly master, but he was too accustomed to city life to remain long in Auchinleck. In 1786 he was admitted to the English bar, and thereafter he spent most of his time in London. Reynolds portrayed him in that year—confident and insolent, with a nose fit to ferret out any secret. At times his wife accompanied him to London, but usually she lived at Auchinleck. There she died in 1789, aged fifty-one, worn out by the care she had given Boswell and his children. He survived her by six years—years of deepening degradation. He tried again and again to overcome his need for liquor, but failed. He died in London May 19, 1795, aged fifty-six, and his body was taken to Auchinleck for burial. His sins are at present in the public mind, but we shall forget them when we read again the greatest of all biographies.

Looking back over this eighteenth century in English literature, we perceive that it was above all a century of prose, from Addison, Swift, and Defoe to Sterne, Gibbon, and Johnson, just as the seventeenth century was an age of poetry, from *Hamlet* and Donne to Dryden and *Paradise Lost*. The rise of science and philosophy, the decline of religion and mystery, the revival of classic unities and restraints, had chilled the warmth and clogged the flow of imagination and aspiration; and the triumph of reason was the defeat of poetry, in France as well as in England. Nevertheless the vitality and versatility of England's prose literature in the eighteenth century amply compensated for the frigid formality prevailing in its verse. Through Richardson and Fielding the novel, which had been, before them, an episodic concatenation of picaresque adventures, became a description and criticism of life, a study of manners, morals, and character, more illuminating than the records of the historians, who lost the people in the state. And what literary influence could equal, in that age, the effect of Richardson on Prévost, Rousseau, Diderot, and Goethe?

If the literature of England in the eighteenth century could not equal that of the seventeenth, or match the Elizabethan flight, the total life of England recovered its upward swing after the failure of national courage and policy in the Restoration. Not since the defeat of the Armada had England felt such a surge of enterprise and politics; the years from the rise of Chatham to the death of his son saw the Industrial Revolution put England far ahead of its rivals in economic inventiveness and power, and saw the English Parliament conquering continents while checking its kings. Now the immense British Empire was built, now the halls of the House of Commons rang with such eloquence as Europe had not heard since Cicero. Now, while France bankrupted itself to free America, and decapitated itself to realize its dreams, England brought all its resources of mind and will to evolve without revolution, and enter the nineteenth century, in economy and statesmanship, victorious and supreme.

BOOK VII

THE COLLAPSE OF FEUDAL FRANCE

1774–89

CHAPTER XXXIV

The Final Glory

1774–83

I. THE HEIRS TO THE THRONE: 1754–74

LOUIS XVI was the third son of the Dauphin Louis de France, who was the only legitimate son of Louis XV. The Dauphin was called Louis the Fat, for he liked to eat. He tried to overcome his obesity by hunting, swimming, felling trees, sawing wood, and busying himself with manual arts.[1] He retained through life his reverence for the Church; his dearest friends were priests, and he was deeply ashamed of his father's adulteries. He read much, including Montesquieu and Rousseau; he adopted the view that "the monarch is nothing but the steward of the state's revenues";[2] he denied himself a trip through France because "my whole person is not worth what it would cost the poor people."[3] It is remarkable how much of his character, habits, and ideas passed down to Louis XVI.

His wife, Marie-Josèphe of Saxony, virtuous and strong, bore him eight children, including Louis-Joseph, Duc de Bourgogne, who was killed by an accident in 1761; Louis-Auguste, Duc de Berry, born on August 23, 1754, who was to be Louis XVI; Louis-Stanislas, Comte de Provence, born in 1755, who was to be Louis XVIII; and Charles-Philippe, Comte d'Artois, born in 1757, who was to be Charles X. When their father died, in 1765, Louis-Auguste, aged eleven, became heir to the throne.

He was a sickly child, timid and shy, but years of country life and simple food gave him health and strength. Like his father he was good rather than bright. He envied the superior cleverness of his brothers, who quite ignored his seniority. Too modest to fight back, he absorbed himself in sports and crafts. He learned to shoot with perfect accuracy, and to rival workingmen in using his hands and tools. He admired the skills of the artisans who served the court; he liked to talk and work with them, and he took on something of their manners and speech. But also he loved books. He developed a special fondness for Fénelon; at the age of twelve he installed a printing press in the palace at Versailles, and, with the help of his brothers (then nine and eleven), he set the type for a little volume which he published in 1766 as *Maximes morales et politiques tirées de Télémaque*. His grandfather did not like the maxims. "Look at that big boy," said Louis XV. "He will be the ruin of France and of himself, but at any rate I shall not live to see it."[4]

How could this princely workingman be transformed into a king? Could a stimulating mate be found to give him courage and pride, and to bear him future Bourbons? The present ruler was too busy with Mme. du Barry to attend to this matter; but Choiseul, minister for foreign affairs, remembered his days at the court of Vienna, and a lively archduchess, Maria Antonia Josepha, then (1758) three years old; perhaps her marriage with Louis-Auguste would give new life to that Austrian alliance which had been weakened by France's separate peace with England (1762). Prince von Kaunitz had confided similar ideas to Count Florimund Mercy d'Argentau, a Liège aristocrat of great wealth and good heart, who was Austrian ambassador at Versailles. Louis XV took their concerted advice, and sent (1769) a formal request to Maria Theresa asking the hand of Maria Antonia for Louis-Auguste. The Empress was happy to sanction a union which she too had long ago designed. The Dauphin, who had not been consulted in the matter, obediently accepted the choice made for him. When he was told that his fiancée was a beautiful princess, he said quietly, "If only she has good qualities."[5]

She was born in Vienna November 2, 1755. She was not a pretty child; her forehead was too high, her nose was too long and sharp, her teeth were irregular, her lower lip was too full. But she soon knew that her blood was royal; she learned to walk like a destined queen, and nature, with the mysterious fluids of puberty, refashioned her winsomely until, with silken blond hair, and complexion "of lilies and roses,"[6] and sparkling, playful blue eyes, and a "Grecian neck," she became, if not a morsel for a king, at least a dainty for a dauphin. Three of her five older sisters had been maneuvered by the Empress into cozy berths: Maria Christina had married Prince Albert of Saxony, who became duke of Saxe-Teschen; Maria Amalia had married Ferdinand, duke of Parma; Maria Carolina had become queen of Naples. Brother Joseph was co-emperor of the Holy Roman Empire, and brother Leopold was grand duke of Tuscany. There was nothing left for Maria Antonia but to become queen of France.

As the youngest of Maria Theresa's surviving children, she had been somewhat neglected. At thirteen she had learned some Italian, but she could write neither German nor French correctly, she knew almost nothing of history, and, though Gluck was her teacher, she had made only modest progress in music. When Louis XV decided to accept her as a granddaughter he insisted that she be inoculated against smallpox, and he sent the Abbé Vermond to accelerate her education. Vermond reported that "her character, her heart are excellent," and "she is more intelligent than has been generally supposed," but "she is rather lazy and extremely frivolous, and hard to teach. . . . She would learn only so long as she was being amused."[7] But she loved to dance, and to romp in the woods with her dogs.

The careworn Empress knew that she was entrusting the fate of the alliance to hands too frail for such a responsibility. For two months before the contemplated marriage she had Maria Antonia sleep in the same room with her, so that in the intimacy of their nights she might instill into her daughter something of the wisdom of life and the art of royalty. She drew up for her a list of regulations to guide her conduct in morals and politics. She wrote to Louis XV asking his indulgence for the shortcomings of the immature bride she was sending to his grandson. To the Dauphin she addressed a letter warm with a mother's solicitude and fears:

As she has been my delight, so I hope she will be your happiness. I have brought her up for this, because for a long time I have foreseen that she would share your destiny. I have inspired in her a love for her duties to you, a tender attachment, and the ability to know and practice the means of pleasing you. . . . My daughter will love you, I am sure of it, because I know her. . . . Adieu, my dear Dauphin; be happy, make her happy. . . . I am all bathed in tears. . . . Your tender mother.[8]

On April 19, 1770, in the Church of the Augustines at Vienna, the radiant, thoughtless girl, aged fourteen, was married by proxy to Louis-Auguste of France; her brother Ferdinand took the Dauphin's place. Two days later a long cavalcade of fifty-seven carriages and 366 horses led the Dauphine past the Palace of Schönbrunn, and the Empress bade her a last goodbye. "Be so good to the French," she whispered, "that they can say that I have sent them an angel."[9] The cortege included 132 persons—ladies in waiting, hairdressers, dressmakers, pages, chaplains, surgeons, apothecaries, cooks, servants, and thirty-five men to take care of the horses, which were changed four or five times a day on the long journey to Paris. In sixteen days the procession reached Kehl, on the Rhine opposite Strasbourg. On an island in the river Maria changed her Austrian attire for French garments; her Austrian attendants left her to return to Vienna, and were replaced by an entourage of French ladies and servants; henceforth Maria Antonia was Marie Antoinette. After much ceremony she was brought into Strasbourg while cannon pealed and church bells rang and all the people cheered. She wept and smiled and went through the long ritual patiently. When the burgomaster began a speech in German she interrupted him: "Do not speak German, gentlemen; from today I understand no language but French." Having allowed her a day of rest, the pageant began its transit of France.

It had been arranged that the King and the Dauphin, with much of the court, should go to Compiègne, fifty-two miles northeast of Paris, to meet the Dauphine's cortege. This arrived on May 14. The bride leaped from her coach, ran to Louis XV, bowed to the ground, and remained so till the King raised her and put her at her ease with a gracious remark: "You are already a member of the family, madame, for your mother has the soul of Louis XIV."[10] After kissing her on both cheeks he introduced the Dauphin, who did likewise but with perhaps less relish. On May 15 the combined processions started for Versailles. There, on May 16, 1770, an official marriage confirmed the proxy wedding of a month before. That night there was a great feast in the new opera house. The King warned Louis-Auguste that he was eating too much. The Dauphin replied, "I always sleep better after a good supper."[11] He did, falling asleep soon after entering the marriage bed.

He slept with the same readiness on successive nights, and on successive mornings he rose early to go hunting. Mercy d'Argentau suggested that the recent rapid growth of Louis-Auguste had retarded his sexual development, and that there was nothing to do but wait. Maria Theresa, informed of the situation, wrote to her daughter: "You are both so young! As far as your health is concerned it is all for the best. You will both gain strength."[12] Some of the Dauphin's physicians made matters worse by telling him that exercise and good meals would stimulate amorous development; on the contrary, they made him stouter and sleepier. Finally, late in 1770, the Dauphin tried to consummate the marriage, but failed; the only result was a disenchanting pain. The Count of Aranda, the Spanish ambassador, reported to his King: "They say that an impediment under the foreskin makes the attempt at coitus too painful," or "that the foreskin is so thick that it cannot expand with the elasticity necessary to an erection."[13] Surgeons offered to remove the difficulty by an operation akin to circumcision, but the Dauphin refused.[14] He made repeated attempts, with no effect but to agitate and humiliate himself and his wife. This situation continued till 1777. The sense of his marital deficiency deepened the Dauphin's feeling of inferiority, and may have shared in making him so hesitating and diffident a king.

Probably those seven years of marital frustration affected the character and conduct of Marie Antoinette. She knew that the men and women of the court made merciless fun of her misfortune, and that most of France, not knowing the cause, charged her with barrenness. She consoled herself with trips to the opera or the theater in Paris, and indulged herself in costly extravagance of dress. She rebelled against frequent mingling with the court, with all its ceremony and protocol; she preferred intimate friendships with sympathetic souls like the Princesse de Lamballe. For a long time she refused to speak to Mme. du Barry, whether through distaste for her morals or through envy that another woman should be so competently loved and so influential with the King.

On May 10, 1774, Louis XV died. The courtiers rushed to the apartments of the Dauphin. They found him and the Dauphine on their knees weeping and praying. "O God," the nineteen-year-old youth cried, "protect us! We are too young to rule!" And to a friend he said, "What a burden! I have learned nothing. It seems that the universe will fall upon me."[15] All day long, through Versailles and Paris, and then as far in France as the news was carried, men, women, and children cried joyfully, "*Le Roi est mort, vive le Roi!*" Some hopeful Parisian inscribed upon a statue of Henry IV the word *Resurrexit;*[16] the great King had risen from the dead to rescue France again from chaos, corruption, bankruptcy, and defeat.

II. THE GOVERNMENT

What was wrong with the government? It was not as despotic as Prussia's, not as corrupt as England's; its bureaucracy and provincial administration contained some good and many able men. Nevertheless the Bourbon monarchy had failed to keep up with the economic and intellectual development of the people. Revolution came to France sooner than elsewhere because the middle classes had reached a higher stage of intelligence than in any other contemporary nation, and the alert and aroused mind of her citizenry made sharper demands upon the state than any government of the time had to meet.

Frederick II and Joseph II, devotees of philosophy and absolute monarchy, had brought into the political management of Prussia and Austria a degree of order and competence not then present in a France that loved a Latin laxity and ease. "Confusion and chaos reigned everywhere."[17] At Versailles the King's Council conflicted in jurisdiction with the departmental ministers, who conflicted with one another because their functions overlapped, because they competed for the same public funds, and because no authority was superimposed to bring their policies into accord. The nation was divided in one way (*bailliages* or *sénéchaussées*) for the judiciary; in another (*généralités*) for finance, in another (*gouvernements*) for the army, in another (*paroisses* and *provinces*) for the Church. In each *généralité* the intendant conflicted with the governor and the regional *parlement*. Throughout France the interests of rural producers conflicted with those of urban consumers, the rich conflicted with the poor, the nobles with the bourgeoisie, the *parlements* with the king. A unifying cause and a commanding will were needed; the cause did not come till 1792, the will not till 1799.

One of the worst aspects of French life was the law, and yet one of the best was the judiciary. South France kept Roman law, north France kept common and feudal law. "Justice," said de Tocqueville, was "complicated, costly, and slow"[18]—though this is a universal plaint. Prisons were filthy, punishments were barbarous; judicial torture was still allowed in 1774. The judges were irremovable, usually unbribable and just; Sir Henry Maine thought that the jurists of France, "in all the qualities of the advocate, the judge, and the legislator, far excelled their compeers throughout Europe."[19] They held their office for life, and were entitled to transmit it to a son. The ablest among them found their way into the regional *parlements*, and the most wealthy and influential were chosen to the Parlement of Paris. By 1774 the "nobility of the robe"—the hereditary magistrates—had come to consider itself only slightly below the "nobility of the sword" in dignity and deserts. It admitted to the *parlements* only persons born into one or the other of the two aristocracies.

Montesquieu had argued that "intermediate bodies" between the king and the people would be useful brakes on autocratic power; he had specified the landed nobility and the magistracy as two such powers. In order to serve this braking function the *parlements* claimed authority to ratify (*régistrer*) or reject any royal decree as in their judgment it accorded or conflicted with established laws and rights. Several provincial *parlements*, especially those of Grenoble, Rouen, and Rennes, voiced semidemocratic doctrines, sometimes with Rousseauian phrases about "the general will" and "the free consent of the nation"; so the Parlement of Rennes in 1788 proclaimed "that man is born free, that originally men are equal," and "that these truths have no need of proof."[20] Generally, however, the *parlements* were strong defenders of class distinctions and privileges. Their contests with the royal power shared in preparing the Revolution, but as this approached they sided with the Old Regime, and fell with its fall.

Theoretically the royal power was absolute. By Bourbon tradition the king was the sole legislator, the chief executive, and the supreme court. He could have any person in France arrested and indefinitely confined without giving a reason or allowing a trial; even the kindly Louis XVI sent out such *lettres de cachet*. The King had inherited a costly establishment, which considered itself indispensable to the administration and prestige of the government. In 1774 the court at Versailles included the royal family and 886 noblemen, with their wives and children; add 295 cooks, fifty-six hunters, forty-seven musicians, eight architects, sundry secretaries, chaplains, physicians, couriers, guards . . . ; altogether some six thousand persons, with ten thousand soldiers stationed nearby. Each member of the royal family had his or her separate court; so did some special nobles, like the Princes de Condé and de Conti and the Ducs d'Orléans and de Bourbon. The King maintained several palaces—at Versailles, Marly, La Muette, Meudon, Choisy, St.-Hubert, St.-Germain, Fontainebleau, Compiègne, and Rambouillet. It was customary for him to move from palace to palace, with parts of the court following him and requiring to be housed and fed. The expenses of the King's table in 1780 ran to 3,660,491 livres.[21]

The salaries of court officials were moderate, but the perquisites were elastic; so M. Augeard, a secretary in one of the ministries, was paid only nine hundred livres a year, but admitted that the post netted him 200,000 livres annually. A hundred sinecures brought the courtiers money while subordinates did the work; M. Machault received eighteen thousand livres for signing his name twice a year.[22] A hundred pensions totaling 28,000,000 livres annually went to persuasive nobles or their protégés.[23] A hundred intrigues were carried on to determine who should receive the careless bounty of the King. He was expected to relieve old titled families fallen into straitened finances, and to provide dowries for noble daughters on their marriage. Each of Louis XV's surviving children received approximately 150,000 livres per year. Each minister of state was paid up to 150,000 livres as annual salary, for he was expected to entertain expansively. All this prodigality, these pensions, gifts, salaries, and sinecures were paid out of revenues drawn from the economic life of the nation. In sum the court cost France fifty million livres a year—a tenth of the total income of the government.[24]

III. THE VIRGIN QUEEN

Marie Antoinette was the most extravagant member of the court. Attached to an impotent husband, cheated of romance, indulging in no liaisons, she amused herself, till 1778, with costly dresses, gems, and palaces, with operas, plays, and balls. She lost fortunes in gambling, and gave fortunes to favorites in reckless generosity. She spent 252,000 livres on her wardrobe in one year (1783).[25] Designers brought her fancy garments named "Indiscreet Pleasures," "Stifled Signs," or "Masked Desires."[26] Hairdressers worked for hours over her head, training her hair to such heights that her chin seemed to be the mean point of her height; this *haute coiffure*, like almost everything about her, set a fashion for the ladies of the court, then of Paris, then of the provincial capitals.

Her longing for jewelry became almost a mania. In 1774 she bought from Böhmer, official jeweler to the Crown, gems valued at 360,000 livres.[27] Louis XVI gave her a set of rubies, diamonds, and bracelets costing 200,000 livres.[28] In 1776 Mercy d'Argentau wrote to Maria Theresa:

> Although the King has given the Queen, on various occasions, more than 100,000 écus' worth of diamonds, and although her Majesty already has a prodigious collection, she nevertheless resolved to acquire . . . chandelier earrings from Böhmer. I did not conceal from her Majesty that under present economic conditions it would have been wiser to avoid such a tremendous expenditure, but she could not resist—although she handled the purchase carefully, keeping it a secret from the King.[29]

Maria Theresa sent her daughter a stern reproof; the Queen compromised by wearing her jewelry only on state occasions; but the public never forgave her this intemperate expenditure of its taxes, and later it would believe the story that she had agreed to buy the famous diamond necklace.

The King indulged his wife in her foibles because he admired and loved her, and because he was grateful for her patience with his impotence. He paid her gambling debts out of his own purse. He encouraged her trips to the Paris opera, though he knew that her gaiety in public disturbed a people accustomed to royal dignity and reserve. The government paid for three theatrical performances, two balls, two formal suppers almost every week at court; in addition the Queen attended masked balls in Paris or in private homes. These years, 1774–77, were a period of what her mother frankly called dissipation. Deriving nothing but aroused and unsatisfied passion from her husband's nocturnal approaches, the Queen encouraged him to go to sleep early (sometimes setting the clock ahead to advance his retirement), so that she could join her friends in games that might last all night. She took no interest in literature, little in art, more in drama and music; she sang and acted well, played the harp, and performed some Mozart sonatas on the clavichord.[30]

In all these faults only one was fundamental—a thoughtless extravagance derived from boredom and frustration, and from a childhood and youth accustomed to riches and ignorant of poverty. The Prince de Ligne (who may have been more of a gentleman than an historian) claimed that she soon outgrew her love of costly raiment, that her gambling losses were exaggerated, and that her debts were due as much to unwise generosity as to reckless expenditure.[31] The court and the salons were hostile to her as an Austrian; the alliance with Austria had never been popular; Marie Antoinette, called "L'Autrichienne," personified that alliance, and was suspected, with some reason, of favoring Austrian interests, sometimes at the cost of France. Even so, her youthful vitality, her gaiety and kindliness, won many hearts. Mme. Vigée-Lebrun, many months pregnant, came to paint her portrait (1779); while at work the artist dropped some tubes of color; the Queen at once told her not to stoop, for "you are too far along," and herself picked up the tubes.[32] Antoinette was usually considerate, but occasionally, in her thought-less merriment, she made fun of other people's mannerisms or defects. And she responded too readily to every appeal; "she did not yet know the danger of yielding to every gracious impulse."[33]

So vivacious a creature, to whom life and movement were synonyms, was not made for the slow and careful pace of court etiquette. Soon she rebelled against it, and sought simplicity and ease in and around the Petit Trianon, a mile from the Palace of Versailles. In 1778 Louis XVI offered the Queen undisputed possession of this trysting place; there she might retire with her intimates, and Louis promised that he would not intrude upon them except by invitation. As there were only eight rooms in the building, the Queen had some cottages built near it for her friends. She had the surrounding gardens designed in the "natural" style—with winding paths, varied trees, surprises, and a brook, and for this she had water piped in from Marly at great cost. To complete the illusion of a Rousseauian return to nature, she had eight small farms set up in the adjoining park, each with its rustic cottage, peasant family, dung heap, and cows. There she dressed like a shepherdess in white gown, gauze kerchief, and straw hat, and loved to see milk coaxed from choice udders into vessels of Sèvres porcelain. Within the Petit Trianon she and her friends played music or games, and on the lawn they gave banquets to the King or to distinguished visitors. There, as well as in the royal palace, the Queen staged dramas, in some of which she played major roles— Suzanne in *Le Mariage de Figaro*, Colette in *Le Devin du village*, delighting the King with her versatility and charm.

Fearing scandal if she mingled too freely with men, she formed with women some friendships so close that scandal took another line. First came Marie-Thérèse de Savoie-Carignan, Princesse de Lamballe, gentle, sad, and frail. Twenty-one, she was already two years a widow. Her husband, son of Louis XIV's grandson the Duc de Penthièvre, went off to mistresses or prostitutes soon after his marriage; he contracted syphilis and died of it after confessing his sins to his wife in revolting detail. She never recovered from the long ordeal of that marriage; she suffered from nervous convulsions and fainting spells until, in 1792, she was torn to pieces by a Revolutionary mob. Marie Antoinette first took to her out of pity, then learned to love her fervently, seeing her every day, writing to her letters of endearment sometimes twice a day. In October, 1775, she made the Princess superintendent of the Queen's Household, and persuaded the King, over Turgot's protests, to pay her a yearly salary of 150,000 livres. Moreover, the Princess had relatives and friends, who begged her to use her influence with the Queen, and through her with the King, to obtain posts or gifts. Antoinette, after a year, let her love fade, and took another friend.

Yolande de Polastron, wife of Comte Jules de Polignac, was of ancient family and straitened means; pretty, petite, natural; no one would, seeing her, suspect her of such financial voracity that Turgot despaired of balancing the budget while the Queen found pleasure in her witty company. When the Countess neared childbirth the Queen persuaded her to move to La

Muette, a royal villa near the Versailles Palace; there she visited her daily, almost always bearing gifts. When the Comtesse became a mother nothing could be refused her: 400,000 livres to settle her debts, a dowry of 800,000 livres for her daughter, an embassy for her father, money, jewels, furs, works of art for herself, and finally (1780) a dukedom and the estate of Bitche—for the Count longed to be a duke. At last Mercy d'Argentau informed the Queen that she was being exploited, and that the new Duchess did not return her devotion. He proposed, and the Queen accepted, as a test, that she ask Mme. de Polignac to dismiss from her entourage the Comte de Vaudreuil, who was distasteful to Antoinette; Madame refused, and Marie turned to other friendships. The Polignacs joined her enemies, and became a source of the slanders with which the court and the pamphleteers besmirched the name of the Queen.

Almost everything that she did made her enemies. The courtiers regretted the gifts she gave to her favorites, since this meant less for themselves. They complained that she so often absented herself from court functions that these lost glamour and attendance. Many who had condemned the costly wardrobe of her earlier years now censured her for setting a new fashion of simplicity in dress; the silk merchants of Lyons and the couturiers of Paris would be ruined.[34] She had induced the King to dismiss the Duc d'Aiguillon (1775), who had led the supporters of Mme. du Barry; the Duke had many sympathizers, and these formed another nucleus of foes. After 1776 the Paris pamphleteers—many of whom received material and money from members of the court[35]—engaged in a campaign of merciless vituperation against the Queen.[36] Some writers described her as the mistress, at one time or another, of every available male at Versailles.[37] "How many times," asked a pamphlet entitled *A Reprimand to the Queen*, "have you left the nuptial bed and the caresses of your husband to abandon yourself to bacchantes or satyrs, and to become one with them through their brutal pleasures?"[38] Another pamphlet illustrated her extravagance by describing a wall in the Petit Trianon as covered with diamonds.[39] Rumor accused her of saying, during the bread riots of 1788, "If they have no bread let them eat cake"; historians agree that she was never guilty of that heartless remark;[40] on the contrary, she contributed abundantly from her own purse to public relief. Even more cruel was the general opinion, among the populace, that she was barren. Mme. Campan, first lady of the bedchamber to the Queen, relates:

> When in 1777 a son was born to the Comte d'Artois, the market women and fishwives, asserting their prerogative to enter the royal palace at times of royal births, followed the Queen to the very door of her apartments, shouting in the coarsest and most vulgar terms that it was up to her, not to her sister-in-law, to provide heirs to the French crown. The Queen hurried to close the door upon these licentious harridans, and closeted herself in her room with me to weep over her plight.[41]

How could she explain to the people that the King was impotent?

France waited for the Emperor of the Holy Roman Empire to come and clear this impasse. In April, 1777, Joseph II arrived at Versailles under the pseudonym of Count von Falkenstein. He fell in love with the Queen. "If you were not my sister," he told her, "I should not hesitate to marry again in order to have such a charming companion."[42] And to their brother Leopold he wrote:

> I have spent hour after hour with her, and not noticed their passing. . . . She is a charming and honorable woman, somewhat young, a little thoughtless, but essentially decent and virtuous. . . . She also has spirit and a keenness which surprised me. Her first reaction is always correct; if she would only act according to it, . . . and pay less attention to the gossips, . . . she would be perfect. She has a strong desire for pleasure, and since her tastes are known, advantage is taken of her weakness. . . .
> But she thinks only of her own pleasure, has no love for the King, and is drunk with the extravagance of this country. . . . She drives the King by force to the things he does not wish to do. . . . In short, she does not fulfill the duties of either a wife or a queen.[43]

She explained why she and the King slept in separate rooms; he wished to go to sleep early, and they both found it wise to avoid sexual excitement. Joseph visited the King, and liked him well. "This man," he wrote to Leopold, "is a little weak, but not an imbecile. He has ideas and a sound judgment, but his mind and body are apathetic. He converses reasonably, but he has no wish to learn, and no curiosity; . . . in fact the *fiat lux* has not yet come; the matter is still without form."[44] The Emperor talked to Louis as no one had dared speak to him; he pointed out that the impediment in the royal prepuce could be removed by a simple, though painful, operation, and that the King owed it to his country to have children. Louis promised to submit to the knife.

Before leaving Versailles Joseph wrote a sheet of "Instructions" for the Queen. It is a remarkable document:

> You are getting older, and no longer have youth as an excuse. What will become of you if you delay any longer [to reform]? . . . When the King caresses you, when he speaks to you, do you not show irritation, even repugnance? Have you ever thought what effect your intimacies and friendships . . . must have on the public? . . . Have you weighed the terrible consequences of games of chance, the company they bring together and the tone they set? . . .

And of her fondness for the masked balls in Paris:

> Why mingle with a crowd of libertines, prostitutes, and strangers, listening to their remarks, and perhaps making similar ones? How indecent! . . . The King is left alone all night at Versailles, and you mix in society and mingle with the riffraff of Paris! . . . I really tremble for your happiness, for it cannot turn out well in the long run, and there will be a cruel revolution [*une révolution cruelle*] unless you take steps against it.[45]

The Queen was moved by his reproaches. After he had gone she wrote to her mother: "The Emperor's departure has left a gap I cannot fill. I was so happy during that short time that now it all seems like a dream. But what will never be a dream for me is all the good counsel . . . he gave me, which is engraved in my heart forever."[46] What really reformed her was not advice but motherhood. For Louis, in that summer of 1777, submitted, apparently without anesthetic of any kind, to an operation which proved completely successful. He celebrated his twenty-third birthday (August 23, 1777) by at last consummating his marriage. He was proud and happy. "I very much enjoy this pleasure," he confided to one of his maiden aunts, "and I am sorry to have been deprived of it for so long."[47] However, it was not till April, 1778, that the Queen became pregnant. She announced this to the King in her frolicsome way: "Sire, I have come to complain that one of your subjects has been so bold as to kick me in the belly."[48] When Louis caught her meaning he clasped her in his arms. Now more than ever he indulged her whims and granted her requests. Ten times a day he visited her apartments for the latest communiqué on the progress of the expected heir. And Marie Antoinette, undergoing a mysterious transformation of body and soul, told the King, "Henceforth I want to live otherwise than before. I want to live as a mother, nurse my own child, and devote myself to its education."[49]

After grievous suffering, made worse by a clumsy *accoucheur*, the Queen gave birth, December 19, 1778. The parents regretted that the child was a girl, but the King was happy that the gates of life had been opened, and confident that a son would come forth in time. The young mother rejoiced that at last she had been fulfilled. To Maria Theresa (now entering her final year) she wrote in 1779: "Dear Mamma may be very satisfied as to my conduct. If I was formerly to blame, it was because I was childish and giddy. Now, however, I am much more sensible, and I am very well aware what my duty is."[50] Neither the court nor the populace believed it, but "it is an accepted fact," wrote the Comte de Ségur, "that after the birth of her first child she gradually began to lead a more regular existence, and to occupy herself seriously. She is more careful to avoid anything that might give rise to scandal. Her gay parties are less frequent, less lively. . . . Extravagance gives place to simplicity; sumptuous robes are replaced by little linen frocks."[51] It was part of Marie Antoinette's long punishment that the people of France would not realize that the spoiled and reckless girl had become a tender and conscientious mother. Nothing is lost, but everything has to be paid for.

She knew that French law excluded women from the throne. She welcomed a second pregnancy, and prayed for a son; but she suffered a miscarriage so agonizing that she lost most of her hair.[52] She tried again, and on October 22, 1781, she gave birth to a boy, who was named Louis-Joseph-Xavier. Cynics questioned the child's paternity, but the happy King ignored them. "My son the Dauphin!" he cried. "My son!"

IV. *LE ROI BONHOMME*[53]

Except in age Louis was everything that his wife was not. She was graceful, agile, mobile, playful, impulsive, effervescent, frivolous, extravagant, self-assertive, proud, always a queen; he was clumsy, inert, hesitant, serious, quiet, industrious, thrifty, modest, diffident, every inch not a king. He loved the day, his work, and the hunt; she loved the night, the card table, and the dance. And yet, after those early tentative years, it was not an unhappy marriage; the Queen was faithful, the King was fond, and when grief came it made them firmly one.

His features were regular; he might have been handsome if he had controlled his weight. He was tall, and might have been royal had he not walked with swinging shoulders and heavy tread. His eyesight was poor, which contributed to his awkwardness. His hair was seldom in order; "his person was greatly neglected," reported Mme. Campan.[54] He was muscular and strong; he lifted one of his pages with one arm. He ate avidly. He drank moderately, but sometimes became drunk with food, and had to be helped to his bed.[55] He had few passions, few ecstasies of pleasure, few extremes of pain.

He was ill at ease with the Frenchmen who surrounded him, and who were trained in alertness of mind and witty readiness of speech; however, in private converse, he impressed men like Joseph II with his wide knowledge and sane judgment. Hear Prince Henry of Prussia, brother to Frederick the Great:

> The King surprised me. . . . I had been told that his education had been neglected, that he knew nothing, had little spirit. I was astonished, in talking with him, to see that he knew geography very well, that he had sound ideas in politics, that the happiness of his people was always in his thoughts, and that he was full of good sense, which is worth more in a prince than a brilliant intellect; but he distrusted himself too much.[56]

Louis had a good library, and used it. He read and in part translated Gibbon's *Decline and Fall of the Roman Empire*,[57] but he put it aside when he perceived its anti-Christian tendency. He read and reread Clarendon's *History of the Rebellion*, as if in premonition that he would repeat the fate of Charles I. "Had I been in his place," he said, "I should never have drawn the sword against my people."[58] For the guidance of La Pérouse's Pacific expedition (1785) he composed detailed instructions which his ministers ascribed to the savants of the Académie des Sciences.[59] He kept in close touch with the various ministries, especially on foreign affairs. Washington and Franklin admired his judgment.[60] His weaknesses were rather of will than of mind, and may have been allied to his heaviness of diet and flesh. Basic was his incapacity to resist persuasion, or to conclude from reflection to action. He himself practiced economy, but he was too amiable to force it upon others, and he signed away hundreds of thousands of francs at the behest of his wife.

He had no lack of virtues. He took no mistress, and he was faithful in friendship, perhaps except with Turgot. "It is quite probable that, next to Turgot, he is the man of his day who loved the people most."[61] On the day of his accession he bade the Controller General of Finance distribute 200,000 francs among the poor, and he added, "If, considering the needs of the state, you find this too much, you will take it out of my pension."[62] He forbade collection of the "coronation tax" which made the beginning of a reign a new burden for the nation. In 1784, when Paris was suffering from inundations and epidemics, he allotted three million francs for public aid. During a severe winter he allowed the poor, day after day, to invade his kitchen and help themselves. He was a Christian in title, in fact, and in observance; he followed all the ritual and regulations of the Church scrupulously; and though he loved food, he kept all the fasts of Lent. He was religious without fanaticism or display; it was he, orthodox and pious, who gave civil rights to the Protestants of France. He tried to reconcile Christianity with government, which is the most difficult thing in the world.

Despite his love of simplicity he had to live externally like a king: to go through the formal levee, let himself be dressed by pages and courtiers, recite his morning prayers in their presence, give audience, preside in council, issue edicts, attend dinners, receptions, balls—though he did not dance. But so far as his position and appetite allowed, he lived like any good citizen. He agreed with Rousseau that every man should learn a manual craft; he learned several, from lockmaking to masonry. Mme. Campan tells us that "he admitted into his private apartment a common locksmith, with whom he made keys and locks; and his hands, blackened by that sort of work, were often, in my presence, the subject of remonstrances, and even sharp reproaches, from the Queen."[63] He was fascinated by all that concerned construction; he helped the palace workingmen to move materials, girders, paving blocks. He liked to make repairs in his apartment with his own hands; he was a good middle-class husband. One of his rooms contained geographical paraphernalia, globes, maps—some of which he had drawn himself; another held instruments for working in wood; another was equipped with a forge, anvils, and a great variety of iron tools. He labored for months to manufacture a giant clock that would record months, phases of the moon, seasons, and years. Several rooms were occupied by his library.

France loved him, even to his death and beyond, for it was Paris, not France, that guillotined him in 1793. In those early years the acclaim was almost universal. "You have a very good king," wrote Frederick the Great to d'Alembert, "and I congratulate you with all my heart. A king who is wise and virtuous is more to be feared by his rivals than a prince who has only courage." And d'Alembert replied: "He loves goodness, justice, economy, and peace. . . . He is just what we ought to desire as our king, if a propitious fate had not given him to us."[64] Voltaire concurred: "All that Louis has done since his accession has endeared him to France."[65] Goethe in old age recalled the auspicious beginning:

> In France a new and benevolent sovereign evinced the best intentions of devoting himself to the removal of so many abuses, and to the noblest ends— of introducing a regular and efficient system of political economy, of dispensing with all arbitrary power, and of ruling by law and justice alone. The brightest hopes spread over the world, and confident youth promised itself and to all mankind a bright and noble future.[66]

V. THE MINISTRY OF TURGOT: 1774–76

The first task of Louis XVI was to find capable and upright ministers who would repair the chaos in administration and finance. The people were clamoring for the recall of the banished *parlements;* he recalled them, and dismissed Maupeou, who had tried to replace them. For his chief minister he brought back to Versailles Jean-Frédéric Phélypeaux, Comte de Maurepas, who had been minister of state from 1738 to 1749, had been deposed for lampooning Mme. de Pompadour, and now returned to power at the age of seventy-three. It was a benevolent but unfortunate choice, for Maurepas, living for a decade on his rural estate, had lost touch with the development of France in economy and thought, and had more wit than wisdom. For foreign affairs the twenty-year-old King chose Charles Gravier, Comte de Vergennes; for the war ministry Comte Claude-Louis de Saint-Germain; and for minister of marine Anne-Robert-Jacques Turgot, Baron de l'Aulne.

We have in previous pages seen him as a seminarian, a lecturer on Christianity and progress, a friend of physiocrats and *philosophes*, an enterprising and beneficent intendant in Limoges. The *dévots* at the court warned Louis that Turgot was an unbeliever, who had contributed articles to the *Encyclopédie;*[67] nevertheless, on August 24, 1774, the King advanced him to the most critical post in the government—controller general of finance. Turgot's place at the navy was taken by Gabriel de Sartine, who spent prodigally in building the fleets that were to help free America, and who relied on Turgot to find the funds.

Turgot was such a Frenchman as Louis XIV had had in Colbert, dedicated to the service of his country, farseeing in his views, tireless, incorruptible. He was tall and handsome, but he lacked the graces of men polished in the salons—though he was welcomed ardently by Mlle. de Lespinasse. His health had been sacrificed to his work; much of the time when he was laboring to remake the French economy he was confined to his rooms with gout. He tried to compress a quarter century of reforms into one brief ministry because he felt that his tenure of office was precarious. He was forty-seven when he came to power, forty-nine when he lost it, fifty-four when he died.

He believed with the physiocrats that industry and trade should be left as free as possible from regulation by government or guilds; that land was the only source of wealth; that a single tax on land was the fairest and most practical way of raising revenue; and that all indirect taxes should be abolished. From the *philosophes* he took their religious skepticism and toleration, their trust in reason and progress, their hope for reform through an enlightened king. If the monarch was a man of intelligence and good will, and would accept philosophy as his guide, this would be a peaceful revolution, far better than a violent and chaotic uprising which might destroy not only old abuses but social order itself. Now this *thèse royale* of Voltaire was to be put to the test. So the *philosophes* joined with the physiocrats in rejoicing over Turgot's rise to power.

At Compiègne on August 24, 1774, Turgot went to thank Louis XVI for appointment to the Ministry of Finance. "I give myself not to the king," he said, "but to the honest man." Louis, taking Turgot's hands in his own, replied, "You shall not be deceived."[68] That evening the minister sent to the King a letter stating the essentials of his program:

> No bankruptcy, either avowed or disguised. . . .
> No increase in taxes, the reason for this lying in the condition of your people. . . .
> No loans, . . . because every loan necessitates, at the end of a given time, either bankruptcy or the increase of taxes. . . .
> To meet these three points there is but one means. It is to reduce expenditure below revenue, and sufficiently below it to insure each year a saving of twenty millions, to be applied to the redemption of the old debts. Without that, the first gunshot will force the state into bankruptcy.[69]

(Necker later resorted to loans, and the war of 1778 led France to bankruptcy.)

After noting that the annual revenue of the government was 213,500,000 francs, and the annual expenditure 235,000,000 francs, Turgot ordered various economies, and issued instructions that no payment should be made from the treasury, for any purpose, without his knowledge and consent. He sought to stimulate the economy by establishing, step by step, freedom of enterprise, production, and trade. He began with an attempt to restore agriculture. Usually, to avoid discontent in the cities, the government had controlled the trade in grain, regulating its sale by the farmer to the wholesaler and by the wholesaler to the retailer, and limiting the price of bread. But low prices to the peasant discouraged him from growing more grain, and deterred others from farming; vast cultivable areas of France lay unsown, and the potential wealth of the nation was being checked at its source. The restoration of agriculture seemed to Turgot the first step in reviving France. Freedom of the farmer to sell his grain at whatever price he could get would raise his income, status, and purchasing power, and lift him out of the primitive and bestial life that La Bruyère had described in the heyday of Louis XIV.[70]

So, on September 13, 1774, Turgot issued through the Royal Council an edict freeing the grain trade everywhere except in Paris, where the urban reaction would be critical. Du Pont de Nemours had written for the edict a preamble explaining its purpose: "To animate and extend the cultivation of the land, whose produce is the most real and certain wealth of the state; to maintain abundance by granaries and the entry of foreign grain; . . . and to remove monopoly . . . in favor of full competition." Such an explanatory preface was itself an innovation, reflecting the rise of public opinion as a political power. Voltaire hailed the edict as the beginning of a new economic era, and predicted that it would soon raise the nation's prosperity.[71] He sent a note to Turgot: "The old invalid of Ferney thanks nature for having made him live long enough to see the decree of September 13, 1774. He presents his respects to the author, and prays for his success."[72]

There was an ominous exception to the applause. In the spring of 1775 Jacques Necker, a Swiss banker living in Paris, came to Turgot with a manuscript *Sur la Législation et le commerce des grains*, and asked if it might be published without detriment to the government. Necker's pamphlet argued that some measure of governmental control over the economy was necessary if the superior cleverness of the few was not to concentrate wealth at one end and intensify poverty at the other. He proposed that if free trade should raise the price of bread beyond a stated figure the government should resume regulation. Turgot, confident in his theories, and favoring freedom of the press, told Necker to publish and let the people judge.[73] Necker published.

The city populace did not read him, but it agreed with him. As the price of bread rose in the spring of 1775, riots broke out in several cities. In the districts around Paris, controlling the flow of grain into the capital, men went from town to town, rousing the people to revolt. Armed bands burned down the granges of farmers and merchants and threw the stored grain into the Seine; they tried to prevent imported grain from proceeding from Le Havre to Paris; and on May 2 they led a crowd to the gates of the palace at Versailles. Turgot believed that these bands were employed by the municipal or provincial officials who had lost their posts through the end of regulation, and who aimed to create in Paris a scarcity of grain that would raise the price of bread and compel a return to controlled trade.[74] The King appeared on a balcony and tried to speak; the noise of the crowd drowned out his words. He forbade his troops to fire upon the people, and ordered a reduction in the price of bread.

Turgot protested that this interference with the laws of supply and demand would ruin the attempt to test them; he was confident that, if they were left free to operate, the competition among merchants and bakers would soon bring down the price of bread. The King rescinded his order for reducing the price. On May 3 angry crowds gathered in Paris and began to pillage the bakeries. Turgot ordered the Paris militia to protect the bakeries and granaries, and to fire upon any person who offered violence. Meanwhile he saw to it that foreign grain reached Paris and the markets. Monopolists who had held their grain in expectation of high prices were compelled, by this imported competition, to release their stores; the price of bread fell, and the rebellion subsided. Several of its leaders were arrested; two were hanged by order of the police. Turgot emerged victorious from this "Guerre des Farines," but the King's faith in *laissez-faire* had been shaken, and he mourned those two hangings in the Place de Grève.

He was pleased, however, with the reforms that Turgot was effecting in the finances of the government. Only a day after the grain edict the hurried minister began to issue ordinances for economy in state expenditures, for the more efficient collection of taxes, and stricter control of the farmers general; for transferring to the state the hitherto private monopolies in diligences, post carriages, and the manufacture of gunpowder. He proposed, but had no time to establish, a "Caisse d'Escompte," a bank to discount commercial paper, receive deposits, make loans, and issue notes payable on presentation; this bank served as a model for the Bank of France organized by Napoleon in 1800. By the end of 1775 Turgot had reduced expenses by 66,000,000 livres, and had lowered the interest on the national debt from 8,700,000 to 3,000,000 livres. The credit of the government was so restored that he was able to borrow 60,000,000 livres from Dutch financiers at four per cent, and so discharge debts on which the treasury had been paying from seven to twelve per cent. He came close to balancing the budget, and he did this not by raising taxes but by lessening corruption, extravagance, incompetence, and waste.

In these and other reforms he received little aid from Maurepas, but much from Chrétien de Malesherbes, whom we have met as protector of the *Encyclopédie* and Rousseau. Now president of the Cours des Aides (which dealt with indirect taxes), he sent to Louis XVI (May 6, 1775) a memoir—*Remontrance*—explaining the injustices involved in the collection of taxes by the farmers general, and warning the King of the hatred generated by their operation. He advised a simplification and clarification of the laws; "there are no good laws," he said, "except simple laws." The King grew fond of Malesherbes, and made him minister of the King's Household (July, 1775). The aging liberal urged Louis to support Turgot, but advised Turgot not to attempt too many reforms at once, for each reform would arouse new foes. The Controller General answered, "What would you have me do? The needs of the people are enormous, and in my family we die of gout at fifty."[75]

In January, 1776, Turgot startled France with six edicts issued in the name of the King. One extended to Paris the freedom of trade in grain, and ended a multitude of offices connected with that trade; the functionaries so dislodged joined his enemies. Two of the edicts canceled or modified the taxes on cattle and tallow; the peasants rejoiced. Another abolished the *corvée*—the twelve or fifteen days of unpaid labor exacted from peasants yearly to maintain bridges, canals, and roads; henceforth this work was to be paid for by a tax upon all non-ecclesiastical property; the peasants rejoiced, the nobles complained. Turgot aroused further resentment by the preamble that he placed in the mouth of the King:

> With the exception of a small number of provinces, . . . nearly all the roads of the kingdom have been built by the unpaid labor of the poorest part of our subjects. The whole burden has therefore fallen on those who have nothing but their hands and are interested only in a very secondary degree in the roads; those really interested are the landowners, almost all of them privileged persons, the value of whose property is increased by the roads. When the poor man alone is forced to maintain these roads, when he is forced to give his time and his work without pay, the only resource he has against misery and hunger is taken from him to make him work for the profit of the rich.[76]

When the Paris Parlement indicated that it would refuse to register this edict, Turgot almost proclaimed class war:

> While as unfriendly to despotism as ever, I shall say constantly to the King, to the Parlement, and, if necessary, to the whole nation, that this is one of those matters that must be decided by the absolute will of the King, and for this reason: at bottom this is a lawsuit between the rich and the poor. Now, of what is the Parlement made up? Of men wealthy as compared with the masses, and all noble, since their offices carry nobility. The court, whose clamor is so powerful—of what is it composed? Of great lords, the majority of whom own estates that will be subject to the tax. . . . Consequently neither the remonstrance of the Parlement . . . nor even the clamor of the court should in any wise prejudice the case. . . . So long as the people shall have no voice in the *parlements* the King, after hearing these, must judge for himself, and he must judge in favor of the people, for this class is the most unhappy.[77]

The last of the six edicts abolished the guilds. These had become an aristocracy of labor, for they controlled nearly all the crafts, they limited admission by requiring high entrance fees, and they still further restricted eligibility to mastership. They obstructed invention, and hampered trade by tolls or embargoes on competitive products entering their commune. The rising class of entrepreneurs—men who supplied initiative, capital, and organization, but demanded liberty to hire any worker, whether guildsman or not, and to sell their wares in any market they could reach—denounced the guilds as monopolies in restraint of trade; and Turgot, anxious to promote industrial development by freeing invention, enterprise, and commerce, felt that the national economy would benefit by the suppression of the guilds. The preamble of this edict read, in part:

> In almost all towns the exercise of the different arts and trades was centered in the hands of a small number of masters united in guilds, who alone had the freedom to manufacture and sell the articles of the particular industry of which they had the exclusive privilege. He who devoted himself to any part or trade could not exercise it freely until after attaining the mastership, to which he could be admitted only by submitting to long, tedious, and superfluous tasks, and at the cost of multiplied exactions depriving him of a part of the capital requisite for establishing a business or for fitting up a workshop. Those who could not afford these expenses were reduced to a precarious existence under the sway of the masters, with no choice but to live in penury, . . . or to carry to some foreign land an industry that might have been useful to their country.[78]

So far as we know, these charges against the guilds were justified. But Turgot went on to prohibit all masters, journeymen, and apprentices from forming any union or association.[79] He believed completely in freedom of enterprise and trade, and did not foresee that the right of organization might be the only means by which the workers could pool their individual weakness into a collective strength capable of bargaining with organized employers. He felt that in the long run all classes would benefit by the liberation of the businessman from feudal, guild, and governmental restraints on enterprise. All persons in France—even foreigners—were declared free to engage in any industry or trade.

On February 9, 1776, the six edicts were submitted to the Paris Parlement. It agreed to only one, which abolished certain minor offices; it refused to approve or register the rest, and it especially opposed, as an infringement of feudal rights,[80] the ending of the *corvée*. By this vote the Parlement, which had professed to protect the people against the king, declared itself the ally and voice of the nobility. Voltaire entered the lists with a pamphlet attacking the *corvée* and the Parlement and supporting Turgot; Parlement ordered the pamphlet suppressed. Some of the King's ministers defended the Parlement; Louis, in a moment of fortitude, rebuked them, saying, "I see well that there is no one here but Monsieur Turgot and myself who love the people."[81] On March 12 he summoned the Parlement to a "bed of justice" at Versailles, and ordered it to register the edicts. Parades of workingmen celebrated Turgot's victory.

Exhausted by repeated crises, the Controller General slowed his revolution. When he extended freedom of internal trade to the wine industry (April, 1776) only the monopolists complained. He urged the King to establish religious liberty. He instructed Du Pont de Nemours to draw up a plan for electoral assemblies in each parish, chosen by men who owned land to the value of six hundred livres or more; these local assemblies would elect representatives to a cantonal assembly, which would elect representatives to a provincial assembly, which would elect deputies to a national assembly. Believing that France was not ready for democracy, Turgot proposed to give these assemblies only advisory and administrative functions; legislative power would remain solely in the king; but through these assemblies the ruler would be informed of the condition and needs of the realm. Turgot also offered the King a sketch of universal education as the necessary prelude to an enlightened citizenship. "Sire," he said, "I venture to assert that in two years your nation will no longer be recognizable, and through enlightenment and good morals . . . it will rise above all other states."[82] The minister had no time, the King had no money, to bring these ideas to fulfillment.

Turgot's edicts—and their preambles—had inflamed all the influential classes against him except the merchants and manufacturers, who flourished in the new freedom. Actually he was attempting to bring about peaceably that emancipation of the businessman which was the basic economic result of the Revolution. Yet some merchants secretly opposed him because he had interfered with their monopolies. The nobility opposed him because he wished to put all taxes upon the land, and was setting the poor against the rich. The Parlement hated him for persuading the King to override its vetoes. The clergy distrusted him as an unbeliever who rarely went to Mass and was advocating religious liberty. The farmers general fought him because he wished to replace them with governmental agents in collecting indirect taxes. Financiers resented his getting loans from abroad at four per cent. Courtiers disliked him because he frowned upon their extravagance, their pensions, and their sinecures. Maurepas, his superior in the ministry, looked with no pleasure upon the growing power and independence of the Controller General of Finance. "Turgot," wrote the Swedish ambassador, "finds himself the butt of a most formidable coalition."[83]

Marie Antoinette had at first favored Turgot, and had tried to adjust her expenditures to his economies. But soon she resumed (till 1777) her extravagances in gowns and gifts. Turgot did not conceal his dismay at her drafts upon the treasury. To please the Polignacs the Queen had secured the appointment of their friend the Comte de Guines to the French embassy in London; there he engaged in questionable financial dealings; Turgot joined Vergennes in advising the King to recall him; the Queen vowed revenge.

Louis XVI had his own reasons for losing confidence in his revolutionary minister. The King respected the Church, the nobility, even the *parlements;* these institutions had been mortised in tradition and sanctified by time; to disturb them was to loosen the foundations of the state; but Turgot had alienated them all. Could Turgot be right and all the others wrong? Louis secretly complained about his minister: "Only his friends have merit, and only his own ideas are good."[84] Almost daily the Queen or a courtier sought to influence him against the Controller. When Turgot appealed to him to resist these pressures and Louis made no answer, Turgot returned to his home and wrote to the King (April 30, 1776) a letter that sealed his own fate:

> SIRE:
>
> I will not conceal from you the fact that my heart is deeply wounded by your Majesty's silence last Sunday. . . . So long as I could hope to retain your Majesty's esteem by doing right, nothing was too hard for me. Today what is my recompense? Your Majesty sees how impossible it is for me to make head against those who injure me by the evil they do me, and by the good they keep me from doing by thwarting all my measures; yet your Majesty gives me neither aid nor consolation. . . . I venture to say, Sire, that I have not deserved this. . . .
>
> Your Majesty . . . has pleaded the lack of experience. I know that at the age of twenty-two, and in your position, you have not the training in the judging of men which private individuals obtain from habitual association with equals; but will you have more experience in a week, in a month? And is your mind not to be made up until this slow experience has come? . . .
>
> Sire, I owe to M. Maurepas the place your Majesty has given me; never shall I forget it, never shall I be wanting in due deference to him. . . . But, Sire, do you know how weak is the character of M. de Maurepas?—how much he is governed by the ideas of those around him? Everyone knows that Mme. de Maurepas, who has infinitely less mind but much more character, constantly inspires his will. . . . It is this weakness that moves him to fall in so readily with the clamor of the court against me, and that deprives me of almost all power in my department. . . .
>
> Forget not, Sire, that it was weakness that brought to the block the head of Charles I, . . . that made Louis XIII a crowned slave, . . . and that brought about all the misfortunes of the last reign. Sire, you are deemed weak, and upon occasion I have feared lest your character had this defect; nevertheless I have seen you, upon other more difficult occasions, exhibit genuine courage. . . . Your Majesty cannot, without being untrue to yourself, yield out of complaisance for M. de Maurepas. . . .[85]

To this letter the King made no reply. He felt that now he had to choose between Maurepas and Turgot, and that Turgot was asking almost complete submission of the government to his own will. On May 12, 1776, he sent Turgot an order to resign. On the same day, yielding to the Queen and the

Polignacs, he made the Comte de Guines a duke. Malesherbes, hearing of Turgot's removal, handed in his own resignation. "You are a fortunate man," Louis told him; "would that I too could leave my post."[86] Soon most of Turgot's appointees were discharged. Maria Theresa was shocked by these developments, and agreed with Frederick and Voltaire that the fall of Turgot presaged the collapse of France;[87] she deplored the part that her daughter had played in the matter, and would not believe the Queen's disclaimer of responsibility. Voltaire wrote to Laharpe: "Nothing is left for me but to die, now that M. Turgot has gone."[88]

After his dismissal Turgot lived quietly in Paris, studying mathematics, physics, chemistry, and anatomy. He often saw Franklin, and wrote for him a *Mémoire sur l'impôt*. His gout became so severe that after 1778 he walked only with crutches. He died on March 18, 1781, after years of pain and disappointment. He could not foresee that the nineteenth century would accept and implement most of his ideas. Malesherbes summed him up lovingly: "He had the head of Francis Bacon and the heart of L'Hôpital."[89]

VI. NECKER'S FIRST MINISTRY: 1776–81

Turgot was succeeded as controller of finances by Clugny de Nuis, who re-established the *corvée* and many guilds, and did not enforce the grain edicts. The Dutch bankers canceled their agreement to lend France sixty million livres at four per cent; and the new minister discovered no better way of luring money into the treasury than by establishing a national lottery (June 30, 1776). When Clugny died (October), the bankers of Paris persuaded the King to call to his service the man who had been the ablest critic of Turgot.

Jacques Necker was a Protestant, born at Geneva in 1732. His father, professor of law in the Geneva Academy, sent him to Paris to work as a clerk in the bank of Isaac Vernet. When Vernet retired he advanced some funds to Necker to start a bank of his own. Necker pooled his resources with another Swiss; they prospered through loans to the government and speculation in grains. At the age of thirty-two Necker was rich, dignified, and unmarried. His desire now was not for more wealth but for high place, a chance for distinguished service and national renown. For this he needed a wife and a home as a *point d'appui*, or base of operations. He courted the widowed Marquise de Vermenoux; she refused him, but brought from Geneva the pretty and talented Suzanne Curchod, who had recently escaped marriage with Edward Gibbon. Necker fell in love with Suzanne, and married her in 1764. Their mutual devotion through an eventful life is one of the bright colors in the kaleidoscope of that troubled age. They made a home over his bank, and there she opened a salon (1765) to which she invited writers and men of affairs, hoping that these friendships would smooth and illuminate her husband's way.

Necker himself itched to write. He began in 1773 with an *Éloge de Col-*

bert, which was crowned by the French Academy. Now he retired from business, and entered the political fray with that essay *Sur la Législation des grains* which countered Turgot's policy of *laissez-faire*. The little book won praise from Diderot, who may have relished a paragraph in which the banker (who had read Rousseau) spoke like a socialist. Necker assailed

> the power of the owning class, in exchange for labor, to pay the lowest possible wage, that which merely suffices for strict necessaries. . . . Almost all civil institutions have been made by property owners. One might say that a small number of men, having divided the earth among themselves, made laws as a union and guarantee against the multitude. . . . The latter could say: "Of what import to us are your laws of property?—we have no property; or your laws of justice?—we have nothing to defend; or of liberty?—if we do not work tomorrow we shall die!"[90]

On October 22, 1776, on Maurepas' recommendation, Louis XVI appointed Necker "director of the Royal Treasury." It was an apologetic appellation. Some prelates protested against letting a Swiss Protestant rule the nation's money; Maurepas replied, "If the clergy will pay the debts of the state they can share in choosing the ministers."[91] To cover the reality a French Catholic, Taboureau de Réau, was made controller general of finance as formally Necker's superior. Clerical opposition subsided as Necker made his piety conspicuous. On June 29, 1777, Taboureau resigned, and Necker was named director general of finance. He refused any salary; on the contrary, he lent to the treasury two million livres of his own.[92] He was still denied the title of minister, and was not admitted to the Royal Council.

He did well within the limits of his character and his power. He had been trained to deal with problems of banking rather than of state; he could multiply money more successfully than he could manage men. In the financial administration he established better order, accountability, and economy; he abolished over five hundred sinecures and superfluous posts. Having the confidence of the financial community, he was able to float loans that brought to the treasury 148,000,000 livres within a year. He promoted some minor reforms, reducing inequities in taxation, improving hospitals, and organizing pawnshops to lend money to the poor at low interest. He continued Turgot's endeavors to check the expenditures of the court, the King's household, and the Queen. The collection of indirect taxes was restored to the farmers general (1780), but Necker reduced their number, and subjected them to sharper scrutiny and control. He prevailed upon Louis XVI to allow the establishment of provincial assemblies in Berry, Grenoble, and Montauban, and he set an important precedent by arranging that in these gatherings the representatives of the Third Estate (the middle and lower classes) should equal those of the nobility and the clergy combined. The King, however, chose the members of these assemblies, and allowed them no legislative authority. Necker won a substantial victory by inducing the King to free all remaining serfs on the royal domain, and to invite all feudal lords to do likewise. When they refused, Necker advised Louis to abolish all serfdom in France, with indemnities to the masters, but the King, imprisoned in his traditions, replied that property rights were too basic an institution to be annulled by a decree.[93] In 1780, again on Necker's prompting, he ordered an end to judicial torture, the disuse of subterranean prisons, and the separation of prisoners duly convicted of crimes from those not yet tried, and both of these groups from those arrested for debt. These and other achievements of Necker's first ministry deserve more acknowledgment than they have generally received. If we ask why he did not cut deeper and faster, we should remember that Turgot had been censured for going too fast and making too many simultaneous enemies. Necker was criticized for floating loans instead of raising taxes, but he felt that the people had been taxed enough.

Mme. Campan, always close to the developing drama, summarized well the attitude of the King to his ministers: "Turgot, Malesherbes, and Necker judged that this prince, modest and simple in his habits, would willingly sacrifice the royal prerogative to the solid greatness of his people. His heart disposed him to reform, but his prejudices and fears, and the clamor of pious and privileged persons, intimidated him, and made him abandon plans which his love for the people had suggested."[94] Yet he dared to say, in a public proclamation (1780) probably prepared by Necker, that "the taxes of the poorest part of our subjects" had "increased in proportion much more than all the rest," and he expressed his "hopes that rich people will not think themselves wronged when, put back to the general level [of taxation], they will have to meet the charges which long since they should have shared more equally with others."[95] He shuddered at the thought of Voltaire, but his liberal spirit, unwittingly, had been formed by the work that Voltaire, Rousseau, and the *philosophes* in general had done to expose old abuses and to stir to new life the humanitarian sentiments formerly associated with Christianity. In this first half of his reign Louis XVI began reforms which, if continued and gradually expanded, might have averted revolution. And it was under this weak king that France, despoiled and humiliated by England under his predecessors, struck boldly and with success at proud Britain, and, in the process, helped to free America.

VII. FRANCE AND AMERICA

Philosophy for once agreed with diplomacy: the writings of Voltaire, Rousseau, Diderot, Raynal, and a hundred others had prepared the French mind to support colonial as well as intellectual liberation, and many American leaders—Washington, Franklin, Jefferson—were sons of the French Enlightenment. So, when Silas Deane came to France (March, 1776) to seek a loan for the rebellious colonies, public opinion was strongly sympathetic. The ebullient Beaumarchais sent memoir after memoir to Vergennes, urging him to help America.

Vergennes was a nobleman who believed in monarchy and aristocracy, and was no friend of republics or revolutions; but he longed to avenge

France against England. He would not sanction any open aid to America, for the British navy was still stronger than the French despite Sartine's outlays, and in open war it could soon destroy French shipping. But he advised the King to permit some secret aid. If (he argued) Britain crushed the revolt, it would have, in or near America, a fleet capable of taking at will the French and Spanish possessions in the Caribbean. If the revolt could be prolonged, France would be strengthened, England would be weakened, and the French navy could complete its renewal. Louis trembled at the thought of helping a revolution, and he warned Vergennes against any overt act that might lead to war with England.[96]

In April Vergennes wrote to Beaumarchais:

> We will secretly give you one million livres. We will try to obtain an equal sum from Spain. [This was obtained.] With these two millions you will establish a commercial firm, and at your risk and peril you will supply the Americans with arms, munitions, equipment, and all other things that they will need to maintain the war. Our arsenal will deliver to you arms and munitions, but you will either replace them or pay for them. You will not demand money from the Americans, since they have none, but you will ask in return the produce of their soil, which we will help you sell in this country.[97]

With this money Beaumarchais bought cannon, muskets, gunpowder, clothing, and equipment for 25,000 men; these stores he sent to a port where Deane had assembled and refitted several American privateers. The arrival or assurance of this aid encouraged the colonists to issue their Declaration of Independence (July 4, 1776). Translated into French, and circulated with the tacit consent of the French government, this pronouncement was greeted with enthusiasm and joy by the *philosophes,* and by Rousseau's disciples, who recognized in it some echoes of the *Contrat social.* In September the American Congress appointed Benjamin Franklin and Arthur Lee to proceed as commissioners to France, join Deane, and seek not only more supplies, but, if possible, open alliance.

It was by no means Franklin's first appearance in Europe. In 1724, not yet nineteen, he went to England; he worked as a printer, published a defense of atheism,[98] returned to Philadelphia and deism, married, joined the Freemasons, and won international renown as inventor and scientist. In 1757 he was sent to England to represent the Pennsylvania Assembly in a tax dispute. He stayed in England five years, met Johnson and other notables, visited Scotland, met Hume and Robertson, received a degree from the University of St. Andrews, and was henceforth Dr. Franklin. He was again in England from 1766 to 1775, addressed the House of Commons in opposition to the Stamp Tax, attempted conciliation, and went back to America when he saw that war was imminent. He shared in drafting the Declaration of Independence.

He reached France in December, 1776, bringing two grandchildren with him. He was now seventy years old, and looked like wisdom itself; all the world knows that massive head, the sparse white hair, the face like the full moon at its beaming rise. The scientists covered him with honors, the philosophers and the physiocrats claimed him as their own, the admirers of ancient Rome saw in him Cincinnatus, Scipio Africanus, and both Catos, all reborn. The ladies of Paris dressed their hair in a curly mass to imitate his beaver cap; doubtless they had heard of his many amours. The courtiers were startled by his simplicity of manners, dress, and speech; but instead of his seeming ridiculous in his almost rustic garb, it was their own display of velvet, silk, and lace that appeared now as a vain attempt to cover reality with show. Yet they too accepted him, for he paraded no utopias, talked with reason and good sense, and showed full awareness of the difficulties and the facts. He realized that he was a Protestant, a deist, and a republican seeking help from a Catholic country and a pious King.

He went about his task cautiously. He offended no one, delighted everyone. He paid his respects not only to Vergennes but to Mirabeau *père* and Mme. du Deffand; his bald head shone at the salons and at the Académie des Sciences. A young noble, the Duc de La Rochefoucauld, was proud to be his secretary. Crowds ran after him when he appeared in the streets. His books, translated and published as *Oeuvres complètes,* had a wide welcome; one volume, *La Science du bonhomme Richard (Poor Richard's Almanac),* went through eight editions in three years. Franklin attended the Neuf Soeurs Lodge of the Freemasons, and was made an honorary member; the men he met there helped him to win France to an alliance with America. But he could not ask at once for open support from the government. Washington's army was in retreat before Sir William Howe, and its morale seemed shattered. While waiting for more propitious events Franklin settled down in Passy, a pleasant suburb of Paris, and studied, negotiated, wrote propaganda under pseudonyms, entertained Turgot, Lavoisier, Morellet, and Cabanis, and flirted with Mme. d'Houdetot at Sannois and Mme. Helvétius at Auteuil; for these women had a charm that made them agelessly attractive.

Meanwhile Beaumarchais and others were sending supplies to the colonies, and French army officers were enlisting for service under Washington. Silas Deane wrote in 1776: "I am well-nigh harassed to death with applications of officers to go out to America. . . . Had I ten ships here I could fill them all with passengers for America."[99] All the world knows how the Marquis de Lafayette, nineteen years old, left a devoted and pregnant wife to go (April, 1777) and serve without pay in the colonial army. He confessed to Washington, "The one thing for which I thirst is glory."[100] In that quest he faced many dangers and humiliations, was wounded at Brandywine, shared the hardships of Valley Forge, and earned warm affection from the usually reserved Washington.

On October 17, 1777, a force of five thousand British soldiers and three thousand German mercenaries, coming down from Canada, was overwhelmed at Saratoga by a colonial army of twenty thousand men, and surrendered. When news of this American victory reached France the plea of Franklin, Deane, and Lee for an alliance found more acceptance among the King's advisers. Necker opposed it, unwilling to see his almost balanced budget upset by the expenses of a war. Vergennes and Maurepas won reluctant consent from Louis XVI by warning him that England—long since aware and resentful of French aid to America—might make peace with her colonies and turn her full military force against France. On February 6, 1778, the French government signed two treaties with "the United States of America": one established relations of trade and assistance, the other secretly stipulated that if England should declare war upon France the signatories would join in defense; neither would make peace without the other's consent, and both would continue to fight England until American independence had been won.

On March 20 Louis received the American envoys; Franklin put on silk stockings for this occasion. In April John Adams arrived to replace Deane; he lived with Franklin at Passy, but found the old philosopher so occupied with women that little time was left for official business. He quarreled with Franklin, tried to have him recalled, failed, and returned to America. Franklin was made minister plenipotentiary to France (September, 1779). In 1780, aged seventy-four, he proposed, in vain, to Mme. Helvétius, aged sixty-one.

The war was popular with almost every Frenchman except Necker. He had to raise the great sums that France lent to America: a million livres in 1776, three million more in 1778, another million in 1779, four in 1780, four in 1781, six in 1782.[101] He entered into private negotiations with Lord North (December 1, 1779) in the hope of finding a formula of peace.[102] In addition to these loans he had to raise money to finance the French government, army, navy, and court. Altogether he borrowed, from bankers and the public, 530,000,000 livres.[103] He coaxed the clergy into lending fourteen million, repayable in installments of a million livres a year. He still refused to raise taxes, though the prosperity of the upper classes might have made this comparatively painless; his successors were to complain that he left to them this unavoidable necessity. The financiers favored him because he allowed them, on their loans, the high interest rates which they demanded on the ground that they were running increasing risks of never being repaid.

To foster confidence in the financial community, Necker, with the King's consent, published in January, 1781, a *Compte rendu au Roi,* which purported to inform the King and the nation of the government's revenues and expenses. It brightened the picture by excluding military outlays and other "extraordinary" charges, and ignoring the national debt. The *Compte rendu* was bought by the public at the rate of thirty thousand copies in twelve months. Necker was acclaimed as a wizard of finance who had saved the government from bankruptcy. Catherine the Great asked Grimm to assure Necker of her "infinite admiration for his book and for his talents."[104] But the court was angry that the *Account Rendered to the King* had exposed so many fiscal abuses of the past, and so many pensions that went out from the treasury. Some attacked the document as merely a eulogy of the minister by himself. Maurepas became as jealous of Necker as he had been of Turgot, and joined several others in recommending his dismissal. The Queen, though she had been vexed by Necker's economies, defended him, but Vergennes called him a revolutionist,[105] and the intendants, who feared that Necker planned to undermine them by establishing more provincial assemblies, joined in the cry and hunt. Necker contrived his own fall by declaring that he would resign unless given the full title and authority of a minister, with a seat on the Conseil du Roi. Maurepas told the King that if this were done all the other ministers would abandon their posts. Louis yielded, and let Necker go (May 19, 1781). All Paris except the court mourned his fall. Joseph II sent condolences; Catherine invited him to come and direct the finances of Russia.[106]

On October 12, 1779, Spain joined France against England, and the combined French and Spanish fleets, 140 ships of the line, now almost equaled the 150 vessels of the British navy,[107] and interrupted Britannia's rule of the waves. This change in the balance of naval power vitally affected the American war. The main British army in America, seven thousand men under Lord Cornwallis, held a fortified position at Yorktown on the York River near Chesapeake Bay. Lafayette with five thousand men and Washington with eleven thousand (including three thousand Frenchmen under the Comte de Rochambeau) had converged on Yorktown and had captured all feasible land approaches. On September 5, 1781, a French fleet under the Comte de Grasse defeated an English squadron in the bay, and then shut off all escape by water for Cornwallis' outnumbered force. Having exhausted his provisions, Cornwallis surrendered with all his men (October 19, 1781). France was able to say that de Grasse, Lafayette, and Rochambeau had played major roles in what proved to be the decisive event of the war.

England asked for terms. Shelburne sent separate missions to the French government and to the American envoys in France, hoping to play one ally against the other. Vergennes had already (1781) meditated peace with England on the basis of partitioning most of North America among England, France, and Spain.[108] He entered into an understanding with Spain to keep the Mississippi Valley under European control.[109] In November, 1782, he proposed to support the English in their endeavor to exclude the American states from the Newfoundland fisheries.[110] These negotiations were quite in line with diplomatic precedents, but the American envoys, learning of them, felt warranted in operating with similar secrecy. Vergennes and Franklin agreed that each ally might deal separately with England, but that neither should sign any treaty of peace without the other's consent.[111]

The American negotiators—chiefly John Jay and Franklin—played the diplomatic game brilliantly. They won for the United States not only independence but also access to the Newfoundland fisheries, half of the Great Lakes, and all the vast and rich area between the Alleghenies and the Mississippi; these were far better terms than the American Congress had expected to obtain. On November 30, 1782, Jay, Franklin, and Adams signed a preliminary treaty with England. Formally this violated the agreement with Vergennes, but it stipulated that it was not to have validity until England had made peace with France. Vergennes complained, then accepted the situation. On September 3, 1783, the definitive treaty was signed—"in the name of the most Holy and undivided Trinity"[112]—between England and America at Paris, between England, France, and Spain at Versailles. Franklin remained in France as United States ambassador till 1785. When he died in Philadelphia, April 17, 1790, the French Constituent Assembly wore mourning for three days.

The French government was made bankrupt by the war, and that bankruptcy led to the Revolution. Altogether France had spent a billion livres on the conflict, and the interest on the national debt was dragging the treasury down day by day toward insolvency. Nevertheless that debt was an affair between the government and the rich; it hardly affected the people, many of whom had prospered from the stimulation of industry. The monarchy was critically injured, but not the nation; otherwise how could history explain the success with which the economy and the armies of Revolutionary France withstood half of Europe from 1792 to 1815?

Certainly the spirit of France was uplifted. Statesmen saw in the peace of 1783 a triumphant resurrection from the debasement of 1763. The *philosophes* hailed the result as a victory for their views; and indeed, said de Tocqueville, "The Americans seemed to have executed what our writers had conceived."[113] Many Frenchmen saw in the achievement of the colonies an inspiring presage of democracy spreading through Europe. Democratic ideas infected even the aristocracy and the *parlements*. The Declaration of Rights issued by the Virginia constitutional convention on June 12, 1776, and the Bill of Rights added to the American Constitution, became part models for the Declaration of the Rights of Man promulgated by the French Constituent Assembly on August 26, 1789.

It was the final glory, the culminating chivalry, of feudal France that it died in helping to establish democracy in America. It is true that most French statesmen thought in terms of revitalizing France. But the enthusiasm of nobles like Lafayette and Rochambeau was real; they risked their lives time and again in serving the newborn state. "I was far from being the only one," wrote the young Comte de Ségur, "whose heart palpitated at the sound of the awakening of liberty, struggling to shake off the yoke of arbitrary power."[114] The famous surrender of feudal rights by the aristocrats in the Constituent Assembly (August 4, 1789) was here prefigured and prepared. It was a brave hara-kiri. France gave money and blood to America, and received in return a new and powerful impulse to freedom.

CHAPTER XXXV

Death and the Philosophers

1774–1807

I. VOLTAIRE FINALE

1. Twilight in Ferney

HE was eighty in 1774. He had some fainting spells in these years; we call them little strokes, he called them *petites avertissements*. He shrugged them off, being long since accustomed to dying; he lived on and savored the adulation of kings and queens. Catherine the Great called him "the most illustrious man of our age."[1] Frederick the Great reported in 1775: "People tear at one another in the struggle for the busts of Voltaire at the manufactory of porcelain" in Berlin, "where they do not turn them out fast enough to meet the demand."[2] Ferney had long since become a goal of pilgrimage for intellectual Europe; now it was almost a religious shrine. Hear Mme. Suard after her visit in 1775: "I have seen M. de Voltaire. The transports of St. Theresa never surpassed those which I experienced on seeing this great man. It seemed to me that I was in the presence of a god, a god cherished and adored, to whom I had at last been able to show all my gratitude and all my respect."[3] When he passed through Geneva in 1776 he was nearly stifled by the enthusiastic crowd that surrounded him.[4]

He continued, even in his eighties, to take an interest in politics and literature. He celebrated the accession of Louis XVI with an *Éloge historique de la raison* in which, by the device of prediction, he suggested some reforms that might endear the new ruler to posterity:

> The laws will be made uniform. . . . Pluralities [several benefices held by one ecclesiastic], superfluous expenditure, will be cut away. . . . To the poor who work hard will be given the immense riches of certain idle men who have taken a vow of poverty. The marriages of a hundred thousand [Protestant] families useful to the state will no longer be regarded as concubinage, nor the children held illegitimate. . . . Minor offenses will no longer be punished as great crimes. . . . Torture will no longer be employed. . . . There will cease to be two powers [state and Church], because there can exist but one—that of the king's law in a monarchy, that of the nation in a republic. . . . Lastly, we shall dare to pronounce the word *tolerance*.[5]

Louis accomplished many of these reforms, barring the ecclesiastical. Sincerely pious, and convinced that the loyalty of the Church was an indispensable support of his throne, he deplored the influence of Voltaire. In July, 1774, his government instructed the intendant of Burgundy to keep watch on the aged heretic, and to seize all his papers immediately after his death; Marie Antoinette sympathized with Voltaire, wept at a performance of his

Tancrède, and said she would like to "embrace the author";[6] he sent her some pretty verses.

He had an optimistic spell when his friend Turgot was made controller general of finance; but when Turgot was dismissed he fell into a dark Pascalian pessimism about human affairs. He recovered happiness by adopting a daughter. Reine Philiberte de Varicourt was introduced to him in 1775 as a girl whose family, too poor to provide her with a dowry, was planning to send her to a nunnery. Her innocent beauty warmed the old man's bones; he took her into his ménage, called her "Belle et Bonne," and found a husband for her—the young and moneyed Marquis de Villette. They were married in 1777, and spent their honeymoon at Ferney. "My young lovers are a joy to see," he wrote; "they are working night and day to make a little philosopher for me."[7] The childless octogenarian rejoiced at the thought of being a father, if only by proxy.

Meanwhile he composed his last drama, *Irène*, and sent it to the Comédie-Française. Its reception (January, 1778) created a problem. The custom of the company was to stage each play in the order of its acceptance; two other dramas had been received and approved before Voltaire's—one by Jean-François de Laharpe, one by Nicolas Barthe. Both authors at once waived their prior rights to performance. Barthe wrote to the company:

> A new play by Monsieur de Voltaire has been read to you. You were on the point of considering *L'Homme personnel*. There is only one thing for you to do: do not think of my play any longer. I am aware . . . of the prescribed procedure. But what writer would dare to call upon the rule in a case like this? Monsieur stands above the law like a king. If I am not to have the honor of making my contribution to the pleasure of the public, the least I can do is not to stand in the way of the public delight that will surely be occasioned by a new drama from the pen that created *Zaïre* and *Mérope*. I hope you will stage this play as soon as possible. May its author, like Sophocles, continue to write tragedies until he is a hundred years old, and may he die as you, messieurs, live —flooded with applause.[8]

When news of this reached Voltaire he played lovingly with the idea of going to Paris to direct the staging of his play. After all, there was no official or express prohibition of his coming to Paris. What if the clergy should attack him in their pulpits? He was accustomed to that. What if they persuaded the King to send him to the Bastille? Well, he was accustomed to that too. What a joy it would be to see the great city again, now the capital of the Enlightenment! How it must have changed since his last flight from it twenty-eight years ago! And besides, Mme. Denis, who had long since tired of Ferney, had often begged him to take her back to Paris. The Marquis de Villette offered to put him up in comfort in his *hôtel* on the Rue de Beaune. A dozen messages from Paris cried out: Come!

He decided to go. If the trip killed him it would only advance the inevitable triflingly; it was time to die. The servants of his household, the caretakers of his farm, the peasants on his land, the workers in his industrial colony, protested and mourned; he promised to return in six weeks, but they were sadly sure that they would never see him again; and what successor would treat them as kindly as he had done? When the caravan left Ferney (February 5, 1778) his dependents gathered about him; many of them wept, and he himself could not hold back his tears. Five days later, after a three-hundred-mile trip, he sighted Paris.

2. Apotheosis

At the city gates the officials checked the carriage for contraband. "By my faith, gentlemen," Voltaire assured them, "I believe there is nothing here contraband except myself."[9] Wagnière, his secretary, assures us that his master "had enjoyed all the way the best of health. I never saw him in a more agreeable humor; his gaiety was delightful."[10]

Rooms had been prepared for him in the residence of M. de Villette at the corner of the Rue de Beaune and the Quai des Théatins on the left bank of the Seine. Immediately after alighting from his coach Voltaire walked along the quay to the nearby home of his friend d'Argental, now seventy-eight years old. The Count was not at home, but he soon appeared at the Hôtel Villette. "I have left off dying to come and see you," said Voltaire. Another ancient friend sent a note of welcome; he replied with his usual obituary flourish: "I arrive dead, and I wish to be revived only to throw myself at the knees of Madame la Marquise du Deffand."[11] The Marquis de Jaucourt brought word that Louis XVI was furious at Voltaire's coming to Paris, but Mme. de Polignac came to assure him that Marie Antoinette would protect him.[12] The clergy wished to have him expelled, but no official ban forbidding Voltaire's visit could be found in the records, and Louis confined himself to rejecting the Queen's plea that the world-famous writer be allowed to present himself at court.[13]

When news spread through Paris that the man who had set the intellectual tone of the century had come out of his long exile, the room at the Hôtel Villette was turned into a veritable court and throne. On February 11, it was said, over three hundred persons called, including Gluck, Piccini, Turgot, Talleyrand, Marmontel, and Mesdames Necker, du Barry, and du Deffand. Franklin came with a seventeen-year-old grandson, and asked the blessing of the patriarch for him; Voltaire raised his hands over the boy's head, and said in English, "My child, God and liberty; remember these two words."[14] When the stream of visitors continued day after day Dr. Tronchin wrote to the Marquis de Villette: "Voltaire is living now on his principal rather than his interest, and his strength will soon be exhausted by such a way of living." This note was published in the *Journal de Paris* on February 19, apparently to keep the curious away.[15] Voltaire himself, at Ferney, had predicted what this triumph would cost him: "I would be dead in four days if I had to live as a man of the world."[16]

Some clergymen thought it would be a good stroke to secure his reconciliation with the Catholic Church. He was half willing, for he knew that only those who had died in the arms of the Church could be buried in consecrated ground; and all the cemeteries in France were consecrated ground.

So he welcomed a letter sent him on February 20 by Abbé Gaultier asking for an interview. The abbé came on the twenty-first. They talked for a while, to no known theological result; Mme. Denis begged the abbé to go; Voltaire told him he might come again. On the twenty-fifth Voltaire suffered a severe hemorrhage, spouting blood through mouth and nose when he coughed. He bade his secretary summon Gaultier. Wagnière confesses: "I avoided sending my letter, not wishing to have it said that M. de Voltaire had shown weakness. I assured him that the abbé could not be found."[17] Wagnière knew that the skeptics in Paris were hoping that Voltaire would not surrender to the Church at the last moment; and perhaps he had heard of Frederick the Great's prediction, "He will dishonor us all."[18]

Tronchin came and stopped the hemorrhage, but for the next twenty-two days Voltaire spat blood. On the twenty-sixth he wrote to Gaultier: "I beg you to come as soon as you can."[19] Gaultier came the next morning, found Voltaire sleeping, and went away. On the twenty-eighth Voltaire handed to Wagnière a confession of faith: "I die adoring God, loving my friends, not hating my enemies, and detesting persecution."[20] Gaultier returned on March 2; Voltaire asked to be confessed; the abbé answered that Jean de Tersac, curé of St.-Sulpice, had required him to get a retraction before hearing the confession. Wagnière protested. Voltaire asked for pen and paper, and wrote with his own hand:

> I, the undersigned, having been attacked for four months past with vomiting blood, and being, at the age of eighty-four, no longer able to drag myself to church; and the curé of St.-Sulpice, having wished to add to his good works this of having sent M. l'Abbé Gaultier, priest; I have confessed myself to him; and [declare] that if God disposes of me, I die in the Catholic religion in which I was born, hoping in the divine mercy that it will pardon all my faults; and that if I have ever scandalized the Church, I ask pardon of God and her. —Signed, VOLTAIRE, the 2nd of March, 1778, in the home of M. le Marquis de Villette.[21]

M. de Vielleville and Abbé Mignot (a nephew of Voltaire) signed the statement as witnesses. Gaultier brought it to the Archbishop at Conflans (a suburb) and to the curé of St.-Sulpice, both of whom pronounced it inadequate.[22] Nevertheless Gaultier prepared to administer Communion to Voltaire, but Voltaire suggested that this should be deferred, saying, "I am continually coughing blood; we must guard against mingling my blood with that of the good God."[23] We do not know in what spirit—pious or whimsical —this was said.

On March 3 Diderot, d'Alembert, and Marmontel came to see the sick man. When Gaultier called on that day, with instructions from his superior to get a "less equivocal and more detailed" confession, he was told that Voltaire was in no condition to receive him. Gaultier returned several times, but was each time turned away by the Swiss guard at the door. On March 4 Voltaire wrote to the curé of St.-Sulpice, apologizing for having dealt with a subordinate. On March 13 the curé was received, but apparently nothing came of this visit except an exchange of courtesies.[24] Meanwhile the hemorrhages had ceased; Voltaire felt his strength returning, and his piety declined.

On March 16 *Irène* was performed at the Théâtre-Français. Nearly all the court came, including the Queen. The play was not up to Voltaire's standard, but it was acclaimed nevertheless as a marvelous production for a man of eighty-four. Voltaire, too ill to attend, was kept notified, act by act, of the audience's reaction; and on the seventeenth a deputation from the French Academy brought him congratulations. By March 21 he felt well enough to go out riding. He visited Suzanne de Livry, Marquise de Gouvernet, who had been his mistress sixty-three years before. On the twenty-eighth he visited Turgot.

March 30 was his supreme day. In the afternoon he went to the Louvre for a meeting of the Academy. "As he drove out from his house," reported Denis von Visin, a Russian writer then in Paris, "the carriage was accompanied as far as the Academy by an endless throng of people who kept on applauding. All the Academicians came out to meet him."[25] D'Alembert welcomed him with a speech that brought tears to the old man's eyes. Voltaire was placed in the presidential chair, and was elected by acclamation president for the April quarter. The session over, he was escorted to his carriage, which then moved with difficulty to the Théâtre-Français through an immense crowd that repeatedly cried out, "*Vive Voltaire!*"

When he entered the theater, audience and actors alike rose to greet him. He found his way to the loge where Mme. Denis and the Marquise de Villette were awaiting him. He sat behind them; the audience appealed to him to make himself more visible; he took a seat between the ladies. An actor came to the loge and placed a laurel wreath on Voltaire's head; he took it off and put it upon the head of the Marquise; she insisted on his accepting it. Voices were heard in the audience: "Hail Voltaire!" "Hail Sophocles!" "Honor to the philosopher who teaches men to think!" "Glory to the defender of Calas!"[26] "This enthusiasm," said eyewitness Grimm, "this general delirium, lasted more than twenty minutes."[27] Then *Irène* was performed for the sixth time. At the close the audience demanded a few words from the author; Voltaire complied. The curtain rose again; the actors had taken a bust of Voltaire from the foyer and placed it on the stage; now they crowned it with laurels, and Mme. Vestrice, who had played Irène, read to Voltaire some laudatory verses:

Aux yeux de Paris enchanté	Before the eyes of enchanted Paris
Reçois en ce jour un hommage	Receive on this day a homage
Que confirmera d'âge en âge	Which a severe posterity will
La sévère postérité.	Confirm from age to age.
Non, tu n'as pas besoin	No, you need not
d'atteindre au noir rivage	reach the dark shore
Pour jouir de l'honneur	To enjoy the honor
de l'immortalité.	of immortality.
Voltaire, reçois la couronne	Voltaire, receive the crown
Que l'on vient de te présenter;	Which has been offered you;
Il est beau de la mériter	It is beautiful to merit it
Quand c'est la France qui la donne.[28]	When it is France that gives it.

The audience asked that the verses be repeated; they were. During the applause Voltaire left his seat; all made way for him; he was led to his carriage amid an enthusiastic multitude. Torches were brought, the coachman was persuaded to drive slowly, and a crowd accompanied the carriage to the Hôtel de Villette.[29] So far as we know, there had never been such a scene in all the history of French literature.

Mme. Vigée-Lebrun, who had witnessed all this, wrote: "The celebrated old man was so thin and frail that I feared such strong emotions would cause him mortal harm."[30] Tronchin advised him to return to Ferney as soon as possible; Mme. Denis begged her uncle to make Paris his home. Intoxicated by the reception given him, he agreed with her. He praised the people of Paris as the gayest, most polite, enlightened, and indulgent in the world, with the finest tastes, amusements, and arts;[31] for a moment he forgot the "canaille." Soon he was driving about Paris looking for a house; on April 27 he bought one. Tronchin raged. "I have seen many fools in my life," he said, "but never one madder than he. He is reckoning on a hundred years."[32]

On April 7 Voltaire was taken to the "Nine Sisters" Lodge of the Freemasons. He was initiated into membership without being required to pass through the usual preliminary stages. A laurel wreath was put upon his head, and the chairman made a speech: "We swear to help our brothers, but you have been the founder of an entire colony which adores you and which overflows with your benefactions. . . . You, much beloved brother, have been a Freemason before you received the degree, . . . and you have fulfilled the obligations of a Freemason before you promised to keep them."[33] On the eleventh he returned Mme. du Deffand's visit by going to see her in her apartment at the Convent of St.-Joseph. She felt his face with her seeing hands, and found only bones, but on the twelfth she wrote to Horace Walpole: "He is as animated as ever. He is eighty-four, and verily I think he will never die. He enjoys all his senses, none is weakened. He is a singular being, and in truth far superior."[34] When the nuns heard of his visit they denounced the Marquise for desecrating their cloister with the presence of a man condemned by both Church and state.[35]

On April 27 he went again to the Academy. The discussion turned on the Abbé Delille's version of Pope's *Epistle to Dr. Arbuthnot;* Voltaire had read the original, and complimented the abbé on his translation. He took the occasion to suggest that the *Dictionary* of the Academy be revised to enrich the accredited language with hundreds of new words that had come into respectable usage. On May 7 he returned to the Academy with a plan for the new dictionary. He offered to take charge of all words beginning with *A*, and proposed that each member undertake a letter. On adjourning he thanked them "in the name of the alphabet"; the Marquis de Chastellux replied, "And we thank you in the name of letters."[36] That evening he attended, incognito, a performance of his *Alzire;* at the end of Act IV the audience applauded the actor Larive; Voltaire joined audibly in the acclaim by crying out, "*Ah, que c'est bien!*" (Ah, that is well done!) The audience recognized him, and for forty-five minutes the frenzy of March 30 was renewed.

Perhaps he did well to enjoy those last weeks of life at the expense of his health, instead of shrinking into privacy to gain a few painful days. He worked so ardently on his plan for a new dictionary, and drank so much coffee—sometimes twenty-five cups in a day—that he could not sleep at night. Meanwhile his stricture worsened; urination became more painful and incomplete; toxic elements that should have been eliminated passed into the blood, producing uremia. The Duc de Richelieu sent him a solution of opium, recommending it as an anodyne. Misunderstanding the directions, Voltaire drank a whole flask of it at once (May 11). He fell into a delirium that lasted forty-eight hours. His face was deformed with suffering. Tronchin was summoned, and gave him some relief, but for several days Voltaire uttered no word and could hold no food. He begged to be taken back to Ferney, but it was too late.

On May 30 Abbé Gaultier and the curé of St.-Sulpice came, prepared to administer the final sacrament of the Church if Voltaire would add, to his previous confession of faith, belief in the divinity of Christ. An uncorroborated story by Condorcet[37] described Voltaire as crying out, "In God's name, do not talk to me of that man!" Laharpe reported Voltaire's response as "Let me die in peace." Desnoiresterres accepted the usual account: the priests found Voltaire delirious, and departed without offering him the sacrament.[38] Tronchin claimed that the last hours of the philosopher were marked by extreme agony and cries of fury.[39] Peace came at eleven o'clock that night.

The Abbé Mignot, anticipating that his uncle's corpse would be refused interment in a Paris cemetery, seated it upright in a carriage, and drove with it 110 miles out to the Abbey of Scellières in the village of Romilly-sur-Seine. There a local priest gave the body the traditional religious ceremony, sang a High Mass over it, and allowed its burial in the vault of the church.

An order of Louis XVI forebade the press to mention Voltaire's death.[40] The French Academy asked the Franciscan friars to have a Mass said for the dead man; permission could not be obtained. Frederick the Great, as one skeptic for another, arranged to have a Mass said for Voltaire in a Catholic Church at Berlin; and he composed a warm eulogy of his friend and foe, which was read to the Berlin Academy on November 26, 1778. Catherine the Great wrote to Grimm:

> I have lost two men whom I never saw, who liked me, and whom I honored—Voltaire and Milord Chatham. Not for a very long time, perhaps never, will they—especially the former—find their equals, and never their superiors. . . . A few weeks ago Voltaire was publicly honored, and now they do not dare to bury him. What a man! The first of his nation. Why did you not take possession of his body in my name? You should have sent it to me embalmed. He would have the most splendid tomb. . . . If possible, buy his library and his papers, including his letters. I will pay his heirs a good price.[41]

Mme. Denis received 135,000 livres for the library, which was transported to the Hermitage in St. Petersburg.

In July, 1791, by order of the Constituent Assembly of the Revolution, the remains of Voltaire were removed from the Abbey of Scellières, were taken to Paris, were carried through the city in a triumphal procession, and were deposited in the Church of Ste.-Geneviève (soon to be renamed the Panthéon). In the same year the Quai des Théatins was officially rechristened the Quai de Voltaire. In May, 1814, during the Bourbon Restoration, a group of pious ghouls secretly removed the bones of Voltaire and Rousseau from the Panthéon, put them in a sack, and buried them in a dumping ground on the outskirts of Paris. No trace of them remains.

3. The Influence of Voltaire

It began with the anticlerical moments in *Oedipe* (1718); it operates almost ecumenically today. We have seen it moving sovereigns: Frederick II, Catherine II, Joseph II, Gustavus III, and in less degree Charles III of Spain through Aranda, and Joseph II of Portugal through Pombal. In the intellectual world of the last two hundred years it has been equaled only by the influence of Rousseau and Darwin.

Whereas Rousseau's moral influence was toward tenderness, sentiment, and the restoration of family life and marital fidelity, the moral influence of Voltaire was toward humanity and justice, toward the cleansing of French law and custom from legal abuses and barbaric cruelties; he, more than any other individual, spurred on the humanitarian movement that became one of the credits of the nineteenth century. To feel the influence of Voltaire on literature we need only recall Wieland, Kellgren, Goethe, Byron, Shelley, Heine, Gautier, Renan, Anatole France. Without Voltaire Gibbon would have been impossible; and historians acknowledge his lead and inspiration in giving less attention to the crimes of men and governments and more to the development of knowledge, morals, manners, literature, and art.

Voltaire shared in begetting the French Revolution by weakening the respect of the intellectual classes for the Church, and the belief of the aristocracy in its feudal rights. But after 1789 Voltaire's political influence was overwhelmed by Rousseau's. Voltaire seemed too conservative, too scornful of the masses, too much of the seigneur; Robespierre rejected him; and for two years the *Social Contract* was the bible of the Revolution. Bonaparte felt the two influences in the usual sequence: "Until I was sixteen," he recalled, "I would have fought for Rousseau against the friends of Voltaire; today it is the opposite. . . . The more I read Voltaire the more I love him. He is a man always reasonable, never a charlatan, never a fanatic."[42] After the restoration of the Bourbons the writings of Voltaire became an instrument of bourgeois thought against the revived nobility and clergy. Between 1817 and 1829 there were twelve editions of Voltaire's collected works; in those twelve years over three million volumes by Voltaire were sold.[43] The Communist crusade under Marx and Engels once more gave the leadership to Rousseau. In general the revolutionary movements since 1848 have followed Rousseau rather than Voltaire in politics, Voltaire rather than Rousseau in religion.

The most profound and lasting influence of Voltaire has been on religious belief. Through him and his associates France bypassed the Reformation, and went directly from the Renaissance to the Enlightenment. Perhaps that is one reason why the change was so violent; there was no pause at Protestantism. Some enthusiasts felt that the Enlightenment as a whole was a deeper reformation than that which Luther and Calvin had effected, for it challenged not merely the excesses of sacerdotalism and superstition, but the very fundamentals of Christianity, even of all supernatural creeds. Voltaire gathered into one voice all the varieties of anti-Catholic thought; he gave them added force by clarity, repetition, and wit; and for a time it seemed as if he had pulled down the Temple in which he had been reared. The intellectual classes throughout Christendom were moved by the *philosophes* to a polite deism or a secret atheism. In Germany the youth of Goethe's generation were profoundly influenced. Goethe thought that "Voltaire will always be regarded as the greatest man in the literature of modern times, and perhaps of all times."[44] In England a brilliant minority—Godwin, Paine, Mary Wollstonecraft, Bentham, Byron, Shelley—felt Voltaire's influence, but by and large English deism had anticipated him and dulled his point; moreover, English gentlemen felt that no cultured mind would attack a religion that gave such calming solace to the weaker classes and the weaker sex. In America the founding fathers were almost all disciples of Voltaire. There and in England the influence of Darwin and modern biology has overlaid that of Voltaire in impairing religious belief; and in our times the Christian theology suffers most of all from the unparalleled barbarity of our wars, and the victorious audacities of sciences that invade the very heavens that once housed deities and saints.

To Voltaire, more than to any other individual, we owe the religious toleration that now precariously prevails in Europe and North America. The people of Paris thought of him not as the author of epochal books but as the defender of the Calas and the Sirvens. After him no tribunal in Europe would have dared to break a man on the wheel on such charges and evidence as had condemned Jean Calas. Books like *Emile* were still banned and burned, but their ashes helped to disseminate their ideas. Religious censorship declined until it tacitly admitted defeat. If, as seems possible, our children may have to fight all over again the battle for the freedom of the mind, let them seek inspiration and encouragement in the ninety-nine volumes of Voltaire. They will not find there one dull page.

II. ROUSSEAU EPILOGUE: 1767–78

1. The Haunted Spirit

Arriving in France May 22, 1767, after his unhappy sojourn in England, Rousseau, almost at the end of his sanity, found some comfort in the welcome given him by the cities through which he and Thérèse passed. Though he traveled under the pseudonym of Jean-Joseph Renou, and was still legally under the ban decreed against him in 1762, he was nevertheless recognized and honored; Amiens gave him a triumphal reception, and other towns sent him the *vin de ville*.

Many Frenchmen—all nobles—offered him a home. First, Mirabeau *père*, who gave him a choice of twenty estates; Rousseau chose Fleury-sous-Meudon, near Paris. But the Marquis pestered him to read the Marquis' books; Rousseau fled, and took refuge with Louis-François de Bourbon, Prince de Conti, at Trye-le-Château, near Gisors (June 21, 1767). The Prince put the entire castle at Jean-Jacques' disposal, and even sent musicians to play soft music for him; Rousseau interpreted this as an imputation on his sanity. He thought that Choiseul and the Comtesse de Boufflers (mistress of the Prince) had joined Voltaire, Diderot, and Grimm in conspiring against him; and indeed Voltaire had accused him of setting fire to the theater at Geneva, which burned to the ground on January 29, 1768.[45] Rousseau believed that everyone in Gisors looked upon him as a criminal. He longed to be restored to Geneva, and wrote to Choiseul asking him to persuade the Genevan Council to make reparation to Rousseau for past injuries.[46] Choiseul sent him an official permit to travel anywhere in France, to leave it and to return to it at will.[47] Rousseau now thought of going back to England; he wrote to Davenport inquiring would he be allowed to occupy the house at Wooton again; Davenport answered, By all means.

Fearing for his life at Trye, Rousseau fled from it in June, 1768, leaving Thérèse at the château for her own safety. He went by public coach to Lyons, and lived there for a while with relatives of the Daniel Roguin who had given him a refuge in Switzerland in 1762. Soon, however, he isolated himself in the Golden Fountain Inn at Bourgoin-en-Dauphiné. On the door of his room there he wrote a list of the people whom he believed to be conspiring against him. He sent for Thérèse, received her with joy and tears, and decided at last to marry her. It was done by a civil ceremony at the inn on August 30, 1768.

In January, 1769, they moved to a farmhouse at Mouquin, near Grenoble. There he composed the final, half-insane pages of the *Confessions*, and cooled his nerves with botany. Thérèse found his temper more and more difficult; she herself was suffering from rheumatism and the vague ills sometimes accompanying "change of life." The newlyweds had a quarrel so serious that Rousseau departed on a long botanizing trip, leaving her a letter that advised her to enter a convent (August 12, 1769).[48] When he returned and found her waiting for him their love was renewed. Now he regretted that he had disposed of her offspring. "Happy the man," he felt, "who can rear his children under his own eyes!"[49] To a young mother he wrote: "The sweetest way of life that can possibly exist is that of the home. . . . Nothing is more strongly, more constantly, identified with us than our family and our children. . . . But I who speak of family, children—. . . madame, pity those whose iron fate deprives them of such happiness; pity them if they are merely unfortunate; pity them more if they are guilty!"[50]

The winter at Mouquin was hard to bear in a farmhouse subject to all the winds. Thérèse begged for Paris. On April 10, 1770, the couple resumed their odyssey. They spent a pleasant month at Lyons, where Rousseau's operetta, *Le Devin du village,* was performed as part of a celebration in his honor. They moved by slow stages through Dijon, Montbard, Auxerre. At last, on June 24, 1770, they reached Paris. They took rooms on the fourth floor of his former lodgings at the Hôtel Saint-Esprit, Rue Platrière—now called the Rue Jean-Jacques Rousseau—in one of the noisiest quarters of the city.

He lived modestly and quietly, copying music for income, and studying botany; now (September 21, 1771) he wrote his letter of homage to Linnaeus.[51] When it became known that he was in Paris, old friends and new devotees came to visit him: the Prince de Ligne (who offered him a home on his estate near Brussels), Grétry and Gluck (who came to discuss music with him), Goldoni the dramatist, Sophie Arnould the singer, Gustavus the Crown Prince of Sweden, and young authors like Jean-Joseph Dusaulx and Jacques-Henri Bernardin de Saint-Pierre. In 1777 he received what Voltaire had coveted and missed—a visit from the Emperor Joseph II.[52] His free entry to the Opéra (as a composer) was restored, and he went there occasionally, especially to hear Gluck. Bernardin de Saint-Pierre described him (now sixty years old) as slender, well-proportioned, with "lofty brow, and eyes full of fire; . . . profound sadness in the wrinkles of the brow, and a keen and even caustic gaiety."[53]

Despite the promise he had made in 1762 to write no more books, Rousseau had been stung into renewed composition by the continued attacks of his enemies. To answer these, and all the hostile gossip of Paris and Geneva, he had undertaken the *Confessions* (1765). Now (November, 1770) this was complete, and Rousseau, though as yet unwilling to publish it in its entirety, was resolved that certain parts, relevant to the attacks, should be made known in Paris. So in December he read to Dusaulx and others, in his room, long passages from his greatest book; the reading lasted seventeen hours, interrupted by two hasty collations.[54] In May, 1771, he held another reading, before the Comte and Comtesse d'Egmont, Prince Pignatelli d'Egmont, the Marquise de Mesme, and the Marquis de Juigné. He concluded with a fiery challenge:

> I have written the truth. If any person has heard of things contrary to those I have just stated, were they a thousand times proved, he has heard calumny and falsehood; and if he refuses thoroughly to examine and compare them with me while I am alive, he is not a friend to justice or truth. For my part I openly and without the least fear declare that whoever, even without having read my works, shall have examined with his own eyes my disposition, character, manners, inclinations, pleasures, and habits, and pronounces me a dishonorable man, is himself one who deserves a gibbet.[55]

Those who heard him concluded from his intense emotion that he was nearing mental disorder. Dusaulx pronounced Rousseau's suspicions and recriminations unworthy of "the generous, the virtuous Jean Jacques"; this criticism ended their friendship.[56] Other hearers carried echoes of these readings into the salons of Paris, and some sensitive souls felt that Rousseau had maligned them. Mme. d'Épinay wrote to the lieutenant general of police:

> I must inform you again that the person of whom I spoke to you yesterday morning read his work to Messrs. Dorat, de Pezay, and Dusaulx. Since he is using these men as confidants of a libel, you have the right to let him know what you think of it. I feel that you ought to speak to him with enough kindness so that he should not complain, but with firmness enough so that he won't repeat his fault. If you secure his word of honor I believe he will keep it. Pardon me a thousand times, but my peace of mind was at stake.[57]

The police asked Rousseau to give no more readings; he agreed. He concluded that he could never get a fair hearing in his lifetime, and this feeling of frustration helped to unhinge his mind. After 1772 he closed his door to nearly all visitors but Bernardin de Saint-Pierre. On his solitary walks he suspected an enemy in almost everyone whom he passed. Aside from such specters of hostility his essential good nature remained. He subscribed, over Voltaire's resistance, to the fund for a statue to Voltaire. When an abbé sent him a brochure denouncing Voltaire he rebuked the writer: "Voltaire," he told him, "is without doubt a bad man, whom I do not intend to praise; but he has said and done so many good things that we should draw the curtain over his irregularities."[58]

When he could take his mind off the "conspiracy" that he saw around him, he could write with as much clarity as before, and with surprising conservatism and practicality. We have seen how the Polish convention of 1769 asked his suggestions for a new constitution. He began his *Considérations sur le gouvernement de la Pologne* in October, 1771, and finished it in April, 1772. Our first impression of it is that it violates all the principles for which he had fought so passionately. On rereading it in old age we are comforted to see that Rousseau (then sixty) could also age and, as the old would like to put it, mature. The same man who had cried out, "Man is born free, and is everywhere in chains," now warned the Poles, whose "free veto" had condemned them to anarchy, that freedom is a trial as well as a dispensation, and requires a self-discipline far more arduous than obedience to external commands.

> Liberty is a strong food, but it needs a stout digestion. . . . I laugh at those degraded peoples who rise in revolt at a word from an intriguer; who dare to speak of liberty while in total ignorance of what it means; and who . . . imagine that, to be free, it is enough to be a rebel. High-souled and holy liberty! If these poor men could only know thee; if they could only learn what is the price at which thou art won and guarded; if they could only be taught how far sterner are thy laws than the hard yoke of the tyrant![59]

Life and Montesquieu had taught Rousseau that such discussions as his *Social Contract* are flights *in vacuo*, abstract theories without a hinge on reality. All states, he now admitted, are rooted in history and circumstance, and will die if their roots are indiscriminately cut. So he advised the Poles to make no sudden changes in their constitution. They should keep their elective monarch but should limit their *liberum veto;* they should keep Catholicism as the state religion but develop an educational system independent of the Church.[60] Poland, in the existing condition of its communications and transport, seemed to him too large to be ruled from one center; better divide it into three states federated only in mutual contacts and foreign affairs. He who had once denounced private property as the source of all evils now sanctioned Polish feudalism; he proposed to tax all land, but to leave present property rights intact. He hoped that serfdom would one day be abolished, but he did not advocate its early end; that, he thought, should wait until the serf had had more education. Everything, he insisted, depended upon the extension of education; to promote freedom faster than intelligence and moral character would be an open sesame to chaos and partition.

The partition was effected before Rousseau could finish his essay; in Poland, as in Corsica, *Realpolitik* ignored his philosophical legislation. This double frustration shared in embittering his final years, and it intensified his scorn of those *philosophes* who had praised as enlightened despots and philosopher kings those rulers—Frederick II, Catherine II, and Joseph II—who were dismembering Poland.

In 1772 he began another attempt to answer his enemies. He called it *Dialogues: Rousseau juge de Jean-Jacques.* He worked on this 540-page book, on and off, for four years, and his mind darkened more and more as he proceeded. The foreword begged the reader to read all three dialogues thoroughly; "consider that this grace, which is asked of you by a heart burdened with sorrow, is a debt of justice which Heaven imposes upon you."[61] He admitted the "long-windedness, the repetitions, the verbiage, and the disorder of this composition,"[62] but for fifteen years past (he said) there had been a conspiracy to defame him, and he must clear himself before dying. He denied any contradiction between the individualism of the *Discourses* and the collectivism of the *Social Contract;* he reminded his readers that he had never wished to destroy the sciences and the arts and return to barbarism. He described his works—especially *Julie* and *Émile*—as rich in virtue and tenderness, and asked how such books could have been written by so diseased a roué as his detractors had pictured him to be.[63] He charged his enemies with burning him in effigy, and with serenading him in mockery.[64] Even now, he complained, they kept watch on all his visitors, and stirred up his neighbors to insult him.[65] He repeated the story of his birth, family, and youth, and described the gentleness and integrity of his character, but he confessed to laziness, "a taste for reverie,"[66] and a tendency to create, on his solitary walks, an imaginary world in which for the moment he could be happy. He comforted himself with the prediction, "A day will come, I am confident, when good and honorable people will bless my memory and will weep over my fate."[67]

To the final dialogue he added a chapter entitled "The History of This Work." He told how, to bring his book to the attention of Paris and Versailles, he resolved to deposit a copy of the manuscript, with an address to Providence, on the high altar in the Cathedral of Notre-Dame. This he tried to do on February 24, 1776. Finding the sanctuary barred by a railing, he sought side entrances to it; finding these locked, he grew dizzy, ran out of the church, and wandered in the streets in semi-delirium for hours before reaching his rooms.[68] He composed a plea to the French people, entitled it "To All Frenchmen Who Still Love Justice and Truth," copied it on hand-bills, and distributed these to passers-by in the streets. Several of these refused it, saying that it was not addressed to them.[69] He gave up his efforts, and resigned himself to defeat.

His excitement abated now that he was reconciled. He wrote at this time (1777–78) his most beautiful book, *Rêveries d'un promeneur solitaire*. He told how the people of Môtiers had rejected him and had stoned his house, and how he had retired to the Île de St.-Pierre in the Lake of Bienne. There he had found happiness; and now, looking back upon that retreat, he pictured the quiet water, the inflowing streams, the verdure-covered island, and the polymorphous sky. He struck a new romantic note by suggesting that the meditative spirit may always find in nature something responsive to its mood. As we read those pages we ask ourselves, Could a man half insane write so well, so lucidly, at times so serenely? But then the old plaints recur, and Rousseau mourns again that he had cast off his children, that he had not had the simple courage to bring up a family. He saw a child playing; he returned to his room and "wept and expiated."[70]

In those last years at Paris he envied the religious faith that lifted the life of the common people about him into a drama of death and resurrection. Sometimes he attended Catholic services. He visited a hermitage with Bernardin de Saint-Pierre, and heard the monks reciting a litany. "Ah, how happy the man who can believe!"[71] He could not believe,[72] but he tried to behave like a Christian, giving alms, visiting and comforting the sick.[73] He read and annotated Thomas a Kempis' *The Imitation of Christ*.

Bitterness diminished in him as he approached death. When Voltaire arrived in Paris and received so many honors, Rousseau was jealous, but spoke well of his old enemy. He rebuked an acquaintance who had ridiculed the coronation of Voltaire at the Théâtre-Français: "How dare you mock the honors rendered to Voltaire in the temple of which he is the god, and by the priests who for fifty years have been living off his masterpieces?"[74] When he heard that Voltaire was dying he predicted, "Our lives were linked to each other; I shall not survive him long."[75]

When the spring of 1778 began to flower he asked that someone offer him a home in the country. Marquis René de Girardin invited him to occupy a cottage near his château at Ermenonville, some thirty miles from Paris. Jean-Jacques and Thérèse went on May 20. There he gathered botanical specimens, and taught botany to the Marquis' ten-year-old son. On July 1 he dined heartily with the family of his host. The next morning he suffered an apoplectic stroke, and fell to the floor. Thérèse lifted him onto his bed, but he fell from it, and struck the tiled floor so sharply that his head was cut and blood poured out. Thérèse cried out for help; the Marquis came, and found Rousseau dead.

Falsehoods pursued him to the end. Grimm and others spread the tale that Rousseau had committed suicide; Mme. de Staël later added that he had killed himself in grief over discovering Thérèse's infidelity. This was an especially cruel story, for Thérèse's comment, soon after his death, revealed her love for him: "If my husband was not a saint, who could be one?" Other gossip described Rousseau as dying insane; all who were with him in those final days described him as serene.

On July 4, 1778, he was buried on the Isle of Poplars in a small lake on the Girardin estate. For a long time this Île des Peupliers was a goal of pious pilgrimage; all the world of fashion—even the Queen—went out to worship at Rousseau's tomb. On October 11, 1794, his remains were removed to the Panthéon, and were laid near those of Voltaire. From that haven of neighborly peace their spirits rose to renew their war for the soul of the Revolution, of France, and of Western man.

2. The Influence of Rousseau

So we end as we began, by contemplating, now in substantiation, the incredible effect of Rousseau upon the literature, pedagogy, philosophy, religion, morals, manners, art, and politics of the century that began with his death. Today much that he wrote seems exaggerated, sentimental, or absurd; only the *Confessions* and the *Rêveries* move us; but till yesterday his every word was being heard in one or another field of European or American thought. Rousseau, said Mme. de Staël, "invented nothing, but he set everything on fire."[76]

First of all, of course, he was the mother of the Romantic movement. We have seen many others sowing its seed: Thomson, Collins, Gray, Richardson, Prévost, and Christianity itself, whose theology and art are the most marvelous romance of all. Rousseau matured the seeds in the hothouse of his emotions, and delivered the offspring, full-grown and fertile from birth, in the *Discourses*, *La Nouvelle Héloïse*, the *Contrat social*, *Émile*, and the *Confessions*.

But what shall we mean by the Romantic movement? The rebellion of feeling against reason, of instinct against intellect, of sentiment against judgment, of the subject against the object, of subjectivism against objectivity, of solitude against society, of imagination against reality, of myth and legend against history, of religion against science, of mysticism against ritual, of poetry and poetic prose against prose and prosaic poetry, of neo-Gothic against neoclassical art, of the feminine against the masculine, of romantic love against the marriage of convenience, of "Nature" and the "natural" against civilization and artifice, of emotional expression against conventional restraints, of individual freedom against social order, of youth against authority, of democracy against aristocracy, of man versus the state—in short, the revolt of the nineteenth century against the eighteenth, or, more precisely, of 1760–1859 against 1648–1760: all these are waves of the great Romantic tide that swept Europe between Rousseau and Darwin.

Now nearly every one of these elements found voice and sanction in Rousseau, and some support in the needs and spirit of the time. France had wearied of classic reason and aristocratic restraint. Rousseau's exaltation of feeling offered liberation to suppressed instincts, to repressed sentiment, to oppressed individuals and classes. The *Confessions* became the bible of the Age of Feeling as the *Encyclopédie* had been the New Testament of the Age of Reason. Not that Rousseau rejected reason; on the contrary, he called it a divine gift, and accepted it as final judge;[77] but (he felt) its cold light needed the warmth of the heart to inspire action, greatness, and virtue. "Sensibility" became the watchword of women and men. Women learned to faint, men to weep, more readily than before. They oscillated between joy and grief, and mingled both in their tears.

The Rousseauian revolution began at the mother's breasts, which were now to be freed from stays; this part of the revolution, however, proved the hardest of all, and was won only after more than a century of alternating imprisonment and release. After *Émile* French mothers nursed their infants, even at the opera, between arias.[78] The child was freed from swaddling clothes, and was brought up directly by the parents. When it went to school it enjoyed—more in Switzerland than in France—education à la Rousseau. Since man was now considered good by nature, the pupil was to be viewed not as an imp of the perverse but as an angel whose wishes were the voice of God. His senses were no longer condemned as the instruments of Satan, but as doors to illuminating experiences and a thousand harmless delights. Classrooms were no longer to be prisons. Education was to be made natural and pleasant, through the unfolding and encouragement of inherent curiosities and powers. The stuffing of the memory with facts, the stifling of the mind with dogmas, were to be replaced by training in the arts of perceiving, calculating, and reasoning. As far as possible children were to learn not from books but from things—from plants in the field, rocks in the soil, clouds and stars in the skies. Enthusiasm for Rousseau's educational ideas stimulated Pestalozzi and Lavater in Switzerland, Basedow in Germany, Maria Montessori in Italy, John Dewey in America; "progressive education" is part of the legacy of Rousseau. Inspired by Rousseau, Friedrich Froebel established the kindergarten system in Germany, whence it spread throughout the Western world.

Some breath of the Rousseauian afflatus reached art. The exaltation of children influenced Greuze and Mme. Vigée-Lebrun; the paintings of the Pre-Raphaelites in England reflected the cult of pathos and mystery. Deeper was the effect on morals and manners. There was some growth in the warmth and fidelity of friendship, in mutual sacrifices and solicitude. Romantic love captured literature and made its way into life. Husbands could now love their wives without flouting convention; parents could love their children; the family was restored. "People had been smiling at adultery; Rousseau dared to make it a crime"[79]; it continued, but was no longer *de rigueur*. The idolatry of courtesans was replaced by pity for prostitutes. Contempt for convention resisted the tyranny of etiquette. Bourgeois virtues came into repute: industry, thrift, simplicity of manners and dress. Soon France would lengthen its *culottes* into trousers and be sans-culottes in pants as well as in politics. Rousseau shared with English horticulture in changing French gardens from Renaissance regularity to romantic curves and surprising turns, and sometimes to wild and "natural" disarray. Men and women went out from the city to the country, and married the moods of Nature to their own. Men climbed mountains. They sought solitude and fondled their egos.

Literature surrendered almost en masse to Rousseau and the Romantic wave. Goethe bathed *Werther* in love, nature, and tears (1774), and made Faust compress half of Rousseau in three words: *"Gefühl ist Alles"*—feeling is all. "*Émile* and its sentiments," he recalled in 1787, "had a universal influence on the cultivated mind."[80] Schiller stressed the revolt against law in *The Robbers* (1781); he hailed Rousseau as a liberator and martyr, and compared him with Socrates.[81] Herder, at a similar stage in development, cried, "Come, Rousseau, and be my guide."[82] The eloquence of Rousseau helped to free French poetry and drama from the rules of Boileau, the tradition of Corneille and Racine, and the rigors of classic style. Bernardin de Saint-Pierre, fervent disciple of Rousseau, achieved a romantic classic in *Paul et Virginie* (1784). After the Napoleonic interlude the literary influence of Jean-Jacques triumphed in Chateaubriand, Lamartine, Musset, Vigny, Hugo, Gautier, Michelet, and George Sand. It mothered a brood of confessions, reveries, and novels of sentiment or passion. It favored the conception of genius as innate and lawless, the victor over tradition and discipline. In Italy it moved Leopardi; in Russia, Pushkin and Tolstoi; in England, Wordsworth, Southey, Coleridge, Byron, Shelley, and Keats; in America, Hawthorne and Thoreau.

Half the philosophy of the century between *La Nouvelle Héloïse* (1761) and Darwin's *Origin of Species* (1859) is colored with the revolt of Rousseau against the rationalism of the Enlightenment. Indeed, in a letter of 1751 to Bordes, Rousseau had already expressed his scorn of philosophy.[83] He based this contempt on what he felt to be the impotence of reason to teach men virtue. Reason seems to have no moral sense; it will labor to defend any desire, however corrupt. Something else is needed—an inborn consciousness of right and wrong; and even this conscience has to be warmed with feeling if it is to engender virtue and make not a clever calculator but a good man.

This, of course, had been said by Pascal, but Pascal had been rejected by Voltaire, and in Germany the "rationalism" of Wolff was rising in the universities. When Immanuel Kant became professor at Königsberg he had already been convinced by Hume and the *philosophes* that reason alone could give no adequate defense of even the fundamentals of the Christian theology. In Rousseau he found a way to save those fundamentals: deny the validity of reason in the suprasensible world; affirm the independence of mind, the primacy of will, and the absoluteness of innate conscience; and deduce the freedom of the will, the immortality of the soul, and the existence of God from man's feeling of unconditional obligation to the moral law.

Kant acknowledged his debt to Rousseau, hung a picture of him on his study wall, and declared him the Newton of the moral world.[84] Other Germans felt the spirit of Rousseau upon them: Jacobi in his *Gefühlphilosophie*, Schleiermacher in his web-weaving mysticism, Schopenhauer in his enthronement of the will. The history of philosophy since Kant has been a contest between Rousseau and Voltaire.

Religion began by banning Rousseau, and went on to use him as its savior. Protestant leaders joined Catholic in declaring him an infidel; he was classed with Voltaire and Bayle as "spreading the poison of error and impiety."[85] Yet even in his lifetime there were laymen and clergymen who took comfort in hearing that the Savoyard Vicar had accepted with ardor the cardinal doctrines of Christianity, and had counseled doubters to return to their native faiths. On his flight from Switzerland in 1765 Rousseau was welcomed by the bishop of Strasbourg. After his return from England he found some French Catholics gratefully quoting him against unbelievers, and holding hopes for his triumphant conversion.

The theorists of the French Revolution tried to establish a morality independent of religious creeds; Robespierre, following Rousseau, gave up this attempt as a failure, and sought the support of religious beliefs in maintaining moral order and social content. He condemned the *philosophes* as rejecting God but keeping kings; Rousseau (said Robespierre) had risen above these cowards, had bravely attacked all kings, and had spoken in defense of God and immortality.[86]

In 1793 the rival legacies of Voltaire and Rousseau came to decision in the struggle between Jacques-René Hébert and Maximilien Robespierre. Hébert, a leader of the Paris Commune, followed Voltairean rationalism, encouraged the desecration of churches, and set up the public worship of the Goddess of Reason (1793). Robespierre had seen Rousseau in the philosopher's final stay in Paris. He apostrophized Jean-Jacques: "Divine man! . . . I looked upon your august features; . . . I understood all the griefs of a noble life devoted to the worship of truth."[87] When Robespierre rose to power he persuaded the National Convention to adopt the Profession of Faith of the Savoyard Vicar as the official religion of the French nation; and in May, 1794, he inaugurated, in memory of Rousseau, the Festival of the Supreme Being. When he sent Hébert and others to the guillotine on a charge of atheism, he felt that he was following to the letter the counsels of Rousseau.

The agnostic Napoleon agreed with Robespierre on the need of religion, and realigned the French government with God (1802). The Catholic Church was fully restored with the French Bourbon Restoration (1814); it won the powerful pens of Chateaubriand, de Maistre, Lamartine, and Lamennais; but now the old faith leaned more and more on the rights of feeling rather than the arguments of theology; it fought Voltaire and Diderot with Pascal and Rousseau. Christianity, which had seemed moribund in 1760, flourished again in Victorian England and Restoration France.

Politically we are only now emerging from the age of Rousseau. The first sign of his political influence was in the wave of public sympathy that supported active French aid to the American Revolution. Jefferson derived the Declaration of Independence from Rousseau as well as from Locke and Montesquieu. As ambassador to France (1785–89) he absorbed much from both Voltaire and Rousseau; he echoed Jean-Jacques in supposing that the North American Indians "enjoy in their general mass an infinitely greater degree of happiness than those who live under European governments."[88] The success of the American Revolution raised the prestige of Rousseau's political philosophy.

According to Mme. de Staël, Napoleon ascribed the French Revolution more to Rousseau than to any other writer.[89] Edmund Burke thought that in the French Revolutionary Constituent Assembly (1789–91)

> there is a great dispute, among their leaders, which of them is the best re-semblance of Rousseau. In truth, they all resemble him. . . . Him they study, him they meditate; him they turn over in all the time they can spare from the laborious mischief of the day or the debauches of the night. Rousseau is their canon of Holy Writ; . . . to him they erect their first statue.[90]

Mallet Dupan in 1799 recalled that

> Rousseau had a hundred times more readers among the middle and lower classes than Voltaire. He alone inoculated the French with the doctrine of the sovereignty of the people. . . . It would be difficult to cite a single revolution-ist who was not transported over these anarchical theories, and who did not burn with ardor to realize them. . . . I heard Marat in 1788 read and comment on the *Contrat social* in the public streets to the applause of an enthusiastic auditory.[91]

Throughout France orators quoted Rousseau in preaching the sovereignty of the people; it was partly the ecstatic welcome given to this doctrine that enabled the Revolution to survive for a decade despite its enemies and its excesses.

Through all the alternations of revolutions and reaction, Rousseau's influ-ence on politics continued. Because of his contradictions, and because of the force and passion with which he proclaimed them, he served as prophet and saint to anarchists and socialists alike; for both these opposed gospels found nourishment in his condemnation of the rich and his sympathy for the poor. The individualism of the first *Discourse*, and its rejection of "civilization," inspired rebels from Paine, Godwin, and Shelley to Tolstoi, Kropotkin, and Edward Carpenter. "At fifteen," said Tolstoi, "I carried around my neck, instead of the usual cross, a medallion with Rousseau's portrait."[92] The egali-tarianism of the second *Discourse* provided a basic theme for the variations of socialist theory from "Gracchus" Babeuf through Charles Fourier and Karl Marx to Nikolai Lenin. "For a century now," said Gustave Lanson, "all the progress of democracy, equality, universal suffrage, . . . all the claims of extreme parties that may be the wave of the future, the war against wealth and property, all the agitations of the working and suffering masses, have been in a sense the work of Rousseau."[93] He had not appealed to the learned and lofty with logic and argument; he had spoken to the people at large with feeling and passion in language that they could understand; and

the ardor of his eloquence proved, in politics as in literature, mightier than
the scepter of Voltaire's pen.

III. *MARCHE FUNÈBRE*

Diderot, after seeing Voltaire in 1778, asked a friend, "Why must he
die?"[94] The funeral march of the *philosophes*, from the death of Helvétius
in 1771 to that of Morellet in 1819, seemed to be a sardonic commentary on
vanity and pride, but we might also wonder why some of these men lived
so long, inviting all the pains and humiliations of senility.

The more fortunate among them died before the Revolution, comforted
by a hundred signs that their ideas were approaching victory. Condillac
disappeared in 1780, Turgot in 1781. D'Alembert reluctantly survived the
death of Mlle. de Lespinasse. She had left her papers to his care, and from
them it was evident that during the last twelve years of her life her love had
been given to Mora or Guibert, leaving for himself only a friendship sometimes tinged with irritation. "D'Alembert is badly hit," Condorcet told Turgot; "my whole hope for him now is that his life may prove bearable."[95] He
returned to his studies, but he wrote nothing more of importance. He attended some of the salons, but the life had gone out of his once brilliant
conversation. He rejected Frederick's invitation to Potsdam, and Catherine's
invitation to St. Petersburg. He wrote to Frederick: "I feel like a man with
a long stretch of desert in front of him and the precipice of death at its end,
and no hope of coming across a single soul who would grieve if he saw him
fall into it, or give himself another thought after he had disappeared."[96]

He was mistaken; many cared, if only those to whom he regularly sent
part of his income. Hume, in his will, left £200 to d'Alembert,[97] confident
that it would be spread around. Despite various pensions, d'Alembert lived
simply to the last. In 1783 both he and Diderot were stricken with serious
illnesses—Diderot with pleurisy, d'Alembert with a disorder of the bladder.
Diderot recovered; d'Alembert died (October 29, 1783), aged sixty-seven.

Diderot had returned from his Russian adventure in October, 1774. The
long trip in a confining carriage had weakened him, but he correctly predicted that he had "ten years of life left in his sack."[98] He worked on a *Plan
of a University for the Government of Russia* (which was not published
till 1813); anticipating pedagogical developments by 150 years, he advocated
predominant attention to science and technology, and placed Greek, Latin,
and literature almost at the end of the list, with philosophy between. In 1778
he began an *Essai sur les règnes de Claude et de Néron, et sur la vie et les
écrits de Sénèque*. He digressed to beg the victorious Americans, in their
new commonwealth, to "prevent the enormous increase and unequal distribution of wealth and luxury, idleness, and the corruption of morals."[99] And
in the section on Seneca he made place for a hot defense of Grimm, Mme.
d'Épinay, and himself against the charges that Rousseau had made in public
readings of the *Confessions*:

If, by a bizarrerie without exception, there should ever appear a work where honest people are pitilessly torn to pieces by a clever criminal [*un artificieux scélérat*], . . . look ahead and ask yourselves if an impudent fellow, . . . who has confessed a thousand misdeeds, can be . . . worthy of belief. What can calumny cost such a man?—what can one crime more or less add to the secret turpitude of a life hidden during more than fifty years behind the thickest mask of hypocrisy? . . . Detest the ingrate who speaks evil of his benefactors; detest the atrocious man who does not hesitate to blacken his old friends; detest the coward who leaves on his tomb the revelation of secrets confided to him. . . . As for me, I swear that my eyes shall never be sullied by reading his work; I protest that I would prefer his invectives to his praise.[100]

In 1783 Mme. d'Épinay died. Diderot felt this loss deeply, for he had enjoyed her friendship and her salon. Grimm and d'Holbach were alive, but his relations with them were tepid; each of the three was sinking into the narrow egoism of old age; all they could talk of to each other was their pains. Diderot's assortment included nephritis, gastritis, gallstones, and inflammation of the lungs; he could no longer climb the stairs from his fourth-floor rooms to his fifth-floor library. He felt lucky now to have a wife; he had reduced his infidelities to wistful memories, and she had worn out her vocabulary; they lived in a peace of mutual exhaustion.

In 1784 he fell seriously ill. Jean de Tersac, the curé of St.-Sulpice, who had failed with Voltaire, tried to redeem himself with Diderot, visited him, begged him to return to the Church, and warned him that unless he received the sacraments he could not enjoy burial in a cemetery. Diderot answered, "I understand you, Monsieur le Curé. You refused to bury Voltaire because he did not believe in the divinity of the Son. Well, when I am dead, they can bury me wherever they like, but I declare that I believe neither in the Father nor in the Holy Ghost, nor in any of the Family."[101]

Hearing of his infirmities, the Empress Catherine secured for him and his wife a splendid suite of rooms in the Rue de Richelieu. They moved into it about July 18. He smiled as he saw new furniture being carried in; he could use it, he said, for only a few days. He used it for less than two weeks. On July 31, 1784, he ate a hearty meal, had an attack of coronary thrombosis, and died at the table, aged seventy-one. His wife and his son-in-law persuaded a local priest to give Diderot a church burial despite his notorious atheism. The corpse was buried in the Church of St.-Roch, from which, at some unknown time, it mysteriously disappeared.

The procession continued. Mably died in 1785, Buffon in 1788, d'Holbach in 1789. Raynal, as we have seen, outlived the Revolution, denounced its barbarities, and surprised himself by dying a natural death (1796). Grimm met all strokes of fortune with Teutonic patience. In 1775 Joseph II made him a baron of the Holy Roman Empire, and in 1776 the Duke of Saxe-Gotha made him minister to France. His *Correspondance littéraire*, after 1772, was mostly written by his secretary Jakob Meister, but Grimm contributed trenchant articles on literature, art, religion, morals, politics, and philosophy. He was the only thorough skeptic among the *philosophes*, for he doubted philosophy too, and reason, and progress. While Diderot and others of the faithful looked toward posterity with utopia mirrored in their eyes, Grimm noted that this was a very ancient mirage, "an illusion which has been handed down from generation to generation"; and we have noted his prediction, in 1757, of an imminent "fatal revolution."[102] When the Revolution came and became murderous, he returned to his native Germany and settled in Gotha (1793). Catherine relieved his poverty and made him her minister at Hamburg (1796). On the death of his imperial benefactress he went to live with Émilie de Belsunce, granddaughter of his beloved Mme. d'Épinay. He survived till 1807, chiefly on memories of those exciting days when the mind of France was leading Europe to the dizzy brink of freedom.

IV. THE LAST *PHILOSOPHE*

Jean-Antoine-Nicolas Caritat, Marquis de Condorcet, descendant of an ancient family in Dauphiné, was born in Picardy (1743), was educated by the Jesuits at Reims and Paris, and for many years thought only of becoming a great mathematician. At the age of twenty-six he was elected to the Académie des Sciences. Later, as its permanent secretary, he composed *éloges* of departed members, as Fontenelle had done for the French Academy. Voltaire liked these memorial eulogies so well that he told Condorcet: "The public wishes that an Academician might die every week or so that you might have a chance to write about him."[103] He visited Voltaire at Ferney (1770), edited an edition of Voltaire's works for Beaumarchais, and wrote for it an ardent *Vie de Voltaire*. D'Alembert persuaded him to contribute to the *Encyclopédie*, and introduced him to Julie de Lespinasse, at whose receptions he became, despite his shyness, a principal figure. Indeed, in Julie's view, he stood next only to d'Alembert in the range of his intellect, and perhaps above him in the warmth of his benevolence. He was among the first to join the campaign against slavery (1781). Julie helped to free him from his hopeless love for Mlle. d'Ussé, a coquette who took advantage of his devotion but did not return it. He consoled himself with the friendship of Jean-Baptiste Suard and Mme. Suard, and lived with them in a contented *ménage à trois*.

In 1785 he published an *Essai sur l'application de l'analyse aux probabilités*. In this he anticipated Malthus' theory that the growth of population tends to outrun the production of food; but instead of advocating sexual abstinence as a remedy, he proposed birth control.[104]

He welcomed the Revolution as opening the door to a future of universal education, justice, and prosperity. In 1790 he was chosen to the municipal council that had taken over the administration of Paris. He was elected to the Legislative Assembly that ruled France from October 1, 1791, to September 20, 1792. As chairman of the Committee on Public Instruction he drew up a report advocating and outlining a national system of primary and secondary education, universal, free, equal for both sexes, and removed from ecclesiastical influence.[105] He laid down the principle of the "welfare state": "All social institutions should have for their aim the physical, intellectual, and moral betterment of the most numerous and poorest class" of the population.[106] The report was presented to the Assembly on April 21, 1792; action on it was deferred by the Revolutionary Wars; but when Napoleon had established his power he made Condorcet's report the basis of his epochal reorganization of education in France.

In the National Convention that replaced the Legislative Assembly Condorcet had less prominence, for he was distrusted by the conservative Girondins as a republican, and by the radical Jacobins as an aristocrat who was trying to keep the Revolution under middle-class control.[107] He voted to condemn Louis XVI as guilty of treason, but voted against his execution. Appointed with eight others to a commission to formulate a new constitution, he submitted a draft that was rejected as too favorable to the bourgeoisie. When the Convention, dominated by the Jacobins, adopted a more radical constitution, Condorcet wrote an anonymous pamphlet advising the citizens to repudiate it. On July 8, 1793, the Convention ordered his arrest.

For nine months he hid himself in a pension kept by the widow of the painter Claude-Joseph Vernet. There, to distract his mind from fear of apprehension, he wrote the little book that served both as a summary of the Enlightenment and as a blueprint of the coming utopia. The manuscript bears the title *Prospectus d'un tableau historique des progrès de l'esprit humain*.[108] He called it also *Esquisse*—a sketch; apparently he hoped someday to write a fuller exposition of his philosophy.

He took his inspiration from the lecture in which Turgot, then a seminarian (December 11, 1750), had outlined "The Successive Advances of the Human Mind."[109] Condorcet divided history into ten stages: (1) the union of families into tribes; (2) pastoralism and agriculture; (3) invention of writing; (4) the flowering of Greek culture to the time of Alexander; (5) the development of knowledge during the rise and decline of Rome; (6) the Dark Ages, from A.D. 476 to the Crusades; (7) the growth of science between the Crusades and the invention of printing; (8) from Gutenberg to Bacon, Galileo, and Descartes, who "shook off the yoke of authority"; (9) from Descartes to the foundation of the American and French republics; (10) the age of the liberated mind.[110]

Condorcet, like Voltaire, had no appreciation of the Middle Ages; he thought of them as the domination of European thought by the Church, the hypnotism of the people by the magic of the Mass, and the resurrection of polytheism through the worship of the saints.[111] Though, again like Voltaire, he retained a deistic belief in God, he relied on the progress and dissemination of knowledge to undermine the power of the Church, to extend democracy, and even to improve morals; sin and crime, he felt, were largely the result of ignorance.[112] "The time will come when the sun will shine only upon free men who know no other master but their reason."[113] He lauded Voltaire for emancipating the mind, and Rousseau for inspiring men to build a juster social order. He pictured the cornucopia that would flow in the nineteenth and twentieth centuries from the labors of the eighteenth: universal education, freedom of thought and expression, liberation of colonies, equality before the law, and the redistribution of wealth. He vacillated a bit on universal suffrage: generally he wished to limit the vote to owners of property, however little this might be;[114] at times he feared that the simplicity of the masses would enable a moneyed minority to indoctrinate them at will, and so create a bourgeois oligarchy behind a democratic front;[115] but the flight of Louis XVI and Marie Antoinette to Varennes, and fear that the powers would seek to restore autocratic monarchy in France, led him back to the advocacy of universal suffrage, including women.[116]

From his hunted isolation he looked out in imagination upon a future of glorious fulfillments. He predicted the rise of journalism as a check on governmental tyranny; the development of a welfare state through national insurance and pensions; the stimulation of culture by the emancipation of women; the lengthening of human life by the progress of medicine; the spread of federation among states; the transformation of colonialism into foreign aid by developed to underdeveloped countries; the lessening of national prejudices by the spread of knowledge; the application of statistical research to the illumination and formation of policies; and the increasing association of science with government.[117] Since each age would add new goals to its achievements, there could be no foreseeable end to progress; not that man will ever become perfect, but that he will endlessly seek improvement. "Nature has set no term to the perfection of human faculties; the perfectibility of man is indefinite; and the progress of this perfectibility— henceforth independent of any power that might wish to halt it—has no other limit than the duration of the globe upon which nature has cast us."[118]

Toward the end of the *Prospectus* Condorcet faced the problem that Malthus was to pose four years later in *An Essay on the Principle of Population* (1798):

> Might there not come a moment . . . when, the number of people in the world exceeding the means of subsistence, there will in consequence ensue a continual diminution of happiness, . . . or at best an oscillation between good and bad? Will it not show that a point has been reached beyond which still further improvement is impossible—that the perfectibility of the human race has, after long years, arrived at a term beyond which it may never go? . . .
> Who will take it upon himself to predict the condition to which the art of converting the elements to the use of man may in time be brought? . . . Even if we agree that the limit will one day arrive, . . . consider that, before all this comes to pass, the progress of reason will have kept pace with that of the sciences, and that the absurd prejudices of superstition will have ceased to corrupt and degrade the moral code by its harsh doctrines. . . . We can assume that by then men will know that they have a duty toward those that are not yet born, a duty not to give them [mere] existence but happiness.[119]

Condorcet's optimism was not quite blind. "We still see the forces of enlightenment in possession of no more than a very small portion of the globe, and the truly enlightened vastly outnumbered by the great mass of men, who are still given over to ignorance and prejudice. We still see vast areas in which men groan in slavery."[120] But "the friend of humanity" must not lose hope in the face of these difficulties; think of the many noble things that have already been done, of the immense development of knowledge and enterprise; what may not a continuance and dissemination of these accomplishments produce? And so Condorcet ended his book with a vision that provided his support in adversity, and served him, and a million others, in place of a supernatural faith. This is the final and culminating word of the Enlightenment:

> How consoling for the philosopher—who laments the errors, the crimes, the injustices which still pollute the earth, and of which he is so often the victim— is this view of the human race, emancipated from its shackles, . . . advancing with a firm and sure step along the path of truth, virtue, and happiness! It is the contemplation of this prospect that rewards him for all his efforts to assist the progress of reason and the defense of liberty. . . . Such contemplation is for him an asylum into which the memory of his persecutors cannot pursue him. There he lives in thought with man restored to his natural right and dignity, and forgets man tormented and corrupted by greed, fear, or envy. There he lives with his peers in an Elysium created by reason, and graced by the purest pleasures known to the love of mankind.[121]

This profession of faith was almost the cry of a man conscious that death was seeking him. Fearing that Mme. Vernet might suffer if she were found sheltering him, Condorcet deposited his manuscript with her, and, over her protests, left her house in disguise. After wandering on the outskirts of Paris for several days, he asked for food at an inn. His appearance, and his lack of identifying papers, aroused suspicion; he was soon identified as an aristocrat, was arrested, and was taken to a jail in the town of Bourg-la-Reine (April 7, 1794). The next morning he was found dead in his cell. His first biographer thought that Condorcet had carried poison in a ring, and had swallowed the poison; but the report of the medical officer who examined the body ascribed Condorcet's death to a clot in a blood vessel.[122] The Convention, having secured and read the *Prospectus*, ordered three thousand copies of it to be printed by the state, and to be disseminated throughout France.

V. THE PHILOSOPHERS AND THE REVOLUTION

Burke, de Tocqueville,[123] and Taine[124] agreed that the philosophers of France, from Bayle to Mably, were a major factor in bringing on the Revolution. Can we accept the conclusions of these brilliant conservatives?

All the prominent philosophers were opposed to revolution against the existing governments of Europe; on the contrary, several of them put their faith in kings as the most practical instruments of reform; Voltaire, Diderot, and Grimm maintained relations of friendship, if not of adoration, for one or the other of the most absolute contemporary rulers—Frederick II, Catherine II, Gustavus III; and Rousseau was happy to receive Joseph II of Austria. Diderot, Helvétius, and d'Holbach declaimed against kings in general, but never, in their extant works, advocated the overthrow of the French monarchy.[125] Marmontel and Morellet explicitly opposed revolution;[126] Mably, the socialist, declared himself a royalist;[127] Turgot, idol of the *philosophes*, labored to save, not to destroy, Louis XVI. Rousseau advanced republican ideas, but only for small states; the Revolution accepted his theories and neglected his warning. When the revolutionists made France a republic they did so in terms not of the French philosophers but of Plutarch's Greek and Roman heroes; their idol was not Ferney but Sparta and republican Rome.

The philosophers provided the ideological preparation for the Revolution. The causes were economic or political, the phrases were philosophical; and the operation of the basic causes was smoothed by the demolition work of the philosophers in removing such obstacles to change as belief in feudal privileges, ecclesiastical authority, and the divine right of kings. Until 1789 all European states had depended upon the aid of religion in inculcating the sanctity of governments, the wisdom of tradition, the habits of obedience, and the principles of morality; some roots of earthly power were planted in heaven, and the state considered God as the chief of its secret police. Chamfort, while the Revolution was in process, wrote that "the priesthood was the first bulwark of absolute power, and Voltaire overthrew it."[128] De Tocqueville in 1856 thought that "the universal discredit into which all religious belief fell at the end of the eighteenth century exercised, without doubt, the greatest influence upon the whole course of the Revolution."[129]

Gradually the skepticism that had riddled the old theology passed to the scrutiny of secular institutions and affairs. The philosophers denounced poverty and serfdom as well as intolerance and superstition, and labored to reduce the power of feudal lords over the peasantry. Some aristocrats acknowledged the force of the satires that attacked them, and many lost confidence in their inborn superiority and traditional rights. Hear Comte Louis-Philippe de Ségur:

> We were scornful critics of the old customs, of the feudal pride of our fathers and their severe etiquette. . . . We felt disposed to follow with enthusiasm the philosophical doctrines professed by witty and bold writers. Voltaire attracted our intellect, and Rousseau touched our hearts. We took secret pleasure in seeing them assail the old framework. . . . We enjoyed at the same time the advantages of the patriciate and the amenities of a plebeian philosophy.[130]

These conscience-stricken nobles included such influential persons as Mirabeau *père* and *fils*, La Rochefoucauld-Liancourt, Lafayette, Vicomte Louis-Marie de Noailles, and "Philippe Égalité," Duc d'Orléans; and recall the aid and comfort given to Rousseau by the Maréchal de Luxembourg and Louis-François de Bourbon, Prince de Conti. This liberal minority, spurred by peasant raids on feudal property, led the seigneurs, in the Constituent Assembly, to renounce, for redemptions, most of their feudal dues (August 4, 1789). Even the royal family was touched by the semirepublican ideas that the philosophers had helped to spread. The father of Louis XVI memorized many passages from Montesquieu's *Spirit of Laws*, read Rousseau's *Social Contract*, and judged it "largely sound" except for its criticism of Christianity. He taught his sons (three of whom became kings) that "the distinctions which you enjoy were not given you by nature, which has created all men equal."[131] Louis XVI, in his edicts, acknowledged "natural law" and "the rights of man"[132] as following from man's nature as a rational being.

The American Revolution gave added prestige to republican ideas. That Revolution, too, took its force from economic realities like taxation and trade, and its Declaration of Independence owed as much to English thinkers as to French; but it was noted that Washington, Franklin, and Jefferson had been molded to free thought by the *philosophes*. Through those American sons of the French Enlightenment, republican theories graduated into a government victorious in arms, recognized by a French King, and proceeding to establish a constitution indebted in some measure to Montesquieu.

The French Revolution had three phases. In the first the nobles, through the *parlements*, tried to recapture from the monarchy that dominance which they had lost to Louis XIV; those nobles were not inspired by the philosophers. In the second stage the middle classes won control of the Revolution; they had been deeply permeated by the notions of the philosophers, but what they meant by "equality" was the equality of the bourgeois with the aristocrat. In the third stage the directors of the city populace seized the mastery. The masses remained pious, but their leaders had lost respect for priests and kings; the masses loved Louis XVI to the end, but the leaders cut off his head. After October 6, 1789, the Jacobins controlled Paris, and Rousseau was their god. On November 10, 1793, the triumphant radicals celebrated in the Cathedral of Notre-Dame the Feast of Reason. At Tours the revolutionaries replaced the statues of saints with new figures called Mably, Rousseau, and Voltaire. At Chartres in 1795, in the famous cathedral, a Feast of Reason was opened by a drama in which Voltaire and Rousseau were shown united in a campaign against fanaticism.[133]

Therefore we cannot doubt that the philosophers profoundly affected the ideology and the political drama of the Revolution. They had not intended to produce violence, massacre, and the guillotine; they would have shrunk in horror from those bloody scenes. They could properly say that they had been cruelly misunderstood; but they were responsible insofar as they had underestimated the influence of religion and tradition in restraining the animal instincts of men. Meanwhile, under those striking pronouncements and visible events, the real revolution was proceeding, as the middle classes, using philosophy as one among a hundred instruments, took from the aristocracy and the king the control of the economy and the state.

CHAPTER XXXVI

On the Eve

1774-89

I. RELIGION AND THE REVOLUTION

FINANCIALLY the Catholic Church was the soundest institution in the country. It owned some six per cent of the land, and other property, valued in sum at from two to four billion livres, with an annual income of 120,000,000 livres.[1] It received an additional 123,000,000 in tithes levied on the produce and livestock of the soil.[2] These revenues, in the view of the Church, were needed for its various functions of promoting family life, organizing education (before 1762), forming moral character, supporting social order, distributing charity, tending the sick, offering to meditative or unpolitical spirits a monastic refuge from the confusion of the crowd and the tyranny of the state, and inculcating a judicious mixture of fear, hope, and resignation in souls condemned, by the natural inequality of men, to poverty, hardship, or grief.

All this it claimed to do through its clergy, which constituted about one half of one per cent of the population. Their number had fallen since 1779,[3] and the monasteries were in serious decline. "Many monks," we are told, "were favorable to the new ideas, and read the writings of the philosophers."[4] Hundreds of monks abandoned the monastic life, and were not replaced; between 1766 and 1789 their number in France fell from 26,000 to 17,000; in one monastery from eighty to nineteen, in another from fifty to four.[5] A royal edict of 1766 closed all monasteries having fewer than nine inmates, and raised the permitted age for taking vows from sixteen to twenty-one for men, to eighteen for women. Monastic morals were lax. The Archbishop of Tours wrote in 1778: "The Gray Friars [Franciscans] are in a state of degradation in this province; the bishops complain of their debaucheries and disorderly life."[6] On the other hand the nunneries were in good condition. There were 37,000 nuns in the 1,500 convents of France in 1774;[7] their morals were good, and they actively fulfilled their tasks of educating girls, serving in hospitals, and offering asylum to widows, spinsters, and women broken in the battle of life.

The secular clergy prospered in the sees and languished in the parishes. There were many devoted and industrious bishops, some worldly idling ones. Burke, visiting France in 1773, found a few prelates guilty of avarice, but the great majority impressed him by their learning and integrity.[8] An historian familiar with the literature of scandal concluded: "It may be broadly stated that the vices which had infected the whole body of the clergy during the sixteenth century had disappeared by the eighteenth. Despite the law of celibacy the country curates were, as a rule, moral, austere, virtuous men."[9] These parish priests complained of the pride of class in the bishops, who were all nobles; of the requirement to transmit to the bishop the greater part of the tithes, and of the consequent poverty that compelled the curates to till the soil as well as serve the Church. Louis XVI was moved by their protests, and arranged that their salaries should be raised from five hundred to seven hundred livres per year. When the Revolution came many of the lower clergy supported the Third Estate. Some bishops, too, favored political and economic reform, but most of them remained adamant against any changes in the Church or the state.[10] When the treasury of France neared bankruptcy the wealth of the Church offered a tempting contrast, and bondholders, worried about the ability of the government to pay interest or principal on their loans, began to see in the expropriation of church property the only road to national solvency. The spreading rejection of the Christian creed concurred with this economic urge.

Religious belief flourished in the villages, waned in the towns; and in these the women of the middle and lower classes kept their traditional piety. "My mother," Mme. Vigée-Lebrun recalled, "was very pious. I too was pious at heart. We used always to hear High Mass and attend the services of the Church."[11] The churches were crowded on Sundays and holydays.[12] But among the men unbelief had captured half the leading spirits. In the nobility a gay skepticism had become fashionable, even among the women. "The fashionable world for ten years past," wrote Mercier in his *Tableau de Paris* in 1783, "has not attended Mass"; or, if they did go, it was "so as not to scandalize their lackeys, who know that it is on their account."[13] The upper middle class followed the lead of the aristocracy. In the schools "many teachers were infected with unbelief after 1771";[14] many students neglected Mass, and read the *philosophes*. In 1789 Father Bonnefax declared: "The gravest scandal, and that which will entail the most fatal consequences, is the almost absolute abandonment of religious teaching in the public schools."[15] In one college, it was said, "only three imbeciles" believed in God.[16]

Among the clergy belief varied inversely with income. The prelates "accepted the 'utilitarian morality' of the *philosophes*, and kept Jesus only as a discreet front."[17] There were hundreds of abbés like Mably, Condillac, Morellet, and Raynal, who themselves were *philosophes*, or adopted the current doubts. There were bishops like Talleyrand, who made little pretense to Christian belief; there were archbishops like Loménie de Brienne, of whom Louis XVI complained that he did not believe in God.[18] Louis refused to have a priest teach his son, lest the boy lose religious faith.[19]

The Church continued to demand censorship of the press. In 1770 the bishops sent to the King a memoir on "the dangerous consequences of liberty of thinking and printing."[20] The government had relaxed, under Louis XV, the laws against the entry of Protestants into France; hundreds of them were now in the kingdom, living under political disabilities, in marriages unrecognized by the state, and in daily fear that the old laws of Louis XIV would at any moment be enforced. In July, 1775, an assembly of the Catholic clergy petitioned the King to forbid Protestant meetings, marriages, or education, and to exclude Protestants from all public office; it also asked that the age of permitted monastic vows be restored to sixteen.[21] Turgot pleaded with Louis XVI to ignore these proposals, and to relieve the Protestants of their disabilities; the hierarchy joined in the campaign to displace him. In 1781 the second edition of Raynal's *Histoire philosophique des deux Indes* was burned by order of the Parlement of Paris, and the author was banished from France. Buffon was attacked by the Sorbonne for outlining a natural evolution of life. In 1785 the clergy demanded life imprisonment for persons thrice condemned of irreligion.[22]

But the Church, weakened by a century of attacks, could no longer dominate public opinion, and it could no longer rely on the "secular arm" to implement its decrees. Louis XVI, after much worry about his coronation oath to stamp out heresy, yielded to the pressure of liberal ideas, and issued in 1787 an edict of toleration prepared by Malesherbes: "Our justice does not permit us to exclude any longer, from the rights of the civil state, those of our subjects who do not profess the Catholic religion."[23] The edict still excluded non-Catholics from public office, but it gave them all other civil rights, admitted them to the professions, legitimized their marriages past and future, and allowed them to celebrate their religious services in private homes. We should add that a Catholic bishop, M. de La Luzerne, vigorously supported the emancipation of the Protestants, and full freedom of religious worship.[24]

No class in the cities of France was so disliked by the educated male minority as the Catholic clergy. The Church was hated, said de Tocqueville, "not because the priests claimed to regulate the affairs of the *other* world, but because they were landed proprietors, lords of manors, tithe owners, and administrators in *this* world."[25] A peasant wrote to Necker in 1788: "The poor suffer from cold and hunger while the canons [cathedral clergy] feast and think of nothing but fattening themselves like pigs that are to be killed for Easter."[26] The middle classes resented the exemption of church wealth from taxation.

Most previous revolutions had been against the state *or* the Church, rarely against both at once. The barbarians had overthrown Rome, but they had accepted the Roman Catholic Church. The Sophists in ancient Greece, the Reformers in sixteenth-century Europe, had rejected the prevailing religion, but they had respected the existing government. The French Revolution attacked both the monarchy and the Church, and undertook the double task and jeopardy of removing both the religious and the secular props of the existing social order. Is it any wonder that for a decade France went mad?

II. LIFE ON THE EDGE

The philosophers had recognized that, having rejected the theological foundations of morality, they were obligated to find another basis, another system of belief that would incline men to decent behavior as citizens, husbands, wives, parents, and children.[27] But they were not at all confident that the human animal could be controlled without a supernaturally sanctioned moral code. Voltaire and Rousseau finally admitted the moral necessity of popular religious belief. Mably, addressing to John Adams in 1783 some *Observations sur le gouvernement . . . des États unis d'Amérique*, warned him that indifference in matters religious, however harmless it might be in enlightened and rational individuals, is fatal to the morals of the masses. A government, he suggested, must control and direct the thought of these "children" just as parents do with the young.[28] Diderot, in the second half of his life, pondered how to devise a natural ethic, and admitted his failure: "I have not even dared to write the first line; . . . I do not feel myself equal to this sublime work."[29]

What sort of morality prevailed in France after forty years of attacks upon supernatural beliefs? In answering this question we must not idealize the first half of the eighteenth century. Fontenelle, shortly before his death in 1757, said he wished he could live sixty years more "to see what universal infidelity, depravity, and dissolution of all ties would turn to."[30] If that statement (which was probably unfair to the middle and lower classes) gave a true picture of upper-class morals in France before the *Encyclopédie* (1751), we should hardly be justified in ascribing to the *philosophes* the defects of morality in the second half of the century. Other factors than the decline of religious belief were weakening the old moral code. The growth of wealth enabled men to finance sins that had been too costly before. Restif de La Bretonne showed a good bourgeois lamenting the deterioration of French character by the passage of population from villages and farms to cities;[31] young men escaped from the discipline of the family, the farm, and the neighborhood to the corrosive contacts and opportunities of city life, and the protective anonymity of city crowds. In *Les Nuits de Paris* Restif described the Paris of the 1780s as a maelstrom of juvenile delinquents, petty thieves, professional criminals, and prostitutes female and male. Taine supposed that the France of 1756–88 was diseased with "vagrants, mendicants, every species of refractory spirit, . . . foul, filthy, haggard, and savage, engendered by the system; and upon each social ulcer they gathered like vermin."[32] This human waste of the social organism was the product of human nature and Bourbon rule, and can hardly be ascribed to philosophy or the decay of religious belief.

Possibly some of the gambling that flourished in Paris (as in London) was connected with unbelief; but everybody joined in it, pious and impious alike. In 1776 all private lotteries were suppressed to be merged in the Loterie Royale. Nevertheless, some part of the sexual chaos in the upper classes could reasonably be attributed to atheism. In Choderlos de Laclos' *Les Liaisons dangereuses* (1782) we find fictional aristocrats exchanging notes on the art of seduction, laying plans to have a fifteen-year-old girl deflowered as soon as she left the convent, and professing a philosophy of moral nihilism. The protagonist, the Vicomte de Valmont, argues that all men are equally evil in their desires, but that most men fail to effect them because they allow moral traditions to intimidate them. The wise man, Valmont holds, will pursue whichever sensations promise him most pleasure, and will disdain all moral inhibitions.[33] Some Greek Sophists, we recall, reached similar conclusions after discarding the gods.[34]

This philosophy of amoralism, as all the world now knows, was carried *ad nauseam* by the Comte—usually miscalled Marquis—de Sade. Born in Paris in 1740, he served twelve years in the army, was arrested and condemned to death for homosexual offenses (1772), escaped, was captured, escaped again, was captured again, and was committed to the Bastille. There he wrote several novels and plays, as obscene as his imagination could make them: chiefly *Justine* (1791) and *Histoire de Juliette, ou Les Prospérités du vice* (1792). Since there is no God, he argued, the wise man will seek to realize every desire so far as he can without incurring earthly punishment. All desires are equally good; all moral distinctions are delusions; abnormal sexual relations are legitimate, and are not really abnormal; crime is delightful if you avoid detection; and there are few things more delicious than beating a pretty girl. Readers were shocked less by de Sade's amoralism than by his suggestion that the total destruction of the human race would afflict the cosmos so little that "it would no more interrupt its course than if the entire species of rabbits or hares were extinguished."[35] In 1789 de Sade was removed to a lunatic asylum at Charenton; he was released in 1790, was recommitted as incurable in 1803, and died in 1814.

The philosophers might plead that this amoralism was a sickly *non sequitur* from their criticism of the Christian theology, and that a sane mind would recognize moral obligations with or without religious belief. Many people did. And among the normal population of France—even of Paris—there were in these years many elements of moral regeneration: the rise of sentiment and tenderness; the triumphs of romantic love over marriages of convenience; the young mother proudly nursing her child; the husband courting his own wife; the family restored to unity as the soundest source of social order. These developments were often allied with some remnants of the Christian creed, or with the semi-Christian philosophy of Rousseau; but the atheist Diderot gave them enthusiastic support.

The death of Louis XV was followed by a reaction against his sensuality. Louis XVI gave good example by his simple dress and life, his fidelity to his wife, and his condemnation of gambling. The Queen herself joined in the fashion of simplicity, and led the revival of sensibility and sentiment. The French Academy annually awarded a prize for outstanding virtue.[36] Most literature was decent; the novels of Crébillon *fils* were put aside, and Bernardin de Saint-Pierre's *Paul et Virginie* set the tone of moral purity in love. Art reflected the new morality; Greuze and Mme. Vigée-Lebrun celebrated children and motherhood.

Christianity and philosophy together nourished a humanitarianism that spread a thousand works of philanthropy and charity. During the hard winter of 1784 Louis XVI devoted three million livres to relief of the poor; Marie Antoinette contributed 200,000 from her own purse; many others followed suit. King and Queen helped to finance the Deaf and Dumb School established by the Abbé de L'Épée in 1778 to teach his new deaf-and-dumb alphabet, and the School for Blind Children organized by Valentin Haüy in 1784. Mme. Necker founded (1778) an asylum and hospital for the poor, which she personally superintended for ten years. The churches, monasteries, and convents distributed food and medicines. It was in this reign that a campaign took form to abolish slavery.

Manners, like morals, reflected the age of Rousseau; never, under the Bourbons, had they been so democratic. Class distinctions remained, but they were tempered with greater kindliness and wider courtesy. Untitled men of talent, if they had learned to wash and bow, were welcomed in the most pedigreed homes. The Queen leaped from her carriage to help a wounded postilion; the King and his brother the Comte d'Artois put their shoulders to the wheel to help a workman disengage his cart from the mud. Dress became simpler: wigs disappeared, and gentlemen discarded, except at court, their embroideries, laces, and swords; by 1789 it was difficult to tell a man's class from his garb. When Franklin captured France even the tailors surrendered to him; people appeared in the streets "dressed à la Franklin, in coarse cloth . . . and thick shoes."[37]

The ladies of the bourgeoisie dressed quite as handsomely as those of the court. After 1780 the women abandoned the clumsy hoopskirt, but fortified themselves with stiff petticoats worn one over the next like a Chinese puzzle. Bodices were cut low in front, but the bosom was usually covered with a triangular kerchief called a *fichu* (fastening); these could be thickened to conceal underdevelopment; so the French called them *trompeurs* or *menteurs*—deceivers or liars.[38] Coiffures continued high, but when Marie Antoinette lost much of her hair during one of her confinements she replaced the tower style with curls, and the new fashion spread through the court to Paris. There were two hundred styles of women's hats; some were precarious edifices of wire, feathers, ribbons, flowers, and artificial vegetables; but in their easier hours women followed the style affected by the Queen at the Petit Trianon, covering the head with a simple scarf. In the greatest revolution of all, some women wore low heels or comfortable mules.[39]

A healthier way of life accompanied the change to easier dress. A growing minority went in for "natural living": no corsets, no servants, more outdoor living, and, whenever possible, a retreat from the city to the country. Arthur Young reported: "Everybody that have country seats is at them, and those who have not visit those who have. This revolution in French manners is certainly one of the best features they have taken from England. Its introduction was the easier because of the magic of Rousseau's writings."[40] But much of this "return to nature" was talk or sentiment rather than action or reality; life in Paris still ran a dizzy race with concerts, operas, plays, horse races, water sports, card games, dances, balls, conversation, and salons.

III. THE *SALONNIÈRES*

French women adorned the decline of feudalism not only with the charms of their persons and their dress, but also with their unrivaled ability to make French society no mere gathering of gossips but a vital part of the nation's intellectual life. Gibbon, after renewing in 1777 his acquaintance with the salons of Paris, wrote:

> If Julian could now revisit the capital of France [where he had been born in A.D. 331], he might converse with men of science and genius capable of understanding and instructing a disciple of the Greeks; he might excuse the graceful follies of a nation whose martial spirit has never been enervated by the indulgence of luxury; and he must applaud the perfection of that inestimable art which softens and refines and embellishes the intercourse of social life.[41]

And in a letter he added: "It has always seemed to me that in Lausanne, as well as in Paris, the women are far superior to the men."[42]

The older *salonnières* were reluctantly leaving the scene. Mme. Geoffrin, as we have seen, died in 1777. Mme. du Deffand almost spanned the century by entering history as one of the Regent's mistresses[43] and opening a salon that continued from 1739 to 1780. She had lost most of the literary lions to Julie de Lespinasse and the new salons, and Horace Walpole, coming to her for the first time in 1765, found her assortment of aging aristocrats unexciting. "I sup there twice a week, and bear all her dull company for the sake of the Regent"[44]—i.e., for her lively memories of that remarkable interregnum which had set the tone of French society and morals for the next sixty years. But (Horace added) she herself "is delicious [at sixty-eight], as eager about what happens every day as I am about the last century."

He admired her mind so rapturously—having never met such brilliance in the still-suppressed women of England—that he went to her every day, and paid her compliments that seemed to restore her golden days. She gave him a special chair, which was always reserved for him; she had him pampered with every form of womanly solicitude. Herself somewhat masculine, she was not displeased by his almost effeminate delicacy. Unable to see him, she could mold her image of him close to her heart's desire, and fell in love with that image. Able to see her, he could never forget her age and her physical helplessness. When he went back to England she wrote him letters almost as warm with devotion as those of Julie de Lespinasse to Guibert, and written in as fine a prose as that age could show. His replies tried to check her elation; he shivered at the thought of what the Selwyns of England would do with such a juicy morsel for satire. She suffered his reproofs, reaffirmed her love, agreed to call it friendship, but assured him that in France friendship was often deeper and stronger than love. "I belong to you more than to myself. . . . I wish I could send you my soul instead of a letter. I would willingly give up years of my life to be sure of being alive when you come back to Paris." She compared him to Montaigne, "and this is the highest praise I could give you, for I find no mind as just or as clear as his."[45]

He went to Paris again in August, 1767. She awaited him with virginal excitement. "At last, at last, no sea divides us. I cannot make myself believe that a man of your importance, with his hands on the wheel of a great government, and therefore of Europe, could . . . leave everything to come and see an old sibyl in the corner of a convent. It is really too absurd, but I am enchanted. . . . Come, my tutor! . . . It is not a dream—I know I am awake—I shall see you today!" She sent her carriage for him; he went to her at once. For six weeks he gladdened her with his presence and saddened her with his cautions. When he had gone back to England she could think only of his returning to Paris. "You will make my sunset far more beautiful and happy than my noon or my dawn. Your pupil, who is as submissive as a child, only wishes to see you."[46]

On March 30, 1773, he asked her to write no more.[47] Then he relented, and the correspondence was resumed. In February, 1775, he asked her to return all his letters. She complied, with a delicate suggestion that he reciprocate. "You will have enough to light your fires for a long time if you add to yours all those you have received from me. That would be only fair, but I leave it to your prudence."[48] Of his eight hundred letters to her only nineteen have survived; all of hers were preserved, and were published after Walpole's death. When he heard that her pension had been discontinued he offered to replace it out of his own income; she did not think it necessary.

The collapse of her romance darkened the natural pessimism of a woman who missed the colors of life but knew its shallows and depths. Even in her blindness she could see through all gallant surfaces to the indefatigable selfishness of the self. "My poor tutor," she asked Walpole, "have you met only monsters, crocodiles, and hyenas? As for me I see only fools, idiots, liars, envious and sometimes perfidious people. . . . Everyone I see here dries up my soul. I find no virtue, no sincerity, no simplicity, in anyone."[49] Little religious belief survived to comfort her. Yet she continued her suppers, usually twice a week, and often dined out, if only to avoid the boredom of days as dark as the nights.

At last she, who had learned to hate life, stopped clutching at it, and reconciled herself to death. The illnesses that plague old age had mounted and combined, and she felt too weak, at eighty-three, to combat them. She summoned a priest and made, without much faith, her surrender to hope. In August, 1780, she sent her last letter to Walpole:

> I am worse today. . . . I cannot think that this condition means anything but the end. I am not strong enough to be frightened, and as I am not to see you again I have nothing to regret. . . . Amuse yourself, my friend, as well as you can. Do not distress yourself about my condition. . . . You will regret me, for one is glad to know that one is loved.[50]

She died on September 23, having left to Walpole her papers and her dog.

Many other *salonnières* continued the great tradition: Mesdames d'Houdetot, d'Épinay, Denis, de Genlis, Luxembourg, Condorcet, Boufflers, Choiseul, Gramont, Beauharnais (wife of an uncle to Josephine). Add to all these

the last great pre-Revolutionary salon—Mme. Necker's. About 1770 she began her Friday receptions; later she received also on Tuesdays, when music
ruled; there the Gluck-Piccini war divided the diners, and Mlle. Clairon
united them by reciting passages from her favorite roles. On Fridays one might
meet there Diderot, Marmontel, Morellet, d'Alembert (after Julie's death),
Saint-Lambert, Grimm (after Mme. d'Épinay's death), Gibbon, Raynal,
Buffon, Guibert, Galiani, Pigalle, and Suzanne's special literary friend, Antoine Thomas. It was at one of these gatherings (April, 1770) that the idea
was broached of a statue to Voltaire. There Diderot muzzled his heresies,
and became almost refined. "It is regrettable to me," he wrote to Mme.
Necker, "that I did not have the good fortune of knowing you sooner. You
would certainly have inspired in me a sense of pureness and delicacy that
would have passed from my soul into my works."[51] Others did not report so
favorably. Marmontel, though he remained her friend for twenty-five years,
described Suzanne in his *Memoirs:* "Unacquainted with the manners and
customs of Paris, she had none of the charms of a young Frenchwoman. . . .
She had no taste in her dress, no ease in her demeanor, no charm in her politeness, and her mind, as well as the expression of her face, was too completely adjusted to possess grace. Her most attractive qualities were those of
decorum, sincerity, and kindliness of heart."[52] Aristocratic ladies did not take
to her; the Baroness d'Oberkirch, who visited the Neckers with Grand Duke
Paul in 1782, put her down as "simply nothing more than a governess";[53]
and the Marquise de Créqui tore her to shreds in some charmingly spiteful
pages.[54] Mme. Necker must have had many good qualities to win the lasting
love of Gibbon, but she never quite overcame her Calvinist heritage; she remained prim and puritan amid her wealth, and never acquired the sophisticated gaiety that Frenchmen expected of women.

In 1766 she gave birth to the future Mme. de Staël. Germaine Necker,
growing up among philosophers and statesmen, became a pundit at ten. Her
precocious intelligence made her the pride of her parents until her willful
and excitable temperament proved hard on her mother's nerves. Suzanne,
more conservative every day, subjected Germaine to strict discipline; the
daughter rebelled, and discord in the elegant home rivaled the chaos in the
finances of the state. Necker's difficulties in trying to stave off governmental
bankruptcy despite the American war, and Mme. Necker's resentment of
every criticism that he received in the press, added to the mother's unhappiness, and Suzanne began to long for the calm life that she had led in Switzerland.

In 1786 Germaine married, and took over part of the duties of hostess in
her mother's salon. But the French salon was now in decline; literary discussion was giving way to eager and partisan politics. "I have no literary news to
give you," Suzanne wrote to a friend in 1786. "Such conversation is no
longer the fashion; the crisis is too great; people do not care to play chess on
the edge of a precipice."[55] In 1790 the family moved to Coppet, a château
which Necker had bought on the north shores of the Lake of Geneva. There
Mme. de Staël reigned, and Mme. Necker suffered for years a painful nervous disease, which put an end to her life in 1794.

IV. MUSIC

"As far as music is concerned," Mozart wrote from Paris on May 1, 1778, "I am surrounded by mere brute beasts. . . . Ask anyone you like—provided he is not a Frenchman born—and if he knows anything about the matter he will say exactly the same. . . . I shall thank Almighty God if I escape with my taste unspoiled."[56] These were hard words, but Grimm and Goldoni agreed with them;[57] however, all three critics were foreigners. The musical taste of the upper-class Parisians reflected their manners, inclining to restraint of expression and regularity of form; it still echoed the age of Louis XIV. Yet it was precisely in these first years of the new reign that half of Paris lost restraint, and perhaps good manners, in the excitement of the battle over Piccini and Gluck. And note Julie de Lespinasse's letter of September 22, 1774: "I go constantly to *Orfé et Eurydice*. I long to hear a dozen times a day that air which rends me, . . . 'J'ai perdu mon Eurydice.' "[58] Paris was not dead to music, though it imported more than it produced.

In 1751 François-Joseph Gossec, aged seventeen, came from his native Hainaut to Paris with a letter of introduction to Rameau. The old master secured for him a post as conductor of the private orchestra maintained by Alexandre-Joseph de La Popelinière. For that "band" Gossec composed (1754 f.) symphonies antedating Haydn's first by five years, and in 1754 he published quartets antedating Haydn's by a year. In 1760 he presented in the Church of St. Roch his *Messe des Morts*, which originated the idea of playing the wind instruments of the *Tuba mirum* outside the church. There was no end to Gossec's enterprise and versatility. In 1784 he founded the Ecole Royale du Chant, which became the nucleus of the renowned Paris Conservatoire de Musique. He achieved a moderate success in opera, comic and serious. He adjusted himself to the Revolution, and composed some of its most famous songs, including the "Hymn to the Supreme Being" for Robespierre's celebration (June 8, 1794). He survived all political modulations, dying in 1829 at the age of ninety-five.

The dominant figure in the French opera of this period was André Grétry. Like so many others prominent in French music in the eighteenth century, he was an alien, born at Liège in 1741, son of a violinist. On the day of his first Communion, he tells us, he asked God to let him die at once unless he was destined to be a good man and a great musician. That day a rafter fell on his head and severely wounded him; he recovered, and concluded that a noble future was divinely promised him.[59] From the age of sixteen he suffered periodically from internal hemorrhages, vomiting six cups of blood in a day; he was subject to fevers and occasional delirium, and at times he went almost mad from inability to stop some strain of music from turning round and round in his head. Even bad music could be forgiven to a man who was so tormented and yet kept his good cheer through seventy-two years.

At the age of seventeen he composed six symphonies, good enough to secure from a cathedral canon the means of going to Rome. If we may believe the engaging *Mémoires* which he published in 1797, he walked all the way.[60] During his eight years in Italy he was influenced by the success of Pergolesi to compose comic operas. Coming to Paris (1767), he received encouragement from Diderot, Grimm, and Rousseau. He studied the dramatic art of Mlle. Clairon, developed a special skill in adjusting his music to the accents and inflexions of dramatic speech, and achieved in his operas a lyric delicacy and tenderness that seemed to reflect the spirit of Rousseau, and the return to simplicity and sentiment in French life. He continued to be popular throughout the Revolution, which ordered his works to be published at the government's expense; arias from his operas were sung by revolutionary crowds. Napoleon gave him a pension. Everybody liked him because he had so few of the stigmata of genius: he was kindly, affectionate, sociable, modest, spoke well of his rivals, and paid his debts. He loved Rousseau, though Rousseau had offended him; in his old age he bought the Hermitage, where Rousseau had lived. In that cottage, on September 24, 1813, while Napoleon was fighting all Europe, Grétry died.

V. ART UNDER LOUIS XVI

Now the *style Louis Seize*, which had begun almost with the birth of Louis XVI (1754), continued its reaction against the sinuous irregularities of baroque and the feminine delicacies of rococo, and moved toward the masculine lines and symmetrical proportions of a neoclassical art inspired by the excavations at Herculaneum and the Greco-Roman fervor of Winckelmann. The most famous example of the new style in architecture is the Petit Trianon; it is amusing that Mme. du Barry and Marie Antoinette, who were not on speaking terms, agreed in enjoying this modest tribute to classical order and simplicity. Another pretty example is the present Palais de la Légion d'Honneur, built as the Hôtel Salm (1782) by Pierre Rousseau on the left bank of the Seine. A more massive product of the style is the Palais de Justice as rebuilt in 1776, with its magnificent wrought-iron grille fronting the Cour de Mai. The Théâtre National de l'Odéon (1779) took a somber Doric form; more amiable is the theater raised at Amiens (1778) by Jacques Rousseau in a union of classical and Renaissance. At Bordeaux Victor Louis built (1775) on classical lines an immense theater which Arthur Young described as "by far the most magnificent in France; I have seen nothing that approaches it."[61]

Interior decoration retained French elegance. Tapestry was going out of fashion except as covering for armchairs and sofas; painted wallpaper was coming in from China, but was used chiefly in bedrooms; the walls of salons were generally divided into panels of treated wood, carved or painted with figures or floral arabesques rivaling the best in Italy. The finest furniture in the France of Louis XVI was designed and made by two Germans, Jean-

Henri Riesener and David Roentgen; the Wallace Collection has some enviable examples made for Marie Antoinette and the Petit Trianon.

Sculpture flourished. Pigalle, Falconet, and Jean-Jacques Caffieri lived on from the days of Louis XV. Augustin Pajou, who had begun work in that reign, now came into his own. Under commissions from Louis XVI he carved decorations for the Palais-Royal and the Palais-Bourbon. In his *Psyche Abandoned*,[62] he tried to reconcile two elements in the new age—tender sentiment and classic form. He transmitted his art—and gave his daughter in marriage—to Clodion, whose real name was Claude Michel. Clodion carved a way to prosperity with terra-cotta groups slightly erotic, and reached his zenith with a statue of Montesquieu.[63] All the ecstasy of the flesh sings in the *Nymph and Satyr* now in the Metropolitan Museum of Art in New York.

The supreme sculptor of the age was Jean-Antoine Houdon. His father was a porter, but in an art school. Born in Versailles, Jean breathed sculpture from the statues with which Louis XIV had peopled the gardens of Le Nôtre. After studying with Pigalle he won the Prix de Rome at twenty, and sallied off to Italy (1760). The *St. Bruno* that he carved in Rome so pleased Clement XIV that he commented, "The Saint would speak, were it not that the rules of his order impose silence."[64] In Paris he carved or cast a succession of Dianas; one in bronze, in the Huntington Collection, is a marvel of classic features and French grace. More famous is the bronze *Diane Nue* now in the Louvre; it was refused a place in the Salon of 1785, perhaps because (said a critic) "she was too beautiful and too nude to be exposed to the public,"[65] more probably because the statue violated the traditional conception of Diana as chaste.

Houdon, like so many artists of the eighteenth century, found more profit in contemporary portraits than in inviolable goddesses. Nevertheless he resolved to be fair with the facts, and to show a character rather than a face. He spent many hours in the dissecting rooms of medical schools, studying anatomy. When possible he made careful measurements of the sitter's head, and carved or cast the statue to correspond. When question arose as to whether a corpse that had been exhumed in Paris was really, as claimed, that of John Paul Jones, the shape and measurements of the skull were compared with those of the portrait that Houdon had cast in 1781, and the agreement was so close that the identity was accepted as confirmed.[66] He cut into the marble of his *Mirabeau* all the ravages of smallpox, and showed every shadow and wrinkle, even the fire and depth of the eyes, and the lips parted in readiness to speak.

Soon all the Titans of the upheaval were glad to sit for him, and he transmitted them to us with a fidelity that turned marble and bronze into the flesh and soul of history. So we now can see Voltaire, Rousseau, Diderot, d'Alembert, Buffon, Turgot, Louis XVI, Catherine II, Cagliostro, Lafayette, Napoleon, Ney. When Voltaire came to Paris in 1778 Houdon made several statues of him: a bronze bust now in the Louvre, showing exhaustion and weariness; a similar marble bust now in the Victoria and Albert Museum;

another in the Wallace Collection; an idealized smiling head ordered by Frederick the Great; and, most famous of all, the statue presented by Mme. Denis to the Comédie-Française: Voltaire seated in a flowing robe, bony fingers grasping the arms of the chair, thin lips, toothless mouth, some gaiety still in the wistful eyes—this is one of the great statues in the history of art. In that same year, hearing of Rousseau's death, Houdon hurried to Ermenonville and took a death mask of Voltaire's rival; from this he made the bust now in the Louvre; this too is a masterpiece.

There were American heroes also, and Houdon made such lifelike heads of them that coins of the United States still bear his likenesses of Washington, Franklin, and Jefferson. When Franklin returned to America in 1785 Houdon went with him; he hastened to Mt. Vernon and persuaded the busy and impatient Washington to sit for him, on and off, for a fortnight; so he made the statue that adorns the state capitol at Richmond, Virginia—a man of granite, sombered with costly victories and remaining tasks. Here again is that union of body and soul which is the sign and seal of Houdon's art.

Such sculpture would have made painting a minor delicacy had it not been that Greuze and Fragonard continued to work throughout the reign and the Revolution, and that Jacques-Louis David, a painter, in a career as meteoric as Napoleon's, rose to a dictatorship over all the arts in France. He learned his technique from his great-uncle François Boucher, and became a first-rate draftsman, a master of line and composition rather than of color. Boucher perceived that the change of morals since Pompadour and Du Barry to Marie Antoinette was reducing the market for bosoms and buttocks; he advised David to go and pick up the chaste neoclassical style in the studio of Joseph Vien, who was painting Roman soldiers and heroic women. In 1775 David accompanied Vien to Rome. There he felt the influence of Winckelmann and Mengs, of the antique sculptures in the Vatican Gallery, of the ruins exhumed at Herculaneum and Pompeii. He accepted the neoclassical principles, and took Greek statuary as a model for his painting.

Back in Paris, he exhibited a succession of classical subjects severely drawn: *Andromache Weeping over the Dead Body of Hector* (1783), *The Oath of the Horatii* (1785), *The Death of Socrates* (1787), *Brutus Returning from Condemning His Sons to Death* (1789).[67] (In the legend as told by Livy, Lucius Junius Brutus, as praetor of the young Roman Republic (509 B.C.), sentenced his own sons to death for conspiring to restore the kings.) David had painted this last picture in Rome; when he offered it to the Academy in Paris its exhibition was forbidden; the art public protested; finally the canvas was shown, and added to the revolutionary fever of the time. Paris saw in these paintings, and in the stern ethic they conveyed, a double revolt—against aristocratic rococo and royal tyranny. David became the radical hero of the Paris studios.

During the Revolution he was elected to the Convention, and in January, 1793, he voted for the execution of the King. Another deputy who had so voted was slain by a royalist (January 20, 1793); the body was exhibited to the public as that of a republican martyr; David painted *The Last Moments of Lepeletier;* the Convention hung it in its chamber. When Marat was slain by Charlotte Corday (July 13, 1793), David pictured the dead man lying half immersed in his bath; seldom had art been so realistic, or so calculated to arouse feeling. These two paintings established the martyrology of the Revolution. David worked enthusiastically for Danton and Robespierre; in return he was made director of all art in Paris.

When Napoleon took power with the Roman title of consul, David painted for him as zealously as he had done for the leaders of the Terror. He saw Bonaparte as the Son of the Revolution, fighting to keep the kings of Europe from restoring their like to France. When Napoleon made himself emperor (1804) David's adoration was not subdued; and Napoleon made him painter to the imperial court. The artist produced for him several famous pictures: *Napoleon Crossing the Alps, The Coronation of Josephine by Napoleon,* and *The Distribution of the Eagles;* these immense paintings were later placed on the walls of rooms in the palace at Versailles. Meanwhile David displayed his versatility with excellent portraits of Mme. Récamier and Pope Pius VI.[68] When the Bourbons were restored David was banished as a regicide; he retired to Brussels, where his wife (who had left him in 1791 because of his revolutionary ardor) came to share his exile. Now he returned to classical subjects, and to the sculptural style of painting favored by Mengs. In 1825, aged seventy-seven, he ended one of the most spectacular careers in the history of art.

Among his portraits is one of Mme. Vigée-Lebrun, who rejected revolution and preferred kings and queens. Toward the end of her eighty-seven years (1755–1842) she published memoirs giving a pleasant account of her youth, a sad story of her marriage, an itinerary of her artistic odyssey, and a picture of a good woman shocked by the violence of history. Her father, a portrait painter, died when she was thirteen, leaving no fortune, but Élisabeth had been so apt a pupil that by the age of sixteen she was earning a good income from her portraits. In 1776 she married another painter, Pierre Lebrun, grandnephew of the Charles Le Brun who had been master of arts for Louis XIV. Her husband (she tells us) squandered her fortune and his through "his unbridled passion for women of bad morals, joined to his fondness for gambling."[69] She bore him a daughter (1778), and soon thereafter left him.

In 1779 she painted Marie Antoinette, who so fancied her as to sit for twenty portraits. The two women became such friends that they sang together the tender airs with which Grétry was drawing tears from Paris eyes. This royal favor, and the genteel elegance of her work, opened all doors to the attractive painter. She made every woman beautiful, putting roses into faded cheeks; soon every moneyed lady itched to sit. She received such high fees that she was able to maintain an expensive apartment and a salon frequented by the best musicians of Paris.

Despite her friendship with the Queen, she went out three times to portray Mme. du Barry at Louveciennes. On the third occasion (July 14, 1789) she heard the sound of cannon firing in Paris. She returned to the city to find

that the Bastille had been taken, and that the victorious populace was carrying noble heads on bloody pikes. On October 5, while another mob was
tramping to Versailles to make the King and Queen their captives, she gathered what she could of her belongings and began thirteen years of voluntary
exile. In Rome she made the familiar portrait of herself and her daughter.[70]
At Naples she pictured Lady Hamilton as a bacchante.[71] She painted in
Vienna, Berlin, and St. Petersburg; and when the Revolution had run its
course she returned to France (1802). There, triumphant over all vicissitudes, she lived another forty years, wisely dying before revolution was renewed.

VI. LITERATURE

In the brief period between 1774 and 1789 French literature produced
some memorable works that still find readers and move minds: the *Maximes*
of Chamfort, the *Paul et Virginie* of Bernardin de Saint-Pierre, the *Liaisons
dangereuses* of Choderlos de Laclos (of which we have said enough), and
the chaotic but revealing volumes of Restif de La Bretonne.

These were islands erupting from a literary sea of schools, libraries, reading circles, lectures, newspapers, magazines, pamphlets, and books—such a
froth and ferment of ink as the world had never known before. Only a small
minority of the French people could read;[72] nevertheless millions of them
were thirsty for knowledge and bursting with ideas. Encyclopedias, com-
pendiums of science, outlines of knowledge, were in wide demand. The *philosophes* and the reformers were investing high hopes in the spread of education.

Though the Jesuits were gone and the schools were now controlled by the
state, most of the teaching was still in the hands of the clergy. The universities, rigidly orthodox in religion and politics, had fallen into torpor and
disrepute, and were only beginning, at the end of the century, to notice the
sciences. But public lectures on science were eagerly attended, and technical
schools were multiplying. In the colleges nearly all the students were of the
middle class; young nobles went rather to one or another of the twelve military academies that Saint-Germain had set up in or after 1776. (In one of
these, at Brienne, Napoleon Bonaparte was studying.) College students, we
are told, "frequently formed organizations to support political demonstrations";[73] and as there were at this time more college graduates than the
French economy could use, the placeless ones became voices of discontent;
such men wrote pamphlets that stoked the fires of revolt.

The rich had private libraries, enviably housed, of books luxuriously
bound and sometimes read. The middle and lower classes used circulating libraries, or bought their books—nearly all paperbacks—from stalls or stores.
In 1774 the sale of books in Paris was estimated to be four times that of much
more populous London.[74] Restif de La Bretonne reported that reading had
made the workers of Paris "intractable."[75]

Newspapers were growing in number, size, and influence. The old *Gazette de France*, established in 1631, was still the official—and distrusted—purveyor of political news. The *Mercure de France*, which had begun in 1672 as the *Mercure galant*, had in 1790 a circulation of thirteen thousand copies, which was thought excellent; Mirabeau called it the ablest of the French newspapers.[76] The *Journal de Paris*, the first French daily, began publication in 1777; the more famous *Moniteur* did not appear till November 24, 1789. There were many provincial newspapers, like the *Courier de Provence*, which was edited by Mirabeau *fils*.

Pamphlets were an inundation that finally swept everything before them. In the last months of 1788 some 2,500 were published in France.[77] Some had historic effect, like the Abbé Sieyès' *Qu'est-ce que le Tiers-état?* or Camille Desmoulins' *La France libre*. By July, 1789, the press was the strongest force in France. Necker described it, in 1784, as "an invisible power which, though without wealth, without weapons, and without an army, dictates alike to town and court, and even in the palaces of kings."[78] Songs played a part in the agitation; Chamfort called the government a monarchy limited by popular airs.[79]

Chamfort himself was snatched up into the revolutionary current, and passed from being *persona grata* at court to taking part in storming the Bastille. Born the son of a village grocer (1741), he came to Paris and lived on his wits and wit. Women housed and fed him merely to have the stimulus of his conversation. He wrote several dramas, one of which, performed at Fontainebleau, so pleased Marie Antoinette that she persuaded the King to give him a pension of twelve hundred livres. He was made secretary to a sister of Louis XVI, and received an additional two thousand livres a year. Everything seemed to bind him to the royal cause, but in 1783 he met Mirabeau, and was soon changed into a caustic critic of the government. It was he who gave Sieyès the catching title for his famous pamphlet.

Meanwhile, inspired by La Rochefoucauld, Vauvenargues, and Voltaire, he jotted down "maxims" expressing his sardonic view of the world. Mme. Helvétius, who for years kept him as a house guest at Sèvres, said, "Whenever I had a conversation with Chamfort in the morning, I was saddened for the rest of the day."[80] He thought life a hoax upon hope. "Hope is a charlatan that always deceives us; and as for myself, my happiness began only when I abandoned hope."[81] "If the cruel truths, the sad discoveries, the secrets of society, which compose the knowledge of a man of the world who has reached the age of forty, had been known to this same man at the age of twenty, either he would have fallen into despair or he would have deliberately become corrupt."[82] Coming at the end of the Age of Reason, Chamfort laughed at reason as less a master of passion than a tool of evil. "Man, in the actual state of society, seems more corrupted by his reason than by his passions."[83] As for women, "whatever evil a man can think of them, there is no woman who does not think still worse of them than he does."[84] Marriage is a snare. "Marriage and celibacy are both of them troublesome; we should prefer that one whose inconveniences are not without remedy."[85]

"Women give to friendship only what they borrow from love,"[86] and "love, such as it exists in society, is nothing but an exchange of fantasies and the contact of two skins [*contact de deux épidermes*]."[87]

When Chamfort stepped out of palaces and mansions into the streets of Paris his pessimism was intensified. "Paris, city of amusement and pleasure, where four fifths of the people die of grief, . . . a place that stinks and where no one loves."[88] The only cure for these slums would be childlessness. "It is unfortunate for mankind, fortunate for tyrants, that the poor and miserable do not have the instinct or pride of the elephant, who does not reproduce in captivity."[89]

Chamfort at times indulged in an ideal. "It is necessary to unite contraries: the love of virtue with indifference to public opinion; the taste for work with indifference to fame; and the care of one's health with indifference to life."[90] For some years he thought to give meaning to life by dedicating himself to revolution, but five years of dealing with Mirabeau, Danton, Marat, and Robespierre regenerated his despair. It seemed to him then that the Revolutionary motto "Liberty, equality, fraternity" had come to mean "Be my brother or I'll kill you."[91] He cast in his lot with the Girondins, and lashed the more radical leaders with his reckless wit. He was arrested, but was soon released. Threatened again with arrest, he shot and stabbed himself. He lingered till April 13, 1794, and died after saying to Sieyès, "I go at last out of this world, where the heart must break or make itself bronze [*Je m'en vais enfin de ce monde, où il faut que le cœur se brise ou se bronze*]."[92]

If the influence of Voltaire predominated in Chamfort, that of Rousseau was complete and avowed in Jacques-Henri Bernardin de Saint-Pierre. At the age of thirty-one (1768) he went as an engineer on a governmental commission to the Île de France, now called Mauritius. In that mountainous, rainy, fruitful island he found what he thought was Rousseau's "state of nature"—men and women living close to the earth and free from the vices of civilization. Returning to France (1771), he became a devoted friend of Jean-Jacques, learned to tolerate his tantrums, and to think of him as another saviour for mankind. In a *Voyage à l'Île de France* (1773) he described the simple life and sustaining religious faith of the island's population. The bishop of Aix saw in this book a wholesome reaction against Voltaire, and secured for the author a royal pension of a thousand livres. Bernardin responded with *Études de la nature* (1784) and *Les Harmonies de la nature* (1796), in which he described the wonders of plant and animal life, and argued that the many instances of apparent adaptation, purpose, and design prove the existence of a supreme intelligence. He went beyond Rousseau in exalting feeling above reason. "The further reason advances, the more it brings us evidence of our nothingness; and far from calming our sorrows by its researches, it often increases them by its light. . . . But feeling . . . gives us a sublime impulsion, and in subjugating our reason it becomes the noblest and most gratifying instinct in human life."[93]

To a second edition of the *Études* (1788) Bernardin appended a romance,

Paul et Virginie, which has remained a classic of French literature through a dozen shifts of taste. Two pregnant Frenchwomen come to Mauritius, one whose husband has died, the other whose lover has deserted her. One gives birth to Paul, the other to Virginie. The children grow up in a mountain valley, amid majestic scenery scented with natural flowers. Their morals are formed by maternal devotion and religious teaching. As soon as they reach puberty they fall in love with each other—no one else being around. Virginie is sent to France to collect an inheritance—which does not often happen in a state of nature. She is offered marriage and great fortune if she will stay in France, but she rejects them to return to Mauritius and Paul. He runs down to the shore to see her ship approaching; he is overjoyed with thoughts of love and happiness; but the vessel runs into shallows, is grounded, and is shattered by a storm; Virginie is drowned in trying to reach the shore. Paul dies of grief.

The little book is a prose poem, told with a simplicity of style and a purity and music of language nowhere surpassed in French literature. Its piety and sentiment fell in with the mood of the time, and no one was disturbed by the fact that these virtuous women and children had slaves.[94] Bernardin was hailed as the authentic successor of Rousseau; women wrote to him in the same tone of devout admiration with which they had comforted the author of *Émile.* Like him, Bernardin did not take advantage of his fame; he shunned society, and lived quietly among the poor. The Revolution left him unharmed. Amid its violence he married, at fifty-five, Félicité Didot, aged twenty-two; she gave him two children, who were named Paul and Virginie. After Félicité's death he married again, at sixty-three, a young woman, Désirée de Pellepou, who took care of him lovingly till his death in 1814. Before he departed he saw the rise of Chateaubriand, who took the torch of French romanticism and piety from his hands, and carried it into the nineteenth century.

There were in this age some minor books which are no longer read, but which shared in giving voice and color to the time. Abbé Jean-Jacques Barthélemy published at the age of seventy-two (1788), after working on it for thirty years, *Voyage du jeune Anacharsis en Grèce,* which purported to describe the physical appearance, the antiquities, institutions, customs, and coins of Greece in the fourth century before Christ, as seen by a Scythian traveler; it came on the crest of the classic wave, and was one of the outstanding literary successes of the age. It almost established the science of numismatics in France.

Its popularity was rivaled by *Les Ruines, ou Méditations sur les révolutions des empires,* which Comte Constantin de Volney issued in 1791 after four years of travel in Egypt and Syria. Seeing the shattered remnants of ancient civilizations, he asked, "Who can assure us that a like desolation will not one day be the lot of our country?" We should now hesitate to give an optimistic answer to this question, but Volney, coming at the close of the Age of Reason, and inheriting, like Condorcet, all its hopes for mankind, informed his readers that the collapse of those old empires had been due to the ignorance of their peoples, and that this had been due to the difficulty of transmitting knowledge from man to man and from generation to generation. But now these difficulties had been overcome by the invention of printing. All that is needed henceforth to avert the ruin of civilization is the wide dissemination of knowledge, which leads men and states to reconcile their unsocial impulses with the common good. In this equilibrium of forces war will give way to arbitration, and "the whole species will become one *great society*, a single family governed by the same spirit and by common laws, enjoying all the felicity of which human nature is capable."[95]

We come to the incredible career of Nicolas-Edme Restif de La Bretonne, called, by some contemporaries, "the Rousseau of the gutter" and "the Voltaire of the chambermaids"; author of some two hundred volumes, many of them printed by his own hand and press, some deliberately pornographic, all constituting a detailed picture of the morals and manners of the lower classes in the reign of Louis XVI.

In *La Vie de mon père* (1779) he gave a tenderly idealized account of his father, Edmond, whom he remembered as having "the air of a Hercules and the gentleness of a girl."[96] The son recorded his own life in sixteen meandering volumes entitled *Monsieur Nicolas* (1794–97), fact and fiction about his vicissitudes, amours, and ideas. He was born in a farmhouse (1737) in Sacy (one section of which was called La Bretonne), twenty miles from Auxerre. At the age of eleven, he assures us, he first became a father.[97] At fourteen he fell in love with Jeannette Rousseau, seventeen, and began his lifelong adoration of female feet. "My feeling for her was as pure and tender as it was intense. . . . Her pretty foot was irresistible to me."[98] Perhaps to disengage him from such entanglements he was sent to Auxerre (1751) to serve as apprentice to a printer. He soon seduced his master's wife; but for this he is the sole authority. By the age of fifteen, he tells us, he had had fifteen "mistresses." After four years of this pursuit he moved to Paris; there he was employed as a journeyman printer, earning two and a half francs a day, which enabled him to eat, and to pay for an occasional prostitute; sometimes, when his funds were low, he slept with charcoal women.[99] In 1760, aged twenty-six, he married a woman almost as experienced as himself, Agnès Lebèque; each proved unfaithful. They were divorced in 1784, not because of these peccadilloes, but because both had fallen into authorship, and they were competing for paper, ink, and fame.

Nicolas had begun his career as a writer in 1767, with *Le Pied de Fanchette*, in which the *pièce de résistance* was the lass's foot. His first literary success was *Le Paysan perverti* (1775). It tells in letter form how the peasant Edmond, moving to Paris, is perverted by city life and irreligion. A freethinker, Gaudit d'Arras, teaches him that God is a myth and morality a sham, that all pleasures are legitimate, that virtue is an unwarranted imposition upon the natural rights of our desires, and that our prime obligation is to live as fully as possible.[100] Arras is arrested; Edmond tells him, "There is a God"; Arras is hanged impenitent. One contemporary called the book "the *Liaisons dangereuses* of the people";[101] Restif thought it would live as long as the French language.[102] In a companion volume, *La Paysanne per-vertie* (1784), he continued his attack upon amoralism and the corruptions of city life. He used his royalties to raise himself a notch or two on the social scale of adultery.

Restif's most significant work was *Les Contemporaines*, which ran to sixty-five volumes (1780-91). These short stories had an attractive subtitle: "Aventures des plus jolies femmes de l'âge présent"—the lives, loves, and manners of flower girls, chestnut sellers, charcoal vendors, seamstresses, hair-dressers, described so realistically and accurately that actual persons recognized themselves, and cursed the author when they met him in the streets.[103] Not till Balzac was so large a panorama of human life presented in French literature. Critics condemned Restif's addiction to "low subjects," but Sé-bastien Mercier, whose *Tableau de Paris* (1781-90) was offering a more systematic survey of the city, pronounced him "incontestably our greatest novelist."[104]

Just before the Revolution Restif began to record, in *Les Nuits de Paris* (1788-94), the incidents that he witnessed (or imagined) on his nightly walks. Again he noted chiefly the lower depths of Paris—beggars, porters, pickpockets, smugglers, gamblers, drunkards, kidnapers, thieves, deviates, prostitutes, pimps, and suicides. He claimed to have seen little happiness, much misery, and he pictured himself as in many cases a rescuing hero. He visited the cafés near the Palais-Royal, and saw the Revolution taking form; he heard Camille Desmoulins' famous call to arms; saw the victorious mob parading the severed head of de Launay, warden of the Bastille; saw the women marching to capture the King at Versailles.[105] Soon he tired of the violence, the terror, the insecurity of life. He was several times in danger of arrest, but escaped by professions of revolutionary faith. Privately he de-nounced it all, and wished that "good Louis XVI could be restored to power."[106] He berated Rousseau for having unleashed the passions of the young, the ignorant, and the sentimental. "It is *Émile* that has brought us this arrogant generation, stubborn and insolent and willful, which speaks loudly, and silences the elderly."[107]

So he grew old, and repented the ideas, but not the sins, of his youth. In 1794 he was again a poor man, rich only in memories and grandchildren. He drew up in Volume XIII of *Monsieur Nicolas* a *calendrier* of the men and women in his life, including several hundred paramours, and he reaffirmed his belief in God. In 1800 the Comtesse de Beauharnais told Napoleon that Restif was living in poverty, without heat in his room; Napoleon sent him money, a servant, and a guard, and (1805) gave him a place in the ministry of police. On February 8, 1806, Restif died, aged seventy-two. The Countess and several members of the Institute de France (which had refused him ad-mission) joined the eighteen hundred commoners who followed his funeral.

VII. BEAUMARCHAIS

"The more I see of the French theater," wrote Arthur Young in 1788, "the more I am forced to acknowledge its superiority to our own, in the number of its good performers, . . . in the quality of dancers, singers, and persons on whom the business of the theater depends, all established on a grand scale."[108] At the Théâtre-Français, rebuilt in 1782, and in many provincial theaters, performances were given every night, including Sundays. In acting there was now an interregnum: Lekain died, and Sophie Arnould retired, in 1778; Talma, future favorite of Napoleon, made his debut with the Comédie-Française in 1787, and earned his first triumph in Marie-Joseph Chénier's *Charles IX* in 1789. The most popular playwright of the time was Michel-Jean Sedaine, who wrote sentimental comedies that kept the French stage for a century. We salute him and pass on to the man who, with the help of Mozart and Rossini, gave life to Figaro, and (as he saw it) freedom to America.

Pierre-Augustin Caron, like Voltaire, lived twenty-four years without knowing his historic name. His father was a watchmaker in the St.-Denis suburb of Paris. After some rebellion he resigned himself to follow the paternal trade. At the age of twenty-one he invented a new type of escapement which enabled him to make "excellent watches as flat and as small as may be thought fit."[109] He pleased Louis XV with a sample, and for Mme. de Pompadour made one so small that it fitted into her ring; this, he claimed, was the smallest watch ever constructed. In 1755 he bought from its aging holder, M. Franquet, a place among the "controllers of the royal pantry," who waited upon the King at his meals; it was no very exalted post, but it gave Pierre entry to the court. A year later Franquet died; Pierre married the widow (1756), six years older than himself; and, as she owned a small fief, Pierre added its name to his own, and became Beaumarchais. When his wife died (1757) he inherited her property.

He had never received any secondary education, but everyone—even the aristocrats who resented his agile climb—recognized the alertness of his mind and the quickness of his wit. In the salons and the cafés he met Diderot, d'Alembert, and other *philosophes*, and imbibed the Enlightenment. An improvement that he had made in the pedal arrangement of the harp caught the attention of Louis XV's unmarried daughters; in 1759 he began to give them lessons on the harp. The banker Joseph Paris-Duverney asked Beaumarchais to enlist the aid of Mesdames Royales in securing the support of Louis XV for the École Militaire, of which the financier was a director; Pierre succeeded in this, and Paris-Duverney gave him stocks worth sixty thousand francs. "He initiated me," said Beaumarchais, "into the secrets of finance. . . . I commenced making my fortune under his direction; by his advice I undertook several speculations, in some of which he assisted me with his money or his name."[110] So Beaumarchais, following in this as in so many other ways the precedents set by Voltaire, became a millionaire philosopher. By 1871 he was rich enough to buy one of the titular secretaryships to the king, which brought him a title of nobility. He took a fine house in the Rue de Condé, and installed in it his proud father and sisters.

Two other sisters were living in Madrid—one married, the other, Lisette, engaged to José Clavigo y Fajardo, editor and author, who for six years repeatedly postponed the marriage. In May, 1764, Beaumarchais began a long ride by stagecoach, day and night, to the Spanish capital. He found Clavigo, who promised to marry Lisette soon, but then eluded Beaumarchais by moving from place to place. Pierre finally caught up with him, and demanded his signature for a contract of marriage; José excused himself on the ground that he had just taken a purgative, and Spanish law held invalid any contract signed by a person in such a condition. Beaumarchais threatened him; Clavigo set the forces of government against him; the clever Frenchman was defeated by *mañana*. Abandoning that chase, he took up the pursuit of business and organized several companies, one for supplying Negro slaves to Spanish colonies. (He forgot that only a year earlier he had written a poem condemning slavery.[111]) All these plans foundered on the Spanish gift for procrastination. Meanwhile, however, Pierre enjoyed good company and a titled mistress, and learned enough about Spanish manners to write his plays about a barber of Seville. Lisette found another lover, and Beaumarchais returned to France with nothing gained but experience. He composed fascinating memoirs of his trip, from which, as we have seen, Goethe made a drama, *Clavigo* (1775).

In 1770 Paris-Duverney died, after making a will acknowledging that he owed Beaumarchais fifteen thousand francs. The chief heir, the Comte de La Blache, contested this clause as a forgery. The matter was referred to the Paris Parlement, which appointed Councilor Louis-Valentin Goëzman to pass on it. At this juncture Beaumarchais was in jail as a result of a violent fracas with the Duc de Chaulnes about a mistress. Temporarily released, he sent a "present" of a hundred louis d'or, and a diamond-studded watch, to Mme. Goëzman as inducements to get him a hearing before her husband; she asked an additional fifteen louis d'or for a "secretary"; he sent them. He secured the interview; the Councilor decided against him; Mme. Goëzman returned all but the fifteen louis d'or; Beaumarchais insisted on her returning these too; Goëzman charged him with bribery. Pierre put the matter before the public in a series of *Memoirs* so vivacious and witty that they won him wide acclaim as a brilliant debater if not quite an honest man. Voltaire said of them: "I have never seen anything stronger, bolder, funnier, more interesting, more humiliating for his foes. He fights a dozen of them at a time, and mows them down."[112] The Parlement ruled against his claim to the inheritance (April 6, 1773), in effect charged him with forgery, and condemned him to pay 56,300 livres in damages and debts.

Released from jail (May 8, 1773), Beaumarchais engaged himself to Louis XV as a secret agent on a mission to England to prevent the circulation of a scandalous pamphlet against Mme. du Barry. He succeeded, and continued in secret service under Louis XVI, who commissioned him to return to London and bribe Guglielmo Angelucci to refrain from publishing a pamphlet against Marie Antoinette. Angelucci surrendered the manuscript for 35,000 francs and departed for Nuremberg; Beaumarchais, suspecting him to have another copy, pursued him through Germany, caught up with him near Neustadt, and forced him to surrender the copy. Two brigands attacked him; he fought them off, was wounded, made his way to Vienna, was arrested as a spy, spent a month in jail, was freed, and rode back to France.

His next exploit has more right to a place in history. In 1775 Vergennes sent him to London to report on the growing crisis between England and America. In September Beaumarchais dispatched to Louis XVI a report predicting the success of the American revolt, and emphasizing the pro-American minority in England. On February 29, 1776, he addressed to the King another letter, recommending secret French aid to America, on the ground that France could protect herself from subjection only by weakening England.[113] Vergennes concurred with this view, and, as we have seen, arranged to finance Beaumarchais in providing war materials to the English colonies. Beaumarchais gave himself wholeheartedly to the enterprise. He organized the firm of Rodrigue Hortalez and Company, and went from one French port to another, buying and equipping ships, loading them with provisions and weapons, recruiting experienced French officers for the American army, and spending (he claimed) several million livres of his own in addition to the two million supplied him by the French and Spanish governments. Silas Deane reported to the American Congress (November 29, 1776): "I should never have completed my mission but for the generous, indefatigable, and intelligent exertion of M. de Beaumarchais, to whom the United States are, on every account, more indebted than to any other person on this side of the ocean."[114] At the end of the war Silas Deane calculated that America owed Beaumarchais 3,600,000 francs. The Congress, having assumed that all the material was a gift from allies, rejected the claim, but in 1835 it paid 800,000 livres to Beaumarchais' heirs.

During this feverish activity he found time to write more memorials, addressed to the public, protesting the decree of Parlement of April 6, 1773. On September 6, 1776, that decree was annulled, and all of Beaumarchais' civil rights were restored. In July, 1778, a court at Aix-en-Provence ruled in his favor in the matter of Paris-Duverney's will, and Beaumarchais could feel that at last he had cleared his name.

All his enterprises in love, war, business, and law were not enough for Beaumarchais. There was a world of words, ideas, and print not yet quite conquered. In 1767 he offered to the Comédie-Française his first play, *Eugénie*; it was presented on January 29, 1769, was well received by the audience, but was rejected by the critics. Another play, *Les Deux Amis* (January 13, 1770), failed despite the customary preparation; "I had filled the pit with the most excellent workers, with hands like paddles, but the efforts of the cabal" prevailed against him.[115] The literary confraternity, led by Fréron, opposed him as an intruder, a jailbird turned dramatist, just as the court at

Versailles was against him as a watchmaker turned noble. So, in his next play, he made Figaro describe "the republic of letters" as "the republic of wolves, continually at one another's throats; . . . all the insects, gnats, mosquitoes, and critics, all the envious journalists, booksellers, censors."[116]

On the stage, as in life, Beaumarchais encountered a swarm of enemies, and defeated them all. In the most creative moment of his multiform genius he conceived Figaro: barber, surgeon, philosopher, dressed in satin vest and breeches, his guitar slung over his shoulder, his quick mind ready to resolve any difficulty, his wit piercing the cant, pretenses, and injustices of his time. In one sense Figaro was not a creation, being a new name and form for the stock figure of the clever servant in Greek and Roman comedy, in the Commedia dell' Arte of Italy, in Molière's Sganarelle; but as we know him all but the music is Beaumarchais'. Even the music was originally his; he first composed *Le Barbier de Séville* as a comic opera, which he presented to the Comédie-Italienne in 1772; it was rejected, but Mozart became acquainted with this music while he was in Paris.[117] Beaumarchais remodeled the opera into a comedy; this was accepted by the Comédie-Française, and was scheduled for production when the author's imprisonment (February 24, 1773) compelled a postponement. On his release it was again prepared for presentation, but was adjourned because the author was under indictment by the Parlement. The success of Beaumarchais' public self-defense in his *Memoirs* led the theater again to plan the production; it was announced for February 12, 1774; "all the boxes," Grimm reported, "were sold up to the fifth performance."[118] At the last moment the government forbade the play on the ground that it might prejudice the case still pending in the Parlement.

Another year passed; a new King came, whom Beaumarchais served valiantly at the repeated risk of his life; permission was given; and on February 23, 1775, *The Barber of Seville* finally reached the stage. It did not go well; it was too long; and the preliminary excitement had led the audience to expect too much. In one day Beaumarchais revised and shortened it in a chef-d'oeuvre of surgery; the comedy was cleared from confusing complications, the wit was freed from excessive discourse; as Beaumarchais put it, he removed the fifth wheel from the carriage. On the second evening the play was a triumph. Mme. du Deffand, who was there, described it as "an extravagant success, . . . applauded beyond all bounds."[119]

The Prince de Conti challenged Beaumarchais to write a continuation play which would show Figaro as a more developed character. The author was now absorbed in his role as savior of America, but when that had been accomplished he returned to the stage and produced a comedy that made more dramatic history than even the *Tartuffe* of Molière. In *The Marriage of Figaro* the Count Almaviva and the Rosina of *The Barber of Seville* have lived through several years of marriage; he has already tired of the charms that lured him through so many complications; his present enterprise is to seduce Suzanne, maid to his Countess and affianced to Figaro, who has become premier valet to the Count and major-domo of the château. Chérubin, a thirteen-year-old page, provides a graceful obbligato to the central theme by his calf love for the Countess, who is twice his age. Figaro has become a philosopher; Beaumarchais describes him as *"la raison assaisonnée de gaiété et de saillies"*—reason seasoned with gaiety and sallies[120]—which is almost a definition of the *esprit gaulois*, and of the Enlightenment.

"I was born to be a courtier," he tells Suzanne; and when she supposes this "is a difficult art," he replies, "Not at all. To receive, to take, to ask— behold the secret in three words."[121] And in the soliloquy which Rossini has made to resound throughout the world, he addresses the nobles of Spain (and France) with almost revolutionary scorn: "What have you done for so much good fortune? You gave yourselves the trouble to be born, and nothing more; for the rest you are sufficiently ordinary! While I, lost in the common crowd, have had to use more science and calculation merely to subsist than have gone into governing all Spain these hundred years past."[122] He laughs at soldiers who "kill and get themselves killed for interests quite unknown to them. As for me, I want to know *why* I am furious."[123] Even the human race gets its comeuppance: "To drink without being thirsty, and to make love at all seasons—this alone distinguishes us from other animals."[124] There were miscellaneous strokes against the sale of public offices, the arbitrary power of ministers, the miscarriages of justice, the condition of prisons, the censorship and persecution of thought. "Provided in my writings I mention neither the authorities nor the state religion, nor politics, nor morals, nor the officials, nor finances, nor the opera, nor . . . any person of consequence, I may print whatever I like, subject to inspection by two or three censors."[125] A passage which the actors deleted, perhaps as coming too close to their own recreations, accused the male sex as responsible for prostitution: men by their demands create the supply, and by their laws punish the women who meet the demand.[126] The plot itself did not merely show the servant cleverer than his master—this was too traditional to offend—but it revealed the noble count as an arrant adulterer.

The Marriage of Figaro was accepted by the Comédie-Française in 1781, but it could not be produced till 1784. When it was read to Louis XVI he bore with tolerant humor the incidental satire, but when he heard the soliloquy, with derision of the nobility and the censorship, he felt that he could not allow these basic institutions to be publicly abused. "This is detestable," he exclaimed; "it must never be played. To allow its representation would be equivalent to destroying the Bastille. This man laughs at everything that ought to be respected in a government."[127] He forbade the staging of the piece.

Beaumarchais read parts of the play in private homes. Curiosity was aroused. Some courtiers arranged that it be performed before the court; but at the last minute this too was prohibited. At last the King yielded to protests and requests, and agreed to sanction public performances after careful expurgation of the text by censors. The première (April 27, 1784) was an historic event. All Paris seemed bent on attending the first night. Nobles fought with commoners for admission; iron gates were broken down, doors were smashed, three persons were suffocated. Beaumarchais was there, happy in the fracas. The success was so great that the play was performed sixty times running, nearly always to a full house. The receipts were unprecedented. Beaumarchais gave all of his share—41,999 livres—to charity.[128]

History has thought of *The Marriage of Figaro* as a harbinger of revolution; Napoleon described it as "the Revolution already in action."[129] Some of its lines entered into the ferment of the time. In the preface later attached to the published play Beaumarchais denied any revolutionary intent, and he quoted from his writings passages in defense of monarchy and aristocracy. He asked not for the destruction of existing institutions but for the removal of abuses attached to them; for equal justice to all classes, for greater freedom of thought and press, for protection of the individual against *lettres de cachet* and other excesses of monarchical power. Like his idol, Voltaire, he rejected revolution as an invitation to chaos and the mob.

Through all the varied turbulence that enveloped him he continued to study the works of Voltaire. He recognized the similarities, though perhaps not the distance, between himself and the patriarch: the same combination of feverish intellectual activity with canny financial skill, the same scorn of scruples and of moral delicacy, the same courage in fighting injustice and adversity. He resolved to preserve and disseminate the works of Voltaire in a collected and complete edition. He knew that this could not be done in France, where many of Voltaire's writings were prohibited. He went to Maurepas and told him that Catherine II had proposed to bring out a French edition in St. Petersburg; he argued that this would be a disgrace to France; the minister saw the point, and promised to allow the circulation of a complete edition. Charles-Joseph Pancoucke, a Paris bookseller, had secured the rights to Voltaire's unpublished manuscripts; Beaumarchais bought these for 160,000 francs. He collected all the published works of Voltaire that he could find. He imported Baskerville type from England, and purchased paper mills in the Vosges. He secured Condorcet as an editor and biographer. He leased an old fort at Kehl, across the Rhine from Strasbourg, installed presses, and, despite a thousand tribulations, brought out two editions, one in seventy volumes octavo, the other in ninety-two volumes duodecimo (1783–90). This was the largest publishing enterprise yet attempted in Europe, not excepting the *Encyclopédie*. Expecting a ready sale, Beaumarchais printed fifteen thousand sets; he sold only two thousand, partly because of campaigns against the enterprise by the Parlement and the clergy,[130] partly because of the political turmoil of 1788–90, and partly because the instability of personal fortunes deterred individuals from buying so expensive a set. Beaumarchais claimed to have lost a million livres in the venture. However, he produced also an edition of Rousseau.

The Revolution which he had helped to prepare proved a misfortune for him. In 1789 he built for himself and his third wife a costly mansion opposite the Bastille; he filled it with fine furniture and art, and surrounded it with two acres of land. The mobs that repeatedly rioted in the area looked askance at such luxury; twice his house was invaded, and Beaumarchais, now deaf and prematurely old, was threatened as an aristocrat. He sent a petition to the Commune of Paris professing his faith in the Revolution; nevertheless he was arrested (August 23, 1792); though soon set free, he lived in daily fear of assassination. Then the wheel of fortune turned, and he was commissioned by the Revolutionary government (1792) to go to Holland and buy guns for the republic. The negotiations failed; and during his absence his property was seized, and his wife and daughter were arrested (July 5, 1794). He rushed back to Paris, secured their release, and was allowed to recover his property. He lived three years more, broken in body but not in spirit, and hailed the rise of Napoleon. He died on May 18, 1799, of an apoplectic stroke, at the age of sixty-seven. Seldom even in French history had a man led so full and varied and adventurous a life.

CHAPTER XXXVII

The Anatomy of Revolution

1774-89

WE HAVE examined the mind of France on the eve of the Revolution —its philosophy, religion, morals, manners, literature, and art. But these were frail flowers growing from an economic ground; we cannot understand them without a knowledge of their roots. Much less can we understand the political convulsion that ended the Old Regime without examining in turn, however briefly, each organ of the French economy, and inquiring how its condition made for the great debacle.

In dealing once more with agriculture, industry, commerce, and finance, we should remember that they are not dismal abstractions but living and sensitive human beings: nobles and peasants organizing the production of food; managers and workers manufacturing goods; inventors and scientists forging new methods and tools; towns throbbing with shops and factories, worried housewives and rebellious mobs; ports and ships alive with merchants, navigators, sailors, and adventurous spirits; bankers risking, gaining, losing money like Necker, life like Lavoisier; and, through all the agitated mass, the flow and pressure of revolutionary ideas and discontent. It is a complex and tremendous picture.

I. THE NOBLES AND THE REVOLUTION

France was 24,670,000 men, women, and children; so Necker reckoned the population in 1784.[1] The number had grown from 17,000,000 in 1715 through greater food production, better sanitation, and the absence of foreign invasion and civil war. The nation as a whole experienced a rise of prosperity during the eighteenth century, but most of the new affluence was confined to the middle class.[2]

All but two millions of the French were rural. Agricultural life was directed by royal intendants, provincial administrators, and parish priests, and by seigneurs—feudal lords—estimated in 1789 at some 26,000. These and their sons served their country in war in their gallant, old-fashioned way (swords were now more an ornament than a weapon). Only a small minority of the nobles remained at the court; the majority lived on their estates, and claimed to earn their keep by providing agricultural management, police surveillance, courts, schools, hospitals, and charity. Most of these functions, however, had been taken over by agents of the central government, and the peasant proprietors were developing their own institutions for local administration. So the nobility had become a vestigial organ, taking much blood from the social organism, and giving little but military service in return. Even this service aroused a public grievance, for the nobility persuaded Louis XVI (1781) to exclude all but men with four generations of aristocracy behind them from every major office in the army, the navy, and the government.

It was further alleged against the nobles that they left vast areas of their estates uncultivated, while thousands of city dwellers were hungering for bread. True of many parts of France was Arthur Young's description of the Loire and Cher River sections: "The fields are scenes of pitiable manage-ment, as the houses are of misery. Yet all this country [is] highly improv-able, if they knew what to do with it."[3] * Not a few of the nobles were themselves poor, some through incompetence, some through misfortune, some through the exhaustion of their soil. Many of these appealed to the King for help, and several received grants from the national purse.

Serfdom, in the sense of a person bound by law to a piece of land, and permanently subject to its owner for dues and services, had largely disap-peared from France by 1789; about a million serfs remained, chiefly on monastic properties. When Louis XVI freed the serfs on the royal domain (1779), the Parlement of Franche-Comté (in eastern France) delayed nine months before registering his edict. The Abbey of Luxeuil and the Priory of Fontaine, owning together eleven thousand serfs, and the Abbey of St.-Claude in the present department of the Jura, with twenty thousand serfs, refused to follow the King's example, despite appeals in which several ec-clesiastics joined with Voltaire.[5] Gradually these serfs bought their freedom, or gained it by flight; and Louis XVI, in 1779, abolished the owner's right to pursue fugitive serfs outside his own domain.

Though ninety-five per cent of the peasants were free in 1789, the great majority of these were still subject to one or more feudal dues, varying in degree from region to region. They included a yearly rental (doubled in the eighteenth century), a fee for the right to bequeath goods, and payment for use of the lord's grist mills, bake ovens, wine presses, and fishponds—on all of which he maintained a monopoly. He reserved the right to hunt his game even into the peasant's crops. He enclosed more and more of the common ground on which the peasant had formerly grazed his cattle and cut wood. The *corvée*, in most of France, had been commuted for a money payment, but in Auvergne, Champagne, Artois, and Lorraine the peasant was still re-quired to give the local seigneur three or more days of unpaid labor every year for the maintenance of roads, bridges, and waterways.[6] In sum and on the average the surviving feudal dues took ten per cent of the peasant's produce or income. The ecclesiastical tithe took another eight to ten per cent. Add the taxes paid to the state, the market and sales taxes, and the fees

---

* Arthur Young, English gentleman farmer, traveled on the Continent in 1787, 1788, and 1789, and reported his observations in *Travels in France* (1792). He had some English prejudices ("Take the mass of mankind, and you have more good sense in half an hour in England than in half a year in France"[4]); but he seems to have given a fair and reliable account of what he saw. We shall find him reporting prosperity as well as poverty. His chief criticisms of France were of its technological backwardness and its excessively centralized, ubiquitous, and autocratic government.

paid to the parish priest for baptism, marriage, and burial, and the peasant was left about half the fruit of his toil.

As the money payments received by the lords were reduced in value by depreciation of the currency, the seigneurs sought to protect their income by increasing the dues, by reviving dues long fallen into disuse, and by enclosing more of the common lands. The collection of dues was usually farmed out to professional agents, who were often heartless in their work. When the peasant questioned the right to certain requisitions he was told that they were listed on the rolls or registers of the manors. If he challenged the authenticity of these rolls the matter was submitted to the manorial court or the provincial *parlement*, whose judges were controlled by the seigneurs.[7] When Boncerf, secretly encouraged by Turgot, published (1776) a brochure, *The Disadvantages of the Feudal Rights*, recommending the reduction of such rights, he was censured by the Parlement of Paris. Voltaire, aged eighty-two, rose again to battle. "To propose the abolition of feudal rights," he wrote, "is tantamount to attacking the holdings of the gentlemen of the Parlement themselves, most of whom possess fiefs. . . . It is a case of the Church, the nobility, and the members of the Parlement . . . united against the common enemy—i.e., the people."[8]

Something could be said for the feudal dues. From the noble's point of view they were a mortgage freely assumed by the peasant as part of the price at which he bought a parcel of land from its legal owner—who in many cases had bought it in good faith from its previous possessor. Some poor nobles depended upon the dues for their sustenance. The peasant suffered far more from taxes, tithes, and the demands and ravages of war than from feudal dues. Hear the greatest and noblest of French socialists, Jean Jaurès: "If there had been, in the society of eighteenth-century France, no other abuse than the despicable remains of that [feudal] system, there would have been no need of a revolt to heal the sore; a gradual reduction of feudal rights, a liberation of the peasantry, would have accomplished the change peaceably."[9]

The most remarkable feature of the French nobility was its acknowledgment of guilt. Not only did many nobles join the *philosophes* in rejecting the old theology; some, as we have seen, laughed at the outdated prerogatives of their caste.[10] A year before the Revolution thirty nobles offered to renounce their pecuniary feudal privileges.[11] All the world knows the idealism of the young Lafayette, who not only fought for America, but, on returning to France, vigorously engaged in the struggle for peaceful reform. He denounced slavery, and devoted part of his fortune to freeing the slaves in French Guiana.[12] The profession of liberal principles, and the advocacy of reform, became fashionable in a section of the aristocracy, especially among titled ladies like Mesdames de La Marck, de Boufflers, de Brienne, and de Luxembourg. Hundreds of nobles and prelates took an active part in campaigns for equalizing taxes, checking governmental extravagance, organizing charities, ending the *corvée*.[13] Some nobles, like the Duchesse de Bourbon, gave most of their wealth to the poor.[14]

All this, however, was only a graceful ornament on the visible fact that the French nobility had ceased to earn its keep. Many nobles tried to fulfill their traditional responsibilities, but the contrast between the luxurious idleness of rich seigneurs and the hardships of a populace repeatedly on the verge of famine aroused hostility and scorn. Long ago a great noble himself had passed sentence of death upon his caste. Hear René-Louis de Voyer, Marquis d'Argenson, secretary of state (1744–47), writing about 1752:

> The race of great lords must be destroyed completely. By great lords I understand those who have dignities, property, tithes, offices, and functions, and who, without deserts and without necessarily being adults, are none the less great, and for this reason often worthless. . . . I notice that a breed of good hunting dogs is preserved, but once it deteriorates it is done away with.[15]

It was these lords, rich, proud, and often functionless, who initiated the Revolution. They looked fondly back to the days before Richelieu, when their order was the ruling power in France. When the *parlements* asserted their right to annul royal edicts, the nobilities of race and sword joined with the nobility of the robe—the hereditary magistrates—in an attempt to subordinate the king. They cheered the *parlement* orators who raised the cry for *liberté;* they encouraged the people and the pamphleteers to denounce the absolute power of Louis XVI. We cannot blame them; but by weakening the authority of the monarch they made it possible for the National Assembly of 1789, controlled by the bourgeoisie, to seize the sovereignty in France. The nobles threw the first spadeful of earth that dug their grave.

II. THE PEASANTS AND THE REVOLUTION

On the fifty-five per cent of the French soil owned by the nobility, the clergy, and the king, most of the agricultural work was done by métayers, who received stock, tools, and seed from the owner, and paid him, usually, half the yield. These sharecroppers were so poor generally that Arthur Young pronounced the system "the curse and ruin of the whole country";[16] not so much because the owners were cruel, but because incentives were weak.

The majority of the peasant proprietors who tilled forty-five per cent of the soil were condemned to poverty by the small size of their holdings, which limited the profitable use of machinery. Agricultural technology in France lagged behind that of England. There were schools of agriculture, and model farms, but only a few farmers took advantage of them. Probably sixty per cent of the peasant proprietors owned less than the five hectares (about thirteen acres) needed to support a family, and the men were driven to hire themselves out as laborers on large farms. Wages of farm laborers rose twelve per cent between 1771 and 1789, but in the same period prices rose sixty-five per cent or more.[17] While agricultural production rose during the reign of Louis XVI, the hired laborers grew poorer, and formed a rural proletariat which, in periods of slack employment, served as a breeding ground for a multitude of beggars and vagabonds. Chamfort thought it "incontestable that there are in France seven million men who beg alms, and twelve million who are unable to give alms."[18]

Probably the poverty of the peasants was exaggerated by travelers because they noticed chiefly the visible conditions, and did not see the currency and goods concealed to avoid the eye of the tax assessor. Contemporary estimates conflict. Arthur Young found areas of poverty, brutality, and filth, as in Brittany, and areas of prosperity and pride, as in Béarn.[19] By and large, poverty in rural France in 1789 was not as bad as in Ireland, no worse than in Eastern Europe or in the slums of some "affluent" cities of our time, but worse than in England or in the ever bountiful valley of the Po. The latest studies indicate that "there was, at the end of the Old Regime, an agrarian crisis."[20] When drought and famine came, as in 1788–89, the sufferings of the peasantry, particularly in the south of France, were such that only the charities distributed by the government and the clergy kept half the population from starving.

The peasant had to pay for the state, the Church, and the aristocracy. The taille, or land tax, fell almost entirely upon him. He supplied almost all the manpower of the army's infantry. He bore the brunt of the government's monopoly on salt. His labor maintained roads, bridges, and canals. He might have paid the tithe more cheerfully, for he was a pious "God-fearing" man, and the tithe was collected with mercy, and seldom took a literal tenth;[21] but he saw most of the tithe leaving the parish to support a distant bishop, or an ecclesiastical idler at the court, or even a layman who had bought a share of future tithes. The direct tax burden on the peasant was reduced by Louis XVI; the indirect taxes were in many districts increased.[22]

Was the poverty of the peasants the cause of the Revolution? It was a dramatic factor in a complex of causes. The very poor were too weak to revolt; they could cry out for relief, but they had neither the means nor the spirit to organize rebellion, until they were aroused by the more prosperous farmers, by the agents of the middle class, and by uprisings of the Paris populace. Then, however, when the powers of the state had been reduced by the intellectual development of the people, when the army was dangerously infected with radical ideas, and local authorities could no longer rely on military support from Versailles—then the peasants became a revolutionary force. They assembled, exchanged complaints and vows, armed themselves, attacked the châteaux, burned the homes of unyielding seigneurs, and destroyed the manorial rolls which were quoted as sanctioning the feudal dues. It was that direct action, threatening a nationwide destruction of seignorial property, that frightened the nobles into surrendering their feudal privileges (August 4, 1789), and so bringing a legal end to the Old Regime.

III. INDUSTRY AND THE REVOLUTION

Here especially the pre-Revolutionary picture is complex and obscure. (1) Domestic industry—of men, women, and children in the home—served merchants who provided the material and bought the product. (2) Guilds—masters, journeymen, and apprentices—produced handicraft goods, chiefly for local needs. The guilds survived till the Revolution, but by 1789 they had been fatally weakened by the growth of (3) capitalistic free enterprise —companies free to collect capital from any source, to hire anybody, to invent and apply new methods of production and distribution, to compete with anybody, and to sell anywhere. These establishments were usually small, but they were multiplying; so Marseilles alone, in 1789, had thirty-eight soap factories, forty-eight for hats, eight for glass, twelve sugar refineries, ten tanneries.[23] In textiles, building, mining, and metallurgy, capitalism had expanded into large-scale enterprises, usually through joint-stock companies—*sociétés anonymes*.

France was slow to adopt the textile machines that were inaugurating the Industrial Revolution in England, but large textile factories were operating in Abbeville, Amiens, Reims, Paris, Louviers, and Orléans, and the silk industry flourished at Lyons. The building trades were raising those massive blocks of apartment houses that still give French cities their characteristic physiognomy. Shipbuilding employed thousands of workers in Nantes, Bordeaux, Marseilles. Mining was the most advanced of French industries. The state kept all rights to the subsoil, leased the mines to concessionaires, and enforced a code of safety for the miners.[24] Companies sank shafts to depths of three hundred feet, installed expensive equipment for ventilation, drainage, and transport, and made millionaires. The Anzin firm (1790) had four thousand workmen, six hundred horses, and twelve steam engines, and mined 310,000 tons of coal per year. The mining of iron and other metals supplied material for an expanding metallurgical industry. In 1787 the Creusot stock company raised ten million livres of capital to apply the latest machinery in the production of ironware; steam engines operated bellows, hammers, and drills, and railways enabled one horse to pull what had required five horses before.

Some startling inventions were developed by Frenchmen in these years. In 1776 the Marquis de Jouffroy d'Abbans amused crowds along the River Doubs with a sidewheeler boat propelled by a steam engine, thirty-one years before Fulton's *Clermont* steamed up and down the Hudson. Even more spectacular were the first steps in the conquest of the air. In 1766 Henry Cavendish had shown that hydrogen has a lower density than air; Joseph Black concluded that a bladder filled with hydrogen would rise. Joseph and Étienne Montgolfier worked on the principle that air loses density when heated; on June 5, 1783, at Annonay, near Lyons, they filled a balloon with heated air; it rose to a height of sixteen hundred feet, and descended ten minutes later when its air had cooled. A hydrogen-filled balloon, designed by Jacques-Alexandre Charles, made an ascent from Paris on August 27, 1783, before 300,000 cheering spectators; when it came down fifteen miles away a village crowd tore it to pieces on the theory that it was a hostile invader from the sky.[25] On October 15 Jean-François Pilâtre de Rozier made the first recorded human flight, using a Montgolfier balloon with heated air; this ascent lasted four minutes. On January 7, 1785, François Blanchard, a

Frenchman, and John Jeffries, an American physician, flew in a balloon from England to France. People began to talk of flying to America.[26]

Nourished with industry and commerce, the towns of France prospered during the fatal reign. Lyons hummed with shops, factories, and enterprise. Arthur Young was amazed by the splendor of Bordeaux. Paris was now a business rather than a political center; it was the hub of an economic complex that controlled half the capital, and so half the economy, of France. In 1789 it had a population of some 600,000.[27] It was not then an especially beautiful city; Voltaire described much of it as worthy of Goths and Vandals.[28] Priestley, visiting it in 1774, reported: "I cannot say that I was much struck with anything except the spaciousness and magnificence of the public buildings, and to balance this I was exceedingly offended by the narrowness, dirt, and stench of almost all the streets."[29] Young gave a similar account:

> The streets are nine-tenths dirty, and all without foot pavements. Walking, which in London is so pleasant and so clean that ladies do it every day, is here a toil and a fatigue to a man, and an impossibility to a well-dressed woman. The coaches are numerous, and what is much worse, there are an infinity of one-horse cabriolets, which are driven by young men of fashion and their imitators, . . . with such rapidity as to . . . render the streets exceedingly dangerous. . . . I have been myself many times blackened with mud.[30]

In the cities and towns a proletariat was taking form: men, women, and children working for wages with tools and materials not their own. There are no statistics of them, but they have been estimated, for the Paris of 1789, at 75,000 families, or 300,000 individuals;[31] and there were proportionate masses in Abbeville, Lyons, and Marseilles. Hours of work were long and wages were low, for a ruling of the Paris Parlement (November 12, 1778) forbade the workers to organize. Between 1741 and 1789 wages rose twenty-two per cent, prices sixty-five per cent;[32] the condition of the workers seems to have deteriorated in the reign of Louis XVI.[33] When demand slackened, or (as in 1786) foreign competition became severe, workingmen in great number were discharged, and became a burden on charity. A rise in the price of bread—which constituted half the food of the Parisian populace[34]—put thousands of families close to starvation. At Lyons in 1787 thirty thousand persons were on public relief; at Reims in 1788, after an inundation, two thirds of the population were destitute; at Paris, in 1791, a hundred thousand families were listed as indigent.[35] "In Paris," wrote Mercier about 1785, "the [common] people are weak, pallid, diminutive, stunted, and apparently a class apart from other classes in the state."[36]

Defying prohibitions, laborers formed unions and went on strike. In 1774 the silk workers of Lyons quit work, alleging that the cost of living was rising much faster than wages, and that the unregulated laws of supply and demand were driving workers to a level of mere subsistence. The employers, with well-stocked larders, waited for hunger to bring the strikers to terms. Frustrated, many workers left Lyons for other towns, even for Switzerland or Italy; they were halted at the frontier and were brought back by force to their homes. The workers rose in revolt, seized municipal offices, and established a brief dictatorship of the proletariat over the commune. The government called in the army; the revolt was suppressed; two leaders were hanged; the strikers returned to their shops beaten, but hostile now to the government as well as to their employers.[37]

In 1786 they struck again, protesting that even with eighteen hours' work per day they could not support their families, and complaining that they were treated "more inhumanly than domestic animals, for even these are given enough to keep them in health and vigor."[38] The city authorities agreed to a rise in pay, but forbade any meeting of more than four persons. A battalion of artillery took charge of enforcing this prohibition; soldiers fired upon the strikers, killing several. The strikers returned to work. The increase in pay was later revoked.[39]

Riots against the cost of living occurred sporadically throughout the second half of the eighteenth century. In Normandy there were six between 1752 and 1768; in 1768 the rioters captured control of Rouen, sacked the public granaries, pillaged the stores. Similar riots occurred at Reims in 1770, Poitiers in 1772, Dijon, Versailles, Paris, Pontoise in 1775, Aix-en-Provence in 1785, and again at Paris in 1788 and 1789.[40]

What role did the poverty of the proletariat, or of the urban populace in general, play in bringing on the Revolution? On the surface it was a proximate cause; the bread shortages and consequent riots in Paris in 1788–89 raised the fever of the people to a point where they were willing to risk their lives in defying the army and attacking the Bastille. But hunger and wrath can give motive force; they do not give leadership; it is likely that the riots would have been calmed by a lowering of the price of bread if leadership from higher strata had not directed the rioters to take the Bastille and march on Versailles. The masses had as yet no idea of overturning the government, of deposing the King, of establishing a republic. The proletariat talked hopefully of natural equality, but it did not dream of taking possession of the state. It demanded, whereas the bourgeoisie opposed, state regulation of the economy, at least to fixing the price of bread; but this was a return to the old system, not an advance toward an economy dominated by the working class. It is true that when the time for action came it was the populace of Paris which, moved by hunger and roused by orators and agents, took the Bastille and thereby deterred the King from using the army against the Assembly. But when that Assembly remade France it was under the guidance, and for the purposes, of the bourgeoisie.

IV. THE BOURGEOISIE AND THE REVOLUTION

The outstanding feature of French economic life in the eighteenth century was the rise of the business class. It had begun to prosper under Louis XIV and Colbert; it benefited most from the excellent roads and canals that facilitated trade; it grew rich on commerce with the colonies; it rose to prominence in administrative posts (till 1781); it controlled the finances of the state.

But it was harassed to the point of revolt by the tolls exacted for seigneurs or the government on roads and canals, and by the time-consuming examination of the cargo at each toll station. There were from thirty-five to forty such tolls to be paid by a boat carrying cargo from south France to Paris.[41] Businessmen demanded free trade within frontiers, but they were not sure that they wanted it between nations. In 1786, moved by physiocratic theories, the government reduced tariffs on textiles and hardware from England, in return for reduction of English tariffs on French wines, glassware, and other products. One result was a blow to the French textile industry, which could not meet the competition of English mills equipped with later machinery. Unemployment in Lyons, Rouen, and Amiens reached an explosive point.

Nevertheless, the lowering of tariffs promoted foreign trade, and filled the coffers of the merchant class. That trade almost doubled between 1763 and 1787, rising to over a billion francs in 1780.[42] The port cities of France swelled with merchants, shippers, sailors, warehouses, refineries, distilleries; in those towns the business class was supreme long before the Revolution sanctioned its national supremacy.

Part of mercantile prosperity, as in England, came from the capture or purchase of African slaves, their transport to America, and their sale there for work on the plantations. In 1788 French slave dealers shipped 29,506 Negroes to St.-Domingue (Haiti) alone.[43] French investors owned most of the soil and industries there and in Guadeloupe and Martinique. In St.-Domingue thirty thousand whites used 480,000 slaves.[44] A Société des Amis des Noirs was formed in Paris in 1788, under the presidency of Condorcet, and including Lafayette and Mirabeau *fils*, for the abolition of slavery, but the shippers and planters overwhelmed the movement with protests. In 1789 the Chamber of Commerce of Bordeaux declared· "France needs its colonies for the maintenance of its commerce, and consequently it needs slaves in order to make agriculture pay in this quarter of the world, at least until some other expedient may have been found."[45]

Industrial, colonial, and other enterprises required capital, and generated a spreading breed of bankers. Joint-stock companies offered shares, the government floated loans, speculation developed in the sale and purchase of securities. Speculators hired journalists to disseminate rumors designed to raise or lower the price of stocks.[46] Members of the ministries joined in the speculation, and so became subject to pressure or influence by the bankers. Every war made the state more dependent upon the financiers, and made the financiers more vitally concerned with the policy and solvency of the state. Some bankers enjoyed a personal credit superior to that of the government; hence they could borrow at a low rate, lend to the government at a higher rate, and increase their wealth merely by bookkeeping—provided their judgment was good and the state paid its debts.

The farmers general (financiers who bought, by an advance to the state, the right to collect indirect taxes) were especially rich and especially hated, for the indirect taxes, like sales taxes in general, were most burdensome to those who had to spend much of their income on the necessaries of daily life. Some of these *fermiers généraux*, like Helvétius and Lavoisier, were men of relative integrity and public spirit, contributing abundantly to charity, literature, and art.[47] The government recognized the evils of the tax-farming system, and reduced the number of farmers general from sixty to forty in 1780, but public animosity continued. The tax farm was abolished by the Revolution, and Lavoisier's was one of the heads that fell in the process.

As taxation played a leading role among the causes of the Revolution, we must once more call to mind the various taxes paid by Frenchmen. (1) The taille was a tax on land and personal property. Nobles were exempted from it because of their military service; the clergy were excused because they maintained social order and prayed for the state; magistrates, head administrators, and university officials were exempt; almost all the taille fell upon the landowners of the Third Estate—therefore chiefly upon the peasants. (2) The capitation, or poll, tax was laid upon every head of a household; here only the clergy were exempt. (3) The *vingtième*, or twentieth, was a tax on all property, real or personal; but the nobles escaped a large part of this and the poll tax by using private influence, or engaging lawyers to find loopholes in the law; and the clergy avoided the *vingtième* by making a voluntary payment periodically to the state. (4) Every town paid a tax (*octroi*) to the government, and passed it on to its citizens. (5) Indirect taxes were levied through (a) transport tolls; (b) import and export dues; (c) excise taxes (*aides*) on wines, liquors, soap, leather, iron, playing cards, etc.; and (d) governmental monopolies on the sale of tobacco and salt. Every individual was required to buy annually a stated minimum of salt from the government at a price fixed by it, always higher than the market price. This salt tax (gabelle) was one of the chief miseries of the peasant. (6) The peasant paid a tax to escape the *corvée*. Altogether the average member of the Third Estate paid from forty-two to fifty-three per cent of his income in taxes.[48]

If we take together merchants, manufacturers, financiers, inventors, engineers, scientists, minor bureaucrats, clerks, tradesmen, chemists, artists, booksellers, teachers, writers, physicians, and untitled lawyers and magistrates as constituting the bourgeoisie, we can understand how by 1789 it had become the richest and most energetic part of the nation. It probably owned as much rural land as the nobility,[49] and it could acquire nobility merely by buying a noble fief or a post as one of the many "secretaries" to the king. While the nobility lost numbers and wealth through idleness, extravagance, and biological decay, and the clergy lost ground through the rise of science, philosophy, and an urban epicurean life and code, the middle classes grew in money and power by the development of industry, technology, commerce, and finance. They filled with their products or imports the *boutiques*, or stores, whose splendor astonished foreign visitors to Paris, Lyons, Reims, or Bordeaux.[50] While wars were bankrupting the government they enriched the bourgeoisie, which provided transport and matériel. The growing prosperity was almost confined to the towns; it eluded the peasantry and the proletariat, and appeared most visibly in merchants and financiers. In 1789 forty French merchants had a combined wealth of sixty million livres;[51] and one banker, Paris-Montmartel, amassed a hundred million.[52]

The essential cause of the Revolution was the disparity between economic reality and political forms—between the importance of the bourgeoisie in the production and possession of wealth and its exclusion from governmental power. The upper middle class was conscious of its abilities and sensitive to its slights. It was galled by the social exclusiveness and insolence of the nobility—as when the brilliant Mme. Roland, invited to stay for dinner in an aristocratic home, found herself served in the servants' quarters.[53] It saw the nobility milking the coffers of the state for extravagant expenditures and feasts while denying political or military office or promotion to those very men whose inventive enterprise had expanded the tax-yielding economy of France, and whose savings were now supporting the treasury. It saw the clergy absorbing a third of the nation's income in maintaining a theology that almost all educated Frenchmen considered medieval and infantile.

The middle classes did not wish to overthrow the monarchy, but they aspired to control it. They were far from desiring democracy, but they wanted a constitutional government in which the intelligence of all classes could be brought to bear upon legislation, administration, and policy. They demanded freedom from state or guild regulation of industry or commerce, but they were not averse to state subsidies, or to support from the peasants and the city populace in achieving middle-class aims. The essence of the French Revolution was the overthrow of the nobility and the clergy by a bourgeoisie using the discontent of peasants to destroy feudalism, and the discontent of urban masses to neutralize the armies of the king. When, after two years of revolution, the Constituent Assembly had become supreme, it abolished feudalism, confiscated the property of the Church, and legalized the organization of merchants, but forbade all organizations or gatherings of workingmen (June 14, 1791).[54]

Specifically and immediately the financiers were alarmed by the possibility that the government to which they had lent so much money might declare bankruptcy—as it had done, in whole or in part, fifty-six times since Henry IV.[55] The holders of government bonds lost faith in Louis XVI; contractors who worked on state enterprises were uncertain of their payment, or of its value when it came. Businessmen in general felt that the only escape from national bankruptcy was (and so it proved to be) the full taxation of all classes, especially of the wealth accumulated by the Church. When Louis XVI hesitated to extend the taille to the privileged classes, lest he lose their support for his shaking throne, the bondholders, almost unconsciously, and despite their generally conservative principles, became a revolutionary force. The Revolution was due not to the patient poverty of the peasants but to the endangered wealth of the middle class.

V. THE GATHERING OF THE FORCES

All these revolutionary forces were subject to the influence of ideas, and used them to clothe and warm desires. In addition to the propaganda of the philosophers and the physiocrats, there were scattered communists who continued and extended the socialism expounded in the preceding generation by Morelly, Mably, and Linguet.[56] Brissot de Warville, in *Recherches philosophiques sur le droit de propriété* (1780), anticipated Pierre Proudhon's *"La propriété, c'est le vol"* by arguing that private property is theft of public goods. There is no "sacred right . . . to eat the food of twenty men when one man's share is not enough." The laws are "a conspiracy of the stronger against the weaker, of the rich against the poor."[57] Brissot later apologized for his early books as schoolboy ebullitions; he became a leader of the Girondins, and was guillotined for moderation (1793).

In 1789, shortly before the taking of the Bastille, François Boissel issued a *Catéchisme du genre humain*, which went the whole distance to communism. All evils are due to "the mercenary, homicidal, and antisocial class which has governed, degraded, and destroyed men till now."[58] The strong have enslaved the weak, and have established the laws to govern them. Property, marriage, and religion have been invented to legitimize usurpation, violence, and deceit, with the result that a small minority own the land, while the majority live in hunger and cold. Marriage is private property in women. No man has a right to more than he needs; everything above this should be distributed to each according to his need. Let the rich idlers go to work or cease to eat. Turn the monasteries into schools.[59]

The most interesting and influential of these radicals was François-Émile Babeuf. After serving nobles and clergy in their assertion of feudal rights against the peasants,[60] he sent to the Academy of Arras (March 21, 1787) a proposal that it offer a prize for the best essay on the question "With the general sum of knowledge now acquired, what would be the condition of a people whose social instincts were such that there should reign among them the most perfect equality; . . . where everything should be in common?"[61] The Academy did not respond; so Gracchus Babeuf (as he later called himself), in a letter of July 8, 1787, explained that by nature all men are equal, and in the state of nature all things were in common; all later history was degeneration and deceit. During the Revolution he gathered a numerous following, and was about to lead a revolt against the Directory when he was arrested by its agents and sentenced to death (1797).

Such ideas played only a modest part in engendering the Revolution. There was hardly a trace of socialist sentiment in the *cahiers* (bills of grievances) that came to the States-General from all quarters of France in 1789; none of them contained attacks upon private property or the monarchy. The middle class was in control of the situation.

Were the Freemasons a factor in the Revolution? We have noted the rise of this secret society in England (1717), and its first appearance in France (1734). It spread rapidly through Protestant Europe; Frederick II favored it in Germany, Gustavus III in Sweden. Pope Clement XII (1738) forbade ecclesiastic or secular authorities to join or help the Freemasons, but the Paris Parlement refused to register this bull, so depriving it of legal effect in France. In 1789 there were 629 Masonic lodges in Paris, usually with fifty to a hundred members.[62] These included many nobles, some priests, the broth-

ers of Louis XVI, and most leaders of the Enlightenment.[63] In 1760 Helvétius founded the Loge des Sciences; in 1770 the astronomer Lalande expanded this into the Loge des Neuf Soeurs, or Lodge of the Nine Sisters
(i.e., the Muses). Here gathered Berthollet, Franklin, Condorcet, Chamfort,
Greuze, Houdon, and, later, Sieyès, Brissot, Desmoulins, Danton.[64]

Theoretically the Freemasons excluded the "godless libertine" and the
"stupid atheist";[65] every member had to profess belief in "the Great Architect of the Universe." No further religious creed was required, so that in
general the Freemasons limited their theology to deism. They were apparently influential in the movement to expel the Jesuits from France.[66] Their
avowed purpose was to establish a secret international brotherhood of men
bound in fellowship by assemblage and ritual, and pledged to mutual aid,
religious toleration, and political reform. Under Louis XVI they entered
actively into politics; several of their aristocratic members—Lafayette, Mirabeau *père et fils*, the Vicomte de Noailles, the Duc de La Rochefoucauld-
Liancourt, and the Duc d'Orléans—became liberal leaders in the National
Assembly.[67]

Last came the definitely political clubs. Organized at first on the English
model—for eating, conversation, and reading—they became, toward 1784,
centers of semi-revolutionary agitation. There, said a contemporary, "they
hold forth loudly and without restraint on the rights of man, on the advantages of freedom, on the great abuses of inequality of condition."[68] After the
assembling of the States-General the deputies from Brittany formed the
Club Breton; this soon widened its membership to include non-Bretons like
Mirabeau *fils*, Sieyès, and Robespierre. In October, 1789, it moved its headquarters to Paris, and became the Société des Jacobins.

So, as with most pivotal events in history, a hundred diverse forces converged to produce the French Revolution. Fundamental was the growth of
the middle classes in number, education, ambition, wealth, and economic
power; their demand for a political and social status commensurate with
their contribution to the life of the nation and the finances of the state; and
their anxiety lest the treasury render their governmental securities worthless
by declaring bankruptcy. Subsidiary to this factor, and used by it as aids and
threats, were the poverty of millions of peasants crying out for relief from
dues and taxes and tithes; the prosperity of several million peasants strong
enough to defy seigneurs, tax collectors, bishops, and regiments; and the
organized discontent of city masses suffering from the manipulation of the
bread supply, and from the lag of wages behind prices in the historic spiral
of inflation.

Add to this a maze of contributory factors: the costly extravagance of
the court; the incompetence and corruption of the government; the weakening of the monarchy by its long struggle with the *parlements* and the nobility; the absence of political institutions through which grievances could be
legally and constructively expressed; the rising standards of administration
expected by a citizenry whose intellect had been sharpened beyond that of
any contemporary people by schools and books and salons, by science,

philosophy, and the Enlightenment. Add the collapse of press censorship under Louis XVI; the dissemination of reform or revolutionary ideas by Voltaire, Rousseau, Diderot, d'Alembert, d'Holbach, Helvétius, Morellet, Morelly, Mably, Linguet, Mirabeau *père*, Turgot, Condorcet, Beaumarchais, Mirabeau *fils*, and a thousand other writers whose sum and brilliance and force had never been equaled, and whose propaganda penetrated into every class but the peasantry, into the barracks of the army, the cells of monasteries, the palaces of the nobility, the antechambers of the King. Add the catastrophic decline of faith in the credibility of a Church that had upheld the status quo and the divine right of kings, had preached the virtues of obedience and resignation, and had amassed a hoard of enviable wealth while the government could not find the means to finance its expanding tasks. Add the spread of belief in a "natural law" that required a humane justice for every rational being regardless of birth, color, creed, or class, and in a bountiful "state of nature" in which all men had once been equal, good, and free, and from which they had fallen because of the development of private property, war, and caste-oriented law. Add the rise and multiplication of lawyers and orators ready to defend or attack the status quo, and to arouse and organize public sentiment; the profusion and fury of pamphleteers; the secret activity of political clubs; the ambition of the Duc d'Orléans to replace his cousin on the throne of France.

Bring all these factors together in the reign of a gentle and benevolent, weak and vacillating King bewildered by the maze of conflicts about him, and the contradictory motives within him; let them operate upon a people more keenly conscious of its grievances, more passionate, excitable, and imaginative than almost any other people known to history; and all that would be needed to unite and ignite these forces in a disruptive explosion would be some event affecting multitudes, and reaching deeper than thought to the most powerful instincts of men. Perhaps that was the function of the drought and famine of 1788, and the cruel winter of 1788–89. "Hunger alone will cause this great revolution," the Marquis de Girardin had predicted in 1781.[69] Hunger came to the countryside, to the towns, to Paris; it was sharp enough in the masses to overcome tradition, reverence, and fear, and to provide an instrument for the aims and brains of well-fed men. The dykes of law and custom and piety broke, and the Revolution began.

CHAPTER XXXVIII

The Political Debacle

1783–89

I. THE DIAMOND NECKLACE: 1785

IN June, 1783, Axel von Fersen, after gallant fighting for America, and having earned distinction at Yorktown, returned to France, and found Marie Antoinette as fascinating as when he had left her three years before. Even in 1787, when she was thirty-two, Arthur Young thought her "the most beautiful woman" he had seen at the court that day.[1] She readily seconded the request of Gustavus III that Louis XVI appoint the handsome Fersen colonel of the Royal Swedish Regiment in the French army—which would allow him to spend considerable time at Versailles. Axel confessed to his sister Sophie that he loved the Queen, and he believed that his love was returned. Certainly she felt a warm affection for him, and eight years later, after his brave attempt to get her and the King out of France, they exchanged tender letters; but her invitation to Sophie to come and live near him suggests a resolve to keep her feeling for him within proper bounds.[2] Hardly anyone at the court except her husband believed her innocent. A song popular among the populace admitted no doubt of her guilt:

Veux-tu connaître	Would you know
Un cocu, un bâtard, une catin?	A cuckold, a bastard, a whore?
Voyez le Roi, la Reine,	See the King, the Queen,
Et Monsieur le Dauphin.[3]	And Monsieur the Dauphin.

Louis-Philippe de Ségur summed up the matter: "She lost her reputation but preserved her virtue."[4]

On March 25, 1785, Marie Antoinette gave birth to a second son, who was named Louis-Charles. The King was so pleased that he gave her the Palace of St.-Cloud, which he had bought from the Duc d'Orléans for six million livres. The court condemned the extravagance of his appreciation, and Paris nicknamed the Queen "Madame Deficit."[5] She used her power over her husband to influence his appointment of ministers, ambassadors, and other dignitaries. She tried, and failed, to change his distaste for the alliance with Austria, and her efforts increased her unpopularity.

Only against the background of this public hostility to "L'Autrichienne" can we understand the credence given to the story of the diamond necklace. This *collier* was itself incredible: a string of 647 diamonds allegedly weighing 2,800 carats.[6] * Two court jewelers, Charles Böhmer and Paul Bassenge,

---

* At the 1965 valuation of $1,200 per carat the diamond necklace would be worth $3,360,000.

had bought diamonds from half the world to make a necklace for Mme. du Barry, confident that Louis XV would buy it for her. But Louis XV died, and who now would buy so expensive an adornment? The jewelers offered it to Marie Antoinette for 1,600,000 livres; she rejected it as too costly.[7] Cardinal Prince Louis-René-Édouard de Rohan came to the fore.

He was a ripe product of one of France's oldest and richest families; he had, it was said, an income of 1,200,000 livres per year. Ordained a priest in 1760, he was appointed coadjutor to his uncle, the Archbishop of Strasbourg; in that capacity he officially welcomed Marie Antoinette when she first entered France (1770). Finding Strasbourg too narrow a field for his ambitions, Rohan lived mostly in Paris, where he joined the faction hostile to Austria and the Queen. In 1771 Louis XV sent him to Vienna as special envoy to ferret out Austrian maneuvers in the partition of Poland. Maria Theresa was offended by the lavish fetes that he gave, and by his dissemination of scandalous gossip about the new Dauphine. Louis XVI recalled him to Paris, but powerful relatives induced the King to make him grand almoner —head disburser of the royal alms (1777). A year later the gay and handsome priest was raised to the cardinalate, and in 1779 he became archbishop of Strasbourg. There he met Cagliostro, and was charmed into believing the impostor's magic claims. Having risen so high so soon, it seemed to Rohan that he might aspire to be chief minister to Louis XVI, if only he could atone for his years of opposition to the Queen.

Among his amusements in Paris was the attractive and ingenious Mme. de La Motte-Valois. Jeanne de St.-Rémy de Valois claimed descent from Henry II of France by a mistress. Her family lost its property, and Jeanne was reduced to begging in the streets. In 1775 the government confirmed her royal lineage, and gave her a pension of eight hundred francs. In 1780 she married Antoine de La Motte, an army officer with a penchant for intrigue. He had deceived her about his income; their marriage, as she put it, was a union of drought with famine.[8] He appropriated the title of count, which made Jeanne the Comtesse de La Motte. As such she fluttered around Paris and Versailles, making conquests by what she called her "air of health and youth (which men call radiance), and an extraordinarily vivacious personality."[9] Having become mistress to the Cardinal (1784),[10] she pretended to high intimacy at the court, and offered to win the Queen's approval of his aims. She engaged Rêtaux de Villette to imitate her Majesty's handwriting, and brought to the Cardinal affectionate letters allegedly from Marie Antoinette; finally she promised to arrange an interview. She trained a prostitute, the "Baroness" d'Oliva, to impersonate the Queen. In the "Grove of Venus" at Versailles, in the dark of night, the Cardinal briefly met this woman, mistook her to be Antoinette, kissed her foot, and received from her a rose as token of reconciliation (August, 1784); or so the "Countess" relates.[11]

Mme. de La Motte now ventured upon a bolder plan which, if successful, would put an end to her poverty. She forged a letter from the Queen authorizing Rohan to buy the necklace in her name. The Cardinal presented this letter to Böhmer, who surrendered the gems to him (January 24, 1785) on his written promise to pay 1,600,000 francs in installments. Rohan took the brilliants to the Countess, and at her request he turned them over to an alleged representative of the Queen. Their further history is uncertain; apparently they were taken by the "Comte" de La Motte to England and sold piece by piece.[12]

Böhmer sent a bill for the necklace to the Queen, who replied that she had never ordered it and had never written the letter that bore her name. When the date arrived for payment of the first installment (July 30, 1785), and Rohan offered only thirty thousand of the 400,000 francs then due, Böhmer laid the matter before the Baron de Breteuil, minister of the King's Household. Breteuil informed the King. Louis summoned the Cardinal and invited him to explain his actions. Rohan showed him some supposed letters from the Queen. The King saw at once that they were forgeries. "This," he said, "is not in the Queen's handwriting, and the signature is not even in proper form."[13] He suspected that Rohan and others of the faction hostile to his wife had plotted to discredit her. He ordered the Cardinal to the Bastille (August 15), and bade the police find Mme. de La Motte. She had fled to a succession of hiding places, but she was apprehended, and she too was sent to the Bastille. Also arrested were "Baronne" d'Oliva, Rêtaux de Villette, and Cagliostro, who was wrongly suspected of having planned the intrigue; actually he had done his best to discourage it.[14]

Believing that an open trial was necessary to convince the public of the Queen's innocence, Louis submitted the case to his enemies, the Paris Parlement. The trial was the *cause célèbre* of the century in France, as that of Warren Hastings became in England three years later. The judgment of the Parlement was pronounced on May 31, 1786. Cardinal Rohan was declared innocent, as more deceived than deceiving, but the King deprived him of his state offices and exiled him to the Abbey of La Chaise-Dieu. Two accomplices received sentences of imprisonment; Cagliostro was freed. Mme. de La Motte was publicly stripped and whipped in the Cour de Mai before the Palais de Justice; she was branded with a *V* (for *voleuse*, thief), and was condemned for life to the notorious Salpêtrière women's prison. After a year in this maddening confinement she escaped, joined her husband in London, wrote an autobiography explaining everything, and died in 1791.

The nobility and the Paris populace rejoiced over the acquittal of the Cardinal, and blamed the Queen for bringing the matter to a public trial; the general feeling was that her known appetite for jewelry had excused the Cardinal for believing the forged letters. Gossip went so far as to accuse her of being Rohan's mistress,[15] though she had not seen him in the ten years before his arrest. Once more she had preserved her virtue and suffered damage to her reputation. "The Queen's death," said Napoleon, "must be dated from the Diamond Necklace Trial."[16]

II. CALONNE: 1783–87

On November 10, 1783, the King appointed Charles-Alexandre de Calonne controller general of finance. Calonne had served successfully as intendant at Metz and Lille, and had earned repute for engaging manners, buoyant spirits, and monetary skill—though he himself, like the government that he was called to rescue, was hopelessly in debt.[17] He found only 360,000 francs in the treasury, against a floating debt of 646,000,000, increasing by fifty million francs a year. Like Necker he decided against additional taxation, fearing that this would arouse revolt and depress the economy; instead he negotiated a lottery, which brought in a hundred million livres. He appealed to the clergy, and won from it a *don gratuit* of eighteen million livres on his promise to suppress Beaumarchais' edition of Voltaire. He reminted the gold coins, making a profit of fifty million for the treasury. He borrowed 125,000,000 from the bankers. Hoping to stimulate business, he allotted great sums for city sanitation and the improvement of roads, canals, and harbors; Le Havre, Dunkirk, Dieppe, and La Rochelle benefited; the great docks at Cherbourg began. On the theory that a government must always put up a prosperous front, he allocated funds readily to courtiers, and asked no questions about the expenses of the King's brothers and the Queen. The King himself, despite good intentions, allowed the outlay for his household to rise from 4,600,000 livres in 1775 to 6,200,000 in 1787.[18]

The more Calonne spent, the more he borrowed; the more he borrowed, the more interest had to be paid on the debt. In August, 1786, he confessed to the bewildered King that all expedients had been exhausted, that the national debt and the annual deficit were greater than ever, and that only the extension of taxation in the nobility and the clergy could save the government from financial disaster. Knowing that the Paris Parlement, now in undisguised alliance with the nobility of the sword, would resist this suggestion, he proposed that a group of distinguished men, to be chosen by him from all three classes throughout France, be summoned to Versailles to consult for the financial salvation of the state. The King agreed.

The Assembly of Notables convened on February 22, 1787: forty-six nobles, eleven ecclesiastics, twelve members of the Royal Council, thirty-eight magistrates, twelve deputies from the *pays d'état* (regions enjoying special privileges), and twenty-five municipal officials; 144 in all. Calonne addressed them with courageous candor about abuses which, however deeply rooted in time and prejudice, must be abolished because "they bear heavily upon the most productive and laborious class." He condemned the general inequality of subsidies, and "the enormous disproportion in the contributions of different provinces and subjects of one same sovereign."[19] He expounded proposals more radical than Turgot's, and presented them as having been approved by the King. Had they been adopted they might have averted the Revolution. Some of them, carried over from Turgot, were accepted by the Notables: a reduction in the salt tax, the removal of tolls on internal commerce, the restoration of free trade in grains, the establishment of provincial assemblies, and an end to the *corvée*. But his request for a new and universal tax on land was rejected. The noble and ecclesiastical members argued that this *subvention territoriale* would require a survey of all land, and a census of all landowners, in France; this would take a year, and could have no effect on the current crisis.

Calonne appealed to the people by publishing his speeches; neither the nobles nor the clergy relished this resort to public opinion. The Assembly retaliated by demanding from Calonne a full account of revenues and expenditures during his ministry. He refused to comply, knowing that a revelation of his methods and outlays would ruin him. The Assembly insisted that economy in expenditures was more needed than a revision of the tax structure; moreover, it questioned its authority to establish a new system of taxation; such authority belonged only to a States-General (États Généraux— i.e., a national conference of deputies chosen by the three *états*, or classes). No such meeting had been called since 1614.

Lafayette, one of the Notables, approved most of Calonne's proposals, but distrusted the man. He accused Calonne of having sold some of the royal lands without the King's knowledge; Calonne challenged him to prove the charge; Lafayette proved it.[20] Louis XVI had resented Calonne's appeal to the public over the heads of the government; he realized, from a succession of disclosures, that Calonne had deceived him about the condition of the treasury, and he saw that he could get no co-operation from the Notables as long as Calonne was controller. When Calonne asked for the dismissal of his critic the Baron de Breteuil, who was a personal friend of Marie Antoinette, she advised the King to dismiss Calonne instead. Wearied with the turmoil, he took her advice (April 8, 1787). Calonne, learning that the Parlement of Paris was planning to investigate his administration and his private affairs, decamped to England. On April 23 Louis sought to appease the Notables by promising governmental economies, and publicity of state finances. On May 1, again on the advice of the Queen, he appointed one of the Notables to be chief of the Council of Finance.

III. LOMÉNIE DE BRIENNE: 1787–88

He was archbishop of Toulouse, but so notoriously a freethinker that the *philosophes* hailed his advent to power. When, six years before, he had been recommended to succeed Christophe de Beaumont in the metropolitan see, Louis XVI had protested, "We must at least have an archbishop of Paris who believes in God."[21] One of his most satisfying coups as minister of finance was to have himself transferred to the archbishopric of Sens, which was much richer than that of Toulouse. He persuaded the Notables to approve his plan for raising eighty million francs by a loan, but when he asked consent to the new land tax they again pleaded lack of authority. Seeing that the Notables would do no more, Louis politely dismissed them (May 25, 1787).

Brienne attempted economies by asking cuts in the expenditures of each department; the departmental heads resisted; the King did not sustain his minister. Louis reduced his household expenses by a million francs, and the Queen accepted a similar reduction (August 11). Brienne had the courage to refuse monetary demands by the court, by the friends of the Queen, by a brother of the King. It is to his credit that he carried through the reluctant

Parlement (January, 1788), against the resistance of most of his fellow prelates, the royal edict extending civil rights to Protestants.

He was unfortunate in having come to power at a time when crop failures and the competition of British imports had spread an economic recession that lasted till the Revolution. In August, 1787, hungry rioters in Paris shouted revolutionary slogans and burned some ministers in effigy. "The feeling of everybody," noted Arthur Young on October 13, "seems to be that the Archbishop will not be able to exonerate the state from the burden of its present situation; . . . that something extraordinary will happen; and a bankruptcy is an idea not at all uncommon."[22] And on the seventeenth: "One opinion pervaded the whole company, that they are on the eve of some great revolution in the government; . . . a great ferment in all ranks of men, who are eager for some change; . . . and a strong leaven of liberty, increasing every hour since the American Revolution."[23]

The reforms which Calonne and Brienne had advocated, and which the King had accepted, had yet to be registered and recognized as law by the *parlements*. The Paris Parlement agreed to freeing the grain trade and commuting the *corvée* into a monetary payment, but it refused to sanction a stamp tax. On July 19, 1787, it sent to Louis XVI a declaration that "the Nation, represented by the States-General, alone has the right of granting to the King the resources which might prove indispensable."[24] The Paris public approved this pronouncement, forgetting that the States-General, as thus far known in French history, was a feudal institution heavily weighted in favor of the privileged classes. Not forgetting this, the nobility of the sword approved the declaration, and henceforth allied itself with the *parlements* and the *noblesse de robe* in that *révolte nobiliaire* which prepared the Revolution. Louis hesitated to call the States-General, lest it should end the absolutism of the Bourbon monarchy by asserting legislative powers.

In August, 1787, he presented to the Parlement an edict for a tax on all land in all classes. The Parlement refused to register it. Louis summoned the members to a *lit de justice* at Versailles, and ordered the registration; the members, returning to Paris, declared the registration void, and again demanded a States-General. The King banished them to Troyes (August 14). The provincial *parlements* rose in protest; riots broke out in Paris; Brienne and the King yielded, and the Parlement was recalled (September 24) amid popular rejoicing.

The conflict was renewed when the Parlement refused to sanction Brienne's proposal to raise a loan of 120,000,000 livres. The King called a "royal session" of the Parlement (November 11, 1787), at which his ministers presented arguments for registering the measure. The Parlement still refused, and the Duc d'Orléans cried out, "Sire, it is illegal!" Louis, in an unusually reckless burst of temper, answered, "That makes no difference! It is legal because I wish it"—thus plainly asserting absolutism. He ordered the edict registered; it was done; but as soon as he had left the hall the Parlement revoked the registration. Informed of this, Louis exiled the Duc d'Orléans to Villers-Cotterêts, and sent two of the magistrates to the Bastille (November

20). Protesting these and other arrests without trial, the Parlement sent to the King (March 11, 1788) "remonstrances" containing words that pleased nobles and commoners alike: "Arbitrary acts violate irremovable rights. . . . Kings rule either by conquest or by law. . . . The nation asks from his Majesty the greatest good that a king can give to his subjects—liberty."[25]

The ministry thought to pacify the Parlement by yielding to its demand for publication of the government's revenues and expenditures. This made matters worse by revealing a deficit of 160,000,000 livres. The bankers refused to lend more to the state unless the Parlement sanctioned the loan; the Parlement vowed it would not. On May 3, 1788, it issued a "Declaration of Rights" which reminded Louis XVI and his ministers that France was "a monarchy governed by the king, following the laws," and that Parlement must not surrender its ancient right to register royal edicts before these could become laws. It again called for a States-General. The ministers ordered the arrest of two Parlement leaders, d'Éprémesnil and Goislard (May 4); this was done amid wild confusion in the hall and angry protests in the street. On May 8 Brienne announced the intention of the government to establish new courts, headed by a Cour Plénière which alone would henceforth have the power of registering royal edicts; the *parlements* were to be restricted to purely judicial functions, and the whole structure of French law was to be reformed. Meanwhile the Paris Parlement was "put on vacation"—in effect suspended from operation.

It appealed to the nobility, the clergy, and the provincial *parlements*. All came to its support. Dukes and peers sent to the King protests against abrogating the traditional rights of the Parlement. An assembly of the clergy (June 15) condemned the new Plenary Court, reduced its "gratuitous gift" from a past average of twelve million livres to 1,800,000, and refused any further aid until the Parlement should be restored.[26] One after another the provincial *parlements* rose against the King. The Parlement of Pau (capital of Béarn) declared it would register no edicts rejected by the Parlement of Paris; and when force was threatened against the magistrates the people took up arms to protect them. The Parlement of Rouen (capital of Normandy) denounced the ministers of the King as traitors, and outlawed all persons who should use the new courts. The Parlement of Rennes (capital of Brittany) issued similar decrees; when the government sent soldiers to dismiss it these were faced by the armed retainers of the local nobility.[27] At Grenoble (capital of Dauphiné), when the military commander proclaimed a royal edict dissolving the local *parlement*, the populace of the town, reinforced by peasants summoned by the tocsin, pelted the reluctant troops with tiles from the roofs, and compelled the commander, on pain of being hanged from his chandelier, to withdraw the edict of the King (June 7, 1787, the "Journée des Tuiles," or Day of Tiles). The magistrates, however, obeyed a royal order to go into exile.

The Grenoble community made history by its reaction. Nobles, clergy, and commonalty resolved to re-establish the old Estates of Dauphiné for a meeting on July 21. Since the Third Estate had led the victory on the "Day of Tiles," it was accorded representation equal to that of the two other orders combined; and it was agreed that in the new assembly voting should be by individuals and not by classes; these agreements set precedents that played a part in the organization of the national States-General. Forbidden to meet at Grenoble, the Dauphiné Estates met at Vizille, a few miles away; and there, under the leadership of a young lawyer, Jean-Joseph Mounier, and a young orator, Antoine Barnave, the five hundred deputies drew up resolutions (August, 1788) upholding the registration rights of the *parlements*, demanding abolition of *lettres de cachet*, calling for a States-General, and pledging itself never to consent to new taxes unless a States-General sanctioned them. Here was one beginning of the French Revolution: an entire province had defied the King, and had declared, in effect, for a constitutional monarchy.

Overcome by the almost nationwide revolt against the royal authority, the King surrendered, and decided to summon a States-General. But, as 174 years had passed since the last meeting of this body, and the growth of the Third Estate made it impossible to use the old forms of procedure, Louis XVI issued to the people (July 5, 1788) an extraordinary appeal as an order of the Royal Council:

> His Majesty will endeavor to approximate earlier practices; but when these cannot be determined he wishes to offset the deficiency by ascertaining the will of his subjects. . . . Accordingly the King has decided to command that all possible researches concerning the aforementioned matters be made in all the depositories of each and every province; that the results of such investigations be transmitted to the provincial estates and assemblies, . . . which in turn shall apprise his Majesty of their wishes. . . . His Majesty invites all scholars and educated persons in his kingdom . . . to direct to the Keeper of the Seals all information and memoirs connected with matters contained in the present decree.[28]

On August 8 Louis summoned the three classes of France to send deputies to a States-General which was to meet at Versailles on May 1, 1789. On the same day he suspended the Cour Plénière, which soon faded from history. On August 16 the government in effect acknowledged its bankruptcy by announcing that till December 31, 1789, the obligations of the state would be paid not all in currency but partly in paper, which all citizens should accept as legal payment. On August 25 Brienne resigned, loaded with favor and wealth, while the Paris public burned him in effigy. He retired to his rich see at Sens, and there, in 1794, he killed himself.

IV. NECKER AGAIN: 1788–89

Reluctantly the King asked Necker to return to the government (August 25). Now he gave him the title of secretary of state and a seat in the Royal Council. Everyone, from the Queen and the clergy to the bankers and the populace, applauded the appointment. A multitude gathered in the courtyard of the Versailles Palace to welcome him; he came out and told them,

"Yes, my children, I remain; be comforted." Some fell on their knees and kissed his hands.[29] He wept, in the manner of the time.

Disorder in the administration, in the streets, in the official and the public mind had come so close to political disintegration that the best that Necker could do was to maintain stability until the States-General convened. As a gesture to restore confidence, he put two million francs of his own into the treasury, and pledged his personal fortune as partial guarantee of the state's engagements.[30] He revoked the order of August 16 requiring bondholders to accept paper instead of money; government bonds rose thirty per cent on the market. The bankers advanced the treasury sufficient funds to tide over the crisis for a year.

On Necker's advice the King again recalled the Parlement (September 23). Intoxicated with its triumph, it made the mistake of declaring that the coming States-General should operate as in 1614—sitting as separate classes and voting in class units, which would automatically reduce the Third Estate to political impotence. The general public, which had credited the Parlement's claim to be defending liberty against tyranny, perceived that the liberty intended was that of the two privileged classes to overrule the king. The Parlement, by so ranging itself on the side of the feudal regime, forfeited the support of the powerful middle class, and henceforth ceased to be a factor in shaping events. The *révolte nobiliaire* had shown its limits and run its course; now it gave place to the bourgeois revolution.

Necker's task was made harder by the drought of 1788, which was ended by hailstorms that ruined the stunted crops. The winter of 1788–89 was one of the bitterest in the history of France; at Paris the thermometer fell to 18 degrees below zero Fahrenheit; the Seine froze solid from Paris to Le Havre. Bread rose in price from nine sous in August, 1788, to fourteen in February, 1789. The upper classes did their best to relieve the suffering; some nobles, like the Duc d'Orléans, spent hundreds of thousands of livres feeding and warming the poor; the Archbishop gave 400,000 livres; one monastery fed twelve hundred persons daily for six weeks.[31] Necker forbade the export of grain, and imported seventy million livres' worth; famine was averted. He left to his successors or to the States-General the task of repaying the loans that he raised.

Meanwhile he persuaded the King, over the opposite advice of powerful nobles, to decree (December 27, 1788) that in the coming States-General the deputies of the Third Estate should equal in number those of the other states combined. On June 24, 1789, he sent out to all districts an invitation to vote for representatives. In the Third Estate every Frenchman above the age of twenty-four who paid any tax was entitled—and even commanded—to vote; so were all professional men, businessmen, guildsmen; in effect all the commonalty except paupers and the poorest laborers had the vote.[32] The successful candidates met as an electoral committee which chose a deputy for the district. In the First Estate every priest or curate, every monastery or convent, voted for a representative in the electoral assembly of the district; archbishops, bishops, and abbots were members of that assembly *ex officio;*

this assembly chose an ecclesiastical deputy to the States-General. In the Second Estate every nobleman above the age of twenty-four was automatically a member of the electoral assembly which chose a deputy to represent the nobility of his district. In Paris only those who paid a poll tax of six or more livres had the vote; there most of the proletariat was left out.[33]

Each electoral assembly in each class was invited by the government to draw up a *cahier des plaintes et doléances*—a statement of complaints and grievances—for the guidance of its deputy. The district *cahiers* were summarized for each class in provincial *cahiers*, and these, in whole or in synopsis, were presented to the King. The *cahiers* of all classes united in condemning absolutism, and in demanding a constitutional monarchy in which the powers of the king and his ministers would be limited by law, and by a nationally elected assembly meeting periodically and alone authorized to vote new taxes and to sanction new laws. Nearly all deputies were instructed to vote no funds for the government until such a constitution had been secured. All classes denounced the financial incompetence of the government, the evils associated with the indirect taxes, and the excesses of royal power, as in *lettres de cachet*. All demanded trial by jury, privacy of the mails, and reform of the law. All pleaded for liberty, but in their own fashion: the nobles for the restoration of their pre-Richelieu powers; the clergy and the bourgeoisie for freedom from all state interference; the peasantry for freedom from oppressive taxes and feudal dues. All accepted in principle the equal taxation of all property. All expressed loyalty to the King, but none mentioned his "divine right" to rule;[34] that, by common consent, was dead.

The *cahiers* of the nobility stipulated that in the States-General each of the classes should meet separately and vote as a united class. The *cahiers* of the clergy rejected toleration, and asked that the civil rights recently granted to Protestants be revoked. Some *cahiers* called for a greater portion of the tithe to be left to the parish, and for access of all priests to positions in the hierarchy. Nearly all the ecclesiastical *cahiers* deplored the immorality of the age in art, literature, and the theater; they ascribed this deterioration to excessive freedom of the press, and called for exclusive control of education by the Catholic clergy.

The *cahiers* of the Third Estate voiced chiefly the views of the middle class and the peasant proprietors. They pleaded for the abolition of feudal rights and transport tolls. They demanded career open to talent for all classes to all posts. They condemned the wealth of the Church and the costly idleness of monks. One *cahier* suggested that to meet the deficit the King should sell the lands and rents of the clergy; another proposed the confiscation of all monastic property.[35] Many complained of the devastation of farms by the animals and hunts of the nobility. They asked for universal free education, for the reform of hospitals and prisons, for the complete extinction of serfdom and the trade in slaves. A typical *cahier* of the peasants asserted: "We are the principal prop of the throne, the true support of the armies. . . . We are the source of riches for others, and we ourselves remain in poverty."[36]

All in all, this election of the States-General was a proud and generous moment in the history of France. Almost, for a while, Bourbon France became a democracy, with probably a larger proportion of the people voting than go to the polls in an American election today. It was a fair election, not as disorderly as might have been expected in so novel an operation; it was apparently freer from corruption than most of the elections held in the later democracies of Europe.[37] Never before, so far as we know, had a government issued so broad an invitation to its people to instruct it in modes of procedure, and to communicate to it their complaints and desires. Taken altogether, these *cahiers* gave the government a more complete view of conditions in France than it had ever before possessed. Now, if ever, France had the materials for statesmanship; now she had freely chosen her best men, from every class, to meet with a King who had already made brave overtures to change. All France was filled with hope as these men, from every part of the country, made their way to Paris and Versailles.

V. ENTER MIRABEAU

One of them was a noble elected by the commonalty of both Aix-en-Provence and Marseilles. Distinguished by this anomalous and double dignity, Honoré-Gabriel-Victor Riqueti, Comte de Mirabeau, ugly and fascinating, became a dominant figure in the Revolution from his arrival in Paris (April, 1789) till his premature death (1791).

We have celebrated his father—Victor Riqueti, Marquis de Mirabeau—as physiocrat and "Friend of Man," i.e., of everybody except his wife and children. Vauvenargues described this "Ami de l'homme" as "of an ardent, melancholy temper, prouder and more restless . . . than the sea, with a sovereign insatiability for pleasure, knowledge, and glory."[38] The Marquis admitted all this, and added that "immorality was for him a second nature." At twenty-eight he resolved to discover if one woman could be enough; he asked for the hand of Marie de Vessan, whom he had never seen, but who was heiress apparent to a sizable fortune. After marrying her he found that she was a slovenly and incompetent termagant; but she gave him in eleven years eleven children, of whom five survived infancy. In 1760 the Marquis was imprisoned in the Château de Vincennes for seditious writings, but was released after a week. In 1762 his wife left him and returned to her mother.

Honoré-Gabriel, the eldest son, grew up amid this domestic drama. One of his grandmothers died insane, one of his sisters and one of his brothers were subject to occasional insanity; it is a marvel that Gabriel himself, buffeting one calamity after another, did not go mad. He had two teeth at birth, as a warning to the world. At three he suffered an attack of smallpox, which left his face scarred and pitted like a battlefield. He was an exuberant, quarrelsome, and willful boy; his father, who was exuberant, quarrelsome, and willful, beat him frequently, generating filial hate. The Marquis was glad to get rid of him by sending him, aged fifteen (1764), to a military academy in

Paris. There Gabriel acquired mathematics, German, and English, and read eagerly, being consumed with a passion for achievement. He read Voltaire and lost religion; he read Rousseau and learned to feel for the commonalty. In the army he stole the mistress of his commanding officer, fought a duel, took part in the French invasion of Corsica, and won such commendation for courage that his father momentarily loved him.

At twenty-three he married, frankly for money, Émilie de Marignac, who expected to inherit 500,000 francs. She bore a son to Gabriel, and took a lover; he discovered her infidelity, concealed his own, and forgave her. He quarreled with a M. de Villeneuve, broke an umbrella over his back, and was accused of intent to kill. To have him escape arrest his father secured a *lettre de cachet* by which Gabriel was forcibly confined in the Château d'If, on an island off Marseilles. He asked his wife to join him; she refused; they exchanged letters of rising wrath, until he bade her, "Farewell forever" (December 14, 1774). Meanwhile he kept warm by sleeping occasionally with the wife of the château's commandant.

In May, 1775, his father had him transferred to laxer custody at the Château de Joux, near Pontarlier and the Swiss border. His jailer, M. de Saint-Mauris, invited him to a party, where he met Sophie de Ruffey, the nineteen-year-old wife of the seventy-year-old Marquis de Monnier. She found Mirabeau more satisfying than her husband; his face was deterring, his hair was woolly, his nose was massive, but his eyes were on fire, his disposition was "sulfurous," and he could seduce any woman with his speech. Sophie gave herself to him completely. He escaped from Pontarlier, fled to Thonon in Savoy, and seduced a cousin there. In August, 1776, Sophie joined him at Verrières in Switzerland, for, she said, to live apart from him was "to die a thousand times a day."[39] Now she vowed, "Gabriel or death!" She proposed to go to work, for Gabriel was penniless.

He went with her to Amsterdam, where Rousseau's publisher, Marc Rey, hired him as a translator. Sophie served as his amanuensis, and taught Italian. He wrote several minor works, in one of which he spoke of his father: "He preaches virtue, beneficence, and frugality, while he is the worst of husbands, and the hardest and most spendthrift of fathers."[40] Mirabeau *père* thought this a breach of etiquette. He united with Sophie's parents in arranging the extradition of the couple from Holland. They were arrested (May 14, 1777) and brought to Paris. Sophie, having failed in an attempt at suicide, was sent to a house of correction; Gabriel, raging, was imprisoned in the Château de Vincennes, following in the footsteps of his father and Diderot. There he languished for forty-two months. After two years he was allowed to have books, paper, pen, and ink. To Sophie he sent letters of passionate devotion. On January 7, 1778, she gave birth to a daughter, presumably his. In June mother and child were transferred to a convent at Gien, near Orléans.

Mirabeau appealed to his father to forgive him and have him freed. "Let me see the sun," he begged; "let me breathe a freer air; let me see the face of my kind! I see nothing but dark walls. My father, I shall die from the tortures of nephritis!"[41] To alleviate his misery, to make some money for Sophie, and to keep from going mad, he wrote several books, some erotic. Most important was the *Lettres de cachet*, which described the injustices of arrest without warrant and detention without trial, and demanded reform of prisons and the law. Published in 1782, the little volume so moved Louis XVI that in 1784 he ordered the release of all the prisoners held at Vincennes.[42]

Mirabeau's jailers took pity on him, and after November, 1779, he was allowed to walk in the gardens of the château and to meet visitors; in some of these he found outlets for his overflowing sexual energy.[43] His father agreed to have him liberated if he would apologize to his wife and resume cohabitation with her, for the old Marquis was anxious to have a grandson to carry on the family. Gabriel wrote to his wife asking forgiveness. On December 13, 1780, he was released under custody of his father, who invited him to the paternal mansion at Le Bignon. He had some liaisons in Paris, and visited Sophie in her convent; apparently he told her that he intended to rejoin his wife. Then he went to Le Bignon, and charmed his father. Sophie received money from her husband, moved to a house near the convent, engaged in works of charity, and agreed to marry an ex-captain of cavalry. He died before the marriage could take place, and on the next day (September 9, 1789) Sophie killed herself.[44]

Mirabeau's wife refused to see him; he sued her for desertion; he lost his case, but astonished friends and foes with the eloquence of his five-hour speech pleading his own impossible cause. His father disowned him; he sued his father, and obtained from him an allowance of three thousand francs a year. He borrowed money and lived sumptuously. In 1784 he took a new mistress, Henriette de Nehra. With her he went to England and Germany (1785–87). En route he had tangential liaisons, which Henriette forgave, for, she said, "If a woman made him the least advances he took fire at once."[45] He met Frederick twice, and learned enough about Prussia to compose (from material supplied him by a Prussian major) the book *De la Monarchie prussienne* (1788); this he dedicated to his father, who described it as "the enormous compilation of a frenzied workman." Calonne commissioned him to send some secret dispatches about German affairs; he sent seventy, which amazed the minister by their keen perception and forceful style.

Back in Paris, he perceived that public discontent was nearing revolutionary ardor. In a letter to the minister Montmorin he warned that unless a States-General met by 1789, revolution would come. "I ask if you have reckoned with the convulsive energy of hunger acting on the genius of despair. I ask who will dare make himself responsible for the safety of all who surround the throne, nay, of the King himself?"[46] He was caught up in the agitation, and rushed into the current. He achieved a tenuous reconciliation with his father (who died in 1789), and offered himself at Aix-en-Provence as a candidate for the States-General. He invited the nobles of the district to choose him; they refused; he turned to the Third Estate, which welcomed him. Now he left his conservative cocoon and took wings as a democrat. "The right of sovereignty rests solely . . . with the people; the sovereign . . . can be no more than the first magistrate of the people."[47] He wished to keep the monarchy, but only as a protection of the people against the aristocracy; meanwhile he urged that all male adults should have the vote.[48] In a discourse to the Estates of Provence he threatened the privileged classes with a general strike: "Take care; do not disdain this people, which produces everything; this people, which, to be formidable, need only be immobile."[49]

A bread riot arose in Marseilles (March, 1789); the authorities sent for Mirabeau to come and calm the people, for they knew his popularity. The populace gathered in a crowd of 120,000 to acclaim him.[50] He organized a patrol to prevent violence. In an *Avis au peuple marseillais* he advised the commonalty to be patient till the States-General should have time to find a balance between producers wanting high prices and consumers wanting low. The rioters obeyed him. By the same persuasiveness he pacified an uprising at Aix. Both Aix and Marseilles chose him as their deputy; he thanked the electors, and decided to represent Aix. In April, 1789, he left for Paris and the States-General.

VI. THE LAST REHEARSAL: 1789

He passed through a country facing famine and rehearsing revolution. In several districts, in the spring of 1789, there were repeated revolts against taxes and the cost of bread. In Lyons the populace invaded the offices of the tax collector and destroyed his registers. At Agde, near Montpellier, the people threatened a general pillage unless the prices of commodities were reduced; they were reduced. Villages fearing a shortage of grain forcibly prevented the export of grain from their districts. Some peasants talked of burning all châteaux and killing the seigneurs (May, 1789).[51] At Montlhéry the women, hearing that the price of bread had been raised, led a mob into the granaries and bakeries, and seized all available bread and flour. Similar scenes at Bray-sur-Seine, Bagnols, Amiens, almost everywhere in France. In town after town orators aroused the people by telling them that the King had postponed all tax payments.[52] A report ran through Provence in March and April that "the best of kings desires tax equality; that there are to be no more bishops, nor seigneurs, nor tithes, nor dues, no more titles or distinctions."[53] After April 1, 1789, feudal dues were no longer paid. The "voluntary" surrender of these dues by the nobility on August 4 was not an act of self-sacrifice but the recognition of an accomplished fact.

In Paris the excitement mounted almost daily as the meeting of the States-General approached. Pamphlets poured from the press, oratory lifted its voice at the cafés and clubs. The most famous and powerful pamphlet in all history appeared in January, 1789, written by the freethinking Abbé Emmanuel-Joseph Sieyès, vicar general of the diocese of Chartres. Chamfort had written, *"Qu'est-ce que le Tiers état?—Tout. Qu'a-t-il?—Rien."* ("What is the Third Estate? Everything. What does it have? Nothing.")

Sieyès made this explosive epigram into an arresting title, and turned it into three questions that soon half of France was asking:

> What is the Third Estate? Everything.
> What has it been, till the present, in the political order? Nothing.
> What does it ask? To become something.[54]

Of the 26,000,000 souls in France, Sieyès pointed out, at least 25,000,000 belonged to the Third Estate—the untitled laity; in effect the Third Estate was the nation. If, in the States-General, the other classes should refuse to sit with it, it would be justified in constituting itself the "Assemblée Nationale." That phrase endured.

Hunger was even more eloquent than words. As relief stations were set up in Paris by the government, the clergy, and the rich, beggars and criminals flocked in from the hinterland to eat and to risk their nothing in acts of desperation. Here and there the populace took matters into its own hands; it threatened to hang at the nearest lamppost any merchant hiding grain or charging too much for it; often it stopped and sacked convoys of grain before these could reach the market; sometimes it mobbed the markets and took by force, without pay, the grain that peasants had brought in to sell.[55] On April 23 Necker issued through the Royal Council a decree empowering judges and police to take inventory of private granaries, and to compel them, where bread was running short, to send their grain to the market; but this order was loosely enforced. Such was the picture of Paris in the spring.

In these angry mobs the Duc d'Orléans saw a possible instrument for his ambitions. He was the great-grandson of that Philippe d'Orléans who had been regent of France (1715–23). Born in 1747, named Duc de Chartres at five, he married at twenty-two Louise-Marie de Bourbon-Penthiévre, whose wealth made him the richest man in France.[56] In 1785 he succeeded to the title of Duc d'Orléans; after 1789, through his advocacy of popular causes, he was known as Philippe Égalité. We have seen him challenging the King in the Parlement and exiled to Villers-Cotterêts. Soon back in Paris, he determined to make himself an idol of the people, hoping that he might be chosen to succeed his cousin Louis XVI in case the harassed King should abdicate or be deposed. He gave largesse to the poor, recommended nationalization of ecclesiastical property,[57] and threw open to the public the garden and some rooms of his Palais-Royal in the very heart of Paris. He had the graces of a generous aristocrat and the morals of his ancestor the Regent. Mme. de Genlis, governess of his children, served him as liaison with Mirabeau, Condorcet, Lafayette, Talleyrand, Lavoisier, Volney, Sieyès, Desmoulins, Danton. His fellow Freemasons gave him substantial support.[58] The novelist Choderlos de Laclos, his secretary, acted as his agent in organizing public demonstrations and revolts. In the gardens, cafés, gambling houses, and brothels near his palace the pamphleteers exchanged ideas and formed plans; here thousands of people, of all classes, joined in the agitations of the hour. The Palais-Royal, as a name for all this complex, became the hub of the Revolution.

It is alleged and probable, but not certain, that the money of the Duke, and the activity of Choderlos de Laclos, played a part in organizing the attack upon the Réveillon factory in the Rue St.-Antoine. Réveillon was leading a revolution of his own: replacing wall paintings and tapestry with vellum paper painted by artists in a technique developed by him, and producing what an English authority has called "undoubtedly the most beautiful wallpapers that have ever been made."[59] His factory employed three hundred men, whose minimum wage was twenty-five sous ($1.56?) per day.[60] At a meeting of the electoral assembly of Ste.-Marguerite a dispute arose between middle-class electors and workingmen; there was some apprehension that wages might be cut,[61] and a false[62] report was spread that Réveillon had said, "A workingman with wife and children can live on fifteen sous a day." On April 27 a crowd gathered before the manufacturer's house and, unable to find him, burned him in effigy. On the twenty-eighth, reinforced and armed, it invaded his home, sacked it, made bonfires of its furniture, drank the liquor from its cellar, and appropriated currency and silver plate. The rioters moved on to the factory and plundered it. Troops were sent against them; they defended themselves in a battle that raged for several hours; twelve soldiers and over two hundred rioters were killed. Réveillon closed his factory and moved to England.

This was the mood of Paris as the elected deputies and their substitutes arrived for the States-General at Versailles.

VII. THE STATES-GENERAL: 1789

On May 4 the deputies moved in a stately procession to hear Mass in the Church of St. Louis: the Versailles clergy in front, then the representatives of the Third Estate, dressed in black, then the noble delegates, colorful and plumed, then the ecclesiastical deputies, then the King and Queen, surrounded by the royal family. The townspeople crowded the streets, the balconies, and the roofs; they applauded the commoners, the King, and the Duc d'Orléans, and received with silence the nobles, the clergy, and the Queen. For a day everyone (except the Queen) was happy, for what so many had hoped for had come to pass. Many, even among the nobles, wept at the sight of the divided nation apparently made one.

On May 5 the deputies assembled in the immense Salle des Menus Plaisirs (Hall of Minor Diversions), about four hundred yards from the royal palace. There were 621 commoners, 308 clergy, 285 nobles (including twenty of the *noblesse de robe*). Of the ecclesiastical deputies some two thirds were of plebeian origin; many of these later threw in their lot with the commoners. Nearly half the deputies of the Third Estate were lawyers, five per cent were professional men, thirteen per cent were businessmen, eight per cent represented the peasantry.[63] Among the clergy was Charles-Maurice de Talleyrand-Périgord, bishop of Autun. Mirabeau, anticipating Napoleon's phrase about "mud in a silk stocking," described Talleyrand as "a vile, greedy, base, intriguing fellow, whose one desire is mud and money;

for money he would sell his soul; and he would be right, for he would be exchanging a dunghill for gold";[64] which hardly did justice to Talleyrand's flexible intelligence. Among the nobles were several men who advocated substantial reforms: Lafayette, Condorcet, Lally-Tollendal, the Vicomte de Noailles, the Ducs d'Orléans, d'Aiguillon, and de La Rochefoucauld-Liancourt. Most of these joined Sieyès, Mirabeau, and other deputies of the Third Estate in forming Les Trentes, a "Society of Thirty" which acted as an organizing group for liberal measures. Prominent in the delegation of the Third Estate were Mirabeau, Sieyès, Mounier, Barnave, Jean Bailly the astronomer, and Maximilien Robespierre. All in all this was the most distinguished political assembly in French annals, perhaps in all modern history. Generous spirits throughout Europe looked to this gathering to raise a standard to which the oppressed in every nation might repair.

The King opened the first session with a brief address frankly confessing the financial distress of his government, ascribing this to "a costly but honorable war," asking for an "augmentation of taxes," and deploring "an exaggerated desire for innovation." Necker followed with a three-hour speech admitting a deficit of 56,150,000 livres (it was really 150,000,000), and asking sanction for a loan of 80,000,000 livres. The deputies fidgeted over the brain-taxing statistics; most of them had expected the liberal minister to expound a program of reform.

The struggle of the classes began the next day, when the nobles and the clergy went to separate halls. The general public now forced its way into the Salle des Menus Plaisirs; soon it was influencing votes by its vigorous—and usually organized—expression of approval or dissent. The Third Estate refused to acknowledge itself a separate chamber; it waited resolutely for the other estates to join it and vote man by man. The nobles replied that voting by classes—each class one vote—was an unalterable part of the monarchical constitution; to merge the three classes in one and allow individual voting, in an assembly where the Third Estate was already half the total and could readily win some support from the lower clergy, would be to surrender the intelligence and character of France to mere number and bourgeois dictation. The clerical delegates, divided between conservatives and liberals, took no stand, waiting to be guided by events. A month passed.

Meanwhile the price of bread continued to rise despite Necker's attempts to regulate it, and the danger of public violence increased. The flood of pamphlets mounted. Arthur Young wrote on June 9:

> The business going forward at present in the pamphlet shops of Paris is incredible. I went to the Palais Royal to see what new things were published, and to procure a catalogue of all. Every hour produces something new. Thirteen came out today, sixteen yesterday, ninety-two last week. . . . Nineteen twentieths of these productions are in favor of liberty, and commonly violent against the clergy and the nobility. . . . Nothing in reply appears.[65]

On June 10 the deputies of the Third Estate sent a committee to the nobles and the clergy again inviting them to a joint meeting, and declaring that if the other orders continued to meet separately the Third Estate would proceed without them to legislate for the nation. The break in the contest of collective wills came on June 14, when nine parish priests came over to the commoners. On that day the Third Estate elected Bailly its president, and organized itself for deliberation and legislation. On the fifteenth Sieyès proposed that since the delegates in the Salle des Menus Plaisirs represented ninety-six per cent of the nation, they should call themselves the "Assembly of the Recognized and Verified Representatives of the French Nation." Mirabeau thought this too broad a term, which the King would surely reject. Instead of retreating, Sieyès simplified the proposed name to Assemblée Nationale. It was so voted, 491 to 89.[66] This declaration automatically changed the absolute monarchy into a limited one, ended the special powers of the upper classes, and constituted, politically, the beginning of the Revolution.

But would the King accept this demotion? To so incline him the National Assembly decreed that all existing taxes should be paid as formerly until the Assembly should be dissolved; that thereafter no taxes should be paid except those that had been authorized by the Assembly; that the Assembly would as soon as possible consider the causes and remedies of the bread shortage; and that after a new constitution had been accepted the Assembly would assume and honor the debts of the state. One of these measures aimed to quiet the rioters; another sought the support of the bondholders; all were cleverly designed to reduce the resistance of the King.

Louis consulted his Council. Necker warned him that unless the privileged orders yielded, the States-General would collapse, taxes would not be paid, and the government would be bankrupt and helpless. Other ministers protested that individual voting would mean dictatorship by the Third Estate, and the reduction of the nobility to political impotence. Feeling that his throne depended upon the nobles and the clergy, Louis decided to resist the National Assembly. He announced that he would address the Estates on June 23. Necker, defeated, offered to resign; the King, knowing that the public would resent such a move, prevailed upon him to stay.

For the scheduled *séance royale* the Salle des Menus Plaisirs had to be prepared by some new physical arrangements. Orders for this were sent to the palace artisans, without notification to the Assembly. When the deputies of the Third Estate tried to enter the hall on June 20 they found its doors shut and the interior occupied by workingmen. Believing that the King was planning to dismiss them, the deputies moved to a nearby tennis court (Salle du Jeu de Paume), and took an oath that made history:

> The National Assembly, considering that it has been summoned to establish the constitution of the kingdom, to effect the regeneration of public order, and to maintain the true principles of monarchy, that nothing can prevent it from continuing its deliberations in whatever place it may be forced to establish itself, and, finally, that wheresoever its members are assembled, *there* is the National Assembly, decrees that all members of this Assembly shall take a solemn oath not to separate, and to reassemble wherever circumstances may require, until the condition of the kingdom is established, and consolidated upon firm foundations; and that, the said oath taken, all members, and each one of them individually, shall ratify this steadfast resolution by signature.[67]

All but two of the 557 deputies and twenty alternates who were present signed; fifty-five more and five priests signed later. When news of these events reached Paris an angry multitude gathered around the Palais-Royal and swore to defend the National Assembly at whatever cost. At Versailles it became dangerous for a nobleman or a prelate to appear in the streets; several were manhandled, and the Archbishop of Paris saved himself only by promising to join the Assembly. On June 22 the sworn deputies met in the Church of St. Louis; there they were joined by a few nobles and 149 of the 308 ecclesiastical delegates.

On June 23 the three estates met in the Salle des Menus Plaisirs to hear the King. The hall was surrounded by troops. Necker was conspicuously absent from the royal retinue. Louis spoke briefly, and then delegated a secretary of state to read his decision. This rejected as illegal and void the assumption of the deputies who had declared themselves a National Assembly. It allowed a united meeting of the three orders, and individual voting on affairs not affecting the class structure of France; but nothing was to be done to impair "the ancient and constitutional rights . . . of property, or the honorific privileges . . . of the first two orders"; and matters concerning religion or the Church must receive the approval of the clergy. The King conceded to the States-General the right to veto new taxes and loans; he promised equality of taxation if the privileged orders voted for it; he offered to receive recommendations for reform, and to establish provincial assemblies in which voting would be individual. He agreed to end the *corvée, lettres de cachet,* tolls on internal trade, and all vestiges of serfdom in France. He concluded the session with a brief display of authority:

> If you abandon me in this great enterprise I will work alone for the welfare of my people. . . . I will consider myself alone their true representative. . . . None of your plans or proceedings can become law without my express approval. . . . I command you to separate at once, and to proceed tomorrow morning each to the hall of his own order to renew your deliberations.[68]

When the King had gone, most of the nobles and a minority of the clergy departed. The Marquis de Brézé, grandmaster of ceremonies, announced to those deputies who remained that it was the King's will that all should leave the hall. Mirabeau made a famous reply: "Monsieur, . . . you have here no place nor voice nor right to speak. . . . If you have been charged to make us leave this hall, you will have to seek orders to employ force, . . . for we shall not leave our places except by the power of the bayonet."[69] This declaration was seconded by a general cry: "That is the will of the Assembly." De Brézé withdrew. Orders were given to local troops to clear the hall, but some liberal nobles persuaded them to take no action. Told of the situation, the King said, "Oh, well, the devil with it; let them stay."[70]

On June 24 Young noted in his diary: "The ferment at Paris is beyond conception; ten thousand people have been all this day in the Palais Royal. . . . The constant meetings there are carried to a degree of licentiousness, and fury of liberty, that is scarcely credible."[71] The municipal authorities were unable to maintain order, for they could not rely upon the local "French Guards"; many of these had relatives who expounded the popular cause to them; some of these soldiers fraternized with the throngs around the Palais-Royal; in one regiment at Paris there was a secret society pledged to obey no orders hostile to the National Assembly. On June 25 the 407 men who had elected the deputies of the Third Estate for Paris met and substituted themselves for the royal government of the capital; they chose a new municipal council, nearly all of the middle class, and the old council abandoned to them the task of protecting life and property. On that same day forty-seven nobles, led by the Duc d'Orléans, moved over to the Salle des Menus Plaisirs. The victory of the Assembly seemed secure. Only force could dislodge it.

On June 26, over Necker's opposition, the conservatives in the King's ministry informed him that the local troops in Versailles and Paris could no longer be trusted to obey orders, and they persuaded him to send for six provincial regiments. On the twenty-seventh, veering to Necker's advice, Louis bade the noble and ecclesiastical deputations to unite with the rest. They did, but the nobles refused to take part in the voting, on the ground that the mandates of their constituents forbade them to vote individually in the States-General. Most of them, in the next thirty days, retired to their estates.

On July 1 the King summoned to Paris ten regiments, mostly Germans and Swiss. In the first weeks of July six thousand troops under the Maréchal de Broglie occupied Versailles, and ten thousand men under the Baron de Besenval took up positions around Paris, chiefly in the Champ de Mars. The Assembly and the people believed that the King was planning to disperse or intimidate them. Some deputies were so fearful of arrest that they slept in the Salle des Menus Plaisirs instead of going to their homes at night.[72]

Amid this terror the Assembly appointed a committee to draw up plans for a new constitution. The committee brought in a preliminary report on July 9, and from that day the deputies called themselves the "National Constituent Assembly." The dominant sentiment was for a constitutional monarchy. Mirabeau argued for "a government more or less like England's," in which the Assembly would be the legislature, but he continued, in the two years left to him, to urge the retention of a king. He praised Louis XVI for a good heart and generous intentions, occasionally confused by shortsighted counselors, and he asked:

> Have these men studied, in the history of any people, how revolutions commence and how they are carried out? Have they observed by what a fatal chain of circumstances the wisest men are driven far beyond the limits of moderation, and by what terrible impulses an enraged people is precipitated into excesses at the very thought of which they would have shuddered?[73]

The Assembly suspected that Mirabeau was being paid by the King or the Queen to defend the monarchy, but essentially it followed his advice. The delegates, now predominantly middle class, felt that the populace was becoming dangerously unmanageable, and that the only way to prevent a general disintegration of social order was to maintain, for some time to come, the present executive structure of the state.

They were not so well disposed toward the Queen. It was known that she participated actively in support of the conservative faction in the Royal Council, and was wielding political power far beyond her competence. During these critical months she had borne a bereavement that may have impaired what capacity she might have had for calm and prudent judgment. Her older son, the Dauphin Louis, suffered so severely from rickets and curvature of the spine that he could not walk without help,[74] and on June 4 he died. Broken by grief and fear, Marie Antoinette was no longer the captivating woman who had frolicked through the first years of the reign. Her cheeks were pale and thin, her hair was turning gray, her smiles were wistful, remembering happier days; and her nights were darkened with consciousness of the crowds cursing her name in Paris and protecting and frightening the Assembly in Versailles.

On July 8 Mirabeau put through a motion asking the King to remove from Versailles the provincial troops that were making the gardens of Le Nôtre an armed camp. Louis answered that no harm was intended to the Assembly, but on July 11 he showed his hand by dismissing Necker and ordering him to leave Paris at once. "All Paris," Mme. de Staël recalled, "flocked to visit him in the twenty-four hours allowed him to prepare for his journey. . . . Public opinion transformed his disgrace into a triumph."[75] He and his family left quietly for the Netherlands. Those who had supported him in the ministry were discharged at the same time. On July 12, in complete surrender to the advocates of force, Louis appointed the Queen's friend, Baron de Breteuil, to replace Necker, and de Broglie was made secretary for war. The Assembly and its incipient revolution seemed doomed.

They were saved by the people of Paris.

VIII. TO THE BASTILLE

Many factors were leading the populace to pass from agitation to action. The price of bread was an irritating issue with housewives, and there was a widespread suspicion that some wholesalers were keeping their grain from the market in hopes of still higher prices.[76] The new municipal authorities, fearing that hunger would take to indiscriminate pillage, sent soldiers to protect the bakeries. With the men of Paris the burning issue was the knowledge that out-of-town regiments, not yet won to the popular cause, were threatening the Assembly and the Revolution. The sudden fall of Necker—the only man in the government whom the people had trusted—brought the anger and fear of the populace to a point where only a word was needed to arouse a violent response. On the afternoon of July 12 Camille Desmoulins, a Jesuit graduate but now a radical lawyer, aged twenty-nine, leaped upon a table outside the Café de Foy near the Palais-Royal, denounced the dismissal of Necker as a betrayal of the people, and cried out, "The Germans [the troops] in the Champ de Mars will enter Paris tonight to butcher the inhabitants!" Then, flourishing both a pistol and a sword, he called "To arms!"[77] Part of his audience followed him to the Place Vendôme, carrying busts of Necker and the Duc d'Orléans; there some troops put them to flight. In the evening a crowd gathered in the Tuileries Gardens; a regiment of German troops charged it, was resisted with bottles and stones, fired upon it and wounded many. Dispersed, the crowd reassembled at the Hôtel de Ville, forced its way in, and seized all the weapons it could find. Beggars and criminals joined the rioters, and together they pillaged several homes.

On July 13 the crowd gathered again. They entered the Monastery of St.-Lazare, appropriated its store of grain, and carried this to the market at Les Halles. Another crowd opened the prison of La Force and liberated the inmates, mostly debtors. Everywhere the people searched for guns; finding only a few, they forged fifty thousand pikes.[78] Fearing for their homes and possessions, the middle classes in Paris formed and armed their own militia; yet at the same time agents of the rich continued to encourage, finance, and arm revolutionary crowds, hoping thereby to deter the King from using force on the Assembly.[79]

Early on July 14 a crowd of eight thousand men invaded the Hôtel des Invalides, and captured 32,000 muskets, some powder, and twelve pieces of artillery. Suddenly someone cried out, "To the Bastille!" Why the Bastille? Not to release its prisoners, who were only seven; and generally, since 1715, it had been used as a place of genteel confinement for the well-to-do. But this massive fortress, one hundred feet high, with walls thirty feet thick, and surrounded by a moat seventy-five feet wide, had long been a symbol of despotism; it stood in the public mind for a thousand prisons and secret dungeons; some of the *cahiers* had already demanded its destruction. Probably what moved the crowd was the knowledge that the Bastille had pointed some cannon at the Rue and Faubourg St.-Antoine, a quarter seething with revolutionary sentiment. Perhaps most important of all, the Bastille was said to contain a great store of arms and ammunition, especially powder, of which the rebels had little. In the fortress was a garrison of eighty-two French soldiers and thirty-two Swiss Guards, under the command of the Marquis de Launay, a man of mild temper[80] but popularly reported to be a monster of cruelty.[81]

While the crowd, composed mainly of shopkeepers and artisans, converged upon the Bastille, a deputation from the municipal council was received by de Launay. It asked him to withdraw the threatening cannon from their positions, and not to take any hostile action against the people; in return it promised to use its influence to dissuade the crowd from attacking the fortress. The commandant agreed, and entertained the deputation for lunch. Another committee, from the besiegers themselves, received de Launay's pledge that his soldiers would not fire upon the people unless there was an attempt at forcible entry. This did not satisfy the excited assemblage; it was resolved to capture the ammunition without which its muskets could not resist the expected advance of Besenval's foreign troops into the city. Besenval was not anxious to move into Paris, for he suspected that his men would refuse to fire upon the people. He waited for orders from de Broglie; none came.

About one o'clock in the afternoon eighteen of the rebels climbed the wall of an adjoining structure, leaped into the forecourt of the Bastille, and lowered two drawbridges. Hundreds crossed over the moat; two other drawbridges were lowered; soon the court was filled with an eager and confident crowd. De Launay commanded them to withdraw; they refused; he ordered his soldiers to fire upon them. The attackers fired back, and set fire to some wooden structures attached to the stone walls. Toward three o'clock some members of the radical French Guard joined the besiegers, and began to bombard the fortress with five of the cannon that had been taken that morning at the Hôtel des Invalides. In four hours of fighting, ninety-eight of the attackers and one of the defenders were killed. De Launay, seeing the multitude always increasing with new arrivals, receiving no word of help from Besenval, and having no supply of food to stand a siege, bade his soldiers to cease fire and hoist a white flag. He offered to surrender if his troops were allowed to march out, with their arms, to safety. The crowd, infuriated by the sight of its dead, refused to consider anything but unconditional surrender.[82] De Launay proposed to blow up the fortress; his men prevented him. He sent down to the assailants the key to the main entrance. The crowd rushed in, disarmed the soldiers, slew six of them, seized de Launay, and freed the bewildered prisoners.

While many of the victors took what weapons and ammunition they could find, part of the crowd led de Launay toward the Hôtel de Ville, apparently intending to have him tried for murder. On the way the more ardent among them knocked him down, beat him to death, and cut off his head. With this bleeding trophy held aloft on a pike, they marched through Paris in a triumphal parade.

That afternoon Louis XVI returned to Versailles from a day's hunting, and entered a note into his diary: "July 14: Nothing." Then the Duc de La Rochefoucauld-Liancourt, arriving from Paris, told him of the successful attack upon the Bastille. "Why," exclaimed the King, "this is a revolt!" "No, Sire," said the Duke, "it is a revolution."

On July 15 the King went humbly to the Assembly and assured it that the provincial and foreign troops would be sent away from Versailles and Paris. On July 16 he dismissed Breteuil and recalled Necker to a third ministry. Breteuil, Artois, de Broglie, and other nobles began the exodus of émigrés from France. Meanwhile the populace, with pickaxes and gunpowder, demolished the Bastille. On July 17 Louis, escorted by fifty deputies of the Assembly, went to Paris, was received at the Hôtel de Ville by the municipal council and the people, and affixed to his hat the red-white-and-blue cockade of the Revolution.

Envoi

SO we end our survey, in these last two volumes, of the century whose conflicts and achievements are still active in the life of mankind today. We
have seen the Industrial Revolution begin with that Mississippi of inventions
which may, by the year two thousand, realize Aristotle's dream of machines
liberating men from all menial toil. We have recorded the advances of a
dozen sciences toward a better understanding of nature and a more effective
application of her laws. We have welcomed the passage of philosophy from
futile metaphysics to the tentative pursuit of reason in the mundane affairs
of men. We have followed with living concern the attempt to free religion
from superstition, bigotry, and intolerance, and to organize morality without supernatural punishments and rewards. We have been instructed by the
efforts of statesmen and philosophers to evolve a just and competent government, and to reconcile democracy with the simplicity and natural inequality
of men. We have enjoyed the diverse creations of beauty in baroque, rococo,
and neoclassical art, and the triumphs of music in Bach, Handel, and Vivaldi,
in Gluck, Haydn, and Mozart. We have witnessed the flowering of literature
in Germany with Schiller and Goethe, in England with the great novelists
and the greatest of historians, in Scotland with Boswell and Burns, in Sweden
with the outburst of song under Gustavus III; and in France we have
wavered between Voltaire defending reason with wit and Rousseau pleading with tears for the rights of feeling. We have heard the applause on which
Garrick and Clairon lived. We have admired the succession of fascinating
women in the salons of France and England, and the brilliant reigns of women
in Austria and Russia. We have watched philosopher kings.

It seems absurd to end our story just when so many historic events were
about to enliven and incarnadine the page. We should have been happy to
advance through the turmoil of the Revolution, to contemplate that volcanic
eruption of energy known as Napoleon, and then feast upon the wealth of
the nineteenth century in literature, science, philosophy, music, art, technology, and statesmanship. Still more we should have enjoyed coming home
to America, South as well as North, and trying to weave the complex tapestry of American life and history into one united and moving picture. But
we must reconcile ourselves to mortality, and leave to fresher spirits the task
and risk of adding experiments in synthesis to the basic researches of historical and scientific specialists.

We have completed, as far as we could go, this Story of Civilization; and
though we have devoted the best part of our lives to the work, we know
that a lifetime is but a moment in history, and that the historian's best is soon
washed away as the stream of knowledge grows. But as we followed our
studies from century to century we felt confirmed in our belief that his-

toriography has been too departmentalized, and that some of us should try to write history whole, as it was lived, in all the facets of the complex and continuing drama.

Forty years of happy association in the pursuit of history have come to an end. We dreamed of the day when we should write the last word of the last volume. Now that that day has come we know that we shall miss the absorbing purpose that gave meaning and direction to our lives.

We thank the reader who has been with us these many years for part or all of the long journey. We have ever been mindful of his presence. Now we take our leave and bid him farewell.

Bibliographical Guide

to editions referred to in the Notes

ABBOTT, G. F., *Israel in Europe*. London, 1907.

ABRAHAMS, ISRAEL, *Jewish Life in the Middle Ages*. Philadelphia, 1896.

ACTON, JOHN EMERICH, LORD, *Lectures on Modern History*. London, 1950.

ALDIS, JANET, *Madame Geoffrin: Her Salon and Her Times*. New York, 1905.

ALFIERI, VITTORIO, *Autobiography*. Lawrence, Kansas, 1953. References are to "epoch" and chapter.

———, *Of Tyranny*. Toronto, 1961. References are to book and section.

ALTAMIRA, RAFAEL, *History of Spain*. Princeton, 1955.

———, *History of Spanish Civilization*. London, 1930.

ANDERSON, EMILY, *Letters of Mozart and His Family*, 3v. London, 1938.

ANDERSSON, INGVAR, *A History of Sweden*. London, 1956.

ANONYMOUS, *Tiepolo*. "Masters in Art" series.

ASHTON, T. S., *Economic History of England: The Eighteenth Century*. New York, 1959.

AULARD, A., *The French Revolution*, 4v. New York, 1910.

BABBITT, IRVING, *Spanish Character and Other Essays*. Boston, 1940.

BAEDEKER, KARL, *Northern Italy*. London, 1913.

BAILEY, JOHN, *Dr. Johnson and His Circle*. Oxford University Press, 1957.

BAIN, R. NISBET, *Gustavus III*, 2v. London, 1894.

———, *The Last King of Poland*. London, 1909.

BANCROFT, GEORGE, *Literary and Historical Miscellanies*. New York, 1957.

BARNES, HARRY ELMER, *Economic History of the Western World*. New York, 1942.

BARON, SALO W., *Social and Religious History of the Jews*, 3v. New York, 1937.

BARTHOU, LOUIS, *Mirabeau*. New York: Dodd, Mead, n.d.

BARTON, MARGARET, *Garrick*. London, 1948.

BATIFFOL, LOUIS, ed., *The Great Literary Salons*. New York, 1930.

BEARD, CHARLES and MARY, *The Rise of American Civilization*, 2v. New York, 1927.

BEARD, MIRIAM, *History of the Business Man*. New York, 1938.

BEARNE, MRS., *A Court Painter and His Circle*. London, 1913.

BEAUMARCHAIS, PIERRE-AUGUSTIN CARON DE, *Oeuvres: Théâtre et Mémoires*. Paris, 1906.

BECKER, CARL, *The Heavenly City of the Eighteenth-Century Philosophers*. New Haven, 1951.

BECKFORD, WILLIAM, *Travel Diaries*, 2v. Cambridge, England, 1928.

BELL, AUBREY, *Portuguese Literature*. Oxford, 1922.

BENTHAM, JEREMY, *A Fragment on Government* and *Introduction to Principles of Morals and Legislation.* Oxford, 1948.

BERNAL, J. D., *Science in History.* London, 1957.

BERNARDIN DE SAINT-PIERRE, J.H., *Paul et Virginie.* Paris: Librairie Gründ, n.d.

BERTAUT, J., *Napoleon in His Own Words.* Chicago, 1916.

BERTRAND, JOSEPH, *D'Alembert.* Paris, 1889.

BESANT, SIR WALTER, *London in the Eighteenth Century.* London, 1903.

BIANCOLLI, LOUIS, *The Mozart Handbook.* New York, 1962.

BLACK, J. B., *The Art of History.* New York, 1926.

BLACKSTONE, SIR WILLIAM, *Commentaries on the Laws of England,* ed. George Chase. New York, 1914.

BLOK, PETRUS J., *History of the People of the Netherlands,* Part V. New York, 1912.

BLOM, ERIC, *Mozart.* New York, 1962.

BOEHN, MAX VON, *Modes and Manners,* Vol. IV: *The Eighteenth Century.* Philadelphia: Lippincott, n.d.

BOSANQUET, BERNARD, *History of Aesthetic.* New York, 1957.

BOSWELL, JAMES, *Journal of a Tour to the Hebrides with Samuel Johnson.* Everyman's Library.

———, *Life of Samuel Johnson.* Modern Library.

———, *Note Book, 1776–1777.* London, 1925.

Boswell for the Defense. New York, 1959.

Boswell in Holland. New York, 1952.

Boswell in Search of a Wife. New York, 1956.

Boswell on the Grand Tour: Germany and Switzerland, 1764. New York, 1953.

Boswell on the Grand Tour: Italy, Corsica and France, 1765–66. New York, 1955.

Boswell's London Journal, 1762–1763. New York, 1956.

Boswell: The Ominous Years, 1774–1776, New York, 1963.

BOTSFORD, J. B., *English Society in the Eighteenth Century.* New York, 1924.

BOYD, WILLIAM, *Educational Theory of Jean Jacques Rousseau.* London, 1911.

BRANDES, GEORG, *Creative Spirits of the Nineteenth Century.* New York, 1923.

———, *Wolfgang Goethe,* 2v. New York, 1924.

———, *Voltaire,* 2v. New York, 1930.

BROCKWAY, WALLACE, and WEINSTOCK, HERBERT, *The Opera: A History.* New York, 1941.

BROCKWAY, WALLACE, and WINER, BART K., *Second Treasury of the World's Great Letters.* New York, 1941.

BROOKE, HENRY, *The Fool of Quality.* London, 1906.

BROWN, HILTON, *There Was a Lad: An Essay on Robert Burns.* London, 1906.

BROWNE, EDWARD G., *Literary History of Persia,* 4v. Cambridge, Eng., 1929 f.

BROWNE, LEWIS, *The Wisdom of Israel.* New York, 1945.

BRÜCKNER, A., *Literary History of Russia.* London, 1908.

BRUFORD, W. H., *Germany in the Eighteenth Century.* Cambridge, Eng., 1939.

BRUNETIÈRE, FERDINAND, *A Manual of the History of French Literature.* New York, 1898.

BUCKLE, HENRY T., *An Introduction to the History of Civilization in England,* 2v in 4. New York, 1913.

BURKE, EDMUND, *On Taste, and On the Sublime and Beautiful.* New York, 1937.

———, *Reflections on the French Revolution.* Everyman's Library.

——, *Speeches and Letters on American Affairs.* Everyman's Library.
——, *A Vindication of Natural Society, or A View of the Miseries Arising to Mankind from Every Species of Artificial Society,* in *Works,* Vol. I.
BURNEY, CHARLES, *General History of Music,* 2v. New York, 1957.
BURNEY, FANNY, *Diary.* Everyman's Library.
——, *Evelina.* Everyman's Library.
BURNS, ROBERT, *The Merry Muses of Caledonia.* New York, 1964.
——, *Works,* 2v. in 1. Philadelphia, 1830.
—— and "CLARINDA," *Correspondence.* New York, 1843.
—— and MRS. DUNLOP, *Correspondence.* London, 1898.
BURTON, JOHN HILL, *Life and Correspondence of David Hume,* 2v. Edinburgh, 1846.
BURTON, SIR RICHARD, *Personal Narrative of a Pilgrimage to Al-Madinah and Meccah,* 2v. London, 1893.
BURY, J. B., *History of Freedom of Thought.* New York: Home University Library, n.d.
——, *The Idea of Progress.* New York, 1955.
BUTTERFIELD, HERBERT, *George III and the Historians.* London, 1957.

CALVERT, A. F., *Goya.* London, 1908.
——, *Royal Palaces of Spain.* London, 1909.
Cambridge History of English Literature [*CHE*], 14v. New York, 1910.
Cambridge History of Poland [*CHP*], 2v. Cambridge, Eng., 1950.
Cambridge Modern History [*CMH*], original ed., 12v. Cambridge, Eng., 1907 f.
CAMPAN, MME. JEANNE-LOUISE, *Memoirs of the Court of Marie Antoinette,* 2v. Boston: Grolier Society, n.d.
CAMPBELL, THOMAS J., *The Jesuits.* New York, 1921.
CARLYLE, THOMAS, *Works,* 19v. New York, 1901.
——, *History of Friedrich the Second,* 7v. New York, 1901.
CARUS, PAUL, *Goethe.* Chicago, 1915.
CASANOVA, JACQUES, *Memoirs,* 2v. London, 1922.
CASSIRER, ERNST, *The Philosophy of the Enlightenment,* Princeton, 1951.
——, *The Question of Jean-Jacques Rousseau.* New York, 1954.
——, *Rousseau, Kant, and Goethe.* Hamden, Conn., 1961.
CASTELOT, ANDRÉ, *Queen of France: Marie Antoinette.* New York, 1957.
CASTÉRA, J. H., *History of Catherine II.* London, 1800.
CATHERINE THE GREAT, *Memoirs.* New York, 1955.
CHADOURNE, MARC, *Restif de La Bretonne.* Paris, 1958.
CHAMFORT, SÉBASTIEN, *Maximes, Pensées, Anecdotes, Caractères, et Dialogues.* Brussels, 1957.
CHAPONNIÈRE, PAUL, *Voltaire chez les calvinistes.* Paris, 1936.
CHATTERTON, THOMAS, *Complete Poetical Works.* London, 1906.
CHEKE, MARCUS, *Dictator of Portugal: A Life of the Marquis of Pombal.* London, 1938.
CHESTERFIELD, PHILIP DORMER STANHOPE, 4th EARL OF, *Letters to His Son,* 2v. in 1. New York, 1901.
CHURCHILL, WINSTON S., *History of the English-Speaking Peoples.* 4v. London, 1957.
CLARK, BARRETT H., *Great Short Biographies of the World.* New York, 1928.
CLARK, GEORGE NORMAN, *The Seventeenth Century.* Oxford, 1929.

CLARK, ROBERT T., *Herder: His Life and Thought*. University of California Press, 1955.

COBBAN, ALFRED, *Historians and the Causes of the French Revolution*. London, 1958.

———, *History of Modern France*, 2v. Penguin Books, 1957.

———, *In Search of Humanity*. New York, 1960.

———, *Rousseau and the Modern State*. London, 1934.

COLLINS, JOHN CHURTON, *Bolingbroke, and Voltaire in England*. New York, 1886.

CONDORCET, ANTOINE-NICOLAS CARITAT, MARQUIS DE, *Sketch for a Historical Picture of the Progress of the Human Mind*. London, 1955.

CORTI, EGON C., *Rise of the House of Rothschild*, 2v. New York, 1928.

COWPER, WILLIAM, *Poems*. Everyman's Library.

COXE, WILLIAM, *History of the House of Austria*, 3v. London, 1847.

———, *Memoirs of the Kings of Spain of the House of Bourbon*, 5v. London, 1813.

———, *Travels in Poland, Russia, Sweden, and Denmark*, 5v. London, 1802.

CRAVEN, THOMAS, *Treasury of Art Masterpieces*. New York, 1952.

CRÉBILLON, CLAUDE-PROSPER JOLYOT DE (CRÉBILLON *fils*), *The Sofa*. London, 1927.

CRÉQUI, MARQUISE DE, *Souvenirs*. New York, 1904. Of doubtful authenticity.

CROCE, BENEDETTO, *The Philosophy of Giambattista Vico*. New York, 1913.

CROCKER, LESTER G., *An Age of Crisis*. Baltimore, 1950.

———, *The Embattled Philosopher: A Biography of Denis Diderot*. East Lansing, Mich., 1954.

———, *Rousseau et la philosophie politique*. Paris, 1965.

CROSS, WILBUR, *Life and Times of Laurence Sterne*, 2v. New Haven, Conn., 1925.

CRU, ROBERT LOYALTY, *Diderot as a Disciple of English Thought*. New York, 1913.

CUMMING, IAN, *Helvétius*. London, 1955.

CURRIE, JAMES, *Life of Robert Burns, with His General Correspondence*, in Burns, *Works*, Vol. II. Philadelphia, 1830.

DAKIN, DOUGLAS, *Turgot and the Ancien Régime in France*. London, 1939.

D'ALTON, E. A., *History of Ireland*, 6v. Dublin: Gresham, n.d.

DAVIDSON, WILLIAM L., *Political Thought in England: The Utilitarians*. London, 1947.

DAVIS, BERTRAM H., *Johnson before Boswell*. New Haven, 1961.

DAY, CLIVE, *History of Commerce*. London, 1926.

DE SANCTIS, FRANCESCO, *History of Italian Literature*, 2v. New York, 1959.

DESNOIRESTERRES, GUSTAVE, *Voltaire et la société française au xviiie siècle*. Paris, 1871.

DIDEROT, DENIS, *Dialogues*. New York, 1927.

———, *Oeuvres complètes*. Paris, 1935.

———, *The Paradox of Acting*. New York, 1957.

———, *Salons*, 3v. Paris, 1821.

DILKE, LADY EMILIA, *French Architects and Sculptors of the Eighteenth Century*. London, 1900.

DILLON, EDWARD, *Glass*. New York, 1907.

DORN, WALTER L., *Competition for Empire*. New York, 1940.

DOUGHTY, CHARLES M., *Travels in Arabia Deserta*, 2v. New York, 1923.

DRINKWATER, JOHN, *Charles James Fox*. New York, 1928.

DUBNOW, S. M., *History of the Jews in Russia and Poland*, 3v. Philadelphia, 1916.

DUCLOS, CHARLES PINOT, *Considérations sur les moeurs*. Cambridge, Eng., 1939.

DUCROS, LOUIS, *French Society in the Eighteenth Century*. London, 1926.

DU DEFFAND, MARIE DE VICHY-CHAMROND, MARQUISE, *Lettres à Voltaire*. Paris, 1922.

DU HAUSSET, MME., *Memoirs of Madame de Pompadour*. New York, 1928.

ECKERMANN, JOHANN PETER, and SORET, M., *Conversations with Goethe*. London, 1882.

EINSTEIN, ALFRED, *Gluck*. London, 1954.

——, *Mozart*. Oxford, 1945.

ELLIS, HAVELOCK, *The New Spirit*. London: Walter Scott, n.d.

——, *Sexual Inversion*. Philadelphia, 1908.

Encyclopaedia Britannica, 14th ed.

ÉPINAY, LOUISE DE LA LIVE D', *Memoirs and Correspondence*, 3v. London, 1899.

ERCOLE, LUCIENNE, *Gay Court Life: France in the Eighteenth Century*. New York, 1932.

FAGUET, ÉMILE, *Dix-huitième Siècle: Études littéraires*. Paris, Boivin, n.d.

——, *Literary History of France*. New York, 1907.

——, *Rousseau artiste*. Paris, Société Française, n.d.

——, *Rousseau penseur*. Paris, Société Française, n.d.

——, *Vie de Rousseau*. Paris, Société Française, n.d.

FANIEL, STÉPHANE, *French Art of the Eighteenth Century*. New York, 1957.

FAŸ, BERNARD, *La Franc-Maçonnerie et la révolution intellectuelle du dix-huitième siècle*. Paris, 1935.

——, *Franklin, the Apostle of Modern Times*. Boston, 1929.

——, *Louis XVI, ou La Fin d'un monde*. Paris, 1955.

FINKELSTEIN, LOUIS, ed., *The Jews: Their History, Culture, and Religion*, 2v. New York, 1949.

FITZMAURICE-KELLY, JAMES, *History of Spanish Literature*. New York, 1928.

FLORINSKY, MICHAEL T., *Russia: A History and an Interpretation*, 2v. New York, 1955.

FORD, MIRIAM ALLEN DE, *Love Children*. New York, 1931.

FRANCKE, KUNO, *A History of German Literature*. New York, 1901.

FRANKEL, CHARLES, *The Faith of Reason*. New York, 1948.

FREDERICK THE GREAT, *Histoire de la guerre de Sept Ans*, in *Mémoires*, Vol. II.

——, *Mémoires*, 2v. Paris, 1866.

FREEDLEY, G., and REEVES, J., *History of the Theatre*. New York, 1941.

FRENCH, SIDNEY J., *Torch and Crucible: The Life and Death of Antoine Lavoisier*. Princeton, 1941.

FRIEDELL, EGON, *Cultural History of the Modern Age*, Vol. I. New York, 1930.

FRIEDLÄNDER, LUDWIG, *Roman Life and Manners under the Early Empire*, 4v. London, 1928.

FUGLUM, PER, *Edward Gibbon*. Oslo, 1953.

FÜLOP-MILLER, RENÉ, *The Power and Secret of the Jesuits*. New York, 1930.

FUNCK-BRENTANO, FRANTZ, *L'Ancien Régime*. Paris, 1926.

FUNK, F. X., *A Manual of Church History*, 2v. London, 1910.

GAMBIER-PARRY, MARK, *Madame Necker: Her Family and Her Friends*. Edinburgh, 1913.
GARLAND, H. B., *Lessing*. Cambridge, Eng., 1949.
GARNETT, RICHARD, *History of Italian Literature*. New York, 1898.
———, and GOSSE, EDMUND, *English Literature*, 4v. New York, 1908.
GARRISON, F., *History of Medicine*. Philadelphia, 1929.
GAY, PETER, *Voltaire's Politics*. Princeton, 1959.
GEIRINGER, KARL, *Haydn*. New York, 1946.
GEORGE, M. DOROTHY, *England in Transition*. London, 1931.
———, *London Life in the Eighteenth Century*. London, 1925.
GERSHOY, LEO, *From Despotism to Revolution: 1763–89*. New York, 1944.
G. G. S., *Life of R. B. Sheridan*, in Sheridan, *Dramatic Works*. London, 1881.
GHÉON, HENRI, *In Search of Mozart*. New York, 1934.
GIBBON, EDWARD, *The Decline and Fall of the Roman Empire*, 7v, ed. J. B. Bury. London, 1900.
———, Same, 6v, ed. Dean Milman. New York: Nottingham Society, n.d. References are to this edition unless otherwise stated.
———, Same. Everyman's Library.
———, *Journal*, ed. D. M. Low. New York: Norton, n.d.
———, *Memoirs*. London, 1900.
———, *Miscellaneous Writings*. New York, 1907.
GILBERT, O. P., *The Prince de Ligne*. New York: McDevitt-Wilson, n.d.
GILLET, LOUIS, *La Peinture, xviie et xviiie siècles*. Paris, 1913.
GOETHE, JOHANN WOLFGANG VON, *Works*, 14v in 7. New York, 1902.
GOLDONI, CARLO, *Memoirs*. New York, 1926.
———, *Three Comedies*, and ALFIERI, VITTORIO, *Three Tragedies*. London, 1907.
GOLDSMITH, OLIVER, *Select Works*. London, 1929.
GONCOURT, EDMOND and JULES DE, *French Eighteenth-Century Painters*. New York, 1948.
———, *Madame de Pompadour*. Paris, n.d.
———, *The Woman of the Eighteenth Century*. New York, 1927.
GOOCH, G. P., *Catherine the Great and Other Studies*. New York, 1954.
———, *Frederick the Great*. New York, 1947.
———, *Maria Theresa and Other Studies*. London, 1951.
GOODWIN, A., ed., *The European Nobility in the Eighteenth Century*. London, 1953.
GOYA, FRANCISCO DE, *The Disasters of War*. Garden City, N.Y., 1956.
———, *Drawings from the Prado*. London, 1947.
GOZZI, CARLO, *Memoirs*, 2v. London, 1890.
GRAETZ, HEINRICH, *History of the Jews*, 6v. Philadelphia, 1891.
GREENE, DONALD J., *The Politics of Samuel Johnson*. New Haven, 1960.
GRIMM, MELCHIOR, et al., *Correspondance littéraire, philosophique, et critique*, 16v. Paris, 1877–82.
GROUT, DONALD J., *A Short History of Opera*. New York, 1954.
Grove's Dictionary of Music, 5v. New York, 1927.
GUÉRARD, ALBERT, *Life and Death of an Ideal: France in the Classical Age*. New York, 1928.
GUSTAFSON, ALRIK, *History of Swedish Literature*. Minneapolis, 1961.

HALSBAND, ROBERT, *The Life of Lady Mary Wortley Montagu*. Oxford, 1957.

HAMMOND, J. L. and BARBARA, *The Rise of Modern Industry*. New York, 1926.

——, *The Village Labourer, 1760–1832*. London, 1927.

HAUSER, ARNOLD, *The Social History of Art*, 2v. New York, 1952.

HAVENS, GEORGE R., *The Age of Ideas*. New York, 1955.

HAWKINS, SIR JOHN, *Life of Samuel Johnson*. New York, 1961.

HAZARD, PAUL, *European Thought in the Eighteenth Century*. New Haven, 1954.

HAZLITT, WILLIAM CAREW, *The Venetian Republic*, 2v. London, 1900.

HEARNSHAW, F. J., ed., *Social and Political Ideas of Some Great French Thinkers of the Age of Reason*. New York, 1950.

HEISELER, BERNT VON, *Schiller*. London, 1962.

HELVÉTIUS, CLAUDE-ADRIEN, *Treatise on Man*, 2v. London, 1810.

HENDEL, CHARLES W., *Citizen of Geneva: Selections from the Letters of Jean-Jacques Rousseau*. Oxford, 1937.

——, *Jean-Jacques Rousseau, Moralist*, 2v. London, 1934.

HENSEL, SEBASTIAN, *The Mendelssohn Family*, 2v. New York, 1882.

HERBERT, SYDNEY, *The Fall of Feudalism in France*. London, 1921.

HEROLD, J. CHRISTOPHER, *Love in Five Temperaments*. New York, 1961.

——, *Mistress to an Age: A Life of Madame de Staël*. Indianapolis, 1958.

——, *The Swiss without Halos*. New York, 1958.

HERR, RICHARD, *The Eighteenth-Century Revolution in Spain*. Princeton, 1958.

HIGGS, HENRY, *The Physiocrats*. London, 1897.

HILL, GEORGE BIRKBECK, ed., *Johnsonian Miscellanies*, 2v. Oxford, 1897.

HILL, J. C., *Love Songs and Heroines of Robert Burns*. London, 1961.

History Today magazine, London.

HÖFFDING, HARALD, *Jean Jacques Rousseau and His Philosophy*. New Haven, 1930.

HOLBERG, LUDWIG, *The Journey of Niels Klim to the World Underground*. Lincoln, Neb., n.d.

——, *Selected Essays*. Lawrence, Kan., 1955.

——, *Seven One-Act Plays*. Princeton, 1950.

HOPKINS, MARY ALDEN, *Hannah More and Her Circle*. New York, 1947.

HORN, F. W., *History of the Literature of the Scandinavian North*. Chicago, 1884.

HOWE, IRVING, and GREENBERG, ELIEZER, *A Treasury of Yiddish Stories*. New York, 1958.

HUME, DAVID, *Essays, Literary, Moral, and Political*. London: Ward, Lock & Co., n.d.

——, *Treatise of Human Nature*. Everyman's Library.

HUME, MARTIN, *Spain: Its Greatness and Decay*. Cambridge, Eng., 1899.

IRVING, WASHINGTON, *Oliver Goldsmith*. Boston, 1903.

JACOB, H. E., *Joseph Haydn*. New York, 1950.

JAHN, OTTO, *Life of Mozart*, 3v. London, 1891.

JAMES, E. E. C., *Bologna*. London, 1909.

JAURÈS, JEAN, *Histoire socialiste de la Révolution française*, 8v. Paris, 1922.

JEFFERSON, D. W., ed., *Eighteenth-Century Prose*. Pelican Books, 1956.

JOHNSON, SAMUEL, *Lives of the English Poets*, 2v. Everyman's Library.
————, *The Rambler*. Everyman's Library.
————, *Works*, 12v. London, 1823.
Johnson's Dictionary: A Modern Selection, ed. E. L. McAdam, Jr., and George Milne. New York, 1963.
JOSEPHSON, MATTHEW, *Jean-Jacques Rousseau*. London, 1932.
"JUNIUS," *Letters*, ed. C. W. Everett. London, 1927.

KANT, IMMANUEL, *Critique of Judgment*, 2v in 1, ed. James C. Meredith. Oxford, 1957.
————, *Critique of Practical Reason*. Translation by T. K. Abbott, London, 1954. References are to pages in Vol. VIII of Kant's *Works*, edited by Rosenkranz and Schubert.
————, *Critique of Pure Reason*. Translation by Norman Kemp Smith, London, 1956. References are to pages of the first German edition unless otherwise noted.
————, *Education*. Ann Arbor, Mich., 1960.
————, *Fundamental Principles of the Metaphysics of Ethics*. Translation by T. K. Abbott, London, 1929. References are to Vol. VIII of the Rosenkranz and Schubert ed.
————, *A Philosophical Treatise on Perpetual Peace*. London: Hodder & Stoughton, n.d.
————, *Prolegomena to Any Future Metaphysics That Will Be Able to Present Itself as a Science*. Manchester, Eng., 1953.
————, *Religion within the Limits of Reason Alone*, tr. T. M. Greene and H. H. Hudson. Chicago, 1934.
KANY, CHARLES E., *Life and Manners in Madrid, 1750–1800*. Berkeley, Calif., 1932.
KEITH, CHRISTINA, *The Russet Coat* (Burns). London, 1956.
KIRKPATRICK, RALPH, *Domenico Scarlatti*. Princeton, 1953.
KLINGENDER, F. D., *Goya in the Democratic Tradition*. London, 1948.
KLINKE, WILLIBALD, *Kant for Everyman*. London, 1952.
KLOPSTOCK, FRIEDRICH GOTTLIEB, *The Messiah*, 2v. London, 1826.
KLUCHEVSKY, V. O., *History of Russia*, 5v. London, 1912.
Kobbé's Complete Opera Book, ed. the Earl of Harewood. New York, 1961.
KÖHLER, CARL, *A History of Costume*. New York, 1928.
KOVEN, ANNA DE, *Horace Walpole and Madame du Deffand*. New York, 1929.
KROPOTKIN, P. A., *The Great French Revolution*. New York, 1909.
KRUTCH, JOSEPH WOOD, *Samuel Johnson*, New York, 1945.

LACLOS, PIERRE CHODERLOS DE, *Les Liaisons dangereuses*. London: Routledge, n.d.
LACROIX, PAUL, *The Eighteenth Century in France*. London: Bickers, n.d.
LA FONTAINERIE, F. DE, *French Liberalism and Education in the Eighteenth Century*. New York, 1932.
LANE, EDWARD W., *Manners and Customs of the Modern Egyptians*. London, 1846.
LANE-POOLE, STANLEY, *Cairo*. London, 1895.
————, *The Story of Turkey*. New York, 1895.
LANFREY, PIERRE, *L'Église et les philosophes au dix-huitième siècle*. Paris, 1857.

————, *Histoire philosophique des papes*. Paris, 1873.

Láng, P. H., *Music in Western Civilization*. New York, 1941.

Lanson, Gustave, *Histoire de la littérature française*. Paris, 1912.

————, *Voltaire*. Paris, 1906.

Laski, Harold, *Political Thought in England, Locke to Bentham*. Oxford, 1950.

Lassaigne, Jacques, *Spanish Painting: From Velázquez to Picasso*. New York, 1952.

Lea, Henry C., *History of the Inquisition in Spain*, 4v. New York, 1906.

Lecky, William E., *History of England in the Eighteenth Century*, 8v. London, 1887.

Lee, Vernon (Violet Paget), *Studies of the Eighteenth Century in Italy*. Chicago, 1908.

Lefebvre, Georges, *The Coming of the French Revolution*. New York: Vintage Books, n.d.

Lemaître, Jules, *Jean-Jacques Rousseau*. London, 1908.

Lespinasse, Julie de, *Letters*. London, 1903.

Lessing, Gotthold Ephraim, *Dramatic Works*. London, 1910.

————, *Laocoön*. London: Routledge, n.d.

Levey, Michael, *Painting in Eighteenth-Century Venice*. London, 1959.

Levron, Jacques, *Pompadour*. New York, 1963.

Lewes, George H., *Life of Goethe*, 2v, in Goethe, *Works*. New York, 1902.

Lewinski-Corwin, E. H., *Political History of Poland*. New York, 1917.

Lewis, D. B. Wyndham, *Four Favorites*. New York, 1949.

Lewis, W. S., *Horace Walpole*. Pantheon Books, 1960.

Lewisohn, Ludwig, *Goethe: The Story of a Man*, 2v. New York, 1949.

Lichtenberger, André, *Le Socialisme et la Révolution française*. Paris, 1895.

Lipson, E., *The Growth of English Society*. London, 1949.

Litchfield, Frederick, *Illustrated History of Furniture*. Boston, 1922.

Loménie, Louis de, *Beaumarchais and His Times*. New York, 1857.

Loomis, Stanley, *Du Barry*. London, 1960.

Lovejoy, Arthur O., *Essays in the History of Ideas*. Baltimore, 1948.

————, *The Great Chain of Being*. Cambridge, Mass., 1953.

Low, D. M., *Edward Gibbon*. New York, 1937.

Ludwig, Emil, *Goethe*. New York, 1928.

Lyashchenko, Peter, *History of the National Economy of Russia*. New York, 1949.

Macaulay, Thomas Babington, *Critical and Historical Essays*, 2v. Everyman's Library.

MacCoby, S., *The English Radical Tradition*. London, 1952.

————, *The Development of Muslim Theology, Jurisprudence, and Constitutional Theory*. New York, 1903.

Macdonald, Duncan B., *The Religious Attitude to Life in Islam*. Chicago, 1909.

Macdonald, Frederika, *Jean Jacques Rousseau: A New Criticism*, 2v. New York, 1906.

Mack, M. P., *Jeremy Bentham*. New York, 1963.

MacLaurin, C., *Mere Mortals*, 2v. New York, 1925.

Macpherson, James, *The Poems of Ossian*. Edinburgh, 1896.

Magnus, Rudolf, *Goethe as a Scientist*. New York, 1949.

MAHAN, A. T., *The Influence of Sea Power upon History, 1660–1783.* New York, 1950.

MAINE, SIR HENRY, *Ancient Law.* Everyman's Library.

MALRAUX, ANDRÉ, *Saturne, Essai sur Goya.* Paris, 1950.

MANN, THOMAS, *Three Essays.* New York, 1932.

MANTOUX, PAUL, *The Industrial Revolution in the Eighteenth Century.* London, 1955.

MANTZIUS, KARL, *History of Theatrical Art*, 6v. New York, 1937.

MARITAIN, JACQUES, *Three Reformers: Luther, Descartes, Rousseau.* London, 1950.

MARMONTEL, JEAN-FRANÇOIS, *Memoirs.* New York, n.d.

——, *Moral Tales.* London, 1895.

MARTIN, HENRI, *The Age of Louis XIV*, 2v. Boston, 1865.

——, *Histoire de France*, 16v. Paris, 1865.

MARTIN, KINGSLEY, *The Rise of French Liberal Thought.* New York, 1956.

MASSON, *Memoirs of Catherine II and Her Court.* Boston: Grolier Society, n.d.

MASSON, PIERRE M., *La Religion de Rousseau*, 3v. Paris, 1916.

MATHIEZ, ALBERT, *The French Revolution.* New York, 1964.

MATTHEWS, BRANDER, *Chief European Dramatists.* Boston, 1916.

MAVOR, JAMES, *Economic History of Russia*, 2v. London, 1925.

McCABE, JOSEPH, *A Candid History of the Jesuits.* New York, 1913.

——, *Crises in the History of the Papacy.* New York, 1916.

McKINNEY, H. D., and ANDERSON, W. R., *Music in History.* Cincinnati, 1940.

MICHELET, JULES, *The French Revolution.* London, 1890.

——, *Histoire de France*, 5v. Paris: Hetzel & Cie., n.d.

MILLAR, OLIVER, *Thomas Gainsborough.* New York, 1959.

MITFORD, NANCY, *Madame de Pompadour.* Penguin Books, 1958.

MOLMENTI, POMPEO, *Tiepolo.* Paris, 1911.

——, *Venice*, Part III: *The Decadence*, 2v. London, 1906.

MONROE, PAUL, *Text-book in the History of Education.* New York, 1928.

MONTAGU, LADY MARY WORTLEY, *Letters and Works*, 2v. London, 1893 f.

MOORE, THOMAS, *Memoirs of the Life of the Rt. Hon. Richard Brinsley Sheridan*, 2v. New York, 1866.

MORE, HANNAH, *Letters.* New York, 1926.

MORLEY, JOHN, *Burke.* New York: Harper & Brothers, n.d.

——, *Burke: A Historical Study.* New York, 1924.

——, *Diderot*, 2v. London, 1923.

——, *Rousseau and His Era*, 2v. London, 1923.

MORNET, DANIEL, *Les Origines intellectuelles de la Révolution française.* Paris, 1933.

MORRIS, R. B., *The Peacemakers: The Great Powers and American Independence.* New York, 1965.

MOSSIKER, FRANCES, *The Queen's Necklace.* New York, 1961.

MOSSNER, ERNEST C., *Life of David Hume.* Austin, Tex., 1954.

MOUSNIER, ROLAND, and LABROUSSE, ERNEST, *Le Dix-huitième Siècle.* Paris, 1953.

MOWAT, R. B., *The Age of Reason.* Boston, 1934.

MÜLLER-LYER, F., *History of Social Development.* London, 1923.

MUMFORD, LEWIS, *The Condition of Man.* New York, 1944.

MUTHER, RICHARD, *History of Modern Painting*, 4v. London, 1907.

NAMIER, SIR LEWIS, *Crossroads of Power*. London, 1962.
———, *The Structure of Politics at the Accession of George III*. London, 1961.
NEILSON, WILLIAM A., *Robert Burns*. Indianapolis, 1917.
NETTLE, PAUL, *Mozart and Masonry*. New York, 1957.
NEVILL, JOHN C., *Thomas Chatterton*. London, 1948.
New Cambridge Modern History [*New CMH*], Vols. VII and VIII. Cambridge, Eng., 1957.
NICOLSON, HAROLD, *The Age of Reason*. London, 1960.
NIETZSCHE, FRIEDRICH, *Thus Spake Zarathustra*. New York, 1915.
NOYES, ALFRED, *Voltaire*. New York, 1936.
NUSSBAUM, F. L., *History of the Economic Institutions of Modern Europe*. New York, 1937.

OECHSLI, WILHELM, *History of Switzerland*. Cambridge, Eng., 1922.
OGG, DAVID, *Europe in the Seventeenth Century*. London, 1956.
Oxford History of Music, 7v. London, 1929 f.

PADOVER, SAUL K., *The Life and Death of Louis XVI*. New York, 1963.
———, *The Revolutionary Emperor: Joseph II*. London, 1934.
PAINE, THOMAS, *The Rights of Man*. Everyman's Library.
PALACHE, JOHN G., *Four Novelists of the Old Regime*. New York, 1926.
PARTON, JAMES, *Daughters of Genius*. Philadelphia, 1888.
———, *Life of Voltaire*, 2v. Boston, 1882.
PASCAL, ROY, *The German Sturm und Drang*. Manchester, Eng., 1953.
PATER, WALTER, *The Renaissance*. Modern Library.
PAULSEN, FRIEDRICH, *German Education*. New York, 1908.
———, *Immanuel Kant*, New York, 1963.
PEARSON, HESKETH, *Johnson and Boswell*. London, 1958.
Penguin Book of German Verse. Baltimore, 1961.
PETERSON, HOUSTON, ed., *Treasury of the World's Great Speeches*. New York, 1954.
PIJOAN, JOSEPH, *History of Art*, 3v. New York, 1927.
PINCHERLE, MARC, *Vivaldi*. New York, 1962.
PIOZZI, HESTER LYNCH THRALE, *Anecdotes of the Late Samuel Johnson*. Cambridge, Eng., 1925.
PLUMB, J. H., *Men and Places*. London, 1963.
POMEAU, RENÉ, *La Religion de Voltaire*. Paris, 1958.
POORE, CHARLES, *Goya*. New York, 1939.
POPE, ARTHUR UPHAM, *An Introduction to Persian Art*. London, 1930.
———, *A Survey of Persian Art*, 6v. Oxford, 1938.
POUGIN, ARTHUR, *A Short History of Russian Music*. London, 1915.
PRATT, W. S., *History of Music*. New York, 1927.
PUTNAM, G. H., *The Censorship of the Church of Rome*, 2v. New York, 1906.

QUENNELL, MARJORIE and CHARLES, *History of Everyday Things in England, 1733–1851*. New York, 1934.

RAMBAUD, ALFRED, *History of Russia*, 3v. Boston, 1879.
RANKE, LEOPOLD, *History of the Popes*, 3v. London, 1878.

Réalités magazine, Paris.

RÉAU, LOUIS, *L'Art russe*, 2v. Paris, 1921.

REDDAWAY, W. F., *Frederick the Great and the Rise of Prussia*. London, 1947.

REID, THOMAS, *Works*, 2v, ed. Sir William Hamilton. Edinburgh, 1852.

RENARD, GEORGES, *Guilds in the Middle Ages*. London, 1918.

————, and WEULERSEE, G., *Life and Work in Modern Europe*. London, 1926.

RESTIF DE LA BRETONNE, NICOLAS-EDME, *Les Contemporaines*. Paris: Charpentier, n.d.

————, *Monsieur Nicolas*, 3v. Paris: Rasmussen, n.d.

————, *Les Nuits de Paris*. New York, 1964.

————, *La Vie de mon père*. Paris, 1924.

REYNOLDS, SIR JOSHUA, *Fifteen Discourses*. Everyman's Library.

————, *Portraits*. New York, 1952.

RICHARD, ERNST, *History of German Civilization*. New York, 1911.

RIEDL, FREDERICK, *History of Hungarian Literature*. New York, 1906.

ROBERTSON, JOHN MACKINNON, *Gibbon*. London, 1925.

————, *Short History of Freethought*, 2v. London, 1914.

ROBINSON, JAMES HARVEY, *Readings in European History*. Boston, 1906.

ROGERS, J. E. THOROLD, *Six Centuries of Work and Wages*. New York, 1890.

ROLLAND, ROMAIN, *Essays in Music*. New York, 1959.

————, *A Musical Tour through the Land of the Past*. London, 1922.

ROSEBERY, ARCHIBALD PHILIP PRIMROSE, 5TH EARL OF, *Pitt*. London, 1908.

ROTH, CECIL, *The Jewish Contribution to Civilization*. Oxford, 1945.

ROUSSEAU, JEAN-JACQUES, *Collection complète des oeuvres de Jean-Jacques Rousseau*, 11v. Neuchâtel, 1775.

————, *Les Confessions de Jean-Jacques Rousseau*, 2v. Lausanne, 1960.

————, *The Confessions of Jean-Jacques Rousseau*. London, n.d.

————, *Émile*. Everyman's Library.

————, *Julia, or The New Eloisa*, 3v. Edinburgh, 1794.

————, *Julie, ou La Nouvelle Héloïse*. Paris: Garnier, n.d.

————, *Politics and the Arts*. Glencoe, Ill., 1960.

————, *Reveries of a Solitary*. London, 1927.

————, *Rousseau juge de Jean-Jacques*, 2v. London, 1782.

————, *The Social Contract and Discourses*. Everyman's Library.

RUSSELL, BERTRAND, *History of Western Philosophy*. New York, 1945.

SAINTE-BEUVE, CHARLES-AUGUSTIN, *English Portraits*. New York, 1875.

————, *Portraits of the Eighteenth Century*, 2v. in 1. New York, 1905.

SAINTSBURY, GEORGE, *History of the French Novel*, 2v. London, 1917.

SANGER, WILLIAM, *History of Prostitution*. New York, 1910.

SAY, LÉON, *Turgot*. Chicago, 1888.

SCHAPIRO, J. SALWYN, *Condorcet and the Rise of Liberalism*. New York, 1934.

SCHILLER, FRIEDRICH, *Works*, 7v. London, 1901.

————, and GOETHE, JOHANN WOLFGANG VON, *Correspondence*, 2v. London, 1877.

————, and KÖRNER, CHRISTIAN GOTTFRIED, *Correspondence*, 3v. London, 1849.

SCHOENFELD, HERMANN, *Women of the Teutonic Nations*. Philadelphia, 1908.

SCHUSTER, M. LINCOLN, *Treasury of the World's Great Letters*. New York, 1940.

SÉE, HENRI, *Economic and Social Conditions in France during the Eighteenth Century*. New York, 1935.

————, *Les Idées politiques en France aux xviiiᵉ siècle*. Paris, 1920.

SEEBOHM, FREDERICK, *The Age of Johnson*. London, 1899.

SÉGUR, MARQUIS DE, *Julie de Lespinasse*. New York, 1927.

————, *Marie Antoinette*. New York, 1928.

SHERIDAN, RICHARD BRINSLEY, *Dramatic Works*. London, 1881.

SHERWIN, OSCAR, *A Gentleman of Wit and Fashion: The Life and Times of George Selwyn*. New York, 1963.

SIME, JAMES, *Lessing*, 2v. London, 1879.

SITWELL, SACHEVERELL, *German Baroque Art*. New York, 1928.

————, *The Netherlands*. London: Botsford, n.d.

————, *Southern Baroque Art*. London, 1951.

SMITH, ADAM, *Inquiry into the Nature and Cause of the Wealth of Nations*, 2v. Everyman's Library.

————, *Moral and Political Philosophy*. New York, 1948.

SMITH, D. E., *History of Mathematics*, 2v. Boston, 1923.

SMITH, NORMAN KEMP, *Commentary to Kant's "Critique of Pure Reason."* London, 1923.

SMITH, PRESERVED, *The Age of the Reformation*. New York, 1920.

————, *History of Modern Culture*, 2v. New York, 1930.

SMOLLETT, TOBIAS, *Travels through France and Italy*. London, 1919.

SNYDER, FRANKLIN B., *Life of Robert Burns*. New York, 1932.

SOMBART, WERNER, *The Jews and Modern Capitalism*. Glencoe, Ill., 1951.

STAËL, MADAME DE, *Germany*, 2v. New York, 1861.

STEPHEN, SIR LESLIE, *History of English Thought in the Eighteenth Century*, 2v. New York, 1902.

STEPHENS, H. MORSE, *The Story of Portugal*. New York, 1893.

STEWART, JOHN HALL, *A Documentary Survey of the French Revolution*. New York, 1951.

STIRLING-MAXWELL, SIR WILLIAM, *Annals of the Artists of Spain*, 4v. London, 1891.

STOKES, HUGH, *Francisco Goya*. New York, 1914.

STRACHEY, LYTTON, *Books and Characters*. New York, 1922.

STRYIENSKI, CASIMIR, *The Eighteenth Century*. London, 1916.

SYKES, SIR PERCY, *History of Persia*, 2v. London, 1921.

TAINE, HIPPOLYTE, *The Ancient Regime*. New York, 1891.

————, *The French Revolution*, 3v. New York, 1931.

————, *History of English Literature*, New York, 1873.

TALMAN, J. L., *Origins of Totalitarian Democracy*. Boston, 1952.

TEXTE, JOSEPH, *Jean-Jacques Rousseau and the Cosmopolitan Spirit in Literature*. London, 1899.

THACKERAY, WILLIAM MAKEPEACE, *English Humourists*. Boston: Dana Estes, n.d.

————, *The Four Georges*. Boston: Dana Estes, n.d.

THOMSON, DERICK S., *The Gaelic Sources of Macpherson's "Ossian."* Edinburgh, 1951.

TICKNOR, GEORGE, *History of Spanish Literature*, 3v. New York, 1854.

Time magazine, New York.

TOCQUEVILLE, ALEXIS DE, *L'Ancien Régime*. Oxford, 1927.

TORREY, NORMAN L., *The Spirit of Voltaire*. New York, 1938.

TOTH, KARL, *Woman and Rococo in France*. Philadelphia, 1931.

TOYNBEE, ARNOLD J., *A Study of History*, 10v. Oxford, 1935 f.

TRAILL, HENRY DUFF, ed., *Social England*, 6v. New York, 1902.

TREITSCHKE, HEINRICH VON, *Life of Frederick the Great*. New York, 1915.

TREVOR-ROPER, H. R., *Historical Essays*. London, 1957.

TURBERVILLE, A. S., ed., *Johnson's England*, 2v. Oxford, Eng., 1952.

TURGOT, ANNE-ROBERT-JACQUES, BARON DE L'AULNE, *Reflections on the Formation and the Distribution of Wealth*. New York, 1898.

ÜBERWEG, FRIEDRICH, *History of Philosophy*, 2v. New York, 1871.

UNGAR, FREDERICK, *Friedrich Schiller: An Anthology*. New York, 1960.

———, *Goethe's World View, Presented in His Reflections and Maxims*. New York, 1963.

USHER, A. P., *An Introduction to the Industrial History of England*. Boston, 1920.

VAIHINGER, HANS, *The Philosophy of "As If."* New York, 1924.

VALLENTIN, ANTONIA, *This I Saw: The Life and Times of Goya*. New York, 1957.

VAMBÉRY, ÁRMIN, *The Story of Hungary*. New York, 1894.

VAN DOREN, MARK, *Anthology of World Poetry*. New York, 1928.

VAUGHN, C. E., *Political Writings of Rousseau*, 2v. Cambridge, Eng., 1915.

VAUSSARD, MAURICE, *La Vie quotidienne en Italie au xviiie siècle*. Paris: Hachette, n.d.

VENTURI, LIONELLO, *Italian Painting from Caravaggio to Modigliani*. New York, 1959.

VICO, GIAMBATTISTA, *Autobiography*. Ithaca, N. Y., 1944.

———, *The New Science*. Ithaca, N. Y., 1948.

VIGÉE-LEBRUN, MME. MARIE-ANNE-ÉLISABETH, *Memoirs*. New York, 1927.

VOLTAIRE, *Age of Louis XIV*. Everyman's Library.

———, *Age of Louis XV*, 2v. Glasgow, 1771.

———, *Love Letters of Voltaire to His Niece*, ed. and tr. Theodore Besterman. London, 1958.

———, *Oeuvres complètes*. Paris, 1825 f.

———, *Philosophical Dictionary*, in *Works*, Vols. III–VI.

———, *Works*, 44v. in 22. New York, 1927.

——— and FREDERICK THE GREAT, *Letters*. New York, 1927.

WALISZEWSKI, K., *History of Russian Literature*. New York, 1900.

———, *Peter the Great*. London, 1898.

———, *Poland the Unknown*. London, 1919.

———, *The Romance of an Empress: The Life of Catherine II of Russia*. New York, 1929.

WALPOLE, HORACE, *Letters*, 9v. London, 1880.

———, *Memoirs of the Last Ten Years of the Reign of George the Second*, 2v. London, 1822.

———, *Memoirs of the Reign of King George III*, 4v. London, 1894.

WARWICK, CHARLES F., *Mirabeau and the French Revolution*. Philadelphia, 1905.

WATERHOUSE, ELLIS, *Gainsborough*. London, 1958.

———, *Reynolds*. London, 1941.

WATSON, J. STEVEN, *The Reign of George III*. Oxford, 1960.

WATSON, PAUL B., *Some Women of France*. New York, 1936.

WEBB, SIDNEY and BEATRICE, *History of Trade Unionism*. New York, 1920.

WEINSTOCK, HERBERT, *Handel*. New York, 1959.

WESTERMARCK, EDWARD, *Origin and Development of the Moral Ideas*, 2v. London, 1917.

WHARTON, GRACE and PHILIP, *The Wits and Beaux of Society*, 2v. Philadelphia, 1860.

WHERRY, E. M., *Commentary on the Quran*, with Sale's translation, 4v. London, 1896.

WIELAND, CHRISTOPH MARTIN, *History of Agathon*, 4v. London, 1773.

———, *Oberon*. New York, 1940.

WIENER, LEO, *Anthology of Russian Literature*, 2v. New York, 1902.

WILENSKI, R. H., *English Painting*. London, 1946.

WILHELMINE, MARGRAVINE OF BAYREUTH, *Memoirs*. London, 1887.

WILLIAMS, H. S., *History of Science*, 5v. New York, 1909.

WILSON, A. M., *Diderot: The Testing Years, 1713–59*. New York, 1957.

WILSON, E. C., *Immanuel Kant*, New Haven, 1925.

WILSON, P. W., *William Pitt the Younger*. New York, 1934.

WINCKELMANN, JOHANN JOACHIM, *History of Ancient Art*, 4v. in 2. Boston, 1880.

WITTE, WILLIAM, *Schiller*. Oxford, 1949.

———, *Schiller and Burns*. Oxford, 1959.

WOLF, A., *History of Science, Technology, and Philosophy in the Eighteenth Century*. New York, 1939.

WYZEWA, T. DE, and SAINT-FOIX, G. DE, *W. A. Mozart*, 5v. Paris, 1936.

YOUNG, ARTHUR, *Travels in France during the Years 1787, 1788, 1789*. London, 1906.

ZWEIG, STEFAN, *Marie Antoinette*. New York, 1933.

Notes

CHAPTER I

1. Rousseau, *The Confessions of Jean-Jacques Rousseau*, I, 22.
2. *Ibid.*, 4.
3. I, 156-57; II, 70, 321.
4. Saintsbury, *History of the French Novel*, I, 391.
5. Sainte-Beuve, *Portraits of the 18th Century*, I, 174.
6. Lanson, G., *Histoire de la littérature française*, 801.
7. *Encyclopaedia Britannica*, XIX, 587a.
8. Rousseau, *The Confessions*, I, 3.
9. *Ibid.*, 8.
10. 9.
11. 11.
12. 13.
13. 9.
14. 16.
15. 22.
16. 41.
17. 44.
18. *Ibid.*; Lemaître, *Jean-Jacques Rousseau*, 290; Mann, Thomas, *Three Essays*, 156.
19. Masson, P. M., *La Religion de Rousseau*, I, 51 f.
20. Rousseau, *The Confessions*, I, 69.
21. Rousseau, *Les Confessions*, I, 140.
22. *The Confessions*, I, 117-19.
23. *Ibid.*, 76.
24. 76.
25. 106.
26. 91.
27. 92.
28. 96.
29. 104.
30. 107.
31. 116.
32. 122.
33. 130.
34. 154.
35. 138.
36. 148.
37. 160.
38. 178.
39. *Les Confessions*, I, 238.
40. *Ibid.*; *The Confessions*, I, 178.
41. *Ibid.*, 224.
42. 195.
43. Josephson, *J.-J. Rousseau*, 111.
44. *Ibid.*, 113-14.
45. *The Confessions*, I, 247, 250.
46. *Ibid.*, 259.
47. 262.
48. 265.
49. *Ibid.*
50. 296.
51. 295.
52. 300.
53. Josephson, 132.
54. *Ibid.*, 133.
55. *The Confessions*, I, 305.
56. Letter of Frederick, 1762, in Gooch, *Frederick the Great*, 145.
57. *The Confessions*, I, 309.
58. *Ibid.*, 310.
59. *Ibid.*, II, 139.
60. Martin, Henri, *Histoire de France*, XVI, 83; Collins, J. C., *Bolingbroke, and Voltaire in England*, 209.
61. Josephson, 140.
62. Morley, John, *Rousseau and His Era*, I, 127; Hendel, C. W., *Citizen of Geneva*, 208.
63. Diderot, *Essai sur les règnes de Claude et Néron*, Ch. 67.
64. Marmontel, *Memoirs*, I, 321.
65. *The Confessions*, II, 21.
66. *Ibid.*, 32.
67. Rousseau, *Discourse on Arts and Sciences*, in *Social Contract and Discourses*, 130.
68. *Ibid.*, 132.
69. 134.
70. 134.
71. 146.
72. 151.
73. 142.
74. 151.
75. 135.
76. 139.
77. 153.
78. 153.
79. Rousseau, preface to *Narcisse*.
80. Michelet, *Histoire de France*, V, 371.
81. Grimm, *Correspondance littéraire*, IX, 49.
82. Bayle, Pierre, *Réponse aux questions d'un provincial*.
83. Rousseau, *Reveries of a Solitary*, Book VI, pp. 127-32.
84. *The Confessions*, II, 21.
85. Lemaître, 92.
86. Letter of July 15, 1756, in Hendel, *Citizen of Geneva*, 142.
87. Marmontel, *Memoirs*, I, 321.
88. *The Confessions*, II, 34.
89. *Ibid.*, 48.
90. 49.
91. 51.
92. 56; Goncourt, E. and J. de, *Madame de Pompadour*, 143.
93. Faguet, *Rousseau artiste*, 192.
94. Grimm, II, 307.

95. Rousseau, *Reveries*, 111.
96. In Faguet, *Rousseau artiste*, 193.
97. Musée, St.-Quentin.
98. Levey, Michael, *Painting in 18th-Century Venice*, 155.
99. Marmontel, *Memoirs*, I, 169.
100. Épinay, Mme. d', *Memoirs and Correspondence*, II, 52.
101. *Ibid.*; Masson, *La Religion de Rousseau*, I, 184-85.
102. Preface to *Narcisse*.
103. Masson, I, 182.
104. Michelet, *Histoire de France*, V, 428.
105. *The Confessions*, II, 63.
106. *Ibid.*, 58.
107. Rousseau, *Discourse on the Origin of Inequality*, in *Social Contract . . .* , 157.
108. *Ibid.*, 159.
109. 160.
110. 239.
111. Nietzsche, *Thus Spake Zarathustra*, 129.
112. Rousseau, *Discourse on the Origin of Inequality*, *loc. cit.*, 181.
113. *Ibid.*, 169.
114. 175.
115. 222.
116. Rousseau, *Social Contract*, Book I, Ch. ii.
117. Second *Discourse*, in *Social Contract . . .* , 214.
118. *Ibid.*, 207.
119. 220-22.
120. 238.
121. 242-44.
122. *Rousseau juge de Jean-Jacques*, in Cassirer, *The Question of Rousseau*, 54.
123. Second *Discourse*, *loc. cit.*, 236.
124. End of second *Discourse*.
125. Mumford, Lewis, *The Condition of Man*, 275.
126. Helvétius, *Treatise on Man*, II, xx.
127. Duclos, *Considérations sur les moeurs*, 11.
128. Lemaître, 122.
129. Second *Discourse*, *loc. cit.*, 175, 246.
130. Voltaire, *Works*, XXIa, 227-30.
131. *Ibid.*
132. *The Confessions*, II, 65.
133. *Social Contract*, 271.
134. *Ibid.*, 272.
135. 281.
136. 269.
137. 262.
138. 253.
139. 260.
140. 256.
141. *The Confessions*, II, 40.
142. *Ibid.*
143. Masson, I, 181.
144. Sainte-Beuve, *Portraits of the 18th Century*, II, 181.
145. *The Confessions*, II, 40.
146. Grimm, *Correspondance*, II, 239.
147. Sainte-Beuve, II, 195n.
148. *Ibid.*, 180.

149. 191.
150. 213.
151. Morley, *Rousseau*, I, 272.
152. Macdonald, Frederika, *Jean Jacques Rousseau*, II, 83.
153. Source lost.
154. Toth, Karl, *Woman and Rococo in France*.
155. Hobbes, *De Corpore*, Ch. xxv.
156. Toth, 194; Josephson, 194; Faguet (*Vie de Rousseau*, 214) thought Mme. d'Épinay had been infected by Dupin de Francueil.
157. Épinay, II, 85.
158. *Ibid.*, 130.
159. Josephson, 149.
160. *The Confessions*, II, 81.
161. *Ibid.*, 66.
162. Letter to Malesherbes, Jan. 26, 1762.
163. Épinay, II, 128; Sainte-Beuve, II, 187; Morley, *Rousseau*, I, 274.

CHAPTER II

1. Frederick the Great, *Mémoires*, I, 4.
2. Frederick the Great, *Histoire de la guerre de Sept Ans*, 388.
3. Dorn, W. L., *Competition for Empire*, 306.
4. Mahan, A. T., *Influence of Sea Power upon History*, 74.
5. Aldis, Janet, *Madame Geoffrin*, 200.
6. Goodwin, A., *The European Nobility in the 18th Century*, 113.
7. Coxe, Wm., *History of the House of Austria*, III, 346.
8. Walpole, H., *Memoirs of . . . the Reign of George the Second*, II, 73; Marmontel, *Memoirs*, I, 175.
9. Carlyle, *History of Friedrich the Second*, V, 72.
10. Levron, Jacques, *Pompadour*, 174.
11. Treitschke, H. von, *Life of Frederick the Great*, 149.
12. Mann, Thos., *Three Essays*, 163.
13. Dorn, *Competition for Empire*, 15.
14. Treitschke, *Frederick*, 181.
15. Carlyle, *Friedrich*, V, 263-69; Martin, H., *Histoire de France*, XV, 497; Reddaway, *Frederick the Great*, 198; Coxe, *History of . . . Austria*, III, 370.
16. Reddaway, 199.
17. Gooch, G. P., *Frederick the Great*, 334.
18. Reddaway, 201.
19. Dorn, 300; *Cambridge Modern History*, VI, 251.
20. Gooch, *Frederick*, 334.
21. *CMH*, VI, 402.
22. Coxe, *History of . . . Austria*, III, 369.
23. *Ibid.*
24. Padover, *The Revolutionary Emperor*, 33.
25. Gooch, *Frederick*, 43.

26. Coxe, 379.
27. Sainte-Beuve, *Portraits of the 18th Century*, II, 369; Carlyle, *Friedrich*, V, 479.
28. *Ibid.*, 523.
29. 527.
30. 534; Sainte-Beuve, II, 373
31. *Ibid.*, I, 219; Brandes, *Voltaire*, II, 77.
32. Sainte-Beuve, II, 372.
33. Martin, H., *France*, XV, 522.
34. Michelet, *Histoire de France*, V, 402.
35. Dorn, 323.
36. Michelet, V, 402.
37. Carlyle, VI, 22.
38. *Ibid.*, V, 547.
39. Jahn, *Life of Mozart*, I, 47.
40. Carlyle, VI, 42; Robinson, J. H., *Readings in European History*, 395.
41. Macaulay, *Critical and Historical Essays*, II, 173.
42. Acton, Lord, *Lectures on Modern History*, 297.
43. Carlyle, VI, 63.
44. Martin, XV, 527.
45. *Ibid.*, 528.
46. Carlyle, VI, 63.
47. Dorn, 338.
48. Carlyle, VI, 115.
49. *CMH*, VI, 290.
50. Wilhelmine, *Memoirs*, vii.
51. *Ibid.*, ix.
52. Frederick, *Guerre de Sept Ans*, 44.
53. Carlyle, VI, 265.
54. Coxe, *History*, III, 407.
55. Voltaire and Frederick the Great, *Letters*, 259.
56. Carlyle, VI, 322, 386.
57. Martin, XV, 533.
58. Dorn, 363.
59. Voltaire and Frederick, *Letters*, 262; Carlyle, VI, 399.
60. Martin, XV, 565.
61. Voltaire and Frederick, *Letters*, 271.
62. Coxe, III, 425.
63. Dec. 25, 1761, by the Russian calendar.
64. Frederick, *Guerre de Sept Ans*, 229.
65. *Ibid.*, 227.
66. 295.
67. Gooch, *Frederick*, 64.
68. Frederick, *Guerre de Sept Ans*, 305.
69. Macaulay, *Essays*, II, 185.
70. Voltaire and Frederick, *Letters*, 245; Mann, *Three Essays*, 210.
71. Gooch, *Frederick*, 64.
72. Sainte-Beuve, *Portraits of the 18th Century*, II, 192.

CHAPTER III

1. Du Hausset, *Memoirs of Mme. de Pompadour*, 97.
2. Goncourts, *Madame de Pompadour*, 338-42.
3. *Ibid.*, 200.
4. Aldis, *Madame Geoffrin*, 129.
5. Lewis, D. B. Wyndham, *Four Favorites*, 42.
6. Goncourts, *Mme. de Pompadour*, 317.
7. *Ibid.*, 319; Sainte-Beuve, *Portraits of the 18th Century*, I, 451.
8. Mitford, Nancy, *Madame de Pompadour*, 234.
9. Levron, Jacques, *Pompadour*, 260.
10. Bancroft, George, *Literary and Historical Miscellanies*, 91.
11. See Stryienski, *Eighteenth Century*, 189.
12. Mitford, *Pompadour*, 234.
13. Ercole, Lucienne, *Gay Court Life*, 236.
14. Mitford, 234-35.
15. Taine, H., *Ancient Regime*, 338.
16. Tocqueville, *L'Ancien Régime*, 181-82; Martin, H., *France*, XVI, 236.
17. Barnes, H. E., *Economic History of the Western World*, 253.
18. Nussbaum, F. L., *History of the Economic Institutions of Modern Europe*, 213.
19. Martin, H., *Age of Louis XIV*, I, 54.
20. Mousnier and Labrousse, *Le Dix-huitième Siècle*, 135.
21. Du Hausset, *Memoirs*, 27.
22. Voltaire, *Age of Louis XIV*, 352.
23. Rousseau, *La Nouvelle Héloïse*, in Ducros, Louis, *French Society in the 18th Century*, 193.
24. Parton, James, *Life of Voltaire*, II, 329.
25. Voltaire, *Works*, VIIb, 56.
26. Goldoni, *Memoirs*, 359.
27. Taine, *Ancient Regime*, 308.
28. Cru, R. L., *Diderot as a Disciple of English Thought*, 61.
29. Ducros, *French Society*, 325.
30. Martin, H., *France*, XVI, 163; Acton, *Lectures on Modern History*, 326.
31. Higgs, Henry, *The Physiocrats*, 18.
32. Say, Léon, *Turgot*, 47, 67.
33. Turgot, *Éloge de Gournai*, in Martin, *France*, XVI, 165.
34. Mirabeau *père* in Higgs, 21
35. Higgs, 24.
36. Wolf, A., *History of Science, Technology, and Philosophy in the 18th Century*, 730.
37. Higgs, 37.
38. Warwick, C. F., *Mirabeau and the French Revolution*, 146.
39. Higgs, 68.
40. In Sée, Henri, *Les Idées politiques en France au xviiie siècle*, 161.
41. Pomeau, René, *La Religion de Voltaire*, 405.
42. Hume, letter to Morellet, July 10, 1769.
43. Voltaire, *Works*, Ib, 247-48, 265.
44. In Gay, Peter, *Voltaire's Politics*, 169n.
45. Smith, Adam, *Wealth of Nations*, Book IV, Ch. ix.
46. Higgs, 135.

47. In Frankel, Charles, *The Faith of Reason*, 121.
48. Bury, J. B., *The Idea of Progress*, 157.
49. Say, *Turgot*, 27.
50. Dakin, *Turgot*, 10.
51. Say, 29.
52. Dakin, 19.
53. Turgot, *Reflections on the Formation and the Distribution of Wealth*, No. 6.
54. *Ibid.*, No. 68.
55. See *The Age of Voltaire*, Ch. xviii, Sec. III.
56. Morelly, *Code de la nature*, in Hearnshaw, F. J., ed., *Social and Political Ideas of Some Great French Thinkers of the Age of Reason*, 224.
57. In Tocqueville, *L'Ancien Régime*, 173.
58. Martin, H., *France*, XVI, 147.
59. In Martin, Kingsley, *The Rise of French Liberal Thought*, 254.
60. *Ibid.*
61. 256.
62. Talman, J. L., *Origins of Totalitarian Democracy*, 58.
63. Hazard, Paul, *European Thought in the 18th Century*, 178.
64. Hearnshaw, 238.
65. Jaurès, Jean, *Histoire socialiste de la Révolution française*, I, 158.
66. Martin, Kingsley, 247.
67. Hearnshaw, 243.
68. *Ibid.*, 244.
69. Mornet, Daniel, *Les Origines intellectuelles de la Révolution française*, 233.
70. Hearnshaw, 217.
71. Marquis d'Argenson in Taine, *Ancient Regime*, 82.
72. Crocker, L. G., *The Embattled Philosopher*, 78.
73. Ducros, 81.
74. Sainte-Beuve, *Portraits of the 18th Century*, I, 452.
75. Loomis, Stanley, *Du Barry*, 33.
76. *Ibid.*, 57.
77. Ercole, 263-66.
78. Parton, II, 394.
79. Loomis, *Du Barry*, 175.
80. Michelet, *Histoire*, V, 454.
81. Diderot, *Salons*, in *Oeuvres complètes*, II, 357.
82. Loomis, 89.
83. Lefebvre, *Coming of the French Revolution*, 41.
84. Stryienski, *Eighteenth Century*, 162.
85. *Ibid.*, 163.
86. Lecky, W. E., *History of England in the 18th Century*, V, 327.
87. Voltaire, *Works*, XVIa, 234.
88. *Ibid.*, 232.
89. 236.
90. Dorn, 352.
91. Voltaire, XVIa, 231.
92. *Ibid.*, 226.

93. Cobban, A., *History of Modern France*, I, 127.
94. Voltaire, XVIa, 227.
95. See *Age of Voltaire*, pp. 765 f.
96. Martin, H., *France*, XVI, 243.
97. *Ibid.*
98. Voltaire, letter to Thieriot, Aug. 9, 1769.
99. Crocker, *Embattled Philosopher*, 352.
100. Martin, H., XVI, 281.
101. *Ibid.*
102. 283.
103. Voltaire, letter to Mignot, June 24, 1771.
104. Crocker, *Embattled Philosopher*, 352.
105. Walpole, H., letters of Oct. 19 and 28, 1765.
106. Collins, J. C., *Bolingbroke . . . 47*; Cumming, Ian, *Helvétius*, 168.
107. Grimm, *Correspondance*, January, 1768.
108. Loomis, 131.
109. *Ibid.*, 140.
110. Du Hausset, *Memoirs*, 36.
111. *Ibid.*
112. Loomis, 151.
113. Martin, H., *France*, XVI, 308.
114. Loomis, 154.

CHAPTER IV

1. Funck-Brentano, F. (*L'Ancien Régime*, 180), gives another form: "*Qui n'a pas vécu avant 1789 n'a pas connu la douceur de vivre.*"
2. Wilson, A. M., *Diderot: The Testing Years*, 135.
3. Hazard, *European Thought*, 256.
4. Goncourts, *Woman of the 18th Century*, 112.
5. Crébillon *fils*, *The Sofa*, introduction.
6. Ségur, *Julie de Lespinasse*, 237.
7. Goncourts, *Woman*, 143.
8. *Ibid.*, 142; Michelet, *Histoire*, V, 454.
9. Ellis, Havelock, *Sexual Inversion*, 207.
10. Westermarck, *Origin and Development of the Moral Ideas*, II, 482.
11. Rousseau, *Émile*, 145.
12. Smollett, *Travels through France and Italy*, Letter xv.
13. Toth, *Woman and Rococo*, 271.
14. Casanova, *Memoirs*, I, 51.
15. Boehn, *Modes and Manners*, IV, 196.
16. *Ibid.*, 211.
17. Ducros, *French Society*, 340.
18. La Fontainerie, *French Liberalism and Education*, 63.
19. Vigée-Lebrun, Mme., *Memoirs*, 27.
20. Láng, *Music in Western Civilization*, 722.
21. Jahn, *Life of Mozart*, I, 38.
22. Rolland, *Essays in Music*, 194.
23. Voltaire, *Mélanges littéraires*, in Tiersot, Jean, *Gluck and the Encyclopedists*.
24. Goncourts, *Woman*, 87.
25. Taine, *Ancient Regime*, 154.
26. Herold, *Love in Five Temperaments*, 264.

27. *Ibid.*, 267.
28. 277.
29. Diderot, *Paradox of Acting*, 15.
30. Herold, *Love in Five Temperaments*, 281.
31. *Ibid.*, p. 288.
32. 326.
33. Mornet, *Origines intellectuelles*, 121.
34. In Aldis, *Madame Geoffrin*, 223.
35. Marmontel, *Memoirs*, I, 102, 120.
36. Marmontel, *Moral Tales*, I, 18.
37. In Martin, Kingsley, *Rise of French Liberal Thought*, 101.
38. Hazard, 63.
39. Brunetière, *Manual of the History of French Literature*, 371.
40. Faniel, *French Art of the 18th Century*, 119D.
41. Litchfield, *Illustrated History of Furniture*, 240.
42. This statue has disappeared.
43. Letter of May 11, 1770.
44. Grimm, *Correspondance*, VII, 23.
45. Diderot, *Salons*, I, 370.
46. Louvre. Another form in Huntington Art Gallery, San Marino, Calif.
47. Louvre.
48. Huntington Art Gallery.
49. Louvre.
50. In Muther, *History of Modern Painting*, I, 98.
51. *Ibid.*
52. Dilke, Lady E., *French Architects and Sculptors of the 18th Century*, 36.
53. Diderot, *Dialogues*, 163.
54. Vigée-Lebrun, 160.
55. Both in the Louvre.
56. Goncourts, *French 18th-Century Painters*, 213.
57. *Ibid.*, 233.
58. Prado.
59. Turin.
60. Victoria and Albert Museum.
61. Musée Condé, Chantilly.
62. National Gallery, Edinburgh.
63. Goncourts, *French Painters*, 216.
64. Louvre.
65. Louvre.
66. Wallace Collection.
67. Louvre.
68. Diderot, *Salons*, I, 243.
69. Louvre.
70. Goncourts, 224.
71. *Ibid.*, 228.
72. 239.
73. École des Beaux-Arts, Paris.
74. Goncourts, 266.
75. Catalogue of the Fragonard Exhibition, Bern, 1954, Plate XIII.
76. Diderot, *Salons*, I, 544.
77. Leningrad.
78. All in the Louvre.
79. Louvre.
80. Louvre.

81. Hume in Mossner, *Life of David Hume*, 449.
82. Aldis, 11.
83. Batiffol, *The Great Literary Salons*, 155.
84. *Ibid.*, 131.
85. Goncourts, *Woman*, 321.
86. Musée de Montpellier.
87. Batiffol, 158.
88. Aldis, 198.
89. Toth, 269.
90. Aldis, 287.
91. *Ibid.*, 356.
92. 355.
93. 357.
94. Koven, Anna de, *Horace Walpole and Mme. du Deffand*, 81; Lespinasse, Julie de, *Letters*, introd. by Sainte-Beuve, 25.
95. Ségur, *Julie de Lespinasse*, 129.
96. Bertrand, J., *D'Alembert*, 101.
97. *Ibid.*, 59-60.
98. 86.
99. Koven, 76.
100. Ségur, *Lespinasse*, 98.
101. *Ibid.*, 103.
102. 102.
103. 104.
104. 83.
105. 125.
106. Du Deffand, Marquise, *Lettres à Voltaire*, 12.
107. *Ibid.*, 26.
108. Ségur, *Lespinasse*, 132.
109. *Ibid.*, 133.
110. 134.
111. In Lespinasse, *Letters*, 1.
112. *Ibid.*, 33.
113. Mossner, *Life of Hume*, 477.
114. Marmontel, *Memoirs*, I, 259.
115. Miranda in *The Tempest*.
116. Ségur, *Lespinasse*, 336.
117. *Ibid.*, 293.
118. 296.
119. 295.
120. Lespinasse, 44 (letter of May 15, 1773).
121. *Ibid.*, 45 (May 23, 1773).
122. In Ford, Miriam de, *Love Children*, 212.
123. Lespinasse, 52.
124. Ségur, *Lespinasse*, 211, 321-22.
125. *Ibid.*, 271.
126. Lespinasse, 204.
127. Ségur, 322.
128. Lespinasse, 234 (letter of July 3, 1775).
129. Ségur, 387.
130. Lespinasse, 327.
131. Ségur, 395.
132. *Ibid.*, 398.

CHAPTER V

1. Chaponnière, *Voltaire chez les calvinistes*, 202.
2. Parton, *Life of Voltaire*, II, 262.
3. *Ibid.*, 263-65.

4. Besterman in Voltaire, *Love Letters to His Niece*, 9.
5. Chaponnière, 203.
6. Parton, II, 475.
7. Letter of July 4, 1782, in Desnoiresterres, *Voltaire*, VI, 288.
8. *Boswell on the Grand Tour: Germany and Switzerland*, 283.
9. *Ibid.*, 293.
10. 302.
11. Low, D. M., *Edward Gibbon*, 144.
12. Desnoiresterres, VI, 290; Chaponnière, 202.
13. Parton, *Life of Voltaire*, II, 481.
14. *Ibid.*
15. Desnoiresterres, I, 131.
16. Noyes, A., *Voltaire*, 550.
17. Torrey, N. L., *The Spirit of Voltaire*, 189.
18. Desnoiresterres, VII, 335.
19. *Ibid.*, 335.
20. Parton, II, 480.
21. Voltaire, *Philosophical Dictionary*, art. "Malady—Medicine."
22. Molière, *Le Malade imaginaire*.
23. Chaponnière, 202; Parton, II, 480.
24. Voltaire, art. "Malady."
25. Parton, I, 529.
26. Chaponnière, 202.
27. Brandes, *Voltaire*, II, 312.
28. Parton, II, 263.
29. Desnoiresterres, V, 324.
30. Parton, II, 471.
31. Chaponnière, 202.
32. Lanson, *Voltaire*, 197.
33. Desnoiresterres, VII, 482.
34. Torrey, *Spirit of Voltaire*, 201.
35. Faguet, *Literary History of France*, 507.
36. Lanson, *Voltaire*, 197.
37. Torrey, 34.
38. Lanson, 197.
39. Voltaire, *Oeuvres complètes*, XXXIX, 546.
40. *Works*, VIIIb, 286.
41. *Philosophical Dictionary*, art. "Ancients and Moderns."
42. Michelet, *Histoire*, V, 426.
43. Parton, II, 489.
44. Brunetière, 361.
45. Torrey, 176.
46. Letter of Mar. 12, 1766.
47. Voltaire, *Age of Louis XV*, II, Ch. xxxix.
48. Lanfrey, *L'Église et les philosophes*, 335.
49. Letter of Frederick to Voltaire, June 10, 1759.
50. Letter of July 2, 1759.
51. Voltaire and Frederick, *Letters*, 266.
52. *Ibid.*, 358.
53. 363.
54. Brandes, II, 241.
55. Desnoiresterres, VI, 391.
56. *Phil. Dict.*, art. "Peter the Great."

57. Robespierre, speech of 18 Floréal, Year II, in Hazard, *European Thought*, 265.
58. Parton, II, 260.
59. Chaponnière, 238.
60. Gibbon, *Memoirs*, 154n.
61. Parton, II, 556.
62. Voltaire, *Mémoires*, in Parton, I, 141.
63. Letter to Frederick, January, 1737, in Voltaire and Frederick, 41.
64. *Phil. Dict.*, art. "Property."
65. *Ibid.*
66. *Ibid.*
67. Letter to Dr. Daquir in Sainte-Beuve, *Portraits of the 18th Century*, I, 228.
68. *Phil. Dict.*, art. "Equality."
69. Lacroix, Paul, *The Eighteenth Century in France*, 47.
70. *Phil. Dict.*, art. "Country" ("Pays").
71. Voltaire, *L'A, B, C*, in Sée, *Les Idées politiques*, 84.
72. *Phil. Dict.*, art. "Laws."
73. *Essai sur les moeurs*, xii, 161, in Gay, *Voltaire's Politics*, 181.
74. *Mérope*, Act. II, Sc. ii.
75. Michelet, *French Revolution*, 47.
76. In Parton, II, 544.
77. Desnoiresterres, VI, 240.
78. Casanova, *Memoirs*, II, 406-7.
79. Letter of Oct. 28, 1773.
80. *Phil. Dict.*, art. "Democracy."
81. Letter of Sept. 20, 1760.
82. In Gay, 236.
83. *Phil. Dict.*, art. "Government," Sec. 3.
84. *Ibid.*, Sec. 6, slightly transposed.
85. *Phil. Dict.*, art. "Equality."
86. Voltaire, *Age of Louis XIV*, 415.
87. Quoted in Black, *Art of History*, 48.
88. *Phil. Dict.*, art. "Law, Civil and Ecclesiastical."
89. In Hearnshaw, *Social . . . Ideas of Some Great French Thinkers*, 157.
90. Art. "Execution."
91. Art. "Torture."
92. In Gay, 307.
93. Art. "Wit."
94. Sainte-Beuve, *Portraits of the 18th Century*, II, 146.
95. *Ibid.*, 228.
96. Black, 29.
97. *Candide*, last chapter.
98. In Pomeau, 261.
99. Desnoiresterres, V, 24.
100. Brandes, *Voltaire*, I, 118.
101. Torrey, 10.
102. Letter of Aug. 28, 1751.
103. Brandes, *Creative Spirits of the 19th Century*, 138.
104. *Ibid.*, 142; Höffding, H., *Jean Jacques Rousseau and His Philosophy*, 80; Desnoiresterres, VI, 310.
105. *Ibid.*
106. Mme. de Graffigny in Parton, I, 392.

107. Hume, letter of Apr. 26, 1764, in Gay, 81.
108. Torrey, 131.
109. Letter to Thieriot, Dec. 10, 1738.
110. Torrey, 131.
111. *Ibid.*
112. Voltaire, *English Notebooks*, in Gay, 353.
113. *Phil. Dict.*, art. "Solomon."
114. Desnoiresterres, V, 157; Parton I, 106.
115. See letter of March, 1737, to Moussinot, in *Works*, XXIa, 190.
116. Parton, II, 520.
117. *Ibid.*, I, 507.
118. *Ibid.*, 144.
119. Morley, *Voltaire*, in Voltaire, *Works*, XXIb, 96.
120. Parton, II, 600.
121. In Noyes, *Voltaire*, 536.
122. Voltaire, *Age of Louis XIV*, 61.
123. Pomeau, 462.
124. Desnoiresterres, II, 239.
125. In Torrey, 197.
126. Desnoiresterres, VI, 287.
127. Torrey, 91.

CHAPTER VI

1. Rousseau, *Émile*, p. 371.
2. *The Confessions*, II, 84.
3. Josephson, 190.
4. *Ibid.; The Confessions*, II, 84.
5. *The Confessions*, II, 88.
6. Diderot, *Le Fils naturel*, Act. IV, Sc. iii.
7. Brockway, W., and Winer, B., *Second Treasury of the World's Great Letters*, 195.
8. *Ibid.*, 201.
9. *The Confessions*, II, 107.
10. *Ibid.*, 99.
11. Rousseau, *Collection complète des oeuvres*, I, 424.
12. *Ibid.*, I, 428.
13. 431.
14. 438.
15. 442.
16. 449.
17. 443.
18. Desnoiresterres, V, 141.
19. *The Confessions*, II, 105.
20. Épinay, Mme. d', *Memoirs*, II, 329.
21. *Ibid.*, 334.
22. *The Confessions*, II, 102.
23. Josephson, 213.
24. *The Confessions*, II, 114-15, 110.
25. *Ibid.*, 113.
26. 114-16.
27. Josephson, 220.
28. *The Confessions*, II, 118.
29. *Ibid.*, 121.
30. Sainte-Beuve, *Portraits of the 18th Century*, II, 195.
31. *The Confessions*, II, 133. Several of Mme. d'Houdetot's letters to Rousseau survive,

and a few of his to her; see Martin, H., *France*, XVI, 91n.
32. *The Confessions*, II, 136.
33. Sainte-Beuve, II, 213.
34. *The Confessions*, II, 144.
35. *Ibid.*, 146.
36. 147.
37. Épinay, III, 130-32; Josephson, 249.
38. Épinay, III, 140-42.
39. *Ibid.*, 186.
40. *The Confessions*, II, 154.
41. Josephson, 252.
42. *The Confessions*, II, 155.
43. Letter of Nov. 26, 1758, in Hendel, *Citizen of Geneva*, 160.
44. Lemaître, *Rousseau*, 174.
45. Josephson, 308.
46. *The Confessions*, II, 165.
47. Rousseau, *Politics and the Arts*, 7.
48. *Ibid.*, 121.
49. 125 26.
50. *The Confessions*, II, 165.
51. Torrey, *Spirit of Voltaire*, 97, 105.
52. Hendel, *Citizen of Geneva*, 169; Desnoiresterres, VI, 85.
53. Chaponnière, 169; Josephson, 278.
54. Masson, P. M., *La Religion de Rousseau*, III, 33.
55. Josephson, 279.
56. *Rousseau juge de Jean-Jacques*, Part I, Letter I.
57. Letter II.
58. Letter IV.
59. Letter V.
60. Letter XIV.
61. *Rousseau juge*, p. 139.
62. *Ibid.*, Part IV, Letter XVII.
63. Part V, Letter V.
64. *Rousseau juge*, p. 186.
65. *Ibid.*, Part V, Letter X.
66. *The Confessions*, II, 163.
67. In Hendel, *J.-J. Rousseau, Moralist*, II, 47.
68. *Rousseau juge*, Part VI, Letter VI.
69. Part V, Letter V.
70. *The Confessions*, I, 101.
71. Kant, Fragment 618, in Cassirer, *Rousseau, Kant, and Goethe*, 6.
72. Texte, J., *Rousseau and the Cosmopolitan Spirit*, 236.
73. Desnoiresterres, VI, 87.
74. Michelet, *Histoire*, V, 427.
75. *Ibid.*
76. *The Confessions*, II, 213.
77. *Ibid.*, 211.
78. Maritain, *Three Reformers: Luther, Descartes, Rousseau*, 119.
79. Taine, *Ancient Regime*, 271.

CHAPTER VII

1. Hendel, *Citizen of Geneva*, 179.
2. *Ibid.*, 195.

3. Rousseau, *Social Contract*, Book I, Ch. v.
4. *Ibid.*, IV, ii.
5. IV, i.
6. I, vii.
7. I, viii.
8. I, vii.
9. II, iv.
10. I, viii.
11. Vaughn, *Political Writings of Rousseau*, I, 81.
12. *Social Contract*, Book III, Ch. v.
13. III, iv.
14. III, xv.
15. III, xviii.
16. III, i.
17. I, ix.
18. II, xi.
19. I, end.
20. II, i.
21. Letter to Mme. d'Étang, in Cobban, *Rousseau and the Modern State*, 193.
22. Cobban, *Rousseau*, 211.
23. *Social Contract*, IV, viii.
24. II, vii.
25. IV, viii.
26. *Ibid.*
27. *Ibid.*
28. *Ibid.*
29. *Ibid.*
30. IV, vi.
31. In Cobban, *Rousseau*, 55.
32. *Émile*, p. 157.
33. *Ibid.*
34. Cobban, *In Search of Humanity*, 168.
35. Voltaire, *Works*, XXIb, 332.
36. Havens, *Voltaire's Marginalia*, 68, in Gay, *Voltaire's Politics*, 268.
37. Cf. *Social Contract*, II, iv; Talman, *Origins of Totalitarian Democracy;* Crocker, *Rousseau et la philosophie politique*, p. 111.
38. *Social Contract*, 11, v.
39. Faguet, *Rousseau penseur*, 397.
40. *Ibid.*
41. *Émile*, preface.
42. Boyd, *Educational Theory of Jean Jacques Rousseau*, 297.
43. Rousseau, *Émile*, 13.
44. *Ibid.*, 216.
45. 26.
46. 256.
47. 118.
48. 133.
49. 27.
50. 92.
51. 50.
52. 21-22, 46.
53. 56-58.
54. 341.
55. 253.
56. 251.
57. 254.

58. 53.
59. 58.
60. 167.
61. 149, 306.
62. 160.
63. Martin, H., *France*, XVI, 98.
64. Rousseau, *Émile*, 158.
65. *Ibid.*, 220.
66. 230.
67. 261-62.
68. 263.
69. 257.
70. 272.
71. 232.
72. *Ibid.*
73. 238-49.
74. 245-47.
75. Letter of Oct. 5, 1758, in Hendel, *Citizen of Geneva*, 152.
76. *Émile*, 261.
77. 223.
78. 275.
79. See Robertson, J. M., *Short History of Freethought*, II, 256.
80. *Émile*, 272.
81. 271-72.
82. 179.
83. 192.
84. 298-99.
85. Letter of Nov. 5, 1758, in Hendel, *Citizen*, 158.
86. In Faguet, *Rousseau penseur*, 111.
87. *Émile*, 351; Hendel, *J.-J. Rousseau*, II, 23.
88. *Émile*, 330, 370.
89. 340.
90. 341, 371.
91. 337, 350.
92. 350.
93. 349.
94. 320.
95. 357.
96. 443.
97. 444.
98. Staël, Mme. de, *Germany*, I, 125.
99. Seillière, *J. J. Rousseau*, 132, in Maritain, *Three Reformers*, 125.
100. Rousseau, *Collection complète des oeuvres*, IXb, 157.
101. Plato, *Republic*, No. 592.

CHAPTER VIII

1. Hendel, *Citizen of Geneva*, 232.
2. *The Confessions*, II, 243.
3. *Collection complète*, IXa, pp. v-x.
4. *The Confessions*, II, 253.
5. *Collection*, IXb, 4.
6. *The Confessions*, II, 255.
7. In Torrey, *Spirit of Voltaire*, 110.
8. Masson, P. M., *La Religion de Rousseau*, III, 33.
9. Voltaire, letter of July 26, 1764.

10. In Brandes, *Voltaire*, II, 97.
11. *Ibid.*, 98; Desnoiresterres, VI, 320-23.
12. Hendel, *J.-J. Rousseau*, II, 252.
13. *The Confessions*, II, 257.
14. *Boswell on the Grand Tour: Germany and Switzerland*, 226.
15. In Gooch, *Frederick the Great*, 138.
16. *The Confessions*, II, 264.
17. Hendel, *Citizen of Geneva*, 252.
18. *The Confessions*, II, 265.
19. *Ibid.*, 259.
20. 270.
21. 265-66.
22. Letter of July 22, 1764, in Masson, P. M., *La Religion*, III, 171.
23. In Goncourts, *Woman of the 18th Century*, 287.
24. Sainte-Beuve, *Portraits of the 18th Century*, II, 138.
25. Masson, III, 73-75.
26. 2 Timothy iii, 1 f.
27. *Collection complète*, IXa, pp. *xi-xiii*.
28. *Ibid.*, p. *xiii*.
29. P. *xiv*.
30. P. *xvi*.
31. P. *xxxix*.
32. P. 1.
33. 2.
34. 4.
35. 7.
36. 8.
37. 26-28.
38. 55.
39. 63.
40. 65-66.
41. 70-71.
42. 121-22.
43. 8.
44. 15.
45. 42.
46. 44.
47. 47.
48. 50.
49. 83.
50. 86.
51. 87-89.
52. Exodus vii, 9-12.
53. Matthew xxiv, 24.
54. *Collection complète*, IXa, 201-2.
55. *Ibid.*, 210-12.
56. 244-45.
57. 334.
58. Letter of Mar. 8, 1765, in Masson, P. M., *La Religion*, III, 206-7.
59. *Collection complète*, IXa, 184-85.
60. Morley, *Voltaire*, in Voltaire, *Works*, XXIb, 97.
61. In Faguet, *Vie de Rousseau*, 318-20.
62. *Rousseau juge de J.-J.*, I, *ii-iv*.
63. Grimm, *Correspondance*, May 15, 1763, Dec. 15, 1763, Jan. 15, 1765; see also Masson, P. M., II, 126-40.

64. Boileaux-Despréaux, Nicolas, *L'Art poétique*, lines 37-38.
65. Goethe, *Faust*, Part I, Everyman's Library translation, p. 116.
66. *Collection complète*, I, 196n.
67. Horace Walpole, letter of Dec. 31, 1769, to Horace Mann.
68. *Boswell on the Grand Tour: Germany and Switz.*, 150.
69. *Ibid.*, 215.
70. 217.
71. 219.
72. 229.
73. 230-31.
74. 254.
75. 258-68.
76. In Vaughn, *Political Writings of Rousseau*, II, 293.
77. Macdonald, Frederika, *Jean Jacques Rousseau*, II, 118.
78. Vaughn, II, 369n.
79. *Ibid.*, 350.
80. 338.
81. Letter of Feb. 26, 1770.
82. Morley, *Rousseau and His Era*, II, 94.
83. Letter of Mar. 10, 1765.
84. Letter of Mar. 29, 1765.
85. Macdonald, F., II, 123.
86. *The Confessions*, II, 301.
87. *Ibid.*
88. Letter of Oct. 1, 1765.
89. *The Confessions*, II, 302.
90. *Ibid.*
91. Rousseau, *Reveries*, 106.
92. *Ibid.*, 108; cf. *The Confessions*, 308.
93. Morley, *Rousseau*, II, 117.
94. *The Confessions*, II, 312.
95. Hendel, *Citizen of Geneva*, 326.
96. Burton, *Life of David Hume*, II, 299.
97. Macdonald, F., II, 166.
98. *Ibid.*, 213-14.
99. Walpole, Letter of Jan. 12, 1766.
100. Macdonald, II, 168.
101. Lemaître, 322; Macdonald, II, 172.
102. *Ibid.*, II, 171.
103. Morellet, *Mémoires*, in Mossner, *Life of Hume*, 575.
104. *Ibid.*, 517.
105. 518.
106. Faguet, *Vie de Rousseau*, 332.
107. In Burton, *Hume*, II, 304, 309.
108. Hume, letter to Lord Charlemont, in Mossner, 523.
109. Mossner, 519.
110. *Boswell on the Grand Tour: Italy, Corsica, France*, 279.
111. But summarized by Col. Robert Isham, who read them before their destruction by the executors.
112. *Boswell on the Grand Tour: Italy . . .*, 277-81.
113. Mossner, 521.

114. *Ibid.*, 523.
115. Letter of May 10, 1766, in Hendel, *Citizen of Geneva*, 336.
116. Letter of Apr. 24, 1766, in Hendel.
117. Josephson, 460.
118. Macdonald, F., II, 186-209.
119. Mossner, 529.
120. Macdonald, II, 171.
121. *Ibid.*, 174.
122. Josephson, 464; Morley, *Rousseau*, II, 133.
123. Josephson, 467.
124. Morley, II, 135.
125. *Ibid.*
126. Josephson, 471.
127. Faguet, *Vie de Rousseau*, 361; Ségur, *Julie de Lespinasse*, 203.

CHAPTER IX

1. Vaussard, *La Vie quotidienne en Italie au xviiie siècle*, 27.
2. *Ibid.*, 107.
3. 105.
4. 125.
5. Smith, D. E., *History of Mathematics*, I, 519.
6. Baedeker, *Northern Italy*, 471.
7. James, E. E., *Bologna*, 178-80.
8. Casanova, *Memoirs*, I, 14.
9. Rolland, Romain, *Musical Tour through the Land of the Past*, 167.
10. *Ibid.*
11. *Ibid.*
12. *Réalités*, November, 1954, p. 45.
13. Láng, *Music in Western Civilization*, 354.
14. Grout, D. J., *Short History of Opera*, 196.
15. Kirkpatrick, R., *Domenico Scarlatti*, 94.
16. Einstein, Alfred, *Gluck*, 101.
17. Lee, Vernon, *Studies of the 18th Century in Italy*, 206.
18. Vaussard, 82.
19. De Sanctis, *History of Italian Literature*, II, 825.
20. Vaussard, 83.
21. *Ibid.*, 86.
22. 88.
23. Campbell, T. J., *The Jesuits*, 424.
24. McCabe, Jos., *Candid History of the Jesuits*, 287.
25. Renard and Weulersee, *Life and Work in Modern Europe*, 276.
26. Chesterfield, *Letters*, Feb. 28, 1749.
27. Einstein, *Gluck*, 15.
28. Gatti-Cazazza Collection, Venice.
29. Private collection, Venice.
30. *Ibid.*
31. Museo Civico, Bassano.
32. Voltaire, *Works*, VIIIa, 5.
33. Molmenti, P., *Venice*, Part III: *The Decadence*, I, 37.

34. *Ibid.*, 49.
35. Molmenti, *The Decadence*, II, 17, 146.
36. *Ibid.*, 48.
37. 49.
38. Rousseau, *The Confessions*, I, 301; Molmenti, II, 93.
39. Vaussard, 180.
40. Goldoni, *Memoirs*, 178.
41. Rousseau, *The Confessions*, I, 292.
42. Molmenti, I, 169; Vaussard, 195.
43. *Grove's Dictionary of Music*, III, 314.
44. Pincherle, *Vivaldi*, 16.
45. *Ibid.*, 17.
46. Rolland, *Musical Tour*, 187.
47. Pincherle, 67.
48. E. g., Violin Concerto in E, Concerto Grosso in D Minor.
49. Pincherle, 61.
50. *Ibid.*, 229-32.
51. *Time*, Nov. 29, 1963.
52. Lord Walpole Collection.
53. Brera Gallery, Milan.
54. Boston Museum of Fine Arts; Wallace Collection.
55. National Gallery, London.
56. Wallace Collection.
57. London, Vienna, Geneva.
58. New York.
59. Turin.
60. Louvre.
61. Duke of Devonshire Collection.
62. Levey, *Painting in 18th-Century Venice*, 92.
63. Anon., *Tiepolo*, 34.
64. Ospedaletto, Venice.
65. E.g., Sitwell, S., *Southern Baroque Art*, 35.
66. Molmenti, *Tiepolo*, 19; Venturi, L., *Italian Painting from Caravaggio to Modigliani*, 74.
67. Letter of Mar. 13, 1734, in Rolland, *Musical Tour*, 149.
67a. Goldoni, *Memoirs*, 184.
68. Casanova, *Memoirs*, II, 276.
69. Kirkpatrick, *Scarlatti*, 29; Vaussard, 193.
70. Goldoni, *Memoirs*, 1, 4.
71. *Ibid.*, 179.
72. 183.
73. Garnett, R., *History of Italian Literature*, 323.
74. Gozzi, Carlo, *Memoirs*, II, 110 f.
75. Molmenti, *Venice: Decadence*, I, 168.
76. Goldoni, *Memoirs*, 346.
77. *Ibid.*, introd., *xi*.
78. Gibbon, Edward, *Memoirs*, 7.
79. Goldoni, *Memoirs*, xxi.
80. Sitwell, S., *German Baroque Art*, 70.
81. Gibbon, *Decline and Fall of the Roman Empire*, VI, 675.
82. Ranke, *History of the Popes*, III, 472.
83. *New Cambridge Modern History*, VII, 284.

84. Funk, F. X., *Manual of Church History*, II, 180.
85. Macaulay, Essays, II, 179.
86. De Brosses in McCabe, Jos., *Crises in the History of the Papacy*, 354.
87. *Correspondance de Benoît XIV*, II, 268, in McCabe, *Crises*, 354.
88. *CMH*, VI, 591.
89. Ford, Miriam de, *Love Children*, 205.
90. Lanfrey, P., *L'Église et les philosophes*, 190.
91. Putnam, G. H., *Censorship of the Church of Rome*, II, 60.
92. Sime, James, *Lessing*, I, 92.
93. Stirling-Maxwell, *Annals of the Artists of Spain*, IV, 1393.
94. Gershoy, Leo, *From Despotism to Revolution*, 146.
95. *CMH*, VI, 598.
96. *Ibid.*, 599.
97. Robertson, *Short History of Freethought*, II, 369.
98. Vico, Giambattista, *Autobiography*, 111.
99. Croce, B., *Philosophy of Giambattista Vico*, 252.
100. Vico, *The New Science*, No. 31.
101. *Ibid.*, Nos. 916–18; we have ventured to improve the translation.
102. Nos. 922–24.
103. 925–27.
104. Vico, *Autobiography*, 171.
105. *The New Science*, No. 1104.
106. 1105.
107. 417–24.
108. 873–80.
109. 361.
110. *Autobiography*, 173.
111. *The New Science*, No. 1110.
112. Croce, *Philosophy of Vico*, 269.
113. *Ibid.*, 274.
114. Croce, *Filosofia di G. B. Vico* (1911).
115. Grout, *Opera*, 200.
116. *Ibid.*, 208.
117. *Oxford History of Music*, IV, 185.
118. Burney, Charles, *General History of Music*, II, 917.
119. *Grove's Dictionary*, II, 785.
120. *Ibid.*
121. *Ibid.*
122. Beckford, Wm., *Travel Diaries*, II, 167.
123. Lee, Vernon, *Studies*, 194.
124. Kirkpatrick, *Scarlatti*, 21.
125. *Ibid.*, 32.
126. 33.
127. Introd. to the Victor Album of Scarlatti's Sonatas.
128. Kirkpatrick, 58.
129. *Ibid.*, 103.
130. Especially delightful: Nos. 13, 23, 25, 104, and 338, in the Longo numbering.
131. Coxe, Wm., *Memoirs of the Kings of Spain*, IV, 231.

CHAPTER X

1. Beckford, *Travel Diaries*, II, 171.
2. Cheke, Marcus, *Dictator of Portugal*, 4.
3. Day, Clive, *History of Commerce*, 186; *History Today*, November, 1955, p. 730.
4. Frederick the Great, *Mémoires*, I, 28; Stirling-Maxwell, IV, 1385.
5. *New CMH*, VII, 289.
6. Stephens, H. M., *Story of Portugal*, 354.
7. *Enc. Brit.*, XX, 681b.
8. *History Today*, November, 1955, p. 731.
9. Campbell, *The Jesuits*, 431.
10. Cheke, 50.
11. *Ibid.*, 111.
12. *History Today*, November, 1955, p. 733.
13. See *The Age of Reason Begins*, 249-51.
14. Cheke, 106.
15. McCabe, *The Jesuits*, 262.
16. Lanfrey, *L'Église et les philosophes*, 258; Cheke, 114.
17. Our account follows Cheke, 118 f.
18. Lanfrey, 259.
19. Cheke, 132.
20. Lanfrey, 260.
21. McCabe, *Jesuits*, 263.
22. Campbell, *Jesuits*, 462.
23. Gershoy, *From Despotism to Revolution*, 152; Cheke, 140.
24. Voltaire, *Works*, XVIa, 243.
25. Cheke, 155.
26. *Ibid.*, 157.
27. Voltaire, XVIa, 243.
28. Gershoy, 153; Cheke, 204.
29. Gershoy, 154.
30. Stephens, *Portugal*, 367.
31. Lea, H. C., *History of the Inquisition in Spain*, III, 310n.
32. Bell, Aubrey, *Portuguese Literature*, 277.
33. Cheke, 251.
34. *Ibid.*, 268.
35. *Ibid.*

CHAPTER XI

1. Altamira, R., *History of Spain*, 482, 466; Ogg, D., *Europe in the 17th Century*, 22; *New CMH*, VII, 271.
2. Herr, Richard, *The Eighteenth-Century Revolution in Spain*, 106; see also Altamira, 467-68.
3. Herr, 96.
4. Altamira, 460; Stokes, Hugh, *Francisco Goya*, 187.
5. Klingender, F. D., *Goya in the Democratic Tradition*, 4n.
6. *Ibid.*, 4-5; Campbell, *Jesuits*, 424.
7. Kany, C. E., *Life and Manners in Madrid*, 1750-1800, 375.
8. Vallentin, A., *This I Saw*, 26.
9. Lea, *Inquisition in Spain*, III, 308-10; IV, 523.

10. Martin, H., *France*, XV, 114-15.
11. Ticknor, Geo., *History of Spanish Literature*, III, 244.
12. Lea, IV, 530.
13. Buckle, H. T., *Introd. to the History of Civilization in England*, IIa, 61.
14. *CMH*, VI, 124.
15. Voltaire, XIXa, 214.
16. Burney, Charles, *History of Music*, II, 815-16.
17. Kany, 392.
18. Coxe, *Memoirs of the Kings of Spain*, IV, 141-43.
19. Trevor-Roper, *Historical Essays*, 268.
20. Herr, 75.
21. Letter of d'Alembert to Voltaire, May 13, 1773, in Robertson, J. M., *Short History of Freethought*, II, 372.
22. Herr, 63.
23. *Ibid.*, 77.
24. Ségur, *Lespinasse*, 254.
25. Altamira, 508.
26. Lea, *Inquisition*, IV, 307.
27. Herr, 210.
28. Michelet, *Histoire de France*, V, 439.
29. Stokes, *Goya*, 147.
30. Coxe, *Kings of Spain*, IV, 235.
31. Letters of an English officer, 1788, in Buckle, IIa, 92.
32. Coxe, IV, 236.
33. Hume, Martin, *Spain: Its Greatness and Decay*, 397.
34. Coxe, IV, 408.
35. Gershoy, *From Despotism to Revolution*, 163.
36. Coxe, IV, 341.
37. *Ibid.*, 361.
38. Campbell, *Jesuits*, 511-12.
39. *Ibid.*; Lanfrey, *L'Église et les philosophes*, 280.
40. Coxe, IV, 362.
41. *Ibid.*, 363.
42. Lanfrey, 282.
43. Campbell, 517-18.
44. *Ibid.*, 519; Lanfrey, 281.
45. Coxe, IV, 368.
46. Herr, 23.
47. *Ibid.*
48. 205.
49. 29.
50. 208.
51. Kany, 356-57.
52. Buckle, IIa, 86; Robertson, *Freethought*, II, 372.
53. Herr, 210; Robertson, 373.
54. Herr, 35; Trevor-Roper, 264.
55. Coxe, IV, 412-16; Casanova, *Memoirs*, II, 344.
56. Altamira, 438.
57. Fitzmaurice-Kelly, *History of Spanish Literature*, 357.
58. Rev. Geo. Edmundsen, in *CMH*, VI, 384.
59. Vallentin, 5.
60. Herr, 54.
61. *Ibid.*, 57.
62. Buckle, IIa, 98.
63. *Ibid.*, 94.
64. Herr, 128.
65. *CMH*, VI, 383.
66. Herr, 148.
67. *Ibid.*, 141-42.
68. 150.
69. Kany, 24; Vallentin, 26.
70. Kany, 38.
71. *Ibid.*, 18.
72. Hume, Martin, *Spain*, 411.
73. Stokes, 188; Kany, 214.
74. Laborde, *Spain*, in Buckle, IIa, 114.
75. Kany, 24.
76. *Ibid.*, 280.
77. Casanova, II, 348.
78. Kirkpatrick, *Scarlatti*, 132.
79. Altamira, *History of Spanish Civilization*, 183.
80. Trevor-Roper, 264.
81. Kany, 345; Buckle, IIa, 95.
82. Ticknor, III, 256; Herr, 165.
83. Ticknor, III, 262.
84. *Ibid.*, 273.
85. Vallentin, 144.
86. Calvert, A. F., *Royal Palaces of Spain*, 97.
87. Cathedral of Salamanca.
88. Prado.
89. Private collection, Zurich.
90. Prado.
91. Poore, Charles, *Goya*, 156.
92. Calvert, *Goya*, 55.
93. Poore, 48.
94. One in Frick Collection, New York.
95. Prado.
96. Prado.
97. Vallentin, 93.
98. Trevor-Roper, 266.
99. Vallentin, 111.
100. *Ibid.*, 112.
101. E.g., Malraux in Goya, *Drawings from the Prado*, xiv.
102. Lassaigne, J., *Spanish Painting: From Velázquez to Picasso*, 89.
103. Vallentin, 112.
104. *Ibid.*, 119.
105. Duke of Alba Collection.
106. Goya, *Drawings*, Plate 4.
107. Collection of the Hispanic Society, New York.
108. Vallentin, 195.
109. *Ibid.*, 203.
110. Prado.
111. Vallentin, 183.
112. Academy of San Fernando, Madrid.
113. National Gallery, Washington.
114. Academy of San Fernando, Madrid.
115. Klingender, *Goya*, 92.
116. Goya, *Drawings*, 123.

117. *Ibid.*, 130.
118. 170.
119. Academy of San Fernando.
120. Goya, *Drawings*, 112.
121. *Ibid.*, 89-117.
122. 118.
123. Vallentin, 223.
124. Both in the Prado.
125. Metropolitan Museum of Art, New York.
126. In Goya, *The Disasters of War*, No. 23.
127. *Ibid.*, No. 12.
128. No. 44.
129. No. 47.
130. No. 18.
131. These pictures from the Quinta del Sordo are in the Prado.
132. Lassaigne, *Spanish Painting: From Velázquez to Picasso*, 106.

CHAPTER XII

1. Goethe, *Letters from Italy*, Sept. 16, 1786.
2. *Ibid.*, Sept. 12 and 17, 1786.
3. Gozzi, Carlo, *Memoirs*, II, 7.
4. *Ibid.*, 100-03.
5. Hazlitt, W. C., *The Venetian Republic*, II, 323.
6. Casanova, *Memoirs*, II, 110.
7. Renard and Weulersee, *Life and Work in Modern Europe*, 275.
8. Pearson, Hesketh, *Johnson and Boswell*, 171.
9. Goethe, *Letters from Italy*, Oct. 25, 1786.
10. *CMH*, VI, 601.
11. Winckelmann, J., *History of Ancient Art*, I, 48.
12. Goethe, *Letters from Italy*, Mar. 17, 1787.
13. Vaussard, 74.
14. Friedländer, Ludwig, *Life and Manners under the Early Empire*, II, 78.
15. Goethe, Oct. 27, 1786.
16. Vaussard, 84.
17. *Ibid.*, 89.
18. Bury, J. B., *History of Freedom of Thought*, 122.
19. McCabe, *The Jesuits*, 346.
20. E.g., Lanfrey, *Histoire politique des papes*, 384; *id.*, *L'Église et les philosophes*, 305.
21. Campbell, *Jesuits*, 536.
22. McCabe, *Jesuits*, 346.
23. Ranke, *History of the Popes*, II, 449-50.
24. Campbell, 538.
25. *Ibid.*, 541.
26. McCabe, 355.
27. Campbell, 563.
28. Mozart, letter of Aug. 4, 1770, in Anderson, Emily, *Letters of Mozart*, I, 227.
29. Jahn, *Life of Mozart*, I, 151.
30. Blom, Eric, *Mozart*, 57.
31. Goethe, *Letters from Italy*, Nov. 24, 1786.
32. Vaussard, 141-43.

33. Beccaria, *Dei delitti e delle pene* (1766 ed.), p. 11.
34. Carlyle, "Count Cagliostro," in *Essays* (*Works*, III), 187-92.
35. Goethe, *Letters*, Apr. 13 and 14, 1787.
36. Casanova, I, 13.
37. *Ibid.*, 14.
38. 123.
39. Introd. *xx*.
40. 210.
41. 211.
42. 219.
43. 287.
44. 330.
45. 406-7.
46. II, 370, 393.
47. *Ibid.*, 340.
48. Gilbert, O. P., *The Prince de Ligne*, 157.
49. Winckelmann, I, 3.
50. *Ibid.*, 9.
51. 18.
52. 21.
53. Pater, Walter, *The Renaissance*, 155.
54. In Brandes, *Goethe*, II, 244.
55. Winckelmann, I, 31.
56. In Muther, *History of Modern Painting*, I, 81.
57. Pater, *Renaissance*, 148.
58. Winckelmann, I, 46.
59. *Ibid.*, 60.
60. II, 319.
61. I, 64.
62. *Ibid.*
63. *Ibid.*
64. *Ibid.*
65. I, 70.
66. 287.
67. 77.
68. 76, 84.
69. 86.
70. In Pater, 147.
71. Both in Museo Correr, Venice.
72. Good examples in Morgan Library, New York, and Metropolitan Museum of Art.
73. Levey, *Painting in Venice*, 103.
74. Poldi-Pezzoli Museum, Milan.
75. Louvre.
76. Ältere Pinakothek, Munich.
77. Muther, I, 86.
78. Winckelmann, I, 407.
79. Prado.
80. Jahn, *Mozart*, III, 1, 15.
81. Burney, Fanny, *Diary*, 72-73.
82. Burney, Charles, *History of Music*, II, 886-91.
83. Einstein, Albert, *Gluck*, 151.
84. *Grove's Dictionary*, IV, 174.
85. *Ibid.*, 509.
86. Einstein, *Gluck*, 149.
87. *Grove's*, I, 650.
88. Translation by Richard Garnett (*History of Italian Literature*, 300).

89. In De Sanctis, II, 831.
90. Alfieri, Vittorio, *Autobiography*, Epoch I, Ch. i.
91. *Ibid.*, Epoch II, Ch. iv.
92. III, iii.
93. III, xii.
94. Alfieri, *Of Tyranny*, 102.
95. *Ibid.*, Book I, Section 1.
96. II, vii.
97. II, viii.
98. I, ix.
99. I, viii.
100. "Forethought" to *Of Tyranny*.
101. *Autobiography*, Epoch IV, Ch. viii.
102. Epoch I, Ch. viii.
103. IV, v.
104. IV, xx.
105. IV, xvi.

CHAPTER XIII

1. Gilbert, *Prince de Ligne*, 29, 57.
2. *Ibid.*, 135.
3. Mowat, R. B., *Age of Reason*, 96.
4. Frederick the Great, *Guerre de Sept Ans*, 386.
5. Gooch, G. P., *Maria Theresa*, 3.
6. Jahn, *Mozart*, I, 65.
7. Voltaire, *Works*, XVIa, 167.
8. Gershoy, *From Despotism to Revolution*, 89.
9. Campbell, *Jesuits*, 433.
10. Paulsen, F., *German Education*, 147-49.
11. Schoenfeld, Hermann, *Women of the Teutonic Nations*, 297.
12. Padover, *The Revolutionary Emperor*, 100.
13. Casanova, *Memoirs*, I, 147.
14. Frederick, *Guerre de Sept Ans*, 387.
15. Renard and Weulersee, *Life and Work in Modern Europe*, 305.
16. Padover, 20.
17. Stryienski, *Eighteenth Century*, 64.
18. *Ibid.*
19. *Jahn*, I, 67.
20. Frederick, *Guerre de Sept Ans*, 387.
21. Casanova, I, 148.
22. *Enc. Brit.*, XIII, 151b.
23. Padover, 34.
24. *Enc. Brit.*, 1. c.
25. Padover, 34.
26. *Ibid.*, 37.
27. 41.
28. Gooch, *Maria Theresa*, 14.
29. Padover, 47.
30. Mann, Thos., *Three Essays*, 165.
31. Gooch, 21-29; Padover, 67.
32. Gooch, 29.
33. Padover, 134.
34. *Ibid.*, 134, 30.
35. 136.
36. 84; Gooch, 29.

37. Padover, 89.
38. Gooch, 65.
39. *Ibid.*, 66.
40. Padover, 77.
41. Gooch, 41.
42. Padover, 90-93.
43. Lewis, D. B. Wyndham, *Four Favorites*, 202.
44. Gershoy, 89.
45. Riedl, Frederick, *History of Hungarian Literature*, 77-81.
46. Hazard, *European Thought*, 109.
47. Padover, 73.
48. *Ibid.*, 74.
49. 81.
50. Gooch, 70.
51. Martin, *France*, XVI, 392.
52. *Ibid.*, 391.
53. Padover, 94; *CMH*, VI, 628.
54. Parton, James, *Daughters of Genius*, 402.
55. Cf. Coxe, *History of the House of Austria*, III, 485-86.
56. Richard, Ernst, *History of German Civilization*, 380.
57. Padover, 181.
58. *Ibid.*, 178.
59. 279.
60. 281.
61. 285; Gershoy, 100.
62. Gershoy, 101.
63. Padover, 286.
64. Coxe, *House of Austria*, III, 491n.
65. Lanfrey, *L'Église et les philosophes*, 356.
66. Padover, 212.
67. Jahn, *Mozart*, II, 401.
68. Padover, 214-15.
69. *Ibid.*
70. *History Today*, September, 1955, p. 615.
71. Padover, 246.
72. Coxe, III, 493.
73. Padover, 243.
74. Vambéry, *The Story of Hungary*, 385.
75. Padover, 299.
76. *Ibid.*, 311.
77. Coxe, III, 526.
78. Padover, 329.
79. *Ibid.*, 345.
80. 373.
81. 360.
82. 364.
83. 383.
84. *History Today*, September, 1955, p. 620.
85. Gilbert, O. P., *Prince de Ligne*, 193.
86. Coxe, III, 541.
87. Carlyle, *History of Friedrich the Second*, VII, 492.
88. Padover, 287.

CHAPTER XIV

1. Jahn, *Mozart*, II, 202.
2. Weinstock, Herbert, *Handel*, 268.

3. Rolland, *Musical Tour*, 208.
4. Rolland, *Essays in Music*, 176.
5. Einstein, *Gluck*, 59.
6. In Brockway and Weinstock, *The Opera*, 66.
7. Einstein, *Gluck; Grove's Dictionary of Music*, II, 401.
8. Láng, P. H., *Music in Western Civilization*, 659.
9. Faguet, E., *Rousseau artiste*, 191; Einstein, *Gluck*, 137.
10. Brockway and Weinstock, *Opera*, 97.
11. Einstein, 138.
12. Faguet, *Rousseau artiste*, 191.
13. *Grove's*, II, 400.
14. Rolland, *Essays*, 197-98.
15. *Kobbé's Complete Opera Book*, 42.
16. Rolland, *Essays*, 179.
17. Einstein, 146.
18. Burney, C., *History of Music*, II, 973.
19. Einstein, 151.
20. Vigée-Lebrun, Mme., *Memoirs*, 70.
21. *Kobbé's*, 52.
22. *Grove's*, IV, 174.
23. Einstein, 182.
24. Pratt, W. S., *History of Music*, 362.
25. Clark, Robert, *Herder*, 108, 429.
26. *Grove's*, II, 566.
27. Geiringer, Karl, *Haydn*, 44.
28. *Grove's*, II, 568.
29. Geiringer, 52-54.
30. *Ibid.*, 55.
31. *Grove's*, II, 570.
32. Jahn, II, 349.
33. Geiringer, 77.
34. *Ibid.*, 89.
35. 99.
36. *Grove's*, II, 574.
37. Geiringer, 108.
38. *Ibid.*, 110.
39. 121.
40. Jacob, H. E., *Joseph Haydn*, 222.
41. *Ibid.*, 267.
42. Geiringer, 168.
43. *Ibid.*, 167.
44. McKinney and Anderson, *Music in History*, 465.
45. *Grove's*, II, 582.

CHAPTER XV

1. Jahn, *Mozart*, II, 437.
2. *Ibid.*, I, 21n.
3. I, 28.
4. 33.
5. Blom, *Mozart*, 26.
6. Biancolli, *Mozart Handbook*, 129.
7. Jahn, I, 39.
8. *Ibid.*, 107.
9. 119.
10. 129.
11. 132.

12. 137.
13. *Ibid.*
14. Wyzewa and Saint-Foix, *W. A. Mozart*, I, 470.
15. *Ibid.*, 474.
16. Jahn, I, 149.
17. *Ibid.*, 344.
18. Anderson, E., *Letters of Mozart*, I, 403.
19. *Ibid.*, 395.
20. Einstein, *Mozart*, 41.
21. Anderson, II, 686-88.
22. *Ibid.*, 695.
23. 681-83.
24. 700-09.
25. Einstein, *Mozart*, 30-31.
26. Anderson, II, 925.
27. Blom, 88; Jahn, II, 65-66.
28. Letter of May 6, 1781, in Einstein, 54.
29. Jahn, II, 171.
30. *Ibid.*, 176.
31. 179
32. 184.
33. Anderson, II, 1100.
34. Letter of July 25, 1781, in Anderson, II, 1121.
35. Anderson, III, 1166-69.
36. Einstein, 458.
37. Jahn, II, 413.
38. *Ibid.*, 419.
39. 420.
40. 439.
41. 337, 422.
42. Einstein, 238.
43. Letter of Leopold Mozart, Feb. 14, 1785, in Anderson, III, 1321.
44. Anderson, 1329.
45. Letter of Apr. 10, 1784, in Einstein, 265.
46. *Grove's*, III, 563.
47. Einstein, 223
48. Biancolli, 343.
49. Einstein, 214.
50. Biancolli, 355.
51. *Ibid.*, 374.
52. 367-69; Blom, 183.
53. Einstein, 280.
54. Goethe, *Poetical Works*, 120. In *Works*.
55. "His Master's Voice" Record C 2736.
56. Jahn, II, 440; Nettle, Paul, *Mozart and Masonry*, 112.
57. Biancolli, 132.
58. Rolland, *Essays*, 246.
59. *Ibid.*
60. E.g., in the letter of Nov. 5, 1777: "I wish you good night, but first shit into your bed." And on Nov. 13: "I've been shitting, so 'tis said, nigh twenty-two years through the same old hole, which is not yet frayed one bit." (Anderson, II, 525, 546).
61. Letter of Jan. 31, 1778.
62. Letter of Sept. 26, 1777.
63. Nettle, 122.

64. Jahn, II, 269-71.
65. *Ibid.*
66. E.g., letters of Apr. 13, 1789, and Sept. 30, 1790.
67. Letter of June 7, 1783.
68. Letter of Feb. 20, 1784.
69. Letter of July 31, 1782.
70. Anderson, II, 826.
71. Nettle, 115; Ghéon, *In Search of Mozart,* 216.
72. Anderson, III, 1450.
73. Jahn, II, 304; Nettle, 120.
74. Einstein, 57.
75. Jahn, II, 295.
76. *Ibid.*
77. 298.
78. Einstein, 57.
79. Anderson, III, 1253.
80. *Ibid.,* 1296.
81. In Biancolli, 138.
82. Jahn, II, 412.
83. Einstein, 442.
84. Jahn, III, 134.
85. *Ibid.,* 140.
86. Goethe to Schiller, Dec. 30, 1797.
87. Anderson, III, 1360.
88. Blom, 138.
89. *Ibid.*
90. Letters of Dec. 14, 1789, in Anderson, III, 1383-85.
91. Brockway and Weinstock, *Opera,* 91.
92. Anderson, III, 1398-99.
93. Jahn, II, 278-80.
94. Nettle, 116.
95. Biancolli, 421.
96. Jahn, III, 285.
97. Einstein, 363.
98. Grout, *Short History of Opera,* 294.
99. Biancolli, 554.
100. Nettle, 117.
101. Stendhal in Clark, B. H., *Great Short Biographies of the World,* 999.

CHAPTER XVI

1. Montagu, Lady Mary W., *Letters,* I, 372; *cf.* Macdonald, Duncan, *The Religious Attitude to Life in Islam,* 126.
2. Lane, Edward W., *Manners and Customs of the Modern Egyptians,* I, 148; Macdonald, Duncan, *Development of Muslim Theology,* 283; Wherry, E. M., *Commentary on the Quran,* I, 281.
3. Macdonald, D., *Religious Attitude,* 126.
4. Doughty, Charles M., *Travels in Arabia Deserta,* II, 99.
5. Halsband, Robert, *Life of Lady Mary Wortley Montagu,* 73.
6. Lane-Poole, Stanley, *Story of Turkey,* 319.
7. Burton, Sir Richard, *Personal Narrative*

of a Pilgrimage to Al-Madinah and Meccah, II, 94.
8. Letter of Apr. 18, 1717, in Montagu, *Letters,* I, 318.
9. Letter of Apr. 1, 1717, in same, 286.
10. Friedländer, L., *Roman Life and Manners,* II, 201.
11. Frederick, *Mémoires,* I, 55.
12. Sir Wm. Petty, *Political Arithmetic* (1683).
13. Halsband, 74.
14. See *The Age of Louis XIV,* 425-26.
15. Lane, I, 272.
16. Lane-Poole, *Cairo,* 180.
17. Lane, I, 98.
18. *Ibid.,* 66.
19. *Enc. Brit.,* I, 618a.
20. *Ibid.,* XV, 816d.
21. Toynbee, *A Study of History,* I, 162.
22. Browne, Edward G., *Literary History of Persia,* IV, 135.
23. *Ibid.,* 136; Sykes, Sir Percy, *History of Persia,* II, 260.
24. *Ibid.,* 267.
25. *Enc. Brit.,* XII, 705b; Pope, Arthur U., *Survey of Persian Art,* IV, 470, 497-506.
26. Sykes, II, 201.
27. Pope, Arthur U., *Introduction to Persian Art,* 140.
28. Browne, E. G., IV, 282.
29. *Ibid.,* 292-96.

CHAPTER XVII

1. Frederick the Great, *Mémoires,* I, 207.
2. Lyashchenko, Peter, *History of the National Economy of Russia,* 271-73.
3. *Ibid.*
4. Réau, Louis, *L'Art russe,* II, 88.
5. Florinsky, M. T., *Russia: A History and an Interpretation,* I, 575.
6. Mavor, James, *Economic History of Russia,* I, 477.
7. Réau, II, 88.
8. Mavor, I, 498-99.
9. Bernal, J. D., *Science in History,* 360.
10. Coxe, Wm., *Travels in Poland, Russia, Sweden, and Denmark,* I, 281-82.
11. Castéra, J., *History of Catherine II,* 174.
12. Dorn, *Competition for Empire,* 70.
13. Florinsky, I, 600; Brückner, A., *Literary History of Russia,* 113.
14. Coxe, *Travels,* I, 322.
15. Masson, *Memoirs of Catherine II and Her Court,* 250.
16. Pougin, Arthur, *Short History of Russian Music,* 10 f.
17. Réau, II, 55.
18. Brückner, 78.
19. Waliszewski, K., *History of Russian Literature,* I, 57.

20. Wiener, Leo, *Anthology of Russian Literature*, I, 224-29.
21. Rambaud, Alfred, *History of Russia*, II, 170.
22. Waliszewski, *Peter the Great*, 224.
23. Waliszewski, *Russian Literature*, 83.
24. *Ibid.*
25. 85.
26. Catherine the Great, *Memoirs*, 60.
27. Waliszewski, *Romance of an Empress*, 47.
28. *Ibid.*
29. 25.
30. Kluchevsky, V. O., *History of Russia*, IV, 354.
31. Catherine, *Memoirs*, 58.
32. Gooch, G. P., *Catherine the Great*, 11.
33. *CMH*, VI, 317.
34. Carlyle, *History of Frederich the Second*, V, 294.
35. Waliszewski, *Romance of an Empress*, 34.
36. Kluchevsky, IV, 358.
37. Casanova, *Memoirs*, I, 33-34.
38. *CMH*, VI, 658.
39. Catherine, *Memoirs*, 28.
40. *Ibid.*, 44-45.
41. 29-30.
42. 54.
43. 62.
44. 63.
45. 65.
46. *CMH*, VI, 659.
47. Waliszewski, *Romance*, 78.
48. *Ibid.*
49. Kluchevsky, IV, 360.
50. Castéra, 122-23.
51. Waliszewski, *Romance*, 91.
52. Catherine, *Memoirs*, 203.
53. Castéra, 89.
54. Walpole, H., *Memoirs of the Reign of King George III*, I, 145.
55. Catherine, *Memoirs*, 208.
56. Gooch, *Catherine*, 8.
57. Catherine, 301.
58. *Ibid.*, 240.
59. 255 f.
60. Waliszewski, *Romance*, 102; Crocker, *The Embattled Philosopher*, 378.
61. Catherine, 271-74; Waliszewski, *Romance*, 119.
62. *Ibid.*, 125.
63. Catherine, 282.
64. Waliszewski, *Romance*, 145.
65. *Enc. Brit.*, XVII, 645b.
66. Castéra, 153.
67. Rambaud, II, 175.
68. Kluchevsky, IV, 366.
69. Castéra, 147, 157.
70. *Ibid.*, 156; *CMH*, VI, 328.
71. Kluchevsky, IV, 362.
72. Castéra, 152.
73. Waliszewski, *Romance*, 166.
74. *Ibid.*, 166; Castéra, 158.
75. Waliszewski, 166.
76. *Ibid.*, 164.
77. Gooch, *Catherine*, 16.
78. Catherine, 343.
79. *Ibid.*
80. Waliszewski, *Romance*, 176.

CHAPTER XVIII

1. Letter of Catherine to Potemkin, Aug. 2, 1762, in Catherine, *Memoirs*, 347.
2. Kluchevsky, IV, 371.
3. Catherine, 345.
4. Kluchevsky, IV, 371.
5. Catherine, 345.
6. Florinsky, I, 502.
7. *CMH*, VI, 663.
8. Waliszewski, *Romance of an Empress*, 199.
9. *Ibid.*
10. Catherine, 370.
11. Gershoy, *From Despotism to Revolution*, 303.
12. Rambaud, II, 207.
13. Florinsky, I, 504.
14. Brandes, *Voltaire*, 253.
15. Florinsky, I, 504.
16. Catherine, 263-72.
17. Masson, *Memoirs of Catherine II and Her Court*, 97.
18. Waliszewski, *Romance*, 383-88; Gooch, *Catherine*, 38.
19. Waliszewski, 4-6.
20. Masson, *Memoirs*, 98.
21. *Ibid.*
22. Catherine, 360.
23. *Ibid.*, 20.
24. Lewis, D. B. W., *Four Favorites*, 197.
25. Catherine, 376.
26. *Ibid.*, 48.
27. Gooch, *Catherine the Great*, 45.
28. Masson, *Memoirs*, 116.
29. Waliszewski, *Romance*, 448.
30. Masson, 118.
31. Parton, *Life of Voltaire*, II, 386; Gooch, 58.
32. Voltaire, letter of May 18, 1767, in Desnoiresterres, VI, 380.
33. Parton, II, 388.
34. Desnoiresterres, VI, 380.
35. Letter of Sept. 7, 1764.
36. Crocker, *Embattled Philosopher*, 373.
37. Diderot, *Oeuvres*, 28.
38. In Ellis, Havelock, *The New Spirit*, 47.
39. Morley, John, *Diderot*, II, 113.
40. *Ibid.*, 114.
41. In Faguet, *Dix-huitième Siècle*, 242.
42. Crocker, 380.
43. Sainte-Beuve, *Portraits of the 18th Century*, II, 215.

44. Padover, *Revolutionary Emperor*, 161.
45. Sainte-Beuve, II, 216.
46. Catherine, 365.
47. Castéra, 226; cf. Waliszewski, *Romance*, 371-82.
48. Coxe, *Travels in Poland*, III, 156; Castéra, 385.
49. Quoted by Voltaire in *Philosophical Dictionary*, II, 102.
50. Florinsky, I, 511; *CMH*, VI, 686.
51. In Gooch, *Catherine*, 69.
52. Voltaire to Catherine, Feb. 26, 1769.
53. In Rambaud, II, 206.
54. Voltaire, *Phil. Dict.*, art. "Power."
55. Mavor, *Economic History of Russia*, I, 241; Rambaud, II, 211.
56. Waliszewski, *Romance*, 365.
57. Garrison, F., *History of Medicine*, 400.
58. Castéra, *Catherine*, 297; Rambaud, II, 212.
59. Mavor, I, 313-14.
60. *Ibid.*, 472.
61. *CMH*, VI, 690.
62. Waliszewski, *Romance*, 298.
63. Lyashchenko, 273.
64. Mavor, I, 204-08.
65. Gershoy, 125.
66. Catherine, *Memoirs*, 385.
67. Gershoy, 123.
68. Florinsky, I, 567-68.
69. Waliszewski, *Romance*, 321.
70. *Ibid.*
71. Rambaud, II, 192; *Cambridge History of Poland*, II, 103.
72. Gooch, *Catherine*, 63.
73. Rambaud, II, 192.
74. *CMH*, VI, 674.
75. Quoted by George Bancroft in *Literary and Historical Miscellanies*, 359.
76. Gooch, *Catherine*, 51.
77. Lewis, *Four Favorites*, 213.
78. *Ibid.*, 179.
79. 215; Bain, R. N., *The Last King of Poland*, 175.
80. Florinsky, I, 531.
81. Catherine, 15.
82. Gilbert, *Prince de Ligne*, 139; Waliszewski, *Romance*, 209.
83. Castéra, 575.
84. Gooch, *Catherine*, 96.
85. Reddaway, *Frederick the Great*, 340.
86. Waliszewski, *Romance*, 233, 287.
87. *Ibid.*, 388.
88. Catherine, 377.
89. *CMH*, VI, 696.
90. Waliszewski, *Romance*, 237.
91. Wiener, *Anthology of Russian Literature*, I, 272-76.
92. *Ibid.*, 385.
93. 390.
94. 381.
95. Waliszewski, *History of Russian Literature*, 103.
96. Brückner, *Literary History of Russia*, 102.
97. *Ibid.*, 115.
98. 116.
99. 105-07.
100. Waliszewski, *Romance of an Empress*, 342.
101. Réau, *L'Art russe*, II, 111.
102. *Ibid.*, 68.
103. Waliszewski, *Romance*, 349.
104. *Enc. Brit.*, XIX, 747b.
105. Waliszewski, *Romance*, 346.
106. Réau, II, 76.
107. *Ibid.*
108. 79.
109. Masson, *Memoirs of Catherine II and Her Court*, 93.
110. Gilbert, *Prince de Ligne*, 143.
111. Brückner, 112.
112. Morley, John, *Diderot*, II, 128; Rambaud, II, 245.
113. *Ibid.*, 247.
114. Masson, *Memoirs*, 303-06.
115. Catherine, 20.
116. Masson, 66.
117. Gooch in introd. to Catherine, *Memoirs*, 10.
118. Otto Hötzsch in *CMH*, VI, 701.

CHAPTER XIX

1. Gershoy, *From Despotism to Revolution*, 37.
2. Goodwin, *The European Nobility*, 161.
3. Waliszewski, *Poland the Unknown*, 127.
4. Bain, R. Nisbet, *The Last King of Poland*, 22; Friedländer, L., *Roman Life and Manners*, II, 162.
5. Bain, 43.
6. *Cambridge History of Poland*, II, 75.
7. *Ibid.*, 76-77; Coxe, Wm., *Travels in Poland*, II, 125.
8. *New CMH*, VII, 374; Lewinski-Corwin, E. H., *Political History of Poland*, 286.
9. Staël, Mme. de, *Germany*, I, 73.
10. Bain, *Last King of Poland*, 100.
11. *Ibid.*, 59.
12. 31-32.
13. See *The Age of Louis XIV*, 374, 385-87.
14. *CHP*, II, 24.
15. Lewinski-Corwin, 289.
16. Bain, *Last King*, 55.
17. *Ibid.*, 56.
18. Aldis, *Madame Geoffrin*, 248.
19. Florinsky, *Russia*, I, 517.
20. Aldis, 251.
21. *Ibid.*, 282.
22. *CHP*, II, 116; Bain, 161.
23. Bain, *Last King*, 121.
24. Rambaud, *History of Russia*, II, 188.
25. *CHP*, II, 118.
26. *CHP*, II, 97-98; Bain, 77-78.

27. Rambaud, II, 188.
28. Bain, *Last King*, 78.
29. *CHP*, II, 120.
30. Voltaire, *Philosophical Dictionary*, art. "Superstition," Sec. III.
31. Martin, H., *Histoire de France*, XVI, 267.
32. *CHP*, II, 102.
33. *Ibid.*, 103.
34. *Ibid.*; Bain, 108.
35. Bain, *Last King*, 108.
36. *Ibid.*, 2.
37. *Enc. Brit.*, XVIII, 143d.
38. Treitschke, *Life of Frederick the Great*, 164.
39. *CMH*, VI, 670.
40. Lewis, D. B. W., *Four Favorites*, 202.
41. Gershoy, 180.
42. Morley, John, *Life of Voltaire*, in Voltaire, *Works*, XXIb, 346; Florinsky, I, 537.
43. Coxe, *Travels in Poland*, I, 159.
44. Bain, *Last King*, 121.
45. *CHP*, II, 181-82.
46. Bain, 102.
47. *CHP*, II, 181-83.
48. *Ibid.*, 135.
49. Bain, *Last King*, 249.
50. *Ibid.*, 278.
51. *CHP*, II, 155.

CHAPTER XX

1. In Gooch, *Frederick the Great*, 65.
2. MacLaurin, C., *Mere Mortals*, 195.
3. Mowat, R. B., *The Age of Reason*, 61.
4. Gooch, *Frederick*, 141.
5. Mann, Thos., *Three Essays*, 213.
6. Sir James Harrison in Gooch, *Frederick*, 149.
7. In Rolland, *Musical Tour*, 214.
8. *New York Times*, Mar. 10, 1929.
9. Frederick, letter of Oct. 30, 1770, in Voltaire and Frederick, *Letters*, 314.
10. Crocker, Lester, *Age of Crisis*, 133.
11. Gooch, *Frederick*, 138.
12. Gershoy, *From Despotism to Revolution*, 86.
13. Voltaire and Frederick, *Letters*, 249.
14. Frederick to Voltaire, July 2, 1759, and Oct. 31, 1760, in *Letters*, 256, 270.
15. Bertaut, J., *Napoleon in His Own Words*, 463.
16. Treitschke, *Life of Frederick*, 182.
17. In Hazard, Paul, *European Thought in the 18th Century*, 333.
18. *Sainte-Beuve, Portraits of the 18th Century*, II, 344.
19. *Ibid.*, 347.
20. In Mowat, 105.
21. Morley, in Voltaire, *Works*, XXIb, 195.
22. Sainte-Beuve, I, 220-21.
23. Voltaire and Frederick, *Letters*, 282.

24. Carlyle, *History of Friedrich the Second*, IV, 179n.
25. Frederick to Voltaire, Feb. 10, 1767.
26. Chesterfield to his son, *Letters*, June 23, 1752.
27. Schoenfeld, *Women of the Teutonic Nations*, 299.
28. Staël, Mme. de, *Germany*, I, 106; Gershoy, 75.
29. Paulsen, *German Education*, 142.
30. Gershoy, 284.
31. Carlyle, *Friedrich*, VII, 201.
32. Gershoy, 76; Renard and Weulersee, *Life and Work in Modern Europe*, 297.
33. *Ibid.*, 299.
34. Bruford, W. H., *Germany in the 18th Century*, 186.
35. *CMH*, VI, 718.
36. Gershoy, 84.
37. Frederick, *Testament* (1768), in *CMH*, VI, 723.
38. Bruford, 22.
39. Casanova, *Memoirs*, I, 349.
40. Burke, *Thoughts on French Affairs*, in *Reflections on the French Revolution*, 296.
41. Pascal, Roy, *The German Sturm und Drang*, 75-76.
42. Goethe, *Truth and Fiction*, I, 163.
43. Sime, James, *Lessing*, II, 131.
44. Schiller, *Poems*, 219-20. In *Works*.
45. Eckermann and Soret, *Conversations with Goethe*, 79.
46. Staël, Mme. de, *Germany*, I, 44.
47. Bruford, 39.
48. *Enc. Brit.*, IX, 132b.
49. Padover, *Revolutionary Emperor*, 289; Campbell, Thos., *The Jesuits*, 611.
50. Smith, Preserved, *History of Modern Culture*, II, 404.
51. Smith, N. K., *Commentary to Kant's "Critique of Pure Reason,"* 6.
52. Eckermann, introduction.
53. Staël, Mme. de, *Germany*, I, 118.
54. *Ibid.*, 116-17.
55. Goethe, *Truth and Fiction*, II, 251. In *Works*.
56. F. C. Schlosser in Monroe, Paul, *Textbook in the History of Education*, 580.
57. Morley in Voltaire, *Works*, XXIb, 153.
58. Nettle, *Mozart and Masonry*, 9.
59. Robertson, J. M., *Short History of Freethought*, II, 318.
60. *Ibid.*
61. 331.
62. Sime, *Lessing*, I, 27.
63. Garland, H. B., *Lessing*, 154.
64. *Ibid.*, 118.
65. Lessing, *Laocoön*, 190; Ch. xxvi, *ad. init.*
66. Bosanquet, *History of Aesthetic*, 221n.
67. Lessing, *Laocoön*, 56.
68. *Ibid.*, 57.

69. Sime, II, 4.
70. *Ibid.*, 55.
71. Lessing, *Hamburgische Dramaturgie*, No. 70, in Garland, 64.
72. Lessing, *Sämtliche Schriften*, X, 53, in Sime, II, 206.
73. Sime, II, 85.
74. Casanova, II, 271.
75. See *The Age of Voltaire*, 502.
76. Sime, II, 348.
77. Lessing, *Education of the Human Race*, No. 74 (Harvard Classics, Vol. XXXII, 212).
78. *Ibid.*, Nos. 85–86.
79. Brandes, *Goethe*, I, 434; Cassirer, *Philosophy of the Enlightenment*, 190.
80. Sime, II, 300; Brandes, *Goethe*, I, 434.
81. Sime, II, 346.
82. *Ibid.*, 330.
83. Klopstock, *The Messiah, ad finem.*
84. Goethe, *Truth and Fiction*, I, 79; II, 5. In *Works*.
85. *Penguin Book of German Verse*, 175.
86. *Ibid.*, 178-90.
87. Goethe, *Truth and Fiction*, II, 350. In *Works*.
88. Eckermann, 370 (Feb. 18, 1829).
89. Boehn, Max von, *Modes and Manners*, IV, 238.
90. Pascal, Roy, *The German Sturm und Drang*, 5.
91. *Ibid.*, 31.
92. Francke, Kuno, *History of German Literature*, 312.
93. *Ibid.*, 310.
94. Boehn, 124.
95. Schloss Tiefurt, near Weimar.
96. Schlossmuseum, Weimar.
97. Sanssouci Palace, Potsdam.
98. Winckelmann, II, 36.
99. Leipzig, Museum der Bildenden Künste.
100. Munich, Neue Pinakothek.
101. Dresden Gemäldegalerie.
102. Winterthur, Museum des Kunstvereins.
103. Schlossmuseum, Weimar.
104. Dresden Gemäldegalerie.
105. Weimar Museum.
106. Jahn, *Mozart*, III, 235.
107. Láng, P. H., *Music in Western Civilization*, 589.
108. *Grove's Dictionary of Music*, I, 175.
109. Jahn, II, 65.
110. *Grove's*, I, 145-55, 177-81.
111. Gooch, *Frederick*, 298.
112. Frederick, *Mémoires*, I, 56 f.
113. Gooch, 309.
114. *Ibid.*, 305.
115. 319.
116. 323.
117. Frederick, *Mémoires*, I, 56.
118. Gooch, *Frederick*, 319.
119. *Ibid.*, 280.
120. 292.
121. 287.
122. 287.
123. 291.
124. 89.
125. 294.
126. In Hauser, Arnold, *Social History of Art*, II, 602.
127. Pascal, Roy, *Sturm und Drang*, 42.
128. MacLaurin, *Mere Mortals*, 201.
129. Gooch, *Frederick*, 110.

CHAPTER XXI

1. Paulsen, *Immanuel Kant*, 26n.
2. Überweg, F., *History of Philosophy*, II, 139.
3. T. M. Greene in introd. to Kant, *Religion within the Limits of Reason Alone*, xxviii.
4. *Ibid.*, xxx.
5. Paulsen, *Kant*, 37.
6. Wilson, E. C., *Immanuel Kant*, 3.
7. Herder, *Briefe zur Beförderung der Humanität*, in Paulsen, *Kant*, 40.
8. Williams, H. S., *History of Science*, III, 27-28.
9. Lovejoy, Arthur, *The Great Chain of Being*, 266.
10. Harlow Shapley in Wilson, *Immanuel Kant*, 51.
11. Kant, *Critique of Judgment*, II, 78; Paulsen, 272n.
12. Überweg, II, 150.
13. Paulsen, 272n.
14. In Smith, N. K., *Commentary, xix.*
15. Kant, *Critique of Pure Reason*, 1st ed., 13 (preface).
16. *Critique of Judgment*, I, 3.
17. *Pure Reason*, 1st German ed., 10 (preface).
18. *Pure Reason*, 2d German ed., *xliii.*
19. *Ibid., xxx, xxxiv.*
20. *Prolegomena to Any Future Metaphysics*, 9 (preface).
21. In Paulsen, 96.
22. *Pure Reason*, 1st Germ. ed., 112.
23. *Ibid.*, 125; *Prolegomena*, No. 36.
24. *Pure Reason*, 42.
25. *Ibid.*, 307, 375.
26. *Pure Reason*, 2d Germ. ed., 131-33, 136, 139, 143.
27. *Ibid.*, 428.
28. First ed., 622-23.
29. *Ibid.*, 627.
30. 671-73, 675.
31. 468.
32. 683-92, 698.
33. 700.
34. Karl Reinhold in Paulsen, 114.
35. *Prolegomena*, 13 (preface).
36. *Pure Reason*, first ed., 298, 752.

37. Robertson, J. M., *Short History of Freethought*, II, 337.
38. *Pure Reason*, 2d ed., *xxx, xxxiv*.
39. Kant, *Fundamental Principles of the Metaphysics of Ethics*, 35.
40. Kant, *Critique of Practical Reason*, 313.
41. *Ibid.*, 248, 259.
42. 142.
43. *Fundamental Principles*, 68.
44. *Ibid.*, 57.
45. *Practical Reason*, 108-9, 146.
46. *Pure Reason*, 2d ed., 571-73.
47. *Ibid.*, *xxviii*, 566-69, 580-81; *Practical Reason*, 164 f.
48. *Ibid.*, 259 f.
49. 260.
50. *Pure Reason*, 1st ed., 819.
51. Cassirer, *Rousseau, Kant, and Goethe*, 25.
52. Heine, H., *Religion and Philosophy in Germany*, in Paulsen, 8a.
53. *Critique of Judgment*, I, 18, 15.
54. *Ibid.*
55. 46.
56. *Critique of Judgment*, II, 89.
57. *Ibid.*, 117.
58. Kant, *Werke*, VI, 129, in Cassirer, *Rousseau, Kant, and Goethe*, 39.
59. Überweg, II, 141.
60. Kant, *Religion within the Limits of Reason Alone*, 3.
61. *Ibid.*, 8.
62. 8.
63. 28.
64. 29.
65. Kant, *Education*, No. 19.
66. Kant, *Religion*, 35.
67. Kant, "Conjectural Beginning of the History of Man," in Überweg, II, 186.
68. Kant, *Religion*, 51.
69. *Ibid.*, 147, 159-61.
70. 142-43.
71. 91.
72. 63.
73. 117.
74. 57, 134.
75. 186.
76. 183-85.
77. 153, 164-65, 168, 112.
78. *Ibid.*, *xxxiv*.
79. Kant, *A Philosophical Treatise on Perpetual Peace*, 10.
80. *Ibid.*, 28.
81. 32.
82. *Practical Reason*, 341n.
83. *Perpetual Peace*, 78.
84. Paulsen, 351.
85. *Perpetual Peace*, 29-30; Smith, N. K., *Commentary*, lvii.
86. *Education*, No. 30.
87. *Ibid.*, No. 7.
88. Paulsen, 374.
89. *Practical Reason*, 326n.

90. *Ibid.*, introd. by T. G. Abbott, *xliii*.
91. *Ibid.*, *xliv*.
92. Paulsen, 45.
93. *Ibid.*, 47; Klinke, *Kant for Everyman*, 105.
94. Stuckenberg, *Life of Kant*, 340-54, in Robertson, J. M., *Freethought*, II, 343.
95. Robertson, II, 345.
96. Letter of Apr., 1766, in *Religion within the Limits of Reason Alone*, introd., *xxxvi*.
97. Paulsen, 52.
98. Vaihinger, *The Philosophy of "As if,"* 313.
99. *Ibid.*, 316-17.
100. Witte, *Schiller*, 46.
101. Schiller, *Poems*, 290.
102. Eckermann, 79 (Apr. 14, 1824).
103. Emerson, lecture of 1842 on "The Transcendentalist," in Wilson, E. C., *Immanuel Kant*, 23.

CHAPTER XXII

1. Eckermann, 138 (Apr. 27, 1825).
2. Lewisohn, L., *Goethe*, I, 134.
3. Schiller to Körner, Aug. 8 and Sept. 10, 1787, in Schiller and Körner, *Correspondence*, I, 140-43.
4. Brandes, *Goethe*, I, 307.
5. Staël, Mme. de, *Germany*, I, 101.
6. Francke, *History of German Literature*, 253.
7. Wieland, *History of Agathon*, I, *xxiv*.
8. Francke, 255.
9. *Agathon*, I, 123 (Book III, Ch. ii).
10. *Ibid.*, Book III, Ch. iii.
11. In Francke, 258.
12. Eckermann, 285 (Sept. 26, 1827).
13. Mann, Thos., *Three Essays*, 8.
14. Goethe, *Truth and Fiction*, I, 385. In *Works*.
15. *Ibid.*, 155 f.
16. 209-30.
17. 178.
18. 175.
19. 233.
20. 318.
21. Goethe, *Works*, VII, 27.
22. *Truth and Fiction*, I, 306. In *Works*.
23. *Ibid.*, 367.
24. 368.
25. Brandes, *Goethe*, I, 71.
26. Autobiography of Heinrich Jung-Stilling in Lewisohn, I, 49.
27. In Ludwig, Emil, *Goethe*, 31.
28. *Truth and Fiction*, I, 407.
29. In Ludwig, 42.
30. Eckermann, 291 (Oct. 8, 1827).
31. E.g., *Truth and Fiction*, II, 43.
32. *Ibid.*, 75.
33. Letter of June, 1771, in Lewisohn, I, 57.

34. *Truth and Fiction*, II, 120.
35. *Ibid.*, 143.
36. Brandes, I, 140.
37. Ludwig, 57.
38. Goethe, *Götz von Berlichingen*, Act I, Sc. ii.
39. *Truth*, II, 167.
40. From Kestner's diary, in Lewisohn, I, 71.
41. *Truth*, II, 188.
42. *Ibid.*, 214
43. 214.
44. Brandes, I, 273.
45. In Ludwig, 87.
46. Lewisohn, I, 101.
47. *Truth*, II, 216-17.
48. Eckermann, 52 (Jan. 2, 1824).
49. Goethe, *Werther*, letters of July 19 and 21 and Aug. 30, 1771.
50. Goethe, letter to Kestner, Nov. 20, 1774, in Lewisohn, I, 105.
51. Sime, *Lessing*, II, 200.
52. Lewisohn, I, 101.
53. Kestner, letter to Hennings, Nov. 18, 1772, in Pascal, *German Sturm und Drang*, 108.
54. *Truth*, Book XII.
55. In Ludwig, 94.
56. Lavater's diary, June 28, 1774, in Lewisohn, I, 99.
57. Goethe's letter of Nov. 12, 1816, in Lewisohn, II, 262.
58. Lewisohn, I, 295.
59. *Truth*, II, 261, 309.
60. Translation in Carus, Paul, *Goethe*, 245-47.
61. *Truth*, II, 318, 327.
62. *Ibid.*, 366.
63. Clark, Robert, *Herder*, 160.
64. *Truth*, II, 11.
65. *Ibid.*, 16.
66. In Pascal, *German Sturm und Drang*, 225.
67. Heiseler, B. von, *Schiller*, 49.
68. Schiller, *Poems*, 7. In *Works*.
69. *Ibid.*, 9.
70. Carlyle, *Life of Schiller*, 15. In *Works*.
71. Schiller, *The Robbers*, Act I, Sc. ii.
72. *Ibid.*, II, iii.
73. *Ibid.*
74. V, i.
75. Heiseler, 47.
76. Ungar, Frederick, *Friedrich Schiller*, 34.
77. Witte, *Schiller*, 131.
78. Heiseler, 83.
79. Schiller, *Philosophical Letters*, p. 376 (Letter I). In *Works*.
80. *Ibid.*, 385 (Letter IV).
81. Schiller and Körner, *Correspondence*, I, 12.
82. *Ibid.*, 13-16.
83. Heiseler, 85.
84. *Ibid.*
85. Schiller and Körner, *Correspondence*, I, 30-33.
86. Körner to Schiller, July 8, 1785, in *Correspondence*, I, 36.

CHAPTER XXIII

1. Einstein, *Mozart*, 19.
2. Goethe, *Truth and Fiction*, I, 291. In *Works*.
3. Schiller to Körner, July 28 and Aug. 29, 1787.
4. Schiller and Körner, *Correspondence*, I, 85.
5. *Ibid.*, 90, 168.
6. Wieland, *Oberon*, introd.
7. Brandes, *Goethe*, II, 266-69.
8. Lewisohn, II, 209.
9. Schiller and Körner, I, 85.
10. Pascal, *German Sturm und Drang*, 17.
11. *Ibid.*, 18.
12. 17.
13. Goethe to Jacobi, Nov. 12, 1783.
14. Goethe to Lavater, December, 1783.
15. Schiller and Körner, I, 85.
16. Clark, *Herder*, 240.
17. Bancroft, Geo., *Literary and Historical Miscellanies*, 173.
18. Herder to Hamann, Jan. 13, 1777, in Pascal, 95.
19. Clark, *Herder*, 274-77.
20. Herder to Jacobi, Feb. 6 and Dec. 30, 1784, in Pascal, 104.
21. Pascal, 104.
22. Clark, 340.
23. Pascal, 106.
24. Clark, 303.
25. *Ibid.*, 322.
26. 357.
27. 368.
28. Lewisohn, I, 133.
29. *Ibid.*
30. 153.
31. Eckermann, 285 (Sept. 26, 1827).
32. Lewisohn, I, 134.
33. *Ibid.*, 135.
34. 137-40.
35. 141.
36. 146.
37. 150.
38. Goethe to Charlotte von Stein, May 24, 1776.
39. Lewisohn, I, 151.
40. *Ibid.*, 156.
41. 222.
42. Brandes, I, 335.
43. Lewisohn, I, 327.
44. *Ibid.*, 236.
45. 271.
46. 306.
47. Eckermann, 251 (Apr. 25, 1827).
48. Goethe's diary, in Lewisohn, I, 215.
49. Ludwig, 440.
50. Translation by Longfellow.
51. Lewisohn, I, 232.

52. See *The Age of Reason Begins*, 259-65.
53. Goethe, *Tasso*, Act I, Sc. ii.
54. *Ibid.*, II, i.
55. I, ii.
56. *Ibid.*
57. Letter of Apr. 24, 1783, in Lewisohn, I, 266.
58. Ludwig, 155.
59. Lewisohn, I, 309.
60. Ludwig, 217.
61. Letter of Oct. 8, 1786, in *Letters from Italy*, 177.
62. Ludwig, 222.
63. Städelsches Museum, Frankfurt.
64. Lewisohn, I, 320.
65. *Ibid.*, 322.
66. Eckermann, 133, 201 (Jan. 30, 1825, and Jan. 18, 1827).
67. *Letters from Italy*, Dec. 3, 1786, and Feb. 16, 1787.
68. *Ibid.*, Dec. 1 and 3, 1786.
69. Feb. 3, 1787, in Lewisohn, I, 327.
70. In McKinney and Anderson, *Music in History*, 511.
71. Eckermann, 213 (Jan. 29, 1827).
72. Taine, *Philosophy of Art*, in Brandes, *Goethe*, I, 457.
73. Letter of Dec. 13, 1786, in Lewisohn, I, 323.
74. Lewisohn, I, 353.
75. Brandes, I, 469.
76. Lewisohn, I, 257.
77. Goethe, *Poetical Works*, 34-42. In *Works*.
78. Lewisohn, I, 368.
79. Ludwig, 300.
80. Brandes, II, 50.
81. Letter of Jan. 3, 1781, in Lewisohn, I, 229.
82. Examples in Lewisohn, I, 101-2, 186-88, 196-97, 229, 379.
83. Ludwig, 246.
84. Schiller and Körner, *Correspondence*, I, 112.
85. *Ibid.*, 89 (Aug. 28, 1787).
86. Letters of July 28 and Aug. 18, 1787.
87. *Don Carlos*, Act III, Sc. x.
88. Schiller to Körner, Apr. 15, 1786.
89. Körner to Schiller, November, 1788.
90. Schiller to Körner, Sept. 12, 1788.
91. Schiller and Körner, *Correspondence*, II, 330.
92. Letter of May 28, 1789.
93. Carlyle, *Life of Schiller*, 103. In *Works*.
94. Letter of Dec. 7, 1787.
95. Heiseler, 114.
96. Letter of Mar. 1, 1790.
97. Heiseler, 119.
98. Schiller to Körner, Feb. 22, 1791.
99. Letter of May 24, 1791.
100. Schiller, *Essays*, 203. In *Works*.
101. *On the Aesthetic Education of Mankind*, Letters VII and x in *Essays*, 45, 53.
102. Letter of May 5, 1792.

103. Ludwig, 326.
104. Schiller, *Poems*, 272. In *Works*.
105. Schiller to Goethe, Aug. 17, 1795, in Schiller and Goethe, *Correspondence*, I, 88-89.
106. *On Naïve and Sentimental Poetry*.
107. Eckermann, Oct. 7, 1827.
108. *Cf.* letter to Körner, Aug. 29, 1787.
109. Schiller to Goethe, Aug. 23, 1794.
110. Schiller to Goethe, Aug. 31, 1794.
111. Goethe, "Happy Incident," in Carlyle, *Life of Schiller*, 305. In *Works*.
112. Schiller and Goethe, *Correspondence*, I, 1.
113. *Ibid.*, 5.
114. 6.
115. Schiller to Körner, Feb. 1, 1796.
116. In Ungar, *Schiller*, 129.
117. *Ibid.*, 140.
118. Schiller, *Essays*, 286, 321. In *Works*.
119. *Wilhelm Meisters Lehrjahre*, I, 324.
120. Schiller to Körner, Dec. 9, 1794, Feb. 22, 1795, June 15, 1795, July 2, 1796.
121. Letters of July 2-9, Oct. 9, and Oct. 23, 1796.
122. Goethe to Schiller, July 7, 1796.
123. Eckermann, Mar. 23, 1829.
124. Ludwig, 385-86.
125. Eckermann, Mar. 22, 1825.
126. Lewes, G. H., *Life of Goethe*, II, 202.
127. Goethe to Schiller, Jan. 18, 1797.
128. *Hermann and Dorothea*, 56-57. In *Works*.
129. Brandes, II, 470.
130. Schiller to Körner, Jan. 5, 1800.
131. Eckermann, July 23, 1827.
132. Heiseler, 143.
133. Ludwig, 386.
134. Schiller to Charlotte Schimmelmann.
135. Goethe to Schiller, Feb. 28, 1801.
136. Eckermann, Oct. 7, 1827.
137. Lewisohn, I, 61.
138. Letter of Jan. 20, 1801.
139. Heiseler, 170.
140. Staël, Mme. de, *Germany*, I, 182.
141. Schiller to Goethe, Dec. 21, 1803, in Lewisohn, II, 92.
142. *Ibid.*
143. Staël, 23-24.
144. Lewisohn, II, 293.
145. Heiseler, 189.
146. Eckermann, Jan. 18, 1827.
147. Witte. *Schiller*, 38.
148. Goethe to Zelter, June 1, 1805, in Lewisohn, II, 107.

CHAPTER XXIV

1. *Cf.* final lines of *Faust*, Part II.
2. Brandes, *Goethe*, II, 250.
3. Recollections of Friedrich von Müller, in Lewisohn, II, 161.
4. Brandes, 263-64.
5. *Ibid.*

6. Eckermann, Mar. 15, 1829.
7. For the historical background of the Faust legend see *The Reformation*, 852.
8. Goethe, *Truth and Fiction*, II, 21-22. In *Works*.
9. Lewisohn, I, 123.
10. *Ibid.*
11. Eckermann, Feb. 10, 1829.
12. Brandes, 305.
13. In the *Gesamtausgabe* by Breitkopf and Härtel.
14. Translation by Albert Latham in Everyman's Library ed. of *Faust*.
15. Eckermann, Jan. 10, 1825.
16. Latham's translation, p. 52.
17. *Ibid.*, 117-19.
18. 116.
19. Brandes, 229.
20. Lewisohn, II, 174.
21. *Elective Affinities*, English tr., 335. In *Works*.
22. *Ibid.*, 180.
23. 218.
24. Ludwig, 427.
25. *Ibid.*, 429.
26. 453.
27. Lewisohn, II, 202-4.
28. Ludwig, 445.
29. Lewisohn, II, 250.
30. *Ibid.*, 303.
31. 334.
32. 306-8.
33. Ungar, Frederick, *Goethe's World View*, 9.
34. Magnus, Rudolf, *Goethe as a Scientist*, 221.
35. *Ibid.*, xvi-xviii, 209.
36. 167.
37. 178.
38. Goethe's letter of May 17, 1787.
39. Magnus, 73.
40. *Ibid.*, 78; Brandes, 462.
41. *Ibid.*, 429.
42. Magnus, 42.
43. Ludwig, 188.
44. Magnus, 136.
45. Eckermann, Apr. 16, 1825.
46. Ungar, *Goethe's World View*, 31.
47. *Ibid.*, 77.
48. *Faust*, Part II, line 1754.
49. Ungar, *Goethe's World View*, 9, 105.
50. Letter of Jan. 6, 1798.
51. Ungar, 99.
52. Goethe, *Truth and Fiction*, II, 108. In *Works*.
53. Quoted in Mann, *Three Essays*, 49.
54. *Truth and Fiction*, Part III, Book II.
55. Ludwig, 3.
56. Ungar, *Goethe's World View*, 47.
57. *Ibid.*
58. *Truth and Fiction*, II, 272-73.
59. Lewisohn, I, 255.
60. *Truth and Fiction*, Book XIV.

61. Ungar, *Goethe's World View*, 47.
62. *Ibid.*, 41.
63. 37.
64. 37.
65. 43-45; Smith, Preserved, *Age of the Reformation*, 712.
66. *Truth and Fiction*, II, 311 f.
67. Ungar, *Goethe's World View*, 55.
68. Ludwig, 206.
69. *Ibid.*, 457.
70. Recollections of Johann Falk, in Lewisohn, II, 210.
71. Goethe to Zelter, May 11, 1820.
72. Brandes, I, 437.
73. Ungar, *Goethe's World View*, 81.
74. *Ibid.*, 6.
75. Eckermann, Apr. 2, 1829.
76. Ungar, 167.
77. *Ibid.*, 129.
78. 139.
79. 16.
80. 89.
81. *Truth and Fiction*, I, 421.
82. *Wilhelm Meisters Lehrjahre*, Book VII, Ch. iii.
83. *Ibid.*, Book V, Ch. iii.
84. Carus, *Goethe*, 168.
85. *Faust*, Part II, Act II.
86. Eckermann, Jan. 4, 1824.
87. Ungar, *Goethe's World View*, 59.
88. Eckermann, Feb. 13, 1829.
89. Ungar, 141.
90. *Ibid.*
91. 91.
92. Lewisohn, II, 438.
93. *Faust*, Part II, p. 341.
94. *Ibid.*, 407.
95. Friedrich von Müller, in Lewisohn, II, 370.
96. *Ibid.*, 371.
97. 376.
98. 430.
99. Goethe to Zelter, Dec. 14, 1830.
100. Lewisohn, II, 411.
101. Ungar, *Goethe's World View*, 131.
102. Mann, *Three Essays*, 63.
103. *Truth and Fiction*, II, 246.
104. Ludwig, 293.
105. *Ibid.*, 472.
106. In Mann, 47.
107. Lewisohn, II, 254.
108. In Friedell, Egon, *Cultural History of the Modern Age*, I, 272.
109. In Mann, 64.
110. We have followed the account given by K. W. Müller in 1832, in Lewisohn, II, 449 f.
111. Eckermann, 572.

CHAPTER XXV

1. In Masson, P. M., *La Religion de Rousseau*, II, 240.

2. See "Sermon of Rabbi Akib," and art. "Jews" in *Philosophical Dictionary*.
3. *Ibid.*, Sec. III.
4. Sec. IV.
5. See *The Age of Voltaire*, Ch. xiii, Sec. VII.
6. *Cf.* Black, J. B., *The Art of History*, 49-50.
7. Graetz, H., *History of the Jews*, V, 346.
8. Gay, *Voltaire's Politics*, 352.
9. Graetz, V, 347.
10. Rousseau, *Émile*, 267-68.
11. Sombart, W., *The Jews and Modern Capitalism*, 56.
12. Lea, H. C., *History of the Inquisition in Spain*, III, 308-11.
13. Altamira, *History of Spain*, 462.
14. Parton, *Life of Voltaire*, I, 161.
15. Bell, Aubrey, *Portuguese Literature*, 280.
16. Lea, III, 310.
17. Abbott, G. F., *Israel in Europe*, 209.
18. Abrahams, I., *Jewish Life in the Middle Ages*, 224.
19. *Ibid.*
20. Padover, *The Revolutionary Emperor*, 252.
21. *Jewish Encyclopedia*, XII, 434; Padover, 253 f; Graetz, V, 357.
22. Padover, 257.
23. Letter of May 17, 1717, in Montagu, Lady Mary W., *Letters and Works*, II, 321.
24. Dubnow, S. M., *History of the Jews in Russia and Poland*, I, 255-58; Florinsky, *Russia*, I, 490.
25. Dubnow, I, 307.
26. *Ibid.*, 189.
27. 169-71.
28. 173.
29. 172-79.
30. 179-80.
31. 182-86.
32. Roth, Cecil, *The Jewish Contribution to Civilization*, 28.
33. Sombart, 23.
34. *Jew. Enc.*, XIX, 418a.
35. *Ibid.*, 415-18.
36. Corti, Egon C., *Rise of the House of Rothschild*, I, 19.
37. George, M. Dorothy, *London Life in the 18th Century*, 127.
38. Besant, Sir Walter, *London in the 18th Century*, 178.
39. Roth, 242.
40. Finkelstein, Louis, ed., *The Jews*, I, 260.
41. Besant, 180.
42. Browne, Lewis, *The Wisdom of Israel*, 551.
43. Dubnow, I, 233.
44. *Ibid.*, 222 f.; Baron, Salo, *Social and Religious History of the Jews*, II, 54 f.: Graetz, V, 374 f; Howe and Greenberg, *Treasury of Yiddish Stories*, 15 f.

45. Graetz, V, 294.
46. Hensel, S., *The Mendelssohn Family*, 4.
47. Sime, *Lessing*, I, 133.
48. Graetz, V, 298.
49. In Wolf, A., *History of Science . . . in the 18th Century*, 781.
50. Graetz, V, 309.
51. *Ibid.*, 311.
52. Hensel, 10.
53. Graetz, V, 317.
54. *Jew. Enc.*, VIII, 482d.
55. Graetz, V, 365.
56. *Ibid.*, 355.

CHAPTER XXVI

1. Voltaire, *Works*, 1b, 302.
2. In Herold, J., *The Swiss without Halos*, 106.
3. Oechsli, W., *History of Switzerland*, 290.
4. Parton, *Life of Voltaire*, II, 458.
5. Lewisohn, II, 238-39.
6. Goethe, *Truth and Fiction*, II, 240-46, 252, 375, 398-404. In *Works*.
7. Holberg, Ludwig, *Selected Essays*, p. 48 (Epistle 48).
8. Lady Mary Wortley Montagu, letters of Aug. 3 and 5, 1716, in *Letters and Works*, II, 226-27.
9. Desnoiresterres, *Voltaire et la société française*, I, 237.
10. *Boswell in Holland*, 288.
11. Cumming, Ian, *Helvétius*, 50.
12. Smith, Adam, *Wealth of Nations*, I, 81.
13. Parton, *Life of Voltaire*, I, 152.
14. Blok, P. J., *History of the People of the Netherlands*, Part V, 174 f.; Robertson, J. M., *Short History of Freethought*, II, 353.
15. Blok, V, 183.
16. *Ibid.*, 92.
17. 86.
18. Dillon, Edw., *Glass*, 295 f.; Sitwell, S., *The Netherlands*, 147.
19. George Dempter to Boswell, Aug. 26, 1763.
20. *Boswell in Holland*, 93.
21. *Ibid.*, 317.
22. Herold, *Mistress to an Age*, 143.
23. *Ibid.*, 144.
24. Blok, V, 56.
25. *Ibid.*, 108.
26. Horn, F. W., *History of the Literature of the Scandinavian North*, 187.
27. Freedley and Reeves, *History of the Theatre*, 268.
28. Holberg, *Seven One-Act Plays*, 165-87.
29. Matthews, Brander, *The Chief European Dramatists*, 705.
30. Holberg, *Journey of Niels Klim to the World Underground*, 10.
31. *Ibid.*, 18.
32. 32.

33. 109.
34. 191.
35. 109.
36. Translation by Longfellow, in Van Doren, Mark, *Anthology of World Poetry*, 981.
37. Horn, *Scandinavian Literature*, 217.
38. Goodwin, A., *European Nobility*, 136.
39. *CMH*, VI, 762.
40. Bain, R. N., *Gustavus III*, I, 56.
41. *CMH*, VI, 768.
42. Bain, *Gustavus III*, I, 124.
43. Andersson, Ingvar, *History of Sweden*, 281.
44. Higgs, *The Physiocrats*, 87.
45. Bain, *Gustavus III*, I, 163.
46. *CMH*, VI, 776.
47. *Enc. Brit.*, XXI, 653d; Smith, Preserved, *History of Modern Culture*, II, 460, 108.
48. Gustafson, Alrik, *History of Swedish Literature*, 112, 136.
49. Bain, *Gustavus III*, I, 260; Horn, 355.
50. Bain, II, 239.
51. Horn, 359 f.
52. Gustafson, 139 f.
53. Bain, *Gustavus III*, II, 286-88; Gustafson, 139 f.
54. Horn, 369.
55. Bain, II, 210.
56. *Ibid.*, I, 38.
57. *Ibid.*, II, 157.

CHAPTER XXVII

1. Shakespeare, *Richard II*, Act II, Sc. i.
2. Nussbaum, *History of the Economic Institutions of Modern Europe*, 130.
3. Namier, Sir Lewis, *Crossroads of Power*, 175.
4. Ashton, T. S., *Economic History of England*, 179.
5. Watson, J. S., *Reign of George III*, 28.
6. Nussbaum, 73.
7. Hammond, J. L. and Barbara, *The Village Labourer*, 17.
8. Usher, A. P., *An Introd. to the Industrial History of England*, 323.
9. Quennell, M. and C., *History of Everyday Things in England*, 79.
10. Mantoux, Paul, *The Industrial Revolution in the 18th Century*, 258.
11. Samuel Smiles, *Lives of the Engineers*, in *History Today*, April, 1956, 263.
12. *Ibid.*, 263, 265.
13. *The Age of Voltaire*, 517.
14. Mantoux, 326.
15. Usher, *Introd. to Industrial History*, 326.
16. Boswell, *Life of Johnson*, 598.
17. Lipson, E., *Growth of English Society*, 190.
18. Mantoux, 385; George, *London Life*, 206-7.

19. Smith, Adam, *Wealth of Nations*, I, 73.
20. Mantoux, 439; Smith, 60.
21. Ashton, 203.
22. Mantoux, 70.
23. Arthur Young in Turberville, *Johnson's England*, I, 218.
24. Müller-Lyer, F., *History of Social Development*, 221.
25. Mantoux, 420.
26. *Ibid.*, 421.
27. Barnes, H. E., *Economic History of the Western World*, 313.
28. Webb, Sidney and Beatrice, *History of Trade Unionism*, 51.
29. Ashton, 235.
30. Traill, H. D., *Social England*, V, 336.
31. Mantoux, 411.
32. *Ibid.*, 413.
33. 413.
34. Lecky, *History of England*, III, 135-36.
35. Smith, *Wealth of Nations*, I, 59.
36. Rogers, J. E. T., *Six Centuries of Work and Wages*, 89.

CHAPTER XXVIII

1. George, M. D., *England in Transition*, 218 f.
2. *Ibid.*, 219.
3. 218.
4. Namier, *Structure of Politics at the Accession of George III*, 80.
5. New *CMH*, VII, 245.
6. Lecky, *History of England*, III, 172.
7. Wilson, P. W., *William Pitt the Younger*, 6.
8. Plumb, J. H., *Men and Places*, 22.
9. Namier, *Structure of Politics*, 77-79.
10. *Ibid.*, 150.
11. Lecky, III, 171.
12. Blackstone, Sir W., *Commentaries on the Laws of England*, 17 (p. 50 of orig. ed.).
13. Namier, *Crossroads of Power*, 133.
14. Thackeray, *The Four Georges*, 62.
15. Cf. Butterfield, *George III and the Historians*, 175; Morley, John, *Burke: a Historical Study*, 9.
16. Lecky, III, 11; Namier in *History Today*, September, 1953, p. 615.
17. Watson, J. S., *The Reign of George III*, 6.
18. *Age of Voltaire*, Ch. iii, Sec. IX; present volume, Ch. ii, Secs. II, IV.
19. Walpole, Horace, *Memoirs of the Reign of George III*, II, 331.
20. Burke, Edmund, speech on American Taxation, in *Speeches and Letters on American Affairs*, 28.
21. Burke, *Vindication of Natural Society*, 9.
22. *Ibid.*
23. 12-20.
24. 20.

25. 22.

26. 44.

27. 21.

28. 48.

29. 50.

30. Morley, John, *Burke*, 13.

31. *Vindication*, 4 (preface).

32. Burke, *On Taste, and On the Sublime and Beautiful*, 45 f.

33. *Ibid.*

34. 93.

35. 95.

36. Macaulay, *Essays*, I, 454.

37. Morley, *Burke*, 30.

38. *Ibid.*, 104.

39. Boswell, *Journal of a Tour to the Hebrides*, 141.

40. Stephen, Sir Leslie, *History of English Thought in the 18th Century*, I, 222.

41. *Parliamentary History*, XXXVII, 363, in Buckle, H. T., *An Introd. to the History of Civilization in England*, I, 327.

42. Piozzi, Hester Thrale, *Anecdotes of the Late Samuel Johnson*, 138.

43. Morley, *Burke*, 107.

44. In *Cambridge History of English Literature*, XI, 9.

45. *Enc. Brit.*, XI, 644d.

46. Moore, Thomas, *Memoirs of the Life of Sheridan*, I, 78.

47. Drinkwater, John, *Charles James Fox*, 9, 11.

48. Staël, Mme. de, *Germany*, I, 277.

49. Thackeray, *Four Georges*, 87.

50. *Enc. Brit.*, IX, 568b.

51. Drinkwater, 195.

52. Walpole, Horace, *Letters*, Feb. 4, 1778.

53. Lecky, III, 468.

54. Gibbon, Edward, *Memoirs*, 54.

55. National Gallery, London; Dulwich College; National Gallery, Washington.

56. Moore, *Sheridan*, I, 17.

57. *The Rivals*, Act I, Sc. ii.

58. *Ibid.*, III, iii.

59. In Taine, II., *English Literature*, 355.

60. *Enc. Brit.*, XVII, 973b.

61. Wilson, P. W., *William Pitt*, 58.

62. Dorn, W. L., *Competition for Empire*, 75.

63. Walpole, letter of Oct. 31, 1760.

64. Laski, Harold, *Political Thought in England, Locke to Bentham*, 144.

65. Butterfield, *George III*, 173.

66. Lecky, III, 61.

67. Macaulay, *Essays*, I, 431.

68. Wilson, *William Pitt*, 44.

69. Gibbon, Edward, *Journal*, 145.

70. *Enc. Brit.*, XXIII, 602b.

71. *Ibid.*

72. Sherwin, *A Gentleman of Wit and Fashion: The Life and Times of George Selwyn*, 47-53.

73. Jefferson, D. W., *Eighteenth-Century Prose*, 140.

74. Walpole, *Memoirs of Reign of George III*, I, 248.

75. *Enc. Brit.*, XXIII, 603d.

76. Walpole, *Reign of George III*, I, 263.

77. *Boswell on the Grand Tour: Italy, Corsica and France*, 5.

78. Walpole, *Reign of George III*, III, 239.

79. Lecky, III, 151.

80. S. MacCoby, ed., *The English Radical Tradition*, 2.

81. Lecky, III, 175-76.

82. *Ibid.*, 152.

83. MacCoby, 2.

84. Lecky, III, 153.

85. Junius, *Letters*, 3-6.

86. Junius, letter of Nov. 29, 1769.

87. *Letters*, pp. 134, 148.

88. *Ibid.*, p. 29.

89. Lecky, II, 468.

90. Walpole, *Reign of George III*, IV, 78; Lecky, III, 143.

91. MacCoby, 31.

92. *Enc. Brit.*, XXIII, 603d.

93. *CMH*, VIII, 714.

94. Lecky, III, 268.

95. *Ibid.*, 300.

96. Watson, *Reign of George III*, 174.

97. Ashton, 158; Traill, V, 115.

98. Hammond, J. L. and Barbara, *Rise of Modern Industry*, 32.

99. Lecky, III, 299.

100. Drinkwater, 94.

101. *CMH*, VIII, 521.

102. Lecky, III, 331.

103. Beard, Charles and Mary, *Rise of American Civilization*, I, 212.

104. Peterson, Houston, *Treasury of the World's Great Speeches*, 102-22.

105. Lecky, III, 530.

106. *Ibid.*, 531.

107. 545.

108. Peterson, 143-46.

109. *CHE*, IX, 6.

110. Sherwin, 205.

111. Burke, *Speeches and Letters on American Affairs*, 84.

112. *Ibid.*, 118-19.

113. Drinkwater, 145.

114. Walpole, letter of Sept. 11, 1775.

115. Lecky, IV, 82.

116. Churchill, Sir Winston, *History of the English-Speaking Peoples*, II, 116.

117. Lecky, IV, 221.

118. Namier, *Crossroads*, 130.

119. *Enc. Brit.*, V, 833d.

120. Namier, *Crossroads*, 164.

121. Walpole, letter of Mar. 5, 1772.

122. Lecky, III, 491.

123. *CMH*, VI, 570.

124. *Ibid.*, 572.

125. 578-80.
126. Walpole, letter of Mar. 2, 1773.
127. Wilson, *William Pitt*, 171.
128. Morley, *Burke*, 33; Namier, *Crossroads*, 165-67.
129. Watson, *Reign of George III*, 319.
130. Morley, *Burke*, 125.
131. G. G. S., *Life of R. B. Sheridan*, 113.
132. Macaulay, *Essays*, I, 633.
133. Peterson, *Great Speeches*, 179.
134. Gibbon, *Memoirs*, 334.
135. Macaulay, I, 644.
136. Burke, *Observations on the State of the Nation* (1769), in Lecky, V, 335n.
137. Burke, speech on "Relief of Protestant Dissenters" (1773), in Morley, *Burke*, 69.
138. Wilson, *William Pitt*, 226.
139. Stephen, *English Thought in the 18th Century*, I, 279.
140. Lecky, V, 449; Wilson, 235.
141. Burke, *Reflections on the French Revolution*, 8.
142. *Enc. Brit.*, IV, 418c.
143. Burke, *Reflections*, 35.
144. *Ibid.*, 18 f.
145. 36.
146. 73.
147. *Enc. Brit.*, IV, 418d.
148. *CHE*, X, 285.
149. Morley, *Burke*, 179.
150. *Ibid.*, 15.
151. Burke, *Reflections*, 93.
152. *Ibid.*, 6.
153. *CHE*, XI, 11.
154. *Letter to a Member of the National Assembly*, in *Reflections*, 279.
155. Burke, 87.
156. Lecky, III, 218-19; Stephen, *English Thought in the 18th Century*, I, 251-52; Laski, 159, 171.
157. Laski, 147.
158. Sherwin, *Selwyn*, 275.
159. Taine, *English Literature*, 416.
160. Wilson, 325.
161. G. G. S., *Life of Sheridan*, 155.

CHAPTER XXIX

1. Eckermann and Soret, *Conversations with Goethe*, Mar. 12, 1827.
2. Lecky, *England in the 18th Century*, VI, 139.
3. Quennell, *Everyday Things*, 93.
4. George, *London Life*, 103.
5. Quennell, 90.
6. George, 26.
7. Boswell, *Hebrides*, 31.
8. Lecky, VI, 153.
9. Nussbaum, *History of Economic Institutions*, 128.
10. Boswell, *Life of Johnson*, 1, 781.
11. Sherwin, *George Selwyn*, 34.
12. *Ibid.*, 125.
13. Drinkwater, *Charles James Fox*, 13.
14. Lecky, VI, 152.
15. Boswell, *Johnson*, 978.
16. *Age of Voltaire*, Ch. ii, Sec. vi.
17. *Wealth of Nations*, II, 276.
18. Stephen, *English Thought*, I, 421.
19. Besant, *London*, 282-83.
20. Sherwin, 288.
21. *Vicar of Wakefield*, Ch. xxiv.
22. Boswell, *Johnson*, 338.
23. Lecky, VI, 268; Drinkwater, 131.
24. Lecky, VI, 269.
25. Boswell, *Johnson*, 846.
26. Walpole, Mar. 22, 1780.
27. *CMH*, VI, 187.
28. Buckle, *An Introd. to the History . . . of England*, I, 321n.
29. George, *London Life*, 135.
30. Botsford, J. B., *English Society in the 18th Century*, 332 f.
31. Blackstone, *Commentaries*, 128-29.
32. *Enc. Brit.*, XX, 780a.
33. *Ibid.*, 780d.
34. Faÿ, Bernard, *Franklin*, 77.
35. Mowat, *Age of Reason*, 61.
36. Quennell, 9.
37. Watson, P. B., *Some Women of France*, 77.
38. Walpole, *Memoirs of the Reign of George III*, IV, 158.
39. Boswell, *Johnson*, 597.
40. Burke, *Reflections*, 86.
41. *Boswell on the Grand Tour: Italy . . .*, 184.
42. Robertson, *Short History of Freethought*, II, 206.
43. *Boswell in Holland*, 62.
44. Gibbon, *Decline and Fall of the Roman Empire*, V, 554.
45. Faÿ, *La Franc-Maçonnerie*, 273.
46. *Age of Voltaire*, pp. 528, 580.
47. Cowper, *The Task*, ii, lines 378-94.
48. Stephen, *English Thought*, II, 375.
49. Walpole, June 3, 1780.
50. Walpole, June 7, 1780.
51. June 16, 1780.
52. Lecky, V, 189.
53. Sir F. D. McKinnon, in Turberville, *Johnson's England*, II, 289.
54. Bentham, Jeremy, *A Fragment on Government*, 22.
55. Blackstone, *Commentaries*, Vol. I, p. 3.
56. *Commentaries* (orig. ed.), Book I, Ch. vii.
57. *Commentaries* (1914 ed.), Vol. II, p. 129.
58. Lecky, VI, 261.
59. *Ibid.*, 255-58; Turberville, I, 17-21; Johnson, *The Idler*, Jan. 6, 1759.
60. Besant, *London*, 608.
61. Bentham, *Fragment*, 10.
62. *Ibid.*

63. Ch. iv, No. 20.
64. Bentham, *Fragment*, 3.
65. *Ibid.*, 56.
66. *Age of Voltaire*, 139, 149, 529, 687.
67. Mack, M. P., *Jeremy Bentham*, 102-5.
68. Bentham, *Introduction to Principles of Morals and Legislation*, 189.
69. Clark, G. N., *Seventeenth Century*, 127.
70. Davidson, W. L., *Political Thought in England: The Utilitarians*, 26.
71. Turberville, II, 178.
72. Mantzius, Karl, *History of Theatrical Art*, V, 388.
73. Krutch, *Samuel Johnson*, 272.
74. Barton, Margaret, *Garrick*, 53.
75. *Ibid.*, 59.
76. 50.
77. Burney, Fanny, *Diary*, 12.
78. Hawkins, Sir John, *Life of Samuel Johnson*, 189.
79. Pearson, Hesketh, *Johnson and Boswell*, 282.
80. Johnson, Samuel, *Works*, I, 196.
81. Krutch, 37.
82. George, *London Life*, 288.
83. *Boswell: The Ominous Years*, 118.
84. Turberville, I, 195.
85. George, *London*, 171.
86. *Ibid.*, 24.
87. Turberville, I, 171.
88. *Boswell's London Journal*, 81.
89. Boswell, *Johnson*, 733.

CHAPTER XXX

1. Geiringer, *Haydn*, 95.
2. *Ibid.*, 103.
3. Burney, Charles, *History of Music*, II, 868.
4. Walpole, June 23, 1789.
5. National Portrait Gallery, London.
6. Burney, II, 9.
7. Sherwin, *Selwyn*, 110.
8. Lewis, W. S., *Horace Walpole*, 107.
9. Turberville, II, 110.
10. Dillon, *Glass*, 299.
11. Samuel Smiles in Mantoux, *Industrial Revolution*, 385.
12. London, Royal Academy of Arts.
13. Turberville, II, 10.
14. *Ibid.*, 91.
15. Wilson, *William Pitt*, 97.
16. Collection of Lady Ford.
17. Greenwich, Eng., National Maritime Museum.
18. London, National Gallery. (Unallocated pictures are in private collections.)
19. National Portrait Gallery.
20. *Ibid.*
21. Reynolds, Sir Joshua, *Portraits*, 110.
22. National Portrait Gallery.
23. *Ibid.*

24. San Marino, Calif., Huntington Art Gallery.
25. Waterhouse, *Reynolds*, 110.
26. *Ibid.*, 127.
27. 79.
28. 87.
29. 63.
30. 267.
31. 291; London, National Gallery.
32. Waterhouse, 57.
33. Wallace Collection, London.
34. Reynolds, *Fifteen Discourses*, 3.
35. Wilenski, R. H., *English Painting*, 150.
36. Reynolds, *Portraits*, 167.
37. Boswell, *Johnson*, 651.
38. National Portrait Gallery.
39. Royal Academy of Arts.
40. Reynolds, *Fifteen Discourses*, 78 (Discourse VI), 8 (I).
41. *Ibid.*, 7 (I).
42. 14 (II).
43. *Ibid.*
44. 30 (III).
45. *Ibid.*
46. 264 (XV).
47. Wilenski, 113.
48. Allan Cunningham in Clark, B. H., *Great Short Biographies*, 789.
49. Gillet, Louis, *La Peinture, xviie et xviiie siècles*, 416.
50. Washington, National Gallery.
51. Edinburgh, National Gallery.
52. Millar, Oliver, *Thomas Gainsborough*, 11.
53. Clark, B. H., *Biographies*, 796.
54. Craven, Thomas, *Treasury of Art Masterpieces*, 214.
55. Reynolds, *Fifteen Discourses*, 230 (XIV).
56. Waterhouse, *Gainsborough*, 36.
57. Pijoan, Joseph, *History of Art*, III, 479.
58. Reynolds, *Fifteen Discourses*, 227 (XIV).

CHAPTER XXXI

1. Lecky, *England in the 18th Century*, IV, 314.
2. *New CMH*, VIII, 28.
3. *Ibid.*, 714.
4. Lecky, IV, 317.
5. D'Alton, E. A., *History of Ireland*, IV, 545; *Enc. Brit.*, X, 659d.
6. Faÿ, *La Franc-Maçonnerie*, 399.
7. Smith, Adam, *Wealth of Nations*, I, 70.
8. Johnson, *Works*, II, 271, 345.
9. Boswell, *Hebrides*, 135.
10. *Enc. Brit.*, XX, 169d.
11. Snyder, F. B., *Life of Robert Burns*, 189.
12. *Age of Voltaire*, 184.
13. *Ibid.*, 507-86.
14. 586-602.
15. 139-61.
16. Reid, Thomas, *Works*, I, 7, 81, 91.

17. *Ibid.*, 12.
18. 106.
19. Hume, David, *Treatise of Human Nature*, I, 254.
20. Reid, *Works*, 423.
21. Boswell's Journal, Sept. 16, 1769 (*Boswell in Search of a Wife*, 293).
22. London National Portrait Gallery.
23. Edinburgh National Gallery.
24. Private Collection.
25. Carlyle, *Schiller*, 103.
26. Walpole, July 11, 1759.
27. Gibbon, *Memoirs*, 122.
28. Stewart, Dugald, *Life of Robertson* (1811), 305.
29. Gibbon, *Memoirs*, Appendix 22, p. 296.
30. Black, *Art of History*, 15.
31. Brandes, *Goethe*, I, 84.
32. See *The Age of Faith*, 498.
33. Thomson, Derick, *The Gaelic Sources of Macpherson's "Ossian,"* 4-5, 80.
34. Macpherson, James, *Poems*, 40 (*Fingal*, Book I).
35. *Ibid.*, 49, 52, 54.
36. 415-16.
37. Johnson, *Works*, XII, 375; Boswell, *Hebrides*, 163.
38. Boswell, *Johnson*, 496.
39. Thomson, Derick, 16 f.
40. Buckle, Ib, 347.
41. Smith, Adam, *Moral and Political Philosophy*, 75.
42. *Ibid.*, 255.
43. 191.
44. Laski, *Political Thought in England*, 99, 101, 188; see also *Age of Voltaire*, 155.
45. Smith, *Wealth of Nations*, II, 107.
46. *Ibid.*, 113.
47. 121.
48. See *Age of Voltaire*, 138.
49. *Wealth of Nations*, II, 180.
50. *Ibid.*, I, 26, 29.
51. I, 119.
52. 129.
53. 129.
54. 42.
55. 75, 2.
56. 73.
57. 72, 345.
58. Rosebery, Lord, *Pitt*, 4.
59. Waterhouse, *Reynolds*, 329.
60. Burns's autobiographical letter to John Moore, in Neilson, W. A., *Robert Burns*, 1.
61. In Snyder, *Burns*, 54.
62. *Ibid.*, 67.
63. 67.
64. 239.
65. See "The Ordination."
66. Witte, *Schiller and Burns*, 10.
67. Hill, J. C., *Love Songs and Heroines of Robert Burns*, vii-x.
68. Burns, Robert, *Works*, I, 85, 75.
69. *Ibid.*, 101.
70. Witte, *Schiller and Burns*, 10.
71. "The Rigs o' Barley."
72. Burns, *Works*, I, 85, 77.
73. *Ibid.*, 50.
74. Brown, Hilton, *There Was a Lad*, 23, 50.
75. Carlyle, *Essay on Burns*, in *Works*, XIII, 294-96.
76. Burns, *Works*, I, 162.
77. Keith, Christina, *The Russet Coat*, 81.
78. Burns, *Works*, I, 141.
79. Brown, Hilton, 26.
80. Snyder, 297.
81. *Ibid.*, 308.
82. Hill, J. C., 102.
83. Snyder, 360, 374, 379, 390.
84. Burns, Robert, and Mrs. Dunlop, *Correspondence*, 11, *viii*.
85. Burns, *Works*, I, 24.
86. Currie, James, *Life of Robert Burns*, in Burns, *Works*, II, 58.
87. Robert Chambers in Snyder, 432.
88. Snyder, 432-35.
89. *Ibid.*, 430.
90. *Boswell's London Journal*, 108.
91. Pearson, 107.
92. *Boswell's London Journal*, 66.
93. *Ibid.*, 93.
94. 66.
95. 93.
96. 137.
97. 206-9.
98. *Boswell on the Grand Tour: Germany and Switzerland*, 44.
99. Boswell, *Johnson*, 237-40.
100. *Boswell's London Journal*, 251, 281.
101. *Boswell in Holland*, Sept. 18, 1763.
102. *Ibid.*, 387-90.
103. 46.
104. 157.
105. 259-61.
106. 314.
107. 328.
108. 330.
109. 349.
110. 368.
111. *Boswell on the Grand Tour: Germany*, 134.
112. *Ibid.*, 117.
113. 164-66.
114. 241.
115. *Boswell in Search of a Wife*, 24.
116. *Ibid.*, 36-37.
117. 76.
118. 207.
119. 240.
120. *Boswell for the Defense*, 140.
121. *Boswell: The Ominous Years*, 34-48.
122. *Ibid.*, 304-7.
123. Macaulay, *Essays*, II, 539-41.
124. *Boswell: The Ominous Years*, 338.

125. *Boswell in Search of a Wife*, 40.
126. *Boswell: The Ominous Years*, Introd., *x*.

CHAPTER XXXII

1. Johnson, *The Idler*, No. 40.
2. Brooke, Henry, *The Fool of Quality*, 80.
3. Cross, Wilbur, *Life and Times of Laurence Sterne*, 99.
4. *Ibid.*, 179.
5. *Ibid.*
6. 183.
7. Parton, *Life of Voltaire*, II, 267.
8. Mossner, E. C., *Life of David Hume*, 503.
9. Sterne, Laurence, *Tristram Shandy*, Book VIII, Ch. ii.
10. *Ibid.*, Book IV, Ch. xxxviii.
11. Cross, 263.
12. Sterne, *Letters to Eliza*, x.
13. *Ibid.*, letter of Apr. 14, 1767.
14. Sterne, *Journal*, Apr. 24, 1767.
15. Moore, Thomas, *Life of Lord Byron*, in Taine, *English Literature*, 477.
16. Macaulay, *Essays*, II, 565.
17. Burney, Fanny, *Diary*, 17.
18. Burney, Fanny, *Evelina*, 22.
19. Letter of Mar. 5, 1772.
20. Walpole, Feb. 28, 1769.
21. See *Age of Voltaire*, 95-98.
22. Lewis, *Horace Walpole*, 12n; Wharton, Grace and Philip, *Wits and Beaux of Society*, II, 28.
23. Walpole, "Reminiscences," in *Letters*, I, xciii.
24. Letter of Mar. 2, 1773.
25. Nicolson, Harold, *The Age of Reason*, 249.
26. Walpole, *Memoirs of the Reign of George III*, II, 154.
27. Letter of Nov. 24, 1774.
28. Nicolson, 248.
29. *Ibid.*, 249.
30. Letter of July 24, 1756.
31. Letter of Dec. 2, 1762.
32. Sherwin, *Selwyn*, 104.
33. Letter of Nov. 11, 1766.
34. Walpole, *Memoirs of the Last Ten Years of the Reign of George the Second*, p. xl.
35. Letter of June 15, 1768.
36. Oct. 1, 1782.
37. Nov. 11, 1763.
38. Lewis, *Horace Walpole*, 5.
39. Feb. 7, 1772.
40. Jan. 12, 1766.
41. Letter to John Chute, January, 1766.
42. Lewis, 20.
43. Wharton, II, 83.
44. Lewis, 81.
45. Jan. 18, 1759.
46. Gibbon, *Memoirs*, introd. by G. B. Hill, xxi; Robertson, J. M., *Gibbon*, 1.
47. *Memoirs*, 20.

48. *Age of Voltaire*, 127.
49. *Memoirs*, 45.
50. *Ibid.*, 51, 54.
51. 65.
52. 69.
53. 105.
54. 106, 156.
55. Gambier-Parry, M., *Madame Necker*, 16.
56. Gibbon, *Journal*, introd., *lxxii*.
57. *Memoirs*, 107.
58. *Ibid.*, 120.
59. Gibbon, *Essai sur l'étude de la littérature*, in *Miscellaneous Writings*, No. 1.
60. *Ibid.*, liii.
61. *Memoirs*, 143.
62. *Journal*, 22.
63. *Ibid.*, 136.
64. *Memoirs*, 153.
65. Robertson, J. M., *Gibbon*, 117; *Memoirs*, 158.
66. *Ibid.*, 167.
67. *Decline and Fall of the Roman Empire*, final page.
68. *Memoirs*, Appendix 30.
69. *Ibid.*, 172.
70. 189.
71. 191n.
72. 193.
73. Robertson, *Gibbon*, 119; Drinkwater, *Charles James Fox*, 206.
74. Low, D. M., *Edward Gibbon*, 282.
75. *Memoirs*, 190.
76. *Ibid.*, 195.
77. 195.
78. *Decline and Fall*, I, 316. Renan agreed with Gibbon about the Antonines; see his *Marc Aurèle*, 479, Calmann-Lévy, Paris, n.d.
79. *Decline and Fall*, I, 316.
80. *Ibid.*, 250.
81. 9 and 10 William III, c. 22.
82. *Decline and Fall*, II, 72-73.
83. *Ibid.*
84. 102-5.
85. 182.
86. 244; see Voltaire's view in *The Age of Voltaire*, 486.
87. Low, 260.
88. Sainte-Beuve, *English Portraits*, 152-53.
89. Low, 258.
90. Gibbon, *Miscellaneous Writings*, 277.
91. Walpole, Jan. 27, 1781.
92. *Memoirs*, 211.
93. *Decline and Fall*, 432-33.
94. *Memoirs*, 213.
95. *Ibid.*, 215.
96. Low, 302.
97. *Memoirs*, 214.
98. Walpole, June 5, 1788.
99. *Decline and Fall*, VI, 656.
100. *Memoirs*, 225.
101. *Ibid.*, 89n.

102. Fuglum, Per, *Edward Gibbon*, 15.
103. *Memoirs*, 240.
104. Boswell, *Johnson*, Mar. 19, 1781.
105. Low, 222-23.
106. *Memoirs*, 230-31.
107. Low, 320.
108. *Memoirs*, 228, 234; G. G. S., *Life of Sheridan*, 122.
109. *Memoirs*, Appendix 55.
110. *Ibid.*, 241n.
111. Appendix 66.
112. Sainte-Beuve, *English Portraits*, 159.
113. *Memoirs*, Appendix 66.
114. *Ibid.*, 339 and Appendix 62.
115. Gibbon, *Correspondence*, II, 93, 298, in *Memoirs*, 339.
116. *Correspondence*, II, 255, in Robertson, *Gibbon*, 120.
117. Gibbon, *Autobiography*, Everyman's Library ed., in Gay, P., *Voltaire's Politics*, 259.
118. *Memoirs*, introd. by G. B. Hill, *xii.*
119. Low, 344.
120. Gibbon, letter of Nov. 11, 1793.
121. *Decline and Fall*, 1776 ed., I, 206.
122. Bury, J. B., in *Enc. Brit.*, X, 331d.
123. *Decline and Fall*, ed. J. B. Bury, I, *xli.*
124. *Ibid.*, *xlvii*; Robertson, *Gibbon*, 15; Black, *Art of History*, 161.
125. *Decline and Fall*, IV, 673.
126. *Ibid.*, 99.
127. I, 314.
128. Voltaire, *Works*, XVIa, 250-51.
129. *Decline and Fall*, III, 97.
130. VI, 337.
131. Cf. Fuglum, 136.
132. *Decline and Fall*, Ch. lxiv.
133. V, 237.
134. *Ibid.*, 423.
135. III, 522.
136. Preface to Milman ed., p. 6.
137. *CHE*, X, 445.
138. Seebohm, Frederick, *The Age of Johnson*, 228.
139. Walpole, letter of Nov. 15, 1764; *Reign of George III*, II, 25.
140. Nevill, J. C., *Thomas Chatterton*, 96.
141. Chatterton, *Complete Poetical Works*, 207.
142. *Ibid.*, 64.
143. Walpole, letters of June 19, 1777, and July 24, 1778.
144. Irving, Washington, *Oliver Goldsmith*, 266.
145. Stanza xlv.
146. Cowper, William, *Poems*, 135.
147. Sainte-Beuve, *English Portraits*, 173.
148. Cowper, 188.
149. *CHE*, XI, 89.
150. Sainte-Beuve, *English Portraits*, 176-77.
151. Cowper, 87.
152. See *Age of Voltaire*, 331.

153. Cowper, *The Task*, Book I, line 749.
154. *Ibid.*, line 718.
155. II, lines 1-7.
156. II, 11-28.
157. 206.
158. Cowper, *Poems*, 172.
159. *Enc. Brit.*, X, 495a (by Macaulay).
160. Boswell, *Johnson*, 252.
161. *Ibid.*, 305.
162. Goethe, *Truth and Fiction*, II, 37, 170.
163. Thackeray, *English Humourists*, in *Works*, 281n.
164. Irving, 170.
165. *Vicar of Wakefield*, preface.
166. Boswell, *Johnson*, 449.
167. Barton, *Garrick*, 256.
168. E.g., Reynolds, *Portraits*, 38.
169. Irving, 121.
170. Garnett and Gosse, *English Literature*, III, 342; Irving, 320.
171. *Boswell for the Defense*, 167.
172. Thackeray, *English Humourists*, 291.
173. *Ibid.*
174. Goldsmith, Oliver, *Select Works*, 194.

CHAPTER XXXIII

1. Boswell, *Johnson*, 17.
2. Boswell, *Hebrides*, 142.
3. Krutch, *Johnson*, 12.
4. Pearson, *Johnson and Boswell*, 6.
5. Krutch, 10.
6. Boswell, *Johnson*, 564.
7. *Enc. Brit.*, XIII, 109d.
8. Hill, G. Birkbeck, *Johnsonian Miscellanies*, II, 309; Greene, Donald, *Politics of Samuel Johnson*, 133.
9. Johnson, *London*, line 202.
10. Hawkins, *Life of Samuel Johnson*, 55-57.
11. Krutch, 49.
12. *Ibid.*
13. Turberville, *Johnson's England*, I, 318n.
14. Boswell, *Johnson*, 94.
15. *Enc. Brit.*, XIII, 110a.
16. Boswell, *Johnson*, 1177.
17. Hawkins, 66.
18. Hume, David, *Essays, Literary, Moral, and Political*, 52.
19. Johnson, *Works*, I, 213.
20. *Ibid.*, 215.
21. 217.
22. Hawkins, 98.
23. Johnson, *The Rambler*, 257-64.
24. Boswell, *Holland Journal*, Sept. 23, 1763.
25. Davis, Bertram, *Johnson before Boswell*, 72.
26. Hill, G. B., *Miscellanies*, I, 136.
27. Boswell, *Johnson*, 165.
28. *Ibid.*, 242.
29. Schuster, M. L., *Treasury of the World's Great Letters*, 130.
30. Boswell, *Johnson*, 992.

31. *Ibid.*, 157.
32. *Boswell for the Defense*, 55 (Mar. 23, 1772).
33. *Johnson's Dictionary*, preface; p. 20.
34. *Ibid.*, 284.
35. Boswell, *Johnson*, 179.
36. Arthur Murphy in Johnson, *Works*, I, 89.
37. *Works*, V, 419.
38. *Rasselas*, Ch. vi.
39. *Ibid.*, Ch. xix.
40. Ch. xxviii.
41. Ch. xli.
42. Boswell, *Johnson*, 228.
43. *Ibid.*, 260.
44. Wharton, Grace and Philip, *Wits and Beaux of Society*, I, 366.
45. Krutch, 264.
46. Pearson, 184.
47. Boswell, *Johnson*, 272.
48. Bailey, John, *Dr. Johnson and His Circle*, 35.
49. Boswell, 542.
50. *Boswell for the Defense*, 175.
51. Boswell, *Hebrides*, 189.
52. Pearson, 195.
53. *Boswell's London Journal*, 234.
54. Piozzi, *Anecdotes of the Late Samuel Johnson*, 190.
55. National Portrait Gallery.
56. National Gallery, London.
57. Hawkins, 293.
58. Turberville, I, 384.
59. Boswell, *Johnson*, 283; Hawkins, 147.
60. Boswell, *Hebrides*, 136.
61. Boswell, *Johnson*, 49.
62. Pearson, 81.
63. *Boswell: The Ominous Years*, 264.
64. Bailey, 29.
65. Boswell, *Johnson*, 955.
66. *Ibid.*, 1197.
67. 293.
68. Piozzi, 181.
69. Hawkins, 122.
70. *Rasselas*, Ch. xliii.
71. Hawkins, 132.
72. Boswell, 586.
73. Turberville, II, 198.
74. Krutch, 369.
75. This is Hume's report, in Krutch, 221, and Pearson, 48; the phraseology was made more decorous in Boswell.
76. Boswell, *Hebrides*, 144.
77. Walpole, May 26, 1791.
78. Irving, *Goldsmith*, 183.
79. Piozzi, 70.
80. *Ibid.*, 57.
81. Boswell, *Johnson*, 1124.
82. *Ibid.*, 1126.
83. Bailey, 30.
84. Boswell, 351.
85. Krutch, 366.

86. Boswell, *Hebrides*, 200.
87. Boswell, *Johnson*, 343.
88. *Boswell: The Ominous Years*, 133.
89. Low, *Gibbon*, 223.
90. Lovejoy, Arthur, *Essays in the History of Ideas*, 39.
91. Walpole, Mar. 28, 1786.
92. In Gibbon, *Memoirs*, 220n.
93. Boswell, *Hebrides*, 11.
94. Boswell, *Johnson*, 222.
95. *Hebrides*, 140.
96. *Johnson*, 988.
97. Pearson, 262.
98. Greene, Donald, *Politics of Samuel Johnson*, 270.
99. Boswell, *Johnson*, 744.
100. *Ibid.*, 1025.
101. 807.
102. 362.
103. Bailey, 104.
104. Boswell, *Johnson*, 807.
105. *Ibid.*, 410.
106. 363.
107. 525.
108. 274.
109. Hawkins, 208.
110. Boswell, *Johnson*, 267, 414, 469, 514, 740; *Boswell's London Journal*, 276, 281.
111. *Ibid.*, 253; Johnson, *Works*, XII, 111.
112. Boswell, *Johnson*, 787.
113. *Ibid.*, 341.
114. 309.
115. 486.
116. Greene, 161.
117. *Ibid.*, 167.
118. *Taxation No Tyranny*, in *Works*, XII, 225.
119. Boswell, *Johnson*, 508.
120. Johnson, *Works*, XII, 198n.
121. Hawkins, 222.
122. Boswell, *Johnson*, 505.
123. *Ibid.*, 507.
124. 654.
125. In Greene, 195.
126. Boswell, *Johnson*, 33, 1051; Piozzi, 14.
127. Boswell, *Johnson*, 1102-3.
128. *Ibid.*, 282.
129. 421; Bailey, 103.
130. Pearson, 252.
131. *Ibid.*, 251.
132. *Lives of the English Poets*, I, 63 ("Milton").
133. *Rasselas*, Ch. xxxi; Hawkins, 131.
134. *Lives*, I, 63.
135. Pearson, 248.
136. Boswell, *Johnson*, 352, 807.
137. *Ibid.*, 309.
138. 308.
139. Hopkins, Mary A., *Hannah More*, 61.
140. Hawkins, 198.
141. Johnson, *Works*, X, 169.
142. *Ibid.*, 137, 149.

143. Krutch, 289.
144. Boswell, *Hebrides*, 178.
145. *Ibid.*, 268.
146. *Works*, XII, 413.
147. Pearson, 237.
148. Boswell, *Johnson*, 685n.
149. *Lives*, I, 93.
150. Walpole, Feb. 19, 1781.
151. Walpole, Apr. 14, 1781.
152. Piozzi, 186.
153. Krutch, 522.
154. *Ibid.*, 509.
155. Schuster, *Treasury of the World's Great Letters*, 133.
156. Burney, Fanny, *Diary*, 92.
157. Boswell, *Johnson*, 1109.
158. Krutch, 547.
159. Boswell, *Johnson*, 1059.
160. Hawkins, 255.
161. *Ibid.*, 259.
162. Krutch, 551.
163. Boswell, *Johnson*, 1181.
164. Davis, Bertram, *Johnson before Boswell*, vii.
165. *CHE*, X, 213.
166. *Boswell: The Ominous Years*, 103.
167. E.g., Boswell, *Note Book*, xvii, 1, 23; Krutch, *Johnson*, 384.
168. E.g., *Boswell: The Ominous Years*, 111.
169. Boswell, *Johnson*, x.
170. Hannah More, *Letters*, 102.
171. *CHE*, X, 213.
172. Letter of May 26, 1791.

CHAPTER XXXIV

1. Gooch, *Maria Theresa*, 124.
2. *Ibid.*, 7.
3. 8.
4. Bearne, Mrs., *A Court Painter*, 323.
5. Ercole, *Gay Court Life*, 272.
6. Castelot, André, *Queen of France*, 20.
7. Zweig, Stefan, *Marie Antoinette*, 5.
8. Padover, Saul, *Life and Death of Louis XVI*, 30.
9. Gooch, *Maria Theresa*, 122.
10. Padover, 30.
11. Castelot, 37.
12. *Ibid.*, 40.
13. Zweig, 21.
14. Castelot, 64.
15. *Ibid.*, 73; Dakin, *Turgot and the Ancien Régime*, 19.
16. Walpole, July 10, 1774.
17. Mathiez, Albert, *The French Revolution*, 9.
18. Tocqueville, *L'Ancien Régime*, 122.
19. Maine, Sir Henry, *Ancient Law*, 48.
20. Cobban, Alfred, *History of Modern France*, I, 127.
21. Taine, *The Ancient Regime*, 95.
22. *Ibid.*, 68-69.
23. Mathiez, 5.
24. Taine, *Ancient Regime*, 118, 98.
25. Ercole, 370.
26. Castelot, 85.
27. Campan, Mme., *Memoirs*, I, 317.
28. Mossiker, Frances, *The Queen's Necklace*, 201.
29. *Ibid.*, 163.
30. Castelot, 66, 158.
31. Lacroix, *The Eighteenth Century*, 35.
32. Vigée-Lebrun, Mme., *Memoirs*, 56.
33. Desnoiresterres, *Voltaire et la société française*, VIII, 294.
34. Castelot, 174.
35. Cobban, Alfred, *Historians and the Causes of the French Revolution*, 5, 14.
36. Mme. Campan gives several examples (*Memoirs*, I, 190-94).
37. Cobban, *History of Modern France*, I, 115.
38. Castelot, 123.
39. Faÿ, Bernard, *Louis XVI, ou La Fin d'un monde*, 311.
40. Havens, G. R., *The Age of Ideas*, 392.
41. In Mossiker, *Queen's Necklace*, 160.
42. Castelot, 119.
43. Padover, *The Revolutionary Emperor*, 119, 125.
44. *Ibid.*, 119.
45. Castelot, 122.
46. *Ibid.*, 121.
47. 124.
48. Zweig, *Marie Antoinette*, 137.
49. Padover, *Louis XVI*, 102.
50. Ségur, Marquis de, *Marie Antoinette*, 104.
51. *Ibid.*
52. Michelet, *Histoire de France*, V, 491.
53. "The Good-natured King."
54. Campan, Mme., *Memoirs*, I, 178.
55. Padover, *Louis XVI*, 118-19.
56. Funck-Brentano, *L'Ancien Régime*, 545.
57. Gibbon, *Decline and Fall*, ed. J. B. Bury, IV, 529.
58. Padover, *Louis XVI*, 23.
59. Campan, Mme., I, 185n.
60. Faÿ, *Louis XVI*, 8.
61. Taine, *Ancient Regime*, 304.
62. Funck-Brentano, 546.
63. Campan, I, 180.
64. Stryienski, *Eighteenth Century*, 213.
65. Gooch, *Catherine the Great*, 230.
66. Goethe, *Truth and Fiction*, II, 350.
67. Dakin, *Turgot*, 126.
68. Say, Léon, *Turgot*, 101.
69. Robinson, J. H., *Readings in European History*, 426.
70. See *Age of Louis XIV*, 160.
71. Voltaire, *Works*, XXIb, 347.
72. Parton, *Life of Voltaire*, II, 535.
73. Martin, H., *Histoire de France*, XVI, 340.
74. Dakin, 187; Padover, *Louis XVI*, 75.
75. Say, 12.

76. Dakin, 152; Tocqueville, 190.
77. Tocqueville, 190.
78. Say, 161-66; Funck-Brentano, 554.
79. Renard, Georges, *Guilds in the Middle Ages*, 125.
80. Martin, H., *France*, XVI, 371.
81. *Ibid.*, 372.
82. Taine, *Ancient Regime*, 237.
83. Padover, *Louis XVI*, 92.
84. Dakin, 221.
85. Say, 185-91.
86. Dakin, 263; Martin, H., *France*, XVI, 379.
87. Michelet, *Histoire de France*, V, 480.
88. Say, 43.
89. Warwick, *Mirabeau and the French Revolution*, 104. On L'Hôpital see *The Age of Reason Begins*, 337-45.
90. Jaurès, Jean, *Histoire socialiste de la Révolution française*, I, 159.
91. Martin, H., *France*, XVI, 387.
92. Taine, *Ancient Regime*, 302.
93. Michelet, *Histoire de France*, V, 488.
94. Campan, Mme., I, 181.
95. Tocqueville, 191.
96. Lecky, *History of England in the 18th Century*, V, 39-41.
97. Padover, *Louis XVI*, 108; Martin, H., *France*, XVI, 416.
98. Becker, Carl, *The Heavenly City of the 18th-Century Philosophers*, 77.
99. Lecky, IV, 50.
100. *History Today*, October, 1957, 659.
101. Martin, H., *France*, XVI, 428.
102. Morris, R. B., *The Peacemakers*, 104-7.
103. *CMH*, VIII, 93.
104. Gooch, *Catherine the Great*, 97.
105. Martin, H., *France*, XVI, 500-1.
106. *Ibid.*, 504.
107. Mahan, A. T., *Influence of Sea Power upon History*, 337.
108. Morris, *Peacemakers*, 178-81.
109. Lecky, IV, 256-59.
110. *Ibid.*
111. Morris, 277.
112. *Ibid.*, 461.
113. Tocqueville, 155.
114. *Ibid.*, 119.

CHAPTER XXXV

1. Parton, *Life of Voltaire*, II, 491.
2. *Ibid.*, 496.
3. Pomeau, *La Religion de Voltaire*, 427.
4. Chaponnière, *Voltaire chez les calvinistes*, 262.
5. Faguet, *Literary History of France*, 508.
6. Lanson, Gustave, *Voltaire*, 158.
7. Torrey, N. L., *The Spirit of Voltaire*, 150.
8. Brandes, *Voltaire*, II, 317.
9. Wagnière in Parton, II, 564.
10. *Ibid.*
11. Note to Walpole, *Letters*, VII, 35.

12. Brandes, *Voltaire*, II, 322; Parton, II, 367.
13. Desnoiresterres, *Voltaire et la société française*, VIII, 199-200; Campan, I, 323; Martin, H., *Histoire de France*, XVI, 393.
14. Parton, *Life of Voltaire*, II, 568.
15. Brandes, II, 324.
16. Pomeau, 263.
17. Noyes, *Voltaire*, 583.
18. Pomeau, 307.
19. Desnoiresterres, VIII, 230.
20. Lanson, *Voltaire*, 200.
21. Desnoiresterres, VIII, 232-33.
22. *Ibid.*, 235.
23. 236.
24. 245.
25. Wiener, Leo, *Anthology of Russian Literature*, I, 357.
26. Noyes, 600.
27. Brandes, *Voltaire*, II, 336.
28. *Ibid.*, 337.
29. Desnoiresterres, VIII, 283-91.
30. Vigée-Lebrun, *Memoirs*, 199.
31. Ducros, *French Society in the 18th Century*, 121.
32. Desnoiresterres, VIII, 302.
33. *Ibid.*, 306; Brandes, *Voltaire*, II, 340.
34. Strachey, Lytton, *Books and Characters*, 121n.
35. Brandes, II, 341.
36. Desnoiresterres, VIII, 334, 365.
37. Pomeau, 447.
38. Desnoiresterres, VIII, 359.
39. *Ibid.*, 366; Créqui, Marquise de, *Souvenirs*, 235n.
40. Brandes, *Voltaire*, II, 348.
41. Gooch, *Catherine the Great*, 70.
42. In Brandes, *Voltaire*, II, 94n.; the order has been slightly changed.
43. *Ibid.*, 354.
44. Parton, II, 494.
45. Voltaire, *La Guerre de Genève*, in Josephson, *Rousseau*, 479.
46. Hendel, Charles, *Citizen of Geneva*, 92.
47. Josephson, 481.
48. Hendel, *Citizen*, 98.
49. *Ibid.*, 99 (letter of Oct. 10, 1769).
50. *Ibid.*, 101 (letter of Jan. 17, 1770).
51. See *Age of Voltaire*, 565.
52. Michelet, *Histoire de France*, V, 485.
53. Morley, *Rousseau*, II, 156.
54. Josephson, 495.
55. Rousseau, *The Confessions*, II, end.
56. Josephson, 501.
57. *Ibid.*
58. Desnoiresterres, VII, 488.
59. Vaughn, C. E., *Political Writings of Rousseau*, II, 445.
60. *Ibid.*, 376, 381.
61. Rousseau, *Rousseau juge de Jean-Jacques*, p. x.
62. *Ibid.*, 19.

63. 64-67.
64. 120, 124.
65. 117-18.
66. 292, 302, 327.
67. Third Dialogue.
68. *Rousseau juge*, 319 f.
69. Josephson, 508.
70. *Reveries of a Solitary*, Ninth Promenade.
71. Josephson, 518.
72. Masson, P. M., *La Religion de Rousseau*, II, 213-15, 301-2.
73. *Ibid.*, 246.
74. Josephson, 502; Faguet, *Vie de Rousseau*, 399.
75. Josephson, 527.
76. Babbitt, Irving, *Spanish Character and Other Essays*, 225.
77. Cassirer, *The Question of Rousseau*, 39.
78. Lemaître, *Rousseau*, 247.
79. Lanson, *Histoire de la littérature française*, 798.
80. Goethe, *Truth and Fiction*, II, 236.
81. Schiller, "Rousseau," in *Poems*, 25. In *Works*.
82. In Maritain, *Three Reformers*, 225.
83. *Collection complète des oeuvres*, I, 186.
84. Cassirer, *Question of Rousseau*, 39.
85. Pomeau, 340.
86. Masson, P. M., *La Religion de Rousseau*, III, 239-44.
87. *Ibid.*, 74.
88. In Morley, *Rousseau and His Era*, II, 273.
89. Masson, *La Religion*, III, 227.
90. Burke, "Letter to a Member of the National Assembly," in *Reflections on the French Revolution*, 262.
91. Taine, *Ancient Regime*, 317.
92. Lemaître, 361.
93. Lanson, *Histoire de la littérature française*, 798.
94. Crocker, *The Embattled Philosopher*, 310.
95. Ségur, *Julie de Lespinasse*, 402.
96. Letter of Feb. 27, 1777, in Hazard, *European Thought*, 323.
97. Ford, Miriam de, *Love Children*, 212.
98. Havens, *Age of Ideas*, 351.
99. Crocker, *Embattled Philosopher*, 400.
100. *Rousseau juge de Jean-Jacques*, "Avertissement," *v-vi*.
101. Crocker, *Embattled Philosopher*, 433.
102. Sainte-Beuve, *Portraits of the 18th Century*, II, 213.
103. Schapiro, J. S., *Condorcet*, 69.
104. Russell, Bertrand, *History of Western Philosophy*, 722.
105. Schapiro, *Condorcet*, 91.
106. Martin, H., *France*, XVI, 525.
107. Schapiro, 96-97.
108. So reads the ms. in the Bibliothèque de l'Institut.
109. See *The Age of Voltaire*, 775.

110. Condorcet, *Sketch for a Historical Picture of the Progress of the Mind*, p. v.
111. *Ibid.*, 105.
112. 10.
113. 179.
114. Aulard, A., *The French Revolution*, I, 123.
115. Schapiro, 80, 88.
116. Condorcet, 193.
117. *Ibid.*, *x-xi*, 175.
118. 4.
119. 188.
120. 169.
121. 202.
122. Schapiro, 107.
123. Tocqueville, 8.
124. Taine, *Ancient Regime*, 317.
125. Aulard, I, 83.
126. Robertson, J. M., *Short History of Freethought*, II, 284.
127. Aulard, I, 83.
128. Robertson, J. M., *Short History*, 288.
129. Tocqueville, 165.
130. In Sée, Henri, *Economic and Social Conditions in France during the 18th Century*, 107.
131. Padover, *Louis XVI*, 6, 7, 11.
132. Tocqueville, 156.
133. Masson, P. M., *La Religion de Rousseau*, III, 237.

CHAPTER XXXVI

1. Sée, *Economic and Social Conditions*, 61; Jaurès, *Histoire socialiste*, I, 60; Taine (*The French Revolution*, I, 168) estimated the value of church property at four billion livres.
2. Herbert, Sydney, *The Fall of Feudalism in France*, 40.
3. Mornet, Daniel, *Les Origines intellectuelles de la Révolution française*, 278.
4. *Ibid.*, 274; Sée, 66.
5. *Ibid.*; Taine, *French Revolution*, I, 162-63.
6. Sée, 66.
7. Taine, *French Revolution*, I, 167.
8. Burke, Edmund, *Reflections on the French Revolution*, 142.
9. Sanger, W., *History of Prostitution*, 131.
10. Sée, 23; Mornet, 276.
11. Vigée-Lebrun, *Memoirs*, 14.
12. Lacroix, Paul, *The Eighteenth Century in France*, 346.
13. Taine, *Ancient Regime*, 291.
14. Mornet, 335.
15. Lacroix, 265.
16. Mornet, 331.
17. Faÿ, *Louis XVI*, 280.
18. Martin, H., *Histoire de France*, XVI, 512.
19. Faÿ, 280.
20. Lecky, *England in the 18th Century*, V, 308.

21. Martin, H., *France*, XVI, 353.
22. Mornet, 212.
23. Funck-Brentano, *L'Ancien Régime*, 554.
24. Martin, H., *France*, XVI, 585.
25. Tocqueville, 9.
26. Herbert, S., *Fall of Feudalism*, 84.
27. See *Age of Voltaire*, 776-80.
28. In Crocker, *Age of Crisis*, 392.
29. In Becker, *Heavenly City*, 80.
30. Carlyle, *Essay on Diderot*.
31. Restif de La Bretonne, *La Vie de mon père*, 90 f.
32. Taine, *Ancient Regime*, 380.
33. Laclos, Choderlos de, *Les Liaisons dangereuses*, Letter LXVI.
34. See Plato, *The Republic*, Nos. 338-44.
35. De Sade, Comte, *Juliette*, in Crocker, *Age of Crisis*, 15.
36. Guérard, Albert, *Life and Death of an Ideal*, 294.
37. Mme. d'Oberkirch in Taine, *Ancient Regime*, 163.
38. Köhler, Carl, *History of Costume*, 366.
39. Boehn, *Modes and Manners*, IV, 215.
40. In Loomis, *Du Barry*, 169.
41. *Decline and Fall of the Roman Empire*, near end of Ch. xix.
42. Gibbon, *Correspondence*, II, 46, in *Memoirs*, 222n.
43. See *Age of Voltaire*, 301-2.
44. Walpole, Dec. 2, 1765.
45. Koven, Anna de, *Horace Walpole and Mme. du Deffand*, 102, 116.
46. *Ibid.*, 127.
47. Watson, Paul, *Some Women of France*, 90.
48. *Ibid.*
49. 89; Koven, 157.
50. *Ibid.*, 195.
51. Crocker, *Embattled Philosopher*, 354.
52. Gambier-Parry, *Madame Necker*, 78.
53. *Ibid.*, 215.
54. Créqui, Marquise de, *Souvenirs*, 192-94.
55. Gambier-Parry, 250.
56. Anderson, E., *Letters of Mozart*, II, 787.
57. Einstein, *Mozart*, 356.
58. Lespinasse, *Letters*, 138.
59. Rolland, Romain, *Essays in Music*, 147.
60. *Grove's Dictionary of Music*, II, 456.
61. Young, Arthur, *Travels in France*, 67.
62. Louvre.
63. In the Institute, Paris.
64. Dilke, Lady Emilia, *French Architects and Sculptors*, 130. It is now in the École des Beaux-Arts in Paris.
65. *Time* magazine, Jan. 31, 1764, p. 44.
66. *Ibid.*
67. All in the Louvre.
68. Both in the Louvre.
69. Vigée-Lebrun, 42.
70. Louvre.
71. Private collection.

72. Taine, *French Revolution*, I, 141; Mornet, *Origines intellectuelles*, 419; La Fontainerie, *French Liberalism*, 23.
73. Mornet, 443.
74. Lecky, V, 394.
75. Mornet, 426.
76. *Enc. Brit.*, XVI, 349d.
77. Lecky, V, 425.
78. Ducros, *French Society*, 314.
79. *Ibid.*
80. Faguet, *Literary History*, 539.
81. Chamfort, Sébastien, *Maximes*, 25.
82. *Ibid.*, 27.
83. 6.
84. 71.
85. 67.
86. 69.
87. 62.
88. 87.
89. 89.
90. 26.
91. 539.
92. *Ibid.*, preface, p. 50.
93. In Masson, *La Religion de Rousseau*, III, 137-38.
94. Bernardin de Saint-Pierre, *Paul et Virginie*, 15, 34, 58.
95. In Bury, J. B., *The Idea of Progress*, 200; italics ours.
96. Restif de La Bretonne, *La Vie de mon père*, 75.
97. Palache, *Four Novelists of the Old Regime*, 172.
98. *Ibid.*, 191.
99. Restif, *La Vie de mon père*, 14.
100. Chadourne, *Restif de La Bretonne*, 185.
101. *Ibid.*, 354.
102. Palache, 246.
103. Chadourne, 223.
104. *Ibid.*, 219.
105. Restif, *Les Nuits de Paris*, Nos. 109-114.
106. Ibid., No. 112.
107. No. 103.
108. Young, Arthur, 143.
109. Beaumarchais, letter of June 16, 1755, in Loménie, *Beaumarchais and His Times*, 55.
110. *Ibid.*, 78.
111. 94.
112. Voltaire, letter of Jan. 3, 1774.
113. Loménie, *Beaumarchais*, 263, 269 f.
114. Havens, *Age of Ideas*, 368.
115. Beaumarchais, *The Barber of Seville*, Act I, in Matthews, *Chief European Dramatists*, 332.
116. *Ibid.*
117. Blom, Eric, *Mozart*, 119n.
118. Loménie, *Beaumarchais*, 250.
119. *Ibid.*, 252.
120. *Le Mariage de Figaro*, directions to the players, in Beaumarchais, *Oeuvres*, 184.
121. *Ibid.*, Act II, Sc. ii.

122. V, vii.
123. V, xii.
124. II, xxi.
125. V, iii.
126. Preface, *Oeuvres*, 172.
127. Loménie, *Beaumarchais*, 351.
128. *Ibid.*, 383-84.
129. Havens, 382.
130. Loménie, 348.

CHAPTER XXXVII

1. Sée, *Economic and Social Conditions*, 8.
2. Labrousse, C. E., in Cobban, *Historians and . . . the French Revolution*, 35.
3. Young, Arthur, *Travels in France*, 70.
4. *Ibid.*, 19.
5. Herbert, *Fall of Feudalism*, 5-10.
6. *Ibid.*, 12, 15.
7. Lefebvre, Georges, *Coming of the French Revolution*, 121.
8. Sée, *Economic Conditions*, 54.
9. Jaurès, *Histoire socialiste*, I, 36.
10. Mornet, *Origines intellectuelles de la Révolution*, 143.
11. Michelet, *Histoire de France*, V, 548.
12. Martin, H., *France*, XVI, 512n.
13. Tocqueville, 193; Taine, *Ancient Regime*, 300 f.; Taine, *French Revolution*, I, 157.
14. Goodwin, *The European Nobility*, 41.
15. Argenson, Marquis d', *Pensées sur la réformation de l'état*, in Sée, *Economic Conditions*, 109.
16. Young, 24.
17. Herbert, *Fall of Feudalism*, 58; Sée, 5; Gershoy, *From Despotism to Revolution*, 310.
18. Chamfort, *Maximes*, 90.
19. Young, 125, 61.
20. Lefebvre, 116; see also Taine, *Ancient Regime*, 335-36.
21. Lefebvre, 118.
22. *Ibid.*
23. Jaurès, I, 76.
24. *New CMH*, VII, 237.
25. Mousnier and Labrousse, *Le Dix-huitième Siècle*, 137.
26. Stryienski, *Eighteenth Century*, 271.
27. Lefebvre, 87.
28. Lacroix, *Eighteenth Century in France*, 340.
29. French, Sidney, *Torch and Crucible: The Life and Death of Antoine Lavoisier*, 87.
30. Young, 103.
31. Lefebvre, 97.
32. *Ibid.*, 21.
33. Sée, 183; Renard and Weulersee, *Life and Work in Modern Europe*, 198.
34. Mousnier and Labrousse, 186.
35. Taine, *Ancient Regime*, 387.
36. *Ibid.*, 388.
37. Jaurès, *Histoire socialiste*, I, 109.

38. *Ibid.*, 110.
39. *Ibid.*
40. Taine, *Ancient Regime*, 334.
41. *Ibid.*, 361.
42. Lecky, V, 394; Gershoy, 308.
43. Jaurès, I, 69.
44. *Ibid.*, 68.
45. Sée, 148.
46. Cobban, *History of Modern France*, I, 123.
47. Jaurès, I, 62; Sée, 197-98.
48. Taine, *Ancient Regime*, 351-52.
49. Lefebvre, 14.
50. Jaurès, I, 62.
51. *Ibid.*, 98.
52. Beard, Miriam, *History of the Business Man*, 404.
53. Taine, 320.
54. Beard, Miriam, 352.
55. Lecky, V, 484.
56. See above, Ch. iii, Sec. v.
57. Lichtenberger, André, *Le Socialisme et la Révolution française*, 35; Martin, Kingsley, *Rise of French Liberal Thought*, 252.
58. Lichtenberger, 447.
59. *Ibid.*, 446-50.
60. *Enc. Brit.*, II, 238b.
61. Lichtenberger, 442 f.
62. Mornet, 360.
63. *Ibid.*, 364; Lefebvre, 43.
64. Cumming, Ian, *Helvétius*, 126-28.
65. *Ibid.*, 119.
66. Fülop-Miller, R., *Power and Secret of the Jesuits*, 436.
67. Faÿ, *La Franc-Maçonnerie*, 242.
68. Georgel, *Memoirs*, II, 310, in Buckle, Ib, 665.
69. Mornet, 450.

CHAPTER XXXVIII

1. Young, Arthur, *Travels in France*, 15.
2. Ségur, *Marie Antoinette*, 121; Castelot, 184.
3. Faÿ, *Louis XVI*, 293.
4. Gooch, *Maria Theresa*, 168.
5. Vigée-Lebrun, *Memoirs*, 57.
6. Mossiker, *Queen's Necklace*, 36.
7. *Ibid.*, 37, 200. 203.
8. 105.
9. *Vie de Jeanne de Valois*, by herself, in Mossiker, 63.
10. *Enc. Brit.*, VII, 321a.
11. Mossiker, 183-84.
12. *Ibid.*, 226.
13. 273.
14. 269.
15. Faÿ, *Louis XVI*, 275.
16. Mossiker, *ix*.
17. Martin, H., *France*, XVI, 539.

18. Taine, *Ancient Regime*, 92.
19. Martin, H., XVI, 573.
20. Paine, Thomas, *The Rights of Man*, 80.
21. Stryienski, *Eighteenth Century*, 286.
22. Young, Arthur, 92.
23. *Ibid.*, 97.
24. Guérard, A., *Life and Death of an Ideal*, 308.
25. Martin, H., *France*, XVI, 597.
26. Lefebvre, 29; Cobban, *History of Modern France*, I, 128.
27. Martin, H., XVI, 608.
28. Stewart, J. H., *Documentary Survey of the French Revolution*, 27-29; Martin, H., XVI, 612.
29. Michelet, *The French Revolution*, 118.
30. Michelet, *Histoire de France*, V, 545.
31. Faÿ, *Louis XVI*, 308; Taine, *French Revolution*, I, 2.
32. Aulard, I, 129; Michelet, *French Revolution*, 73.
33. Lichtenberger, 20; Martin, H., XVI, 630n.
34. Tocqueville, 121.
35. Herbert, *Fall of Feudalism*, 76, 87.
36. *Ibid.*, 76.
37. *CMH*, VIII, 128.
38. Barthou, Louis, *Mirabeau*, 11.
39. *Ibid.*, 62.
40. 68.
41. Michelet, *Histoire de France*, V, 515.
42. Crocker, *Embattled Philosopher*, 436.
43. Barthou, 91.
44. *Ibid.*, 97.
45. 118.
46. 138.
47. 162.
48. 163; Martin, H., *France*, XVI, 624.
49. Jaurès, I, 77.

50. Michelet, *Histoire de France*, V, 554.
51. Herbert, *Fall of Feudalism*, 95.
52. Taine, *French Revolution*, I, 17.
53. Taine, *Ancient Regime*, 378.
54. Martin, H., *France*, XVI, 625.
55. Lefebvre, 94.
56. *Enc. Brit.*, XVI, 909d.
57. Faÿ, *Louis XVI*, 312.
58. *Ibid.*, 305.
59. *Enc. Brit.*, XII, 491b.
60. Taine, *French Revolution*, I, 28.
61. *Enc. Brit.*, XII, 491b.
62. Taine, I, 28.
63. *CMH*, VIII, 133; Cobban, *History of Modern France*, I, 140.
64. Barthou, 171.
65. Young, Arthur, 153.
66. Lefebvre, 72.
67. Young, 176.
68. Lefebvre, 76.
69. Young, 176.
70. Lefebvre, 77.
71. Young, 177.
72. Michelet, *French Revolution*, 137; Lefebvre, 80-81.
73. Speech of July 8, 1789, in Barthou, 186.
74. Mme. Campan, *Memoirs*, I, 358.
75. Mme. de Staël, *Considérations sur la Révolution française*, in Ducros, *French Society*, 316.
76. Kropotkin, Peter, *The Great French Revolution*, 61-63.
77. Michelet, *French Revolution*, 133.
78. *Ibid.*, 141.
79. Lefebvre, 86.
80. Taine, *French Revolution*, I, 42.
81. Michelet, *French Revolution*, 150.
82. Lefebvre, 101.

Index

Dates in parentheses following a name are of birth and death except when preceded by *r.*, when they indicate duration of reign for popes and rulers of states. A single date preceded by *fl.* denotes a *floruit*. A footnote is indicated by an asterisk. Italicized page numbers indicate principal treatment. All dates are A.D. unless otherwise noted.

Abbas I, Shah of Persia (r. 1587–1629), 421
Abbas III, Shah of Persia (r. 1732–36), 149, 418
Abbaye, Béardé de l', 454
Abbeville, 932-33
A,B,C, L' (Voltaire), 143
Abduction from the Seraglio (Mozart), 367
Abdul-Hamid I, Ottoman Sultan (r. 1774–89), 415, 460
Abélard, Pierre (1079–1142), 112
Aberdeen, University of, 763
Abhandlung über den Ursprung der Sprache (Herder), 569
Abington, Frances, nee Barton (1737–1815), 740
Abo, University of, 659
Abrégé chronologique de l'histoire de France (Hénault), 123
Abt, Thomas (fl. 1763), 638
abu'l-Ahahab (fl. 1771), 415
academic freedom, 358
Académie de Peinture, 235
Académie des Sciences, 894, 896
Académie Française, *see* French Academy
Academy of Arts, Russian, 432, 466, 468
Academy of Dijon, 19-20, 22, 28
Academy of Mines, Russian, 453
Academy of San Fernando, 297, 299
Accademia della Crusca, 824
Accademia di Pittura e Scultura, Venice, 236
Accademia Filarmonica, 245, 386-87
Accademia Granelleschi, 242
Account of Corsica, The Journal of a Tour of That Island, and Memoirs of Pascal Paoli (Boswell), 783
Account of the Latest Herculaneum Discoveries (Winckelmann), 328
actors, *see* theater
Adam, James (d. 1794), 747-48, 765
Adam, John, 747-48, 765
Adam, Lambert-Sigisbert (1700–59), 247
Adam, Père (fl. 1765), 133
Adam, Robert (1728–92), 699, 747-48, 765
Adam, William (fl. 1770), 694, 732, 747-48, 765
Adams, Mrs. (Rousseau's landlady, 1766), 210
Adams, John (1735–1826), 870
Adams, John Quincy (1767–1848), 576
Adams, Samuel (1722–1803), 709
Adams, Dr. William (1706–89), 838
Addison, Joseph (1672–1719), 320, 485, 842
Adélaïde de France, Madame (1732–1800), 96
Adolphus Frederick of Holstein-Gottorp, King of Sweden (r. 1751–71), 655

Adonais (Shelley), 810
adultery, 97, 731
"Advantages that the Establishment of Christianity Has Conferred Upon the Human Race, The" (Turgot), 77
Adventures of Mr. Nicholas Find-Out, The (Krasicki), 485
advertisements, newspaper, 786
Aegean Isles, 411
Afghanistan, 417-18
Africa, 356
African Company, 732
African slavery, *see* slavery and slave trade
Agde, riots in, 954
Agnesi, Maria Gaetana (1718–99), 219
agriculture: in Austria, 345, 356; in England, 670-71, 680, 682; in France, 859, 861, 927-31; in Holland, 646; in Italy, 217; in Hungary, 341; in Poland, 472-73; in Spain, 273-74, 287-88
Agrigento, 589
Agrippa, Marcus Vipsanius (63–12 B.C.), 110
Ahmad Hatif, Sayyid (fl. 1750), Persian poet, 421
Ahmed III, Ottoman Sultan (r. 1703–30), 414-15
Ahmed Khan Durani, Shah of Afghanistan (r. 1747–73), 420
aides, 936
Aiguillon, Anne-Charlotte de Crussol de Florensac, Duchesse d', 118
Aiguillon, Armand de Vignerot, Duc d' (b. 1750), deputy in States-General, 957
Aiguillon, Emmanuel-Armand de Vignerot, Duc d' (1720–82), French statesman, 89, 92-93, 853
Aims of Jesus and His Disciples, The (Reimarus), 513
Aix-en-Provence, riots in, 934
Aix-la-Chapelle, Treaty of (1748), 38, 40, 58, 279, 648
Ajaccio, 312
Alam, *see* Shah Alam
Alba, Duke of (1508–82), *see* Alva
Alba, Don José de Toledo Osorio, Duke of (d. 1796), 274, 280, 303
Alba, Teresa Cayetana María del Pilar, Duchess of (1762–1803), 291, *303-4*
Albani, Alessandro, Cardinal (1692–1779), 328
Albani, Villa, 249, 331
Albania, 415
Albany, Count of, *see* Stuart, Charles Edward
Albany, Louise Caroline of Stolberg-Gedern, Countess of (1752–1824), 339-40

Alberoni, Giulio, Cardinal (1664–1752), 277-78

Albert (1738–1822), Duke of Saxe-Teschen, 361, 846

Albon, Comtesse Julie d' (fl. 1732), 122

Alcázar, 297

Alceste (Gluck), 369-71, 373

Alembert, Jean Le Rond d' (1717–83), 108, 118, 120, *123-30*, 172, 190, 214, 280, 485, 567, 636, 656, 769, 824, 894, 908, 920; Abarca's intimacy with, 281; abilities of, 127; Catherine II and, 447, 892; contributions to *Encyclopédie*, 123, 162; death of, 892; deference to royalty, 176; Diderot and, 892; Mme. du Deffand and, 123-25; early life of, 123; on expulsion of Spanish Jesuits, 284; Frederick II and, 124, 497-98, 892; French Revolution and, 940; Genevan clergy and, 198; on German literature, 506; Goldoni and, 798; Hume and, 892; Julie de Lespinasse and, *122-28*, *130*, 892; later years of, 892; on Louis XVI, 857; nature and, 169; poverty of, 126; Rousseau and, *163*, 191; supporter of Puccini, 372; Voltaire and, 125, 138, 876-77

Alexander I, Czar of Russia (r. 1801–25), 462, 466, 468

Alexander Palace, Tsarskoe Selo, 468

Alexander the Great, King of Macedon (r. 336–323 B.C.), 895

Alexis Petrovich, Czarevich (1690–1713), 429

Alfieri, Benedetto (1700–67), architect, 226

Alfieri, Vittorio, Conte di Cortemilia (1749–1803), dramatist, 310, *336-40*

Alfonso II d'Este, Duke of Ferrara (r. 1559–97), 584-85

Algarotti, Conte Francesco (1712–64), 238, 254, 370

Algeria, 411

Ali Bey (1728–73), 415

'Ali Hazin, Shaykh (1692–1767), 421

Allegri, Gregorio (1582–1652), 386

Allgemeine Naturgeschichte und Theorie des Himmels (Kant), 533

Allgemeine Preussische Landrecht (1791), 500

Allgemeine Schulordnung (1774), 352

Almada e Mendonça, Francisco de (d. 1804), 263

Alps, 169

Altham, machine-wrecking at, 679

Altona, Jews in, 635

Alva, Duke and Duchess of (18th cent.), *see* Alba

Alva, Fernando Álvarez de Toledo, Duke of (1508–82), 592

A Marilia (Gonzaga), 269

Amelia, Princess (1782–1810), dau. of George III, 727

America: English colonies in, *see* American colonies, English; French colonies in, *see* French America; Portuguese colonies in, 262-63, 269; Seven Years' War and, 57-58; slave trade and, *see* slavery and slave trade; Spanish colonies in, 80, 83, 262, 288; Voltaire's influence on, 881

"America libera" (Alfieri), 340

American colonies, English, 669; commerce and, 57, 708-9, 732-33; early conflicts with England, 708-11; population of, 708; revolt of, *see* American Revolution; slave trade and, 57, 708, 732-33

American Indians, 709, 833; accounts of, 31; Jefferson on, 891; Jesuit communists and, 80, 83, 262

American Revolution, 78, 683; aided by European powers, 354, 711, *867-72*, 922; battles in, 713-14, *869*, *871;* Beaumarchais' services to, *867-69*, 922; Burke's support to, 693, 711-14; early predictions of, 708; English reactions to, 689, 693, 704, 711-14, 833; France and, 354, 711, *867-72;* French Revolution and, 872; George III and, 687; German mercenaries and, 504; Gustavus III's fear of, 662; influence of, 520, *872*, 899; Johnson's opposition to, 833; Kant's support for, 548; Lafayette's aid to, 869, 871-72; outbreak of, 711; peace treaties (1782–83), 871-72; *philosophes* and, 867-68; Pitt the Elder and, 689; Rousseau's influence on, 891; Spain and, 290; surrender at Yorktown (1781), 761

Ami des hommes, ou Traité de la population, L' (Mirabeau the Elder), 74

Amiens: factories in, 932; Peace of (1802), 726; riots in, 954; unemployment in, 935

Amigoni, Jacopo (1675–1752), 235, 298

Amleto (Scarlatti), 257

Amsterdam, 361, 646; Jews in, 637; publishing in, 647

An die Freude (Schiller), 574-75

An die Freunde Lessings (Mendelssohn), 640

Anabaptists, 646

Anacreon (563–478 B.C.), 18

anarchism, 178

anatomy, Goethe's work on, 617

Anaxagoras (500?–428? B.C.), 176

Ancre, Maréchal d' (Concino Concini; d. 1617), 93

Andalusia, 273

Andrews, Dr. (fl. 1762), 798

Anecdotes of the Late Samuel Johnson, LL.D., during the Last Twenty Years of His Life (Thrale), 828, 840

Anecdotes of Painting in England (Walpole), 794

Anet, Claude (d. 1734), 12-13

Angelucci, Guglielmo (fl. 1773), 922

Anglican Church, 261, 711, 734-35

Anhalt, in League of Princes (1785), 362

Anhalt-Zerbst, Prince of, *see* Christian August

Anhalt-Zerbst, Princess of, *see* Johanna Elisabeth

Ankarström, Jakob (1762–92), 664-65

Anna Amalie, Dowager Duchess and Regent of Saxe-Weimar (r. 1758–75), 552, 580, 591, 600

Anna Ivanovna, Empress of Russia, (r. 1730–40), 425; reign of, 429-30

Anna Leopoldovna (1718–46), Regent of Russia (r. 1740–41), 430-31

Anna Petrovna (d. 1728), 429, 432
Annales politiques (Linguet), 82
Annalia d'Italia (Muratori), 244
Anne, Princess, Regent of Holland (r. 1751–59), 648
Anne, Queen of Great Britain (r. 1702–14), 818
Anne of Saxe-Lauenburg (fl. 1697), 228
Année littéraire, L', 372
Ansbach, 354; in League of Princes (1785), 362
Ansbach and Bayreuth, Margrave of, *see* Christian Friedrich Karl Alexander
anti-Semitism: decline in, 629; Voltaire's, 149-50, 629-30; *see also* Jews
Anton Ulrich of Brunswick, Prince (1714–76), 430
Antony, Mark (Marcus Antonius; 83?–30 B.C.), 31, 238
Antwerp, 342, 361, 364
Anville, Madame d', 118
Anzin firm episode, French Revolution, 932
Aphorisms for Women, by a Shepherdess of the North (Nordenflycht), 660
Apology for Suicide (Frederick the Great), 54
Apraksin, Count Stepan (1702–60), 48-49, 432
Aquinas, Saint Thomas (1225–74), 241
Arabia, 411-12, 415
Aranda, Pedro Abarca, Conde de (1718–99), 274, *280-81*, 292, 848; background of, 282; conflict with Jesuits, 283-84; fall of, 286; as father of Spanish Enlightenment, 287; foreign policy of, 290; political diplomacy of, 282; reforms of, 142, 286
Arblay, Gen. Alexandre d' (d. 1818), 791
Arcadian Academy, 256
Arcangeli, Francesco (d. 1768), 330
Archimedes (287?–212 B.C.), 672
Archinto, Alberico, Cardinal (1698–1758), 326, 328
architecture: baroque, 111; classical, 110, 747; in England, 747-48; in France, 109-11, 910; in Germany, 524-25; Industrial Revolution and, 682; in Italy, 247; in Russia, 426, 432, *467-69*; in Scotland, 765; in Spain, 297; in Turkey, 414
Archytas of Tarentum (fl. 400–365 B.C.), 555
Arco, Count, 344
Ardinghello (Heinse), 522
Argens, Jean-Baptiste de Boyer, Marquis d' (1704–71), 59
Argenson, Marc-Pierre de Voyer, Comte d' (1696–1764), 67
Argenson, Marc-René d', *see* Voyer, Marquis de
Argenson, René-Louis de Voyer, Marquis d' (1694–1757), 81; dismissal of, 85; on French nobility, 930; predicts American Revolution, 708; on revolutionary sentiment of Parisians, 91, 92
Argental, Charles-Augustin de Ferriol, Comte d' (1700–88), 875
Argentau, Mercy d', *see* Mercy d' Argentau
aristocracy, *see* nobility
Aristomène (Marmontel), 105
Aristophanes (450?–385 B.C.), 136, 241

Aristotelian unities, 296
Aristotle (384–322 B.C.), 163, 294, 511
Arkwright, Sir Richard (1732–92), 673
Arlechino (comic character), 232, 241
Armed Neutrality, Declaration of (1780), 713; –, League of, 457, 648, 713
Armenia, 418
Armentières, Marquis d' (fl. 1758), 161
Armide (Gluck), 372
Arminians, 646
Armour, Jean, *see* Burns, Jean
Armstead, Elizabeth (b. 1750), 726
Arnaud, Abbé François (1721–84), 371, 372-73
Arnim, Bettina von, nee Brentano (1785–1859), 562, *611*
Arnim, Henrietta von (fl. 1787), 575
Arnould, Sophie (1744–1802), 113, 370-71, 373, 883, 920
Arran, James Hamilton, 2d Earl of (1517?–75), 779
Artamène, ou Le Grand Cyrus (Scudéry), 169
Artarin, publisher, 402
Artois, 928
Artois, Comte d', *see* Charles X
Ascanio in Alba (Mozart), 387
Ashkenazi Jews, 630
Ashraf, Shah of Persia (r. 1725–30), 418
Asia Minor, 411; *see also* Islam
Assemblée Nationale, *see* National Assembly, French
Assembly of Notables (1787), 75, *944-45*
Astarabad, 419
Astrée, L' (Urfé), 169
atheism, 734; *philosophes* and, 183; Rousseau denounces, 183
Athens, ancient, 21, 579, 690
atmospheric engine, 674
Attempt by J. W. Goethe, Privy Councilor of the Duchy of Saxe-Weimar, to Explain the Metamorphosis of Plants, An (Goethe), 617
Auch eine Philosophie der Geschichte (Herder), 569
Auchinleck, Laird of, *see* Boswell, Alexander
Audenaarde, 361
Aufklärung (German Enlightenment), sources of, 507-8
Aufklärungspartei, 351
Augeard, Jacques-Matthieu (1731–1805), 850
Augereau, Maréchal Pierre-François-Charles (1757–1816), Duc de Castiglione, 606
Augsburg, Diet of, 176
Augusta of Saxe-Coburg-Gotha, Princess of Wales (d. 1772), 687
Augustine, Saint (354-430), 4
Augustinian friars, 285, 294
Augustus (Caius Octavius), Emperor of Rome (r. 27 B.C.–A.D. 14), 31, 252
Augustus II the Strong, King of Poland (r. 1697–1704, 1709–33), Elector of Saxony as Frederick Augustus I (r. 1694–1733), 475-76, 633
Augustus III, King of Poland (r. 1734–63),

Elector of Saxony as Frederick Augustus II
(r. 1733–63), *502;* in alliance against Frederick II, 43, 45, 46, 48, 502; Frederick invades
Saxon kingdom of, 44-45, 249, 502; Jews
under, 633; and Mengs, 248, 249; Polish
throne acquired by, 430; promiscuity of, 344,
436

"Auld Lang Syne" (additional passages by
Burns), 777

Aumont, Duc Louis-Marie-Augustin d' (1709–
82), 25

Austen, Jane (1775–1817), 791

Austerlitz, battle of (1805), 726

Austin, Lady (fl. 1785), 811

Australia, 669

Austria, *341-408;* abolition of torture and capital punishment in, 352, 356; academic freedom
in, 358; agriculture in, 345, 356; army of, 38-
39, 311, 344, 356; Bavaria and, 353-54, 362;
Catholic Church in, 343, 348, 351-52, *358-60;*
censorship in, 343, 348, 358; economy of, 344-
45, 349, 356-57, 456; education in, 343, 352,
358, 360; empire of, 38, 341-42, 354, 357, 360-
64; England and, 277-78; Enlightenment in,
343-46, *348-53, 355-61;* feudalism in, 345, 349,
356, 365; France and, 488, 846; as Holy Roman Empire, 341; independence of Netherlands from, *see* Austrian Netherlands; Inquisition in, 343; in Italy, 217, 227, 228, 249, 279,
311, 312, 313-14; Jansenists in, 359; and Jesuits,
318, 351-52; Jews in, 343, 352, 357, *631-32,* 641-
42; Joseph II's reforms in, 348-53, 355-61, 364-
66; legal reform in, 344, 356; literature in,
345-46; morality in, 344, 348; music in, *367-
408;* Poland and, 475, 482-83; population of,
357; prostitution in, 344; Protestants in, 343,
352, 357; religious toleration in, 348, 351-52,
357, 361, 641; Revolution of 1848 in, 366;
Russia and, 349, 362-63, 432; social classes in,
344-45, 349, 356-57; Spain and, 277-78; Turkey
and, 61, 363, 365, 411, 414-15, 430; War of the
Spanish Succession and, 273
FOREIGN POLICY AND AGREEMENTS, *353-54;* Convention of St. Petersburg (1757), 45; expansionist diplomacy, 362-63; First Treaty of
Versailles (1756), 42; in League of Armed
Neutrality (1780), 457; in Quadruple Alliance (1718), 278; Second Treaty of Versailles
(1757), 42
IN SEVEN YEARS' WAR (1756–63): campaign in
Bohemia, 47; campaign in Saxony, 45; coalition against Frederick II, 59-60; diplomacy
leading to, 38-42; end of French subsidies, 61;
peace negotiations, 62; results of conflict, 62-
63

Austrian Netherlands (Belgium), 42, 45, 341, 342,
361-64, 461; declares independence (1790), 364

Austrian Succession, War of the (1740–48), 15,
38, 40, 58, 240, 279, 648

autos-da-fé, 276, 279, 285

automobile, Cugnot's, 70

Auvergne, 928

Avant-Courier, 114

Aviero, Dom José de Mascarenhas, Duke of
(1708–59), 272; conflict with Pombal, 263;
philosophes and, 267-68; trial and execution
of, 265

Avignon, 317

Avis au peuple marseillais (Mirabeau *fils*), 654

Azov, 430, 458

Baal Shem-Tob (Israel ben Eliezer; 1700?–60),
636

Babeuf, François-Émile "Gracchus" (1760–97),
938; Morelly's influence on, 80-81; Rousseau's
influence on, 891

Babuti, Gabrielle, 112-13

Bach, Johann Christian, the "Milan [or London]
Bach" (1735–82), *526-27,* 755; in London, 746;
Mozart and, 384

Bach, Johann Christoph Friedrich, the "Bückeburg Bach" (1732–95), 526, 568

Bach, Johann Ernst, of Weimar (1722–77), 526

Bach, Johann Sebastian (1685–1750), 221-22, 234,
256, 373, 395; family of, 100, *526-27*

Bach, Karl Philipp Emanuel, the "Berlin Bach"
(1714–88), 374, 380, 399, *526;* contribution to
music, 528

Bach, Veit (d. 1619), 527

Bach, Wilhelm Friedemann, the "Halle Bach"
(1710–84), 526-27

Bach, Wilhelm Friedrich Ernst (1759–1845),
526-27

Bacon, Anthony, ironmaster (fl. 1785), 672

Bacon, Sir Francis (1561–1626), 251, 294, 427,
794

Baden, 362

Baggesen, Jens (1764–1826), 594, 650

Baghavand, battle of (1735), 419

Bagnols, riots in, 954

"Bahabec" (Voltaire), 151

Bahamas, 669

Bahrdt, Karl Friedrich (1764–1826), 507

Baia, 327

Bailey, Nathaniel (d. 1742), 820-21

Bailly, Jean-Sylvain (1736–93), 957-58

Bakhchisarai, 430

Baku, 419, 470

balalaikas, 425

Balder's Death (Ewald), 652

Balkh, 417

balloons, airborne, 932

Balsamo, Giuseppe, *see* Cagliostro

Balzac, Honoré de (1799–1850), 104, 919

Bamberg, Prince-Bishop of (fl. 1525), 560

Banco di San Carlos, 288

Banco di San Giorgio, 227

Bank of France, Turgot's model for, 860-61

banking: in England, 670; in France, 235, 860-61;
in Holland, 646; in Italy, 227, 288; in Switzerland, 643

Baptists, 735, 760

Bar, Confederation of, 481-83

Barbados, 669

Barbarossa, Frederick I, Holy Roman Emperor (r. 1152–90), 239
Barbary States, 417-18
Barbauld, Anna, nee Aikin (1743–1825), 787
Barber, Francis (1745?–1801), 822
Barber of Seville, The (Beaumarchais), 334, 923
Barbiere di Siviglia, Il (Mozart and Paisiello), 334
Barcelona, 288-89
Barnave, Antoine-Pierre-Joseph (1761–93), 948, 957
Baroccio, Federigo (1528–1612), 115
Baron Munchausen's Travels (Raspe), 534, 568
Baronius, Henriette (fl. 1789), 405
baroque architecture, 111
Barré, Isaac (1726–1802), 704
Barry, Mme. du, *see* Du Barry, Mme.
Barry, Spranger (1719–77), 740
Barthe, Nicolas (fl. 1778), 874
Barthélemy, Abbé Jean-Jacques (1716–95), 917
Bas Bleu Society, 730
Basedow, Johann Bernhard (1724?–90), 506-7, 612, 888
Basel, 643; Congress of (1795), 547
Bashkir tribes, 455
Basnage, Jacques (1653–1725), 641
Bassano, 229
Bassenge, Paul, jeweler (fl. 1785), 941-42
Bassi, Laura (1711–78), Professor at University of Bologna, 219
Bastille, fall of, 311, 364, 580, 934, *962-63*
Batavian Republic, formation of, 694; *see also* Switzerland
Bath, 740
Bath, Earl of, *see* Pulteney, William
Baumgarten, Alexander Gottlieb (1714–62), 532
Bavaria: Austria and, 362; conflict between Joseph II and Frederick II over, 353-54; secret societies outlawed in, 507; united with Palatinate, 354
Bayeu y Subias, Francisco (1734–95), *299*, 303
Bayle, Pierre (1647–1706), 10, 13, 139, 183, 280, 326, 427, 435, 557; clerical condemnation of, 890
Bayreuth, 354, 525
Bazhenev, Vasili (1737–99), 469
Beatrice of Burgundy (d. 1184), 239
Beauclerk, Lady Diana (1734–1808), 841
Beauclerk, Topham (1739–80), 827, 839
Beauharnais, Fanny, Comtesse de (1738–1813), 919; salon of, 907
Beauharnais, Joséphine de, nee Marie-Josèphe-Rose Tascher de La Pagerie (1763–1814), 907
Beaumarchais, Pierre-Augustin Caron de (1732–99), 149, 852, *920-26*, 944; aid to American Revolution, 867-69, 922; death of, 926; early life and education of, 920; in French Revolution, 925-26, 940; jailed for bribery, 921; *philosophes* and, 920; plays of, 922-25; publishes Voltaire's collected works, 925; in Spain, 921; writes *The Barber of Seville*, 923; writes *The Marriage of Figaro*, 403-4, *923-25*

Beaumont, Christophe de (1703–81), Archbishop of Paris, 90-91; Rousseau persecuted by, 189, *193-97*
Beauregard, Captain (fl. 1722), 150
Beauvau, Mme. de, 118
Beccaria, Cesare Bonesana, Marchese di (1738–94), 312, *320-21*, 451; academic career of, 321; economic theories of, 321; ethics of, 739; influence of, 145, 336; influence of French Enlightenment on, 320; legal reforms proposed by, 320-2
Beckford, William (1760-1844), author, 255; on beggars of Portugal, 259
Beckford, William (1709–70), Lord Mayor of London, 704, 809
Bécu, Anne, 86
Bedford, John Russell, 4th Duke of (1710–71), 62
Bedouins, 411
Beethoven, Ludwig van (1770–1827), 334, 528; Goethe's views on, 613; Haydn and, 378-80; Mozart compared with, 397-98
Beggars Opera, The (Gay), 696
Beiträge zur Optik (Goethe), 615-16
Belgium, *see* Austrian Netherlands
Belgrade, 415, 460
Bélisaire (Marmontel), 106, 463
Belisarius (505?–565), 804
Belisarius (Goldoni), 242
Bellamy, Georgeanne (1731?–88), 740
Bellarmine, Robert, Cardinal (1542–1621), 177
Bellmann, Karl Mikael (1740–95), 660-61
Belluno, 229
Belsunce, Émilie de (fl. 1796), 894
Benda, Georg (1722–95), 342
Bender, 460
Benedict XIII (Pietro Francesco Orsini), Pope (r. 1724–30), 246, 260
Benedict XIV (Prospero Lambertini), Pope (r. 1740–58), 225; aid to Jews, 633; death of, 264; enlightened policies of, 246–47; gentleness of, 319–20; Portuguese Jesuits and, 263-64
Benedictines, 294
Benevento, 244, 317
Bengal, 715-17
Bentham, Jeremy (1748–1832), 320, *738-39*; on Blackstone, 737; Voltaire's influence on, 881
Benucci, Francesco (fl. 1786), 404
Berengar of Tours (998–1088), 513
Berezovsky, Sozonovich (1745?–77), 425
Berg, Baron Friedrich Reinhold von, 328
Bergamo, 218, 228
Bergen, battle of (1759), 54
Bergman, Torbern Olof (1735–84), 612, 658
Berkeley, George (1685–1753), 183, 531, 759, 764, 834
Berlichingen, Gottfried (Götz) von (1480–1562), 561
Berlin, 63, 500, 530; architecture in, 524; factories in, 501; Jews in, 634; population growth in, 501; in Seven Years' War, 49, 55, 60, 510
Berlioz, Hector (1803–69), 627

Bern, 643–44; revolts in, 645; Rousseau expelled from, 191, 206–7

Bernacchi, Antonio (1685–1756), 222, 232

Bernard, Abraham, cousin of Rousseau, 6

Bernard, Gabriel, uncle of Rousseau, 6

Bernard, Samuel, banker (1651–1739), 16

Bernardin de Saint-Pierre, Désirée, nee de Pellepou, 917

Bernardin de Saint-Pierre, Félicité, nee Didot, 917

Bernardin de Saint-Pierre, Jacques-Henri (1737–1814), 883–84, 886, 889, 904, *916-17*

Bernhard, Isaac (fl. 1750), 638

Bernini, Giovanni Lorenzo (1598–1680), 235, 247

Bernis, François-Joachim de Pierre, Cardinal de (1715–94), 41, 67, 317-18

Bernstorff, Count Andreas Peter von (1735–97), 653

Bernstorff, Count Johann Hartwig Ernst von (1712–72), 517, *652*

Berthollet, Claude-Louis (1748–1822), 939

Besenval, Mme. de (fl. 1742), 16

Besenval, Baron Pierre-Victor de (1722–91), 960, 962-63

Bessarabia, 411

Bessenyei, György (1747–1811), 351

Besterman, Theodore, 138

Bestuzhev-Ryumin, Alexei (1693–1766), 431-32, 442

Betsky, Ivan (1704–95), 453, 466

Bevilacqua, Palazzo, 245

Beyer, Karl Friedrich Wilhelm (d. 1806), 345

Bibiena, Alessandro Galli da (1687–1769), 245

Bibiena, Antonio Galli da (1700–44), 245

Bibiena, Ferdinando Galli da (1657–1743), 245

Bibiena, Francesco Galli da (1659–1739), 245

Bibiena, Giuseppe Galli da (1696–1756), 245

Biblioteca Ambrosiana, 219

Biblioteca Magliabechiana, 219

Bibliothek der Schönen Wissenschaften und der Freien Künste, 638

Bijoux, Les (Diderot), 596

Bilderdijk, Willem (1756–1831), 647

Bill of Rights, American Constitution, 872

"Bill of Rights" of 1689, English, 699

Birmingham: growth of, 681; iron industry in, 672; theater in, 740

Biron, Ernst Johann von, Duke of Kurland (1690–1772), 429-30

Bismarck, Otto von (1815–98), 502

Black, Joseph (1728–99), 674-75, 763-64, 932

Black Hole of Calcutta (1756), 715

Black Plague, 312

Black Sea, 456-58, 483

Blackstone, Sir William (1723–80), 832, *736-38;* on conversion of Protestants to Catholicism, 797; on English political structure, 686-87

Blagden, Sir Charles (1748-1820), 841

Blair, Catherine (fl. 1768), 783

Blair, Hugh (1718–1800), 767, 768, 776

Blake, William (1757–1827), 658

Blanchard, François (1753–1809), 932-33

Blenheim Gardens, 748

Blondel, Jacques-François (1705–74), 110

Blot, Mme. de (fl. 1760), 193

Bobrinsky, Alexis (b. 1762), 437

Bocage, Manuel Maria Barbosa du (1765–1805), 270

Boccaccio, Giovanni (1313–75), 515

Boccage, Marie-Anne Fiquet du, nee Le Page (1710–1802), 799

Boccherini, Luigi (1743–1805), 292, *333*, 377

Bodmer, Johann Jakob (1698–1783), 566

Boerhaave, Hermann (1668–1738), 647

Boguslawski, Wojciecz (1760–1829), 486

Bohemia, 354; Austria and, 38, 341, 350, 358, 365-66; culture in, 342; early history of, 341-42; Jews in, *631-32*, 641; metal industry in, 344; population of, 342; revolt of serfs in, 350; Seven Years' War in, 47-48; Thirty Years' War in, 342

Böhme, Frau Hofrat, 524

Böhmer, Charles, jeweler (fl. 1785), 941-43

Boileau-Despréaux, Nicolas (1636–1711), 136, 169, 201, 528, 889

Boisgelin de Cucé, Raymond de (1732–1804), 126

Boisguillebert, François de (1592–1662), 72

Boismont, Nicolas Thyrel de (1715–86), 126

Boissel, François (fl. 1789), 938

Boissieu, Jean-Jacques (1736–1810), 116*

Boizot, Louis-Simon (1743–1809), 106

Bokhara, Emir of (1740), 420

bolero, 292

Bolingbroke, Henry St. John, Viscount (1678–1751), 687

Bologna, 244-45, 310; Goethe in, 587; ratio of priests to lay population in, 224; university in, 219

Bolton, machine-wrecking in, 679

Bolzano, 229

Bombay, 58

Bonaparte, Joseph (1768–1844), 296, 334; in Spain, 296-98

Bonaparte, Napoleon, *see* Napoleon I

Boncerf, Pierre-François (1745–94), 929

Bonnefax, Father (fl. 1789), 901

Bonnot de Condillac, *see* Condillac

Bonnot de Mably, *see* Mably

Book of Lismore, The (compiled by James Magregor), 767

Bordeaux, 107, 932-33

Bordes, Professor (fl. 1740), 14, 23

Bordeu, Théophile de (1722–76), 130

Bordoni, Faustina (1693–1783), 223, 232

Borovikovsky, Vladimir (1757–1825), 466

Bortniansky, Dmitri Stephanovich (1751–1825), 426

Boscawen, Mrs., 730

Boscawen, Edward (1711–61), 57-58

Bosch, Hieronymus (1450?–1516), 305

Bosnia, 411

Bosporus, 458

Bossuet, Jacques Bénigne (1627–1704), 569, 796-97

Boston, 710

Boston Tea Party (1773), 711

Boswell, Alexander, Laird of Auchinleck (d. 1782), 778, 784, 836

Boswell, Euphemia, Lady Auchinleck, nee Erskine (d. 1766), 779, 783

Boswell, James (1740–95), 214, 729-31, 744, 753-54, 763-64, 778-85, 828, 964; bouts with venereal disease, 779-80, 782-83, 785; on Burke, 692; conversion to Catholicism, 779; death of, 842; death of wife, 842; dependence on alcohol, 784-85, 842; description of, 842; on Dutch women, 647; early life and education of, 779-80; in Edinburgh, 783-85; fame as "Corsican Boswell," 784; family background of, 778-79; on Gibbon, 805; on Goldsmith, 817; his honesty about himself, 785; on lack of religion in England, 734; as Laird of Auchinleck, 841; later years of, 841-42; in London, 745, 779-80, 785, 841-42; love affairs of, 647-48, 779-83, 785; marries Margaret Montgomerie, 784; meets English celebrities, 780; on Neuchâtel, 191; Paoli and, 782-83; Rousseau and, 133, 152, 201-4, 210, 782-83; on Soho factory, 675; supports American Revolution, 833; Thérèse Levasseur and, 202-4, 783; on towns in Holland, 646; travels abroad, 781-83; Voltaire and, 133-34, 782; Wilkes and, 703, 782
    JOHNSON AND, 837; conversations and opinions, 785, 820, 826-35, 839; journey to Litchfield and Oxford, 839; length of their association, 827; they meet for the first time, 780; tour of the Hebrides, 785, 835-36, 840; writing of The Life of Samuel Johnson, 840-41

Boswell, John, brother of James, 779

Boswell, Margaret, nee Montgomerie (1738–89), 784, 842

botany, Goethe's work on, 617

Bouchardon, Edme (1698–1762), 107, 120, 247

Boucher, François (1703–70), 23, 106, 113, 117, 120, 912; influences on, 235; sensuality of, 97

Boufflers, Duchesse de, see Luxembourg, Maréchale de

Boufflers, Marie-Charlotte-Hippolyte de Saujon, Comtesse de (1725–c.1800), 125, 161, 907, 929; Rousseau and, 161, 209, 213-14, 882

Boufflers, Marie-Françoise-Catherine de Beauvau-Craon, Marquise de (1711–87), 161*

Boulton, Matthew (1728–1809), 675, 734

Boulton and Watt, engine company, 675-76

Bourbon, Abbé de (b. 1762), 68

Bourbon, Duchesse de, 929

Bourbon, Duc Louis-Henri-Joseph de (1756–1830), 850

Bourbon monarchs: Hapsburg rivalry with, 273; restoration in France (1814), 890

bourgeoisie, see middle class

Bourgogne (Burgundy), Louis-Joseph de France, Duc de (1751–61), grandson of Louis XV, 71, 845

Bourru bienfaisant, Le (Goldoni), 244

Bouverie, Mrs. Edward (fl. 1770), 753

Bowles, Miss, 753

Boyd, Mary Ann (fl. 1769), 783-84

Brabant, 342, 361; Estates of, defiance of Joseph II, 362, 364

Brabantane, Marquis de (fl. 1766), 209

Bracci, Pietro (1700–73), 247

Bragadino, Zuan (fl. 1750), 323

Brahms, Johannes (1833–97), 381, 399

Brandenburg, 54, 484

Brandenburger Tor, 525

Brandywine, battle of (1777), 869

Braschi, Giovanni, see Pius VI

Braut von Messina, Die (Schiller), 604

Bray-sur-Seine, riots in, 954

Brazil, Jesuits in, 263

breast-feeding, 180

Bremen, duchy of, 653

Brentano, Bettina, see Arnim, Bettina von

Brentano, Maximiliana, nee von La Roche, 611

Brentano, Peter (fl. 1773), 611

Breslau, 51-52, 60

Breteuil, Louis-Auguste Le Tonnelier, Baron de (1730–1807): Diamond Necklace Affair and, 943; as emigré, 963; ministry of (1789), 961-63; on Peter III's mistreatment of Catherine, 439

Breton Club, 939

Brézé, Marquis Henri-Evrard de (1766–1829), 959

"Bride of Corinth, The" (Goethe), 599

Bride of Messina, The (Schiller), 604

Bridgewater, Francis Egerton, 3d Duke of (1736–1803), 670, 672

Brief Observations Concerning Trade and Interest (Child), 72

Briefe die neueste Literatur betreffend (issued by Nikolai), 507, 510

Briefe über die ästhetische Erziehung des Menschen (Schiller), 595

Briefe über die Empfindungen (Mendelssohn), 638

Briefe zur Beförderung der Humanitat (Herder), 580

Brienne, Mme. de, 929

Brienne, Loménie de, see Loménie de Brienne, Étienne

Brighella (comic figure), 241

Brindley, James (1716–72), 672

Brindley-Bridgewater canal, 672

Brion, Friederike (1752–1813), 521, 559-60, 608

Brissot de Warville, Jacques-Pierre (1754–93), 88, 938-39

Bristol, George William Hervey, 2d Earl of (1721–75), 282

Bristol: growth of, 681; as port city, 669; theater in, 740; voting population in, 685

Britannicus (Racine), 103

British East India Company: Clive and, 715-16; corruption in, 716-18; Hastings trial and, 719-21; regulation of, 719

British Museum, 750
Briton, The (periodical), 702
Brody, Jews in, 632
Broglie, Mme. de, 118
Broglie, Maréchal Duc Victor-François de
    (1718–1804), 54, 963; defeat at Minden, 55;
    as secretary of war, 961; States General and,
    960
Brook Farm, 81
Brooke, Henry (1703?–83), 786
Broschi, Carlo, *see* Farinelli
Brosses, Charles de (1709–77),149, 218-20, 250
Brown, Agnes, 772
Brown, Lancelot "Capability" (1715–83), 748
Browning, Robert (1812–89), 658
Bruges, 361
Brühl, Count Heinrich von (1700–63), 466
Brummell, George Bryan "Beau" (1778–1840),
    753
Brummell, William, 753
Brunetière, Ferdinand (1849–1906), 138
Brunn, university at, 360
Brunswick: in League of Princes (1785), 362;
    Seven Years' War in, 60
Brunswick, Duke Ferdinand of, *see* Ferdinand
    of Brunswick
Brunswick, Karl Wilhelm Ferdinand, Duke of,
    see Karl Wilhelm Ferdinand
Brunswick-Bevern, August Wilhelm, Duke of
    (1715–81), 47, 51
Brunswick-Wolfenbüttel, Prince Ludwig Ernst
    of, *see* Ludwig Ernst
Brussels, 342, 361, 364
Bruto primo (Alfieri), 338
Bruto secondo (Alfieri), 338
Brutus, Lucius Junius (fl. 510 B.C.), 912
Buccleuch, Henry Scott, 3d Duke of (1746–
    1812), 769
Buchanan, George (1506–82), 177
Bucharest, 458
Buckle, Henry Thomas (1821–62), 769
Budapest, 341, 364
Buen Retiro, 288
Buff, Charlotte, *see* Kestner, Charlotte
Buffon, Georges-Louis Leclerc, Comte de (1707–
    88), 73, 99, 147, 353, 636, 908; clerical attacks
    on, 902; death of, 893; on sensuality, 97
Bug River, 430
Bühren, Ernst von, *see* Biron
Bulgarelli, Marianna (La Romanina; 1686–1734),
    240
Bulgaria, 411
bullfights, 291
Bünau, Count Heinrich von (1697–1762), 326
Bunbury, Henry, 817
Buonaparte, Carlo (1746–85), 313
Buonaparte, Napoleone, *see* Napoleon I
Bureau de Roi, 107
Bürger, Gottfried (1747–94), 519–20
Burgoyne, John (1722–92), 713
Burgundy, Duke of, *see* Bourgogne, Duc de
Büring, Johann Gottlieb (1723–c.1789), 524

Burke, Edmund (1729–97), 683, *689-93*, 696, 700-1,
    721-25, 730, 747-48, 754, 759, 761-62, 828, 832,
    839, 897; cultural tastes of, 689; death of, 725;
    early life and education of, 689; economic
    policies of, 693; election to Parliament, 692;
    esthetic views of, 696; on German principali-
    ties, 503; Goldsmith and, 817; in Hastings' trial,
    719-21; issues *Reflections on the French Revo-*
    lution, 722-23, 806; Johnson and, 692, 827, 839-
    41; on lack of religion in England, 734; later
    conservatism of, 690, 692-93, 722-25; love affairs
    of, 689; Marie Antoinette and, 722-23; marriage
    to June Nugent, 691; in ministry, 714-15;
    morality of, 694; opposition to French Revo-
    lution, 690, 693, 721-25; opposition to slave
    trade, 693, 733; policy toward Catherine II,
    689, 736; policy toward Catholics, 689, 736;
    on Polish constitution, 487-88; predicts French
    Revolution, 721-22; quality as speaker, 692;
    rapprochement with George III, 725; refuses
    peerage offer, 725; on religion, 725; respect for
    French clergy, 900; rising career of, 691-92;
    on Rousseau, 891; social, political views of,
    692-93; supports American Revolution, 693,
    711-14; views on property and state, 724-25;
    youthful radicalism of, 690
Burke, June, nee Nugent, 691
Burke, Richard, brother of Edmund, 719
Burke, William (fl. 1780), cousin of Edmund,
    719
Burkersdorf, battle of (1762), 61
Burlador de Seville, El (Tirso de Molina), 404
Burnes, Agnes, nee Brown, 772
Burnes, William (d. 1784), 772
Burney, Charles (1726–1814), 133, 233, 333, 746-
    47, 790, 828; description of Gluck, 368; on
    Duke of Brunswick, 50; on Frederick II, 496;
    on Gluck-Puccini rivalry, 372; in "the Club,"
    827; on Venetian music, 220; on Voltaire's ap-
    pearance, 134
Burney, Fanny (1752–1840), 333, 730, 743, 787,
    790-91, 839
Burns, Gilbert, brother of Robert, 773
Burns, Jean, nee Armour (d. 1834), 763, 774-77
Burns, Robert (1759–96), 732, 762, 764, *772-78*,
    964
Burr, Margaret, 755
Burslem, potteries at, 749
Burton, Robert (1577–1640), 788
Bury, John Bagnell (1861–1927), 807
Busoni, Ferruccio Benvenuto (1866–1924), 243*
Bussy, Mme, de, 118
Bute, John Stuart, 3d Earl of (1713–92), 61, 688,
    693; conflicts with Wilkes, 702; ministry of,
    698-700, 702; Samuel Johnson and, 826-27;
    Seven Years' War and, 62, 699
Bute, Mary, Countess of, nee Montagu (1718–
    1794), 688
Buttafuoco, Matteo (1731–1806), 204
Buttal, Jonathan, 756
Byng, John, Admiral (1704–57), 42-43
Byron, George Gordon, Lord (1788–1824), 340,

623, 627; Rousseau's influence on, 3; on Sterne, 790; Voltaire's influence on, 880-81

Byzantine Greeks, 312

Cabala, 620, 635, 637
Cabanis, Pierre-Jean (1757–1808), 869
Cabarrús, Conde Francisco de (1752–1810), 288
Cabinet Dictionary (Sheraton), 748
Cadíz, 288-89
Caduta de' giganti, La (Gluck), 368
Caesar, Caius Julius (100–44 B.C.), 48, 529
Caffarelli (Gaetano Majorano; 1703–83), 254
Caffè, ll, 320
Caffieri, Jacques (1678–1755), 106-7
Caffieri, Jean-Jacques (1725–92), *109,* 911
Cagliostro, "Count" Alessandro di (Giuseppi Balsamo; 1743–95), *321-22,* 645; in Affair of the Diamond Necklace, 322, 942-43
Cagliostro, "Countess" Seraphina di (Lorenza Feliciani Balsamo), 321-22
Cagliostro démasqué (author not cited), 322
cahiers des plaintes et doléances, 950
Cahusac, Louis de (d. 1759), 33
Cain, Henri-Louis, *see* Lekain, Henri-Louis
Cairo, 415-16
Calas, Jean (1698–1762), 90, 146, 881
Calas family, 88, 146, 151, 498, 881
Calatrava College at Salamanca, 301
Calcutta: Black Hole of (1756), 715; English stronghold at, 58
Caldwell, Thomas, bookseller (fl. 1776), 800
Caliste (Charrière), 648
Calonne, Charles-Alexandre de (1734–1802), *943-45,* 946
Calvin, John (1509–64), 143, 177, 360, 881
Calvinism: in Holland, 646; Rousseau and, 5-6, 27, 177, 185, 192, 195-99; in Scotland, 763
Calzabigi, Raniero da (1715–95), 368-70
Cambis, Mme. de, 118
Camelford, Lord, 685
Cameron, Charles, architect, 468
Camões, Luiz Vaz de (1524–80), 259, 269
Campan, Jeanne-Louise-Henriette, nee Genêt (1752–1822), 853-57
Campanelli, Cardinal (fl. 1760), 633
Campbell, Mary (d. 1786), 775
Campoformio, Treaty of (1797), 311
Campomanes, Conde Pedro Rodríguez de (1723–1802), 283, 286, *293,* 302
Canada, 89, 698, 709; English conquest of, 57, 62, 68
Canaletto (Antonio Canale; 1697–1768), 236, 332
Canaletto, Bernardo Bellotto (1720–80), 236
canals: in England, 672; in Russia, 456; in Scotland, 762
Candide (Voltaire), 34, 155, 825
Cannabich, Christian (1731–98), 525
Canova, Antonio (1757–1822), 479, 750; monument to Alfieri, 340
Cant, Anna, nee Reuter, 531
Cant, Johann Georg, 531

Cantemir, Prince (fl. 1758), 120
Cantemir, Prince Antioch (1709?–44), 427
Canterbury, Archbishop of (1737–47), *see* Potter, John
Cantillon, Richard (1680?–1734), 72
Cape Breton Island, 57
Capion, Étienne (fl. 1720), 650
capital punishment: abolition in Austria, 356;—in England, 733; —in France, 146; —in Russia, 431, 451; Voltaire's opposition to, 145-46
capitalism: in Austria, 356; in England, *see* Industrial Revolution; in France, 70, 936; in Italy, 218, 230; physiocratic theory and, 71; in Prussia, 501; Adam Smith's attitude toward, 771; *see also* middle class
Cappella Giulia, 257
Caps (Swedish party), 654, 656-67
Caraccioli, Marchese Domenico di (1715–89), 315
Carinthia, 341, 358
Carli, Conde Giovanni Rinaldo (1720–95), 312
Carlisle, Frederick Howard, 5th Earl of (1748–1825), 753
Carlisle, Georgiana, Countess of, 753
Carlos, Don (1545–68), son of Philip II, 338
Carlos of Bourbon, Don, *see* Charles III, King of Spain
Carlton House, 748
Carlyle, Thomas (1795–1881), 50, 627, 658, 823; Kant's influence on, 551; on Kaunitz, 41; on Schiller's *The Robbers,* 570
Carmelites, 294
Carmer, Johann Heinrich Casimir von (fl. 1780), 500
Carmona, Luis Salvador (1709–67), 298
Carniola, 341, 358
carnivals, 232
Caroline Matilda (1751–75), Queen of Christian VII of Denmark, 652-53
Caron, Lisette, 921
Carpenter, Edward (1844–1929), 891
Carriera, Rosalba (1675–1757), 235, 792
Carstens, Asmus Jakob (1754–98), 524
Cartas eruditas y curiosas (Feijóo), 294
Carter, Elizabeth (1717–1806), 730
Carthaginians, 312
Cartwright, Edmund (1743–1823), 673
Carvajal, Don José de (d. 1754), 279
Carvalho, Paul de, 267
Carvalho, Dona Teresa de, nee Noronha (d. 1745), 261
Calasi-Dugnani, Palazzo, 237
Casanova, Giovanni Jacopo (1725–98), 219, 310, *322-25;* adventures in Italy and France, 323-24; on *commedia dell' arte,* 241; death of, 325; early life and education of, 322; joins Freemasons, 326; on Maria Theresa, 344; occultist interests of, 324; on Parma, 311-12; returns to Italy, 325; on Spanish dancing, 292; visit to Rousseau, 324; —to Voltaire, 133, 138, 143, 324; on Wolfenbüttel library, 512; writes his *Memoirs,* 325; on Württemberg court, 502-3

Casas y Nova, Fernando de (fl. 1751), 297
Caserta, palace at, 250
Casimir III the Great, King of Poland (r. 1333–1370), 475
Cassel, 525
Castéra, J. H. (fl. 1800), 444; on Catherine II, 461-62; on Elizaveta Vorontsova, 439; on Peter III, 435-36
Castile, 288
Castle of Otranto (Walpole), 691, 794, 809
castrati in Italy, 222
Castro, Machado de, *see* Machado de Castro, Joaquim
Catalogue of the Royal and Noble Authors of England (Walpole), 794
Catalonia, 288
Catéchisme du genre humain (Boissel), 938
Catherine I, Empress of Russia (r. 1725–27), 429
Catherine II the Great, Empress of Russia (r. 1762–96), 121, 334, 337, 342, 353, 425-28 *passim*, 657, 749, 880, 885, 897; abilities of, 342, 434-35, 442-43, 450-54; absolutism of, 443; achievements of, 470-71; d'Alembert and, 447, 892; Austria and, 349; Beccaria's influence on, 321; children of, 436-37, 462; conflicts with Peter III, 435-36, 439; conspiracies against, 443-44, 469; death of, 470; deposes Peter III, 439-40; Diderot and, 446-50, 462-63, 466, 893; dismemberment of Poland and, 350, 481-85, 487-92; Enlightenment and, 34, 446-50, 452-53, 462-63; early life and education of, 433-34; early unpopularity of, 441; economic policies of, 454-56; Elizabeth Petrovna and, 434; estimates of, 471; Falconet and, 109; foreign policy of, 456-61, 469-70; Frederick II and, 434, 442, 457-58, 462, 484; French Revolution and, 465, 469; Grimm and, 447, 449, 452-53, 463, 466, 894; illnesses of, 433, 435; Joseph II and, 363, 483; journey to Crimea, 459-60; later years of, 469-70; literary activities of, 463-64; love affairs of, 436, 442, 444-46; marries Peter III, 434-35; musical interests of, 334; Necker and, 870-71; Paul I and, 441; personality of, 461-63; policy toward Jews, 632-33; Poniatowski and, 478; reactionary policies in later life, 469-70; reforms of, 142, 146, 452-53; Rousseau and, 173; Russian culture and, 463-69; Sweden and, 656, 664; Voltaire and, 135, 139-40, 434, 442, 447-48, 451, 457-58, 462, 469, 873, 879; withdraws from Seven Years' War, 61
Catholic Church: in Austria, 343, 358-60; basis of power and influence, 316; Burke and, 689, 736; charitable activities of, 905; conflicts with Catholic monarchs, 317-18; conservative role of, 290; in England, 684, 735-36, 762; in France, 142, 900-2; in Germany, 499, 504-5; in Holland, 646-47; Index of, 247, 285, 316, 358; in Ireland, 283, 760-62; in Italy, 225; Jansenism and, *see* Jansenists; Jesuits and, *see* Jesuits; Johnson and, 834; nationalism and, 316; in Poland, 472, 475,

480-81; popular superstitions and, 316; in Portugal, 260, 267-68, 317; Rousseau and, 175, 185; in Russia, 452; in Scotland, 763; in Spain, 281, 283-86, 290; *see also* Inquisition; papacy
Catholic relief laws in England, 735-36, 762
Cattaro, 229
Catullus, Caius Valerius (84?–54? B.C.), 21
Caucasus, 422
"Causes of Barometric Fluctuations, The" (Goethe), 615
Cavalli, Pietro Francesco (1602–76), 232
Cave, Edward (1691–1754), 819-20, 822
Cavendish, Lord, 726
Cavendish, Henry (1731–1810), 932
Caylus, Anne-Claude-Philippe de Tubières, Comte d (1692–1765), 110, 120, 218, 467, 749
Ceán-Bermúdez, Juan Augustín (1749–1829), 298
Cecchina, La (Piccini), 333
celibacy, Rousseau's critique of, 168-69
censorship: in Austria, 343, 348, 358; Goethe's support for, 623; in Italy, 220, 225; in Portugal, 268; in Spain, 285
Cephalonia, 229
Cervantes Saavedra, Miguel de (1547–1616), 788
Chait Singh, Rajah of Benares (r. 1773–80), 717
Chamberlaine, Frances, *see* Sheridan, Frances
Chambers, Sir William (1726–96), 747-48
Chamfort, Sébastien-Roch-Nicolas de (1741–94), 898, 914, *915-16*, 930-31, 939
Chamier, Anthony (1725–80), 827
Champagne, 928
Champ de Mars, 961
Chandernagore, 58
Chapel of the Malta Order, 468
Chapuis, M. (fl. 1755), 31
Chardin, Jean-Baptiste-Siméon (1699–1779), 23, 112-13, 117, 120, 466
charity, 905
Charles (Charles Augustus Christian), Duke of Zweibrücken, 354, 362
Charles I, King of England, Scotland, and Ireland (r. 1625–49), 90, 699, 705, 709, 711; Louis XVI on, 856
Charles II, King of England, Scotland, and Ireland (r. 1660–85), 462
Charles II, King of Spain (r. 1665–1700), 273
Charles III (Don Carlos of Bourbon), King of Spain (r. 1759–88), Duke of Parma and Piacenza (r. 1731–34), King of Naples and Sicily as Charles IV (r. 1731–34), 249-50, 281-90
  ACQUIRES PARMA, THEN NAPLES, 228, 278
  AS KING OF NAPLES, 249-50, 254, 258, 315
  AS KING OF SPAIN, 281-90, 291, 298, 377, 848; accession of, 258, 281, 315; appearance and character of, 281, 290, 301; death of, 290, 302; economic reforms of, 76, 286-89; foreign policy of, 89, 290; Goya and, 301, 306; Inquisition and, 285-86; Jesuits expelled by, 281, 283-85; Jews and, 285, 631; Madrid improved by, 282, 289-90; Naples and, 315; papacy and, 283, 318; po-

litical reforms of, 281-83; schools established by, 293; Tiepolo and, 239, 299

Charles IV, King of Naples and Sicily, *see* Charles III, King of Spain

Charles IV, King of Spain (r. 1788–1808), 292, 302, 304, 306

Charles V, Holy Roman Emperor (r. 1519–56), and King of Spain (as Charles I), 297

Charles VI, Holy Roman Emperor (r. 1711–40), 235, 278

Charles VIII, King of France (r. 1483–98), 21

Charles IX (Chénier), 920

Charles X (Charles-Philippe, Comte d'Artois), King of France (b. 1757, r. 1824–30), 111, 845; democratic attitudes of, 905; as emigré, 963

Charles XII, King of Sweden (r. 1697–1718), 433, 821; defeat at Poltawa (1709), 476; Poland and, 475

Charles XII (Voltaire), 137

Charles, Jacques-Alexandre (1746–1823), 932

Charles Alexander of Lorraine, *see* Charles of Lorraine

Charles Augustus, Duke of Saxe-Weimar, *see* Karl August

Charles Emmanuel I, King of Sardinia (r. 1730–1773), 226, 342, 530

Charles Martel (668?–741), Frankish ruler, 808

Charles of Lorraine, Prince (1712–80), 47, 51-52, 383-84

Charles Theodor, Elector, *see* Karl Theodor

Charlotte Sophia (1744–1818), Queen of George III of England, 384, 698, 795

Charrière, Isabella de ("Zélide"), nee Isabella van Tuyll (1740–1805), 647-48

Charrière, Saint-Hyacinthe de, 647

Chartres, Duc de (in 1752–85), *see* Orléans, Louis-Philippe-Joseph, Duc d'

Chastellux, Marquis François-Jean de (1734–88), 125-27, 878

Chastity Commissioners, Austrian, 344

Chateaubriand, François-René de (1768–1848), 889-90

Châteauroux, Marie-Anne de Nesle de La Tournelle, Duchesse de (1714–44), 102

Chatham, Lady, nee Grenville, 698

Chatham, Lord, *see* Pitt, William, the Elder

Châtillon, Duchesse de (fl. 1764), 125

Chatterton, Thomas (1752–70), 809-10

Chaulnes, Marie-Joseph d'Albert d'Ailly, Duc de (1741–93), 921

Chauvelin, Marquis Bernard-Louis de (1716–1773), 144

Chelsea, potteries at, 748

Chénier, Marie-Joseph (1764–1811), 244, 920

Chenonceaux, Madame de, nee Dupin (fl. 1762), 178

Cheremetyev, Count Boris Petrovich (1652–1719), 428

Cheremetyev, Count Peter, 422-23

Cherubini, Salvatore (1760–1842), 312, 380

Chesmé, battle of (1770), 458

Chesterfield, Philip Dormer Stanhope, 4th Earl of (1694–1773), 690, 786, 789; on Frederick II's court, 499; Johnson and, 821, 823

Chiari, Abate Pietro (1720–88), 243

Child, Sir Josiah (1630–99), 72

child labor, 671, 678, 682

child rearing: in Egypt, 416; Rousseau's theories on, 97, 888

China, Jesuits in, 225, 318

"Chinese Letters" (Goldsmith), 814

Chioggia, 229

Chios, battle of (1770), 458

Chippendale, Thomas (1718–79), 748

Chippendale furniture, 523

Chiswick, Rousseau's stay in, 210-11

Chiusano, Conte Caissotti di (fl. 1770), 316

chivalry in France, 98

Choderlos de Laclos, *see* Laclos

Chodowiecki, Daniel Nicholas (1726–1801), 523-24

Choglokov, Russian officer (1768), 443-44

Choglokova, Maria (fl. 1750), 436

Choiseul, César de, *see* Praslin, Duc de

Choiseul, Duc Étienne-François de (1719–85), 57, 67, 87, 92, 137, 447, 846, 882; achievements of, 88-89; art collection of, 466; dismissal of, 85, 94; Du Barry and, 88; early life of, 88; exile of, 89, failures of, 89; liberal tendencies of, 931; peace negotiations in Seven Years' War, 60, 62; Polish partition and, 482; reforms of, 142, 144; ultimatum to papacy, 318; Voltaire and, 132

Choiseul, Louise-Honorine Crozat, Duchesse de (1735–1801), 98, 118, 125, 447, 907

Cholmondeley, Lord, 726

Chotek, Johann Rudolf (1749–1824), 344-45

"Christ Is Being Born" (Karpiński), 486

Christian VI, King of Denmark (r. 1730–46), 652

Christian VII, King of Denmark (r. 1766–1808), 652-63; correspondence with Voltaire, 139

Christian August, Prince of Anhalt-Zerbst (d. 1746), 438

Christian Friedrich Karl Alexander, Margrave of Ansbach and Bayreuth (r. 1757–91), 103, 354

Christianity: Gibbon's critique of, 801-2; Goethe's views on, 619-20; Herder's views on, 579; Lessing's views on, 515-16; Reimarus's views on, 513-14; Schiller's views on, 596; Voltaire's views on, *see* Voltaire, RELIGION AND

Christina, Queen of Sweden (r. 1632–54), 256

Chubb, Thomas (1679–1747), 734

Chubin, Russian sculptor, 467

Church of the Virgin del Pilar, 297

church music: in Germany, 525; in Italy, 332

Church Synod, Russian, 440

Churchill, Charles (1731–64), 699, 702, 808-9

Cibber, Colley (1671–1757), 742

Cibber, Susannah Maria, nee Arne (1714–66), 740

Cicero, Marcus Tullius (106–43 B.C.), 294, 842

Cimarosa, Domenico (1749–1801), 312, 334-35, 466

Citizen of the World, The (Goldsmith), 814

Clairon, Mlle. (Claire-Josèphe Léris de La Tude; 1723–1803), 102-4, 136, 910, 964

Clarendon, Edward Hyde, 1st Earl of (1609–74), 794, 856

Clarendon Press, 786

Clarissa (Richardson), 167, 169–70, 509, 563

classicism, 315; in architecture, 110, 747; Italy and, 325-31; in literature, 588, 593, 627; in painting, 248-49, 329-30, 524, 910, 911-13; in sculpture, 329, 510, in social values, 118

Claudius, Matthias (1740–1815), 519

Clavigo y Fajardo, José (1726–1806), 921

Clement XI (Giovanni Francesco Albani), Pope (r. 1700–21), 245, 277, 320

Clement XII (Lorenzo Corsini), Pope (r. 1730–1740), 220, 246-47, 938

Clement XIII (Carlo della Torre Rezzonico), Pope (r. 1758–69), 330, 337; bull against Parma; death of, 317; Jesuits and, 264, 266, 284, 317

Clement XIV (Lorenzo Ganganelli), Pope (r. 1769–74), 911; abolishes Jesuit order (1773), 318, 351, 452; conflicts with Catholic monarchs, 318; election of, 317; Portugal and, 268

Clément, Abbé (fl. 1768), 280

Clementi, Muzio (1752–1832), 332-33

Clemenza di Tito, La (Mozart), 407

Cleopatra (Cimarosa), 334

Clerici, Felice (1719–74), 226

Clerici, Palazzo, 237

Clerici, Rho (fl. 1755), 226

Clerks of the Holy Cross and Passion of Our Lord, 226

Clermont, Abbé Comte de (d. 1771), 53

Cleves, 48

Clive, Kitty, nee Catherine Raftor (1711–85), 740

Clive, Robert (1725–74), 85, 715-16

clocks, French, 106

Clodion (Claude Michel; 1738–1814), 106, 911

clothing: changing styles in, 889; in France, 905; in Spain, 282

"Club, the," 817, 827, 840

Club Breton, 939

Clugny de Nuis (d. 1776), 865

Clyde River, 762

coal industry: in England, 671, 675; in France, 932

Cobenzl, Count Johann Ludwig Joseph von (1753–1809), 459

Cocceji, Baron Samuel von (1679–1755), 500

Cochin, Charles-Nicolas (1715–90), 116*, 120

Code de la Nature (Morelly), 80-82

Code Napoléon (1807), 147

coffeehouses, 729

Coimbra, bishop of (fl. 1768), 271

Colbert, Jean-Baptiste (1619–83), 72, 344, 934

Coleridge, Samuel Taylor (1772–1834), 551, 658

College of Pharmacy, Moscow, 453

Collegium Fredericianum, at Königsberg, 531

Collegium Nobilium, Polish, 475

Collier, Jeremy (1650–1726), 163

Collini, secretary to Voltaire, 150

Collins, Anthony (1676–1729), deist, 507, 734

Collins, William (1721–59), poet, 518, 887

Colloredo, Hieronymus von Paula, Count von (fl. 1782), Archbishop of Salzburg, 387-89, 393-95, 504-5

Collot, Marie-Anne (fl. 1768), 467

Colman, George (1732–94), 742, 815

Cologne, 341, 503-5

color, Goethe's work on, 615-16

Columbine (comic character), 232

Comedia nueva (Moratín), 296

Comédie-Française, 101-2, 922

commedia dell' arte, 240-41, 923

Commentaire sur le livre des delits et des peines (Voltaire), 145

Commentaries on Arabic Poetry (Jones), 412

Commentaries on the Laws of England (Blackstone), 736

Commons, House of, see House of Commons

Commune of Paris in French Revolution, 926

communist theories: in France, 80-84, 262, 937-38; of Paraguayan Jesuits, 80, 83, 262

Compagnie des Indes (French East India Company), 630

Comprehensive Study of Tactics (Guibert), 128

Compte rendu au Roi (Necker's financial account), 870

Comte, Auguste (1798–1857), 254

concerto grosso, 222, 528

Concerts Spirituels, 100

Condé, Louis-Joseph de Bourbon, Prince de (1736–1818), 385, 850

Condillac, Étienne Bonnot de (1715–80), 14, 126, 220, 294, 892, 901

Condorcet, Antoine-Nicolas Caritat, Marquis de (1743–94), 894-97, 939, 955; on d'Alembert, 892; in antislavery movement, 894, 935; and Julie de Lespinasse, 126, 131, 895; optimism of, 896-97, 917; in Revolution, 894-95, 897, 940; in States-General, 957; on Voltaire's death, 879; as Voltaire editor and biographer, 895, 925

Condorcet, Sophie de Grouchy, Marquise de (1764–1822), 907

Conegliano, Emmanuele, see Ponte, Lorenzo da

Confederation of Bar, 481-83

Confederation of Targowica, 488-90

Confessions (Rousseau), 18, 214, 336, 887; completion of, 882; debate over truthfulness of, 5*, on Diderot, 15; on Discours sur les arts et les sciences, 24; influence of, 888; on iniquity of powerful, 17; on love of nature, 11; on masochistic feelings, 6; publication of, 171; Rousseau's readings from, 883; Rousseau starts writing, 193; on theft of ribbons, 9; on Thérèse Levasseur, 17-18; uniqueness of, 4; on Voltaire's poetry, 154; on Mme. de Warens, 12-13;

on women, 8; on writing of *La Nouvelle Heloïse*, 155

Confucius (551–479 B.C.), 507

Congiura dei Pazzi, La (Alfieri), 338

Congregation of the Most Holy Redeemer, 225

Congress of Basel (1795), 547

Congress of Utrecht (1713), 547

conscription, military, 62

conseils supérieurs, 94

Consejo de Castilla, 277, 282, 286

Conservatorio di San Onofrio, 334

Conservatorio di Santa Maria di Loreto, 334

Considerations of a Good Citizen (Poniatowski), 480

Considérations sur le gouvernement de la Pologne (Rousseau), 884-85

Considérations sur les causes de la grandeur des Romains et de leur décadence (Montesquieu), see *Greatness and Decadence of the Romans*

Constable, John (1776–1837), 332

Constant, Benjamin (1767–1830), 648

Constantine I, Emperor of Rome (r. 306–337), 803

Constantine Pavlovich, Grand Duke (1779–1831), 458

Constantinople, 413-14

Constituent Assembly (France, 1789–91), see National Assembly

constitutions: American, see United States Constitution; Polish (1791), 487

Contades, Maréchal Duc Louis-Georges de (1704–95), 53, 55

Contemporaines, Les (Restif de La Bretonne), 919

Contes moraux (Marmontel), 102, 105

Conti, Louis-François de Bourbon, Prince de (1717–76), 161, 208, 850, 882, 923

Contrat social, see *Social Contract, The*

Convention, National (France), see National Convention

convents, see nunneries

Conversations with Goethe (Eckermann), 555-56, 559, 581, 600, 603, 607, 609, 612, 618, 620, 622, 625-26

Conway, Lord George, 209, 753

Conway, Henry Seymour (1721–95), 208, 793

Cook, Capt. James (1728–79), 669

Copenhagen, Bank of, 652

Corday, Charlotte (1768–93), 137

Corelli, Arcangelo (1653–1713), 254

Corfu, 229

Corneille, Marie (fl. 1770), 136-37, 150

Corneille, Pierre (1606–84), 104, 136-37, 511, 889

Cornwallis, Charles, 1st Marquis Cornwallis (1738–1805), 714, 729, 761, 871

Corrado, painter, 298

Correggio (Antonio Allegri; 1494–1534), 248

Correspondance littéraire, 34-35, 95, 201, 893

Corsica, 207, 284, 313, 885; early history of, 312; French occupation of (1739–48), 205, 312; French Revolution and, 313; under Paoli, 313;

782-83; re-occupation by French, (1769), 313; Rousseau's constitution for, 178, 202; sold to French by Genoa, 313

Cortona, Pietro da (1596–1669), 115

corvée, 80, 928, 936; Assembly of Notables and, 944; Turgot ends, 863

Cosimo II de' Medici, Grand Duke of Tuscany (r. 1609–20), 228

Cosimo III de' Medici, Grand Duke of Tuscany (r. 1670–1723), 227-28

cosmetics, 99

Cossacks, 451, 455, 633-34

Costa, Bartolomeu da (fl. 1775), 270

Costillares, bullfighter, 291

cotton industry, 672-73

Council of Castille, 277, 282, 286

Council of General Administration, Austrian Netherlands, 362

Council of State, French, 90-91, 94

Council of Ten, Venetian, 229, 255

Council of Trent, 361

Council of Twenty-five, Genevan, 190, 197-99

Cour Plénière, 947-48

Courier de Provence, 915

Cour des Aides, French, 92

Cours de philosophie positive (Comte), 254

Courtrai, 361

Coustou, Guillaume II (1716–77), 107

Covent Garden Theatre, 695, 740, 815

Cowper, Theodora (fl. 1748), 810

Cowper, William (1731–1800), 735, *810-13*; attempts suicide, 810, 812; attitude toward England, 812; death of, 813; early life of, 810; lives with Unwin family, 811-13; opposes slave trade, 730; religiosity of, 811, 813; retreats to Huntingdon, 810-11; writes *The Task*, 811-12

Coxe, William (1747–1828), 472

Cracow: Prussians capture, 491; University of, 485

crafts, 748-50

"Cranes of Ibycus" (Schiller), 599

Crawshay, Richard, ironmaster (fl. 1780), 672

Creation, The (Haydn), 376, 380

Crébillon *fils* (Claude Prosper Jolyot de Crébillon; 1707–77), 97

credit societies, 500

Creech, William (1745–1815), 763

Créqui, Renée-Caroline de Froullay, Marquise de (1714–1803), 189, 908

Crespi, Giuseppe Maria "Lo Spagnuolo" (1665–1747), 245

Crete, 411, 414

Creutz, Count Gustaf Philip (1731–85), 660

Crewe, Master, 753

Crewe, Frances, nee Greville (fl. 1776), 752

crime: in England, 733; in France, 903; in Italy, 319

Crimea, 459-60; Russian conquest of, 430, 459, 461; Turkish domination of, 411

Cristofori, Bartolommeo (1655–1731), 221

Critic, The (Sheridan), 696

Critical Review, The, 786
Critique of Judgment (Kant), 543-44
Critique of Practical Reason (Kant), 540-43
Critique of Pure Reason (Kant), 531, 535-40, 640, 808; influence of Rousseau on, 518
Croce, Benedetto (1866-1952), 254
Crochallan Fencibles, Scottish club, 776
Crompton, Samuel (1753-1827), 673
Crompton's mule, 673
Crosby, Brass, Lord Mayor of London (fl. 1771), 707
Crousaz, Madame de, 805
Crozat, Mlle., see Choiseul, Duchesse de
Crozat, Pierre (1661-1740), 235, 466
Crussol, Madame de, 118
Cruz, Ramón Francisco de la (1731-94), 296
Cugnot, Joseph (1725-1804), 70
cuisine, French, 99
Cumae, 327
Cumberland, William Augustus, Duke of (1721-1765), 48, 50
Cunha, João Anastasio da (1744-87), 269
Curchod, Suzanne, see Necker, Suzanne
Curzon, George Nathaniel, 1st Marquis Curzon of Kedleston (1859-1925), 420
Cüstrin, 53
Cuvillier, Charles-Étienne (fl. 1780), 53
Cuzzoni, Francesca (1700?-70), 223, 232
Cyrus the Great, King of Persia (r. 550-529 B.C.), 22
Czartoryski, Prince Adam Kazimierz (1734-1823), 479
Czartoryski, Prince Alexander Augustus (1696-1782), 473, 479
Czartoryski, Prince Fryderyk Michal (1695?-1775), 473, 479
Czartoryski, Prince Kazimierz (d. 1741), 473
Czartoryski, Isabella, nee Morstin, 473
Czartoryski, Konstantia, see Poniatowski, Konstantia
Czechs, see Bohemia
Czernichev, General (fl. 1762), 61
Czestochowa, oath at (1768), 481-82

Daily Universal Register, The, 786
Dalberg, Johann Friedrich Hugo von (1760-1812), 579-80
Dalberg, Wolfgang Heribert von (1750-1806), 571-72
Dalin, Olof von (1708-63), 659
Dalmatia, 411, 415
Damiens, Robert-François (1715-57), 67, 91
dancing: in Egypt, 416; in Spain, 291-92; in Vienna, 345
Dannecker, Johann Heinrich von (1758-1814), 523
Dante Alighieri (1265-1321), 242, 750, 793
Danton, Georges-Jacques (1759-94), 916, 939, 955
Danube River, 356

Danzig, 472, 483-84
Daquin, Pierre-Louis (d. 1797), 147
Daran, Dr. Jacques (1701-84), 152, 200
Darby, Abraham I (fl. 1754), 671
Darby, Abraham II (1750-91), 672
Darmstadt, 518
Darnley, Henry Stuart, Lord (1545-67), 779
Darwin, Charles (1809-92), 880, 889
Darwin, Erasmus (1731-1802), 617, 734
Dashkova, Princess Ekaterina Romanovna (1743-1810), 439
Dashwood, Sir Francis (1708-81), 702
Daun, Count Leopold von (1705-66), 40, 53, 59; in battle of Hochkirch (1758), 54; in battle of Kolin (1757), 47; captures Dresden (1758), 54-56, 60; occupation of Silesia by, 51
Dauphiné, Estates of, 948
Davenport, Richard (fl. 1766), 211-12, 214, 882
David, Jacques-Louis (1748-1825), 117, 331, 912-913
Davies, Henry E. (1757-84), 802
Davies, Thomas (1712?-85), 780, 786
Day of Tiles (1787), 947-48
Dayer, Edmund (1763-1804), 750
deaf and dumb: school for, 905; sign language for, 636
Deane, Silas (1737-89), 867-69, 922
Debussy, Claude (1862-1918), 381
Declaration of Independence (1776), 868; influence of, 899; Rousseau's influence on, 891
Declaration of Rights, Paris Parlement (1788), 947
Declaration of Rights, Virginia Assembly (1776), 872
Declaration of Rights of Man, French National Assembly, (1789), 642, 872
Decline and Fall of the Roman Empire, The (Gibbon), 746, 764, 786, 800-4, 806-8; criticism of Christianity, 801-2; evaluation of, 806-8; expanded to cover Byzantine Empire, 803-4; Gibbon replies to critics of, 802; importance of, 808; influences on, 801-2; scholarship in, 807; scope of, 807; success of, 800, 805
Deferrari, Palazzo, 227
Deffand, Marquise du, see Du Deffand
Defoe, Daniel (1659?-1731), 31, 182, 485, 730, 842
Dei Pugni, 320
deism: in England, 734; in Germany, 507, 528
De l'Allemagne (Staël), 604
De la Monarchie prussienne sous Frédéric le Grand (Mirabeau fils), 501
De l'Esprit (Helvétius), 162, 324
Delft, 646, 749
Delhi, 419
Delille, Abbé Jacques (1738-1813), 121, 878
Delinquente honrado (Jovellanos), 296
Della tirannide (Alfieri), 337-40
Demetrius (Schiller), 605
democracy: American Revolution and, 872; Burke's early views on, 690; in England, 681; Goethe's distrust of, 622-23; Johnson's opposi-

tion to, 833; oligarchy and, 142; Rousseau's views on, 28, 32, 173-74; Vico's theory of, 252; Voltaire's views on, 142-45

De Mundis sensibiles et intelligibiles Forma et principiis (Kant), 534

Denis, Marie-Louise, nee Mignot (1712–90), 98, 132-34, 148, 874, 876-79 *passim*, 907

Denmark, 438-39, *649-53;* clergy and religion in, 649, 653; drama in, 650-51; economy of, 652; education in, 652; feudalism in, 649, 653; French subsidies to, 89; Italian opera in, 224; Jews in, 635; in League of Armed Neutrality, 457, 713; literature in, 649-52; Poland and, 480; population of, 649; reaction led by Guldberg in, 653; reforms of Struensee, 652-53; reign of Christian VI, 652; reign of Christian VII, 652-53; reign of Frederick V, 652; slave trade abolished by, 649, 653; social classes in, 649, 653; Sweden and, 654, 663-64; trade treaties with Russia, 456

Den svenska Argus (periodical), 659

Denys le Tyran (Marmontel), 105

Deputy's Return, The (Niemcewicz), 486

Derbent, 419; Russian conquest of, 470

Derby, Edward Stanley, 12th Earl of (1752–1834), 726

Derby, potteries at, 748

De rerum natura (Lucretius), 691

Derwentwater, Sir James Radcliffe, 3d Earl of (1689–1716), 728

Derzhavin, Gavril Romanovich (1743–1816), 464

Descartes, René (1596–1650), 251, 294, 532

Description of Denmark and Norway, A (Holberg), 650

Description of the Torso in the Belvedere (Winckelmann), 328

Deserted Village, The (Goldsmith), 753, *813-15*

Desfontaines, Pierre-François Guyot (1685–1745), 149

Desmoulins, Camille (1760–94), 915, 919; calls Parisians to arms (1789), 961-62; Duc d'Orléans and, 955; as Freemason, 939

Desnoiresterres, Gustave (1817–92), 879

De Statu Ecclesiae et legitima Potestate romani Pontificus (Febronius), 504

Detroit, French forts, 57

Deux Amis, Les (Beaumarchais), 922

development and return, Machiavelli's law of, 253

Devin du village, Le (Rousseau), 24-25, 101, 164, 852, 883

Devonshire, Lady Georgiana Spencer, Duchess of (1757–1806), 753

Devonshire, William Cavendish, 4th Duke of (1640–1707), 235

Dewey, John (1859–1952), 888

De Witt brothers, 143

Deyverdun, Georges (d. 1789), 803, 805

Dialoghi sul commercio dei grani (Galiani), 75, 251

Dialogues: Rousseau juge de Jean-Jacques (Rousseau), 171, 885-86

Diamond Necklace Affair (1785), 941-43

Diario de los literatos de España (periodical), 280

Diario de Madrid, 302

Diary (Burney), 333

Dichtung und Wahrheit (Goethe), 503, 613

Dickens, Charles (1812–70), 738

Dictionary (Johnson), 786, 820, *823-25*

Dictionnaire (French Academy), 824, 878

Dictionnaire de la musique (Rousseau), 25, 154

Dictionnaire historique et critique (Bayle), 10, 13, 326, 557

Dictionnaire philosophique (Voltaire), 144, 267, 630

Diderot, Denis (1713–84), 18, 24-25, 73, 104, 108, 175, 182, 208, 250, 280, 370, 435, 464, 485, 559, 567, 636, 641, 824, 842, 882, 908, 910, 920; d'Alembert and, 892; American Revolution and, 867; on ancient art, 110; antimonarchical views of, 95, 897; atheism of, 183; biological speculations of, 147; bones stolen from Panthéon, 880, 893; Catherine II and, 446-50, 462-63, 466, 893; Chardin and, 112; on Choiseul, 88-89; death of, 893; defense of *parlements*, 93-94; deference to royalty, 176, 897; description of, 34; dramatic theories of, 104; eroticism of, 596; ethical views of, 903-4; on Fragonard, 116; French Revolution and, 940; at Mme. Geoffrin's salon, 120; Gibbon and, 798; Greuze and, 112-14; Grimm and, 34; on Index Expurgatorius, 316; influence of, 230; later years of, 892-93; Lessing's admiration for, 509; love for Babuti, 113; on marriage, 97; as most German of Frenchmen, 793; musical theories of, 100-01; nature and, 169; at Mme. Necker's salon, 908; in *Ossian* controversy, 768; Pigalle's statue of, 107; plan for university, 892; on Mme. de Pompadour, 69; on religious burials, 893; Richardson and, 136, 169; Rousseau and, *see* Rousseau, Jean-Jacques, DIDEROT AND; Sterne and, 789; trip to Russia, 892; on Vernet, 111; Voltaire and, 876, 892; writings of, 31, 101, 103-4

Didone abbandonata (Metastasio), 240, 254

Dieppe, 944

Diet, Polish, 472, 485; dissolves Permanent Council, 487; factional conflicts in, 479; first Polish partition and, 484; "Four Years'," 487; last (1793), 490-91; *liberum veto* of, 473, 476-77, 480-81, 484; structure of, 487; yields to Catherine (1768), 481

Diet, Swedish, 654

Diet of Augsburg, 176

Diniz da Cruz e Silva, Antônio (1731–99), 269

Disadvantages of the Feudal Rights, The (Boncerf), 929

Discalced Carmelites, 294

Discourses (Reynolds), 748

"Discours sur l'économie politique" (Rousseau), 32

Discours sur les arts et les sciences (Rousseau), *20-24*, 32, 94, 168, 171, 177, 179, 887, 891

Discours sur l'origine . . . de l'inégalité (Rousseau), *28-32*, 80, 94, 171, 174, 177, 887, 891

Discurso sobre el fomento de la industria popular (Campomanes), 287

Discurso sobre la educación popular de los artesanos y su fomento (Campomanes), 293

Disraeli, Benjamin (1804–81), 725

Dittersdorf, Karl Ditters von (1739–99), 374

"Diverting History of John Gilpin, The" (Cowper), 811

divorce in England, 732

Dmitri I (the "false Dmitri"), Czar of Russia (r. 1605–06), 605

Dnieper River, 430

Dniester River, 430

Dodd, Dr. William (1729–77), 830

Dodington, George Bubb (1691–1762), 702

Dodsley, Robert (1703–64), 786, 794, 814, 819, 821-22

Doge of Venice, 229, 231, 331

Dohm, Christian Wilhelm (1751–1820), 642

Dohna, Count zu (fl. 1758), 53

Doig, Peggy (fl. 1761), 779

Dolgorukaya, Natalia Borisovna (1714–71), 428

Dolgoruki, Ivan Mikhailovich (1764–1823), 428-29

Dolgoruki, Vasili Lukich (1670–1739), 428-29, 458

Dominicans, 275

Dominus ac Redemptor Noster (Clement XIV), 318

Don Carlos (Schiller), 572-73, 592

Don Giovanni (Mozart), 342, 376, 388, 396-97, 402

Don Giovanni Tenorio (Goldoni), 404

Don River, 430

Don Sylvio von Rosalva (Wieland), 553

Donizetti, Gaetano (1797–1848), 245

Donna di garbo, La (Goldoni), 242

Donne, John (1573–1631), 810, 842

Donner, Georg Raphael (1693–1741), 345

Dorat, Claude-Joseph (1734–80), 884

Dos de Mayo (1808), 307

Doughty, Charles Montagu (1843–1926), 412

drama, *see* theatre

Draper, Elizabeth (fl. 1767), 790

Draper, Sir William (fl. 1769), 706

Dresden: beautification of, 476; Jews in, 639; in Seven Years' War, 45, 54-56, 60, 502, 552; Treaty of (1745), 44

Dreux-Brézé, Marquis de, *see* Brézé

Drone, The (Novikov), 464

Drouais, François-Hubert (1727–75), *111*, 120

Drury Lane Theatre, 695, 696, 740, 741, 742-43

Dryden, John (1631–1700), 842

Du Barry, Comte Guillaume (fl. 1768), 86-7

Du Barry, Chevalier Jean (1723–94), 86

Du Barry, Marie-Jeanne Bécu, Comtesse (1743?–1793), *86-88*, 90, 656, 910, 921, 942; d'Aiguillon and, 93, 853; Choiseul and, 88, 89; Marie Antoinette and, 88, 848; Pajou and, 109; relations with Louis XV, 85, 86-88, 95, 845; Voltaire and, 87-88, 875

Dubienka, battle of (1792), 489

Dublin: education in, 759; theater in, 740

du Bocage, du Boccage, *see* Bocage *and* Boccage

Dubois, Guillaume, Cardinal (1656–1723), 148

Du Châtelet-Lomont, Gabrielle-Émilie Le Tonnelier de Breteuil, Marquise (1706–49), 26

Duclos, Charles Pinot (1705–72), 18, 31, 35, 73

Du Deffand, Marquis, 122

Du Deffand, Marie de Vichy-Chamrond, Marquise (1697–1780), 31, 118, *122-25*, 353, 447, 656, 875, *906-7*, 923; d'Alembert and, 123-25; death of, 907; description of, 878; Franklin and, 869; on individuality of English, 733; late years of, 906-7; Julie de Lespinasse and, 122-23; Voltaire and, 135, 138; Walpole and, 125, 794-95, *906-7*

dueling, 732

Duenna, The (Sheridan), 696

Du Hausset, Mme. (b.c. 1720), 95

Dumesnil (Marie-François Marchand; 1711–1803), 102

Dumonceux, Monsieur (fl. 1748), 86

Dumouriez, Charles-François (1739–1823), 481

Dunkirk, 361, 944

Dunlop, Frances (1730–1815), 777

Dunning, John, Baron Ashburton (1731–83), 714

Du Peyrou, printer, 206

Dupin, Mme. (1706–95), 16, 18, 118

Dupin de Francueil, Claude (1715–87), 16, 18, 24, 35

Dupoirier, Citizen (fl. 1801), 103

Du Pont de Nemours, Pierre-Samuel (1739–1817), 72, 75, 78, 863; on free trade in grain, 859

Dupré, P. (fl. 1759), 97*

Duquesne, Fort, 57

Durante, Francesco (1684–1755), 254, 334

Durão, Salvador (fl. 1758), 264

Durazzo, Count Marcello (fl. 1754), 368

Du Rollet, Marie-François Gand-Leblanc, Marquis (1716–86), 370, 371

Duru, porcelain sculptor, 108

Du Ry, Simon-Louis (1726–99), 525

Dusaulx, Jean-Joseph (1728–99), 883-84

Dutch East India Company, 646

Dutch republic, *see* Holland

Du Tillot, Guillaume-Léon (1711–74), 312

East Prussia, Seven Years' War in, 48, 49, 53

Eberhard, Johann (1739–1809), 507

Écho et Narcisse (Gluck), 373

Eckermann, Johann Peter (1792–1854), 505; Goethe's conversations with, 555-56, 559, 581, 600, 603, 607, 609, 612, 618, 620, 622, *625-26*; on Goethe's corpse, 627-28; as Goethe's secretary, 625-26; women authors, 504

École Royale du Chant, 909

Écossaise, L' (Voltaire), 136

Edict of Toleration, Austrian (1781), 357, 361-62

education: in Austria, 343, 352, 358, 360; in Denmark, 652; in England, 681; in France, 3, 863, 895, 900, 914; in Germany, 505-6; in Holland, 647; in Ireland, 759; Islamic, 412; in Italy, 219; Jesuits and, 219; Kant's theories of, 548-49; in Prussia, 500; Rousseau's theories on, see Rousseau, Jean-Jacques, EDUCATIONAL THEORIES OF; in Russia, 432, 453; in Scotland, 763; in Spain, 275-76; in Sweden, 657, 659; in Switzerland, 644, 888; see also schools; universities

Edinburgh: anti-Catholic riots in (1779), 735; Royal Society of, 763; theater in, 740; University of, 763

"Editto sopra gli Ebrei" (Pius VI), 631

Eglinton, Alexander Montgomerie, 10th Earl of (fl. 1760), 779

Egmont, Comte Casimir d', 883

Egmont, Prince Pignatelli d', 883

Egmont, Septimanie de Richelieu, Comtesse d' (1740–73), 883

Egmont (Goethe), 584, 589, 593

Egremont, Sir Charles Wyndham, 2d Earl of (1710–63), 685, 702

Egypt, 21, 411, *415-17*

Einstein, Alfred (1880–1952), 385*

Eisen, Charles (1720–78), 116*

Ekaterinoslav, 633

El Azhar, mosque of, 416

Elbe River, 356

Electa, Padre Joaquín de, 299

Elective Affinities (Goethe), 612

"Elegy" (Gray), 837

Elementa metaphysicae (Giannone), 250

Elijah ben Solomon of Wilna (1720–97), 636

Eliot, Edward, later Lord Eliot (1727–1804), 796

Elisabeth Christine of Brunswick-Bevern (1715–97), Queen of Frederick II of Prussia, 495

Elisabeth Christine of Brunswick-Wolfenbüttel (1691–1750), Empress, wife of Emperor Charles VI, 235

Elizabeth I, Queen of England, 342

Elizabeth Farnese, see Farnese, Elizabeth

Elizaveta (Elizabeth) Petrovna, Empress of Russia (r. 1741–62), 42, 43, 67, 428, 430, *431-32*, 466, 530, 654; appearance and habits, 431; death of, 61, 437; Jews expelled by, 632; reign of, 431-37; selects Peter III for heir, 433; Seven Years' War and, 39; Sweden and, 654-55; Voltaire and, 137

Elizabeth of Valois (1545–68), Queen of Philip II of Spain, 592

Éloge de Colbert (Necker), 865-66

Éloge de Crébillon (Voltaire), 149

Éloge de Richardson (Diderot), 169

Elysée Palace, 68

Emerson, Ralph Waldo (1803–82), 551, 658

Émile (Rousseau), 9, 14, 18, 98, 149, 152, 168, *178-99*, 531, 644, 881, 887; Archbishop of Paris and, 194-97; atheism denounced in, 183; attitude toward Bible, 185; banning of, 190; breast-feeding stressed in, 180; burnings of,

280, 643; clerical attacks on, 185, 189, 192-99, 205; education of girls, 186; emphasis on freedom, 179-180; influence of, 179, 181, 881; instincts and, 181; marriage in, 186–87; models for characters in, 183; moral instruction in, 180; *philosophes* and, 182-83, 189; physical training in, 180-81; publication of, 171, 178; religious instruction in, 182-85; role of nature in, 180-81; Rousseau's earnings from, 178; unitarian beliefs in, 163

Ems, Punctation of (1786), 505

Emilia Galotti (Lessing), 513

Empfindsamkeit cult, 518

Encyclopédie, ou Dictionnaire raisonné des sciences, des arts, et des métiers (1751 f.), 20, 67, 102, 104, 155, 250, 453, 464, 655, 824, 858, 903, 925; d'Alembert's contribution to, 123, 132; attempts to suppress 162-63, 193; Catherine II's offer to print, 447; Choiseul and, 88; Condorcet's contribution to, 894; Mme. Geoffrin's aid to, 120; influence of, 94, 220, 280-81, 888; Malsherbes' aid to, 861; on marriage, 97; publication in Turin, 310; Quesnay's contribution to, 73; Rousseau and, 3, 25, 33; suppression of, 94, 164; Turgot's contribution to, 78

Encyclopédie des citations (Dupré), 97*

Endymion (Keats), 810

Engels, Friedrich (1820–95), 880

England (Great Britain), 364, *669-842;* agriculture in, 670-71, 680, 682, *816;* alliance of European powers against (1779–80), 713-14; American Revolution and, see American Revolution; amusements and sports in, 729-30; architecture in, 747-48; army in, 686; art in, 750-58, 888; Austria and, 277-278; banking in, 670; books and bookshops in, 786-87; Catholics in, 684, *735-36;* clergy and religion in, 64, 142, 684, *735-36;* crafts and furniture in, 744, 748-50; Denmark and, 713; economy of, 72, 456, 668-71, 709, 719; education in, 681; France and, 39, 89, 669, 713, 761; Freemasons in, 938; free trade in, 670-71; French Revolution and, 683, *721-26;* gardens and parks in, 748; guilds in, 670; health and public sanitation in, 728; historical writing in, 795-808, 815; Holland and, 277, 648, 669, 714; Industrial Revolution in, see Industrial Revolution; influences on German culture, 507; Ireland and, 671, *759-62;* Jews in, 635, 684; labor unions in, 679-80; land enclosures in, 670-71; literature in, 518, *786-95, 808-42,* 889; lusty vigor of, 733; manners and morals in, 682, 707, *728-34,* 786; music in, 223-24, 368, 746-47; natural resources of, 671; navy of, 40, 57, 669; opera in, 223-24; pauperism in, 684; periodicals in, 786; population of, 43, 684; Portugal and, 259; prisons in, 737-38; prostitution in, 731-32; radicals in, 704; riots in, 700, 735-36; Romantic movement in, 170; Rousseau in, 209-14; Russia and, 432, 456, 458, 460-61, 700, 713; salons in, 729; Scotland and, 699, *762;* skepticism in, 734; slave trade and, 693,

732-33; social classes in, 669-71, 676-82, *684-85*, 706, 728, 732, 734, 814-16; Spain and, 273, 277-78, 390, 669, 713, 761; Sweden and, 713; taxation in, 686; theater in, 695-96, 739-43; Turkey and, 363; urbanization of, 670-71, 681; Voltaire and, 144, 881; War of the Spanish Succession and, 669; women in, 728, 730-31, 787

EMPIRE OF: command of the seas and, 669; expansion of, 57-59, 63, 669; French rivalry, 39, 57-59; *see also* American colonies; Canada; India

FOREIGN ALLIANCES AND AGREEMENTS: with Prussia (1756 f.), 39-40, 46, 53, 60-61, 432; in Quadruple Alliance (1718), 278; with Russia (1755), 39

GOVERNMENT AND POLITICS IN: Bute ministry, 698-700, 702-3; conflict of George III with Parliament, 687-88, 697-701; corruption in, 707, 733, 848; democracy in, 681, 706-7; development of parliamentary government in, 683-84, 709, 718; Fox-North coalition ministry, 715, 718; Grafton ministry (1768-70), 700, 703, 705-6, 710; Grenville ministry, 700, 709-10; legal reform in, 736-38; Newcastle ministry, 698; North ministry, 700-1, 706, 710-14, 761; Pitt the Elder, de facto ministry of, 700; Pitt the Younger, ministry of, 718-19; political structure in England, 683-87; Rockingham ministries, 700, 703, 710, 714, 761; Shelburne ministry, 714-15; *see also names of British monarchs*

SEVEN YEARS' WAR (1756-63), 798; aid to Frederick II, 50, 53; declares war on France (1756), 43; diplomacy leading to, 38-44; dismissal of Pitt the Younger, 46; England's naval growth and, 669; expansion of Empire and, 57-59, 63; naval operations against France, 42-43; peace negotiations, 62; regiments in Hanover, 47-48, 50; results of conflict, 63-64

English America, *see* American colonies

English East India Company, *see* British East India Company

English Palace at Peterhof, 468

engraving, 750

Enlightenment: American Revolution and, 867; in Austria, 343-46; in France, *see* Encyclopédie; philosophes; French Revolution and, 898-99; in Germany, 507-8; Herder's critique of, 569; in Italy, 220, 230, 250-51; Jews and, 637-42; Kant and, 531; Pope Benedict XIV and, 246-47; in Portugal, 269-70; response of papacy to, 246-47, 316; in Scotland, 764-78; in Sweden, 658-62; in Switzerland, 645

Enquiry concerning the Human Understanding (Hume), 536

Enquiry into the State of Polite Learning in Europe (Goldsmith), 814

Ensenada, Zenón de Somodevilla, Marqués de la (1702-81), 279

Entführung aus dem Serail, Die (Mozart), 395

Entretiens sur la pluralité des mondes (Fontenelle), 427

Epaminondas of Thebes (418?-362 B.C.), 52

Epée, Abbé Charles-Michel de L' (1712-89), 905

Éphémérides, 78

Epictetus (50?-120?), 730

Epicurus (342?-270 B.C.), 251

Épinay, Denis-Joseph Lalive d', 35

Épinay, Louise-Florence Lalive d', nee Tardieu d'Esclavelles (1726-83), 35-37, 118, 390, 656, 892; aids Mozart, 392; death of, 893; early life of, 35; Grimm and, 35-37, 156-57, 159-61, 449; Rousseau and, 4, 5*, 18, 26, 36-37, 153, *156-61*, 884; salon of, 907; visit to Geneva, 159-61

Epistle to Dr. Arbuthnot (Pope), 878

Épître à Boileau (Voltaire), 136

Épître au Cardinal Dubois (Voltaire), 148

Éprémesnil, Jean-Jacques Duval d' (1746-94), 947

equalitarianism: Helvétius' belief in, 141; Rousseau's support for, 141; Voltaire's opposition to, 141-42; *see also* communist theories

Erasmus, Desiderius (1466?-1536), 806

Erfurt, 606

Erivan, 419

Erlach, Fischer von, *see* Fischer von Erlach, Johann Bernhard

Ermita de Jesús in Murcia, 298

Ermolov, Alexis (fl. 1785), 446

Ernesti, Johann August (1707-81), 33

Erreurs sur la musique dans l'Encyclopédie (Rameau), 25

Erskine, John (1695-1768), 763

Erskine, Thomas (1750-1823), 763

Erziehung der Menschengeschlechts, Die (Lessing), 515

Escorial, 250, 261

espionage, Prussian, 43

Esprit des lois, L', *see* Spirit of Laws

Essai sur l'application de l'analyse aux probabilités (Condorcet), 894

Essai sur les moeurs (Voltaire), 137, 528, 630, 781, 797

Essai sur les règnes de Claude et de Néron (Diderot), 892

Essai sur l'étude de la littérature (Gibbon), 798

Essay on the History of Civil Society (Ferguson), 766

Essay on Man (Pope), 703

Essay on the Nature of Commerce (Cantillon), 72

Essay on the Principle of Population, An (Malthus), 896

Essay on the Whole Art . . . of Painting (Richardson), 751

Essay on Women (Potter and Wilkes), 703

Essays (Montaigne), 179

Estates of Brabant, 362, 364

Esterházy, Count (fl. 1788), 363

Esterházy, Countess, 344

Esterházy, Prince Anton (d. 1795), 377-78

Esterházy, Prince Miklós Jozsef (1714-90), 341, 375-76

Esterházy, Prince Miklós II, 379
Esterházy, Prince Pál (1635–1713), 341
Esterházy, Prince Pál Anton (d. 1762), 375
Esthonia, 422, 653
Esthonia, 422, 653
Estrées, Louis-Charles-César Le Tellier, Maréchal Duc d', 37, 48
États Généraux, *see* States-General, French
Ethics (Spinoza), 565
ethics, theories of: Bentham's, 738-39; Diderot's, 903-4; Hume's, 739; Kant's, 540-43; Adam Smith's, 769
Etruscans, 312
Études de la nature (Bernardin de Saint-Pierre), 916
Eugene of Savoy (1663–1736), 414-15
Eugénie (Beaumarchais), 922
Euler, Leonhard (1707–83), 532
Euripides (480–406 B.C.), 136, 372, 588
Evelina, or A Young Lady's Entrance into the World (Burney), 791
"Evening Song" (Karpiński), 486
Evidences of Christianity (Paley), 735
Ewald, Johannes (1743–81), 651-62
Ewige Jude, Der (Goethe), 562
Exposé succinct de la contestation qui s'est élevée entre M. Hume et M. Rousseau (Hume), 214
Exposition of the Catholic Doctrine (Bossuet), 796-97
Exposure of the Jewish Ceremonies (Serafimovich), 633
Ex quo singulari (Benedict XIV), 225
Eybenberg, Marianne von (fl. 1810), 612-13

Fable of the Bees (Mandeville), 770
Fables (Iriarte y Oropesa), 295
Fables and Parables (Krasicki), 485
Fabricius, Johann Albert (1668–1736), 326
factory system: in England, 676-80, 682, 732; in France, 932-33; in Spain, 288
Faguet, Émile (1847–1916), 5*
Falconet, Étienne-Maurice (1716–91), 106-7, 108-9, 467, 911
family life: Industrial Revolution and, 682; in Italy, 218-19; Rousseau's influence on, 888
Farinelli (Carlo Broschi; 1705–82), 240, 257; early life and fame of, 222-23; in Spain, 278-79, 292, 296
farmers general in France, 935-36
Farnese, Elizabeth (Isabella), Queen of Philip V of Spain (b. 1692–d. 1766), 276-77, 279, 296-97
Fasch, Karl Friedrich Christian (1736–1800), 527
Faubourg St.-Antoine, 962
Faust (Goethe), 557, 585, 608-11, 620, 622, 626: Sturm und Drang movement and, 522
Faust, ein Fragment (Goethe), 608
Fausts Leben (Muller), 522
Feast of Reason (1793), 899
Febronius, Justinus, *see* Hontheim, Johann Nikolaus von

Feijóo y Montenegro, Benito Jerónimo (1676–1764), 294
Fel, Mlle. Marie (1713–94), 33, 100
Felipe (Philip), Duke of Parma (r. 1748–65), 311, 348
Felipe, son of Charles III of Spain, 302
Felipe Quinto, *see* Philip V, King of Spain
fellaheen, Egyptian, 415
Feltre, 229
Fénelon, François de Salignac de la Mothe- (1651–1715), 179, 450, 845
Ferdinand, Archduke (b. 1754–d. 1806), Duke of Modena, 346, 350, 387, 847
Ferdinand III, Duke of Parma (r. 1765–1801), 317, 846
Ferdinand IV, King of Naples (r. 1759–1806, 1815–25), King of Sicily as Ferdinand III (r. 1806–15), 315, 334-35, 377
Ferdinand VI, King of Spain (r. 1746–59), 263, 279-81; accession of, 279; becomes insane, 279-80; death of, 258; mild policies toward Jews, 276
Ferdinand VII, King of Spain (r. 1808, 1814–1833), 306-7
Ferdinand of Brunswick, Duke (b. 1721–d. 1792), 50, 53, 54, 60, 507
Ferguson, Adam (1723–1816), 764, 765-66, 767, 775
Fermor, Count William of (1704–71), 53, 60, 435
Ferney, Voltaire, *see* Voltaire AT FERNEY
Ferrara, 641; Goethe in, 587
Ferrara, Duke of (Tasso's patron), Alfonso II (r. 1559–97), 244-45
Ferreira, Antônio (d. 1759), 265
Fersen, Count Frederik Axel von (1719–94), 664
Fersen, Count Hans Axel von (1755–1810), 664, 941
Fersen, Sophie von, 941
Festes de Ramire, Les (Rameau, Voltaire and Rousseau), 18
Festin de Pierre, Le (Molière), 404
Festival of the Supreme Being (1794), 890
feudalism: in Austria, 345; in Denmark, 649, 653; in France, 849, 861-63, 872, 927-29, 931, 937, 954; in Prussia, 43, 500-1; in Russia, 424, 451, 454-55; Adam Smith's critique of, 770
Fiabe (Gozzi), 243, 244
Fichte, Johann Gottlieb (1762–1814), 550-51, 618, 620
Fielding, Henry (1707–54), 723, 835, 842
Fielding, Sarah (1710–68), 787
Filangieri, Gaetano (1752–88), 336
Filippo (Alfieri), 338, 340
Filmer, Sir Robert (d. 1653), 177
Fils naturel, Le (Diderot), 153
Fingal, an Ancient Epic Poem in Six Books, . . . Composed by Ossian, the Son of Fingal (Macpherson), 767-68
Finland, 422, 460; Gustavus III's policy toward, 663; Russian acquisition of, 654
Finta Fracastana, La (Leo), 255

Finta giardiniera, La (Mozart), 388

Firdausi, Persian poet (940?–1020?), 613

Firmian, Count Karl Joseph von (1716–82), 312; aids Mozart, 386-87; Parini aided by, 335-36

First Estate: role in States–General, 956-61; structure of, 949-50

Fischer von Erlach, Johann Bernhard (1656–1723), 345, 426

Fischerström, Johan (1735–96), 660

Fisher, William, 773

Fishers, The (Ewald), 652

Fitzherbert, Alleyn, Baron St. Helens (1758–1839), 459

Fitzherbert, Maria Ann, nee Smythe (1756–1871), 721

Flachsland, Caroline, *see* Herder, Caroline

Flanders, 342

Flaubert, Gustave (1821–80), 104

Flaxman, John (1755–1826), 750

Fleury, André Hercule de, Cardinal (1653–1743), 40

Fleury, Maître Omer Joly de, *see* Joly de Fleury, Omer

Flood, Henry (1732–91), 761

Florence: Accademia della Crusca of, 824; Freemasons in, 220; French Revolutionary Army in (1799), 340; Goethe in, 587, 589; under Grand Duke Leopold, 310; history and achievements, 227-28; library in, 219; theaters in, 220; university in, 219

Florida, 62, 709, 714

Floridablanca, José Moñina, Conde de (1728–1808), 286, *287*, 302

flying shuttle, 673

Fontaine, Priory of, 928

Fontainebleau, Peace of (1762), 62

Fontenailles, Marquise de, 68

Fontenelle, Bernard Le Bovier de (1657–1757), 15, 105, 119-20, 139, 427, 894, 903

Fonthill Abbey, 809

Foote, Samuel (1720–77), 740

Forcalquier, Mme. de, 118

Force, La, prison of, 962

Fordyce, Lord, 525

Formey, Jean-Louis-Samuel (1711–97), 23

Formont, Jean-Baptiste-Nicolas de (d. 1758?), 122

Forth River, 762

Four Ages of Man (González), 295

"Four Seasons" (Naruszewicz), 485

Fourier, François-Marie-Charles (1772–1837), 81, 891

Fourmantelle, Catherine (fl. 1759), 787

Fox, Charles James (1749–1806), 133, 683, *693-694*, 701, 724, 750, 777, 833; and American colonies, 711, 713-14; appearance and habits of, 694; on Burke, 692; in coalition ministry, 715, 718; death of, 726; duels with Adams, 694, 732; early life of, 693; and French Revolution, 722, 724, 726; in Hastings trial, 696, 719-20; and India bills, 718-19; liberal views of, 694; marries

Mrs. Armstead, 726; in Ministry of All the Talents, 726; opposes slave trade, 726, 732-33; in Rockingham ministry, 761

Fox, George (1624–91), 732

Fox, Henry, 1st Baron Holland (1705–74), 364, 693

Frage, ob die Welt veralte, Die (Kant), 532-33

Fragment on Government (Bentham), 738

Fragonard, Jean-Honoré (1732–1806), 97, 112, *115-18*, 911

France, *67-408*, *845-963*; agriculture in, 859, 861, *927-31*; aid to American Revolution, 354, 711, 842, *867-72*; American empire of, *see* French America; anti-religious feeling in, 64, 183; architecture in, 109-11; army in, 686; art in, *106-18*, *910-14*; Austria and, 488, 846; Austrian Netherlands and, 45; ballet in, 100; banking in, 861; book publishing in, 71; Breteuil's ministry (1789), 961-63; cafés in, 99; capital punishment in, 146; clergy and religion in, 67, 92, 142, 857, *900-2*, 931, 949-50, 956-61; clothing and grooming in, 99, 889, *905*; commerce and trade in, 70-77, 80, 709, 859-60, 872, 931-35; communist theories in, 80-84; Corsica and, 205, *312-13*; crime in, 903; cuisine in, 99; drought of 1788 in, 949; economic inequality in, 936-37; education in, 3, 863, 895, 900, 914; England and, 39, 89, 669, 713, 761; on eve of Revolution, 954-56; famine in, 954-55; feudalism in, 849, 861-63, *927-29*, 931, 937, 954; financial problems of, 90, 859-61; First Coalition against, 591; Freemasons in, 94, *938-39*; free trade and, 935; guilds in, 72, 862, 932; Holland and, 648-49; in Holy Roman Empire, 341; home furnishings in, 106-7; India and 58-59, 715; Industrial Revolution in, 931-34; internal tolls in, 935; Italy and, 217; Jansenists in, 85, 91, 193, 246; Jews in, 91, 630, 642; law in, 849, 947-48; libraries in, 914; literature in, 889, *914-19*; marriage in, 97; morality and grace in, 97-100, 902-5; music in, *100-1*, 368, 370-73, *909-10*, 915; Napoleonic, *see* Napoleon I; Napoleonic Wars, 627, 726, 872; navy of, 40, 57; opera in, 26; oratory in, 99; palaces in, 850; papacy and, 317-18; *parlements* in, *see parlements* and Paris, Parlement of; pauperism in, 930-31; periodicals and pamphlets in, 94, *915*; Poland and, 476, 482; political clubs in, 939; population of, 927; prostitution in, 98, 903; Protestants in, 91, *857*, *901-2*, 950; Prussia and, 488; ratio of priests to lay population, 224; recognizes United States, 713; religious toleration in, 144; riots in, 98, 934, 954-55, 956, 961; Romantic movement in, 170; Russia and, 430, 432, 457-58; salons in, 118-31, 906-8; Senegal given to, 714; slave trade and, 58, 935; social classes in, *67-82*, *84-96*, 848-50, 858-59, 861, 863-64, 872, 898-99, 901-4, 914, *927-31*, *934-37*, 944-48, 954-61; Spain and, 277-78, 280, 293, 296, *306-7*; tariff policy of, 935; taxation in, 69, 92, *931*, *935-36*, 944, 946, 959; theater in, *101-6*, 920-26; transportation in, 70; women in, 906-8

FOREIGN ALLIANCES AND AGREEMENTS: alliances against England, 870-71; alliance with the United States (1778), 870; First Treaty of Versailles (1756), 42; Mme. de Pompadour and, 67; in Quadruple Alliance (1718), 278; Second Treaty of Versailles (1757), 45; subsidies to foreign countries, 61, 89

GOVERNMENT AND POLITICS IN: administrative jurisdictions, 849; Assembly of Notables (1787), 75, *944-45;* authority of royal power, 849-50 (*see also* Louis XV; Louis XVI; Marie-Antoinette); Bourbon restoration, 890; Breteuil ministry, 961-63; Brienne ministry, 945-48; Calonne ministry, 943-45; chaos in governmental operations, 848-50; expenses of court, 84, 850; Maurepas ministry, 85, 97, 104; Necker ministries, see Necker, Jacques; Nuis ministry (1776), 865; *parlements* and, *see parlements* and Paris, Parlement of; States-General and, *see* States-General, French; Turgot ministry, 858-65

IN SEVEN YEARS' WAR, 45-46, 48-64 *passim;* diplomacy leading to war, 38-44; European land operations, 48, 49-50, 51, 53-55 *passim,* 60; losses in America and India, 45, *57-59*, 62-63, 68, 709; naval war with England, 42-43, 56, *57-59;* peace negotiations, 60-62

France, Anatole (1844-1924), 880

France libre, La (Desmoulins), 915

Francueil, Dupin de, see Dupin de Francueil, Claude

Franche-Comté, 928

franchise: in England, 685; in Switzerland, 643-644

Francis I (Francis of Lorraine), Holy Roman Emperor (r. 1745-65), 46, 313, 346, 383

Francis II, Holy Roman Emperor (r. 1792-1806), Emperor of Austria as Francis I (r. 1804-35), 378, 379

Francis, Sir Philip (1740-1818), 705-6, 717-19, 723

Franciscans, 224, 902

Franck, Johann Matthais (fl. 1738), 373-74

Frank, Jacob (Jankiew Leibowicz; 1726-91), 636

Frankfurt: fairs in, 556; Jews in, 634, 642; population of, 556; social classes in, 556

Frankfurter gelehrte Anzeigen, 506, 521

Frankl, August (1810-94), 613

Franklin, Benjamin (1706-90), 120, 201, 802, 856; on corruption in English Parliament, 733; death of, 872; in England, 868; in France, 868-72; as Freemason, 939; French America and, 57; French Enlightenment and, 867; French Revolution and, 84; influence of *philosophes* on, 899; Turgot and, 865; Voltaire and, 875

Franks, 312

Franquet, M. (d. 1756), 920

Franyó, Remigius, 363

Frederick I, King of Sweden (r. 1720–51), 654

Frederick I, Barbarossa, Holy Roman Emperor (r. 1152–90), 239

Frederick II the Great, King of Prussia (r. (1740-86), *42-57, 59-64,* 107, 136, 142-43, 249, 337, 433, *495-502, 528-30,* 657, 782, 880, 885, 897; abilities of 43, 46, 529-30, 849; achievements of, 502; d'Alembert and, 124, 892; appearance and habits of, 495, 499-500; attitude toward religion, 498-99; attitude toward royalty, 342, 502, 530; bribes Bestuzhev, 432; Catherine II and, 434, 442, 457-58, 462, 484, condemns Goethe's *Götz von Berlichingen,* 561; curbs freedom of press, 530; death of, 461, 530; death of sister, 47, 54; deism of, 498-99, *528;* economic policies of, 500-1; in first partition of Poland, 350; Freemasons and, 507, 938; George III and, 60; Grimm's *Correspondance littéraire* and, 34-35; Jesuits and, 319; Jewish bankers aid, 53; on John V of Portugal, 260; Joseph II and, 349, 353-54, 361-62; on Kaunitz, 40; legal reforms of, 500; literary works of, 44, 49, 54, *528-29;* Louis XV and, 40; on Louis XVI, 857; love for music, 496, 526; on Maria Theresa, 38-39, 342, 344, 350, 352, 529-30; militarism of, 500, 529; moral probity of, 355; Napoleon on, 530; national pride in, 506; parsimony of, 499-500; personality of, 495-96, 530; Peter III of Russia and, 438, 440; *philosophes* and, 496-98; Pitt the Elder's support for, 698; Poland and, 350, 479-84; prophecies of, 530; reforms of, 142, 321, 500; returns from Seven Years' War, 495; Rousseau and, 173, 497; social and philosophical views of, 496-97, *528-30;* Voltaire and, 108, 139, *496-99,* 528, 873, 876, 879

IN SEVEN YEARS' WAR, *44-64;* appeal to troops, 51-52; army of, 43; in battle of Leuthen (1757), 51-52; in battle of Rossbach (1757), 50, in battle of Torgau (1760), 60; in battle of Zorndorf (1758), 53; bombards Dresden, 60, 502; campaign in Bohemia, 47-48; campaigns in Saxony, 44-45, 49-50, 54, 60, 61; campaigns in Silesia, 51-53, 55, 60-61; coalitions against, 45-46; contemplates suicide, 54; defeat at Kunersdorf (1759), 55; diplomacy leading to, 39-40, 42; espionage system of, 43-44; letters to Voltaire, 59-60; peace negotiations, 47-48, 63-64; pessimism over victory, 46-49; poems written during, 49-50, 59; prestige of, 63; refuses French peace feelers, 56-57; strategy of, 44; in winter of 1759-60, 56, 59

Frederick II, Landgrave of Hesse-Cassel (r. 1760-85), 504, 525

Frederick IV, King of Denmark (r. 1699-1730), 235, 650

Frederick V, King of Denmark (r. 1746-66), 517, 651, 652

Frederick VI, King of Denmark (r. 1784-1808 as regent; 1808-39 as king), 653

Frederick Augustus I, Elector of Saxony, *see* Augustus II the Strong, King of Poland

Frederick Augustus II, Elector of Saxony, *see* Augustus III, King of Poland

Frederick Augustus III, Elector of Saxony (r. 1768–1806), 406, 502

Frederick Louis, Prince of Wales (1707–51), 687

Frederick William I, King of Prussia (r. 1713–1740), 426, 526

Frederick William II, King of Prussia (r. 1786–97), 333, 377, 405, 461, 540; alliance with Turkey (1785), 363; betrays and invades Poland, 489-90; death of, 547; Frederick II's doubts on, 530; Kant threatened by, 545-46

Frederick William III, King of Prussia (r. 1797–1840), liberal policies of, 547

Frederick William, Great Elector of Brandenburg, (r. 1640–88), 528

Fredman, Jan (1712–67), 660

Fredmans Epistlar (Bellmann), 660

Freemasonry, 322, 567; in Austria, 358; Casanova and, 323; doctrines of, 939; in England, 734, 938; in France, 94, 869, *938-39;* in German states, 507, 938; in Italy, 220; Jesuits and, 939; in Russia, 465; spread of, 938

free trade: Austria rejects, 344-45; in England, 670-71; France and, 859-60, 935; in Portugal, 269; in Russia, 455; in Sweden, 657; in Tuscany, 313

Free Trade Act (1779) for Ireland, 761

free trade doctrines, *see* Smith, Adam; physiocrats

Freiberg, Saxony, battle of (1762), 61

Freiburg, university at, 360

Freidenkerlexikon, 507

Freigeist, Der (Lessing), 508-9

French Academy (Académie Française, Forty Immortals), 353, 824, 894; emulation of, 280, 569; Voltaire and, 137, 877, 879

French America, 38-39, 58, 68, 89, 698, 709, 935; English conquest of, 57-58, 62, 68; Martinique restored to France, 62

French Guards, 959, 963

French Guiana, 89

French Revolution, 286, 333, 336, 363, 490, 496, 634, *900-63;* American Revolution and, 872; art and, 117-18, 912-13; attacks on châteaux in, 931; basic purpose of, 937; Burke's opposition to, 722-23, 806; Catherine II and, 465, 469, Church and, 902, *931,* 937, *940;* city populace and, 899; communist theorists in, 80, *937-38;* Condorcet's contribution to, 894-95; Corsica and, 313; court and, 939-40; Declaration of the Rights of Man and, 642, 872; defiance of Dauphiné Estates and, 948; economic inequality and, 937; emigrés from, 963; England and, 683, *721-26;* eve of, 954-56; feudalism abolished by, 872, 937; fraternization of troops with people in, 959-60; Freemasons and, 938-39; German Enlightenment and, 590-91 ; Gibbon's fear of, 805-6; Goethe's opposition to, 622; government corruption and, 939; Holland and, 364, 648-49; hunger and, 940; industry and, 931-34; Italy and, 311; Jews and, 642; Kant's enthusi-asm for, 548; middle class and, 899, *934-37,* 939; nobles and, 899, *927-30;* peasants and, 927-31; phases of, 725, *899; philosophes* and, 143, 880, *959-60, 937-38,* 940; political clubs and, 939; press censorship and, 940; religious tolerance and, 642; Réveillon factory riot and, 956; role of Paris in, 961-63; Rousseau and, 3, 177, 880, *890;* socialism and, 938; Sweden and, 662, 664; Switzerland and, 644-45, 805-6; terrorist period of, 725, 899; Voltaire and, 143, 880; wars of, 488, 872; workers and, 933-34

French West Indies, 709

Fréron, Élie (1719–76), 108, 136, 149, 922

Friederike of Mecklenburg-Strelitz, Princess, 523

Friedrich Christian (1765–1814), Duke of Holstein-Augustenburg, 594

Friesen, Count von (fl. 1750), 33

Friuli, 229

Froebel, Friedrich (1782–1852), 888

Fuga, Ferdinando (1699–1781), 247

Fullerton, duel with Shelburne, 732

Fulton, Robert (1765–1815), 932

Funeral of Danish Comedy, The (Holberg), 650

Fürnberg, Karl Joseph von (fl. 1755), 374

furniture: English, *523,* 748; French, 106-7, *910;* German, 523

Fürstenbund (League of Princes), 362-63

gabelle, 936

Gabriel, Jacques-Ange (1698–1782), 87, 111

Gabrielli, Caterina (1730–96), 333

Gaime, Abbé (fl. 1728), 183

Gainsborough, Thomas (1727–88), 740, *755-57;* Bath period, 756; as colorist, 757; death of, 757; early life of, 755; in London, 756-57; marriage to Margaret Burr, 755; nature paintings of, 756-57; personality of, 755, 757; Reynolds and, 756-57

Galiani, Abbé Ferdinando (1728–87), 75, 120, 251, 327, 333, 587, 908

Galicia: Jews in, *632,* 641; salt deposits in, 344

Galilei, Alessandro (1691–1736), 247

Galilei, Galileo (1564–1642), 294

Gallatin, Mme. de (fl. 1776), 136

Galuppi, Baldassare (1706–85), 232-33, 333, 426, 466

Galvani, Luigi (1737–98), 310

Gama, Vasco da (1469?–1524), 259, 270

gambling, 230-31, 850, 903

Gandzha, 419

gardens: in England, 748; in France, 99; Rousseau's influence on, 889

Garibaldi, Giuseppe (1807–82), 340

Garrick, David (1717–79), 696, 730, 340, *741-43,* 747-48, 750, 780, 791, 808, 828, 964; acting at Drury Lane, 742; appearance and personality of, 741, 756; death of, 743, 839; early life and education of, 741; Goldsmith and, 813-17; innovations of, 742; Johnson and, 741-42, 818, 822, 830; love affairs and marriage, 742-43;

management of Drury Lane, 742-43; on Paris, 71; popularity as actor, 741-42; Rousseau and, 209, 211

Garrick, Eva Maria, nee Weigel (1724–1822), 743

Garve, Christian (1742–98), 536*

Gassendi, Pierre (1592–1655), 294

Gatchina Palace, 468

Gâtier, Abbé (fl. 1729), 9, 183

Gaultier, Abbé (fl. 1778), 876, 879

Gautier, Théophile (1811–72), 880, 889

Gazette de France, 915

Gazzaniga, Giuseppe (1743–1818), 404

Gebler, Tobias von (1726–86), 355

Gedanken über die Nachahmung der griechischen Werke in Mahlerei und Bildhauerkunst (Winckelmann), 327

Gedanken von der wahren Schätzung der lebendigen Kräfte (Kant), 532

Geelvinck, Mme. (fl. 1763), 781

Gefühlsphilosophie (Jacobi), 890

Gelderland, 62

Gelders, 342

Gellert, Christian Fürchtegott (1715–69), 782

Geminiani, Francesco (d. 1762), 221, 746

General Dictionary of the English Language (Sheridan), 695

General History of Music (Burney), 333, 746-47

General History of the Science and Practise of Music (Hawkins), 746

general will, Rousseau's concept of, 172

Generallandschulreglement (1763), 500

Geneva, 176, 643; conflict of middle class with patricians, 143; Rousseau and, 27-28, 163-64, 177, 179, 190; theater in, 163

Genlis, Mme. Stéphanie Félicité de (1746–1830), 805, 955

Genoa, 205, 312; Austria and, 312; Freemasonry in, 220, French control of, 217; history and achievements of, 227; Jesuit colleges in, 219; sells Corsica to French, 313; theaters in, 220; universities in, 219

Genovesi, Antonio (1712–69), 250-51

Gentile, Anna, 219

Gentile, Maria, 257

Gentleman and Cabinet Maker's Director, The (Chippendale), 748

Gentleman's Magazine, The, 786, 819-20

Geoffrin, Marie-Thérèse, nee Rodet (1699–1777), 104-5, 118-125, 126-27, 131, 208, 251, 656; aid to *Encyclopédie*, 120; Betsky and, 453; correspondence of, 121, 447; Diderot and, 120; early life of, 118-19; Gibbon and, 799; husband of, 119; on lack of erudition, 119; piety of, 121; Poniatowski and, 477-78; salon of, 120-21; visit to Warsaw, 121

Geoffroy Saint-Hilaire, Étienne (1772–1844), 617

geology, Goethe's work in, 615

George I (George Louis), King of Great Britain and Ireland (r. 1714–27) and Elector of Hanover (r. 1698–1727), 699

George II, King of Great Britain and Ireland, and Elector of Hanover (r. 1727–60), 687, 794; death of, 60, 697; distaste for politics, 697

George III, King of Great Britain and Ireland, (r. 1760–1820), Elector and (from 1815), King of Hanover, 214, 384, 656, 687-89, 697-701, 722, 737-38, 750, 791, 794; American Revolution and, 687, 711, 713; appearance of, 698; attempts to shackle press, 701; Burns's criticism of, 777; Bute ministry and, 698-700, 702-3; calamity of reign, 688; conflict with Parliament, 61, 683, 686-88, 697-701; death of, 727; distaste for Seven Years' War, 698; early life of, 687; fits of insanity, 700, 721, 726-27; Fox-North coalition ministry and, 718; Federick II and, 60; French Revolution and, 687; Gibbon's praise of, 803; Grafton ministry and, 700; Grenville ministry and, 700; Junius and, 706; marries Charlotte Sophia of Mecklenburg-Strelitz, 698; Napoleonic Wars and, 687; Newcastle ministry and, 698; North ministry and, 700-01, 706, 710-14; partition of Poland and, 484; personality of, 687-88; Pitt ministry and, 700, 718-19, 726; powers of, 686; privy purse of, 686; Rockingham ministry and, 700, 714, 761; slave trade and, 732; Wilkes and, 702

George IV (George Augustus Frederick, Prince of Wales), King of Great Britain and Ireland (r. 1811–20 as prince regent, 1820–30 as king), 379, 721, 727, 777

George, Henry (1839–97), 76

George, Lake, 58

Georgia, 418

Gerl, Viennese basso (fl. 1791), 408

German courts, morality of, 504

German language, 506-7

Germany (German states): anti-religious feeling in, 64, 507; architecture in, 524-25; art in, 523-24; books and periodicals in, 506; clergy and religion in, 502-5, 507-8, 513-14; education in, 505-6; Enlightenment in, 505-17; family life in, 503-4; folk music in, 503; Freemasonry in, 507; Goethe's contempt for, 627; historical writing in, 578-80; in Holy Roman Empire, 341; Jews in, 507, 517, 634, 639, 642; libraries in, 506-22, 553-78, 584-605, 608-11, 623-25, 889; literature in, 509-11, 513-21, 557-65, 584-90, 592, 599-605, 608-11, 623-25; mercenaries in, 504; mildness of governments in, 503; music in, 367, 517-18, 525-28, 552; Napoleon remakes (1808), 666; opera in, 223-24, 527-28; philosophy in, 531-51, 618-23, 889-90; poverty in, 503; principalities of, 502-5; Protestantism in, 64, 142; Romantic movement in, 170, 508, 517-20; social classes in, 503-4; theater in, 509-10, 513-15, 560-61, 584-85, 588, 592, 601-3, 604-5; unification of, 502; village life in, 503

Gerstenberg, Heinrich von (1737–1823), 518

Gerusalemme liberata (Tasso), 464

Geschichte der Kunst des Alterthums (Winckelmann), see *History of Ancient Art*

Geschichte des Abfalls der Vereinigten Nieder-

lande (Schiller), 592

Geschichte des Agathon (Wieland), 553-55

Geschichte des Dreissigjährigen Krieges (Schiller), 593, 601

Geschichte des Instrumentalkonzerts (Schering), 234

Gespräche mit Goethe (Eckermann), *see Conversations with Goethe*

Gessner, Salomon (1730–88), 519-20, 645

Gesuati, Church of, 238

Gewandhaus orchestra, 525

Ghent, 361

Ghislandi, Vittore (1655–1743), 228

Gian (Giovan) Gastone de' Medici, Grand Duke of Tuscany (r. 1723–37), 227-28

Giannone, Pietro (1676–1748), 250

Gibbon, Catherine, 796

Gibbon, Edward (1666–1736), grandfather of the historian, 796

Gibbon, Edward (1707–70), father of the historian, 796, 798-99

Gibbon, Edward (1737–94), historian, 175, 280, 353, 530, 594, 694, 720, 729, 746-47, 772, 794-800, 842, 856, 908; ancestry of, 796; appearance of, 804; appetite of, 804-5; attitude toward Middle Ages, 804; autobiographies of, 795-96; on Bernese oligarchy, 643; on charm of Rome, 245; as Child of Enlightenment, 807-8; "the Club," 805, 827; continental tour of, 799-800; death of, 806; *Decline and Fall of the Roman Empire, see Decline and Fall of the Roman Empire;* early aspirations to be a historian, 798, 800; early life and education of, 796-99; fear of the French Revolution, 805-6; flight from Switzerland, 806; on Goldoni's *Memoirs,* 244; he becomes a Catholic, 797; as a historian, 806-8; Hume and, 799-800; influence of French rationalism on, 797, 880; on intellectual life of Paris, 906; Samuel Johnson and, 805, 831; meets *philosophes,* 797-99; opposes American Revolution, 711; in Parliament, 799-800, 803; relationship with Suzanne Curchod, 797-99, 865; residence in London, 799, 805-6; residence in Switzerland, 797-98, 805-6; on Robertson, 766; scholarship of, 807; in Seven Years' War, 798-99; stay in Buriton, 798-99; style as writer, 806; on Voltaire's theater, 134; on Wilkes, 701

Gibbon, Hester (1705–89), 796

Gibraltar, 273, 278, 290

Gideon, Simon (1699–1762), 635

Gilan, 419

Gillet, Nicolas-François (d. 1791), 467

Gillray, James (1757–1815), 729

Giornale dei letterati d'Italia, 220

Girardin, Marquis René de (fl. 1728), 886, 940

Girgenti, Goethe in, 589

Girondins, 895, 915

Glarus, 643

Glasgow: anti-Catholic riots in (1780), 735; growth of, 762; as port city, 669; University of, 674, 769

glass industry, 230

Glatz, 48; Prussia retains, 62

Gluck, Christoph Willibald (1714–87), 25, 100, 220, 291, 334, *367-73,* 374, 395, 846, 875, 883, 909, 964; appearance and personality of, 368, 371; collaboration with Calzabigi, 368-70; death of, 373; early years and education of, 367; "glass harmonica" compositions of, 368; his *L'innocenza giustificata* première, 368; his *Orfeo* première, 369; lieder of, 373; in London, 368; marriage to Marianne Pergia, 368; in Milan, 227; operatic reforms of, 335, 368-70; in Paris, *101,* 368, 370-73; Piccini rivalry, 333, 371-72, 908; in Vienna, 367-72

"God and the Bayadere, The" (Goethe), 599

Godoy, Manuel de (1767–1851), 302, 304-6

Godunov, Boris Feodorovich, Czar of Russia (r. 1598–1605), 425

Godwin, William (1756–1836), 881, 891

Goethe, August von (1789–1830), 614, 626

Goethe, Christiane, nee Vulpius (1765–1816), 589-90, 603, 605-6, 611-14

Goethe, Cornelia (1750–77), 556

Goethe, Johann Kaspar (1710–82), 556

Goethe, Johann Wolfgang von (1749–1832), 63, 321, 347, 379, 400, 471, 502-3, 519, 530, 545, 550, 552, 555-67, 580-91, 596-628, 639, 641, 645, 661, 767, 842, 964; appearance and personality, 587; at battle of Valmy (1792), 591; children of, 589; Christiane Vulpius and, *see* Goethe, Christiane; contribution to Romantic movement, 889; on crime in Italy, 319; on English people, 728; esthetic theories of, 588, 593, 627; fascination with Cagliostro, 322*; as Freemason, 507; on German village life, 503; Herder and, 559, 561-62, 568-69, 577, 580, 586, 591, 600, 608, 613; illnesses of, 603; 605; on Lessing, 517; on Louis XVI, 857; love for Greece, 623-24; love of nature, 584, 619; on Merck, 521; on Mozart, 383, 405, 408; Napoleon and, 623; opposes French Revolution, 590-91; opposes Pestalozzi's schools, 644; in *Ossian* controversy, 768; on papacy, 316; philosophical views of, 564, 618-23; poetry of, 557-58, 584-86, 599, 601; Rousseau's influence on, 518, 889; satires of, 598-99; Schiller and, 591, 593, 595-605; scientific work and theories of, 596-97, 615-18; social views of, 581, 590-91, 622-23; on Tiepolo's frescoes, 239; version of Lessing's *Nathan der Weise,* 515; on *The Vicar of Wakefield,* 815; views on European unity, 607; views on French culture, 607; views on religion, 564-66; Voltaire's influence on, 880-81; Wieland and, 576-77; Winckelmann's influence on, 326*, 331

EARLY YEARS (1749–75): appearance of, 558-60; description of, 561; family life and education of, 556-57; in Frankfurt, 556-58, 560-67; he thinks of suicide, 562; he writes *The Sorrows of Young Werther,* 563-64; interest in Jews, 556, 562; Jacobi and, 563-64; leaves Frankfurt for Weimar, 567; Lessing and, 563-64; literary tastes of, 557; love affairs of, 556-62, 566; meets Duke Karl August, 566; minor literary proj-

ects, 562-63; parents of, 556; in Strasbourg, 558-60; in Sturm und Drang movement, 520-21, 560-61; views on religion, 564-66; writes drama on Prometheus, 564-65; writes *Götz von Berlichingen*, 560-61
AS COUNCILOR (1775-86): acquires status of noble, 581; appointed to Privy Council, 581; dramas of, 584-85; love affair with Charlotte von Stein, *see* Stein, Charlotte von; love of nature, 584; poems of, 584-86; Weimar court life and, 581
IN ITALY (1786-88), 310; architectural studies in, 587; art work in, 587-88; impressions of Italy, 232, 313-15; literary activities in, 588; love affairs, 588; love for Italy, 586; writes *Römische Elegien*, 590
MATURE YEARS OF (1805-25): death of wife, 614; deference to nobility, 622; domestic life, 613; Felix Mendelssohn and, 614-15; love affairs of, 611-15; love of Greece, 623-24; marries Christiane Vulpius, 606, 611; meetings with Napoleon; social views of, 622-23; views on Beethoven, 613; views on marriage, 612; views on religion and morality, 619-22; writes autobiography, 613; writes *Faust*, 608-11, 620, 622-26
LAST YEARS OF (1825-32): appearance in death, 628; completes *Wilhelm Meisters Lehrjahre*, 599-601; death of, 627-28; death of Charlotte von Stein, 626; death of son, 626; international fame, 627
Goethe, Katharina Elisabeth, nee Textor (1731-1803), 556, 606
Goethe, Ottilie von, nee Pogwisch (1796-1872), 614-15, 627
Goethes Briefwechsel mit einem Kinde (Goethe-Brentano), 611
Goeze, Johann Melchior (1717-86), 514, 563
Goëzman, Louis-Valentin (fl. 1770), 921
Goislard de Montsabert, Anne-Louis (1763-1814), 947
Goldene Spiegel, Der (Wieland), 555
Goldoni, Carlo (1707-93), 237, 239-40, 494, 883; attitude toward French music, 909; death of, 244; declining years of, 244; early life of, 241; in Paris, 71, 244; rivalry with Gozzi, 242-43; theatrical reforms of, 242
Goldsmith, Henry, 813
Goldsmith, Oliver (1728-74), 730, 739, 753, 759, 786, 813-17, 827, 828; appearance and personality of, 817; on Burke's oratory, 692; Chatterton's poems and, 810; death of, 817, 839; defense of English peasantry, 814-16; early life and education of, 813-14; early literary works of, 814; fame of, 814-15; Garrick and, 814-17; historical writing of, 815; Samuel Johnson and, 814-17, 831, 840
Golitsyn, Alexander (fl. 1770), 458
Gonçalves Pereira, Dr. Pedro (fl. 1758), 264
Goncourt, Edmond de (1822-96), and Jules de (1830-70), 342

Gontard, Karl Philipp Christian von (1731-91), 524
Gonzaga, Tomaz Antônio (1744-1807), 269
González, Diego (1734?-94), 295
Good-Natured Man, The (Goldsmith), 815, 817
Gordon, Lord George (1751-93), 735-36
Gordon Riots (1780), 735-36
Göschen, G. J. (1752-1828), 573
Gospel Triumphant, The (Olavide), 286
Gospels, 629
Gossec, François-Joseph (1734-1829), 909
Gossen, Stephen (1554-1624), 163
Gotha, 362
Gott, einige Gespräche (Herder), 578
Götter Griechenlands, Die (Schiller), 595
"Gottlieb, Das" (Goethe), 619
Gottsched, Johann Christoph (1700-66), 49, 327, 782
Götz von Berlichingen (Goethe), 506, 521, 560-61, 588, 627
Gougenot, Abbé (fl. 1755), 112
Gounod, Charles-François (1818-93), 611
Gournay, Jean-Claude-Vincent de (1712-59), 72-73, 78
Gouthière, Pierre (1740-1806), 87, 106
Gouveia, Marquis of (d. 1759), 265
Gouvernet, Suzanne de Livry, Marquise de, 877
Goya, Eugracía Lucientes, 300
Goya, José (Goya's father), 300
Goya y Lucientes, Camilo, 300
Goya y Lucientes, Francisco José de (1746-1828), 227, 276, 298-99, 300-9; *caprichos* of, 305; as court painter, 302, 304; deafness of, 303; death of, 297, 309; death of wife, 307; as director of painting in Academy, 302, 304; early life and personality of, 300; growth of, 300-2; Joseph Bonaparte and, 297; later years of, 302, 308; love affairs of, 302-3; *majas* of, 291, 303-5; marriage to Josefa Bayeu, 300; nudes of, 305; portraiture of, 305; rationalism of, 306; social views of, 306-8; in Spanish war of liberation, 307-8; war paintings of, 307-8
Goya y Lucientes, Javier de (b. 1784), 304, 308
Goya y Lucientes, Josefa, nee Bayeu, 300-3, 307
Goya y Lucientes, Mariano de, 308-9
Gozzi, Bettina, 322
Gozzi, Carlo (1720-1806), 239, 242-43, 310-11
Gozzi, Gasparo (1713-86), 242
Gozzi, Padre (fl. 1740), 322
Grabowska, Pani, 479
Gradot café, 99
Graff, Anton (1736-1813), 524
Graffigny, Françoise d'Issembourg d'Happoncourt de, 78
Grafton, Augustus Henry Fitzroy, 3d Duke of (1735-1811), 731-32; Junius' attacks on, 705-6; ministry of, (1760-70), 700, 703, 705-6; 710
Graham, Mrs. (fl. 1777), 756
"Grains" (Quesnay), 73
Gramont, Béatrixe de Choiseul, Duchesse de (1731-94), 907
Gran Consiglio (Great Council) of Venice, 229

"Grandes Remontrances" of Paris *parlement*, 91

Grand Trunk Canal, 672

Granja, La (Palace of San Ildefonso), 297

Grasse, Comte François-Joseph-Paul de (1722–1788), 117, 669, 871

Grattan, Henry (1746–1820), 759, 760, *761-62*

Gravina, Gian Vincenzo (1664–1718), 240

Gray, Thomas (1716–71), 228, 700, 741-42, 815, 887; Chatterton's poem and, 809; death of, 795; Samuel Johnson's views on, 837; Horace Walpole and, 792

Graz, university at, 360

Great Lakes, French control of, 57

Great Rebellion of 1688, 735

Greatness and Decadence of the Romans (Montesquieu), 254, 801

Greco, El (1541?–1614), 227

Greece, ancient, 21; art of, 510; Goethe's admiration for, 593, 623-24; influence of, 118; poetry of, 599; Winckelmann's analysis of, 510

Greece, modern, 411; Turkish conquest of (1715), 415; war of liberation (1821), 623

Greek Orthodox Church, 452, 472, 475, 480

Greeks, Byzantine, 312

Greenland, 652

Grégoire, Abbé Henri (1750–1831), 642

Greiffenklau, Karl Philipp von, Prince-Bishop of Würzburg (fl. 1750), 239

Grenoble, 849, 947-48

Grenville, George (1712–70), 696; ministry of, 700; policies toward American colonies, 709-710

Grétry, André-Ernest-Modeste (1741–1813), 883, *909-10*

Greuze, Gabrielle, nee Babuti (b. 1726), 112-13

Greuze, Jean-Baptiste (1725–1805), *111-15*, 116-17, 120, 235, 888, 904, 911; as Freemason, 939; portrait of Gluck, 371; sensuality of, 116

Grimaldi, Marchese Geronimo de' (1761), 282, 286, 325

Grimm, Friedrich Melchior, later Baron von Grimm (1723–1807), 18, 27, 104, 108, 656, 882, 892-93, 908, 910; on d'Alembert, 127; attitude toward French music, 909; on ancient monuments, 110; becomes baron, 813; Catherine II and, 447, 449, 452, 463, 466, 894; death of, 894; Diderot and, 34; early life of, 33; edits *Correspondance littéraire*, 34-35; Mme. d'Épinay and, *35-37*, 156-57, 159-61, 449; on French music, 100; friendship with monarchs, 897; Mme. Geoffrin and, 120-21; goes to Seven Years' War, 36; on inevitability of revolution in France, 95; influence in Germany, 507; later years of, 893-94; on *Lettre sur la musique français*, 26; Mozart and, 384-85, 390, 392; personality of, 35; on Prussia after Seven Years' War, 63; returns to Germany, 894; Rousseau and, 3-4, 5*, 18, 23, 153, 159-62, 170, 201, 207-8, 212; skepticism of, 893-94; on Voltaire's visit to Paris, 877

Gros, Father (fl. 1729), 10

Gross-Jägersdorf, battle of (1757), 432

Gross-Jägersdorf, convention of, 48

Grosskophta, Der (Goethe), 322*

Grote, George (1794–1871), 739

Grotius, Hugo (1583–1645), 171, 177, 251, 427

Grundlegung zur Metaphysik der Sitten (Kant), 540-41

Guadagni, Gaetano (1725?–92), 369

Guadalajara, 288

Guadeloupe, 58, 62, 89, 935

Guardi, Francesco (1712–93), 236, 332

Guardi, Giovanni Antonio (1698–1760), 332

Guarini, Giovanni Battista (1537–1612), 637

Guarneri, Giuseppe Antonio "del Gesù" (1687?–1745), 221

Guglielmi, Gregorio (1714–73), painter, 345

Guglielmi, Pietro (1727–1804), composer, 333

Guibert, Alexandrine-Louise Boutinonde de Courcelles, Comtesse de, 130, 131*

Guibert, Comte Jacques-Antoine de (1743–90), *128-30*, 131*, 892, 906, 908

Guicciardini, Francesco (1483–1540), 766

guilds: in Austria, 344, 356; in England, 676-77; in France, 72, 862, 932; in Spain, 289

Guilford, Francis North, 1st Earl of (1704–90), 701

Guillard, Nicolas-François (fl. 1778), 372

Guillemardet, Ferdinand, 305

guillotine, 899

Guines, Comte de, later Duc de (fl. 1776), 392, 864

guitar, 417

Guizot, François (1787–1874), 97*

Guldberg, Ove Hoegh- (1731–1808), 653

Gunpowder Plot (1605), 735

Gustaf Adolf Adelmod (Gustavus III), 659

Gustaf Adolf och Ebba Brahe (Gustavus III), 659

Gustaf Vasa (Gustavus III), 659

Gustavus I Vasa, King of Sweden (r. 1523–60), 655

Gustavus II Adolphus, King of Sweden (r. 1611–32), 655

Gustavus III, King of Sweden (r. 1771–92), 121, 655-66, 883, 897, 941, 964; army mutiny against, 663; assassination of, 665; conflict with nobles, 663-64; correspondence with Voltaire, 139; coup against Riksdag, 657; diplomacy of, 460; early popularity of, 656; fear of French Revolution, 662, 664; Freemasons and, 938; influence of French culture on, 655-56; Jews protected by, 635; later reactionary policies of, 662; literary works of, 659; loses confidence of people, 662; marriage to Princess Sophia Magdalena, 655; personality and education of, 655-56; physiocrats and, 76; reforms of, 657-58; Swedish Enlightenment and, 658-60; war against Russia and Denmark, 663-64

Gustavus Adolphus, Prince of Stolberg-Gedern (fl. 1750), 339

Gutenberg, Johann (1400?–68), 895

Gyllenborg, Count Carl (1679–1746), 654

Gyllenborg, Gustaf Fredrik (1731–1808), 660
Gymnasien, 352
gypsies, 684

Haarlem, 361
Hadik, Andreas, Count Hadik von Futak (1710–1790), 49
Haffner, Sigismund (fl. 1782), 398
Hafiz (1320–89), Persian poet, 613-14
Hague, The, 361
haidamacks, 633
Haidar Ali (1722–82), Maharajah of Mysore, 717
Hainaut, 342
hair styles, 99
Haiti, 935
Hales, Stephen (1677–1761), 671
Halevy, Jehuda (1086?–1141?), 637
Halifax, George Montagu Dunk, 2d Earl of (1716–71), 702-3
Haller, Albrecht von (1708–77), 11, 169, 645
Hamadan, battle of (1731), 418
Hamann, Johann Georg (1730–88), 518-19, 567
Hamburg: Freemasonry in, 507; Jews in, 634; opera in, 558
Hamburgische Dramaturgie (Lessing), 511
Hamilton, Emma, Lady, nee Lyon (1765–1815), 758
Hamilton, Gavin (fl. 1785), 773
Hamlet (Shakespeare), 511, 742, 842
Hamond, Walter (fl. 1640), 31
Hanbury-Williams, Sir Charles (1708–59), 436, 478
Handel, George Frederick (1685–1759), 100, 222, 234, 256, 334, 368, 396, 517, 742; Commemoration Concert (1784), 746; Haydn on, 377
Hanover, 653; England and, 38; French evacuation of, 53; in League of Princes (1785), 362; Seven Years' War in, 46, 60
Hanoverian dynasty, 699
Hansard, Luke (1752–1828), 707
Hapsburgs, Spanish, last of, 273
Harewood House, 748
Hargreaves, James (d. 1778), 673
harim (harem), 413
Harlequin (comic figure), 241
Harmonies de la nature, Les (Bernardin de Saint-Pierre), 916
Harrach, Count von (fl. 1792), 378
Harsch, General (fl. 1758), 54
Haschka, Leopold (fl. 1796), 379
Hasenkampf, J. C. (fl. 1774), 564
Hasidism, 636
Haskalah movement, 641-42
Hasse, Johann Adolf (1699–1783), 220, 240, 386; Mozart's rivalry with, 387
Hastenbeck, battle of (1757), 48
Hastings, Warren (1732–1818), 59, 696, 716-18, 943; exploitation of India, 717-18; trial of, 719-21, 805

Hats (Swedish party), 654, 657
Haugwitz, Count Ludwig (fl. 1753–80), 374; domestic policies of, 344
Hauptschulen, 352
Haüy, Valentin (1745–1822), 905
Havana, 62
Havre, Le, 944
Hawkins, Sir John (1719–89), 827-28, *840*
Hawthorne, Nathaniel (1804–64), 889
Haydn, Franz Joseph (1732–1809), 100, 227, 341, *373-81*, 526, 964; Beethoven and, 378-80; contribution to music, 380, 528; death of, 380; early life and education of, 373; in England, 377-78, 746; with Esterházy family, 375-77, 379; in Kantorei, 374; marriage, 375; in Melk, 374; Mozart and, 376-78, 397; as music teacher, 373; Napoleon and, 380; personality of, 374; operas of, 376, 379-80; oratorios of, 377; religiosity of, 380-81; social context of music, 381; string quartets of, 374, 380; symphonies of, 376-78, 380-81; in Vienna, 374-77; writes *Schöpfung* oratorio, 379
Haydn, Johann Michael (1737–1806), 374, 385
Haydn, Maria Anna, 375
Heathfield, George Augustus Eliott, Baron (1717–90), 752
Heaven and Its Wonders and Hell (Swedenborg), 658
Hébert, Jacques-René (1757–94), 890
Hebrews, 578; *see also* Jews
Hebrides: Johnson-Boswell tour of, 785, 835-38, 840; Macpherson's tour of, 767
Hegel, Georg Wilhelm Friedrich (1770–1831), 331, 551, 618
Heine, Heinrich (1797–1856), 543, 880
Heinse, Wilhelm (1749–1803), 522
Hell-Fire Club, 702
Helmholtz, Hermann von (1821–94), 618
Helvetic Republic, proclaimed (1798), 645; *see also* Switzerland
Helvetische Gesellschaft, 643
Helvétius, Anne-Catherine, nee de Ligniville d'Autricourt (1719–1800), 869, 915
Helvétius, Claude-Adrien (1715–71), 31, 73, 105, 119, 162, 219, 220, 280, 294, 324, 501, 641, 769; atheism of, 183; death of, 892; equalitarianism of, 141; ethics of, 739; Franklin and, 870; French Revolution and, 84, 940; Gibbon and, 799; on Index Expurgatorius, 316; influence of, 230, 320; opposition to monarchy, 897; as tax farmer, 936
Hénault, Charles-Jean-François (1685–1770), 123, 125
Henriade (Voltaire), 10, 149, 528, 629, 655
Henry, Patrick (1736–99), 709
Henry II, King of France (r. 1547–99), 942
Henry IV, King of France (r. 1589–1610), 142, 462
Henry VI, King of England (r. 1422–61, 1470–71), 698
Henry VIII, King of England (r. 1509–47), 266, 360

Henry of Prussia, Prince (1726–1802), 54-56, 59, 483; attitude toward Frederick II, 495; in battle of Freiberg, 61; on Louis XVI, 856
Henry the Navigator, Prince (1394–1460), 142
Hepplewhite, George (d. 1786), 748
Herat, 417-18, 421
Herbert, Lord, 753
Herculaneum, excavations at, 110, 248, 910
Herder, Caroline, nee Flachsland (1750–1809), 568-69, 577
Herder, Johann Gottfried (1744–1803), 503, 506-7, 567-69, 577-80, 589, 628, 639, 641, 645, 815; death of, 580; description of Kant, 532; early life of, 567; Enlightenment and, 567, 569; esthetic theories of, 567-68; *Frankfurter gelehrte Anzeigen* and, 52; as Freemason, 507; on Gluck, 373; goes to Weimar, 569; Goethe and, 559, 561-62, 568-69, 577, 580, 591, 600, 608, 613; hatred of Prussia, 530; historical theories of, 578-80; historical writings of, 569; Kant and, 549, 567; marriage of, 569; in *Ossian* controversy, 768; philosophical views of, 580; responsibilities at Weimar, 577; Rousseau's influence on, 518, 889; Sturm und Drang and, 522, 569; views on religion, 578-79; visit to Italy, 579-80; welcomes French Revolution, 590; Winckelmann's influence on, 331; writings on literature, 567
Hermann und Dorothea (Goethe), 601, 627
Hermitage, Catherine II's, 468
Hermitage, L', Rousseau's stay at, *see* Rousseau, Jean-Jacques, AT HERMITAGE
Hero of Alexandria (fl. A.D. 200), 673
Heroic Life of St. Anne (Malagrida), 267
Herschel, Sir William (1738–1822), 791
Hertford, Lady, 729
Hervey, Carr, Lord (1691–1723), 792
Hervey, Frederick Augustus (1730–1803), bishop of Derry, 761
Hervey, John, Baron Hervey of Ickworth (1696–1743), 792
Hervey, Mary, Lady, nee Lepell (1700–68), 792
Herz, Henrietta, nee de Lemos (1764–1847), 640-41
Herz, Marcus (1747–1803), 640-41
Herzlieb, Wilhelmine (1789–1865), 611-12
Hesketh, Harriet, Lady, nee Cowper (1733–1807), 813
Hesse, Andreas von (fl. 1770), 568
Hesse-Cassel: in League of Princes (1785), 362; mercenary troops of, 504
Hesse-Cassel, Landgrave of (r. 1760–85), *see* Frederick II, Landgrave of Hesse-Cassel
Hesse-Darmstadt, Prince [Ludwig] of (fl. 1773), 34, 449
hidalgos, 274
"Highland Mary" (Burns), 775
Hildebrandt, Johann Lukas von (1668–1745), 341
Hirsch, Abraham (fl. 1750), 509, 630
Histoire de Jenni (Voltaire), 138
Histoire de Juliette (Sade), 904

Histoire de la guerre de Sept Ans (Frederick II), 529
Histoire de la Russie sous Pierre le Grand (Voltaire), 137, 432
Histoire du Parlement de Paris (Voltaire), 92-93
Histoire générale (Voltaire), *see Essai sur les moeurs*
Histoire philosophique des deux Indes (Raynal), 902
Historia del famoso predicador Fray Gerundio (Isla), 295
Historic Doubts on the Life and Reign of King Richard III (Walpole), 794
historiography: in England, 795-808, 815; in Germany, 578-80; in Scotland, 765-66
History of Agathon, The (Wieland), 553-55
History of Ancient Art (Winckelmann), 110, 329, 332, 588
History of Animated Nature (Goldsmith), 815
History of Denmark, A (Holberg), 650
History of England (Hume), 766
History of Rasselas, Prince of Abyssinia, The (Johnson), 819, 825-26, 829
History of Rome (Niebuhr), 253
History of Russia (Tatishchev), 427
History of Scotland during the Reigns of Queen Mary and of James VI (Robertson), 766
History of the Jews, A (Holberg), 650
History of the Protestant Variations (Bossuet), 797
History of the Rebellion (Clarendon), 856
History of the Reign of the Emperor Charles V (Hume), 766
History of the Religion of the Jews (Basnage), 641
History of the Russian Empire under Peter the Great (Voltaire), *see Histoire de la Russie sous Pierre le Grand*
History of the Thirty Years' War (Schiller), *see Geschichte des Dreissigjährigen Krieges*
Hobbema, Meindert (1638–1709), 647
Hobbes, Thomas (1588–1679), 172, 280, 294
Hochkirch, battle of (1758), 54
Hofdemel, Franz (fl. 1789), 405
Hofer, Franz (fl. 1770), 407-8
Hoffmeister, music publisher, 402
Hogarth, William (1697–1764), 524, 724
Hogland, battle of (1788), 663
Hohenberg, Johann Friedrich von (1732–1816), 345
Hohenzollerns, rising power of, 63
Holbach, Baron Paul-Henri-Dietrich d' (1723–1789), 104, 118, 168, 220, 496, 572, 618-19, 641, 893; atheism of, 183; death of, 893; French Revolution and, 940; at Mme. Geoffrin's salon, 120; Gibbon and, 799; on Index Expurgatorius, 316; opposition to monarchy, 897; Rousseau and, 18, 27-28, 153, 209
Holberg, Ludvig von (1684–1754), 645-46, 649-51

Holland, 143, *645-49;* agriculture in, 646; aid to Turkey, 363; art in, 647; decline in naval supremacy, 57; description of, 645-46; economy of, 646; education in, 647; England and, 277, 648, 699, 714; France and, 648-49; French Revolution and, 364, 648-49; India and, 715; Jews in, *635,* 646-47; in League of Armed Neutrality (1780), 648; literature in, 647; oligarchy in, 142; Patriot party in, 648-49; political unrest in, 648; prisons in, 738; Protestantism in, 142; in Quadruple Alliance (1718), 278; religious tolerance in, 646-47; Revolutionary War and, 648; in War of the Austrian Succession (1743), 648

Holland, Caroline, Lady, nee Lennox, 693

Holland, Henry Fox, 1st Baron (1705–74), 364, 693

Holstein-Augustenburg, Duke of, *see* Friedrich Christian, Duke

Holstein-Gottorp, Karl Friedrich, Duke of, *see* Karl Friedrich

Holstein-Gottorp, Karl Friedrich Ulrich, Duke of, *see* Peter III, Czar of Russia

Holstein-Gottorp, Prince of (fl. 1770), 568

"Holy Fair" (Burns), 773

Holy Roman Empire: structure and scope of, 341, 502; *see also* Austria

"Holy Willie's Prayer" (Burns), 773-74

Homage à Haydn (Debussy), 381

Homberg, Herz (fl. 1778), 639

Home, Henry, *see* Kames, Henry Home, Lord

Home, John (1722–1808), Scottish playwright, 699, 764

home furnishings, *see* furniture

Homer (9th cent. B.C.), 253, 485, 519, 528, 599, 750, 837

Homme aux quarante écus, L' (Voltaire), 75-76, 136, 143

Homme machine, L' (La Mettrie), 246-47

Homme personnel, L' (Barthe), 874

homosexuality, 731

Hontheim, Johann Nikolaus von (Justinus Febronius; 1701–90), 351, 504-5, 560

Horace (65 B.C.–8 B.C.), 528

Horen, Die (periodical), 597

Horn, Count Arvid Bernhard (1664–1742), 654

Horn, Count Karl (d. 1823), 664-65

hospitals, 353, 453

Hôtel-Dieu, 353

Hôtel des Invalides, 962

Hôtel Salm, 910

Houasse, Michel-Ange (d. 1730), 298

Houasse, René-Antoine (1645–1710), 298

Houdetot, Comte d', 156

Houdetot, Élisabeth-Sophie de Bellegarde, Comtesse d' (1730–1813), 118, 152, *156-58, 162,* 164, 167, 869; as model for Julie, 157; salon of, 907

Houdon, Jean-Antoine (1741–1828), 466, *911-12,* 939

House of Commons, 683, 699; appointive places in administration, 686; corruption in, 685-86; enactment of legislation in, 686-87; parties in,

see Tories *and* Whigs; press freedom and, 707; privileges of, 685; representation in, 685

House of Lords, 703; enactment of legislation by, 685-86

Houses of Parliament, architecture of, 748; *see also* Parliament, English

Howard, Castle, 235

Howard, John (1726?–90), 737-38

Howe, Sir William, 8th Viscount Howe (1729–1814), 869

Huber, Ludwig Ferdinand (1764–1804), 572-73

Hubertusburg, armistice of (1763), 62

Hudson, Thomas (1701–79), 751

Hugo, Victor (1802–85), 104, 889

Huguenots, 88

Hulegaard, Arense (fl. 1759), 651

Humbert I, Count of Savoy, *see* Umberto I

Humboldt, Alexander von (1769–1859), 273

Humboldt, Wilhelm von (1767–1835), 641

Hume, David (1711–76), 120, 125, 183, 280, 531-32, 537, 594, 762, 764, 766, 773, 794-95, 797; d'Alembert and, 127, 892; ethics of, 739; Gibbon and, 799-800; as an historian, 766; influence of, 536, 543, 768-69, 889; Samuel Johnson's attitude toward, 834; in Lespinasse salon, 126; on physiocrats, 75; Reid and, 764-65; Rousseau and, 207, 209, *211-14;* supports American colonies, 711; tranquillity in face of death, 838; on *Tristram Shandy,* 788; on Voltaire, 149

Hummel, Johann Nepomuk (1778–1837), 380, 525

Hungary, 354; agriculture in, 341; Austria and, 341; disorder in, 461; gold mines in, 344; Jews in, 631; Joseph II's reforms in, 358; population of, 341; revolt against Joseph II, 360-61, 363-64; revolt of nobles in, 357; social classes in, 341; taxation in, 341; Turkey and, 62, 415

Hunter, John (1728–93), 764

Hunter, William (1718–83), 764

Husein, Shah of Persia (r. 1694–1722), 418

Huss, John (Jan Hus; 1369?–1415), 342

Hutcheson, Francis (1694–1746), 320, 733, 764

Hutchinson, Thomas (1711–80), 710

Hutton, James (1726–97), 764

Hyde Park, 744

"Hymn to the Sun" (Naruszewicz), 485

Ibrahim Pasha, Turkish Vizier (d. 1730), 415

Idea of a Patriot King (Bolingbroke), 687

Ideas of Beauty and Virtue (Hutcheson), 320

Ideen zu einer allemeinen Geschichte (Kant), 548

Ideen zur Philosophie der Geschichte der Menschheit (Herder), 578-80

Iffland, August Wilhelm (1759–1814), 571

Iglesia Metropolitana della Nuestra Señora del Pilar, 300

Ignorant Philosopher, The (Voltaire), 138

Île de St.-Pierre, Rousseau at, 206

Iliad (Homer), 528; Pope's translation of, 837

Illuminati, Order of, 507

Imhof, Baron (fl. 1768), 717

Imhof, Marion, Baroness, 717

Imitation of Christ, The (Thomas a Kempis), 886

Imperial Diet, Holy Roman Empire, 502

Impey, Sir Elijah (1732–1809), 717

Important Examination of Milord Bolingbroke (Voltaire), 138

Inchbald, Elizabeth, nee Simpson (1753–1821), 787

Independents (Puritans), 735, 760

Index Expurgatorius (Index Librorum Prohibitorum), 247, 285, 316, 358

India, 698; England and, 39, 57-59, 669, 689, 693, 717-18; France and, 38-39, 57-59, 62, 68, 715; Holland and, 715; Mysore revolt in, 717-18; Persian invasion of, 419; Seven Years' War and, 57-59

India Reform Bill (1783), 718

Indians, American, *see* American Indians

Industrial Revolution, *669-79*, 842, 964
    IN ENGLAND: causes of, 669-71; consequences, 680-82; factory system, 676-80, 682, 732; machine-wrecking by workers, 679; pauperism and, 677, 679; science and, 669, 671, 681; social effects, 670-71, 676-80; technological elements, 671-76; transportation and, 672; wages and, 677
    IN FRANCE, 932
    IN SCOTLAND, 763

Industrious Bee, The (periodical), 464-65

industry and French Revolution, 931-34

Informe sobre un proyecto de ley agraria (Jovellanos), 287

Ingénu, L' (Voltaire), 31, 138

Ingermanland, 653

Innocent XIII (Michelangelo dei Conti), Pope (r. 1721–24), *245-46,* 278

Innocenza giustificata, L' (Gluck and Durazzo), 368

Innsbruck, University of, 358, 360

inoculation, *see* smallpox inoculation

Inquiry into the Human Mind on the Principles of Common Sense (Reid), 764

Inquiry into the Nature and Causes of the Wealth of Nations (Smith), *see* Wealth of Nations

Inquisition, 253; in Austria, 343; Casanova and, 323; in Italy, 225, 229, 252, 316; Jews and, *630-31,* 633; Johnson's support for, 834; in Portugal, 260, *267-70;* in Spain, *275-76,* 279-80, 292, 294-95, 302, 306

Institutes (Calvin), 177

Instructions (Catherine the Great), 450-51

internationalism of papacy, 316

Introduction to the Principles of Morals and Legislation, An (Bentham), 739

inventions: in France, 932; Industrial Revolution and, 671-76

Iphigenia in Tauris (Guillard), 372

Iphigénie (Racine), 370

Iphigenie auf Tauris (Goethe), 584, 587-88, 601, 627

Iphigénie en Aulide (Gluck), 101, 335, 370-71

Iphigénie en Tauride (Gluck), 372

Iphigénie en Tauride (Piccini), 373

Iran, *see* Persia

Ireland, *759-62;* agriculture in, 759-60; Burke's support for, 693; Catholic Church in, 283, 760-62; commerce and industry in, 759, 761; culture in, 759-60; England and, 671, 704, 726, *759-62;* marriage in, 759; population of, 759-60; poverty and crime in, 759; Protestants in, 759-62; rebellion of "Whiteboys" in, 760

Irene (Johnson), 819, 830

Irène (Voltaire), 136, 874

Iriarte y Oropesa, Don Tomás de (1750–91), 291

iron industry in England, 671-72

iron law of wages, 79

Irving, Sir Henry (1838–1905), 740

Irving, Washington (1783–1859), 815

Isabella of Parma (d. 1763), 1st wife of Emperor Joseph II, 347

Isfahan, 419

Isham, Col. Ralph Heyward, 779*

Isla, José Francisco de (1703–81), 294-95

Islam, *411-21;* adultery in, 413; art in, 414; child-rearing in, 416; crafts in, 416, 421; education in, 412; geographic area of, 411; Gibbon's treatment of, 808; morality in, 416; music in, 416-17; poetry in, 412-13, *421;* prostitution in, 416; public baths in, 413; in Russia, 452; science in, 412; sects in, 411-12; slavery in, 413-14, 420; *see also* Afghanistan; Egypt; Mohammedanism; Persia; Turkey

Ismailovsky Regiment, 439

Israel ben Eliezer, *see* Baal Shem-Tob

Istoria civile del regno di Napoli (Giannone), 250

Istria, 229

Italian nationalism and Alfieri, 340

Italy, 19, *310-40;* academies and universities in, 218-19; agriculture in, 217; architecture in, 247; aristocracy in, 230; art in, 227, 235-39, 247-48, *331-32;* Austria and, 38, 341; capitalism in, 230; censorship in, 220, 225; comedy in, 239-44; commerce and industry in, 218; crime in, 319; description of, 217-18; Enlightenment in, 220, 230; Freemasonry in, 220; French Revolution and, 311; happiness of, 217; heresies in, 220; in Holy Roman Empire, 341; Inquisition in, 229, 316; intellectual life in, 218-20; Jesuits and education in, 219; Jews in, 250; legal reform in, 320-21; libraries in, 219; literature in, 220, 239-44, *335-36;* marriage and family life in, 218-19, 230; moral laxity of, 225; music in, 220-24, 226-27, *332-35,* 373, 367; Napoleon and, 311; neoclassical style and, 325-31; opera houses in, 223; opera in, 222-24, 254-57, *333-35, 527-38;* periodicals in, 220; population of, 217; poverty in, 217; prostitution in, 218, 225, 230; religion in, 224-26; singing in, 220, 222-24, 333; social classes in, 218, 230; Spanish ambitions in, 277-78; theater in, 220, *336-40;* wars of succession in, 217; *see also* papacy

Iuvara, Filippo (1676?–1736), 226, 297

Ivan V Alexeevich, Czar of Russia (r. 1682–99), 429

Ivan VI, Czar of Russia (r. 1740–41), 430; murder of, 443, 447

Ivy House Works, 749

Ivy Lane Club, 822, 840

Izmail, battle of (1790), 461

Jacobi, Friedrich Heinrich (1743–1819), 516, 562, 565, 578, 613, 895, 899; Goethe and, 563-64; philosophy of, 519; Rousseau's influence on, 890

Jacobins, 939

Jafar, Mir, *see* Mir Jafar

Jahn, Otto (1813–69), 407

Jamaica, 669

James, William (1842–1910), 739

James I, King of England (r. 1603–25), King of Scotland as James VI (r. 1567–1625), 779

James II, King of England, Scotland, and Ireland (r. 1685–88), 705, 711, 735

James II, King of Scotland (r. 1437–60), 779

"James III," of England, *see* Stuart, James Francis Edward

James VI, King of Scotland, *see* James I, King of England

Janissaries, 414

Jansen, Cornelis (1585–1638), 646

Jansenists: in Austria, 359; in France, 85, 90-91, 193, 246; in Holland, 646; in Italy, 225; Jesuits and, 246

Jassy, Treaty of (1792), 461, 488

Jaucourt, Chevalier (later Marquis) Louis de (1704–79), 102, 875

Jaurès, Jean-Léon (1859–1914), 929

Jay, John (1745–1829), 871

Jean-Jacques Rousseau, Citoyen de Genève, à Christophe de Beaumont, Archevêque de Paris (Rousseau), 195, 197

Jefferson, Thomas (1743–1826): on American Indians, 891; French Enlightenment and, 76, 867, 891, 899

Jeffries, John (1744–1819), 933

Jehan, Shah, *see* Shah Jehan

Jena: battle of (1808), 530, 606, 627; Museum of Mineralogy at, 615; University of, 545, 618

Jeppe of the Hill (Holberg), 650

Jerome of Prague (1360?–1416), 342

Jerusalem, Karl Wilhelm (d. 1772), 561-63

Jerusalem (Mendelssohn), 640

Jesuits, 241, 310, 914; abolition of order by Clement XIV (1773), 318, 351; accounts of Indians by, 31; attacks against Rousseau, 185; in Austria, 351-52; in Brazil, 263; in China, 225, 318; communistic practices in Paraguay, 80, 83, 262; competition with other orders, 285; conflict with kings, 226; in France, 89, 185; Frederick II and, 319; Freemasons and, 939; in Italy, 219, *224-26,* 230, 310; Jansenists

and, 246; origin and purposes of, 283; in Paraguay, 80, 83, 262, 281, 283; popularity of, 284-85; in Portugal, 260, *262-68,* 271-72; in Prussia, 499; reproved by Benedict XIV, 225; restoration by Pius VII, 319; in Russia, 452; in Spain, 281, *283-85,* 293-94; structure of, 507; Voltaire on, 137

EXPULSIONS OF: from France, 88, 92, 266; from Naples, 284, 315; papacy and, 316-18; from Parma, 284, 317; from Philippines, 284; from Portugal, *266-67,* 317; from Spain, 266, 281, *283-85,* 293, 317; from Spanish America, 284

Jesus Christ, loyalty to Judaism, 629

Jews, 252, *629-42;* art and literature of, 636-37, 641; in Austria, 343, 352, 357, *631-32,* 641-42; in banking and finance, 630; in Bohemia, *631-32,* 641; castes among, 630; in Denmark, 635; in England, *635,* 684; in France, 91, 630, 642; French Revolution and, 642; in Galicia, *632,* 641; in Germany, 499, 507, 517, 632, *634,* 639, 642; Gibbon's discussion of, 802; Goethe's interest in, 556, 562; Hasidism among, 636; Haskalah movement among, 641-42; in Holland, *635,* 637, 642, 646-47; in Hungary, 631; influence of religion on, 629; Inquisition and, *630-631,* 633; intellectual liberation of, 637-42; in Islam, 632; in Italy, 250, 631, 642; Lessing's views on, 514-15; massacres by Cossacks, 633-34; messianism among, 635-37; in Moravia, 632, mystical movements among, 635-37; Napoleon and, 631; papacy and, *631,* 633; in Poland, 472, 475, 482, *632-34,* 636, 641; in Portugal, 260, 631; in Prussia, 499; ritual-murder trials against, 633; Rousseau on, 629-30; in Russia, 452, *632-33,* 641; Seven Years' War and, 53; in Silesia, 632; in Spain, 275-76, 285, *287, 630-31;* in Sweden, 635, 657; in Switzerland, 639; in Turkey, 632; in United States, 642, Voltaire's attitude toward, 629 30

Johanna Elisabeth of Holstein-Gottorp (1720–60), Princess of Anhalt-Zerbst, 121, 433

John, King of England (r. 1199–1216), 683

John III (Jan) Sobieski, King of Poland (r. 1674–96), 256, 411

John V, King of Portugal (r. 1706–50), 257, *260-61, 269;* appoints Pombal to ministry, 262

Johnson, Elizabeth, nee Porter (1688–1752), 818, 822

Johnson, Michael (1656–1731), 818, 819

Johnson, Samuel (1709–84), 701, 728-30, 740-41, 745, 747, 750, 762, 791, 810, *818-42;* on adultery, 731-32, 745; aid from government, 826-27; appearance of, 753, 818-19, 828-29; biographical writings of, 819-20, 836-37, 840-41; boarding school of, 819; Boswell and, *see* Boswell, James, JOHNSON AND; Burke and, 692, 827, 839-41; Cave and, 819-20, 822; on Chatterton, 810; Chesterfield and, 821, 823; on consumption of alcohol, 729; conversational ability of, 819, 830-31; death of, 839; *Dictionary* of, 786; dramatic works of, 819, 822; early years and education of, 818-19; fear of hell,

818, 838; first marriage of, 818, 822; on flying, 825; founds Ivy Lane Club, 822; friendships of, 827, 839-40; Garrick and, 741-42, 818, 822, 830; George III and, 826, 830, 835; on Gibbon, 805; goes to London, 819; Goldsmith and, *814-17*, 830; household of, 822-23; invents Parliamentary debates, 820; issues edition of Shakespeare, 835; journalistic writings of, 819, 822, 825; on London, 743; on newspaper advertisements, 786; opposes American Revolution, 711, 833; opposes French Enlightenment, 834-35; opposes slavery, 733, 832; in *Ossian* controversy 768; personality of, 818, 839-40; poems of, 819, 821; public honors for, 835; relations with Anna Williams, 822; religious views of, 834; Reynolds and, 827; rudeness of, 771; Savage and, 820; Sheridan's aid to, 694-95; social and political conservatism of, 692; Mrs. Thrale and, 828, 837-38; views on poets, 836-37; wisdom of, 839; writes *Dictionary*, 820, 823-25; writes *Rasselas*, 825-26
Johnson, Sarah, nee Ford (1669–1759), 818
"Jolly Beggars, The" (Burns), 776
Joly de Fleury, Omer (1715–1810), 189
Jommelli, Niccolò (1714–74), 100, 223, 254, *255*, 333, 335, 368
Jones, John Paul (1747–92), 911
Jones, Sir William (1746–94), 412
Jonson, Ben (1573?–1637), 744
Joseph I (José Manoel), King of Portugal (r. 1750–77): ascends throne, 261; assassination attempt against, 264, 283; confirms appointment of Pombal to cabinet, 261; illness and death of, 270-71; Jesuits and, 264, 266; mistress of, 263
Joseph II, Holy Roman Emperor (r. 1765–90), 334, 342, *346-66*, 387, 453, 457-58, 499, 504, 556, 581, 802, 846, 880, 885; abilities of, 355; absolutist views of, 355; administrative competence of, 849; attitude toward Jesuits, 351-52; capitulation to Hungarian nobles, 364; Catherine II and, 363, 462, 483; Church and, 358-62; conflict with papacy, 318, 359-60; crowned King of the Romans, 347; death of, 365, 461; early life and education of, 346-47, 367; educational policies of, 352; as enlightened despot, 354-60; failure of, 364-66; foreign policy of, 353; Frederick II and, 62, 349, 353-54, 361-63; historical importance of, 365-66; influence of Enlightenment on, 346-47, 351-52, 354-60; Jews and, 631-32; journey to Russia, 459-60; jurisdiction during coregency, 348; Kaunitz and, 348-52, 355, 359; League of Princes against (1785), 362-63; Louis XVI and, 353-54; makes Grimm a baron, 893; Maria Theresa and, 343, 346, *348-54*; Marie Antoinette and, 352-54, 362, 853-54; marriage to Isabella of Parma, 347; marriage to Josepha of Bavaria, 347-48; memorandum on policies, 348-49; moral probity of, 355; Moravian Protestants and, 353; Mozart and, 404-5; musical interests of, 334; partition of Poland and, 483; personality and appearance of, 347;

philosophes and, 353; popular hatred of, 364; Protestant alliance against, 363; reforms of, 348-53, 355-61, 364-66; regulation of serfdom by, 350; religious toleration of, 348, 351-52, 357, 361-62; rescinds all reforms, 364; revolt of Hungary against, 360-61, 363-64; revolt of Netherlands against, 361-62, 364; supports Leopold's policies in Tuscany, 313-14; turns throne over to Leopold, 365; visit to Paris, 353; visit to Rousseau, 883, 897; war with Turkey (1788), 363
Josepha of Bavaria (d. 1767), 2d wife of Emperor Joseph II, 347-48
Josephine, Empress, *see* Beauharnais, Joséphine de
Josephson, Matthew, 5*
Joshagan, 421
Jouffroy d' Abbans, Marquis Claude-François de (1751–1832), 932
Journal de Paris, 875, 915
Journal des savants, 280
Journal of a Tour to the Hebrides (Boswell), 836, 840
Journals of the House of Commons, 707
Journée des Tuiles (1787), 947-48
Journey from St. Petersburg to Moscow (Radishchev), 465
Journey to the Western Islands of Scotland, A (Johnson), 768, 836
Jovellanos, Gaspar Melchor de (1744–1811), *286-87*, 293, 302; comedies of, 296; Meléndez and, 295-96; poetry of, 295; on Spanish sales taxes, 288
Joyeuse Entrée, 361
Judaism, 629; *see also* Jews
Juden, Die (Lessing), 509
Juigné, Marquis de (fl. 1771), 883
Julian the Apostate (Flavius Claudius Julianus), Roman Emperor (r. 361–63), 803
Julie, ou La Nouvelle Héloïse (Rousseau), 27, 113, 128, 149, *165-70*, 177-79, 197, 521, 563, 887, 889; *Clarissa* compared with, 169-70; defects of, 168; educational ideas in, 168; letter form of, 166; models for, 157, 168; *philosophes* and, 170; plot of, 166-67; popularity of, 168-69; publication of, 178; Romantic movement and, 169; writing of, 155, 158, *165*
Julli, M. de, 36
Jung, Heinrich (1740–1817), 503
Jungfrau von Orleans, Die (Schiller), 602
"Junius" (fl. 1768–72), 669, 701, 705-6
Junker, 497
Justine (Sade), 904
Juvenal (59–c.140), 295

Kabale und Liebe (Schiller), 572
Kabul, 417, 419
Kagul, battle of (1770), 458
Kalb, Charlotte von (1761–1843), 573, 575, 591-592, 594
Kames, Henry Home, Lord (1696–1782), 768

Kandahar, 417-19

Kant, Immanuel (1724–1804), 183, *531-51;* 557, 594, 618, 628, 639, 641, 643, 808; aesthetic philosophy of, 543, 595; appearance of, 549; attitude toward Frederick II, 540; *Critique of Judgment,* 543-44, 551; *Critique of Practical Reason,* 540-43; *Critique of Pure Reason,* 517, 535-40, 542-43; early career as teacher, 505, 532; early life and education of, 531-32; Goethe's attitude toward, 580; Herder and, 567, 580; on human nature, 545-46; Hume's influence on, 536; 543; influence of Enlightenment on, 521, 531, 550-51; liberal political views of, 547-49; moral philosophy of, 540-43; personality of, 532, 549; physical decline and death of, 550; posthumous writings of, 550; professorship in University of Königsberg, 534; regularity of daily life, 531; Romantic influences on, 531; Rousseau's influence on, 3, 179, 181, 518, 542-43, *889-90;* scientific writings of, 532-33; threatened by Frederick William II, 546-47; views on education, 548-49; Voltaire's influence on, 542

Kantemir, *see* Cantemir

Karelia, 460, 653, 663

Karim Khan, Persian ruler (r. 1750–79), 420

Karl Alexander, Duke of Württemberg (r. 1733–37), 634

Karl August, Duke (later Grand Duke) of Saxe-Weimar (r. 1775–1828), 34, 373, 503, 507, 521, 523, *552-53;* death of, 626; French Revolution and, 590; Goethe and, 545, 552, 566-67, 580, 581, 584-85, 586, 589, 590-91, 606, 615, 626; Herder and, 567, 577, 579, 580; Schiller and, 573, 575, 594, 602, 604, 605; in wars against French, 580, 591, 606, 607

Karl Eugen, Duke of Württemberg (r. 1737–1793), 133, 255, 502-3

Karl Friedrich, Duke of Holstein-Gottorp (fl. 1725), 429, 432

Karl Friedrich Ulrich, Duke of Holstein-Gottorp, *see* Peter III, Czar

Karl Theodor, Elector Palatine (r. 1733–99), Elector of Bavaria (r. 1778–99), 48, 133, 245, 353-54, 362, 390, 393, 507

Karl Wilhelm Ferdinand (1735–1806), Prince and later Duke of Brunswick (r. 1780–1806), 512, 517

Karnal, battle of (1739), 419

Károlyi, Count (fl. 1788), 363

Karpiński, Franciszek (1741?–1825), 486

Katt, de (fl. 1758), 54

Kauffmann, Angelica (1741–1807), 580, 587, *644-45*

Kaufmann, Christoph, 520

Kaunitz, Count Wenzel Anton von (1711–94), *40-42,* 61, 120, 330; Joseph II and, 347-52, 355, 359; Seven Years' War and, 40-42, 44-46

Kay, John (fl. 1733–64), 673

Kazan, 455

Kazvin, 418-19

Keats, John (1795–1821), 810

Keene, Sir Benjamin (1697–1757), 279

Keith, George, 10th Earl Marischal (1693?–1778), 191-92, 214

Keith, James Francis Edward, Marshal (1696–1758), 43

Kellgren, Johan Henrik (1751–95), 659, *661;* Voltaire's influence on, 880

Kemal Atatürk Pasha (1881–1938), 415

Kemble, John Philip (1757–1823), 740

Kemble, Sarah, *see* Siddons, Sarah

kemengeh, 416

Kepler, Johann (1571–1630), 532

Keppel, Augustus, Viscount (1725–86), 751

Kerch, 458

Kerman, 421

Kermanshah, battle of (1726), 418

Kéroualle, Louise-Renée de, Duchess of Portsmouth (1649–1734), 693

Kestner, Charlotte ("Lotte"), nee Buff (1753–1828), 524, 559, 561-63, 613

Kestner, Georg Christian (1741–1800), *561 64*

Kew Gardens, 748

Keyserling, Count (fl. 1763), 457

Kherson, Jews in, 633

Khurasan, 418

Khiva, Khan of (fl. 1740), 420

Kiellström, Maria (1744–98), 660

Kiev, anti-Semitic massacres in, 634

Kilburun, 415, 458

Kimbolton Castle, 235

kindergartens, establishment of, 888

"King Christian Stood by the Lofty Mast" (Ewald), 652

King Lear (Shakespeare), 511

Kirghiz tribes, 455

Klauer, Ludwig (b. 1782), 523

Klauer, Martin (1742–1801), 523

Kleist, Ewald von (1715–59), 55

Kleist, Heinrich von (1777–1811), 507

Klettenberg, Susanne von (1723–74), 558

Klinger, Friedrich Maximilian von (1752–1831), 521-22, 581

Klopstock, Friedrich Gottlieb (1724–1803), 327, 373, 517, 520, 553, 581, 652, 661; criticism of Goethe, 267; as Freemason, 507; writes *The Messiah,* 517-18

Klopstock, Margareta, nee Moller (d. 1758), 517

Kloster-Zeven, Convention of (1757), 48, 50

Knebel, Karl Ludwig von (1744–1834), 619

Kniaznin, Franciszek Dyonizy (1750–1807), 486

Knox, John (1505–72), 773

Knutzen, Martin (1713–51), 532

Köchel, Ludwig Alois Friedrich (1800–77), 385, 396

Kolin, battle of (1757), 47

Kollontaj, Hugo (1750–1812), 486

Komarczewski, Pan, 474

Komische Erzählungen (Wieland), 553

Konarski, Stanislas (1700–73), 475

König, Eva (d. 1778), 503, 512-13

Königliche Bibliothek, Berlin, 524-25

Königsberg, University of, 505, 532

Konstantin, Duke of Saxe-Weimar (d. 1758), 552

Koran, 412

Korff, Ivan (1696–1766), 429

Korff, Nikolai, 439

Körner, Christian Gottfried (1756–1831), 572-575, 592

Kosciusko, Thaddeus (1746–1817), 488-89, *491-492*

Koslov, 430

Kozlovsky, M. I. (1753–1802), 467

Krasicki, Ignacy (1735–1801), 485-86

Krasiński, Adam, bishop of Kamieniec (fl. 1768), 481

Krefeld, battle of (1758), 53

Kremlin, 469

Kritik der praktischen Vernunft (Kant), *see Critique of Practical Reason*

Kritik der reinen Vernunft (Kant), *see Critique of Pure Reason*

Kritik der Urteilskraft (Kant), *see Critique of Judgment*

Kritische Wälder (Herder), 568

Kronborg, Castle of, 653

Kropotkin, Peter (1842–1921), 819

Kuban River, 430

Kuchuk Kainarji, Treaty of (1774), 415, 458

kulaki, 422

Kunersdorf, battle of (1759), 55

Künstler, Die (Schiller), 595

Kurakin, Princess Elena, 437

Kurland, 492

La Barre, Chevalier Jean-François Lefebre de (1747–66), 90

Labat, Père Jean-Baptiste (1663–1738), 217

La Blache, Comte de, 921

labor unions: in England, 679-80; in France, 933

La Bruyère, Jean de (1645–96), 859

Lacat, M., 23

La Chalotais, Louis-René de (1701–85), 92

Laclos, Pierre Choderlos de (1741–1803), 903-4, 914, 955-56

Lacy, James (d. 1774), 742

Lafayette, Marie-Joseph-Paul-Gilbert du Motier, Marquis de (1757–1834), 898; in American Revolution, 869, 871-72; as Freemason, 939; idealism of, 929; liberalism of, 957; opposition to slavery, 935; Duc d'Orléans and, 955

La Fayette, Marie-Madeleine Pioche de la Vergne, Comtesse de (1634–93), 169

La Ferté-Imbault, Marquise de, nee Geoffrin (b. 1715), 121

La Fontaine, Jean de (1621–95), 486

La Force, prison of, 962

Lagos, battle of (1759), 57

La Guépière, Philippe de (1715–73), 525

Laguerre, Marie-Joséphine (d. 1783), 373

Laharpe, Frédéric-César de (1754–1838), Swiss politician, 127, 470, *645*

Laharpe, Jean-François de (1739–1803), French poet, 127, 133, 149-50, 372, 874, 879

laissez faire policy, defined, 72; *see also* free trade

Lalande, Joseph-Jérôme Le François de (1732–1807), 254

Laleli-Jamissi, mosque of, 414

La Live de Jully, Ange-Laurent de (1725–75), 112

Lally, Comte Thomas-Arthur de, Baron de Tollendal (1702–66), 59, 957

La Luzerne, César-Guillaume de (1738–1821), bishop of Langres, 902

La Marck, Mme. de, 929

Lamarck, Jean-Baptiste de Monet, Chevalier de (1744–1829), 617

Lamartine, Alphonse de (1790–1869), 889-90

Lamballe, Prince de (d. 1767), 852

Lamballe, Marie-Thérèse de Savoie-Carignan, Princesse de (1749–92), 95, 848, 852

Lamennais, Félicité de (1782–1854), 890

La Mettrie, Julien Offroy de (1709–51), 220, 246-47, 316

La Mothe, Jean-Baptiste Vallin de (1729–1800), 468

La Motte, "Comte" Marc-Antoine-Nicolas de (1754–1831), 942

La Motte, Jeanne de St.-Rémy de Valois, Comtesse de (1756–91), 942-43

Lampe (servant of Heine), 543

land enclosures in England, 816

Landeshut, battle of (1760), 60

land reform, 287-88

Lane, Edward William (1801–81), 416

Lange, Joseph (fl. 1781), 394

Langhans, Karl Gotthard (1732–1808), 525

Langton, Bennet (1737–1801), 827, 839

Lannes, Jean, Marshal of France (1769–1809), 606

Lanskoi, Alexis (d. 1784), 444, 446

Lanson, Gustave (1857–1934), 5

Laokoon (Lessing), 510, 557, 691

La Pérouse, Jean-François de Galaup, Comte de (1741–1788?), 856

Laplace, Pierre-Simon (1749–1827), 533

La Popelinière, Alexandre-Joseph de (1692–1762), 70-71, 102

Larive, Jean Maudit de (1747–1827), 878

La Roche, Georg von, 562

La Roche, Maximiliane von (fl. 1772), 562

La Roche, Sophie von, nee Gutermann (1731–1807), 562, 611

La Rochefoucauld, Dominique de, Cardinal (1713–1800), 91

La Rochefoucauld, Duc François de (1613–80), 915, 939

La Rochefoucauld d'Enville, Duc Louis-Alexandre de (1743–92), 869

La Rochefoucauld-Liancourt, Duc François-Alexandre de (1747–1827), 898, 957, 963

Last Testament (Frederick II), 529-30

La Tour, Mme. de, 191, 214

La Tour, Père de, 148

La Tour, Maurice-Quentin de (1704–88), 23, 26, 120, 135, 235
La Tour d'Auvergne, Comte Nicolas de, 323
La Trémoille, Marie-Anne de, Princesse des Ursins (1642?–1722), 276
Laudon, Baron Gideon Ernst von (1717–90), 55, 59-60, 363, 365
Launay, Marquis Bernard-René de (1740–89), 919, 962-63
La Vallière, Mme. de, salonnière, 118
Lavater, Johann Kaspar (1741–1801), 562-63, 565-67, 613, 639, 645, 888
Lavoisier, Antoine-Laurent de (1741–1801), 869, 936, 955
law: Burke's early views on, 690; Vico's theory of, 252; see also legal reform
Law, John (1671–1729), financier, 630
Law, William (1686–1761), 796
Laws (Plato), 177
La-Yesharim Tehilla (Luzzatto), 637
Lazienski Palace, 479
League of Princes, German (1785), 362-63
Lebel, valet of Louis XVI (1768), 86
Lebèque, Agnès, 918
Lebon, Philippe (1767–1804), 676
Le Brun, Charles (1619–90), 913
Lebrun, J.-B.-Pierre (1748–1813), 913
Le Clerc, Jean (1657–1736), 253
Lecouvreur, Adrienne (1692–1730), 102
Lee, Arthur (1740–92), 869
Leeds, 681
legal reform: in Austria, 344; in England, 736-38; in Prussia, 500; in Russia, 450–52; in Sweden, 657
Leghorn, 220, 228
Légion d'Honneur, Palais de la, 910
Legislative Assembly, French, see National Assembly, French
Legros (Le Gros), Joseph (1730–93), 370-71, 392
Leibniz, Gottfried Wilhelm von (1646–1716), 13, 294, 531-32, 534, 536, 637
Leibowicz, Jankiew (Jacob Frank; 1726–91), 636
Leiden, 361; University of, 647
Leiden des jungen Werthers, Die (Goethe), see Sorrows of Young Werther
Leilan, battle of (1733), 419
Leipzig: authors in, 506; orchestra in, 525; University of, 557
Leipziger Liederbuch, Das, 557
Leipziger Zeitung, Die, 506
Leitmeritz, Frederick II at, 47
Lekain (Cain), Henri-Louis (1728–78), 101-2, 136, 920
Lemaître, Jules (1853–1914), 5*
Le Maître, Nicoloz (fl. 1729), 10
Lemberg, university at, 360
Lemercier de la Rivière (1720–94), 74-75, 657
Lemoyne, Jean-Baptiste (1704–78), 107
Lengefeld, Caroline von, 594
Lengefeld, Charlotte von (1766–1826), 594
Lenin, Nikolai (1870–1924), 891

Lenngren, Anna Maria, nee Malmstedt (1754–1817), 662
Lenngren, Karl Peter, 661
Lennox, Caroline, Lady Holland, 693
Lennox, John Stuart, 3d Earl of (d. 1526), 779
"Lenore" (Bürger), 519-20
Lenz, Jakob Michael Reinhold (1751–92), 503, 521, 562, 581, 612
Leo, Leonardo (1694–1744), 240, 254-55, 333
Leo XIII (Gioacchino Vincenzo Pecci), Pope (r. 1878–1903), 247
Leopold II, Holy Roman Emperor (r. 1790–92), Grand Duke of Tuscany as Leopold I (r. 1765–90): as Grand Duke, 76, 310, 313-14, 346, 354, 363, 846; as Holy Roman Emperor, 314, 334, 365, 406, 407, 664
Leopold, Carl Gustaf af (1756–1829), 661
Leopold of Brunswick, Prince, 513
Lepanto, battle of (1571), 229
Lepeletier de Saint-Fargeau, Louis-Michel (1760–93), 913
Le Roy, Julien-David (1724–1803), 110
Lespinasse, Julie de (1732–76), 118, 120, 122-31, 656, 858, 894; d'Alembert and, 122-28, 130, 892; death of, 130-31; description of, 127; Mme. du Deffand and, 122-23; early life of, 122; on Gluck's Orfeo, 909; illness of, 125-26; letters to Guibert, 128-30, 131*; love for Guibert, 128-30; love for Mora, 127-28; popularity of, 123, 125; salon of, 126-27, 906
Lessing, Gotthold Ephraim (1729–81), 331, 507-8; 557, 567-68, 578, 628, 641, 691; aesthetic theories of, 510-11; appearance and personality of, 512; conflicts with theologians, 513-16; criticism of Goethe, 627; death of, 640; early life and education of, 508-9; early literary activities of, 508-9; Eva König and, 512-13; as first German professional writer, 506; as Freemason, 507; friendship with Elise Reimarus, 512; Goethe and, 563-64; influence of, 517, 520; influences on, 510; in Italy, 513; later years and death of, 517; liberating influence on literature, 511; as librarian of Prince of Brunswick, 512-13; as literary critic, 506; marriage and death of wife, 513; Moses Mendelssohn and, 509, 515, 637-38, 640; National Theater and, 511; opposition to aristocratic privilege, 513; philosophical views of, 516; plays of, 509-11, 513-15; on Prussian despotism, 530; publishes Reimarus manuscript, 513; on truth, 512; views on religion, 515-16; Voltaire and, 509, 512; writes Laokoon, 510; writes Nathan the Wise, 514-15
Leszczinska, Marie, see Marie Leszczinska
Leszczyński, Stanislas, see Stanislas I
Letter to a Member of the National Assembly (Burke), 724
Letter to Christophe Beaumont (Rousseau), 195, 197
Letter to Dr. J.-J. Pansophe (Rousseau), 212
Lettere filosofiche (Gentile), 219

Letters from the Mountain (Rousseau), *see Lettres écrites de la montagne*
Letters of an Anonymous Writer to the President of the Diet (Kollontaj), 486
Letters on a Regicide Peace (Burke), 725
Letters on the Aesthetic Education of Mankind (Schiller), 551
Letters on the Antiquity of Herculaneum (Winckelmann), 328
Letters to and from the Late Samuel Johnson (Thrale), 840
"Letters to Eliza" (Sterne), 790
Letters to His Son (Chesterfield), 283
Lettre à M. d'Alembert sur les spectacles (Rousseau), 162-64
Lettre sur la musique française (Rousseau), 372
"Lettre sur la Providence" (Rousseau), 154-55
lettres de cachet, 850, 948, 950
Lettres de cachet (Mirabeau *fils*), 953
Lettres écrites de la campagne (Tronchin), 197
Lettres écrites de la montagne (Rousseau), 184, 188, 197, 199, 205
Lettres provinciales (Pascal), 139, 514
Lettres sur la danse et les ballets (Noverre), 100
Lettres sur La Nouvelle Héloïse (Voltaire), 170
Leuthen, battle of (1757), 51-52
Levasseur, Thérèse (b. 1722), *17-18*, 152, 156-57, 161, 178; Boswell and, 202-4, 783; children sent to foundling asylum, 18, 24, 201; in England, 210-11, 214; Rousseau's final years with in France, 881-83, 886-87; in Switzerland, 192, 202-7 *passim;* Voltaire on, 200
Levellers, 80
Levett, Robert (1705-82), 823
Levetzow, Amalie von, 614
Levetzow, Ulrike von (1804-99), 614
Leviathan (Hobbes), 172
Levitsky, Dmitri (1735-1822), 466-67
Lezioni di commercio (Genovesi), 250
L'Hôpital, Michel de (1507-73), 865
Liaisons dangereuses, Les (Laclos), 903, 914
liberum veto of Polish Diet, 473, 476-77, 480-81, 484, 488, 885
libraries: in France, 914; in Italy, 219-20; in German states, 506
Libya, 411
Lichnowsky, Prince Karl von (fl. 1789), 405
Lidner, Bengt (1758-93), 661-62
Liechtenstein, Joseph Wenzel, Prince of (b. 1696–d. 1772), 38
lieder, 525
Liège, 342
Liegnitz, battle of (1760), 60
Life and Letters of Gray (Mason), 841
Life and Opinions of Tristram Shandy, The (Sterne), 787-89
Life of Johnson (Hawkins), 282
Life of Richard Savage, The (Johnson), 820
Life of Samuel Johnson, The (Boswell), 753 840-41
Life of Swift (Sheridan), 695
Life of Voltaire (Goldsmith), 814

Ligne, Prince Charles-Joseph de (1735-1814), 101, 133, 342, 365, 459-60, 883; on Catherine II, 11, 461; description of Voltaire, 134; of St. Petersburg, 469; on Voltaire, 135
Liguori, St. Alfonso de' (1696-1787), 225
Lillo, George (1693-1739), 509
Lima, Ignez Elena de, 261
Limburg, 342
Limoges, Turgot's reforms in, 79-80
Linguet, Simon-Nicolas-Henri (1736-94), 80, *82;* French Revolution and, 938, 940
Linley, Thomas (1732-95), 695
Linnaeus, Carolus (Carl von Linné; 1707-78), 206, 565, 658
Linz, woolen mills in, 344
Lionhard und Gertrude (Pestalozzi), 644
Lippe, Count Wilhelm zu, 568
Lisbon, *259,* 260, 267, 270; earthquake of, *261,* 263, 533
Lister, Thomas, 752
lit de juseice, 946
Literary Magazine, The, 786
literature: in Austria, 345-46; in Denmark, *649-52;* in England, 518, *786-840;* in France, *104-6, 914-26,* (see also Rousseau; Voltaire); in Germany, 507, *509-22, 552-628;* in Holland, 647; in Italy, 220, *239-44, 335-40;* of Jews, 636-37; in Persia, 421; in Poland, 485-86; in Portugal, 260, 269-70; Rousseau's influence on, 3-4, 889; in Russia, 889; in Scotland, 767-68, *772-85,* 841-42; in Spain, 295-96; in Sweden, 659-62; in United States, 889
Lithuania, 492
Litta, Conte Cavaliere Agostino (fl. 1754), 527
Little Dorrit (Dickens), 738
Little Theatre, 740
Liverpool: growth of, 681; as port city, 669; slave market in, 732; theater in, 740
Lives of Eminent Persons (Johnson), 819
Lives of the Poets, The (Johnson), 820, 830, *836-37*
Livonia, 39, 422, 653, 663
Lloyd's Evening News, 212
Lobkowitz, Prince Ferdinand von, 367
Lobositz, battle of (1756), 45
Lobstein, Dr. (fl. 1770), 568
Locandera, La (Goldoni), 242
Locatelli, Pietro (1695-1764), 228
Locke, John (1632-1704), 171-72, 177, 179-80, 250, 280, 294-95, 427, 485, 487, 531, 637, 725, 891
Loménie de Brienne, Étienne-Charles (1724-94), 126, 901, *945-48*
Lomonosov, Mikhail Vasilievich (1711-65), 427
London: administration of city, 744; appearance of, 743-44; brothels in, 744; commerce in, 745; complexity of, 745; Gordon Riots in (1780), 735-36; Jews in, 635; music in, 368; population of, 745; as port city, 669; prostitution in, 744-45; revolutionary spirit of, 705; Rousseau's flight to, 209-10; slums in, 745; theater in, 740; voting population in, 685

London (Johnson), 819
London Chronicle, The (periodical), 783
London Journal (Boswell), 778*, 780
London Merchant, The (Lillo), 509
London Packet, 817
London Symphonies Nos. 93-104 (Haydn), 378, 381
Longhi, Alessandro (1733–1813), 331
Longhi, Pietro (1702–85), 236, 331
looms, power, 673
Lords, House of, *see* House of Lords
Lorrain, Claude (Claude Gellée; 1600–82), 327, 751
Lorraine, 928
Losenko, Anton Pavlovich (1737–73), 466-67
Lotti, Antonio (1667?–1740), 232-33
Louis, Dauphin of France, *see* Louis de France, Dauphin
Louis, Victor (1731–1800), 101
Louis I King of Spain, *see* Luis I
Louis XIV, King of France (r. 1643–1715), 95, 273, 331; bourgeoisie and, 934; Spain and, 293
Louis XV, King of France (r. 1715–74), *84-96*, 116, 235, 278, 664, 911; abolishes tolls, 76; assassination attempt against, 67, 91; Austrian alliance and, 40-42, 45, 347, 846; Beaumarchais and, 920-22; Choiseul and, 53, 56, 88-89, 94, 656; conflict with Paris Parlement, *90-95;* death of, 95-96, 352, 454, 848, 904; defense of d'Aiguillon, 93; on execution of Malagrida, 267; extravagance of, 84; Frederick II and, 40-41; grief for Mme. de Pompadour's death, 69; household expenditures of, 84; immorality of, 85-86, 344, 429; invites Rousseau for audience, 25; Jansenists and, 85; Louis XVI and, 845-47; Mozart programs for, 384; personality of, 85; popular hatred of, 84-85, 96; Protestants and, 901; reign of, *67-96;* religiosity of, 67; Seven Years' War and, 45, 53, 56-57; Voltaire and, 88, 137
Louis XVI (Louis-Auguste), King of France (r. 1774–92), 353, 802, *845-72;* aids parish priests, 901; American Revolution and, 870; appeals to people (1788), 948; appearance of, 845, *856;* authority of, 850; Beaumarchais' services for, 922; becomes father, 855; bondholders and, 937; Brienne ministry and, *945-48;* Calonne ministry and, 943-45; charity of, 904-5; conflicts with *parlements* (1787–88), 946-48; conflicts with States-General (1789), 958-61; democratic attitudes of, 905; Diamond Necklace Affair and, *942;* difficulty in consummating marriage, 847-48, 853-54; diplomatic considerations in marriage, 846; early liberalism of, 867; execution of, 469, 725, 726, 857, 895; extravagance of, 944; flight to Varennes, 896; frees royal serfs, 928; French Revolution and, 896, 900-63 *passim;* Gustavus III's aid to, 664; issues edict of religious toleration (1787), 902; Joseph II and, 353-54, 854, 856; kindness of, 851-52, 856-57; Louis XV and, 845, 847; love for crafts, *857;* love of masses for, 899; Marie Antoinette and, 436, 847, 851-52; Maurepas'

ministry and, 858; Necker's first ministry and, 867; Necker's second ministry and, *948;* personality of, 845-46, 856; popularity of, *857;* Protestants and, 902; refuses to have priest teach Dauphin, 901; religiosity of, 857; second dismissal of Necker, 961; simplicity of, 904; summons States-General (1788), 948; trial before Convention, 895; Turgot's ministry and, 859-60, 863-65; Voltaire and, 873, 875, 879; weaknesses of will, 856; wedding of, 244
Louis XVII (Louis-Charles de France; b. 1785), titular King of France (1793–95), 941
Louis XVIII (Louis-Stanislas-Xavier, Comte de Provence), King of France (r. 1814–15, 1815–1824), 845
Louis-Auguste, Duc de Berry, *see* Louis XVI
Louis-Charles de France (b. 1785), Dauphin, *see* Louis XVII
Louis de France (1661–1711), "Le Grand Dauphin," son of Louis XIV, 276
Louis de France (1729–65), Dauphin, son of Louis XV, 68, 109, 845, 898-99
Louis-Joseph, Duc de Bourgogne, *see* Bourgogne, Duc de
Louis-Joseph-Xavier de France (1781–89), Dauphin, son of Louis XVI, 855, 961
Louis-Stanislas-Xavier, Comte de Provence, *see* Louis XVIII
Louisa Ulrika (1720–82), Queen of Adolphus Frederick of Sweden, 34, 655, 658
Louisbourg, British siege of, 57
Louise, Queen of Prussia, *see* Luise of Mecklenburg-Strelitz
Louise-Élisabeth de France, Duchess of Felipe of Parma, 311
Louise-Marie de France (1737–87), 95
Louisiana, Spain acquires, 62
Louvain, 342, 361, 364
Louvain, University of, 360, 362
Louveciennes, Château of, 87
Louviers, factories in, 932
Love of the Three Oranges, The (Prokofiev), 243*
Löwenwolde (lover of Anna Ivanovna), 429
Lowther, Sir James (1736–1802), 697
Loyola, St. Ignatius of (1491–1556), 267, 283
Lubomirska, Elizabeth, 479
Lucca, 220, 310
Lucio Silla (Mozart), 388
Lucretius (96?–55 B.C.), 251, 486, 532, 691
Ludwig, of Württemberg, Prince (fl. 1762), 489
Ludwig Ernst of Brunswick-Wolfenbüttel, Regent of Holland (r. 1759–66), 648
Ludwigsburg, 523
Luis I, King of Spain (r. 1724), 283
Luise (Voss), 519, 601
Luise of Hesse-Darmstadt, Duchess of Karl August of Saxe-Weimar, 552
Luise (Louise) of Mecklenburg-Strelitz (1776–1810), Queen of Frederick William III of Prussia, 523
Lully, Jean-Baptiste (1632–87), 372

Lumley, Elizabeth, *see* Sterne, Elizabeth

Lunar Society, 734

Lund, University of, 659

Lutf 'Ali Beg Adar (1711–81), 421

Luther, Martin (1483–1546), 360, 561, 620, 628, 881

Luttrell, Henry (1743–1821), 704

Luxembourg, 342

Luxembourg, Charles-François de Montmorency, Maréchal Duc de (1702–64), 97, 125, 201; Rousseau and, 161-62, 189, 898

Luxembourg, Madeleine-Angélique, Maréchale Duchesse de, earlier Duchesse de Boufflers (1707–87), 118, 161-62, 907, 929

Luxeuil, Abbey of, 928

Luzán y Martínez, José (1710–85), 300

Luze, Jean-Jacques de (fl. 1765), 209-10

Luzzatto, Moses Chayim (1707–47), 636-37

Lycurgus (7th cent. B.C.), 253

Lyons: industry in, 933; poverty in, 933; proletariat in, 933; riots in, 954; stores in, 936; strikes in, 933-34; unemployment in, 934; workers' revolt in, 933-34

Mably, Gabriel Bonnot de (1709–85), 14, 80, *82-84*, 220, 901; death of, 893; French Revolution and, 84, 938, 940; influence of, 94; in Lespinasse salon, 126; sees need for popular religion, 903; writes a constitution for Poland (1770–71), 482

Mably, Jean Bonnot de, grand provost of Lyons (fl. 1740), 14, 82

Mably family, Rousseau as tutor for, 178

Macaulay, Thomas Babington (1800–59), 246, 725, 785, 793

Macbeth (Shakespeare), 740

Macdonald, Frederika, 5*

Macedo, José Agostinho de (1761–1831), 269-70

Macgregor, James (fl. 1512), 767

Machado de Castro, Joachim (1731–1822), 270

Machault d'Arnouville, Jean-Baptiste (1701–94), 850

Machiavelli, Niccolò (1469–1527), 251, 548, 766; influence of, 338; law of development and return, 253

Maciejowice, battle of (1794), 491-92

Mackenzie, Henry (1745–1831), 790

Macklin, Charles (1697?–1797), 740

M'Lehose, Agnes, nee Craig (1759–1841), 776

McLeod, Lady, 831-32

Macpherson, James (1736–96), 559, 567, 764, 767-68, 809; influence in Germany, 518

Madama, Palazzo, 226

Madras: English stronghold at, 58; French siege of, 59

Madrasa-i-Shah-Husein, 420

Madrid, 293, beautification of, 289-90; cleaning up of, 282; factories in, 288; growth of, 289; merchant guilds in, 289; revolt of (1766), 282; royal palace in, 297; war of liberation in, 307

Maffei, Francesco Scipione di (1675–1755), 220, *228-29*

Mafra, Convent of, 261

Magellan, Ferdinand (1480?–1521), 259

magic, 356

Magic Flute, The (Mozart), 376, 528

Magna Carta (1215), 683, 709

Magnasco, Alessandro (1667?–1749), 227

Magyar nobles, 341

Mahmud, Mir of Afghanistan (r. 1717–25), Shah of Persia (r. 1722–25), 418

Mahmud I, Sultan of Turkey (r. 1730–54), 415

Mahomet (Voltaire), 246

Maimonides (Moses ben Maimon; 1135–1204), 637, 642

Maine, Sir Henry (1822–88), 849

Maini, Giovanni Battista (1690–1752), 247

Maintenon, Françoise d'Aubigné, Marquise de (1635–1719), 453

Mainz, *503;* archbishops of, 504-5; in Holy Roman Empire, 341; Jews in, 642; in League of Princes (1785), 362

Maistre, Joseph-Marie de (1753–1821), 725, 890

majas and *majos*, Spanish, 291

Malachowski, Stanislas (1735–1809), 490

Malagrida, Father Gabriel (1689–1761): arrest of, 265; conflict with Pombal, 265, 267-68; execution of, 267; hatred of, 270; missionary activities in Brazil, 263

Malesherbes, Chrétien-Guillaume de Lamoignon de (1721–94), 92, 98, 178; aids *Encyclopédie*, 861; Jews and, 642; as minister of Louis XV's household, 861; reforms of, 144; Rousseau and, 189; Turgot and, 861, 865

Malines, 361

Mallet du Pan, Jacques (1749–1800), 891

Malmesbury, Sir James Harris, 1st Earl of (1746–1820), 500

Malone, Edmund (1741–1812), 835

Malongei, Emerich, 363

Malory, Sir Thomas (fl. 1450), 768

Malouin, Dr. Paul-Jacques (1701–78), 200

Malthus, Thomas R. (1766–1834), 321, 894

Mamonov, Alexis (fl. 1786), 444, 446, 459

Manassah ben Israel (1604–57), 640

Manchester: growth of, 681; industry in, 672; theater in, 740

Mandeville, Bernard (1670?–1733), 770

mandolin, 417

Manger, Heinrich (1728–89), 524

Manila, 62

Manin, Lodovico, Doge of Venice (r. 1789–97), 311

Mann, Sir Horace (1701–86), 792

Mannheim, orchestra in, 525

Man of Feeling, The (Mackenzie), 790

Manon Lescaut (Prévost), 169

Mansfield, William Murray, 1st Earl of (1705–93), 736

Mantua, 245

Manzuoli, Giovanni (b. 1725), 746

Maragha, 418

Marat, Jean-Paul (1743–93), 891, 916; in Panthéon, 110

Maratha tribes, 717

Marcello, Alessandro (1684?–1750?), 233

Marcello, Benedetto (1686–1739), 223, 233, 234, 368

Marchais, Mme. de, 118

Marchionni, Carlo (1702–86), 331

Marcus Aurelius Antoninus, Emperor of Rome (r. 161–180), 496, 800-1

María I (María Francisca), Queen of Portugal (r. 1777–1816), 270-72

Maria Amalia of Austria (d. 1804), Duchess of Ferdinand III of Parma, 846

Maria Amalia of Austria (d. 1759), Queen of Charles III of Spain, 281

María Ana Victoria of Spain (b. 1719), Queen of Joseph I of Portugal, 270, 278

Maria Antonia, Archduchess, see Marie Antoinette, Queen

María Barbara of Portugal (d. 1758), Queen of Ferdinand VI of Spain, 257, 278

Maria Carolina of Austria (1752–1814), Queen of Ferdinand IV of Naples, 315, 346, 846

Maria Christina of Austria, Duchess of Saxe-Teschen (d. 1798), 361-62, 846

Maria Feodorovna, nee Sophia Dorothea Augusta of Württemberg, 2d wife of Paul I of Russia, 377, 462, 468

Mariage de Figaro (Beaumarchais), 403-4, 852, 923-25

María Josefa, Infanta, 305

Maria Josepha, Dauphine of France, see Marie-Josèphe of Saxony

Maria Josepha of Austria, Archduchess (d. 1767), 385-86

Maria Kazimiera (1641–1716), Queen of John I Sobieski of Poland, 256

María Luisa Gabriela of Savoy (1688–1714), Queen of Philip V of Spain, 276

María Luisa of Parma (1751–1819), Queen of Charles IV of Spain, 302

Mariana, Juan de (1536–1624), 177

Maria Stuarda (Alfieri), 338

Maria Theresa, ruler of Austria, Hungary, and Bohemia (r. 1740–80), *38-48*, 51, 235, 330, *342-54*, 942; abilities of, 38-39, 342-43; accession to Austrian throne, 278; ambitions in Italy, 228; attitude toward Church, 343; choice of able ministers, 344; conflicts with Joseph II, 350-54; co-regency of, *348-54*; death of, 354; delighted by Mozart, 383; Frederick II and, 38-48, 352; Frederick II on, 529-30; Hungarian nobles and, 341; Jews and, 631; Joseph II and, 343, 346, *348-54*; Marie Antoinette and, 343, 346, 846-47, 855; morality of, 344; papacy and, 318; partition of Poland and, 483; personality of, 343; Mme. de Pompadour and, 40-42, 45, 56; problems facing, 344-46; reactionary policies of, 343; relations with Frances of Lorraine, 346; response to Gluck's *Orfeo*, 369; Seven Years' War and, 38-48, 56, 61; Turgot's fall and, 865; upbringing of her children, 346

Marie-Adélaïde of France (Marie-Clotilde-Adélaïde-Xavère; 1759–1802), granddaughter of Louis XV, 111

Marie-Anne of Bavaria (1660–90), Dauphine of France, 118

Marie Antoinette (Maria Antonia; 1755–93), Queen of Louis XVI of France, 111, 369, 383, *846-48*, *850-56*, 887, 910, 922; aid to Chamfort, 915; aid to Gluck, 370-71; appearance of, 846, *854, 941;* Burke and, 722-23; Calonne ministry and, 945; charity of, 904-5; children of, 855, 941; democratic attitudes of, 905; diamond necklace episode and (1785), 941-43; difficulty in consummating marriage, 847-48, 853-54; Du Barry and, 88, 848; early life and education, 846; execution of, 270, 469, 725; extravagance of, 850-52, 944; fashions set by, 905; faults of, 850-52; first pregnancy of, 855; flight to Varennes, 896; friendships of, 848, 852-53; gaiety of, 851; Joseph II and 352-54, 362, 853-54, kindness of Louis XVI to, 851-52; Louis XVI and, 436, 847, 851-52; Maria Theresa and, 343, 346, 846-47, 855; marriage to Louis XVI, 244, 847; Necker's second ministry and (1788–89), 948; nicknamed "L'Autrichienne" and "Madame Deficit," 941; personality of, *846, 848, 850-51, 855-56;* popular hostility toward, 851, 853, 941; pretensions to naturalism, 852; States-General and, 961; theatricals of, 101; Turgot and, 863-65; Voltaire and, 873-75

Marie-Josèphe of Saxony (1731–67), Dauphine of France, 45, 48, 107, 845

Marie Leszczinska (1703–68), Queen of Louis XV of France, 86, 384

Marignac, Émilie de, 952

Marigny, Abel Poisson, Marquis de (1727–81), brother of Mme. de Pompadour, 105, 114

Marivaux, Pierre Carlet de Chamblain de (1688–1763), 15, 104

Marmontel, Jean-François (1723–99), 24, 27, 102, *104-106*, 108, 119-20, 149-50, 353, 371, 463, 656, 908; on d'Alembert's poverty, 126; on Mme. Geoffrin's piety, 121; Julie de Lespinasse and, 126-27; on Suzanne Necker, 908; opposition to Revolution, 898; Rousseau meets, 18; as supporter of Puccini, 372; visits ill Voltaire, 875, 876

marriage: in Austria, 348; in England, 731; in France, 97; in Italy, 218-19, 230; Rousseau's views on, 152, 186-87; in Spain, 290-91; Voltaire's views on, 146-47

Marriage of Figaro, The (Beaumarchais), 403-4, 852, 923-25

Marriage of Figaro, The (Mozart), 376, 388, 403-4

Marseilles: bread riot in, 954; factories in, 70; proletariat in, 933; shipbuilding in, 932

Marsilius of Padua (1290?–1343?), 177

Martel, Charles, see Charles Martel

Martin, Samuel (fl. 1763), 703

Martínez, Sebastián (fl. 1792), 302

Martini, Anton von (fl. 1780), 355

Martini, Padre Giovanni Battista (1706–84), 220, 245, 255, 386, 426

Martinique, 58, 89, 935; restored to France, 62

Martín y Solar (later Martini), Vicente (1754–1806), 292

Martos, Ivan Petrovich (1752–1835), 467

Marx, Karl (1818–83), 771, 880; Rousseau's influence on, 3, 891

Mary II, Queen of England, Scotland, and Ireland (r. 1689–94), 683

Mary Stuart, Queen of Scots (r. 1542–67), 338, 602, 766

Maskelyne, Nevil (1732–81), 764

Mason, William (1724–97), 809, 841

Massachusetts, conflicts with England, 709

Masson, Frédéric (1847–1923), 444, 469

Matrimonio segreto, Il (Cimarosa), 335

Mattino, Il (Parini), 335

Maubert, M. (fl. 1790), 117

Maupeou, René-Nicolas de (1714–92), 89, 93-94, 858

Maupertuis, Pierre-Louis Moreau de (1698–1759), 139, 427

Maurepas, Jean-Frédéric Phélypeaux, Comte de (1701–81), 858, 864, 925; American Revolution and, 870; death of, 97; dismissal of, 85; opposition to Necker, 870-71

Maximes (Chamfort), 914

Maximes morales et politiques tirées de Télémaque (Louis XVI), 845

Maximilian, Archduke (1756–1801), 389

Maximilian I, Holy Roman Emperor (r. 1493–1519), 560

Maximilian III Joseph, Elector of Bavaria (r. 1745–77), 353, 383, 388, 389

Mazanderan, 419

Mazarin, Jules, Cardinal (1602–61), 119

Mazzini, Giuseppe (1805-72), 340

Mazzolini, Signora (d. 1774), 219

Mecca, 415

Mecklenburg, in League of Princes (1785), 362

medical schools, 360

Medici, Anna Maria Ludovica de' (1667–1743), 228

Medici, Cosimo II *and* Cosimo III de', *see* Cosimo II *and* Cosimo III

Medici, Prince Ferdinand de' (1663–1715), 227

Medici, Giovan Gastone de', *see* Gian Gastone

Medici, Giuliano de' (1453–78), 338

Medici, Lorenzo de' (1449–92), 338, 620

Medici family, 228, 313

medicine, 276

Medina, London banker, 630

Medinaceli, Duke of (fl. 1785), 274

Medmenham Abbey, 809

"Mein Glaube" (Schiller), 595

Meissen, 749

Meissen factories, 523

Meister, Jakob, 893

Mélanges (Ligne), 342

Meléndez, Luis (1716-80), 299

Meléndez Valdés, Juan (1754–1817), 295-96

Melzi, Prince Francesco (fl. 1737), 227, 367

Mémoire justificatif (Gibbon), 800

Mémoire sur l'impôt (Turgot), 865

Mémoires (Brissot), 88

Mémoires (Grétry), 910

Mémoires d'un père (Marmontel), 104, 106, 908

Mémoires pour servir à l'histoire de la maison de Brandebourg (Frederick II), 528

Memoirs (Ali Hazin), 421

Memoirs (Beaumarchais), 921, 923

Memoirs (Carlo Gozzi), 243

Memoirs (Casanova), 219, 322-23

Memoirs (Catherine II of Russia), 433

Memoirs (Mme. d'Épinay), 26, 159

Memoirs (Gibbon), 766, 795-96, 798, 804

Memoirs (Goldoni), 241, 244

Menander (343?–291? B.C.), 241

Mendel, Menachem (fl. 1725), 637

Mendelssohn, Abraham (1776–1835), 641

Mendelssohn, Dorothea (1764–1839), 641

Mendelssohn, Felix (1809–47), 614-15, 637, 641

Mendelssohn, Fromet, nee Guggenheim, 638

Mendelssohn, Henrietta (1768–1831), 641

Mendelssohn, Moses (1729–86), 507, 637-41, 645; children of, 641; death of, 640; early life and education of, 637; influence of, 640-41; Kant and, 637; Lavater and, 639; Lessing and, 509, 515, 549, 637-38, 640; loyalty to Judaism, 639; marriage to Fromet Guggenheim, 638; pessimism of, 549; philosophical works of, 638-39; spreads Enlightenment among Jews, 640; writes *Phaidon*, 638; writings on Judaism, 640

Mendonça, Francisco de Almada e, *see* Almada e Mendonça, Francisco

Mengozzi-Colonna, Girolamo (fl. 1750), 238-39

Mengs, Anton Raphael (1728–79), 248-49, 258, 510, 523, 524, 912; artistic authority of, 332; death of, 332; revives classical style, 315; in Spain, 299, 300-1; Winckelmann and, 248-49, 327, 329, 331

Mengs, Margarita, nee Guazzi (d. 1778), 248, 332

Menshikov, Prince Alexander Danilovich (1672–1729), 429

mercantilism, 72, 770

mercenary troops, German, 504

Mercier, Louis-Sébastien (1740–1814), 919; on skepticism of upper classes, 901

Merck, Johann Heinrich (1741–91), 506, 521, 612

Mercure de France, 105, 370, 915

Mercure galant, 915

Mercy d'Argentau, Count Florimund (1727–94), 847, 851

Merlini, Domenico, 479

Merope (Maffei), 228

Mérope (Voltaire), 143, 228-29

Merry Muses of Caledonia, The, 776

Meslier, Jean (1678–1733), 80

Mesmer, Franz Anton (1734–1815), 645

Mesmes, Marquise de (fl. 1771), 883

Messiah (Handel), 742

Messiah (Haydn), 377, 379
Messiah, The (Klopstock), 517-18
Mesta (wool association), 273, 287-88
metal industry, 932
"Metamorphosis of Animals, The" (Goethe), 617
Metamorphosis of Plants, The (Goethe), 596, 617
Metastasio (Pietro Trapassi; 1698–1782), 223, 239, 254, 333, 368-69, 374, 407
meteorology, Goethe's contribution to, 615
Methodists, 636, 711, 735, 834
Metternich, Prince Clemens Wenzel von (1773–1859), 366
Meyerbeer, Giacomo (1791–1864), 525
Mezzogiorno, Il (Parini), 335
Michel, Claude, *see* Clodion
Michelangelo Buonarroti (1475–1564), 248, 751
Michelet, Jules (1798–1874), 137, 143*, 254, 889
Middle Ages, 809, 895
middle class: in art forms, 113-14; in Austria, 356; in Austrian Netherlands, 362; drama and, 104; in England, 670, 676-77, 680-81, 706; in France, 848-49, 902, 914, 956-61; French Revolution and, 899, 934-37, 939; in Geneva, 143; in Germany, 503; in Italy, 218, 230; love of music, 367; in Naples, 249; physiocrats and, 77; in Poland, 474, 491; in Prussia, 497; in Russia, 423, 455-56; in Scotland, 762; in Spain, 274, 277, 280, 289; Sturm und Drang movement and, 522; in Switzerland, 643
Middleton, Conyers (1683–1750), 792
Mignot, Abbé (nephew of Voltaire), 879
Milan: Austrian control of, 217; Beccaria in, 310; churches in, 224; Goethe in, 589; history and achievements, 226-27; industry in, 218, 312; Jesuit colleges in, 219; library in, 219; prostitution in, 218; theaters in, 220; university in, 219
Mill, James (1773–1836), 739
Mill, John Stuart (1806–73), 738-39
Milton, John (1608–74), 177, 518, 773, 837, 842
Mina Löjen (Kellgren), 661
Minden: battle of (1758), 54-55; Frederick II reoccupies, 53
mining, 932
Ministry of All the Talents, 726
Minna von Barnhelm (Lessing), 511
Minorca, 714; battle of (1756), 42-43, 57; Spain loses, 273; Spain recaptures, 290
Mirabeau (*fils*), Honoré-Gabriel-Victor Riqueti, Comte de (1749–91), 641, 951-54; in Club Breton, 939; criticism of Prussian economic controls, 501; domestic problems of, 952-53; early life and education of, 951-52; edits *Courier de Provence*, 915; as Freemason, 939; French Revolution and, 940; gains support of Third Estate, 953; in Holland, 952; imprisonments of, 952-53; Jews and, 642; literary works of, 952-54; love affairs of, 952-53; marriage to Émilie de Marignac, 952; opposition to slavery, 935; Duc d'Orléans and, 955; personality of,

951; social policies of, 953-54; in States-General, 957-61; travels abroad, 953
Mirabeau (*père*), Victor Riqueti, Marquis de (1715–89), 47, 73-74, 78, 657, 898; appearance of, 951; economic theories of, 72, 73-74; Franklin and, 869; as Freemason, 939; French Revolution and, 940; imprisonment at Vincennes, 951; Jews and, 642; marries Marie de Vessan, 951; personality of, 951; Rousseau's stay with, 882
Mirandola, Pico della, *see* Pico della Mirandola, Giovanni
Mirepoix, Duchesse de, nee Beauvau (b. 1717), 118
Mir Jafar (1691–1765), plot of, 715
Mir Mahmud, *see* Mahmud, Mir
Mirovich, Vasili (d. 1764), 443
Mir Vais, *see* Vais, Mir
Mirra (Alfieri), 340
Misanthrope, Le (Molière), 163
Misenum, 327
Misón, Luis (d. 1766), 292
Miss Sara Sampson (Lessing), 509
Mitridate, re di Ponto (Mozart), 387
M'Lehose, Agnes, nee Craig (1759–1841), 776
Modena, 217, 244
Moguls, decline of, 58; *see also* India
Mohammed (570–632), 796, 808
Mohammed II, Ottoman Sultan (r. 1451–81), 804
Mohammedanism: clergy of, 412; mosques of, 416; science and, 412; sects in, 411-12; skepticism toward, 412
Mohammed ibn-Abd-al-Wahab (1703?–91), 412
Mohammed Shah, Mogul Emperor of India (r. 1451–81), 419-20
Mohocks gang, 261
Moldavia, 411, 483
Molière (Jean-Baptiste Poquelin, 1622–73), 104, 136, 163, 244, 295, 296, 404, 650, 923; influence on Goldoni, 242
Mollwitz, 529
Molmenti, Pompeo Gherardo (1852–1928), 243
Moluccas, 648
Momolo cortesan (Goldoni), 242
Monaco, Mme. de, 99
monarchy: Blackstone on, 737; Burke's defense of, 723; conflict with Jesuits, 226; Diderot's opposition to, 95, 897; *philosophes* and, 897-898; Voltaire's support for, 142-43
monasteries: in Austria, 343, 358-59; in France, 902; in Italy, 225, 250; regulation in Belgium, 361-62; in Russia, 452; in Spain, 275
Monboddo, James Burnett, Lord (1714–99), 764
Monckton, Mrs. Jane, 730
Moñina, José, *see* Floridablanca, Conde de
Monitor, The, 786
Monnier, Sophie de Ruffey, Marquise de (1756–89), 952-53
monopolies: in Austria, 344; in Prussia, 501; in Russia, 423
Monrepos, Palace of, 525

Mons, 361

Monsieur Nicolas (Restif de La Bretonne), 918, 919

Montagnana, Domenico (1700–40), 221

Montagu, Edward (d. 1775), 730

Montagu, Edward Wortley, *see* Wortley Montagu, Edward

Montagu, Elizabeth, nee Robinson (1720–1800), 730, 787, 841

Montagu, Lady Mary Wortley (1689–1762), 228, 730, 793; on appearance of Holland, 646; on Jews in Turkey, 632; on Mohammedanism, 412

Montaigne, Michel Eyquem de (1533–92), 23, 125, 179

Montaigu, Comte Pierre-Auguste de (fl. 1743), 16-17

Mont Blanc, 645

Montcalm, Marquis Louis-Joseph de (1712–59), 58

Montenegro, 411, 414

Montenegro, Benito Jerónimo Feijóo y (1676–1764), 294

Montesquieu, Charles-Louis de Secondat, Baron de La Brède et de (1689–1755), 104, 119, 172, 220, 254, 280, 295, 337, 427, 451, 478, 485, 487, 725, 797, 801, 845, 884, 891, 899; Catherine II and, 435; at Mme. Geoffrin's salon, 120; importance of *L'Esprit des Lois*, 808; influence on Beccaria, 320; predicts American Revolution, 708; on Turin, 226

Montessori, Maria (1870–1952), 888

Monteverdi, Claudio (1567–1643), 232

Montgolfier, Étienne (1745–99), 793, 932

Montgolfier, Joseph (1740–1810), 793, 932

Montgomerie, Margaret, *see* Boswell, Margaret

Montlhéry, riots in, 954

Montmorency, Duchesse de (fl. 1758), 161

Montmorin, Comte Armand-Marc de (1745?–92), 953

Montsauge, Jeanne de (fl. 1772), 128-29

Monumenti antichi inediti (Winckelmann), 330

Moors, 283, 287

Mora, Marquês de, *see* Mora y Gonzaga, Marquês José de

Moral Tales (Marmontel), 102, 105

morals: in Austria, 344; of Christians, Gibbon's interpretation, 801; in England, 682, 730-34; in France, 19, 97-100, *902-5*; Goethe's views on, 619-22; Industrial Revolution and, 682; Islamic, 416; in Italy, 225; of popes, 540-43; Rousseau's views on, 21, 180; in Scotland, 763; in Spain, 290-91

Morand, Dr. (fl. 1765), 200

Moratín, Leandro Fernández de (1760–1828), 296-97

Moratín, Nicolás Fernández de (1737–80), 295

Moravia: Protestants in, 353; Seven Years' War in, 53

Moravian Brethren, 558, 636, 646-47

Mora y Gonzaga, Marquês José de (1744-74), 127-28, 129, 892

More, Hannah (1745–1833), 730, 743, 787, 795, 835

Morellet, André (1727–1819), 80-81, 108, 121, 221, 321, 869, 901, 908; French Revolution and, 940; at Mme. Geoffrin's salon, 120; in Lespinasse salon, 126; opposition to revolution, 898

Morelly (socialist, fl. 1755), *80-82*, 83-84; French Revolution and, 938, 940; influence of, 94

Morgan, Thomas (d. 1743), deist, 734

Morgenstunden (Mendelssohn), 640

Moriscos, expulsion from Spain, 287

Morley, John, Viscount Morley of Blackburn (1838–1923), 725

Morning Chronicle, The, 377, 786

Morning Herald, The, 786

"Morning Song" (Karpiński), 486

Morocco, 411

Mort de César (Voltaire), 607

Morte d'Arthur, Le (Malory), 768

Morzin, Count Maximilian von (fl. 1759), 374-75

Mosaic Code, 629, 636

Moscow: plague in, 458; size and population, 423

Moscow, University of, 453

Moslems, 312; in Corsica, 312; in Spain, 285; *see also* Afghanistan; Egypt; Mohammedanism; Persia; Turkey

mosques, 414

Môtiers-Travers, Rousseau at, 161-65, 170

Moultou, Paul (fl. 1760), 164

Mounier, Jean-Joseph (1758–1806), 948, 957

mountain-climbing, 645, 889

Mountstuart, John Stuart, Lord (fl. 1765), 782

Mount Edgcumbe, Emma Gilbert, Countess of, 752

Mousiad (Krasicki), 415

Mozart, Anna Maria, nee Pertl (d. 1778), 382-86, 387, 389-92, 393

Mozart, Constanze, nee Weber (1763–1842), 391, 394-95, 403, 405-8

Mozart, Franz Zaver Wolfgang (1791–1844), 407

Mozart, Johann Georg Leopold (1719–87), 397, 403; advice to son, 390-92, 396, 400-1; affection for son, 382; death of, 404; exploits son, 383, 390; *Kapellmeister* for Colloredo, 393; opposes son's marriage, 394-95; on Parisian cosmetics, 99; tours with family, 383-85; on Viennese public, 346

Mozart, Karl Thomas (1784-1858), Wolfgang's 2d son, 403

Mozart, Maria Anna ("Nannerl"; 1751–1829), 382-87, 389, 390, 391

Mozart, Maria Anna Thekla (1758–1841), 389, 401

Mozart, Wolfgang Amadeus (1756–91), 100, 220, 222, 227, 255, 332-34, 342, 358, 367, 373, 376, 380, *382-409*, 525, 527, 744, 920, 964; appearance of, 400; arrogance toward nobility, 393, 401; on K. P. E. Bach, 526; children of, 406-7; Colloredo and, 389, 393-94; concerts in

London, 384; concerts in Paris, 384, 392-93; concerts in Vienna, 385; on crime in Italy, 319; death of mother, 392; dislike of *philosophes*, 392, 402; in England, 746; foresees his death, 408; on French music, 909; Grimm and, 384-85, 390, 392; Haydn and, 376-78, 397-98; illness of, 385-86; Joseph II and, 404-5; lack of formal education, 402; love affairs of, 390-91, 401; personality of, 400-2; polyphony subordinated to melody, 335; on Wieland, 576

CHILDHOOD PRODIGY (1756-66): concert tours, 383-85; exploitation by father, 383; musical training, 382-83, 385; parents, 382; precosity of, 384

ADOLESCENCE (1766-77): admitted to Accademia Filarmonica, 385-87; commissions, 388; concert tours, 385-89; first *opera seria* performed, 387; rivalry with Hasse, 387

YOUTH (1777-78): love for Maria Anna Thekla Mozart, 389; in Mannheim, 390; in Munich, 389; relations with Weber family, 390-92; tours with mother, 389-92

IN SALZBURG AND VIENNA (1779-82): home in Vienna, 402; marries Constanze Weber, 395; quits Colloredo's service, 394; stagnation in Salzburg, 393

SUCCESS (1782-87): appointed court *Kammermusikus*, 404; birth of children, 403; increasing income, 402, 404; spendthrift, 403, 405

MISFORTUNES (1788-90): death, 408; grave unknown, 408; illnesses, 406, 408; lack of work, 406; loans, 405-6; poverty, 405, 407

COMPOSITIONS: abilities to play and compose, 396-97; aristocratic context of music, 400; *Barber of Seville*, 923; cantatas, 387; childhood works, 384; concertos, 389, 392, 399; *Don Giovanni*, 396-97, 404-5; *Eine kleine Nachtmusik*, 398; inspiration from Italy, 395; influences, 395-97; *Jupiter* symphony, 398; Köchel's catalogue of, 396; *Magic Flute*, 407; *Marriage of Figaro*, 403-4; methods of composing, 396-97; operas, 387-89, 393, 395, 404, 407; orchestral music, 389, 398-99; quintets, 397-98; religious music, 400; *Requiem*, 407; songs, 399-400; symphonies, 384, 392, 398, 405

Muette, La (villa), 853
Mulai Ismail, Sultan of Morocco (r. 1672-1727), 417
Müller, Friedrich "Maler" (1749-1825), 522
Müller, Friedrich von (fl. 1808), 606
Müller, Johannes von (1752-1809), 642, 645
Munich, poverty in, 503
Münnich, Count Christoff von (1683-1767), 429, 430, 438, 442, 459
Münster, 503
Münster, Treaty of (1648), 361
Murano, glass industry of, 230
Murat, Joachim (1767-1815), 306, 334
Muratori, Lodovico Antonio (1672-1750), 223, 244
Murcia, 273, 298
Murdock, William (1754-1839), 676

Murray-Pulteney, Sir James (fl. 1797), 772
Musenalmanach, Der, 598
Muses galantes, Les (Rousseau), 18
music: in Austria, 367-408; church, *see* church music; in England, 368, 746-47; in France, 100-1, 368, 370-73, 909-10, 915; Frederick II's love of, 496, in Germany, 503, 517-18, 525-28, 552; growth of instrumental, 527; Islamic, 416-17; in Italy, 220-24, 226-27, 232-235, 254-58, 332-35, 373; melody and polyphony in, 335; Romantic movement in, 399; in Russia, 425-26, 466; in Spain, 292; violin, 221
musical instruments, 221
Musset, Alfred de (1810-57), 889
Mustafa III, Ottoman Sultan (r. 1757-74), 415, 458
Mutozilite sect, 411
Mylius, Christlob (1722-54), 508
Myron (5th cent. B.C.), 329
Mysliveček, Josef (1737-81), 227
Mysteries of Udolpho (Radcliffe), 691

nabobs, 686
Nadir Kuli, Shah of Persia (r. 1736-47), 417-20
Namur, 342, 361
Nancy, 107, 245
Nanine (Voltaire), 136
Nantes: commercial decay of, 58; shipbuilding in, 932
Naples, 249-51, 256, 290, 310, 315; Austria and, 249; churches in, 224; conflict with papacy, 317-18; cultural life of, 250-51; Enlightenment in, 250-51; expulsion of Jesuits from, 317; Freemasons in, 220; Goethe in, 588-89; Inquisition in, 252; Jesuit colleges in, 219; Jesuits expelled from, 315; liveliness of, 315; music in, 232, 254-57; papal concordat with, 246; priesthood in, 224; prostitution in, 218; social classes in, 249-50; Spain and, 217, 228, 250, 273, 277-78, 315; theaters in, 220; war against papacy (1768), 317
Naples, University of, 219, 250
Napoleon I, Emperor of the French (r. 1804-14, 1815), 63, 89, 103, 107, 128, 336, 627, 791, 794, 910; on battle of Leuthen, 52; birth of, 313; bombardment of Vienna (1809) by, 380; Condorcet's influence on, 895; David and, 913; defeats Prussians at Jena (1806), 502, 530, 606; on Diamond Necklace Affair, 943; education of, 914; educational reforms of, 895; France's power and, 872; Goethe and, 606-7, 623; Haydn and, 380; Italy and, 311; Jewish emancipation and, 631; musical interests of, 334, 380; papacy and, 319; plot to assassinate, 726; religious policy of, 890; Rousseau's influence on, 880, 891; on royal palace in Madrid, 297-98; Spanish policies of, 306-7; on *The Marriage of Figaro*, 925; Tuscany and, 314; victory at Austerlitz (1802), 726; Voltaire's influence on, 880; Wieland and, 576
Napoleon III, Emperor of the French (r. 1852-71), 89, 107

Narciso (Scarlatti), 257
Narcisse (Rousseau), 15, 27, 164
Nardini, Pietro (1722–93), 332
Naruszewicz, Adam (1733–96), 485-86
Narva, 423
Nascimento, Francisco Manoel do (1734–1819), 269
Nasrulla (fl. 1739), son of Nadir Kuli, 420
Nathan der Weise (Lessing), 514-15, 640
natifs, Swiss, 643-44
National Assembly, French, 313, 642, 895, 960; Condorcet in, 895; feudalism abolished by, 937; formation of (1789), 958; honors to Voltaire, 879-80; liberal leaders in, 939; middle-class control of, 930
National Convention, French, 244, 313, 890, 913; Louis XVI's trial before, 895
nationalism and Catholic Church, 316
National Theater at Hamburg, 511
Nattier, Jean-Marc (1685–1766), 120
Natur, Die (Goethe), 565-66, 584
nature, 889; Goethe's love of, 584, 619; Rousseau's love of, 11, 14, 180-81
Natürliche Tochter, Die (Goethe), 580, 604
Naufrage des îles flottantes (Morelly), 81
navy, English and French compared, 57
Necker, Jacques (1732–1804), 98, *865-67*, 944, *948-51*, 962; Catherine II and, 870-71; critique of free trade in grains, 860; early banking career of, 865; literary works of, 860, 865-66; marriage to Suzanne Curchod, 265; on power of press, 915
FIRST MINISTRY OF (1777–81), *865-67*; American Revolution and, 869-70; attempts to eliminate serfdom, 866-67; *Compte rendu au Roi* (1781), 870; financial reforms, 866; Louis XVI and, 867; opponents of, 870-71; penal reforms, 867; resignation (1781), 871
SECOND MINISTRY OF (1788–89), *948-51*; controls over grain export, 949; dismissal of second ministry, 961; early enthusiasm for, 948-49; economic policies of, 949, 955; financial policies of, 949; pledges personal fortune to state, 949; policies in States-General, 957-58; prepares meeting of States-General, 949-51
THIRD MINISTRY OF (1789–90), 963
Necker, Suzanne, nee Curchod (1737–94), 103, 107, 118, 126, 353, 656, *797-99*, 875; charity of, 905; Gibbon and, 865; marries Jacques Necker, 802, 865; personality and appearance of, *908*; salon in Paris (1765), 865, *908*
Nedim, Ottoman poet, 412-13
Negapatam, 648
Negroes, 732, 935; *see also* slavery and slave trade
Nehra, Henriette de (fl. 1784), 953
Nelson, Horatio, Viscount Nelson (1758–1805), 750
Nelson's Festivals and Fasts, 734
Neuchâtel, 643; Rousseau's residence near, 191-92
Neue teutsche Merkur, 576

Neues Palais, Potsdam, 523, 524
Neuf Soeurs Lodge, Freemasons, 869, 939
Neumann, Johann Balthasar (1687–1753), 238, 426
Neveu de Rameau, Le (Diderot), 101
Newbery, John (1713–67), 814
Newcastle, Thomas Pelham-Holles, 1st Duke of (1693–1768), 691
Newcastle, growth of, 681
Newcomen, Thomas (1663–1729), 674
"New Doctrine of Motion and Rest" (Kant), 533
Newgate Gaol, 739
New Jerusalem Church, 658
New Marshalsea Prison, 738
newspapers: in Austria, 346; in England, 786; in France, 915
New Testament, 185, 194
Newton, Sir Isaac (1642–1727), 13, 219, 280, 293-94, 532, 616
Newton, John (1725–1807), 811
Newton, Lord, 766
New York, anti-British riots in, 710
New Zealand, 669
Ney, Michel, Maréchal (1769–1815), 606
Nicholas II, Czar of Russia (r. 1894–1917), 468*
Nicolai Klimii Iter subterraneum (Holberg), 650-51
Niebuhr, Barthold Georg (1776–1831), 253, 808
Niemcewicz, Julian Ursyn (1757–1841), 486
Niemetschek, 396
Nietzsche, Friedrich Wilhelm (1844–1900), 29*
Nikolai, Christoph Friedrich (1733–1811), 507, 510, 567, 638.
Nivernois, Louis-Jules Mancini Mazarini, Duc de (1716–98), 208
Noailles, Maréchal Duc Adrien-Maurice de (1678–1766), 648
Noailles, Vicomte Louis-Marie de (1756–1804), 898, 939
nobility: in Austria, 351; in Austrian Netherlands, 362; Burke's defense of, 723; in Denmark, 649, 653; in England, 669-70, 684, 732; in France, 84, 280, 849, 850, 863, 872, 898-99, 903-4, 936, 944-48, 956-61; Frederick II's views on, 497; French Revolution and, 899, *927-30;* in Germany, 497, 503, 504; in Hungary, 341; in Italy, 230, 249-50; love of music, 367; Mozart's disdain for, 393, 401; in Poland, 472-74, 476-77, 480-82, 484-85, 491; in Portugal, 263-65, 268; in Prussia, 497; Rousseau attacks, 17; in Russia, 422, 425, 429-30, 438, 443, 454-56, 470; in Spain, 274, 290; Sturm und Drang movement and, 522; in Sweden, 654-55, 657, 663-64
noble savage, legend of, 31
Nollekens, Joseph (1737–1823), 750, 817
Noot, Henri van den (1750–1827), 364
Nordenflycht, Hedvig (1718–63), 659-60
Normandy, bread riots in, 934
North, Frederick, Lord, 2d Earl of Guilford (1732–92), 700-1, 794, 803; American Revolution and, 711, 713-14; Irish policies of, 761;

ministry of, 700-1, 706, 710-14, 761; ministry with Fox, 715, 718; on parliamentary debates, 701*; policies toward American colonies, 710-11; policy toward Catholics, 735; policy toward India, 716; resignation from government, 714

North Briton, The, 702-3, 705, 786

Norway, population of, 649

Notebook (Boswell), 841

Notes on Russian History (Catherine II), 463

Notte, La (Parini), 335

Nottingham, theater in, 740

Nouveaux Essais sur l'entendement humain (Leibniz), 534

Nouvelle Héloïse, La (Rousseau), see *Julie, ou La Nouvelle Héloïse*

Nouvelles de la république des lettres, 253-54

Nouvelles littéraires, 34

novel, development of, 842

Noverre, Jean-Georges (1727–1810), 100, 255, 368

Novikov, Nikolai Ivanovich (1744–1818), 464-65, 469

Nozze di Figaro, Le (Mozart), 404

Nugent, Dr. Christopher (d. 1775), 827

Nuits de Paris, Les (Restif de La Bretonne), 903, 919

Nuncomar (d. 1775), 717

nunneries: in Austria, 343, 358-59; in France, 900; in Russia, 452

Nuri-Osmanieh, mosque of, 414

Nymphenburg, 523

Nystad, Peace of (1721), 653

Oberkirch, Henriette-Louise, Baroness d', 908

Oberon (Wieland), 576

Observations on the Feeling of the Beautiful and Sublime (Kant), 534

Observations sur le gouvernement . . . des États-unis d'Amérique (Mably), 903

Ochakov, 415, 430; siege of, 460

Ochs, Peter (fl. 1797), 645

Oehlenschläger, Adam Gottlob (1779–1850), 650

"Ode by Samuel Johnson to Mrs. Thrale upon Their Supposed Nuptials" (Boswell), 837

Ode to Joy (Schiller), 574-75

"Ode to the Duty" (Derghavin), 464

Oder River, 356

Odessa, 459

Odoardo II Farnese, Duke of Parma, 276

Oeben, Jean-François (1685–1765), 107

Oedipe a Colone (Sacchini), 334

Oedipus (Sophocles), 604

Oeser, Adam Friedrich (1717–99), 523, 557

Oeuvres du philosophe de Sans-Souci (Frederick the Great), 59

Ohio River Valley, French control of, 57

O Hissope (Cruz e Silva), 269

Olavide, Pablo (1726–1803), 280, 285-86, 288

Old Believers, 438, 455

Old Pretender, see Stuart, James Francis Edward

Old Testament: Rousseau and, 185; Voltaire's attitude toward, 150

Oldenburg, Duke of, 523

Oleg (Catherine II), 463

oligarchies: in Holland, 142; in Switzerland, 142

Olimpiade (Metastasio), 333

Olimpiade, L' (Pergolesi), 256

Oliva, "Baronne" d' (fl. 1785), 942-43

"Olney Hymns" (Cowper), 811

"O my luve's like a red, red rose" (Burns), 777

"On Cannibals" (Montaigne), 23

On Ecclesiastical and Civil Tolerance (Tamburini), 316

On Grace and Dignity (Schiller), 594

On Grace in Works of Art (Winckelmann), 328

"On Instructions of Her Imperial Majesty . . . for the Drawing up of Laws" (Diderot), 448

Only Possible Ground for Proving the Existence of God, The (Kant), 534

On Mendelssohn and the Political Reform of the Jews (Mirabeau), 642

On Music (Iriarte y Oropesa), 295

Onslow, Col. George, later 1st Earl of Onslow (1731–1814), 706-7

Ontario, Lake, French control of, 58

"On the Contest Between the Good and Evil Principles for the Control of Man" (Kant), 545

"On the Effects of Poetry upon the Customs and Morals of the Nations" (Herder), 577-78

On the Failure of All Philosophical Attempts at Theodicy (Kant), 544

"On the Power of the Mind to Master the Feeling of Illness by Force of Resolution" (Kant), 549

"On the Spirit of Hebrew Poetry" (Herder), 578

On the Teachings of Spinoza (Jacobi), 565

O Oriente (Macedo), 269-70

opera, 923; in Austria, 367-73, 376, 379-80; in England, 223-24, 746; in France, 25-26, 99, 256, 909-10; in Germany, 223-24, 525, 527-28; Gluck's reforms in, 368-70; influence of Italian, 224; in Italy, 222-24, 254-56, 333-35; melody versus action in, 335; origins of, 224; poetry and, 223; Rousseau's definition of, 26; in Russia, 425, 466; in Spain, 292

opera buffa, 100, 223, 255, 367

Opéra-Comique, establishment of, 100

opera seria, 100, 255, 367

Opie, Amelia (1769–1853), 787

opium, 729

Oppenheimer, Joseph (1692?–1738), 634

Opticks (Newton), 219, 616

optics, Goethe's work on, 615-16

Opus postumum (Kant), 549-50

oratory: English, 707; French, 99

orchestras, 525-26

Orfeo ed Euridice, libretto (Calzabigi), 369

Orfeo ed Euridice (Gluck), 368-69, 371, 373, 909

Orford, Margaret Walpole, Countess of, 328
Origin of Species (Darwin), 889
Orléans, Louis, Duc d' (1703–52), 17
Orléans, Louise-Marie de Bourbon-Penthièvre, Duchesse d' (1753–1821), 955
Orléans, Louis-Philippe, Duc d' (1725–85), 94, 123, 850
Orléans, Louis-Philippe-Joseph ("Philippe-Égalité), Duc d' (1747–93), 898, 962; aid to revolutionaries, 955-56; early life, 955; exiled by Louis XVI, 946; as Freemason, 939; liberalism of, 957; marriage, 955; in States General, 960
Orléans, Philippe II, Duc d', Regent of France (r. 1715–23), 90, 277, 906, 955
Orléans, factories in, 932
Orlov, Alexei Grigorievich (1737–1809), 439, 458; aids Catherine II coup, 439-40; in death of Peter III, 442
Orlov, Feodor Grigorievich (1741–90), 439
Orlov, Grigori Grigorievich (1734–83), 437, 457, 468; aids Catherine's coup, 439-40; arrests Choglokov, 443-44; as Catherine's lover, 442, 445; Catherine's rewards, 442; policies of, 445
Orphan of China (Voltaire), 103
Orpheus, 253
Orry, Jean (1652–1719), 277
Orsini-Rosenberg, Count Franz (1723–96), 395
Os Burros (Macedo), 270
Osorio de Zuñiga, Don Manuel, 305
ospedali singers, 232
Ossian, The Works of (Macpherson), 559, 567, 767-68, 809
Ossory, Lord (fl. 1765), 209
Ostend, 361
Ostermann, Count Andrei Ivanovich (1686–1747), 429-31
Osuña, Duchess of, 291
Osuña, Duke of, 274, 301
Oswego, Fort, capture of (1756), 58
Othello (Shakespeare), 511
Ottoboni, Pietro, Cardinal (fl. 1708), 256
Ottoman Turks, 411, 414; *see also* Turkey
Otway, Thomas (1652–85), 741
Oudh, begums of, 718, 720
Oudh, Nawab of, 718
Oudry, Jean-Baptiste (1689–1755), 120
"Outline and Announcement of a Course of Lectures on Physical Geography" (Kant), 533
Oxford Symphony (Haydn), 377, 381

Pacassi, Niccolo (1716–90), 345
Pacchierotti, Gasparo (1744–1821), 333
Pacte de Famille (1761), 60, 76, 89
"Pacte de Famine," 76
Padua, 220, *229;* theaters in, 220; university in, 219
Paestum, Greek temples of, 248, 327
Paine, Thomas (1737–1809), 340, 725; Rousseau's influence on, 891; Voltaire's influence on, 881
painting: bourgeois, 113-114; in England, 750-58, 888; in France, *911-14;* in Germany, *523-24;*
in Holland, 647; in Italy, 227, *235-39,* 248, *331-332;* neoclassical, *912-13;* in Portugal, 261; in Russia, 466-67; in Scotland, 765; in Spain, *298-309;* in Sweden, 662
Paisiello, Giovanni (1740–1816), *334,* 388, 466
Pajou, Augustin (1730–1809), 106, 107, *109,* 911
Palais-Bourbon, 911
Palais de Justice, 910
Palais-Royal, 911, *955*
Palatinate, Bavaria united with, 354
Palatine College in Milan, 321
Palermo, 589; university in, 219; witch-burnings in, 316
Palestine, 411
Paley, William (1743–1805), 730, *735*
Palissot de Montenoy, Charles (1730–1814), 108, 120
Palladio, Andrea (1518–80), 229, *248,* 587, 747
pamphleteering in France, 94, *915*
Panckoucke, Charles-Joseph (1736–98), 925
Panin, Nikita Ivanovich (1718–83), 439, 457, 483
Panin, Piotr Ivanovich (1721–89), 455
Pannini, Giuseppe (fl. 1762), 247
Pantalone (comic character), 232, 243
pantaloons, 231
Panthéon, 880
Paoli, Pasquale di (1725–1807), 207, *312-13;* Boswell and, 782-83; conflicts with French, 313; early life of, 312; French depose, 205; leads rebellion against Genoa, 313
papacy, 310; Austria and, 343; basis of power and influence, 316; conflicts with Catholic monarchs, *317-18;* factional conflicts in, 317; Germany and, 504-5; Goethe on, 316; internationalism of, 316; Jesuit expulsions and, *316-18;* Jews and, *631;* material interests of, 316; Napoleon and, 319; nationalism and, 316; Portugal's break with, 267; response to Enlightenment, *316;* restoration of Jesuit order by, 319; Spanish concordat with, 279; Turkey and, 457; under Clement XIII, *317;* under Clement XIV, *317-19;* under Pius IV, 319
Papal States, 217; congestion of expelled Jesuits in, 317; Jesuit colleges in, 219; opera houses in, 223; popes and, 246-47; size of, 244; *see also* papacy; Rome
Papin, Denis (1647–1712), 673
Paradise Lost (Milton), 773, 842
Paradox of the Actor, The (Diderot), 103
Paraguay: communistic practices of Jesuits in, 80, 83, 262; Indian revolt in, 262; Jesuits in, 281, 283
Paret y Alcázar, Luis (1746–99), 299
Paride ed Elena (Gluck), 370
Parini, Giuseppe (1729–99), 335-36
Paris: book trade in, 71; Chamfort on, 915; dirt in, 933; economic activity in, 932-33; great salons in, 118-31; Hôtel-Dieu, 353; hunger in, 71, 860, 933, *961;* intellectual life in, 906; key role in French Revolution, 961-63; life in, 15, 71; Louis XVI's aid to, 857; morals of, 19, 903; music in, 368, 370-73; population of, 71, 933;

press in, 915; proletariat in, 933; revolutionary ferment in, *954-57, 959-62;* riots in, 934, 946, 956, *961-63;* stores in, 936; theater audience in, 241; wealth of, 71
Paris, Peace of (1763), 62
Paris, Treaty of (1782-83), 648, 714
Paris, Parlement of, *90-91,* 353, 849; alliance with nobility, 944; banishments of, 91, 946; burns *Émile,* 190; conflicts with Brienne, 946-48; conflicts with Louis XV, 93-94; conflicts with Turgot, *861-63;* "Declaration of Rights" of (1787), 947; Diamond Necklace Affair and, 943; Diderot's defense of, 93; orders arrest of Rousseau, 189-90; organization of States General and, 949; prohibits labor unions, 933; Voltaire's attack on, 92-93
Paris Conservatoire de Musique, 909
Paris-Duverney, Joseph (1684–1770), 920, 922
Paris-Montmartel, Jean (1690–1766), 936
Park, Anna (fl. 1790), 777
parks in England, 748
parlements, 89-95, 928, 930; allegiance to nobility, 949; attack on Cour Plénière (1787), 947-948; authority of, 849; conservatism of, 90, 93; functions of, 90; hatred of Mme. de Pompadour, 67; Louis XV and, 90-95; Louis XVI and, 858, 946-48; as supporters of nobility, 849; see also Paris, Parlement of
Parliament, British, *683-707;* buying up of seats in, 670, 685; demands for annual, 704; destruction of machines and, 679; economic policies of, 67; electoral districts and, 684-85; forbids labor unions, 680; George III's conflict with, 61, 683, 686-88, 693, 697-701; Irish question in, 760-62; *parlements* compared with, 90; powers of, 686, 709-10; rotten boroughs and, 685, *733;* taxation of American colonies and, 709-10; voting procedures in elections of, 685
Parliament, Irish, 760-61
Parma, duchy of, 228, 239, 278; church lands in, 224; expulsion of Jesuits from, 317; Inquisition abolished in, 316; social reforms in, 311-12; Spanish control of, 217
Parma, Duke of: in 1748-65, see Felipe, Duke of Parma; in 1765-1801, see Ferdinand III
Parsons, Nancy, 731-32
Pascal, Blaise (1623–62), 23, 139, 294, 514, 889, 890
Pasch, Johan (1706–69), 662
Pasch, Lorenz, the Elder (1702–66), 662
Pasch, Lorenz, the Younger (1773–1805), 662
Pasch, Ulrica (1735–96), 662
Passek, Lieut. P. B. (fl. 1762), 439
Passerowitz, Treaty of (1718), 415
Passionei, Cardinal (fl. 1754), 326-27
Passionerna (Thorild), 661
Passionist Order, 225
Pater, Walter (1839–94), 326*
Paton, Betty (fl. 1785), 774
Patriarcha (Filmer), 177
particians in Geneva, 143
Patrick, Saint (389?–461?), 767

Patriot, The (Johnson), 833
Pau, Parlement of, 947
Paul, Lewis (fl. 1738), 673
Paul, Saint (d. 67), 194
Paul I (Grand Duke Paul), Czar of Russia (r. 1796–1801), 441, 462, 465-66, 468, 492, 908
Paul et Virginie (Bernardin de Saint-Pierre), 904, 917
Paul of the Cross, Saint (Paolo Danei; 1694–1775), 225
Pavia, 310; university in, 219
Pavilliard, Pastor (fl. 1753), 797, 804
Paysan perverti, Le (Restif de La Bretonne), 918
Peacock Throne, 419
peasant revolts: in Russia, 423, 455; in Wallachia, 361
peasantry, 12; in Austria, 345; in Egypt, 415; in England, 669-71, 732, 814-16; in France, 859, 861, 902, 954; French Revolution and, *927-31;* in Germany, 501, 503; in Hungary, 341; in Italy, 217-18, 249; Mirabeau *père's* tribute to, 74; in Poland, 472, 474, 487, 491; in Prussia, 501; revolts of, see peasant revolts; Rousseau's opinion of, 174; in Russia, 142, 422, 451, 454-56, 469; in Spain, 274, 287; Sturm und Drang movement and, 522; in Sweden, 654-55, 657, 663; in Switzerland, 27
Pechlin, Baron Karl Fredrik von (fl. 1789), 662, 664
Peder Paars (Holberg), 650
Pedro III, King of Portugal (r. 1777–86), 271
Peel, Robert (1750–1830), 678-79
Peel, Sir Robert (1788–1850), 678
Pellegrini, Giovanni Antonio (1675–1741), 235
Pembroke, Lord, 745
Pembroke, Elizabeth Spencer, Countess of, 753
Pennsylvania Assembly, 868
Pentateuch, 629, 639
Penthièvre, Louis de Bourbon, Duc de (1725–1793), 852
Percy, Thomas (1729–1811), 518, 568, 767, *809,* 817
Pereira, Dr. Pedro Gonçalves, see Gonçalves Pereira, Pedro
Péreire, Jacob Rodrigue (1715–80), 636
Perekop, 430
Perfektibilisten (secret society), 507
Pergolesi, Giovanni Battista (1710–36), 100, 223, 240, 254, *255-56,* 333
Permanent Council, Polish, 485, 487
Persia, 411, *417-21;* disorder after Nadir's death, 420; invasion of India (1739), 419; invasion of Uzbekistan (1740), 420; poetry in, 421; Safavid dynasty in, 417; taxation in, 420; Turkey and, 417-19; war with Russia (1722–23), 419
Persian rugs, 421
Pertl, Anna Maria, see Mozart, Anna Maria
Perugia, 244
perversions in France, 98
Peshawar, 419

Pest, university at, 360
Pestalozzi Johann Heinrich (1746–1827), 888
Peter I the Great, Czar of Russia (r. 1682–1725), 39, 142, 425-26, 433, 456, 632-63; escape from Turks, 414; nobility and, 438; statue of, 467; war with Persia (1722–23), 419; Westernization of Russia, 470-71
Peter II (Piotr Alexeevich), Czar of Russia (r. 1727–30), 429
Peter III (Piotr Feodorovich, orig. Karl Friedrich Ulrich of Holstein-Gottorp) Czar of Russia (r. 1762), 432-40, 456; aids Frederick II, 438; Catherine deposes, 61, 439-40; conflicts with Catherine, 435-36, 439; death of, 442; early life and personality of, 432-33; habits of, 435-36; imprisoned by Catherine, 440-42; love affairs of, 436; meets and marries Catherine, 434-35; popular sympathy for, 441; Pugachev's pretensions as, 45; reforms of, 142, 437-39; reign of, 437-40; unpopularity of, 439
Peterwardein, battle of (1718), 414
Petit, Abbé (fl. 1750), 27
Petit Trianon, 111, 852, 910
Petty, Sir William (1737–1805), see Shelburne, 2d Earl of
Pezay, Alexandre-Frédéric-Jacques Masson, Marquis de (1741–77), 884
Phaedrus, (1st cent. A.D.), 486
Phaidon (Mendelssohn), 638-39
Phèdre (Racine), 169
Philalethie (Basedow), 507
Philanthropinum of Dessau, 506
Philidor, François-André Danican- (1726–95), 16, 100
Philip, Duke of Parma, see Felipe, Duke of Parma
Philip II, King of Spain (r. 1556-98), 279
Philip IV, King of Spain (r. 1621-65), 297, 305
Philip V, King of Spain (r. 1700–46), 273, 276-79, 297, 298, 301; centralization of Spanish state, 277; death of, 279; Farinelli and, 278-79, 296; he becomes insane, 278-79; international conflicts of, 277-78; marriages of, 276-77; personality of, 276-77; presides over auto-da-fé, 276
Philip of Orléans, Regent, see Orléans, Philippe II, Duc d'
Philippe-Égalité, see Orléans, Louis-Philippe-Joseph, Duc d'
Philippines, population of, 273
philosophes, 94-95, 280, 286, 487, 536, 549, 867, 889; American Revolution and, 867-68, 872; Archbishop of Paris and, 193; atheism and, 183; attitudes toward religion and morality, 183, 902-3; Brienne and, 945; Catherine II and 446-50, 452-53; Choiseul and, 88, 89; classical ancient ideals of, 898; clergy and, 901; deaths of, 892-97; declining influence of, 170; fear of revolutionary action, 898; Frederick II and, 496-98; French Revolution and, 890-91, 897-99, 937-38, 940; friendships with monarchs, 897-98; Joseph II and, 353; last of 894-97;

Louis XVI and, 867; Mme. de Pompadour's friendship for, 67; moderate views of, 95, 897-98; Mozart's dislike of, 392; on music, 100; Paris Parlement and, 90; physiocrats and, 75; Pombal and, 267-68; prudence of, 31; Robespierre's rejection of, 890-91; Rousseau and, 162-65, 182-83, 195, 214; Russia and, 140; Turgot and, 78-79, 858-59, 863, 865; views on communism, 82; see also names of individual philosophes
Philosophes, Les (Palissot), 120
Philosophical Dictionary (Voltaire), see Dictionnaire philosophique
Philosophical Enquiry into the Origin of the Sublime and Beautiful, A (Burke), 691
Philosophie rurale (Mirabeau père), 74
Philosophische Briefe (Schiller), 572
Philosophische Gespräche (Mendelssohn), 638
Phocaeans, 312
physiocrats, 356, 455, 678, 858; influence of, 76-77, 287, 769-71; philosophes and, 75; theories of, 71-77
Physiognomische Fragmente, 563, 645
Piacenza, 278
piano: importance in musical evolution, 527; mechanical improvements in, 525
pianoforte: improvement of, 332; invention of, 221
Piazza di Spagna, 247
Piazzetta, Giovanni Battista (1682–1754), 235-36
Piccini, Niccolò (1728–1800), 100, 291, 333, 334, 373, 386, 388, 875; death of, 333; personality of, 333; rivalry with Gluck, 371-72, 908; sympathy for French Revolution, 333; writes musical score to Metastasio's Olimpiade, 333
Piccolomini, Die (Schiller), 601-2
Pico della Mirandola, Giovanni (1463–94), 620
Pied de Fanchette, Le (Restif de La Bretonne), 918
Piedmont, Jesuit colleges in, 219
Pietism, 465, 531, 636
Pigage, Nikolaus von (1723–96), 525
Pigalle, Jean-Baptiste (1714–85), 106, 107, 280, 908, 911
Pilâtre de Rozier, Jean-François (1756–85), 932
Pinto, Isaac (1715–87), 630
Piozzi, Gabriel Mario (1740–1809), 837-38
Piozzi, Hester Lynch, see Thrale, Hester Lynch
Piranesi, Giovanni Battista (1720–78), 248, 479, 747
Pirna, siege of (1756), 45
Piron, Alexis (1689–1773), 121
Pisa, 312; university in, 219
Pisano, Benedetto, 323
Pisiani library, 219
Pitt, William, the Elder, Earl of Chatham (1708–78), 342, 683, 725, 741, 794, 812, 842; accepts peerage as Earl of Chatham, 700; American Revolution and, 689, 708, 710-12; basic policies of, 57, 689; de facto ministry of, 700; death of, 713; personality of, 688-89; refuses peerage, 698

SEVEN YEARS' WAR (1756–63): 40, 698; denounces convention of Kloster-Zeven, 50; dismissal of Pitt (1757), 46, 60-61; refuses French peace feelers, 60; support for Frederick II, 39, 698-99

Pitt, William, the Younger (1759–1806), 461, 680, *696-97, 718-19*, 734, 750: Adam Smith's influence on, 772; consumption of alcohol, 726; death of, 726; duel with Tierney, 732; early life and education of, 696-97; economic policies of, 719, 726; enters Parliament, 697; establishes "cabinet government," 718; forms ministry, 718-19; leads war against revolutionary France, 726; personality of, 697; policies toward India, 719-20; policies toward Ireland, 726; resoluteness of, 697; Samuel Johnson and, 833; support for American colonies, 714

Pittoni, Giambattista (1687–1767), 235

Pittsburgh region, French forts in, 57

Pius VI (Giovanni Angelo Breschi), Pope (r. 1775–99), conflict with Joseph II, 359-60; Jews and, 631; Ricci imprisoned by, 314

Pius VII (Luigi Barnaba Chiaramonti), Pope (r. 1800–23), 319

Plains of Abraham, battle of (1759), 58

Plan for a Dictionary of the English Language (Johnson), 821

Plan of a University for the Government of Russia (Diderot), 892

Planché, John Robinson (1796–1880), 576

Plassey, battle of (1757), 58, 716-17

Plato (427?–347 B.C.), 171, 177, 188, 251-52, 294, 435

Platon (Peter Levshin; 1737–1812), 465

Plautus, Titus Maccius (254?–184 B.C.), 241, 508, 650

plays, see theater

Pleyel, Camille (1788–1855), 380

Pleyel, Ignaz (1757–1831), 380

Plus Beaux Monuments de la Grèce, Les (Le Roy), 110

Plutarch (46?–120? A.D.), 435

pocket boroughs: in England, 685, *733;* in Ireland, 760

Pococke, George, Admiral (fl. 1758), 58

Podolia, 492, 634

Podstatsky, Count (fl. 1767), 386

Poesie drammatiche (Metastasio), 369

poetry: in Denmark, 652; in England, 518, *808-17;* in France, 104, 889; in Germany, 511, *517-21*, 557-58, 564-65, 584-86, 590, 595, 599, 601, 603, 608-11, 623-25; Islamic, 412-13, 421; in Italy, 220, *335-36;* Jewish, 641; opera and, 223; in Persia, 421; in Poland, 485-86; in Portugal, 269-70; in Russia, 427-28, 464; in Scotland, 767-68; in Spain, 295-96; in Sweden, 659-62

Poetry and Truth (Goethe), 626

Poggio Bracciolini, Giovanni Francesco (1380–1459), 804

Poisson, Mme. (d. 1745), 86

Poland, 89, 656; agriculture in, 472-73; army in, 485, 487; art in, 479; Austria and, 475, 482-83; clergy and religion in, 472, 480-81; constitution adopted for (1791), 487-88; culture in, 475; decay of towns, 474; Denmark and, 480; Diet of, 475-76, 479-81, 484, 490-91; dress in, 474; education in, 475, 485; England and, 480, 484; Enlightenment in, 484-87; feudalism in, 472-73, 487; final dismemberment of (1794), 491-92; first partition of (1768-72), 350, 481-85; France and, 476, 482; governmental weakness of, 472-73, 476-77, 480-82, 484-85, 487; in Holy Roman Empire, 341; industry and commerce in, 473-74; Jews in, 472, 475, 482, *632-34*, 636, 641; last stand against dismemberment (1794), 491-92; minorities in, 472, 480, 484; morality in, 474; partriarchalism in, 473; population of, 485; Prussia and, 474, 479-84, 487-88, 490-92; religious tolerance in, 481, 487; Rousseau's constitution for, 178; *884-85;* Russia and, 430, 456, 470, 474, 479-84, 487-92; Saxon kings of (1697-1763), 475-77; second partition of (1792), 490-91; size of, 472; social classes in, 472-74, 476-77, 480-82, 484-85, 487, 491; Sweden and, 475-76; trade treaties with Russia, 456; Treaty of Versailles (1756) and, 42; Turkey and, 415, 458, 475, 482; women in, 474

Polignac, Duc Jules-François de (1745–1817), 864-65

Polignac, Yolande de Polastron, Duchesse de (1749?–93), *852-53*, 875

Polish Succession, War of the (1733–35), 430, 476, 630

political clubs and French Revolution, 939

political economy, first university chair in, 250

Political Law of the Polish Nation, The (Kollantaj), 486

poll tax in France, 936

Poltawa, battle of (1709), 476

Polzelli, Luigia (1780–1832), 376

Pombal, Sebastião José de Carvalho e Mello, Marquês de (1699–1782), *261-72*, 631, 880; attitude toward religion, 268; conflict with Jesuits, 262-68; conflict with nobles, 263-65; reforms of, 142, 268-70

Pomerania, 653; promised to Sweden, 45-46; Seven Years' War in, 48, 54

Pomfret, Henrietta Louisa, Countess of, 228, 793

Pompadour, Jeanne-Antoinette Poisson, Marquise de (1721–64), 73, 87, 105-7, 111, 137, 858, 920; aid to Mirabeau *père*, 74; conference with von Starhemberg, 41-42; death of, 68; Diderot on, 69; Falconet and, 109; friendship for *philosophes*, 67; Kaunitz and, 41; love for Louis XV, 85; Maria Theresa and, 40-42, 45, 56; Mozart performs for, 384; physiocrats and, 71; Pigalle and, 108; popular hatred of, 67-69; reforms of, 144; role in French government, 67; Rousseau and, 25; Seven Years' War and, 40, 41-42, 45, 53, 56; Voltaire on, 69

Pompeii, excavations at (1748-63), 110, *248*, 328, 589

Pondicherry, 58-59

Poniatowski, Prince Józef Antoni (1763–1813), 488-92

Poniatowski, Princess Konstantia, nee Czartoryski, 473

Poniatowski, Prince Stanislas (1676–1762), 473

Poniatowski, Stanislas II, see Stanislas II Augustus, King of Poland

Pont-de-Veyle, Antoine de Ferriol, Comte de (fl. 1768), 125

Ponte, Lorenzo da (Emmanuele Caneglianos 1749–1838), 403, 404, 406, 408

Pontecorvo, 317

Pontejos, Marquesa de (fl. 1785), 301

Pontenuovo, battle of (1769), 313

Pontoise, riots in, 934

Pontverre, Père Benoît de (fl. 1728), 7

Poor Richard's Almanac (Franklin), 869

Pope, the: in 1740–58, see Benedict XIV; in 1758–69, see Clement XIII; in 1769–74, see Clement XIV; in 1775–99, see Pius VI; in 1800–23, see Pius VII

Pope, Alexander (1688–1744), 13, 269, 703, 741, 786, 810, 813, 839, 878; opposes slave trade, 732; Samuel Johnson's views on, 837

Pope ein Metaphysiker! (Mendelssohn), 638

pornography, 98

Porpora, Niccolò (1686–1766), 220, 222, 232, 240, 254, 374

Porson, Richard (1759–1808), 694

Portugal, 259-72; abolition of slavery in, 269; American colonies of, 262-63, 269; breaks relations with Vatican, 267; commerce and industry of, 259-60, 269; control over Church in, 268; culture in, 260-61, 269-70; diplomacy of, 259-60; England and, 259; Enlightenment in, 269-70; expulsion of Jesuits from, 317; Inquisition in, 260, 267-68, 269-70; Italian opera in, 224; Jesuits in, 260, 262-68, 271-72; Jews, in, 260, 631; in League of Armed Neutrality (1780), 457; literature in, 260, 269-70; Negro slavery in, 259; nobles in, 263-65, 268; Old Christians and New Christians in, 268; papal concordat with, 246; Pombal's dictatorship in, see Pombal; poverty in, 259; reasons for decline of, 259; reform of Pombal in, 268-70; Seven Years' War and, 62; Spain and, 262-63, 268; wealth of Church in, 260

Potemkin, Grigori Alexandrovich (1739–91), 322, 444-46, 464, 467, 469; as administrator, 459; death of, 461; generalship against Turks, 459-61

Potemkin villages, 459-60

Potocki, Antoni (fl. 1744), 475

Potocki, Count Stanislas Felix (1752–1805), 473, 488, 490

Potsdam, 523-24

Potter, John (d. 1747), Archbishop of Canterbury, 703

Potter, Thomas (d. 1759), 703

Pottle, Frederick A., 779*

Poussin, Gaspard (Gaspard Dughet; 1613–75), 248

Poussin, Nicolas (1594–1665), 327, 466, 750

power looms, 673

Pozzuoli, 327

Prado (Madrid), 289, 290

Praga, 490, 492

Prague, 641; culture in, 342; siege of (1757), 47; university at, 360

Praslin, César-Gabriel de Choiseul, Duc de (1712–85), 88, 447

Pratt, Sir Charles (1714–94), 703

Prayers and Meditations (Johnson), 734

Précis du siècle de Louis XV (Voltaire), 137

Précis sur M. Rousseau (La Tour), 214

Preobrazhensky Regiment, 440

Pre-Raphaelites, 888

Presbyterians, 735, 760, 763

press, freedom of: in England, 706-7; French Revolution and, 940; Goethe's opposition to, 623; Voltaire's support for, 146; see also censorship

Pressburg, 360

Prete Rosso, Il, see Vivaldi

Preveza, 229

Prévost, Abbé (Antoine-François Prévost d'Exiles; 1697–1763), 119, 169, 842, 887

Price, Richard (1723–91), 722-23

Priestley, Joseph (1733–1804), 734; ethics of, 739; on Paris, 933

Prince Khlor (Catherine II), 463, 464

Princesse de Babylone, La (Voltaire), 136

Princesse de Clèves, La (La Fayette), 169

Principi di una scienza nuova . . . (Vico), 251, 254

Principles of Moral and Political Philosophy (Paley), 735

printing press, 266

prisons: in England, 737-38; in France, 867; in Holland, 738; in Rome, 245

Pritchard, Hannah, nee Vaughn (1711–68), 740

Privy Council of Weimar, 581, 589

Procope (café), 99

Profession de foi d'un théiste (Voltaire), 136

Profession de foi en musique française (Arnaud), 372

progressive education, 888

Projet concernant de nouveaux signes pour la notation musicale (Rousseau), 15

Projet de constitution pour la Corse (Rousseau), 204-5

Prokofiev, Sergei (1891–1953), 243*

Prolegomena to Every Future Metaphysic That Will Be Able to Appear as Science (Kant), 539-40

Prolegomena to Homer (Wolf), 253

proletariat: in France, 933-34; in Naples, 249; Rousseau's opinion of, 173; in Spain, 274; Voltaire's opinion of, 174; see also workers

Prometheus (Goethe), 620

property: French Revolution and, 937-38; Rous-

seau's views on, 29-30, 32-34, 174; Voltaire's views on, 141; *see also* communist theories
Propriété, c'est le vol, La (Proudhon), 938
Prospectus d'un tableau historique des progrès de l'esprit humain (Condorcet), 895-97
prostitution: in Austria, 344; in England, 731-32, 744-45; in France, 98, 903; in Italy, 218, 225, 230; Romantic Movement and, 888; in Scotland, 763
Protestant Association, 735
Protestantism: in Austria, 343, 352, 357; in England, 142; in France, 91, 857, 950; in Germany, 64, 142, 502; Goethe's views on, 620; in Holland, 142, 646; in Ireland, 759-62; in Moravia, 353; in Poland, 472, 475, 480; Rousseau and, 5-6 26-27, 184-85; in Scotland, 763; in Spain, 285; territory held by, 316
Proudhon, Pierre-Joseph (1809–65), 174, 938
Provence, 954
Provence, Comte de, *see* Louis XVIII
Prussia, 356, 364; acquisition of Bayreuth and Ansbach, 354; agriculture in, 500-1; alliance with England (1756), 432; alliance with Turkey (1790), 363; army of, 43, 62, 497, 500, 686; censorship abolished in 547; clergy and religion in, 499; conscription in, 62; despotism in, 530, 848; economy of, 43, 500-1; education in, 500; espionage system of, 43; feudalism in, 43, 500-1; fragmentation of, 43; Jews in, 499; in League of Armed Neutrality (1780), 457; in League of Princes (1785), 362; legal reform in, 500; in Napoleonic wars, 530, 606; Poland and, 474, 479-84, 487-88, 490-92; population of, 43, 63; reign of Frederick the Great, *see* Frederick II the Great; religious tolerance in, 499, 540; Revolutionary France and, 488; Russia and, 460-61, 484; in Seven Years' War, *see* Frederick II the Great, IN SEVEN YEARS' WAR; state monopolies in, 501; social classes in, 497, 500-1; Sweden and, 653-54, 663; taxation in, 500-1; territorial acquisitions of, 653; torture abolished in, 321; West, 484
Prynne, William (1600–69), 163
Public Advertiser, The, 705-6, 786
Public Ledger, The, 786, 814
public libraries, 914; *see also* libraries
public sanitation, 728
Puccini, Giacomo (1858–1924), 243*
Puchberg, Michael (fl. 1788), 405-6
Pufendorf, Samuel von (1632–94), 171, 177
Pugachev, Emelyan Ivanovich (1726–75), 455, 464, 469
Pugnani, Gaetano (1731–98), 332-33
Pulaski, Casimir (1748?–79), 481
Pulaski, Józef (fl. 1750), 481
Pulcinello (comic figure), 241
Pulteney, William, Earl of Bath (1684–1764), 698
Punch, 241
Puritans (Independents), 735, 760
Pushkin, Alexander Sergeevich (1799–1837), 427, 464

Pyrrhonisme de l'histoire, Le (Voltaire), 136
Pythagoras, 254

quadrille, 292
Quadruple Alliance (1718), 278
Quakers, 684, 733, 834
Qualtenburg, Franz Kressel von (1720–1801), 355
Quantz, Johann Joachim (1697–1773), 234
Quarenghi, Giacomo (1744–1817), 468
quartet, 528
Quebec, English conquest of, 58
Quesnay, François (1694–1774), 72, 78, 769, aid to Mirabeau *père*, 74; death of, 77; devotion of disciples to, 74; Genovesi and, 251; influence on Adam Smith, 769; personality of, 76; practical program of, 76; theories of, 73-74, 250
Qu'est-ce que le Tiers-état? (Sieyès), 915, 954-55
Quiberon Bay, battle of (1759), 57
Quinault, Philippe (1635–88), 371

Rabelais, François (1495–1553), 788
Rachmaninov (Russian translator of Voltaire), 463
Racine, Jean-Baptiste (1639–99), 103-4, 136, 169, 427, 511, 528, 588, 661, 889
Råd, Swedish, 654
Radcliffe, Ann, nee Ward (1764–1823), 691
Radishchev, Alexander Nikolaevich (1749–1802), 465-66, 469
Radziwill, Helen, 479
Radziwill, Prince Karol (1734–90), 473
Raeburn, Sir Henry (1756–1823), 762, 765
Raison par alphabet, La (Voltaire), 138
Rambler, The (Johnson), 786, 822, 825
Rameau, Jean-Philippe (1683–1764), 18, 368, 372, 909
Ramírez, Juan (fl. 1760), 300
Ramsay, Allan (1686–1758), poet, 765
Ramsay, Allan (1713–84), painter, 699, 729, 765
Ranc, Jean 298
Rançon, M. (fl. 1757), 86
Ranelagh, 744
Ranke, Leopold von (1795–1886), on Pope Innocent III, 245-46
Raphael (Raffaello Sanzio; 1483–1520), 248, 327, 466, 751
Raskolniki, religious dissenters, 452
Rasmus Montanus (Holberg), 650
Raspe, Rudolph Erich (1737–94), 534, 568
Rasselas, Prince of Abyssinia, History of (Johnson), 819, 825-26, 829
Rastrelli, Bartolomeo (1700–71), 426
Rastrelli, Carlo Bartolomeo (d. 1744), 426
Räuber, Die (Schiller), 521, 570-71, 589
Rauch, Father (fl. 1755), 327
Rautenstrauch, Franz, 343
Ravenna, 244
Ravensburg, 48
Raynal, Guillaume-Thomas-François (1713–96),

34, 108, 220, 280, 361, 798, 901, 908; American Revolution and, 867; clerical attacks on, 902; death of 893; later life of, 893; at Mme. Geoffrin's salon, 120
Razumovsky, Alexis (fl. 1742), 431
Razumovsky, Kirill, 439
Real Academia Española, 280
Réaumur, René-Antoine Ferchault de (1683–1757), 501
Récamier, Jeanne-Françoise, nee Bernard (1777–1849), 118
Recherches philosophiques sur le droit de propriété (Brissot de Warville), 938
Recueil d'antiquités égyptiennes, étrusques, grecques, romaines, et gauloises (Caylus), 110, 749
Redemptionists, 225
Reflections (Pinto), 630
Reflections on the Revolution in France (Burke), 690, 722-23, 806
Réflexions sur la formation et la distribution des richesses (Turgot), 79
Reform Bill (1832; England), 739
Reformation, 504, 620
regaliste faction, 317
Regulated Company, 732
Reichstag of Holy Roman Empire, 502
Reid, Thomas (1710–96), 763, 764-65
Reimarus, Elise (fl. 1768), 512
Reimarus, Hermann Samuel (1694–1768), 512-514, 578
Reims: factories in, 932; poverty in, 933; riots in, 934; statues in, 107; stores in, 936
Reinhold, Karl Leonhard (1758–1823), 539, 551, 594
Religion within the Limits of Reason Alone (Kant), 531, 545
religious toleration: in Austria, 348, 351-52, 357, 641-42; in Austrian Netherlands, 361; in Holland, 646-47; in France, 863, 902; French Revolution and, 642; Jews and, *see* Jews; in Poland, 481, 487; in Prussia, 499, 540; Rousseau demands, 175-76; in Russia, 438, 451-52; in Sweden, 657
Reliques of Ancient English Poetry (Percy), 518, 568, 676, 809
Remarks upon the Architecture of the Ancients (Winckelmann), 328
Rembrandt Harmensj von Rijn (1606–69), 466
Remigius Franyó (fl. 1788), 363
Renan, Joseph-Ernest (1823–92), 880
Rennes, 107; Parlement of, 92-93, 849, 947
Renoir, Pierre-Auguste (1841–1919), 235
Re pastore (Mozart), 389
Repnin, Nikolai Vasilievich (1734–1801), 480, 481-82
Reprimand to the Queen, A, 853
Requiem, Mozart's, 370, 380, 408
Rerum italicarum scriptores (Muratori), 244
Restif de La Bretonne, Nicolas-Edme (1734–1806), 918-19; descriptions of Paris, 908; on reading by workers, 914

Re Teodoro (Paisiello), 334
Re Turandote (Weber, Busoni, and Puccini), 243*
Reutter, Georg (1656–1738), 374
Réveillon factory riot, 956
Rêveries d'un promeneur solitaire, Les (Rousseau), 23-24, 26, 171, 206, 886, 887
Rey, Marc-Michel (fl. 1770), 178
Reynolds, Frances (1729–1807), 745, 751
Reynolds, Richard (fl. 1763), 671
Reynolds, Sir Joshua (1723–92), 238, 645, 699, 720, 728-29, 740, 750, 751-54, 772, 789, 812, 828, 839; description of Boswell by, 842; in "the Club," 827; on development of artist, 754; early life of, 751; earnings of, 753; esthetic theories of, 754; fame of, 753-54, 756; Gainsborough and, 756-57; Goldsmith and, 816-17; illness and death of, 754-55; Samuel Johnson and, 840-41; paean to Michelangelo, 754; paintings of women and children of, 752-53; president of Royal Academy of Arts, 754; scope of portraiture of, 751-53; studies in Italy, 751
Ricardo, David (1772–1823), 739
Ricci, Father, 283
Ricci, Lorenzo (1703–75), 267, 317-18; arrest and death of, 318
Ricci, Marco (1676–1729), 235
Ricci, Scipione de (1741–1810), bishop of Pistoia, 313-14
Ricci, Sebastiano (1660–1734), 235
Ricci, Teodora, 243
Richard III (Shakespeare), 741-42
Richardson, Jonathan (1665–1745), 751
Richardson, Samuel (1689–1761), 136, 167, 169, 509, 518, 563, 661, 790, 793, 814, 825, 842, 887
Richelieu, Armand-Jean du Plessis de, Cardinal (1585–1642), 268, 344
Richelieu, Louis-François-Armand de Vignerot de Plessis, Maréchal Duc de (1696–1788), 42-43, 53, 87, 89, 133, 879
Richelieu, Marie-Élizabeth-Sophie de Guise, Duchesse de (d. 1740), 98
Richmond, Charles Lennox, 3d Duke of (1735–1806), 713
Richmond, Mary Bruce, Duchess of, 752
Richter, Jean Paul (1763–1825), 611
Riddarhus, Swedish, 654
Riddell, Maria (fl. 1793), 778
Ridolfo, Palazzo, 228
Riesener, Jean-Henri (1734–1806), 107, 523, 910-11
Riga, 423
Righini, Vincente (1756–1812), 404
Rights of Man, The (Paine), 340, 725
Riksdag, Swedish, 654-57, 662, 664
Rimnik, battle of (1789), 460
Rimsky-Korsakov, Ivan (fl. 1778), 444, 446
Rinaldi, Antonio (1709–90), 468
Rinaldo di Capua (c.1710–c.1780), 254
riots: in England, 735-36; in France, 98, 934, 946, 956, 961
Risorgimento and Alfieri, 340

Rivals, The (Sheridan), 695
Riza Kuli (fl. 1740), son of Nadir, 419-20
Robbers, The (Schiller), *see Räuber, Die*
Robert, Hubert (1733–1808), *111*, 117, 120, 248
Robertson, William (1721–93), 594, 762-64, *766*, 767, 733, 800, 835
Robespierre, Maximilien de (1758–94), 915; in Club Breton, 939; rejects *philosophes*, 880, 890; Rousseau's influence on, 890; in States General, 957
Robinson, Mary (Perdita), nee Darby (1758–1800), 740
Robinson Crusoe (Defoe), 182
Robison, Sir James (fl. 1758), 674
Rochambeau, J.-B.-Donatien de Vimeur, Comte de (1725–1807), 871, 872
Rochelle, La, 944
Rockingham, Charles Watson-Wentworth, Marquis of (1730–82), 691, 700, 789; ministries of, 700, 703, 710, 714, 761
Rodney, George Brydges, Admiral (1719–92), 669
Rodríguez, Ventura (1754), 297
Roebuck, John (1718–94), 675
Roentgen, David (1743–1807), 523, 911
Roguin, Daniel (fl. 1760), 190, 882
Rohan, Cardinal Prince Louis-René-Édouard de (1734–1803), 322, *942-43*
Rohikhand war, 717, 719
Roland, Jeanne-Manon, nee Phlipon (1754–93), 937
Roland (Gluck), 371
Roland (Piccini), 371
Roland (Quinault), 371
Rolf Krage (Ewald), 651
Rollin, Charles (1661–1741), 179
Roman Elegies (Goethe), 598
Romania, *see* Wallachia
Romanina, La, *see* Bulgaretti, Marianna
Romans, Mlle. de (fl. 1761), 68
romantic love, 888
Romantic movement, 768; Alfieri and, 340; definition of, 887; in England, 809, 813; in France, 3, 128, 157, 887; in Germany, 508, 517-20; Goethe on, 588; influence of Middle Ages on, 809; Kant and, 531, 551; letters of Julie de Lespinasse and, 128; in music, 399; Rousseau and, 3, 157, 887; spread of, 170, *888-89*
Rome, ancient, 21, 690; influence of, 118, 315; *philosophes* and, 898
Rome, modern, *244-49*, 256, 310; architecture in, 247; cosmopolitanism of, 314-15; cultural stagnation of, 247; Freemasons in, 220; Goethe in, 587-88; Jews in, *631*, 642; population of, 245; prison reforms in, 245; prostitution in, 218; ratio of priests to lay population, 224; theaters in, 220; university in, 219; Winckelmann in, 327-28
Romeo and Juliet (Shakespeare), 740
Romero, bullfighter, 291
Romische Elegien (Goethe), 590

Romney, George (1734–1802), 740, *757-58*
Rosciad, The (Churchill), 808
Rosebery, Archibald Philip Primrose, 5th Earl of (1847–1929), 772
Rosicrucians, 324, 465
Rossbach, battle of (1757), 50, 67
Rossini, Gioacchino Antonio (1792–1868), 245, 920; *Barber of Seville* libretto and, 334; on Mozart's *Don Giovani*, 404
Rothschild, Meyer Amschel (1743–1812), 634
Rotrou, Jean de (1609–50), 109
rotten boroughs, 685
Rotterdam, 361
Rouelle, Guillaume-François (1695–1762), 813
Rouen: bread riots in, 934; unemployment in, 935; Parlement in, 849, 947
Rousseau, Mme. (foster mother of d'Alembert), 126
Rousseau, Isaac (father of Jean-Jacques), 5
Rousseau, Jacques (1733–1801), 910
Rousseau, Jeanette (fl. 1748), 918
Rousseau, Jean-Jacques (1712–78), *3-37*, 99, 104, 113, 128, 136, *152-70*, 280, 286, 336-37, 353, 465, 478, 485, 496, 532, 545, 559, 563, 636, 641, 643, 656, 661, 690, 725, 790, 808, 845, 852, 857, *881-92*, 895, 910, 916, 919, 952, 964; aid from nobles, 161, 898; aid to Swiss middle class, 643; d'Alembert and, 163, 191; American Revolution and, 867; appearance of, 26, 202; Armenian costume of, 192, 209; attitude toward reason, 169, 888; attitude toward women, 8; Bernardin de Saint-Pierre and, 883-84, 886, 916-17; Boswell and, *133*, 152, 782; Catherine II and, 173; Casanova and, 324; *Confessions* of, *see Confessions;* constitutions for Poland and Corsica, 178, 202, 482; critique of celibacy, 168-69; descriptions of, 207-8, 209-10, 211; *Émile* of, *see Émile; Encyclopédie* and, 3, 25, 33; exhortations on nursing, 97, 180; Frederick II and, 173, *191-92*, 202, 207-8, 212-13, 497; French Revolution and, 84, 899, 940; on friendship, 153; Geneva and, 163-64, 177, 197; Gluck and, 368, *370-71*, 372; Grimm and, 3-4, *5**, 18, 23, 153, 159-62, 170, 201, 207-8, 212; hatred of injustice, 6, 12, hatred of Paris, 153, 168; d'Holbach and, 153; Houdon's bust of, 912; Hume and, 207, 209, *211-14;* influence of, 3-4, 230, 508, 518, 520-21, 880, *887-92*, 898; on Index Expurgatorius, 316; on Jews, 629-30; Samuel Johnson's dislike of, 834-35; La Tour's painting of, 26; literary style of, 169-70; Louis XVI and, 867; love of nature, 7, 11, 30, 169; Mme. d'Épinay and, 4, *5**, 18, 26, 36-37, 153, *156-61*, 178, 884; Mme. de Warens and, 7, *9-15;* Mme. d'Houdetot and, 152, *156-58*, 162, 164; Malesherbes and, 189; on marriage, 152; morality of, 21, 180, 880; musical theories of, 100, 154, 232; music-copying work of, 17-18, 192, 201; needlework of, 192; *Nouvelle Héloïse, La,* of, *see Julie, ou La Nouvelle Héloïse;* in Panthéon, 110; personality of, 6, 26, 152, 208-9; *philosophes* and, 161-65, 182-83, 195, 214 (*see also be-*

low Rousseau, DIDEROT AND; Rousseau, VOLTAIRE AND); Plato's influence on, 177, 188; popularity of, 890-91; primacy of feeling in, 169; on reception of *Julie*, 170, Romantic movement and, 3, 157, 887; Saint-Lambert and, 164; sensitivity of, 152, 208-9; sexual problems of, 6, 8, 14-15, 16; *Social Contract* of, *see Social Contract;* status as a musical composer, 25; support for French opera, 372; theories of theater, 163; timidity of, 6, 26; views on marriage, 186-87; visit by Joseph II, 897; vows never to write again, 205; Walpole's hoax on, 208-9, 212-14

EARLY LIFE AND WANDERINGS OF (1712-40): birth, 5; education and readings, 6-7; early loves, 6-7, 9-11, 13; apprenticeship, 7; relations with Mme. de Warens, 7, 9-10, 12-14; conversion to Catholicism, 7; as footman, 8-9; studies for priesthood, 9; love of nature, 11; teaches music, 11; passion for walking, 11-12; exposure to Enlightenment, 13-14; pantheistic beliefs, 14

IN LYONS, PARIS, AND VENICE (1740-44): tutors Mably children, 14, 178; offers marriage to Suzanne Serre, 14; dismissed by Mably, 15; *Narcisse* read by Marivaux, 15; meets Diderot in Paris, 15-16; visits Parisian salons, 16; secretary to French Embassy in Venice, 16; dismissal and appeals, 16-17

IN PARIS AND GENEVA (1744-56): copies music in Paris, 17-18; lives with Thérèse Levasseur, 17-18; sends children to foundling asylum, 18, 24, 178; revises *Les Muses galantes*, 18-19; corresponds with Voltaire, 18-19, 31-32; writes *Discours sur les arts et les sciences*, 20-23, 171; controversy over *Discours*, 23-24; success of *Le Devin du village*, 24-25; refuses King's invitation, 25; writes for *Encyclopédie*, 25; writes *Dictionnaire de la musique*, 25-26; writes *Lettre sur la musique française*, 25-26; *Narcisse* performed, 27; quarrels with *philosophes*, 27; visits Geneva (1754), 27; resumes friendship with *philosophes*, 27-28; writes *Discours sur l'origine et les fondements de inégalité parmi les hommes*, 28-30; controversy over *Discours*, 31-32; "Discours sur l'économie politique" published, 32-33, 171; friendship with Grimm, 33-36; meets Mme. d'Épinay, 36; leaves Paris for Hermitage, 36-37

IN HERMITAGE (1756-57): Rousseau's arrival, 36-37; family problems, 152; writings, 154-55; love affairs, 156-59; conflicts with friends, 153-55, 158-61; aid from *philosophes*, 153; leaves Hermitage, 161

IN MÔTIERS-TRAVERS (1757-62): poverty, 161-62; relation with Maréchal de Luxembourg, 161-62; break with friends, 162-65; conflict with *philosophes*, 164-65, 170

PERSECUTION OF (1762-67): clerical attacks on books, *185*, 189, 192-99; *philosophes* attack *Émile*, 189; arrest ordered by Paris Parlement, 189; flees to Switzerland, 189; *Émile* and *Social Contract* banned, 190; arrest ordered by Geneva Council of Twenty-five, 190; Voltaire's sympathy for Rousseau, *190-91*, 199-200; expelled from Bern, 191, 206-7; appeal to Frederick the Great, 191-92; residence near Neuchâtel, 191-92; conflict with Archbishop of Paris, 193-97; conflict with Genevan Calvinists, 197-99; conflict with Voltaire, *200-1;* meetings with Boswell, 201-4; writes constitution for Corsica, 204-5; leaves Môtiers-Travers for Île de St.-Pierre, 206; leaves Île de St.-Pierre for Paris, 207-9; leaves Paris for England, 209; meets Hume, 207; Boswell brings Thérèse to London, 210

IN ENGLAND (1766-67): stay in London, 209-10; residence in Chiswick and Wootton, 210-212; dislike for England, 214; return to France, 214

LATER YEARS OF (1767-78): returns to France, 881; wanderings in France, 882; in Paris, 883-86; readings from *Confessions*, 883-84; works on constitution for Poland, 884-85; writes *Dialogues*, 885-86; writes *Rêveries d'un promeneur solitaire*, 886; death of, 886; rumors and attacks against, 887; aftermath of death, 887; conflicts with *philosophes*, 882-83, 885; Voltaire and, 882, 884, 886; fears and suspicions of, 882-84; mourns loss of children, 882, 886; restraints placed on readings, 884; political conservatism of, 884

DIDEROT AND, 22, 24, 27, 153, 201, 212; conflicts between them, 3, 4, 5*, 25, 153, 158, 159-60; Diderot encourages Rousseau to write first *Discours*, 20; Diderot reproves Rousseau, 25, 892-93; final rupture in relations, 162-63; financial aid to Rousseau, 153; first meeting between, 15-16; repudiation by Rousseau, 3; Rousseau on Diderot, 15; suspicions of Rousseau against, 4, 5*

EDUCATIONAL THEORIES OF, 3, 644; in *Émile, see Émile;* emphasis on freedom, 179-80; instruction of Mably children, 14; moral instruction, 180; physical training, 180-81; rearing of girls, 180; religious instruction, 182-85; role of instincts, 181; role of nature, 180-81; sex education, 185-86

RELIGION AND, 3, *162-63;* accepted by clergy, 890; advice to women on religion, 193; belief in afterlife, 184; on Biblical miracles, 198; calls for "civil religion," 175; Calvinism and, 5-6, 19, 26, 177, 184-85; Catholicism and, 7; denounces atheism, 26; denunciation of atheism, 183; early pantheism, 13-14; Genevan creed of, 184-85; religious tolerance, 175-76

SOCIAL VIEWS OF: agriculture, 205; attacks nobility, 17; attacks social inequality, 17, 28-30; attitude toward "enlightened despots," 173; concept of general will, 32-33; *172;* in constitution for Corsica, 205; criticism of civilization, 19-24; democracy, *173-74*, 205; equalitarianism, 141; family life, 205; Geneva as model, 27; ideal type of government, *173*, 205; justifies revolution, 30; justifies social inequality, 32; for limitations on democracy, 28, 32; private property, 29-30, 32, *174*, *205*; radicalism of, 176, 205; republican ideals, 898; socialism, 174; taxation, 174; views on law, *172-73*

VOLTAIRE AND, 108, 149, 151, 203-4, 212, 882, 884, 886; attitude toward *Julie and Émile*, 149, 182; both men compared, 172, 175, *201*, 518; conflicts between them, 163-65, 200-1, 214; correspondence between them, 154-55; Rousseau on Voltaire's poetry, 154; Voltaire on Rousseau's *Julie*, 170; —on *Social Contract*, 177

Rousseau, Pierre (1750-c. 1792), 910

Rousseau, Suzanne, nee Bernard (d. 1712), mother of Jean-Jacques, 5

Rousseau juge de Jean-Jaques, see Dialogues

Rovigo, 229

Rowlandson, Thomas (1756-1827), 750

Rowley, Thomas, "myth" of, 809

Royal Academy of Arts, London, 645, 750, 751, 756

Royal Academy of Belles-Lettres, Swedish, 658-59

Royal Academy of Fine Arts, Swedish, 658

Royal Academy of History, Portuguese, 260

Royal Academy of Sciences, Swedish, 658

Royal Society of Edinburgh, 763

Rozier, Pilâtre, de, *see* Pilâtre de Rozier, Jean-François

Rudbeck, Governor-General (fl. 1782), 656

Ruffey, Sophie de, *see* Monnier, Marquise de

Ruggiero (Hasse), 387

Ruines, ou Méditations sur les révolutions des empires (Volney), 917

Rukh, Shah, *see* Shah Rukh

rum, American trade in, 57

Rumiantsev, Piotr Alexandrovich (1725-96), 458, 460

Russia, 89, 353, *422-71;* architecture in, 426, 432, *467-69;* army in, 432, 438, 441-42, 459, 686; art in, 426, 432, 466-69; Austria and, 349, 362-63, 432; bureaucratic corruption in, 424; clergy and religion in, 424-25, 438, 451-52; clothing and dress in, 425; commerce and industry in, 423, 455-56; conflicts with Turkey, 140, 411, 414-15, 430, 457-61, 470, 483, 663; Denmark and, 456; Diderot in, 892; education in, 432, 453; England and, 432, 458, 460-61, 700; Enlightenment in, 426-27, 432, 446-50; expansion of empire, 429-30, 457-61, 470, 653; feudalism in, 424, 451, 454-55; Finland and, 456, 654-55; France and, 430, 432, 457-58, 469-70; Freemasons in, 465; French cultural influence in, 450, 467; government in, 424, 431, 459-60; influence of Germans in, 429; Italian opera in, 224; Jews in, 452, *632-33,* 641; legal reforms in, 431, 450-52, 470; literature in, 426-28, *463-66,* 889; minorities in, 422, 452; music in, 224, 425-26, 466; palace coups in, 431, 439-40; *philosophes* and, 140; Poland and, 430, 456, 470, 474, 479-84, 487-92; Prussia and, 456, 460-61, 484; public health and medicine in, 453-

54; reign of Anna Ivanovna (1730-40), 429-30; reign of Catherine I (1725-27), 429; reign of Catherine II, *see* Catherine II the Great; reign of Elizabeth Petrovna (1741-62), 431-437; reign of Peter II (1727-30), 429; reign of Peter III (1762), 432-40; religious toleration in, 438, 451-52; size and geography of, 422, 470; social classes in, 142, 422-25, 429-30, 438, 443, 451, 454-56, 469-70; Sweden and, 456, 458, 460, 653-54; taxation in, 424, 470; torture abolished in, 321; war with Persia (1722-23), 419; Westernization of, 470-71

IN SEVEN YEARS' WAR (1756-63): 432, 438, 456; Brandenburg ravaged by, 54; coalition against Frederick II, 60; difficulties in East Prussia, 49; diplomacy leading to, 39-44; invasions of East Prussia, 48, 53, 55; occupation of Berlin, 60; results of war, 63; withdraws from war, 61

FOREIGN ALLIANCES AND AGREEMENTS OF, 457-58; Conventions of St. Petersburg (1757), 45; in Declaration of Armed Neutrality (1780), 713; Peace of Jassy (1792), 488; treaty with England (1755), 39

Russian Orthodox Church, 422, *424-25,* 452

Sabbatai Zevi (1626-76), 635-36

Sacchetti, Giovanni Battista (fl. 1737-64), 297

Sacchini, Antonio (1730-86), 333-34

Sacharissa (Lady Dorothy Sidney; 1617-84), 790

Sade, Comte Donatien-Alphonse-François de (1740-1814), 904

Safavid dynasty, 417

St. Andrews University, 763

St.-Antoine, Faubourg, 962

Saint-Aubin, Gabriel de (1724-80), 116*

St. Bartholomew's Day Massacre, 93

St.-Cloud, Abbey of, 928

St.-Cyr (school), 453

St.-Domingue, 58, 89, 935

Sainte-Beuve, Charles Augustin (1804-69), 5*, 34, 127, 648, 793, 805

Ste.-Geneviève, Church of, 880

Ste.-Marguerite district in Paris, 956

Saint-Évremond, Charles de Marguetel de Saint-Denis, Seigneur de (d. 1703), 125

St. Gallen, 643

Saint-Germain, Claude-Louis de (1707-78), 858

Saint-Hilaire, Geoffroy, *see* Geoffroy Saint-Hilaire, Étienne

St. James Chronicle, 212

St. James's Palace, 745

Saint-Lambert, Marquis Jean-François de (1716-1803), 26, 27, 104, 156-57, 163, 168, 908; in Mlle. Lespinasse's salon, 126; at Mme. Geoffrin's salon, 120; Rousseau and, 164, 207

St. Lawrence River, French control of, 57

St.-Lazare, Monastery of, 962

Saint-Mauris, M. de (fl. 1775), 952
St. Petersburg, 423-24, 469
St. Petersburg, Convention of (1757), 45
Saint-Pierre, Abbé de (Charles-Irénée Castel; 1658–1743), 153, 547, 643
St.-Rémy de Valois, Comtesse Jeanne de, 942
Saisons, Les (Saint-Lambert), 104
Salamanca, University of, 294
Saldanha, Cardinal de (fl. 1758), patriarch of Lisbon, 264
Salieri, Antonio (1750–1825), 334-35, 466
Salle des Menus Plaisirs, 956-57, 959-60
Salm, Hôtel, 190
Salomon, Johann Peter (1745–1815), 377
salons: in England, 729; in France, 103, 118-31, 906-8; in Italy, 219
Saltykov, Count Piotr Semionovich (1698?–1772), 54-55, 59, 435
Saltykov, Sergei (fl. 1751), 436
Salvi, Niccolò (1697–1751), 247
Salzburg, 382
Samarra, battle of (1733), 418-19
Sammartini, Giovanni Battista (1701–75), 221, 226-27, 380-81, 386
Sancho Pança (Philidor), 100
Sanctis, Francesco de, 247
Sand, George (Aurore Dupin; 1803–76), 889
Sandby, Paul (1725–1809), 750
Sandwich, Edward Montagu, 1st Earl of (1625–1672), 730
Sandwich, John Montagu, 4th Earl of (1718–1792), 703, 729
San Fernando, 288
San Ildefonso, 288
San Ildefonso, Palace of, 297
San Marino, 217
Sansedoni, Porzia (fl. 1765), 782
Santa Maria del Rosario, 238
Santa Maria Maggiore, 247
Santiago de Compostela, cathedral of, 297
Santissima Trinità dei Monti, 247
Saragossa, 275
Saratoga, battle of (1777), 713, 869
Saratov, 455
Sardinia, 246, 273, 277, 644
Sartine, Gabriel de (1729–1801), 858, 868
Satires (Naruszewicz), 485
saturnalia, 232
Saudi Arabia, 412
Saul (Alfieri), 340
Saul (Voltaire), 136
Saurau, Count Franz von (1760–c. 1830), 379
Saussure, Horace-Bénédict de (1740–99), 645
Savage, Richard (1697?–1743), 820
Savery, Thomas (1650?–1715), 674
Savile, Sir George (1726–84), 735
Savoy, 217, 277; Genoa and, 227; territorial acquisition from War of the Spanish Succession, 273
Savoy, house of, 226
Saxe, Maréchal Comte Hermann Maurice de (1696–1750), 99, 107

Saxe-Gotha, Duke of, 893
Saxe-Hildburghausen, Duke of, 49-50
Saxe-Meiningen, Duke of, 594
Saxe-Weimar-Eisenach, 503; in League of Princes (1785), 362; see also Weimar
Saxony, 356, 476, 502-3; in League of Princes (1785), 362, Seven Years' War in, 44-45, 49-50, 54, 60, 61
Scala di Spagna, 247
Scarlatti, Alessandro (1660–1725), 240, 256
Scarlatti, Domenico (1685–1757), 221, 240, 256-58, 333; death of, 257; Handel and, 256; instrumental works of, 257; marriage of, 257; operas of, 256-57; in Rome, 256-57; in Spain, 257, 279, 292; in Venice, 256
Scarlatti, Francesco (fl. 1719), 240
Scarlatti, Pietro (1679–1750), 240
Scarlatti, Tommaso (1670?–1760), 240
Scarron, Paul (1610–60), 790, 839
Schack, Mme. (fl. 1791), 408
Schadow, Johann Gottfried (1764–1850), 523, 525
Schardt, Charlotte von, see Stein, Charlotte von, nee Schardt
Schaumburg-Lippe, Count Wilhelm of (1724–1777), 527, 568
Scheele, Karl Wilhelm (1742–86), 658
Scheldt River, 361
Schelling, Friedrich Wilhelm Joseph von (1775–1834), 551, 618
Schering, Arnold (b. 1877), 234
Schikaneder, Johann Emanuel (1751–1812), 407
Schiller, Charlotte, nee von Lengefeld (1766–1826), 594
Schiller, Johann Christian Friedrich (1759–1805), 63, 379, 502-3, 517, 545, 569-71, 589, 591-605, 628, 641, 766, 964; appearance of, 596; contribution to Romantic Movement, 889; death of, 580, 605; early life and education of, 569-70; edits Die Horen, 596; esthetic theories of, 593, 595; estimates of, 602-3; family life of, 594; friendship with Christian Gottfried Kröner, 572-75; friendship with Wieland, 576; on German family life, 503-4; goes to Weimar, 575; Goethe and, 591, 593, 595-605; historical writings of, 592-94; illnesses of, 594, 596, 605; in Jena, 593-603; Kant's influence on, 551; love affairs of, 573, 575; marriage of, 594; meets Duke Karl August, 573; minor dramatic works of, 571-72; philosophical writings, 572; poetry of, 599, 603; première of Don Carlos, 592; returns to Weimar, 602; Rousseau's influence on, 3, 518, 889; satires of, 598-99; in Sturm und Drang movement, 521-22, 570-71, 593; success of, 605; version of Lessing's Nathan der Weise, 515; views on religion, 595; in Weimar, 591-93; writes Ode to Joy, 574; writes plays on Wallenstein, 601-2; writes The Robbers, 570-71; writes William Tell, 604-5
Schimmelmann, Count Ernst von, 594
Schlegel, August Wilhelm von (1767–1845), 601

Schlegel, Friedrich (1772–1829), 611, 641
Schleiermacher, Friedrich (1768–1834), 641, 890
Schleswig, duchy of, 439
Schloss Benrata, 525
Schloss Esterházy, 341
Schloss of Landgrave of Hesse-Cassel, 525
Schlüsselberg Fortress, 465
Schmettau, Kurt von, 56
Schobert, Johann (1720?–67), 525
Schönbrunn Palace, 345
Schönemann, Lili (1758–1817), 566
Schönkopf, Annette (fl. 1768), 558
School for Blind Children, French, 905
School of Commerce, Russian, 453
School for Scandal, The (Sheridan), 696, 740
Schopenhauer, Arthur (1788–1860), 3, 550-51, 616
Schrattenbach, Sigismund von, Prince Archbishop of Salzburg (r. 1753–71), 382-87 *passim*
Schreiben an den Herrn Diaconus Lavater (Mendelssohn), 639
Schröder, Friedrich Ludwig (1744–1816), 511
Schroeter, Johanna (fl. 1791), 378
Schröter, Korona (1751–1802), 524
Schubart, Christian Friedrich Daniel (1739–91), 527
Schubert, Franz (1797–1828), 399
Schulenburg, Count von der, 344
Schulz, Johann H. (fl. 1784), 507-8
Schulz, Johann Peter (1747–1800), 525
Schumann, Robert (1810–56), 398
"Schutzschrift für die Vernunftigen Verehrer Gottes" (Reimarus), 513-14
Schwarzenberg, Prince Karl Philipp von (1771–1820), 379
Schweidnitz, 51, 53, 60, 61
Schwerin, Count Kurt Christoph von (1684–1757), 43 44, 47
science: in Germany, 532-33, 596-97, 615-18; Industrial Revolution and, 669, 671, 680; in Sweden, 658-59
Scienza della legislazione, La (Filangieri), 336
Scienza nuova (Vico), 251, 254
"Scotia, my dear, my native soil!" (Burns), 775
Scotland, 670, 762-85; agriculture in, 762; anti-Catholic riots in, 735; architecture in, 765; art in, 765; Catholics in, 763; England and, 762; Enlightenment in, 764-78; France and, 39; historians in, 765-66; Industrial Revolution in, 763; morality in, 763; philosophy in, 764-65; poetry in, 767-68, 772-78; population of, 762; Protestants in, 763; social classes in, 762
Scotland, Church (Kirk) of, 763, 766, 774, 779
"Scots wha' hae wi' Wallace bled" (Burns), 777
Scott, Sir Walter (1771–1832), 765, 775, 815
Scudéry, Madeleine de (1607–1701), 169
sculpture: in England, 750; in France, 106-9, 911; in Germany, 523; in Italy, 247; in Portugal, 270; in Russia, 426, 467; in Spain, 298; in Sweden, 662
Scuola degli Incurabili, 255
Scuola di San Rocco, 238

Seasons, The (Haydn), 379
Seasons, The (Thompson), 379
Second Estate in States-General, 956-61
Sedaine, Michel-Jean (1719–97), 920
Segeste, 589
Segovia, 288
Ségur, Comte Louis-Philippe de (1753–1830), 423, 459-60; on American Revolution, 872; on Marie Antoinette, 855, 941; on pre-revolutionary skepticism, 898
Sejm, Polish, 472-73
Select Society, 764
Selwyn, George (1718–91), 702, 729, 730, 734, 747
Seminario Musicale dell' Ospedale della Pietà, 233-34
Semiramide (Sacchini), 334
Semler, Johann Salomo (1725–91), 507
Senate: Polish, 487; Russian, 424, 440; Venetian, 229, 231
"Senate of Magna Lilliputa" (Johnson), 819-20
Senegal, 714
Senesino (Francesco Bernardi; 1690?–1750?), 223
sensibility cult in Germany, 518
Sentimental Journey (Sterne), 465
Sentiments des citoyens (Voltaire), 200-1
Sephardic Jews, 630
September Massacres, French Revolution, 496, 725
Serafinovich (fl. 1716), 633
Serbia, 411
serfdom: in Austria, 345, 349-50, 356; in Denmark, 649; in France, 928; in Germany, 500-1, 503; in Hungary, 341; Joseph II's policies toward, 349-50; in Poland, 472-73, 487; in Prussia, 500-1; revolt in Bohemia, 350; Rousseau on, 885; in Russia, 422-23, 438, 451, 454-55, 470; Voltaire's opposition to, 135
Sergel, Johan Tobias (1740–1814), 662
Sermon des cinquantes, 199
Sermons of Mr. Yorick (Sterne), 789
Serre, Suzanne (d. 1748?), 14
Serva padrona, La (Pergolesi), 100, 223, 333
Servetus, Michael (1511–33), 176
Sevastopol, 459
Seven Last Words of Christ, The (Haydn), 380
Seven Years' War (1756–63), 38-64, 290, 556, 646, 698-99, 798; in America and India, 57-59, 709; efficiency of Prussian army, 43; events leading to, 38-44; George III's attitude toward, 698; results of, 62-64, 552; start of, 44; Voltaire's views on, 149
  DIPLOMACY OF, 699; coalition against Frederick, 45-46, 59-60: Convention of St. Petersburg (1757), 45; effects of battle of Rossbach on, 50; English treaty with Russia (1755), 39; First Treaty of Versailles (1756), 42; Frederick publishes Saxon documents, 45; Frederick's peace efforts, 47-48; French peace feelers, 60; German principalities and Frederick, 45; Kaunitz's diplomacy, 40-42; Maria Theresa's policies, 38, 40-44, 48; "Pacte de

Famille," 60; peace negotiations, 62-64; Pitt's diplomacy, 39; Russia establishes peace, 61; Russia withdraws from war, 61, 457; Second Treaty of Versailles (1757), 45; Spanish alliance with France, 60; territorial pledges, 45-46; Treaty of Westminster (1756), 39-40 LAND CAMPAIGNS OF: battle of Leuthen, 51-52; battle of Rossbach and, 50; in Bohemia, 47-48; in East Prussia, 48-49, 55, 59-60; final victories of Frederick the Great, 61; in India, 57-59; in Moravia, 53; in North America, 57-58; in Saxony, 44-45, 49-50, 54, 60, 61; in Silesia, 51-53, 55, 60-61 NAVAL OPERATIONS OF: battle of Lagos (1759), 57; battle of Minorca (1756), 42-43, 57; seige of Louisbourg, 57-58

Sévigné, Marie de Rabutin-Chantal, Marquise de (1626-96), 138, 792

Seville, 288-89

Sèvres, 106, 749

sex education, Rousseau's views on, 185-86

Seydlitz, Friedrich Wilhelm von (1721-73), 43, 53

Sganarel's Journey to the Land of the Philosophers (Halberg), 650

Shaftesbury, Anthony Ashley Cooper, 3d Earl of (1671-1713), 595

Shah Alam, Mogul Emperor (r. 1759-1806), 716-17

Shah Jehan, Mogul Emperor (r. 1628-58), 419

Shah Rukh, Persian ruler (r. 1748-96), 420

Shakespeare, William (1564-1616), 464, 486, 511, 553, 559-60, 561, 565, 599, 659, 661, 794, 842; influence on Germany, 511, 519; revival of, 739-43; Voltaire's condemnation of, 835

Shakespeare festival, 743

Sharp, Granville (1735-1813), 733

Shaw, George Bernard (1856-1950), 748

Shchedrin, F. F. (1751-1825), 467

She Stoops to Conquer (Goldsmith), 816

Sheffield, 681

Sheffield, John Baker Holroyd, 1st Earl of (fl. 1780), 795

Shelburne, Sir William Petty, 2d Earl of (1737-1805), 759, 871; duel with Fullerton, 732; ministry of, 714-15

Shelley, Percy Bysshe (1792-1822), 810; Rousseau's influence on, 3, 891; Voltaire's influence on, 880, 881

Sheraton, Thomas (1751-1806), 748

Sheraton furniture, 523

Sherbatov, Princess (fl. 1789), 446

Sheridan, Charles, 695

Sheridan, Elizabeth Ann, nee Linley (1754-92), 695, 696, 727

Sheridan, Frances, nee Chamberlaine (1724-66), 694, 696

Sheridan, Richard Brinsley (1751-1816), 486, 694-96, 683, 701, 714, 739, 747, 757, 759, 761; aid to American colonies, 727; death of, 727; early life of, 694-95; enters Parliament, 696; in Hastings' trial, 719-20, 805; on Johnson,

831; liberal views of, 696; literary activities of, 695; marries Elizabeth Linley, 695; in ministry, 714-15; partnership in Drury Lane Theatre, 743; personality and appearance of, 695-96; in "the Club," 827

Sheridan, Thomas, the Elder (1687-1738), 694

Sheridan, Thomas, the Younger (1719-88), 694-696, 780

Shi'a sect, 412, 419

ships, iron, 672

Shiraz, 420-21

Shuvalov, Ivan, 432

Shuvalov, Piotr, Count (d. 1762), 137, 432, 437

Siberia, 422

Sicily, 226, 278; Caraccioli's reforms in, 315; Jesuit colleges in, 219; Spanish loss of, 273

Siddons, Sarah, nee Kemble (1755-1831), 720, 740-41

Siddons, William (fl. 1773), 741

Sidney, Algernon (1622-83), 177

Siècle de Louis XIV, Le (Voltaire), 528

Sievers, Yakov Efimovich (1731-1808), 489-90

Sieyès, Emmanuel-Joseph (1748-1836), 915; in Club Breton, 939; Duc d'Orleans and, 955; as Freemason, 939; as spokesman for Third Estate, 954-55; in States-General, 957

Silesia, 48; excused from taxes, 500; Frederick II regains, 52; mining in, 501; Prussia and, 38, 62; Seven Years' War in, 51-53, 55, 60-61

Silhouette, Étienne de (1709-67), 56

silk industry, 230, 501

Silva, Antônio José da (1705-39), 260, 631

Simon, Richard (1638-1712), 641

Simonides of Ceos (6th century B.C.), 510

Singspiel, 367, 525, 528

Siraj-ud-daula (1728?-57), 715-16

Sirvens family, 140, 146, 151, 498, 881

skepticism: in England, 734; French Revolution and, 898

"Sketch of My Life" (Boswell), 203

slavery and slave trade: American colonies and, 57, 708, 732-33; Beaumarchais and, 921; Denmark and abolition of, 649, 653; England and, 57, 670, 693, 732-33; France and, 58, 935; in Moslem countries, 413-14, 420; Portugal and, abolition of, 259, 269; Wilberforce's opposition to, 726

smallpox inoculation, 93, 348, 434, 454, 846

Smeaton, John (1724-92), 671, 674

Smith, Adam (1723-90), 214, 321, 719, 764, 766, 768-72, 786, 808, 827; Burke and, 693, 832; on class conflict, 680; death of, 772; early life and education of, 768-69; economic theories of, 769-71; ethical theories of, 769; on Gibbon, 805; habits of, 771-72; on Hume, 834; influence of, 287, 772; influences on, 769-70; in London, 772; on morality, 730-31; opposes slave trade, 733; on overwork in factories, 677; philosophes and, 769; physiocrats and, 75-76, 78, 769; at University of Glasgow, 763, 769, 779; on wealth of Holland, 646; writes Theory *of Moral Sentiments,* 769; writes *Wealth of Nations,* 769

Smollett, Tobias (1721–71), 699, 702, 820, 824; on French officers, 98

Smolny Institute, 453

Sobieska, Maria Clementina (1702–35), 247, 320

Sobieski, Jan, *see* John III Sobieski

Social Contract, The (Rousseau), 27, 33, *171-78,* 191, 268, 465, 808, 884-85, 887, 891, 898; American Revolution and, 868; attitude toward peasantry in, 174; attitude toward proletariat in, 174; banning of, 190; concept of general will in, 172; on Corsican independence, 204; critics of, 177; democracy and, 173-74, 198-99; "enlightened despotism" and, 173; French Revolution and, 880; ideal type of government in, 173; importance of law in, 172-73; inconsistencies in, 176-77; influence of, 177; middle classes in, 174; private property and, 174; publication of, 171, 178; radicalism of, 176; religion and, 174-76; Rousseau's earnings from, 178; socialism and, 174; state of nature in, 172; taxes and, 174

socialism: French Revolution and, *938;* Prussia and, 501; Rousseau and, 174, 891

Sociedades Económicas de los Amigos del País, 280, 287

Société des Amis des Noirs, 935

Société du Printemps, 797

Society for the Abolition of Slavery, 749

Society of Arts, 750

Society for Commemorating the Revolution (of 1688), 722-23

Society for the Encouragement of Art, Manufacture, and Commerce, The, 750

Society of Jesus, *see* Jesuits

Society of Supporters of the Bill of Rights, 704, 722

Society of Thirty, 957

Socinians in Holland, 646

Socrate (Voltaire), 136

Socrates (470?–399 B.C.), 834, 839

sodomy, legislation against, 98

Sogno di Scipione, Il (Mozart), 388

Soho, 675

Soldaten, Die (Lenz), 521

Soler, Antonio (1729–83), 292

Solimena, Francesco (1657–1747), 115

Soloviev, Sergei Mikhailovich (1820–79), 435

Soltyk, Kajetan (fl. 1766), bishop of Cracow, 480-81

Some Thoughts on Education (Locke), 179

Something More from the Papers of the Anonymous Writer, concerning Revelation (Reimarus), 513

Somodevilla, Zenón de, Marqués de la Ensenada (1702–81), 279

"Song of the Bell" (Schiller), 503-4, 599

Sonnenfels, Joseph von (1732–1817), 355

Sophia (1630–1714), Electoress of Hanover, 683

Sophia Dorothea (1687–1757), Queen of Frederick William I of Prussia, 47

Sophia Magdelena of Denmark, Queen of Gustavus III of Sweden, 655

Sophia Matilda, Princess (1733–1804), 683

Sophie Augusta Frederika, *see* Catherine II the Great

Sophists, Greek, 902, 904

Sophocles (496?–406 B.C.), 136, 528, 604

Sorau, Marquis de, 111

Sorrows of Young Werther, The (Goethe), *563-64,* 588, 601, 627, 767, 889; influence of, 521

Soubise, Charles de Rohan, Prince de (1715–87), 48-49, 53, 67; extravagance of, 84; tactics of, 50

Soufflot, Jacques-Germain (1713–80), *110,* 120

South Africa, 646

South Carolina, 708

Southey, Robert (1774–1843), 631

South Sea "Bubble," 796

South Sea Company, 279

Souvré, General, 95

Spa, 342, 361

Spain, *273-309;* agriculture in, 273-74, *287-88;* Alberoni's reforms, 277; alliance against England (1779), *871;* ambitions in Italy, 277-78; American colonies of, 273, 288, 871; American Revolution and, 290, 713; architecture in, 297; art in, 285-86, 297-309; Austria and, 277-78; Austrian Netherlands and, 45; Catholic Church in, 246, 274-76, 279, 281, *283-85,* 290, *292-95,* 302, 306, 317; censorship in, 285; concordat with papacy, 246, 279; conflict with papacy, 318; drama in, *296;* dress in, 291; dynastic conflicts in, 273; education in, *275-76,* 287, 293-94; England and, 273, 277-78, 290, 669, 713, 761; Enlightenment in, 280-81; expulsion from Florida, 709; expulsion of Jesuits from, 281, *283-85,* 293, 317; Farinelli in, 223, 279, 292; Florence and, 228; Florida returned to (1783), 714; France and, *277-78,* 280, 293, 296-98, *306-7;* geography of, 273; Gibraltar and, 290; guilds in, 289; individualism in, 293; industries, commerce, and natural resources of, 273-74, *286-89;* Inquisition in, 275-76, 279, 280, 292, 294-95, 302, 306; intellectual activity in, 293-97; Italian opera in, 224, 292; Italy and, 217, 226; Jesuits in, 275, 281, *283-85,* 293, 317; Jews in, 275-76, 285, 287, *630-31;* Joseph Bonaparte in, 296-98, *306-7;* land reform in, 287-88; Liberals in, 306; literature in, *295-96;* Milan and, 226; Minorca returned to (1783), 714; morality and marriage in, 290-91; Moslems in, 283, 285; music and dancing in, 224, 291-92; Naples and, 217, 228, 250, 273, 277-78, 315; national character of, 290-92; Peace of Versailles (1783) and, 290; population of, 273; Portugal and, 262-63, 268; Protestants in, 285; reign of Charles III, 281-90, 291; reign of Charles IV, 302-4, 306; reign of Ferdinand VI, 279-81; reign of Ferdinand VII, 306-7; reign of Philip V,

276-79; religious orders in, 294, 295; Scarlatti in, 257, 279, 292; in Seven Years' War, 60, 62, 290; social classes in, 274, 280, *289-90;* taxation in, 288; Treaty of Versailles (1756) and, 42; Turkey and, 288; war against Moors in, 283; war against papacy (1768) in, 317; war of liberation in, 296, 306-7; *see also* Spanish Succession, War of the

Spanish Academy, 295

Spanish America, 273, 288, 871

Spanish Armada, 842

Spanish Hapsburgs, 273

Spanish Netherlands, 273

Spanish Succession, War of the (1702-13), 42, 273, 297, 630, 646, 669

Sparta, 21, 253; influence on Rousseau, 177; *philosophes* and, 898

Spectator, 320

Spencer, Lord Robert, 753

spinning jenny, 673

spinning wheel, 673

Spinoza, Baruch (1632-77), 510, 557, 562, 565, 578, 619; anti-rationalist reaction to, 519; Lessing's views on, 516; Moses Mendelssohn adheres to, 638

Spirit of Laws, The (Montesquieu), 320, 797, 808; Catherine II on, 435

Sprecher (commander of Breslau), 52

Sprüche in Prosa (Goethe), 618

Squillaci, Marchese de' (fl. 1761), 282

Stackelberg, Count Otto von (fl. 1764), 479

Stadion, Count Johann Philipp von (1763-1824), 553

Staël, Germaine de, nee Necker, Baronne de Staël-Holstein (1766-1817), 103, 118, 188, 506, 644, 647, 891, *908,* 961; on Austria, 345; on culture in Weimar, 553; death of, 908; early life of, 908; Gibbon and, 802; on Guibert, 128; on *La Nouvelle Héloïse,* 170; on morality of German courts, 504; on Rousseau, 887; salon of, 908; on Schiller, 604

Staffordshire, potteries in, 749

Stamitz, Johann (1717-57), 221, 380-81

Stamp Act (1765), 700-1, 709-10, 868

Stanislas I Leszczyński, King of Poland (r. 1704-9, 1733-35), ruler of Lorraine and Bar (r. 1737-66), 23, 24, 34, 86, 430, 475-76

Stanislas II Augustus (Stanislas Poniatowski), King of Poland (r. 1764-95), 120, 473, *477-90;* aid from Russia, 478-81, 483-84; appearance and personality of, 477-78, 489-92; attempts to strengthen monarchy, 476, 480; Catherine II and, 436-37, 460, 478-81, 487, 489; Confederation of Bar and, 482-83; conflict with Russians, 488-89; correspondence with Voltaire, 139; death of, 492; difficulties with nobility, 479; early life of, 477-78; election to kingship, 477; final dismemberment and, 491-92; first partition of Poland and, 484; foils Frederick II's partition plan, 479-81; Mme. Geoffrin and, 121, 477-78; intellectual interest of, 478-79; literature and, 485-86; love affairs of, 479; pro-

motes Enlightenment in Poland, 485; second partition and, 488-91; succession to, 487

Starhemberg, Count Georg Adam von (fl. 1753), 41-42

Starov, Ivan (1743-1808), 469

State of Prisons in England and Wales, . . . and an Account of Some Foreign Prisons (Howard), 738

States-General, French (1789), 84, 938; *cahiers* of, 950-51; conflict between classes in, 957-61; conflicts with King, 958-61; declares itself National Assembly, 958; demands for, 945-47; disputes over organization of, 949; early demands of, 92; electoral arrangements for, 949-51; as feudal institution, 946; national hopes for, 951; number of deputies in, 956; opening of (1789), 956; summoning of (1788), 948

Statute of Popular Schools (1786), Russian, 453

steam engines, 70, *673-76, 932*

Steele, Sir Richard (1672-1729), 732

Steevens, George (1736-1800), 830

Stein, Charlotte von, nee von Schardt (1742-1827), 521, 588, 589, 590, 600, 603; appearance of, 582; death of, 626; in Goethe's *Tasso,* 584-85; love affair with Goethe, 582-84, 586; Schiller and, 591

Stein, Fritz von (b. 1773), 583, 588

Stein, Johann Andreas (1728-92), 390

Stein, Baron Josias Gottlob von (1735-93), 582-83

Sterne, Elizabeth, nee Lumley, 787, 789

Sterne, Laurence (1713-68), 465, 750, *787-90,* 791, 793, 842; death of, 790; Diderot and, 789; domestic difficulties of, 787; early life and education of, 787; Elizabeth Draper and, 789-90; influence of, 518; love affairs of, 787, 789-90; success as author, 789; tour of France, 789; writes *Sentimental Journey,* 789-90; writes *Tristram Shandy,* 787-89

Sterne, Lydia, 787

Sterne, Richard (1596?-1683), Archbishop of York, 787

Stillingfleet, Benjamin (1702-71), 730

Stock, Dorothea (1760-1832), 572-73

Stock, Minna (1762-1843), 572-73

Stockholm, Treaties of (1719-20), 653

Stockholmsposten, 661-62

Stoke-on-Trent, 749

Stolberg, Count Christian zu (1748-1821), 566; on Weimar court, 552

Stolberg, Count Friedrich Leopold zu (1750-1819), 566

Stormont, David Murray, Lord (1728?-83), 730

Stosch, Baron Philipp von (1690-1757), 328

Stradivari, Antonio (1644?-1737), 221

Strahan, William (1715-85), 212, 786, 800

Stratford-on-Avon, 743

Stravaganze del conte (Cimarosa), 334

Strawberry Hill at Twickenham, 747, 793, 795, 809

Streicher, Andreas, 571-72

Streit der Fakultäten, Der (Kant), 547
strikes, labor, 933-34
Strinasacchi, Regina (1764-c.1823), 396-97
Struensee, Johann Friedrich (1737-72), 652-53
Stuart, Charles Edward, Count of Albany, the Young Pretender (1720-88), 51, 53, 137, 635; marriage and death of, 339
Stuart, James Francis Edward ("James III"), the Old Pretender (1688-1766), 247
Stuart dynasty and Tories, 699
Study of Works of Art, The (Winckelmann), 328
Sturm und Drang (Klinger), 521-22
Sturm und Drang movement, 63, 345, 388, 511, 520-22, 661; aims of, 520, 522; Goethe and, 560-61; Herder and, 569; Kant's influence on, 551; Schiller and, 570-71, 593; social concepts of, 522; Wieland and, 576
Styria, 341, 358
Suard, Jean-Baptiste (1733-1817), 131, 214, 894
Suard, Mme., nee Panckoucke (1750-1830), 873, 894
Suárez, Francisco (1548-1617), 177
Subterranean Journey of Niels Klim (Holberg), 650-51
Sudbury, sale of votes in, 685
Sumarokov, Alexis Petrovich (1718-77), 427-28
Summa theologiae (St. Thomas Aquinas), 241
Sunni sect, 412, 418-19
superstition and Catholic Church, 316
Supplément au Voyage de Bougainville (Diderot), 31
Sur la législation et la commerce des grains (Necker), 860, 867
Sur la régéneration physique, morale, et politique des Juifs (Grégoire), 642
Süssmayr, Franz Xaver (1766-1803), 408
Sutherland, Elizabeth Gordon, Countess of, 758
Suvorov, Aleksander Vasilievich (1729-1800), 455, 460, 470; in dismemberment of Poland, 491-92; tomb of, 467
Svarez, K. G. (1780), 500
Svea Rikes Historia (Dalin), 659
Svensksund, battle of (1790), 664
Sweden, 653-65; aid to Turkey, 363; army reforms in, 657; art in, 662; coup against Riksdag, 657; Denmark and, 654, 663-64; drama in, 659; economy of, 657, 662; education in, 657, 659; Enlightenment in, 658-62; France and, 89, 654; free press in, 657; government structure of, 654; growing power of nobles of, 654-55; Jews in, 635, 657; in League of Armed Neutrality (1780), 457, 713; legal reforms in, 657; literature in, 659-62; Poland and, 475-76; Prussia and, 653-54, 663; reign of Adolphus Frederick, 655; reign of Charles XII, 653; reign of Frederick I, 654; reign of Gustavus III, 655-65; religious tolerance in, 657; Russia and, 458, 460, 653-56, 663-64; science in, 658-59; social classes in, 654-55, 657,

663-64; taxation in, 654; territorial losses of, 653-54; Turkey and, 460; weakening of monarchy of, 654-55
IN SEVEN YEARS' WAR: invasion of Pomerania, 54; pledge to Austria, 45-46; Pomerania promised to Sweden, 45-46, 48; results of conflict, 63
Swedenborg, Emmanuel (1688-1772), 658
Swieten, Gerhard van (1700-72), 343, 355
Swieten, Baron Gottfried van (1734-1803), 379, 395-96
Swift, Jonathan (1667-1745), 485, 759, 790, 842
Switzerland, 143, *643-45;* art in, 644-45; banking in, 643; cantonal confederation in, 643; conflict of middle class with patricians, 143; conflicts over franchise in, 643-44; education in, 644, 888; Enlightenment in, 645; French Revolution and, 644, 645, 805-6; French subsidies to, 89; internal divisions in, 643; Jews in, 639; manufacturing and commerce in, 643; oligarchy in, 143; peasants in, 27; population of, 643; Rousseau's flight to, 189
symphonic music: evolution of, 221, 528; rise of, 526
Syria, 411
Système de la nature (Holbach), 572, 618
Szczekociny, battle of (1794), 491

Tableau de Paris (Mercier), 901, 919
Tableau économique (Quesnay), 73-74
Tableau philosophique des progrès successifs de l'esprit humain (Turgot), 77
Taboureau de Réau (fl. 1776), 866
Tacitus, Caius Cornelius (55?-120?), 435
Taganrog, 458
Tahmasp II, Shah of Persia (r. 1730-32), 418
Taine, Hippolyte (1828-93), 588, 897
Talavera, 288
Talleyrand-Périgord, Charles-Maurice de (1754-1838), 606, 644, 875, 955, *957-58*
Talma, François Joseph (1763-1828), 607, 920
Talmont, Mme. de, 118
Talmud, 629, 635
Tambirini, Pietro (1737-1827), 316
Tambroni, Clotilda (1758-1817), 219
Tancrède (Voltaire), 136, 874
Tanucci, Marchese Bernardo di (1698-1783), 249, 250, *315*, 327; Goethe on, 589; reforms of, 142; seizes papal cities, 317
tapestry, 910
Targowica, Confederation of, 488-90
tariffs: Austrian, 344; French, 935
Tartaglia (comic figure), 241, 243, 452, 455-56
Tartini, Giuseppe (1692-1770), 221, *229*
Tartuffe (Molière), 923
Task, The (Cowper), 811-12
Tasso, Torquato (1544-95), 464
Tatishchev, Vasili Nikitich (1686-1750), 426-27
Taurida, Jews in, 633
Taurida Palace, 469
Tavares de Sequeira, Dr. Eusebio (fl. 1758), 265

Tavora, Dom Francisco de Assiz, Marquis of (d. 1759), 263-65

Tavora, Dona Leonor, Marchioness of (d. 1759), 263

Tavora, Dom Luis Bernardo de Assiz, "Younger Marquis" of (d. 1759), 263

taxation: in American colonies, 709-10; in Austria, 356-57; in England, 686; in France, *931, 935-36*, 944, 959; in Hungary, 341; in Persia, 420; physiocratic theory of, 73; in Prussia, 500-01; Rousseau's theory of, 174; in Russia, 424, 470; in Spain, 288; in Sweden, 654; Voltaire's views on, 147

Taxation No Tyranny (Johnson), 833

tax farmers in France, 935-36

Taylor, Dr. John (1711–88), 822

tea drinking in England, 729

Teatro alla moda, 223, 234

Teatro alla Scala, 312

Teatro Capranico, 257

Teatro crítico (Feijóo y Montenegro), 294

Teatro Filarmonico of Verona, 245

Teatro Reale, 245

Teatro San Carlo of Naples, 250

technology: Industrial Revolution and, *671-76;* machine-wrecking and, 679

Télémaque (Fénelon), 179, 450

Telemann, Georg Philipp (1681–1767), 526

Teller, Wilhelm Abraham (1734–1804), 507

tenant farmers, 274

Tencin, Claudine-Alexandrine Guérin, Marquise de (1681–1749), 119, 123

Tencin, Pierre Guérin, Cardinal de (1679–1758), 47-48, 246

Tennis Court Oath (1789), 958-59

Terence (184?–159? B.C.), 241, 508, 650

Teresapol, battle of (1794), 491

Terray, Abbé Joseph-Marie (1715–78), 89-90

Terror, Reign of, 496, 725

Tersac, Jean de (fl. 1778), 876, 879, 893

Teschen, Treaty of (1779), 354

Tessin, Count Carl Gustaf (1695–1770), 654, 658, 662

Tessin, Nicodemus (1654–1728), 662

Testa, bishop of Monreale (d. 1773), 316

Test Act (1673), 760, 761

Testament (Messlier), 80, 141

Teutonic Order, 484

teutsche Merkur, Der, 506, 555, 591

textile industry: in England, 672-73, 676, 678; in France, *932*

Textor, Johann Wolfgang, 556

Thames River, 745

theater, 245; in Austria, 346; bourgeoisie and, 104; in Denmark, 650-51; in England, 695-96, *739-43*, 815-16; in France, *101-6, 920-26;* in Germany, *509-10, 513-15*, 560-61, 584-85, 588, 592, 601-3, 604-5; in Italy, 220, 232, *239-44, 336-40;* in Poland, 486; in Portugal, 260; Rousseau's theories of, 163; in Russia, 463-65; in Sweden, 659; Voltaire's contribution to, 136-37

Theatines, 224

Théâtre des Italiens, 113, 244

Théâtre-Français, 101, 102, 147, 256, 920

Théâtre National de l'Odéon, 910

Theophrastus (d. c. 287 B.C.), 508

Théorie de l'impôt (Mirabeau *père*), 74

Theory of Moral Sentiments (Smith), 769

"Theory of the Weather, The" (Goethe), 615

Theresa, Saint (1515–82), 267

Theresianische Halsgerichts-ordnung, 344

Thetis och Pelée (Gustavus III and Willander), 659

Thicknesse, Philip (1720?–92), 755

Thierry, Dr. (fl. 1765), 200

Third Estate: *cahiers* of, 950; composition of, 956; declares itself National Assembly, 958; growth of, 948; leads Day of Tiles (1787), 947-48; representation in States-General, 949; Sieyès' pamphlet on, 954-55; size in population, 955; in States-General, *956-61;* tennis court oath of (1789), 958-59

Third Partition Treaty (1797), 492

Thirty Years' War, 38, 342

Thomas, Ambroise (1811–96), 600

Thomas, Antoine-Léonard (1732–85), 908

Thomas a Kempis (1380–1471), 886

Thomasius, Christian (1655–1728), 528

Thomson, James (1700–48), 104, 169, 379, 518, 661, 732, 887

Thoreau, Henry David (1817–62), 206, 551

Thorild, Thomas (1759–1808), 661

Thorn, 484; confederacy at, 480

Thorwaldsen, Albert Bertel (1770–1844), 331

Thrale, Henry (1728–81), 837

Thrale (later Piozzi), Hester, nee Lynch (1741–1821), 791, 841; issues *Anecdotes of the Late Samuel Johnson, LL.D., during the Last Twenty Years of His Life*, 828, 840; Johnson and, 828, 837-38

Thun, Count von (fl. 1783), 403

Thun, Countess von (fl. 1756), 374

Thurlow, Edward, 1st Baron Thurlow (1731–1806), 736

Ticonderoga, battle of (1775), 58

Tieffen, Franz (fl. 1703), 226

Tiepolo, Domenico (1727–1804), 239, 258, *331-32*

Tiepolo, Giambattista (1696–1770), 235-36, *237-39*, 258, *298-99*, 300

Tierney, George (1761–1830), 732

Tiflis, 419

Tillot, Guillaume, du, *see* Du Tillot, Guillaume

Times, The, 786

Tindal, Matthew (1657–1733), 507

Tingry, Prince de, 161

Tipu Sahib (1751–99), 717

Tiral, 341

Tirso de Molina (1571–1648), 404

Tischbein, Johann Friedrich August (1750–1812), 523

Tischbein, Johann Heinrich (1722–89), 523

Tischbein, Johann Heinrich Wilhelm (1751–1829), 523, 587, 588

tithes: in France, 931; in Spain, 274

"To a Louse on Seeing One on a Lady's Bonnet at Church" (Burns), 775

"To All French Who Still Love Justice and Truth" (Rousseau), 886

"To My Mind" (Kantemir), 427

"To the Liberty and Independence of the United States" (Nascimento), 269

"To Mary in Heaven" (Burns), 775

tobacco, 729

Tocqueville, Alexis Clérel de (1805–59), 897; on French justice, 849; on popular hatred of Church, 902; on pre-revolutionary skepticism, 898

Toland, John (1670–1722), 507

Toledo, Archbishop of, 285, 298

Toleration Act of 1689, 760

Toleration of Deists, . . . by an Anonymous Writer (Reimarus), 513

toll roads in England, 672

tolls in France, 935, 944

Tolstoi, Count Lev Nikolaevich (1823–1910), 3, 891

Tom Jones (Fielding), 835

Tom Jones (opera by Philidor), 100

Tomé, Narciso (fl. 1721), 298

tonado and tonadillo, 292

Tooke, John Horne (1736–1812), 704

Topal Osman (Turkish general), 419

Torgau, battle of (1760), 60

Tories, 692, 711; Stuart dynasty and, 699; support for George III, 699; Whigs compared with, 685

Torquato Tasso (Goethe), 584-85, 587, 588, 601

Torrigiani, Cardinal, papal secretary, 284

Torstenson, Lennart (1603–51), 659

torture: abolished in Austria, 352; abolished in France, 867; abolished in Russia, 146, 321, 431, 451-52; Voltaire's opposition to, 146

Torún (Thorn), 474

Toscanini, Arturo (1867–1957), 234

Toulouse, Parlement of, 92

Tourney, Voltaire's workshops at, 135

Townsend, Joseph (1740–1815), 274

Townshend, Charles (1725–67), 710

Townshend Acts (1767), 710-12

Traëtta, Tommaso (1727–79), 223, 335, 368

tragedy, middle class development of, 104

Traité des qualités d'un grand roi (Morelly), 81

Transcendentalist movement, 551

transportation, 672

Trapassi, Pietro, see Mestastasio, Pietro

Tratado de la regalia de l'amortización (Campomanes), 282-83

Trattato dei delitti e delle pene (Beccaria), 145, 320

Trattato della moneta (Galiani), 251

Trauttmansdorff (friend of Tamburini), 316

Traveller, or A Prospect of Society, The (Goldsmith), 815

Travels in France (Young), 928*

Treatise on Civil Architecture (Chambers), 747

Treatise on Crimes and Penalties (Beccaria), 320

Treatise on Human Nature (Hume), 756, 769

Treatise on the Capability of the Feeling for Beauty (Winckelmann), 328

Treatise on Toleration (Voltaire), 357

Treatise on Toleration (Voltaire), 357

Trembecki, Stanislas (1737?–1812), 486

Trentes, Les, 957

Trento, 229

Trescho, Sebastian, 567

Trevi, Fontana di, 247

Treviso, 229, 239

Trier, 341, 503

Trier, Archbishop-Elector of (fl. 1788), 504-5

Trieste, 641

Trinity College (in Ireland), 759

Tristram Shandy (Sterne), 787-89

Troisième Entretien sur Le Fils naturel (Diderot), 101

Tronchin, François (author and painter), 212, 213

Tronchin, Jean-Robert (1710–93), 197

Tronchin, Dr. Théodore (1709–81), 103, 159-60, 875-76; 878; on last hours of Voltaire, 879

Troost, Cornelis (1697–1750), 647

Trudaine de Montigny, Jean-Charles-Philibert (1733–77), 73

Truffaldino (comic figure), 241

Tsarskoe Selo, Palace of, 426, 468

Tschoudi, Baron Jean-Baptiste de (b. 1734), 372

Tubières, Anne-Claude de, Comte de Caylus (1692–1765), 110, 120, 218, 467, 749

Tucker, Josiah (1712–99), 676

Tugenbund, 641

Tuileries Gardens, 107, 962

Tunisia, 411

Türckheim, Bernhard Friedrich von (d. 1831), 566

Turenne, Henri de La Tour d' Auvergne, Maréchal Vicomte de (1611–75), 109

Turgot, Anne-Robert-Jacques, Baron de l'Aulne (1727–81), 72-73, 98, 125, 143*, 214, 769, 858-65, 869, 929; advocates religious toleration, 863; agricultural reforms of, 859; appearance of, 858; Assembly of Notables and, 944; attack on feudalism, 861-63; attempts to save monarchy, 898; bread crisis in Paris and, 860; conflicts with Paris Parlement, 861-63; conflicts with privileged classes, 858, 863-64; as controller general of finance, 858; early life of, 77-79; early official career of, 79; economic reforms of, 859-60; fall of, 75; financial reforms of, 859-61; French Revolution and, 940; influence of physiocrats on, 858; later years and death of, 865; in Lespinasse salon, 126; Louis XVI and, 859-60, 863-65; love for the people, 856; Marie Antoinette and, 863-65;

ministry of, 858-65; *philosophes* and, 78-79, 858-59, 863, 865; reforms of, 80, 144, 863; resignation from ministry (1776), 864-65; Swedish economic reform and, 657; theories of, 77-78; tries to help Protestants, 902; Voltaire and, 874, 875

Turin, 256; churches in, 224; Enlightenment in, 310; history and achievements of, 226; industry in, 218; ratio of priests to lay population in, 224; theaters in, 220; universities in, 219

Turkey, 356; architecture in, 414; art in, 414; Austria's conflicts with, 61, 363, 365, 411, 414-15, 430; cleanliness and sanitation in, 413; commerce, 456; culture in, 412; Hungary invaded by, 62; Jews in, 632; papacy and, 457; Peace of Jassy (1792), 488; Persia and, 417-19; poetry in, 412-13; Poland and, 415, 458, 475, 482; Protestant aid to, 363; repulsed from Vienna (1683), 411; reign of Abdul-Hamid I, 415; reign of Mahmud I, 415; Russia's conflicts with, 140, 414-15, 430, 457-61, 470, 483, 663; slavery in, 413; Spain and, 288; Sultanate in, 414; Sweden and, 460; Venice's conflict with, 414; women in, 413

EMPIRE OF: conquest of Crete and Greece (1715), 414; decline, 414-15; European, 414-15; North African, 415-17; size, 411

turnpikes in England, 672

Tuscany, 228, 278-79, 312; Austria and, 217, 228; church lands in, 224; early history of, 313; Inquisition abolished in, 316; Napoleon I in, 314; reforms of Grand Duke Leopold, 313-14; triumph of reaction in, 314

Tuscany, Grand Duke of (r. 1765-90), *see* Leopold II, Emperor

Tuyll, Isabella van, *see* Charrière, Isabelle de

Über die bürgerliche Verbesserung der Juden in Deutschland (Dohn), 642

Über naive und sentimentalische Dichtung (Schiller), 599

Über die neuere deutsche Literatur (Herder), 567

Udine, 229

Uffizi Gallery, 228

Uhlfeld, Count von (fl. 1742), 40

Ukraine, 460

Ulrika Eleanora, Queen of Sweden (r. 1719-20), 654

Ulster, 760

Uman, massacres in, 634

Umberto I Biancamano (970?-1050?), Count of Savoy, 226

Una delle ultime sere di Carnevale (Goldoni), 244

Unger, Georg Christian (1743-1812), 524

Uniates, 475; *see also* Greek Orthodox Church, in Poland

Unigenitus (Pope Benedict XIV), 246

Union of 1707 (Scotland and England), 762

Unitarianism, Rousseau's belief in, 163

United Company of Merchants of England

trading to the East Indies, *see* British East India Company

United Provinces, *see* Holland

United States, 487; French recognition of, 713; Jews in, 642; literature in, 889; physiocratic influence in, 77; treaty of alliance with France (1778), 870

United States Constitution, Bill of Rights of, 872

United States of Belgium, 364

Universal Chronicle, The, 825

Universal Church History (Holberg), 650

Universal Etymological English Dictionary, An (Bailey), 820-21

universities, 218-19, 276, 294, 301, 358, 360, 362, 453, 505-6, 532, 647, 659, 674, 763, 769

Unwin, Mary (1724-96), 811-13

Unwin, Rev. Morley (d. 1767), 811

Unwin, Susannah, 811

Unwin, William, 811

Upsala, University of, 659

"Urbarian Law" (1774), 350

Urfaust (Goethe), 608

Ursins, Marie-Anne de La Trémoille, Princesse des (1642?-1722), 276

Ussé, Mlle. d', 894

Utilitarianism, 738-39

Utrecht, 361, 647

Utrecht, Treaty of (1713), 57, 226, 277, 547

Uzbekistan, Persian invasion of (1740), 420

Uzbeks, 417, 418, 420

Vais (d. 1715), Mir of Kandahar, 418

Valdés, Juan Meléndez, *see* Meléndez Valdés, Juan

Valencia, 273; growth of, 289

Valencia, University of, 294

Valentinois, Comtesse de (fl. 1758), 161

Valhynia, anti-Semitic massacres in, 634

Valle, Filippo della (1696-1768), 247

Valley Forge, Americans at, 869

Vallin de La Mothe, Jean-Baptiste (1729-1800), 468

Valmarana, Villa, 239

Valmy, battle of (1792), 580, 591

Vandyck, Sir Anthony (1599-1641), 466

Vanity of Human Wishes, The (Johnson), 821

Vanloo, Carle (1705-65), 115, 120

Vanloo, Louis-Michel (1707-71), 298

Vanvitelli (Italian painter), 298

Vanvitelli, Luigi (1700-73), 250

Värälä, Treaty of (1790), 664

Varicourt, Mlle., *see* Villette, Marquise de

Vasco da Gama, *see* Gama, Vasco da

Vassilchik, Alexis (fl. 1772), 445

Vathek (Beckford), 809

Vatican School of Painting, 248

Vauban, Sébastien Le Prestre, Seigneur de (1633-1707), 72

Vaud, revolts in, 645

Vaudreuil, Louis-Philippe de Rigaud, Comte de (1724-1802), 853

Vaudreuil-Cavagnal, Pierre-François de Rigaud, Marquis de (1698–1765), 58

Vaughn, C. E., 5*

Vauvenargues, Luc de Clapiers, Marquis de (1715–47), 150, 915

Vauxhall, 744

"Veilchen, Das" (Goethe), 400

Velázquez, Diego Rodríguez de Silva y (1599–1660), 301, 305

Vendôme, Louis-Joseph de Bourbon, Duc de (1654–1712), 277

Venezianishche Epigramme (Goethe), 590

Venice, 217, 229, 239, 310, 641; Casanova in, 323, 325; clothing in, 231; daily life and entertainment in, 230-32; decay of (1760–89), 310-11; economy of, 229–30; French occupation of (1797), 311; gain by Treaty of Passerowitz (1718), 415; Goethe in, 590; government of, 229; instrumental music in, 254; Jesuit colleges in, 219; Jews in, 631; libraries in, 219; literature of, 239-44; music in, 220, *232-33*; painting in, 331-32; population of, 229; prostitution in, 230; religion in, 230; Scarlatti in, 256; size of, 229; theaters in, 220, 241; war with Turkey (1715), 414; wealth of clergy in, 224

Venice Preserved (Otway), 741

Ventimiglio, Monsignor, bishop of Catania (fl. 1760), 316

Veracini, Francesco Maria (c. 1685?–1750), 228

Verdelin, Mme. de (fl. 1765), 209

Verdi, Giuseppe (1813–1901), 335

Verevkin (translator), 463-64

Vergara, Francisco, the Younger (1713–61), 298

Vergennes, Charles Gravier, Comte de (1717–87), 656, 858, 864, 922; American Revolution and, 867-68, 870, 871; Franklin and, 869; predicts American Revolution, 708

Vermenoux, Marquise de, 865

Vermond, Abbé Matthieu-Jacques de (d. after 1789), 846

Vernes, Jacob or Jacques (1728–91), Swiss pastor, 190, 200

Vernet, Claude-Joseph (1714–89), French painter, 111, 120, 466

Vernet, Isaac (fl. 1750), Swiss banker, 865

Vernet, Mme., wife of Claude-Joseph, 895, 897

Verney, Ralph, 2d Earl Verney (fl. 1765), 692, 719

Verona, *228-29*, 245

Verona illustrata (Maffei), 229

Veronese, Paolo (1528–88), 238, 239

Verri, Pietro (fl. 1770), *312*, 320

Verrières, Geneviève Rinteau de (b. 1731), 35

Verrières, Marie Rinteau de (1728–75), 35

Versailles: court in, 849-50; palaces at, 85, 250; riots in, 934; women's march to, 919, 934

Versailles, Peace of (1783), 290

Versailles, Treaty of: first (1756), 42; second (1757), 45

Verschwörung des Fiesko zu Genua, Die (Schiller), 571-72

"Versuch, aus der vergleichenden Knochenlehre . . ." (Goethe), 617

Vesey, Elizabeth (1715?–91), *730, 789*

Vespro, Il (Parini), 335

Vessan, Marie de, 951

Vestris, Gaétan (1729–1808), 370

Vestris or Vestrice, Marie-Rose, nee Gourgaud-Dugason (1746–1804), 877

Vesuvius, Goethe climbs, 588-89

Vicar of Wakefield, The (Goldsmith), 814-15

Vicenza, *229;* Goethe in, 587; industry in, 218; theaters in, 220

Vichy, Diane de, nee d'Albon (b. 1716), 122

Vichy, Gaspard de, 122, 131

Vico, Gennaro, Charles IV's aid to, 254

Vico, Giambattista (1668–1744), *251-54;* early life of, 251; failure to gain attention, 253-54; philosophy of history, 251-53; rediscovery of, 254; secularism of, his analysis, 253

Vicq-d'Azyr, Félix (1748–94), 617

Victor Amadeus II, Duke of Savoy (r. 1675–1732), King of Sardinia as Victor Amadeus I (r. 1720–30), 226

Vie de mon père, La (Restif de La Bretonne), 918

Vie de Voltaire (Condorcet), 894

Vieira, Francisco (1699–1783), 261

Vielleville, M. de (fl. 1778), 876

Vien, Joseph-Marie (1716–1809), 912

Vienna, 245, 256; beauty of, 345; as capital city, 341; dancing in, 345; industries in, 344; Jews in, 631-32; music in, 345, 367-72; Napoleon's bombardment of (1809), 380; newspapers in, 346; theaters in, 346; Turks repulsed from (1683), 411

Vienna, University of, 343, 352, 360

Vigée-Lebrun, Marie-Anne Élisabeth (1755–1842), 99, 111, 372, 467, 644, 851, 888, *913-14;* on acclamation of Voltaire, 878; celebrates children and motherhood, 904; on religious piety, 901

Vigny, Alfred de (1797–1863), 889

Viladomat, Antonio (1678–1755), 298

Villa Albani, 249, 331

Villa Malmarana, 239

Villanueva, Juan de (1739–1811), 289

Villars, Duc Honoré-Armand de (1702–70), 133

Villeneuve, M. de, 952

Villeroi, François de Neufville, Duc de (1644–1730), 161

Villette, Marquis Charles de (1736–93), 874-75

Villette, Reine-Philiberte de Varicourt, Marquise de, 150, 874, 877

Villette, Retaux de (1785), 942-43

Vincennes: Diderot in, 19-20; Mirabeau *fils* in, 952-53

Vinci, Leonardo (1690–1730), composer, 240, 254

Vindication of the Jews (Manasseh ben Israel), 640

Vindication of Natural Society, or a View of

the *Miseries and Evils Arising to Mankind from Every Species of Artificial Society, A* (Burke), 690-91

Vindication of Some Passages in the Fifteenth and Sixteenth Chapters of the History of the Decline and Fall of the Roman Empire, A (Gibbon), 802

vingtième, 936

violin, popularity of, 332

Viotti, Giovanni Battista (1753–1824), 332-33

Virgil (70–19 B.C.), 519, 793

Virginia Assembly, 872

Vischer, Luise (fl. 1780), 570

Visin, Denis Ivanovich von (1744–92), 464

Vistula River, 472

Vita di Vittorio Alfieri . . . scritta da esso (Alfieri), 336

Vitruvius, Goethe in, 587

Vitruvius Pollio, Marcus (1st century B.C.), 747

Vivaldi, Antonio (1675?–1741), 232, *233-34*

Vocabolario (Accademia della Crusca of Florence), 824

Vogler, Abt Georg Josef (1749–1814), 252

Volga Tartars, 452

Volhynia, 492

Volkschulen, 352

Volkslieder (Herder), 577

Volney, Comte Constantin de (1757–1820), 917-18, 955

Volta, Alessandro (1745–1827), 310

Voltaire (François-Marie Arouet; 1694–1778), 40, 43, 59, 67, *132-51*, 156, 207, 220, 246, 269, 280, 286, 295, 336-37, 351, 357, 372, 422, 427, 432, 435, 463, 478, 481, 485, 511, 531, 550, 553, 559-60, 561, 607, 608, 641, 650, 655, 660, 693, 725, 769, 781, 825, 832, *873-81*, 889, 894, 895, 915-16, 925, 928, 952, 964; Abarca's visit to, 281; adulation of, 34; on age of Louis XV, 137-38; d'Alembert and, 123, 125, 138, 876-77; appearance of, 134, 148; attitude toward activity, 135; attitude toward rivals, 149; bones stolen from Panthéon, 880; Boswell and, *133-34*, 204, 782; bourgeois values of, 148; caned by Beauregard, 150; Casanova's visit to, 138, 143, *324;* Catherine II and, 434, 442, 447-48, 451, 457-58, 462, 469, 873; Choiseul and, 88, 132; Clairon and, 102, 104; collected works published, 925; condemnation of Shakespeare, 835; death of Wilhelmine and, 54; deference to royalty, 176; description of Paris, 933; Diderot and, 876, 892; Du Barry and, 87-88; Mme. du Deffand and, 125; energy of, 135; enthusiasm for England, 144; epigrammatic style of, 170; Frederick II and, 47, 49, 56, 59-60, 496-99, 528, 873, 876, 879; French Academy and, 877, 879; friendship with monarchs, 897; generosity of, 150; Gluck's operatic views and, 368; Goldsmith's biography of, 814; on Gustavus III, 657; on *Histoire du Parlement de Paris, par M. l'abbé Big*, 92; historical writings of, 528; on history, 807*; Houdon's bust of, 911-12; humanity of, 151; imitation of Maffei's *Merope*, 228-29; on Index Expurgatorius, 316; influence of, 230, 346-47, 542, *880-81;* Samuel Johnson's dislike of, 834; Lekain discovered by, 101-102; Lessing and, 509, 512; lies of, 148-49; Lisbon earthquake and, 533; Louis XV and, 88; Louis XVI and, 857, 867, 875, 879; love of luxury, 141; love of money, 148; loyalty to friends, 150; on Marie Theresa, 343; Marie Antoinette and, 873-74, 875; meets Gibbon, 797; mocks legend of noble savage, 31; moral courage of, 150-51; Mozart's dislike of, 392, 402; nature and, 169; on opera, 101; in Panthéon, 110; on Paris, 71; partition of Poland and, 484; personality of, 135, 141, *147-51;* physical cowardice of, 149; Pigalle's statue of, 107-8, 280; on Mme. de Pompadour, 69; praise for Goldoni, 242; predicts French Revolution, 143; preface to Beccaria's book, 321; rancor of, 149; Rousseau and, *see* Rousseau, Jean-Jacques, VOLTAIRE AND; scholarship of, 148; sees need for popular religion, 903; Seven Years' War and, 56-57; on *Tristram Shandy*, 788; tributes to, 108; Turgot and, 78-79, 859, 865; use of cosmetics, 134; vanity of, 149; views on drama, 136; wealth of, 140-41; Wilkes's visit to, 703

AT LES DÉLICES (1755–58), 27, 132

AT FERNEY (1758–78): agricultural activities, 135; daily routine, 134-35; ill health, 134-35; last years, 873-74; management of estate, 132-33; moves to, 164; personal habits, 134; relations with employees, 135-36; theater, 134; visitors to, 133-34; workshops at, 135

FINAL YEARS OF (1774–78): adopts Reine Philiberte de Varicourt, 874; appearance of, 878; burial and aftermath, 879-80; fame and adulation, 873; final illness and death, 879; goes to Paris, 774-75; he suggests reforms to Louis XVI, 873; he writes *Irène*, 274; illnesses, 876; last writings, 873-74; performance of *Irène*, 877; reception in Paris, 875-79; seeks to be confessed, 876; Turgot and, 874, 875; visits of clergy to, 875-76

RELIGION AND, 646; anticlerical views, 145; attends religious services, 452; Catholic Church and, 138, 890, 893; defense of Calas, 90, 146, 151, 881; skeptical outlook, 148

POLITICAL VIEWS AND ACTIVITIES (1758–78): aid to Swiss *natifs*, 634-44; on Alberoni's reforms, 277; anti-Semitism of, 149-50; attack on Paris Parlement, 92-95; Beccaria's influence on, 145; belief in monarchism, 142-43; contempt for masses, 147; French Revolution and, 84, 880, 890-91, 899, 940; opposition to equalitarianism, 141-42; opposition to revolutions, 144-45; opposition to serfdom, 135; predicts French Revolution, 143; reforms advocated by, 145-47; support for property, 141; sychophancy toward royalty, 140, 148; views on democracy, 142-45

WRITINGS OF (1758–78), 75-76; anti-clerical, 138;

correspondence, 138-40; denies authorship of controversial writings, 149; histories, 137-38; Italian translation of Voltaire's works, 219; philosophical works, 138; plays, 101-3, 136-37; poem on Lisbon earthquake, 154; variety of, 136-37

Volumina legum (Konarski), 475

Volunteers, Irish Protestant, 760-61

Vorontsov, Mikhail Ilarionovich (1714-67), 432

Vorontsova, Elizaveta (fl. 1760), 436-37, 439-40

Voss, Johann Heinrich (1751-1826), 519, 601, 605

Vossische Zeitung, 506

Voyage à l'Île de France (Bernardin de Saint-Pierre), 916

Voyage du jeune Anacharsis en Grèce (Barthélemy), 917

Voyer, Marc-René d'Argenson, Marquis de (1722-82), 135

Vulpius, Christiane, *see* Goethe, Christiane

wages: of English workers, 677, 679; of French workers, 933

Wagner, Richard (1813-83), 26, 335

Wagnière, Jean-Louis (1739-after 1787), 133; on Voltaire and clergy, 876; on Voltaire's appearance and habits, 134-35; on Voltaire's trip to Paris, 875

Wahabite sect, 412

Wahlverwandtschaften, Die (Goethe), 612

Wäldchen (Herder), 568

Waldegrave, James, 2d Earl Waldegrave (1715-63), 687, 795

Wales, 670

Wales, George Augustus Frederick, Prince of, *see* George IV

"Walk, The" (Schiller), 599

Wallace, Robert (fl. 1750), Scottish clergyman, 763

Wallachia, 411, 483; ceded by Turks to Austria (1718), 415; peasant revolt in, 361

Wallensteins Lager (Schiller), 601-2

Wallensteins Tod (Schiller), 601-2

wallpaper, 910, 956

Walpole, Horace, 4th Earl of Orford (1676-1745), 118, 120, 201, 228, 436, 447, 723, 729-30, 736, 740, 742, 746, 748, 785, 786, 791-95, 809, 824; on Boswell's *Life of Johnson*, 841; Chatterton and, 809-10; death of, 795; Mme. du Deffand and, 125, 794-95, 906-7; early life and education of, 792; elected to Parliament, 792-93; family background of, 791; on French authors, 104; on George III, 698; Gibbon and, 800, 803-4; on historians, 795; hoax on Rousseau, 208, 212-14; on individuality of England, 733-34; influence of Burke on, 691; on Johnson, 830, 831; Julie de Lespinasse and, 906-7; literary tastes of, 793-94; memoirs and letters of, 795; opposes slave trade, 733; personality of, 793; on *philosophes*, 95; policies in Parliament, 793; policy toward India, 716; as pub-

lisher, 793; on Robertson, 766; support for American colonies, 711, 713; tour of Italy, 792; visit to France, 794-95; wealth of, 795; writings of, 794

Walpole, Sir Robert, 1st Earl of Orford (1676-1745), 466, 792, 819

Warburton, William (1698-1779), 690, 703, 737

Warens, Françoise-Marie de La Tour, Baronne de (1699-1762), 27, 167; early life of, 7; Rousseau and, 7, 9-15

"War of the Buffoons," 101

Warsaw, 474-75, 490; acquired by Prussia, 492; last stand against partition, 491-92

Warton, Thomas (1728-90), 824

Washington, George (1732-99), 701, 714, 856; attack on Fort Duquesne, 57; French Enlightenment and, 867; Houdon's bust of, 912; influence of *philosophes* on, 899; retreat before Howe, 869; victory at Yorktown (1781), 871

Was ist Aufklärung? (Kant), 540

Watelet, Claude-Henri (1718-86), 126

water frame, 673

Waterloo, battle of (1815), 627

water power and factories, 673

waterways, trade on, 672

Watson, Charles, Admiral (fl. 1757), 58

Watt, James (1736-1819), 674-76, 734, 763-64

Watteau, Antoine (1684-1721), 116, 235

Wealth of Nations, The (Smith), 746, 786, 808; anticipates Marx's theories, 771; basic concepts of, 769-71; influence of, 772

Weber, Aloysia (1761?-1839), 390-91, 393, 399

Weber, Constanze, *see* Mozart, Constanze

Weber, Fridolin (fl. 1778), 390

Weber, Josepha (1758-1819), 390

Weber, Karl Maria von (1786-1826), 243*, 380, 575, 576

Webster, Noah, 824

Wedgwood, Josiah (1739-95), 733-34, 749-50

Weigel, Eva Maria, *see* Garrick, Eva Maria

Weimar, 581; court life in, 552-53; cultural life in, 552; Napoleon in, 606-7; population of, 552

Weishaupt, Adam (1748-1830), 507

Weisweiler, Adam (d. 1809), 523

Wellington, Arthur Wellesley, Duke of (1769-1852), Madrid liberated by, 307

Werner (Byron), 627

Werner, Abraham (1750-1817), 615

Werner, Gregor (d. 1766), 375

Werther (Goethe), *see* Sorrows of Young Werther, The (Goethe)

Wesel, Prussia retains, 62

Wesley, John (1703-91), 658, 711, 731-32, 749

West Indies, 58, 732

Westminster, Treaty of (1756), 39-40

Westminster, voting population in, 685

Westminster Convention (1689), 683

Westöstlicher Diwan (Goethe), 641

Westphalia, Frederick II occupies, 53

Westphalia, Treaty of (1648), 38, 46

West Prussia, 484

"What Is, and to What End Does One Study, Universal History?" (Schiller), 593

"Whether the Metaphysical Sciences Are Susceptible of Such Evidence as the Mathematical" (Mendelssohn), 638

Whigs, 692, 711; Hanoverian dynasty and, 699; Hastings' trial and, 719; opposition to George III, 699; Tories compared with, 685

Whiston, William (1667–1752), 507

"Whiteboys," rebellion of (Irish Catholic bands), 760

White Russia, 484

"Wiegenlied bei Mondenschein zu singen" (Claudius), 519

Wieland, Christoph Martin (1733–1813), 503, 506, 562, 567, 611, 628, 641, 766; appearance of, 576; contribution to literature, 555; death of, 576-77, 580; early life of, 553; as Freemason, 507; on Goethe, 580-81; on Herder, 577; literary activities of, 576; philosophy of life, 553-55; Sturm und Drang and, 576; Voltaire's influence on, 880; in Weimar, 552; welcomes French Revolution, 590

Wiener Zeitung, 346

wigs, 231

Wilberforce, William (1759–1833), 726, 733

Wilhelm of Hanau, ruler of Hesse-Cassel (r. 1785–1803) as landgrave, (r. 1803–21) as elector, 634

Wilhelm Meister (Goethe), 585, 620-21

Wilhelm Meisters Lehrjahre (Goethe), 558, 599–601

Wilhelmine, Margravine of Bayreuth (1709–1758), sister of Frederick II, 47-48, 54, 529

Wilkes, John (1727–97), 699, 700, *701-4,* 722, 734, 833; Boswell and, 782; conflict with Bute ministry, 702; death of, 708; duel with Martin, 703; early life and education of, 701-2; enters House of Commons, 702; expelled from House of Commons (1764), 701, 703; flight to Europe of, 703; Goldsmith and, 817; in Gordon Riots, 736; imprisonment of, 702, 704; as leader of parliamentary "radicals," 708; in Medmenham Abbey, 809; in Naples, 330; personality of, 701, 703; popular support for, 703-4, 707; release from jail, 707; retains parliament seat, 706-7; riots in support of, 704; second expulsion from House of Commons (1769), 704; support for American colonies, 711; third expulsion from House of Commons (1769), 704

Wilkinson, John (1728–1808), 672, 675

Willander, Johan (fl. 1782), 659

Wille, Johann Georg (1715–1807), 113

Willemer, Johann Jakob von (1760–1838), 613-14

Willemer, Marianne von, nee Jung (1784–1860), 613-14

William I, King of the Netherlands (r. 1815–40), 649

William III, Stadholder of Holland (r. 1672–1702), King of England, Scotland, and Ireland (r. 1689–1702), 648, 683

William IV, Stadholder of Holland (r. 1747–51), 648

William V, Stadholder of Holland (r. 1751–95), 648-49

William Frederick, Prince (1776–1834), Duke of Gloucester, 753

William Henry, Fort, 58

William of Ockham (1300?–40), 177

William Tell (Schiller), 604-5

Williams, Anna (1706–83), 780, 822

Williams (London printer; fl. 1763), 702

Wilna, Elijah, *see* Elijah ben Solomon

Wilno, 489, 491

Wilson, Richard (1714–82), 750-51

Winckelmann, Johann Joachim (1717–68), *325-31, 337, 467, 523,* 557, 588, 595, 703, 747, 782, 910, 912; early life and education of, 325-26; enters Catholic Church, 326; esthetic theories of, 328-29; Gluck's operatic views and, 368; hatred of Prussia, 530; honors given to, 330; influence of, 110, 118, 329-30, 524; Lessing and, 510; limitations of, 330-31; Mengs and, 248-49, 327, 329, 331-32; murder of, 330; on Oeser's paintings, 523; paganism of, 326*; revives classical style, 315; in Rome, 314, 327-28; views on Laocoön statue, 510

Winter Palace, Russia, 426

witchcraft, 276, 316, 356

Woffington, Peg (1714–60), 689, 740, 742

Wolf, Friedrich August (1759–1824), classical philologist, 253

Wolfe, James (1727–59), 58

Wolfenbüttel: library at, 512; Seven Years' War in, 60

Wolfenbüttel Fragments (Reimarus), 578

Wolff, Caspar Friedrich (1733–94), biologist, 616*

Wolff, Christian von (1679–1754), as philosopher-mathematician, 294, 507, 532, 536, 538, 567, 637; influence of, 531-32, 889; philosophy of, 508

Wöllner, Johann Christian von (1730?–1800), 547

Wollstonecraft, Mary (1759–97), 881

Wolzogen, Frau Henrietta von (fl. 1782), 572

Wolzogen, Lotte von, 572

women, 896; in England, 678, 682, 728, 730-31, 787; in factories, 671, 678, 682; in France, 97, 99, *906-8;* in Germany, 503-4; in Italy, 218-19; in Moslem countries, 413; in Poland, 474; Rousseau's views on, 186; in Spain, 290-91; Sturm und Drang movement and, 522

Woodfall, Henry Sampson (1739–1805), 706

Woodward, Henry (1714–77), 741

Wootton, Rousseau's stay in, 211-12

Wordsworth, William (1770–1850), 3, 809, 813

workers: in England, 670-71, 673, 676-82; in France, 914; French Revolution and, *933-34;* in Russia, 423; Smith's support for, 771

Works of Ossian, The (Macpherson), 559, 567, 767-68, 809
World as Will and Idea, The (Schopenhauer), 550
Wortley Montagu, Edward (1678–1761), 412, 413, 730
Writings and Genius of Shakespeare, The (Montagu), 730
Württemberg, 502-3
Württemberg, Duke of: in 1733–37, *see* Karl Alexander, Duke; in 1737–93, *see* Karl Eugen, Duke
Württemberg, Prince of, 246
Württemberg, Princess of, 246
Würzburg-Bamberg, 503
Würzburg Residenz, 239

Xenien (Goethe and Schiller), 598-99

Yankovich, Theodor (fl. 1786), 453
"Ye banks an' braes o' bonnie Doon" (Burns), 777
Yenikale, 458
York, theater in, 740
Yorktown, battle of (1781), 714, 761, 871
Young, Arthur (1741–1820), 912, 931; description of Paris, 933; on emerging revolutionary movement in French, 946; on French agriculture, 928; on manners in France, 905; on Marie Antoinette, 941; observations of, 933; on poverty in England, 677; on unrest in Paris, 957, 959
Young, Edward (1683–1765), 518, 661

Young Pretender, *see* Stuart, Charles Edward
Ypres, 361
Yverdon, 190

Zaddikim, 636
Zaluski, Józef Andrzej, bishop of Kiev, 475, 481
Zand dynasty, 420
Zante, 229
Zapater, Goya's friend (fl. 1788), 303
Zarcillo y Alcáraz, Francisco (1707–81), 298
Zavadovsky, Piotr (fl. 1776), 446
Zedlitz, Karl Abraham von (1731–93), 505, 535, 540
zelanti faction, 317
Zelter, Karl Friedrich (1758–1832), 614-15
Zeno, Apostolo (1668–1750), 220, 223, 239
Ziegesar, Silvie von (fl. 1810), 612-13
Zielence, battle of (1792), 488-89
Ziethen, Johann (Hans) Joachim von (1699–1786), 60
Zimmermann, Dr. Johann Georg (1728–95), 530, 582, 608
Zoffany, John (1733–1810), 746
Zorich, Simon (fl. 1777), 446
Zorndorf, battle of (1758), 53, 437
Zubov, Platon (b. 1764), 446, 470
Zubov, Valerian (b. 1765), 470
Züllichau, battle of, 55
Zur Farbenlehre (Goethe), 616
Zurich, 643, 645
Zweibrücken, Duke Charles of, *see* Charles, Duke of Zweibrücken

About the Authors

WILL DURANT was born in North Adams, Massachusetts, in 1885. He was educated in the Catholic parochial schools there and in Kearny, New Jersey, and thereafter in St. Peter's (Jesuit) College, Jersey City, New Jersey, and Columbia University, New York. For a summer he served as a cub reporter on the New York *Journal*, in 1907, but finding the work too strenuous for his temperament, he settled down at Seton Hall College, South Orange, New Jersey, to teach Latin, French, English, and geometry (1907–11). He entered the seminary at Seton Hall in 1909, but withdrew in 1911 for reasons which he has described in his book *Transition*. He passed from this quiet seminary to the most radical circles in New York, and became (1911–13) the teacher of the Ferrer Modern School, an experiment in libertarian education. In 1912 he toured Europe at the invitation and expense of Alden Freeman, who had befriended him and now undertook to broaden his borders.

Returning to the Ferrer School, he fell in love with one of his pupils, resigned his position, and married her (1913). For four years he took graduate work at Columbia University, specializing in biology under Morgan and Calkins and in philosophy under Woodbridge and Dewey. He received the doctorate in philosophy in 1917, and taught philosophy at Columbia University for one year. In 1914, in a Presbyterian church in New York, he began those lectures on history, literature, and philosophy which, continuing twice weekly for thirteen years, provided the initial material for his later works.

The unexpected success of *The Story of Philosophy* (1926) enabled him to retire from teaching in 1927. Thenceforth, except for some incidental essays, Mr. and Mrs. Durant gave nearly all their working hours (eight to fourteen daily) to *The Story of Civilization*. To better prepare themselves they toured Europe in 1927, went around the world in 1930 to study Egypt, the Near East, India, China, and Japan, and toured the globe again in 1932 to visit Japan, Manchuria, Siberia, Russia, and Poland. These travels provided the background for *Our Oriental Heritage* (1935) as the first volume in *The Story of Civilization*. Several further visits to Europe prepared for Volume II, *The Life of Greece* (1939) and Volume III, *Caesar and Christ* (1944). In 1948, six months in Turkey, Iraq, Iran, Egypt, and Europe provided perspective for Volume IV, *The Age of Faith* (1950). In 1951 Mr. and Mrs. Durant returned to Italy to add to a lifetime of gleanings for Volume V, *The Renaissance* (1953); and in 1954 further studies in Italy, Switzerland, Germany, France, and England opened new vistas for Volume VI, *The Reformation* (1957).

Mrs. Durant's share in the preparation of these volumes became more and more substantial with each year, until in the case of Volume VII, *The Age of Reason Begins* (1961), it was so pervasive that justice required the union of both names on the title page. The name Ariel was first applied to his wife by Mr. Durant in his novel *Transition* (1927) and in his *Mansions of Philosophy* (1929) —now reissued as *The Pleasures of Philosophy*.

With the publication of Volume X, *Rousseau and Revolution*, the Durants have concluded over four decades of work.

NORTH SEA

KINGDOM OF DENMARK

Tönning • Slesvik • Kiel
• Rendsburg
HOLSTEIN
Cuxhaven • Lübeck
• Hamburg
DUCHY OF BREMEN
• Bremen
Lauenburg
ELECTORATE OF HANOVER
• Salzwede
MEC

Norwich •
Ipswich •

Groningen •
PRINCIPALITY OF EAST FRIESLAND
• Oldenburg
BISHOPRIC OF Lingen
• Nienburg
• Minden
Hanover •
Brunswick •
ALT-MAR
DUCHY OF MAGDEBURG

Alkmaar •
Amsterdam •
The Hague • Leiden •
Rotterdam • Utrecht •
UNITED NETHERLANDS
Bentheim •
BISHOPRIC OF MÜNSTER
Münster •
• Arnheim
• Cleves
Dortmund •
• Paderborn
DUCHY OF BRUNSWICK
• Göttingen
• Cassel
• Mühlhausen

Dover •
Dunkerque
Calais •
Boulogne •
Lille •
LANDGRAVATE OF THE GENERALITY
Bruges • Ghent •
AUSTRIAN Antwerp
Brussels •
Mons •
BISHOPRIC OF LIÈGE
Cologne •
Düsseldorf •
Aix-la-Chapelle
Bonn •
DUCHY OF WESTPHALIA
LANDGRAVATE OF HESSE-CASSEL
• Gotha • Weima
SAXON DUCHIES
ELEC

Abbeville •
Amiens •
Douai •
Marienbourg •
NETHERLANDS
Luxenburg
• Coblenz
ARCHBISHOPRIC OF TREVES
• Bergen
Frankfurt am Main
BISHOPRIC OF WÜRZBURG
• Coburg
Bamberg

Laon •
Reims •
Châlons •
Verdun •
Metz •
Treves •
Worms •
PALATINATE
Heidelberg •
Rothenburg •
• Nuremberg
• Ansbach

Paris •
Versailles •
KINGDOM OF FRANCE
Bar-le-Duc •
Toul •
Nancy
LORRAINE to France 1735, 1766
Saarbrücken •
MARGRAVATE OF BADEN
DUCHY OF WÜRTTEMBERG
• Stuttgart
• Ellwangen
• Nördlingen
• Ulm

Fontainebleau •
Troyes •
Langres •
Épinal •
Strasbourg •
Salm •
Colmar •
Mulhouse •
Rothweil •
Biberech •
Ostrach •
Augsburg •
• Munich

Bourges •
Nevers •
Chalon •
Montbéliard (to Württemberg)
Besançon •
Neuenburg (to Prussia)
Berne •
Basel •
Baden •
Zurich •
Lucerne •
Glarus •
Stockach
Constance
COUNTY OF TYROL
• Innsbruck
• Brixen
• Botzen

Clermont-Ferrand •
Lyons •
St. Etienne •
Geneva •
Martigny •
Lausanne •
SWITZERLAND
Airolo •
Bormio •
Sondrio •
• Trent

DUCHY OF SAVOY
KINGDOM OF SARDINIA
to Sardinia 1703 1743
PRINCIPALITY OF PIEDMONT
DUCHY OF MILAN
• Como
Milan •
• Bergamo
VENETIAN